Easy Learning Spanish Dictionary

HarperCollinsPublishers

Second edition/Segunda edición 2001

First reprint 2001

HarperCollins Publishers
Westerhill Road, Bishopbriggs, Glasgow G64 2QT,
Great Britain

The HarperCollins website address is
www.**fire**and**water**.com

ISBN 0-00-472417-8

---

general editor/dirección
Jeremy Butterfield

contributors/colaboradores
Teresa Álvarez, Cordelia Lilly, Fernando León Solís, Gerry Breslin, Malihé Forghani-Nowbari, Jane Horwood, Anna Jené Palat, Lesley Johnston, Victoria Ordóñez Diví, Carol Styles, Eduardo Vallejo, José María Ruiz Vaca

editorial coordination/coordinación editorial
Sharon J. Hunter, Val McNulty, Emma Aeppli

second edition/segunda edición
Sharon J. Hunter, Caitlin McMahon

computing staff/informática editorial
Jane Creevy, Ann Rautenbach

concept development/proyecto editorial
Michela Clari, Ray Carrick

illustrations/ilustraciones
Richard Anderson

series editor/directora de la colección
Lorna Sinclair

Corpus Acknowledgements

We would like to acknowledge the assistance of the many hundreds of individuals and companies who have kindly given permission for copyright material to be used in The Bank of English. The written sources include many national and regional newspapers in Britain and overseas; magazine and periodical publishers; and book publishers in Britain, the United States and Australia. Extensive spoken data has been provided by radio and television broadcasting companies; research workers at many universities and other institutions; and numerous individual contributors. We are grateful to them all.

A catalogue record for this book is available from the British Library

Printed and bound in Italy by Amadeus S.p.A.

ÍNDICE

CONTENTS

INTRODUCCIÓN

Collins Easy Learning Spanish Dictionary es un diccionario innovador, especialmente concebido para cualquier persona que empiece a aprender inglés. Queremos agradecer su colaboración a todos los que han participado en la creación de la serie Easy Learning, y especialmente a los profesores y examinadores que nos han cedido valiosas listas de palabras y exámenes que hemos analizado detalladamente para realizar un diccionario que satisfaga plenamente las necesidades de los alumnos.

INTRODUCTION

Collins Easy Learning Spanish Dictionary is an innovative dictionary designed specifically for anyone starting to learn Spanish. We are grateful to everyone who has contributed to the development of the Easy Learning series, and acknowledge the help of the examining boards in providing us with word lists and exam papers, which we carefully studied when compiling this dictionary.

LA PRONUNCIACIÓN INGLESA

▶ VOCALES

calm, part	[ɑː]
hat	[æ]
fiancé	[ɑ̃ː]
egg, set	[ɛ]
above	[ə]
earn, girl	[əː]
hit, fairly	[ɪ]
green, peace	[iː]
rot	[ɔ]
born, jaw	[ɔː]
hut	[ʌ]
full	[u]
pool	[uː]

▶ DIPTONGOS

buy, die, my	[aɪ]
house, now	[au]
pay, mate	[eɪ]
pair, mare	[ɛə]
no, boat	[əu]
here, near	[ɪə]
boy, coin	[ɔɪ]
tour, poor	[uə]

▶ SEMIVOCALES

yet, million	[j]
wet, why	[w]

▶ CONSONANTES

ball	[b]
child	[tʃ]
field	[f]
good	[g]
hand	[h]
just	[dʒ]
kind, catch	[k]
left, little	[l]
mat	[m]
nest	[n]
long	[ŋ]
put	[p]
run	[r]
sit	[s]
shall	[ʃ]
tag	[t]
thing	[θ]
this	[ð]
very	[v]
loch	[x]
ours, zip	[z]
measure	[ʒ]

▶ OTROS SÍMBOLOS

Acento	[ˈ]
R de enlace	[ʳ]

Como guía para pronunciar el inglés correctamente, en la parte de inglés-español aparece la transcripción fonética tras el lema en todas las entradas.

CÓMO USAR ESTE DICCIONARIO

La utilización de un diccionario es una destreza que consigue mejorarse con un poco de práctica y siguiendo algunas reglas básicas. En las páginas siguientes puedes encontrar la información necesaria para sacar el máximo provecho de este diccionario.

Las soluciones a las preguntas de esta sección se encuentran en la página 14.

▶ CÓMO ASEGURARSE DE QUE ESTAMOS EN LA PARTE CORRECTA DEL DICCIONARIO

La parte de español-inglés viene en primer lugar, seguida de la parte de inglés-español. En la esquina superior de cada página puede verse la inscripción **español ~ inglés** o **inglés ~ español**, lo que nos ayuda a identificar de forma inmediata en qué parte del diccionario nos encontramos. Las páginas centrales están bordeadas en azul para que podamos ver dónde acaba una parte y dónde empieza la siguiente.

1 Si queremos encontrar "*la bicicleta*" ¿miraremos en la parte de español-inglés o de inglés-español?

▶ CÓMO ENCONTRAR LA PALABRA QUE BUSCAMOS

Si estamos buscando una palabra, por ejemplo **temprano**, tendremos que ver por qué letra empieza. En este caso, **t-** y por ello nos vamos a la letra **T** de la parte de español-inglés. En la esquina de cada página pueden leerse la primera y la última palabra de cada página. Cuando encontremos la página con las palabras que empiezan por **tem**, tendremos que seguir mirando más abajo hasta que encontremos la palabra que buscamos.

2 ¿En qué página encontraremos la palabra "*ayer*"?
3 ¿Qué viene antes – "*cándido*" o "*centro*"?

▶ CÓMO ASEGURARSE DE QUE ESTAMOS EN LA ENTRADA CORRECTA

Una entrada léxica consta de una **palabra**, sus traducciones y, con frecuencia, de algunos ejemplos que nos sirven de guía en el uso de las traducciones. Si hay más de una entrada para la misma palabra en la parte de inglés-español, entonces aparece un recuadro que nos remite a la otra entrada. Observa el siguiente ejemplo:

flat [flæt] ADJECTIVE
see also **flat** NOUN
llano ◊ *a flat surface* una superficie llana
♦ **flat shoes** zapatos bajos
♦ **I've got a flat tyre.** Tengo una rueda desinflada.

flat [flæt] NOUN
see also **flat** ADJECTIVE
el piso (el apartamento *LatAm*)

> 4 ¿Qué entrada de las dos anteriores habría que consultar para traducir la frase "*My car has a flat tyre*"?

En numerosas ocasiones aparecen también recuadros con información adicional sobre algún punto de interés gramatical o sobre las diferencias culturales entre España y el Reino Unido.

▶ CÓMO ELEGIR LA TRADUCCIÓN CORRECTA

La traducción principal de una palabra aparece subrayada y en una línea aparte a fin de distinguirla del resto de la entrada. Si existe más de una traducción principal para una misma palabra, cada una de ellas aparece numerada y si una entrada continúa en la página siguiente aparece una señal indicándolo ☞.

Con frecuencia aparecen algunos ejemplos en cursiva, precedidos de un rombo blanco ◊, que nos servirán de ayuda a la hora de elegir la traducción que queremos, pues muestran el uso que hay que dar a la traducción que estamos buscando.

> 5 Emplea los ejemplos que aparecen en la entrada "*intención*" para traducir: "*Tenía intención de irme a vivir al extranjero*".

Las palabras suelen tener más de un significado y más de una traducción y cuando estamos traduciendo del español al inglés hay que tener cuidado de usar la palabra que tiene el significado específico que queremos. Este diccionario te facilita toda la ayuda que necesitas para hacerlo.

El siguiente ejemplo muestra la división de una de estas entradas. Las traducciones principales van subrayadas, la numeración advierte que hay más de una traducción y las palabras escritas en cursiva entre paréntesis nos ayudan a elegir el ejemplo correcto.

la **cinta** SUSTANTIVO
1 ribbon (*de adorno, para el pelo*)
2 tape (*para grabar*)
◆ **una cinta de vídeo** a videotape
◆ **cinta aislante** insulating tape
◆ **una cinta transportadora** a conveyor belt

6 ¿Cómo podríamos traducir: "*Tenía una cinta en el pelo*"?

Es importante recordar que nunca hay que tomar la primera traducción que nos encontramos sin antes mirar las demás. Hay que echar siempre un vistazo a toda la entrada para comprobar si hay más de una traducción subrayada.

Los ejemplos que aparecen **en negrita** precedidos de un rombo negro ◆ son construcciones de uso bastante frecuente, que a veces tienen una traducción completamente distinta de la traducción principal; otras veces la traducción puede ser la misma. Por ejemplo:

cancer ['kænsəʳ] NOUN
el cáncer ◊ *He's got cancer.* Tiene cáncer.
◆ **I'm Cancer.** Soy Cáncer.
◆ **a Cancer** un/una Cáncer

el **acuerdo** SUSTANTIVO
agreement ◊ *llegar a un acuerdo* to reach an agreement
◆ **estar de acuerdo con alguien** to agree with somebody
◆ **ponerse de acuerdo** to agree ◊ *Al final no nos pusimos de acuerdo.* In the end we couldn't agree. ◊ *Nos pusimos de acuerdo para prepararle una bienvenida.* We agreed to organize a welcome for him.
◆ **¡De acuerdo!** All right!

Cuando consultamos una palabra conviene mirar siempre más allá de las traducciones principales para comprobar si la entrada contiene algunas frases en negrita.

7 Consulta la entrada "*out*" y traduce al español "*We're out of petrol*".

▶ CÓMO UTILIZAR LOS EJEMPLOS DEL DICCIONARIO

Cuando consultamos una palabra, encontramos con frecuencia no sólo la palabra sino la frase exacta que estamos buscando. Por ejemplo, si queremos decir *"¿qué hora es?"* consultamos la palabra **hora** y encontraremos el ejemplo completo con su traducción.

En otras ocasiones tenemos que adaptar la información que encontramos en el diccionario. Si queremos decir *"nunca viajo en tren"* y miramos la palabra **tren** encontraremos:

> el **tren** SUSTANTIVO
> train
> ◆ **viajar en tren** to travel by train
> ◆ **Tomé un tren directo.** I took a through train.
> ◆ **con este tren de vida** with such a hectic life

Hay que sustituir la forma de infinitivo *to travel* por la forma conjugada *I travel.* Esto ocurrirá con frecuencia, especialmente en el caso de los verbos, en que tendremos que utilizar el pronombre y la forma correspondientes. Conviene consultar la sección dedicada a la tablas de verbos, que nos ayudará en el uso de los mismos.

8 ¿Cómo dirías "*Estamos jugando al fútbol*"?

Los ejemplos que contienen sustantivos también hay que adaptarlos, especialmente si el sustantivo que buscamos tiene un plural irregular, que viene indicado en la entrada.

9 ¿Cómo dirías "*Las flores rojas son muy bonitas*"?

▶ CÓMO HACER UN MEJOR USO DEL DICCIONARIO

Consultar una palabra requiere su tiempo, por lo que aconsejamos reducir el uso del diccionario cuando no sea realmente necesario. Por eso hay también formas de evitar su uso: primero hay que pensar detenidamente en lo que queremos decir y después ver si podemos expresarlo de otra manera, utilizando las palabras que ya conocemos o cambiando la estructura de la frase, para lo que podremos recurrir a los siguientes trucos:

- Utilizar una palabra con un significado parecido. Esto es más fácil con los adjetivos, ya que existen muchas palabras que significan *bueno, malo, grande*, etc y seguramente conoceremos más de una.

- Emplear frases negatives: si la tarta que hemos hecho nos ha salido muy mala, siempre podremos decir que no ha salido muy buena.

- Usar ejemplos concretos en lugar de palabras generales e innecesarias. En lugar de decir: "En nuestra ciudad hay varias instalaciones deportivas" si no conocemos alguna de las palabras del ejemplo, podemos decir en cambio: "En nuestra ciudad hay una piscina y un campo de fútbol".

10 ¿Cómo podrías decir "*Madrid es una ciudad enorme*", sin necesidad de mirar la palabra "*enorme*"?

También podemos tratar de adivinar el significado de una palabra inglesa mediante el uso de otras que nos sirvan de pista. Si vemos la frase "My father drives a red car", a lo mejor no conocemos el significado de la palabra **drives**, pero sabemos que es un verbo, porque va precedida de un sustantivo y sabemos que tiene algo que ver con un coche. Por tanto debe tratarse de algo que podemos hacer con un coche, o sea, ... **conducir**. Así que la traducción sería: *mi padre conduce un coche rojo.*

11 Sin usar el diccionario, intenta averiguar el significado de la palabra "*essay*" en la frase "*We have to write an essay before the exam*".

LAS CATEGORÍAS GRAMATICALES

Si consultamos la palabra **plano**, veremos que hay dos entradas para esta palabra, ya que puede tratarse de un sustantivo o de un adjetivo.

Por ello es importante aprender a distinguir unos tipos de palabras de otros para reconocer la entrada correcta.

A continuación vamos a dar información sobre las distintas categorías gramaticales y algunos consejos que nos ayudarán a traducir correctamente los sustantivos, preposiciones, etc al inglés y a descifrar la función de algunas palabras inglesas que desconocemos cuando las encontramos en un determinado contexto.

▶ SUSTANTIVOS

Los sustantivos son las palabras que sirven para nombrar a personas, animales y cosas. En inglés suelen venir acompañados de palabras como *a*, *the*, *this*, *that*, *your* o *his*:

his ***dog*** *her* ***cat*** *a* ***street***

En la parte de inglés-español aparecen marcados como NOUN.

Si queremos traducir un sustantivo en plural al inglés, lo primero que hay hacer es encontrar en la parte español-inglés la forma en singular. Así, si queremos decir "los cuadros" en inglés, tendremos que buscar "el cuadro".

12 *¿En qué entrada del diccionario podremos encontrar "camiones"?*

El plural se construye en inglés, por regla general, añadiendo una "**s**" a la forma del singular:

many book**s** two house**s**

Los sustantivos acabados en **-s**, **-sh** o **-x** construyen el plural añadiendo "**es**":

many kiss**es** three brush**es** some box**es**

Algunos sustantivos que acaban en **-y** forman el plural cambiando a "**ies**":

several bab**ies** two pupp**ies**

Algunos sustantivos tienen una forma irregular en plural:

two **children** many **mice** six **loaves** of bread

one child **two children**

Si el plural no se construye añadiendo una "**s**" a la forma del singular, la forma del plural aparece en el diccionario. Los plurales irregulares de los sustantivos ingleses tienen además su propia entrada en la parte de inglés-español con una remisión a la forma en singular.

mice [maɪs] PL NOUN *see* **mouse**

Normalmente, los sustantivos vienen en singular. Sin embargo, algunos no tienen esta forma, por lo que aparecen en plural, seguidos por la abreviatura PL NOUN.

French fries [frɛntʃ'fraɪz] PL NOUN
las patatas fritas (las papas fritas *LatAm*)

The children gave their teacher a box of chocolates.

13 ¿Cuántos sustantivos contiene esta frase?
14 ¿Cuántos sustantivos en plural hay en esta frase?
15 ¿Cuál es el singular de "*children*"?
16 Busca en el diccionario el plural de la palabra inglesa "*calf*".

▶ ADJETIVOS

Los adjetivos son palabras que describen las cualidades del sustantivo. En la parte de inglés-español aparecen marcadas como ADJECTIVE. Los adjetivos en español pueden cambiar de género o número, según el sustantivo al que acompañen, pero el adjetivo en inglés no varía:

a **black** cat   **black** dogs   the cat is **black**

¿Qué entrada habría que consultar para traducir las siguientes oraciones: sweet ADJECTIVE o sweet NOUN?

17 The cake is very sweet.
18 Sweets are bad for your teeth.
19 How sweet of you!

▶ PRONOMBRES

Los pronombres son palabras como *yo, tú, él, me*, que pueden ocupar el lugar de un sustantivo en una oración. En la parte de inglés-español aparecen marcadas como PRONOUN.

A diferencia del español, en inglés siempre hay que colocar el pronombre personal (I, you, he, etc) cuando el sujeto de la frase no es un sustantivo.

▶ VERBOS

Los verbos se utilizan para expresar acciones o estados y, como ya hemos dicho, en inglés van precedidos de pronombres personales, o bien de sustantivos. En este diccionario los verbos se distinguen también porque aparecen precedidos de la partícula **to** y además están marcados por la palabra VERB.

¿Qué entrada habría que consultar para traducir las siguientes frases: fight NOUN o fight VERB?

20 He is always fighting with his brothers.
21 Tyson won most of his fights.

Los verbos pueden ir en distintos tiempos, por ejemplo, en presente (**leo un libro**) o en pasado (**leí un libro** o **he leído un libro**). Además, pueden estar en voz activa (**leo un libro**) o pasiva (**el libro es leído**). Todas estas formas verbales se deducen a partir de la forma base o forma de infinitivo, que es la que aparece en el diccionario. Por eso, si tenemos que traducir **ella lee un libro** tendremos que buscar en la entrada correspondiente a **leer**.

¿En qué forma de infinitivo encontraremos las siguientes formas verbales conjugadas?

22 Canté una canción.
23 Es ingeniero.

Al igual que en español, en inglés existen también verbos irregulares. Para facilitar la localización de la forma de infinitivo, las formas de pasado y participio de los verbos irregulares más importantes aparecen como entradas independientes en la parte de inglés-español, con una remisión a la forma de infinitivo.

found [faund] VERB *see* **find**

En la parte de inglés-español aparecen indicadas después del verbo inglés en infinitivo la forma irregular de pasado y de participio de perfecto.

to **sew** [səu] VERB **(sewed, sewn)**

En las páginas 344-355 se puede encontrar más información sobre las formas más importantes de los verbos ingleses.

Traduce las siguientes frases al inglés:

24 Ella va al colegio.
25 Él fue al cine.
26 Ya se han ido.

▶ ADVERBIOS

Los adverbios se utilizan para modificar el sentido de los adjetivos o de los verbos. En la parte de inglés-español del diccionario aparecen marcados como ADVERB y en inglés se reconocen a menudo por terminar en **"ly"**.

Tanto en inglés como en español hay algunos adjetivos que presentan la misma forma que los adverbios, por lo que es importante aprender a distinguirlos para encontrar la traducción correcta.

rápido (1) ADJETIVO
[1] fast (*veloz*) ◇ *un coche muy rápido* a very fast car
[2] quick (*de poca duración*) ◇ *Fue una visita muy rápida.* It was a very quick visit.
rápido (2) ADVERBIO
fast ◇ *Conduces demasiado rápido.* You drive too fast.
◆ **Lo hice tan rápido como pude.** I did it as quickly as I could.
◆ **¡Rápido!** Hurry up!

¿Qué entrada habría que consultar para traducir las siguientes oraciones: rápido ADJETIVO o rápido ADVERBIO?

27 Un tren muy rápido.
28 Ha sido un cambio muy rápido.
29 Se ha marchado muy rápido.

▶ PREPOSICIONES

Las preposiciones son palabras como *sobre*, *por*, *de* en español y *on*, *for*, *of* en inglés y aparecen habitualmente delante de los sustantivos y pronombres. Es importante reconocerlas, ya que a veces pueden tener la misma forma que un adverbio. En la parte de inglés-español aparecen seguidas de la marca PREPOSITION.

> *The party's over.*
> *The shop's just over the road.*
>
> 30 ¿En qué oración es "*over*" una preposición?
> 31 Traduce al inglés: "*Una película sobre África*".

▶ SOLUCIONES

1 en la parte de **español-inglés**
2 61
3 **cándido**
4 Flat **ADJECTIVE**
5 **I intended to go and live abroad.**
6 **She had a ribbon in her hair.**
7 **Se nos ha acabado la gasolina.**
8 **We're playing football.**
9 **The red flowers are very pretty.**
10 **Madrid is a very big city.**
11 **redacción: Tenemos que hacer una redacción antes del examen.**
12 **camión**
13 **4**: children, teacher, box, chocolates
14 **2**: children, chocolates
15 **child**
16 **calves**
17 **ADJECTIVE**
18 **NOUN**
19 **ADJECTIVE**
20 **VERB**
21 **NOUN**
22 **cantar**
23 **ser**
24 **She goes to school.**
25 **He went to the cinema.**
26 **They've already left.**
27 **ADJETIVO**
28 **ADJETIVO**
29 **ADVERBIO**
30 **The shop's just over the road.**
31 **A film about Africa.**

SPANISH PRONUNCIATION

▶ SPANISH VOWELS

Spanish vowels are always clearly pronounced and not relaxed in unstressed syllables as happens in English.

a – Between English ***a*** as in ***hat*** and ***u*** as in ***hut***
e – Similar to English ***e*** in ***pet***
i – Between English ***i*** as in ***pin*** and ***ee*** as in ***been***
o – Similar to English ***o*** in ***hot***
u – Between English ***ew*** as in ***few*** and ***u*** as in ***put***

▶ SPANISH CONSONANTS

Note the pronunciation of the following letters.

b,v – These letters have the same value. At the start of a word, and after written **m** and **n**, the sound is similar to English ***b***oy
– In all other positions the sound is softer, the lips do not touch
c – Before **a**, **o**, **u** or a consonant, like English ***k***eep, but softer
– Before **e** or **i** like English ***th***in, or, in Latin America and parts of Spain, like English ***s***ame
ch – Like English ***ch***ur***ch***
d – At the start of the word and after **l** or **n**, it is pronounced similarly to English ***d***eep
– Between vowels and after consonants (except **l** or **n**), it is pronounced very like English ***th***ough
– At the end of words it is often not pronounced
g – Before **e** or **i**, the sound is similar to English lo***ch***
– At the start of a word and after **n**, it is pronounced like English **g**et
– In other positions it is softer than in **g**et
– Note that in the group **gue**, **gui**, the **u** is silent, as in English g**u**itar unless it is marked by a diaeresis (**güe**, **güi**), when it is pronounced like English **w**alk
h – This is always silent
j – Like the sound in English lo***ch***
ll – Similar to English *-ll-* in mi***ll***ion, but often like English **y**et or plea**s**ure
ñ – As in English o***ni***on
q – Always followed by silent letter **u**, and pronounced as in English ***k***eep, but softer
r – Single trill, like the Scots **r**
– Pronounced like **rr** below at the start of a word and after **l**, **n** or **s**
rr – Strongly trilled, in a way that does not exist in English
s – Except where mentioned below, like English **s**ing
– When followed by **b**, **d**, **g**, **l**, **m**, **n** like English ro**s**e
w – Usually pronounced as English **v**, but sometimes kept as English ***w***
y – Similar to English **y**es, but often like English lei**s**ure
z – Like English ***th***in
– In some parts of Spain and in Latin America, like English **s**end

f, **k**, **l**, **m**, **n**, **p**, **t**, **x** are pronounced as in English.

DICTIONARY SKILLS

Using a dictionary is a skill you can improve with practice and by following some basic guidelines. This section gives you a detailed explanation of how to use this dictionary to ensure you get the most out of it.

The answers to all the questions in this section are on page 25.

▶ MAKE SURE YOU LOOK ON THE RIGHT SIDE OF THE DICTIONARY

The Spanish-English side comes first, followed by the English-Spanish. At the top of the page, you will see either **Spanish ~ English** or **English ~ Spanish**, so you know immediately if you're looking up the side you want. The middle pages of the book have a blue border so that you can see where one side finishes and the other starts.

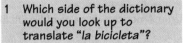

1 Which side of the dictionary would you look up to translate "*la bicicleta*"?

▶ FINDING THE WORD YOU WANT

When looking for a word, for example **feliz**, look at the first letter - **f** - and find the **F** section in the Spanish-English side. At the top of each page, you'll find the first and last words on that page. When you find the page with the words starting with **fe**, scan down the page until you find the word you want. Remember that even if a word has an accent on it, for example *fórmula*, it makes no difference to the alphabetical order. The exception to this rule is **ñ** (*n tilde*), which is treated as a separate letter in Spanish, so that *leña* follows *lento*.

2 On which page will you find the word "*hermana*"?
3 Which comes first – "*francesa*" or "*francés*"?

▶ MAKE SURE YOU LOOK AT THE RIGHT ENTRY

An entry is made up of a **word**, its translations, and, often, example phrases to show you how to use the translations. If there is more than one entry for the same word, then there is a warning box to tell you so. Look at the following example entries:

flat [flæt] ADJECTIVE

| *see also* **flat** NOUN |

llano ◇ *a flat surface* una superficie llana
♦ **flat shoes** zapatos bajos
♦ **I've got a flat tyre.** Tengo una rueda desinflada.

flat [flæt] NOUN

| *see also* **flat** ADJECTIVE |

el piso (el apartamento *LatAm*)

4 Which entry should you look at if you want to translate the phrase "*My car has a flat tyre*"?

Always pay attention to information boxes – they tell you if there is more than one entry for the same word, give you guidance on grammatical points, or tell you about differences between Spanish and British life.

▶ CHOOSING THE RIGHT TRANSLATION

The main translation of a word is shown on a new line and is underlined to make it stand out from the rest of the entry. If there is more than one main translation for a word, each one is numbered. If an entry continues over the page there is a signpost to indicate this ☞. On the English-Spanish side, Latin American equivalents are shown in brackets after the main translation, and are labelled ***LatAm***.

Often you will see phrases in *italics*, preceded by a white diamond ◇. These help you to choose the translation you want because they show how the translation they follow can be used.

5 Use the phrases given at the entry "*hard*" to help you translate: "*This bread is hard*".

Words often have more than one meaning and more than one translation. For example, a **pool** can be a puddle, a pond or a swimming pool; **pool** can also be a game. When you are translating from English into Spanish, be careful to choose the Spanish word that has the particular meaning you want. The dictionary offers you a lot of help with this. Look at the following entry:

pool [pu:l] NOUN
[1] el estanque (*pond*)
[2] la piscina (*swimming pool*)
[3] el billar americano (*game*)
◆ **a pool table** una mesa de billar
◆ **the pools** las quinielas ◊ *I do the pools every week.* Juego a las quinielas todas las semanas.

The underlining highlights all the main translations, the numbers tell you that there is more than one possible translation and the words in brackets in *italics* after the translations help you choose which translation you want.

6 How would you translate "I like playing pool"?

Never take the first translation you see without looking at the others. Always look to see if there is more than one underlined translation.

Phrases in **bold type** preceded by a black diamond ◆ are phrases which are particularly common or important. Sometimes these phrases have a completely different translation from the main translation; sometimes the translation is the same. For example:

cancer ['kænsə^r] NOUN
el cáncer ◊ *He's got cancer.* Tiene cáncer.
◆ **I'm Cancer**. Soy Cáncer.
◆ **a Cancer** un/una Cáncer

el **acuerdo** SUSTANTIVO
agreement ◊ *llegar a un acuerdo* to reach an agreement
◆ **estar de acuerdo con alguien** to agree with somebody
◆ **ponerse de acuerdo** to agree ◊ *Al final no nos pusimos de acuerdo.* In the end we couldn't agree. ◊ *Nos pusimos de acuerdo para prepararle una bienvenida.* We agreed to organize a welcome for him.
◆ **¡De acuerdo!** All right!

When you look up a word, make sure you look beyond the main translations to see if the entry includes any **bold phrases**.

7 Look up "ir" to help you translate the sentence "Voy a casa mañana"?

▶ MAKING USE OF THE PHRASES IN THE DICTIONARY

Sometimes when you look up a word you will find not only the word, but the exact phrase you want. For example, you might want to say *"What's the date today"?* Look up **date** and you will find that exact phrase and its translation.

Sometimes you have to adapt what you find in the dictionary. If you want to say *"I ate a sandwich"* and look up **eat** you will find:

to **eat** [i:t] VERB **(ate, eaten)**
comer ◊ *Would you like something to eat?* ¿Quieres comer algo?

You have to substitute *comí* for the infinitive form *comer*. You will often have to adapt the infinitive in this way, adding the correct ending and choosing the present, future or past form. For help with this, look at the verb tables, **comer** is a regular verb and it is set out on page 361.

8 How would you say "*I don't eat meat*"?

Phrases containing nouns and adjectives also need to be adapted. You may need to make the noun plural, or the adjective feminine or plural. Remember that some Spanish nouns and adjectives change their spelling in the feminine or plural and that this is shown in the entry.

9 How would you say "*The boys are French*"?

▶ DON'T OVERUSE THE DICTIONARY

It takes time to look up words so try to avoid using the dictionary unnecessarily, especially in exams. Think carefully about what you want to say and see if you can put it another way, using words you already know. To rephrase things you can:

- Use a word with a similar meaning. This is particularly easy with adjectives, as there are a lot of words which mean *good*, *bad*, *big* etc and you're sure to know at least one.
- Use negatives: if the cake you made was a total disaster, you could just say it wasn't very good.
- Use particular examples instead of general terms. If you are asked to describe the sports facilities in your area, and time is short, you could say something like "In our town there is a swimming pool and a football ground."

10 How could you say "*Argentina is huge*" without looking up the word "*huge*"?

You can also often guess the meaning of a Spanish word by using others to give you a clue. If you see the sentence *"María lee un buen libro"*, you may not know the meaning of the word **lee**, but you know it's a verb because it's preceded by **María**. Therefore it must be something you can do to a book: **read**. So the translation is: *María is reading a good book*.

11 Try NOT to use your dictionary to work out the meaning of the sentence "*La chica escribe una carta a su amiga en español*".

PARTS OF SPEECH

If you look up the word **flat**, you will see that there are two entries for this word as it can be a noun or an adjective. It helps to choose correctly between entries if you know how to recognize these different types of words.

▶ NOUNS AND PRONOUNS

Nouns often appear with words like *a, the, this, that, my, your* and *his*. They can be singular (abbreviated to SING in the dictionary):

his **dog** *her* **cat** *a* **street**

or plural (abbreviated to PL in the dictionary):

the **facts** *those* **people** *his* **shoes** *our* **holidays**

They can be the subject of a verb:

Vegetables are good for you

or the object of a verb:

I play ***tennis***

Words like *I, me, you, he, she, him, her* and *they* are pronouns. They can be used instead of nouns. You can refer to a person as *he* or *she* or to a thing as *it*.

I bought my mother a box of chocolates.

12 Which three words in this sentence are nouns?
13 Which of the nouns is plural?
14 Which word is a pronoun in this sentence?

Spanish nouns are either masculine or feminine (abbreviated to MASC *or* FEM in the dicitonary). Masculine nouns are shown by **el**:

el hombre ***el*** gato ***el*** fútbol

feminine nouns are shown by **la**:

la mujer *la economía* *la* fábrica

The plural forms of **el** and **la** are **los** and **las**. The plural of most Spanish nouns is made by adding **s** if the word ends in a vowel, or **es** if it ends in a consonant:

*los gato**s*** *las mujer**es***

▶ ADJECTIVES

Flat can be an adjective as well as a noun. Adjectives describe nouns: your tyre can be **flat**, you can have a pair of **flat** shoes.

I'm afraid of the dark.
The girl has dark hair.

15 In which sentence is "*dark*" an adjective?

Spanish adjectives can be masculine or feminine, singular or plural, depending on the noun they describe:

un chico *guapo* (MASCULINE SINGULAR)
une chica *guapa* (FEMININE SINGULAR: replace *-o* of masculine with *-a*)
unos chicos *guapos* (MASCULINE PLURAL = masculine singular + *s*)
unas chicas *guapas* (FEMININE PLURAL = feminine singular + *s*)

Only the masculine singular form of regular adjectives is shown in the dictionary. So if you want to find out what kind of houses **unas casas viejas** are, look under **viejo**.

If the feminine or the plural form of an adjective does not follow these rules, then the irregular form is shown in the dictionary:

francés ADJETIVO (FEM **francesa,** MASC PL **franceses**)
French

French [frɛntʃ] ADJECTIVE
see also **French** NOUN
francés MASC (PL **franceses**)
francesa FEM

There are separate masculine and feminine, singular and plural forms for irregular adjectives of nationality, and those ending in **-án**, **-ín**, **-ón**, eg **español** MASCULINE SINGULAR, **español<u>a</u>**, FEMININE SINGULAR, **español<u>es</u>** MASCULINE PLURAL, **español<u>as</u>** FEMININE PLURAL.

Adjectives ending in **-or** also follow the above pattern unless they are comparatives. The feminine is shown in the dictionary for adjectives of this type.

hablador ADJETIVO (FEM **habladora**)
1 chatty (*parlanchín*)
2 gossipy (*chismoso*)

talkative [ˈtɔːkətɪv] ADJECTIVE
hablador MASC
habladora FEM

Other adjectives ending in a consonant do not have a separate feminine form, but do change in the plural, eg **azul** MASCULINE and FEMININE SINGULAR, **azul<u>es</u>** MASCULINE and FEMININE PLURAL.

feliz ADJETIVO (PL **felices**)
<u>happy</u> ◊ *Se la ve muy feliz.* She looks very happy.
◆ **¡Feliz cumpleaños!** Happy birthday!
◆ **¡Feliz Año Nuevo!** Happy New Year!
◆ **¡Felices Navidades!** Happy Christmas!

happy ['hæpɪ] ADJECTIVE
<u>feliz</u> (PL felices) ◊ *Janet looks happy.* Janet parece feliz.
◆ **to be happy with something** estar* contento con algo ◊ *I'm very happy with your work.* Estoy muy contento con tu trabajo.
◆ **Happy birthday!** ¡Feliz cumpleaños!
◆ **a happy ending** un final feliz

If the masculine form of an adjective ends in **-e** or **-a**, the feminine form is the same, and both the masculine and feminine plurals are formed by adding **-s** to the masculine, eg **verde** MASCULINE and FEMININE SINGULAR, **verde<u>s</u>** MASCULINE and FEMININE PLURAL. Some adjectives remain the same whether they're masculine, feminine or plural. This is also shown in the dictionary:

el **rosa** ADJETIVO, SUSTANTIVO
<u>pink</u> ◊ *Va vestida de rosa.* She's wearing pink.
◆ **Llevaba unos calcetines rosa.** He was wearing pink socks.

16 What is the feminine singular form of "*negro*"?
17 What is the basic form of the adjective in the sentence "*Las flores son hermosas*"?

▶VERBS

She's going to record the programme for me.
His time in the race was a new world record.

Record is a verb in the first sentence, and a noun in the second.

One way to recognize a verb is that it frequently comes with a pronoun such as **I**, **you** or **she**, or with somebody's name. Verbs can relate to the present, the past or the future. They have a number of different forms to show this: **I'm going** (present), **he will go** (future), and **Nicola went by herself** (past). Often verbs appear with **to: they promised to go**. This basic form of the verb is called the infinitive.

In this dictionary, verbs are preceded by "to", so you can identify them at a glance. No matter which of the four previous examples you want to translate, you should look up to **go**, not **going** or **went**. If you want to translate **I thought**, look up to **think**.

18 What would you look up to translate the verbs in these phrases?

I *came* | she'*s crying* | they'*ve done it* | he'*s* out

Verbs have different endings in Spanish, depending on whether you are talking about **yo**, **tú**, **nosotros** etc: **yo hablo**, **tú hablas**, **nosotros hablamos** etc. They also have different forms for the present, future, past etc. **Hablamos** (*we speak* = present), **hemos hablado** (*we spoke* = past), **hablaremos** (*we will speak* = future). **Hablar** is the infinitive and is the form that appears in the dictionary.

Sometimes the verb changes completely between the infinitive form and the **yo**, **tú**, **él** etc form. For example, *to give* is **dar**, but *I give* is **doy**, and **digo** comes from **decir** (*to say*).

On pages 360-363 of the dictionary, you will find tables of regular Spanish verbs. On pages 364-382 you will find tables of the most important irregular verbs, followed by a list of other irregular verbs with the number of the model verb they are like. Irregular Spanish verbs are marked in the dictionary with an asterisk.

to **fulfil** [fulˈfɪl] VERB
realizar* ◊ *He fulfilled his dream to visit China.* Realizó su sueño de viajar a China.
♦**to fulfil a promise** cumplir una promesa

ir* VERBO
1 to go ◊ *Anoche fuimos al cine.* We went to the cinema last night. ◊ *¿A qué colegio vas?* What school do you go to?
♦**ir de vacaciones** to go on holiday
♦**ir a por** to go and get

19 Look up the dictionary to find the imperfect and perfect tenses of "comer".

▶ ADVERBS

An adverb is a word that describes a verb or an adjective:

Write **soon.** | Check your work **carefully.**
The film was **very** good.

In the sentence *"The swimming pool is open daily"*, **daily** is an adverb describing the adjective **open**. In the phrase *"my daily routine"*, **daily** is an adjective describing the noun **routine**. We use the same word in English for both adjective and adverb forms, but to get the right Spanish translation, it is important to know if it's being used as an adjective or an adverb. When you look up **daily** you find:

daily ['deɪlɪ] ADJECTIVE, ADVERB
[1] diario ◊ *daily life* la vida diaria
◆ **It's part of my daily routine.** Forma parte de mi rutina diaria.
◆ **a daily paper** un periódico
[2] todos los días ◊ *The pool is open daily.* La piscina abre todos los días.

The examples show you **daily** being used as an adjective and as an adverb and will help you choose the right Spanish translation.

Take the sentence "The menu changes daily".

20 Is "*daily*" an adverb or an adjective here?

▶ PREPOSITIONS

Prepositions are words like **for**, **with** and **across**, which are followed by nouns or pronouns:

I've got a present ***for*** David. Come ***with*** me. He ran ***across*** the road.

The party's over.
The shop's just over the road.

21 Which sentence shows a preposition followed by a noun?

▶ ANSWERS

1 the Spanish side
2 on page 170
3 **francés** comes first
4 the first (ADJECTIVE) entry
5 **Este pan está duro.**
6 **Me gusta jugar al billar americano.**
7 **I'm going home tomorrow.**
8 **No como carne.**
9 **Los niños son franceses.**
10 **Argentina es muy grande.**
11 **The girl is writing a letter to her friend in Spanish.**
12 **mother**, **box** and **chocolates** are nouns
13 **chocolates** is plural
14 **I** is a pronoun
15 in the second sentence
16 **negra**
17 **hermoso**
18 to **come**, to **cry**, to **do**, to **be**
19 the imperfect tense is **comía**, the perfect tense is **he comido**
20 daily is an **adverb**
21 the second sentence

a PREPOSICIÓN

a + el = al.

1 to

*Se usa **to** hablando de movimiento, dirección.*

◊ *Fueron a Madrid.* They went to Madrid.

Pero a menudo depende de cómo se entienda la dirección: dentro, encima de ..., así como del verbo que la preceda.

♦ **Me caí al río.** I fell into the river.

♦ **Se subieron al tejado.** They climbed onto the roof.

♦ **Marta llegó a la oficina.** Marta arrived at the office.

♦ **Está a 15 km de aquí.** It's 15 km from here.

2 at

*Se usa **at** hablando de la hora, la fecha, la edad, la velocidad.*

◊ *a las 10* at 10 o'clock ◊ *a medianoche* at midnight ◊ *a los 24 años* at the age of 24 ◊ *Íbamos a más de 90 km por hora.* We were going at over 90 km an hour.

♦ **Estamos a 9 de julio.** It's the 9th of July.

♦ **Los huevos están a 300 pesetas la docena.** Eggs are 300 pesetas a dozen.

♦ **una vez a la semana** once a week

*También se usa normalmente **to** delante de un infinitivo.*

◊ *Voy a verle.* I'm going to see him.
◊ *Vine a decírtelo.* I came to tell you.
◊ *Me obligaban a comer.* They forced me to eat.

♦ **Al verlo, lo reconocí inmediatamente.** When I saw him, I recognized him immediately.

♦ **Nos cruzamos al salir.** We bumped into each other as we were going out.

*Cuando **a** forma parte del complemento indirecto también se traduce por **to**, a menos que siga directamente al verbo.*

◊ *Se lo di a Ana.* I gave it to Ana. ◊ *Le enseñé a Pablo el libro que me dejaste.* I showed Pablo the book you lent me.

♦ **Se lo compré a él.** I bought it from him.

En muchas otras ocasiones, como por ejemplo en complementos directos de persona, no se traduce.

♦ **Vi a Juan.** I saw Juan.

♦ **Llamé al médico.** I called the doctor.

♦ **Gira a la derecha.** Turn right.

♦ **Me voy a casa.** I'm going home.

♦ **¡A comer!** Lunch is ready!

la **abadía** SUSTANTIVO

abbey (PL abbeys)

abajo ADVERBIO

1 below ◊ *Los platos y las tazas están abajo.* The plates and cups are below. ◊ *La montaña no parece tan alta desde abajo.* The mountain doesn't seem so high from below.

♦ **Mete las cervezas abajo del todo.** Put the beers at the bottom.

♦ **El estante de abajo.** The bottom shelf.

♦ **La parte de abajo del contenedor.** The bottom of the container.

2 downstairs

*Se usa **downstairs** hablando de los distintos pisos de un edificio.*

◊ *Abajo están la cocina y el salón.* The kitchen and lounge are downstairs. ◊ *Hay una fiesta en el piso de abajo.* There's a party in the flat downstairs.

♦ **más abajo** further down

♦ **ir calle abajo** to go down the street

♦ **Todos los bolsos son de 15.000 pesetas para abajo.** All the bags are 15,000 pesetas or under.

♦ **abajo de** Latin America under

abandonado ADJETIVO

♦ **un pueblo abandonado** a deserted village

abandonar VERBO

1 to leave (*lugar, zona, edificio*)
◊ *Decidieron abandonar el país.* They decided to leave the country.

♦ **Abandonó a su familia.** He deserted his family.

♦ **Mucha gente abandona a sus perros en Navidad.** A lot of people abandon their dogs at Christmas.

2 to give up (*planes, proyecto*) ◊ *Tuve que abandonar la idea de comprarme otro coche.* I had to give up the idea of buying another car.

el **abanico** SUSTANTIVO

fan

abarrotado ADJETIVO

packed ◊ *La sala estaba abarrotada de gente.* The room was packed with people.

la **abarrotería** SUSTANTIVO Mexico

grocer's (PL grocers' shops)

los **abarrotes** SUSTANTIVO Mexico, Chile

groceries

abastecer* VERBO

♦ **abastecer de algo a alguien** to supply somebody with something

♦ **Nos abastecimos bien de comida para el viaje.** We stocked up with food for the trip.

el **abdomen** SUSTANTIVO

stomach

los **abdominales** SUSTANTIVO

sit-ups ◊ *hacer abdominales* to do sit-ups

el **abecedario** SUSTANTIVO

☞

alphabet

la **abeja** SUSTANTIVO
bee

el **abeto** SUSTANTIVO
fir

abierto (1) VERBO *ver* **abrir**

abierto (2) ADJETIVO
1 open ◊ *¿Están abiertas las tiendas?* Are the shops open?
2 on ◊ *No dejes el gas abierto.* Don't leave the gas on.

el **abogado,** la **abogada** SUSTANTIVO
lawyer

abolir VERBO
to abolish

abollar VERBO
to dent ◊ *Me han abollado el coche.* Someone has dented my car.
◆ **abollarse** to get dented

abombarse VERBO Latin America
to go bad

abonar VERBO
1 to pay ◊ *abonar dinero en una cuenta* to pay money into an account
2 to fertilize ◊ *Hay que abonar el terreno antes de sembrar.* The land has to be fertilized before sowing.
◆ **abonarse a (1)** (*canal de televisión*) to take out a subscription to
◆ **abonarse a (2)** (*polideportivo*) to join

el **abono** SUSTANTIVO
1 fertilizer (*para las plantas*)
2 season ticket (*de transporte, fútbol*)

abortar VERBO
1 to have an abortion (*cuando es provocado*)
2 to miscarry (*espontáneamente*)

el **aborto** SUSTANTIVO
1 abortion (*provocado*)
2 miscarriage (*espontáneo*)

abrasar VERBO
to burn ◊ *El fuego le abrasó las manos.* The fire burned his hands.
◆ **abrasarse** to be burned ◊ *Mucha gente se abrasó viva en el incendio.* A lot of people were burned alive in the fire.

abrazar* VERBO
to hug ◊ *Al verme me abrazó.* He hugged me when he saw me.
◆ **¡Abrázame fuerte!** Give me a big hug!
◆ **abrazarse** to hug ◊ *Se abrazaron y se besaron.* They hugged and kissed.

el **abrazo** SUSTANTIVO
hug ◊ *¡Dame un abrazo!* Give me a hug!
◆ **Siempre están dándose besos y abrazos.** They're always hugging and kissing.
◆ **"un abrazo"** (*en cartas*) "with best wishes"

el **abrebotellas** SUSTANTIVO (PL los **abrebotellas**)
bottle opener

el **abrelatas** SUSTANTIVO (PL los **abrelatas**)
tin opener

la **abreviatura** SUSTANTIVO
abbreviation

el **abridor** SUSTANTIVO
1 bottle opener (*de botellas*)
2 tin opener (*de latas*)

abrigar* VERBO
◆ **Esta chaqueta abriga mucho.** This jacket's great for keeping warm.
◆ **Ponte algo que te abrigue.** Put something warm on.
◆ **Abriga bien al niño, que hace frío.** Wrap the baby up well – it's cold.
◆ **abrigarse** to wrap up well

el **abrigo** SUSTANTIVO
coat ◊ *un abrigo de pieles* a fur coat
◆ **ropa de abrigo** warm clothing

abril SUSTANTIVO MASC
Los meses se escriben con mayúscula.
April ◊ *en abril* in April ◊ *Nació el 20 de abril.* He was born on 20 April.

abrir* VERBO
1 to open ◊ *Las tiendas abren a las diez.* The shops open at ten o'clock. ◊ *Abre la ventana.* Open the window.
◆ **¡Abre, soy yo!** Open the door, it's me!
2 to turn on ◊ *¿Has abierto el gas?* Have you turned the gas on?
◆ **abrirse** to open ◊ *De repente se abrió la puerta.* Suddenly the door opened.

abrocharse VERBO
to do up ◊ *Abróchate la camisa.* Do your shirt up.
◆ **Abróchense los cinturones.** Please fasten your seatbelts.

absoluto ADJETIVO
absolute ◊ *Nos dio garantía absoluta.* He gave us an absolute guarantee.
◆ **La operación fue un éxito absoluto.** The operation was a complete success.
◆ **en absoluto** at all ◊ *¿Te molesta que fume? – En absoluto.* Do you mind if I smoke? – Not at all. ◊ *nada en absoluto* nothing at all

absorber VERBO
to absorb

abstemio ADJETIVO
teetotal ◊ *Soy abstemio.* I'm teetotal.

la **abstención** SUSTANTIVO (PL las **abstenciones**)
abstention

abstenerse* VERBO
to abstain (*en una votación*) ◊ *Yo me abstengo.* I'm abstaining.
◆ **abstenerse de hacer algo** to refrain from doing something

abstracto ADJETIVO
abstract

absurdo ADJETIVO
absurd

◆**lo absurdo es que ...** the absurd thing is that ...

la **abuela** SUSTANTIVO
grandmother ◊ *mi abuela* my grandmother
◆**¿Dónde está la abuela?** Where's Gran?

el **abuelo** SUSTANTIVO
grandfather ◊ *mi abuelo* my grandfather
◆**¿Dónde está el abuelo?** Where's Grandad?
◆**mis abuelos** my grandparents

abultado ADJETIVO
bulky

abultar VERBO
to be bulky ◊ *No abulta mucho.* It isn't very bulky.
◆**Tus cosas apenas abultan.** Your things hardly take up any space at all.

abundante ADJETIVO
1 plenty of ◊ *Habrá comida y bebida abundante.* There'll be plenty of food and drink.
2 enormous ◊ *El año pasado tuvimos abundantes pérdidas.* We had enormous losses last year.

aburrido ADJETIVO
1 bored ◊ *Estaba aburrida y me marché.* I was bored so I left.
2 boring ◊ *una película muy aburrida* a very boring film ◊ *No seas aburrida y vente al cine, mujer.* Don't be boring and come to the film.
3 tired (*harto*) ◊ *Estaba aburrido de esperarte, así que me fui.* I was tired of waiting for you, so I left.

el **aburrimiento** SUSTANTIVO
◆**¡Qué aburrimiento!** What a bore this is!
◆**Estoy muerto de aburrimiento.** I'm bored stiff.

aburrirse VERBO
to get bored ◊ *Me aburro viendo la tele.* I get bored watching television.

abusar VERBO
◆**abusar de alguien (1)** (*de su confianza, hospitalidad*) to take advantage of somebody
◆**abusar de alguien (2)** (*sexualmente*) to abuse somebody
◆**Está bien beber de vez en cuando pero sin abusar.** Drinking every so often is fine as long as you don't overdo it.
◆**No conviene abusar del aceite en las comidas.** You shouldn't use too much oil in food.
◆**Abusó de nuestra hospitalidad.** He abused our hospitality.

el **abuso** SUSTANTIVO
abuse ◊ *el abuso de las drogas* drug abuse
◆**los abusos sexuales** sexual abuse SING
◆**Lo que han hecho me parece un abuso.** I think what they've done is outrageous.

acá ADVERBIO
here ◊ *¡Vente para acá!* Come over here!
◆**Hay que ponerlo más acá.** You'll have to bring it closer.

acabar VERBO
to finish ◊ *Cuando acabe esta cerveza me voy.* When I've finished this beer I'm going. ◊ *Ayer acabé de pintar la valla.* Yesterday I finished painting the fence.
◆**acabar con (1)** to put an end to ◊ *Hay que acabar con tanto desorden.* We must put an end to all this confusion.
◆**acabar con (2)** (*agotar*) to finish ◊ *Hemos acabado con todas las provisiones.* We've finished all our provisions.
◆**Acabo de ver a tu padre.** I've just seen your father. ◊ *Acababa de entrar cuando sonó el teléfono.* I had just come in when the phone rang.
◆**acabarse** to run out ◊ *La impresora te avisa cuando se acaba el papel.* The printer tells you when the paper runs out. ◊ *Se me acabó el tabaco.* I ran out of cigarettes.

la **academia** SUSTANTIVO
school ◊ *una academia de idiomas* a language school
◆**una academia militar** a military academy

académico ADJETIVO
academic ◊ *el curso académico* the academic year

la **acampada** SUSTANTIVO
◆**ir de acampada** to go camping

acampar VERBO
to camp

el **acantilado** SUSTANTIVO
cliff

acariciar VERBO
1 to stroke (*pelo, animal*)
2 to caress (*mejilla, niño, amante*)

acaso ADVERBIO
◆**¿Acaso tengo yo la culpa?** Is it MY fault?
◆**por si acaso** just in case
◆**No necesito nada; si acaso, un poco de leche.** I don't need anything; well maybe a little milk.
◆**Si acaso lo vieras, dile que me llame.** If you should see him, tell him to call me.

acatarrarse VERBO
to catch cold

acceder VERBO
◆**acceder a (1)** to agree to ◊ *Al final accedió a venir.* In the end he agreed to come.
◆**acceder a (2)** (*un lugar*) to gain access to

accesible ADJETIVO
1 accessible ◊ *Es un lugar sólo accesible por barco.* The place is only accessible by boat.
2 approachable ◊ *Es una persona muy accesible.* He's very approachable.

el **acceso** SUSTANTIVO
access ◊ *La casa tiene acceso por delante y por detrás.* Access to the house

is from the front and from the rear. ◊ *Tiene acceso a información confidencial.* He has access to confidential information.

♦ **Quieren mejorar los accesos al aeropuerto.** They want to improve access to the airport.

♦ **las pruebas de acceso a la universidad** university entrance exams

el **accesorio** SUSTANTIVO
accessories ◊ *accesorios para el automóvil* car accessories

accidentado ADJETIVO
1 rough (*terreno*)
2 eventful (*viaje*)

el **accidente** SUSTANTIVO
accident ◊ *los accidentes de trabajo* accidents in the workplace

♦ **Han tenido un accidente.** They've had a car accident.

la **acción** SUSTANTIVO (PL las **acciones**)
1 action ◊ *una película llena de acción* an action-packed film

♦ **entrar en acción** to go into action

2 share ◊ *comprar acciones de una empresa* to buy shares in a company

el/la **accionista** SUSTANTIVO
shareholder

el **aceite** SUSTANTIVO
oil

♦ **el aceite de girasol** sunflower oil

♦ **el aceite de oliva** olive oil

aceitoso ADJETIVO
oily

la **aceituna** SUSTANTIVO
olive ◊ *aceitunas rellenas* stuffed olives

el **acelerador** SUSTANTIVO
accelerator

acelerar VERBO
to accelerate ◊ *Aceleré para adelantarlos.* I accelerated to overtake them.

♦ **¡Acelera, que no llegamos!** Speed up or we'll never get there!

♦ **acelerar el paso** to walk faster

las **acelgas** SUSTANTIVO
Swiss chard SING

el **acento** SUSTANTIVO
1 accent (*tilde, pronunciación*) ◊ *"Té" lleva acento cuando significa "bebida".* "Té" has an accent when it means "drink". ◊ *Tiene un acento cerrado del sur.* He has a strong southern accent.
2 stress (*en sílaba sin tilde*) ◊ *¿Qué sílaba lleva el acento en "microphone"?* Which syllable is the stress on in "microphone"?

acentuarse* VERBO
to have an accent ◊ *No se acentúa.* It doesn't have an accent.

aceptable ADJETIVO
acceptable

aceptar VERBO
to accept ◊ *Acepté su invitación.* I accepted his invitation. ◊ *Cuesta aceptar la derrota.* It's hard to accept defeat.

♦ **aceptar hacer algo** to agree to do something

la **acequia** SUSTANTIVO
irrigation channel

la **acera** SUSTANTIVO
pavement

acerca ADVERBIO

♦ **acerca de** about ◊ *un documental acerca de la fauna africana* a documentary about African wildlife

acercar* VERBO
1 to pass ◊ *¿Me acercas los alicates?* Could you pass me the pliers?
2 to bring over ◊ *Acerca la silla.* Bring your chair over here.

♦ **¿Acerco más la cama a la ventana?** Shall I put the bed nearer the window?

♦ **Nos acercaron al aeropuerto.** They gave us a lift to the airport.

♦ **acercarse (1)** to come closer ◊ *Acércate, que te vea.* Come closer so that I can see you.

♦ **acercarse (2)** to go over ◊ *Me acerqué a la ventana.* I went over to the window. ◊ *Acércate a la tienda y trae una botella de agua.* Go over to the shop and get a bottle of water.

♦ **Ya se acerca la Navidad.** Christmas is getting near.

el **acero** SUSTANTIVO
steel ◊ *acero inoxidable* stainless steel

acertar* VERBO
1 to get...right (*pregunta, respuesta, solución*) ◊ *He acertado todas las respuestas.* I got all the answers right.

♦ **No acerté.** I got it wrong.

♦ **Creo que hemos acertado con estas cortinas.** I think these curtains were a good choice.

2 to guess ◊ *Si aciertas cuántos caramelos hay, te los regalo todos.* If you guess how many sweets there are, I'll give you them all.

♦ **Acerté en el blanco.** I hit the target.

ácido ADJETIVO
acid

el **ácido** SUSTANTIVO
acid

acierto VERBO *ver* **acertar**

el **acierto** SUSTANTIVO
1 right answer ◊ *Tuve más aciertos que fallos en el examen.* I got more right answers than wrong ones in the exam.
2 good idea ◊ *Fue un acierto ir de vacaciones a la montaña.* Going to the mountains on holiday was a good idea.

aclarar VERBO

* Verbs marked with this symbol are irregular. See pages 380-382 for further details

1 to rinse ◇ *Aclara la ropa antes de tenderla.* Rinse the washing before hanging it out.
2 to clear up ◇ *Necesito que me aclares unas dudas.* I need you to clear up some doubts for me. ◇ *No me iré hasta que no se aclare este asunto.* I shan't go until this business is cleared up.
♦ **Con tantos números no me aclaro.** There are so many numbers that I can't get it straight.

el **acné** SUSTANTIVO
acne

acobardarse VERBO
♦ **No se acobarda por nada.** He isn't frightened by anything.

acogedor ADJETIVO (FEM **acogedora**)
cosy ◇ *un cuarto muy acogedor* a very cosy room

acoger* VERBO
to receive ◇ *La ciudad acoge todos los años a miles de visitantes.* The city receives thousands of visitors every year.
♦ **Me acogieron muy bien en Estados Unidos.** I was made very welcome in the United States.

la **acogida** SUSTANTIVO
reception ◇ *una fría acogida* a cold reception
♦ **una calurosa acogida** a warm welcome
♦ **tener buena acogida** to be well received

acomodado ADJETIVO
well-off

el **acomodador** SUSTANTIVO
usher

la **acomodadora** SUSTANTIVO
usherette

acompañar VERBO
1 to come with ◇ *Si vas al centro te acompaño.* If you're going to the centre of town I'll come with you.
2 to go with ◇ *Me pidió que la acompañara a la estación.* She asked me to go to the station with her.
♦ **¿Quieres que te acompañe a casa?** Would you like me to see you home?
3 to stay with ◇ *Me acompañó hasta que llegó el autobús.* He stayed with me until the bus arrived.

aconsejar VERBO
1 to advise
♦ **aconsejar a alguien que haga algo** to advise somebody to do something
♦ **Te aconsejo que lo hagas.** I'd advise you to do it.
2 to recommend ◇ *Debe de ser bueno cuando lo aconseja el médico.* It must be good if the doctor recommends it.

el **acontecimiento** SUSTANTIVO
event

acordar* VERBO
to agree on ◇ *Acordamos un precio y unas condiciones.* We agreed on a price and terms.
♦ **acordar hacer algo** to agree to do something

acordarse* VERBO
to remember ◇ *Ahora mismo no me acuerdo.* Right now I can't remember.
♦ **acordarse de** to remember ◇ *¿Te acuerdas de mí?* Do you remember me? ◇ *Acuérdate de cerrar la puerta con llave.* Remember to lock the door.
♦ **acordarse de haber hecho algo** to remember doing something

el **acordeón** SUSTANTIVO (PL los **acordeones**)
accordion

acostado ADJETIVO
♦ **estar acostado** to be in bed

acostarse* VERBO
1 to lie down (*para descansar*)
2 to go to bed (*para dormir*)
♦ **acostarse con alguien** to go to bed with somebody

acostumbrarse VERBO
♦ **acostumbrarse a** to get used to ◇ *No me acostumbro a la vida en la ciudad.* I can't get used to city life.
♦ **acostumbrarse a hacer algo** to get used to doing something ◇ *Ya me he acostumbrado a trabajar de noche.* I've got used to working at night now.

el/la **acróbata** SUSTANTIVO
acrobat

la **actitud** SUSTANTIVO
attitude

la **actividad** SUSTANTIVO
activity (PL activities)

activo ADJETIVO
active ◇ *Es una mujer muy activa.* She's a very active woman.

el **acto** SUSTANTIVO
1 act ◇ *Romper el carnet fue un acto de rebeldía.* Tearing his ID card up was an act of rebellion.
2 ceremony (PL ceremonies) ◇ *Grandes personalidades acudieron al acto.* There were some important people at the ceremony.
♦ **acto seguido** immediately afterwards ◇ *Acto seguido la gente echó a correr.* Immediately afterwards people began running.
♦ **en el acto** instantly
♦ **Te arreglan tus zapatos en el acto.** They will repair your shoes while you wait.

el **actor** SUSTANTIVO
actor

la **actriz** SUSTANTIVO (PL las **actrices**)
actress (PL actresses)

la **actuación** SUSTANTIVO (PL las **actuaciones**)
1 performance ◇ *Fue una actuación muy buena.* It was a very good performance.

☞

2 gig ◊ *Esta noche tenemos una actuación en el Café del Jazz.* Tonight we're doing a gig at the Café del Jazz.

actual ADJETIVO
present ◊ *la situación actual del país* the country's present situation
◆**uno de los mejores pintores del arte actual** one of the greatest painters of today

*No confundir **actual** con la palabra inglesa **actual**.*

la **actualidad** SUSTANTIVO
◆**un repaso a la actualidad nacional** a round-up of the national news
◆**un tema de gran actualidad** a very topical issue
◆**en la actualidad (1)** (*ahora*) currently ◊ *Hay en la actualidad más de 2 millones de parados.* There are currently over 2 million unemployed.
◆**en la actualidad (2)** (*hoy en día*) nowadays ◊ *Eso ya no ocurre en la actualidad.* That doesn't happen nowadays.

actualmente ADVERBIO
1 nowadays (*hoy día*) ◊ *Actualmente apenas se utilizan las máquinas de escribir.* Typewriters are hardly used nowadays.
2 currently (*ahora*) ◊ *Soy geólogo, pero actualmente estoy en paro.* I'm a geologist but I'm currently out of work.

*No confundir **actualmente** con **actually**.*

actuar* VERBO
1 to act ◊ *Es difícil actuar con naturalidad delante de las cámaras.* It's hard to act naturally in front of the cameras.
◆**Hay que actuar con cautela.** We'll have to be cautious.
◆**No comprendo tu forma de actuar.** I can't understand your behaviour.
◆**No actuó en esa película.** He wasn't in that film.
2 to perform (*grupo musical, teatral, humorista*) ◊ *Hoy actúan en el Café del Jazz.* Today they'll be performing at the Café del Jazz.

la **acuarela** SUSTANTIVO
watercolour

el **acuario** SUSTANTIVO
aquarium

Acuario SUSTANTIVO MASC
Aquarius ◊ *Soy Acuario.* I'm Aquarius.

acuático ADJETIVO
◆**esquí acuático** water skiing

acudir VERBO
1 to go ◊ *Acudieron en su ayuda.* They went to her aid. ◊ *Acudió a un amigo en busca de consejo.* He went to a friend for advice.
◆**No tengo a quien acudir.** I have no one to turn to.
◆**acudir a una cita** to keep an appointment
2 to come ◊ *El perro acude cuando lo llamo.* The dog comes when I call.

acuerdo VERBO *ver* **acordar**

el **acuerdo** SUSTANTIVO
agreement ◊ *llegar a un acuerdo* to reach an agreement
◆**estar de acuerdo con alguien** to agree with somebody
◆**ponerse de acuerdo** to agree ◊ *Al final no nos pusimos de acuerdo.* In the end we couldn't agree. ◊ *Nos pusimos de acuerdo para prepararle una bienvenida.* We agreed to organize a welcome for him.
◆**¡De acuerdo!** All right!

la **acupuntura** SUSTANTIVO
acupuncture

acurrucarse* VERBO
to curl up

acusar VERBO
1 to accuse ◊ *Su novia lo acusaba de mentiroso.* His girlfriend accused him of being a liar.
◆**Los otros te acusan a ti de haber roto el jarrón.** The others say it was you who broke the vase.
2 to charge ◊ *Me acusan de homicidio.* They're charging me with homicide.

acústico ADJETIVO
acoustic ◊ *una guitarra acústica* an acoustic guitar

adaptar VERBO
to adapt ◊ *Es la misma receta pero adaptada.* It's the same recipe, but I've adapted it.
◆**adaptarse** to adapt ◊ *No consigo adaptarme a la vida en el campo.* I can't seem to adapt to country life.

adecuado ADJETIVO
1 suitable ◊ *No es la ropa más adecuada para ir de boda.* They aren't the most suitable clothes to wear to a wedding.
2 right ◊ *Has entrado en el momento adecuado.* You've arrived at just the right moment. ◊ *el hombre adecuado para el puesto* the right man for the job

a. de J.C. ABREVIATURA (= *antes de Jesucristo*)
B.C. (= before Christ)

adelantado ADJETIVO
1 advanced ◊ *Suecia es un país muy adelantado.* Sweden is a very advanced country.
◆**los niños más adelantados de la clase** the children who are doing best in the class

[2] fast ◊ *Este reloj va adelantado.* This watch is fast.
♦ **pagar por adelantado** to pay in advance

adelantar VERBO
[1] to bring...forward ◊ *Tuvimos que adelantar la boda.* We had to bring the wedding forward.
[2] to overtake ◊ *Adelanta a ese camión cuando puedas.* Overtake that lorry when you can.
[3] to put...forward ◊ *El domingo hay que adelantar los relojes una hora.* On Sunday we'll have to put the clocks forward an hour.
♦ **Así no adelantas nada.** You won't get anywhere that way.
♦ **Tu reloj adelanta.** Your watch gains.

adelantarse VERBO
to go on ahead ◊ *Me adelanté para coger asiento.* I went on ahead to get a seat.
♦ **adelantarse a alguien** to get ahead of somebody ◊ *Se nos adelantaron los de la competencia.* The competition got ahead of us.

adelante (1) ADVERBIO
forward ◊ *Se inclinó hacia adelante.* He leant forward.
♦ **¿Nos vamos adelante para ver mejor?** Shall we sit near the front to get a better view?
♦ **más adelante (1)** (*más allá*) further on ◊ *El pueblo está más adelante.* The village is further on.
♦ **más adelante (2)** (*después*) later ◊ *Más adelante hablaremos de los resultados.* Later we'll discuss the results.
♦ **adelante de** [Latin America] in front of
♦ **Hay que seguir adelante.** We must go on.
♦ **de ahora en adelante** from now on

adelante (2) EXCLAMACIÓN
[1] come on! (*para animar*)
[2] come in! (*autorizando a entrar*)

el **adelanto** SUSTANTIVO
advance ◊ *los adelantos de la ciencia* the advances in science ◊ *Le pidió un adelanto a su jefe.* He asked his boss for an advance.

adelgazar* VERBO
to lose weight ◊ *¡Cómo has adelgazado!* What a lot of weight you've lost!
♦ **He adelgazado cinco kilos.** I've lost five kilos.

además ADVERBIO
[1] as well ◊ *Es profesor y además carpintero.* He's a teacher and a carpenter as well.
[2] what's more ◊ *El dormitorio es demasiado pequeño y, además, no tiene ventana.* The bedroom's too small and, what's more, it hasn't got a window.
[3] besides ◊ *Además, no tienes nada que perder.* Besides, you've got nothing to lose.
♦ **además de** as well as ◊ *El ordenador es, además de rápido, eficaz.* The computer is efficient as well as fast.

adentro ADVERBIO
inside ◊ *Empezó a llover y se metieron adentro.* It began to rain so they went inside.
♦ **tierra adentro** inland
♦ **adentro de** [Latin America] inside ◊ *desde adentro de la casa* from inside the house

adhesivo ADJETIVO
sticky ◊ *cinta adhesiva* sticky tape

el **adhesivo** SUSTANTIVO
sticker

la **adicción** SUSTANTIVO (PL las **adicciones**)
addiction

la **adición** SUSTANTIVO (PL las **adiciones**)
[River Plate]
bill

adicto ADJETIVO
addicted ◊ *Es adicto a la cafeína.* He is addicted to caffeine.

el **adicto,** la **adicta** SUSTANTIVO
addict ◊ *un adicto a las drogas* a drug addict

adinerado ADJETIVO
wealthy

adiós EXCLAMACIÓN
[1] goodbye! (*para despedirse*)
♦ **decir adiós a alguien** to say goodbye to somebody
[2] hello! (*al pasar*)

el **aditivo** SUSTANTIVO
additive

la **adivinanza** SUSTANTIVO
guess (PL guesses)

adivinar VERBO
to guess ◊ *Adivina quién viene.* Guess who's coming.
♦ **adivinar el pensamiento a alguien** to read somebody's mind
♦ **adivinar el futuro** to see into the future

el **adjetivo** SUSTANTIVO
adjective

adjunto ADJETIVO
[1] enclosed (*en el mismo sobre*)
[2] attached (*con grapas, clips*)
[3] deputy ◊ *el director adjunto* the deputy head

la **administración** SUSTANTIVO (PL las **administraciones**)
[1] administration ◊ *Master de Administración de Empresas* Master of Business Administration
[2] civil service ◊ *Carmen trabaja en la administración.* Carmen works for the civil service.

el **administrador de Web,** la **administradora de Web** SUSTANTIVO
webmaster

administrativo ADJETIVO
administrative ◇ *gastos administrativos* administrative expenses
♦ **trabajo administrativo** clerical work

el **administrativo,** la **administrativa** SUSTANTIVO
clerk

la **admiración** SUSTANTIVO
1 admiration ◇ *Siento profunda admiración por él.* I have great admiration for him.
2 amazement ◇ *para admiración de todos* to everyone's amazement
♦ **Su franqueza causó admiración entre los presentes.** His frankness amazed everyone there.
♦ **signo de admiración** exclamation mark

admirar VERBO
to admire ◇ *Todos la admiran.* Everyone admires her.
♦ **Me admira lo poco que gastas en ropa.** I'm amazed at how little you spend on clothes.

admitir VERBO
1 to admit ◇ *Admite que estabas equivocado.* Admit you were wrong.
2 to accept ◇ *La máquina no admite monedas de 500 pesetas.* The machine doesn't accept 500-peseta coins.
♦ **Espero que me admitan a la universidad.** I hope I'll get a place at university.
3 to allow in ◇ *Aquí no admiten perros.* Dogs aren't allowed in here.

el/la **adolescente** SUSTANTIVO
teenager

adonde CONJUNCIÓN
where
♦ **la ciudad adonde nos dirigimos** the city we're going to

adónde ADVERBIO
where ◇ *¿Adónde ibas?* Where were you going?

la **adopción** SUSTANTIVO (PL las **adopciones**)
adoption

adoptar VERBO
to adopt

adoptivo ADJETIVO
♦ **un hijo adoptivo** an adopted child
♦ **mis padres adoptivos** my adoptive parents

adorar VERBO
1 to adore ◇ *Adora a sus hijos.* He adores his children.
2 to worship ◇ *adorar a Dios* to worship God

adornar VERBO
to decorate

el **adorno** SUSTANTIVO
1 ornament ◇ *Quitó los adornos de la estantería para limpiarla.* He took the ornaments off the shelf to clean it.
2 decoration ◇ *Habían puesto adornos en las calles.* Decorations had been put up in the streets. ◇ *Es sólo de adorno.* It's only for decoration.

adosado ADJETIVO
♦ **un chalet adosado** a semi-detached house

adquirir* VERBO
to acquire ◇ *adquirir conocimientos de algo* to acquire a knowledge of something
♦ **adquirir velocidad** to gain speed
♦ **adquirir fama** to achieve fame
♦ **adquirir una vivienda** to purchase a property
♦ **adquirir importancia** to become important
♦ **Lo podrá adquirir en tiendas especializadas.** You'll be able to get it from specialist shops.

adrede ADVERBIO
on purpose

la **aduana** SUSTANTIVO
customs SING

el **aduanero,** la **aduanera** SUSTANTIVO
customs officer

el **adulto** SUSTANTIVO
adult
♦ **educación de adultos** adult education

el **adverbio** SUSTANTIVO
adverb

el **adversario,** la **adversaria** SUSTANTIVO
opponent

la **advertencia** SUSTANTIVO
warning

advertir* VERBO
1 to warn ◇ *Ya te advertí que no intervinieras.* I warned you not to get involved.
♦ **advertir a alguien de algo** to warn somebody about something
♦ **Te advierto que no va a ser nada fácil.** I must warn you that it won't be at all easy.
2 to notice ◇ *No advertí nada extraño en su comportamiento.* I didn't notice anything strange about his behaviour.

aéreo ADJETIVO
air

> ***air** en este caso va siempre delante del sustantivo.*

◇ *un ataque aéreo* an air raid
♦ **por vía aérea** by air mail
♦ **una fotografía aérea** an aerial photograph

el **aerobic** SUSTANTIVO
aerobics SING

el **aeromozo,** la **aeromoza** SUSTANTIVO

* Verbs marked with this symbol are irregular. See pages 380-382 for further details

Latin America
flight attendant

el **aeropuerto** SUSTANTIVO
airport

el **aerosol** SUSTANTIVO
aerosol

el **afán** SUSTANTIVO (PL los **afanes**)
1 ambition (*deseo*) ◊ *Todo su afán era ser pintora.* Her great ambition was to be a painter.
2 effort (*empeño*)
♦**Trabajan con mucho afán.** They put a lot of effort into their work.

afectado ADJETIVO
upset ◊ *Está muy afectado por la noticia.* He's very upset at the news.

afectar VERBO
to affect ◊ *Esto a ti no te afecta.* This doesn't affect you.
♦**Me afectó mucho la noticia.** The news upset me terribly.

afectivo ADJETIVO
emotional ◊ *problemas afectivos* emotional problems

el **afecto** SUSTANTIVO
affection ◊ *Me cuesta demostrar afecto.* I find it difficult to show affection.
♦**tener afecto a alguien** to be fond of somebody

afectuoso ADJETIVO
affectionate ◊ *Es un chico muy afectuoso.* He's a very affectionate boy.
♦**"Un saludo afectuoso"** (*en cartas*) "With best wishes"

afeitar VERBO
to shave
♦**afeitarse** to shave ◊ *Voy a afeitarme.* I'm going to shave.
♦**Me afeité la barba.** I shaved off my beard.

Afganistán SUSTANTIVO MASC
Afghanistan

el **afiche** SUSTANTIVO Latin America
poster

la **afición** SUSTANTIVO (PL las **aficiones**)
1 hobby (PL hobbies) ◊ *Mi afición es la filatelia.* My hobby is stamp collecting.
◊ *por afición* as a hobby
♦**Tengo mucha afición por el ciclismo.** I'm very keen on cycling.
♦**En este país hay poca afición al teatro.** In this country people aren't very interested in the theatre.
2 fans PL ◊ *la afición del Athletic* the Athletic fans

aficionado ADJETIVO
1 keen ◊ *Es muy aficionada a la pintura.* She's very keen on painting.
2 amateur ◊ *un equipo de fútbol aficionado* an amateur football team

el **aficionado**, la **aficionada** SUSTANTIVO
1 enthusiast ◊ *un libro para los aficionados al bricolaje* a book for DIY enthusiasts
2 lover ◊ *los aficionados al teatro* theatre lovers
3 amateur ◊ *un partido para aficionados* a game for amateurs

aficionarse VERBO
♦**aficionarse a algo (1)** (*como participante*) to take up something ◊ *Raúl se aficionó al billar.* Raúl took up billiards.
♦**aficionarse a algo (2)** (*como espectador*) to become interested in something ◊ *Me he aficionado al teatro.* I've become interested in the theatre.
♦**Me he aficionado al chocolate suizo.** I've developed a taste for Swiss chocolate.

afilado ADJETIVO
sharp

afilar VERBO
to sharpen

afiliarse VERBO
♦**afiliarse a algo** to join something

afinar VERBO
to tune ◊ *afinar un violín* to tune a violin

afirmar VERBO
♦**afirmar que ...** to say that ... ◊ *Afirmaba que no la conocía.* He said that he didn't know her.
♦**Afirma haberla visto aquella noche.** He says that he saw her that night.

afirmativo ADJETIVO
affirmative

aflojar VERBO
to loosen (*cuerda, corbata, tornillo*)
♦**Tengo que aflojarme la corbata.** I must loosen my tie.
♦**aflojarse** to come loose ◊ *Se ha aflojado un tornillo.* A screw has come loose.

el **afluente** SUSTANTIVO
tributary (PL tributaries)

afónico ADJETIVO
♦**Estoy afónico.** I've lost my voice.

el **aforo** SUSTANTIVO
(*de teatro, cine*)
capacity (PL capacities) ◊ *El teatro tiene un aforo de 2.000 personas.* The theatre has a capacity of 2,000 people.

afortunado ADJETIVO
lucky ◊ *Es un tipo afortunado.* He's a lucky guy.

África SUSTANTIVO FEM
Africa

el **africano**, la **africana** ADJETIVO, SUSTANTIVO
African

afrontar VERBO
to face up to ◊ *afrontar un problema* to face up to a problem

afuera ADVERBIO
outside ◊ *Vámonos afuera.* Let's go outside.
♦**afuera de** Latin America outside

las **afueras** SUSTANTIVO
outskirts ◊ *en las afueras de Barcelona* on the outskirts of Barcelona
♦ **un barrio a las afueras de Londres** a London suburb

agacharse VERBO
1 to crouch down (*en cuclillas*)
2 to bend down (*hacia delante*)

la **agarradera** SUSTANTIVO Latin America
handle

agarrado ADJETIVO
stingy (*coloquial*)

agarrar VERBO
1 to grab ◊ *Agarró al niño por el hombro.* He grabbed the child by the shoulder.
2 to hold ◊ *Agarra bien la sartén.* Hold the frying pan firmly.
3 to catch ◊ *Ya han agarrado al ladrón.* They've already caught the thief. ◊ *He agarrado un buen resfriado.* I've caught an awful cold.
4 to take Latin America ◊ *Agarré otro pedazo de pastel.* I took another piece of cake.
♦ **agarrarse** to hold on ◊ *Agárrate a la barandilla.* Hold on to the rail.

la **agencia** SUSTANTIVO
agency (PL agencies) ◊ *una agencia de noticias* a news agency ◊ *una agencia de publicidad* an advertising agency
♦ **una agencia inmobiliaria** an estate agent's
♦ **una agencia de viajes** a travel agent's

la **agenda** SUSTANTIVO
1 (*de notas, trabajo*)
diary (PL diaries)
2 (*de direcciones, teléfonos*)
address book

*No confundir **agenda** con la palabra inglesa **agenda**.*

el/la **agente** SUSTANTIVO
agent (*secreto, de artistas*)
♦ **un agente de bolsa** a stockbroker
♦ **un agente de seguros** an insurance broker
♦ **un agente de policía** a police officer

ágil ADJETIVO
agile

agitado ADJETIVO
hectic

agitar VERBO
1 to stir ◊ *Agitaba su café con una cucharilla.* He was stirring his coffee with a teaspoon.
2 to shake ◊ *Agítese antes de usar.* Shake before use.
3 to wave ◊ *La gente agitaba los pañuelos.* People were waving their handkerchiefs.

aglomerarse VERBO
♦ **La gente se aglomeraba a la entrada.** People were crowding around the entrance.

agobiante ADJETIVO
1 stifling (*calor*)
2 overwhelming (*situación*)
3 exhausting (*trabajo*)

agobiar VERBO
♦ **Le agobian sus problemas.** His problems are getting on top of him.
♦ **agobiarse** to worry ◊ *No te agobies; ya encontraremos una solución.* Don't worry, we'll find a solution.

agosto SUSTANTIVO MASC

Los meses se escriben con mayúscula.

August ◊ *en agosto* in August ◊ *Nació el 8 de agosto.* He was born on 8 August.

agotado ADJETIVO
1 exhausted ◊ *Estoy agotado.* I'm exhausted.
2 sold out ◊ *Ese modelo en concreto está agotado.* That particular model is sold out.

agotador ADJETIVO (FEM **agotadora**)
exhausting

agotar VERBO
1 to use up ◊ *Agotamos todas nuestras reservas de combustible.* We used up all our fuel supplies.
2 to tire out ◊ *Me agota tanto ejercicio.* All this exercise is tiring me out.
♦ **agotarse** to run out ◊ *Se está agotando la leña.* The firewood's running out.
♦ **Se agotaron todas las entradas.** The tickets sold out.

agradable ADJETIVO
nice

agradar VERBO
♦ **Esto no me agrada.** I don't like this.

agradecer* VERBO
♦ **agradecer algo a alguien** to thank somebody for something
♦ **Te agradezco tu interés.** Thank you for your interest.
♦ **Le agradecería me enviara ...** I should be grateful if you would send me ...

agradecido ADJETIVO
♦ **estar agradecido a alguien por algo** to be grateful to somebody for something

agrario ADJETIVO
agricultural ◊ *la política agraria* agricultural policy

agredir VERBO
to attack

la **agresión** SUSTANTIVO (PL las **agresiones**)
1 attack ◊ *una brutal agresión de dos jóvenes* a brutal attack on two young people
2 aggression ◊ *un acto de agresión* an act of aggression

agresivo ADJETIVO

* Verbs marked with this symbol are irregular. See pages 380-382 for further details

aggressive

agrícola ADJETIVO
agricultural

el **agricultor,** la **agricultora** SUSTANTIVO
farmer

la **agricultura** SUSTANTIVO
farming

agridulce ADJETIVO
sweet-and-sour ◇ *salsa agridulce* sweet-and-sour sauce

agrio ADJETIVO
[1] sour (*leche*)
[2] tart (*limón, vino*)

la **agrupación** SUSTANTIVO (PL las **agrupaciones**)
group

agrupar VERBO
[1] to group ◇ *agrupados en distintas categorías* grouped into different categories ◇ *Los insectos se agrupan en varias categorías.* Insects can be grouped into several categories.
[2] to bring together ◇ *una organización que agrupa a varios países* an organization which brings several countries together
◆ **Los ecologistas se han agrupado en varios partidos.** The ecologists have formed several parties.
◆ **Se agruparon en torno a su jefe.** They gathered round their boss.

el **agua** SUSTANTIVO FEM
water
◆ **agua corriente** running water
◆ **agua potable** drinking water
◆ **agua dulce** fresh water
◆ **agua salada** salt water
◆ **agua de colonia** cologne
◆ **agua oxigenada** peroxide

el **aguacate** SUSTANTIVO
avocado (PL avocados)

el/la **aguafiestas** SUSTANTIVO (PL los/las **aguafiestas**)
spoilsport

el **aguanieve** SUSTANTIVO FEM
sleet

aguantar VERBO
[1] to stand ◇ *No aguanto la ópera.* I can't stand opera. ◇ *Su vecina no la aguanta.* Her neighbour can't stand her.
[2] to take ◇ *La estantería no va a aguantar el peso.* The shelf won't take the weight. ◇ *¡No aguanto más!* I can't take any more!
[3] to hold ◇ *Aguántame el martillo un momento.* Can you hold the hammer for me for a moment? ◇ *Aguanta la respiración.* Hold your breath.
[4] to last ◇ *Este abrigo ya no aguanta otro invierno.* This coat won't last another winter.
◆ **No pude aguantar la risa.** I couldn't help laughing.
◆ **Últimamente estás que no hay quien te aguante.** You've been unbearable lately.
◆ **¿Puedes aguantarte hasta que lleguemos a casa?** Can you hold out until we get home?
◆ **Si no puede venir, que se aguante.** If he can't come, he'll just have to lump it.

el **aguante** SUSTANTIVO
◆ **tener aguante (1)** (*paciencia*) to be patient
◆ **tener aguante (2)** (*resistencia*) to have stamina

agudo ADJETIVO
[1] sharp (*oído, dolor*)
[2] high-pitched (*sonido, voz*)
[3] acute (*enfermedad*)
[4] witty (*comentario*)

el **aguijón** SUSTANTIVO (PL los **aguijones**)
sting (*de avispa, escorpión*)

el **águila** SUSTANTIVO FEM
eagle

la **aguja** SUSTANTIVO
needle (*de coser, tocadiscos*)
◆ **las agujas del reloj** the hands of the clock

el **agujero** SUSTANTIVO
[1] hole
◆ **hacer un agujero** to make a hole
[2] pocket (*en billar*)

la **agujeta** SUSTANTIVO Mexico
shoe lace

las **agujetas** SUSTANTIVO
◆ **tener agujetas** to be stiff

ahí ADVERBIO
there ◇ *¡Ahí están!* There they are! ◇ *Ahí llega el tren.* There's the train.
◆ **Ahí está el problema.** That's the problem.
◆ **ahí arriba** up there
◆ **Están ahí dentro.** They're in there.
◆ **Lo tienes ahí mismo.** You've got it right there.
◆ **de ahí que** that's why
◆ **por ahí (1)** (*en ese lugar*) over there ◇ *Tú busca por ahí.* You look over there.
◆ **por ahí (2)** (*en algún lugar*) somewhere ◇ *Nos iremos por ahí a celebrarlo.* We'll go out somewhere to celebrate.
◆ **¿Las tijeras? Andarán por ahí.** The scissors? They must be somewhere around.
◆ **por ahí (3)** (*aproximadamente*) thereabouts ◇ *200 o por ahí* 200 or thereabouts

ahogarse* VERBO
[1] to drown ◇ *Se ahogó en el río.* He drowned in the river.
[2] to suffocate ◇ *Se ahogaron por falta de aire.* They suffocated for lack of air.
[3] to get breathless ◇ *Me ahogo subiendo las cuestas.* I get breathless going uphill.

ahora ADVERBIO
now ◇ *¿Dónde vamos ahora?* Where are we going now?

☞

◆**Ahora te lo digo.** I'll tell you in a moment.
◆**ahora mismo** right now ◊ *Ahora mismo está de viaje.* He's away on a trip right now.
◆**Ahora mismo voy.** I'm just coming.
◆**de ahora en adelante** from now on
◆**hasta ahora (1)** so far ◊ *Hasta ahora nadie se ha quejado.* Nobody has complained so far.
◆**hasta ahora (2)** till now ◊ *Hasta ahora nadie se había quejado.* Nobody had complained till now.
◆**¡Hasta ahora!** See you shortly!
◆**ahora bien** however ◊ *Aceptó las condiciones. Ahora bien, hace falta que las cumpla.* He accepted the conditions. However, he now needs to comply with them.
◆**por ahora** for the moment ◊ *Por ahora no cambies nada.* Don't change anything for the moment.

ahorcar* VERBO
to hang
◆**ahorcarse** to hang oneself

ahorita ADVERBIO Latin America
now

ahorrar VERBO
to save

los **ahorros** SUSTANTIVO
savings

ahumado ADJETIVO
smoked

el **aire** SUSTANTIVO
1 air ◊ *Necesitamos aire para respirar.* We need air to breathe.
◆**aire acondicionado** air conditioning
◆**tomar el aire** to get some fresh air
2 wind ◊ *El aire se le llevó el sombrero.* The wind blew his hat off.
◆**Hace mucho aire.** It's very windy.
◆**al aire libre (1)** outdoors ◊ *Comimos al aire libre.* We had lunch outdoors.
◆**al aire libre (2)** outdoor ◊ *una fiesta al aire libre* an outdoor party

aislado ADJETIVO
isolated ◊ *Es un caso aislado.* It's an isolated case.
◆**El pueblo estaba aislado por la nieve.** The village was cut off by the snow.

el **ajedrez** SUSTANTIVO (PL los **ajedreces**)
1 chess ◊ *jugar al ajedrez* to play chess
2 chess set ◊ *Tráete el ajedrez y echamos una partida.* Get the chess set and we'll have a game.

ajeno ADJETIVO
◆**No respeta la opinión ajena.** He doesn't respect other people's opinions.
◆**por razones ajenas a nuestra voluntad** for reasons beyond our control

ajetreado ADJETIVO
busy ◊ *Ha sido un día muy ajetreado.* It has been a very busy day.

el **ají** SUSTANTIVO River Plate
chili sauce

el **ajo** SUSTANTIVO
garlic

ajustado ADJETIVO
tight ◊ *Lleva ropa muy ajustada.* He wears very tight clothes. ◊ *La falda me queda un poco ajustada.* The skirt's a bit tight on me.

ajustar VERBO
1 to adjust ◊ *Hay que ajustar los frenos.* The brakes need adjusting.
2 to tighten ◊ *Ajusté bien todas las tuercas.* I tightened up all the nuts.
3 to fit ◊ *Esta puerta no ajusta bien.* This door doesn't fit very well.
◆**ajustarse a (1)** to fit in with ◊ *Tendremos que ajustarnos al horario previsto.* We'll have to fit in with the programme. ◊ *Tu versión no se ajusta a la realidad.* Your version doesn't fit in with the facts.
◆**ajustarse a (2)** to keep to ◊ *Nos ajustaremos al presupuesto.* We'll keep to the budget.

al PREPOSICIÓN
(*= a + el*) *ver* **a**

el **ala** SUSTANTIVO FEM
1 wing (*de ave, avión*)
2 brim (*de sombrero*)

alabar VERBO
to praise

la **alambrada** SUSTANTIVO
fence ◊ *una alambrada eléctrica* an electric fence

el **alambre** SUSTANTIVO
wire

el **álamo** SUSTANTIVO
poplar

alardear VERBO
◆**alardear de algo** to boast about something

el **alargador** SUSTANTIVO
extension lead

alargar* VERBO
1 to lengthen ◊ *Hay que alargar un poco las mangas.* We'll need to lengthen the sleeves a little.
2 to extend ◊ *Van a alargar esta línea de metro.* This underground line is going to be extended. ◊ *Decidieron alargar las vacaciones.* They decided to extend their holidays.
3 to stretch out ◊ *Alargué el brazo para apagar la luz.* I stretched out my arm to put out the light.
4 to pass ◊ *¿Me alargas la llave inglesa?* Will you pass me the wrench?

* Verbs marked with this symbol are irregular. See pages 380-382 for further details

◆**alargarse (1)** to get longer ◇ *Ya van alargándose los días.* The days are getting longer.
◆**alargarse (2)** to go on ◇ *La fiesta se alargó hasta el amanecer.* The party went on into the early hours.

la **alarma** SUSTANTIVO
alarm ◇ *Saltó la alarma.* The alarm went off.
◆**dar la voz de alarma** to raise the alarm
◆**alarma de incendios** fire alarm

el **alba** SUSTANTIVO FEM
dawn
◆**al alba** at dawn

el/la **albañil** SUSTANTIVO
1 builder (*más cualificado*)
2 bricklayer (*que sólo pone ladrillos*)

el **albaricoque** SUSTANTIVO
apricot

la **alberca** SUSTANTIVO Latin America
swimming pool

el **albergue** SUSTANTIVO
1 mountain refuge (*de montaña*)
2 hostel (*para gente sin hogar*)
◆**un albergue juvenil** a youth hostel

las **albóndigas** SUSTANTIVO
meatballs

el **albornoz** SUSTANTIVO (PL los **albornoces**)
bathrobe

el **alboroto** SUSTANTIVO
racket ◇ *¡Vaya alboroto que estaban montando los niños!* What a racket the kids were making!

el **álbum** SUSTANTIVO (PL los **álbumes**)
album

la **alcachofa** SUSTANTIVO
1 artichoke (*verdura*)
2 shower head (*de ducha*)
3 rose (*de regadera*)

el **alcalde,** la **alcaldesa** SUSTANTIVO
mayor

el **alcance** SUSTANTIVO
1 range (*de arma, cohete*) ◇ *misiles de largo alcance* long-range missiles
2 scale (*de problema*) ◇ *Se desconoce el alcance de la catástrofe.* The scale of the disaster isn't yet known.
◆**Está al alcance de todos.** It's within everybody's reach.

la **alcantarilla** SUSTANTIVO
1 sewer (*para residuos*)
2 drain (*para la lluvia*)
◆**una boca de alcantarilla** a manhole

alcanzar* VERBO
1 to catch up with ◇ *La alcancé cuando salía por la puerta.* I caught up with her just as she was going out of the door.
2 to reach ◇ *alcanzar la cima de la montaña* to reach the top of the mountain
3 to find ◇ *alcanzar la fama* to find fame
4 to pass ◇ *¿Me alcanzas las tijeras?* Could you pass me the scissors?
◆**Con dos botellas alcanzará para todos.** Two bottles will be enough for all of us.

el **alcaucil** SUSTANTIVO River Plate
artichoke

la **alcoba** SUSTANTIVO
bedroom

*No confundir **alcoba** con **alcove**.*

el **alcohol** SUSTANTIVO
alcohol
◆**cerveza sin alcohol** non-alcoholic beer

alcohólico ADJETIVO
alcoholic

la **aldea** SUSTANTIVO
village

el **aldeano,** la **aldeana** SUSTANTIVO
villager

alegrar VERBO
to cheer up ◇ *Intenté alegrarlos con unos chistes.* I tried to cheer them up with a few jokes.
◆**Me alegra que hayas venido.** I'm glad you've come.
◆**alegrarse** to be glad ◇ *¿Te gusta? Me alegro.* You like it? I'm glad.
◆**alegrarse de algo** to be glad about something ◇ *Me alegro de tu ascenso.* I'm glad about your promotion.
◆**Me alegro de oír que estás bien.** I'm glad to hear that you're well.
◆**alegrarse por alguien** to be happy for somebody ◇ *Me alegro por ti.* I'm happy for you.

alegre ADJETIVO
cheerful (*tela, música, carácter*)
◆**Estoy muy alegre.** I'm feeling very happy.

la **alegría** SUSTANTIVO
◆**Sentí una gran alegría.** I was really happy.
◆**¡Qué alegría!** How lovely!

alejarse VERBO
to move away ◇ *Aléjate un poco del fuego.* Move a bit further away from the fire.
◆**El barco se iba alejando de la costa.** The boat was getting further and further away from the coast.

el **alemán,** la **alemana** ADJETIVO, SUSTANTIVO
German

el **alemán** SUSTANTIVO
German (*idioma*)

Alemania SUSTANTIVO FEM
Germany

alentador ADJETIVO (FEM **alentadora**)
encouraging

la **alergia** SUSTANTIVO
allergy (PL allergies)
◆**la alergia al polen** hay fever

la **alerta** ADJETIVO, SUSTANTIVO, ADVERBIO
alert

☞

♦ **dar la alerta** to give the alert
♦ **estar alerta** to be alert

la **aleta** SUSTANTIVO
1 fin (*de pez*)
2 flipper (*para bucear*)
3 wing (*de automóvil*)

el **alfabeto** SUSTANTIVO
alphabet

la **alfarería** SUSTANTIVO
pottery (PL potteries)

el **alfarero**, la **alfarera** SUSTANTIVO
potter

el **alféizar** SUSTANTIVO
sill

el **alfil** SUSTANTIVO
bishop

el **alfiler** SUSTANTIVO
pin

la **alfombra** SUSTANTIVO
1 rug (*pequeña*)
2 carpet (*más grande*)

la **alfombrilla** SUSTANTIVO
mat

las **algas** SUSTANTIVO
seaweed SING

algo (1) PRONOMBRE
1 something
En oraciones afirmativas y en preguntas si se espera una respuesta afirmativa.
◊ *Algo se está quemando.* Something is burning. ◊ *¿Quieres algo de comer?* Would you like something to eat? ◊ *¿Te pasa algo?* Is something the matter?
♦ **Aún queda algo de café.** There's still some coffee left.
2 anything
En preguntas en general.
◊ *¿Algo más?* Anything else? ◊ *¿Has visto algo que te guste?* Have you seen anything you liked?
♦ **algo así como** a bit like ◊ *Es algo así como una nave espacial.* It's a bit like a spaceship.
♦ **o algo así** or something of the sort
♦ **Por algo será**. There must be a reason for it.

algo (2) ADVERBIO
rather ◊ *La falda te está algo corta, pero puede valer.* The skirt's rather short on you, but it may be all right.

el **algodón** SUSTANTIVO (PL los **algodones**)
cotton ◊ *ropa de algodón* cotton clothes
♦ **Me puse algodones en los oídos.** I put cotton wool in my ears.

alguien PRONOMBRE
1 somebody
En oraciones afirmativas y en preguntas si se espera una respuesta afirmativa.
◊ *Alguien llama a la puerta.* There's somebody knocking at the door. ◊ *¿Necesitas que te ayude alguien?* Do you need somebody to help you?
2 anybody
En preguntas en general.
◊ *¿Conoces a alguien aquí?* Do you know anybody here?

algún ADJETIVO (FEM **alguna,** MASC PL **algunos**)
1 some
En oraciones afirmativas.
◊ *Algún día iré.* I'll go there some day.
2 any
*Se usa **any** en preguntas, con un sustantivo en plural.*
◊ *¿Compraste algún cuadro?* Did you buy any pictures?
♦ **¿Quieres alguna cosa más?** Was there anything else?
♦ **algún que otro** ... the odd ... ◊ *He leído algún que otro libro sobre el tema.* I've read the odd book on the subject.

alguno PRONOMBRE (FEM **alguna**)
1 somebody ◊ *Siempre hay alguno que se queja.* There's always somebody who complains.
♦ **Algunos piensan que no ocurrió así.** Some people think that it didn't happen like that.
2 one ◊ *Tiene que haber sido alguno de ellos.* It must have been one of them. ◊ *Tiene que estar en alguna de estas cajas.* It must be in one of these boxes.
3 some ◊ *Son tantas maletas que alguna siempre se pierde.* There are so many suitcases that some inevitably get lost.
♦ **Sólo conozco a algunos de los vecinos.** I only know some of the neighbours.
4 any ◊ *Necesito una aspirina. ¿Te queda alguna?* I need an aspirin. Have you got any left? ◊ *Si alguno quiere irse que se vaya.* If any of them want to leave, fine. ◊ *¿Lo sabe alguno de vosotros?* Do any of you know?

el **aliado**, la **aliada** SUSTANTIVO
ally (PL allies)

la **alianza** SUSTANTIVO
1 alliance ◊ *formar una alianza* to form an alliance
2 wedding ring (*anillo*)

aliarse* VERBO
♦ **aliarse con alguien** to form an alliance with somebody

los **alicates** SUSTANTIVO
pliers

el **aliento** SUSTANTIVO
breath ◊ *Tengo mal aliento.* I've got bad breath.
♦ **Llegué sin aliento.** I arrived out of breath.

aligerar VERBO

to make...lighter ◊ *aligerar la carga del barco* to make the cargo lighter
◆ **¡Aligera o llegaremos tarde!** Hurry up or we'll be late!
la **alimentación** SUSTANTIVO
diet ◊ *Hay que cuidar la alimentación.* You need to be sensible about your diet.
◆ **una tienda de alimentación** a grocer's shop
alimentar VERBO
to feed ◊ *alimentar a un niño* to feed a child
◆ **Esto no alimenta.** That's not very nutritious.
◆ **alimentarse de algo** to live on something
el **alimento** SUSTANTIVO
food
◆ **alimentos congelados** frozen food SING
◆ **Las legumbres tienen mucho alimento.** Pulses are very nutritious.
la **alineación** SUSTANTIVO (PL las **alineaciones**)
line-up
aliñar VERBO
to season
el **aliño** SUSTANTIVO
dressing
aliviar VERBO
to make...better ◊ *El jarabe te aliviará la tos.* The syrup will make your cough better. ◊ *Estas pastillas te aliviarán.* These pills will make you better.
el **alivio** SUSTANTIVO
relief
◆ **¡Qué alivio!** What a relief!
allá ADVERBIO
there ◊ *allá arriba* up there
◆ **más allá** further on
◆ **Échate un poco más allá.** Move over that way a bit.
◆ **más allá de** beyond
◆ **¡Allá tú!** That's up to you!
◆ **el más allá** the next world
allanar VERBO
to level
allí ADVERBIO
there ◊ *Allí está.* There it is.
◆ **Allí viene tu hermana.** Here comes your sister.
◆ **allí abajo** down there
◆ **allí mismo** right there
◆ **Marta es de por allí.** Marta comes from somewhere around there.
el **alma** SUSTANTIVO FEM
soul
◆ **Lo siento en el alma.** I'm really sorry.
el **almacén** SUSTANTIVO (PL los **almacenes**)
store
◆ **unos grandes almacenes** a department store
almacenar VERBO
to store
la **almeja** SUSTANTIVO
clam
la **almendra** SUSTANTIVO
almond
el **almíbar** SUSTANTIVO
syrup
◆ **en almíbar** in syrup
el **almirante** SUSTANTIVO
admiral
la **almohada** SUSTANTIVO
pillow
la **almohadilla** SUSTANTIVO
cushion
almorzar* VERBO
to have lunch ◊ *No he almorzado todavía.* I haven't had lunch yet.
◆ **¿Qué has almorzado?** What did you have for lunch?
almuerzo VERBO *ver* **almorzar**
el **almuerzo** SUSTANTIVO
lunch (PL lunches)
aló EXCLAMACIÓN Latin America
hello!
alocado ADJETIVO
crazy ◊ *una decisión alocada* a crazy decision
◆ **una chica un poco alocada** a rather silly girl
el **alojamiento** SUSTANTIVO
accommodation
alojarse VERBO
to stay ◊ *¿Dónde os alojáis?* Where are you staying?
la **alpargata** SUSTANTIVO
espadrille
los **Alpes** SUSTANTIVO
the Alps
el **alpinismo** SUSTANTIVO
mountaineering
el/la **alpinista** SUSTANTIVO
mountaineer
alquilar VERBO
1 to rent (*el inquilino*) ◊ *Alquilaremos un apartamento en la playa.* We'll rent an apartment near the beach.
2 to let (*el dueño*) ◊ *Alquilan habitaciones a estudiantes.* They let rooms to students.
◆ **"se alquila"** "to let"
3 to hire (*coche, bicicleta, traje*) ◊ *Alquilamos un coche.* We hired a car.
el **alquiler** SUSTANTIVO
rent ◊ *pagar el alquiler* to pay the rent
◆ **un piso de alquiler** a rented flat
◆ **un coche de alquiler** a hire car
◆ **alquiler de automóviles** car-hire
alrededor ADVERBIO
◆ **alrededor de (1)** around ◊ *El satélite gira alrededor de la Tierra.* The satellite goes around the Earth. ◊ *A su alrededor todos gritaban.* Everybody around him was shouting.

☞

♦ **alrededor de (2)** about ◊ *Deben de ser alrededor de las dos.* It must be about two o'clock.

los **alrededores** SUSTANTIVO

♦ **Ocurrió en los alrededores de Madrid.** It happened near Madrid.

♦ **Hay muchas tiendas en los alrededores del museo.** There are a lot of shops in the area around the museum.

el **alta** SUSTANTIVO FEM

♦ **dar de alta a alguien** (*en hospital*) to discharge somebody

♦ **darse de alta** (*en club, asociación*) to join

el **altar** SUSTANTIVO

altar

el **altavoz** SUSTANTIVO (PL los **altavoces**)

loudspeaker

alterar VERBO

to change ◊ *Alteraron el orden.* They changed the order.

♦ **alterar el orden público** to cause a breach of the peace

♦ **alterarse** to get upset ◊ *¡No te alteres!* Don't get upset!

alternar VERBO

♦ **alternar algo con algo** to alternate something with something

♦ **Alterna con gente del teatro.** He mixes with people from the theatre.

la **alternativa** SUSTANTIVO

alternative

♦ **No tenemos otra alternativa.** We have no alternative.

alterno ADJETIVO

alternate ◊ *en días alternos* on alternate days

♦ **corriente alterna** alternating current

los **altibajos** SUSTANTIVO

ups and downs ◊ *tener altibajos* to have ups and downs

la **altitud** SUSTANTIVO

altitude

alto (1) ADJETIVO

1 tall ◊ *Es un chico muy alto.* He's a very tall boy. ◊ *un edificio muy alto* a very tall building

2 high ◊ *El Everest es la montaña más alta del mundo.* Everest is the highest mountain in the world. ◊ *Sacó notas altas en todos los exámenes.* He got high marks in all his exams.

3 loud ◊ *La música está demasiado alta.* The music's too loud.

♦ **a altas horas de la noche** in the middle of the night

♦ **Celebraron la victoria por todo lo alto.** They celebrated the victory in style.

♦ **alta fidelidad** hi-fi

♦ **una familia de clase alta** an upper-class family

alto (2) ADVERBIO

high ◊ *subir muy alto* to go up very high

♦ **Pepe habla muy alto.** Pepe has got a very loud voice.

♦ **¡Más alto, por favor!** Speak up, please!

♦ **Pon el volumen más alto.** Turn the volume up.

el **alto (3)** SUSTANTIVO

♦ **La pared tiene dos metros de alto.** The wall is two metres high.

♦ **en lo alto de** at the top of

♦ **hacer un alto** to stop ◊ *A las dos haremos un alto para comer.* We'll stop to have lunch at two o'clock.

♦ **pasar algo por alto** to overlook something

♦ **el alto el fuego** ceasefire

alto (4) EXCLAMACIÓN

stop!

el **altoparlante** SUSTANTIVO Latin America

loudspeaker

la **altura** SUSTANTIVO

height ◊ *Volamos a una altura de 15.000 pies.* We're flying at a height of 15,000 feet.

♦ **La pared tiene dos metros de altura.** The wall's two metres high.

♦ **cuando llegues a la altura del hospital** when you reach the hospital

♦ **a estas alturas** at this stage ◊ *A estas alturas no podemos hacer nada.* There's nothing we can do at this stage.

las **alubias** SUSTANTIVO

beans

alucinar VERBO

to be amazed ◊ *Alucino con las cosas que haces.* I'm amazed at the things you do.

el **alud** SUSTANTIVO

avalanche

aludir VERBO

to refer ◊ *No aludió a lo del otro día.* He didn't refer to that business the other day.

♦ **No se dio por aludida.** She didn't take the hint.

el **aluminio** SUSTANTIVO

aluminium

el **alumno,** la **alumna** SUSTANTIVO

pupil

la **alusión** SUSTANTIVO (PL las **alusiones**)

♦ **hacer alusión a** to refer to

la **alverja** SUSTANTIVO Latin America

pea

el **alza** SUSTANTIVO FEM

rise ◊ *un alza de los precios* a rise in prices

♦ **El balonmano es un deporte en alza.** Handball is becoming increasingly popular.

alzar* VERBO

to raise ◊ *alzar la voz* to raise one's voice

* Verbs marked with this symbol are irregular. See pages 380-382 for further details

♦ **alzarse** to rise ◊ *Se alzó el telón.* The curtain rose.
♦ **alzarse en armas** to take up arms

el **ama** SUSTANTIVO FEM
owner
♦ **ama de casa** housewife
♦ **ama de llaves** housekeeper

amable ADJETIVO
kind
♦ **Mi mejor amigo es muy amable.** My best friend is very kind.

amamantar VERBO
1 to breast-feed (*niño*)
2 to suckle (*animal*)

amanecer* VERBO
1 to get light ◊ *Amanece a las siete.* It gets light at seven.
2 to wake up ◊ *El niño amaneció con fiebre.* The boy woke up with a temperature.

el **amanecer** SUSTANTIVO
dawn

el/la **amante** SUSTANTIVO
lover
♦ **amantes del cine** cinema lovers

la **amapola** SUSTANTIVO
poppy (PL poppies)

amar VERBO
to love

amargado ADJETIVO
bitter
♦ **estar amargado por algo** to be bitter about something

amargar* VERBO
to spoil ◊ *Ya me habéis amargado la tarde.* You've spoilt my evening.
♦ **amargar la vida a alguien** to make somebody's life a misery
♦ **amargarse** to get upset ◊ *No te amargues por tan poca cosa.* It's not worth getting upset about such a little thing.

amargo ADJETIVO
bitter

el **amarillo** ADJETIVO, SUSTANTIVO
yellow
♦ **la prensa amarilla** the gutter press

amarrar VERBO
1 to moor (*barco*)
2 to tie up (*animal, persona*)
3 to do up Latin America ◊ *Se amarró los zapatos.* He did up his shoes.

el/la **amateur** ADJETIVO, SUSTANTIVO (PL los/las **amateurs**)
amateur

el **Amazonas** SUSTANTIVO
the Amazon

el **ámbar** SUSTANTIVO
amber

la **ambición** SUSTANTIVO (PL las **ambiciones**)
ambition

ambicioso ADJETIVO
ambitious

el **ambientador** SUSTANTIVO
air freshener

el **ambiente** SUSTANTIVO
atmosphere ◊ *Se respira un ambiente tenso.* There's a tense atmosphere.
♦ **Había un ambiente muy cargado en la habitación.** It was very stuffy in the room.
♦ **Necesito cambiar de ambiente.** I need a change of scene.
♦ **el medio ambiente** the environment

ambiguo ADJETIVO
ambiguous

el **ámbito** SUSTANTIVO
scope

ambos PRONOMBRE (FEM **ambas**)
both ◊ *Vinieron ambos.* They both came. ◊ *Ambos tenéis los ojos azules.* You've both got blue eyes.

la **ambulancia** SUSTANTIVO
ambulance

el **ambulatorio** SUSTANTIVO
out-patients' department

amén EXCLAMACIÓN
amen

amenace VERBO *ver* **amenazar**

la **amenaza** SUSTANTIVO
threat

amenazar* VERBO
to threaten
♦ **amenazar a alguien con hacer algo** to threaten to do something ◊ *Le amenazó con decírselo al profesor.* He threatened to tell the teacher.

ameno ADJETIVO
enjoyable

América SUSTANTIVO FEM
the Americas (*continente*)
♦ **América Central** Central America
♦ **América Latina** Latin America
♦ **América del Sur** South America
♦ **el español de América** Latin American Spanish

la **americana** SUSTANTIVO
1 jacket (*chaqueta*)
2 American (*persona*)

el **americano** ADJETIVO, SUSTANTIVO
American

la **ametralladora** SUSTANTIVO
machine gun

las **amígdalas** SUSTANTIVO
tonsils

el **amigo,** la **amiga** SUSTANTIVO
friend
♦ **hacerse amigos** to become friends
♦ **ser muy amigos** to be good friends

la **amistad** SUSTANTIVO
friendship
♦ **hacer amistad con alguien** to make friends with somebody
♦ **las amistades** friends

amistoso ADJETIVO
friendly

el **amo** SUSTANTIVO
owner ◊ *el amo del perro* the dog's owner

amontonar VERBO
to pile up
◆ **Se me amontona el trabajo.** My work's piling up.

el **amor** SUSTANTIVO
love
◆ **hacer el amor** to make love
◆ **amor propio** self-esteem

amoratado ADJETIVO
[1] blue (*por el frío*)
[2] black and blue (*por los golpes*)

amortiguar* VERBO
[1] to cushion (*golpe*)
[2] to muffle (*ruido*)

ampliar* VERBO
[1] to expand (*negocio*)
[2] to enlarge (*fotografía*)
[3] to extend (*plazo, local*)

el **amplificador** SUSTANTIVO
amplifier

amplio ADJETIVO
[1] wide ◊ *una calle muy amplia* a very wide street
[2] spacious ◊ *una habitación amplia* a spacious room
[3] loose ◊ *ropa amplia* loose clothing

la **ampolla** SUSTANTIVO
blister

amputar VERBO
to amputate

amueblar VERBO
to furnish ◊ *un piso amueblado* a furnished flat
◆ **un piso sin amueblar** an unfurnished flat

analfabeto ADJETIVO
illiterate

el **analgésico** SUSTANTIVO
painkiller

el **análisis** SUSTANTIVO (PL los **análisis**)
[1] (*estudio*)
analysis (PL analyses) ◊ *un análisis de la situación* an analysis of the situation
[2] (*prueba*)
test ◊ *un análisis de sangre* a blood test

analizar* VERBO
to analyse

la **anarquía** SUSTANTIVO
anarchy

la **anatomía** SUSTANTIVO
anatomy

ancho ADJETIVO
[1] wide ◊ *una calle ancha* a wide street
[2] loose ◊ *Le gusta llevar ropa ancha.* He likes to wear loose clothing.
◆ **Me está ancho el vestido.** The dress is too big for me.
◆ **Es ancho de espaldas.** He's broad-shouldered.

el **ancho** SUSTANTIVO
width ◊ *el ancho de la tela* the width of the cloth
◆ **¿Cuánto mide de ancho?** How wide is it?
◆ **Mide tres metros de ancho.** It's three metres wide.
◆ **Le hice un corte a lo ancho.** I cut it crossways.

la **anchoa** SUSTANTIVO
anchovy

la **anchura** SUSTANTIVO
width ◊ *Midió la anchura de la mesa.* He measured the width of the table.
◆ **¿Qué anchura tiene?** How wide is it?
◆ **Tiene tres metros de anchura.** It's three metres wide.

la **anciana** SUSTANTIVO
elderly woman

anciano ADJETIVO
elderly

el **anciano** SUSTANTIVO
elderly man
◆ **los ancianos** the elderly

el **ancla** SUSTANTIVO FEM
anchor

anda EXCLAMACIÓN
[1] hey! ◊ *¡Anda, un billete de 5.000!* Hey, a 5,000-peseta note!
[2] come on (*para animar*) ◊ *¡Anda, ponte el abrigo y vámonos!* Come on, put your coat on and let's go!
◆ **¡Anda ya!** You're not serious!

Andalucía SUSTANTIVO FEM
Andalusia

el **andaluz,** la **andaluza** ADJETIVO, SUSTANTIVO (MASC PL **andaluces**)
Andalusian

el **andamio** SUSTANTIVO
scaffolding ◊ *Ya han quitado los andamios.* They've taken the scaffolding down now.

andar* VERBO
[1] to walk (*caminar*) ◊ *Anduvimos varios kilómetros.* We walked several kilometres.
◆ **Iremos andando a la estación.** We'll walk to the station.
[2] to be ◊ *Últimamente ando muy liado.* I've been very busy lately. ◊ *No sé por dónde anda.* I don't know where he is. ◊ *¿Qué tal andas?* How are you? ◊ *Ando buscando un socio.* I'm looking for a partner.
◆ **andar mal de dinero** to be short of money
◆ **Anda por los cuarenta.** He's about forty.

* Verbs marked with this symbol are irregular. See pages 380-382 for further details

◆ **Siempre andan a gritos.** They're always shouting.
[3] to go (*funcionar*) ◊ *Este reloj anda muy bien.* This watch goes very well.
◆ **¡No andes ahí!** Keep away from there!
◆ **Ándate con cuidado.** Take care.

el **andén** SUSTANTIVO (PL los **andenes**)
platform

los **Andes** SUSTANTIVO
the Andes

anduve VERBO *ver* **andar**

la **anécdota** SUSTANTIVO
anecdote

la **anemia** SUSTANTIVO
anaemia

la **anestesia** SUSTANTIVO
anaesthetic
◆ **poner anestesia a alguien** to give somebody an anaesthetic

el **ángel** SUSTANTIVO
angel

las **anginas** SUSTANTIVO
◆ **tener anginas** to have tonsillitis

el **anglosajón,** la **anglosajona** ADJETIVO, SUSTANTIVO (MASC PL los **anglosajones**)
Anglo-Saxon

el **anglosajón** SUSTANTIVO
Anglo-Saxon (*idioma*)

el **ángulo** SUSTANTIVO
angle
◆ **en ángulo recto** at right angles

el **anillo** SUSTANTIVO
ring
◆ **un anillo de boda** a wedding ring

animado ADJETIVO
[1] cheerful ◊ *Últimamente parece que está más animada.* She has seemed more cheerful lately.
[2] lively ◊ *Fue una fiesta muy animada.* It was a very lively party.
◆ **dibujos animados** cartoons

el **animador,** la **animadora** SUSTANTIVO
[1] entertainments officer (*en centro turístico*)
[2] animator (*gráfico*)

el **animal** SUSTANTIVO
animal
◆ **los animales domésticos** pets

animar VERBO
[1] to cheer up ◊ *Lo ha pasado muy mal y necesita que la animen.* She has had a rough time and needs cheering up.
[2] to cheer on ◊ *Estuvimos animando al equipo.* We were cheering the team on.
[3] to liven up ◊ *Sus chistes animaron la fiesta.* His jokes livened up the party.
◆ **animar a alguien a que haga algo** to encourage somebody to do something
◆ **animarse** to cheer up ◊ *¡Vamos, anímate hombre!* Come on, cheer up mate!
◆ **animarse a hacer algo** to make up one's mind to do something

el **ánimo** SUSTANTIVO
◆ **Está muy mal de ánimo.** He's in very low spirits.
◆ **dar ánimos a alguien (1)** (*si está triste*) to cheer somebody up
◆ **dar ánimos a alguien (2)** (*si necesita apoyo*) to give somebody moral support
◆ **tener ánimos para hacer algo** to feel like doing something

ánimo EXCLAMACIÓN
cheer up! ◊ *¡Ánimo, chaval, que no es el fin del mundo!* Cheer up mate, it's not the end of the world!

el **anís** SUSTANTIVO (PL los **anises**)
anisette (*licor*)

el **aniversario** SUSTANTIVO
anniversary (PL anniversaries) ◊ *su aniversario de boda* their wedding anniversary

anoche ADVERBIO
last night
◆ **antes de anoche** the night before last

anochecer* VERBO
to get dark ◊ *En invierno anochece muy temprano.* It gets dark very early in winter.

anónimo ADJETIVO
anonymous

el **anónimo** SUSTANTIVO
anonymous threat

el **anorak** SUSTANTIVO (PL los **anoraks**)
anorak

anormal ADJETIVO
odd ◊ *Yo no noté nada anormal en su comportamiento.* I didn't notice anything odd about his behaviour.
◆ **¡Soy anormal!** What a fool I am!

anotar VERBO
[1] to take a note of ◊ *Anota mi dirección.* Take a note of my address.
[2] to score ◊ *Jones anotó 34 puntos.* Jones scored 34 points.

la **ansiedad** SUSTANTIVO
anxiety

ansioso ADJETIVO
◆ **estar ansioso por hacer algo** to be eager to do something

el **Antártico** SUSTANTIVO
the Antarctic

ante PREPOSICIÓN
[1] before ◊ *Le da vergüenza aparecer ante tanta gente.* She's shy about appearing before so many people.
[2] in the face of ◊ *Mantuvo la calma ante el peligro.* He remained calm in the face of danger.

el **ante** SUSTANTIVO
suede

anteanoche ADVERBIO
the night before last

anteayer ADVERBIO
the day before yesterday

los **antecedentes** SUSTANTIVO
♦**antecedentes penales** criminal record SING

la **antelación** SUSTANTIVO
♦**hacer una reserva con antelación** to make an advance booking
♦**Deben avisarte con un mes de antelación.** They must give you a month's notice.

antemano ADVERBIO
♦**de antemano** in advance ◊ *Yo lo sabía de antemano.* I knew in advance.

la **antena** SUSTANTIVO
aerial (*de radio, televisión*)
♦**una antena parabólica** a satellite dish

los **anteojos** SUSTANTIVO Latin America
glasses
♦**los anteojos de sol** sunglasses

los **antepasados** SUSTANTIVO
ancestors

anterior ADJETIVO (FEM **anterior**)
1 before ◊ *La semana anterior llovió mucho.* It rained a lot the week before. ◊ *Su boda fue anterior a la nuestra.* Their wedding was before ours.
2 front ◊ *las extremidades anteriores* the front limbs

anteriormente ADVERBIO
previously

antes ADVERBIO
1 before ◊ *Esta película ya la he visto antes.* I've seen this film before. ◊ *Él estaba aquí antes que yo.* He was here before me. ◊ *la noche antes* the night before
♦**El supermercado está justo antes del semáforo.** The supermarket is just before the lights.
♦**antes de** before ◊ *antes de la cena* before dinner ◊ *antes de ir al teatro* before going to the theatre ◊ *antes de que te vayas* before you go
2 first ◊ *Nosotros llegamos antes.* We arrived first.
♦**Antes no había tanto desempleo.** There didn't use to be so much unemployment.
♦**cuanto antes mejor** the sooner the better
♦**lo antes posible** as soon as possible
♦**antes de nada** first and foremost
♦**Antes que verle prefiero esperar aquí.** I'd rather wait here than see him.

el **antibiótico** SUSTANTIVO
antibiotic

anticipado ADJETIVO
early ◊ *convocar elecciones anticipadas* to call early elections
♦**por anticipado** in advance ◊ *pagar por anticipado* to pay in advance

anticipar VERBO
1 to foresee ◊ *Es imposible anticipar lo que va a ocurrir.* It's impossible to foresee what will happen.
2 to bring...forward ◊ *Habrá que anticipar la reunión.* We'll have to bring the meeting forward.
3 to pay...in advance ◊ *Tuvimos que anticipar el alquiler de dos meses.* We had to pay two months' rent in advance.
♦**anticiparse a alguien** to get in before somebody ◊ *Se me anticipó y pagó la cuenta.* He got in before me and paid the bill.
♦**Se anticipó a su tiempo.** He was ahead of his time.

el **anticipo** SUSTANTIVO
advance ◊ *pedir un anticipo* to ask for an advance
♦**ser un anticipo de algo** to be a foretaste of something

el **anticonceptivo** ADJETIVO, SUSTANTIVO
contraceptive

anticuado ADJETIVO
outdated
♦**quedarse anticuado** to become outdated

la **anticuaria** SUSTANTIVO
antique dealer

el **anticuario** SUSTANTIVO
1 antique shop (*tienda*)
2 antique dealer (*persona*)

el **antifaz** SUSTANTIVO (PL los **antifaces**)
mask

antiguamente ADVERBIO
1 in the past ◊ *Antiguamente no se gastaba tanto.* In the past people didn't spend so much money.
2 formerly ◊ *Antiguamente tenía el nombre de Sociedad de Naciones.* Formerly it was called the Society of Nations.

la **antigüedad** SUSTANTIVO
♦**Es un monumento de gran antigüedad.** It's a very old monument.
♦**en la antigüedad** in ancient times
♦**las antigüedades** antiques
♦**una tienda de antigüedades** an antique shop

antiguo ADJETIVO
1 old ◊ *Este reloj es muy antiguo.* This clock is very old.
2 ancient ◊ *Estudia historia antigua.* He studies ancient history.
3 former ◊ *el antiguo secretario general del partido* the former general secretary of the party

las **Antillas** SUSTANTIVO
the West Indies

antipático ADJETIVO
unfriendly

antirrobo ADJETIVO (PL **antirrobo**)

anti-theft ◊ *un sistema antirrobo* an anti-theft system

el **antiséptico** ADJETIVO, SUSTANTIVO
antiseptic

antojarse VERBO
1 to feel like (*apetecer*)
♦ **Siempre hace lo que se le antoja.** He always does what he feels like.
2 to have cravings (*como capricho*) ◊ *Se me ha antojado un helado.* I've got cravings for an ice-cream.

la **antorcha** SUSTANTIVO
torch (PL torches)

la **antropología** SUSTANTIVO
anthropology

anual ADJETIVO
annual

anular VERBO
1 to call off ◊ *Anularon el partido por la lluvia.* The match was called off owing to the rain.
2 to disallow ◊ *El árbitro anuló el gol.* The referee disallowed the goal.
3 to overturn ◊ *El Tribunal Supremo anuló la sentencia.* The Supreme Court overturned the sentence.

el **anular** SUSTANTIVO
ring finger

anunciar VERBO
1 to advertise ◊ *anunciar detergente* to advertise washing powder
2 to announce ◊ *anunciar una decisión* to announce a decision

el **anuncio** SUSTANTIVO
1 advertisement ◊ *Pusieron un anuncio en el periódico.* They put an advertisement in the paper.
♦ **anuncios por palabras** small ads
2 announcement ◊ *Tengo que hacer un anuncio importante.* I have an important announcement to make.

el **anzuelo** SUSTANTIVO
hook

la **añadidura** SUSTANTIVO
♦ **por añadidura** in addition

añadir VERBO
to add

los **añicos** SUSTANTIVO
♦ **hacer algo añicos** to smash something to pieces
♦ **hacerse añicos** to smash to pieces

el **año** SUSTANTIVO
year ◊ *Estuve allí el año pasado.* I was there last year.
♦ **el año que viene** next year
♦ **el año escolar** the school year
♦ **¡Feliz Año Nuevo!** Happy New Year!
♦ **los años 80** the 80s
♦ **¿Cuántos años tiene?** How old is he?
♦ **Tiene 15 años.** He's 15.

apagado ADJETIVO
switched off ◊ *La tele estaba apagada.* The TV was switched off.

apagar* VERBO
1 to switch off ◊ *Apaga la tele.* Switch the TV off. ◊ *No apagues la luz.* Don't switch the light off.
2 to put out ◊ *Por favor, apaguen sus cigarrillos.* Please put your cigarettes out.
♦ **apagar el fuego** to put the fire out

el **apagón** SUSTANTIVO (PL los **apagones**)
power cut

apañado ADJETIVO
resourceful ◊ *¡Qué apañada eres!* You're so resourceful!

apañarse VERBO
to manage ◊ *¿Podrás hacerlo solo? – Ya me apañaré.* Can you do it on your own? – I'll manage.
♦ **apañarse con algo** to make do with something ◊ *Nos apañaremos con la comida que sobró.* We can make do with the leftovers.

el **aparador** SUSTANTIVO
1 sideboard (*mueble*)
2 shop window (*en tienda*) Mexico

el **aparato** SUSTANTIVO
♦ **No sé manejar este aparato.** I don't know how to operate this.
♦ **un aparato de televisión** a television
♦ **los aparatos de gimnasia** the apparatus
♦ **Fabrican aparatos electrónicos.** They make electronic equipment.
♦ **un aparato electrodoméstico** an electrical appliance

el **aparcamiento** SUSTANTIVO
1 car park (*para muchos coches*) ◊ *un aparcamiento subterráneo* an underground car park
2 parking place (*para un coche*) ◊ *buscar aparcamiento* to look for a parking place

aparcar* VERBO
to park
♦ **"prohibido aparcar"** "no parking"

aparecer* VERBO
1 to appear ◊ *De repente apareció la policía.* Suddenly the police appeared.
2 to turn up ◊ *Aparecieron casi una hora tarde.* They turned up nearly an hour late. ◊ *¿Han aparecido ya las tijeras?* Have the scissors turned up yet?
3 to come out ◊ *Su nueva novela aparecerá el mes próximo.* His latest novel will come out next month.

aparentar VERBO
to appear ◊ *Aparentaba no enterarse.* He appeared not to understand.
♦ **Aparenta más edad de la que tiene.** He looks older than he is.

aparente ADJETIVO
apparent

aparentemente ADVERBIO
apparently

la **apariencia** SUSTANTIVO

♦ **Tiene la apariencia de un profesor de universidad.** He looks like a university lecturer.
♦ **En apariencia nada ha cambiado.** On the surface, nothing had changed.
♦ **guardar las apariencias** to keep up appearances

apartado ADJETIVO
isolated ◊ *un lugar apartado* an isolated place
♦ **Vive apartado de todos.** He lives a secluded life.

el **apartado** SUSTANTIVO
section ◊ *en el siguiente apartado* in the following section
♦ **apartado de correos** PO box

el **apartamento** SUSTANTIVO
apartment

apartar VERBO
1 to remove ◊ *Lo apartaron del equipo.* They removed him from the team.
2 to move out of the way ◊ *Aparta todas las sillas.* Move all the chairs out of the way.
♦ **¡Aparta!** Stand back!
3 to set aside ◊ *Hay que apartar algo del sueldo para las vacaciones.* You'll have to set aside some of your pay for the holidays.
♦ **apartarse** to stand back ◊ *Apártense de la puerta.* Stand back from the door.

aparte (1) ADVERBIO
separately ◊ *Cada caso será tratado aparte.* Each case will be dealt with separately.
♦ **La ropa que no valga ponla aparte.** Put the clothes that aren't any use on one side.
♦ **aparte de (1)** (*excepto*) apart from ◊ *Nadie protestó aparte de ella.* Nobody complained apart from her.
♦ **aparte de (2)** (*además de*) as well as ◊ *Aparte de los patines, también quería una bici.* I'd like a bike as well as the skates.
♦ **punto y aparte** full stop, new paragraph

aparte (2) ADJETIVO
separate ◊ *El tuyo es un caso aparte.* You're a separate case.

apasionante ADJETIVO
exciting

apasionar VERBO
♦ **Le apasiona el fútbol.** He's crazy about football.

apdo. ABREVIATURA (= *apartado de correos*)
PO box (= Post Office box)

apearse VERBO
♦ **apearse de** to get off

el **apego** SUSTANTIVO
♦ **tener apego a algo** to be attached to something

apellidarse VERBO
♦ **Se apellida Pérez.** His surname is Pérez.

el **apellido** SUSTANTIVO
surname

apenas ADVERBIO, CONJUNCIÓN
1 hardly ◊ *No tenemos apenas nada de comer.* We've got hardly anything to eat. ◊ *Apenas podía levantarse.* He could hardly stand up.
2 hardly ever

Se usa ***hardly ever*** *cuando se refiere a la frecuencia de una acción.*

◊ *Apenas voy al cine.* I hardly ever go to the cinema.
3 barely

Se usa ***barely*** *cuando precede a un número.*

◊ *Hace apenas 10 minutos que hablé con ella.* I spoke to her barely 10 minutes ago.
♦ **Terminé en apenas dos horas.** It only took me two hours to finish.
4 as soon as ◊ *Apenas me vio, se puso a llorar.* As soon as he saw me he began to cry.

la **apendicitis** SUSTANTIVO
appendicitis

el **aperitivo** SUSTANTIVO
aperitif

la **apertura** SUSTANTIVO
opening ◊ *el acto de apertura* the opening ceremony

apestar VERBO
to stink ◊ *Te apestan los pies.* Your feet stink.
♦ **apestar a** to stink of

apetecer* VERBO
♦ **¿Te apetece una tortilla?** Do you fancy an omelette?
♦ **No, gracias, ahora no me apetece.** No, thanks, I don't feel like it just now.

el **apetito** SUSTANTIVO
appetite ◊ *Eso te va a quitar el apetito.* You won't have any appetite left.
♦ **No tengo apetito.** I'm not hungry.

el **apio** SUSTANTIVO
celery

aplastante ADJETIVO
overwhelming

aplastar VERBO
to squash ◊ *Me senté encima del regalo y lo aplasté.* I sat on the present and squashed it.

aplaudir VERBO
to clap ◊ *Todos aplaudían.* Everyone clapped.

el **aplauso** SUSTANTIVO
applause
♦ **Los aplausos duraron varios minutos.** The applause lasted for several minutes.

aplazar* VERBO

* Verbs marked with this symbol are irregular. See pages 380-382 for further details

to postpone

la **aplicación** SUSTANTIVO (PL las **aplicaciones**)
application ◇ *un producto con muchas aplicaciones* a product with a lot of applications

aplicado ADJETIVO
hard-working ◇ *un alumno aplicado* a hard-working pupil

aplicar* VERBO
[1] to apply ◇ *Aplíquese sobre la zona afectada.* Apply to the affected area.
[2] to enforce ◇ *No se aplicaron las normas.* The rules weren't enforced.

apoderarse VERBO
◆**apoderarse de un lugar** to take over a place
◆**Se apoderaron de las joyas.** They went off with the jewels.

el **apodo** SUSTANTIVO
nickname

el **apogeo** SUSTANTIVO
height ◇ *en el apogeo de su poder* at the height of his power
◆**La fiesta estaba en su apogeo.** The party was in full swing.

aportar VERBO
to provide

aposta ADVERBIO
on purpose

apostar* VERBO
to bet
◆**apostar por algo** to bet on something
◆**¿Qué te apuestas a que ...?** What's the betting that ...?

el **apóstrofo** SUSTANTIVO
apostrophe

apoyar VERBO
[1] to lean ◇ *Apoya el espejo contra la pared.* Lean the mirror against the wall.
[2] to rest ◇ *Apoya la espalda en este cojín.* Rest your back against this cushion.
[3] to support ◇ *Todos mis compañeros me apoyan.* All my colleagues support me.
◆**apoyarse** to lean ◇ *No te apoyes en la mesa.* Don't lean on the table.

el **apoyo** SUSTANTIVO
support

apreciar VERBO
◆**apreciar a alguien** to be fond of somebody ◇ *Lo apreciábamos mucho.* We were very fond of him.
◆**Aprecio mucho mi tiempo libre.** I really value my free time.

el **aprecio** SUSTANTIVO
◆**tener aprecio a alguien** to be fond of somebody

aprender VERBO
to learn ◇ *Ya me he aprendido los verbos irregulares.* I've already learnt the irregular verbs.
◆**aprender a hacer algo** to learn to do something
◆**aprender algo de memoria** to learn something by heart

el **aprendiz,** la **aprendiza** SUSTANTIVO (MASC PL los **aprendices**)
trainee ◇ *Es aprendiz de mecánico.* He's a trainee mechanic.
◆**estar de aprendiz** to be doing an apprenticeship

el **aprendizaje** SUSTANTIVO
learning ◇ *dificultades de aprendizaje* learning difficulties

aprensivo ADJETIVO
overanxious

apresurado ADJETIVO
hasty (*decisión*)

apresurarse VERBO
◆**No nos apresuremos.** Let's not be hasty.
◆**Me apresuré a sugerir que ...** I hastily suggested that ...

apretado ADJETIVO
[1] tight ◇ *Estos pantalones me están muy apretados.* These trousers are very tight on me. ◇ *Tenemos un programa muy apretado.* We've got a very tight programme.
[2] cramped ◇ *Íbamos muy apretados en el autobús.* We were very cramped on the bus.

apretar* VERBO
[1] to tighten ◇ *Aprieta bien los tornillos.* Tighten up the screws.
[2] to press ◇ *Aprieta este botón.* Press this button.
◆**apretar el gatillo** to press the trigger
◆**Me aprietan los zapatos.** My shoes are too tight.
◆**La apretó contra su pecho.** He clasped her to his bosom.
◆**Apretaos un poco para que me siente yo también.** Move up a bit so I can sit down too.
◆**apretarse el cinturón** to tighten one's belt

el **aprieto** SUSTANTIVO
◆**estar en un aprieto** to be in a tight spot

aprisa ADVERBIO
fast ◇ *No vayas tan aprisa.* Don't go so fast.
◆**¡Aprisa!** Hurry up!

aprobar* VERBO
[1] to pass ◇ *aprobar un examen* to pass an exam
◆**Han aprobado una ley antitabaco.** They've passed an anti-smoking law.
◆**aprobar por los pelos** to scrape through
[2] to approve ◇ *La decisión fue aprobada por mayoría.* The decision was approved by a majority.
[3] to approve of ◇ *No apruebo esa conducta.* I don't approve of that sort of behaviour.

apropiado ADJETIVO
suitable

aprovechar VERBO
1 to make good use of ◊ *No aprovecha el tiempo.* He doesn't make good use of his time. ◊ *Mi madre aprovecha toda la comida que sobra.* My mother makes good use of any leftovers.
2 to use ◊ *Aprovecharé los ratos libres para estudiar.* I'll use the free time to study.
◆ **aprovecho la ocasión para decirles ...** I'd like to take this opportunity to tell you ...
◆ **Aprovecharé ahora que estoy solo para llamarle.** I'll call him now while I'm on my own.
◆ **¡Que aproveche!** Enjoy your meal!
◆ **aprovecharse de** to take advantage of ◊ *Me aproveché de la situación.* I took advantage of the situation. ◊ *Todos se aprovechan del pobre chico.* Everyone takes advantage of the poor boy.

aproximadamente ADVERBIO
about

aproximado ADJETIVO
approximate

aproximarse VERBO
to approach ◊ *Se aproximaba un barco.* A boat was approaching.

apruebo VERBO *ver* **aprobar**

apto ADJETIVO
◆ **ser apto para algo** to be suitable for something ◊ *No es apta para el puesto.* She isn't suitable for the job.
◆ **una película no apta para niños** an unsuitable film for children

la **apuesta** SUSTANTIVO
bet ◊ *Hicimos una apuesta.* We had a bet.

apuesto VERBO *ver* **apostar**

apuntar VERBO
1 to write down ◊ *Apúntalo o se te olvidará.* Write it down or you'll forget.
◆ **Apunta mis datos.** Can you take a note of my details?
2 to point ◊ *Apuntó el arma hacia nosotros.* He pointed the gun at us.
◆ **Me apuntó con el dedo.** He pointed at me.
◆ **Luis me apuntó en el examen.** Luis gave me the answers in the exam.
◆ **apuntarse** to put one's name down ◊ *Nos hemos apuntado para el viaje a Marruecos.* We've put our names down for the trip to Morocco.
◆ **apuntarse a un curso** to enrol on a course
◆ **¡Yo me apunto!** Count me in!

No confundir ***apuntar*** *con* ***to appoint.***

los **apuntes** SUSTANTIVO
notes
◆ **tomar apuntes** to take notes

apuñalar VERBO
to stab

apurado ADJETIVO
difficult ◊ *Estábamos en una situación bastante apurada.* We were in rather a difficult situation.
◆ **Si estás apurado de dinero, dímelo.** If you're short of money, tell me.
◆ **estar apurado** (*avergonzado*) to feel embarrassed

apurar VERBO
to finish up ◊ *Apura la cerveza que nos vamos.* Finish up your beer and let's go.
◆ **apurarse (1)** to hurry up ◊ *¡Apúrate!* Hurry up!
◆ **apurarse (2)** to worry ◊ *Yo me encargo; no te apures por nada.* I'll deal with it – don't you worry about anything.

el **apuro** SUSTANTIVO
fix ◊ *El dinero de la herencia los sacó del apuro.* The money they inherited got them out of the fix.
◆ **Pasé muchos apuros para salir del agua.** I had a lot of trouble getting out of the water.
◆ **Me da mucho apuro no llevar ningún regalo.** I feel very embarrassed about not taking a present.
◆ **estar en apuros** to be in trouble

aquel ADJETIVO (FEM **aquella**)
that ◊ *Me gusta más aquella mesa.* I prefer that table.

aquél PRONOMBRE (FEM **aquélla**)
that one ◊ *Éste no, aquél.* Not this one, that one.
◆ **Aquél no era el que yo quería.** That wasn't the one I wanted.

aquello PRONOMBRE
◆ **aquello que hay allí** that thing over there
◆ **Me fui; aquello era insoportable.** I left. It was just unbearable.
◆ **¿Qué fue de aquello del viaje alrededor del mundo?** What ever happened to that round-the-world trip idea?

aquellos ADJETIVO PL (FEM **aquellas**)
those ◊ *¿Ves aquellas montañas?* Can you see those mountains?

aquéllos PRONOMBRE PL (FEM **aquéllas**)
those ones ◊ *Aquéllos de allí son mejores.* Those ones over there are better.
◆ **Aquéllos no eran los que vimos ayer.** Those aren't the ones we saw yesterday.

aquí ADVERBIO
1 here (*en este lugar*) ◊ *Aquí está el informe que me pediste.* Here's the report you asked me for.
◆ **aquí abajo** down here
◆ **aquí arriba** up here
◆ **aquí mismo** right here

* Verbs marked with this symbol are irregular. See pages 380-382 for further details

- **por aquí (1)** around here ◊ *Lo tenía por aquí en alguna parte.* I had it around here somewhere.
- **por aquí (2)** this way ◊ *Pasen por aquí, si son tan amables.* Please come this way.

[2] now (*ahora*)
- **de aquí en adelante** from now on
- **de aquí a siete días** a week from now
- **hasta aquí (1)** up to here ◊ *Hasta aquí el camino es cuesta abajo.* Up to here the path goes downhill.
- **hasta aquí (2)** up to now ◊ *Hasta aquí todos han ido pagando.* Up to now everyone has paid.

el/la **árabe** ADJETIVO, SUSTANTIVO
Arab

el **árabe** SUSTANTIVO
Arabic (*idioma*)

Arabia SUSTANTIVO FEM
- **Arabia Saudí** Saudi Arabia

el **arado** SUSTANTIVO
plough

la **araña** SUSTANTIVO
spider

arañar VERBO
to scratch ◊ *Me arañó el gato.* The cat scratched me. ◊ *Me arañé la cara con las zarzas.* I scratched my face on the brambles.
- **Pedro se arañó las rodillas al caer.** Pedro grazed his knees when he fell over.

el **arañazo** SUSTANTIVO
scratch (PL scratches)

arar VERBO
to plough

el **árbitro,** la **árbitra** SUSTANTIVO
referee

el **árbol** SUSTANTIVO
tree ◊ *un árbol frutal* a fruit tree
- **el árbol de Navidad** the Christmas tree
- **un árbol genealógico** a family tree

el **arbusto** SUSTANTIVO
[1] (*salvaje*)
bush (PL bushes)
[2] (*plantado*)
shrub

el **arca** SUSTANTIVO FEM
chest
- **el Arca de Noé** Noah's Ark

las **arcadas** SUSTANTIVO
- **Me dieron arcadas con el olor.** The smell made me retch.

el **arcén** SUSTANTIVO (PL los **arcenes**)
hard shoulder

el **archivador** SUSTANTIVO
[1] filing cabinet (*mueble*)
[2] file (*carpeta*)

archivar VERBO
to file

el **archivo** SUSTANTIVO
[1] archive (*lugar*)
[2] file (*documento, también informática*)
- **los archivos policiales** police files

la **arcilla** SUSTANTIVO
clay

el **arco** SUSTANTIVO
[1] (*de flechas*)
bow
[2] (*en edificio, monumento*)
arch (PL arches)
- **el arco iris** the rainbow

arder VERBO
to burn ◊ *Ese tronco no va a arder.* That log won't burn.
- **¡La sopa está ardiendo!** The soup's boiling hot!
- **El jefe está que arde.** The boss is seething.

la **ardilla** SUSTANTIVO
squirrel

el **ardor** SUSTANTIVO
passion
- **Defiende sus ideas con ardor.** He defends his ideas passionately.
- **tener ardor de estómago** to have heartburn

el **área** SUSTANTIVO FEM
[1] area ◊ *el área del triángulo* the area of the triangle ◊ *en áreas muy pobladas* in heavily populated areas
- **en distintas áreas del país** in different parts of the country
- **un área de descanso** a lay-by
- **un área de servicios** (*en autopista*) a service area

[2] penalty area ◊ *una falta al borde del área* a foul on the edge of the penalty area

la **arena** SUSTANTIVO
sand
- **arenas movedizas** quicksand SING

el **arenque** SUSTANTIVO
herring
- **arenques ahumados** kippers

Argelia SUSTANTIVO FEM
Algeria

el **argelino,** la **argelina** ADJETIVO, SUSTANTIVO
Algerian

Argentina SUSTANTIVO FEM
Argentina

el **argentino,** la **argentina** ADJETIVO, SUSTANTIVO
Argentinian

la **argolla** SUSTANTIVO
ring

el **argot** SUSTANTIVO (PL los **argots**)
[1] slang (*de la calle*)
[2] jargon (*de una profesión*)

el **argumento** SUSTANTIVO
[1] argument ◊ *los argumentos a favor del desarme* the arguments in favour of disarmament

☞

2 plot ◊ *el argumento de la película* the plot of the film

árido ADJETIVO
arid

Aries SUSTANTIVO MASC
Aries ◊ *Soy Aries.* I'm Aries.

el/la **aristócrata** SUSTANTIVO
aristocrat

el **arma** SUSTANTIVO FEM
1 weapon ◊ *Los guerrilleros entregaron las armas.* The guerrillas handed over their weapons. ◊ *Se prohibió el uso de armas químicas.* The use of chemical weapons was banned.
♦ **un fabricante de armas** an arms manufacturer
2 gun ◊ *Nos apuntaba con un arma.* He pointed a gun at us.
♦ **un arma de fuego** a firearm

la **armada** SUSTANTIVO
navy (PL navies)

la **armadura** SUSTANTIVO
armour
♦ **una armadura medieval** a medieval suit of armour

el **armamento** SUSTANTIVO
arms PL ◊ *negociaciones para la limitación de armamento* talks on arms control

armar VERBO
1 to arm ◊ *No iban armados.* They weren't armed.
2 to assemble ◊ *El armario viene desmontado y luego tú lo armas.* The cupboard comes in pieces and you assemble it.
3 to make ◊ *Los vecinos de arriba arman mucho jaleo.* Our upstairs neighbours make a lot of noise.
♦ **Si no aceptan voy a armar un escándalo.** If they don't agree I'm going to make a fuss.
♦ **armarse un lío** to get in a muddle
♦ **armarse de paciencia** to be patient
♦ **armarse de valor** to summon up one's courage
♦ **Se armó la gorda.** All hell broke loose. (*coloquial*)

el **armario** SUSTANTIVO
1 cupboard
♦ **un armario de cocina** a kitchen cupboard
2 wardrobe (*de ropa*)
♦ **un armario empotrado** a built-in wardrobe

el **armazón** SUSTANTIVO (PL los **armazones**)
frame

la **armonía** SUSTANTIVO
harmony

la **armónica** SUSTANTIVO
mouth organ

el **aro** SUSTANTIVO
1 ring ◊ *los aros olímpicos* the Olympic rings
2 hoop (*para gimnasia, juegos*)

el **aroma** SUSTANTIVO
aroma

la **aromaterapia** SUSTANTIVO
aromatherapy

el **arpa** SUSTANTIVO FEM
harp

la **arqueóloga** SUSTANTIVO
archaeologist

la **arqueología** SUSTANTIVO
archaeology

el **arqueólogo** SUSTANTIVO
archaeologist

el **arquero,** la **arquera** SUSTANTIVO
Latin America
goalkeeper

el **arquitecto,** la **arquitecta** SUSTANTIVO
architect

la **arquitectura** SUSTANTIVO
architecture

arrancar* VERBO
1 to pull up (*planta*) ◊ *Estaba arrancando malas hierbas.* I was pulling up weeds.
♦ **El viento arrancó varios árboles.** Several trees were uprooted by the wind.
♦ **arrancar algo de raíz** to pull something up by the roots
2 to pull out (*clavo, espina*) ◊ *Le arranqué una espina del dedo.* I pulled a thorn out of his finger.
3 to tear out (*hoja, página*) ◊ *Arrancó una hoja del cuaderno.* He tore a page out of the exercise book.
4 to pull off (*cartel, etiqueta, esparadrapo*) ◊ *Me arranqué la tirita.* I pulled off the sticking plaster.
5 to snatch ◊ *Me lo arrancaron de las manos.* They snatched it from me.
♦ **Arranca y vámonos.** Start the engine and let's get going.
♦ **arrancarle información a alguien** to drag information out of somebody

arrasar VERBO
1 to sweep away ◊ *El pueblo fue arrasado por las inundaciones.* The village was swept away by the floods.
2 to destroy ◊ *El fuego arrasó la cosecha.* The harvest was destroyed by fire.
♦ **Los socialistas arrasaron en las elecciones.** The socialists swept the board in the elections.

arrastrar VERBO
1 to drag ◊ *Arrastraba una enorme maleta.* He was dragging an enormous suitcase.
2 to sweep along ◊ *El aire nos arrastraba.* The wind swept us along.

* Verbs marked with this symbol are irregular. See pages 380-382 for further details

3 to trail on the ground ◊ *Las cortinas arrastran un poco.* The curtains trail on the ground slightly. ◊ *Llevas la falda arrastrando.* Your skirt's trailing on the ground.

◆ **arrastrarse** to crawl ◊ *Llegaron hasta la valla arrastrándose.* They crawled up to the fence.

arrebatar VERBO
snatch ◊ *Me lo arrebató de las manos.* He snatched it from me.

el **arrecife** SUSTANTIVO
reef
◆ **los arrecifes de coral** coral reefs

arreglar VERBO
1 to fix (*aparato, mecanismo*) ◊ *¿Sabrás arreglarme el grifo?* Could you fix the tap for me?
◆ **Están arreglando las aceras.** The pavements are being repaired.
2 to do up (*casa, habitación*) ◊ *Este verano hemos arreglado la cocina.* This summer we did up the kitchen.
3 to sort out ◊ *Si tienes algún problema, él te lo arregla.* If you have any problems, he'll sort them out for you.
◆ **Deja tu cuarto arreglado antes de salir.** Leave your room tidy before going out.
◆ **arreglarse (1)** to get ready ◊ *Se arregló para salir.* She got ready to go out.
◆ **arreglarse (2)** to work out ◊ *Ya verás como todo se arregla.* It'll all work out, you'll see.
◆ **arreglarse (3)** to manage ◊ *¿Qué tal te arreglas sin coche?* How are you managing without a car?
◆ **arreglarse el pelo** to do one's hair
◆ **arreglárselas para hacer algo** to manage to do something

el **arreglo** SUSTANTIVO
1 repair ◊ *El tostador sólo necesita un pequeño arreglo.* The toaster only needs a minor repair.
◆ **Esta tele no tiene arreglo.** This TV is unrepairable.
◆ **Este problema no tiene arreglo.** There's no solution to this problem.
2 compromise ◊ *Llegamos a un arreglo.* We reached a compromise.
◆ **con arreglo a** in accordance with

arrepentirse* VERBO
◆ **arrepentirse de algo** to regret something
◆ **arrepentirse de haber hecho algo** to regret doing something

arrestar VERBO
to arrest

el **arresto** SUSTANTIVO
arrest ◊ *un arresto domiciliario* a house arrest

arriba ADVERBIO
above ◊ *Los platos y las tazas están arriba.* The plates and mugs are above. ◊ *Visto desde arriba parece más pequeño.* Seen from above it looks smaller.
◆ **Pon esos libros arriba del todo.** Put those books on top.
◆ **la parte de arriba del biquini** the bikini top

Se usa ***upstairs*** *hablando de los distintos pisos de un edificio.*

◊ *Arriba están los dormitorios.* The bedrooms are upstairs. ◊ *los vecinos de arriba* our upstairs neighbours
◆ **allí arriba** up there
◆ **más arriba** further up
◆ **ir calle arriba** to go up the street
◆ **Tenemos bolsos de 4.000 para arriba.** We've got bags from 4,000 pesetas upwards.
◆ **arriba de (1)** Latin America on top of ◊ *Lo dejé arriba del refrigerador.* I left it on top of the fridge.
◆ **arriba de (2)** Latin America above ◊ *Viven en el departamento arriba del mío.* They live in the flat above mine.
◆ **mirar a alguien de arriba abajo** to look somebody up and down

arriesgado ADJETIVO
risky

arriesgar* VERBO
to risk ◊ *Carlos arriesgó su vida para salvar a su perro.* Carlos risked his life to save his dog.
◆ **arriesgarse** to take a risk ◊ *Se arriesgó pero salió ganando.* He took a risk but he came out on top.
◆ **arriesgarse a hacer algo** to risk doing something ◊ *Me arriesgo a perderlo todo.* I risk losing everything.

arrimar VERBO
to bring...closer ◊ *Arrima tu silla a la mía.* Bring your chair closer to mine.
◆ **Vamos a arrimar la mesa a la pared.** Let's put the table by the wall.
◆ **arrimarse** to get close ◊ *Al aparcar procura arrimarte a la acera.* Try to get close to the pavement when parking.
◆ **Arrímate a mí.** Come closer.

arrodillarse VERBO
to kneel down

arrogante ADJETIVO
arrogant

arrojar VERBO
1 to throw ◊ *Arrojaban piedras y palos.* They were throwing sticks and stones.
◆ **arrojar a alguien de un sitio** to throw somebody out of a place
2 to dump ◊ *"Prohibido arrojar basuras"* "No dumping"
◆ **arrojarse** to throw oneself ◊ *Un hincha se arrojó al campo.* A fan threw himself onto the pitch.

arropar VERBO

1 to tuck in (*en la cama*) ◊ *Voy a arropar al niño.* I'll go and tuck the baby in.
2 to wrap up ◊ *Arrópala bien.* Wrap her up well.
♦ **arrópate bien (1)** (*en la cama*) tuck yourself up warmly
♦ **arrópate bien (2)** (*antes de salir*) wrap up well

el **arroyo** SUSTANTIVO
stream

el **arroz** SUSTANTIVO (PL los **arroces**)
rice
♦ **arroz blanco** white rice
♦ **arroz con leche** rice pudding

la **arruga** SUSTANTIVO
1 wrinkle (*en la piel*)
2 crease (*en la ropa, el papel*)

arrugarse* VERBO
1 to get wrinkled ◊ *La piel se va arrugando.* Skin gets increasingly wrinkled.
2 to get creased ◊ *Se me han arrugado los pantalones.* My trousers have got creased. ◊ *Procura que no se arrugue el sobre.* Try not to let the envelope get creased.

arruinar VERBO
to ruin ◊ *Esto arruinó mis planes.* That ruined my plans.
♦ **arruinarse** to be ruined ◊ *Con aquel negocio se arruinó.* He was ruined thanks to that deal.

el **arte** SUSTANTIVO (PL las **artes**)
1 art ◊ *el arte del Renacimiento* Renaissance art
♦ **el arte abstracto** abstract art
♦ **las artes plásticas** plastic arts
2 flair (*maña*) ◊ *Tiene arte para la cocina.* She has a flair for cooking.
♦ **por arte de magia** by magic

el **artefacto** SUSTANTIVO
device ◊ *un artefacto explosivo* an explosive device

la **arteria** SUSTANTIVO
artery (PL arteries)

la **artesana** SUSTANTIVO
craftswoman (PL craftswomen)

la **artesanía** SUSTANTIVO
♦ **la artesanía local** local crafts
♦ **objetos de artesanía** hand-crafted goods

el **artesano** SUSTANTIVO
craftsman (PL craftsmen)

ártico ADJETIVO
arctic

la **articulación** SUSTANTIVO (PL las **articulaciones**)
joint

el **artículo** SUSTANTIVO
article (*en periódico, de ley*) ◊ *el artículo determinado* the definite article ◊ *el artículo indeterminado* the indefinite article
♦ **artículos de lujo** luxury goods
♦ **artículos de escritorio** stationery
♦ **artículos de tocador** toiletries

artificial ADJETIVO
artificial

el/la **artista** SUSTANTIVO
artist (*pintor, escultor*)
♦ **un artista** actor (*de cine, teatro*)
♦ **una artista** actress (*de cine, teatro*)

la **arveja** SUSTANTIVO Latin America
pea

el **arzobispo** SUSTANTIVO
archbishop

el **as** SUSTANTIVO
ace ◊ *el as de picas* the ace of spades
♦ **ser un as de la cocina** to be a wizard at cooking

el **asa** SUSTANTIVO FEM
handle

asado ADJETIVO
roast ◊ *pollo asado* roast chicken

el **asado** SUSTANTIVO
1 roast (*en horno*)
2 barbecue Latin America

asaltar VERBO
1 to storm ◊ *Los rebeldes asaltaron la embajada.* The rebels stormed the embassy.
2 to raid ◊ *Asaltaron un banco.* They raided a bank.
3 to mug ◊ *Me asaltaron a la salida del banco.* I was mugged coming out of the bank.

el **asalto** SUSTANTIVO
1 raid ◊ *un asalto a una gasolinera* a raid on a petrol station
♦ **durante el asalto al parlamento** during the storming of parliament
2 round (*en boxeo*)

la **asamblea** SUSTANTIVO
1 meeting (*reunión*) ◊ *organizar una asamblea* to organize a meeting
2 assembly (*corporación*) ◊ *una asamblea legislativa* a legislative assembly

asar VERBO
to roast (*al horno*)
♦ **asar algo a la parrilla** to grill something
♦ **Me aso de calor.** I'm boiling.
♦ **Aquí se asa uno.** It's boiling in here.

ascender* VERBO
1 to rise ◊ *El globo comenzó a ascender.* The balloon began to rise.
2 to be promoted ◊ *Ascendió a teniente.* He was promoted to lieutenant.
♦ **ascender a primera división** to go up to the first division

el **ascenso** SUSTANTIVO
promotion (*de empleado, militar*)

* Verbs marked with this symbol are irregular. See pages 380-382 for further details

el **ascensor** SUSTANTIVO
lift
asciendo VERBO *ver* **ascender**
el **asco** SUSTANTIVO
♦ **El ajo me da asco.** I think garlic's revolting.
♦ **¡Puaj! ¡Qué asco!** Yuk! How revolting!
♦ **La casa está hecha un asco.** The house is filthy.
asegurar VERBO
[1] to insure ◊ *Hemos asegurado la casa.* We've insured the house.
[2] to assure ◊ *Te aseguro que es verdad.* I assure you it's true.
♦ **No he sido yo. Te lo aseguro.** It wasn't me, I assure you.
♦ **Ella asegura que no lo conoce.** She says that she doesn't know him.
[3] to fasten securely ◊ *Asegura bien la cuerda.* Fasten the rope securely.
♦ **asegurarse de** to make sure ◊ *Asegúrate de que los grifos están cerrados.* Make sure the taps are turned off.
el **aseo** SUSTANTIVO
♦ **el cuarto de aseo** the toilet
♦ **el aseo personal** personal hygiene
♦ **los aseos** the toilets
asequible ADJETIVO
[1] affordable ◊ *un precio asequible* an affordable price
[2] achievable ◊ *una meta asequible* an achievable goal
la **asesina** SUSTANTIVO
murderer
asesinar VERBO
to murder
el **asesinato** SUSTANTIVO
murder
el **asesino** SUSTANTIVO
murderer
el **asesor,** la **asesora** SUSTANTIVO
consultant
♦ **asesor fiscal** tax consultant
♦ **asesor de imagen** public relations consultant
el **asfalto** SUSTANTIVO
tarmac
la **asfixia** SUSTANTIVO
suffocation
asfixiarse VERBO
to suffocate ◊ *Me asfixio de calor.* I'm suffocating in this heat.
así ADVERBIO
[1] like this ◊ *Se hace así.* You do it like this.
[2] like that ◊ *Es así: como lo hace Jorge.* It's like that: the way Jorge is doing it. ◊ *¿Ves aquel abrigo? Quiero algo así.* Do you see that coat? I'd like something like that.
♦ **un tomate así de grande** a tomato this big
♦ **Así es la vida.** That's life.
♦ **así, así** so-so ◊ *¿Te gusta? – Así, así.* Do you like it? – So-so.
♦ **así es** that's right ◊ *¿Y ocurrió todo en un día? – Así es.* And it all happened the same day? – That's right.
♦ **¿No es así?** Isn't that so?
♦ **así que ...** so ... ◊ *No me gusta, así que lo tiraré.* I don't like it, so I'll throw it away.
♦ **... o así** ... or thereabouts ◊ *mil pesetas o así* a thousand pesetas or thereabouts
♦ **y así sucesivamente** and so on
Asia SUSTANTIVO FEM
Asia
el **asiático,** la **asiática** ADJETIVO, SUSTANTIVO
Asian
el **asiento** SUSTANTIVO
seat
♦ **el asiento delantero** the front seat
♦ **el asiento trasero** the back seat
la **asignatura** SUSTANTIVO
subject
♦ **Tiene dos asignaturas pendientes.** He's got two subjects to retake.
el **asilo** SUSTANTIVO
[1] home
♦ **un asilo de ancianos** an old people's home
♦ **un asilo de pobres** a hostel for the poor
[2] asylum ◊ *asilo político* political asylum
asimilar VERBO
to assimilate ◊ *Hay que asimilar lo aprendido.* You have to assimilate what you've learnt.
♦ **El cambio es grande y cuesta asimilarlo.** It's a big change and it takes getting used to.
la **asistencia** SUSTANTIVO
♦ **asistencia médica (1)** medical attention ◊ *Tuvieron que recibir asistencia médica.* They needed medical attention.
♦ **asistencia médica (2)** medical care ◊ *El seguro cubre la asistencia médica.* The insurance covers medical care.
♦ **asistencia técnica** technical support
la **asistenta** SUSTANTIVO
cleaner
el/la **asistente** SUSTANTIVO
assistant
♦ **asistente social** social worker
♦ **los asistentes al acto** those present at the ceremony
asistir VERBO
[1] to go ◊ *No asistieron a la ceremonia.* They didn't go to the ceremony.
[2] to treat ◊ *Le asistió un médico que había de guardia.* He was treated by a duty doctor.
el **asma** SUSTANTIVO FEM
asthma
la **asociación** SUSTANTIVO (PL las **asociaciones**)
association ◊ *por asociación de ideas* by an association of ideas

asociar VERBO
to associate ◊ *Asocio la lluvia con Londres.* I associate rain with London.
◆ **asociarse** to go into partnership ◊ *Los dos empresarios decidieron asociarse.* The two businessmen decided to go into partnership.

asolearse VERBO Latin America
to sunbathe

asomar VERBO
◆ **Te asoma el pañuelo por el bolsillo.** Your handkerchief's sticking out of your pocket.
◆ **No asomes la cabeza por la ventanilla.** Don't lean out of the window.
◆ **Me asomé a la terraza a ver quién gritaba.** I went out onto the balcony to see who was shouting.
◆ **Asómate a la ventana.** Look out of the window.

asombrar VERBO
to amaze ◊ *Me asombra que no lo sepas.* I'm amazed you don't know.
◆ **Intentaba asombrarnos con sus conocimientos.** He was trying to stun us with his knowledge.
◆ **asombrarse** to be amazed ◊ *Se asombró de lo tarde que era.* He was amazed at how late it was.

el **asombro** SUSTANTIVO
amazement ◊ *La gente la observaba con asombro.* People were looking at her in amazement.

asombroso ADJETIVO
amazing

el **aspecto** SUSTANTIVO
1 appearance ◊ *A ver si cuidas más tu aspecto.* Try taking a bit more trouble with your appearance.
2 aspect ◊ *Nos interesa mucho el aspecto económico.* We are very interested in the financial aspect.
◆ **tener buen aspecto (1)** (*persona*) to look well
◆ **tener buen aspecto (2)** (*comida*) to look good

áspero ADJETIVO
1 rough (*mano, toalla*)
2 harsh (*voz*)

la **aspiradora** SUSTANTIVO
vacuum cleaner

aspirar VERBO
1 to breathe in
◆ **Aspire profundamente.** Take a deep breath.
◆ **aspirar a hacer algo** to hope to do something
2 to hoover Latin America

la **aspirina** SUSTANTIVO
aspirin

asqueroso ADJETIVO
1 disgusting (*comida, olor*)
2 filthy (*cocina, manos*) ◊ *Esta cocina está asquerosa.* This kitchen is filthy.
3 horrible ◊ *Esta gente es asquerosa.* They're horrible people.

la **astilla** SUSTANTIVO
splinter

el **astro** SUSTANTIVO
star

la **astrología** SUSTANTIVO
astrology

el/la **astronauta** SUSTANTIVO
astronaut

la **astronomía** SUSTANTIVO
astronomy

astuto ADJETIVO
clever

asumir VERBO
to accept ◊ *Ya he asumido que no voy a ganar.* I've already accepted that I'm not going to win.
◆ **Asumo toda la responsabilidad.** I take full responsibility.
◆ **No estoy dispuesta a asumir ese riesgo.** I'm not prepared to take that risk.

el **asunto** SUSTANTIVO
matter ◊ *Es un asunto muy delicado.* It's a very delicate matter.
◆ **el ministro de asuntos exteriores** the minister for foreign affairs
◆ **No me gusta que se metan en mis asuntos.** I don't like anyone meddling in my affairs.
◆ **¡Eso no es asunto tuyo!** That's none of your business!

asustar VERBO
1 to frighten ◊ *No me asustan los fantasmas.* I'm not frightened of ghosts.
2 to startle ◊ *¡Huy! Me has asustado.* Goodness! You startled me.
◆ **asustarse** to get frightened ◊ *Se asusta por nada.* He gets frightened over nothing.
◆ **No te asustes.** Don't be frightened.

atacar* VERBO
to attack

el **atado** SUSTANTIVO River Plate
◆ **un atado de cigarrillos** a packet of cigarettes

el **atajo** SUSTANTIVO
short cut ◊ *Cogeremos un atajo.* We'll take a short cut.

el **ataque** SUSTANTIVO
attack ◊ *un ataque contra alguien* an attack on somebody
◆ **un ataque cardíaco** a heart attack
◆ **Le dio un ataque de risa.** He burst out laughing.
◆ **un ataque de nervios** a fit of panic

atar VERBO

* Verbs marked with this symbol are irregular. See pages 380-382 for further details

to tie ◊ *Ata al perro a la farola.* Tie the dog to the lamppost.
◆ **Átate los cordones.** Tie your shoelaces up.

atardecer* VERBO
to get dark ◊ *Está atardeciendo.* It's getting dark.

el **atardecer** SUSTANTIVO
dusk
◆ **al atardecer** at dusk

atareado ADJETIVO
busy

el **atasco** SUSTANTIVO
traffic jam

el **ataúd** SUSTANTIVO
coffin

Atenas SUSTANTIVO FEM
Athens

la **atención** SUSTANTIVO (PL las **atenciones**)
◆ **Hay que poner más atención.** You should pay more attention.
◆ **Escucha con atención.** He listens attentively.
◆ **Me llamó la atención lo grande que era la casa.** I was struck by how big the house was.
◆ **El director del colegio le llamó la atención.** The headmaster gave him a talking-to.
◆ **Estás llamando la atención con ese sombrero.** You're attracting attention in that hat.

atención EXCLAMACIÓN
Attention! (*a los soldados*)
◆ **¡Atención, por favor!** May I have your attention please?
◆ **"¡Atención!"** (*como aviso*) "Danger!"

atender* VERBO
1 to serve (*en un bar, tienda*) ◊ *¿Le atienden?* Are you being served?
2 to attend to (*en un banco, oficina*) ◊ *Tengo que atender a un par de clientes.* I've got a couple of clients to attend to.
3 to look after ◊ *atender a los enfermos* to look after the sick
4 to pay attention to ◊ *Todos en clase atendían al profesor.* Everyone in the class was paying attention to the teacher.
◆ **atender los consejos de alguien** to listen to somebody's advice
◆ **La recepcionista atiende al teléfono.** The receptionist answers the telephone.
◆ **No atendieron nuestra petición.** They didn't take any notice of our petition.

atentamente ADVERBIO
1 Yours sincerely
Se usa cuando se conoce personalmente al destinatario.
2 Yours faithfully
Se usa en cartas más formales cuando no se conoce personalmente al destinatario.

atento ADJETIVO
thoughtful ◊ *Es un chico muy atento.* He's a very thoughtful boy.
◆ **Estaban atentos a las explicaciones del instructor.** They were listening attentively to the instructor's explanations.

el **aterrizaje** SUSTANTIVO
landing
◆ **un aterrizaje forzoso** an emergency landing

aterrizar* VERBO
to land

atestado ADJETIVO
packed ◊ *El local estaba atestado de gente.* The place was packed with people.

atiborrarse VERBO
to stuff oneself ◊ *Se atiborró de pasteles.* He stuffed himself with cakes.

el **ático** SUSTANTIVO
top-floor flat
◆ **un ático de lujo** a luxurious penthouse

atiendo VERBO *ver* **atender**

atlántico ADJETIVO
atlantic
◆ **el océano atlántico** the Atlantic Ocean

el **atlas** SUSTANTIVO (PL los **atlas**)
atlas (PL atlases)

el/la **atleta** SUSTANTIVO
athlete

el **atletismo** SUSTANTIVO
athletics

la **atmósfera** SUSTANTIVO
atmosphere

atolondrado ADJETIVO
scatterbrained

atómico ADJETIVO
atomic

el **átomo** SUSTANTIVO
the atom

atónito ADJETIVO
amazed
◆ **quedarse atónito** to be amazed

el **atracador**, la **atracadora** SUSTANTIVO
1 robber ◊ *un atracador de bancos* a bank robber
2 mugger ◊ *Unos atracadores le robaron el bolso.* She had her bag stolen by muggers.

atracar* VERBO
1 to hold up ◊ *atracar un banco* to hold up a bank
2 to mug ◊ *La atracaron en la plaza.* She was mugged in the square.

la **atracción** SUSTANTIVO (PL las **atracciones**)
attraction ◊ *una atracción turística* a tourist attraction
◆ **sentir atracción por algo** to be attracted to something ◊ *Sentía atracción por él.* I was attracted to him.

el **atraco** SUSTANTIVO

☞

1 hold-up ◊ *un atraco a un banco* a hold-up at a bank
2 mugging ◊ *un atraco en plena calle* a mugging in broad daylight

atractivo ADJETIVO
attractive ◊ *un hombre muy atractivo* a very attractive man

el **atractivo** SUSTANTIVO
attraction
◆ **Es una chica con un atractivo especial.** She's a really charming girl.

atraer* VERBO
to attract ◊ *Si bajamos los precios atraeremos a más clientes.* If we put our prices down we'll attract more customers.
◆ **Esa chica me atrae mucho.** I find that girl very attractive.
◆ **No me atrae mucho lo del viaje a Turquía.** That Turkey trip doesn't appeal to me much.

atrapar VERBO
to catch

atrás ADVERBIO
*Se usa **the back**, como sustantivo, cuando nos referimos a la parte posterior de algo.*
◊ *Los niños viajan siempre atrás.* The children always travel in the back.
◆ **la parte de atrás** the back
◆ **el asiento de atrás** the back seat
*Se usa **back**, como adverbio, cuando se habla de la dirección o de una posición posterior en general.*
◊ *Mirar hacia atrás.* To look back. ◊ *Está más atrás.* It's further back.
◆ **Ir para atrás.** To go backwards.
*Se usa **behind** cuando se habla de una posición posterior en relación a otra delantera.*
◊ *El coche de atrás va a adelantarnos.* The car behind is going to overtake us.
◊ *Yo me quedé atrás porque iba muy cansado.* I stayed behind because I was very tired.
◆ **años atrás** years ago

atrasado ADJETIVO
1 backward ◊ *Es un país muy atrasado.* It's a very backward country.
2 back ◊ *números atrasados de una revista* back numbers of a magazine ◊ *pagos atrasados* back payments
3 behind ◊ *Va bastante atrasado en la escuela.* He's rather behind at school.
◆ **Tengo mucho trabajo atrasado.** I'm very behind with my work.
◆ **El reloj está atrasado.** The clock's slow.
4 late Latin America ◊ *Siempre llega atrasada al trabajo.* She's always late for work.

atravesar* VERBO
1 to cross ◊ *Atravesamos el río.* We crossed the river.
2 to go through ◊ *La navaja le atravesó el hígado.* The blade went through his liver. ◊ *Atravesamos un mal momento.* We're going through a bad patch.

atravieso VERBO *ver* **atravesar**

atreverse VERBO
to dare ◊ *No me atreví a decírselo.* I didn't dare tell him.
◆ **No me atrevo.** I daren't.
◆ **La gente no se atreve a salir de noche.** People are afraid of going out at night.

atrevido ADJETIVO
1 daring ◊ *El periodista le hizo preguntas atrevidas.* The reporter asked him some daring questions. ◊ *un escote muy atrevido* a very daring neckline
2 cheeky ◊ *No seas tan atrevido con el jefe.* Don't be so cheeky to the boss.

atropellar VERBO
to run over ◊ *Un coche atropelló al perro.* The dog was run over by a car.

el/la **ATS** ABREVIATURA (= *Ayudante Técnico Sanitario*)
Registered Nurse

el **atún** SUSTANTIVO (PL los **atunes**)
tuna (PL tuna *o* tunas)

audaz ADJETIVO (PL **audaces**)
daring

la **audiencia** SUSTANTIVO
audience ◊ *Su programa tiene mucha audiencia.* His programme has a large audience.

audiovisual ADJETIVO
audiovisual

el **auditorio** SUSTANTIVO
1 auditorium ◊ *El auditorio estaba lleno.* The auditorium was full.
2 audience ◊ *Todo el auditorio aplaudió a la orquesta.* The whole audience applauded the orchestra.

el **aula** SUSTANTIVO FEM
classroom

aumentar VERBO
to increase ◊ *El gobierno ha aumentado el presupuesto de educación.* The government has increased the education budget.
◆ **aumentar de peso** to put on weight

el **aumento** SUSTANTIVO
increase ◊ *Se ha producido un aumento de la productividad.* There has been an increase in productivity.
◆ **Los precios van en aumento.** Prices are going up.

aun ADVERBIO
even ◊ *Aun sentado me duele la pierna.* Even when I'm sitting down, my leg hurts.
◆ **aun así** even so
◆ **aun cuando** even if

* Verbs marked with this symbol are irregular. See pages 380-382 for further details

aún ADVERBIO
1 still
En oraciones afirmativas o preguntas.
◊ *Aún me queda un poco para terminar.* I've still got a little bit left to finish. ◊ *¿Aún te duele?* Is it still hurting?
2 yet
En oraciones o preguntas negativas.
◊ *Aún no han llegado los periódicos de hoy.* Today's papers haven't arrived yet. ◊ *¿No ha venido aún?* Hasn't he got here yet?
*Cuando se usa de forma enfática en una oración o pregunta negativa se puede usar **still**.*
◊ *Y aún no me has devuelto el libro.* You still haven't given me the book back.
3 even
*Cuando **aún** es parte de una comparación.*
◊ *La película es aún más aburrida de lo que creía.* The film's even more boring than I thought it would be. ◊ *Aquello nos unió aún más.* That brought us even closer together.

aunque CONJUNCIÓN
1 although ◊ *Me gusta el francés, aunque prefiero el alemán.* I like French, although I prefer German.
*Lo mismo puede expresarse de una forma más coloquial con **though**.*
◊ *Estoy pensando en ir, aunque no sé cuándo.* I'm thinking of going, though I don't know when.
2 even though ◊ *Seguí andando, aunque me dolía mucho la pierna.* I went on walking, even though my leg was hurting badly.
♦ **No te lo daré, aunque protestes.** I won't give it to you however much you complain.
3 even if ◊ *Pienso irme, aunque tenga que salir por la ventana.* I shall leave, even if I have to climb out of the window.

el **auricular** SUSTANTIVO
receiver (*del teléfono*)
♦ **los auriculares** (*de radio, aparato de música*) headphones

la **ausencia** SUSTANTIVO
absence

ausente ADJETIVO
absent

Australia SUSTANTIVO FEM
Australia

el **australiano,** la **australiana** ADJETIVO, SUSTANTIVO
Australian

Austria SUSTANTIVO FEM
Austria

el **austriaco,** la **austriaca** ADJETIVO, SUSTANTIVO
Austrian

auténtico ADJETIVO
1 real (*no sintético*) ◊ *Es de cuero auténtico.* It's real leather.
2 genuine (*no falso*) ◊ *El cuadro era auténtico.* The painting was genuine.
♦ **Es un auténtico campeón.** He's a real champion.

el **auto** SUSTANTIVO
car

la **autobiografía** SUSTANTIVO
autobiography (PL autobiographies)

el **autobús** SUSTANTIVO (PL los **autobuses**)
bus (PL buses)
♦ **en autobús** by bus
♦ **un autobús de línea** a coach

el **autocar** SUSTANTIVO
coach (PL coaches)

la **autoedición** SUSTANTIVO
desktop publishing

la **autoescuela** SUSTANTIVO
driving school

el **autógrafo** SUSTANTIVO
autograph

automático ADJETIVO
automatic

el **automóvil** SUSTANTIVO
car

el/la **automovilista** SUSTANTIVO
motorist

la **autonomía** SUSTANTIVO
1 autonomy ◊ *un estatuto de autonomía* a statute of autonomy ◊ *Tengo mucha autonomía en mi trabajo.* I have a lot of autonomy in my work.
2 autonomous region ◊ *Andalucía es una de las autonomías más extensas.* Andalusia is one of the biggest autonomous regions.

autonómico ADJETIVO
regional

autónomo ADJETIVO
1 autonomous ◊ *las comunidades autónomas* the autonomous regions
2 self-employed ◊ *Ser autónomo tiene sus ventajas.* Being self-employed has its advantages.

la **autopista** SUSTANTIVO
motorway
♦ **autopista de peaje** toll motorway

el **autor,** la **autora** SUSTANTIVO
author ◊ *el autor de la novela* the author of the novel
♦ **el autor del cuadro** the painter
♦ **los presuntos autores del crimen** the suspected killers

autorizado ADJETIVO
authorized

autorizar* VERBO
to authorize ◊ *No le han autorizado la entrada al país.* His entry into the country hasn't been authorized.

♦ **Eso no te autoriza a tratarlo así.** That doesn't give you the right to treat him this way.

el **autoservicio** SUSTANTIVO
[1] supermarket ◊ *Sale más económico comprar en el autoservicio.* It's cheaper to shop at the supermarket.
[2] self-service restaurant ◊ *Comimos en un autoservicio.* We ate at a self-service restaurant.

el **autostop** SUSTANTIVO
hitch-hiking
♦ **hacer autostop** to hitch-hike

el/la **autostopista** SUSTANTIVO
hitch-hiker

la **autovía** SUSTANTIVO
dual carriageway

el **auxilio** SUSTANTIVO
help ◊ *una llamada de auxilio* a call for help
♦ **los primeros auxilios** first aid

auxilio EXCLAMACIÓN
help!

avanzar* VERBO
to make progress ◊ *Isabel avanzó mucho el pasado trimestre.* Isabel made a lot of progress last term.
♦ **¿Qué tal avanza el proyecto?** How's the project coming on?

avaro ADJETIVO
miserly

Avda. ABREVIATURA (= *Avenida*)
Ave. (= Avenue)

el **AVE** ABREVIATURA (= *Alta Velocidad Española*)
high-speed train

el **ave** SUSTANTIVO FEM
bird
♦ **un ave de rapiña** a bird of prey
♦ **aves de corral** poultry SING

la **avellana** SUSTANTIVO
hazelnut

la **avena** SUSTANTIVO
oats PL

la **avenida** SUSTANTIVO
avenue

aventajar VERBO
♦ **El Salamanca aventaja en tres puntos al Córdoba.** Salamanca has a three-point lead over Córdoba.

aventar* VERBO Mexico
to throw

el **aventón** SUSTANTIVO (PL los **aventones**)
Mexico
lift ◊ *Le di un aventón.* I gave him a lift.

la **aventura** SUSTANTIVO
[1] adventure ◊ *Te contaré nuestras aventuras en África.* I'll tell you about our adventures in Africa.
[2] affair ◊ *Tuvo una aventura con su vecino.* She had an affair with her neighbour.

avergonzar* VERBO
to embarrass ◊ *Me avergonzaste delante de todos.* You embarrassed me in front of everyone.
♦ **Me avergüenzan estas situaciones.** I find this sort of situation embarrassing.
♦ **No me avergüenza nuestra relación.** I'm not ashamed of our relationship.
♦ **avergonzarse de algo** to be ashamed of something ◊ *No hay de qué avergonzarse.* There's nothing to be ashamed of.
♦ **Me avergüenzo de haberme portado tan mal.** I'm ashamed of myself for behaving so badly.

la **avería** SUSTANTIVO
♦ **El coche tiene una avería.** The car has broken down.

averiarse* VERBO
to break down

averiguar* VERBO
to find out ◊ *La policía no ha conseguido averiguar dónde se escondió el arma.* The police haven't managed to find out where the weapon was hidden.

el **avestruz** SUSTANTIVO (PL los **avestruces**)
ostrich (PL ostriches)

la **aviación** SUSTANTIVO (PL las **aviaciones**)
[1] aviation ◊ *aviación civil* civil aviation
[2] air force ◊ *Es oficial de aviación.* He's an officer in the air force.

aviento VERBO *ver* **aventar**

el **avión** SUSTANTIVO (PL los **aviones**)
plane
♦ **ir en avión** to fly

la **avioneta** SUSTANTIVO
light aircraft

avisar VERBO
[1] to warn ◊ *Ya nos avisaron de que había nieve en la carretera.* They had warned us that there was snow on the roads.
[2] to let...know ◊ *Avísanos si hay alguna novedad.* Let us know if there's any news.
[3] to call ◊ *avisar al médico* to call the doctor ◊ *Avisaron a una ambulancia.* They called an ambulance.

el **aviso** SUSTANTIVO
[1] warning ◊ *El árbitro le dio un aviso.* The referee gave him a warning.
[2] notice ◊ *Había un aviso en la puerta.* There was a notice on the door.
♦ **hasta nuevo aviso** until further notice

la **avispa** SUSTANTIVO
wasp

ay EXCLAMACIÓN

1 ow! ◊ *¡Ay! ¡Me has pisado!* Ow! You've trodden on my toe!
2 oh no! ◊ *¡Ay! ¡Creo que nos han engañado!* Oh no! I think they've cheated us!

ayer ADVERBIO
yesterday
◆ **antes de ayer** the day before yesterday
◆ **ayer por la mañana** yesterday morning
◆ **ayer por la tarde (1)** (*si es de día*) yesterday afternoon
◆ **ayer por la tarde (2)** (*si no es de día*) yesterday evening
◆ **ayer por la noche** last night

la **ayuda** SUSTANTIVO
help
◆ **la ayuda humanitaria** humanitarian aid

el/la **ayudante** SUSTANTIVO
assistant

ayudar VERBO
to help ◊ *¿Me ayudas con los ejercicios?* Could you help me with these exercises?
◆ **ayudar a alguien a hacer algo** to help somebody do something

el **ayuntamiento** SUSTANTIVO
1 council ◊ *El ayuntamiento recauda sus propios impuestos.* The council collects its own taxes.
2 town hall (*en pueblo*) ◊ *¿Dónde está el ayuntamiento?* Where's the town hall?
3 city hall (*en ciudad grande*) ◊ *¿Dónde está el ayuntamiento?* Where's the city hall?

la **azafata** SUSTANTIVO
air-hostess (*de avión*)
◆ **una azafata de congresos** a conference hostess

el **azar** SUSTANTIVO
chance ◊ *Nos encontramos por azar.* We met by chance.
◆ **al azar** at random ◊ *Escoge uno al azar.* Pick one at random.

azotar VERBO
to whip

la **azotea** SUSTANTIVO
roof

el/la **azteca** ADJETIVO, SUSTANTIVO
Aztec

el **azúcar** SUSTANTIVO
sugar
◆ **azúcar moreno** brown sugar
◆ **un caramelo sin azúcar** a sugar-free sweet

el **azul** ADJETIVO, SUSTANTIVO
blue ◊ *una puerta azul* a blue door ◊ *Yo iba de azul.* I was dressed in blue.
◆ **azul celeste** sky blue
◆ **azul marino** navy blue

el **azulejo** SUSTANTIVO
tile

B

el **babero** SUSTANTIVO
bib
el **babi** SUSTANTIVO
smock
la **baca** SUSTANTIVO
roof rack
el **bacalao** SUSTANTIVO
cod
el **bache** SUSTANTIVO
1 pothole (*socavón*)
2 bump (*saliente*)
el **Bachillerato** SUSTANTIVO

> *The **Bachillerato** is a two-year secondary school course leading to university.*

la **bacteria** SUSTANTIVO
bacterium (PL bacteria)
el **bafle** SUSTANTIVO
loudspeaker
la **bahía** SUSTANTIVO
bay (PL bays)
bailar VERBO
to dance
◆ **sacar a bailar a alguien** to ask someone to dance
el **bailarín,** la **bailarina** SUSTANTIVO (MASC PL los **bailarines**)
dancer
el **baile** SUSTANTIVO
dance ◇ *Me han invitado a un baile.* I have been invited to a dance.
la **baja** SUSTANTIVO
◆ **darse de baja** to leave ◇ *Se dieron de baja en el club.* They left the club.
◆ **estar de baja** to be on sick leave
la **bajada** SUSTANTIVO
drop ◇ *Han anunciado una bajada de las temperaturas.* They forecast a drop in temperatures.
◆ **Me caí en la bajada de la montaña.** I fell going down the mountain.
◆ **La bajada hasta la playa es muy pronunciada.** The road down to the beach is very steep.
bajar VERBO
1 to go down
Cuando el hablante está arriba.
◇ *Bajó la escalera muy despacio.* He went down the stairs very slowly.
2 to come down
También cuando el hablante está abajo.
◇ *Baja y ayúdame.* Come down and help me. ◇ *Han bajado los precios.* Prices have come down.
◆ **Los coches han bajado de precio.** Cars have come down in price.
3 to take down
Cuando el hablante está arriba.
◇ *¿Has bajado la basura?* Have you taken the rubbish down?
4 to bring down
Cuando el hablante está abajo.
◇ *¿Me bajas el abrigo? Hace frío aquí fuera.* Could you bring my coat down, it's cold out here.
5 to get down
Cuando no se alcanza algo.
◇ *¿Me bajas la maleta del armario?* Could you get me the suitcase down from the wardrobe?
6 to put down ◇ *¿Bajo la persiana?* Shall I put the blind down? ◇ *Los comercios han bajado los precios.* Businesses have put their prices down.
◆ **¡Baja la voz, que no estoy sordo!** Keep your voice down, I'm not deaf!
7 to turn down ◇ *Baja la radio que no oigo nada.* Turn the radio down, I can't hear a thing.
8 to download (*Internet*)
◆ **bajarse de (1)** to get off (*del autobús, tren, avión*) ◇ *Se bajó del autobús antes que yo.* He got off the bus before me.
◆ **bajarse de (2)** to get out of (*del coche*) ◇ *¡Bájate del coche!* Get out of the car!
◆ **bajarse de (3)** to get down from (*de un árbol, escalera, silla*) ◇ *¡Bájate de ahí!* Get down from there!

bajo (1) ADJETIVO
1 low (*notas, temperaturas, nivel*) ◇ *una silla muy baja* a very low chair
◆ **la temporada baja** the low season
2 short ◇ *Mi hermano es muy bajo.* My brother is very short.
◆ **Viven en la planta baja.** They live on the ground floor.
◆ **Hablaban en voz baja.** They spoke quietly.

bajo (2) PREPOSICIÓN
under ◇ *bajo el título de ...* under the title of ... ◇ *Juan llevaba un libro bajo el brazo.* Juan was carrying a book under his arm.
◆ **bajo tierra** underground

bajo (3) ADVERBIO
1 low ◇ *El avión volaba muy bajo.* The plane was flying very low.
2 quietly ◇ *¡Habla bajo!* Speak quietly!

el **bajo** SUSTANTIVO
1 (*instrumento*)

bass (PL basses) ◊ *Elena toca el bajo en un grupo.* Elena plays bass in a group.
2 (*de un edificio*)
ground floor ◊ *Vivo en un bajo.* I live on the ground floor.

el **bakalao** SUSTANTIVO
techno

la **bala** SUSTANTIVO
bullet

el **balcón** SUSTANTIVO (PL los **balcones**)
balcony (PL balconies)

la **baldosa** SUSTANTIVO
tile

el **baldosín** SUSTANTIVO (PL los **baldosines**)
tile

balear ADJETIVO
Balearic

Baleares SUSTANTIVO FEM PL
the Balearic Islands

la **ballena** SUSTANTIVO
whale

el **ballet** SUSTANTIVO (PL los **ballets**)
ballet

el **balneario** SUSTANTIVO
spa

el **balón** SUSTANTIVO (PL los **balones**)
ball

el **baloncesto** SUSTANTIVO
basketball

el **balonmano** SUSTANTIVO
handball

el **balonvolea** SUSTANTIVO
volleyball

la **balsa** SUSTANTIVO
raft

la **banana** SUSTANTIVO Latin America
banana

bancario ADJETIVO
bank (*cuenta, tarjeta, préstamo*)

***bank** en este caso va siempre delante del sustantivo.*

el **banco** SUSTANTIVO
1 (*para el dinero*)
bank
2 (*de un parque*)
bench (PL benches)
3 (*de iglesia*)
pew

la **banda** SUSTANTIVO
1 band ◊ *Toca la trompeta en la banda del pueblo.* He plays the trumpet in the village band.
2 gang ◊ *La policía ha cogido a toda la banda.* The police have caught the whole gang.
3 sash (PL sashes) ◊ *Las autoridades llevaban una banda azul.* The dignitaries were wearing a blue sash.
◆ **la banda sonora** the soundtrack

la **bandeja** SUSTANTIVO
tray (PL trays)

la **bandera** SUSTANTIVO
flag
◆ **la bandera blanca** the white flag

el **bandido** SUSTANTIVO
bandit

el **bando** SUSTANTIVO
side ◊ *Un bando está a favor y el otro en contra.* One side is in favour and the other is against.

la **banqueta** SUSTANTIVO
1 stool (*asiento*)
2 pavement Mexico

el **banquete** SUSTANTIVO
banquet
◆ **el banquete de bodas** the wedding reception

el **banquillo** SUSTANTIVO
bench (PL benches) ◊ *El entrenador siempre se sienta en el banquillo.* The trainer always sits on the bench.
◆ **el banquillo de los acusados** the dock

el **bañador** SUSTANTIVO
1 swimming trunks PL (*de hombre*)
2 swimming costume (*de mujer*)

bañarse VERBO
1 to have a bath ◊ *Me gusta más bañarme que ducharme.* I prefer having a bath to having a shower.
2 to go for a swim ◊ *Estuve en la playa pero no me bañé.* I was on the beach but I didn't go for a swim.

la **bañera** SUSTANTIVO
bath

el **baño** SUSTANTIVO
bathroom ◊ *¿Podría decirme dónde está el baño?* Could you tell me where the bathroom is?
◆ **darse un baño (1)** to have a bath (*en la bañera*)
◆ **darse un baño (2)** to go for a swim (*en el mar*)

el **bar** SUSTANTIVO
bar

la **baraja** SUSTANTIVO
pack of cards

la **barandilla** SUSTANTIVO
1 banisters PL (*de una escalera*)
2 railing (*de un balcón*)

la **barata** SUSTANTIVO Mexico
sale

barato (1) ADJETIVO
cheap ◊ *Esta marca es más barata que aquélla.* This brand is cheaper than that one.

barato (2) ADVERBIO
cheaply ◊ *Aquí se come muy barato.* You can eat really cheaply here.

la **barba** SUSTANTIVO
beard
◆ **dejarse barba** to grow a beard

la **barbacoa** SUSTANTIVO
barbecue

la **barbaridad** SUSTANTIVO

☞

atrocity (PL atrocities) ◊ *Hicieron barbaridades en la guerra.* They committed atrocities during the war.

♦ **Pablo come una barbaridad.** Pablo eats an awful lot.

♦ **decir barbaridades** to talk nonsense

♦ **¡Qué barbaridad!** Good grief!

la **barbilla** SUSTANTIVO
chin

la **barca** SUSTANTIVO
boat

el **barco** SUSTANTIVO
[1] ship (*más grande*)
♦ **un barco de guerra** a warship
[2] boat (*más pequeño*)
♦ **un barco de vela** a sailing boat

la **barda** SUSTANTIVO Mexico
fence

el **barniz** SUSTANTIVO (PL los **barnices**)
varnish (PL varnishes)

barnizar* VERBO
to varnish

la **barra** SUSTANTIVO
bar ◊ *una barra metálica* a metal bar ◊ *Me tomé un café en la barra.* I had a coffee at the bar.
♦ **una barra de pan** a French loaf
♦ **una barra de labios** lipstick
♦ **las barras paralelas** the parallel bars

la **barraca** SUSTANTIVO
small farmhouse
♦ **una barraca de feria** a fairground stall

el **barranco** SUSTANTIVO
ravine

barrer VERBO
to sweep

la **barrera** SUSTANTIVO
barrier
♦ **una barrera de seguridad** a safety barrier

la **barriga** SUSTANTIVO (*coloquial*)
belly (PL bellies) ◊ *Estás echando barriga.* You're getting a bit of a belly.
♦ **Me duele la barriga.** I have a sore stomach.

el **barril** SUSTANTIVO
barrel

el **barrilete** SUSTANTIVO River Plate
kite

el **barrio** SUSTANTIVO
area ◊ *Ese chico no es del barrio.* That boy's not from this area.
♦ **la pescadería del barrio** the local fishmonger's
♦ **el barrio chino** the red-light district

el **barro** SUSTANTIVO
[1] mud ◊ *Metí el pie en un charco y me llené de barro.* I stood in a puddle and got covered in mud.
[2] clay ◊ *una vasija de barro* a clay pot

el **barrote** SUSTANTIVO
bar ◊ *los barrotes de la ventana* the bars on the window

el **barullo** SUSTANTIVO
[1] racket
♦ **armar barullo** to make a racket
[2] mess ◊ *Esta habitación está hecha un barullo.* This room is a mess.

basarse VERBO
♦ **Mi conclusión se basa en los datos.** My conclusion is based on the facts.
♦ **¿En qué te basas para decir eso?** What grounds have you got for saying that?
♦ **Para la novela me basé en la vida de mi abuela.** I based the novel on the life of my grandmother.

la **báscula** SUSTANTIVO
scales PL

la **base** SUSTANTIVO
[1] base ◊ *la base de la columna* the base of the column
[2] basis (PL bases) ◊ *El esfuerzo es la base del éxito.* Effort is the basis for success.
♦ **las bases del concurso** the rules of the competition
♦ **Lo consiguió a base de mucho trabajo.** She managed it through hard work.
♦ **una base militar** a military base
♦ **una base de datos** a database

básico ADJETIVO
basic

bastante (1) ADJETIVO, PRONOMBRE
[1] enough
Cuando significa suficiente.
◊ *No tengo bastante dinero.* I haven't enough money. ◊ *Ya hay bastantes libros en casa.* There are enough books in the house. ◊ *¿Hay bastante?* Is there enough?
[2] quite a lot of
Cuando significa una cantidad considerable.
◊ *Vino bastante gente.* Quite a lot of people came.
♦ **Se tarda bastante tiempo en llegar.** It takes quite a while to get there.
♦ **Voy a tardar bastante.** I'm going to take quite a while.

bastante (2) ADVERBIO
[1] quite ◊ *Son bastante ricos.* They are quite rich. ◊ *Juegas bastante bien.* You play quite well.
[2] quite a lot ◊ *Sus padres ganan bastante.* Their parents earn quite a lot.

bastar VERBO
to be enough ◊ *Con esto basta.* That's enough. ◊ *¡Basta ya de tonterías!* That's enough of your nonsense!
♦ **¡Basta!** That's enough!

* Verbs marked with this symbol are irregular. See pages 380-382 for further details

◆ **bastarse** to manage ◊ *Yo me basto solo.* I can manage on my own.

basto ADJETIVO
coarse ◊ *Esta tela es muy basta.* It's a very coarse material.
◆ **¡Qué basto eres!** You've got no manners!

el **bastón** SUSTANTIVO (PL los **bastones**)
stick
◆ **un bastón de esquí** a ski stick

los **bastos** SUSTANTIVO
clubs

> **Bastos** *are clubs, one of the suits in the Spanish card deck.*

la **basura** SUSTANTIVO
[1] rubbish ◊ *Eso es basura.* That's rubbish.
◆ **tirar algo a la basura** to put something in the bin
[2] litter ◊ *Hay mucha basura en la calle.* There's a lot of litter in the street.

el **basurero** SUSTANTIVO
[1] (*persona*)
dustman (PL dustmen)
[2] (*vertedero*)
rubbish dump
[3] rubbish bin Chile, Mexico

la **bata** SUSTANTIVO
[1] dressing gown (*de casa*)
[2] lab coat (*de laboratorio*)

la **batalla** SUSTANTIVO
battle

la **batería** SUSTANTIVO
[1] battery (PL batteries) ◊ *Se ha agotado la batería.* The battery is flat.
[2] drums PL ◊ *¿Tocas la batería?* Do you play the drums?
◆ **aparcar en batería** to park at an angle to the kerb
◆ **una batería de cocina** a set of kitchen equipment
[3] (*en grupo*)
drummer ◊ *La batería del grupo se llama Amanda.* The group's drummer is called Amanda.

el **batería** SUSTANTIVO
drummer ◊ *El batería del grupo se llama Juan.* The group's drummer is called Juan.

el **batido** SUSTANTIVO
milkshake ◊ *un batido de fresa* a strawberry milkshake

la **batidora** SUSTANTIVO
mixer

batir VERBO
[1] to beat (*un huevo*)
[2] to whip (*nata*)
[3] to break (*un récord*)

el **baúl** SUSTANTIVO
[1] chest (*para ropa*)
[2] trunk (*para viajar*)
[3] boot (*de un coche*) River Plate

el **bautizo** SUSTANTIVO
christening

la **bayeta** SUSTANTIVO
cloth
◆ **¿Has pasado la bayeta por la mesa?** Have you wiped the table?

el **bebe**, la **beba** SUSTANTIVO River Plate
baby (PL babies)

el **bebé** SUSTANTIVO (PL los **bebés**)
baby (PL babies)

el **bebedero** SUSTANTIVO Chile, Mexico
drinking fountain

beber VERBO
to drink
◆ **Se bebió la leche de un trago.** He drank the milk in one gulp.

la **bebida** SUSTANTIVO
drink
◆ **bebidas alcohólicas** alcoholic drinks

bebido ADJETIVO
drunk
◆ **estar bebido** to be drunk

la **beca** SUSTANTIVO
[1] grant (*ayuda económica general*)
[2] scholarship (*dada por méritos o en concurso*)

el **béisbol** SUSTANTIVO
baseball

el **belén** SUSTANTIVO (PL los **belenes**)
crib

el/la **belga** ADJETIVO, SUSTANTIVO
Belgian

Bélgica SUSTANTIVO FEM
Belgium

la **belleza** SUSTANTIVO
beauty (PL beauties)

bello ADJETIVO
beautiful
◆ **bellas artes** fine art SING

bendecir* VERBO
to bless

la **bendición** SUSTANTIVO (PL las **bendiciones**)
blessing

beneficiar VERBO
to benefit
◆ **beneficiarse de algo** to benefit from something

el **beneficio** SUSTANTIVO
profit ◊ *Obtuvieron un beneficio de 4.000 millones de pesetas.* They made a profit of 4,000 million pesetas.
◆ **No han tenido beneficios este año.** They didn't make any profit this year.
◆ **sacar beneficio de algo** to benefit from something ◊ *Seguro que espera sacar algún beneficio.* He definitely expects to benefit from it.
◆ **a beneficio de** in aid of ◊ *un concierto a beneficio de las víctimas del terremoto* a concert in aid of the earthquake victims

benéfico ADJETIVO

☞

charity (PL charities)

charity en este caso va siempre delante del sustantivo.

◇ *un concierto benéfico* a charity concert

el **berberecho** SUSTANTIVO

cockle

la **berenjena** SUSTANTIVO

aubergine

las **bermudas** SUSTANTIVO

Bermuda shorts

♦ **unas bermudas** a pair of Bermuda shorts

la **berza** SUSTANTIVO

cabbage

besar VERBO

to kiss

♦ **Ana y Pepe se besaron.** Ana and Pepe kissed each other.

el **beso** SUSTANTIVO

kiss (PL kisses)

♦ **dar un beso a alguien** to give somebody a kiss

la **bestia** SUSTANTIVO

beast

bestia ADJETIVO

♦ **¡Qué bestia eres!** You're so rough! (*coloquial*)

♦ **Tiró de él a lo bestia.** He pulled him roughly.

el **besugo** SUSTANTIVO

sea bream

el **betún** SUSTANTIVO

shoe polish

el **biberón** SUSTANTIVO (PL los **biberones**)

baby's bottle

♦ **Voy a dar el biberón al niño.** I'm going to give the baby his bottle.

la **Biblia** SUSTANTIVO

Bible

la **biblioteca** SUSTANTIVO

library (PL libraries)

el **bicarbonato** SUSTANTIVO

bicarbonate

el **bicho** SUSTANTIVO

insect ◇ *Me ha picado un bicho.* I've been bitten by an insect.

♦ **un bicho raro** an oddball (*coloquial*)

la **bici** SUSTANTIVO

bike

la **bicicleta** SUSTANTIVO

bicycle

♦ **una bicicleta de montaña** a mountain bike

el **bidé** SUSTANTIVO (PL los **bidés**)

bidet

el **bidón** SUSTANTIVO (PL los **bidones**)

drum

el **bien** SUSTANTIVO

good ◇ *Lo digo por tu bien.* I'm telling you for your own good.

♦ **los bienes** possessions ◇ *todos los bienes de la familia* all the family's possessions

bien ADVERBIO

1 well ◇ *Habla bien el español.* He speaks Spanish well. ◇ *El traje me está bien.* The suit fits me well.

2 good

Con verbos que expresan una sensación física.

◇ *Huele bien.* It smells good. ◇ *Sabe bien.* It tastes good.

♦ **Has contestado bien.** You gave the right answer.

♦ **Lo pasamos muy bien.** We had a very good time.

3 very

Cuando acompaña a un adjetivo.

◇ *un café bien caliente* a very hot coffee

♦ **¿Estás bien?** Are you OK?

♦ **¡Está bien! Lo haré.** OK! I'll do it.

♦ **Ese libro está muy bien.** That's a very good book.

♦ **Está muy bien que ahorres dinero.** It's good that you're saving.

♦ **¡Eso no está bien!** That's not very nice!

♦ **Hiciste bien en decírselo.** You were right to tell him.

♦ **¡Ya está bien!** That's enough!

♦ **¡Qué bien!** Excellent!

el **bienestar** SUSTANTIVO

well-being

la **bienvenida** SUSTANTIVO

♦ **dar la bienvenida a alguien** to welcome somebody

♦ **una fiesta de bienvenida** a welcome party

bienvenido (1) ADJETIVO

welcome ◇ *Siempre serás bienvenido aquí.* You will always be welcome here.

bienvenido (2) EXCLAMACIÓN

welcome!

el **bife** SUSTANTIVO Chile, River Plate

steak

la **bifurcación** SUSTANTIVO (PL las **bifurcaciones**)

fork

el **bigote** SUSTANTIVO

moustache

el **bikini** SUSTANTIVO

bikini

bilingüe ADJETIVO

bilingual

el **billar** SUSTANTIVO

billiards SING

♦ **el billar americano** pool

el **billete** SUSTANTIVO

1 ticket ◇ *un billete de metro* an underground ticket

♦ **sacar un billete** to buy a ticket

♦ **un billete de ida y vuelta** a return ticket

2 note ◊ *un billete de mil pesetas* a thousand peseta note

el **billón** SUSTANTIVO (PL los **billones**)

♦ **un billón** a million millions

> *La palabra* ***billion*** *equivale a mil millones.*

el **bingo** SUSTANTIVO

1 bingo ◊ *jugar al bingo* to play bingo

2 bingo hall ◊ *Van a abrir un bingo aquí.* They're opening a bingo hall here.

biodegradable ADJETIVO

biodegradable

la **biografía** SUSTANTIVO

biography (PL biographies)

la **biología** SUSTANTIVO

biology

biológico ADJETIVO

1 organic (*alimento*)

2 biological (*ciclo, padre, guerra*)

el **biombo** SUSTANTIVO

folding screen

el **biquini** SUSTANTIVO

bikini (PL bikinis)

la **birome** SUSTANTIVO River Plate

ballpoint pen

la **birria** SUSTANTIVO

♦ **ser una birria** to be rubbish (*coloquial*)

la **bisabuela** SUSTANTIVO

great-grandmother

el **bisabuelo** SUSTANTIVO

great-grandfather

♦ **mis bisabuelos** my great-grandparents

la **bisagra** SUSTANTIVO

hinge

bisiesto ADJETIVO

♦ **un año bisiesto** a leap year

la **bisnieta** SUSTANTIVO

great-granddaughter

el **bisnieto** SUSTANTIVO

great-grandson

♦ **tus bisnietos** your great-grandchildren

el **bistec** SUSTANTIVO (PL los **bistecs**)

steak

la **bisutería** SUSTANTIVO

costume jewellery

♦ **Son de bisutería.** They're costume jewellery.

bizco ADJETIVO

cross-eyed

el **bizcocho** SUSTANTIVO

sponge cake

blanco ADJETIVO

white ◊ *un vestido blanco* a white dress

el **blanco** SUSTANTIVO

white ◊ *Me gusta el blanco.* I like white.

♦ **dar en el blanco** to hit the target

♦ **dejar algo en blanco** to leave something blank

♦ **Cuando iba a responder me quedé en blanco.** Just as I was about to reply my mind went blank.

blando ADJETIVO

1 soft ◊ *Este colchón es muy blando.* This mattress is very soft.

2 easy ◊ *El director es muy blando con sus alumnos.* The headmaster is very easy on his pupils.

el **bloc** SUSTANTIVO (PL los **blocs**)

writing pad

♦ **un bloc de dibujo** a drawing pad

el **bloque** SUSTANTIVO

block

♦ **un bloque de pisos** a block of flats

bloquear VERBO

to block ◊ *La nieve bloqueó las carreteras.* The snow blocked the roads.

la **blusa** SUSTANTIVO

blouse

la **bobada** SUSTANTIVO

♦ **hacer bobadas** to do stupid things

♦ **Este programa es una bobada.** This programme is stupid.

♦ **decir bobadas** to talk nonsense

la **bobina** SUSTANTIVO

reel

bobo ADJETIVO

silly

la **boca** SUSTANTIVO

mouth ◊ *No debes hablar con la boca llena.* You shouldn't talk with your mouth full. ◊ *No abrió la boca en toda la tarde.* He didn't open his mouth all afternoon.

♦ **boca abajo** face down

♦ **boca arriba** face up

♦ **Me quedé con la boca abierta.** I was dumbfounded.

♦ **la boca del metro** the entrance to the underground

la **bocacalle** SUSTANTIVO

♦ **Es una bocacalle del Paseo Central.** It's a side street off the Paseo Central.

♦ **La primera bocacalle a la derecha.** The first road on the right.

el **bocadillo** SUSTANTIVO

♦ **Ya me he comido el bocadillo.** I've already had my roll.

♦ **un bocadillo de queso** a cheese baguette

el **bocado** SUSTANTIVO

1 bite ◊ *Le he dado sólo un bocado a tu tortilla.* I've only had a bite out of your omelette.

♦ **No he probado bocado desde ayer.** I haven't had a bite to eat since yesterday.

2 mouthful ◊ *Intentaba hablar entre bocado y bocado.* I was trying to talk between mouthfuls.

el **bocata** SUSTANTIVO = **bocadillo**

el **bochorno** SUSTANTIVO

♦ **Hace bochorno.** It's muggy.

la **bocina** SUSTANTIVO

☞

1 horn (*del coche*)
2 receiver (*del teléfono*) Chile, River Plate

la **boda** SUSTANTIVO
wedding
◆ **las bodas de oro** golden wedding SING
◆ **las bodas de plata** silver wedding SING

la **bodega** SUSTANTIVO
1 cellar (*de una casa*)
2 wine cellar (*para guardar el vino*)
3 wine shop (*para vender vino*)
4 hold (*de un avión*)

la **bofetada** SUSTANTIVO
slap ◊ *dar una bofetada a alguien* to give somebody a slap

el **boicot** SUSTANTIVO (PL los **boicots**)
boycott
◆ **hacer el boicot a algo** to boycott something

la **boina** SUSTANTIVO
beret

la **bola** SUSTANTIVO
ball
◆ **una bola de nieve** a snowball

la **bolera** SUSTANTIVO
bowling alley

la **boletería** SUSTANTIVO Latin America
ticket office

el **boletín** SUSTANTIVO (PL los **boletines**)
bulletin
◆ **un boletín informativo** a news bulletin

el **boleto** SUSTANTIVO
ticket ◊ *un boleto de lotería* a lottery ticket ◊ *un boleto de quinielas* a pools coupon

el **boli** SUSTANTIVO
pen

el **bolígrafo** SUSTANTIVO
pen

el **bolillo** SUSTANTIVO Mexico
bun

Bolivia SUSTANTIVO FEM
Bolivia

el **boliviano**, la **boliviana** ADJETIVO, SUSTANTIVO
Bolivian

la **bollería** SUSTANTIVO
pastries PL

el **bollo** SUSTANTIVO
1 bun ◊ *Me he comido un bollo para desayunar.* I had a bun for breakfast.
2 dent ◊ *Tengo el coche lleno de bollos.* My car is full of dents.

los **bolos** SUSTANTIVO
1 bowls SING (*juego al aire libre*)
2 tenpin bowling SING (*juego en bolera*)

la **bolsa** SUSTANTIVO
1 bag ◊ *una bolsa de plástico* a plastic bag
◆ **una bolsa de deportes** a sports bag
◆ **una bolsa de viaje** a travel bag
2 handbag Mexico
◆ **la Bolsa** the Stock Exchange

el **bolsillo** SUSTANTIVO
pocket ◊ *Sacó las llaves del bolsillo.* He took the keys out of his pocket.
◆ **un libro de bolsillo** a paperback

el **bolso** SUSTANTIVO
bag

la **bomba** SUSTANTIVO
1 bomb ◊ *la bomba atómica* the atomic bomb
2 pump ◊ *una bomba de agua* a water pump
◆ **pasarlo bomba** to have a brilliant time

la **bombacha** SUSTANTIVO River Plate
panties PL

bombardear VERBO
to bombard
◆ **bombardear a alguien a preguntas** to bombard somebody with questions

el **bombero** SUSTANTIVO
fireman (PL firemen)
◆ **llamar a los bomberos** to call the fire brigade

la **bombilla** SUSTANTIVO
lightbulb

la **bombita** SUSTANTIVO River Plate
lightbulb

el **bombo** SUSTANTIVO
bass drum

el **bombón** SUSTANTIVO (PL los **bombones**)
chocolate

la **bombona** SUSTANTIVO
gas cylinder

la **bondad** SUSTANTIVO
kindness ◊ *un acto de bondad* an act of kindness
◆ **¿Tendría la bondad de ...?** Would you be so kind as to ...?

el **boniato** SUSTANTIVO
sweet potato (PL sweet potatoes)

bonito ADJETIVO
pretty ◊ *una casa muy bonita* a very pretty house

el **bonito** SUSTANTIVO
tuna (PL tuna *o* tunas)

el **bonobús** SUSTANTIVO (PL los **bonobuses**)
bus pass (PL bus passes)

el **boquerón** SUSTANTIVO (PL los **boquerones**)
anchovy (PL anchovies)

el **boquete** SUSTANTIVO
hole ◊ *Abrieron un boquete en el muro.* They made a hole in the wall.

la **borda** SUSTANTIVO
◆ **echar algo por la borda** to throw something overboard

bordar VERBO
to embroider

el **borde** SUSTANTIVO

edge ◇ *al borde de la mesa* at the edge of the table
◆ **estar al borde de algo** to be on the verge of something

borde ADJETIVO
◆ **¡No seas borde!** Don't be so horrible!

el **bordillo** SUSTANTIVO
kerb ◇ *Los coches no pueden subirse al bordillo.* Cars are not allowed onto the kerb.

bordo SUSTANTIVO MASC
◆ **subir a bordo** to get on board

la **borrachera** SUSTANTIVO
◆ **coger una borrachera** to get drunk

borracho ADJETIVO
drunk ◇ *Estás borracho.* You're drunk.

el **borrador** SUSTANTIVO
1 rough draft ◇ *Escribe primero un borrador.* First write a rough draft.
2 duster ◇ *Usó un trapo como borrador.* He used a rag as a duster.

borrar VERBO
1 to rub out ◇ *Borra toda la palabra.* Rub out the whole word.
2 to clean ◇ *Borra la pizarra.* Clean the blackboard.
3 to wipe ◇ *No borres esa cinta.* Don't wipe that tape.
◆ **borrarse de (1)** to take one's name off ◇ *Voy a borrarme de la lista.* I'm going to take my name off the list.
◆ **borrarse de (2)** to leave ◇ *Se borró del club.* He left the club.

la **borrasca** SUSTANTIVO
◆ **Viene una borrasca por el Atlántico.** There's low pressure over the Atlantic.

el **borrón** SUSTANTIVO (PL los **borrones**)
stain

borroso ADJETIVO
blurred ◇ *Lo veo muy borroso.* It looks very blurred.

Bosnia SUSTANTIVO FEM
Bosnia

el **bosnio,** la **bosnia** ADJETIVO, SUSTANTIVO
Bosnian

el **bosque** SUSTANTIVO
1 wood (*pequeño*)
2 forest (*más grande*)

bostezar* VERBO
to yawn

la **bota** SUSTANTIVO
boot
◆ **unas botas de agua** a pair of wellingtons
◆ **una bota de vino** a wineskin

la **botana** SUSTANTIVO Mexico
snack

la **botánica** SUSTANTIVO
botany

botánico ADJETIVO
botanical

botar VERBO
1 to bounce ◇ *Esta pelota no bota.* This ball isn't bouncing.
2 to jump ◇ *Botar de alegría.* To jump with joy.
3 to throw out Latin America ◇ *Boté los libros.* I threw the books out.

el **bote** SUSTANTIVO
1 can (*de bebidas*)
2 tin (*de pintura*)
3 jar (*de mermelada*)
4 boat (*barco*)
◆ **un bote salvavidas** a lifeboat
◆ **pegar un bote** to jump

la **botella** SUSTANTIVO
bottle

el **botellín** SUSTANTIVO (PL los **botellines**)
bottle ◇ *un botellín de cerveza* a bottle of beer

el **botijo** SUSTANTIVO

> ℹ *A **botijo** is an earthenware water container with spouts.*

el **botín** SUSTANTIVO (PL los **botines**)
1 ankle boot (*bota*)
2 haul (*de un robo*)

el **botiquín** SUSTANTIVO (PL los **botiquines**)
1 medicine cupboard (*armario*)
2 first-aid kit (*conjunto de medicinas*)
3 sick bay (*enfermería*)

el **botón** SUSTANTIVO (PL los **botones**)
button ◇ *He perdido un botón de la camisa.* I've lost a button off my shirt.
◆ **pulsar un botón** to press a button

la **bóveda** SUSTANTIVO
vault

el **boxeador,** la **boxeadora** SUSTANTIVO
boxer

boxear VERBO
to box

el **boxeo** SUSTANTIVO
boxing

el **bozal** SUSTANTIVO
muzzle

las **bragas** SUSTANTIVO
knickers
◆ **unas bragas** a pair of knickers

la **bragueta** SUSTANTIVO
fly (PL flies)

la **brasa** SUSTANTIVO
◆ **carne a la brasa** barbecued meat
◆ **las brasas** the embers

el **brasier** SUSTANTIVO Mexico
bra

Brasil SUSTANTIVO MASC
Brazil

el **brasileño,** la **brasileña** ADJETIVO, SUSTANTIVO
Brazilian

el **brasilero,** la **brasilera** ADJETIVO, SUSTANTIVO
Latin America = **brasileño**

bravo (1) ADJETIVO
◆**un toro bravo** a fighting bull

bravo (2) EXCLAMACIÓN
well done!

la **braza** SUSTANTIVO
breaststroke
◆**nadar a braza** to do the breaststroke

el **brazalete** SUSTANTIVO
bracelet

el **brazo** SUSTANTIVO
arm ◇ *Me duele el brazo.* My arm hurts. ◇ *Estaba sentada con los brazos cruzados.* She was sitting with her arms folded.
◆**ir del brazo** to walk arm-in-arm
◆**un brazo de gitano** a swiss roll

la **brecha** SUSTANTIVO
opening (*en un muro*)
◆**Me he hecho una brecha en la cabeza.** I've split my head open.

breve ADJETIVO
1 brief ◇ *por breves momentos* for a few brief moments ◇ *Para no aburrirlos seré breve.* To avoid boring you I will be brief.
2 short ◇ *un relato breve* a short story
◆**en breve** shortly

el **bricolaje** SUSTANTIVO
DIY ◇ *una tienda de bricolaje* a DIY shop

brillante ADJETIVO
1 shiny ◇ *Tenía el pelo brillante.* Her hair was shiny.
◆**El coche estaba brillante.** The car was shining.
◆**blanco brillante** brilliant white
2 outstanding ◇ *un alumno brillante* an outstanding student

el **brillante** SUSTANTIVO
diamond

brillar VERBO
1 to shine (*muebles, metal*) ◇ *Hoy brilla el sol.* The sun is shining today.
2 to sparkle (*diamantes, agua*)

el **brillo** SUSTANTIVO
1 shine (*de muebles, metal*)
2 sparkle (*de joyas*)
◆**La pantalla tiene mucho brillo.** The screen is too bright.
◆**sacar brillo a algo** to polish something

brincar* VERBO
to jump up and down ◇ *¡Deja de brincar!* Stop jumping up and down!
◆**brincar de alegría** to jump for joy

el **brinco** SUSTANTIVO
◆**pegar un brinco** to jump
◆**Bajé tres escalones de un brinco.** I jumped down three steps.

brindar VERBO
◆**brindar por** to drink a toast to
◆**brindarse a hacer algo** to offer to do something ◇ *Se brindó a ayudarme.* He offered to help me.

el **brindis** SUSTANTIVO (PL los **brindis**)
toast
◆**hacer un brindis** to make a toast

la **brisa** SUSTANTIVO
breeze

británico ADJETIVO
British

el **británico**, la **británica** SUSTANTIVO
British person
◆**los británicos** the British

la **brocha** SUSTANTIVO
1 (*para pintar*)
paintbrush (PL paintbrushes)
2 (*para afeitarse*)
shaving brush (PL shaving brushes)

el **broche** SUSTANTIVO
1 (*joya*)
brooch (PL brooches)
2 (*de un collar, pulsera*)
clasp

la **broma** SUSTANTIVO
joke
◆**gastar una broma a alguien** to play a joke on someone
◆**decir algo en broma** to say something as a joke
◆**una broma pesada** a practical joke

bromear VERBO
to joke

el/la **bromista** SUSTANTIVO
joker

la **bronca** SUSTANTIVO
1 row (*pelea*) ◇ *Tuvieron una bronca muy gorda.* They had a huge row.
◆**echar una bronca a alguien** to tell somebody off
2 fuss (*escándalo*)
◆**armar una bronca** to kick up a fuss

el **bronce** SUSTANTIVO
bronze

bronceado ADJETIVO
tanned

el **bronceado** SUSTANTIVO
suntan

el **bronceador** SUSTANTIVO
suntan lotion

la **bronquitis** SUSTANTIVO
bronchitis

brotar VERBO
to sprout

bruces ADVERBIO
◆**Me caí de bruces.** I fell flat on my face.

la **bruja** SUSTANTIVO
witch (PL witches)

el **brujo** SUSTANTIVO
wizard

la **brújula** SUSTANTIVO

compass (PL compasses)

la **bruma** SUSTANTIVO
mist

brusco ADJETIVO
[1] sudden ◊ *un movimiento brusco* a sudden movement
[2] abrupt ◊ *una persona brusca* an abrupt person

bruto ADJETIVO
gross ◊ *el salario bruto* gross salary
♦ **¡No seas bruto!** Don't be so rough!
♦ **Su padre es un diamante en bruto.** Her dad is a rough diamond.

bucear VERBO
to dive

buen ADJETIVO = **bueno**

bueno ADJETIVO
good ◊ *"Don Quijote" es un buen libro.* "Don Quijote" is a good book. ◊ *Hace buen tiempo.* The weather's good. ◊ *Tiene buena voz.* She has a good voice. ◊ *Es buena persona.* He's a good person. ◊ *un buen trozo* a good slice ◊ *Le eché un buen rapapolvo.* I gave him a good telling-off.
♦ **ser bueno para** to be good for ◊ *Esta bebida es buena para la salud.* This drink is good for your health.
♦ **Está muy bueno este bizcocho.** This sponge cake is lovely.
♦ **Lo bueno fue que ni siquiera quiso venir.** The best thing was that he didn't even want to come.
♦ **¡Bueno! (1)** (*para aceptar una sugerencia*) OK!
♦ **¡Bueno! (2)** (*al teléfono*) Mexico Hello!
♦ **Bueno. ¿Y qué?** Well?
♦ **¡Buenas!** Hello!
♦ **Irás por las buenas o por las malas.** You'll go whether you like it or not.

el **buey** SUSTANTIVO
ox (PL oxen)

la **bufanda** SUSTANTIVO
scarf (PL scarves)

el **bufete** SUSTANTIVO
♦ **un bufete de abogados** a legal practice

el **buffet** SUSTANTIVO (PL los **buffets**)
buffet
♦ **buffet libre** free buffet

la **buhardilla** SUSTANTIVO
attic

el **búho** SUSTANTIVO
owl

el **buitre** SUSTANTIVO
vulture

la **bujía** SUSTANTIVO
spark plug

Bulgaria SUSTANTIVO FEM
Bulgaria

el **búlgaro,** la **búlgara** ADJETIVO, SUSTANTIVO
Bulgarian

el **búlgaro** SUSTANTIVO
Bulgarian (*idioma*)

el **bulto** SUSTANTIVO
[1] lump ◊ *Tengo un bulto en la frente.* I have a lump on my forehead.
[2] figure ◊ *Sólo vi un bulto.* I only saw a figure.
♦ **Llevábamos muchos bultos.** We were carrying a lot of bags.

el **buñuelo** SUSTANTIVO
doughnut

BUP SUSTANTIVO MASC (= *Bachillerato Unificado Polivalente*)

> *The **BUP** was a three-year secondary course leading to university.*

el **buque** SUSTANTIVO
ship
♦ **un buque de guerra** a warship

la **burbuja** SUSTANTIVO
bubble ◊ *Este jabón hace muchas burbujas.* This soap makes lots of bubbles.
♦ **un refresco sin burbujas** a still drink
♦ **un refresco con burbujas** a fizzy drink

la **burla** SUSTANTIVO
♦ **hacer burla de alguien** to make fun of someone

burlarse VERBO
♦ **burlarse de alguien** to make fun of someone

el **buró** SUSTANTIVO (PL los **burós**) Mexico
bedside table

la **burocracia** SUSTANTIVO
bureaucracy (PL bureaucracies)

la **burrada** SUSTANTIVO (*coloquial*)
♦ **hacer burradas** to do stupid things ◊ *No hagas burradas con el coche.* Don't do anything stupid with the car.

el **burro** SUSTANTIVO
[1] (*animal*)
donkey (PL donkeys)
[2] (*persona*)
idiot ◊ *Eres un burro.* You're an idiot.

burro ADJETIVO
[1] thick (*estúpido*)
[2] rough (*bruto*)

la **busca** SUSTANTIVO
♦ **en busca de** in search of

el **busca** SUSTANTIVO
bleeper

el **buscador** SUSTANTIVO
search engine

buscar* VERBO
to look for ◊ *Estoy buscando las gafas.* I'm looking for my glasses. ◊ *Ana busca trabajo en un colegio.* Ana's looking for work in a school.
♦ **Te voy a buscar a la estación.** I'll come and get you at the station.

☞

◆ **Mi madre siempre me viene a buscar al colegio en coche.** My mother always picks me up from school in the car.
◆ **buscar una palabra en el diccionario** to look up a word in the dictionary
◆ **Él se lo ha buscado.** He was asking for it.

la **búsqueda** SUSTANTIVO
search (PL searches)

la **butaca** SUSTANTIVO
1 armchair (*sillón*)
2 seat (*en el cine*)

el **butano** SUSTANTIVO
bottled gas
◆ **color butano** bright orange

el **buzo** SUSTANTIVO
diver

el **buzón** SUSTANTIVO (PL los **buzones**)
1 (*en casa*)
letterbox (PL letterboxes)
2 (*en la calle*)
postbox (PL postboxes)
◆ **echar una carta al buzón** to post a letter
◆ **buzón de voz** voice mail

C

C/ ABREVIATURA (= *calle*)
St (= Street)

el **caballero** SUSTANTIVO
gentleman (PL gentlemen) ◊ *damas y caballeros* ladies and gentlemen
◆ **¿Dónde está la sección de caballeros?** Where is the men's department?
◆ **"Caballeros"** (*en aseos*) "Gents"

el **caballo** SUSTANTIVO
1 horse
◆ **¿Te gusta montar a caballo?** Do you like riding?
◆ **un caballo de carreras** a racehorse
2 knight (*en ajedrez*)

la **cabaña** SUSTANTIVO
hut

el **cabello** SUSTANTIVO
hair

caber* VERBO
to fit ◊ *No cabe en mi armario.* It won't fit in my cupboard.
◆ **En mi coche caben dos maletas más.** There's room for two more suitcases in my car.
◆ **No cabe nadie más.** There's no room for anyone else.

la **cabeza** SUSTANTIVO
head ◊ *Se rascó la cabeza.* He scratched his head.
◆ **Al oírlos volví la cabeza.** When I heard them I looked round.
◆ **Se tiró al agua de cabeza.** He dived headfirst into the water.
◆ **estar a la cabeza de la clasificación** to be at the top of the league

la **cabina** SUSTANTIVO
1 (*de teléfonos*)
phone box (PL phone boxes)
2 (*de disc-jockey, intérprete*)
booth (PL booths)
3 (*del piloto*)
cockpit
4 (*en vestuarios*)
cubicle

el **cable** SUSTANTIVO
cable

el **cabo** SUSTANTIVO
1 cape
◆ **Cabo Cañaveral** Cape Canaveral
2 corporal (*en el ejército*)
◆ **al cabo de dos días** after two days
◆ **llevar algo a cabo** to carry something out

la **cabra** SUSTANTIVO
goat
◆ **¡Estás como una cabra!** You're crazy! (*coloquial*)

cabrá VERBO *ver* **caber**

cabreado ADJETIVO
annoyed

cabrear VERBO
◆ **Lo que más me cabrea es que me mientas.** What really annoys me is when you lie to me.
◆ **cabrearse** to get annoyed

la **caca** SUSTANTIVO
◆ **hacer caca (1)** (*en lenguaje infantil*) to do a poo
◆ **hacer caca (2)** (*entre adultos*) to go to the loo (*coloquial*)

el **cacahuate** SUSTANTIVO Mexico
peanut

el **cacahuete** SUSTANTIVO
peanut

el **cacao** SUSTANTIVO
1 cocoa (*polvo*)
2 lipsalve (*para los labios*)

la **cacerola** SUSTANTIVO
saucepan

el **cacharro** SUSTANTIVO
◆ **los cacharros** the pots and pans

el **cachondeo** SUSTANTIVO
◆ **Las clases eran un cachondeo.** (*coloquial*) The classes were a joke.
◆ **No le hagas caso, está de cachondeo.** (*coloquial*) Don't pay any attention to him, he's having you on.

el **cachorro**, la **cachorra** SUSTANTIVO
1 (*de perro*)
puppy (PL puppies)
2 (*de león, lobo*)
cub

el **cactus** SUSTANTIVO (PL los **cactus**)
cactus (PL cacti)

cada ADJETIVO
1 each ◊ *Cada libro es de un color distinto.* Each book is a different colour.
◆ **cada uno** each one
2 every (*con tiempo, números*) ◊ *cada año* every year ◊ *cada vez que la veo* every time I see her ◊ *uno de cada diez* one out of every ten
◆ **Viene cada vez más gente.** More and more people are coming.
◆ **Viene cada vez menos.** He comes less and less often.
◆ **Cada vez hace más frío.** It's getting colder and colder.
◆ **¿Cada cuánto vas al dentista?** How often do you go to the dentist?

el **cadáver** SUSTANTIVO
corpse

la **cadena** SUSTANTIVO
1 chain ◊ *una cadena de oro* a gold chain
◆ **una reacción en cadena** a chain reaction

☞

◆**tirar de la cadena del wáter** to flush the toilet
◆**la cadena de montaje** the assembly line
2 channel ◇ *Por la cadena 3 dan una película.* There's a film on channel 3.
◆**cadena perpetua** life imprisonment

la **cadera** SUSTANTIVO
hip

caducar* VERBO
to expire (*pasaporte, carnet*)
◆**Esta leche está caducada.** This milk is past its sell-by date.

caer* VERBO
to fall ◇ *Me hice daño al caer.* I fell and hurt myself.
◆**El avión cayó al mar.** The plane came down in the sea.
◆**Su cumpleaños cae en viernes.** Her birthday falls on a Friday.
◆**caerse** to fall ◇ *Tropecé y me caí.* I tripped and fell.
◆**El niño se cayó de la cama.** The child fell out of bed.
◆**No te vayas a caer del caballo.** Be careful not to fall off the horse.
◆**Se cayó por la ventana.** He fell out of the window.
◆**Se me cayeron las monedas.** I dropped the coins.
◆**¡No caigo!** I don't get it!
◆**Su hermano me cae muy bien.** I really like his brother.

el **café** SUSTANTIVO (PL los **cafés**)
1 coffee
◆**un café con leche** a white coffee
◆**un café solo** a black coffee
2 café (*establecimiento*)

> *En Gran Bretaña no se venden bebidas alcohólicas en los cafés y éstos cierran, por lo general, a las 5.30 p.m.*

la **cafetera** SUSTANTIVO
coffee pot

la **cafetería** SUSTANTIVO
café

cagar* VERBO
to have a crap (*vulgar*)

la **caída** SUSTANTIVO
fall

caigo VERBO *ver* **caer**

el **caimán** SUSTANTIVO (PL los **caimanes**)
alligator

la **caja** SUSTANTIVO
1 box (PL boxes) ◇ *una caja de zapatos* a shoe box
2 (*de vino, champán*)
case
3 (*de cervezas, refrescos*)
crate
4 (*en supermercado*)
checkout
5 (*en tienda, restaurante*)
till
6 (*en banco*)
cash desk
◆**la caja de ahorros** the savings bank
◆**la caja de cambios** the gearbox
◆**la caja fuerte** the safe

el **cajero** SUSTANTIVO
◆**un cajero automático** a cash dispenser

el **cajero,** la **cajera** SUSTANTIVO
◆**Trabajo de cajera en un supermercado.** I work on the checkout in a supermarket.

el **cajón** SUSTANTIVO (PL los **cajones**)
1 drawer (*de mueble*)
2 crate (*para embalaje*)
3 coffin (*ataúd*) Latin America

la **cajuela** SUSTANTIVO Mexico
boot

la **cala** SUSTANTIVO
cove

el **calabacín** SUSTANTIVO (PL los **calabacines**)
courgette

la **calabacita** SUSTANTIVO Mexico
courgette

la **calabaza** SUSTANTIVO
pumpkin

calado ADJETIVO
soaked ◇ *Estaba calado hasta los huesos.* He was soaked to the skin.

el **calamar** SUSTANTIVO
squid
◆**calamares a la romana** squid fried in batter

el **calambre** SUSTANTIVO
1 cramp ◇ *Tengo un calambre en la pierna.* I've got cramp in my leg.
2 electric shock ◇ *Si tocas el cable te dará calambre.* If you touch the cable you'll get an electric shock.

calar VERBO
to soak ◇ *La lluvia me caló hasta los huesos.* I got soaked to the skin in the rain.
◆**Se le caló el coche.** He stalled the car.

la **calavera** SUSTANTIVO
skull

calcar* VERBO
to trace
◆**Es calcado a su abuelo.** He's the spitting image of his grandfather.

el **calcetín** SUSTANTIVO (PL los **calcetines**)
sock

el **calcio** SUSTANTIVO
calcium

la **calculadora** SUSTANTIVO
calculator

calcular VERBO

* Verbs marked with this symbol are irregular. See pages 380-382 for further details

to calculate ◊ *Calculé lo que nos costaría.* I calculated what it would cost us.
◆ **Calculo que nos llevará unos tres días.** I reckon that it will take us around three days.

el **cálculo** SUSTANTIVO
calculation
◆ **según mis cálculos** according to my calculations

el **caldo** SUSTANTIVO
broth ◊ *Yo tomaré el caldo de verduras.* I'll take the vegetable broth.
◆ **una pastilla de caldo** a stock cube

la **calefacción** SUSTANTIVO
heating ◊ *calefacción central* central heating

el **calendario** SUSTANTIVO
calendar

el **calentador** SUSTANTIVO
heater

el **calentamiento** SUSTANTIVO
◆ **el calentamiento del planeta** global warming
◆ **ejercicios de calentamiento** warm-up exercises

calentar* VERBO
1 to heat up (*comida, agua*) ◊ *¿Quieres que te caliente la leche?* Do you want me to heat up the milk for you?
2 to warm up (*habitación*)
◆ **calentarse (1)** (*comida, agua*) to heat up ◊ *Espera a que se caliente el agua.* Wait for the water to heat up.
◆ **calentarse (2)** (*habitación, persona*) to warm up ◊ *Deja que se caliente el motor.* Let the engine warm up.

la **calentura** SUSTANTIVO
1 temperature ◊ *Tiene un poco de calentura.* He's got a bit of a temperature.
2 cold sore (*en los labios*)

la **calidad** SUSTANTIVO
quality (PL qualities) ◊ *Lo que importa es la calidad.* What matters is quality.

caliente (1) VERBO *ver* **calentar**

caliente (2) ADJETIVO
1 hot
Cuando nos referimos a una temperatura que puede quemar.
◊ *Esta sopa está muy caliente.* This soup is very hot.
2 warm
Cuando nos referimos a algo que está templado, que no quema o que no está suficientemente frío.
◊ *¡Esta cerveza está caliente!* This beer is warm!
◆ **Mi habitación está calentita.** My room is nice and warm.

la **calificación** SUSTANTIVO (PL las **calificaciones**)
mark (*nota escolar*) ◊ *Siempre saca buenas calificaciones.* He always gets good marks.
◆ **boletín de calificaciones** school report

calificar* VERBO
to mark ◊ *El profesor califica los ejercicios.* The teacher marks the exercises.
◆ **Me calificó con sobresaliente.** He gave me an A.

callado ADJETIVO
quiet ◊ *Estuvo callado bastante rato.* He was quiet for quite a while. ◊ *una persona muy callada* a very quiet person

callar VERBO
to be quiet ◊ *Calla, que no me dejas concentrarme.* Be quiet, I can't concentrate.
◆ **callarse (1)** to keep quiet ◊ *Prefirió callarse.* He preferred to keep quiet.
◆ **callarse (2)** to stop talking ◊ *Al entrar el profesor todos se callaron.* When the teacher came in, everyone stopped talking.
◆ **¡Cállate!** Shut up! (*coloquial*)

la **calle** SUSTANTIVO
1 street ◊ *Viven en la calle Peñalver, 13.* They live at number 13, Peñalver Street.
◆ **Hoy no he salido a la calle.** I haven't been out today.
◆ **una calle peatonal** a pedestrian precinct
2 lane (*en circuito, piscina*)

el **callejero** SUSTANTIVO
street map

el **callejón** SUSTANTIVO (PL los **callejones**)
alley (PL alleys)

el **callo** SUSTANTIVO
1 (*en los pies*)
corn
2 (*en las manos*)
callus (PL calluses)
◆ **callos** (*comida*) tripe SING

la **calma** SUSTANTIVO
calm
◆ **Todo estaba en calma.** Everything was calm.
◆ **Logró mantener la calma.** He managed to keep calm.
◆ **Piénsalo con calma.** Think about it calmly.
◆ **Tómatelo con calma.** Take it easy.

el **calmante** SUSTANTIVO
1 painkiller (*para el dolor*)
2 tranquillizer (*para los nervios*)

calmar VERBO
1 to calm down ◊ *Intenté calmarla un poco.* I tried to calm her down a little. ◊ *¡Cálmate!* Calm down!
2 to relieve (*dolor*)

el **calor** SUSTANTIVO
heat ◊ *No se puede trabajar con este calor.* It's impossible to work in this heat.
◆ **Hace calor.** It's hot.

☞

◆ **Tengo calor.** I'm hot.
◆ **entrar en calor** to get warm
la **caloría** SUSTANTIVO
calorie
calvo ADJETIVO
bald
◆ **Se está quedando calvo.** He's going bald.
el **calzado** SUSTANTIVO
footwear
los **calzoncillos** SUSTANTIVO
underpants
◆ **unos calzoncillos** a pair of underpants
los **calzones** SUSTANTIVO Chile
panties (*de mujer*)
la **cama** SUSTANTIVO
bed
◆ **hacer la cama** to make the bed
◆ **Está en la cama.** He's in bed.
◆ **meterse en la cama** to get into bed
la **cámara** SUSTANTIVO
1 camera (*de cine, fotos*)
◆ **a cámara lenta** in slow motion
2 inner tube (*de neumático*)
◆ **la cámara de comercio** the Chamber of Commerce
◆ **música de cámara** chamber music
la **camarera** SUSTANTIVO
1 (*de restaurante*)
waitress (PL waitresses)
2 (*de hotel*)
maid
el **camarero** SUSTANTIVO
1 waiter (*de restaurante*)
2 bellboy (*de hotel*)
cambiar VERBO
1 to change ◇ *No has cambiado nada.* You haven't changed a bit.
◆ **Quiero cambiar este abrigo por uno más grande.** I want to change this coat for a larger size.
◆ **Tenemos que cambiar de tren en París.** We have to change trains in Paris.
◆ **He cambiado de idea.** I've changed my mind.
2 to swap ◇ *Te cambio mi bolígrafo por tu goma.* I'll swap my ballpoint for your rubber.
◆ **Me gusta el tuyo, te lo cambio.** I like yours, let's swap.
◆ **cambiarse** to get changed ◇ *Voy a cambiarme.* I'm going to get changed.
◆ **Se han cambiado de coche.** They have changed car.
◆ **cambiarse de sitio** to move
◆ **cambiarse de casa** to move house
el **cambio** SUSTANTIVO
1 change ◇ *un cambio brusco de temperatura* a sudden change in temperature ◇ *¿Tiene cambio de cien?* Have you got change of a hundred? ◇ *¿Te han dado bien el cambio?* Have they given you the right change?
2 small change ◇ *Necesito cambio.* I need small change.
3 exchange ◇ *¿A cómo está el cambio?* What's the exchange rate?
◆ **Me lo regaló a cambio del favor que le hice.** He gave it to me in return for the favour I did him.
◆ **en cambio** on the other hand
el **camello** SUSTANTIVO
1 camel (*animal*)
2 drug pusher (*coloquial: traficante*)
la **camilla** SUSTANTIVO
1 (*de ambulancia*)
stretcher
2 (*en consultorio médico*)
couch (PL couches)
caminar VERBO
to walk
el **camino** SUSTANTIVO
1 path (*sendero*)
◆ **un camino de montaña** a mountain track
2 way ◇ *¿Sabes el camino a su casa?* Do you know the way to his house?
◆ **A medio camino paramos a comer.** Halfway there, we stopped to eat.
◆ **La farmacia me queda de camino.** The chemist's is on my way.
el **camión** SUSTANTIVO (PL los **camiones**)
1 lorry (PL lorries)
◆ **un camión cisterna** a tanker
◆ **el camión de la basura** the dustcart
2 bus (PL buses) Mexico
el **camionero**, la **camionera** SUSTANTIVO
lorry driver
la **camioneta** SUSTANTIVO
van
la **camisa** SUSTANTIVO
shirt
la **camiseta** SUSTANTIVO
1 T-shirt (*de manga corta*)
2 vest (*ropa interior*)
3 shirt (*de deportes*)
el **camisón** SUSTANTIVO (PL los **camisones**)
nightdress (PL nightdresses)
el **camote** SUSTANTIVO Mexico
sweet potato (PL sweet potatoes)
el **campamento** SUSTANTIVO
camp ◇ *un campamento de verano* a summer camp
la **campana** SUSTANTIVO
bell
la **campaña** SUSTANTIVO
campaign
◆ **la campaña electoral** the election campaign
◆ **una campaña publicitaria** an advertising campaign
el **campeón**, la **campeona** SUSTANTIVO
champion

el **campeonato** SUSTANTIVO
championship

el **campesino,** la **campesina** SUSTANTIVO
[1] *(persona del campo)*
country person (PL country people)
[2] *(labrador pobre)*
peasant

el **camping** SUSTANTIVO (PL los **campings**)
[1] camping ◊ *ir de camping* to go camping
[2] campsite ◊ *Estamos en un camping.* We're at a campsite.

el **campo** SUSTANTIVO
[1] country ◊ *Prefiero vivir en el campo.* I prefer living in the country.
[2] *(paisaje)*
countryside ◊ *El campo se pone verde en primavera.* The countryside turns green in springtime.
♦ **Corrían campo a través.** They were running cross-country.
♦ **el trabajo del campo** farm work
♦ **Ya no se ven bueyes en el campo.** You don't see oxen in the fields any more.
[3] *(de fútbol)*
pitch (PL pitches)
♦ **un campo de deportes** a sports ground
♦ **un campo de golf** a golf course
♦ **un campo de concentración** a concentration camp

la **cana** SUSTANTIVO
grey hair
♦ **Tiene canas.** He's got grey hair.
♦ **Le están saliendo canas.** He's going grey.

Canadá SUSTANTIVO MASC
Canada

el/la **canadiense** ADJETIVO, SUSTANTIVO
Canadian

el **canal** SUSTANTIVO
[1] channel ◊ *Por el canal 2 dan una película.* They're showing a film on channel 2.
♦ **el Canal de la Mancha** the English Channel
[2] canal *(artificial)* ◊ *un canal de riego* an irrigation canal
♦ **el Canal de Panamá** the Panama Canal

el **canapé** SUSTANTIVO (PL los **canapés**)
canapé

Canarias SUSTANTIVO FEM PL
the Canaries
♦ **las Islas Canarias** the Canary Islands

el **canario** SUSTANTIVO
canary (PL canaries)

la **canasta** SUSTANTIVO
basket

cancelar VERBO
to cancel

el **cáncer** SUSTANTIVO
cancer ◊ *cáncer de mama* breast cancer

Cáncer SUSTANTIVO MASC
Cancer ◊ *Soy Cáncer.* I'm Cancer.

la **cancha** SUSTANTIVO
[1] *(de baloncesto, tenis)*
court
[2] *(de fútbol, rugby)*
pitch (PL pitches) Latin America

la **canción** SUSTANTIVO (PL las **canciones**)
song
♦ **una canción de cuna** a lullaby

el **candado** SUSTANTIVO
padlock
♦ **Estaba cerrado con candado.** It was padlocked.

el **candidato,** la **candidata** SUSTANTIVO
candidate
♦ **presentarse como candidato a la presidencia** to stand for president

la **canela** SUSTANTIVO
cinnamon

los **canelones** SUSTANTIVO
cannelloni SING

el **cangrejo** SUSTANTIVO
[1] *(de mar)*
crab
[2] *(de río)*
crayfish (PL crayfish)

el **canguro** SUSTANTIVO
kangaroo

el/la **canguro** SUSTANTIVO
baby-sitter *(de niños)*
♦ **hacer de canguro** to baby-sit

la **canica** SUSTANTIVO
marble
♦ **jugar a las canicas** to play marbles

la **canilla** SUSTANTIVO River Plate
tap

la **canoa** SUSTANTIVO
canoe

cansado ADJETIVO
[1] tired ◊ *Estoy muy cansado.* I'm very tired.
♦ **Estoy cansado de hacer lo mismo todos los días.** I'm tired of doing the same thing every day.
[2] tiring ◊ *Es un trabajo muy cansado.* It's a very tiring job.

el **cansancio** SUSTANTIVO
♦ **¡Qué cansancio!** I'm so tired!

cansar VERBO
♦ **Es un viaje que cansa.** It's a tiring journey.
♦ **cansarse** to get tired ◊ *Está muy débil y enseguida se cansa.* He is very weak and gets tired quickly.
♦ **Me cansé de esperarlo y me marché.** I got tired of waiting for him and I left.

el/la **cantante** SUSTANTIVO
singer

cantar VERBO
to sing

la **cantidad** SUSTANTIVO
[1] amount ◊ *una cierta cantidad de dinero* a certain amount of money

☞

2 quantity (PL quantities) ◊ *La calidad es más importante que la cantidad.* Quality is more important than quantity.
♦ **¡Qué cantidad de gente!** What a lot of people!
♦ **Había cantidad de turistas.** There were loads of tourists.

la **cantimplora** SUSTANTIVO
water bottle

el **canto** SUSTANTIVO
1 edge (*de mesa, moneda*)
2 singing (*arte*) ◊ *Mi hermana estudia canto.* My sister is studying singing.
3 song (*de pájaro*)

la **caña** SUSTANTIVO
cane
♦ **caña de azúcar** sugar cane
♦ **Me tomé dos cañas.** I had two beers.
♦ **una caña de pescar** a fishing rod

la **cañería** SUSTANTIVO
pipe

el **caos** SUSTANTIVO
chaos ◊ *Aquello fue un verdadero caos.* That was absolute chaos.

la **capa** SUSTANTIVO
1 layer (*de nieve, polvo*)
♦ **la capa de ozono** the ozone layer
2 cloak (*prenda*)

la **capacidad** SUSTANTIVO
1 (*aptitud*)
ability (PL abilities) ◊ *Nadie duda de tu capacidad.* No one doubts your ability.
2 (*de recipiente, lugar*)
capacity (PL capacities) ◊ *El teatro tiene capacidad para mil espectadores.* The theatre has a seating capacity of a thousand.

capaz ADJETIVO (PL **capaces**)
capable ◊ *Es capaz de olvidarse el pasaporte.* He's quite capable of forgetting his passport.
♦ **Por ella sería capaz de cualquier cosa.** He would do anything for her.

la **capilla** SUSTANTIVO
chapel

la **capital** SUSTANTIVO
capital

el **capitán**, la **capitana** SUSTANTIVO
captain

el **capítulo** SUSTANTIVO
1 chapter (*de un libro*)
2 episode (*de una serie*)

el **capricho** SUSTANTIVO
whim ◊ *Hacer un crucero fue un puro capricho.* Going on a cruise was just a whim.
♦ **Lo compré por capricho.** I bought it on a whim.
♦ **Decidí viajar en primera para darme un capricho.** I decided to travel first class to give myself a treat.

Capricornio SUSTANTIVO MASC
Capricorn ◊ *Soy Capricornio.* I'm Capricorn.

capturar VERBO
to capture

la **capucha** SUSTANTIVO
1 hood (*de ropa*)
2 top (*de bolígrafo*)

caqui ADJETIVO (PL **caqui**)
khaki

la **cara** SUSTANTIVO
1 face ◊ *Tiene la cara alargada.* He has a long face.
♦ **Tienes mala cara.** You don't look well.
♦ **Tenía cara de pocos amigos.** He looked very unfriendly.
♦ **No pongas esa cara.** Don't look like that.
2 cheek (*coloquial: descaro*) ◊ *¡Qué cara!* What a cheek!
3 side (*de disco, papel*) ◊ *un folio escrito por las dos caras* a sheet written on both sides
♦ **¿Cara o cruz?** Heads or tails?
♦ **Lo echamos a cara o cruz.** We tossed for it.

el **caracol** SUSTANTIVO
1 snail (*de tierra*)
2 winkle (*de mar*)

el **carácter** SUSTANTIVO (PL los **caracteres**)
nature ◊ *Tiene el carácter de su padre.* He has his father's nature.
♦ **tener buen carácter** to be good-natured
♦ **tener mal carácter** to be bad-tempered
♦ **La chica tiene mucho carácter.** The girl has a strong personality.

la **característica** SUSTANTIVO
characteristic

el **caramelo** SUSTANTIVO
sweet

la **caravana** SUSTANTIVO
caravan (*remolque*)
♦ **Había una caravana de dos kilómetros.** There was a two kilometre tailback.

el **carbón** SUSTANTIVO
coal
♦ **carbón de leña** charcoal

la **carcajada** SUSTANTIVO
♦ **soltar una carcajada** to burst out laughing
♦ **reírse a carcajadas** to roar with laughter

la **cárcel** SUSTANTIVO
prison ◊ *Todavía está en la cárcel.* He's still in prison.

el **cardenal** SUSTANTIVO
1 bruise (*moretón*)
2 cardinal (*prelado*)

cardiaco ADJETIVO
cardiac ◊ *ataque cardiaco* cardiac arrest

la **careta** SUSTANTIVO
mask

la **carga** SUSTANTIVO
[1] load ◇ *carga máxima* maximum load
[2] burden ◇ *No quiero ser una carga para ellos.* I don't want to be a burden to them.
[3] refill (*de bolígrafo, pluma*)

cargado ADJETIVO
[1] loaded (*arma, cámara*)
[2] stuffy (*ambiente, habitación*)
[3] strong (*café*)
♦ **Venía cargada de paquetes.** She was laden with parcels.

el **cargamento** SUSTANTIVO
[1] (*de avión, barco*)
cargo (PL cargoes)
[2] (*de camión*)
load

cargar* VERBO
[1] to load ◇ *Cargaron el coche de maletas.* They loaded the car with suitcases.
[2] to fill (*bolígrafo, encendedor*)
[3] to charge (*batería, pilas*)
♦ **Tuve que cargar con todo.** I had to take responsibility for everything.
♦ **cargarse algo** (*coloquial*) to break something ◇ *Te vas a cargar el vídeo.* You're going to break the video.

el **cargo** SUSTANTIVO
post ◇ *un cargo de mucha responsabilidad* a very responsible post
♦ **Está a cargo de la contabilidad.** He's in charge of keeping the books.

el **Caribe** SUSTANTIVO
the Caribbean

el **caribeño**, la **caribeña** ADJETIVO, SUSTANTIVO
Caribbean

la **caricatura** SUSTANTIVO
caricature

la **caricia** SUSTANTIVO
caress (PL caresses)
♦ **Le hacía caricias al bebé.** She was caressing the baby.

la **caridad** SUSTANTIVO
charity (PL charities)

la **caries** SUSTANTIVO (PL las **caries**)
[1] tooth decay ◇ *Es importante prevenir la caries dental.* It's important to prevent tooth decay.
[2] (*agujero*)
cavity (PL cavities)

el **cariño** SUSTANTIVO
affection ◇ *Lo recuerdo con cariño.* I remember him with affection.
♦ **Les tengo mucho cariño.** I'm very fond of them.
♦ **Le ha tomado cariño al gato.** He has become fond of the cat.
♦ **Ven aquí, cariño.** Come here, darling.

cariñoso ADJETIVO
affectionate ◇ *La maestra es muy cariñosa con los niños.* The teacher is very affectionate towards the children.

el **carnaval** SUSTANTIVO
carnival

> *The* ***carnaval*** *is the traditional period of celebrating prior to the start of Lent.*

C

la **carne** SUSTANTIVO
meat ◇ *No como carne.* I don't eat meat.
♦ **carne de cerdo** pork
♦ **carne de puerco** Mexico pork
♦ **carne de cordero** lamb
♦ **carne molida** Latin America mince
♦ **carne picada** mince
♦ **carne de ternera** veal
♦ **carne de vaca** beef
♦ **carne de res** Mexico beef

el **carnet** SUSTANTIVO (PL los **carnets**)
card
♦ **el carnet de identidad** identity card
♦ **un carnet de conducir** a driving licence

la **carnicería** SUSTANTIVO
butcher's (PL butchers' shops) ◇ *Lo compré en la carnicería.* I bought it at the butcher's.

el **carnicero**, la **carnicera** SUSTANTIVO
butcher

caro ADJETIVO, ADVERBIO
expensive ◇ *Las entradas me costaron muy caras.* The tickets were very expensive. ◇ *Aquí todo lo venden tan caro.* Everything is so expensive here.

la **carpeta** SUSTANTIVO
folder

la **carpintería** SUSTANTIVO
[1] carpenter's shop (*taller*)
[2] carpentry (*actividad*)

la **carrera** SUSTANTIVO
[1] race ◇ *una carrera de caballos* a horse race
♦ **Me di una carrera para alcanzar el autobús.** I had to run to catch the bus.
[2] degree ◇ *Está haciendo la carrera de derecho el año que viene.* He's doing a law degree next year.
[3] career ◇ *Estaba en el mejor momento de su carrera.* He was at the height of his career.
[4] ladder ◇ *Tienes una carrera en las medias.* You've got a ladder in your tights.

el **carrete** SUSTANTIVO
[1] film (*de fotos*)
[2] reel (*de hilo*)

la **carretera** SUSTANTIVO
road
♦ **una carretera nacional** an A-road
♦ **una carretera de circunvalación** a bypass

la **carretilla** SUSTANTIVO
wheelbarrow

el **carril** SUSTANTIVO
[1] lane (*de carretera, autopista*)

☞

[2] rail (*de vía de tren*)

el **carril-bici** SUSTANTIVO (PL los **carriles-bici**)
cycle lane

el **carrito** SUSTANTIVO
trolley (PL trolleys)

el **carro** SUSTANTIVO
[1] (*vehículo*)
cart
[2] (*en aeropuerto, supermercado*)
trolley (PL trolleys)
[3] car Latin America
◆ **un carro de combate** a tank

la **carroza** SUSTANTIVO
[1] (*de caballos*)
coach (PL coaches)
[2] (*de carnaval*)
float

la **carta** SUSTANTIVO
[1] letter ◊ *Le he escrito una carta a Juan.* I've written Juan a letter.
◆ **echar una carta** to post a letter
[2] card ◊ *jugar a las cartas* to play cards
[3] menu ◊ *El camarero nos trajo la carta.* The waiter brought us the menu.
◆ **la carta de vinos** the wine list

el **cartel** SUSTANTIVO
[1] poster (*de propaganda*)
[2] sign ◊ *Un cartel que pone "prohibida la entrada".* A sign which says "no entry".

la **cartelera** SUSTANTIVO
[1] billboard (*en un teatro, cine*)
[2] listings PL (*en un periódico*)
◆ **Estuvo tres años en la cartelera.** It ran for three years.

la **cartera** SUSTANTIVO
[1] (*para el dinero*)
wallet
[2] (*para documentos*)
briefcase
[3] (*de colegial*)
satchel
[4] (*bolso de mujer*)
handbag Latin America
[5] (*empleada de Correos*)
postwoman (PL postwomen)

el **cartero** SUSTANTIVO
postman (PL postmen)

el **cartón** SUSTANTIVO (PL los **cartones**)
[1] cardboard ◊ *una caja de cartón* a cardboard box
[2] carton (*de tabaco, leche*)

el **cartucho** SUSTANTIVO
cartridge

la **cartulina** SUSTANTIVO
card

la **casa** SUSTANTIVO
[1] house
Cuando nos referimos al edificio.
◊ *una casa de dos plantas* a two-storey house
[2] home
Cuando nos referimos al hogar.
◊ *Estábamos en casa.* We were at home. ◊ *Le dolía la cabeza y se fue a casa.* She had a headache so she went home.
◆ **Estábamos en casa de Juan.** We were at Juan's.
◆ **una casa de discos** a record company

casado ADJETIVO
married ◊ *una mujer casada* a married woman
◆ **Está casado con una francesa.** He's married to a French woman.

casarse VERBO
to get married ◊ *Quieren casarse.* They want to get married.
◆ **Se casó con una periodista.** He married a journalist.

el **cascabel** SUSTANTIVO
small bell

la **cascada** SUSTANTIVO
waterfall

cascar* VERBO
to crack (*nuez, huevo*)

la **cáscara** SUSTANTIVO
[1] shell (*de huevo, nuez*)
[2] skin (*de plátano, patata*)

el **casco** SUSTANTIVO
helmet ◊ *El ciclista llevaba casco.* The cyclist was wearing a helmet.
◆ **el casco antiguo de la ciudad** the old part of the town
◆ **el casco urbano** the town centre
◆ **los cascos** (*para escuchar música*) headphones

casero ADJETIVO
homemade ◊ *mermelada casera* homemade jam

la **caseta** SUSTANTIVO
[1] kennel (*de perro*)
[2] bathing hut (*en la playa*)
[3] stall (*de feria*)

el **casete** SUSTANTIVO
[1] cassette player (*magnetófono*)
[2] cassette (*cinta*)

la **casete** SUSTANTIVO
cassette

casi ADVERBIO
almost ◊ *Casi me ahogo.* I almost drowned. ◊ *Son casi las cinco.* It's almost five o'clock.
En oraciones afirmativas se pueden usar tanto ***almost*** *como* ***nearly****.*
◊ *Casi me ahogo.* I nearly drowned.
En oraciones negativas se suele usar ***hardly****.*
◊ *Casi no comí.* I hardly ate. ◊ *No queda casi nada en la nevera.* There's hardly anything left in the refrigerator. ◊ *Casi nunca se equivoca.* He hardly ever makes a mistake.

la **casilla** SUSTANTIVO

* Verbs marked with this symbol are irregular. See pages 380-382 for further details

1 (*en formulario*)
box (PL boxes)
2 (*en crucigrama, tablero de ajedrez*)
square
♦ **Casilla de Correos** River Plate post-office box number

el **casino** SUSTANTIVO
casino (PL casinos)

el **caso** SUSTANTIVO
case ◊ *En casos así es preferible callarse.* In such cases it's better to keep quiet.
♦ **en ese caso** in that case
♦ **En caso de que llueva, iremos en autobús.** If it rains, we'll go by bus.
♦ **El caso es que no me queda dinero.** The thing is, I haven't got any money left.
♦ **No le hagas caso.** Don't take any notice of him.
♦ **Hazle caso que ella tiene más experiencia.** Listen to her, she has more experience.

la **caspa** SUSTANTIVO
dandruff

la **cassette** = **casete**

el **cassette** = **casete**

la **castaña** SUSTANTIVO
chestnut

castaño ADJETIVO
chestnut ◊ *Mi hermana tiene el pelo castaño.* My sister has chestnut hair.

las **castañuelas** SUSTANTIVO
castanets

el **castellano**, la **castellana** ADJETIVO, SUSTANTIVO
Castilian

el **castellano** SUSTANTIVO
Spanish (*idioma*)

castigar* VERBO
to punish ◊ *Mi padre me castigó por contestarle.* My father punished me for answering him back.

el **castigo** SUSTANTIVO
punishment ◊ *Tuve que escribirlo diez veces, como castigo.* I had to write it out ten times, as punishment.

Castilla SUSTANTIVO FEM
Castile

el **castillo** SUSTANTIVO
castle

la **casualidad** SUSTANTIVO
coincidence
♦ **¡Qué casualidad!** What a coincidence!
♦ **Nos encontramos por casualidad.** We met by chance.
♦ **Da la casualidad que nacimos el mismo día.** It so happens that we were born on the same day.

el **catalán**, la **catalana** ADJETIVO, SUSTANTIVO (MASC PL los **catalanes**)
Catalan

el **catalán** SUSTANTIVO
Catalan (*idioma*)

el **catálogo** SUSTANTIVO
catalogue

Cataluña SUSTANTIVO FEM
Catalonia

la **catarata** SUSTANTIVO
waterfall
♦ **las cataratas del Niágara** Niagara Falls

el **catarro** SUSTANTIVO
cold ◊ *Vas a pillar un catarro.* You're going to catch a cold.

la **catástrofe** SUSTANTIVO
catastrophe

la **catedral** SUSTANTIVO
cathedral

el **catedrático**, la **catedrática** SUSTANTIVO
1 professor (*de universidad*)
2 principal teacher (*de instituto*)

la **categoría** SUSTANTIVO
category (PL categories) ◊ *Cada grupo está dividido en tres categorías.* Each group is divided into three categories.
♦ **un hotel de primera categoría** a first-class hotel
♦ **un puesto de poca categoría** a low-ranking position

el **católico**, la **católica** ADJETIVO, SUSTANTIVO
Catholic ◊ *Soy católico.* I am a Catholic.

catorce ADJETIVO, PRONOMBRE
fourteen
♦ **el catorce de enero** the fourteenth of January

el **caucho** SUSTANTIVO
rubber

la **causa** SUSTANTIVO
cause ◊ *No se sabe la causa del accidente.* The cause of the accident is unknown.
♦ **a causa de** because of

causar VERBO
to cause ◊ *La lluvia causó muchos daños.* The rain caused a lot of damage.
♦ **Su visita me causó mucha alegría.** His visit made me very happy.
♦ **Rosa me causó buena impresión.** Rosa made a good impression on me.

cavar VERBO
to dig ◊ *cavar un hoyo* to dig a hole

cayendo VERBO *ver* **caer**

la **caza** SUSTANTIVO
1 hunting (*de animales grandes*)
2 shooting (*de aves*)

el **cazador** SUSTANTIVO
hunter

la **cazadora** SUSTANTIVO
1 jacket (*chaqueta*)
2 hunter (*mujer*)

cazar* VERBO
1 to hunt (*animales grandes*) ◊ *Salieron a cazar ciervos.* They went deer-hunting.
2 to shoot (*aves*) ◊ *Cazaron muchas codornices.* They shot a lot of quail.

el **cazo** SUSTANTIVO

☞

1 saucepan (*cacerola*)
2 ladle (*cucharón*)

la **cazuela** SUSTANTIVO
pot

el **CD** SUSTANTIVO (PL los **CDs**)
CD

el **CD-ROM** SUSTANTIVO (PL los **CD-ROMs**)
CD-ROM

la **CE** ABREVIATURA (= *Comunidad Europea*)
EC (= European Community)

el **cebo** SUSTANTIVO
bait

la **cebolla** SUSTANTIVO
onion

la **cebolleta** SUSTANTIVO
1 spring onion
2 pickled onion (*en vinagre*)

la **cebra** SUSTANTIVO
zebra
◆ **un paso de cebra** a zebra crossing

ceder VERBO
1 to give in ◇ *Al final tuve que ceder.* Finally I had to give in.
2 to give way ◇ *La estantería cedió por el peso de los libros.* The shelves gave way under the weight of the books.
◆ **"Ceda el paso"** "Give way"

la **ceguera** SUSTANTIVO
blindness

la **ceja** SUSTANTIVO
eyebrow

la **celda** SUSTANTIVO
cell

la **celebración** SUSTANTIVO (PL las **celebraciones**)
celebration (*fiesta*)

celebrar VERBO
1 to celebrate (*cumpleaños, Navidad*)
2 to hold (*reunión, elecciones*)

el **celo** SUSTANTIVO
Sellotape ®

el **celofán** SUSTANTIVO
cellophane

los **celos** SUSTANTIVO
jealousy SING ◇ *Lo hizo por celos.* He did it out of jealousy.
◆ **Tiene celos de su mejor amiga.** She's jealous of her best friend.
◆ **Lo hace para darle celos.** He does it to make her jealous.

celoso ADJETIVO
jealous ◇ *Está celoso de su hermano.* He's jealous of his brother.

la **célula** SUSTANTIVO
cell

la **celulitis** SUSTANTIVO
cellulite

el **cementerio** SUSTANTIVO
(*para difuntos*)
cemetery (PL cemeteries)
◆ **un cementerio de coches** a scrapyard

el **cemento** SUSTANTIVO
1 cement (*material de construcción*)
◆ **el cemento armado** reinforced concrete
2 glue (*pegamento*) Latin America

la **cena** SUSTANTIVO
dinner ◇ *La cena es a las nueve.* Dinner is at nine o'clock.

cenar VERBO
to have dinner ◇ *No he cenado.* I haven't had dinner.
◆ **¿Qué quieres cenar?** What do you want for dinner?

el **cenicero** SUSTANTIVO
ashtray (PL ashtrays)

la **ceniza** SUSTANTIVO
ash (PL ashes)

la **censura** SUSTANTIVO
censorship

la **centésima** SUSTANTIVO
◆ **una centésima de segundo** a hundredth of a second

centígrado ADJETIVO
centigrade ◇ *veinte grados centígrados* twenty degrees centigrade

el **centímetro** SUSTANTIVO
centimetre

el **céntimo** SUSTANTIVO
cent

central ADJETIVO
central

la **central** SUSTANTIVO
head office (*oficina principal*)
◆ **una central eléctrica** a power-station
◆ **una central nuclear** a nuclear power-station

la **centralita** SUSTANTIVO
switchboard

céntrico ADJETIVO
central ◇ *Está en un barrio céntrico.* It's in a central area.
◆ **Es un piso céntrico.** The flat is in the centre of town.

el **centro** SUSTANTIVO
centre ◇ *en pleno centro de la ciudad* right in the town centre
◆ **Fui al centro a hacer unas compras.** I went into town to do some shopping.
◆ **un centro comercial** a shopping centre
◆ **un centro de deportes** a sports centre
◆ **un centro médico** a hospital

el **centroamericano,** la **centroamericana** ADJETIVO, SUSTANTIVO
Central American

ceñido ADJETIVO
tight
◆ **Esta falda me queda muy ceñida.** This skirt's too tight for me.

cepillar VERBO
to brush (*chaqueta, pelo*)

♦ **Se está cepillando los dientes.** He's brushing his teeth.

el **cepillo** SUSTANTIVO
brush (PL brushes)
♦ **un cepillo de dientes** a toothbrush

la **cera** SUSTANTIVO
wax

la **cerámica** SUSTANTIVO
pottery ◊ *Me gusta la cerámica.* I like pottery.
♦ **una cerámica** a piece of pottery

cerca ADVERBIO
near ◊ *El colegio está muy cerca.* The school is very near.
♦ **¿Hay algún banco por aquí cerca?** Is there a bank nearby?
♦ **cerca de la iglesia** near the church
♦ **cerca de dos horas** nearly two hours
♦ **Quería verlo de cerca.** I wanted to see it close up.

cercano ADJETIVO
nearby ◊ *Viven en un pueblo cercano.* They live in a nearby village.
♦ **una de las calles cercanas a la catedral** one of the streets close to the cathedral
♦ **el Cercano Oriente** the Near East

el **cerdo** SUSTANTIVO
1 pig ◊ *Tienen cerdos.* They keep pigs.
2 pork ◊ *No comemos cerdo.* We don't eat pork.

el **cereal** SUSTANTIVO
cereal
♦ **Los niños desayunan cereales.** The children have cereal for breakfast.

el **cerebro** SUSTANTIVO
brain

la **ceremonia** SUSTANTIVO
ceremony (PL ceremonies)

la **cereza** SUSTANTIVO
cherry (PL cherries)

la **cerilla** SUSTANTIVO
match (PL matches) ◊ *una caja de cerillas* a box of matches

el **cerillo** SUSTANTIVO Mexico
match (PL matches)

el **cero** SUSTANTIVO
zero (PL zeros *o* zeroes)
♦ **Estamos a cinco grados bajo cero.** It's five degrees below zero.
♦ **cero coma tres** zero point three
♦ **Van dos a cero.** The score is two-nil.
♦ **Empataron a cero.** It was a no-score draw.
♦ **quince a cero** (*en tenis*) fifteen-love
♦ **Tuve que empezar desde cero.** I had to start from scratch.

el **cerquillo** SUSTANTIVO Latin America
fringe

cerrado ADJETIVO
closed ◊ *Las tiendas están cerradas.* The shops are closed.
♦ **una curva muy cerrada** a very sharp bend

la **cerradura** SUSTANTIVO
lock

cerrar* VERBO
1 to close ◊ *No cierran al mediodía.* They don't close at noon. ◊ *Cerró el libro.* He closed the book.
*En la mayoría de los casos se puede usar tanto **shut** como **close**.*
◊ *No puedo cerrar la maleta.* I can't shut this suitcase.
2 to turn off (*grifo*) ◊ *Cierra el grifo.* Turn off the tap.
♦ **Cerré la puerta con llave.** I locked the door.
♦ **La puerta se cerró de golpe.** The door slammed shut.
♦ **Se me cierran los ojos.** I can't keep my eyes open.

el **cerrojo** SUSTANTIVO
bolt
♦ **echar el cerrojo** to bolt the door

certificado ADJETIVO
registered (*carta*)
♦ **Mandé el paquete certificado.** I sent the parcel by registered post.

el **certificado** SUSTANTIVO
certificate

la **cervecería** SUSTANTIVO
bar

la **cerveza** SUSTANTIVO
beer ◊ *Fuimos a tomar unas cervezas.* We went to have a few beers.
♦ **la cerveza de barril** draught beer

cesar VERBO
to stop
♦ **No cesa de hablar.** He never stops talking.
♦ **No cesaba de repetirlo.** He kept repeating it.

el **césped** SUSTANTIVO
grass ◊ *"no pisar el césped"* "keep off the grass"

la **cesta** SUSTANTIVO
basket
♦ **una cesta de Navidad** a Christmas hamper

el **cesto** SUSTANTIVO
basket

el **chabacano** SUSTANTIVO Mexico
apricot

la **chabola** SUSTANTIVO
shack
♦ **un barrio de chabolas** a shantytown

el **chaleco** SUSTANTIVO
waistcoat
♦ **un chaleco salvavidas** a life-jacket

el **chalet** SUSTANTIVO (PL **los chalets**)
1 cottage (*en el campo*)
2 villa (*en centro turístico*)
3 house (*adosado*)

el **champán** SUSTANTIVO (PL los **champanes**)
champagne

el **champiñón** SUSTANTIVO (PL los **champiñones**)
mushroom

el **champú** SUSTANTIVO (PL los **champús**)
shampoo (PL shampoos)

el **chancho,** la **chancha** SUSTANTIVO River Plate
pig

la **chancleta** SUSTANTIVO
flip-flop
♦ **unas chancletas** a pair of flip-flops

el **chándal** SUSTANTIVO (PL los **chándals**)
tracksuit

el **chantaje** SUSTANTIVO
blackmail
♦ **hacer chantaje a alguien** to blackmail somebody

la **chapa** SUSTANTIVO
1 badge (*insignia*)
2 top (*de botella*)
3 sheet (*de metal*)
4 panel (*de madera*)
5 number plate (*de coche*) Latin America

chapado ADJETIVO
♦ **chapado en oro** gold-plated

el **chaparrón** SUSTANTIVO (PL los **chaparrones**)
♦ **Anoche cayó un buen chaparrón.** There was a real downpour last night.
♦ **Es sólo un chaparrón.** It's just a shower.

chapotear VERBO
to splash around

la **chapuza** SUSTANTIVO
botched job
♦ **hacer chapuzas** (*arreglos, trabajillos*) to do odd jobs

el **chapuzón** SUSTANTIVO (PL los **chapuzones**)
♦ **darse un chapuzón** to go for a dip

la **chaqueta** SUSTANTIVO
1 cardigan (*de punto*)
2 jacket (*americana*)

la **charca** SUSTANTIVO
pond

el **charco** SUSTANTIVO
puddle

la **charcutería** SUSTANTIVO
delicatessen

la **charla** SUSTANTIVO
1 chat ◊ *Estuvimos de charla.* We had a chat.
2 talk ◊ *Dio una charla sobre teatro clásico.* He gave a talk on classical theatre.

charlar VERBO
to chat

el **chasco** SUSTANTIVO
♦ **llevarse un chasco** to be disappointed

el **chat** SUSTANTIVO
chatroom

la **chatarra** SUSTANTIVO
scrap metal

la **chava** SUSTANTIVO Mexico
girl

el **chavo** SUSTANTIVO Mexico
boy

checar* VERBO Mexico
to check

el **checo,** la **checa** ADJETIVO, SUSTANTIVO
Czech
♦ **la República Checa** the Czech Republic

el **checo** SUSTANTIVO
Czech (*idioma*)

el **chef** SUSTANTIVO (PL los **chefs**)
chef (PL chefs)

el **cheque** SUSTANTIVO
cheque
♦ **los cheques de viaje** traveller's cheques

el **chequeo** SUSTANTIVO
check-up (PL check-ups) ◊ *hacerse un chequeo* to have a check-up

chévere ADJETIVO, ADVERBIO Latin America
great (*coloquial*)

la **chica** SUSTANTIVO
girl

el **chícharo** SUSTANTIVO Mexico
pea

el **chichón** SUSTANTIVO (PL los **chichones**)
bump ◊ *Me ha salido un chichón en la frente.* I've got a bump on my forehead.

el **chicle** SUSTANTIVO
chewing gum

chico ADJETIVO
small

el **chico** SUSTANTIVO
1 boy ◊ *los chicos de la clase* the boys in the class
2 guy ◊ *Me parece un chico muy majo.* He seems like a really nice guy.

Chile SUSTANTIVO MASC
Chile

el **chileno,** la **chilena** ADJETIVO, SUSTANTIVO
Chilean

chillar VERBO
1 to scream (*persona*)
2 to squeak (*ratón*)
3 to squeal (*cerdo*)
4 to screech (*gaviotas*)

la **chimenea** SUSTANTIVO
1 chimney (PL chimneys) ◊ *Salía humo de la chimenea.* There was smoke coming out of the chimney.
2 fireplace ◊ *sentado frente a la chimenea* sitting in front of the fireplace
♦ **Enciende la chimenea.** Light the fire.

el **chimpancé** SUSTANTIVO (PL los **chimpancés**)
chimpanzee

la **china** SUSTANTIVO
1 Chinese woman (*persona*)

* Verbs marked with this symbol are irregular. See pages 380-382 for further details

2 stone ◊ *Se me ha metido una china en el zapato.* I've got a stone in my shoe.

China SUSTANTIVO FEM
China

la **chinche** SUSTANTIVO Mexico, River Plate
drawing pin

la **chincheta** SUSTANTIVO
drawing pin

chino ADJETIVO
Chinese

el **chino** SUSTANTIVO
1 Chinese man (*persona*)
◆ **los chinos** the Chinese
2 Chinese (*idioma*)

Chipre SUSTANTIVO MASC
Cyprus

la **chirimoya** SUSTANTIVO
custard apple

chirriar* VERBO
to squeak

chismorrear VERBO
to gossip

chismoso ADJETIVO
◆ **¡No seas chismoso!** Don't be such a gossip!

el **chiste** SUSTANTIVO
1 joke ◊ *contar un chiste* to tell a joke
◆ **un chiste verde** a dirty joke
2 cartoon ◊ *el chiste del periódico* the newspaper cartoon

chocar* VERBO
◆ **chocar contra (1)** to hit ◊ *El coche chocó contra un árbol.* The car hit a tree.
◆ **chocar contra (2)** (*andando*) to bump into ◊ *Me choqué contra una farola.* I bumped into a lamppost.
◆ **chocar con algo** to crash into something
◆ **Los trenes chocaron de frente.** The trains crashed head-on.
◆ **Me choca que no sepas nada.** I'm shocked that you don't know anything about it.

el **chocolate** SUSTANTIVO
chocolate ◊ *chocolate con leche* milk chocolate
◆ **Nos tomamos un chocolate.** We had a cup of hot chocolate.

la **chocolatina** SUSTANTIVO
chocolate bar

el **chófer**, la **chófer** SUSTANTIVO
1 driver (*de autobús, camión*)
2 chauffeur (*empleado particular*)

el **chopo** SUSTANTIVO
black poplar

el **choque** SUSTANTIVO
1 (*de vehículos*)
crash (PL crashes)
2 (*entre personas, culturas*)
clash (PL clashes)

el **chorizo** SUSTANTIVO

> ***Chorizo** is a kind of spicy sausage.*

el **chorrito** SUSTANTIVO
dash ◊ *Échame un chorrito de leche.* Just a dash of milk, please.

el **chorro** SUSTANTIVO
◆ **salir a chorros** to gush out

la **choza** SUSTANTIVO
hut

el **chubasco** SUSTANTIVO
heavy shower

el **chubasquero** SUSTANTIVO
cagoule

la **chuleta** SUSTANTIVO
chop ◊ *una chuleta de cerdo* a pork chop

chulo ADJETIVO
1 cocky (*coloquial*)
◆ **ponerse chulo con alguien** to get cocky with someone
2 neat (*coloquial*) ◊ *¡Qué mochila más chula!* What a neat rucksack!

chupar VERBO
to suck ◊ *Se chupaba el dedo.* He was sucking his thumb.

el **chupete** SUSTANTIVO
dummy (PL dummies)

el **churro** SUSTANTIVO

> *A **Churro** is a type of fritter typically eaten with a cup of hot chocolate.*

el **cibercafé** SUSTANTIVO
cybercafe

la **cicatriz** SUSTANTIVO (PL las **cicatrices**)
scar ◊ *Me quedó una cicatriz en la cara.* I was left with a scar on my face.

el **ciclismo** SUSTANTIVO
cycling
◆ **Mi hermano hace ciclismo.** My brother is a cyclist.

el/la **ciclista** SUSTANTIVO
cyclist

el **ciclo** SUSTANTIVO
cycle

la **ciega** SUSTANTIVO
blind woman (PL blind women)
◆ **Avanzábamos a ciegas.** We couldn't see where we were going.
◆ **Tomaron la decisión a ciegas.** They took the decision blindly.

ciego ADJETIVO
blind
◆ **quedarse ciego** to go blind

el **ciego** SUSTANTIVO
blind man
◆ **los ciegos** the blind

el **cielo** SUSTANTIVO
1 sky (PL skies) ◊ *No había ni una nube en el cielo.* There wasn't a single cloud in the sky.
2 heaven ◊ *ir al cielo* to go to heaven

cien ADJETIVO, PRONOMBRE
a hundred ◇ *Había unos cien invitados a la boda.* There were about a hundred guests at the wedding. ◇ *cien mil* a hundred thousand
◆ **cien por cien** a hundred percent ◇ *Es cien por cien algodón.* It's a hundred percent cotton.

la **ciencia** SUSTANTIVO
science ◇ *Me gustan mucho las ciencias.* I really enjoy science. ◇ *ciencias sociales* social sciences
◆ **ciencias empresariales** business studies

la **ciencia-ficción** SUSTANTIVO
science fiction ◇ *Me gustan novelas de ciencia-ficción.* I like science fiction novels.

la **científica** SUSTANTIVO
scientist

científico ADJETIVO
scientific

el **científico** SUSTANTIVO
scientist

ciento ADJETIVO, PRONOMBRE
a hundred
◆ **ciento cuarenta y dos libras** a hundred and forty two pounds
◆ **Recibimos cientos de cartas.** We received hundreds of letters.
◆ **el diez por ciento de la población** ten percent of the population

el **cierre** SUSTANTIVO
1 clasp (*de pulsera, bolso*)
2 closing-down (*de empresa, hospital*)
◆ **un cierre relámpago** River Plate a zip

cierro VERBO *ver* **cerrar**

cierto ADJETIVO
1 true (*verdadero*) ◇ *No, eso no es cierto.* No, that's not true.
2 certain ◇ *Viene ciertos días a la semana.* He comes certain days of the week.
◆ **por cierto** by the way

el **ciervo** SUSTANTIVO
deer (PL deer)

la **cifra** SUSTANTIVO
figure ◇ *un número de cuatro cifras* a four-figure number

el **cigarrillo** SUSTANTIVO
cigarette

el **cigarro** SUSTANTIVO
cigarette

la **cigüeña** SUSTANTIVO
stork

la **cima** SUSTANTIVO
top ◇ *Quiere llegar a la cima.* He wants to get to the top.

los **cimientos** SUSTANTIVO
foundations

cinco ADJETIVO, PRONOMBRE
five
◆ **Son las cinco.** It's five o'clock.
◆ **el cinco de enero** the fifth of January

cincuenta ADJETIVO, PRONOMBRE
fifty ◇ *Tiene cincuenta años.* He's fifty.
◆ **el cincuenta aniversario** the fiftieth anniversary

el **cine** SUSTANTIVO
cinema
◆ **ir al cine** to go to the cinema
◆ **una actriz de cine** a film actress

cínico ADJETIVO
cynical

la **cinta** SUSTANTIVO
1 ribbon (*de adorno, para el pelo*)
2 tape (*para grabar*)
◆ **una cinta de vídeo** a videotape
◆ **cinta aislante** insulating tape
◆ **una cinta transportadora** a conveyor belt

la **cintura** SUSTANTIVO
waist ◇ *¿Cuánto mides de cintura?* What's your waist size?

el **cinturón** SUSTANTIVO (PL los **cinturones**)
belt
◆ **el cinturón de seguridad** the safety belt

el **ciprés** SUSTANTIVO (PL los **cipreses**)
cypress

el **circo** SUSTANTIVO
circus (PL circuses)

el **circuito** SUSTANTIVO
1 track (*deportivo*) ◇ *El corredor dio cuatro vueltas al circuito.* The runner ran four laps of the track.
2 circuit (*eléctrico*)
◆ **circuito cerrado de televisión** closed-circuit television

la **circulación** SUSTANTIVO
1 traffic (*de vehículos*) ◇ *un accidente de circulación* a traffic accident
2 circulation (*de la sangre*)

circular VERBO
1 to drive (*en coche*) ◇ *En Australia se circula por la derecha.* In Australia they drive on the left.
◆ **¡Circulen!** Move along please!
2 to circulate (*sangre*)
3 to go round (*rumor*) ◇ *Circula el rumor de que se van a casar.* There's a rumour going round that they're getting married.

el **círculo** SUSTANTIVO
circle ◇ *Las sillas estaban puestas en círculo.* The chairs were set out in a circle.

la **circunferencia** SUSTANTIVO
circumference

la **circunstancia** SUSTANTIVO
circumstance

la **ciruela** SUSTANTIVO
plum
◆ **una ciruela pasa** a prune

la **cirugía** SUSTANTIVO
surgery (PL surgeries)
♦ **hacerse la cirugía plástica** to have plastic surgery

el **cirujano,** la **cirujana** SUSTANTIVO
surgeon

el **cisne** SUSTANTIVO
swan

la **cisterna** SUSTANTIVO
cistern (*del wáter*)

la **cita** SUSTANTIVO
1 appointment (*profesional*) ◊ *Tengo cita con el Sr. Pérez.* I've got an appointment with Mr. Pérez.
2 date (*romántica*) ◊ *No llegues tarde a la cita.* Don't be late for your date.
3 quotation (*textual*) ◊ *una cita de Quevedo* a quotation from Quevedo

citar VERBO
1 to quote (*frase, texto*) ◊ *Siempre está citando a los clásicos.* He's always quoting the classics.
2 to mention ◊ *Citó el caso que ocurrió el otro día.* He mentioned as an example what happened the other day.
♦ **Nos han citado a las diez.** We've been given an appointment for ten o'clock.

la **ciudad** SUSTANTIVO
1 city (PL cities) ◊ *una ciudad como Salamanca* a city like Salamanca
2 town ◊ *una pequeña ciudad al norte de Londres* a small town north of London
♦ **la ciudad universitaria** the university campus

el **ciudadano,** la **ciudadana** SUSTANTIVO
citizen ◊ *ser ciudadano español* to be a Spanish citizen

civil ADJETIVO
civil ◊ *la guerra civil* the Civil War

la **civilización** SUSTANTIVO (PL las **civilizaciones**)
civilization

civilizado ADJETIVO
civilized

la **clara** SUSTANTIVO
white (*de huevo*)

el **clarinete** SUSTANTIVO
clarinet

claro (1) ADJETIVO
1 clear (*explicación, idea*) ◊ *Lo quiero mañana. ¿Está claro?* I want it tomorrow. Is that clear?
♦ **Está claro que esconden algo.** It's obvious that they are hiding something.
♦ **No tengo muy claro lo que quiero hacer.** I'm not very sure about what I want to do.
2 light (*color*) ◊ *una camisa azul claro* a light blue shirt

claro (2) ADVERBIO
clearly ◊ *Lo oí muy claro.* I heard it very clearly.
♦ **Quiero que me hables claro.** I want you to be frank with me.
♦ **No he sacado nada en claro de la reunión.** I'm none the wiser after that meeting.
♦ **¡Claro! (1)** Sure! ◊ *¿Te gusta el fútbol? – ¡Claro!* Do you like football? – Sure!
♦ **¡Claro! (2)** Of course! ◊ *¿Te oyó? – ¡Claro que me oyó!* Did he hear you? – Of course he heard me!

la **clase** SUSTANTIVO
1 class (PL classes) ◊ *A las diez tengo clase de física.* At ten o'clock I have a physics class.
♦ **Mi hermana da clases de inglés.** My sister teaches English.
♦ **Hoy no hay clase.** There's no school today.
♦ **clases de conducir** driving lessons
♦ **clases particulares** private classes
2 (*aula*)
classroom
3 (*tipo*)
kind ◊ *Había juguetes de todas clases.* There were all kinds of toys.
♦ **la clase media** the middle class

clásico ADJETIVO
1 classical ◊ *Me gusta la música clásica.* I like classical music.
2 classic (*típico*) ◊ *Es el clásico ejemplo de malnutrición.* It's the classic case of malnutrition.

la **clasificación** SUSTANTIVO (PL las **clasificaciones**)
classification (*de libros, plantas*)
♦ **estar a la cabeza de la clasificación** to be at the top of the table

clasificar* VERBO
to classify (*libros, plantas*)
♦ **Esperan clasificarse para la final.** They hope to qualify for the final.
♦ **Se clasificaron en tercer lugar.** They came third.

clavar VERBO
♦ **clavar una punta en algo** to hammer a nail into something
♦ **Las tablas están mal clavadas.** The boards aren't properly nailed down.
♦ **Me he clavado una espina en el dedo.** I got a thorn in my finger.
♦ **Aquí te clavan.** (*coloquial*) You get ripped off in this place.

la **clave** SUSTANTIVO
1 code (*de caja fuerte, secreta*)
♦ **un mensaje en clave** a coded message
2 key ◊ *la clave del éxito* the key to success
♦ **la clave de sol** the treble clef

el **clavel** SUSTANTIVO
carnation

la **clavícula** SUSTANTIVO
collar bone

el **clavo** SUSTANTIVO

☞

nail

el **clic** SUSTANTIVO
click
♦ **hacer clic en** to click on

el **cliente,** la **clienta** SUSTANTIVO
1 customer (*de tienda, restaurante*)
2 client (*de empresa, banco*)
3 guest (*de hotel*)

el **clima** SUSTANTIVO
climate ◊ *Es un país de clima tropical.* It's a country with a tropical climate.

climatizado ADJETIVO
1 air-conditioned (*cine*)
2 heated (*piscina*)

la **clínica** SUSTANTIVO
hospital

clínico ADJETIVO
clinical

el **clip** SUSTANTIVO (PL los **clips**)
1 paper clip (*para papeles*)
2 clip (*para el pelo*)

la **cloaca** SUSTANTIVO
sewer

el **cloro** SUSTANTIVO
chlorine

el **club** SUSTANTIVO (PL los **clubs**)
club ◊ *el club de tenis* the tennis club

cobarde ADJETIVO
cowardly ◊ *una actitud cobarde* a cowardly attitude
♦ **¡No seas cobarde!** Don't be such a coward!

el/la **cobarde** SUSTANTIVO
coward

la **cobaya** SUSTANTIVO
guinea-pig

la **cobija** SUSTANTIVO Latin America
blanket

cobrar VERBO
to charge ◊ *Me cobró dos mil pesetas por la reparación.* He charged me two thousand pesetas for the repair.
♦ **cuando cobre el sueldo de este mes** when I get my wages this month
♦ **¿Me cobra los cafés?** How much do I owe for the coffees?
♦ **¡Cóbrese, por favor!** Can I pay, please?
♦ **cobrar un cheque** to cash a cheque

el **cobre** SUSTANTIVO
copper

el **cobro** SUSTANTIVO
♦ **llamar a cobro revertido** to reverse the charges

la **Coca-Cola** ® SUSTANTIVO (PL las **Coca-Colas**)
Coke ®

la **cocaína** SUSTANTIVO
cocaine

cocer* VERBO
1 to boil (*hervir*) ◊ *Cocer las verduras durante tres minutos.* Boil the vegetables for three minutes.
2 to cook (*cocinar*) ◊ *Las zanahorias no están cocidas todavía.* The carrots aren't properly cooked yet.
♦ **Tarda diez minutos en cocerse.** It takes ten minutes to cook.

el **coche** SUSTANTIVO
1 car ◊ *Fuimos a París en coche.* We went to Paris by car.
♦ **un coche de carreras** a racing car
♦ **los coches de choque** the bumper cars
2 pram (*para el bebé*)
3 carriage (*de tren*)
♦ **Fuimos en coche cama.** We took the sleeper.
♦ **un coche de bomberos** a fire engine

cochino ADJETIVO
filthy

el **cochino** SUSTANTIVO
pig

el **cocido** SUSTANTIVO
stew

> ℹ *The* ***cocido madrileño*** *is a stew of chickpeas, vegetables and meat.*

la **cocina** SUSTANTIVO
1 kitchen ◊ *Comemos en la cocina.* We eat in the kitchen.
2 cooker ◊ *una cocina de gas* a gas cooker
♦ **la cocina vasca** Basque cuisine
♦ **un libro de cocina** a cookery book

cocinar VERBO
to cook ◊ *No sabe cocinar.* He can't cook.
♦ **Cocinas muy bien.** You're a very good cook.

el **cocinero,** la **cocinera** SUSTANTIVO
cook ◊ *Soy cocinero.* I'm a cook.

el **coco** SUSTANTIVO
coconut (*fruto*)

el **cocodrilo** SUSTANTIVO
crocodile

el **código** SUSTANTIVO
code
♦ **el código de la circulación** the highway code
♦ **el código postal** the postcode

el **codo** SUSTANTIVO
elbow

la **codorniz** SUSTANTIVO (PL las **codornices**)
quail

coger* VERBO
1 to take (*tomar*) ◊ *Coge el que más te guste.* Take the one which you like best. ◊ *Coja la primera calle a la derecha.* Take the first street on the right.

* Verbs marked with this symbol are irregular. See pages 380-382 for further details

2 to catch (*pillar*) ◊ *¡Coge la pelota!* Catch the ball! ◊ *La cogieron robando.* They caught her stealing.
◆ **coger un resfriado** to catch a cold
3 to pick up (*levantar*) ◊ *Coge al niño, que está llorando.* Pick up the baby, he's crying.
4 to get (*obtener*) ◊ *¿Nos coges dos entradas?* Would you get us two tickets?
5 to borrow (*tomar prestado*) ◊ *¿Te puedo coger el bolígrafo?* Can I borrow your pen?
◆ **Voy a coger el autobús.** I'm going to get the bus.
◆ **Le cogió cariño al gato.** He took a liking to the cat.
◆ **Iban cogidos de la mano.** They were walking hand in hand.

el **cohete** SUSTANTIVO
rocket
◆ **un cohete espacial** a rocket

cohibido ADJETIVO
inhibited
◆ **sentirse cohibido** to feel inhibited

la **coincidencia** SUSTANTIVO
coincidence
◆ **¡Qué coincidencia!** What a coincidence!

coincidir VERBO
to match ◊ *Las huellas dactilares coinciden.* The fingerprints match.
◆ **Coincidimos en el tren.** We happened to meet on the train.
◆ **Es que esas fechas coinciden con mi viaje.** The problem is, those dates clash with my trip.

cojear VERBO
1 to limp ◊ *Todavía cojea un poco.* He's still limping a little.
2 to be lame (*ser cojo*)
◆ **Cojea del pie izquierdo.** He's lame in his left leg.
3 to wobble (*silla, mesa*)

el **cojín** SUSTANTIVO (PL los **cojines**)
cushion

cojo (1) VERBO *ver* **coger**

cojo (2) ADJETIVO
1 lame
◆ **Está cojo.** He's lame.
◆ **Vas un poco cojo.** You're limping a bit.
2 wobbly (*mueble*)

la **col** SUSTANTIVO
cabbage
◆ **las coles de Bruselas** Brussels sprouts

la **cola** SUSTANTIVO
1 tail (*de animal*)
2 queue (*de gente*) ◊ *Había mucha cola para los lavabos.* There was a long queue for the toilets.
◆ **hacer cola** to queue
3 glue (*pegamento*)

colaborar VERBO
◆ **Todo el pueblo colaboró.** Everyone in the village joined in.
◆ **Se negó a colaborar con nosotros.** He refused to cooperate with us.

el **colador** SUSTANTIVO
1 strainer (*para líquidos*)
2 sieve (*para arroz, verduras*)

colar VERBO
to strain (*verduras, té*)
◆ **colarse** (*coloquial*) to push in ◊ *No te cueles.* Don't push in.
◆ **Nos colamos en el cine.** We sneaked into the cinema without paying.

la **colcha** SUSTANTIVO
bedspread

el **colchón** SUSTANTIVO (PL los **colchones**)
mattress (PL mattresses)
◆ **un colchón de aire** an airbed

la **colchoneta** SUSTANTIVO
1 mat (*gimnasia*)
2 air bed (*de aire*)

la **colección** SUSTANTIVO (PL las **colecciones**)
collection

coleccionar VERBO
to collect

la **colecta** SUSTANTIVO
collection
◆ **Hicieron una colecta para comprarle el billete.** They had a collection to buy him the ticket.

el **colectivo** SUSTANTIVO River Plate
bus (PL buses)

el/la **colega** SUSTANTIVO
1 colleague (*de profesión*)
2 mate (*coloquial: amigo*)

el **colegio** SUSTANTIVO
school ◊ *Voy al colegio en bicicleta.* I cycle to school. ◊ *¿Todavía vas al colegio?* Are you still at school? ◊ *Mi hermano estaba en el colegio.* My brother was at school.
◆ **un colegio de curas** a Catholic boys' school
◆ **un colegio de monjas** a convent school
◆ **un colegio público** a state school
◆ **un colegio mayor** a hall of residence

el **colesterol** SUSTANTIVO
cholesterol

la **coleta** SUSTANTIVO
ponytail (*una sólo*)
◆ **La niña llevaba coletas.** The girl wore her hair in bunches.

colgado ADJETIVO
hanging ◊ *Había varios cuadros colgados en la pared.* There were several pictures hanging on the wall.
◆ **Debe de tener el teléfono mal colgado.** He must have the telephone off the hook.

el **colgante** SUSTANTIVO
pendant

colgar* VERBO
to hang ◊ *Colgamos un cuadro en la pared.* We hung a picture on the wall.

☞

◆ **¡No dejes la chaqueta en la silla, cuélgala!** Don't leave your jacket on the chair, hang it up!
◆ **Me colgó el teléfono.** He hung up on me.
◆ **¡Cuelga, por favor, que quiero hacer una llamada!** Hang up, please. I want to use the phone!
◆ **No cuelgue, por favor.** Please hold.

la **coliflor** SUSTANTIVO
cauliflower

la **colilla** SUSTANTIVO
cigarette end

la **colina** SUSTANTIVO
hill

el **collar** SUSTANTIVO
1 necklace (*joya*)
2 collar (*de perro, gato*)

la **colmena** SUSTANTIVO
beehive

el **colmillo** SUSTANTIVO
1 canine tooth (*de persona, perro*)
2 fang (*de vampiro, cobra*)
3 tusk (*de elefante*)

el **colmo** SUSTANTIVO
◆ **¡Esto ya es el colmo!** This really is the last straw!
◆ **Para colmo de males, empezó a llover.** To make matters worse, it started to rain.

colocar* VERBO
1 to put (*poner*) ◇ *Colocamos la mesa en medio del comedor.* We put the table in the middle of the dining room.
2 to arrange (*ordenar*) ◇ *He colocado los libros por temas.* I've arranged the books by subject.
◆ **colocarse (1)** to get a job ◇ *Se colocó de aprendiz en un taller mecánico.* He got a job as an apprentice in a garage workshop.
◆ **colocarse (2)** (*coloquial: con alcohol*) to get plastered
◆ **colocarse (3)** (*coloquial: con drogas*) to get high
◆ **¡Colocaos en fila!** Get into a line!
◆ **El equipo se ha colocado en quinto lugar.** The team are now in fifth place.

Colombia SUSTANTIVO FEM
Colombia

el **colombiano,** la **colombiana** ADJETIVO, SUSTANTIVO
Colombian

la **colonia** SUSTANTIVO
1 (*de buen olor*)
perfume
2 (*de otro país*)
colony (PL colonies)
3 district Mexico
◆ **una colonia de verano** a summer camp

colonizar* VERBO
to colonize

coloquial ADJETIVO
colloquial

el **color** SUSTANTIVO
colour ◇ *¿De qué color son?* What colour are they?
◆ **un vestido de color azul** a blue dress
◆ **una televisión en color** a colour television

colorado ADJETIVO
red
◆ **ponerse colorado** to blush

la **columna** SUSTANTIVO
column
◆ **la columna vertebral** the spine

el **columpio** SUSTANTIVO
swing

la **coma** SUSTANTIVO
comma ◇ *palabras separadas por comas* words separated by commas
◆ **cero coma ocho** zero point eight

el **coma** SUSTANTIVO
coma
◆ **estar en coma** to be in a coma

la **comadrona** SUSTANTIVO
midwife (PL midwives)

el/la **comandante** SUSTANTIVO
major
◆ **el comandante en jefe** the commander in chief

la **comba** SUSTANTIVO
skipping rope (*cuerda*)
◆ **saltar a la comba** to skip

el **combate** SUSTANTIVO
battle ◇ *entrar en combate* to go into battle
◆ **un piloto de combate** a fighter pilot
◆ **un combate de boxeo** a boxing match

combinar VERBO
1 to combine ◇ *Combina los estudios con el trabajo.* He combines his studies with work.
2 to match (*ropa, colores*) ◇ *colores que combinan con el azul* colours which match with blue

el **combustible** SUSTANTIVO
fuel

la **comedia** SUSTANTIVO
comedy (PL comedies)

el **comedor** SUSTANTIVO
1 (*en casa, hotel*)
dining room
2 (*en colegio*)
refectory (PL refectories)
3 (*en lugar de trabajo*)
canteen

comentar VERBO
1 to say ◇ *Comentó que le había parecido muy joven.* He said that she had seemed very young.
2 to discuss ◇ *Comentamos el tema en clase.* We discussed the subject in class.

♦ **Me han comentado que es una película muy buena.** I've been told that is a very good film.

el **comentario** SUSTANTIVO
comment (*observación*) ◊ *No hizo ningún comentario.* He made no comment.
♦ **Fue un comentario desagradable.** It was an unpleasant remark.

el/la **comentarista** SUSTANTIVO
commentator

comenzar* VERBO
to begin
♦ **Comenzó a llover.** It began to rain.

comer VERBO
1 to eat ◊ *¿Quieres comer algo?* Do you want something to eat?
♦ **Me comí una manzana.** I had an apple.
2 to have lunch (*al mediodía*) ◊ *Comimos en el hotel.* We had lunch in the hotel.
♦ **Hemos comido paella.** We had paella for lunch.
♦ **¿Qué hay para comer?** What is there for lunch?
3 to have dinner Latin America
♦ **Le estaba dando de comer a su hijo.** She was feeding her son.
♦ **No te comas el coco por eso.** (*coloquial*) Don't worry too much about it.

comercial ADJETIVO
1 business (*relación, zona, estructura*)
business *en este caso va siempre delante del sustantivo.*
2 trade (*déficit, guerra*)
trade *en este caso va siempre delante del sustantivo.*
3 commercial ◊ *una película muy comercial* a very commercial film

el/la **comerciante** SUSTANTIVO
shopkeeper

el **comercio** SUSTANTIVO
1 trade ◊ *el comercio exterior* foreign trade
♦ **el comercio electrónico** e-commerce
2 shop ◊ *¿A qué hora cierran los comercios?* What time do the shops close?

el **cometa** SUSTANTIVO
comet

la **cometa** SUSTANTIVO
kite

cometer VERBO
1 to commit (*un delito*)
2 to make (*un error*)

el **cómic** SUSTANTIVO (PL los **cómics**)
comic ◊ *un cómic nuevo* a new comic
♦ **un personaje de cómic** a comic-book character

cómico ADJETIVO
1 comical ◊ *Fue muy cómico.* It was very comical.
2 comic ◊ *un actor cómico* a comic actor

la **comida** SUSTANTIVO
1 food ◊ *La comida es muy buena en el hotel.* The food in the hotel is very good.
2 (*al mediodía*)
lunch (PL lunches) ◊ *La comida es a la una y media.* Lunch is at half past one.
3 (*por la noche*)
supper Latin America
4 meal ◊ *Es la comida más importante del día.* It's the most important meal of the day.

comienzo VERBO *ver* **comenzar**

las **comillas** SUSTANTIVO
quotation marks
♦ **entre comillas** in quotation marks

la **comisaría** SUSTANTIVO
police station

la **comisión** SUSTANTIVO (PL las **comisiones**)
1 commission ◊ *una comisión del 20%* a 20% commission
2 committee ◊ *La comisión organizadora del festival.* The festival organizing committee.

el **comité** SUSTANTIVO (PL los **comités**)
committee

como ADVERBIO, CONJUNCIÓN
1 like ◊ *Tienen un perro como el nuestro.* They've got a dog like ours. ◊ *Se portó como un imbécil.* He behaved like an idiot.
♦ **Sabe como a cebolla.** It tastes a bit like onion.
2 as ◊ *Lo hice como me habían enseñado.* I did it as I had been taught. ◊ *Lo usé como cuchara.* I used it as a spoon. ◊ *blanco como la nieve* as white as snow ◊ *Como ella no llegaba, me fui.* As she didn't arrive, I left.
♦ **Hazlo como te dijo ella.** Do it the way she told you.
♦ **Es tan alto como tú.** He is as tall as you.
♦ **tal como lo había planeado** just as I had planned it
♦ **como si** as if ◊ *Siguió leyendo, como si no hubiera oído nada.* He kept on reading, as if he had heard nothing.
3 if ◊ *Como lo vuelvas a hacer se lo digo a tu madre.* If you do it again I'll tell your mother.
4 about ◊ *Vinieron como unas diez personas.* About ten people came. ◊ *Llegó como a las cuatro.* He arrived about four o'clock.

cómo ADVERBIO
how ◊ *¿Cómo se dice en inglés?* How do you say it in English? ◊ *¿Cómo están tus padres?* How are your parents? ◊ *No sé cómo voy a explicárselo.* I don't know how I'm going to explain it to him.
♦ **¿A cómo están las manzanas?** How much are the apples?

☞

- **¿Cómo es de grande?** How big is it?
- **¿Cómo es su novio? (1)** (*de personalidad*) What's her boyfriend like?
- **¿Cómo es su novio? (2)** (*de físico*) What does her boyfriend look like?
- **Perdón, ¿cómo has dicho?** Sorry, what did you say?
- **¡Cómo! ¿Mañana?** What? Tomorrow?
- **¡Cómo corría!** Boy, was he running!

la **cómoda** SUSTANTIVO
chest of drawers (PL chests of drawers)

la **comodidad** SUSTANTIVO
1 comfort ◊ *Sólo le interesa su propia comodidad.* He's only interested in his own comfort.
2 convenience ◊ *la comodidad de vivir en el centro* the convenience of living in the centre

cómodo ADJETIVO
1 comfortable ◊ *un sillón cómodo* a comfortable chair ◊ *Me siento cómodo en tu casa.* I feel comfortable in your house.
2 convenient ◊ *Tener un coche es muy cómodo.* Having a car is very convenient.

el **compact disc** SUSTANTIVO (PL los **compact discs**)
1 compact disc (*disco*)
2 compact disc player (*aparato*)

compadecer* VERBO
to feel sorry for ◊ *Te compadezco.* I feel sorry for you.

el **compañero**, la **compañera** SUSTANTIVO
1 classmate (*de clase*)
2 workmate (*de trabajo*)
3 partner (*pareja*)
- **un compañero de piso** a flatmate

la **compañía** SUSTANTIVO
company (PL companies) ◊ *una compañía de seguros* an insurance company
- **El chico andaba en malas compañías.** The boy was keeping bad company.
- **Ana vino a hacerme compañía.** Ana came to keep me company.
- **una compañía aérea** an airline

la **comparación** SUSTANTIVO (PL las **comparaciones**)
comparison
- **Mi coche no tiene comparación con el tuyo.** There's no comparison between my car and yours.
- **Mi cuarto es pequeñísimo en comparación con el tuyo.** My room is tiny compared to yours.

comparar VERBO
to compare ◊ *Siempre me comparan con mi hermana.* I'm always being compared to my sister.

compartir VERBO
to share

el **compás** SUSTANTIVO (PL los **compases**)
(*para dibujo*)
compass (PL compasses)
- **bailar al compás de la música** to dance in time to the music

compatible ADJETIVO
compatible

compensar VERBO
1 to make up for ◊ *Intentan compensar la falta de medios con imaginación.* What they lack in resources they try to make up for in imagination.
2 to compensate (*económicamente*) ◊ *El gobierno compensará a los agricultores por la mala cosecha.* The government will compensate farmers for the bad harvest.
- **No me compensa con el sueldo que pagan.** It's not worth my while for the salary they pay.
- **No compensa viajar tan lejos por tan poco tiempo.** It's not worth travelling that far for such a short time.
- **No sé si compensa.** I don't know if it's worth it.

la **competencia** SUSTANTIVO
1 rivalry ◊ *la competencia entre dos hermanos* the rivalry between two brothers
2 competition ◊ *Una campaña para desacreditar a la competencia.* A campaign to discredit the competition.
- **una competencia deportiva** Latin America a sports competition
- **No quiere hacerle la competencia a su mejor amigo.** He doesn't want to compete with his best friend.

competente ADJETIVO
competent

la **competición** SUSTANTIVO (PL las **competiciones**)
competition

competir* VERBO
to compete
- **Van a competir contra los mejores del mundo.** They're going to compete against the best in the world.
- **competir por un título** to compete for a title

complacer* VERBO
to please

el **complejo** SUSTANTIVO
complex (PL complexes)
- **Tiene complejo porque es gordo.** He's got a complex about being fat.
- **un complejo deportivo** a sports complex

completar VERBO
to complete

completo ADJETIVO
1 complete ◊ *las obras completas de Lorca* the complete works of Lorca

* Verbs marked with this symbol are irregular. See pages 380-382 for further details

2 full (*lleno*) ◊ *Los hoteles estaban completos.* The hotels were full.

◆ **Me olvidé por completo.** I completely forgot.

complicado ADJETIVO
complicated

complicar* VERBO
to complicate

◆ **complicarse** to get complicated ◊ *La situación se fue complicando cada día más.* The situation was getting more complicated by the day.

◆ **No quiero complicarme la vida.** I don't want to make life more difficult for myself.

el/la **cómplice** SUSTANTIVO
accomplice

componer* VERBO
to compose ◊ *Él compuso la música.* He composed the music. ◊ *El comité se compone de seis miembros.* The committee is made up of six members.

el **comportamiento** SUSTANTIVO
behaviour

comportarse VERBO
to behave

la **compra** SUSTANTIVO
shopping

◆ **hacer la compra** to do the shopping

◆ **Hice unas compras en el centro.** I did some shopping in the centre.

◆ **ir de compras** to go shopping

comprar VERBO
to buy ◊ *Les compré un helado a los niños.* I bought an ice-cream for the children.

◆ **Le compré el coche a mi amigo.** I bought my friend's car.

◆ **Quiero comprarme unos zapatos.** I want to buy a pair of shoes.

comprender VERBO
to understand ◊ *¡No lo comprendo!* I don't understand it!

comprensivo ADJETIVO
understanding

la **compresa** SUSTANTIVO
sanitary towel

el **comprobante** SUSTANTIVO
receipt

comprobar* VERBO
to check

comprometerse VERBO
◊ *Me he comprometido a ayudarlos.* I have promised to help them.

◆ **No quiero comprometerme por si después no puedo ir.** I don't want to commit myself in case I can't go.

el **compromiso** SUSTANTIVO
engagement ◊ *El ministro canceló sus compromisos.* The minister cancelled his engagements. ◊ *Se iban a casar pero rompieron el compromiso.* They were going to get married but they broke off their engagement.

◆ **Puede probarlo sin ningún compromiso.** You can try it with no obligation.

◆ **Iba a ir pero sólo por compromiso.** I was going to go but only out of duty.

◆ **poner a alguien en un compromiso** to put someone in a difficult situation

compruebo VERBO *ver* **comprobar**

compuesto (1) VERBO *ver* **componer**

compuesto (2) ADJETIVO

◆ **un jurado compuesto de seis miembros** a jury made up of six members

el **computador,** la **computadora**
SUSTANTIVO Latin America
computer

◆ **un computador portátil** a laptop

común ADJETIVO
common (*frontera, característica, objetivo*) ◊ *un apellido muy común* a very common surname

◆ **No tenemos nada en común.** We have nothing in common.

◆ **Hicimos el trabajo en común.** We did the work between us.

◆ **las zonas de uso común** the communal areas

la **comunicación** SUSTANTIVO (PL las **comunicaciones**)
communication

◆ **Se ha cortado la comunicación.** We've been cut off.

comunicar* VERBO
to be engaged (*teléfono*) ◊ *Siempre está comunicando.* The line is always engaged.

◆ **comunicarse** to communicate ◊ *Le cuesta comunicarse con los demás.* He finds it hard to communicate with others.

◆ **Los dos despachos se comunican.** The two offices are connected.

la **comunidad** SUSTANTIVO
community (PL communities)

◆ **la Comunidad Europea** the European Community

◆ **una comunidad autónoma** an autonomous region

la **comunión** SUSTANTIVO (PL las **comuniones**)
communion

◆ **Voy a hacer la primera comunión.** I'm going to make my first communion.

el/la **comunista** ADJETIVO, SUSTANTIVO
communist

con PREPOSICIÓN
with ◊ *Vivo con mis padres.* I live with my parents. ◊ *¿Con quién vas a ir?* Who are you going with?

◆ **Lo he escrito con bolígrafo.** I wrote it in pen.

◆ **Voy a hablar con Luis.** I'll talk to Luis.

◆ **café con leche** white coffee

◆ **Ábrelo con cuidado.** Open it carefully.

☞

♦ **Con estudiar un poco apruebas.** With a bit of studying you should pass.
♦ **Con que me digas tu teléfono basta.** If you just give me your phone number that'll be enough.
♦ **con tal de que no llegues tarde** as long as you don't arrive late

el **concejal**, la **concejala** SUSTANTIVO
town councillor

concentrarse VERBO
1 to concentrate ◊ *Me cuesta concentrarme.* I find it hard to concentrate.
♦ **Concéntrate en lo que estás haciendo.** Concentrate on what you're doing.
2 to gather ◊ *Los manifestantes se concentraron en la plaza.* The demonstrators gathered in the square.

concertar* VERBO
to arrange (*entrevista*)

la **concha** SUSTANTIVO
shell (*de molusco*)

la **conciencia** SUSTANTIVO
conscience ◊ *Tengo la conciencia tranquila.* My conscience is clear.
♦ **Le remuerde la conciencia.** His conscience is pricking him.
♦ **Lo han estudiado a conciencia.** They've studied it thoroughly.

el **concierto** SUSTANTIVO
1 concert ◊ *Van a dar varios conciertos en Madrid.* They're going to give several concerts in Madrid.
2 concerto (PL concertos) ◊ *un concierto para violín* a violin concerto

la **conclusión** SUSTANTIVO (PL las **conclusiones**)
conclusion ◊ *Llegamos a la conclusión de que no valía la pena.* We reached the conclusion that it wasn't worthwhile.

concreto ADJETIVO
1 specific ◊ *por poner un ejemplo concreto* to take a specific example
♦ **No hablo de personas concretas.** I don't mean anyone in particular.
2 definite ◊ *Todavía no hay fechas concretas.* There are no definite dates yet.
♦ **este modelo en concreto** this particular model
♦ **No me refiero a nadie en concreto.** I don't mean anyone in particular.
♦ **Todavía no hemos decidido nada en concreto.** We still haven't decided anything definite.

el/la **concursante** SUSTANTIVO
competitor

el **concurso** SUSTANTIVO
1 game show (*de televisión*)
2 competition ◊ *un concurso de poesía* a poetry competition
♦ **un concurso de belleza** a beauty contest

el **conde** SUSTANTIVO
count

la **condecoración** SUSTANTIVO (PL las **condecoraciones**)
decoration

la **condena** SUSTANTIVO
sentence
♦ **cumplir una condena** to serve a sentence

condenar VERBO
to sentence ◊ *Lo condenaron a tres años de prisión.* He was sentenced to three years in prison.

la **condesa** SUSTANTIVO
countess

la **condición** SUSTANTIVO (PL las **condiciones**)
condition
♦ **a condición de que apruebes** on condition that you pass
♦ **El piso está en muy malas condiciones.** The flat is in a very bad state.
♦ **No está en condiciones de viajar.** He's not fit to travel.

el **condón** SUSTANTIVO (PL los **condones**)
condom

conducir* VERBO
1 to drive (*coche*)
♦ **No sé conducir.** I can't drive.
2 to ride (*moto*)
♦ **Enfadarse no conduce a nada.** Getting angry won't get you anywhere.

la **conducta** SUSTANTIVO
behaviour

el **conductor**, la **conductora** SUSTANTIVO
driver

conduzco VERBO *ver* **conducir**

conectar VERBO
to connect ◊ *conectar dos cables* to connect two cables
♦ **Vamos a conectar ahora con el estadio.** Now we go over to the stadium.
♦ **Le cuesta conectar con la gente.** He has trouble relating to people.

el **conejillo** SUSTANTIVO
♦ **un conejillo de Indias** a guinea-pig

el **conejo** SUSTANTIVO
rabbit

la **conexión** SUSTANTIVO (PL las **conexiones**)
connection

la **conferencia** SUSTANTIVO
1 lecture (*de un experto*)
2 conference (*congreso*)
3 long-distance call (*de teléfono*)

confesar* VERBO
1 to confess to ◊ *confesar un crimen* to confess to a crime
2 to admit ◊ *Confesó que había sido él.* He admitted that it had been him.

* Verbs marked with this symbol are irregular. See pages 380-382 for further details

◆**confesarse** to go to confession ◊ *Se confiesa todos los domingos.* He goes to confession every Sunday.

el **confeti** SUSTANTIVO
confetti

la **confianza** SUSTANTIVO
trust ◊ *Han puesto toda su confianza en él.* They have put all their trust in him.
◆**Tengo confianza en ti.** I trust you.
◆**No tiene confianza en sí mismo.** He has no self-confidence.
◆**un empleado de confianza** a trusted employee
◆**Se lo dije porque tenemos mucha confianza.** I told her about it because we're very close.
◆**Los alumnos se toman muchas confianzas con él.** The pupils take too many liberties with him.

confiar* VERBO
to trust ◊ *No confío en ella.* I don't trust her.
◆**Confiaba en que su familia le ayudaría.** He was confident that his family would help him.
◆**No hay que confiarse demasiado.** You mustn't be over-confident.

confidencial ADJETIVO
confidential

confieso VERBO *ver* **confesar**

confirmar VERBO
to confirm

el **conflicto** SUSTANTIVO
conflict

conformarse VERBO
◆**conformarse con** to be satisfied with ◊ *Tengo que conformarme con lo que tengo.* I have to be satisfied with what I've got.
◆**Se conforman con poco.** They're easily satisfied.
◆**Tendrás que conformarte con uno más barato.** You'll have to make do with a cheaper one.

conforme ADJETIVO
satisfied ◊ *No se quedó muy conforme con esa explicación.* He wasn't very satisfied with that explanation.
◆**estar conforme** to agree ◊ *¿Estáis todos conformes?* Do you all agree?

confundir VERBO
1 to mistake ◊ *confundir la sal con el azúcar* to mistake the salt for the sugar ◊ *La gente me confunde con mi hermana.* People mistake me for my sister.
2 to confuse ◊ *Su explicación me confundió todavía más.* His explanation confused me even more.
◆**Confundí las fechas.** I got the dates mixed up.
◆**¡Vaya! ¡Me he confundido!** Oh! I've made a mistake!
◆**Me confundí de piso.** I got the wrong flat.

la **confusión** SUSTANTIVO (PL las **confusiones**)
confusion

confuso ADJETIVO
confused

congelado ADJETIVO
frozen

el **congelador** SUSTANTIVO
freezer

congelar VERBO
to freeze
◆**Me estoy congelando.** I'm freezing.

congestionado ADJETIVO
1 blocked (*nariz*)
2 congested (*carretera*)

el **congreso** SUSTANTIVO
conference
◆**un congreso médico** a medical conference
◆**el Congreso de los Diputados**

> *The Lower Chamber of the Spanish Parliament.*

la **conjunción** SUSTANTIVO (PL las **conjunciones**)
conjunction

el **conjunto** SUSTANTIVO
1 collection ◊ *El libro es un conjunto de poemas de amor.* The book is a collection of love poems.
2 group ◊ *un conjunto de música pop* a pop group
◆**un conjunto de falda y blusa** a matching skirt and blouse
◆**Hay que estudiar esos países en conjunto.** You have to study these countries as a whole.

conmemorar VERBO
to commemorate

conmigo PRONOMBRE
with me ◊ *¿Por qué no vienes conmigo?* Why don't you come with me?
◆**Rosa quiere hablar conmigo.** Rosa wants to talk to me.
◆**No estoy satisfecho conmigo mismo.** I'm not proud of myself.

conmovedor ADJETIVO (FEM **conmovedora**)
moving

conmover* VERBO
to move

el **cono** SUSTANTIVO
cone
◆**el Cono Sur** the Southern Cone

conocer* VERBO
1 to know ◊ *Conozco a todos sus hermanos.* I know all his brothers. ◊ *Conozco un restaurante donde se come bien.* I know a restaurant where the food is very good.
◆**Nos conocemos desde el colegio.** We know each other from school.

☞

♦ **Me encantaría conocer China.** I would love to visit China.
[2] to meet (*por primera vez*) ◊ *La conocí en una fiesta.* I met her at a party.
◊ *¿Dónde os conocisteis?* Where did you first meet?

la **conocida** SUSTANTIVO
acquaintance ◊ *Es una conocida mía.* She's an acquaintance of mine.

conocido ADJETIVO
well-known ◊ *un actor muy conocido* a well-known actor

el **conocido** SUSTANTIVO
acquaintance ◊ *Son conocidos nuestros.* They are acquaintances of ours.

el **conocimiento** SUSTANTIVO
consciousness
♦ **perder el conocimiento** to lose consciousness
♦ **Tengo algunos conocimientos de francés.** I have some knowledge of French.

conozco VERBO *ver* **conocer**

conque CONJUNCIÓN
so ◊ *Hemos terminado, conque podéis iros.* We've finished, so you may leave now.

conquistar VERBO
[1] to conquer ◊ *los países conquistados por los romanos* the countries conquered by the Romans
[2] to win...over ◊ *La conquistó con su sonrisa.* He won her over with his smile.

consciente ADJETIVO
conscious ◊ *El enfermo no estaba consciente.* The patient wasn't conscious.
♦ **Es plenamente consciente de sus limitaciones.** He's fully aware of his shortcomings.

la **consecuencia** SUSTANTIVO
consequence ◊ *Todo es una consecuencia de su falta de disciplina.* Everything is a consequence of his lack of discipline.
♦ **Perdió el conocimiento a consecuencia del golpe.** He lost consciousness as a result of the blow.

consecutivo ADJETIVO
consecutive ◊ *tres semanas consecutivas* three consecutive weeks

conseguir* VERBO
[1] to get (*trabajo, billete*) ◊ *Él me consiguió el trabajo.* He got me the job.
[2] to achieve (*objetivo*) ◊ *Consiguió las mejores calificaciones de la clase.* He achieved the best results in the class.
♦ **Nuestro equipo consiguió el triunfo.** Our team won.
♦ **Después de muchos intentos, al final lo consiguió.** After many attempts, he finally succeeded.
♦ **Finalmente conseguí convencerla.** I finally managed to convince her.
♦ **No conseguí que se lo comiera.** I couldn't get him to eat it.

el **consejo** SUSTANTIVO
advice ◊ *Fui a pedirle consejo.* I went to ask him for advice.
♦ **¿Quieres que te dé un consejo?** Would you like me to give you some advice?

consentir* VERBO
[1] to allow ◊ *No consiento que me faltes al respeto.* I won't allow you to be disrespectful to me.
[2] to spoil ◊ *Su abuela lo consiente demasiado.* His grandmother spoils him too much.

el/la **conserje** SUSTANTIVO
[1] caretaker (*de edificio*)
[2] janitor (*de colegio*)
[3] porter (*de hotel*)

la **conserva** SUSTANTIVO
♦ **No comemos muchas conservas.** We don't eat much tinned food.
♦ **atún en conserva** tinned tuna

conservador ADJETIVO (FEM **conservadora**)
conservative

el **conservante** SUSTANTIVO
preservative

conservar VERBO
[1] to keep ◊ *Debe conservarse en la nevera.* It should be kept in the fridge.
◊ *conservar las amistades* to keep friends
[2] to preserve ◊ *El frío conserva mejor los alimentos.* The cold preserves food better.
♦ **Enrique se conserva joven.** Enrique looks good for his age.

el **conservatorio** SUSTANTIVO
music school

considerable ADJETIVO
considerable

considerado ADJETIVO
considerate ◊ *Es muy considerado con su madre.* He's very considerate towards his mother.
♦ **Está muy bien considerada entre los profesores.** She's very highly regarded among the teachers.

considerar VERBO
to consider ◊ *Lo considero una pérdida de tiempo.* I consider it a waste of time.

consiento VERBO *ver* **consentir**

la **consigna** SUSTANTIVO
left-luggage office

consigo (1) VERBO *ver* **conseguir**

consigo (2) PRONOMBRE
[1] with him (*con él*)

* Verbs marked with this symbol are irregular. See pages 380-382 for further details

2 with her (*con ella*)
3 with you (*con usted, ustedes*)
♦ **No está satisfecho consigo mismo.** He is not proud of himself.

consiguiendo VERBO *ver* **conseguir**

consintiendo VERBO *ver* **consentir**

consistir VERBO
♦ **El menú consiste en tres platos.** The menu consists of three courses.
♦ **¿En qué consiste el trabajo?** What does the job involve?
♦ **En eso consiste el secreto.** That's the secret.

la **consola** SUSTANTIVO
console
♦ **consola de videojuegos** games console

consolar* VERBO
to console ◊ *No conseguíamos consolarla.* We were unable to console her.
♦ **Para consolarme me compré un helado.** I bought an ice cream to cheer myself up.

la **consonante** SUSTANTIVO
consonant

constante ADJETIVO
constant ◊ *el ruido constante de los coches* the constant noise of the cars
♦ **Tienes que ser más constante.** You should keep working at it.

constantemente ADVERBIO
constantly

constar VERBO
♦ **La obra consta de siete relatos.** The work consists of seven stories.
♦ **¡Que conste que yo pagué mi parte!** Don't forget that I paid my share!

constipado ADJETIVO
♦ **estar constipado** to have a cold

*No confundir **constipado** con **constipated**.*

el **constipado** SUSTANTIVO
cold ◊ *coger un constipado* to catch a cold

la **constitución** SUSTANTIVO (PL las **constituciones**)
constitution

la **construcción** SUSTANTIVO (PL las **construcciones**)
construction ◊ *un edificio en construcción* a building under construction
♦ **Trabajan en la construcción.** They work in the building industry.

el **constructor**, la **constructora** SUSTANTIVO
builder ◊ *Es constructor.* He's a builder.

construir* VERBO
to build

consuelo VERBO *ver* **consolar**

el **consuelo** SUSTANTIVO
consolation

el/la **cónsul** SUSTANTIVO
consul

el **consulado** SUSTANTIVO
consulate

la **consulta** SUSTANTIVO
surgery (PL surgeries) ◊ *La doctora no tiene consulta los martes.* The doctor doesn't hold a surgery on Tuesdays.
♦ **horas de consulta** surgery hours
♦ **un libro de consulta** a reference book

consultar VERBO
to consult ◊ *consultar a un médico* to consult a doctor
♦ **Tengo que consultarlo con mi familia.** I must discuss it with my family.

la **consumición** SUSTANTIVO (PL las **consumiciones**)
drink ◊ *Con la entrada tienes una consumición.* The admission price includes a drink.

consumir VERBO
1 to use (*energía, drogas*) ◊ *Mi coche consume mucha gasolina.* My car uses a lot of petrol.
2 to drink (*alcohol*)
♦ **No podemos estar en el bar sin consumir.** We can't stay in the pub without buying a drink.
♦ **Sólo piensan en consumir.** Spending money is all they think about.

el **consumo** SUSTANTIVO
consumption ◊ *el consumo de bebidas alcohólicas* alcohol consumption
♦ **una charla sobre el consumo de drogas** a talk on drug use
♦ **la sociedad de consumo** the consumer society

la **contabilidad** SUSTANTIVO
accountancy ◊ *Estudia contabilidad.* He's studying accountancy.
♦ **Mi madre lleva la contabilidad.** My mother keeps the books.

el/la **contable** SUSTANTIVO
accountant

contactar VERBO
♦ **contactar con alguien** to contact someone

el **contacto** SUSTANTIVO
1 contact ◊ *el contacto físico* physical contact
2 touch ◊ *Nos mantenemos en contacto por teléfono.* We keep in touch by phone. ◊ *Me puse en contacto con su familia la semana pasada.* I got in touch with her family last week.

contado: **al contado** ADVERBIO
♦ **Lo pagué al contado.** I paid cash for it.

el **contador** SUSTANTIVO
meter ◊ *el contador de la luz* the electricity meter

el **contador**, la **contadora** SUSTANTIVO
Latin America
accountant

contagiar VERBO

☞

◆ **No quiero contagiarte.** I don't want to give it to you.
◆ **Tiene la gripe y no quiere que los niños se contagien.** He has the flu and doesn't want the children to catch it.

contagioso ADJETIVO
infectious

la **contaminación** SUSTANTIVO
pollution ◇ *la contaminación del aire* air pollution

contaminar VERBO
to pollute ◇ *El humo contamina la atmósfera.* Smoke pollutes the atmosphere.

contar* VERBO
1 to count (*dinero*) ◇ *Sabe contar hasta diez.* He can count to ten.
2 to tell (*historia*) ◇ *Les conté un cuento a los niños.* I told the children a story. ◇ *Cuéntame lo que pasó.* Tell me what happened.
◆ **Cuento contigo.** I'm counting on you.
◆ **¿Qué te cuentas?** How's things? (*coloquial*)

contendrá VERBO *ver* **contener**

contener* VERBO
to contain ◇ *La caja contenía monedas viejas.* The box contained old coins.
◆ **contenerse** to control oneself

el **contenido** SUSTANTIVO
contents PL ◇ *el contenido de la maleta* the contents of the suitcase

contentarse VERBO
◆ **Se contenta con cualquier juguete.** She is happy with any toy.
◆ **Tuve que contentarme con el segundo premio.** I had to be satisfied with second prize.

contento ADJETIVO
happy ◇ *Estaba contento porque era su cumpleaños.* He was happy because it was his birthday.
◆ **estar contento con algo** to be pleased with something

la **contestación** SUSTANTIVO (PL las **contestaciones**)
reply (PL replies)
◆ **No me des esas contestaciones.** Don't answer back.

el **contestador** SUSTANTIVO
◆ **el contestador automático** the answering machine

contestar VERBO
to answer ◇ *Contesté a todas las preguntas.* I answered all the questions.
◆ **Les he llamado varias veces y no contestan.** I've phoned them several times and there's no answer.
◆ **Me escribieron y tengo que contestarles.** They wrote to me and I have to reply to them.

contigo PRONOMBRE
with you ◇ *Quiero ir contigo.* I want to go with you.
◆ **Necesito hablar contigo.** I need to talk to you.

el **continente** SUSTANTIVO
continent

continuamente ADVERBIO
constantly

continuar* VERBO
to continue ◇ *Continuaremos la reunión por la tarde.* We will continue the meeting in the afternoon. ◇ *Si continúa así habrá que llevarlo al hospital.* If he continues like this, he'll have to be taken to hospital.
◆ **Continuó estudiando toda la noche.** He carried on studying right through the night.

continuo ADJETIVO
1 constant (*viajes, quejas*)
2 continuous (*línea*)

contra PREPOSICIÓN
against ◇ *Eran dos contra uno.* They were two against one. ◇ *El domingo jugamos contra el Málaga.* We play against Malaga on Sunday.
◆ **Me choqué contra una farola.** I bumped into a lamppost.
◆ **Estoy en contra de la pena de muerte.** I'm against the death penalty.

el **contrabajo** SUSTANTIVO
double bass (PL double basses)

el **contrabando** SUSTANTIVO
smuggling ◇ *el contrabando de drogas* drug smuggling
◆ **Lo trajeron al país de contrabando.** They smuggled it into the country.

contradecir* VERBO
to contradict

la **contradicción** SUSTANTIVO (PL las **contradicciones**)
contradiction

contradicho VERBO *ver* **contradecir**

contradigo VERBO *ver* **contradecir**

contradije VERBO *ver* **contradecir**

contradiré VERBO *ver* **contradecir**

contraer* VERBO
1 to tense (*músculo*)
2 to contract (*enfermedad*)
◆ **contraerse** to contract (*material, metal*)

la **contraria** SUSTANTIVO
◆ **llevar la contraria a alguien (1)** (*en discusión*) to contradict somebody
◆ **llevar la contraria a alguien (2)** (*en comportamiento*) to do the opposite of what somebody wants

contrario ADJETIVO
1 opposing (*equipo, argumento*)

* Verbs marked with this symbol are irregular. See pages 380-382 for further details

2 opposite (*dirección, lado*) ◊ *Los dos coches viajaban en dirección contraria.* The two cars were travelling in opposite directions.
◆ **Ella opina lo contrario.** She thinks the opposite.
◆ **Al contrario, me gusta mucho.** On the contrary, I like it a lot.
◆ **De lo contrario, tendré que castigarte.** Otherwise, I will have to punish you.

la **contraseña** SUSTANTIVO
password

contrastar VERBO
to contrast ◊ *El rojo contrasta con el negro.* Red contrasts with black.

el **contraste** SUSTANTIVO
contrast

contratar VERBO
1 to hire (*empleado*)
2 to sign up (*deportista, artista*)

el **contrato** SUSTANTIVO
contract

la **contribución** SUSTANTIVO (PL las **contribuciones**)
1 contribution ◊ *Le agradecemos su contribución.* Thank you for your contribution.
2 tax (PL taxes) ◊ *la contribución municipal* local tax

contribuir* VERBO
to contribute ◊ *Todos contribuyeron al éxito de la fiesta.* Everyone contributed to the success of the party. ◊ *Cada uno contribuyó con mil pesetas para el regalo.* Each person contributed a thousand pesetas towards the present.

el/la **contribuyente** SUSTANTIVO
taxpayer

el/la **contrincante** SUSTANTIVO
opponent

el **control** SUSTANTIVO
1 control ◊ *Nunca pierde el control.* He never loses control.
2 road-block ◊ *Hay un control a 3 kilómetros.* There's a road-block 3 kilometres further on.

controlar VERBO
to control (*situación, personas, impulsos*)
◆ **Tuve que controlarme para no pegarle.** I had to control myself, otherwise I would have hit him.
◆ **No te preocupes, todo está controlado.** Don't worry, everything is under control.

convencer* VERBO
1 to convince ◊ *Su argumento me convenció.* His argument convinced me. ◊ *La convencí de que era necesario.* I convinced her that it was necessary.
◆ **No me convence nada la idea.** I'm not convinced by the idea.
2 to persuade ◊ *La convencimos para que nos acompañara.* We persuaded her to go with us.

convencional ADJETIVO
conventional

conveniente ADJETIVO
convenient (*hora, lugar*) ◊ *Cuando te sea más conveniente.* Whenever is more convenient for you.
◆ **Sería conveniente que se lo dijeras.** It would be advisable to tell him.

convenir* VERBO
1 to suit ◊ *el método que más le convenga* the method that suits you best
2 to be good for ◊ *Te conviene descansar un poco.* It would be good for you to get some rest.
◆ **Quizá convenga recordar que ...** It might be appropriate to recall that ...

la **conversación** SUSTANTIVO (PL las **conversaciones**)
conversation ◊ *Necesito clases de conversación.* I need conversation classes.
◆ **las conversaciones de paz** peace talks

convertir* VERBO
to turn ◊ *Convirtieron la casa en colegio.* They turned the house into a school.
◆ **convertirse** to convert ◊ *Se convirtió al cristianismo.* He converted to Christianity.
◆ **convertirse en (1)** to become ◊ *Se convirtió en un hombre rico.* He became a rich man. ◊ *El convento se convirtió en hotel.* The convent became a hotel.
◆ **convertirse en (2)** to turn into ◊ *Se convirtió en una pesadilla.* It turned into a nightmare. ◊ *La oruga se convierte en mariposa.* The caterpillar turns into a butterfly.

convocar* VERBO
to call (*reunión, huelga*) ◊ *Nos convocó a una reunión.* He called us to a meeting.

el **coñac** SUSTANTIVO (PL los **coñacs**)
brandy (PL brandies)

la **cooperación** SUSTANTIVO
cooperation

cooperar VERBO
to cooperate ◊ *Cooperaron con la policía en el caso.* They cooperated with the police on the case.

la **copa** SUSTANTIVO
1 (*vaso*)
glass (PL glasses) ◊ *Sólo tomé una copa de champán.* I only had one glass of champagne.
2 (*bebida*)
drink
◆ **Fuimos a tomar unas copas.** We went for a few drinks.
3 (*de árbol*)
top
◆ **copas**

> *i* ***copas*** *are goblets, one of the suits in the Spanish card deck.*

C

la **copia** SUSTANTIVO
copy (PL copies) ◊ *hacer una copia* to make a copy
◆ **una copia impresa** (*informática*) a printout

copiar VERBO
to copy
◆ **copiar y pegar** to copy and paste (*informática*)

el **copo** SUSTANTIVO
◆ **un copo de nieve** a snowflake
◆ **copos de avena** rolled oats

el **corazón** SUSTANTIVO (PL los **corazones**)
heart ◊ *Está mal del corazón.* He has heart trouble.
◆ **Tiene muy buen corazón.** He is very kind-hearted.

la **corbata** SUSTANTIVO
tie

el **corcho** SUSTANTIVO
cork
◆ **un tapón de corcho** a cork

el **cordel** SUSTANTIVO
cord

el **cordero** SUSTANTIVO
lamb ◊ *Comimos chuletas de cordero.* We had lamb chops.

el **cordón** SUSTANTIVO (PL los **cordones**)
1 shoelace (*para los zapatos*)
2 cable (*eléctrico*)

la **corneta** SUSTANTIVO
bugle

el **coro** SUSTANTIVO
1 choir (*de iglesia, colegio*)
2 chorus (*en obra musical*)

la **corona** SUSTANTIVO
crown (*de rey*)
◆ **una corona de flores** a garland

el **coronel** SUSTANTIVO
colonel

corporal ADJETIVO
1 body (*temperatura, olor, fluidos*)

> ***body** en este caso va siempre delante del sustantivo.*

2 corporal (*castigo*)
3 personal (*higiene*)

el **corral** SUSTANTIVO
1 farmyard (*para gallinas*)
2 playpen (*para niños*)

la **correa** SUSTANTIVO
1 belt (*cinturón*)
2 lead (*de perro*)
3 strap (*de reloj*)

correcto ADJETIVO
correct ◊ *Las respuestas eran correctas.* The answers were correct.

el **corredor**, la **corredora** SUSTANTIVO
runner

corregir* VERBO
1 to correct (*error, postura*) ◊ *Corrígeme si me equivoco.* Correct me if I get it wrong.
2 to mark ◊ *Tengo que corregir los exámenes.* I have to mark the exams.

el **correo** SUSTANTIVO
post ◊ *Me lo mandó por correo.* He sent it to me by post.
◆ **Correos** post office ◊ *Fui a Correos a comprar unos sellos.* I went to the post office to buy some stamps.
◆ **el servicio de correos** the postal service
◆ **correo electrónico** email

correr VERBO
1 to run ◊ *Tuve que correr para alcanzar el autobús.* I had to run to catch the bus.
◆ **El ladrón echó a correr.** The thief started to run.
2 to hurry ◊ *Corre que llegamos tarde.* Hurry or we'll be late.
◆ **No corras que te equivocarás.** Don't rush or you'll make a mistake.
3 to go fast ◊ *No corras tanto, que hay hielo en la carretera.* Don't go so fast, the road's icy.
4 to move ◊ *Corre un poco la silla para allá.* Move the chair that way a little. ◊ *Córrete un poco hacia la izquierda.* Move a bit to the left.
◆ **¿Quieres que corra la cortina?** Do you want me to draw the curtains?

la **correspondencia** SUSTANTIVO
◆ **un curso por correspondencia** a correspondence course

corresponder VERBO
◆ **Me pagó lo que me correspondía.** He paid me my share.
◆ **Estas fotos corresponden a otro álbum.** These photos belong to another album.
◆ **No me corresponde a mí hacerlo.** It's not for to me to do it.

correspondiente ADJETIVO
relevant (*apropiado*) ◊ *toda la documentación correspondiente* all the relevant documentation
◆ **los datos correspondientes al año pasado** the figures for last year

el/la **corresponsal** SUSTANTIVO
correspondent

la **corrida** SUSTANTIVO
bullfight

corriente ADJETIVO
common ◊ *Pérez es un apellido muy corriente.* Pérez is a very common surname.
◆ **Es un caso poco corriente.** It's an unusual case.
◆ **Tengo que ponerle al corriente de lo que ha pasado.** I have to let him know what has happened.

* Verbs marked with this symbol are irregular. See pages 380-382 for further details

la **corriente** SUSTANTIVO
1 current (*de agua, electricidad*)
◆ **Te va a dar corriente.** You'll get an electric shock.
2 draught (*de aire*)
◆ **Si está de mal humor es mejor seguirle la corriente.** If he's in a bad mood it's best just to humour him.

corrijo VERBO *ver* **corregir**

el **corro** SUSTANTIVO
ring ◇ *Los niños hicieron un corro.* The children formed a ring.

la **corrupción** SUSTANTIVO
corruption

cortado ADJETIVO
1 sour (*leche*)
2 chapped (*piel, labios*)
3 closed (*calle, carretera*)
◆ **Juan estaba muy cortado con mis padres.** Juan was very shy with my parents.

el **cortado** SUSTANTIVO

> ⓘ *A* ***cortado*** *is a small white coffee with only a little milk.*

cortar VERBO
1 to cut (*carne, pastel*) ◇ *Corta la manzana por la mitad.* Cut the apple in half. ◇ *Me corté el dedo con un cristal.* I cut my finger on a piece of broken glass.
◆ **Te vas a cortar.** You're going to cut yourself.
◆ **Estas tijeras no cortan.** These scissors are blunt.
2 to cut off (*agua, luz*) ◇ *Han cortado el gas.* The gas has been cut off.
3 to close (*calle, carretera*)
◆ **Fui a cortarme el pelo.** I went to get my hair cut.
◆ **De repente se cortó la comunicación.** Suddenly we were cut off.

el **cortaúñas** SUSTANTIVO (PL los **cortaúñas**)
nail clippers PL

el **corte** SUSTANTIVO
cut ◇ *Tenía un corte en la frente.* He had a cut on his forehead.
◆ **un corte de pelo** a hair-cut
◆ **Me da corte pedírselo.** I'm embarrassed to ask him.

la **cortesía** SUSTANTIVO
courtesy
◆ **por cortesía** as a courtesy

la **corteza** SUSTANTIVO
1 crust (*del pan*)
2 rind (*del queso*)
3 bark (*de árbol*)

la **cortina** SUSTANTIVO
curtain

corto ADJETIVO
short ◇ *Susana tiene el pelo corto.* Susana has short hair.
◆ **Las mangas me están cortas.** The sleeves are too short for me.
◆ **ser corto de vista** to be short-sighted
◆ **¡Carlos es más corto ...!** (*coloquial*) Carlos is so dim!

el **cortocircuito** SUSTANTIVO
short-circuit

la **cosa** SUSTANTIVO
thing ◇ *¿Qué es esa cosa redonda?* What's that round thing? ◇ *Cogí mis cosas y me fui.* I picked up my things and left.
◆ **cualquier cosa** anything
◆ **¿Me puedes decir una cosa?** Can you tell me something?
◆ **¡Qué cosa más rara!** How strange!
◆ **Son cosas de la edad.** It's just old age.

la **cosecha** SUSTANTIVO
harvest

cosechar VERBO
to harvest

coser VERBO
to sew ◇ *Me estaba cosiendo un botón.* I was sewing on a button.

el **cosmético** SUSTANTIVO
cosmetic

las **cosquillas** SUSTANTIVO
◆ **hacer cosquillas a alguien** to tickle someone
◆ **Tiene muchas cosquillas.** He's very ticklish.

la **costa** SUSTANTIVO
coast ◇ *Pasamos el verano en la costa.* We spend the summer on the coast.
◆ **Vive a costa de los demás.** He lives at the expense of others.

el **costado** SUSTANTIVO
side
◆ **Estaba tumbado de costado.** He was lying on his side.

costar* VERBO
to cost ◇ *Cuesta mucho dinero.* It costs a lot of money. ◇ *¿Cuánto cuesta?* How much does it cost? ◇ *Me costó dos mil pesetas.* It cost me two thousand pesetas.
◆ **Las matemáticas le cuestan mucho.** He finds maths very difficult.
◆ **Me cuesta hablarle.** I find it hard to talk to him.

Costa Rica SUSTANTIVO FEM
Costa Rica

el/la **costarricense** ADJETIVO, SUSTANTIVO
Costa Rican

el **costarriqueño**, la **costarriqueña** ADJETIVO, SUSTANTIVO
Costa Rican

el **coste** SUSTANTIVO
cost ◇ *el coste de la vida* the cost of living

la **costilla** SUSTANTIVO
rib

C

el **costo** SUSTANTIVO
cost

la **costra** SUSTANTIVO
1 scab (*de herida*)
2 crust (*del pan*)

la **costumbre** SUSTANTIVO
1 habit (*de persona*) ◊ *Tiene la mala costumbre de morderse las uñas.* He has the bad habit of biting his nails.
2 custom (*de país, pueblo*) ◊ *una costumbre británica* a British custom
♦ **Se le olvidó, como de costumbre.** He forgot, as usual.
♦ **Nos sentamos en el sitio de costumbre.** We sat in our usual place.

la **costura** SUSTANTIVO
1 seam ◊ *Se te ha descosido la costura de la falda.* Your skirt has come apart at the seam.
2 sewing ◊ *No me gusta la costura.* I don't like sewing.

cotidiano ADJETIVO
everyday
***everyday** en este caso va siempre delante del sustantivo.*
◊ *la vida cotidiana* everyday life

el/la **cotilla** SUSTANTIVO
gossip

cotillear VERBO
to gossip

el **cotilleo** SUSTANTIVO
gossip

COU ABREVIATURA (= *Curso de Orientación Universitaria*)

> *Former term for the final year at school before university.*

el **cráneo** SUSTANTIVO
skull

la **creación** SUSTANTIVO (PL las **creaciones**)
creation

crear VERBO
to create
♦ **No quiero crearme problemas.** I don't want to create problems for myself.
♦ **crearse enemigos** to make enemies

creativo ADJETIVO
creative

crecer* VERBO
1 to grow ◊ *Me crece mucho el pelo.* My hair grows very fast. ◊ *¡Cómo has crecido!* Haven't you grown!
2 to grow up ◊ *Crecí en Sevilla.* I grew up in Seville.

el **crecimiento** SUSTANTIVO
growth

el **crédito** SUSTANTIVO
1 loan ◊ *Pedí un crédito al banco.* I asked for a loan at the bank.
2 credit ◊ *comprar algo a crédito* to buy something on credit

la **creencia** SUSTANTIVO
belief

creer* VERBO
1 to believe ◊ *¿Crees en los fantasmas?* Do you believe in ghosts? ◊ *Nadie me cree.* Nobody believes me.
♦ **Eso no se lo cree nadie.** No one will believe that.
2 to think ◊ *No creo que pueda ir.* I don't think I'll be able to go.
♦ **Se cree muy lista.** She thinks she's pretty clever.
♦ **Creo que sí.** I think so.
♦ **Creo que no.** I don't think so.

creído ADJETIVO
♦ **Es muy creído.** He's so full of himself.

la **crema** SUSTANTIVO
cream ◊ *Me pongo crema en las manos.* I put cream on my hands.
♦ **la crema de afeitar** shaving cream
♦ **crema de champiñones** cream of mushroom soup
♦ **una blusa de color crema** a cream-coloured blouse

la **cremallera** SUSTANTIVO
zip ◊ *Súbete la cremallera.* Pull up your zip.

el **crematorio** SUSTANTIVO
crematorium (PL crematoria)

creyendo VERBO *ver* **creer**

el/la **creyente** SUSTANTIVO
believer

crezco VERBO *ver* **crecer**

la **cría** SUSTANTIVO
1 baby (*criatura*)
♦ **una cría de cebra** a baby zebra
♦ **La leona tuvo dos crías.** The lioness had two cubs.
♦ **La hembra es muy protectora de sus crías.** The female is very protective of her young.
2 girl (*niña*)

la **criada** SUSTANTIVO
maid

el **criado** SUSTANTIVO
servant

criar* VERBO
1 to raise (*ganado*)
2 to breed (*conejos, perros*)
3 to bring up ◊ *Me criaron mis abuelos.* My grandparents brought me up.
♦ **Me crié en Sevilla.** I grew up in Seville.

el **crimen** SUSTANTIVO (PL los **crímenes**)
1 murder ◊ *cometer un crimen* to commit murder
2 crime ◊ *los crímenes de guerra* war crimes

el/la **criminal** SUSTANTIVO

criminal

el **crío** SUSTANTIVO

[1] baby (*criatura*)

♦ **¡no seas crío!** Don't be such a baby

[2] boy (*niño*)

♦ **los críos** the children

la **crisis** SUSTANTIVO (PL las **crisis**)

crisis (PL crises) ◊ *una crisis política* a political crisis

♦ **una crisis nerviosa** a nervous breakdown

el **cristal** SUSTANTIVO

[1] (*vidrio normal*)

glass (PL glasses) ◊ *una botella de cristal* a glass bottle

♦ **Me corté con un cristal.** I cut myself on a piece of broken glass.

♦ **En el suelo había cristales rotos.** There was some broken glass on the floor.

[2] (*de ventana*)

window pane ◊ *Los niños rompieron el cristal.* The children broke the window pane.

♦ **limpiar los cristales** to clean the windows

[3] (*vidrio fino, mineral*)

crystal ◊ *una estatuilla de cristal* a crystal statuette

el **cristiano,** la **cristiana** ADJETIVO, SUSTANTIVO

Christian

Cristo SUSTANTIVO MASC

Christ

la **crítica** SUSTANTIVO

[1] criticism

♦ **No hagas caso de sus críticas.** Pay no attention to his criticism.

[2] review ◊ *La película ha tenido muy buenas críticas.* The film got very good reviews.

[3] critic ◊ *Es crítica de cine.* She's a film critic.

criticar* VERBO

to criticize ◊ *Siempre me está criticando.* He's always criticizing me.

crítico ADJETIVO

critical ◊ *Llegó en un momento crítico.* He arrived at a critical moment.

el **crítico** SUSTANTIVO

critic ◊ *Es crítico de cine.* He's a film critic.

el **croissant** SUSTANTIVO (PL los **croissants**)

croissant

el **cromo** SUSTANTIVO

picture card

crónico ADJETIVO

chronic

cronometrar VERBO

to time

el **cronómetro** SUSTANTIVO

stopwatch (PL stopwatches)

la **croqueta** SUSTANTIVO

croquette ◊ *croquetas de pollo* chicken croquettes

el **cruce** SUSTANTIVO

crossroads ◊ *En el cruce hay un semáforo.* There are traffic lights at the crossroads.

♦ **un cruce de peatones** a pedestrian crossing

crucial ADJETIVO

crucial

el **crucifijo** SUSTANTIVO

crucifix (PL crucifixes)

el **crucigrama** SUSTANTIVO

crossword

crudo ADJETIVO

[1] raw (*sin cocinar*) ◊ *las zanahorias crudas* raw carrots

[2] underdone (*poco hecho*) ◊ *El filete estaba crudo.* The fillet was underdone.

cruel ADJETIVO

cruel

la **crueldad** SUSTANTIVO

cruelty

crujiente ADJETIVO

[1] crunchy (*galletas, zanahoria*)

[2] crusty (*pan*)

crujir VERBO

[1] to rustle (*hojas secas*)

[2] to creak (*ramas, tablas*)

[3] to crunch (*nieve, galletas*)

la **cruz** SUSTANTIVO (PL las **cruces**)

cross (PL crosses)

♦ **la Cruz Roja** the Red Cross

cruzado ADJETIVO

♦ **Había un tronco cruzado en la carretera.** There was a tree trunk lying across the road.

cruzar* VERBO

[1] to cross (*calle, desierto, río*)

[2] to fold (*brazos*)

♦ **Nos cruzamos en la calle.** We passed each other in the street.

el **cuaderno** SUSTANTIVO

notebook

♦ **un cuaderno de ejercicios** an exercise book

la **cuadra** SUSTANTIVO

[1] stable

[2] block Latin America ◊ *Está a dos cuadras de aquí.* It's two blocks from here.

el **cuadrado** ADJETIVO, SUSTANTIVO

square

♦ **dos metros cuadrados** two square metres

cuadrar VERBO

to tally ◊ *Las cuentas no cuadran.* The accounts don't tally.

♦ **Eso no cuadra con lo que ella nos contó.** That doesn't fit in with what she told us.

cuadriculado ADJETIVO

♦ **papel cuadriculado** squared paper

el **cuadro** SUSTANTIVO

☞

1 painting (*pintura*) ◇ *un cuadro de Picasso* a painting by Picasso ◇ *¿Quién pintó ese cuadro?* Who did that painting?
2 picture (*reproducción*) ◇ *Hay varios cuadros en la pared.* There are several pictures on the wall.
◆ **un mantel a cuadros** a checked tablecloth

cuajar VERBO
1 to set (*flan, yogur*)
2 to lie (*nieve*)
◆ **cuajarse** (*leche*) to curdle

cual PRONOMBRE
1 who

Se usa ***who*** *cuando nos referimos a una persona.*

◇ *el primo del cual te estuve hablando* the cousin who I was speaking to you about
2 which

Se usa ***which*** *cuando nos referimos a una cosa.*

◇ *la ventana desde la cual nos observaban* the window from which they were watching us
◆ **lo cual** which ◇ *Se ofendió, lo cual es comprensible.* He took offence, which is understandable.
◆ **con lo cual** with the result that
◆ **sea cual sea la razón** whatever the reason may be

cuál PRONOMBRE
1 what ◇ *¿Cuál es la solución?* What is the solution? ◇ *No sé cuál es la solución.* I don't know what the solution is.
2 which one (*entre varios*) ◇ *¿Cuál te gusta más?* Which one do you like best?

la **cualidad** SUSTANTIVO
quality (PL qualities)

cualquier ADJETIVO *ver* **cualquiera**

cualquiera (1) ADJETIVO
any ◇ *en cualquier ciudad española* in any Spanish town ◇ *Puedes usar un bolígrafo cualquiera.* You can use any pen.
◆ **No es un empleo cualquiera.** It's not just any job.
◆ **cualquier cosa** anything
◆ **cualquier persona** anyone
◆ **en cualquier sitio** anywhere

cualquiera (2) PRONOMBRE
1 anyone (*personas*) ◇ *Cualquiera puede hacer eso.* Anyone can do that.
◆ **cualquiera que le conozca** anyone who knows him
2 any one (*de varias cosas*) ◇ *Me da igual, cualquiera.* It doesn't matter, any one.
◆ **en cualquiera de las habitaciones** in any one of the rooms
◆ **cualquiera que elijas** whichever one you choose
3 either (*entre dos personas o cosas*) ◇ *¿Cuál de los dos prefieres? – Cualquiera.* Which of the two do you prefer? – Either.

cuando CONJUNCIÓN
when ◇ *cuando vienen a vernos* when they come to see us ◇ *Lo haré cuando tenga tiempo.* I'll do it when I have time.
◆ **Puedes venir cuando quieras.** You can come whenever you like.

cuándo ADVERBIO
when ◇ *¿Cuándo te va mejor?* When suits you? ◇ *No sabe cuándo ocurrió.* He doesn't know when it happened.
◆ **¿Desde cuándo trabajas aquí?** Since when have you worked here?

cuanto ADJETIVO, PRONOMBRE (FEM **cuanta**)
◆ **Termínalo cuanto antes.** Finish it as soon as possible.
◆ **Cuanto más lo pienso menos lo entiendo.** The more I think about it, the less I understand it.
◆ **Cuantas menos personas haya mejor.** The fewer people the better.
◆ **En cuanto oí su voz me eché a llorar.** As soon as I heard his voice I began to cry.
◆ **Había sólo unos cuantos invitados.** There were only a few guests.
◆ **en cuanto a** as for

cuánto ADJETIVO, PRONOMBRE (FEM **cuánta**)
1 how much ◇ *¿Cuánto dinero?* How much money? ◇ *¿Cuánto le debo?* How much do I owe you? ◇ *Me dijo cuánto costaba.* He told me how much it was.
2 how many ◇ *¿Cuántas sillas?* How many chairs? ◇ *No sé cuántos necesito.* I don't know how many I need.
◆ **¿A cuántos estamos?** What's the date?
◆ **¡Cuánta gente!** What a lot of people!
◆ **¿Cuánto hay de aquí a Bilbao?** How far is it from here to Bilbao?
◆ **¿Cuánto tiempo llevas estudiando inglés?** How long have you been studying English?

cuarenta ADJETIVO, PRONOMBRE
forty ◇ *Tiene cuarenta años.* He's forty.
◆ **el cuarenta aniversario** the fortieth anniversary

el **cuartel** SUSTANTIVO
barracks (PL barracks)
◆ **el cuartel general** the headquarters

cuarto ADJETIVO, PRONOMBRE (FEM **cuarta**)
fourth ◇ *Vivo en el cuarto piso.* I live on the fourth floor.

el **cuarto** SUSTANTIVO
1 room ◇ *Los niños jugaban en su cuarto.* The children were playing in their room.
◆ **el cuarto de estar** the living room

♦ **el cuarto de baño** the bathroom
[2] quarter ◊ *un cuarto de hora* a quarter of an hour
♦ **Son las once y cuarto.** It's a quarter past eleven.
♦ **A las diez menos cuarto.** At a quarter to ten.
♦ **Es un cuarto para las diez.** [Latin America] It's a quarter to ten.

el **cuate** SUSTANTIVO [Mexico]
[1] twin brother (*hermano*)
[2] guy (*coloquial: tipo*)

cuatro ADJETIVO, PRONOMBRE
four
♦ **Son las cuatro.** It's four o'clock.
♦ **el cuatro de julio** the fourth of July

cuatrocientos ADJETIVO, PRONOMBRE (FEM **cuatrocientas**)
four hundred

Cuba SUSTANTIVO FEM
Cuba

el **cubano,** la **cubana** ADJETIVO, SUSTANTIVO
Cuban

la **cubertería** SUSTANTIVO
cutlery

cúbico ADJETIVO
cubic ◊ *tres metros cúbicos* three cubic metres

la **cubierta** SUSTANTIVO
[1] cover (*de libro*)
[2] tyre (*de neumático*)
[3] deck (*de barco*)

cubierto (1) VERBO *ver* **cubrir**

cubierto (2) ADJETIVO
covered ◊ *Estaba todo cubierto de nieve.* Everything was covered in snow.
♦ **una piscina cubierta** an indoor swimming pool

los **cubiertos** SUSTANTIVO PL
cutlery SING

el **cubito de hielo** SUSTANTIVO
ice-cube

el **cubo** SUSTANTIVO
bucket
♦ **el cubo de la basura** the dustbin
♦ **tres elevado al cubo** three cubed

cubrir* VERBO
to cover ◊ *Son capaces de cubrir grandes distancias.* They can cover great distances.
♦ **Las mujeres se cubren la cara con un velo.** The women cover their face with a veil.
♦ **El agua casi me cubría.** I was almost out of my depth.

la **cucaracha** SUSTANTIVO
cockroach

la **cuchara** SUSTANTIVO
spoon

la **cucharada** SUSTANTIVO
spoonful ◊ *una cucharada de jarabe* a spoonful of syrup

la **cucharilla** SUSTANTIVO
teaspoon

el **cucharón** SUSTANTIVO (PL los **cucharones**)
ladle

cuchichear VERBO
to whisper

la **cuchilla** SUSTANTIVO
blade
♦ **una cuchilla de afeitar** a razor blade

el **cuchillo** SUSTANTIVO
knife (PL knives)

cuclillas
♦ **en cuclillas** ADVERBIO
squatting
♦ **ponerse en cuclillas** to squat down

el **cucurucho** SUSTANTIVO
cone (*helado*)

cuelgo VERBO *ver* **colgar**

el **cuello** SUSTANTIVO
[1] neck (*de persona, botella*)
[2] collar (*de camisa, chaqueta*)

la **cuenta** SUSTANTIVO
[1] bill (*factura*) ◊ *El camarero nos trajo la cuenta.* The waiter brought us the bill.
[2] account (*de banco*)
♦ **una cuenta corriente** a current account
♦ **Ahora trabaja por su cuenta.** He's self-employed now.
♦ **una cuenta de correo** an email account
♦ **darse cuenta (1)** (*enterarse*) to realize ◊ *Perdona, no me daba cuenta de que eras vegetariano.* Sorry, I didn't realize you were a vegetarian.
♦ **darse cuenta (2)** (*ver*) to notice ◊ *¿Te has dado cuenta de que han cortado el árbol?* Did you notice they've cut down that tree?
♦ **tener algo en cuenta** to bear something in mind ◊ *También hay que tener en cuenta su edad.* You must also bear in mind her age.

cuento VERBO *ver* **contar**

el **cuento** SUSTANTIVO
story (PL stories) ◊ *La abuela nos contaba cuentos.* Grandma used to tell us stories.
♦ **un cuento de hadas** a fairy-tale

la **cuerda** SUSTANTIVO
[1] rope (*gruesa*) ◊ *Le ataron las manos con una cuerda.* They tied his hands together with a rope.
[2] string (*fina*) ◊ *Necesito una cuerda para atar este paquete.* I need some string to tie up this parcel. ◊ *La guitarra tiene ocho cuerdas.* The guitar has eight strings.
♦ **la cuerda floja** the tightrope
♦ **dar cuerda a un reloj** to wind up a watch

el **cuerno** SUSTANTIVO
horn

el **cuero** SUSTANTIVO
leather ◊ *una chaqueta de cuero* a leather jacket

el **cuerpo** SUSTANTIVO
body (PL bodies) ◊ *el cuerpo humano* the human body
◆ **el cuerpo de bomberos** the fire-brigade

el **cuervo** SUSTANTIVO
raven

cuesta VERBO *ver* **costar**

la **cuesta** SUSTANTIVO
slope ◊ *una cuesta muy empinada* a very steep slope
◆ **ir cuesta abajo** to go downhill
◆ **ir cuesta arriba** to go uphill
◆ **Llevaba la caja a cuestas.** He was carrying the box on his back.

la **cuestión** SUSTANTIVO (PL las **cuestiones**)
matter ◊ *Eso es otra cuestión.* That's another matter.
◆ **Llegaron en cuestión de minutos.** They arrived in a matter of minutes.

la **cueva** SUSTANTIVO
cave

cuezo VERBO *ver* **cocer**

el **cuidado** SUSTANTIVO
care ◊ *Pone mucho cuidado en su trabajo.* He takes great care over his work.
◆ **Conducía con cuidado.** He was driving carefully.
◆ **Debes tener mucho cuidado al cruzar la calle.** You must be very careful crossing the street.
◆ **¡Cuidado!** Careful!
◆ **Carlos está al cuidado de los niños.** Carlos looks after the children.
◆ **cuidados intensivos** intensive care SING

cuidadoso ADJETIVO
careful

cuidar VERBO
to look after (*libros, plantas, niño*) ◊ *Ella cuida de los niños.* She looks after the children.
◆ **cuidarse** to look after oneself ◊ *Tienes que cuidarte.* Make sure you look after yourself.
◆ **¡Cuídate!** Take care!

la **culebra** SUSTANTIVO
snake

el **culo** SUSTANTIVO
bum (*coloquial*)

la **culpa** SUSTANTIVO
fault ◊ *La culpa es mía.* It's my fault.
◆ **Tú tienes la culpa de todo.** It's all your fault.
◆ **Siempre me echan la culpa a mí.** They're always blaming me.
◆ **por culpa del mal tiempo** because of the bad weather

culpable ADJETIVO
guilty ◊ *Yo no soy culpable.* I'm not guilty. ◊ *Se siente culpable de lo que ha pasado.* He feels guilty about what has happened.

el/la **culpable** SUSTANTIVO
culprit (*de delito*)
◆ **Ella es la culpable de todo.** She is to blame for everything.

cultivar VERBO
1 to grow (*cereales, hortalizas*)
2 to farm (*la tierra*)

culto ADJETIVO
1 cultured (*persona*)
2 formal (*lenguaje*)

la **cultura** SUSTANTIVO
culture

el **culturismo** SUSTANTIVO
body-building

la **cumbre** SUSTANTIVO
summit (*de montaña*)

el **cumpleaños** SUSTANTIVO (PL los **cumpleaños**)
birthday (PL birthdays) ◊ *Mañana es mi cumpleaños.* It's my birthday tomorrow.
◆ **¡Feliz cumpleaños!** Happy birthday!

cumplir VERBO
1 to carry out (*orden, objetivo*)
2 to keep (*promesa*)
3 to observe (*ley*)
4 to serve (*condena*)
◆ **Sólo he cumplido con mi deber.** I have only done my duty.
◆ **Mañana cumplo dieciséis años.** I'll be sixteen tomorrow.
◆ **El viernes se cumple el plazo para entregar las solicitudes.** Friday is the deadline for handing in applications.

la **cuna** SUSTANTIVO
cradle

la **cuneta** SUSTANTIVO
ditch (PL ditches)

la **cuñada** SUSTANTIVO
sister-in-law (PL sisters-in-law)

el **cuñado** SUSTANTIVO
brother-in-law (PL brothers-in-law)

la **cuota** SUSTANTIVO
fee ◊ *La cuota de socio son 10.000 Ptas. anuales.* The membership fee is 10,000 pesetas per year.

cupo VERBO *ver* **caber**

el **cupón** SUSTANTIVO (PL los **cupones**)
1 voucher (*vale*)
2 ticket (*para sorteo*)

la **cura** SUSTANTIVO
1 cure ◊ *No tiene cura.* There is no cure for it.
2 therapy (PL therapies) ◊ *una cura de reposo* rest therapy

el **cura** SUSTANTIVO
priest

curar VERBO
1 to cure (*enfermo, enfermedad*)

* Verbs marked with this symbol are irregular. See pages 380-382 for further details

2 to treat (*herida*)

◆ **Espero que te cures pronto.** I hope that you get better soon.

◆ **Ya se le ha curado la herida.** His wound has already healed.

la **curiosidad** SUSTANTIVO

curiosity

◆ **Lo pregunté por curiosidad.** I asked out of curiosity.

◆ **Tengo curiosidad por saber cuánto gana.** I'm curious to know how much he earns.

curioso ADJETIVO

1 curious ◊ *Tiene una forma muy curiosa.* It's a very curious shape.

◆ **¡Qué curioso!** How odd!

2 nosy ◊ *No seas curioso.* Don't be nosy.

la **curita** SUSTANTIVO Latin America

sticking plaster

cursi ADJETIVO

1 affected (*persona*)

2 twee (*objeto*)

el **cursillo** SUSTANTIVO

course ◊ *un cursillo de cocina* a cookery course

◆ **hacer un cursillo de natación** to have swimming lessons

el **curso** SUSTANTIVO

1 year ◊ *un chico de mi curso* a boy in my year ◊ *Hago segundo curso.* I'm in the second year.

◆ **el curso académico** the academic year

2 course ◊ *Hice un curso de alemán.* I did a German course.

la **curva** SUSTANTIVO

1 bend (*en carretera*) ◊ *Hay algunas curvas muy cerradas.* There are some very sharp bends.

2 curve (*línea*) ◊ *dibujar una curva* to draw a curve

cuyo ADJETIVO

whose ◊ *El marido, cuyo nombre era Ricardo, estaba jubilado.* The husband, whose name was Ricardo, was retired. ◊ *La señora en cuya casa me hospedé.* The lady whose house I stayed in.

C

D

el **dado** SUSTANTIVO
dice (PL dice)
♦ **jugar a los dados** to play dice

la **dama** SUSTANTIVO
lady (PL ladies) ◊ *Damas y caballeros ...* Ladies and gentlemen ...
♦ **las damas** draughts ◊ *jugar a las damas* to play draughts

el **damasco** SUSTANTIVO Latin America
apricot

danés ADJETIVO (FEM **danesa,** MASC PL **daneses**)
Danish

el **danés,** la **danesa** SUSTANTIVO (MASC PL los **daneses**)
Dane

el **danés** SUSTANTIVO
Danish (*idioma*)

el **daño** SUSTANTIVO
damage ◊ *El daño producido no es muy grave.* The damage isn't very serious.
♦ **ocasionar daños** to cause damage ◊ *La sequía ha ocasionado grandes daños.* The drought has caused a lot of damage.
♦ **hacer daño a alguien** to hurt somebody
♦ **hacerse daño** to hurt oneself

dar* VERBO
1 to give ◊ *Le dio un bocadillo a su hijo.* He gave his son a sandwich. ◊ *Se lo di a Teresa.* I gave it to Teresa.
♦ **Me dio mucha alegría verla.** I was very pleased to see her.
♦ **Déme 2 kilos.** 2 kilos please.
2 to strike ◊ *El reloj dio las 6.* The clock struck 6.
♦ **dar a** to look out onto ◊ *Mi ventana da al jardín.* My window looks out onto the garden.
♦ **dar con** to find ◊ *Dimos con él dos horas más tarde.* We found him two hours later.
♦ **Al final di con la solución.** I finally came up with the answer.
♦ **El sol me da en la cara.** The sun's shining in my face.
♦ **¿Qué más te da?** What does it matter to you?
♦ **Se han dado muchos casos.** There have been a lot of cases.
♦ **Se me dan bien las ciencias.** I'm good at science.
♦ **darse un baño** to have a bath
♦ **darse por vencido** to give up

el **dátil** SUSTANTIVO
date

el **dato** SUSTANTIVO
♦ **Ése es un dato importante.** That's an important piece of information.
♦ **Necesito más datos para poder juzgar.** I need more information to be able to judge.
♦ **reunir datos para un proyecto de investigación** to gather data for a research project
♦ **los datos personales** personal details

de (*de + el = del*) PREPOSICIÓN
1 of ◊ *un paquete de caramelos* a packet of sweets
♦ **una copa de vino (1)** (*llena*) a glass of wine
♦ **una copa de vino (2)** (*vacía*) a wine glass
♦ **la casa de Isabel** Isabel's house
♦ **las clases de inglés** English classes
♦ **un anillo de oro** a gold ring
♦ **una máquina de coser** a sewing machine
♦ **es de ellos** it's theirs
♦ **a las 8 de la mañana** at 8 o'clock in the morning
2 from ◊ *Soy de Gijón.* I'm from Gijón.
♦ **salir del cine** to leave the cinema
3 than ◊ *Es más difícil de lo que creía.* It's more difficult than I thought it would be.
♦ **más de 500 personas** over 500 people
♦ **De haberlo sabido ...** If I'd known ...

dé VERBO *ver* **dar**

debajo ADVERBIO
underneath ◊ *Levanta la maceta, la llave está debajo.* Lift up the flowerpot, the key's underneath.
♦ **debajo de** under ◊ *debajo de la mesa* under the table

el **debate** SUSTANTIVO
debate

debatir VERBO
to debate

el **deber** SUSTANTIVO
duty (PL duties) ◊ *Sólo cumplí con mi deber.* I simply did my duty.
♦ **los deberes** (*escolares*) homework SING

deber VERBO
1 must ◊ *Debo intentar verla.* I must try to see her. ◊ *No debes preocuparte.* You mustn't worry.
♦ **Debería dejar de fumar.** I should stop smoking.
♦ **No deberías haberla dejado sola.** You shouldn't have left her alone.
♦ **como debe ser** as it should be
♦ **deber de** must ◊ *Debe de ser canadiense.* He must be Canadian.

* Verbs marked with this symbol are irregular. See pages 380-382 for further details

- **No debe de tener mucho dinero.** He can't have much money.

[2] to owe ◊ *¿Cuánto le debo?* How much do I owe you?

- **deberse a** to be due to ◊ *El retraso se debió a una huelga.* The delay was due to a strike.

debido ADJETIVO
- **debido a** owing to ◊ *Debido al mal tiempo, el vuelo se suspendió.* Owing to the bad weather, the flight was cancelled.
- **Habla como es debido.** Speak properly.

débil ADJETIVO
weak

la **debilidad** SUSTANTIVO
weakness (PL weaknesses)
- **tener debilidad por algo** to have a weakness for something
- **tener debilidad por alguien** to have a soft spot for somebody

debilitar VERBO
to weaken

la **década** SUSTANTIVO
decade

la **decena** SUSTANTIVO
ten ◊ *decenas de miles de* tens of thousands of
- **Habrá una decena de libros.** There must be about ten books.

decente ADJETIVO
decent ◊ *Exigen un sueldo decente.* They are demanding a decent wage.

la **decepción** SUSTANTIVO (PL las **decepciones**)
disappointment

*No confundir **decepción** con **deception**.*

decepcionar VERBO
to disappoint ◊ *Me has decepcionado de nuevo.* You've disappointed me again.
- **La película me decepcionó.** The film was disappointing.

decidido ADJETIVO
determined ◊ *Estoy decidido a hacerlo.* I'm determined to do it. ◊ *Julia es una mujer muy decidida.* Julia is a very determined woman.

decidir VERBO
to decide ◊ *Tú decides.* You decide.
- **decidirse a hacer algo** to decide to do something
- **decidirse por algo** to decide on something
- **¡Decídete!** Make up your mind!

el **decimal** ADJETIVO, SUSTANTIVO
decimal

décimo ADJETIVO, PRONOMBRE (FEM **décima**)
tenth
- **Vivo en el décimo.** I live on the tenth floor.

el **décimo** SUSTANTIVO
- **un décimo de lotería** a tenth part of a lottery ticket

> *In Spain's National Lottery, whole tickets are very expensive so smaller shares such as **décimos** are also sold.*

decir* VERBO
[1] to say ◊ *¿Qué dijo?* What did he say? ◊ *¿Cómo se dice "casa" en inglés?* How do you say "casa" in English?
- **es decir** that's to say
- **es un decir** it's a manner of speaking
- **¡Diga!** (*al teléfono*) Hello?

[2] to tell ◊ *Me dijo que no vendría.* He told me that he wouldn't come.
- **decirle a alguien que haga algo** to tell somebody to do something ◊ *Me dijo que esperara fuera.* He told me to wait outside.
- **¡No me digas!** Really?
- **querer decir** to mean ◊ *No sé lo que quiere decir.* I don't know what it means.

la **decisión** SUSTANTIVO (PL las **decisiones**)
decision ◊ *tomar una decisión* to take a decision

decisivo ADJETIVO
decisive

la **declaración** SUSTANTIVO (PL las **declaraciones**)
[1] statement ◊ *El ministro no quiso hacer ninguna declaración.* The minister didn't want to make a statement.
[2] evidence ◊ *Prestó declaración ante el juez.* He gave evidence before the judge.
- **una declaración de amor** a declaration of love
- **la declaración de la renta** the income tax return

declarar VERBO
[1] to declare ◊ *¿Algo que declarar?* Anything to declare? ◊ *El presidente declaró que apoyaría el proyecto.* The president declared his support for the project.
[2] to give evidence ◊ *declarar en un juicio* to give evidence at a trial
- **declarar culpable a alguien** to find somebody guilty
- **declararse (1)** to declare oneself ◊ *Se declaró partidario de hacerlo.* He declared himself in favour of doing it.
- **declararse (2)** to break out ◊ *Se declaró un incendio en el bosque.* A fire broke out in the forest.
- **declararse a alguien** to propose to somebody

el **decorador**, la **decoradora** SUSTANTIVO
interior decorator

decorar VERBO
to decorate

el **decreto** SUSTANTIVO
decree

el **dedal** SUSTANTIVO
thimble

dedicar* VERBO
1 to devote ◊ *Dedicó su vida a los demás.* He devoted his life to others.
2 to dedicate ◊ *Dedicó el poema a su padre.* He dedicated the poem to his father.
◆ **¿A qué se dedica?** What does he do for a living?
◆ **Ayer me dediqué a arreglar los armarios.** I spent yesterday tidying the cupboards.

la **dedicatoria** SUSTANTIVO
dedication

el **dedo** SUSTANTIVO
1 finger (*de la mano*) ◊ *Lleva un anillo en el dedo meñique.* She wears a ring on her little finger.
◆ **hacer dedo** to hitch a lift
◆ **no mover un dedo** not to lift a finger
2 toe (*del pie*)
◆ **el dedo gordo (1)** (*de la mano*) the thumb
◆ **el dedo gordo (2)** (*del pie*) the big toe

deducir* VERBO
to deduce ◊ *Deduje que había mentido.* I deduced that he'd lied.

el **defecto** SUSTANTIVO
1 defect ◊ *El jarrón tiene un pequeño defecto.* The vase has a small defect.
2 fault ◊ *Le encuentra defectos a todo.* He finds fault with everything.

defender* VERBO
to defend ◊ *Defendió a su amigo de las críticas.* He defended his friend against criticisms.
◆ **defenderse** to defend oneself ◊ *Tenemos que defendernos del enemigo.* We have got to defend ourselves against the enemy.
◆ **Me defiendo en inglés.** I can get by in English.

la **defensa** SUSTANTIVO
defence
◆ **salir en defensa de alguien** to come to somebody's defence
◆ **en defensa propia** in self-defence

el **defensor**, la **defensora** SUSTANTIVO
defender

deficiente ADJETIVO
poor ◊ *Su trabajo es muy deficiente.* His work is very poor.

la **definición** SUSTANTIVO (PL las **definiciones**)
definition

definir VERBO
to define

definitivo ADJETIVO
definitive ◊ *Esta solución no es definitiva.* This is not a definitive solution.
◆ **en definitiva** in short

deformar VERBO
1 to deform (*pie, mano*)
◆ **No cuelgues el jersey así que lo deformarás.** Don't hang the jersey up like that or you'll pull it out of shape.
2 to distort (*imagen, metal*)
◆ **deformarse** (*pie, mano*) to become deformed
◆ **Si lo lavas en la lavadora, se deformará.** If you wash it in the washing machine, it'll lose its shape.

defraudar VERBO
1 to disappoint ◊ *Su comportamiento la defraudó.* His behaviour disappointed her.
2 to defraud ◊ *Defraudar dinero a Hacienda es delito.* It's an offence to defraud the Treasury of money.

dejar VERBO
1 to leave ◊ *He dejado las llaves en la mesa.* I've left the keys on the table. ◊ *Su novio la ha dejado.* Her fiancé has left her. ◊ *Déjame tranquilo.* Leave me alone. ◊ *Dejó todo su dinero a sus hijos.* He left all his money to his children.
◆ **¡Déjalo ya!** Don't worry about it!
◆ **Deja mucho que desear.** It leaves a lot to be desired.
2 to let ◊ *Mis padres no me dejan salir de noche.* My parents won't let me go out at night.
3 to lend ◊ *Le dejé mi libro de matemáticas.* I lent him my maths book.
4 to give up ◊ *Dejó el esquí después del accidente.* He gave up skiing after the accident.
◆ **dejar de** to stop ◊ *dejar de fumar* to stop smoking
◆ **dejarse** to leave ◊ *Se dejó el bolso en un taxi.* She left her bag in a taxi.

del PREPOSICIÓN
(*= de + el*) *ver* **de**

el **delantal** SUSTANTIVO
apron

delante ADVERBIO
in front ◊ *Siéntate delante.* You sit in front.
◆ **de delante** front ◊ *la rueda de delante* the front wheel
◆ **la parte de delante** the front
◆ **delante de (1)** in front of ◊ *No digas nada delante de los niños.* Don't say anything in front of the children.
◆ **delante de (2)** opposite ◊ *Mi casa está delante de la escuela.* My house is opposite the school.
◆ **pasar por delante de** to go past ◊ *Ayer pasé por delante de tu casa.* I went past your house yesterday.
◆ **hacia delante** forward ◊ *Se inclinó hacia delante.* He leaned forward.

delantero ADJETIVO

front ◊ *los asientos delanteros* the front seats
◆ **la parte delantera del coche** the front of the car

delatar VERBO
1 to inform on ◊ *el hombre que delató a los dos secuestradores* the man who informed on the two kidnappers
◆ **Los delató a la policía.** He tipped the police off about them.
2 to give away ◊ *Tu sonrisa te delata.* Your smile gives you away.

la **delegación** SUSTANTIVO (PL las **delegaciones**) Mexico
police station

el **delegado,** la **delegada** SUSTANTIVO
delegate
◆ **el delegado de clase** the class representative

deletrear VERBO
to spell out

el **delfín** SUSTANTIVO (PL los **delfines**)
dolphin

delgado ADJETIVO
1 slim ◊ *Todas las modelos están delgadas.* All models are slim.
2 thin ◊ *Esta tela es demasiado delgada.* This material is too thin.

delicado ADJETIVO
1 delicate ◊ *Estas copas son muy delicadas.* These glasses are very delicate. ◊ *Se trata de un asunto muy delicado.* It's a very delicate subject.
2 thoughtful ◊ *Enviarte flores ha sido un gesto muy delicado.* Sending you flowers was a very thoughtful gesture.

la **delicia** SUSTANTIVO
delight ◊ *¡Qué delicia!* What a delight!
◆ **Este guiso es una delicia.** This stew is delicious.

delicioso ADJETIVO
delicious

el/la **delincuente** SUSTANTIVO
criminal ◊ *Es uno de los delincuentes más buscados.* He's one of the most wanted criminals.
◆ **un delincuente juvenil** a juvenile delinquent

el **delito** SUSTANTIVO
crime

la **demanda** SUSTANTIVO
demand ◊ *la oferta y la demanda* supply and demand
◆ **Se manifestaron en demanda de un aumento salarial.** They demonstrated for a wage increase.
◆ **presentar una demanda contra alguien** to sue somebody

demás (1) ADJETIVO
other ◊ *los demás niños* the other children

demás (2) PRONOMBRE
◆ **los demás** the others
◆ **lo demás** the rest ◊ *Yo limpio las ventanas y lo demás lo limpias tú.* I'll clean the windows and you clean the rest.
◆ **todo lo demás** everything else

demasiado (1) ADJETIVO
too much (PL too many) ◊ *demasiado vino* too much wine ◊ *demasiados libros* too many books

demasiado (2) ADVERBIO
1 too ◊ *Es demasiado pesado para levantarlo.* It's too heavy to lift. ◊ *Caminas demasiado deprisa.* You walk too quickly.
2 too much ◊ *Hablas demasiado.* You talk too much.

la **democracia** SUSTANTIVO
democracy (PL democracies)

democrático ADJETIVO
democratic

el **demonio** SUSTANTIVO
devil
◆ **¡Jaime es un auténtico demonio!** Jaime's a real devil! (*coloquial*)
◆ **¡Demonios!** Hell! (*coloquial*)
◆ **¿Qué demonios será?** What the devil can it be? (*coloquial*)

la **demostración** SUSTANTIVO (PL las **demostraciones**)
1 demonstration (*de funcionamiento, método*)
2 proof (*de teoría*)

demostrar* VERBO
1 to demonstrate (*funcionamiento, método*)
2 to prove (*teoría*) ◊ *Tendrá que demostrar su inocencia.* He will have to prove his innocence.
◆ **Así sólo demuestras tu ignorancia.** That way you only show how ignorant you are.

la **densidad** SUSTANTIVO
density ◊ *la densidad de población* population density

denso ADJETIVO
1 thick (*humo, niebla*)
2 heavy (*novela, discurso*)

la **dentadura** SUSTANTIVO
teeth PL
◆ **la dentadura postiza** false teeth PL

el **dentífrico** SUSTANTIVO
toothpaste

el/la **dentista** SUSTANTIVO
dentist

dentro ADVERBIO
inside ◊ *¿Qué hay dentro?* What's inside?
◆ **por dentro** inside ◊ *Mira bien por dentro.* Have a good look inside.
◆ **Está aquí dentro.** It's in here.

☞

◆ **dentro de** in ◇ *Mételo dentro del sobre.* Put it in the envelope. ◇ *dentro de tres meses* in three months

◆ **dentro de poco** soon

◆ **dentro de lo que cabe** as far as it goes

la **denuncia** SUSTANTIVO

◆ **Voy a ponerle una denuncia por hacer tanto ruido.** I'm going to report him for making so much noise.

◆ **Le pusieron una denuncia por verter residuos en el río.** He was reported to the authorities for tipping waste into the river.

denunciar VERBO

to report (*un delito*)

el **departamento** SUSTANTIVO

1 department (*de grandes almacenes, empresa*)

2 compartment (*de tren*)

3 flat (*apartamento*) Latin America

depender VERBO

◆ **depender de** to depend on ◇ *El precio depende de la calidad.* The price depends on the quality.

◆ **Depende.** It depends.

◆ **No depende de mí.** It's not up to me.

el **dependiente,** la **dependienta** SUSTANTIVO

sales assistant

el **deporte** SUSTANTIVO

sport ◇ *No hago mucho deporte.* I don't do much sport. ◇ *los deportes de invierno* winter sports

deportista ADJETIVO

sporty ◇ *Alicia es poco deportista.* Alicia is not very sporty.

el **deportista** SUSTANTIVO

sportsman (PL sportsmen)

la **deportista** SUSTANTIVO

sportswoman (PL sportswomen)

deportivo ADJETIVO

1 sports (*ropa, coche*)

> **sports** *en este caso va siempre delante del sustantivo.*

◇ *un club deportivo* a sports club

2 sporting (*actitud, espíritu*)

el **depósito** SUSTANTIVO

1 tank (*de agua, gasolina*)

2 deposit (*de dinero*)

la **depresión** SUSTANTIVO (PL las **depresiones**)

1 depression (*enfermedad*)

◆ **tener una depresión** to be suffering from depression

2 hollow (*de terreno*)

deprimido ADJETIVO

depressed

deprimir VERBO

to depress

◆ **deprimirse por algo** to get depressed about something

deprisa ADVERBIO

quickly ◇ *Acabaron muy deprisa.* They finished very quickly.

◆ **¡Deprisa!** Hurry up!

◆ **Lo hacen todo deprisa y corriendo.** They do everything in a rush.

la **derecha** SUSTANTIVO

1 right hand (*mano*) ◇ *Escribo con la derecha.* I write with my right hand.

2 right (*dirección, grupo político*) ◇ *doblar a la derecha* to turn right ◇ *La derecha ganó las elecciones.* The elections were won by the right.

◆ **ser de derechas** to be right-wing ◇ *un partido de derechas* a right-wing party

◆ **a la derecha** on the right ◇ *la segunda calle a la derecha* the second turning on the right

◆ **a la derecha del castillo** to the right of the castle

◆ **conducir por la derecha** to drive on the right

derecho (1) ADJETIVO

1 right ◇ *Me duele el ojo derecho.* I've got a pain in my right eye. ◇ *Escribo con la mano derecha.* I write with my right hand.

◆ **a mano derecha** on the right-hand side

2 straight ◇ *¡Ponte derecho!* Stand up straight!

derecho (2) ADVERBIO

straight ◇ *Vino derecho hacia mí.* He came straight towards me. ◇ *Siga derecho.* Carry straight on.

el **derecho** SUSTANTIVO

1 right ◇ *tener derecho a hacer algo* to have the right to do something ◇ *No tienes derecho a decir eso.* You have no right to say that. ◇ *los derechos humanos* human rights

◆ **¡No hay derecho!** It's not fair!

2 law ◇ *Estudio derecho.* I'm studying law.

◆ **Ponte la camiseta del derecho.** Put your T-shirt on the right way out.

derramar VERBO

to spill ◇ *Derramó vino sobre el mantel.* He spilt wine on the tablecloth.

derrapar VERBO

to skid

derretir* VERBO

to melt

◆ **derretirse** to melt ◇ *El queso se ha derretido.* The cheese has melted. ◇ *El hielo se está derritiendo.* The ice is melting.

◆ **derretirse de calor** to be melting

derribar VERBO

1 to demolish (*construcción*)

2 to shoot down (*avión*)

3 to overthrow (*persona, gobierno*)

la **derrota** SUSTANTIVO

* Verbs marked with this symbol are irregular. See pages 380-382 for further details

defeat ◊ *sufrir una derrota* to suffer a defeat

derrotar VERBO
to defeat

derrumbar VERBO
to pull down ◊ *Han derrumbado el cine.* The cinema has been pulled down.
♦ **derrumbarse** to collapse ◊ *El edificio se derrumbó.* The building collapsed.

desabrochar VERBO
to undo
♦ **desabrocharse (1)** to undo ◊ *Me desabroché la blusa.* I undid my blouse.
♦ **desabrocharse (2)** to come undone ◊ *Se te ha desabrochado la cremallera.* Your zip has come undone.

el **desacuerdo** SUSTANTIVO
disagreement

desafiar* VERBO
to challenge ◊ *Mi hermano me desafió a una carrera.* My brother challenged me to a race.

desafinar VERBO
to go out of tune

el **desafío** SUSTANTIVO
challenge

desafortunado ADJETIVO
unfortunate

desagradable ADJETIVO
unpleasant ◊ *un olor muy desagradable* a very unpleasant smell
♦ **ser desagradable con alguien** to be unpleasant to somebody

desagradecido ADJETIVO
ungrateful

el **desagüe** SUSTANTIVO
1 wastepipe (*de lavabo*)
2 drain (*de patio, terraza*)

desahogarse* VERBO
♦ **Se desahogó conmigo.** He poured out his heart to me.
♦ **Lloraba para desahogarse.** He was crying to let off steam.

desalojar VERBO
to clear ◊ *La policía desalojó a los manifestantes.* The police cleared the demonstrators. ◊ *Los bomberos desalojaron el edificio.* The firemen cleared the building.

desanimado ADJETIVO
1 downhearted (*persona*)
2 dull (*espectáculo, fiesta*)

desanimar VERBO
to discourage ◊ *Me desanimó su falta de interés.* His lack of interest discouraged me.
♦ **desanimarse** to lose heart

desaparecer* VERBO
to disappear ◊ *Me han desaparecido las gafas.* My glasses have disappeared. ◊ *La mancha ha desaparecido.* The stain has disappeared.
♦ **¡Desaparece de mi vista!** Get out of my sight!

la **desaparición** SUSTANTIVO (PL las **desapariciones**)
disappearance

desapercibido ADJETIVO
♦ **pasar desapercibido** to go unnoticed

desaprovechar VERBO
to waste ◊ *Han desaprovechado una gran oportunidad.* They've wasted a great opportunity.

el **desarme** SUSTANTIVO
disarmament ◊ *el desarme nuclear* nuclear disarmament

desarrollar VERBO
to develop ◊ *El estudio desarrolla la mente.* Study develops the mind.
♦ **La UNICEF desarrolla una labor importante.** UNICEF carries out important work.
♦ **desarrollarse (1)** to develop ◊ *La empresa se desarrolla rápidamente.* The business is developing rapidly.
♦ **desarrollarse (2)** to take place ◊ *La reunión se desarrolló sin incidentes.* The meeting took place without incident.

el **desarrollo** SUSTANTIVO
development ◊ *La alimentación es importante para el desarrollo del niño.* Diet is important for a child's development.
♦ **La industria está en pleno desarrollo.** The industry is expanding steadily.
♦ **un país en vías de desarrollo** a developing country

el **desastre** SUSTANTIVO
disaster ◊ *un gran desastre económico* a major economic disaster ◊ *La función fue un desastre.* The show was a disaster.
♦ **Soy un desastre para la gimnasia.** I'm hopeless at gymnastics.
♦ **Siempre va hecho un desastre.** He always looks a mess.

desastroso ADJETIVO
disastrous

desatar VERBO
1 to undo (*nudo, lazo*)
2 to untie (*cordones, cuerda*)
♦ **desatarse (1)** (*nudo, cordones*) to come undone
♦ **desatarse (2)** (*perro*) to get loose
♦ **desatarse (3)** (*tormenta*) to break

desayunar VERBO
1 to have breakfast ◊ *Nunca desayuno.* I never have breakfast.
2 to have...for breakfast ◊ *Desayuné café con leche y un bollo.* I had coffee and a roll for breakfast.

el **desayuno** SUSTANTIVO
breakfast

descalzarse* VERBO
to take one's shoes off

descalzo ADJETIVO

D

barefoot (*fuera de casa*) ◇ *Paseaban descalzos por la playa.* They walked barefoot along the beach.
♦ **No entres en la cocina descalzo.** Don't come into the kitchen in bare feet.

el **descampado** SUSTANTIVO
open space

descansar VERBO
1 to rest ◇ *Tienes que descansar.* You must rest.
♦ **descanse en paz** may he rest in peace
2 to sleep ◇ *¡Que descanses!* Sleep well!

el **descansillo** SUSTANTIVO
landing

el **descanso** SUSTANTIVO
1 rest ◇ *He caminado mucho, necesito un descanso.* I've done a lot of walking, I need a rest.
2 break ◇ *Cada dos horas me tomo un descanso.* I have a break every two hours.
3 relief (*alivio*) ◇ *¡Qué descanso!* What a relief!
4 interval (*en el teatro, cine*)
5 half time (*en un partido*)
♦ **tomarse unos días de descanso** to take a few days off

el **descapotable** SUSTANTIVO
convertible

descarado ADJETIVO
cheeky ◇ *¡No seas descarado!* Don't be cheeky!

la **descarga** SUSTANTIVO
1 unloading (*de mercancías*)
2 discharge (*de electricidad*)

descargar* VERBO
1 to unload ◇ *Me ayudó a descargar los muebles de la camioneta.* He helped me unload the furniture from the van.
2 to take out ◇ *Descarga su mal humor sobre mí.* He takes his bad moods out on me.
3 to download (*informática*)
♦ **descargarse** to go flat (*batería, pila*)

el **descaro** SUSTANTIVO
nerve ◇ *¡Qué descaro!* What a nerve!

descender* VERBO
to go down ◇ *Descendieron por la escalinata.* They went down the staircase. ◇ *Ha descendido el nivel del pantano.* The level of the reservoir has gone down.
♦ **descender de** to be descended from ◇ *Desciende de una familia noble.* He is descended from a noble family.
♦ **Mi equipo ha descendido de categoría.** My team has been relegated.

el/la **descendiente** SUSTANTIVO
descendant

el **descenso** SUSTANTIVO
1 drop ◇ *El descenso de la temperatura ha causado heladas.* The drop in temperature has brought frosts.
2 descent ◇ *Los ciclistas iniciaron el descenso del puerto.* The cyclists began the descent from the mountain pass.
3 relegation ◇ *el descenso a segunda división* relegation to the second division

descolgar* VERBO
1 to take down ◇ *Descolgó las cortinas para lavarlas.* He took down the curtains to wash them.
2 to pick up the phone ◇ *Descolgó y marcó el número.* He picked up the phone and dialled the number.
♦ **descolgar el teléfono** (*para contestar*) to pick up the phone
♦ **descolgarse por una pared** to lower oneself down a wall

descomponerse* VERBO Latin America
to break down

desconcertar* VERBO
to disconcert
♦ **desconcertarse** to be disconcerted ◇ *Se desconcertó al verla allí.* He was disconcerted to see her there.

desconectar VERBO
1 to unplug (*aparato*)
2 to disconnect (*línea*)

desconfiado ADJETIVO
distrustful

la **desconfianza** SUSTANTIVO
distrust

desconfiar* VERBO
♦ **Desconfío de él.** I don't trust him.
♦ **Desconfía siempre de las apariencias.** Always beware of appearances.

descongelar VERBO
to defrost (*comida, nevera*)
♦ **descongelarse** to defrost (*comida, nevera*)

el **desconocido**, la **desconocida** SUSTANTIVO
stranger

desconocido ADJETIVO
unknown ◇ *un actor desconocido* an unknown actor
♦ **Está desconocido.** He's unrecognizable.

descontar* VERBO
to deduct ◇ *Me descuentan un porcentaje del sueldo por impuestos.* A percentage of my salary is deducted for tax.
♦ **Descuentan el 5% si se paga en metálico.** They give a 5% discount if you pay cash.
♦ **Descontaron mil pesetas del precio marcado.** They took a thousand pesetas off the marked price.

descontento ADJETIVO
unhappy ◇ *Están descontentos de mis notas.* They're unhappy with my marks.

descoser VERBO

* Verbs marked with this symbol are irregular. See pages 380-382 for further details

to unpick
♦ **descoserse** to come apart at the seams
descremado ADJETIVO
skimmed
describir* VERBO
to describe
la **descripción** SUSTANTIVO (PL las **descripciones**)
description
el **descubierto** SUSTANTIVO
overdraft (*de cuenta bancaria*)
el **descubrimiento** SUSTANTIVO
discovery (PL discoveries)
descubrir* VERBO
1 to discover ◊ *Colón descubrió América en 1492.* Columbus discovered America in 1492.
2 to find out ◊ *¡Me has descubierto!* You've found me out!
el **descuento** SUSTANTIVO
discount ◊ *Me hicieron un descuento del 3%.* They gave me a 3% discount.
♦ **con descuento** at a discount
descuidado ADJETIVO
1 careless ◊ *Es muy descuidada con sus juguetes.* She's very careless with her toys.
2 neglected ◊ *El jardín estaba descuidado.* The garden was neglected.
descuidar VERBO
to neglect ◊ *Descuidó su negocio.* He neglected his business.
♦ **Descuida, que yo lo haré.** Don't worry, I'll do it.
♦ **descuidarse** to let one's attention wander ◊ *Se descuidó un segundo y el niño cruzó la calle.* He let his attention wander for a second and the child crossed the road.
el **descuido** SUSTANTIVO
oversight ◊ *Me olvidé de invitarla, fue un descuido.* I forgot to invite her, it was an oversight.
desde PREPOSICIÓN
1 from ◊ *Desde Burgos hasta mi casa hay 30 km.* It's 30km from Burgos to my house. ◊ *Le llamaré desde la oficina.* I'll ring him from the office.
2 since ◊ *Desde que llegó no ha salido.* He hasn't been out since he arrived. ◊ *La conozco desde niño.* I've known her since I was a child. ◊ *desde entonces* since then
♦ **¿Desde cuándo vives aquí?** How long have you been living here?
♦ **desde hace tres años** for three years
♦ **desde ahora en adelante** from now on
♦ **desde luego** of course
desdichado ADJETIVO
1 ill-fated (*suceso*)
2 unlucky (*persona*)
desdoblar VERBO
to unfold ◊ *Desdobló el plano.* He unfolded the map.
desear VERBO
to wish ◊ *Te deseo mucha suerte.* I wish you lots of luck.
♦ **Estoy deseando que esto termine.** I'm longing for this to finish.
♦ **¿Qué desea?** What can I do for you?
♦ **dejar mucho que desear** to leave a lot to be desired
desechable ADJETIVO
disposable
los **desechos** SUSTANTIVO
waste SING ◊ *los materiales de desecho* waste material ◊ *los desechos nucleares* nuclear waste
desembarcar* VERBO
1 to disembark ◊ *Fue el primero en desembarcar.* He was the first to disembark.
2 to unload ◊ *Han desembarcado la mercancía.* They've unloaded the goods.
el **desembarco** SUSTANTIVO
landing
desembocar* VERBO
♦ **desembocar en (1)** (*río*) to flow into ◊ *El Ebro desemboca en el Mediterráneo.* The Ebro flows into the Mediterranean.
♦ **desembocar en (2)** (*calle*) to lead into ◊ *Este callejón desemboca en la Avenida Pablo Casals.* This alley leads into Avenida Pablo Casals.
desempacar* VERBO Latin America
to unpack
el **desempate** SUSTANTIVO
play-off
♦ **el partido de desempate** the deciding match
♦ **En el minuto veinte llegó el gol del desempate.** The goal which broke the deadlock came in the twentieth minute.
el **desempleado**, la **desempleada** SUSTANTIVO
unemployed person
♦ **los desempleados** the unemployed
el **desempleo** SUSTANTIVO
unemployment
desenchufar VERBO
to unplug
desengañar VERBO
♦ **Su traición la desengañó.** His betrayal opened her eyes.
♦ **¡Desengáñate! No está interesada en ti.** Stop fooling yourself! She isn't interested in you.
el **desengaño** SUSTANTIVO
disappointment ◊ *¡Qué desengaño!* What a disappointment!
♦ **llevarse un desengaño** to be disappointed
♦ **sufrir un desengaño amoroso** to be disappointed in love
desenredar VERBO

☞

1 to untangle (*pelo*)
2 to resolve (*asunto*)

desenrollar VERBO
1 to unwind (*hilo, cinta*)
2 to unroll (*papel*)

desenroscar* VERBO
to unscrew

desenvolver* VERBO
to unwrap ◊ *Desenvolvió todos los regalos.* He unwrapped all the presents.
◆ **desenvolverse** to cope ◊ *No sabe desenvolverse en este tipo de situaciones.* He can't cope in this sort of situation.
◆ **desenvolverse bien** to do well

el **deseo** SUSTANTIVO
wish (PL wishes) ◊ *Pide un deseo.* Make a wish.

desequilibrado ADJETIVO
unbalanced

desértico ADJETIVO
desert

***desert** en este caso va siempre delante del sustantivo.*

◊ *una región desértica* a desert region

desesperado ADJETIVO
desperate

el **desesperado**, la **desesperada** SUSTANTIVO
◆ **Corría como un desesperado.** He was running like mad. (*coloquial*)

desesperante ADJETIVO
infuriating

desesperar VERBO
1 to drive...mad ◊ *Los atascos me desesperan.* Traffic jams drive me mad.
2 to despair ◊ *No desesperes y sigue intentándolo.* Don't despair, just keep trying.
◆ **desesperarse** to get exasperated

desfavorable ADJETIVO
unfavourable

el **desfiladero** SUSTANTIVO
gorge

desfilar VERBO
to parade

el **desfile** SUSTANTIVO
parade (*de soldados*)
◆ **un desfile de modas** a fashion show

la **desgana** SUSTANTIVO
1 loss of appetite (*falta de apetito*)
2 reluctance (*falta de entusiasmo*)
◆ **hacer algo con desgana** to do something reluctantly

desganado ADJETIVO
◆ **estar desganado (1)** (*sin apetito*) to have little appetite
◆ **estar desganado (2)** (*sin ánimos*) to be lethargic

desgarrar VERBO
to tear up ◊ *Desgarró la sábana para hacer trapos.* He tore up the sheet to make rags.
◆ **desgarrarse** to rip ◊ *La cortina se desgarró.* The curtain ripped.

el **desgarrón** SUSTANTIVO (PL los **desgarrones**)
rip

desgastar VERBO
1 to wear out (*ropa, zapatos*)
2 to wear away (*roca*)
◆ **desgastarse** to get worn out

el **desgaste** SUSTANTIVO
1 wear and tear (*de ropa, zapatos*)
2 erosion (*de roca*)

la **desgracia** SUSTANTIVO
tragedy (PL tragedies) ◊ *La muerte de su marido fue una auténtica desgracia.* Her husband's death was an absolute tragedy.
◆ **Ha tenido una vida llena de desgracias.** He's had a lot of misfortune in his life.
◆ **por desgracia (1)** sadly ◊ *Por desgracia no se salvó nadie.* Sadly there were no survivors.
◆ **por desgracia (2)** unfortunately ◊ *Por desgracia he vuelto a suspender.* Unfortunately I've failed again.
◆ **tener la desgracia de** to be unfortunate enough to ◊ *Tuvo la desgracia de perder un brazo en la guerra.* He was unfortunate enough to lose an arm in the war.
◆ **No hubo desgracias personales.** There were no casualties.

desgraciado ADJETIVO
1 unhappy ◊ *Desde que Ana le dejó ha sido muy desgraciado.* He has been very unhappy since Ana left him.
2 tragic ◊ *Murió en un desgraciado accidente.* He died in a tragic accident.

deshabitado ADJETIVO
1 uninhabited (*edificio*)
2 unoccupied (*zona*)

deshacer* VERBO
1 to untie (*nudo*)
2 to unpack (*maleta*)
3 to melt (*helado, mantequilla*)
4 to unpick (*labor*)
◆ **deshacerse (1)** (*nudo, labor*) to come undone
◆ **deshacerse (2)** (*helado, mantequilla*) to melt
◆ **deshacerse de algo** to get rid of something

deshecho ADJETIVO
1 undone (*nudo, costura*)
2 unmade (*cama*)
3 broken (*matrimonio*)
4 melted (*helado, mantequilla*)
◆ **Estoy deshecho. (1)** (*cansado*) I'm shattered.

* Verbs marked with this symbol are irregular. See pages 380-382 for further details

◆ **Estoy deshecho. (2)** (*apenado*) I'm devastated.

deshidratarse VERBO
to become dehydrated

el **deshielo** SUSTANTIVO
thaw

deshinchar VERBO
to let down (*globo, neumático*)
◆ **deshincharse (1)** (*globo*) to go down
◆ **deshincharse (2)** (*neumático*) to go flat

desierto ADJETIVO
deserted ◇ *El pueblo parecía desierto.* The village seemed deserted.

el **desierto** SUSTANTIVO
desert

desigual ADJETIVO
1 different (*tamaño*)
2 uneven (*escritura, terreno*)
3 unequal (*lucha*)

la **desilusión** SUSTANTIVO (PL las **desilusiones**)
disappointment ◇ *¡Qué desilusión!* What a disappointment!
◆ **llevarse una desilusión** to be disappointed

desilusionar VERBO
to disappoint ◇ *No quiero desilusionarte, pero ...* I don't want to disappoint you, but ...
◆ **Su conferencia me desilusionó.** His lecture was disappointing.
◆ **desilusionarse** to be disappointed

el **desinfectante** SUSTANTIVO
disinfectant

desinfectar VERBO
to disinfect

desinflar VERBO
to let down ◇ *Alguien me ha desinflado los neumáticos.* Somebody has let my tyres down.

el **desinterés** SUSTANTIVO
lack of interest ◇ *Muestra un total desinterés por sus estudios.* He shows a total lack of interest in his studies.

deslizarse* VERBO
to slide ◇ *El trineo se deslizaba por la nieve.* The sledge slid over the snow.

deslumbrar VERBO
to dazzle ◇ *Las luces del coche me deslumbraron.* The car headlights dazzled me. ◇ *Tanta riqueza la deslumbró.* She was dazzled by so much wealth.

desmayarse VERBO
to faint

el **desmayo** SUSTANTIVO
faint
◆ **sufrir un desmayo** to faint

desmemoriado ADJETIVO
forgetful

desmontar VERBO
1 to take apart (*mueble*)
2 to take down (*tienda de campaña*)
3 to strip down (*motor*)
4 to dismount (*jinete*)

desnatado ADJETIVO
1 skimmed (*leche*)
2 low-fat (*yogur*)

desnudar VERBO
to undress
◆ **desnudarse** to get undressed

desnudo ADJETIVO
1 naked ◇ *una escultura de un hombre desnudo* a sculpture of a naked man
◆ **Duerme desnudo.** He sleeps in the nude.
2 bare ◇ *Sin los cuadros la pared parece desnuda.* The wall looks bare without the paintings.

desobedecer* VERBO
to disobey

desobediente ADJETIVO
disobedient

el **desodorante** SUSTANTIVO
deodorant

el **desorden** SUSTANTIVO (PL los **desórdenes**)
mess ◇ *Toda la casa estaba en desorden.* The whole house was in a mess.
◆ **los desórdenes callejeros** street disturbances

desordenado ADJETIVO
untidy

desordenar VERBO
to mess up ◇ *Los niños han desordenado la habitación.* The children have messed up the room.

la **desorganización** SUSTANTIVO
disorganization

desorientar VERBO
to confuse ◇ *Sus consejos la desorientaron todavía más.* His advice confused her even more.
◆ **desorientarse** to lose one's way ◇ *Se desorientó al salir del metro.* He lost his way when he came out of the underground.

despachar VERBO
1 to sell ◇ *También despachamos sellos.* We also sell stamps.
2 to serve ◇ *Me despachó un dependiente muy educado.* I was served by a very polite sales assistant.
3 to dismiss ◇ *Me despachó sin ninguna explicación.* He dismissed me without any explanation.

el **despacho** SUSTANTIVO
1 office
◆ **los muebles de despacho** office furniture
◆ **una mesa de despacho** a desk
2 study (PL studies) ◇ *Cuando llega a casa se encierra en el despacho.* When he gets home he shuts himself away in the study.
◆ **un despacho de billetes** a booking office

despacio ADVERBIO
slowly ◇ *Conduce despacio.* Drive slowly.

☞

♦ **¡Despacio!** Take it easy!

despectivo ADJETIVO

1 contemptuous ◊ *Habla a sus alumnos en un tono muy despectivo.* He speaks to his pupils in a very contemptuous tone.

2 pejorative ◊ *"Mujerzuela" es una palabra despectiva.* "Mujerzuela" is a pejorative term.

la **despedida** SUSTANTIVO

♦ **Le hicimos una buena despedida a Marta.** We gave Marta a good send-off.

♦ **una fiesta de despedida** a farewell party

♦ **una despedida de soltero** a stag party

♦ **una despedida de soltera** a hen party

despedir* VERBO

1 to say goodbye to ◊ *Salí a la calle a despedirla.* I went out into the street to say goodbye to her.

♦ **Fueron a despedirlo al aeropuerto.** They went to the airport to see him off.

2 to dismiss ◊ *Lo despidieron por llegar tarde.* He was dismissed for being late.

♦ **despedirse** to say goodbye ◊ *Se despidieron en la estación.* They said goodbye at the station. ◊ *despedirse de alguien* to say goodbye to somebody

despegar* VERBO

to take off ◊ *Despegó la etiqueta del precio.* He took the price label off. ◊ *El avión despegó con retraso.* The plane took off late.

♦ **despegarse** to come unstuck

el **despegue** SUSTANTIVO

takeoff

despeinar VERBO

♦ **despeinar a alguien** to mess somebody's hair up

♦ **No me toques el pelo, que me despeinas.** Don't touch my hair, you'll mess it up.

♦ **Se despeinó al vestirse.** She messed up her hair getting dressed.

despejado ADJETIVO

clear ◊ *El cielo estaba despejado.* The sky was clear.

♦ **Por las mañanas tengo la mente más despejada.** My head's clearer in the mornings.

despejar VERBO

to clear ◊ *La policía ha despejado la zona.* The police have cleared the area. ◊ *El aire fresco te despejará.* The fresh air will clear your head.

♦ **¡Despejen!** Move along!

♦ **Tomaré un café para despejarme.** I'll have a coffee to wake myself up.

despellejar VERBO

to skin

la **despensa** SUSTANTIVO

larder

desperdiciar VERBO

1 to waste ◊ *Está mal desperdiciar la comida.* It's wrong to waste food.

2 to throw away ◊ *Desperdició la oportunidad de hacerse rico.* He threw away the chance to get rich.

el **desperdicio** SUSTANTIVO

waste ◊ *Tirar toda esta comida es un desperdicio.* It's a waste to throw away all this food.

♦ **los desperdicios** scraps ◊ *Le dimos los desperdicios al perro.* We gave the dog the scraps.

♦ **El libro no tiene desperdicio.** It's an excellent book from beginning to end.

desperezarse* VERBO

to stretch

el **desperfecto** SUSTANTIVO

flaw

♦ **El pantalón tenía un pequeño desperfecto.** There was a slight flaw in the trousers.

♦ **sufrir desperfectos** to get damaged

el **despertador** SUSTANTIVO

alarm clock

despertar* VERBO

1 to wake up ◊ *No me despiertes hasta las once.* Don't wake me up until eleven o'clock.

2 to arouse ◊ *El debate despertó un gran interés.* The debate aroused a lot of interest.

♦ **despertarse** to wake up

el **despido** SUSTANTIVO

dismissal

despierto ADJETIVO

1 awake ◊ *A las siete ya estaba despierto.* He was already awake by seven o'clock.

2 bright ◊ *Es un niño muy despierto.* He's a very bright boy.

el **despistado**, la **despistada** SUSTANTIVO

scatterbrain ◊ *Eres un despistado.* You're a scatterbrain.

despistado ADJETIVO

absent-minded ◊ *Es tan despistado que siempre se olvida las llaves.* He's so absent-minded that he's always forgetting his keys.

despistar VERBO

1 to shake off ◊ *Despistaron al coche que los seguía.* They managed to shake off the car that was following them.

2 to be misleading ◊ *Estas instrucciones más que ayudar despistan.* These instructions are more misleading than helpful.

♦ **Me despisté y salí de la autopista demasiado tarde.** I wasn't concentrating and I turned off the motorway too late.

el **despiste** SUSTANTIVO

absent-mindedness ◊ *Su despiste es conocido por todos.* His absent-mindedness is notorious.

♦ **¡Vaya despiste que tienes!** How absent-minded can you get!

desplegar* VERBO

1 to unfold ◊ *Desplegó el mapa.* He unfolded the map.

2 to spread ◊ *El águila desplegó las alas.* The eagle spread its wings.

♦ **desplegarse** to be deployed ◊ *El ejército se desplegó por la ciudad.* The army was deployed throughout the city.

desplomarse VERBO

to collapse ◊ *Se ha desplomado el techo.* The roof has collapsed.

despreciar VERBO

to despise

el **desprecio** SUSTANTIVO

contempt

♦ **Habló de ellos con desprecio.** He spoke of them contemptuously.

♦ **Le hicieron el desprecio de no acudir.** They snubbed him by not turning up.

desprender VERBO

to give off (*olor, calor*)

♦ **desprenderse** to fall off ◊ *Se desprendió una baldosa.* A tile fell off.

♦ **desprenderse de algo** to give something up ◊ *No quería desprenderse de la casa.* He didn't want to give the house up.

despreocuparse VERBO

to stop worrying ◊ *Despreocúpate porque ya no tiene remedio.* Stop worrying because there's nothing we can do about it now.

♦ **despreocuparse de todo** to show no concern for anything

desprevenido ADJETIVO

♦ **pillar a alguien desprevenido** to catch somebody unawares

después ADVERBIO

1 afterwards ◊ *Después todos estábamos muy cansados.* Afterwards we were all very tired.

♦ **Primero cenaré y después saldré.** I'll have dinner first and go out after that.

2 later ◊ *Ellos llegaron después.* They arrived later. ◊ *un año después* a year later

3 next ◊ *¿Qué viene después?* What comes next?

♦ **después de** after ◊ *Tu nombre está después del mío.* Your name comes after mine. ◊ *Después de comer fuimos de paseo.* After lunch we went for a walk.

♦ **después de todo** after all

♦ **después de que** after ◊ *después de que te acostaras* after you had gone to bed

destacar* VERBO

1 to stress ◊ *Me gustaría destacar la importancia de esto.* I'd like to stress the importance of this.

2 to stand out ◊ *Isabel destacaba por su generosidad.* Isabel's generosity made her stand out.

el **destapador** SUSTANTIVO Latin America

bottle opener

destapar VERBO

1 to open (*botella*)

2 to take the lid off (*cacerola*)

♦ **destaparse** to get uncovered ◊ *El niño se destapa por las noches.* The child gets uncovered at night.

desteñir* VERBO

1 to run ◊ *Estos pantalones destiñen.* These trousers run.

2 to fade ◊ *El sol ha desteñido las cortinas.* The sun has faded the curtains.

♦ **desteñirse** to fade ◊ *Se ha desteñido el jersey.* This jumper has faded.

desternillarse VERBO

♦ **desternillarse de risa** (*coloquial*) to split one's sides laughing

destinar VERBO

1 to post ◊ *Lo han destinado a Madrid.* He has been posted to Madrid.

2 to earmark ◊ *Destinaron los fondos a la compra de maquinaria.* The funds were earmarked for purchasing machinery.

♦ **El libro está destinado al público infantil.** The book is aimed at children.

el **destinatario**, la **destinataria** SUSTANTIVO

addressee

el **destino** SUSTANTIVO

1 destination ◊ *Por fin llegamos a nuestro destino.* We finally arrived at our destination.

♦ **el tren con destino a Valencia** the train to Valencia

♦ **salir con destino a** to leave for

2 posting ◊ *Cada dos años me cambian de destino.* They give me a new posting every two years.

3 use ◊ *Quiero saber qué destino tendrá este dinero.* I want to know what use will be made of this money.

el **destornillador** SUSTANTIVO

screwdriver

destornillar VERBO

to unscrew

la **destreza** SUSTANTIVO

skill

destrozar* VERBO

to wreck ◊ *Tu perro ha destrozado la silla.* Your dog has wrecked the chair.

♦ **La noticia le destrozó el corazón.** The news broke his heart.

los **destrozos** SUSTANTIVO

damage SING ◊ *La lluvia ocasionó grandes destrozos.* The rain caused a lot of damage.

la **destrucción** SUSTANTIVO

destruction

destruir* VERBO

☞

1 to destroy ◇ *Los huracanes destruyen edificios enteros.* Hurricanes can destroy whole buildings.
2 to ruin ◇ *Aquello destruyó su carrera.* That business ruined his career.
3 to demolish ◇ *Con cuatro palabras destruyó todos mis argumentos.* He demolished all my arguments with a few words.

desvalijar VERBO
1 to burgle (*casa*)
2 to rob (*persona*)

el **desván** SUSTANTIVO (PL los **desvanes**)
attic

desvelar VERBO
1 to keep...awake ◇ *El café me desvela.* Coffee keeps me awake.
2 to reveal ◇ *Nos desveló todos sus secretos.* He revealed all his secrets to us.
◆ **Se desvelan por sus hijos.** They're devoted to their children.

la **desventaja** SUSTANTIVO
disadvantage
◆ **estar en desventaja** to be at a disadvantage

la **desviación** SUSTANTIVO (PL las **desviaciones**)
diversion ◇ *una desviación de la circulación* a traffic diversion
◆ **Hicimos una desviación para evitar el tráfico del centro.** We made a detour to avoid the traffic in the town centre.

desviar* VERBO
to divert ◇ *Desviaron la circulación.* Traffic was diverted.
◆ **Quería desviar mi atención.** He wanted to divert my attention.
◆ **desviar la mirada** to look away
◆ **desviarse** to turn off ◇ *No debes desviarte de la carretera principal.* You mustn't turn off the main road. ◇ *Nos estamos desviando del tema.* We're getting off the point.

el **desvío** SUSTANTIVO
1 turning ◇ *Coge el primer desvío a la derecha.* Take the first turning on the right.
2 diversion ◇ *Hay un desvío por obras.* There's a diversion due to roadworks.

el **detalle** SUSTANTIVO
detail ◇ *No recuerdo todos los detalles.* I don't remember all the details.
◆ **No pierde detalle.** He doesn't miss a trick.
◆ **Quiero comprarte un detalle.** I want to buy you a little something.
◆ **tener un detalle con alguien** to be considerate towards somebody
◆ **¡Qué detalle!** How thoughtful!
◆ **vender al detalle** to sell retail

detectar VERBO
to detect

el/la **detective** SUSTANTIVO
detective ◇ *un detective privado* a private detective

detener* VERBO
1 to stop ◇ *¡Detenlos!* Stop them!
2 to arrest ◇ *Han detenido a los ladrones.* They've arrested the thieves.
◆ **detenerse** to stop ◇ *Nos detuvimos en el semáforo.* We stopped at the lights.
◆ **¡Deténgase!** Stop!

el **detergente** SUSTANTIVO
detergent

deteriorar VERBO
to damage ◇ *La lluvia ha deteriorado el tejado.* The rain has damaged the roof.
◆ **deteriorarse** to deteriorate ◇ *Su salud se ha deteriorado.* His health has deteriorated.

la **determinación** SUSTANTIVO
determination ◇ *Luchó contra su enfermedad con gran determinación.* He fought his illness with great determination.
◆ **tomar una determinación** to take a decision

determinado ADJETIVO
1 certain ◇ *En determinadas ocasiones es mejor callarse.* There are certain occasions when it's better to say nothing.
◆ **No hemos quedado a una hora determinada.** We haven't fixed a definite time.
2 particular ◇ *¿Buscas algún libro determinado?* Are you looking for a particular book?

determinar VERBO
1 to determine ◇ *Trataron de determinar la causa del accidente.* They tried to determine the cause of the accident.
2 to fix ◇ *determinar la fecha de una reunión* to fix the date of a meeting
3 to bring about ◇ *Aquello determinó la caída del gobierno.* That brought about the fall of the government.
4 to state ◇ *El reglamento determina que ...* The rules state that ...

detestar VERBO
to detest

detrás ADVERBIO
behind ◇ *El resto de los niños vienen detrás.* The rest of the children are coming on behind.
◆ **detrás de** behind ◇ *Se escondió detrás de un árbol.* He hid behind a tree.
◆ **uno detrás de otro** one after another
◆ **La critican por detrás.** They criticize her behind her back.

la **deuda** SUSTANTIVO

* Verbs marked with this symbol are irregular. See pages 380-382 for further details

debt
- **contraer deudas** to get into debt
- **estar en deuda con alguien** to be in somebody's debt

la **devolución** SUSTANTIVO (PL las **devoluciones**)
[1] return (*de carta, libro*)
[2] repayment (*de dinero*)
- **No se admiten devoluciones.** Goods cannot be returned.

devolver* VERBO
[1] to give back ◊ *¿Me puedes devolver la cinta que te presté?* Could you give me back the tape I lent you?
- **Me devolvieron mal el cambio.** They gave me the wrong change.
- **Te devolveré el favor cuando pueda.** I'll return the favour when I can.

[2] to take back ◊ *Devolví la falda porque me iba pequeña.* I took the skirt back as it was too small for me.
[3] to throw up (*coloquial*) ◊ *Devolvió toda la cena.* He threw up his dinner.

devorar VERBO
to devour ◊ *Los leones devoraron un ciervo.* The lions devoured a deer.
- **devorar un bocadillo** to wolf down a sandwich

di VERBO *ver* **decir**

el **día** SUSTANTIVO
day (PL days) ◊ *Pasaré dos días en la playa.* I'll spend a couple of days at the beach. ◊ *Duerme de día y trabaja de noche.* He sleeps during the day and works at night.
- **Es de día.** It's daylight.
- **¿Qué día es hoy? (1)** (*del mes*) What's the date today?
- **¿Qué día es hoy? (2)** (*de la semana*) What day is it today?
- **el día de mañana** tomorrow
- **al día siguiente** the following day
- **todos los días** every day
- **un día de estos** one of these days
- **un día sí y otro no** every other day
- **¡Buenos días!** Good morning!
- **un día de fiesta** a public holiday
- **un día feriado** Latin America a public holiday
- **un día laborable** a working day
- **pan del día** fresh bread

el **diablo** SUSTANTIVO
devil ◊ *No creo en el diablo.* I don't believe in the devil. ◊ *Juanito es un verdadero diablo.* Juanito's a real little devil.
- **¿Cómo diablos lo has hecho?** How the devil did you do it? (*coloquial*)
- **Hace un frío de mil diablos.** It's hellishly cold. (*coloquial*)

el **diagnóstico** SUSTANTIVO
diagnosis (PL diagnoses)

la **diagonal** ADJETIVO, SUSTANTIVO
diagonal
- **en diagonal** diagonally

el **dialecto** SUSTANTIVO
dialect

dialogar* VERBO
- **dialogar con alguien** to hold talks with somebody ◊ *El ministro dialogará con los sindicatos.* The minister will hold talks with the unions.

el **diálogo** SUSTANTIVO
conversation ◊ *Fue un diálogo interesante.* It was an interesting conversation.
- **No hay diálogo entre los dos bandos.** There's no dialogue between the two sides.

el **diamante** SUSTANTIVO
diamond
- **diamantes** (*en naipes*) diamonds

el **diámetro** SUSTANTIVO
diameter

la **diana** SUSTANTIVO
[1] bull's-eye ◊ *dar en la diana* to get a bull's-eye
[2] dartboard ◊ *En el bar hay una diana y dardos.* There's a dartboard and darts in the bar.

la **diapositiva** SUSTANTIVO
slide

diario ADJETIVO
daily ◊ *la rutina diaria* the daily routine
- **la ropa de diario** everyday clothes
- **a diario** every day ◊ *Va al gimnasio a diario.* He goes to the gym every day.

el **diario** SUSTANTIVO
[1] (*periódico*)
newspaper
[2] (*libro diario*)
diary (PL diaries)

la **diarrea** SUSTANTIVO
diarrhoea

el/la **dibujante** SUSTANTIVO
[1] (*en general*)
artist
[2] (*de dibujos animados*)
cartoonist
[3] (*de dibujo técnico*)
draughtsman (PL draughtsmen)

dibujar VERBO
to draw ◊ *No sé dibujar.* I can't draw. ◊ *Dibujó un árbol en la pizarra.* He drew a tree on the blackboard.

el **dibujo** SUSTANTIVO
drawing ◊ *el dibujo técnico* technical drawing
- **los dibujos animados** cartoons

el **diccionario** SUSTANTIVO
dictionary (PL dictionaries)

dicho (1) VERBO *ver* **decir**

dicho (2) ADJETIVO
- **en dichos países** in the countries mentioned above

☞

◆ **mejor dicho** or rather ◇ *Vendré el lunes, mejor dicho, el martes.* I'll come on Monday, or rather, on Tuesday.
◆ **dicho y hecho** no sooner said than done

el **dicho** SUSTANTIVO
saying

dichoso ADJETIVO
1 happy (*feliz*)
2 lucky (*afortunado*)
◆ **¡Dichoso ruido!** (*coloquial*) Damned noise!

diciembre SUSTANTIVO MASC
Los meses se escriben con mayúscula.
December ◇ *en Diciembre* in December ◇ *Llegaron el 6 de diciembre.* They arrived on 6 December.

diciendo VERBO *ver* **decir**

el **dictado** SUSTANTIVO
dictation ◇ *La maestra nos hizo un dictado.* The teacher gave us a dictation.

el **dictador,** la **dictadora** SUSTANTIVO
dictator

la **dictadura** SUSTANTIVO
dictatorship

dictar VERBO
to dictate ◇ *El maestro nos dictó un párrafo del libro.* The teacher dictated a paragraph of the book to us.
◆ **dictar sentencia** to pass sentence

diecinueve ADJETIVO, PRONOMBRE
nineteen ◇ *Tengo diecinueve años.* I'm nineteen.
◆ **el diecinueve de julio** the nineteenth of July
◆ **en el siglo diecinueve** in the nineteenth century

dieciocho ADJETIVO, PRONOMBRE
eighteen ◇ *Tengo dieciocho años.* I'm eighteen.
◆ **el dieciocho de abril** the eighteenth of April
◆ **en el siglo dieciocho** in the eighteenth century

dieciséis ADJETIVO, PRONOMBRE
sixteen ◇ *Tengo dieciséis años.* I'm sixteen.
◆ **el dieciséis de febrero** the sixteenth of February
◆ **en el siglo dieciséis** in the sixteenth century

diecisiete ADJETIVO, PRONOMBRE
seventeen ◇ *Tengo diecisiete años.* I'm seventeen.
◆ **el diecisiete de enero** the seventeenth of January
◆ **en el siglo diecisiete** in the seventeenth century

el **diente** SUSTANTIVO
(*de persona, sierra*)
tooth (PL teeth) ◇ *lavarse los dientes* to clean one's teeth
◆ **un diente de leche** a milk tooth
◆ **un diente de ajo** a clove of garlic

la **dieta** SUSTANTIVO
diet ◇ *una dieta vegetariana* a vegetarian diet
◆ **estar a dieta** to be on a diet
◆ **ponerse a dieta** to go on a diet
◆ **dietas** (*de viaje, hotel*) expenses

diez ADJETIVO, PRONOMBRE
ten ◇ *Tengo diez años.* I'm ten.
◆ **Son las diez.** It's ten o'clock.
◆ **el diez de agosto** the tenth of August
◆ **el siglo diez** the tenth century

la **diferencia** SUSTANTIVO
difference
◆ **a diferencia de** unlike ◇ *A diferencia de su hermana, a ella le encanta viajar.* Unlike her sister, she loves travelling.

diferenciar VERBO
◆ **¿En qué se diferencian?** What's the difference between them?
◆ **Sólo se diferencian en el tamaño.** The only difference between them is their size.
◆ **Se diferencia de los demás por su bondad.** His kindness sets him apart from the rest.
◆ **No diferencia el color rojo del verde.** He can't tell the difference between red and green.

diferente ADJETIVO
different

difícil ADJETIVO
difficult ◇ *Es un problema difícil de entender.* It's a difficult problem to understand. ◇ *Resulta difícil concentrarse.* It's difficult to concentrate. ◇ *Es un hombre difícil.* He's a difficult man.

la **dificultad** SUSTANTIVO
difficulty (PL difficulties) ◇ *con dificultad* with difficulty
◆ **tener dificultades para hacer algo** to have difficulty doing something
◆ **Nos pusieron muchas dificultades para obtener el visado.** They made it very difficult for us to get a visa.

dificultar VERBO
to make...difficult ◇ *La niebla dificultaba la visibilidad.* The fog made visibility difficult.

digerir* VERBO
to digest

la **digestión** SUSTANTIVO
digestion
◆ **hacer la digestión** to digest

digestivo ADJETIVO
digestive

digital ADJETIVO
digital ◇ *un reloj digital* a digital watch
◆ **una huella digital** a fingerprint

la **dignidad** SUSTANTIVO
dignity ◊ *Se comportó con mucha dignidad.* He behaved with great dignity.

digno ADJETIVO
[1] decent (*sueldo, vivienda*)
[2] honourable (*comportamiento*)
♦ **digno de mención** worth mentioning
♦ **digno de verse** worth seeing

digo VERBO *ver* **decir**

dije VERBO *ver* **decir**

diluir* VERBO
to dilute

diluviar VERBO
♦ **Está diluviando.** It's pouring with rain.

el **diluvio** SUSTANTIVO
downpour ◊ *Cayó un diluvio.* There was a downpour.
♦ **un diluvio de cartas** a flood of letters

la **dimensión** SUSTANTIVO (PL las **dimensiones**)
dimension ◊ *en tres dimensiones* in three dimensions
♦ **un cine de grandes dimensiones** a huge cinema

el **diminutivo** SUSTANTIVO
diminutive

diminuto ADJETIVO
tiny

la **dimisión** SUSTANTIVO (PL las **dimisiones**)
resignation ◊ *presentar la dimisión* to hand in one's resignation

dimitir VERBO
to resign ◊ *Ha dimitido de su cargo.* He has resigned from his post.

Dinamarca SUSTANTIVO FEM
Denmark

dinámico ADJETIVO
dynamic

el **dinero** SUSTANTIVO
money ◊ *No tengo más dinero.* I haven't got any more money.
♦ **una familia de dinero** a wealthy family
♦ **andar mal de dinero** to be short of money
♦ **dinero suelto** loose change

el **dinosaurio** SUSTANTIVO
dinosaur

dio VERBO *ver* **dar**

Dios SUSTANTIVO MASC
God ◊ *¡Gracias a Dios!* Thank God! ◊ *¡Dios mío!* My God!
♦ **¡Por Dios!** For God's sake!
♦ **¡Si Dios quiere!** God willing!
♦ **No vino ni Dios.** (*coloquial*) Nobody turned up.

el **dios** SUSTANTIVO (PL los **dioses**)
god

la **diosa** SUSTANTIVO
goddess (PL goddesses)

el **diploma** SUSTANTIVO
diploma

la **diplomacia** SUSTANTIVO
diplomacy

diplomático ADJETIVO
diplomatic

el **diplomático**, la **diplomática** SUSTANTIVO
diplomat

el **diptongo** SUSTANTIVO
dipthong

el **diputado**, la **diputada** SUSTANTIVO
Member of Parliament

dirá VERBO *ver* **decir**

la **dirección** SUSTANTIVO (PL las **direcciones**)
[1] direction ◊ *Íbamos en dirección equivocada.* We were going in the wrong direction.
♦ **Tienes que ir en esta dirección.** You have to go this way.
♦ **una calle de dirección única** a one-way street
♦ **"dirección prohibida"** "no entry"
♦ **"todas direcciones"** "all routes"
[2] address (PL addresses) ◊ *Apúntame tu dirección aquí.* Can you write your address down here for me?
[3] management ◊ *la dirección de la empresa* the management of the company ◊ *Ha tomado la dirección del proyecto.* He's taken over the management of the project.

directo ADJETIVO
[1] direct ◊ *Hay un tren directo a Valencia.* There's a direct train to Valencia. ◊ *una pregunta directa* a direct question
[2] straight ◊ *Se fue directa a casa.* She went straight home.
♦ **transmitir en directo** to broadcast live

el **director**, la **directora** SUSTANTIVO
[1] manager (*de empresa*)
[2] headteacher (*de colegio*)
[3] director (*de cine*)
[4] conductor (*de orquesta*)
[5] editor (*de periódico*)

el **directorio** SUSTANTIVO
[1] directory (PL directories)
[2] phone book Latin America
[3] (*informática*)
directory

el/la **dirigente** SUSTANTIVO
[1] leader (*de partido político*)
[2] manager (*de empresa*)

dirigir* VERBO
[1] to manage ◊ *Dirige la empresa desde hace diez años.* He has been managing the company for ten years.
[2] to lead ◊ *Dirigirá la expedición.* He'll be leading the expedition.
[3] to aim at ◊ *Este anuncio va dirigido a los niños.* This advertisement is aimed at children.
♦ **no dirigir la palabra a alguien** not to speak to somebody
[4] to direct (*película*)
[5] to conduct (*orquesta*)

☞

◆ **dirigirse a (1)** to address ◊ *El Rey se dirigió a la nación.* The King addressed the nation.
◆ **dirigirse a (2)** to write to ◊ *Me dirijo a ustedes para pedirles información sobre sus cursos de idiomas.* I am writing to you to ask you for information about language courses.
◆ **dirigirse a (3)** to make one's way to ◊ *Se dirigió a la terminal del aeropuerto.* He made his way to the airport terminal.

discapacitado ADJETIVO
disabled

discar* VERBO Latin America
to dial

la **disciplina** SUSTANTIVO
discipline

el **disco** SUSTANTIVO
1 record (*de música*)
2 light (*de semáforo*)
3 discus (*en deporte*)
◆ **un disco compacto** a compact disc
◆ **el disco duro** the hard disk

la **discoteca** SUSTANTIVO
discotheque

la **discreción** SUSTANTIVO
discretion
◆ **Ha actuado con mucha discreción.** He was very discreet.

discreto ADJETIVO
discreet ◊ *No dirá nada porque es muy discreto.* He won't say anything because he's very discreet.
◆ **un color discreto** a sober colour
◆ **un sueldo discreto** a modest salary

la **discriminación** SUSTANTIVO
◊ *la discriminación racial* racial discrimination

la **disculpa** SUSTANTIVO
◆ **pedir disculpas a alguien por algo** to apologize to somebody for something

disculpar VERBO
to excuse ◊ *Disculpa ¿me dejas pasar?* Excuse me, can I go past?
◆ **disculparse** to apologize ◊ *Se disculpó por llegar tarde.* He apologized for being late.

el **discurso** SUSTANTIVO
speech (PL speeches) ◊ *pronunciar un discurso* to make a speech

la **discusión** SUSTANTIVO (PL las **discusiones**)
discussion ◊ *El tema fue sometido a discusión.* The subject came up for discussion.
◆ **tener una discusión con alguien** to have an argument with somebody

discutir VERBO
1 to quarrel ◊ *Siempre discuten por dinero.* They're always quarrelling about money. ◊ *Siempre estaba discutiendo con mi hermana.* He was always quarrelling with my sister.
◆ **Discutió con su madre.** He had an argument with his mother.
2 to discuss ◊ *Tenemos que discutir el nuevo proyecto.* We've got to discuss the new project.

diseñar VERBO
to design

el **disfraz** SUSTANTIVO (PL los **disfraces**)
1 disguise ◊ *Llevaba un disfraz para que no lo reconocieran.* He wore a disguise so as not to be recognized.
2 costume ◊ *un disfraz de vaquero* a cowboy costume
◆ **una fiesta de disfraces** a fancy-dress party

disfrazarse* VERBO
◆ **disfrazarse de (1)** to disguise oneself as ◊ *Se disfrazó de mujer para escapar.* He disguised himself as a woman in order to escape.
◆ **disfrazarse de (2)** to dress up as ◊ *Su hija se disfrazó de hada.* His daughter dressed up as a fairy.

disfrutar VERBO
to enjoy oneself ◊ *Disfruté mucho en la fiesta.* I really enjoyed myself at the party.
◆ **Disfruto leyendo.** I enjoy reading.
◆ **disfrutar de buena salud** to enjoy good health

disgustado ADJETIVO
upset

*No confundir **disgustado** con **disgusted.***

disgustar VERBO
to upset ◊ *Me disgustó su tono.* His tone upset me.
◆ **disgustarse** to get upset ◊ *Me disgusté cuando descubrí que mentía.* I got upset when I found out he was lying.
◆ **disgustarse con alguien** to fall out with somebody

el **disgusto** SUSTANTIVO
◆ **dar un disgusto a alguien** to upset somebody
◆ **llevarse un disgusto** to get upset
◆ **hacer algo a disgusto** to do something unwillingly
◆ **estar a disgusto** to be ill at ease

disimular VERBO
to hide ◊ *Intentó disimular su enfado.* He tried to hide his annoyance.
◆ **No disimules, sé que has sido tú.** Don't bother pretending, I know it was you.

la **disminución** SUSTANTIVO (PL las **disminuciones**)
fall ◊ *una disminución del número de robos* a fall in the number of thefts

el **disminuido**, la **disminuida** SUSTANTIVO

♦**un disminuido mental** a mentally handicapped person
♦**un disminuido físico** a physically handicapped person

disminuir* VERBO
to fall ◊ *Ha disminuido el número de accidentes.* The number of accidents has fallen.

disolver* VERBO
1 to dissolve (*azúcar*)
2 to break up (*manifestación*)
♦**disolverse** (*manifestantes, reunión*) to break up

disparar VERBO
to shoot ◊ *Le dispararon en la pierna.* They shot him in the leg.
♦**disparar a alguien** to shoot at somebody
♦**Disparó dos tiros.** He fired two shots.
♦**dispararse (1)** (*pistola*) to go off
♦**dispararse (2)** (*precios*) to shoot up

el **disparate** SUSTANTIVO
silly thing ◊ *He hecho muchos disparates en mi vida.* I've done a lot of silly things in my life.
♦**decir disparates** to talk nonsense
♦**¡Qué disparate!** How absurd!

el **disparo** SUSTANTIVO
shot

disponer* VERBO
to arrange ◊ *Dispusieron las sillas en un círculo.* They arranged the chairs in a circle.
♦**disponer de** to have ◊ *Disponéis de diez minutos para leer las preguntas.* You have ten minutes to read the questions.
♦**disponerse a hacer algo** to get ready to do something

disponible ADJETIVO
available ◊ *El director no estará disponible hasta las 4.* The manager won't be available until 4 o'clock.

dispuesto ADJETIVO
1 prepared ◊ *estar dispuesto a hacer algo* to be prepared to do something
2 ready ◊ *Todo está dispuesto para la fiesta.* Everything's ready for the party.

el **disquete** SUSTANTIVO
diskette

la **distancia** SUSTANTIVO
distance
♦**mantenerse a distancia** to keep at a distance
♦**¿Qué distancia hay entre Madrid y Barcelona?** How far is Madrid from Barcelona?
♦**¿A qué distancia está la estación?** How far's the station?
♦**a 20 kilómetros de distancia** 20 kilometres away

la **distinción** SUSTANTIVO (PL las **distinciones**)
distinction ◊ *hacer una distinción entre ...* to make a distinction between ...
♦**No hace distinciones entre sus alumnos.** He treats all his pupils the same.

distinguido ADJETIVO
distinguished

distinguir* VERBO
1 to distinguish ◊ *Resulta difícil distinguir el macho de la hembra.* It's difficult to distinguish the male from the female.
♦**No distingue entre el rojo y el verde.** He can't tell the difference between red and green.
♦**No sé distinguir entre un coche u otro.** I can't tell one car from another.
♦**Se parecen tanto que no los distingo.** They're so alike that I can't tell them apart.
2 to make out ◊ *No pude distinguirla entre tanta gente.* I couldn't make her out amongst so many people.
♦**distinguirse** to stand out ◊ *No le gusta distinguirse de los demás.* He doesn't like to stand out.

distinto ADJETIVO
different ◊ *Carlos es distinto a los demás.* Carlos is different from other people.
♦**distintos** several ◊ *distintas clases de coches* several types of car

la **distracción** SUSTANTIVO (PL las **distracciones**)
pastime ◊ *Coser es mi distracción favorita.* My favourite pastime is sewing.
♦**En el pueblo hay pocas distracciones.** There isn't much to do in the village.

distraer* VERBO
1 to keep...entertained ◊ *Les pondré un vídeo para distraerlos.* I'll put a video on to keep them entertained.
2 to distract ◊ *No me distraigas, que tengo trabajo.* Don't distract me. I've got work to do.
♦**Me distrae mucho escuchar música.** I really enjoy listening to music.
♦**Me distraje un momento y me pasé de parada.** I let my mind wander for a minute and missed my stop.

distraído ADJETIVO
absent-minded ◊ *Mi padre es muy distraído.* My father is very absent-minded.
♦**Perdona, estaba distraído.** Sorry, I wasn't concentrating.

la **distribución** SUSTANTIVO (PL las **distribuciones**)
1 layout ◊ *la distribución de las habitaciones* the layout of the rooms
2 distribution ◊ *la distribución de la riqueza* the distribution of wealth

distribuir* VERBO
1 to distribute ◊ *Esta empresa distribuye nuestros productos en el*

☞

extranjero. This company distributes our products abroad.
[2] to hand out ◊ *La profesora distribuyó los folios del examen.* The teacher handed out the exam papers.

distribuyendo VERBO *ver* **distribuir**

el **distrito** SUSTANTIVO
district ◊ *un distrito postal* a postal district
♦ **un distrito electoral** a constituency

la **diversión** SUSTANTIVO (PL las **diversiones**)
entertainment

No confundir ***diversión*** *con* ***diversion.***

diverso ADJETIVO
different ◊ *España y Francia dieron explicaciones muy diversas del incidente.* France and Spain gave very different explanations for the incident.
♦ **diversos** various ◊ *diversos libros* various books

divertido ADJETIVO
[1] funny (*película, cómic*)
[2] enjoyable (*fiesta*)
♦ **Fue muy divertido.** It was great fun.

divertir* VERBO
to entertain ◊ *Nos divirtió con sus anécdotas.* He entertained us with his stories.
♦ **divertirse** to have a good time

dividir VERBO
to divide ◊ *El libro está dividido en dos partes.* The book is divided into two parts. ◊ *Dividió sus tierras entre sus tres hijas.* He divided his land between his three daughters. ◊ *Divide cuatro entre dos.* Divide four by two.
♦ **dividirse (1)** to divide ◊ *Nos dividimos el trabajo entre los tres.* We divided the work between the three of us.
♦ **dividirse (2)** to share ◊ *Se dividieron el dinero.* They shared the money.

divierto VERBO *ver* **divertir**

divino ADJETIVO
divine

la **división** SUSTANTIVO (PL las **divisiones**)
division ◊ *en primera división* in the first division ◊ *Ya sabe hacer divisiones.* He already knows how to do division.

divorciarse VERBO
to get divorced
♦ **Se ha divorciado de su mujer.** He has got divorced from his wife.

el **divorcio** SUSTANTIVO
divorce

divulgar* VERBO
to spread ◊ *divulgar rumores* to spread rumours

el **DNI** ABREVIATURA (= *Documento Nacional de Identidad*)
ID card

doblar VERBO
[1] to double ◊ *Le han doblado el sueldo.* They've doubled his salary.
[2] to fold ◊ *Dobla los pañuelos y guárdalos.* Fold the handkerchieves and put them away.
[3] to turn ◊ *Cuando llegues al cruce, dobla a la derecha.* When you reach the junction, turn right.
[4] to dub ◊ *Doblan todas las películas extranjeras.* All foreign films are dubbed.
[5] to toll ◊ *Las campanas de la iglesia doblan cuando hay un funeral.* The church bells toll when there's a funeral.

doble ADJETIVO
double ◊ *una frase con doble sentido* an expression with a double meaning ◊ *una habitación doble* a double room

el **doble** SUSTANTIVO
twice as much ◊ *Su sueldo es el doble del mío.* His salary's twice as much as mine. ◊ *Comes el doble que yo .* You eat twice as much as I do.
♦ **Trabaja el doble que tú.** He works twice as hard as you do.
♦ **jugar un partido de dobles** to play doubles

doce ADJETIVO, PRONOMBRE
twelve ◊ *Tengo doce años.* I'm twelve.
♦ **Son las doce.** It's twelve o'clock.
♦ **el siglo doce** the twelfth century

la **docena** SUSTANTIVO
dozen

el **doctor**, la **doctora** SUSTANTIVO
doctor

la **doctrina** SUSTANTIVO
doctrine

el **documental** SUSTANTIVO
documentary (PL documentaries)

el **documento** SUSTANTIVO
[1] document ◊ *un documento oficial* an official document
♦ **el documento nacional de identidad** the identity card
[2] document (*informática*)

el **dólar** SUSTANTIVO
dollar

doler* VERBO
to hurt ◊ *Me duele el brazo.* My arm hurts. ◊ *Esta inyección no duele.* This injection won't hurt. ◊ *Me dolió que me mintiera.* I was hurt that he lied to me.
♦ **Me duele la cabeza.** I've got a headache.
♦ **Me duele el pecho.** I've got a pain in my chest.
♦ **Me duele la garganta.** I've got a sore throat.

el **dolor** SUSTANTIVO
pain ◊ *Gritó de dolor.* He cried out in pain.
♦ **Tengo dolor de cabeza.** I've got a headache.

◆ **Tengo dolor de estómago.** I've got stomach ache.
◆ **Tengo dolor de muelas.** I've got toothache.
◆ **Tengo dolor de oídos.** I've got earache.
◆ **Tengo dolor de garganta.** I've got a sore throat.

doméstico ADJETIVO
domestic ◇ *para uso doméstico* for domestic use
◆ **las tareas domésticas** the housework
◆ **un animal doméstico** a pet

el **domicilio** SUSTANTIVO
residence ◇ *su domicilio particular* their private residence
◆ **servicio a domicilio** home delivery

dominar VERBO
1 to dominate ◇ *El padre dominaba totalmente a los hijos.* The father totally dominated his children.
◆ **tener dominado a alguien** to have somebody at one's mercy
2 to control ◇ *No pudo dominar su mal genio.* He couldn't control his temper.
3 to be fluent in ◇ *Mi hermana domina el inglés.* My sister is fluent in English.
4 to bring under control ◇ *Los bomberos tardaron en dominar el incendio.* The fire brigade took a long time to bring the fire under control.
◆ **dominarse** to control oneself

el **domingo** SUSTANTIVO
Los días de la semana se escriben con mayúscula.
Sunday ◇ *La vi el domingo.* I saw her on Sunday. ◇ *todos los domingos* every Sunday ◇ *el domingo pasado* last Sunday ◇ *el domingo que viene* next Sunday ◇ *Jugamos los domingos.* We play on Sundays.

el **dominicano,** la **dominicana** ADJETIVO, SUSTANTIVO
Dominican

el **dominio** SUSTANTIVO
1 command ◇ *Tiene un gran dominio del inglés.* He has a good command of English.
2 rule ◇ *Francia estuvo bajo el dominio romano.* France was under Roman rule.
3 control ◇ *Ejerció un dominio absoluto sobre sus seguidores.* He exercised absolute control over his followers.
◆ **dominio de sí mismo** self-control
◆ **ser del dominio público** to be public knowledge

el **dominó** SUSTANTIVO
1 domino (*pieza*)
2 dominoes SING (*juego*) ◇ *jugar al dominó* to play dominoes

el **don** SUSTANTIVO
gift ◇ *Tiene un don para la música.* He has a gift for music.
◆ **tener don de gentes** to be good with people
◆ **don Juan Gómez** Mr Juan Gómez

> *cuando **don** va seguido sólo del nombre de pila, se traduce por **Mr** más el apellido.*

◆ **Es un don nadie.** He's a nobody.

la **dona** SUSTANTIVO Mexico
doughnut

el/la **donante** SUSTANTIVO
donor ◇ *un donante de órganos* an organ donor

el **donativo** SUSTANTIVO
donation

donde ADVERBIO
where ◇ *La nota está donde la dejaste.* The note's where you left it.

dónde ADVERBIO
where ◇ *¿Dónde vas?* Where are you going? ◇ *Le pregunté dónde estaba la catedral.* I asked him where the cathedral was. ◇ *¿Sabes dónde está?* Do you know where he is?
◆ **¿De dónde eres?** Where are you from?
◆ **¿Por dónde se va al cine?** How do you get to the cinema?

la **doña** SUSTANTIVO
◆ **doña Marta García** Mrs Marta García

> *cuando **doña** va seguido sólo del nombre de pila, se traduce por **Mrs** más el apellido.*

dorado ADJETIVO
golden

dormir* VERBO
to sleep ◇ *Antonio durmió 10 horas.* Antonio slept for 10 hours.
◆ **Se me ha dormido el brazo.** My arm has gone to sleep.
◆ **dormir la siesta** to have a nap
◆ **dormir como un tronco** to sleep like a log
◆ **estar medio dormido** to be half asleep
◆ **dormirse** to fall asleep

el **dormitorio** SUSTANTIVO
1 (*de una casa*)
bedroom
2 (*de un internado*)
dormitory (PL dormitories)

el **dorso** SUSTANTIVO
back ◇ *Se apuntó el teléfono en el dorso de la mano.* He wrote the telephone number on the back of his hand.
◆ **"véase al dorso"** "see over"

dos ADJETIVO, PRONOMBRE
1 two ◇ *¿Tienes los dos libros que te dejé?* Have you got the two books I lent you? ◇ *Tiene dos años.* He's two.
◆ **Son las dos.** It's two o'clock.
◆ **de dos en dos** in twos

☞

◆**el dos de enero** the second of January
◆**cada dos por tres** every five minutes
[2] both (*ambos*) ◊ *Al final vinieron los dos.* In the end they both came. ◊ *Nos han suspendido a los dos.* We have both failed. ◊ *Mis dos hijos han emigrado.* Both of my sons have emigrated. ◊ *Los hemos invitado a los dos.* We've invited both of them.

doscientos ADJETIVO, PRONOMBRE (FEM **doscientas**)
two hundred ◊ *dos cientos cincuenta* two hundred and fifty

la **dosis** SUSTANTIVO (PL las **dosis**)
dose

doy VERBO *ver* **dar**

el **dragón** SUSTANTIVO (PL los **dragones**)
dragon

el **drama** SUSTANTIVO
drama

dramático ADJETIVO
dramatic

la **droga** SUSTANTIVO
drug ◊ *las drogas blandas* soft drugs ◊ *las drogas duras* hard drugs ◊ *el problema de la droga* the drug problem

el **drogadicto**, la **drogadicta** SUSTANTIVO
drug addict

drogar* VERBO
to drug
◆**drogarse** to take drugs

la **droguería** SUSTANTIVO

> *A shop selling cleaning materials, paint and toiletries.*

la **ducha** SUSTANTIVO
shower ◊ *darse una ducha* to have a shower

ducharse VERBO
to have a shower

la **duda** SUSTANTIVO
doubt
◆**Tengo mis dudas.** I have my doubts.
◆**sin duda** no doubt
◆**sin duda alguna** without a doubt
◆**no cabe duda** there's no doubt about it
◆**Tengo una duda.** I have a query.
◆**poner algo en duda** to call something into question
◆**¿Alguna duda?** Any questions?

dudar VERBO
to doubt ◊ *Lo dudo.* I doubt it.
◆**Dudo que sea cierto.** I doubt if it's true.
◆**Dudó si comprarlo o no.** He wasn't sure whether to buy it or not.

dudoso ADJETIVO
[1] doubtful ◊ *Es dudoso que vengan.* It's doubtful whether they'll come.
[2] dubious ◊ *un chiste de dudoso gusto* a joke in dubious taste

duelo VERBO *ver* **doler**

el **dueño**, la **dueña** SUSTANTIVO
owner
◆**ser dueño de sí mismo** to have self-control

duermo VERBO *ver* **dormir**

el **Duero** SUSTANTIVO
the Douro

dulce ADJETIVO
[1] sweet (*pastel*)
[2] gentle (*persona*)

el **dulce** SUSTANTIVO
sweet

el **dúo** SUSTANTIVO
duet
◆**cantar a dúo** to sing a duet

la **duración** SUSTANTIVO
length ◊ *Depende de la duración de la película.* It depends on the length of the film.
◆**una pila de larga duración** a long-life battery

duradero ADJETIVO
[1] lasting (*fe, paz*)
[2] hard-wearing (*material*)

durante ADVERBIO
during ◊ *Laura tuvo que trabajar durante las vacaciones.* Laura had to work during the holidays.
◆**durante toda la noche** all night long
◆**Habló durante una hora.** He spoke for an hour.

durar VERBO
to last ◊ *La película duraba dos horas.* The film lasted two hours. ◊ *Mario sólo duró dos meses como director.* Mario only lasted two months as manager. ◊ *Todavía le dura el enfado.* He's still angry.

el **durazno** SUSTANTIVO Latin America
peach (PL peaches)

la **dureza** SUSTANTIVO
[1] hardness ◊ *la dureza del acero* the hardness of steel
[2] harshness ◊ *la dureza de sus palabras* the harshness of his words
[3] callus (PL calluses) ◊ *Tiene una dureza en la planta del pie.* He has a callus on the sole of his foot.

durmiendo VERBO *ver* **dormir**

duro (1) ADJETIVO
[1] hard ◊ *Los diamantes son muy duros.* Diamonds are very hard.
[2] tough ◊ *Esta carne está dura.* This meat's tough.
[3] harsh ◊ *El clima es muy duro.* The climate is very harsh.
◆**a duras penas** with great difficulty

♦ **ser duro con alguien** to be hard on somebody
♦ **ser duro de oído** to be hard of hearing

duro (2) ADVERBIO
hard ◊ *trabajar duro* to work hard

el **duro** SUSTANTIVO
five-peseta coin
♦ **estar sin un duro** to be broke (*coloquial*)

el **DVD** ABREVIATURA (= *Disco de Vídeo Digital*)
DVD

E

e CONJUNCIÓN

***e* is used instead of *y* in front of words beginning with "i" and "hi", but not "hie".**

and ◊ *Pablo e Inés.* Pablo and Inés.

echar VERBO

[1] to throw (*lanzar*) ◊ *Échame las llaves.* Throw me the keys over.

◆ **Eché la carta en el buzón.** I posted the letter.

[2] to put (*poner*) ◊ *Tengo que echar gasolina.* I need to put petrol in the car.

◆ **¿Te echo más whisky?** Shall I pour you some more whisky?

[3] to throw out (*expulsar*) ◊ *Me echó de su casa.* He threw me out of the house.

[4] to expel ◊ *Lo han echado del colegio.* He's been expelled from school.

◆ **La echaron del trabajo.** They sacked her.

◆ **La chimenea echa humo.** Smoke is coming out of the chimney.

◆ **¿Qué echan hoy en la tele?** What's on TV today?

◆ **echar de menos a alguien** to miss somebody ◊ *Echo de menos a mi familia.* I miss my family.

◆ **¿Cuántos años me echas?** How old do you think I am?

◆ **echar una ojeada (a)** to browse (*informática*)

◆ **echarse (1)** (*tumbarse*) to lie down ◊ *Me eché en el sofá y me quedé dormido.* I lay down on the sofa and fell asleep.

◆ **echarse (2)** (*lanzarse*) to jump ◊ *Los niños se echaron al agua.* The children jumped into the water.

el **eco** SUSTANTIVO

echo (PL echoes)

la **ecología** SUSTANTIVO

ecology

ecológico ADJETIVO

ecological ◊ *un desastre ecológico* an ecological disaster

◆ **un producto ecológico** an environmentally friendly product

ecologista ADJETIVO

environmental ◊ *un grupo ecologista* an environmental group

el/la **ecologista** SUSTANTIVO

environmentalist

la **economía** SUSTANTIVO

[1] economy (PL economies) ◊ *Un país de economía capitalista.* A country with a capitalist economy.

[2] economics SING ◊ *Quiero estudiar economía.* I want to study economics.

económico ADJETIVO

[1] economic (*financiero*) ◊ *una profunda crisis económica* a deep economic crisis

[2] economical (*de poco gasto*)

◆ **un motor económico** an economical engine

[3] inexpensive ◊ *Comimos en un restaurante económico.* We ate in an inexpensive restaurant.

el/la **economista** SUSTANTIVO

economist

economizar* VERBO

to economize ◊ *Economiza en la comida para comprarse joyas.* She economizes on food to buy herself jewels.

Ecuador SUSTANTIVO MASC

Ecuador

el **ecuatoriano,** la **ecuatoriana** ADJETIVO, SUSTANTIVO

Ecuadorean

la **edad** SUSTANTIVO

age ◊ *Tenemos la misma edad.* We're the same age.

◆ **¿Qué edad tienen?** How old are they?

◆ **No tiene edad para votar.** She isn't old enough to vote.

◆ **Está en la edad del pavo.** She's at that difficult age.

la **edición** SUSTANTIVO (PL las **ediciones**)

edition ◊ *una edición de bolsillo* a pocket edition

edificar* VERBO

to build ◊ *Están edificando un centro deportivo.* They're building a sports centre.

el **edificio** SUSTANTIVO

building

Edimburgo SUSTANTIVO MASC

Edinburgh

editar VERBO

to publish (*publicar*)

el **editor,** la **editora** SUSTANTIVO

publisher

la **editorial** SUSTANTIVO

publisher

el **edredón** SUSTANTIVO (PL los **edredones**)

[1] eiderdown (*cubrecama*)

[2] duvet (*nórdico*)

la **educación** SUSTANTIVO

[1] education ◊ *Han aumentado el presupuesto de educación.* They've increased the education budget.

◆ **educación física** PE

[2] upbringing ◊ *Rosa recibió una educación muy estricta.* Rosa had a very strict upbringing.

* Verbs marked with this symbol are irregular. See pages 380-382 for further details

- **Señalar es de mala educación.** It's rude to point.
- **Se lo pedí con educación.** I asked her politely.
- **Es una falta de educación hablar con la boca llena.** It's bad manners to speak with your mouth full.

educado ADJETIVO
polite
- **Me contestó de forma educada.** He answered me politely.
- **Es un chico bien educado.** He's a well-mannered boy.

educar* VERBO
[1] to educate ◊ *Se educó en un colegio alemán.* He was educated in a German school.
[2] to bring up ◊ *Educaron a sus hijos de una manera muy estricta.* They brought their children up very strictly.

educativo ADJETIVO
educational

EE.UU. ABREVIATURA (= *Estados Unidos*)
USA

efectivamente ADVERBIO
◊ *Efectivamente, estaba donde tú decías.* You were right, he was where you said.
◊ *Entonces, ¿Es usted su padre? – Efectivamente.* So, are you his father? – That's right.

efectivo ADJETIVO
effective (*eficaz*) ◊ *un medicamento muy efectivo* a very effective medicine
- **pagar en efectivo** to pay in cash

el **efecto** SUSTANTIVO
effect
- **efectos especiales** special effects
- **hacer efecto** to take effect ◊ *La aspirina enseguida me hizo efecto.* The aspirin took effect on me immediately.
- **Devolvió la pelota con efecto.** He put some spin on the ball.

efectuar* VERBO
to carry out (*operación, maniobra*)

eficaz ADJETIVO
[1] effective ◊ *un remedio eficaz* an effective remedy
[2] efficient (*persona*) ◊ *un funcionario eficaz* an efficient civil servant

eficiente ADJETIVO
efficient

el **egipcio**, la **egipcia** ADJETIVO, SUSTANTIVO
Egyptian

Egipto SUSTANTIVO MASC
Egypt

el **egoísmo** SUSTANTIVO
selfishness

egoísta ADJETIVO
selfish

el/la **egoísta** SUSTANTIVO
◊ *María es una egoísta.* Maria's very selfish.

Eire SUSTANTIVO MASC
Eire

el **eje** SUSTANTIVO
[1] axle (*de ruedas*)
[2] axis (*de la Tierra*)

la **ejecución** SUSTANTIVO (PL las **ejecuciones**)
execution (*de condenado*)

ejecutar VERBO
[1] to carry out ◊ *Ejecutaron el proyecto según lo previsto.* They carried out the project according to plan.
[2] to execute ◊ *La ejecutaron al amanecer.* They executed her at dawn.

el **ejecutivo**, la **ejecutiva** SUSTANTIVO
executive

el **ejemplar** SUSTANTIVO
(*de libro, periódico*)
copy (PL copies)

el **ejemplo** SUSTANTIVO
example ◊ *¿Puedes ponerme un ejemplo?* Can you give me an example?
- **por ejemplo** for example
- **Debes dar ejemplo a tu hermano pequeño.** You must set your younger brother an example.

ejercer* VERBO
- **Ejerce de abogado.** He's a practising lawyer.
- **Ejerce mucha influencia sobre sus hermanos.** He has a lot of influence on his brothers.

el **ejercicio** SUSTANTIVO
exercise ◊ *La maestra nos puso varios ejercicios.* The teacher gave us several exercises to do.
- **hacer ejercicio** to exercise

el **ejército** SUSTANTIVO
army (PL armies)

el **ejote** SUSTANTIVO Mexico
green bean

el ARTÍCULO (FEM SING **la**, PL **los**)
the ◊ *Perdí el autobús.* I missed the bus.
- **el del sombrero rojo** the one with the red hat
- **Yo fui el que lo encontró.** I was the one who found it.

El artículo se traduce por el posesivo en inglés cuando se refiere a una parte del cuerpo, una prenda que se lleva puesta o algo que nos pertenece.

◊ *Ayer me lavé la cabeza.* I washed my hair yesterday. ◊ *Me puse el abrigo.* I put my coat on. ◊ *Tiene un coche bonito, pero prefiero el de Juan.* He's got a nice car, but I prefer Juan's.

El artículo a veces no se traduce en inglés; por ejemplo cuando se refiere a algo en general, con algunas expresiones de tiempo, o con apellidos.

◊ *No me gusta el pescado.* I don't like fish. ◊ *Vendrá el lunes que viene.* He's coming next Monday. ◊ *Ha llamado el Sr. Sendra.* Mr. Sendra called.

él PRONOMBRE
1 he (*como sujeto*) ◇ *Me lo dijo él.* He told me.
2 him (*con preposición, en comparaciones*) ◇ *Se lo di a él.* I gave it to him. ◇ *Su mujer es más alta que él.* His wife is taller than him.
◆ **él mismo** himself ◇ *No lo sabe ni él mismo.* He doesn't even know himself.
◆ **de él** his ◇ *El coche es de él.* The car's his.

elaborar VERBO
to produce (*producto*)

elástico ADJETIVO
◆ **un tejido elástico** a stretchy material
◆ **una goma elástica** an elastic band

la **elección** SUSTANTIVO (PL las **elecciones**)
1 election (*votación*) ◇ *Han convocado elecciones generales.* General elections have been called.
2 choice (*selección*) ◇ *Ésa es una buena elección.* That's a good choice. ◇ *No tuve elección.* I had no choice.

electoral ADJETIVO
◆ **la campaña electoral** the election campaign

la **electricidad** SUSTANTIVO
electricity

el/la **electricista** SUSTANTIVO
electrician ◇ *Mi primo es electricista.* My cousin's an electrician.

eléctrico ADJETIVO
1 electric ◇ *una guitarra eléctrica* an electric guitar
2 electrical ◇ *a causa de un fallo eléctrico* due to an electrical fault

__electric__ se usa para referirnos a objetos que funcionan con electricidad, mientras que __electrical__ es menos frecuente y se emplea en términos de física y mecánica.

el **electrodoméstico** SUSTANTIVO
domestic appliance

la **electrónica** SUSTANTIVO
electronics SING

electrónico ADJETIVO
electronic
◆ **el correo electrónico** email

el **elefante** SUSTANTIVO
elephant

elegante ADJETIVO
smart

elegir* VERBO
1 to choose ◇ *No sabía qué color elegir.* I didn't know what colour to choose.
◆ **Te dan a elegir entre dos modelos.** You're given a choice of two models.
2 to elect ◇ *Me eligieron delegado de curso.* I was elected class representative.

el **elemento** SUSTANTIVO
element

elevado ADJETIVO
high (*terreno, precio, temperatura*)

elevar VERBO
to raise (*nivel, precio, voz*)

eligiendo VERBO *ver* **elegir**

elijo VERBO *ver* **elegir**

eliminar VERBO
1 to remove ◇ *un detergente que elimina las manchas* a washing powder that removes the stains
2 to eliminate ◇ *Fueron eliminados de la competición.* They were eliminated from the competition.

el **elixir bucal** SUSTANTIVO
mouthwash

ella PRONOMBRE
1 she (*como sujeto*) ◇ *Ella no estaba en casa.* She was not at home.
2 her (*con preposición, en comparaciones*) ◇ *El regalo es para ella.* The present's for her. ◇ *Él estaba más nervioso que ella.* He was more nervous than her.
◆ **ella misma** herself ◇ *Me lo dijo ella misma.* She told me herself.
◆ **de ella** hers ◇ *Este abrigo es de ella.* This coat's hers.

ellos PRONOMBRE PL (FEM **ellas**)
1 they ◇ *Ellos todavía no lo saben.* They don't know yet.
2 them (*con preposición, en comparaciones*) ◇ *Yo me iré con ellas.* I'll leave with them. ◇ *Somos mejores que ellos.* We're better than them.
◆ **ellos mismos** themselves ◇ *Me lo dijeron ellos mismos.* They told me themselves.
◆ **de ellos** theirs ◇ *El coche era de ellos.* The car was theirs.

elogiar VERBO
to praise

el **elote** SUSTANTIVO Mexico
1 corncob (*mazorca*)
2 sweetcorn (*granos*)

la **embajada** SUSTANTIVO
embassy (PL embassies)

el **embajador**, la **embajadora** SUSTANTIVO
ambassador

embalar VERBO
to pack

el **embalse** SUSTANTIVO
reservoir

embarazada ADJETIVO
pregnant ◇ *Estaba embarazada de cuatro meses.* She was four months pregnant.
◆ **quedarse embarazada** to get pregnant

No confundir __embarazada__ con __embarrassed__.

embarazoso ADJETIVO
embarrassing

embarcar* VERBO

to board ◊ *Los pasajeros ya estaban embarcando.* The passengers were already boarding.

el **embargo** SUSTANTIVO
embargo (*a un país*)
♦ **sin embargo** nevertheless

embobado ADJETIVO
♦ **Se quedaron mirándola embobados.** They watched her in fascination.
♦ **Está embobado con su novia.** His girlfriend has got him under her spell.

emborracharse VERBO
to get drunk

embotellado ADJETIVO
bottled (*agua, vino*)

el **embotellamiento** SUSTANTIVO
traffic jam

el **embrague** SUSTANTIVO
clutch

embrollarse VERBO
1 to get tangled up ◊ *Las cuerdas se embrollaron.* The ropes got tangled up.
2 to get muddled up ◊ *Me embrollé con tanta información.* With so much information, I got muddled up.

el **embrollo** SUSTANTIVO
tangle (*de hilos, cuerdas*)

embrujado ADJETIVO
haunted ◊ *una casa embrujada* a haunted house

el **embudo** SUSTANTIVO
spout

el **embustero,** la **embustera** SUSTANTIVO
fibber

el **embutido** SUSTANTIVO
cold meats ◊ *No comemos mucho embutido.* We don't eat a lot of cold meats.

la **emergencia** SUSTANTIVO
emergency (PL emergencies)
♦ **la salida de emergencia** the emergency exit
♦ **en caso de emergencia** in case of emergency

emigrar VERBO
1 to emigrate (*personas*)
2 to migrate (*pájaros*)

la **emisión** SUSTANTIVO (PL las **emisiones**)
1 broadcast (*de programa*)
2 emission (*de gases*)

emitir VERBO
1 to broadcast (*programa*)
2 to give off (*gases, olores*)

la **emoción** SUSTANTIVO (PL las **emociones**)
emotion ◊ *Me temblaba la voz de emoción.* My voice was trembling with emotion.
♦ **Su carta me produjo gran emoción.** I was very moved by his letter.
♦ **¡Qué emoción!** How exciting!

emocionado ADJETIVO
1 moved (*conmovido*)
2 excited (*entusiasmado*)

emocionante ADJETIVO
1 moving (*conmovedor*) ◊ *La despedida fue muy emocionante.* The farewell was very moving.
2 exciting (*apasionante*) ◊ *El final del partido fue muy emocionante.* The end of the match was very exciting.

emocionarse VERBO
to be moved ◊ *Me emocioné mucho con la película.* I was very moved by the film.
♦ **Se emocionó al volver a ver a su padre.** She got emotional when she saw her father again.

emotivo ADJETIVO
1 moving (*acto, discurso*)
2 emotional ◊ *La vuelta a casa fue muy emotiva.* It was a very emotional homecoming.

empacharse VERBO
to get a tummy upset ◊ *Me empaché por comer tanto chocolate.* I got a tummy upset through eating so much chocolate.

empalagoso ADJETIVO
sickly (*pastel, dulce*)

empalmar VERBO
1 to connect ◊ *Empalma los dos cables para hacer la conexión.* Connect the two wires to make the connection.
2 to join ◊ *Esta carretera empalma con la autopista.* This road joins the motorway.

la **empanada** SUSTANTIVO
pasty (PL pasties)

empañarse VERBO
to get steamed up ◊ *Se me empañaron las gafas al entrar en el museo.* My glasses got steamed up when I went into the museum.
♦ **Los cristales del dormitorio estaban empañados.** There was condensation on the bedroom windows.

empapar VERBO
to soak ◊ *Cierra la ducha que me estás empapando.* Can you turn the shower off, you're soaking me.
♦ **Se me empaparon los calcetines.** My socks got soaked.
♦ **estar empapado hasta los huesos** to be soaked to the skin

empapelar VERBO
to paper

empaquetar VERBO
to pack ◊ *Empaqueta todos tus libros.* Pack all your books.

el **emparedado** SUSTANTIVO Latin America
sandwich (PL sandwiches)

empastar VERBO
♦ **Me han empastado dos muelas.** I've had two fillings.

el **empaste** SUSTANTIVO
filling

E

empatar VERBO
to draw ◊ *Empatamos a uno y tuvimos que jugar la prórroga.* We drew one-all and had to play extra time. ◊ *Los dos candidatos empataron en la votación.* The two candidates got the same number of votes.

el **empate** SUSTANTIVO
[1] draw (*en partido*) ◊ *un empate a cero* a goalless draw
[2] tie (*en votación, concurso*)

empedernido ADJETIVO
◆ **un fumador empedernido** a chronic smoker
◆ **Es un lector empedernido.** He's a compulsive reader.

empeñado ADJETIVO
determined ◊ *Está empeñado en aprobar el curso.* He's determined to get through the course.
◆ **Está empeñada en que yo soy mayor que ella.** She insists that I'm older than she is.

empeñarse VERBO
◆ **empeñarse en hacer algo (1)** to be determined to do something ◊ *Se había empeñado en irse con él.* She was determined to go with him.
◆ **empeñarse en hacer algo (2)** to insist on doing something ◊ *Se empeñó en que nos quedáramos a cenar.* He insisted that we should stay for dinner.

empeorar VERBO
[1] to get worse (*enfermo, situación*) ◊ *Mi padre empeoró con aquel medicamento.* My father got worse with that medicine.
[2] to make...worse ◊ *Tu comentario sólo emperorará las cosas.* Your comment will only make matters worse.

empezar* VERBO
to start ◊ *Las vacaciones empiezan el 20.* The holidays start on the 20th.
◆ **empezar a hacer algo** to start doing something ◊ *Ha empezado a nevar.* It's started snowing.
◆ **volver a empezar** to start again

empinado ADJETIVO
steep (*calle, pendiente*)

el **empleado,** la **empleada** SUSTANTIVO
[1] employee
[2] shop assistant [Latin America]
◆ **una empleada del hogar** a servant

emplear VERBO
[1] to use ◊ *Puedes emplear cualquier jabón.* You can use any soap.
[2] to employ ◊ *La fábrica emplea a veinte trabajadores.* The factory employs twenty workers.
◆ **Le está bien empleado.** It serves her right.

el **empleo** SUSTANTIVO
job ◊ *Ha encontrado empleo en un restaurante.* He has found a job in a restaurant.
◆ **estar sin empleo** to be unemployed
◆ **"modo de empleo"** "instructions for use"

empollar VERBO
to swot ◊ *Me pasé la noche empollando.* I spent the whole night swotting.

el **empollón ,** la **empollona** SUSTANTIVO (MASC PL los **empollones**)
swot

la **empresa** SUSTANTIVO
firm ◊ *Trabaja en una empresa de informática.* He works in a computer firm.

la **empresaria** SUSTANTIVO
businesswoman (PL businesswomen)

el **empresario** SUSTANTIVO
businessman (PL businessmen)

empujar VERBO
to push ◊ *Tuvimos que empujar al coche.* We had to push the car.

el **empujón** SUSTANTIVO (PL los **empujones**)
◊ *Me dieron un empujón y caí a la piscina.* They pushed me and I fell into the pool.
◆ **abrirse paso a empujones** to shove one's way through

en PREPOSICIÓN
[1] in ◊ *en el armario* in the wardrobe ◊ *Viven en Granada.* They live in Granada. ◊ *Nació en invierno.* He was born in winter. ◊ *Lo hice en dos días.* I did it in two days. ◊ *Hablamos en inglés.* We speak in English. ◊ *Está en el hospital.* She's in hospital.
[2] into (*con verbos que indican movimiento*) ◊ *Entré en el banco.* I went into the bank. ◊ *Me metí en la cama a las diez.* I got into bed at ten o'clock.
[3] on ◊ *Las llaves están en la mesa.* The keys are on the table. ◊ *Lo encontré tirado en el suelo.* I found it lying on the floor. ◊ *La librería está en la calle Pelayo.* The bookshop is on Pelayo street. ◊ *La oficina está en el quinto piso.* The office is on the fifth floor.
◆ **Mi cumpleaños cae en viernes.** My birthday falls on a Friday.
[4] at ◊ *Yo estaba en casa.* I was at home. ◊ *Te veo en el cine.* See you at the cinema. ◊ *Vivía en el número 17.* I was living at number 17. ◊ *en ese momento* at that moment ◊ *en Navidades* at Christmas
[5] by ◊ *Vinimos en avión.* We came by plane.
◆ **ser el primero en llegar** to be the first to arrive

enamorado ADJETIVO

* Verbs marked with this symbol are irregular. See pages 380-382 for further details

◆**estar enamorado de alguien** to be in love with somebody

enamorarse VERBO
to fall in love ◊ *Se ha enamorado de Yolanda.* He's fallen in love with Yolanda. ◊ *Se enamoraron nada más verse.* They fell in love at first sight.

el **enano,** la **enana** SUSTANTIVO
dwarf (PL dwarves)

encabezar* VERBO
to head ◊ *El Betis encabeza la clasificación de Liga.* Betis are heading the League. ◊ *la cita que encabeza el artículo* the quote heading the article

encajar VERBO
1 to fit ◊ *Las piezas no encajan.* The pieces don't fit.
2 to cope with ◊ *Ha encajado muy bien la muerte de su madre.* She's coped very well with her mother's death.

encaminarse VERBO
◆**Nos encaminamos hacia el pueblo.** We headed towards the village.

encantado ADJETIVO
1 delighted (*muy contento*) ◊ *Está encantada con su nuevo coche.* She's delighted with her new car.
2 enchanted (*hechizado*) ◊ *un castillo encantado* an enchanted castle
◆**¡Encantado de conocerle!** Pleased to meet you!

encantador ADJETIVO (FEM **encantadora**)
charming

encantar VERBO
to love ◊ *Me encantan los animales.* I love animals. ◊ *Les encanta esquiar.* They love skiing. ◊ *Me encantaría que vinieras.* I'd love you to come.

el **encanto** SUSTANTIVO
charm
◆**Eugenia es un encanto.** Eugenia is charming.

encarcelar VERBO
to imprison

el **encargado,** la **encargada** SUSTANTIVO
manager ◊ *Quiero hablar con el encargado.* I'd like to talk to the manager.

encargar* VERBO
1 to order ◊ *Encargamos dos pizzas.* We ordered two pizzas.
2 to ask ◊ *Le encargó que le recogiera los documentos.* She asked him to fetch the documents for her.
◆**Yo me encargaré de avisar a los demás.** I'll take care of letting the others know.
◆**Estoy encargada de vender las entradas.** I'm in charge of selling the tickets.

encariñarse VERBO
◆**encariñarse con** to grow fond of

el **encendedor** SUSTANTIVO
lighter

encender* VERBO
1 to light (*vela, hoguera, cigarro*)
2 to switch on (*luz, calefacción*)

encendido ADJETIVO
1 on (*luz, calefacción*) ◊ *La tele estaba encendida.* The telly was on.
2 lit (*fuego, hoguera*) ◊ *El cigarro no está bien encendido.* Your cigarette isn't properly lit.

el **encerado** SUSTANTIVO
blackboard (*pizarra*)

encerrar* VERBO
1 to shut up ◊ *Encerré el gato en la cocina.* I shut the cat up in the kitchen. ◊ *Me encerré en mi cuarto para estudiar.* I shut myself up in my room to study.
2 to lock up ◊ *Lo encerraron en un calabozo.* They locked him up in a cell.
◆**Los manifestantes se encerraron en el ayuntamiento.** The demonstrators held a sit-in in the town hall.

la **enchilada** SUSTANTIVO Mexico
stuffed tortilla

el **enchufado,** la **enchufada** SUSTANTIVO
◆**Amelia es la enchufada del profesor.** Amelia's the teacher's pet. (*coloquial*)

enchufar VERBO
to plug in ◊ *Enchufa la tele.* Plug the TV in.

el **enchufe** SUSTANTIVO
1 plug (*macho*)
2 socket (*hembra*)
◆**Consiguió ese puesto por enchufe.** He got that job through pulling strings.

la **encía** SUSTANTIVO
gum

la **enciclopedia** SUSTANTIVO
encyclopaedia

enciendo VERBO *ver* **encender**

encierro VERBO *ver* **encerrar**

encima ADVERBIO
on ◊ *Pon el cenicero aquí encima.* Put the ashtray on there. ◊ *No llevo dinero encima.* I haven't got any money on me.
◆**encima de (1)** on ◊ *Ponlo encima de la mesa.* Put it on the table.
◆**encima de (2)** on top of ◊ *Mi maleta está encima del armario.* My case is on top of the wardrobe.
◆**Lo leí por encima.** I glanced at it.
◆**por encima de (1)** above ◊ *Los helicópteros volaban por encima de nuestras cabezas.* The helicopters were flying above our heads. ◊ *Las temperaturas han subido por encima de lo normal.* Temperatures have been above average.
◆**por encima de (2)** over ◊ *Tuve que saltar por encima de la mesa.* I had to jump over the table.
◆**¡Y encima no te da ni las gracias!** And on top of it he doesn't even thank you!

la **encina** SUSTANTIVO
oak tree

E

encoger* VERBO
to shrink ◊ *Este jersey ha encogido.* This jumper has shrunk.
♦ **Antonio se encogió de hombros.** Antonio shrugged his shoulders.

encontrar* VERBO
to find ◊ *Mi hermano ha encontrado trabajo.* My brother has found a job. ◊ *Lo encuentro un poco arrogante.* I find him a bit arrogant.
♦ **No encuentro las llaves.** I can't find the keys.
♦ **encontrarse (1)** (*sentirse*) to feel ◊ *Ahora se encuentra mejor.* Now she's feeling better.
♦ **encontrarse (2)** (*verse*) to meet ◊ *Nos encontramos en el cine.* We met at the cinema.
♦ **Me encontré con Manolo en la calle.** I bumped into Manolo in the street.

el **encuentro** SUSTANTIVO
1 (*reunión*)
meeting
♦ **punto de encuentro** meeting point
2 (*partido*)
match (PL matches)

la **encuesta** SUSTANTIVO
survey

enderezar* VERBO
to straighten

endulzar* VERBO
to sweeten

endurecer* VERBO
to tone up (*músculos*)

el **enemigo,** la **enemiga** ADJETIVO, SUSTANTIVO
enemy (PL enemies) ◊ *el ejército enemigo* the enemy army

enemistarse VERBO
to fall out ◊ *Se enemistó con la familia de su mujer.* He fell out with his wife's family.

la **energía** SUSTANTIVO
energy ◊ *ahorrar energía* to save energy
♦ **la energía solar** solar power
♦ **la energía eléctrica** electricity

enérgico ADJETIVO
energetic ◊ *Es una persona muy enérgica.* She's very energetic.

enero SUSTANTIVO MASC
Los meses se escriben con mayúscula.
January ◊ *en enero* in January ◊ *Nació el 6 de enero.* He was born on 6 January.

enfadado ADJETIVO
angry ◊ *Mi padre estaba muy enfadado conmigo.* My father was very angry with me.
♦ **Ana y su novio están enfadados.** Ana and her boyfriend have fallen out.

enfadarse VERBO
to be angry ◊ *Papá se va a enfadar mucho contigo.* Dad will be very angry with you.
♦ **Mi hermana y su novio se han enfadado.** My brother and his girlfriend have fallen out.

el **enfado** SUSTANTIVO
♦ **Ya se le ha pasado el enfado.** He isn't angry anymore.

enfermarse VERBO Latin America
to fall ill

la **enfermedad** SUSTANTIVO
1 illness (PL illnesses) ◊ *Adelgazó mucho durante su enfermedad.* He lost a lot of weight during his illness.
2 disease ◊ *Tiene una enfermedad contagiosa.* He's got an infectious disease.

la **enfermería** SUSTANTIVO
sick bay

el **enfermero,** la **enfermera** SUSTANTIVO
nurse ◊ *Mi madre es enfermera.* My mother's a nurse.

enfermo ADJETIVO
ill ◊ *He estado enferma toda la semana.* I've been ill all week.
♦ **¿Cuándo te pusiste enfermo?** When did you get ill?
♦ **¡Me pones enfermo!** You make me sick!

el **enfermo,** la **enferma** SUSTANTIVO
patient (*en hospital*)
♦ **Los enfermos deben tomar precauciones especiales.** Sick people need to take special precautions.

enfocar* VERBO
1 to focus on ◊ *El fotógrafo enfocó el ciervo.* The photographer focussed on the deer.
2 to approach ◊ *Depende de cómo enfoques el problema.* It depends on how you approach the problem.

enfrentarse VERBO
♦ **enfrentarse a algo** to face something ◊ *Tienes que enfrentarte al problema.* You have to face the problem.

enfrente ADVERBIO
opposite ◊ *Luisa estaba sentada enfrente.* Luisa was sitting opposite.
♦ **La panadería está enfrente.** The baker's is across the street.
♦ **de enfrente** opposite ◊ *la casa de enfrente* the house opposite
♦ **enfrente de** opposite ◊ *Mi casa está enfrente del colegio.* My house is opposite the school.

enfriarse* VERBO
1 to get cold ◊ *La sopa se ha enfriado.* The soup has got cold.
2 to cool down ◊ *Hay que dejar que se enfríe el motor.* We must let the engine cool down.

3 to catch cold ◊ *Ponte el abrigo que te vas a enfriar.* Put your coat on or you'll catch cold.

enganchar VERBO
to hook ◊ *Enganché la correa al collar del perro.* I hooked the lead onto the dog's collar.
♦ **engancharse** to get caught ◊ *Se me enganchó el jersey en la valla.* My jumper got caught on a rosebush.

engañar VERBO
1 to cheat ◊ *Te han engañado; no es de oro.* You've been cheated. It's not gold.
2 to lie ◊ *No me engañes y dime quién lo hizo.* Don't lie to me and tell me who did it.
3 to cheat on ◊ *Su novio la engaña.* Her boyfriend is cheating on her.
♦ **Las apariencias engañan.** Appearances can be deceptive.

el **engaño** SUSTANTIVO
1 con (*coloquial*) ◊ *Fue un engaño.* It was a con.
2 deception ◊ *Carmen siguió manteniendo el engaño.* Carmen continued to keep up the deception.

engordar VERBO
1 to put on weight ◊ *No quiero engordar.* I don't want to put on weight.
♦ **He engordado dos kilos.** I've put on two kilos.
2 to be fattening ◊ *Los caramelos engordan mucho.* Sweets are very fattening.

engreído ADJETIVO
conceited

la **enhorabuena** SUSTANTIVO
♦ **¡Enhorabuena!** Congratulations!
♦ **Me dieron la enhorabuena por el premio.** They congratulated me on winning the prize.

el **enlace** SUSTANTIVO
1 connection (*de trenes, autobuses*)
♦ **Perdí el enlace con Buenos Aires.** I missed the connecting flight to Buenos Aires.
2 link (*informática*)

enlatado ADJETIVO
tinned (*verduras, carne*)

enlazar* VERBO
to connect ◊ *Este vuelo enlaza con el de Moscú.* This flight connects with the Moscow flight.

enloquecer* VERBO
to be crazy about ◊ *Le enloquecen las motos.* He's crazy about motorbikes.

enmarcar* VERBO
to frame

enmoquetado ADJETIVO
carpeted

enojado ADJETIVO
angry ◊ *Mi padre estaba muy enojado conmigo.* My father was very angry with me.
♦ **Ana y su novio están enojados.** Ana and her boyfriend have fallen out.

enojarse VERBO
to be angry ◊ *Mi madre se va a enojar.* My mother will be angry. ◊ *Manolo y su novio se han enojado.* Manolo and his boyfriend have fallen out.

enorme ADJETIVO
enormous ◊ *Tienen una casa enorme.* They have an enormous house.

la **enredadera** SUSTANTIVO
creeper

enredarse VERBO
1 to get tangled up (*hilos, cuerda*) ◊ *Se me ha enredado el pelo.* My hair's got all tangled up.
2 to get into a tangle ◊ *Me enredé haciendo las cuentas.* I got into a tangle with the accounts. (*coloquial*)

enrevesado ADJETIVO
difficult (*problema*)

enriquecerse* VERBO
to get rich ◊ *Se enriquecieron tratando con armas.* They got rich dealing in arms.

enrollar VERBO
1 to roll up ◊ *No dobles el póster, enróllalo.* Don't fold the poster, roll it up.
2 to wind ◊ *Tenía un pañuelo enrollado en la cabeza.* She had a scarf wound round her head.
♦ **Se enrolló con Juan en la discoteca.** She got off with Juan in the disco. (*coloquial*)

enroscar* VERBO
1 to screw in (*tornillo, tuerca*)
♦ **Enrosca bien la tapa.** Screw the top on tight.
2 to coil (*cable, manguera*) ◊ *La manguera se le enroscó en la pierna.* The hose coiled round his leg.

la **ensalada** SUSTANTIVO
salad

la **ensaladilla** SUSTANTIVO
♦ **una ensaladilla rusa** a Russian salad

ensanchar VERBO
to widen ◊ *Están ensanchando la carretera.* They're widening the road.
♦ **ensancharse** to stretch ◊ *Mi jersey se ha ensanchado.* My jumper has stretched.

ensayar VERBO
to rehearse (*obra de teatro, canción*)

el **ensayo** SUSTANTIVO
rehearsal ◊ *Esta tarde tenemos ensayo.* We've got a rehearsal this afternoon.

enseguida ADVERBIO
straight away ◊ *La ambulancia llegó enseguida.* The ambulance arrived straight away.
♦ **Enseguida te atiendo.** I'll be with you in a minute.

la **enseñanza** SUSTANTIVO

1 teaching ◊ *la enseñanza de lenguas extranjeras* the teaching of foreign languages

2 education ◊ *Debería invertirse más dinero en la enseñanza.* More money should be invested in education.

♦ **la enseñanza primaria** primary education

enseñar VERBO

1 to teach ◊ *Ricardo enseña inglés en una academia de idiomas.* Ricardo teaches English at a language school. ◊ *Mi padre me enseñó a nadar.* My father taught me to swim.

2 to show ◊ *Ana me enseñó todos sus videojuegos.* Ana showed me all her video games.

♦ **Les enseñé el colegio.** I showed them round the school.

ensuciar VERBO

to get...dirty ◊ *Vas a ensuciar el sofá.* You'll get the sofa dirty.

♦ **ensuciarse** to get dirty ◊ *No toques la pintura que te vas a ensuciar.* Don't touch the paint or you'll get dirty. ◊ *Me he ensuciado las manos.* I've got my hands dirty.

♦ **Te has ensuciado de barro los pantalones.** You've got mud on your trousers.

entender* VERBO

to understand ◊ *No entiendo el francés.* I don't understand French. ◊ *¿Lo entiendes?* Do you understand?

♦ **¿Entiendes lo que quiero decir?** Do you know what I mean?

♦ **Creo que lo he entendido mal.** I think I've misunderstood.

♦ **Mi primo entiende mucho de coches.** My cousin knows a lot about cars.

♦ **entenderse (1)** (*llevarse bien*) to get on ◊ *Mi hermana y yo no nos entendemos.* My sister and I don't get on.

♦ **entenderse (2)** (*comunicarse*) to communicate ◊ *Se entienden por gestos.* They communicate through sign language.

♦ **Dio a entender que no le gustaba.** He implied that he didn't like it.

el **entendido**, la **entendida** SUSTANTIVO

expert ◊ *No soy un entendido en el tema.* I'm not an expert on the subject.

enterarse VERBO

1 to find out (*averiguar*) ◊ *Me enteré por Manolo.* I found out from Manolo. ◊ *Entérate bien de todos los detalles.* Make sure you find out about all the details.

♦ **Se enteraron del accidente por la tele.** They heard about the accident on the TV.

♦ **Me sacaron una muela y ni me enteré.** They took out a tooth and I didn't notice a thing.

2 to understand (*comprender*) ◊ *No me hables en francés que no me entero.* Don't talk to me in French – I won't understand.

entero ADJETIVO

whole ◊ *Se comió el paquete entero de galletas.* He ate the whole packet of biscuits. ◊ *Se pasó la noche entera estudiando.* He spent the whole night studying.

♦ **la leche entera** full-cream milk

enterrar* VERBO

to bury

entiendo VERBO *ver* **entender**

entierro VERBO *ver* **enterrar**

el **entierro** SUSTANTIVO

funeral (*ceremonia*)

entonces ADVERBIO

1 then ◊ *Si no es tu padre, ¿entonces quién es?* If he isn't your father, then who is he? ◊ *Me recogió y entonces fuimos al cine.* He picked me up and then we went to the cinema. ◊ *Iban andando porque entonces no tenían coche.* They would walk because they didn't have a car then.

2 so ◊ *¿Entonces, vienes o te quedas?* So, are you coming or staying?

♦ **desde entonces** since then

♦ **para entonces** by then

el **entorno** SUSTANTIVO

surroundings PL

la **entrada** SUSTANTIVO

1 entrance ◊ *Nos vemos en la entrada.* I'll see you at the entrance.

♦ **"entrada libre"** "free admission"

2 ticket ◊ *Tengo entradas para el teatro.* I've got tickets for the theatre.

3 entry (PL entries) ◊ *La entrada de España en la Comunidad Europea.* Spain's entry into the European Community.

♦ **"prohibida la entrada"** "no entry"

4 deposit ◊ *Pagamos una entrada de diez mil pesetas.* We paid a deposit of ten thousand pesetas.

el **entrante** SUSTANTIVO

starter

entrar VERBO

1 to go in

> *Se traduce por* **go** *cuando indica dirección diferente a donde está el hablante.*

◊ *Abrí la puerta y entré.* I opened the door and went in. ◊ *Mi amiga entró al banco.* My friend went into the bank.

♦ **Pedro entra a trabajar a las 8.** Pedro starts work at 8 o'clock.

♦**No me dejaron entrar por ser menor de 16 años.** They wouldn't let me in because I was under 16.

[2] to come in

Se traduce por **come** *cuando indica dirección hacia el hablante.*

◊ *¿Se puede? – Sí, entra.* May I? – Yes, come in. ◊ *Entraron en mi cuarto mientras yo dormía.* They came into my room while I was asleep.

[3] to fit ◊ *Estos zapatos no me entran.* These shoes don't fit me. ◊ *La maleta no entra en el maletero.* The case won't fit in the boot.

♦**El vino no entra en el precio.** The wine is not included in the price.

♦**Le entraron ganas de reír.** She wanted to laugh.

♦**De repente le entró sueño.** He suddenly felt sleepy.

♦**Me ha entrado hambre al verte comer.** Watching you eat made me hungry.

entre PREPOSICIÓN

[1] between (*dos personas o cosas*) ◊ *Lo terminamos entre los dos.* Between the two of us we finished it. ◊ *Vendrá entre las diez y las once.* He'll be coming between ten and eleven.

[2] among (*más de dos personas o cosas*) ◊ *Había un baúl entre las maletas.* There was a trunk in among the cases. ◊ *Las mujeres hablaban entre sí.* The women were talking among themselves.

♦**Le compraremos un regalo entre todos.** We'll buy her a present between all of us.

[3] by ◊ *15 dividido entre 3 es 5.* 15 divided by 3 is 5

entreabierto ADJETIVO

ajar (*puerta*)

entregar* VERBO

[1] to hand in (*deberes, trabajo*) ◊ *Marta entregó el examen.* Marta handed her exam paper in.

[2] to deliver (*carta, pedido*) ◊ *El cartero entregó el paquete.* The postman delivered the parcel.

[3] to present with (*premio, condecoración*) ◊ *El director le entregó la medalla.* The director presented him with the medal.

♦**El ladrón se entregó a la policía.** The thief gave himself up.

los **entremeses** SUSTANTIVO

appetizers

el **entrenador**, la **entrenadora** SUSTANTIVO

coach (PL coaches)

el **entrenamiento** SUSTANTIVO

training

entrenarse VERBO

to train

entretener* VERBO

[1] to entertain (*divertirse*)

♦**La tele entretiene mucho.** TV is very entertaining.

[2] to keep (*retener*) ◊ *Una vecina me entretuvo hablando en las escaleras.* A neighbour kept me talking on the stairs.

♦**entretenerse** (*divertirse*) to amuse oneself ◊ *Se entretienen viendo los dibujos animados.* They amuse themselves by watching cartoons.

♦**No os entretengáis jugando.** Don't hang about playing.

entretenido ADJETIVO

entertaining ◊ *La película es muy entretenida.* The film is very entertaining.

E

la **entrevista** SUSTANTIVO

interview

♦**hacer una entrevista a alguien** to interview somebody ◊ *Le hicieron una entrevista por la radio.* They interviewed her on the radio.

el **entrevistador**, la **entrevistadora** SUSTANTIVO

interviewer

entrevistar VERBO

to interview

entrometerse VERBO

to meddle ◊ *No te entrometas en mis asuntos.* Don't meddle in my affairs.

entusiasmado ADJETIVO

excited ◊ *Estaba entusiasmado con su fiesta de cumpleaños.* He was excited about his birthday party.

entusiasmarse VERBO

to get excited ◊ *Se entusiasmó con la idea de hacer una fiesta.* He got very excited about the idea of having a party.

el **entusiasmo** SUSTANTIVO

enthusiasm

♦**con entusiasmo** enthusiastically

enumerar VERBO

to list

el **envase** SUSTANTIVO

container ◊ *Viene en envases de plástico.* It comes in a plastic container.

♦**"envase no retornable"** "non-returnable bottle"

envejecer* VERBO

to age ◊ *Sus padres han envejecido mucho.* His parents have aged a lot.

enviar* VERBO

to send ◊ *Envíame las fotos.* Send me the photos.

♦**Juan me envió el regalo por correo.** Juan posted me the present.

la **envidia** SUSTANTIVO

envy

♦**¡Qué envidia!** I'm so jealous!

♦**Le tiene envidia a Ana.** She's jealous of Ana.

♦**Le da envidia que mi coche sea mejor.** He's jealous that my car is better.

envidiar VERBO

to envy ◊ *¡No te envidio!* I don't envy you!

envidioso ADJETIVO
envious
envolver* VERBO
to wrap up ◊ *Llevaba al niño envuelto en una manta.* She carried the baby wrapped up in a blanket.
♦ **¿Desea que se lo envuelva para regalo?** Would you like it gift-wrapped?
envuelto VERBO *ver* **envolver**
la **epidemia** SUSTANTIVO
epidemic
el **episodio** SUSTANTIVO
episode
la **época** SUSTANTIVO
time ◊ *En aquella época vivíamos en Alicante.* At that time we were living in Alicante. ◊ *en esta época del año* at this time of year
equilibrado ADJETIVO
balanced (*persona, dieta*)
el **equilibrio** SUSTANTIVO
balance ◊ *Perdí el equilibrio y me caí.* I lost my balance and fell over. ◊ *Luis podía mantener el equilibrio en la cuerda floja.* Luis managed to keep his balance on the tightrope.
el **equipaje** SUSTANTIVO
luggage
♦ **equipaje de mano** hand luggage
el **equipo** SUSTANTIVO
1 team ◊ *un equipo de baloncesto* a basketball team
2 equipment ◊ *Me robaron todo el equipo de esquí.* They stole all my skiing equipment.
♦ **el equipo de música** the stereo
la **equitación** SUSTANTIVO
riding
equivaler* VERBO
♦ **equivaler a algo** to be equivalent to something
la **equivocación** SUSTANTIVO (PL las **equivocaciones**)
mistake
♦ **He marcado otro número por equivocación.** I dialled another number by mistake.
equivocado ADJETIVO
wrong ◊ *Estás equivocada.* You're wrong. ◊ *Elena me dio el número equivocado.* Elena gave me the wrong number.
equivocarse* VERBO
1 to make a mistake ◊ *Me equivoqué muchas veces en el examen.* I made a lot of mistakes in the exam.
2 to be wrong ◊ *Si crees que voy a dejarte ir, te equivocas.* If you think I'm going to let you go, you're wrong.
♦ **Perdone, me he equivocado de número.** Sorry, wrong number.
♦ **Se equivocaron de tren.** They caught the wrong train.
era VERBO *ver* **ser**
eres VERBO *ver* **ser**
el **erizo** SUSTANTIVO
hedgehog
♦ **un erizo de mar** a sea urchin
el **error** SUSTANTIVO
mistake ◊ *Fue un error contárselo a Luisa.* Telling Luisa about it was a mistake. ◊ *Cometí muchos errores en el examen.* I made a lot of mistakes in the exam.
eructar VERBO
to burp
el **eructo** SUSTANTIVO
burp
es VERBO *ver* **ser**
esa ADJETIVO *ver* **ese**
ésa PRONOMBRE *ver* **ése**
esbelto ADJETIVO
slender
escabullirse* VERBO
1 to slip away ◊ *Se escabulló de la fiesta.* He managed to slip away from the party.
2 to wriggle out of ◊ *No debes escabullirte de tus deberes.* You mustn't try to wriggle out of your responsibilities.
la **escala** SUSTANTIVO
1 scale ◊ *a escala nacional* on a national scale
2 stopover ◊ *Tenemos una escala de tres horas en Bruselas.* We've got a three-hour stopover in Brussels.
♦ **Hicimos escala en Roma.** We stopped over in Rome.
escalar VERBO
to climb
la **escalera** SUSTANTIVO
stairs PL ◊ *bajar las escaleras* to go down the stairs
♦ **una escalera de mármol** a marble staircase
♦ **una escalera de mano** a ladder
♦ **la escalera de incendios** the fire escape
♦ **una escalera mecánica** an escalator
el **escalofrío** SUSTANTIVO
♦ **Tengo escalofríos.** I'm shivering.
♦ **La escena te produce escalofríos.** The scene makes you shudder.
el **escalón** SUSTANTIVO (PL los **escalones**)
step
la **escama** SUSTANTIVO
scale (*de pez*)
escandalizarse* VERBO
to shock ◊ *Mi abuela se escandalizó.* My grandmother was shocked.
el **escándalo** SUSTANTIVO
1 scandal

* Verbs marked with this symbol are irregular. See pages 380-382 for further details

♦ **La boda produjo un gran escándalo.** The wedding caused a huge scandal.
[2] racket ◊ *¿Qué escándalo es éste?* What's all this racket?

escandaloso ADJETIVO
noisy

el **escandinavo,** la **escandinava** ADJETIVO, SUSTANTIVO
Scandinavian
♦ **un escandinavo** a Scandinavian
♦ **una escandinava** a Scandinavian
♦ **los escandinavos** the Scandinavians

el **escáner** SUSTANTIVO
[1] scanner (*aparato*)
[2] scan (*imagen*) ◊ *hacerse un escáner* to have a scan

escapar VERBO
to escape ◊ *Conseguí escapar de la fiesta.* I managed to escape from the party.
♦ **No quiero dejar escapar esta oportunidad.** I don't want to let this opportunity slip.
♦ **escaparse** to escape ◊ *El ladrón se escapó de la cárcel.* The thief escaped from prison. ◊ *El calor se escapa por esta rendija.* The heat escapes through this grill.
♦ **Se me escapó un eructo.** I let out a burp.

el **escaparate** SUSTANTIVO
shop window (*de tienda*)

el **escape** SUSTANTIVO
leak ◊ *Había un escape de gas.* There was a gas leak.

escaquearse VERBO
♦ **escaquearse de clase** to skip school

el **escarabajo** SUSTANTIVO
beetle

escarbar VERBO
to dig ◊ *Los niños escarbaban en la arena.* The children were digging in the sand.

la **escarcha** SUSTANTIVO
frost

la **escasez** SUSTANTIVO
shortage ◊ *Hay escasez de medicamentos.* There is a shortage of medicine.

escaso ADJETIVO
scarce ◊ *Los alimentos están muy escasos.* Food is scarce.
♦ **Habrá escasa visibilidad en las carreteras.** Visibility on the roads will be poor.
♦ **Duró una hora escasa.** It lasted barely an hour.

la **escayola** SUSTANTIVO
plaster (*para fracturas*) ◊ *Mañana me quitan la escayola.* I'm getting my plaster taken off tomorrow.

escayolar VERBO
♦ **Le escayolaron la pierna.** They put his leg in plaster.

la **escena** SUSTANTIVO
scene

el **escenario** SUSTANTIVO
stage

escéptico ADJETIVO
sceptical

el **esclavo,** la **esclava** SUSTANTIVO
slave

la **escoba** SUSTANTIVO
broom

escocer* VERBO
to sting ◊ *Me escuecen los ojos.* My eyes are stinging.

escocés ADJETIVO (FEM **escocesa,** MASC PL **escoceses**)
Scottish
♦ **el whisky escocés** Scotch whisky
♦ **una falda escocesa** a kilt

el **escocés** SUSTANTIVO (MASC PL los **escoceses**)
Scotsman (PL Scotsmen) ◊ *los escoceses* Scottish people

la **escocesa** SUSTANTIVO
Scotswoman (PL Scotswomen)

Escocia SUSTANTIVO FEM
Scotland

escoger* VERBO
to choose ◊ *Yo escogí el azul.* I chose the blue one.

escolar ADJETIVO
school

> ***school** en este caso va siempre delante del sustantivo.*

◊ *el uniforme escolar* school uniform

los **escombros** SUSTANTIVO
rubble SING

esconder VERBO
to hide ◊ *Lo escondí en el cajón.* I hid it in the box.
♦ **Me escondí debajo de la cama.** I hid under the bed.

las **escondidas** SUSTANTIVO
♦ **jugar a las escondidas** [Latin America] to play hide-and-seek
♦ **a escondidas** in secret ◊ *Beben alcohol a escondidas.* They drink in secret.

el **escondite** SUSTANTIVO
♦ **jugar al escondite** to play hide-and-seek

la **escopeta** SUSTANTIVO
shotgun

Escorpio SUSTANTIVO MASC
Scorpio
♦ **Soy Escorpio.** I'm Scorpio.

el **escorpión** SUSTANTIVO (PL los **escorpiones**)
scorpion

escribir* VERBO
to write ◊ *Les escribí una carta.* I wrote them a letter. ◊ *Escribe pronto.* Write soon.
♦ **Nos escribimos de vez en cuando.** We write to each other from time to time.
♦ **¿Cómo se escribe tu nombre?** How do you spell your name?

☞

◆ **escribir a máquina** to type
escrito ADJETIVO
written ◇ *un examen escrito* a written exam
el **escritor,** la **escritora** SUSTANTIVO
writer ◇ *Pablo es escritor.* Pablo's a writer.
el **escritorio** SUSTANTIVO
1 desk (*mueble*)
2 office (*oficina*) Latin America
la **escritura** SUSTANTIVO
writing
escrupuloso ADJETIVO
fussy ◇ *No come en los bares porque es muy escrupuloso.* He doesn't eat in bars because he's very fussy.
escuchar VERBO
to listen ◇ *Juan escuchaba con atención.* Juan was listening attentively. ◇ *Escucha el consejo de tus padres.* Listen to your parents' advice. ◇ *Me gusta escuchar música.* I like listening to music.
el **escudo** SUSTANTIVO
1 shield (*de soldado*)
2 badge (*en la solapa*)
la **escuela** SUSTANTIVO
school ◇ *Hoy no tengo que ir a la escuela.* I don't have to go to school today.
◆ **la escuela primaria** primary school
◆ **Escuela Oficial de Idiomas**

> *The* ***Escuelas Oficiales*** *are state-run language schools where you can study a wide range of foreign languages. The qualification obtained is highly regarded.*

esculcar* VERBO Mexico
to search
la **escultura** SUSTANTIVO
sculpture
escupir VERBO
to spit
escurridizo ADJETIVO
slippery (*jabón, piel*)
el **escurridor** SUSTANTIVO
1 colander (*para pasta, verduras*)
2 plate rack (*para los platos*)
escurrir VERBO
1 to wring (*ropa*)
2 to drain (*verdura, pasta*)
ese ADJETIVO (FEM **esa**)
that ◇ *Dame ese libro.* Give me that book.
◆ **A partir de ese momento empezó a mejorar.** From then on it began to get better.
ése PRONOMBRE (FEM **ésa**)
that one ◇ *Prefiero ésa.* I prefer that one.
◆ **¿Quién es ése?** Who's that?
esencial ADJETIVO
essential
◆ **He entendido lo esencial de la conversación.** I understood the main points of the conversation.
esforzarse* VERBO
to make an effort ◇ *Tienes que esforzarte si quieres ganar.* You have to make an effort if you want to win.
◆ **Se esforzó todo lo que pudo por aprobar el examen.** He did all he could to pass the exam.
el **esfuerzo** SUSTANTIVO
effort ◇ *Tuve que hacer un esfuerzo para comer.* I had to make an effort to eat.
esfumarse VERBO
to vanish (*persona, dinero*)
la **esgrima** SUSTANTIVO
fencing
el **esguince** SUSTANTIVO
sprain
◆ **Me hice un esguince en el tobillo.** I've sprained my ankle.
el **esmalte** SUSTANTIVO
◆ **el esmalte de uñas** nail varnish
esmerarse VERBO
◆ **Se esmeró para que todo saliera bien.** He went to a lot of trouble so that everything would come out right.
◆ **No necesitas esmerarte tanto en la presentación.** You don't need to make such an effort with the presentation.
esnob ADJETIVO (PL **esnobs**)
snobbish
la **ESO** ABREVIATURA (= *Enseñanza Secundaria obligatoria*)

> *ESO is the compulsory secondary education course done by 12 to 16 year-olds.*

eso PRONOMBRE
that ◇ *Eso es mentira.* That's a lie. ◇ *¡Eso es!* That's it!
◆ **a eso de las cinco** at about five
◆ **En eso llamaron a la puerta.** Just then there was a ring at the door.
◆ **Por eso te lo dije.** That's why I told you.
◆ **¡Y eso que estaba lloviendo!** And it was raining and everything!
esos ADJETIVO PL (FEM **esas**)
those ◇ *Trae esas sillas aquí.* Bring those chairs over here.
ésos PRONOMBRE PL (FEM **ésas**)
those ones ◇ *Ésos de ahí son mejores.* Those ones over there are better.
◆ **Ésos no son los que vimos ayer.** Those aren't the ones we saw yesterday.
espabilar VERBO = **despabilar**
el **espacio** SUSTANTIVO

* Verbs marked with this symbol are irregular. See pages 380-382 for further details

[1] room (*sitio*) ◊ *No hay espacio para tantas sillas.* There isn't room for so many chairs. ◊ *El piano ocupa mucho espacio.* The piano takes up a lot of room.
[2] space (*entre dos cosas, palabras*) ◊ *Deja más espacio entre las líneas.* Leave more space between the lines.
♦ **un espacio en blanco** a gap
♦ **viajar por el espacio** to travel in space

la **espada** SUSTANTIVO
sword
♦ **espadas**

> *Espadas are swords, one of the suits in the Spanish card deck.*

*No confundir **espada** con **spade.***

los **espaguetis** SUSTANTIVO
spaghetti SING

la **espalda** SUSTANTIVO
back ◊ *Me duele la espalda.* My back aches.
♦ **Estaba tumbada de espaldas.** She was lying on her back.
♦ **Ana estaba de espaldas a mí.** Ana had her back to me.
♦ **Le dispararon por la espalda.** They shot him from behind.
♦ **Me encanta nadar a espalda.** I love swimming backstroke.

el **espantapájaros** SUSTANTIVO (PL los **espantapájaros**)
scarecrow

espantoso ADJETIVO
awful ◊ *un monstruo espantoso* an awful monster ◊ *Los niños hicieron un ruido espantoso.* The children made an awful noise.
♦ **Hacía un frío espantoso.** It was awfully cold.

España SUSTANTIVO FEM
Spain

español ADJETIVO (FEM **española**)
Spanish

el **español,** la **española** SUSTANTIVO
Spaniard
♦ **los españoles** the Spanish

el **español** SUSTANTIVO
Spanish (*idioma*)

el **esparadrapo** SUSTANTIVO
plaster ◊ *Me puse un esparadrapo en el dedo.* I put a plaster on my finger.

el **espárrago** SUSTANTIVO
asparagus ◊ *¿Te gustan los espárragos?* Do you like asparagus?
♦ **La mandé a freir espárragos.** I told her to buzz off. (*coloquial*)

la **especia** SUSTANTIVO
spice

especial ADJETIVO
special ◊ *Fue un día muy especial.* It was a very special day.
♦ **en especial** particularly ◊ *¿Desea ver a alguien en especial?* Is there anybody you particularly want to see?

la **especialidad** SUSTANTIVO
speciality (PL specialities) ◊ *la especialidad de la casa* the speciality of the house

el/la **especialista** SUSTANTIVO
specialist

especializarse* VERBO
♦ **Rosario se especializó en pediatría.** Rosario specialized in paediatrics.

especialmente ADVERBIO
[1] especially (*sobre todo*) ◊ *Me gusta mucho el pan, especialmente el integral.* I love bread, especially wholemeal bread.
[2] specially (*expresamente*) ◊ *un vestido diseñado especialmente para ella* a dress designed specially for her

la **especie** SUSTANTIVO
species (*animal, planta*)

específico ADJETIVO
specific

espectacular ADJETIVO
spectacular

el **espectáculo** SUSTANTIVO
performance (*función*) ◊ *El espectáculo empieza a las ocho.* The performance starts at eight.
♦ **Dio el espectáculo delante de todo el mundo.** He made a spectacle of himself in front of everyone.

el **espectador,** la **espectadora** SUSTANTIVO
spectator (*en estadio, pista de tenis*)
♦ **los espectadores** (*en teatro, concierto*) the audience

el **espejo** SUSTANTIVO
mirror ◊ *Me miré en el espejo.* I looked at myself in the mirror.
♦ **el espejo retrovisor** rearview mirror

espeluznante ADJETIVO
hair-raising

la **espera** SUSTANTIVO
wait ◊ *tras una espera de tres horas* after a three-hour wait
♦ **estar a la espera de algo** to be expecting something

la **esperanza** SUSTANTIVO
hope
♦ **No tengo esperanzas de aprobar.** I have no hope of passing.
♦ **No pierdas las esperanzas.** Don't give up hope.

esperar VERBO
[1] to wait ◊ *Espera en la puerta. Ahora mismo voy.* Wait at the door. I'm just coming.
♦ **Espera un momento, por favor.** Hang on a moment, please.
[2] to wait for ◊ *No me esperéis.* Don't wait for me.
♦ **Me hizo esperar una hora.** He kept me waiting for an hour.

☞

[3] to expect ◇ *Llegaron antes de lo que yo esperaba.* They arrived sooner than I expected. ◇ *Esperaban que Juan les pidiera perdón.* They were expecting Juan to apologize. ◇ *Llamará cuando menos lo esperes.* He'll call when you're least expecting it. ◇ *No esperes que venga a ayudarte.* Don't expect him to come and help you.
◆ **esperar un bebé** to be expecting a baby
◆ **Me espera un largo día de trabajo.** I've got a long day of work ahead of me.
◆ **Era de esperar que no viniera.** He was bound not to come.
[4] to hope ◇ *Espero que no sea nada grave.* I hope it isn't anything serious.
◆ **¿Vendrás a la fiesta? – Espero que sí.** Are you coming to the party? – I hope so.
◆ **¿Crees que Carmen se enfadará? – Espero que no.** Do you think Carmen will be angry? – I hope not.
◆ **Fuimos a esperarla a la estación.** We went to the station to meet her.

espeso ADJETIVO
thick (*salsa, chocolate*)

el/la **espía** SUSTANTIVO
spy (PL spies)

espiar* VERBO
to spy on ◇ *Los vecinos nos estaban espiando.* The neighbours were spying on us.

la **espina** SUSTANTIVO
[1] thorn (*de rosal*)
[2] bone (*de pez*)
◆ **espina dorsal** backbone

la **espinaca** SUSTANTIVO
spinach ◇ *No me gustan las espinacas.* I don't like spinach.

la **espinilla** SUSTANTIVO
[1] shin (*de la pierna*)
[2] blackhead (*grano*)

el **espionaje** SUSTANTIVO
spying
◆ **una novela de espionaje** a spy story

espirar VERBO
to breathe out

el **espíritu** SUSTANTIVO
spirit

espiritual ADJETIVO
spiritual

espléndido ADJETIVO
splendid (*día, comida*)

la **esponja** SUSTANTIVO
sponge

esponjoso ADJETIVO
spongy

espontáneo ADJETIVO
spontaneous ◇ *Fue una reacción espontánea.* It was a spontaneous reaction.
◆ **de manera espontánea** spontaneously

la **esposa** SUSTANTIVO
wife (PL wives)
◆ **las esposas** (*para detenidos*) handcuffs

el **esposo** SUSTANTIVO
husband

la **espuma** SUSTANTIVO
[1] foam (*de jabón, champú*)
[2] head (*de cerveza*)
◆ **la espuma de afeitar** shaving cream

espumoso ADJETIVO
◆ **vino espumoso** sparkling wine

el **esqueleto** SUSTANTIVO
skeleton

el **esquema** SUSTANTIVO
[1] outline (*resumen*)
[2] diagram (*croquis*)

el **esquí** SUSTANTIVO (PL los **esquís**)
[1] (*deporte*)
skiing ◇ *Me gusta mucho el esquí.* I enjoy skiing a lot.
◆ **el esquí acuático** water skiing
◆ **una pista de esquí** a ski slope
[2] (*tabla*)
ski (PL skis)

esquiar* VERBO
to ski ◇ *¿Sabes esquiar?* Can you ski?

el/la **esquimal** ADJETIVO, SUSTANTIVO
Eskimo (PL Eskimos)

la **esquina** SUSTANTIVO
corner
◆ **doblar la esquina** to turn the corner

esquivar VERBO
to dodge (*coche, golpe*)

esta ADJETIVO *ver* **este**

ésta PRONOMBRE *ver* **éste**

está VERBO *ver* **estar**

estable ADJETIVO
stable

establecer* VERBO
to establish (*relación*) ◇ *Se ha establecido una buena relación entre los dos países.* A good relationship has been established between the two countries.
◆ **Han logrado establecer contacto con el barco.** They've managed to make contact with the boat.
◆ **La familia se estableció en Madrid.** The family settled in Madrid.

el **establecimiento** SUSTANTIVO
establishment
◆ **un establecimiento comercial** a commercial establishment

el **establo** SUSTANTIVO
stable

la **estación** SUSTANTIVO (PL las **estaciones**)
[1] station ◇ *la estación de autobuses* the bus station
[2] season ◇ *las cuatro estaciones del año* the four seasons of the year

* Verbs marked with this symbol are irregular. See pages 380-382 for further details

◆ **una estación de esquí** a ski resort
◆ **una estación de servicio** a service station

estacionar VERBO
to park (*coche*)

estacionarse VERBO
Chile, River Plate, Mexico
to park

la **estadía** SUSTANTIVO Latin America
stay

el **estadio** SUSTANTIVO
stadium

el **estado** SUSTANTIVO
state ◊ *La carretera está en mal estado.* The road is in a bad state.
◆ **El Estado Español** The Spanish State
◆ **estado civil** marital status
◆ **María está en estado.** María is expecting.

los **Estados Unidos** SUSTANTIVO PL
the United States ◊ *en Estados Unidos* in the United States
A menudo se les llama simplemente "The States".

el/la **estadounidense** ADJETIVO, SUSTANTIVO
American

estafar VERBO
to swindle ◊ *Les estafaron 8 millones de pesetas.* They swindled 8 million pesetas out of them.

estallar VERBO
1 to explode (*bomba*)
2 to burst (*neumático, globo*)
3 to break out (*guerra, revolución*)

la **estampilla** SUSTANTIVO Latin America
stamp

estancado ADJETIVO
stagnant (*agua*)

la **estancia** SUSTANTIVO
1 (*permanencia*)
stay
2 (*rancho*)
ranch (PL ranches)

el **estanco** SUSTANTIVO
tobacconist's

estándar ADJETIVO
standard ◊ *Éstos son los modelos estándar.* These are the standard models.

el **estanque** SUSTANTIVO
pond

el **estante** SUSTANTIVO
shelf (PL shelves) ◊ *Puse los libros en el estante.* I put the books on the shelf.

la **estantería** SUSTANTIVO
1 shelves PL ◊ *la estantería de la cocina* the kitchen shelves
2 bookshelves PL (*para libros*)
3 shelf unit (*mueble*)

el **estaño** SUSTANTIVO
tin

estar* VERBO
indicando una posición
1 to be
*El verbo **to be** en presente suele usarse en las formas contraídas, particularmente al hablar.*
◊ *En la cama se está muy bien.* It's nice being in bed. ◊ *¿Dónde estabas?* Where were you? ◊ *Madrid está en el centro de España.* Madrid is in the centre of Spain.
◆ **¿Está Mónica?** Is Mónica there?
Indicando una situación o estado.
◊ *¿Cómo estás?* How are you? ◊ *Estoy muy cansada.* I'm very tired. ◊ *¿Estás casado o soltero?* Are you married or single? ◊ *Estamos de vacaciones.* We're on holiday.
◆ **Hoy no estoy para bromas.** I'm not in the mood for jokes today.
Indicando el aspecto de algo.
2 to look ◊ *¡Qué guapa estás esta noche!* You look really pretty tonight! ◊ *Ese vestido te está muy bien.* That dress looks very good on you.
Indicando el precio de algo.
◊ *¿A cuánto está el kilo de naranjas?* What price are oranges per kilo?
Con fechas y temperaturas.
◊ *Estamos a 30 de enero.* It's 30 January. ◊ *Estábamos a 40°C.* The temperature was 40°C.
*Cuando **estar** va seguido de un gerundio o un participio también se traduce por **to be**.*
◊ *Estamos esperando a Manolo.* We're waiting for Manolo. ◊ *María estaba sentada en la arena.* María was sitting on the sand. ◊ *La radio está rota.* The radio's broken.
◆ **¡Ya está! Ya sé lo que podemos hacer.** That's it! I know what we can do.
◆ **estarse** to be ◊ *¡Estáte quieto!* Keep still!

estas ADJETIVO *ver* **estos**

éstas PRONOMBRE *ver* **éstos**

estatal ADJETIVO
state
***state** en este caso va siempre delante del sustantivo.*
◊ *un colegio estatal* a state school

la **estatua** SUSTANTIVO
statue

la **estatura** SUSTANTIVO
height ◊ *¿Cuál es tu estatura?* What height are you? ◊ *Mide casi dos metros de estatura.* He's over six and half feet tall.

el **este** SUSTANTIVO, ADJETIVO
east ◊ *el este del país* the east of the country ◊ *en la costa este* on the east coast ◊ *en el este de España* in the East of Spain
◆ **vientos del este** easterly winds
◆ **los países del Este** the Eastern bloc countries

este ADJETIVO (FEM **esta**)
this ◊ *este libro* this book

éste PRONOMBRE (FEM **ésta**)
this one ◇ *Ésta me gusta más.* I prefer this one.
◆ **Éste no es el que vi ayer.** This is not the one I saw yesterday.

esté VERBO *ver* **estar**

la **estera** SUSTANTIVO
mat

el **estéreo** SUSTANTIVO (PL los **estéreos**)
stereo (PL stereos)

esterlina ADJETIVO
◆ **diez libras esterlinas** ten pounds sterling

estético ADJETIVO
◆ **Se ha hecho la cirugía estética.** He's had plastic surgery.

el **estiércol** SUSTANTIVO
manure (*abono*)

el **estilo** SUSTANTIVO
style ◇ *Ése no es mi estilo.* That's not my style.
◆ **un estilo de vida similar al nuestro** a similar lifestyle to ours
◆ **Tiene mucho estilo vistiendo.** He dresses very stylishly.

la **estima** SUSTANTIVO
◆ **Lo tengo en gran estima.** I think very highly of him.

estimulante ADJETIVO
stimulating (*trabajo*)

estimular VERBO
1 to encourage (*persona*) ◇ *Es una forma de estimular a los jugadores a esforzarse más.* It's a way of encouraging the players to try harder.
2 to stimulate (*economía*)

estirar VERBO
to stretch ◇ *Voy a salir a estirar las piernas.* I'm going to go out and stretch my legs.

esto PRONOMBRE
this ◇ *¿Para qué es esto?* What's this for?
◆ **En esto llegó Juan.** Just then Juan arrived.

el **estofado** SUSTANTIVO
stew

el **estómago** SUSTANTIVO
stomach ◇ *Me dolía el estómago.* I had stomach ache.

estorbar VERBO
to be in the way ◇ *Estas maletas estorban aquí.* These cases are in the way here.

estornudar VERBO
to sneeze

estos ADJETIVO PL (FEM **estas**)
these
◆ **estas maletas** these cases

éstos PRONOMBRE PL (FEM **éstas**)
these ones ◇ *Éstos son los míos.* These ones are mine.
◆ **Éstos no son los que vimos ayer.** These are not the ones we saw yesterday.
◆ **un día de éstos** one of these days

estoy VERBO *ver* **estar**

estrafalario ADJETIVO
1 eccentric (*persona, ideas*)
2 outlandish (*ropa*)

estrangular VERBO
to strangle

estratégico ADJETIVO
strategic

estrechar VERBO
to take in ◇ *¿Me puedes estrechar esta falda?* Can you take in this skirt for me?
◆ **La carretera se estrecha en el puente.** The road gets narrower over the bridge.
◆ **Se estrecharon la mano.** They shook hands.

estrecho ADJETIVO
1 narrow (*calle, pasillo*)
2 tight ◇ *La falda me va muy estrecha.* The skirt is very tight on me.

el **estrecho** SUSTANTIVO
strait
◆ **el estrecho de Gibraltar** the straits of Gibraltar

la **estrella** SUSTANTIVO
star
◆ **una estrella de cine** a film star
◆ **una estrella de mar** a starfish

estrellarse VERBO
to smash ◇ *El camión se estrelló contra un árbol.* The lorry smashed into a tree.

estrenar VERBO
to premiere ◇ *La película se estrenó en Junio.* The film was premiered in June.
◆ **Mañana estrenaré el vestido.** I'll wear the dress for the first time tomorrow.

el **estreno** SUSTANTIVO
premiere (*de película*)

estreñido ADJETIVO
constipated

el **estrés** SUSTANTIVO
stress

estricto ADJETIVO
strict

estridente ADJETIVO
loud

el **estropajo** SUSTANTIVO
scourer

estropeado ADJETIVO
1 broken (*lavadora, tele, radio*)
2 broken down (*coche, motor*)

estropear VERBO
1 to break (*juguete, lavadora*)
2 to ruin ◇ *Ese detergente me estropeó la ropa.* That detergent ruined my clothes. ◇ *La lluvia nos estropeó las vacaciones.* The rain ruined our holidays.

♦**estropearse** to break ◊ *Se nos ha estropeado la tele.* The TV's broken.
♦**Se me estropeó el coche en la autopista.** My car broke down on the motorway.
♦**La fruta se está estropeando con este calor.** The fruit's going off in this heat.

la **estructura** SUSTANTIVO
structure

estrujar VERBO
[1] to squeeze (*limón, naranja*)
[2] to wring (*bayeta, trapo*)

el **estuche** SUSTANTIVO
case (*de gafas, lápices*)

el/la **estudiante** SUSTANTIVO
student

estudiar VERBO
[1] to study ◊ *Quiere estudiar medicina.* She wants to study medicine.
[2] to learn ◊ *Tengo que estudiar cuatro lecciones para el examen.* I have to learn four lessons for the exam.

el **estudio** SUSTANTIVO
[1] studio (*de televisión*)
[2] studio flat (*apartamento*)
♦**Ha dejado los estudios.** He's given up his studies.

estudioso ADJETIVO
studious

la **estufa** SUSTANTIVO
[1] heater ◊ *una estufa eléctrica* an electric heater
[2] stove Mexico

estupendamente ADVERBIO
♦**Me encuentro estupendamente.** (*coloquial*) I feel great.
♦**Nos lo pasamos estupendamente.** (*coloquial*) We had a great time.

estupendo ADJETIVO
great (*coloquial*) ◊ *Pasamos unas Navidades estupendas.* We had a great Christmas.
♦**¡Estupendo!** Great!

la **estupidez** SUSTANTIVO (PL las **estupideces**)
♦**No dice más que estupideces.** He just talks rubbish.
♦**Lo que hizo fue una estupidez.** What he did was stupid.

estúpido ADJETIVO
stupid

el **estúpido**, la **estúpida** SUSTANTIVO
idiot ◊ *Ese tío es un estúpido.* That guy's an idiot.

estuve VERBO *ver* **estar**

la **etapa** SUSTANTIVO
stage ◊ *Lo hicimos por etapas.* We did it in stages.

etc. ABREVIATURA (= *etcétera*)
etc.

eterno ADJETIVO
eternal

la **ética** SUSTANTIVO
[1] ethics (*asignatura*)
[2] ethics PL (*principios morales*)

ético ADJETIVO
ethical

Etiopía SUSTANTIVO FEM
Ethiopia

la **etiqueta** SUSTANTIVO
label
♦**traje de etiqueta** formal dress

étnico ADJETIVO
ethnic

ETT ABREVIATURA (= *Empresa de Trabajo Temporal*)
temp agency

eufórico ADJETIVO
ecstatic

el **euro** SUSTANTIVO
euro

Europa SUSTANTIVO FEM
Europe

el **europeo**, la **europea** ADJETIVO, SUSTANTIVO
European

Euskadi SUSTANTIVO
the Basque Country

el **euskera** SUSTANTIVO
Basque

> *Basque is one of Spain's four official languages, and there is Basque-language radio and television. It is not from the same family of languages as Spanish.*

evacuar* VERBO
to evacuate

evadir VERBO
[1] to avoid (*peligro, pregunta*)
[2] to evade (*impuestos*)

la **evaluación** SUSTANTIVO (PL las **evaluaciones**)
assessment ◊ *evaluación continua* continuous assessment

evaluar* VERBO
to assess (*pérdidas, daños, estudiante*)

el **evangelio** SUSTANTIVO
gospel

evaporarse VERBO
to evaporate

evasivo ADJETIVO
evasive

eventual ADJETIVO
♦**un trabajo eventual** a temporary job

la **evidencia** SUSTANTIVO
evidence
♦**Ante la evidencia de las hechos, se confesó culpable.** Faced with the evidence, he pleaded guilty.
♦**La puso en evidencia delante de todos.** He showed her up in front of everyone.

evidente ADJETIVO
obvious
♦**Era evidente que estaba agotada.** She was obviously exhausted.

evidentemente ADVERBIO
obviously

evitar VERBO
1 to avoid (*eludir*) ◊ *Quiero evitar ese riesgo.* I want to avoid that risk. ◊ *Intento evitar a Luisa.* I'm trying to avoid Luisa.
♦ **No pude evitarlo.** I couldn't help it.
2 to save (*ahorrar*) ◊ *Esto nos evitará muchos problemas.* This will save us a lot of problems.

la **evolución** SUSTANTIVO (PL las **evoluciones**)
progress ◊ *Seguimos de cerca la evolución del paciente.* We are keeping a close watch on the patient's progress.
♦ **la teoría de la evolución** the theory of evolution

evolucionar VERBO
1 to develop ◊ *Este país no ha evolucionado en la última década.* This country hasn't developed in the last decade.
♦ **El enfermo evoluciona favorablemente.** The patient is making good progress.
2 to evolve (*especie*)

ex PREFIJO
ex
♦ **su ex-marido** her ex-husband

exactamente ADVERBIO
exactly

la **exactitud** SUSTANTIVO
♦ **No lo sabemos con exactitud.** We don't know exactly.

exacto ADJETIVO
1 exact ◊ *el precio exacto* the exact price
♦ **El tren salió a la hora exacta.** The train left bang on time.
2 accurate ◊ *Tus conclusiones no son muy exactas.* Your conclusions aren't very accurate.
♦ **Tenemos que defender nuestros derechos. – ¡Exacto!** We have to stand up for our rights. – Exactly!

la **exageración** SUSTANTIVO (PL las **exageraciones**)
exaggeration

exagerado ADJETIVO
exaggerated (*descripción*)
♦ **¡No seas exagerada, no era tan alto!** Don't exaggerate! He wasn't that tall.
♦ **El precio me parece exagerado.** I think the price is excessive.

exagerar VERBO
to exaggerate

el **examen** SUSTANTIVO (PL los **exámenes**)
exam
♦ **el examen de conducir** driving test

examinar VERBO
to examine ◊ *El médico la examinó.* The doctor examined her. ◊ *Nos examinaron dos profesores.* We were examined by two teachers.
♦ **Mañana me examino de inglés.** Tomorrow I've got an English exam.

la **excavadora** SUSTANTIVO
digger

excavar VERBO
to dig ◊ *Los niños excavaban en la arena.* The children were digging in the sand. ◊ *Están excavando un túnel.* They're digging a tunnel.

excelente ADJETIVO
excellent

excéntrico ADJETIVO
eccentric

la **excepción** SUSTANTIVO (PL las **excepciones**)
exception
♦ **a excepción de** except for

excepcional ADJETIVO
exceptional

excepto PREPOSICIÓN
except for ◊ *todos, excepto Juan* everyone, except for Juan

excesivo ADJETIVO
excessive

el **exceso** SUSTANTIVO
♦ **Anoche bebí en exceso.** Last night I drank to excess.
♦ **exceso de equipaje** excess luggage
♦ **Me multaron por exceso de velocidad.** They fined me for speeding.

excitarse VERBO
◊ *Se excitó mucho en la discusión.* He got very worked up in the argument.

exclamar VERBO
to exclaim

excluir* VERBO
to exclude ◊ *Me excluyeron de la lista.* They excluded me from the list.

exclusivo ADJETIVO
exclusive (*club, diseño*)

excluyendo VERBO *ver* **excluir**

la **excursión** SUSTANTIVO (PL las **excursiones**)
trip ◊ *Mañana vamos de excursión con el colegio.* Tomorrow we're going on a school trip.

la **excusa** SUSTANTIVO
excuse

la **exhibición** SUSTANTIVO (PL las **exhibiciones**)
exhibition (*de arte*)

exhibir VERBO
to exhibit (*obras de arte*)
♦ **Le gusta mucho exhibirse.** He likes drawing attention to himself.

exigente ADJETIVO
demanding ◊ *El jefe es muy exigente con nosotros.* The boss is very demanding with us.

exigir* VERBO

1 to demand ◇ *Exigió hablar con el encargado.* He demanded to speak to the manager.
♦ **La maestra nos exige demasiado.** Our teacher is too demanding.
2 to require ◇ *Ese puesto exige mucha paciencia.* This job requires a lot of patience.
♦ **Exigen tres años de experiencia para el puesto.** They're asking for three years' experience for the job.

el **exiliado,** la **exiliada** SUSTANTIVO
exile

existir VERBO
to exist ◇ *¿Existen los fantasmas?* Do ghosts exist?
♦ **Existen dos maneras de hacerlo.** There are two ways of doing it.

el **éxito** SUSTANTIVO
success (PL successes) ◇ *Esa novela será un gran éxito.* That novel will be a great success.
♦ **Su película tuvo mucho éxito.** His film was very successful.
♦ **Acabaron con éxito el proyecto.** They completed the project successfully.
*No confundir **éxito** con **exit**.*

exótico ADJETIVO
exotic

la **expansión** SUSTANTIVO (PL las **expansiones**)
expansion

la **expedición** SUSTANTIVO (PL las **expediciones**)
expedition

el **expediente** SUSTANTIVO
file (*documentación*)
♦ **expediente académico** student record
♦ **Le han abierto expediente por mala conducta.** He has been disciplined for bad behaviour.

el **expendio** SUSTANTIVO Latin America
shop (*tienda*)

expensas SUSTANTIVO FEM PL
♦ **a expensas de su salud** at the cost of her health
♦ **vivir a expensas de alguien** to live at somebody's expense

la **experiencia** SUSTANTIVO
experience ◇ *"Se requiere experiencia laboral"* "Work experience required"
♦ **con experiencia** experienced
♦ **sin experiencia** inexperienced

experimental ADJETIVO
experimental

experimentar VERBO
1 to experiment ◇ *experimentar con animales* to experiment on animals
2 to experience (*dolor, alegría*)

el **experimento** SUSTANTIVO
experiment

el **experto,** la **experta** SUSTANTIVO
expert
♦ **Es un experto en informática.** He's a computer expert.

la **explanada** SUSTANTIVO
open area

la **explicación** SUSTANTIVO (PL las **explicaciones**)
explanation

explicar* VERBO
to explain
*La preposición **to** debe aparecer delante del objeto indirecto.*
◇ *Le expliqué cómo se hacía una paella.* I explained to her how to make a paella.
♦ **Antonio se explica muy bien.** Antonio is very good at expressing himself.
♦ **¿Me explico?** Do I make myself clear?
♦ **No me lo explico.** I can't understand it.

el **explorador,** la **exploradora** SUSTANTIVO
explorer

explorar VERBO
to explore

la **explosión** SUSTANTIVO (PL las **explosiones**)
explosion
♦ **El artefacto hizo explosión.** The device exploded.

el **explosivo** SUSTANTIVO
explosive

la **explotación** SUSTANTIVO (PL las **explotaciones**)
exploitation

explotar VERBO
1 to exploit (*tierra, trabajador*) ◇ *Sabe cómo explotar sus posibilidades.* He knows how to exploit his potential.
2 to explode ◇ *La caldera explotó.* The boiler exploded.

exponer* VERBO
1 to display (*cuadro, productos*)
2 to present (*idea*)

la **exportación** SUSTANTIVO (PL las **exportaciones**)
export

exportar VERBO
to export

la **exposición** SUSTANTIVO (PL las **exposiciones**)
exhibition ◇ *montar una exposición* to put on an exhibition

expresamente ADVERBIO
1 specifically ◇ *Mencioné expresamente tu nombre.* I specifically mentioned your name.
2 specially ◇ *Fui expresamente a devolvérselo.* I went specially to give it back to him.

expresar VERBO
to express ◇ *No sabe expresarse.* He doesn't know how to express himself.

la **expresión** SUSTANTIVO (PL las **expresiones**)
expression

expresivo ADJETIVO
expressive

E

el **expreso** SUSTANTIVO
1 express (*tren*)
2 espresso (*café*)
exprimir VERBO
to squeeze (*limón, naranja*)
expuesto VERBO *ver* **exponer**
expulsar VERBO
1 to expel ◊ *La expulsaron del colegio.* They expelled her from school.
2 to send off ◊ *El árbitro lo expulsó del terreno de juego.* The referee sent him off the pitch.
la **expulsión** SUSTANTIVO (PL las **expulsiones**)
expulsion (*de colegio, territorio*)
♦ **La expulsión del jugador fue injusta.** Sending the player off was unfair.
exquisito ADJETIVO
delicious ◊ *El postre estaba exquisito.* The dessert was delicious.
el **éxtasis** SUSTANTIVO
ecstasy
extender* VERBO
to spread (*mantequilla, pintura*) ◊ *Extendí la toalla sobre la arena.* I spread the towel out on the sand. ◊ *El fuego se extendió rápidamente.* The fire spread quickly.
♦ **extender los brazos** to stretch one's arms out
extendido ADJETIVO
outstretched (*brazos, alas*)
la **extensión** SUSTANTIVO (PL las **extensiones**)
area ◊ *una enorme extensión de tierra* an enormous area of land
♦ **¿Me pone con la extensión 212, por favor?** Can you put me through to extension 212, please?
extenso ADJETIVO
extensive (*superficie, conocimientos*)
exterior ADJETIVO (FEM **exterior**)
1 outside (*pared, superficie*)
2 foreign (*política, comercio*)
el **exterior** SUSTANTIVO
outside
♦ **Salimos al exterior para ver qué pasaba.** We went outside to see what was going on.
externo ADJETIVO
1 outside (*influencia*)
2 outer (*superficie*)
extiendo VERBO *ver* **extender**
la **extinción** SUSTANTIVO
putting out (*de incendio*)
♦ **una especie en vías de extinción** an endangered species
el **extinguidor** SUSTANTIVO Latin America
fire extinguisher
extinguir* VERBO
to put out (*fuego*)
♦ **extinguirse** to become extinct (*volcán*)
♦ **El fuego se fue extinguiendo lentamente.** The fire was slowly going out.
extinto ADJETIVO
extinct
el **extintor** SUSTANTIVO
fire extinguisher
extra ADJETIVO
extra ◊ *una manta extra* an extra blanket
♦ **chocolate de calidad extra** top quality chocolate
el/la **extra** SUSTANTIVO
extra (*de cine*)
el **extractor** SUSTANTIVO
extractor fan ◊ *un extractor de humos* a smoke extractor
extraer* VERBO
1 to extract ◊ *El dentista me ha extraído la muela.* The dentist has extracted my tooth.
2 to draw (*conclusiones*)
extraescolar ADJETIVO
♦ **actividades extraescolares** extracurricular activities
extraigo VERBO *ver* **extraer**
extranjero ADJETIVO
foreign
el **extranjero**, la **extranjera** SUSTANTIVO
foreigner (*persona*)
♦ **vivir en el extranjero** to live abroad
♦ **viajar al extranjero** to travel abroad
extrañar VERBO
to miss ◊ *Extraña mucho a sus padres.* He misses his parents a lot.
♦ **Me extraña que no haya llegado.** I'm surprised he hasn't arrived.
♦ **¡Ya me extrañaba a mí!** I thought it was strange!
♦ **extrañarse de algo** to be surprised at something ◊ *Se extrañó de vernos juntos.* He was surprised to see us together.
la **extrañeza** SUSTANTIVO
♦ **Nos miró con extrañeza.** He looked at us in surprise.
extraño ADJETIVO
strange
♦ **¡Qué extraño!** How strange!
extraordinario ADJETIVO
extraordinary
extravagante ADJETIVO
extravagant
extraviado ADJETIVO
1 lost (*objeto*)
2 missing (*persona, animal*)
extraviar* VERBO
to mislay ◊ *Me extraviaron el equipaje en el aeropuerto.* They mislaid my luggage at the airport.
el/la **extremista** ADJETIVO, SUSTANTIVO

extremist

extremo ADJETIVO

extreme ◊ *Ése es un caso extremo.* That's an extreme case.

◆ **la extrema derecha** the far Right

◆ **extremo derecho** (*jugador*) right winger

◆ **el Extremo Oriente** the Far East

el **extremo** SUSTANTIVO

end (*punta*) ◊ *Cogí la cuerda por un extremo.* I took hold of one end of the rope.

◆ **pasar de un extremo a otro** to go from one extreme to the other

◆ **en último extremo** as a last resort

extrovertido ADJETIVO

outgoing ◊ *José es muy extrovertido.* José is very outgoing.

exuberante ADJETIVO

lush (*vegetación*)

F

la **fábrica** SUSTANTIVO
factory (PL factories)
◆ **una fábrica de cerveza** a brewery
*No confundir **fábrica** con **fabric**.*

el/la **fabricante** SUSTANTIVO
manufacturer

fabricar* VERBO
to make
◆ **"fabricado en China"** "made in China"

la **fachada** SUSTANTIVO
◆ **la fachada del edificio** the front of the building

fácil ADJETIVO
easy ◊ *El examen fue muy fácil.* The exam was very easy.
◆ **Es fácil de entender.** It's easy to understand.
◆ **Es fácil que se le haya perdido.** He may have lost it.

la **facilidad** SUSTANTIVO
◆ **Se me rompen las uñas con facilidad.** My nails break easily.
◆ **Pepe tiene facilidad para los idiomas.** Pepe has a gift for languages.
◆ **Te dan facilidades de pago.** They offer credit facilities.

facilitar VERBO
to make...easier ◊ *Un ordenador facilita mucho el trabajo.* A computer makes work much easier.
◆ **El banco me facilitó la información.** The bank provided me with the information.

el **factor** SUSTANTIVO
factor ◊ *La edad del paciente es un factor importante.* The age of the patient is an important factor.

la **factura** SUSTANTIVO
bill ◊ *la factura del gas* the gas bill

facturar VERBO
to check in (*en el aeropuerto*)

la **facultad** SUSTANTIVO
1 faculty (PL faculties) ◊ *Mi abuela está perdiendo facultades.* My grandmother is losing her faculties.
◆ **la Facultad de Derecho** the Law Faculty
2 university
◆ **ir a la facultad** to go to university

la **falda** SUSTANTIVO
skirt

fallar VERBO
to fail (*frenos, motor, vista*) ◊ *Le falla la memoria.* His memory is failing.
◆ **Fallé el tiro.** I missed.

fallecer* VERBO
to die

el **fallo** SUSTANTIVO
1 fault (*defecto leve*) ◊ *un pequeño fallo eléctrico* a small electrical fault
2 failure (*defecto grave*) ◊ *debido a un fallo de motor* due to engine failure
3 mistake (*error*) ◊ *¡Qué fallo!* What a stupid mistake!
◆ **Fue un fallo humano.** It was human error.

falsificar* VERBO
to forge (*firma, documento*)

falso ADJETIVO
1 false (*nombre, pasaporte*)
2 forged (*billete*)
◆ **Los diamantes eran falsos.** The diamonds were fakes.
◆ **Eso es falso.** That's not true.

la **falta** SUSTANTIVO
1 lack (*carencia*) ◊ *la falta de dinero* lack of money
2 foul (*en fútbol, baloncesto*) ◊ *Ha sido falta.* It was a foul.
◆ **Tiene cinco faltas de asistencia.** He has been absent five times.
◆ **Eso es una falta de educación.** That's bad manners.
◆ **una falta de ortografía** a spelling mistake
◆ **Me hace falta un ordenador.** I need a computer.
◆ **No hace falta que vengáis.** You don't need to come.

faltar VERBO
to be missing ◊ *Me falta un bolígrafo.* One of my pens is missing.
◆ **Faltan varios libros del estante.** There are several books missing from the shelf.
◆ **No podemos irnos. Falta Manolo.** We can't go. Manolo isn't here yet.
◆ **A la sopa le falta sal.** There isn't enough salt in the soup.
◆ **Falta media hora para comer.** There's half an hour to go before lunch.
◆ **¿Te falta mucho?** Will you be long?
◆ **faltar al colegio** to miss school

la **fama** SUSTANTIVO
fame
◆ **llegar a la fama** to become famous
◆ **tener mala fama** to have a bad reputation
◆ **Tiene fama de mujeriego.** He has a reputation for being a womanizer.

la **familia** SUSTANTIVO
family (PL families)
◆ **una familia numerosa** a large family

familiar ADJETIVO
1 family

* Verbs marked with this symbol are irregular. See pages 380-382 for further details

family en este caso va siempre delante del sustantivo.

◊ *la vida familiar* family life

[2] familiar ◊ *Su cara me es familiar.* Your face is familiar.

el/la **familiar** SUSTANTIVO
relative ◊ *un familiar mío* a relative of mine

famoso ADJETIVO
famous

el/la **fan** SUSTANTIVO (PL los **fans**)
fan

la **fantasía** SUSTANTIVO
fantasy (PL fantasies) ◊ *un mundo de fantasía* a fantasy world ◊ *Son fantasías infantiles.* They're just children's fantasies.
♦ **las joyas de fantasía** costume jewellery SING

el **fantasma** SUSTANTIVO
ghost

fantástico ADJETIVO
fantastic

el **farmacéutico**, la **farmacéutica** SUSTANTIVO
chemist

la **farmacia** SUSTANTIVO
chemist's (PL chemists' shops) ◊ *Lo compré en la farmacia.* I bought it at the chemist's.
♦ **una farmacia de guardia** a duty chemist's

el **faro** SUSTANTIVO
[1] lighthouse (*en la costa*)
[2] headlight (*de coche, moto*)
[3] lamp (*de bicicleta*)
♦ **los faros antiniebla** foglamps

el **farol** SUSTANTIVO
[1] streetlamp (*en la calle*)
[2] lantern (*en el jardín*)

la **farola** SUSTANTIVO
[1] streetlamp (*lámpara*) ◊ *a la luz de las farolas* by the light of the streetlamps
[2] lamppost (*poste*) ◊ *El coche dio contra una farola.* The car hit a lamppost.

el **fascículo** SUSTANTIVO
part ◊ *el primer fascículo del libro* the first part of the book

fascinante ADJETIVO
fascinating

el/la **fascista** ADJETIVO, SUSTANTIVO
fascist

la **fase** SUSTANTIVO
phase

fastidiar VERBO
[1] to annoy ◊ *Lo que más me fastidia es tener que decírselo.* What annoys me most is having to tell him.
♦ **Esa actitud me fastidia mucho.** I find this attitude very annoying.
[2] to pester ◊ *¡Deja ya de fastidiarme!* Will you stop pestering me!
[3] to spoil ◊ *El accidente nos fastidió las vacaciones.* The accident spoilt our holidays.

el **fastidio** SUSTANTIVO
♦ **¡Qué fastidio!** What a nuisance!

fatal (1) ADJETIVO
awful ◊ *Nos hizo un tiempo fatal.* We had awful weather. ◊ *Me siento fatal.* I feel awful. ◊ *La obra estuvo fatal.* The play was awful.
♦ **Me parece fatal que le trates así.** I think it's rotten of you to treat him like that.

fatal (2) ADVERBIO
♦ **Lo pasé fatal.** I had an awful time.
♦ **Lo hice fatal.** I made a mess of it.

el **favor** SUSTANTIVO
favour ◊ *¿Puedes hacerme un favor?* Can you do me a favour?
♦ **por favor** please
♦ **¡Haced el favor de callaros!** Will you please be quiet!
♦ **estar a favor de algo** to be in favour of something

favorecer* VERBO
to suit (*vestido, peinado*) ◊ *Esa chaqueta te favorece mucho.* That jacket really suits you.

favorito ADJETIVO
favourite ◊ *¿Cuál es tu color favorito?* What's your favourite colour?

el **fax** SUSTANTIVO (PL los **fax**)
fax (PL faxes)
♦ **mandar algo por fax** to fax something

la **fe** SUSTANTIVO
faith
♦ **tener fe en algo** to have faith in something

febrero SUSTANTIVO MASC
Los meses se escriben con mayúscula.
February ◊ *en febrero* in February ◊ *Ella nació el 28 de febrero.* She was born on 28 February.

la **fecha** SUSTANTIVO
date ◊ *¿A qué fecha estamos?* What's the date today?
♦ **La carta tiene fecha del 21 de enero.** The letter is dated the 21st of January.
♦ **la fecha de caducidad** (*de alimentos*) the use-by date
♦ **la fecha límite** (*para solicitud*) the closing date
♦ **la fecha tope** the deadline
♦ **su fecha de nacimiento** his date of birth

la **felicidad** SUSTANTIVO
happiness ◊ *Carmen lloraba de felicidad.* Carmen was crying with happiness.
♦ **¡Felicidades! (1)** (*por cumpleaños*) Happy birthday!
♦ **¡Felicidades! (2)** (*enhorabuena*) Congratulations!

la **felicitación** SUSTANTIVO (PL las **felicitaciones**)

☞

congratulations PL ◊ *Mi felicitación al ganador.* My congratulations to the winner.
◆ **He recibido muchas felicitaciones.** Lots of people have congratulated me.

felicitar VERBO
to congratulate ◊ *La felicité por sus notas.* I congratulated her on her exam results.
◆ **¡Te felicito!** Congratulations!
◆ **felicitar a alguien por su cumpleaños** to wish somebody a happy birthday

feliz ADJETIVO (PL **felices**)
happy ◊ *Se la ve muy feliz.* She looks very happy.
◆ **¡Feliz cumpleaños!** Happy birthday!
◆ **¡Feliz Año Nuevo!** Happy New Year!
◆ **¡Felices Navidades!** Happy Christmas!

el **felpudo** SUSTANTIVO
doormat

femenino ADJETIVO
1 feminine (*modales, vestido*) ◊ *una chica muy femenina* a very feminine girl
2 female (*cuerpo, órganos*) ◊ *el sexo femenino* the female sex
3 women's (*equipo, deporte*) ◊ *el tenis femenino* women's tennis

el **femenino** SUSTANTIVO
feminine ◊ *El femenino de "lobo" es "loba".* The feminine of "lobo" is "loba".

fenomenal ADJETIVO, ADVERBIO
great (*coloquial*) ◊ *Nos hizo un tiempo fenomenal.* We had great weather.
◆ **Lo pasé fenomenal.** I had a great time.

feo ADJETIVO
ugly ◊ *un edificio muy feo* a very ugly building

el **féretro** SUSTANTIVO
coffin

la **feria** SUSTANTIVO
1 fair
◆ **una feria de muestras** a trade fair
2 small change (*cambio*) Mexico
3 street market (*mercado*) Chile, River Plate

la **ferretería** SUSTANTIVO
ironmonger's (PL ironmongers' shops) ◊ *Lo compré en la ferretería.* I bought it at the ironmonger's.

el **ferrocarril** SUSTANTIVO
railway

fértil ADJETIVO
fertile

el **fertilizante** SUSTANTIVO
fertilizer

festejar VERBO Latin America
to celebrate

el **festival** SUSTANTIVO
festival

festivo ADJETIVO
festive (*ambiente*)
◆ **un día festivo** a holiday

el **feto** SUSTANTIVO
foetus (PL foetuses)

fiable ADJETIVO
reliable

los **fiambres** SUSTANTIVO
cold meats

la **fianza** SUSTANTIVO
deposit ◊ *Dejé una fianza de 2.000 pesetas.* I left a 2,000 peseta deposit.

fiar* VERBO
◆ **Es un hombre de fiar.** He's completely trustworthy.
◆ **fiarse de alguien** to trust somebody ◊ *No me fío de él.* I don't trust him.

la **fibra** SUSTANTIVO
fibre ◊ *fibras artificiales* man-made fibres

la **ficha** SUSTANTIVO
1 (*tarjeta*)
index card
2 (*en juegos de mesa*)
counter
◆ **una ficha de dominó** a domino (PL dominoes)

fichar VERBO
1 to clock in (*al entrar al trabajo*)
2 to clock out (*al salir del trabajo*)
3 to sign up (*jugador*)

el **fichero** SUSTANTIVO
1 filing cabinet (*archivador*)
2 card index (*caja con fichas*)
3 file (*informática*)

los **fideos** SUSTANTIVO
1 noodles (*para sopa*)
2 pasta SING River Plate

la **fiebre** SUSTANTIVO
1 temperature (*síntoma*) ◊ *Le bajó la fiebre.* His temperature came down.
◆ **tener fiebre** to have a temperature
2 fever (*enfermedad*) ◊ *la fiebre amarilla* yellow fever

fiel ADJETIVO
faithful
◆ **ser fiel a alguien** to be faithful to somebody

la **fiera** SUSTANTIVO
wild animal

la **fiesta** SUSTANTIVO
1 party (PL parties) ◊ *Voy a dar una fiesta para celebrarlo.* I'm going to have a party to celebrate.
◆ **una fiesta de cumpleaños** a birthday party
2 holiday ◊ *El lunes es fiesta.* Monday is a holiday.
◆ **El pueblo está en fiestas.** There's a fiesta on in the town.

la **figura** SUSTANTIVO

* Verbs marked with this symbol are irregular. See pages 380-382 for further details

figure ◊ *una figura de porcelana* a porcelain figure

figurar VERBO
to appear ◊ *Su nombre no figura en la lista.* His name doesn't appear on the list.
♦**figurarse** to imagine ◊ *Figúrate lo que debió sufrir.* Just imagine how he must have suffered.
♦**¡Ya me lo figuraba!** I thought as much!

fijar VERBO
to fix ◊ *Tienes que fijar la fecha.* You must fix the date.
♦**fijarse (1)** (*prestar atención*) to pay attention ◊ *Tienes que fijarte más en lo que haces.* You must pay more attention to what you're doing.
♦**fijarse (2)** to notice ◊ *No me fijé en la ropa que llevaba.* I didn't notice what she was wearing.
♦**¡Fíjate en esos dos!** Just look at those two!

fijo ADJETIVO
[1] fixed ◊ *Gano un sueldo fijo.* I earn a fixed salary.
[2] permanent (*empleo, contrato*)
♦**Está fija en la empresa.** She's got a permanent job in the company.

la **fila** SUSTANTIVO
[1] row (*de asientos*) ◊ *Estábamos sentados en segunda fila.* We were sitting in the second row.
[2] line (*de personas*) ◊ *Los niños se pusieron en fila.* The children got into line.

el **filete** SUSTANTIVO
[1] steak ◊ *un filete con patatas fritas* steak and chips
[2] fillet ◊ *un filete de merluza* a hake fillet

Filipinas SUSTANTIVO FEM PL
the Philippines

filmar VERBO
to film ◊ *Mi hermano filmó nuestra boda.* My brother filmed our wedding.
♦**filmar una película** to shoot a film

el **filo** SUSTANTIVO
♦**Tiene poco filo.** It isn't very sharp.

filoso ADJETIVO Latin America
sharp

la **filosofía** SUSTANTIVO
philosophy

filtrar VERBO
to filter ◊ *Hay que filtrar el agua.* The water needs filtering.
♦**filtrarse (1)** (*agua*) to seep ◊ *El agua se filtraba por las paredes.* Water was seeping in through the walls.
♦**filtrarse (2)** (*luz*) to filter ◊ *La luz se filtraba por las rendijas.* Light was filtering in through the cracks.

el **filtro** SUSTANTIVO
filter

el **fin** SUSTANTIVO
end ◊ *el fin de una era* the end of an era
♦**a fines de** at the end of ◊ *a fines de abril* at the end of April
♦**al fin** finally ◊ *Al fin llegaron a un acuerdo.* They finally reached an agreement.
♦**al fin y al cabo** after all
♦**En fin, ¡qué le vamos a hacer!** Oh well, what can we do about it!
♦**por fin** at last ◊ *¡Por fin hemos llegado!* We've got here at last!
♦**el fin de año** New Year's Eve
♦**el fin de semana** the weekend

final ADJETIVO
final ◊ *el resultado final* the final result

el **final** SUSTANTIVO
end (*de pasillo, película*) ◊ *Al final de la calle hay un semáforo.* At the end of the street there's a set of traffic lights.
♦**a finales de mayo** at the end of May
♦**al final** in the end ◊ *Al final tuve que darle la razón.* In the end I had to admit that he was right.
♦**un final feliz** a happy ending

la **final** SUSTANTIVO
final ◊ *la final de la copa* the cup final

la **finca** SUSTANTIVO
country house (*casa de campo*)

fingir* VERBO
to pretend ◊ *Fingió no haberme oído.* He pretended not to have heard me.

finlandés ADJETIVO (FEM **finlandesa,** MASC PL **finlandeses**)
Finnish

el **finlandés,** la **finlandesa** SUSTANTIVO (MASC PL los **finlandeses**)
Finn

el **finlandés** SUSTANTIVO
Finnish (*idioma*)

Finlandia SUSTANTIVO FEM
Finland

fino ADJETIVO
[1] thin (*papel, capa*)
[2] fine (*arena, punta, pelo*)
[3] slender (*dedos, cuello*)

la **firma** SUSTANTIVO
signature

firmar VERBO
to sign

firme ADJETIVO
[1] steady (*mesa, andamio*) ◊ *Mantén la escalera firme.* Can you hold the ladder steady?
[2] firm (*persona*) ◊ *Se mostró muy firme con ella.* He was very firm with her.

el/la **fiscal** SUSTANTIVO
public prosecutor

fisgar* VERBO
to snoop (*coloquial*) ◊ *La encontré fisgando en mi bolso.* I found her snooping in my bag.

la **física** SUSTANTIVO

1 physics SING (*asignatura, ciencia*)
2 physicist (*científica*)

físico ADJETIVO
physical

el **físico** SUSTANTIVO
physicist (*científico*)

flaco ADJETIVO
thin

la **flama** SUSTANTIVO Mexico
flame

el **flamenco** SUSTANTIVO
flamenco

el **flan** SUSTANTIVO
crème caramel

el **flash** SUSTANTIVO (PL los **flashes**)
flash (PL flashes)

la **flauta** SUSTANTIVO
1 recorder (*dulce*)
2 flute (*travesera*)

la **flecha** SUSTANTIVO
arrow

el **flechazo** SUSTANTIVO
♦ **Fue un flechazo.** It was love at first sight.

los **flecos** SUSTANTIVO
fringe SING ◊ *los flecos de la cortina* the curtain fringe

el **flequillo** SUSTANTIVO
fringe

flexible ADJETIVO
flexible

flojo ADJETIVO
1 loose (*nudo, tornillo*)
2 slack (*elástico*)
3 weak (*té, café*)
4 lazy (*persona*) Latin America
♦ **Todavía tengo las piernas muy flojas.** My legs are still very weak.
♦ **Está flojo en matemáticas.** He's weak at maths.

la **flor** SUSTANTIVO
flower ◊ *un ramo de flores* a bunch of flowers

el **florero** SUSTANTIVO
vase

la **floristería** SUSTANTIVO
florist's (PL florists' shops) ◊ *Las compré en la floristería.* I bought them at the florist's.

el **flotador** SUSTANTIVO
1 rubber ring (*para la cintura*)
2 armband (*para el brazo*)

flotar VERBO
to float

flote ADVERBIO
♦ **a flote** afloat ◊ *La barca se mantuvo a flote.* The boat stayed afloat.

fluir* VERBO
to flow

fluorescente ADJETIVO
fluorescent

fluyendo VERBO *ver* **fluir**

la **foca** SUSTANTIVO
seal

el **foco** SUSTANTIVO
1 spotlight (*de teatro*)
2 floodlight (*de estadio, monumento*)
3 headlight (*de coche*) Latin America
4 light bulb (*bombilla*) Mexico
♦ **el foco de atención** the focus of attention

el **folio** SUSTANTIVO
sheet of paper (PL sheets of paper)
♦ **un documento de 20 folios** a 20-page document
♦ **un sobre de tamaño folio** an A4-size envelope

el **folklore** SUSTANTIVO
folklore

el **folleto** SUSTANTIVO
1 brochure (*libro*)
2 leaflet (*hoja*)

fomentar VERBO
to promote (*turismo, industria*)

la **fonda** SUSTANTIVO
1 boarding house (*pensión*)
2 restaurant (*restaurante*)

el **fondo** SUSTANTIVO
1 bottom (*parte más honda*) ◊ *el fondo de la cazuela* the bottom of the pan
♦ **en el fondo del mar** at the bottom of the sea
2 end (*parte trasera*) ◊ *Mi habitación está al fondo del pasillo.* My room's at the end of the corridor.
♦ **estudiar una materia a fondo** to study a subject in depth
♦ **un corredor de fondo** a long-distance runner
♦ **en el fondo** deep down
♦ **recaudar fondos** to raise funds

el **fontanero**, la **fontanera** SUSTANTIVO
plumber

el **footing** SUSTANTIVO
jogging ◊ *Hago footing todas las mañanas.* I go jogging every morning.

forestal ADJETIVO
forest

forest en este caso va siempre delante del sustantivo.

◊ *un incendio forestal* a forest fire

la **forma** SUSTANTIVO
1 shape (*contorno*) ◊ *Me gusta la forma de esa mesa.* I like the shape of that table.
♦ **en forma de pera** pear-shaped
2 way (*manera*) ◊ *Me miraba de una forma extraña.* She was looking at me in a strange way.
♦ **de todas formas** anyway
♦ **estar en forma** to be fit

la **formación** SUSTANTIVO (PL las **formaciones**)
training (*educación*)

◆ **formación profesional** vocational training

formal ADJETIVO
responsible ◇ *un chico muy formal* a very responsible boy
◆ **Sé formal y pórtate bien.** Be good and behave yourself.

formar VERBO
to start ◇ *Quieren formar una orquesta.* They want to start an orchestra.
◆ **Se formó una cola enorme en la puerta.** A huge queue formed at the door.
◆ **estar formado por** to be made up of
◆ **formar parte de algo** to be part of something

formidable ADJETIVO
fantastic (*coloquial*) ◇ *Pedro tiene un coche formidable.* Pedro has got a fantastic car. ◇ *Desde el despacho hay una vista formidable.* There's a fantastic view from the office.

la **fórmula** SUSTANTIVO
formula ◇ *una fórmula mágica* a magic formula
◆ **coches de Fórmula 1** Formula 1 cars

el **formulario** SUSTANTIVO
form ◇ *Hay que rellenar un formulario.* You have to fill in a form.

forrar VERBO
[1] to line (*chaqueta*)
[2] to cover (*libro, sofá*)

el **forro** SUSTANTIVO
[1] lining (*de chaqueta*)
[2] cover (*de libro, sillón*)

la **fortuna** SUSTANTIVO
fortune ◇ *Vale una fortuna.* It's worth a fortune.
◆ **por fortuna** luckily

forzar* VERBO
to force (*puerta, sonrisa*)
◆ **Estás forzando la vista.** You're straining your eyes.

la **fosa** SUSTANTIVO
[1] (*zanja*)
ditch (PL ditches)
[2] (*tumba*)
grave

la **foto** SUSTANTIVO
photo (PL photos) ◇ *Les hice una foto a los niños.* I took a photo of the children.

la **fotocopia** SUSTANTIVO
photocopy (PL photocopies) ◇ *Hice dos fotocopias del recibo.* I made two photocopies of the receipt.

fotocopiar VERBO
to photocopy

la **fotógrafa** SUSTANTIVO
photographer

la **fotografía** SUSTANTIVO
[1] photograph (*retrato*) ◇ *una fotografía de mis padres* a photograph of my parents
[2] photography (*arte*) ◇ *un curso de fotografía* a photography course

el **fotógrafo** SUSTANTIVO
photographer

fracasar VERBO
to fail

el **fracaso** SUSTANTIVO
failure

la **fracción** SUSTANTIVO (PL las **fracciones**)
fraction

la **fractura** SUSTANTIVO
fracture

frágil ADJETIVO
fragile

el **fraile** SUSTANTIVO
friar

la **frambuesa** SUSTANTIVO
raspberry (PL raspberries)

francés ADJETIVO (FEM **francesa,** MASC PL **franceses**)
French

el **francés** SUSTANTIVO (MASC PL los **franceses**)
[1] (*persona*)
Frenchman (PL Frenchmen)
◆ **los franceses** the French
[2] (*idioma*)
French

la **francesa** SUSTANTIVO
Frenchwoman (PL Frenchwomen)

Francia SUSTANTIVO FEM
France

franco ADJETIVO
frank (*persona*)
◆ **para serte franco ...** to be frank with you ...

el **franco** SUSTANTIVO
franc (*moneda*)

el **franqueo** SUSTANTIVO
postage

el **frasco** SUSTANTIVO
bottle ◇ *un frasco de perfume* a bottle of perfume

la **frase** SUSTANTIVO
sentence (*oración*)
◆ **una frase hecha** a set phrase

el **fraude** SUSTANTIVO
fraud

la **frazada** SUSTANTIVO Latin America
blanket

la **frecuencia** SUSTANTIVO
frequency (PL frequencies) ◇ *¿En qué frecuencia está?* What frequency is it on?
◆ **Nos vemos con frecuencia.** We often see each other.
◆ **¿Con qué frecuencia tienen estos síntomas?** How often do they get these symptoms?

frecuente ADJETIVO
[1] common (*común*) ◇ *un error bastante frecuente* a fairly common mistake

☞

2 frequent (*reiterado*) ◊ *los frecuentes viajes al extranjero del ministro* the minister's frequent trips abroad

el **fregadero** SUSTANTIVO
sink (*de la cocina*)

fregar* VERBO
to wash ◊ *Tengo que fregar la cazuela.* I've got to wash the pan.
◆ **fregar los platos** to wash the dishes
◆ **Yo estaba en la cocina fregando.** I was in the kitchen washing the dishes.
◆ **fregar el suelo** to mop the floor

la **fregona** SUSTANTIVO
mop

freír* VERBO
to fry ◊ *No sabe ni freír un huevo.* He can't even fry an egg.

frenar VERBO
to brake

el **frenazo** SUSTANTIVO
◆ **Tuve que dar un frenazo.** I had to brake suddenly.

el **freno** SUSTANTIVO
brake ◊ *Me quedé sin frenos.* My brakes failed.
◆ **el freno de mano** the handbrake

la **frente** SUSTANTIVO
forehead ◊ *Tiene una cicatriz en la frente.* He has a scar on his forehead.

el **frente** SUSTANTIVO
front ◊ *un frente frío* a cold front ◊ *un frente común* a united front
◆ **frente a** opposite ◊ *Frente al hotel hay un banco.* There's a bank opposite the hotel.
◆ **Los coches chocaron de frente.** The cars collided head on.
◆ **Viene un coche de frente.** There's a car coming straight for us.
◆ **hacer frente a algo** to face up to something

la **fresa** SUSTANTIVO
strawberry (PL strawberries)

fresco ADJETIVO
1 cool (*lugar, tela, bebida*)
2 fresh (*pescado, verdura*)
◆ **hace fresco (1)** (*desagradable*) it's chilly
◆ **hace fresco (2)** (*agradable*) it's cool

el **fresco** SUSTANTIVO
◆ **Hace fresco.** It's a bit chilly.

friego VERBO *ver* **fregar**

el **frigorífico** SUSTANTIVO
fridge

el **frijol** SUSTANTIVO Latin America
bean

frío (1) VERBO *ver* **freír**

frío (2) ADJETIVO
cold ◊ *Tengo las manos frías.* My hands are cold.
◆ **Estuvo muy frío conmigo.** He was very cold towards me.

el **frío** SUSTANTIVO
◆ **Hace frío.** It's cold.
◆ **Tengo mucho frío.** I'm very cold.

frito (1) VERBO *ver* **freír**

frito (2) ADJETIVO
fried ◊ *huevos fritos* fried eggs

la **frontera** SUSTANTIVO
border ◊ *Nos pararon en la frontera.* We were stopped at the border.

el **frontón** SUSTANTIVO (PL los **frontones**)
1 pelota court (*pista*)
2 pelota (*juego*)

frotar VERBO
to rub ◊ *¿Te froto la espalda?* Shall I rub your back for you?
◆ **El niño se frotaba las manos para calentarse.** The child was rubbing his hands to get warm.

fruncir* VERBO
◆ **fruncir el ceño** to frown

frustrado ADJETIVO
frustrated ◊ *Se siente frustrado.* He feels frustrated.

la **fruta** SUSTANTIVO
fruit ◊ *La fruta está muy cara.* Fruit is very expensive.

la **frutería** SUSTANTIVO
greengrocer's (PL greengrocers' shops) ◊ *Lo compré en la frutería.* I bought it at the greengrocer's.

la **frutilla** SUSTANTIVO River Plate
strawberry (PL strawberries)

el **fruto** SUSTANTIVO
fruit ◊ *el fruto de nuestro trabajo* the fruit of our labours
◆ **los frutos secos** nuts

fue VERBO *ver* **ir, ser**

el **fuego** SUSTANTIVO
fire ◊ *encender el fuego* to light the fire
◆ **prender fuego a algo** to set fire to something
◆ **Puse la cazuela al fuego.** I put the pot on to heat.
◆ **cocinar algo a fuego lento** to cook something on a low heat
◆ **¿Tiene fuego, por favor?** Have you got a light, please?
◆ **fuegos artificiales** fireworks

la **fuente** SUSTANTIVO
1 (*en la calle*)
fountain
2 (*plato*)
dish (PL dishes)

fuera (1) VERBO *ver* **ir, ser**

fuera (2) ADVERBIO
1 outside ◊ *Los niños estaban jugando fuera.* The children were playing outside. ◊ *Por fuera es blanco.* It is white on the outside.
◆ **¡Estamos aquí fuera!** We are out here!

♦ **Hoy vamos a cenar fuera.** We're going out for dinner tonight.
[2] away ◊ *Mis padres llevan varios días fuera.* My parents have been away for several days.
♦ **El enfermo está fuera de peligro.** The patient is out of danger.
♦ **fuera de mi casa** outside my house

fuerte (1) ADJETIVO
[1] strong (*material, olor, carácter*)
[2] loud (*ruido, voz*)
[3] hard (*golpe*)
[4] bad (*dolor, resfriado*)
♦ **"un beso muy fuerte"** "lots of love"

fuerte (2) ADVERBIO
loudly ◊ *Hablaba fuerte.* He was talking loudly.
♦ **Agárrate fuerte.** Hold on tight.
♦ **No le pegues tan fuerte.** Don't hit him so hard.

la **fuerza** SUSTANTIVO
strength ◊ *No le quedaban fuerzas.* He had no strength left.
♦ **tener mucha fuerza** to be very strong
♦ **Sólo lo conseguirás a fuerza de practicar.** You'll only manage it by practising.
♦ **No te lo comas a la fuerza.** Don't force yourself to eat it.
♦ **la fuerza de gravedad** the force of gravity
♦ **la fuerza de voluntad** willpower

fuerzo VERBO *ver* **forzar**

fugarse* VERBO
to escape

fui VERBO *ver* **ir, ser**

el **fumador,** la **fumadora** SUSTANTIVO
smoker
♦ **sección para no fumadores** non-smoking section

fumar VERBO
to smoke ◊ *Quiero dejar de fumar.* I want to give up smoking.

la **función** SUSTANTIVO (PL las **funciones**)
[1] function (*de máquina, organismo*) ◊ *Los insectos desempeñan una función muy importante.* Insects perform a very useful function.
[2] role (*de persona, institución*) ◊ *la función de la policía en la sociedad* the role of the police in society
[3] show (*espectáculo*) ◊ *Los niños representan una función en el colegio.* The children are putting on a show at school.

funcionar VERBO
to work ◊ *El ascensor no funciona.* The lift isn't working.
♦ **"No funciona."** "Out of order."
♦ **Funciona con pilas.** It runs on batteries.

el **funcionario,** la **funcionaria** SUSTANTIVO
civil servant

la **funda** SUSTANTIVO
cover (*de raqueta, cojín*)
♦ **una funda de almohada** a pillowcase

fundamental ADJETIVO
basic ◊ *Hay dos tipos fundamentales de personas.* There are two basic types of people.
♦ **Es fundamental que entendamos el problema.** It is essential that we understand the problem.

fundar VERBO
to found (*hospital, colegio*)

fundirse VERBO
to melt ◊ *La nieve se está fundiendo.* The snow's melting.
♦ **Se han fundido los fusibles.** The fuses have blown.

el **funeral** SUSTANTIVO
funeral

la **funeraria** SUSTANTIVO
undertaker's

la **furgoneta** SUSTANTIVO
van

la **furia** SUSTANTIVO
fury

furioso ADJETIVO
furious ◊ *Mi padre estaba furioso conmigo.* My father was furious with me.

furtivo ADJETIVO
♦ **la pesca furtiva** poaching
♦ **un cazador furtivo** a poacher

el **fusible** SUSTANTIVO
fuse ◊ *Han saltado los fusibles.* The fuses have blown.

el **fusil** SUSTANTIVO
rifle

el **fútbol** SUSTANTIVO
football ◊ *jugar al fútbol* to play football

el **futbolín** SUSTANTIVO (PL los **futbolines**)
table football

el/la **futbolista** SUSTANTIVO
footballer ◊ *Quiere ser futbolista.* He wants to be a footballer.

el **futuro** ADJETIVO, SUSTANTIVO
future ◊ *su futuro marido* your future husband
♦ **El futuro de "comes" es "comerás".** The future of "comes" is "comerás".
♦ **la futura madre** the mother-to-be

F

G

la **gabardina** SUSTANTIVO
raincoat

el **gabinete** SUSTANTIVO
1 office (*profesional*)
◆ **el gabinete de prensa** press office
2 cabinet (*de ministros*)

las **gafas** SUSTANTIVO
1 glasses ◊ *Tengo que llevar gafas.* I have to wear glasses.
◆ **Había unas gafas encima de la mesa.** There was a pair of glasses on the table.
◆ **las gafas de sol** sunglasses
2 goggles (*de nadador, esquiador*)

la **gaita** SUSTANTIVO
bagpipes PL ◊ *tocar la gaita* to play the bagpipes
◆ **¡Menuda gaita!** What a pain! (*coloquial*)

los **gajes** SUSTANTIVO
◆ **Son gajes del oficio.** They're occupational hazards.

el **gajo** SUSTANTIVO
segment

la **galaxia** SUSTANTIVO
galaxy (PL galaxies)

la **galería** SUSTANTIVO
(*en edificio, teatro, mina*)
gallery (PL galleries) ◊ *una galería de arte* an art gallery
◆ **una galería comercial** a shopping centre

Gales SUSTANTIVO MASC
Wales
◆ **el País de Gales** Wales

galés ADJETIVO (FEM **galesa,** MASC PL **galeses**)
Welsh

el **galés** SUSTANTIVO (PL los **galeses**)
1 (*persona*)
Welshman (PL Welshmen) ◊ *los galeses* the Welsh
2 (*idioma*)
Welsh

la **galesa** SUSTANTIVO
Welshwoman (PL Welshwomen)

el **galgo** SUSTANTIVO
greyhound ◊ *una carrera de galgos* a greyhound race

Galicia SUSTANTIVO FEM
Galicia

el **gallego,** la **gallega** ADJETIVO, SUSTANTIVO
Galician

el **gallego** SUSTANTIVO
Galician (*idioma*)

la **galleta** SUSTANTIVO
biscuit
◆ **una galleta salada** a cracker

la **gallina** SUSTANTIVO
hen
◆ **Sólo pensarlo me pone la carne de gallina.** It gives me goosepimples just thinking about it.
◆ **jugar a la gallinita ciega** to play blind man's buff

el/la **gallina** SUSTANTIVO
◆ **¡Eres un gallina!** You're chicken! (*coloquial*)

el **gallinero** SUSTANTIVO
1 henhouse (*para las gallinas*)
2 madhouse (*coloquial*) ◊ *La clase era un gallinero.* The class was a madhouse.

el **gallo** SUSTANTIVO
cock (*ave*)
◆ **en menos que canta un gallo** in an instant

galopar VERBO
to gallop

la **gama** SUSTANTIVO
range ◊ *una amplia gama de ordenadores* a wide range of computers

la **gamba** SUSTANTIVO
prawn

el **gamberro,** la **gamberra** SUSTANTIVO
hooligan

la **gana** SUSTANTIVO
◆ **Me visto como me da la gana.** I dress the way I want to.
◆ **¡No me da la gana!** I don't want to!
◆ **Hazlo como te dé la gana.** Do it however you like.
◆ **hacer algo de mala gana** to do something reluctantly
◆ **tener ganas de hacer algo** to feel like doing something
◆ **Tengo ganas de que llegue el sábado.** I'm looking forward to Saturday.

la **ganadería** SUSTANTIVO
◆ **Se dedican a la ganadería.** They raise cattle.

el **ganado** SUSTANTIVO
livestock ◊ *alimento para el ganado* livestock feed
◆ **el ganado vacuno** cattle

ganador ADJETIVO (FEM **ganadora**)
winning ◊ *el equipo ganador* the winning team

el **ganador,** la **ganadora** SUSTANTIVO
winner

la **ganancia** SUSTANTIVO
profit ◊ *las pérdidas y las ganancias* profits and losses

ganar VERBO
1 to earn (*en un trabajo*) ◊ *Gana un buen sueldo.* He earns a good wage.
◆ **ganarse la vida** to earn a living

[2] to win (*premio, competición, guerra*) ◇ *¿Quién ganó la carrera?* Who won the race? ◇ *Lo importante no es ganar.* Winning isn't the most important thing.
[3] to beat (*contrincante*) ◇ *Ganamos al Olimpic tres a cero.* We beat Olimpic three-nil.
♦ **Con eso no ganas nada.** You won't achieve anything by doing that.
♦ **ganar tiempo** to save time
♦ **¡Te lo has ganado!** You deserve it!
♦ **salir ganando** to do well ◇ *Salí ganando con la venta del coche.* I did well out of the sale of the car.

el **ganchillo** SUSTANTIVO
crochet ◇ *una aguja de ganchillo* a crochet hook
♦ **hacer ganchillo** to crochet

el **gancho** SUSTANTIVO
[1] hook ◇ *Colgué el cuadro de un gancho.* I hung the picture on a hook.
♦ **Maradona tiene gancho.** Maradona is a crowd-puller.
[2] hanger (*para la ropa*) Latin America

gandul ADJETIVO (FEM **gandula**)
lazy

el **gandul,** la **gandula** SUSTANTIVO
good-for-nothing ◇ *Su marido es un gandul.* Her husband is a good-for-nothing.

la **ganga** SUSTANTIVO
bargain ◇ *A ese precio es una ganga.* It's a real bargain at that price.

el **gángster** SUSTANTIVO (PL los **gángsters**)
gangster

el **ganso,** la **gansa** SUSTANTIVO
goose (PL geese)

el **garabato** SUSTANTIVO
[1] doodle (*dibujo*) ◇ *una página llena de garabatos* a page full of doodles
♦ **Me pasé la clase haciendo garabatos.** I spent the whole class doodling.
[2] scribble (*escritura*) ◇ *una hoja cubierta de garabatos ininteligibles* a page full of unintelligible scribbles
♦ **Mientras pensaba iba haciendo garabatos en una libreta.** As I was thinking I scribbled away in my notebook.

el **garaje** SUSTANTIVO
garage ◇ *Metí el coche en el garaje.* I put the car in the garage.
♦ **una plaza de garaje** a parking space

la **garantía** SUSTANTIVO
guarantee ◇ *La lavadora está todavía bajo garantía.* The washing machine is still under guarantee.

garantizar* VERBO
to guarantee ◇ *No te lo puedo garantizar.* I can't guarantee it.

el **garbanzo** SUSTANTIVO
chick pea

la **garganta** SUSTANTIVO
throat ◇ *Me duele la garganta.* I've got a sore throat.

la **gargantilla** SUSTANTIVO
necklace

las **gárgaras** SUSTANTIVO
♦ **hacer gárgaras** to gargle

la **garita** SUSTANTIVO
sentry box (PL sentry boxes)

la **garra** SUSTANTIVO
[1] claw (*de tigre, gato*)
[2] talon (*de águila*)

la **garrafa** SUSTANTIVO
carafe (*pequeña*)

> ℹ *A **garrafa** is also a large bottle with handles.*

♦ **vino de garrafa** cheap wine

la **garúa** SUSTANTIVO Latin America
drizzle

el **gas** SUSTANTIVO (PL los **gases**)
gas ◇ *¿No hueles a gas?* Can you smell gas?
♦ **agua mineral sin gas** still mineral water
♦ **una bebida sin gas** a still drink
♦ **agua mineral con gas** sparkling mineral water
♦ **los gases del tubo de escape** exhaust fumes
♦ **gases lacrimógenos** tear gas SING
♦ **El niño tiene muchos gases.** The baby's got a lot of wind.
♦ **Pasó una moto a todo gas.** A motorbike shot past at full speed.

la **gasa** SUSTANTIVO
gauze

la **gaseosa** SUSTANTIVO

> ℹ *A **gaseosa** is a drink of sweet fizzy water.*

el **gasoil** SUSTANTIVO
diesel oil

el **gasóleo** SUSTANTIVO
diesel oil

la **gasolina** SUSTANTIVO
petrol ◇ *Tengo que poner gasolina.* I have to fill up with petrol.
♦ **gasolina súper** four-star petrol
♦ **gasolina sin plomo** unleaded petrol

la **gasolinera** SUSTANTIVO
petrol station

gastado ADJETIVO
worn ◇ *La moqueta está muy gastada.* The carpet is very worn.

gastar VERBO
[1] to spend
♦ **Javier gasta mucho en ropa.** Javier spends a lot of money on clothes.
[2] to use (*gasolina, electricidad*) ◇ *Gastamos mucha agua.* We use a lot of water.

☞

- **Gasté toda una caja de cerillas.** I used up a whole box of matches.
- **¿Qué numero de zapato gastas?** What size shoes do you take?
- **Le gastamos una broma a Juan.** We played a joke on Juan.
- **Se han gastado las pilas.** The batteries have run out.
- **Se me han gastado las suelas.** The soles of my shoes have worn out.

el **gasto** SUSTANTIVO
expense ◊ *Es un gasto tremendo.* It's a horrendous expense. ◊ *Este año hemos tenido muchos gastos.* We've had a lot of expenses this year.
- **gastos de envío** postage and packing SING
- **el gasto público** public spending

la **gata** SUSTANTIVO
cat
- **andar a gatas** to crawl ◊ *El niño todavía anda a gatas.* The baby is still crawling.
- **Tienes que subir las escaleras a gatas.** You have to go up the stairs on all fours.

gatear VERBO
to crawl

el **gato** SUSTANTIVO
1 cat (*animal*)
2 jack (*para coche*)

la **gaviota** SUSTANTIVO
seagull

el **gay** ADJETIVO, SUSTANTIVO (PL los **gays**)
gay

el **gazpacho** SUSTANTIVO

> *Gazpacho is a refreshing soup made from tomatoes, cucumber, garlic, peppers, oil and vinegar and served cold.*

el **gel** SUSTANTIVO
gel ◊ *gel de baño* bath gel

la **gelatina** SUSTANTIVO
jelly (PL jellies)

el **gemelo,** la **gemela** ADJETIVO, SUSTANTIVO
identical twin ◊ *Son gemelos.* They're identical twins. ◊ *mi hermano gemelo* my identical twin

los **gemelos** SUSTANTIVO
1 binoculars (*prismáticos*)
2 cufflinks (*de camisa*)

Géminis SUSTANTIVO MASC
Gemini
- **Soy Géminis.** I'm Gemini.

el **gen** SUSTANTIVO
gene

la **generación** SUSTANTIVO (PL las **generaciones**)
generation

general ADJETIVO
general ◊ *medicina general* general medicine
- **en general** in general
- **por lo general** generally ◊ *Por lo general me acuesto temprano.* I generally go to bed early.

el/la **general** SUSTANTIVO
general

generalizar* VERBO
to generalize ◊ *No se puede generalizar.* You can't generalize.

generalmente ADVERBIO
generally

generar VERBO
to generate

el **género** SUSTANTIVO
1 gender (*de sustantivo, adjetivo*)
2 kind ◊ *¿Qué género de música prefieres?* What kind of music do you prefer?
3 material ◊ *Para las cortinas necesitamos un género más grueso.* We need a thicker material for the curtains.
- **el género humano** the human race

la **generosidad** SUSTANTIVO
generosity

generoso ADJETIVO
generous

genial ADJETIVO
brilliant ◊ *Antonio tuvo una idea genial.* Antonio had a brilliant idea. ◊ *El concierto estuvo genial.* It was a brilliant concert.

el **genio** SUSTANTIVO
1 temper ◊ *¡Menudo genio tiene tu padre!* Your father has got such a temper!
- **tener mal genio** to have a bad temper

2 genius (PL geniuses) ◊ *¡Eres un genio!* You're a genius!
3 (*de la botella*)
genie

los **genitales** SUSTANTIVO
genitals

el **genoma** SUSTANTIVO
genome

la **gente** SUSTANTIVO
people
El verbo va siempre en plural.
◊ *Había poca gente en la sala.* There were few people in the room. ◊ *La gente está cansada de promesas.* People are tired of promises.
- **Son buena gente.** They're good people.
- **Óscar es buena gente.** Óscar's a good sort.
- **la gente de la calle** the people in the street

la **geografía** SUSTANTIVO
geography

la **geología** SUSTANTIVO
geology

* Verbs marked with this symbol are irregular. See pages 380-382 for further details

la **geometría** SUSTANTIVO
geometry

el **geranio** SUSTANTIVO
geranium

el/la **gerente** SUSTANTIVO
manager ◊ *Isabel es gerente de ventas.* Isabel is a sales manager.

el **germen** SUSTANTIVO (PL los **gérmenes**)
germ

germinar VERBO
to germinate

el **gesto** SUSTANTIVO
◆ **Hizo un gesto de alivio.** He looked relieved.
◆ **Me hizo un gesto para que me sentara.** He made a sign for me to sit down.

la **gestoría** SUSTANTIVO

> *A **gestoría** is a private agency which deals with government departments on behalf of its clients.*

Gibraltar SUSTANTIVO MASC
Gibraltar

el **gibraltareño**, la **gibraltareña** ADJETIVO, SUSTANTIVO
Gibraltarian

el/la **gigante** SUSTANTIVO
giant

gigantesco ADJETIVO
gigantic

la **gimnasia** SUSTANTIVO
gymnastics SING ◊ *Después del recreo tenemos gimnasia.* After break we have gymnastics.
◆ **Mi madre hace gimnasia todas las mañanas.** My mother does exercises every morning.

el **gimnasio** SUSTANTIVO
gym

el/la **gimnasta** SUSTANTIVO
gymnast

la **ginebra** SUSTANTIVO
gin

el **ginecólogo**, la **ginecóloga** SUSTANTIVO
gynaecologist ◊ *Soy ginecóloga.* I'm a gynaecologist.

la **gira** SUSTANTIVO
tour ◊ *Hicimos una gira por toda Europa.* We did a tour all round Europe.
◆ **estar de gira** to be on tour

girar VERBO
1 to turn ◊ *Al llegar al semáforo gira a la derecha.* When you get to the lights turn right. ◊ *Giré la cabeza para ver quién era.* I turned my head to see who it was.
2 to rotate ◊ *La Tierra gira alrededor de su eje.* The Earth rotates on its axis.
◆ **La Luna gira alrededor de la Tierra.** The moon revolves around the Earth.

el **girasol** SUSTANTIVO
sunflower

el **giro** SUSTANTIVO
1 turn ◊ *El avión dio un giro de 90 grados.* The plane did a 90 degree turn.
2 postal order ◊ *Voy a mandarte un giro de 15.000 pesetas.* I'll send you a 15,000 peseta postal order.

el **gitano**, la **gitana** SUSTANTIVO
gypsy (PL gypsies)

la **glándula** SUSTANTIVO
gland

global ADJETIVO
global ◊ *una solución global* a global solution

el **globo** SUSTANTIVO
balloon (*de juguete, para volar*)
◆ **un globo terráqueo** a globe

la **glorieta** SUSTANTIVO
roundabout

glotón ADJETIVO (FEM SING **glotona,** MASC PL **glotones**)
greedy

gobernar* VERBO
to govern

el **gobierno** SUSTANTIVO
government

el **gol** SUSTANTIVO
goal
◆ **meter un gol** to score a goal

el **golf** SUSTANTIVO
golf
◆ **jugar al golf** to play golf

el **golfo** SUSTANTIVO
gulf ◊ *el Golfo pérsico* the Persian Gulf

la **golondrina** SUSTANTIVO
swallow

la **golosina** SUSTANTIVO
sweet

goloso ADJETIVO
◆ **ser goloso** to have a sweet tooth ◊ *Soy muy golosa.* I've got a very sweet tooth.

el **golpe** SUSTANTIVO
knock ◊ *Oímos un golpe a la puerta.* We heard a knock at the door.
◆ **Me he dado un golpe en el codo.** I banged my elbow.
◆ **Se dio un golpe contra la pared.** He hit the wall.
◆ **El coche de atrás nos dio un golpe.** The car behind ran into us.
◆ **Di unos golpecitos a la puerta antes de entrar.** I tapped on the door before going in.
◆ **de golpe** suddenly ◊ *De golpe decidió dejar el trabajo.* He suddenly decided to give up work.
◆ **La puerta se cerró de golpe.** The door slammed shut.
◆ **no dar golpe** to be bone idle

golpear VERBO

G

1 to hit (*pegar*) ◊ *Me golpeó en la cara con su raqueta.* He hit me in the face with his racquet.
2 to bang (*objeto*) ◊ *El maestro golpeó el pupitre con la mano.* The teacher banged the desk with his hand.
♦ **Me golpeé la cabeza contra el armario.** I banged my head on the cupboard.

la **goma** SUSTANTIVO
1 eraser ◊ *¿Me prestas la goma?* Can you lend me your eraser?
♦ **una goma de borrar** an eraser ◊ *unos guantes de goma* a pair of rubber gloves
2 elastic band ◊ *Necesito una goma para el pelo.* I need an elastic band for my hair.

gordo ADJETIVO
1 fat ◊ *Estoy muy gordo.* I'm very fat.
2 thick (*libro, jersey*)
3 big (*problema*) ◊ *Debe de ser algo bastante gordo.* It must be something pretty big.
♦ **Su mujer me cae gorda.** I can't stand his wife.

el **gorila** SUSTANTIVO
gorilla

la **gorra** SUSTANTIVO
cap
♦ **de gorra** for free ◊ *Entramos de gorra.* We got in for free.

el **gorrión** SUSTANTIVO (PL los **gorriones**)
sparrow

el **gorro** SUSTANTIVO
hat ◊ *Llevaba un gorro de lana.* He wore a woollen hat.
♦ **un gorro de baño** a swimming cap
♦ **Ya estoy hasta el gorro.** I'm absolutely fed up.

el **gorrón**, la **gorrona** SUSTANTIVO (MASC PL los **gorrones**)
scrounger

la **gota** SUSTANTIVO
drop ◊ *Sólo bebí una gota de vino.* I only had a drop of wine.
♦ **Están cayendo cuatro gotas.** It's spitting.

gotear VERBO
1 to drip (*grifo*)
2 to leak (*cañería*)

la **gotera** SUSTANTIVO
leak ◊ *Tenemos goteras en la cocina.* We've got some leaks in the kitchen.

gozar* VERBO
♦ **gozar de algo** to enjoy something ◊ *Quiere gozar de la vida.* He wants to enjoy life. ◊ *Mis abuelos gozan de buena salud.* My grandparents enjoy good health.

la **grabación** SUSTANTIVO (PL las **grabaciones**)
recording

la **grabadora** SUSTANTIVO
recorder

grabar VERBO
1 to tape ◊ *Quiero grabar esta película.* I want to tape this film.
2 to record ◊ *Lo grabaron en vivo.* It was recorded live.
3 to engrave (*en madera, metal*) ◊ *Grabó sus iniciales en la medalla.* He engraved his initials on the medal.
♦ **Lo tengo grabado en la memoria.** It's etched on my memory.

la **gracia** SUSTANTIVO
♦ **tener gracia** to be funny ◊ *Sus chistes tienen mucha gracia.* His jokes are very funny.
♦ **Yo no le veo la gracia.** I don't see what's so funny.
♦ **Me hizo mucha gracia.** It was so funny.
♦ **No me hace gracia tener que salir con este tiempo.** I'm not too pleased about having to go out in this weather.
♦ **¡Muchas gracias!** Thanks very much!
♦ **dar las gracias a alguien por algo** to thank somebody for something ◊ *Vino a darme las gracias por las flores.* He came to thank me for the flowers.
♦ **Ni siquiera me dio las gracias.** He didn't even say thank you.
♦ **gracias a** thanks to ◊ *Gracias a él me encuentro con vida.* Thanks to him I'm still alive.

gracioso ADJETIVO
funny ◊ *¡Qué gracioso!* How funny!

las **gradas** SUSTANTIVO
terraces

el **grado** SUSTANTIVO
degree ◊ *Estaban a diez grados bajo cero.* It was ten degrees below zero. ◊ *quemaduras de primer grado* first-degree burns

graduado ADJETIVO
♦ **gafas graduadas** prescription glasses

gradual ADJETIVO
gradual

graduar* VERBO
to adjust (*volumen, temperatura*)
♦ **Tengo que graduarme la vista.** I've got to have my eyes tested.
♦ **Se graduó en Medicina hace dos años.** He graduated in Medicine two years ago.

la **gráfica** SUSTANTIVO
graph

gráfico ADJETIVO
graphic

el **gráfico** SUSTANTIVO
table

la **gramática** SUSTANTIVO
grammar ◊ *un libro de gramática inglesa* a book on English grammar

el **gramo** SUSTANTIVO
gram

> **i** *En los países anglosajones el peso a menudo se expresa en onzas* ***ounces****. Una onza equivale a 28.35 gramos.*

gran ADJETIVO *ver* **grande**

la **granada** SUSTANTIVO
pomegranate (*fruta*)
♦ **una granada de mano** a hand grenade

granate ADJETIVO
maroon ◊ *una bufanda granate* a maroon scarf

Gran Bretaña SUSTANTIVO FEM
Great Britain

grande ADJETIVO
1 big (*de tamaño*) ◊ *Viven en una casa muy grande.* They live in a very big house.
♦ **¿Cómo es de grande?** How big is it?
♦ **La camisa me está grande.** The shirt is too big for me.
2 large (*de cantidad*) ◊ *un gran número de visitantes* a large number of visitors ◊ *grandes sumas de dinero* large sums of money
3 great (*en importancia, grado*) ◊ *un gran pintor* a great painter ◊ *Es una ventaja muy grande.* It's a great advantage.
♦ **Me llevé una alegría muy grande.** I felt very happy.
♦ **Lo pasamos en grande.** We had a great time.
♦ **unos grandes almacenes** a department store

granel ADVERBIO
♦ **a granel** in bulk ◊ *Venden las aceitunas a granel.* They sell olives in bulk.

el **granero** SUSTANTIVO
barn

el **granizado** SUSTANTIVO

> **i** *A* ***granizado*** *is a crushed ice drink.*

granizar* VERBO
to hail ◊ *Está granizando.* It's hailing.

el **granizo** SUSTANTIVO
hail

la **granja** SUSTANTIVO
farm
♦ **una granja avícola** a poultry farm

el **granjero**, la **granjera** SUSTANTIVO
farmer

el **grano** SUSTANTIVO
1 grain (*de arena, arroz, azúcar*)
2 bean (*de café*)
3 spot ◊ *Me ha salido un grano en la frente.* I've got a spot on my forehead.
♦ **ir al grano** to get to the point

la **grapa** SUSTANTIVO
staple

la **grapadora** SUSTANTIVO
stapler

la **grasa** SUSTANTIVO
1 fat ◊ *No me va bien tanta grasa.* So much fat isn't good for me.
2 grease (*suciedad*)
♦ **La cocina está llena de grasa.** The cooker's really greasy.

grasiento ADJETIVO
greasy

graso ADJETIVO
greasy ◊ *Tengo el cutis graso.* I've got greasy skin.

gratis ADJETIVO, ADVERBIO (PL **gratis**)
1 free ◊ *La entrada es gratis.* Entry is free.
2 for free ◊ *Te lo arreglarán gratis.* They'll fix it for free.

gratuito ADJETIVO
free

la **grava** SUSTANTIVO
gravel

grave ADJETIVO
1 serious (*enfermedad, herida*) ◊ *Tenemos un problema grave.* We've got a serious problem.
♦ **Su padre está grave.** His father is seriously ill.
2 low (*nota, sonido*)

la **gravedad** SUSTANTIVO
gravity ◊ *la ley de la gravedad* the law of gravity
♦ **estar herido de gravedad** to be seriously injured

gravemente ADVERBIO
seriously
♦ **estar gravemente enfermo** to be seriously ill

Grecia SUSTANTIVO FEM
Greece

el **griego**, la **griega** ADJETIVO, SUSTANTIVO
Greek

el **griego** SUSTANTIVO
Greek (*idioma*)

la **grieta** SUSTANTIVO
crack

el **grifo** SUSTANTIVO
tap ◊ *abrir el grifo* to turn on the tap ◊ *cerrar el grifo* to turn off the tap

el **grillo** SUSTANTIVO
cricket

la **gripe** SUSTANTIVO
flu ◊ *tener la gripe* to have the flu

el **gris** ADJETIVO, SUSTANTIVO
grey ◊ *una puerta gris* a grey door

gritar VERBO
1 to shout (*dar voces*)
♦ **El público le gritaba al árbitro.** The crowd were shouting at the referee.
♦ **Niños, no gritéis tanto.** Children, stop shouting so much.
2 to scream (*dar un chillido*) ◊ *El enfermo no podía dejar de gritar.* The patient couldn't stop screaming.

el **grito** SUSTANTIVO

☞

[1] shout ◊ *gritos de protesta* shouts of protest
♦ **¡No des esos gritos!** Stop shouting like that!
[2] scream (*chillido*) ◊ *Oímos un grito en la calle.* We heard a scream outside.
♦ **Dando gritos a viva voz.** Screaming at the top of his voice.
♦ **Es el último grito.** It's all the rage.

la **grosella** SUSTANTIVO
redcurrant

grosero ADJETIVO
rude

el **grosor** SUSTANTIVO
thickness
♦ **La pared tiene 30cm de grosor.** The wall is 30cm thick.

la **grúa** SUSTANTIVO
crane (*para construcción*)
♦ **La grúa se ha llevado el coche.** My car was towed away.

grueso ADJETIVO
[1] thick (*jersey, pared, libro*)
[2] stout (*persona*)

el **grumo** SUSTANTIVO
lump

gruñir* VERBO
to grumble ◊ *El abuelo siempre está gruñendo.* Grandad is always grumbling.

el **grupo** SUSTANTIVO
[1] group ◊ *Se dividieron en grupos.* They divided into groups.
♦ **el grupo sanguíneo** blood group
♦ **Los alumnos trabajan en grupo.** The students work in groups.
[2] band ◊ *uno de los mejores grupos de rock* one of the best rock bands

el **guacho,** la **guacha** SUSTANTIVO [Andes, River Plate]
homeless child

el **guajolote** SUSTANTIVO [Mexico]
turkey

el **guante** SUSTANTIVO
glove ◊ *Uso guantes de goma.* I use rubber gloves.
♦ **unos guantes** a pair of gloves

la **guantera** SUSTANTIVO
glove compartment

guapo ADJETIVO
[1] handsome (*hombre*)
[2] pretty (*mujer*)
[3] beautiful (*bebé*)
♦ **¡Ven, guapo!** (*a un niño*) Come here, love!

el/la **guarda** SUSTANTIVO
keeper (*de parque, zoo*)
♦ **guarda jurado** armed security guard

el **guardabarros** SUSTANTIVO (PL los **guardabarros**)
mudguard

el/la **guardaespaldas** SUSTANTIVO (MASC PL los/las **guardaespaldas**)
bodyguard

guardar VERBO
[1] to put away (*recoger*) ◊ *Los niños guardaron los juguetes.* The children put away their toys. ◊ *Guardé los documentos en el cajón.* I put the documents away in the drawer.
♦ **Raúl se guardó el pañuelo en el bolsillo.** Raúl put the handkerchief in his pocket.
[2] to keep ◊ *Guarda el recibo.* Keep the receipt. ◊ *No sabe guardar un secreto.* He can't keep a secret.
♦ **No les guardo rencor.** I don't bear them a grudge.
♦ **guardar las apariencias** to keep up appearances
♦ **guardar un fichero** to save a file (*informática*)

el **guardarropa** SUSTANTIVO
cloakroom

la **guardería** SUSTANTIVO
nursery (PL nurseries)

la **guardia** SUSTANTIVO
♦ **de guardia** on duty ◊ *Me atendió el médico de guardia.* I was seen by the doctor on duty. ◊ *Estoy de guardia.* I'm on duty.
♦ **la Guardia Civil** the Civil Guard

el/la **guardia** SUSTANTIVO
police officer

el **guarro,** la **guarra** SUSTANTIVO (*coloquial*)
♦ **¡Eres un guarro!** You're disgusting!

guay ADJETIVO
cool (*coloquial*) ◊ *¡Qué moto más guay!* What a cool bike!

güero ADJETIVO [Mexico]
blonde

la **guerra** SUSTANTIVO
war ◊ *la Segunda Guerra Mundial* the Second World War
♦ **declarar la guerra a un país** to declare war on a country
♦ **estar en guerra** to be at war

el/la **guía** SUSTANTIVO
guide ◊ *El guía vino a recogernos al aeropuerto.* The guide came to pick us up at the airport.

la **guía** SUSTANTIVO
guidebook (*libro*) ◊ *Compré una guía turística de Londres.* I bought a tourist guidebook of London.
♦ **una guía de hoteles** a hotel guide
♦ **una guía telefónica** a telephone directory

guiar* VERBO
to guide ◊ *Mi amigo nos guió a la estación.* My friend guided us to the station.

♦ **Nos guiamos por un mapa que teníamos.** We found our way using a map that we had.

el **guijarro** SUSTANTIVO
pebble

la **guinda** SUSTANTIVO
cherry (PL cherries)

la **guindilla** SUSTANTIVO
chilli pepper

guiñar VERBO
to wink
♦ **Me guiñó el ojo.** He winked at me.

el **guión** SUSTANTIVO (PL los **guiones**)
[1] hyphen (*en palabras compuestas*)
♦ **La palabra "self-defence" lleva guión.** The word "self-defence" is hyphenated.
[2] dash (*para indicar un diálogo*)
[3] script (*de una película*)

el **guisante** SUSTANTIVO
pea

guisar VERBO
to cook

la **guitarra** SUSTANTIVO
guitar

el **gusano** SUSTANTIVO
[1] worm
♦ **un gusano de seda** a silk worm
[2] maggot (*de mosca*)
[3] caterpillar (*de mariposa*)

gustar VERBO
♦ **Me gustan las uvas.** I like grapes.
♦ **¿Te gusta viajar?** Do you like travelling?
♦ **Me gustó como hablaba.** I liked the way he spoke.
♦ **Me gustaría conocerla.** I would like to meet her.
♦ **Me gusta su hermana.** I fancy his sister.
♦ **Le gusta más llevar pantalones.** She prefers to wear trousers.

el **gusto** SUSTANTIVO
taste ◊ *No tiene gusto para vestirse.* He has no taste in clothes. ◊ *Me he decorado la habitación a mi gusto.* I've decorated the room to my taste.
♦ **un comentario de mal gusto** a tasteless remark
♦ **Le noto un gusto a almendras.** It tastes of almonds.
♦ **¡Con mucho gusto!** With pleasure!
♦ **¡Mucho gusto en conocerle!** I'm very pleased to meet you!
♦ **sentirse a gusto** to feel at ease

G

H

ha VERBO *ver* **haber**

el **haba** SUSTANTIVO
broad bean

Habana SUSTANTIVO
◆ **La Habana** Havana

haber* VERBO
to have

*El verbo **to have** suele usarse en las formas contraídas, particularmente al hablar.*

◊ *He comido.* I've eaten. ◊ *Hemos comido.* We've eaten. ◊ *Había comido.* I'd eaten. (*= had*) ◊ *Se ha sentado.* She's sat down. (*= has*)

◆ **De haberlo sabido, habría ido.** If I'd known, I would have gone.
◆ **¡Haberlo dicho antes!** You should have said so before!
◆ **hay**

***Hay** seguido de complemento singular se traduce por **there is**.*

◊ *Hay una iglesia en la esquina.* There's a church on the corner. ◊ *Hubo una guerra.* There was a war.

***Hay** seguido de complemento plural se traduce por **there are**.*

◊ *Hay treinta alumnos en mi clase.* There are thirty pupils in my class. ◊ *¿Hay entradas?* Are there any tickets?

◆ **¡No hay de qué!** Don't mention it!
◆ **¿Qué hay?** (*¿Qué tal?*) How are things? (*coloquial*)
◆ **¿Qué hubo?** Mexico How are things? (*coloquial*)
◆ **hay que ...**

*La expresión impersonal **hay que** se traduce normalmente utilizando el pronombre **you**, a menos que esté claro quien realiza la acción.*

◆ **Hay que ser respetuoso.** You must be respectful.
◆ **¡Habrá que decírselo!** We'll have to tell him!

hábil ADJETIVO
skilful (*diestro*) ◊ *Es un jugador muy hábil.* He's a very skilful player.
◆ **Es muy hábil con las manos.** He's very good with his hands.
◆ **Es muy hábil para los negocios.** He's a very able businessman.

la **habilidad** SUSTANTIVO
skill ◊ *Ha demostrado una gran habilidad para los negocios.* He's shown great business skill.
◆ **Tiene mucha habilidad para los idiomas.** She's very good at languages.

la **habitación** SUSTANTIVO (PL las **habitaciones**)
1 bedroom (*dormitorio*)
2 room (*en hotel*)
◆ **una habitación doble** a double room
◆ **una habitación individual** a single room

el/la **habitante** SUSTANTIVO
inhabitant
◆ **los habitantes de la zona** people living in the area

habitar VERBO
to live in ◊ *los que habitaban en la zona* those who lived in the area
◆ **La casa está todavía sin habitar.** The house is still unoccupied.

el **hábito** SUSTANTIVO
habit ◊ *Fumar es un mal hábito.* Smoking is a bad habit.

habitual ADJETIVO
usual ◊ *No es habitual verlos juntos.* It's not usual to see them together.
◆ **un cliente habitual** a regular customer

el **habla** SUSTANTIVO
speech
◆ **Ha perdido el habla.** He's lost the power of speech.
◆ **países de habla inglesa** English-speaking countries
◆ **¿Señor López? – Al habla.** Señor López? – Speaking.

hablador ADJETIVO (FEM **habladora**)
1 chatty (*parlanchín*)
2 gossipy (*chismoso*)

las **habladurías** SUSTANTIVO
gossip SING

el/la **hablante** SUSTANTIVO
speaker

hablar VERBO
1 to speak ◊ *¿Hablas español?* Do you speak Spanish?
◆ **¿Quién habla?** (*al teléfono*) Who's calling?
2 to talk ◊ *Estuvimos hablando toda la tarde.* We were talking all afternoon.
◆ **hablar con alguien (1)** to speak to someone ◊ *¿Has hablado ya con el profesor?* Have you spoken to the teacher yet?
◆ **hablar con alguien (2)** to talk to someone ◊ *Necesito hablar contigo.* I need to talk to you.
◆ **hablar de algo** to talk about something
◆ **¿Vas a ayudarle en la mudanza? – ¡Ni hablar!** Are you going to help him with the move? – No way!

habré VERBO *ver* **haber**

hacer* VERBO
1 to make ◊ *Tengo que hacer la cama.* I've got to make the bed. ◊ *Voy a hacer*

* Verbs marked with this symbol are irregular. See pages 380-382 for further details

una tortilla. I'm going to make an omelette. ◊ *Están haciendo mucho ruido.* They're making a lot of noise.
[2] to do ◊ *¿Qué haces?* What are you doing? ◊ *Estoy haciendo los deberes.* I'm doing my homework. ◊ *Hago mucho deporte.* I do a lot of sport. ◊ *¿Qué hace tu padre?* What does your father do?
[3] to be (*hablando del tiempo atmosférico*) ◊ *Hace calor.* It's hot. ◊ *Ojalá haga buen tiempo.* I hope the weather's nice. ◊ *Hizo dos grados bajo cero.* It was two degrees below zero.
♦ **hace ... (1)** ago ◊ *Terminé hace una hora.* I finished an hour ago. ◊ *Ha estado aquí hasta hace poco.* He was here a few minutes ago.
♦ **hace ... (2)** for ◊ *Hace un mes que voy.* I've been going for a month.
♦ **¿Hace mucho que esperas?** Have you been waiting long?
♦ **hacer hacer algo** to have something done ◊ *Hicieron pintar la fachada del colegio.* They had the front of the school painted.
♦ **hacer a alguien hacer algo** to make someone do something ◊ *Hace estudiar a los alumnos.* He makes the pupils study.
♦ **hacer clic en** to click on (*informática*)
♦ **hacerse** to become ◊ *Quiere hacerse famoso.* He wants to become famous. ◊ *Se hicieron amigos.* They became friends.
♦ **Ya se está haciendo viejo.** He's getting old now.

el **hacha** SUSTANTIVO
axe

hacia PREPOSICIÓN
[1] towards ◊ *Venía hacia mí.* He was coming towards me. ◊ *su actitud hacia sus padres* his attitude towards his parents
[2] at about ◊ *Volveremos hacia las tres.* We'll be back at about three.
♦ **hacia adelante** forwards
♦ **hacia atrás** backwards
♦ **hacia dentro** inside
♦ **hacia fuera** outside
♦ **hacia abajo** down
♦ **hacia arriba** up

el **hada** SUSTANTIVO
fairy (PL fairies)
♦ **un hada madrina** a fairy godmother
♦ **un cuento de hadas** a fairy tale

hago VERBO *ver* **hacer**

hala EXCLAMACIÓN
come on!

halagar* VERBO
to flatter

hallar VERBO
to find
♦ **hallarse** to be ◊ *Se halla fuera del país.* He's out of the country.

la **hamaca** SUSTANTIVO
[1] hammock
[2] deckchair (*asiento plegable*)
[3] swing (*columpio*) River Plate

el **hambre** SUSTANTIVO
hunger
♦ **tener hambre** to be hungry ◊ *Tengo mucha hambre.* I'm very hungry.

la **hamburguesa** SUSTANTIVO
hamburger

el **hámster** SUSTANTIVO (PL los **hámsters**)
hamster

el **hardware** SUSTANTIVO
hardware

haré VERBO *ver* **hacer**

la **harina** SUSTANTIVO
flour
♦ **harina de trigo** wheat flour

hartar VERBO
♦ **hartarse** to get fed up ◊ *Me harté de estudiar.* I got fed up with studying.
♦ **Me harté de pasteles.** I stuffed myself with cakes. (*coloquial*)
♦ **¡Me estás hartando!** You're getting on my nerves!

harto (1) ADJETIVO
[1] fed up
♦ **estar harto de algo** to be fed up with something ◊ *Estábamos hartos de repetirlo.* We were fed up with repeating it. ◊ *¡Me tienes harto!* I'm fed up with you!
[2] a lot of Latin America ◊ *Había harta comida.* There was a lot of food.

harto (2) ADVERBIO Latin America
[1] very ◊ *Es un idioma harto difícil.* It's a very difficult language.
[2] a lot ◊ *Tenemos harto que estudiar.* We've got a lot to study.

hasta (1) ADVERBIO
even ◊ *Estudia hasta cuando está de vacaciones.* He even studies when he's on holiday.

hasta (2) PREPOSICIÓN, CONJUNCIÓN
[1] till ◊ *Está abierto hasta las cuatro.* It's open till four o'clock.
♦ **¿Hasta cuándo?** How long? ◊ *¿Hasta cuándo te quedas? – Hasta la semana que viene.* How long are you staying? – Till next week.
♦ **Hasta ahora no ha llamado nadie.** No one has called up to now.
♦ **hasta que** until ◊ *Espera aquí hasta que te llamen.* Wait here until you're called.

> ***Till** sustituye a "until" en la lengua hablada e informal.*

[2] up to ◊ *Caminamos hasta la puerta.* We walked up to the door.

☞

3 as far as ◊ *Desde aquí se ve hasta el pueblo vecino.* From here you can see as far as the next town.
♦ **¡Hasta luego!** See you!
♦ **¡Hasta el sábado!** See you on Saturday!

hay VERBO *ver* **haber**

haz VERBO *ver* **hacer**

he VERBO *ver* **haber**

la **hebilla** SUSTANTIVO
buckle

el **hebreo,** la **hebrea** ADJETIVO, SUSTANTIVO
Hebrew

el **hebreo** SUSTANTIVO
Hebrew (*idioma*)

el **hechizo** SUSTANTIVO
spell

hecho (1) VERBO *ver* **hacer**

hecho (2) ADJETIVO
made ◊ *¿De qué está hecho?* What's it made of?
♦ **hecho a mano** handmade
♦ **hecho a máquina** machine-made
♦ **Me gusta la carne bien hecha.** I like my meat well done.
♦ **un filete poco hecho** a rare steak
♦ **¡Bien hecho!** Well done!
♦ **un hombre hecho y derecho** a fully grown man

el **hecho** SUSTANTIVO
1 fact ◊ *el hecho de que ...* the fact that ...
♦ **el hecho es que ...** the fact is that ...
2 event (*acontecimiento*) ◊ *un hecho histórico* an historic event
♦ **de hecho** in fact

la **helada** SUSTANTIVO
frost

la **heladera** SUSTANTIVO River Plate
refrigerator

la **heladería** SUSTANTIVO
ice-cream parlour

helado ADJETIVO
1 frozen ◊ *El lago está helado.* The lake's frozen over.
2 freezing ◊ *Este cuarto está helado.* This room's freezing. ◊ *¡Estoy helado!* I'm freezing!

el **helado** SUSTANTIVO
ice cream ◊ *un helado de chocolate* a chocolate ice cream

helar* VERBO
to freeze ◊ *El frío ha helado las tuberías.* The cold has frozen the pipes. ◊ *Esta noche va a helar.* It's going to freeze tonight.
♦ **helarse** to freeze ◊ *Me estoy helando.* I'm freezing.
♦ **Anoche heló.** There was a frost last night.

el **helecho** SUSTANTIVO
fern

el **helicóptero** SUSTANTIVO
helicopter

la **hembra** ADJETIVO, SUSTANTIVO
female ◊ *un elefante hembra* a female elephant

hemos VERBO *ver* **haber**

heredar VERBO
to inherit

la **heredera** SUSTANTIVO
heiress (PL heiresses)

el **heredero** SUSTANTIVO
heir

la **herencia** SUSTANTIVO
inheritance

la **herida** SUSTANTIVO
1 wound ◊ *una herida de bala* a bullet wound ◊ *una herida de cuchillo* a stab wound
2 injury (PL injuries) ◊ *Murió a causa de las heridas del accidente.* He died from injuries received in the accident.

herido ADJETIVO
1 wounded (*por un arma*)
2 injured (*en un accidente*)

herir* VERBO
1 to wound ◊ *Lo hirieron en el pecho.* He was wounded in the chest.
2 to injure ◊ *Resultó gravemente herido en la caída.* He was seriously injured in the fall.

la **hermana** SUSTANTIVO
sister

la **hermanastra** SUSTANTIVO
stepsister

el **hermanastro** SUSTANTIVO
stepbrother
♦ **mis hermanastros (1)** (*varones*) my stepbrothers
♦ **mis hermanastros (2)** (*varones y mujeres*) my stepbrothers and sisters

el **hermano** SUSTANTIVO
brother
♦ **mis hermanos (1)** (*varones*) my brothers
♦ **mis hermanos (2)** (*varones y mujeres*) my brothers and sisters

hermético ADJETIVO
airtight

hermoso ADJETIVO
beautiful

la **hermosura** SUSTANTIVO
beauty ◊ *el secreto de su hermosura* the secret of her beauty
♦ **¡Qué hermosura de paisaje!** What a beautiful landscape!

el **héroe** SUSTANTIVO
hero (PL heroes)

la **heroína** SUSTANTIVO
heroine

* Verbs marked with this symbol are irregular. See pages 380-382 for further details

el **heroinómano**, la **heroinómana** SUSTANTIVO
heroin addict

la **herradura** SUSTANTIVO
horseshoe

la **herramienta** SUSTANTIVO
tool

el **herrero** SUSTANTIVO
blacksmith

hervir* VERBO
to boil ◊ *El agua está hirviendo.* The water's boiling.
◆ **hervir agua** to boil water

el/la **heterosexual** ADJETIVO, SUSTANTIVO
heterosexual

hice VERBO *ver* **hacer**

hielo VERBO *ver* **helar**

el **hielo** SUSTANTIVO
ice

la **hierba** SUSTANTIVO
1 grass (*césped*)
2 herb (*para infusión*)
◆ **una mala hierba** a weed

la **hierbabuena** SUSTANTIVO
mint

el **hierbajo** SUSTANTIVO
weed

el **hierro** SUSTANTIVO
iron ◊ *una caja de hierro* an iron box

el **hígado** SUSTANTIVO
liver

la **higiene** SUSTANTIVO
hygiene

higiénico ADJETIVO
hygienic
◆ **poco higiénico** unhygienic

el **higo** SUSTANTIVO
fig
◆ **un higo chumbo** a prickly pear

la **higuera** SUSTANTIVO
fig tree

la **hija** SUSTANTIVO
daughter
◆ **Soy hija única.** I'm an only child.
◆ **Sí, hija mía, tienes razón.** Yes, my dear, you're right.

la **hijastra** SUSTANTIVO
stepdaughter

el **hijastro** SUSTANTIVO
stepson
◆ **mis hijastros (1)** (*varones*) my stepsons
◆ **mis hijastros (2)** (*varones y mujeres*) my stepsons and daughters

el **hijo** SUSTANTIVO
son ◊ *Su hijo mayor.* His oldest son.
◆ **mis hijos (1)** (*varones*) my sons
◆ **mis hijos (2)** (*varones y mujeres*) my children
◆ **Soy hijo único.** I'm an only child.

la **hilera** SUSTANTIVO
1 row ◊ *una hilera de casas* a row of houses
2 line ◊ *ponerse en hilera* to get into a line

el **hilo** SUSTANTIVO
1 thread ◊ *hilo de coser* sewing thread
2 linen ◊ *un traje de hilo* a linen suit
◆ **los hilos del teléfono** the telephone wires

el **himno** SUSTANTIVO
hymn
◆ **el himno nacional** the national anthem

el/la **hincha** SUSTANTIVO
fan ◊ *los hinchas del fútbol* football fans

hinchado ADJETIVO
swollen

el **hipermercado** SUSTANTIVO
hypermarket

el **hipo** SUSTANTIVO
hiccups ◊ *Tengo hipo.* I've got hiccups. ◊ *Me ha dado hipo.* It's given me hiccups.

hipócrita ADJETIVO
hypocritical
◆ **¡No seas hipócrita!** Don't be such a hypocrite!

el/la **hipócrita** SUSTANTIVO
hypocrite

el **hipódromo** SUSTANTIVO
racecourse

el **hipopótamo** SUSTANTIVO
hippo (PL hippos)

la **hipoteca** SUSTANTIVO
mortgage

hiriendo VERBO *ver* **herir**

hirviendo VERBO *ver* **hervir**

hispanohablante ADJETIVO
Spanish-speaking ◊ *los países hispanohablantes* Spanish-speaking countries

el/la **hispanohablante** SUSTANTIVO
Spanish-speaker

la **historia** SUSTANTIVO
1 history ◊ *la historia de España* Spanish history
2 story (PL stories) ◊ *El libro cuenta la historia de dos niños.* The book tells the story of two children.
◆ **la misma historia de siempre** the same old story

el **historial** SUSTANTIVO
record

histórico ADJETIVO
1 historic ◊ *una ciudad histórica* a historic city
2 historical ◊ *un personaje histórico* a historical character

la **historieta** SUSTANTIVO
comic strip

hizo VERBO *ver* **hacer**

el **hobby** SUSTANTIVO
hobby (PL hobbies)
◆ **Lo hago por hobby.** I do it as a hobby.

☞

*The "h" in **hobby** is pronounced like Spanish "j".*

el **hockey** SUSTANTIVO
hockey
◆ **el hockey sobre hielo** ice hockey
*The "h" in **hockey** is pronounced like Spanish "j".*

el **hogar** SUSTANTIVO
home ◊ *en todos los hogares españoles* in every Spanish home
◆ **productos para el hogar** household products

la **hoguera** SUSTANTIVO
bonfire

la **hoja** SUSTANTIVO
1 (*de árbol*)
leaf (PL leaves)
2 sheet ◊ *una hoja de papel* a sheet of paper
◆ **una hoja de cálculo** a spreadsheet
3 page ◊ *las hojas de un libro* the pages of a book
◆ **una hoja de afeitar** a razor blade

el **hojaldre** SUSTANTIVO
puff pastry

hojear VERBO
to leaf through

hola EXCLAMACIÓN
hello!

Holanda SUSTANTIVO FEM
Holland

holandés ADJETIVO (FEM **holandesa,** MASC PL **holandeses**)
Dutch

el **holandés** SUSTANTIVO (PL los **holandeses**)
1 (*persona*)
Dutchman (PL Dutchmen)
◆ **los holandeses** the Dutch
2 (*idioma*)
Dutch

la **holandesa** SUSTANTIVO
Dutchwoman (PL Dutchwomen)

holgazán ADJETIVO (FEM **holgazana,** MASC PL **holgazanes**)
lazy

el **hollín** SUSTANTIVO
soot

el **hombre** SUSTANTIVO
man (PL men)
◆ **un hombre de negocios** a businessman
◆ **la historia del hombre sobre la tierra** the history of mankind on earth

el **hombro** SUSTANTIVO
shoulder
◆ **encogerse de hombros** to shrug one's shoulders

el **homenaje** SUSTANTIVO
tribute
◆ **en homenaje a** in honour of

el/la **homosexual** ADJETIVO, SUSTANTIVO
homosexual

hondo ADJETIVO
deep ◊ *un pozo muy hondo* a very deep well ◊ *Se ha tirado por la parte honda de la piscina.* He dived into the deep end of the pool.

Honduras SUSTANTIVO FEM
Honduras

el **hondureño,** la **hondureña** ADJETIVO, SUSTANTIVO
Honduran

la **honestidad** SUSTANTIVO
1 honesty (*honradez*)
2 decency (*decoro*)

honesto ADJETIVO
honest (*honrado*) ◊ *un vendedor honesto* an honest salesman

el **hongo** SUSTANTIVO
1 fungus (*bacteria*)
2 mushroom (*seta*) Latin America

el **honor** SUSTANTIVO
honour

la **honradez** SUSTANTIVO
honesty

honrado ADJETIVO
honest ◊ *Es una persona muy honrada.* He's a very honest person.

la **hora** SUSTANTIVO
1 hour ◊ *El viaje dura una hora.* The journey lasts an hour.
2 time ◊ *¿Qué hora es?* What's the time? ◊ *¿Tienes hora?* Have you got the time?
◆ **¿A qué hora llega?** What time is he arriving?
◆ **llegar a la hora** to arrive on time
◆ **la hora de cenar** dinner time
◆ **a última hora** at the last minute
3 period
◆ **Después de inglés tenemos una hora libre.** After English we have a free period.
4 appointment ◊ *Tengo hora para el dentista.* I've got an appointment at the dentist's.
◆ **horas extras** overtime SING
◆ **en mis horas libres** in my spare time

el **horario** SUSTANTIVO
timetable
◆ **el horario de trenes** the train timetable
◆ **horario de visitas** visiting hours PL

la **horchata** SUSTANTIVO

> ℹ ***Horchata** is a milky looking drink made from tiger nuts and served with ice.*

horizontal ADJETIVO
horizontal

el **horizonte** SUSTANTIVO
horizon ◊ *en el horizonte* on the horizon

la **hormiga** SUSTANTIVO

ant

el **hormigón** SUSTANTIVO
concrete

el **hormigueo** SUSTANTIVO
pins and needles ◊ *Tengo un hormigueo en la pierna.* I've got pins and needles in my leg.

el **horno** SUSTANTIVO
oven ◊ *¡Este lugar es un horno!* This place is like an oven!
♦ **pescado al horno** baked fish
♦ **pollo al horno** roast chicken
♦ **un horno microondas** a microwave oven

el **horóscopo** SUSTANTIVO
horoscope

la **horquilla** SUSTANTIVO
hairgrip (*para el pelo*)

horrible ADJETIVO
awful ◊ *El tiempo ha estado horrible.* The weather has been awful.

el **horror** SUSTANTIVO
horror ◊ *los horrores de la guerra* the horrors of war
♦ **tener horror a algo** to be terrified of something ◊ *Les tengo horror a las arañas.* I'm terrified of spiders.
♦ **¡Qué horror!** How awful!

horroroso ADJETIVO
1 horrific ◊ *un accidente horroroso* a horrific accident
2 hideous ◊ *¡Qué camisa mas horrorosa!* What a hideous shirt!

la **hortaliza** SUSTANTIVO
vegetable

hortera ADJETIVO
naff (*coloquial*) ◊ *Tiene un gusto muy hortera.* He's got really naff taste.

hospedarse VERBO
to stay ◊ *Se hospedaron en un hotel.* They stayed in a hotel.

el **hospital** SUSTANTIVO
hospital ◊ *La tuvieron que llevar al hospital.* She had to be taken to hospital.

la **hospitalidad** SUSTANTIVO
hospitality

el **hostal** SUSTANTIVO
small hotel

la **hostia** SUSTANTIVO
host

el **hotel** SUSTANTIVO
hotel

hoy ADVERBIO
today ◊ *Hoy no tenemos clases.* We haven't got any classes today. ◊ *el periódico de hoy* today's paper ◊ *los jóvenes de hoy* young people today
♦ **desde hoy en adelante** from now on
♦ **hoy en día** nowadays
♦ **hoy por la mañana** this morning

el **hoyo** SUSTANTIVO
hole

hube VERBO *ver* **haber**

la **hucha** SUSTANTIVO
moneybox

hueco ADJETIVO
hollow

el **hueco** SUSTANTIVO
1 space ◊ *Deja un hueco para la respuesta.* Leave a space for the answer.
♦ **Hazme un hueco para sentarme.** Make a bit of room so that I can sit down.
2 free period ◊ *Los lunes tengo un hueco entre clase y clase.* I have a free period between classes on Mondays.
♦ **Entró por un hueco que había en la valla.** He got in through a gap in the fence.

la **huelga** SUSTANTIVO
strike ◊ *una huelga general* a general strike
♦ **estar en huelga** to be on strike
♦ **declararse en huelga** to go on strike

el/la **huelguista** SUSTANTIVO
striker

la **huella** SUSTANTIVO
footprint (*pisada*)
♦ **huellas** tracks (*de animal, vehículo*)
♦ **Desapareció sin dejar huella.** He disappeared without trace.
♦ **huella digital** fingerprint

huelo VERBO *ver* **oler**

huérfano ADJETIVO
♦ **un niño huérfano** an orphan
♦ **ser huérfano** to be an orphan
♦ **es huérfano de padre** he's lost his father
♦ **quedarse huérfano** to be orphaned

el **huérfano**, la **huérfana** SUSTANTIVO
orphan

la **huerta** SUSTANTIVO
1 vegetable garden (*de hortalizas*)
2 orchard (*de árboles frutales*)

el **huerto** SUSTANTIVO
1 kitchen garden (*de hortalizas*)
2 orchard (*de árboles frutales*)

el **hueso** SUSTANTIVO
1 bone (*de humano, animal*)
2 stone (*de fruta*)
♦ **aceitunas sin hueso** pitted olives
♦ **La profesora de francés es un hueso.** (*coloquial*) The French teacher's a real dragon.

el/la **huésped** SUSTANTIVO
guest

el **huevo** SUSTANTIVO
egg
♦ **un huevo duro** a hard-boiled egg
♦ **un huevo escalfado** a poached egg
♦ **un huevo frito** a fried egg
♦ **huevos revueltos** scrambled eggs
♦ **un huevo pasado por agua** a soft-boiled egg

huir* VERBO
to escape ◊ *Huyó de la cárcel.* He escaped from prison.
♦ **Huyeron del país.** They fled the country.
♦ **salir huyendo** to run away

el **hule** SUSTANTIVO
1 oilcloth (*mantel*)
2 rubber (*goma*) Mexico ◊ *una liga de hule* a rubber band

la **humanidad** SUSTANTIVO
humanity

humano ADJETIVO
◊ *el cuerpo humano* the human body
◆ **los seres humanos** human beings

el **humano** SUSTANTIVO
human being

la **humareda** SUSTANTIVO
cloud of smoke

la **humedad** SUSTANTIVO
1 dampness (*de la ropa, las paredes*)
2 humidity (*del aire*)

húmedo ADJETIVO
1 damp (*ropa, pared*) ◊ *La ropa está todavía húmeda.* The clothes are still damp.
2 humid (*clima*) ◊ *El día estaba muy húmedo.* It was a very humid day.

humilde ADJETIVO
humble ◊ *Era de familia humilde.* She was from a humble background.

el **humo** SUSTANTIVO
smoke ◊ *El humo de la chimenea.* The smoke from the chimney.
◆ **darse humos** to brag (*coloquial*)
◆ **bajar los humos a alguien** to take someone down a peg or two
◆ **Estaba que echaba humo.** She was absolutely fuming. (*coloquial*)

el **humor** SUSTANTIVO
mood ◊ *No está de humor para bromas.* He's not in the mood for jokes.
◆ **estar de buen humor** to be in a good mood
◆ **estar de mal humor** to be in a bad mood
◆ **Tiene un gran sentido del humor.** He has got a good sense of humour.
◆ **humor negro** black humour

hundirse VERBO
1 to sink ◊ *El barco se hundió durante la tormenta.* The boat sank during the storm.
2 to collapse ◊ *El techo se hundió con el peso.* The ceiling collapsed under the weight.

el **húngaro,** la **húngara** ADJETIVO, SUSTANTIVO
Hungarian

el **húngaro** SUSTANTIVO
Hungarian (*idioma*)

Hungría SUSTANTIVO FEM
Hungary

el **huracán** SUSTANTIVO
hurricane

hurgar* VERBO
to rummage ◊ *La encontré hurgando en los cajones.* I found her rummaging through the drawers. ◊ *Hurgó en sus bolsillos buscando las llaves.* He rummaged in his pockets for the keys.
◆ **hurgarse la nariz** to pick one's nose

huyendo VERBO *ver* **huir**

I

I.B. ABREVIATURA (= *Instituto de Bachillerato*)

> ❶ *In Spain the* ***Institutos de Bachillerato*** *are state secondary schools for 12- to 18-year-olds.*

iba VERBO *ver* **ir**

el **iberoamericano**, la **iberoamericana** ADJETIVO, SUSTANTIVO
Latin American

el **iceberg** SUSTANTIVO (PL los **icebergs**)
iceberg

el **icono** SUSTANTIVO
icon

la **ictericia** SUSTANTIVO
jaundice

la **ida** SUSTANTIVO
single ◊ *¿Cuánto cuesta la ida?* How much does a single cost?
♦ **¿Me da uno de ida y vuelta para Londres, por favor?** A return to London please.
♦ **un billete de ida y vuelta** a return ticket
♦ **un boleto de ida y vuelta** [Latin America] a return ticket
♦ **a la ida** on the way there
♦ **El viaje de ida duró dos horas.** The journey there took two hours.

la **idea** SUSTANTIVO
idea ◊ *¡Qué buena idea!* What a good idea! ◊ *No tengo ni idea.* I haven't the faintest idea.
♦ **Mi idea era que nos juntáramos en mi casa.** I thought that we could meet at my house.
♦ **Ya me voy haciendo a la idea.** I'm beginning to get used to the idea.
♦ **cambiar de idea** to change one's mind ◊ *He cambiado de idea.* I've changed my mind.

ideal ADJETIVO
ideal ◊ *el lugar ideal para pasar el verano* the ideal place to spend the summer

el **ideal** SUSTANTIVO
ideal ◊ *los ideales democráticos* democratic ideals ◊ *Mi ideal sería trabajar cuatro horas diarias.* My ideal would be to work four hours a day.

idear VERBO
to devise ◊ *Idearon un nuevo sistema.* They devised a new system.

idéntico ADJETIVO
identical ◊ *Tiene una falda idéntica a la mía.* She has an identical skirt to mine.
♦ **Es idéntica a su padre.** (*coloquial*) She's the spitting image of her father.

identificar* VERBO
to identify ◊ *Ya han identificado a la víctima.* They've already identified the victim.
♦ **identificarse con alguien** to identify with somebody

el **idioma** SUSTANTIVO
language ◊ *Habla tres idiomas a la perfección.* He speaks three languages perfectly.

idiota ADJETIVO
stupid ◊ *¡No seas tan idiota!* Don't be so stupid!

el/la **idiota** SUSTANTIVO
idiot

la **idiotez** SUSTANTIVO (PL las **idioteces**)
♦ **Deja de decir idioteces.** Stop talking nonsense.

el **ídolo** SUSTANTIVO
idol

la **iglesia** SUSTANTIVO
church (PL churches) ◊ *Voy a la iglesia todos los domingos.* I go to church every Sunday.
♦ **la Iglesia católica** the Catholic Church

ignorante ADJETIVO
ignorant

ignorar VERBO
1 not to know ◊ *Ignoramos su paradero.* We don't know his whereabouts.
2 to ignore ◊ *Es mejor ignorarla.* It's best to ignore her.

igual (1) ADJETIVO
1 equal ◊ *Se dividieron el dinero en partes iguales.* They divided the money into equal shares.
♦ **X es igual a Y.** X is equal to Y.
2 the same ◊ *Todas las casas son iguales.* All the houses are the same.
♦ **Es igual a su madre. (1)** (*físicamente*) She looks just like her mother.
♦ **Es igual a su madre. (2)** (*en la personalidad*) She's just like her mother.
♦ **Tengo una falda igual que la tuya.** I've got a skirt just like yours.
♦ **ir iguales** to be even
♦ **Van quince iguales.** It's fifteen all.
♦ **Es igual hoy que mañana.** Today or tomorrow, it doesn't matter.
♦ **Me da igual.** I don't mind.

igual (2) ADVERBIO
1 the same (*de la misma forma*) ◊ *Se visten igual.* They dress the same.
2 maybe (*a lo mejor*) ◊ *Igual no lo saben todavía.* Maybe they don't know yet.
3 anyway (*de todas formas*) ◊ *No hizo nada pero la castigaron igual.* She didn't

☞

do anything but they punished her anyway.

la **igualdad** SUSTANTIVO
equality ◊ *la igualdad racial* racial equality
◆ **la igualdad de oportunidades** equal opportunities

igualmente ADVERBIO
the same to you ◊ *¡Feliz Navidad! – Gracias, igualmente.* Happy Christmas! – Thanks, the same to you.

ilegal ADJETIVO
illegal

ilegible ADJETIVO
illegible ◊ *Tiene una letra ilegible.* His handwriting's illegible.

ileso ADJETIVO
unhurt ◊ *Salió ileso del accidente.* He escaped unhurt from the accident.
◆ **Todos resultaron ilesos.** No one was hurt.

la **iluminación** SUSTANTIVO
lighting (*de habitación, calle*) ◊ *La iluminación de las calles es muy deficiente.* The street lighting is poor.
◆ **Se cortó la iluminación del estadio.** The stadium floodlighting went out.

iluminar VERBO
to light ◊ *los faroles que iluminan la calle* the streetlamps that light the street ◊ *Unas velas iluminaban la habitación.* The room was lit by candles.
◆ **El flash le iluminó el rostro.** The flash lit up his face.
◆ **Esta lámpara ilumina muy poco.** This lamp gives out very little light.
◆ **Se le iluminó la cara.** His face lit up.

la **ilusión** SUSTANTIVO (PL las **ilusiones**)
1 hope ◊ *Llegó aquí con muchísima ilusión.* He arrived here full of hope. ◊ *No te hagas muchas ilusiones.* Don't build your hopes up.
2 dream ◊ *Mi mayor ilusión es llegar a ser médico.* My greatest dream is to become a doctor.
3 illusion ◊ *una ilusión óptica* an optical illusion
◆ **Le hace mucha ilusión que vengas.** He's really looking forward to you coming.
◆ **Tu regalo me hizo mucha ilusión.** I was delighted to get your present.
◆ **¡Qué ilusión!** How wonderful!

ilusionar VERBO
◆ **Me ilusiona mucho la idea.** I'm really excited about the idea.
◆ **ilusionarse** to build up one's hopes ◊ *No te ilusiones demasiado.* Don't build up your hopes too much.
◆ **ilusionarse con algo** to get really excited about something

la **ilustración** SUSTANTIVO (PL las **ilustraciones**)
illustration

la **imagen** SUSTANTIVO (PL las **imágenes**)
1 image ◊ *Han decidido cambiar de imagen.* They've decided to change their image.
◆ **ser la viva imagen de alguien** to be the spitting image of somebody
2 picture ◊ *Las películas dan una imagen falsa de América.* Films give a false picture of America.

la **imaginación** SUSTANTIVO (PL las **imaginaciones**)
imagination ◊ *Tiene mucha imaginación.* He has a vivid imagination.
◆ **Esas son imaginaciones tuyas.** You're imagining things.
◆ **Ni se me pasó por la imaginación.** It never even occurred to me.

imaginarse VERBO
to imagine ◊ *No te imaginas lo mal que me sentí.* You can't imagine how bad I felt. ◊ *Me imagino que seguirá en Madrid.* I imagine that he's still in Madrid.
◆ **Me imagino que sí.** I imagine so.
◆ **Me imagino que no.** I wouldn't think so.
◆ **¿Se enfadó mucho? – ¡Imagínate!** Was he very angry? – What do you think!

el **imán** SUSTANTIVO (PL los **imanes**)
magnet

imbécil ADJETIVO
stupid ◊ *¡No seas imbécil!* Don't be stupid!

la **imitación** SUSTANTIVO (PL las **imitaciones**)
1 impression ◊ *Es muy buena haciendo imitaciones.* She's very good at doing impressions.
2 imitation ◊ *Aprendemos a hablar por imitación.* We learn to speak by imitation. ◊ *los diamantes de imitación* imitation diamonds ◊ *Es imitación cuero.* It's imitation leather.

imitar VERBO
to copy ◊ *Imita todo lo que hace su hermano.* He copies everything his brother does.
◆ **imitar a alguien** to do an impression of somebody ◊ *Imita muy bien a la directora.* She does a very good impression of the headmistress.
◆ **imitar un acento** to imitate an accent

impaciente ADJETIVO
impatient ◊ *Se estaba empezando a poner impaciente.* He was beginning to get impatient. ◊ *Estarás impaciente por saberlo.* You'll be impatient to know.

impar ADJETIVO (FEM **impar**)
odd ◊ *un número impar* an odd number

el **impar** SUSTANTIVO
odd number

imparcial ADJETIVO

* Verbs marked with this symbol are irregular. See pages 380-382 for further details

impartial

impecable ADJETIVO
impeccable ◊ *Su comportamiento siempre ha sido impecable.* His behaviour has always been impeccable.
♦ **Siempre va impecable.** He is always impeccably dressed.

impedir* VERBO
1 to prevent ◊ *Trataron de impedir la huida de los presos.* They tried to prevent the prisoners' escape. ◊ *impedir que alguien haga algo* to prevent somebody from doing something
2 to stop ◊ *A mí nadie me lo va a impedir.* Nobody is going to stop me.
3 to block ◊ *Un camión nos impedía el paso.* A lorry was blocking our way.

el **imperdible** SUSTANTIVO
safety pin

el **imperio** SUSTANTIVO
empire

impermeable ADJETIVO
waterproof ◊ *una tela impermeable* waterproof material

el **impermeable** SUSTANTIVO
raincoat

impersonal ADJETIVO
impersonal

impertinente ADJETIVO
impertinent

impidiendo VERBO *ver* **impedir**

impido VERBO *ver* **impedir**

imponer* VERBO
to impose ◊ *Le impusieron una multa de 5.000 pesetas.* They imposed a 5,000-peseta fine on him.
♦ **imponerse (1)** to triumph ◊ *El corredor nigeriano se impuso en la segunda carrera.* The Nigerian runner triumphed in the second race.
♦ **imponerse (2)** to assert oneself ◊ *Sabe imponerse.* He knows how to assert himself.

la **importación** SUSTANTIVO (PL las **importaciones**)
import ◊ *una empresa de importación/exportación* an import-export business
♦ **los artículos de importación** imported goods
♦ **Está prohibida su importación.** There's a ban on importing it.

la **importancia** SUSTANTIVO
importance ◊ *un asunto de suma importancia* a matter of great importance
♦ **dar importancia a algo** to attach importance to something ◊ *Les da demasiada importancia a los detalles.* He attaches too much importance to details.
♦ **darse importancia** to give oneself airs
♦ **La educación tiene mucha importancia.** Education is very important.
♦ **¡Me he olvidado tu libro! – No tiene importancia.** I've forgotten your book! – It doesn't matter.
♦ **cuestiones sin importancia** unimportant matters

importante ADJETIVO
important
♦ **lo importante** the important thing ◊ *Lo importante es que vengas.* The important thing is that you come.

importar VERBO
1 to import ◊ *Importa whisky de Escocia.* He imports whisky from Scotland.
2 to matter ◊ *¿Y eso qué importa?* And what does that matter?
♦ **no importa (1)** it doesn't matter ◊ *No importa lo que piensen los demás.* It doesn't matter what other people think.
♦ **no importa (2)** never mind ◊ *No importa, podemos hacerlo mañana.* Never mind, we can do it tomorrow.
♦ **No me importa levantarme temprano.** I don't mind getting up early. ◊ *¿Le importa que fume?* Do you mind if I smoke?
♦ **¿Y a ti qué te importa?** What's it to you?
♦ **Me importan mucho mis estudios.** My studies are very important to me.
♦ **Me importa un bledo.** I couldn't care less.

imposible ADJETIVO
impossible ◊ *Es imposible predecir quién ganará.* It's impossible to predict who will win. ◊ *Es imposible de predecir.* It's impossible to predict. ◊ *El abuelo está imposible hoy.* Granddad is being impossible today.
♦ **Me es imposible comprenderla.** I can't understand her.
♦ **Es imposible que lo sepan.** They can't possibly know.

el **impostor**, la **impostora** SUSTANTIVO
impostor

la **impresión** SUSTANTIVO (PL las **impresiones**)
impression ◊ *Le causó muy buena impresión a mis padres.* He made a very good impression on my parents.
♦ **Tengo la impresión de que no va a venir.** I have a feeling that he won't come.
♦ **Me dio mucha impresión verlo tan delgado.** I was shocked to see him looking so thin.

impresionante ADJETIVO
1 impressive (*hazaña*) ◊ *una colección de sellos de lo más impresionante* a most impressive stamp collection
2 amazing (*éxito, memoria*) ◊ *una cantidad impresionante de coches* an amazing number of cars
3 striking (*belleza*) ◊ *El parecido es impresionante.* The likeness is striking.
♦ **paisajes de una belleza impresionante** strikingly beautiful landscapes

I

impresionar VERBO
1 to shock ◇ *Me impresionó mucho su palidez.* I was really shocked at how pale he was.
2 to impress ◇ *Unos poemas me impresionaron más que otros.* Some poems impressed me more than others.
♦ **Impresiona lo rápido que es.** His speed is impressive.
♦ **impresionarse** to be impressed ◇ *Se impresiona con facilidad.* He's easily impressed.

el **impreso** SUSTANTIVO
form ◇ *un impreso de solicitud* an application form

la **impresora** SUSTANTIVO
printer ◇ *una impresora láser* a laser printer

imprevisible ADJETIVO
1 unforeseeable ◇ *acontecimientos imprevisibles* unforeseeable events
2 unpredictable ◇ *Tiene unas reacciones totalmente imprevisibles.* His reactions are completely unpredictable.

imprevisto ADJETIVO
unexpected

el **imprevisto** SUSTANTIVO
♦ **si no surge algún imprevisto** if nothing unexpected comes up

imprimir* VERBO
to print

improvisar VERBO
to improvise

la **imprudencia** SUSTANTIVO
♦ **Saltar la tapia fue una imprudencia.** It was unwise to jump over the wall.
♦ **El accidente fue debido a una imprudencia del conductor.** The accident was caused by reckless driving.

imprudente ADJETIVO
unwise ◇ *Sería imprudente nadar aquí.* It would be unwise to go swimming here.
♦ **conductores imprudentes** reckless drivers

impuesto VERBO *ver* **imponer**

el **impuesto** SUSTANTIVO
tax (PL taxes)
♦ **el impuesto sobre la renta** income tax
♦ **el impuesto sobre el valor añadido** value-added tax
♦ **el impuesto sobre el valor agregado** Latin America value-added tax
♦ **libre de impuestos** duty-free ◇ *Lo compré en la tienda libre de impuestos.* I bought it at the duty-free shop.

impulsar VERBO
to drive ◇ *Está impulsado por un motor eléctrico.* It's driven by an electric motor. ◇ *La ambición la impulsó a mentir.* Ambition drove her to lie.
♦ **una política destinada a impulsar el comercio** a policy designed to boost trade

el **impulso** SUSTANTIVO
impulse ◇ *Actué por impulso.* I acted on impulse.
♦ **Mi primer impulso fue salir corriendo.** My first instinct was to run away.
♦ **Tomó impulso antes de saltar.** He took a run up before jumping.

inaceptable ADJETIVO
unacceptable

inadecuado ADJETIVO
unsuitable

inadvertido ADJETIVO
♦ **pasar inadvertido** to go unnoticed ◇ *Tu ausencia no pasó inadvertida.* Your absence didn't go unnoticed.

inapropiado ADJETIVO
unsuitable ◇ *Esos zapatos son inapropiados para caminar por el bosque.* Those shoes are unsuitable for walking in the woods.

la **inauguración** SUSTANTIVO (PL las **inauguraciones**)
opening ◇ *Había mucha gente en la inauguración.* There were a lot of people at the opening. ◇ *la ceremonia de inauguración* the opening ceremony

inaugurar VERBO
to open ◇ *Mañana inauguran el nuevo hospital.* The new hospital is being opened tomorrow.

el/la **inca** ADJETIVO, SUSTANTIVO
Inca

la **incapacidad** SUSTANTIVO
inability ◇ *debido a su incapacidad para concentrarse* owing to his inability to concentrate
♦ **la incapacidad física** physical disability
♦ **la incapacidad mental** mental disability

incapaz ADJETIVO (PL **incapaces**)
incapable ◇ *Es incapaz de estarse callado.* He is incapable of keeping quiet.
♦ **Hoy soy incapaz de concentrarme.** I can't concentrate today.

incendiarse VERBO
to catch fire ◇ *Se le incendió el coche.* His car caught fire.

el **incendio** SUSTANTIVO
fire ◇ *Se declaró un incendio en el hotel.* A fire broke out in the hotel.

el **incentivo** SUSTANTIVO
incentive ◇ *No tengo incentivo para estudiar.* I have no incentive to study.

el **incidente** SUSTANTIVO
incident ◇ *La reunión transcurrió sin incidentes.* The meeting passed off without incident.

* Verbs marked with this symbol are irregular. See pages 380-382 for further details

incierto ADJETIVO
uncertain ◊ *un porvenir incierto* an uncertain future
inclinar VERBO
to tilt ◊ *Inclina un poco más la sombrilla.* Can you tilt the sun umbrella a bit more?
◆**inclinar la cabeza** to nod
◆**inclinarse (1)** to bend down ◊ *Se inclinó para besarlo.* She bent down to kiss him.
◆**inclinarse (2)** to lean ◊ *inclinarse sobre algo* to lean over something ◊ *inclinarse hacia delante* to lean forward ◊ *inclinarse hacia atrás* to lean back
◆**inclinarse (3)** to bow ◊ *inclinarse ante alguien* to bow to somebody
incluido ADJETIVO
included ◊ *El servicio no está incluido en el precio.* Service is not included.
incluir* VERBO
to include ◊ *El precio incluye las comidas.* The price includes meals.
◆**El examen no incluye este tema.** This topic doesn't come into the exam.
inclusive ADVERBIO
1 inclusive ◊ *Está abierto de lunes a sábado inclusive.* It's open from Monday to Saturday inclusive.
2 including ◊ *hasta el capítulo diez inclusive* up to and including chapter ten
incluso ADVERBIO
even ◊ *He tenido que estudiar incluso los domingos.* I've even had to study on Sundays.
incluyendo VERBO *ver* **incluir**
incómodo ADJETIVO
uncomfortable ◊ *Este asiento es muy incómodo.* This seat is very uncomfortable. ◊ *Se siente muy incómoda cuando está con él.* She feels very uncomfortable with him.
incompetente ADJETIVO
incompetent
incompleto ADJETIVO
incomplete
incomprensible ADJETIVO
incomprehensible
inconsciente ADJETIVO
1 unconscious ◊ *estar inconsciente* to be unconscious ◊ *Quedó inconsciente con el golpe.* The force of the blow left him unconscious. ◊ *un deseo inconsciente* an unconscious desire
2 thoughtless ◊ *¡Qué inconsciente eres!* You're so thoughtless!
inconveniente ADJETIVO
inconvenient ◊ *a una hora inconveniente* at an inconvenient time
el **inconveniente** SUSTANTIVO
1 problem ◊ *Ha surgido un inconveniente.* A problem has come up.
2 drawback ◊ *El plan tiene sus inconvenientes.* The plan has its drawbacks.
◆**No tengo ningún inconveniente.** I have no objection.
◆**No tengo inconveniente en preguntárselo.** I don't mind asking him.
◆**¿Tienes algún inconveniente en que le dé tu teléfono?** Do you mind if I give him your telephone number?
incorrecto ADJETIVO
1 incorrect ◊ *una respuesta incorrecta* an incorrect answer
2 impolite ◊ *Has estado muy incorrecto.* You were very impolite.
increíble ADJETIVO
incredible
inculto ADJETIVO
ignorant (*persona*)
incurable ADJETIVO
incurable
indeciso ADJETIVO
indecisive ◊ *Es una persona muy indecisa.* She's very indecisive.
◆**Estoy indecisa, no sé cuál comprar.** I can't make up my mind, I don't know which to buy.
indefenso ADJETIVO
defenceless
la **indemnización** SUSTANTIVO (PL las **indemnizaciones**)
compensation ◊ *Recibieron mil dólares de indemnización.* They received a thousand dollars compensation.
◆**la indemnización por daños y perjuicios** damages PL
indemnizar* VERBO
to compensate ◊ *El gobierno indemnizará a las víctimas.* The government will compensate the victims.
◆**Nos tienen que indemnizar.** They've got to pay us compensation.
la **independencia** SUSTANTIVO
independence
independiente ADJETIVO
1 independent ◊ *Es una chica muy independiente.* She's a very independent girl.
2 self-contained ◊ *Son apartamentos independientes.* They are self-contained flats.
independientemente ADVERBIO
independently ◊ *Los dos motores funcionan independientemente.* The two engines work independently.
◆**Iremos, independientemente de lo que hayan decidido.** We'll go, regardless of what they have decided.
independizarse* VERBO
to become independent ◊ *Quiero independizarme.* I want to become independent.
la **india** SUSTANTIVO
Indian woman (PL Indian women)
India SUSTANTIVO FEM
◆**La India** India

I

la **indicación** SUSTANTIVO (PL las **indicaciones**)
sign
◆ **Nos hizo una indicación para que siguiéramos.** He signalled to us to go on.
◆ **indicaciones (1)** instructions ◇ *Hay que seguir las indicaciones del manual.* You'll need to follow the instructions in the manual.
◆ **indicaciones (2)** directions ◇ *Me dio indicaciones de cómo llegar.* He gave me directions for getting there.

indicar* VERBO
1 to indicate ◇ *El termómetro indicaba treinta grados.* The thermometer indicated thirty degrees. ◇ *Todo indica que ...* Everything indicates that ...
2 to tell ◇ *¿Puede indicarme dónde hay una gasolinera?* Please can you tell where there's a petrol station? ◇ *Un guardia me indicó el camino.* A policeman told me the way.
3 to advise ◇ *El médico me indicó que no fumara.* The doctor advised me not to smoke.

el **índice** SUSTANTIVO
1 index (PL indexes *o* indices) ◇ *un índice alfabético* an alphabetical index
◆ **el índice de materias** the table of contents
◆ **el índice de natalidad** the birth rate
2 (*dedo*)
index finger

la **indiferencia** SUSTANTIVO
indifference

indiferente ADJETIVO
indifferent ◇ *Parece indiferente al cariño.* She seems indifferent to affection.
◆ **Es indiferente que viva en Glasgow o Edimburgo.** It makes no difference whether he lives in Glasgow or Edinburgh.
◆ **Me es indiferente hacerlo hoy o mañana.** I don't mind whether I do it today or tomorrow.

indígena ADJETIVO
indigenous ◇ *la población indígena* the indigenous population

el/la **indígena** SUSTANTIVO
native

la **indigestión** SUSTANTIVO
indigestion

indignado ADJETIVO
angry ◇ *Están muy indignados con ella.* They're very angry with her.

indignar VERBO
to infuriate ◇ *Su comportamiento los indignó.* His behaviour infuriated them.
◆ **indignarse por algo** to get angry about something
◆ **indignarse con alguien** to be furious with somebody

el **indio** ADJETIVO, SUSTANTIVO
Indian

la **indirecta** SUSTANTIVO
hint ◇ *lanzar una indirecta* to drop a hint

indirecto ADJETIVO
indirect

indispensable ADJETIVO
essential ◇ *Es indispensable saber inglés.* It's essential to know English.
◆ **Llevaba sólo lo indispensable.** He was carrying only the essentials.

individual ADJETIVO
1 individual (*porción, rasgo*) ◇ *Los venden en paquetes individuales.* They're sold in individual packets.
2 single (*cama, cuarto*) ◇ *Quisiera una habitación individual.* I'd like a single room.

el **individual** SUSTANTIVO
singles PL ◇ *la final del individual femenino* the ladies' singles final

el **individuo** SUSTANTIVO
individual

la **industria** SUSTANTIVO
industry (PL industries) ◇ *la industria pesada* heavy industry ◇ *la industria petrolera* the oil industry

industrial ADJETIVO
industrial

el/la **industrial** SUSTANTIVO
industrialist

ineficiente ADJETIVO
inefficient

inesperado ADJETIVO
unexpected ◇ *una visita inesperada* an unexpected visit

inestable ADJETIVO
1 unsteady (*mueble*)
2 changeable (*tiempo*)

inevitable ADJETIVO
inevitable

inexacto ADJETIVO
inaccurate ◇ *La biografía contiene muchos datos inexactos.* The biography contains a lot of inaccurate details.

inexperto ADJETIVO
inexperienced

inexplicable ADJETIVO
inexplicable

infantil ADJETIVO
1 children's (*parque, ropa*) ◇ *un programa infantil* a children's programme
2 childish (*actitud*) ◇ *¡No seas tan infantil!* Don't be so childish!

el **infarto** SUSTANTIVO
heart attack ◇ *Le dio un infarto.* He had a heart attack.

la **infección** SUSTANTIVO (PL las **infecciones**)

infection ◊ *tener una infección* to have an infection ◊ *Tiene una infección de oídos.* He has got an ear infection.

infeliz ADJETIVO (PL **infelices**)
unhappy

inferior ADJETIVO (FEM **inferior**)
1 lower ◊ *Tenía el labio inferior hinchado.* His lower lip was swollen. ◊ *Las temperaturas han sido inferiores a lo normal.* Temperatures have been lower than normal.
2 inferior ◊ *de calidad inferior* of inferior quality
♦ **un número inferior a nueve** a number below nine

el **infiernillo** SUSTANTIVO
stove

el **infierno** SUSTANTIVO
hell

el **infinitivo** SUSTANTIVO
infinitive

inflable ADJETIVO
inflatable

la **inflación** SUSTANTIVO
inflation ◊ *Hay que reducir la inflación.* Inflation has to be reduced.

inflamable ADJETIVO
inflammable

inflar VERBO
1 to blow up (*globo*)
2 to inflate (*rueda*)

la **influencia** SUSTANTIVO
influence ◊ *Mi abuelo tuvo una gran influencia en mí.* My grandfather had a great influence on me.

influenciar VERBO
to influence

influir* VERBO
♦ **dos hombres que influyeron en su vida** two men who influenced his life
♦ **Mis padres influyeron mucho en mí.** My parents had a great influence on me.
♦ **El cansancio ha influido en su rendimiento.** Tiredness has affected his work.

la **información** SUSTANTIVO (PL las **informaciones**)
1 information ◊ *Quisiera información sobre los cursos de inglés.* I'd like some information on English courses.
♦ **una información muy importante** a very important piece of information
2 news SING ◊ *Este canal tiene mucha información deportiva.* There's a lot of sports news on this channel.
3 directory enquiries ◊ *Llama a información y pide que te den el número.* Call directory enquiries and ask them for the number.
♦ **Pregunta en información de dónde sale el tren.** Ask at the information desk which platform the train leaves from.

informal ADJETIVO
1 informal ◊ *un ambiente muy informal* a very informal atmosphere
♦ **Prefiero la ropa informal.** I prefer casual clothes.
2 unreliable ◊ *Es una persona muy informal.* He's a very unreliable person.

informar VERBO
to inform ◊ *Nos informaron que venía con retraso.* They informed us that it was going to be late.
♦ **Les han informado mal.** You've been misinformed.
♦ **¿Me podría informar sobre los cursos de inglés?** Could you give me some information about English courses?
♦ **informarse de algo** to find out about something

la **informática** SUSTANTIVO
computing ◊ *los avances de la informática* advances in computing
♦ **Quiere estudiar informática.** He wants to study computer science.

informático ADJETIVO
computer

> ***computer** en este caso va siempre delante del sustantivo.*

◊ *un programa informático* a computer program

el **informático** SUSTANTIVO
computer expert

el **informe** SUSTANTIVO
report ◊ *Presentó un informe detallado sobre lo ocurrido.* He gave a detailed report about what had happened.
♦ **según mis informes** according to my information
♦ **pedir informes** to ask for references

la **infusión** SUSTANTIVO (PL las **infusiones**)
herbal tea
♦ **una infusión de manzanilla** a camomile tea

ingeniar VERBO
to devise ◊ *Habían ingeniado un sistema para evadir impuestos.* They had devised a system for evading taxes.
♦ **ingeniárselas** to manage ◊ *No sé cómo se las ingenió para conseguir el dinero.* I don't know how he managed to get the money.

la **ingeniera** SUSTANTIVO
engineer ◊ *Quiere ser ingeniera.* She wants to be an engineer.

la **ingeniería** SUSTANTIVO
engineering

el **ingeniero** SUSTANTIVO
engineer ◊ *Quiere ser ingeniero.* He wants to be an engineer.
♦ **un ingeniero agrónomo** an agriculturist

el **ingenio** SUSTANTIVO
1 ingenuity (*talento*)
2 wit (*agudeza*)
♦ **un ingenio azucarero** Latin America a sugar refinery

ingenioso ADJETIVO
1 ingenious ◊ *¡Qué idea más ingeniosa!* What an ingenious idea!
2 witty ◊ *un comentario ingenioso* a witty comment

ingenuo ADJETIVO
naïve

Inglaterra SUSTANTIVO FEM
England

inglés ADJETIVO (FEM **inglesa,** MASC PL **ingleses**)
English ◊ *la comida inglesa* English food

el **inglés** SUSTANTIVO (PL los **ingleses**)
1 (*persona*)
Englishman (PL Englishmen)
◆ **los ingleses** the English
2 (*idioma*)
English ◊ *El inglés le resulta difícil.* He finds English difficult.

la **inglesa** SUSTANTIVO
Englishwoman (PL Englishwomen)

el **ingrediente** SUSTANTIVO
ingredient

ingresar VERBO
to pay in ◊ *ingresar un cheque en una cuenta* to pay a cheque into an account
◆ **ingresar en el hospital** to go into hospital
◆ **Han vuelto a ingresar a mi abuela.** They've taken my grandmother into hospital again.
◆ **ingresar en un club** to join a club

el **ingreso** SUSTANTIVO
admission (*en institución*)
◆ **un examen de ingreso** an entrance exam
◆ **los ingresos** income SING ◊ *Tiene unos ingresos muy bajos.* He has a very low income.

la **inicial** SUSTANTIVO
initial

la **iniciativa** SUSTANTIVO
initiative ◊ *Lo hizo por iniciativa propia.* He did it on his own initiative.

la **injusticia** SUSTANTIVO
injustice ◊ *Lucharon contra las injusticias sociales.* They fought against social injustices.
◆ **Es una injusticia que lo hayan expulsado.** It was unfair of them to expel him.

injusto ADJETIVO
unfair

inmaduro ADJETIVO
1 immature (*persona*)
2 unripe (*fruta*)

inmediatamente ADVERBIO
immediately

inmediato ADJETIVO
immediate (*instantáneo*)
◆ **inmediato a algo** next to something ◊ *en el edificio inmediato a la embajada* in the building next to the embassy
◆ **de inmediato** immediately

inmenso ADJETIVO
immense
◆ **la inmensa mayoría** the vast majority

la **inmigración** SUSTANTIVO
immigration

el/la **inmigrante** SUSTANTIVO
immigrant

inmoral ADJETIVO
immoral

inmortal ADJETIVO
immortal

inmóvil ADJETIVO
motionless ◊ *Se quedó inmóvil.* He remained motionless.

innecesario ADJETIVO
unnecessary

inocente ADJETIVO
innocent ◊ *Es inocente.* He's innocent.
◆ **El jurado la declaró inocente.** The jury found her not guilty.

inofensivo ADJETIVO
harmless

inolvidable ADJETIVO
unforgettable

inquietante ADJETIVO
worrying

inquieto ADJETIVO
1 worried ◊ *Estaba inquieta porque su hijo no había llegado.* She was worried because her son hadn't come home.
2 restless ◊ *Es un niño muy inquieto y le cuesta dormirse.* He's a very restless boy and finds it hard to get to sleep.

el **inquilino,** la **inquilina** SUSTANTIVO
1 tenant (*de un piso, una casa*)
2 lodger (*de una habitación*)

insatisfecho ADJETIVO
dissatisfied

inscribirse* VERBO
to enrol ◊ *Se inscribió en un curso de idiomas.* He enrolled on a language course.

la **inscripción** SUSTANTIVO (PL las **inscripciones**)
1 enrolment ◊ *Mañana se cierra la inscripción.* Tomorrow is the last day for enrollment.
2 inscription ◊ *Sobre la puerta hay una inscripción con el año.* Above the door there's an inscription with the year on it.

inscrito VERBO *ver* **inscribirse**

el **insecto** SUSTANTIVO
insect

la **inseguridad** SUSTANTIVO
insecurity ◊ *la inseguridad en el trabajo* job insecurity

* Verbs marked with this symbol are irregular. See pages 380-382 for further details

♦ **la inseguridad ciudadana** the lack of safety on the streets

inseguro ADJETIVO
1 insecure (*persona*)
2 unsafe (*lugar*)

insensato ADJETIVO
foolish

insensible ADJETIVO
insensitive ◊ *Se han vuelto insensibles al frío.* They have become insensitive to the cold.
♦ **Es insensible al sufrimiento ajeno.** He is blind to the suffering of others.

insignificante ADJETIVO
insignificant

insinuar* VERBO
to hint at ◊ *No lo dijo pero lo insinuó.* He didn't say it but he hinted at it.
♦ **¿Insinúas que miento?** Are you insinuating that I'm lying?

insípido ADJETIVO
insipid

insistir VERBO
to insist ◊ *insistir en hacer algo* to insist on doing something ◊ *Insiste en que vea a un médico.* He's insisting that I see a doctor.

la **insolación** SUSTANTIVO
sunstroke

insolente ADJETIVO
insolent

insoportable ADJETIVO
unbearable

el **inspector**, la **inspectora** SUSTANTIVO
inspector

las **instalaciones** SUSTANTIVO
facilities ◊ *El hotel tiene unas estupendas instalaciones deportivas.* The hotel has excellent sports facilities.

instalar VERBO
1 to install ◊ *Instaló una alarma en el coche.* He installed an alarm in the car.
2 to set up ◊ *Aquí van a instalar unas oficinas.* They're going to set up offices here.
♦ **instalarse** to settle ◊ *Decidieron instalarse en el centro.* They decided to settle in the town centre.

instantáneo ADJETIVO
instantaneous
♦ **el café instantáneo** instant coffee

el **instante** SUSTANTIVO
moment ◊ *por un instante* for a moment
♦ **A cada instante suena el teléfono.** The phone rings all the time.
♦ **al instante** right away

el **instinto** SUSTANTIVO
instinct

la **institución** SUSTANTIVO (PL las **instituciones**)
institution

el **instituto** SUSTANTIVO
institute ◊ *el Instituto Británico* the British Institute
♦ **un instituto de enseñanza secundaria** a secondary school

las **instrucciones** SUSTANTIVO
instructions

instructivo ADJETIVO
educational

el **instructor**, la **instructora** SUSTANTIVO
instructor ◊ *un instructor de esquí* a ski instructor ◊ *un instructor de autoescuela* a driving instructor

el **instrumento** SUSTANTIVO
instrument

insuficiente ADJETIVO
insufficient ◊ *una cantidad insuficiente de dinero* an insufficient amount of money

el **insuficiente** SUSTANTIVO
♦ **Sacó un insuficiente en francés.** He got an F in French.

la **insulina** SUSTANTIVO
insulin

insultar VERBO
to insult

el **insulto** SUSTANTIVO
insult

el/la **intelectual** ADJETIVO, SUSTANTIVO
intellectual

la **inteligencia** SUSTANTIVO
intelligence

inteligente ADJETIVO
intelligent

la **intención** SUSTANTIVO (PL las **intenciones**)
intention ◊ *No tengo la más mínima intención de hacerlo.* I haven't got the slightest intention of doing it.
♦ **tener intención de hacer algo** to intend to do something ◊ *Tenía intención de descansar un rato.* He intended to rest for a while.
♦ **Lo que cuenta es la intención.** It's the thought that counts.

intencionado ADJETIVO
deliberate ◊ *La patada fue intencionada.* It was a deliberate kick.
♦ **bien intencionado** well-meaning
♦ **mal intencionado** malicious

intensivo ADJETIVO
intensive ◊ *un curso intensivo de inglés* an intensive English course

intenso ADJETIVO
intense

intentar VERBO
to try ◊ *¿Por qué no lo intentas otra vez?* Why don't you try again? ◊ *intentar hacer algo* to try to do something

el **intento** SUSTANTIVO
attempt ◊ *Aprobó al primer intento.* He passed at the first attempt.

intercambiar VERBO

☞

1 to exchange (*impresiones, presos, ideas*)
2 to swap (*sellos, fotos*)

el **intercambio** SUSTANTIVO
exchange

el **interés** SUSTANTIVO (PL los **intereses**)
interest ◊ *Tienes que poner más interés en tus estudios.* You must take more of an interest in your studies. ◊ *El banco da un interés del 5%.* The bank gives 5% interest.
◆ **tener interés en hacer algo** to be keen to do something
◆ **Todo lo hace por interés.** Everything he does is out of self-interest.

interesante ADJETIVO
interesting

interesar VERBO
to interest ◊ *Eso es algo que siempre me ha interesado.* That's something that has always interested me.
◆ **Me interesa mucho la física.** I'm very interested in physics.
◆ **interesarse por algo** to ask about something

el **interfono** SUSTANTIVO
intercom

interior ADJETIVO (FEM **interior**)
1 inside (*bolsillo*)
2 inner (*mundo*)

el **interior** SUSTANTIVO
◆ **El tren se detuvo en el interior del túnel.** The train stopped inside the tunnel.

el/la **interiorista** SUSTANTIVO
interior designer

intermedio ADJETIVO
1 intermediate (*nivel*)
2 medium (*tamaño*)

el **intermedio** SUSTANTIVO
interval

interminable ADJETIVO
endless

intermitente ADJETIVO
1 intermittent (*lluvia*)
2 flashing (*luz*)

el **intermitente** SUSTANTIVO
indicator

internacional ADJETIVO
international

el **internado** SUSTANTIVO
boarding school

el/la **internauta** SUSTANTIVO
internet user

el/la **Internet** SUSTANTIVO
the internet ◊ *en Internet* on the internet

interno ADJETIVO
◆ **estar interno en un colegio** to be a boarder at a school

el **interno**, la **interna** SUSTANTIVO
1 (*alumno*)
boarder
2 (*médico*)
houseman (PL housemen)

la **interpretación** SUSTANTIVO (PL las **interpretaciones**)
interpretation (*de un texto, papel*)
◆ **la interpretación simultánea** simultaneous interpreting
◆ **Todo fue producto de una mala interpretación.** It was all the result of a misunderstanding.

interpretar VERBO
1 to interpret ◊ *Sabe interpretar los sueños.* He knows how to interpret dreams.
2 to play ◊ *Interpreta el papel de Victoria.* She plays the part of Victoria.
3 to perform ◊ *Interpretó una pieza de Mozart.* He performed a piece by Mozart.
◆ **No me interpretes mal.** Don't misunderstand me.

el/la **intérprete** SUSTANTIVO
interpreter ◊ *Quiere ser intérprete.* She wants to be an interpreter.

interrogar* VERBO
to question ◊ *Fue interrogado por la policía.* He was questioned by the police.

interrumpir VERBO
1 to interrupt (*persona*)
2 to cut short (*vacaciones*)
3 to block (*tráfico*) ◊ *Estás interrumpiendo el paso.* You're blocking the way.

la **interrupción** SUSTANTIVO (PL las **interrupciones**)
interruption

el **interruptor** SUSTANTIVO
switch (PL switches)

interurbano ADJETIVO
long-distance (*llamada*)

el **intervalo** SUSTANTIVO
interval (*de tiempo, intermedio*)

intervenir* VERBO
1 to take part (*tomar parte*) ◊ *No intervino en el debate.* He did not take part in the debate.
2 to intervene (*injerirse*) ◊ *La policía intervino para separarlos.* The police intervened to separate them.

la **intimidad** SUSTANTIVO
1 private life ◊ *Protege mucho su intimidad.* He's very protective of his private life.
2 privacy ◊ *En esta casa no tengo ninguna intimidad.* I have no privacy in this house.
◆ **La boda se celebró en la intimidad.** It was a private wedding.

intimidar VERBO
to intimidate

íntimo ADJETIVO

* Verbs marked with this symbol are irregular. See pages 380-382 for further details

intimate ◊ *mis secretos íntimos* my intimate secrets
◆**Es un amigo íntimo.** He's a close friend.

la **introducción** SUSTANTIVO (PL las **introducciones**)
introduction

introducir* VERBO
1 to insert ◊ *Introdujo la moneda en la ranura.* He inserted the coin in the slot.
2 to bring in ◊ *Esperan introducir un nuevo sistema de trabajo.* They're hoping to bring in new working methods.
◆**Han introducido cambios en el horario.** They've made changes to the timetable.

introvertido ADJETIVO
introverted

el **intruso**, la **intrusa** SUSTANTIVO
intruder

la **intuición** SUSTANTIVO
intuition ◊ *la intuición femenina* feminine intuition
◆**por intuición** intuitively

la **inundación** SUSTANTIVO (PL las **inundaciones**)
flood

inundar VERBO
to flood ◊ *El río inundó el pueblo.* The river flooded the village.
◆**inundarse** to be flooded ◊ *Se nos inundó el baño.* Our bathroom was flooded.

inútil ADJETIVO
useless ◊ *La oficina está llena de trastos inútiles.* The office is full of useless rubbish. ◊ *Es inútil tratar de hacerle entender.* It's useless trying to make him understand.
◆**Es inútil que esperes.** There's no point in your waiting.

el/la **inútil** SUSTANTIVO (PL los/las **inútiles**)
◆**¡Es un inútil!** He's useless!

invadir VERBO
to invade

la **inválida** SUSTANTIVO
disabled woman (PL disabled women)

inválido ADJETIVO
disabled ◊ *Quedó inválida después del accidente.* She was left disabled following the accident.

el **inválido** SUSTANTIVO
disabled man (PL disabled men)
◆**los inválidos** the disabled

la **invasión** SUSTANTIVO (PL las **invasiones**)
invasion

inventar VERBO
1 to invent ◊ *Inventaron un nuevo sistema.* They invented a new system.
2 to make up ◊ *Inventó toda la historia.* He made up the whole story.

el **invento** SUSTANTIVO
invention

el **inventor**, la **inventora** SUSTANTIVO
inventor

el **invernadero** SUSTANTIVO
greenhouse
◆**el efecto invernadero** the greenhouse effect

invernar VERBO
to hibernate

inverosímil ADJETIVO
unlikely

la **inversión** SUSTANTIVO (PL las **inversiones**)
investment

inverso ADJETIVO
reverse ◊ *en orden inverso* in reverse order
◆**a la inversa** the other way round

invertir* VERBO
1 to invest (*dinero*) ◊ *He invertido mucho dinero en estas acciones.* I've invested a lot of money in these shares.
2 to spend (*tiempo*) ◊ *Hemos invertido muchas horas en el proyecto.* We've spent a lot of time on this project.
3 to reverse (*orden*)

la **investigación** SUSTANTIVO (PL las **investigaciones**)
1 (*estudio*)
research ◊ *Está haciendo una investigación sobre el envejecimiento.* He's doing some research into aging.
2 (*por la policía*)
investigation
3 (*por una comisión*)
inquiry (PL inquiries) ◊ *Se hará una investigación pública.* There will be a public inquiry.

el **invierno** SUSTANTIVO
winter ◊ *en invierno* in winter ◊ *el invierno pasado* last winter

invisible ADJETIVO
invisible

la **invitación** SUSTANTIVO (PL las **invitaciones**)
invitation

el **invitado**, la **invitada** SUSTANTIVO
guest ◊ *Es el invitado de honor.* He's the guest of honour.

invitar VERBO
to invite ◊ *Me invitó a una fiesta.* He invited me to a party. ◊ *Me gustaría invitarla a cenar.* I'd like to invite her to dinner.
◆**Te invito a un café.** I'll buy you a coffee.
◆**Esta vez invito yo.** This time it's on me.

la **inyección** SUSTANTIVO (PL las **inyecciones**)
injection ◊ *ponerle una inyección a alguien* to give someone an injection

inyectar VERBO
◆**Le tuvieron que inyectar insulina.** They had to give him insulin injections.
◆**inyectarse algo** to inject oneself with something ◊ *Se había inyectado heroína.* He had injected himself with heroin.

ir* VERBO

☞

I

1 to go ◊ *Anoche fuimos al cine.* We went to the cinema last night. ◊ *¿A qué colegio vas?* What school do you go to?
- ♦ **ir de vacaciones** to go on holiday
- ♦ **ir a por** to go and get ◊ *Voy a por el paraguas.* I'll go and get the umbrella. ◊ *Ha ido a por el médico.* She has gone to get the doctor.
- ♦ **Voy a hacerlo mañana.** I'm going to do it tomorrow.
- ♦ **vamos** let's go ◊ *Vamos a casa.* Let's go home.
- ♦ **¡Vamos!** Come on! ◊ *¡Vamos! ¡Di algo!* Come on! Say something!

2 to be ◊ *Iba muy bien vestido.* He was very well dressed. ◊ *Iba con su madre.* He was with his mother. ◊ *como iba diciendo* as I was saying ◊ *Va a ser difícil.* It will be difficult.

3 to come ◊ *¡Ahora voy!* I'm just coming!
- ♦ **¿Puedo ir contigo?** Can I come with you?
- ♦ **ir a pie** to walk
- ♦ **ir en avión** to fly
- ♦ **¿Cómo te va?** How are things?
- ♦ **¿Cómo te va en los estudios?** How are you getting on with your studies?
- ♦ **¡Que te vaya bien!** Take care of yourself!
- ♦ **¡Qué va!** What are you talking about!
- ♦ **¡Vaya! ¿Qué haces tú por aquí?** Well, what a surprise! What are you doing here?
- ♦ **¡Vaya coche!** What a car!
- ♦ **irse (1)** to leave ◊ *Acaba de irse.* He has just left.
- ♦ **irse (2)** to go out ◊ *Se ha ido la luz.* The lights have gone out.
- ♦ **¡Vámonos!** Let's go!
- ♦ **¡Vete!** Go away!
- ♦ **Vete a hacer los deberes.** Go and do your homework.

Irak SUSTANTIVO MASC
Iraq

Irán SUSTANTIVO MASC
Iran

el/la **iraní** ADJETIVO, SUSTANTIVO (PL los/las **iraníes**)
Iranian

el/la **iraquí** ADJETIVO, SUSTANTIVO (PL los/las **iraquíes**)
Iraqi

Irlanda SUSTANTIVO FEM
Ireland ◊ *Irlanda del Norte* Northern Ireland

irlandés ADJETIVO (FEM **irlandesa,** MASC PL **irlandeses**)
Irish ◊ *un café irlandés* an Irish coffee

el **irlandés** SUSTANTIVO (PL los **irlandeses**)
1 (*persona*)
Irishman (PL Irishmen)
- ♦ **los irlandeses** the Irish

2 (*idioma*)
Irish

la **irlandesa** SUSTANTIVO
Irishwoman (PL Irishwomen)

irónico ADJETIVO
ironic

irracional ADJETIVO
irrational

irrelevante ADJETIVO
irrelevant

irresistible ADJETIVO
irresistible

irresponsable ADJETIVO
irresponsible

irritante ADJETIVO
irritating

irritar VERBO
to irritate

irrompible ADJETIVO
unbreakable

la **isla** SUSTANTIVO
island ◊ *una isla desierta* a desert island
- ♦ **la Isla de Pascua** Easter Island

el **Islam** SUSTANTIVO
Islam

islámico ADJETIVO
Islamic

islandés ADJETIVO (FEM **islandesa,** MASC PL **islandeses**)
Icelandic

el **islandés,** la **islandesa** SUSTANTIVO (MASC PL los **islandeses**)
Icelander

el **islandés** SUSTANTIVO
Icelandic (*idioma*)

Islandia SUSTANTIVO FEM
Iceland

el **isleño** SUSTANTIVO
islander

Israel SUSTANTIVO MASC
Israel

el/la **israelí** ADJETIVO, SUSTANTIVO (PL los/las **israelíes**)
Israeli

Italia SUSTANTIVO FEM
Italy

el **italiano,** la **italiana** ADJETIVO, SUSTANTIVO
Italian

el **italiano** SUSTANTIVO
Italian (*idioma*)

el **itinerario** SUSTANTIVO
1 route ◊ *Hicimos el itinerario de costumbre.* We took the usual route.
2 itinerary (PL itineraries) ◊ *Me gustaría incluir Roma en el itinerario.* I'd like to include Rome on our itinerary.

el **IVA (1)** ABREVIATURA (= *Impuesto sobre el Valor Añadido*)
VAT (= Value Added Tax)

el **IVA (2)** ABREVIATURA (= *Impuesto sobre el Valor Agregado*) Latin America

VAT (= Value Added Tax)

izar* VERBO

to hoist ◊ *Izaron la bandera a media asta.* They hoisted the flag to half mast.

la **izquierda** SUSTANTIVO

1 left hand (*mano*)

♦ **Escribo con la izquierda.** I write with my left hand.

2 left ◊ *doblar a la izquierda* to turn left ◊ *La izquierda ganó las elecciones.* The elections were won by the left.

♦ **ser de izquierdas** to be left-wing ◊ *un partido de izquierdas* a left-wing party

♦ **a la izquierda** on the left ◊ *la segunda calle a la izquierda* the second turning on the left

♦ **a la izquierda del edificio** to the left of the building

♦ **conducir por la izquierda** to drive on the left

izquierdo ADJETIVO

left ◊ *Levanta la mano izquierda.* Raise your left hand.

♦ **Escribo con la mano izquierda.** I write with my left hand.

♦ **el lado izquierdo** the left side

♦ **a mano izquierda** on the left-hand side

I

J

el **jabón** SUSTANTIVO (PL los **jabones**)
soap
la **jaiba** SUSTANTIVO Latin America
crab
jalar VERBO Latin America
1 to pull ◇ *No le jales el pelo.* Don't pull his hair.
2 to take ◇ *Jaló un folleto de la mesa.* He took a leaflet from the table.
jamás ADVERBIO
never ◇ *Jamás he visto nada parecido.* I've never seen anything like it.
el **jamón** SUSTANTIVO (PL los **jamones**)
ham ◇ *un bocadillo de jamón* a ham sandwich
◆ **jamón serrano** cured ham
◆ **jamón de York** boiled ham
Japón SUSTANTIVO MASC
Japan
el **japonés**, la **japonesa** ADJETIVO, SUSTANTIVO (MASC PL los **japoneses**)
Japanese
el **japonés** SUSTANTIVO
Japanese (*idioma*)
el **jarabe** SUSTANTIVO
syrup
◆ **jarabe para la tos** cough syrup
el **jardín** SUSTANTIVO (PL los **jardines**)
garden
◆ **el jardín de infancia** nursery school
la **jardinera** SUSTANTIVO
1 gardener (*persona*)
2 window box (*maceta*)
la **jardinería** SUSTANTIVO
gardening
el **jardinero** SUSTANTIVO
gardener
la **jarra** SUSTANTIVO
1 jug (*de leche*)
2 beer glass (*de cerveza*)
el **jarro** SUSTANTIVO
jug
el **jarrón** SUSTANTIVO (PL los **jarrones**)
vase
la **jaula** SUSTANTIVO
cage
el **jefe**, la **jefa** SUSTANTIVO
1 boss (PL bosses) ◇ *Carlos es mi jefe.* Carlos is my boss.
2 head ◇ *El jefe de la empresa dimitió.* The head of the company resigned.
◆ **el jefe del departamento** the head of department
◆ **jefe de estado** head of state
◆ **el jefe del grupo guerrillero** the leader of the guerrilla group

el **jerez** SUSTANTIVO
sherry
la **jeringuilla** SUSTANTIVO
syringe
el **jersey** SUSTANTIVO (PL los **jerséis**)
jumper
Jesús EXCLAMACIÓN
1 Bless you! (*al estornudar*)
2 Good God! (*por asombro*)
el **jinete** SUSTANTIVO
jockey (PL jockeys)
la **jirafa** SUSTANTIVO
giraffe
el **jitomate** SUSTANTIVO Mexico
tomato (PL tomatoes)
la **jornada** SUSTANTIVO
◆ **jornada de trabajo** working day
◆ **trabajar a jornada completa** to work full-time
◆ **trabajar a media jornada** to work part-time
joven ADJETIVO (PL **jóvenes**)
young ◇ *un chico joven* a young boy
el/la **joven** SUSTANTIVO (PL los/las **jóvenes**)
◆ **un joven** a young man
◆ **una joven** a young woman
◆ **los jóvenes** young people
la **joya** SUSTANTIVO
jewel
◆ **Me han robado mis joyas.** My jewellery has been stolen.
la **joyera** SUSTANTIVO
jeweller
la **joyería** SUSTANTIVO
jeweller's (*tienda*)
el **joyero** SUSTANTIVO
1 jeweller (*persona*)
2 jewellery box (*estuche*)
la **jubilación** SUSTANTIVO (PL las **jubilaciones**)
1 retirement ◇ *La edad de jubilación es a los 65 años.* The retirement age is 65.
2 pension ◇ *cobrar la jubilación* to get one's pension
jubilado ADJETIVO
retired
◆ **estar jubilado** to be retired
el **jubilado**, la **jubilada** SUSTANTIVO
pensioner
jubilarse VERBO
to retire
la **judía** SUSTANTIVO
Jew (*hebrea*)
◆ **judía blanca** haricot bean
◆ **judía verde** green bean
judío ADJETIVO
Jewish

el **judío** SUSTANTIVO
Jew
el **judo** SUSTANTIVO
judo
juego VERBO *ver* **jugar**
el **juego** SUSTANTIVO
1 game ◊ *un juego de ordenador* a computer game
♦ **juegos de cartas** card games
♦ **juegos de mesa** board games
2 gambling ◊ *Lo perdió todo en el juego.* He lost everything through gambling.
3 set ◊ *un juego de café* a coffee set
♦ **Las cortinas hacen juego con el sofá.** The curtains go with the sofa.
la **juerga** SUSTANTIVO
♦ **irse de juerga** to go out on the town
el **jueves** SUSTANTIVO (PL los **jueves**)
Los días de la semana se escriben con mayúscula.
Thursday ◊ *La vi el jueves.* I saw her on Thursday. ◊ *todos los jueves* every Thursday ◊ *el jueves pasado* last Thursday ◊ *el jueves que viene* next Thursday ◊ *Jugamos los jueves.* We play on Thursdays.
el **juez,** la **jueza** SUSTANTIVO (MASC PL los **jueces**)
judge
♦ **juez de línea** (*en el fútbol*) linesman (PL linesmen)
el **jugador,** la **jugadora** SUSTANTIVO
player
jugar* VERBO
1 to play ◊ *¿Jugamos una partida de dominó?* Shall we have a game of dominoes?
♦ **jugar al fútbol** to play football
2 to gamble ◊ *Perdió un dineral jugando en el casino.* He lost a fortune gambling at the casino.
♦ **jugar a la lotería** to do the lottery
el **jugo** SUSTANTIVO
1 juice (*de frutas*)
2 gravy (*de carne, como salsa*)
el **juguete** SUSTANTIVO
toy (PL toys)
♦ **un avión de juguete** a toy plane
la **juguetería** SUSTANTIVO
toy shop
el **juicio** SUSTANTIVO
trial ◊ *El juicio empieza mañana.* The trial starts tomorrow.
♦ **llevar a alguien a juicio** to take someone to court
julio SUSTANTIVO MASC
Los meses se escriben con mayúscula.
July ◊ *en julio* in July ◊ *Nació el 4 de julio.* He was born on 4 July.
la **jungla** SUSTANTIVO
jungle
junio SUSTANTIVO MASC
Los meses se escriben con mayúscula.
June ◊ *en junio* in June ◊ *Nací el 20 de junio.* I was born on 20 June.
la **junta** SUSTANTIVO
committee (*comité*)
♦ **La junta directiva tiene la última palabra.** The board of management has the final say.
juntar VERBO
1 to put together ◊ *Vamos a juntar los pupitres.* Let's put the desks together.
2 to gather together ◊ *Consiguieron juntar a mil personas.* They managed to gather together one thousand people.
♦ **juntarse (1)** to move closer together ◊ *Si os juntáis más cabremos todos.* If you move closer together we'll all fit in.
♦ **juntarse (2)** to meet up ◊ *Nos juntamos los domingos para comer.* We meet up for dinner on Sundays.
junto (1) ADJETIVO
1 close together ◊ *Los muebles están demasiado juntos.* The furniture is too close together.
2 together ◊ *Cuando estamos juntos apenas hablamos.* We hardly talk when we're together.
♦ **todo junto** all together ◊ *Ponlo todo junto en una sola bolsa.* Put it all together in one bag.
junto (2) ADVERBIO
♦ **junto a** by ◊ *Hay una mesa junto a la ventana.* There's a table by the window.
♦ **junto con** together with
♦ **Mi apellido se escribe todo junto.** My surname is all in one word.
el **jurado** SUSTANTIVO
1 (*en un juicio*)
jury (PL juries)
2 (*en un concurso*)
panel
jurar VERBO
to swear
la **justicia** SUSTANTIVO
justice
justificar* VERBO
to justify
justo (1) ADJETIVO
1 fair ◊ *Tuvo un juicio justo.* He had a fair trial.
2 right
♦ **Este reloj siempre da la hora justa.** This watch always tells the right time. ◊ *Apareció en el momento justo.* He appeared at the right time.
3 tight ◊ *Me están muy justos estos pantalones.* These trousers are tight on me.
4 just enough ◊ *Tengo el dinero justo para el billete.* I have just enough money for the ticket.

J

justo (2) ADVERBIO
just ◊ *El supermercado está justo al doblar la esquina.* The supermarket is just round the corner. ◊ *La vi justo cuando entrábamos.* I saw her just as we came in.
◆ **Me dio un puñetazo justo en la nariz.** He punched me right on the nose.

juvenil ADJETIVO
1 youth (*paro, centro*)

***youth** en este caso va siempre delante del sustantivo.*

2 junior (*equipo, torneo*)
◆ **la literatura juvenil** young people's literature

la **juventud** SUSTANTIVO
1 youth ◊ *Fue soldado en su juventud.* He was a soldier in his youth.
2 youngsters PL ◊ *La juventud viene aquí a divertirse.* Youngsters come here to have fun.

el **juzgado** SUSTANTIVO
court

juzgar* VERBO
to try ◊ *Lo juzgaron por un delito menor.* He was tried on a minor charge.

* Verbs marked with this symbol are irregular. See pages 380-382 for further details

K

el **kárate** SUSTANTIVO
karate

el **kilo** SUSTANTIVO
kilo ◊ *un kilo de tomates* a kilo of tomatoes

el **kilogramo** SUSTANTIVO
kilogramme

> ℹ *En los países anglosajones el peso a menudo se expresa en libras* ***pounds****. Un kilogramo equivale a 2.2 libras aproximadamente.*

el **kilómetro** SUSTANTIVO
kilometre

> ℹ *En los países anglosajones las distancias se expresan en millas* ***miles****. Un kilómetro equivale a 0.6 millas aproximadamente.*

◊ *Está a tres kilómetros de aquí.* It's three kilometres from here. ◊ *a 90 kilómetros por hora* at 90 kilometres per hour

♦ **¡Caminamos kilómetros y kilómetros!** We walked for miles!

el **kiosco** SUSTANTIVO
news stand

L

la (1) ARTÍCULO
the ◊ *la pared* the wall
♦ **la del sombrero rojo** the girl in the red hat
♦ **Yo fui la que te despertó.** It was I who woke you up.
El artículo se traduce por el posesivo en inglés cuando se refiere a una parte del cuerpo, a una prenda que se lleva puesta o a algo que se posee.
♦ **Ayer me lavé la cabeza.** I washed my hair yesterday.
♦ **Abróchate la camisa.** Do your shirt up.
♦ **Tiene una casa bonita, pero prefiero la de Juan.** He's got a lovely house, but I prefer Juan's.
El artículo a veces no se traduce en inglés; por ejemplo cuando se refiere a algo en general, con algunas expresiones de tiempo, o con apellidos.
♦ **No me gusta la fruta.** I don't like fruit.
♦ **Vendrá la semana que viene.** He'll come next week.
♦ **Me he encontrado a la Sra. Sendra.** I met Mrs Sendra.

la (2) PRONOMBRE
[1] her
Cuando nos referimos a "ella".
◊ *La quiero.* I love her.
♦ **La han despedido.** She has been sacked.
[2] you
Cuando nos referimos a "usted".
◊ *La acompaño hasta la puerta.* I'll see you out.
[3] it
Cuando nos referimos a una cosa.
◊ *No la toques.* Don't touch it.

el **labio** SUSTANTIVO
lip

la **labor** SUSTANTIVO
work ◊ *Mi labor consiste básicamente en regar las plantas.* My work is basically watering the plants.
♦ **las labores domésticas** the housework

laborable ADJETIVO
♦ **día laborable** working day

laboral ADJETIVO
[1] working (*condiciones, jornada*)
[2] labour (*mercado*)
***labour** en este caso va siempre delante del sustantivo.*
[3] industrial (*accidente*)

el **laboratorio** SUSTANTIVO
laboratory (PL laboratories)

la **laca** SUSTANTIVO
[1] hairspray (*para el pelo*)
[2] lacquer (*para los muebles*)
♦ **la laca de uñas** nail varnish

lácteo ADJETIVO
♦ **los productos lácteos** dairy products

la **ladera** SUSTANTIVO
hillside

el **lado** SUSTANTIVO
side ◊ *a los dos lados de la carretera* on both sides of the road
*También se traduce por **-where** en palabras compuestas.*
◊ *Hay gente por todos lados.* There are people everywhere. ◊ *Tiene que estar en otro lado.* It must be somewhere else.
♦ **Mi casa está aquí al lado.** My house is right nearby.
♦ **la mesa de al lado** the next table
♦ **al lado de** beside ◊ *La silla que está al lado del armario.* The chair beside the wardrobe.
♦ **Felipe se sentó a mi lado.** Felipe sat beside me.
♦ **por un lado ..., por otro lado ...** on the one hand ..., on the other hand ...

ladrar VERBO
to bark ◊ *El perro les ladró.* The dog barked at them.

el **ladrillo** SUSTANTIVO
brick

el **ladrón,** la **ladrona** SUSTANTIVO
[1] (*de objetos*)
thief (PL thieves) ◊ *Un ladrón me quitó el bolso.* A thief took my bag.
[2] (*de una casa*)
burglar ◊ *Los ladrones entraron de noche en la casa.* The burglars broke into the house during the night.
[3] (*de un banco*)
robber ◊ *Tres ladrones atracaron el banco.* Three robbers raided the bank.

el **lagarto** SUSTANTIVO
lizard

el **lago** SUSTANTIVO
lake

la **lágrima** SUSTANTIVO
tear

la **laguna** SUSTANTIVO
lake

lamentar VERBO
♦ **Lamento lo ocurrido.** I am sorry about what happened.
♦ **lamentarse** to complain ◊ *De nada vale lamentarse.* There's no use complaining.

lamer VERBO
to lick

la **lámina** SUSTANTIVO

[1] sheet (*de metal*)
[2] plate (*ilustración*)

la **lámpara** SUSTANTIVO
lamp

la **lana** SUSTANTIVO
wool
◆ **una bufanda de lana** a woollen scarf

la **lancha** SUSTANTIVO
motorboat
◆ **una lancha de salvamento** a lifeboat

la **langosta** SUSTANTIVO
[1] lobster (*de mar*)
[2] locust (*insecto*)

el **langostino** SUSTANTIVO
king prawn

lanzar* VERBO
[1] to throw (*piedra, balón, granada*)
◊ *Lanzó una piedra al río.* He threw a stone into the river.
[2] to launch (*cohete, producto*) ◊ *Han lanzado dos satélites al espacio.* They have launched two satellites into space.
◆ **lanzarse** to dive ◊ *Los niños se lanzaron a la piscina.* The children dived into the swimming pool.

el **lapicero** SUSTANTIVO
pencil

la **lápida** SUSTANTIVO
gravestone

el **lápiz** SUSTANTIVO (PL los **lápices**)
pencil ◊ *Escribió mi dirección a lápiz.* He wrote my address in pencil.
◆ **los lápices de colores** crayons
◆ **un lápiz de labios** a lipstick
◆ **un lápiz de ojos** an eyeliner pencil

largo ADJETIVO
long ◊ *Fue una conferencia muy larga.* It was a very long conference. ◊ *Esta cuerda es demasiado larga.* This piece of string is too long.

el **largo** SUSTANTIVO
length ◊ *Nadé cuatro largos de la piscina.* I swam four lengths of the pool.
◆ **¿Cuánto mide de largo?** How long is it?
◆ **Tiene nueve metros de largo.** It's nine metres long.
◆ **a lo largo del río** along the river
◆ **a lo largo de la semana** throughout the week
◆ **Pasó de largo sin saludar.** He passed by without saying hello.

*No confundir **largo** con **large**.*

las (1) ARTÍCULO PL
the ◊ *las paredes* the walls
◆ **las del estante de arriba** the ones on the top shelf

El artículo se traduce por el posesivo en inglés cuando se refiere a una parte del cuerpo, a una prenda que se lleva puesta o a algo que se posee.

◆ **Me duelen las piernas.** My legs hurt.
◆ **Poneos las bufandas.** Put on your scarves.
◆ **Estas fotos son bonitas, pero prefiero las de Pedro.** These photos are nice, but I prefer Pedro's.

El artículo plural a veces no se traduce en inglés; por ejemplo cuando se refiere a algo en general o para expresar la hora.

◆ **No me gustan las arañas.** I don't like spiders.
◆ **Vino a las seis de la tarde.** He came at six in the evening.

las (2) PRONOMBRE
[1] them

Cuando nos referimos a "ellas".

◊ *Las vi por la calle.* I saw them in the street.
◆ **Las han despedido.** They've been sacked.
[2] you

Cuando nos referimos a "ustedes".

◊ *Las acompañaré hasta la puerta, señoras.* I'll see you out, ladies.

el **láser** SUSTANTIVO
laser

la **lástima** SUSTANTIVO
◆ **Me da lástima de ella.** I feel sorry for her.
◆ **Es una lástima que no puedas venir.** It's a shame you can't come.

la **lata** SUSTANTIVO
[1] tin (*de sardinas, anchoas*)
[2] can (*de cerveza, cola*)
◆ **Deja de dar la lata.** Stop being a pain.

lateral ADJETIVO
side

***side** en este caso va siempre delante del sustantivo.*

◊ *la puerta lateral* the side door

el **latido** SUSTANTIVO
beat

el **látigo** SUSTANTIVO
whip

el **latín** SUSTANTIVO
Latin

Latinoamérica SUSTANTIVO FEM
Latin America

el **latinoamericano**, la **latinoamericana** ADJETIVO, SUSTANTIVO
Latin American

latir VERBO
to beat

el **laurel** SUSTANTIVO
laurel
◆ **una hoja de laurel** a bay leaf

el **lavabo** SUSTANTIVO
[1] sink ◊ *Llené el lavabo de agua.* I filled the sink with water.
[2] toilet ◊ *Voy al lavabo.* I'm going to the toilet.

el **lavado** SUSTANTIVO
wash (*de ropa, vehículo*)
◆ **el lavado en seco** dry cleaning

la **lavadora** SUSTANTIVO

☞

washing machine

la **lavandería** SUSTANTIVO
launderette

el **lavaplatos** SUSTANTIVO (PL los **lavaplatos**)
1 dishwasher (*electrodoméstico*)
2 sink Mexico

lavar VERBO
to wash ◊ *Lava estos vasos.* Wash these glasses.
◆ **lavar la ropa** to do the washing
◆ **lavarse** to wash ◊ *Me lavo todos los días.* I wash every day.
◆ **Ayer me lavé la cabeza.** I washed my hair yesterday.
◆ **Lávate los dientes.** Brush your teeth.

el **lavarropas** SUSTANTIVO (PL los **lavarropas**) Mexico
washing machine

el **lavavajillas** SUSTANTIVO (PL los **lavavajillas**)
1 dishwasher (*lavaplatos*)
2 washing-up liquid (*detergente*)

el **lazo** SUSTANTIVO
1 bow (*nudo*)
2 ribbon (*cinta*)

le PRONOMBRE
1 him
Cuando nos referimos a "él".
◊ *Le mandé una carta.* I sent him a letter.
◊ *Le miré con atención.* I watched him carefully.
◆ **Le abrí la puerta.** I opened the door for him.
2 her
Cuando nos referimos a "ella".
◊ *Le mandé una carta.* I sent her a letter.
◆ **No le hablé de ti.** I didn't speak to her about you.
◆ **Le busqué el libro.** I looked out the book for her.
3 you
Cuando nos referimos a "usted".
◊ *Le presento a la Señora Gutiérrez.* Let me introduce you to Mrs. Gutiérrez.
◆ **Le he arreglado el ordenador.** I've fixed the computer for you.
Con partes del cuerpo o con prendas que se llevan puestas se usa el adjetivo posesivo.
◊ *Le huelen los pies.* His feet smell. ◊ *Le arrastra la falda.* Her skirt is trailing on the floor.

la **lealtad** SUSTANTIVO
loyalty (PL loyalties)

la **lección** SUSTANTIVO (PL las **lecciones**)
lesson

la **leche** SUSTANTIVO
milk
◆ **la leche desnatada** skimmed milk
◆ **la leche en polvo** powdered milk

la **lechuga** SUSTANTIVO
lettuce

la **lechuza** SUSTANTIVO
owl

el **lector**, la **lectora** SUSTANTIVO
1 reader ◊ *Varios lectores se quejaron del artículo.* Several readers complained about the article.
2 language assistant ◊ *Es la lectora de francés.* She's the French language assistant.

el **lector** SUSTANTIVO
◆ **un lector de CD** a CD player

la **lectura** SUSTANTIVO
reading ◊ *Me encanta la lectura.* I love reading.

leer* VERBO
to read

legal ADJETIVO
legal

la **legaña** SUSTANTIVO
◆ **tener legañas** to have sleep in one's eyes

la **legumbre** SUSTANTIVO
pulse

lejano ADJETIVO
distant ◊ *un sitio muy lejano* a very distant place

la **lejía** SUSTANTIVO
bleach

lejos ADVERBIO
far ◊ *¿Está lejos?* Is it far? ◊ *No está lejos de aquí.* It's not far from here.
◆ **De lejos parecía un avión.** From a distance it looked like a plane.

la **lencería** SUSTANTIVO
lingerie

la **lengua** SUSTANTIVO
1 tongue ◊ *Me he mordido la lengua.* I've bitten my tongue.
2 language ◊ *Habla varias lenguas.* He speaks several languages.
◆ **mi lengua materna** my mother tongue

el **lenguado** SUSTANTIVO
sole

el **lenguaje** SUSTANTIVO
language

la **lente** SUSTANTIVO
lens (PL lenses)
◆ **las lentes de contacto** contact lenses

la **lenteja** SUSTANTIVO
lentil

los **lentes** SUSTANTIVO Latin America
glasses
◆ **los lentes de sol** sunglasses

la **lentilla** SUSTANTIVO
contact lens

lento (1) ADJETIVO
slow ◊ *un proceso lento* a slow progress

lento (2) ADVERBIO
slowly ◊ *Vas un poco lento.* You're going a bit slowly.

la **leña** SUSTANTIVO

* Verbs marked with this symbol are irregular. See pages 380-382 for further details

firewood

Leo SUSTANTIVO MASC
Leo ◊ *Soy Leo.* I'm Leo.

el **león** SUSTANTIVO (PL los **leones**)
lion

la **leona** SUSTANTIVO
lioness (PL lionesses)

el **leopardo** SUSTANTIVO
leopard

los **leotardos** SUSTANTIVO
woolly tights

les PRONOMBRE
1 them
Cuando nos referimos a "ellos" o "ellas".
◊ *Les mandé una carta.* I sent them a letter. ◊ *Les miré con atención.* I watched them carefully.
◆ **Les abrí la puerta.** I opened the door for them.
◆ **Les eché de comer a los gatos.** I gave the cats something to eat.
2 you
Cuando nos referimos a "ustedes".
◊ *Les presento a la Señora Gutiérrez.* Let me introduce you to Mrs. Gutiérrez.
◆ **Les he arreglado el ordenador.** I've fixed the computer for you.
Con partes del cuerpo o con prendas que se llevan puestas se usa el adjetivo posesivo.
◊ *Les huelen los pies.* Their feet smell.
◊ *Les arrastraban los abrigos.* Their coats were trailing on the floor.

la **lesbiana** SUSTANTIVO
lesbian

la **lesión** SUSTANTIVO (PL las **lesiones**)
injury (PL injuries)

lesionado ADJETIVO
injured ◊ *Está lesionado.* He's injured.

la **letra** SUSTANTIVO
1 letter ◊ *la letra "a"* the letter "a"
2 handwriting ◊ *Tengo muy mala letra.* My handwriting's very poor.
3 lyrics PL ◊ *Él escribe la letra de sus canciones.* He writes the lyrics for his songs.

el **letrero** SUSTANTIVO
sign

levantar VERBO
to lift ◊ *Levanta la tapa.* Lift the lid.
◆ **Levantad la mano si tenéis alguna duda.** Raise your hand if you are unclear.
◆ **levantarse** to get up ◊ *Hoy me he levantado temprano.* I got up early this morning. ◊ *Me levanté y seguí caminando.* I got up and carried on walking.

leve ADJETIVO
minor ◊ *Sólo tiene heridas leves.* He only has minor injuries. ◊ *Cometió una falta leve.* He made a minor mistake.

la **ley** SUSTANTIVO (PL las **leyes**)
law ◊ *la ley de la gravedad* the law of gravity

leyendo VERBO *ver* **leer**

liar* VERBO
1 to tie up (*atar*) ◊ *Lía este paquete con una cuerda.* Tie up this parcel with some string.
2 to confuse (*confundir*) ◊ *Me liaron con tantas explicaciones.* They confused me with all their explanations.
◆ **A mí no me líes en esto.** Don't get me mixed up in this.
◆ **liarse** (*confundirse*) to get muddled up ◊ *Me estoy liando, empezaré otra vez.* I'm getting muddled up, I'll start again.
◆ **Se lió a tortas con su hermano.** He got into a fight with his brother.
◆ **Nos liamos a hablar y se nos pasó la hora.** We got talking and we forgot the time.

Líbano SUSTANTIVO MASC
Lebanon

el/la **liberal** ADJETIVO, SUSTANTIVO
liberal

liberar VERBO
to free

la **libertad** SUSTANTIVO
freedom ◊ *libertad de expresión* freedom of expression
◆ **No tengo libertad para hacer lo que quiera.** I'm not free to do what I want.
◆ **El rehén está en libertad.** The hostage is free.
◆ **poner a alguien en libertad** to release somebody

la **libra** SUSTANTIVO
pound (*moneda, unidad de peso*)

> *En los países anglosajones el peso a menudo se expresa en libras* ***pounds****. Un kilogramo equivale a 2.2 libras aproximadamente.*

◆ **libra esterlina** pound sterling

Libra SUSTANTIVO MASC
Libra ◊ *Soy Libra.* I'm Libra.

librarse VERBO
◆ **librarse de (1)** (*evitar*) to get out of ◊ *¡No te creas que te vas a librar de fregar los platos!* Don't think you're going to get out of doing the washing-up!
◆ **librarse de (2)** to get rid of ◊ *Logré librarme de mi hermana.* I managed to get rid of my sister.
◆ **Se libró del castigo por pura suerte.** He got away with it by pure good luck.

libre ADJETIVO
free ◊ *¿Está libre este asiento?* Is this seat free? ◊ *El martes estoy libre, así que podemos quedar.* I'm free on Tuesday so we can meet up.
◆ **los 100 metros libres** the 100 metres freestyle

L

la **librería** SUSTANTIVO
[1] (*tienda*)
bookshop
[2] (*estantería*)
bookshelf (PL bookshelves)
*No confundir **librería** con **library**.*

el **librero** SUSTANTIVO [Chile, Mexico]
bookcase

la **libreta** SUSTANTIVO
notebook
◆ **una libreta de ahorros** a savings book

el **libro** SUSTANTIVO
book
◆ **un libro de bolsillo** a paperback
◆ **un libro de texto** a text book

la **licencia** SUSTANTIVO
licence ◊ *una licencia de armas* a gun licence
◆ **la licencia de obras** planning permission
◆ **estar de licencia** [Latin America] to be on leave

el **licenciado**, la **licenciada** SUSTANTIVO
graduate ◊ *un licenciado en historia* a history graduate

la **licenciatura** SUSTANTIVO
degree

el **licor** SUSTANTIVO
liqueur (*bebida dulce*) ◊ *un licor de pera* a pear liqueur
◆ **Bebimos cerveza y licores.** We drank beer and spirits.

el/la **líder** SUSTANTIVO
leader

la **liebre** SUSTANTIVO
hare

la **liga** SUSTANTIVO
[1] league (*en deportes*)
[2] garter (*para medias*)

ligar* VERBO
◆ **Ayer ligué con una chica.** (*coloquial*) I got off with a girl yesterday.

ligero ADJETIVO
[1] light ◊ *Me gusta llevar ropa ligera.* I like to wear light clothing. ◊ *Comimos algo ligero.* We ate something light.
[2] slight ◊ *Tengo un ligero dolor de cabeza.* I have a slight headache.
◆ **Andaba a paso ligero.** He walked quickly.

la **lila** SUSTANTIVO
lilac

la **lima** SUSTANTIVO
[1] file (*herramienta*) ◊ *una lima de uñas* a nail file
[2] lime (*fruta*)

limitar VERBO
to limit ◊ *Limitaron el tiempo de examen a dos horas.* The exam time was limited to two hours.
◆ **España limita con Francia.** Spain has a border with France.
◆ **Yo me limité a observar.** I just watched.

el **límite** SUSTANTIVO
[1] limit ◊ *el límite de velocidad* the speed limit
◆ **fecha límite** deadline
[2] boundary (PL boundaries) ◊ *Está dentro de los límites de la finca.* It's within the boundaries of the estate.

el **limón** SUSTANTIVO (PL los **limones**)
lemon

la **limonada** SUSTANTIVO
lemonade

la **limosna** SUSTANTIVO
◆ **pedir limosna** to beg

el **limpiaparabrisas** SUSTANTIVO (PL los **limpiaparabrisas**)
windscreen-wiper

limpiar VERBO
[1] to clean ◊ *El sábado voy a limpiar la casa.* I'm going to clean the house on Saturday.
[2] to wipe (*con la mano, con un trapo*) ◊ *¿Has limpiado la mesa?* Have you wiped the table? ◊ *Límpiate la nariz.* Wipe your nose.

la **limpieza** SUSTANTIVO
cleaning ◊ *Yo hago la limpieza y tú paseas al perro.* I'll do the cleaning and you can walk the dog.
◆ **limpieza en seco** dry cleaning

limpio ADJETIVO
clean ◊ *El baño está muy limpio.* The bathroom's very clean.
◆ **Voy a pasar esto a limpio.** I'm going to write this out neat.

lindo ADJETIVO
[1] pretty (*bonito*) ◊ *sus lindos ojos* her pretty eyes
[2] nice (*agradable*) [Latin America] ◊ *un día muy lindo* a very nice day

la **línea** SUSTANTIVO
line ◊ *Dibujó una línea recta.* He drew a straight line.
◆ **Vaya en línea recta.** Go straight ahead.
◆ **una línea aérea** an airline
◆ **en línea** online

el **lino** SUSTANTIVO
linen

la **linterna** SUSTANTIVO
torch (PL torches)

el **lío** SUSTANTIVO
◆ **En mi mesa hay un lío enorme de papeles.** My desk is in a real muddle with all these papers.
◆ **hacerse un lío** to get muddled up ◊ *Se hizo un lío con tantos nombres.* He got muddled up with all the names.
◆ **Esta ecuación es un lío.** This equation is a real headache.

◆ **Si sigues así te vas a meter en un lío.** If you carry on like that you'll get yourself into a real mess.

el **líquido** ADJETIVO, SUSTANTIVO
liquid

Lisboa SUSTANTIVO FEM
Lisbon

liso ADJETIVO
1 smooth (*superficie*)
2 straight (*pelo*)
3 plain (*tela, color*)

la **lista** SUSTANTIVO
list ◊ *la lista de espera* the waiting list
◆ **pasar lista** to call the register
◆ **la lista de correo** mailing list

listo ADJETIVO
1 clever ◊ *Es una chica muy lista.* She's a very clever girl.
2 ready ◊ *¿Estás listo?* Are you ready?

la **litera** SUSTANTIVO
1 bunk bed (*en dormitorio*)
2 berth (*en barco, tren*)

la **literatura** SUSTANTIVO
literature

el **litro** SUSTANTIVO
litre

> *En los países anglosajones el volumen a menudo se expresa en pintas,* **pints**. *Una pinta equivale a 0.6 litros.*

liviano ADJETIVO
light

la **llaga** SUSTANTIVO
sore

la **llama** SUSTANTIVO
flame

la **llamada** SUSTANTIVO
call
◆ **hacer una llamada telefónica** to make a phone call

llamar VERBO
1 to call ◊ *Me llamaron mentiroso.* They called me a liar. ◊ *llamar a la policía* to call the police
2 to ring (*al timbre*)
3 to knock (*a la puerta*)
◆ **llamar por teléfono a alguien** to phone somebody
◆ **¿Cómo te llamas?** What's your name?
◆ **Me llamo Adela.** My name's Adela.

llano ADJETIVO
flat

la **llanta** SUSTANTIVO
1 wheel rim (*metálica*)
2 tyre Latin America

la **llave** SUSTANTIVO
1 key ◊ *las llaves del coche* the car keys
◆ **Echa la llave de la puerta cuando salgas.** Lock the door when you go out.
◆ **una llave inglesa** a spanner
2 tap (*grifo*) Latin America

el **llavero** SUSTANTIVO
keyring

la **llegada** SUSTANTIVO
1 arrival (*de tren, avión, viajeros*)
2 finish (*meta*)

llegar* VERBO
1 to get to

> *Cuando se menciona dónde se llega, se suele usar* **get to**.

◊ *Cuando llegamos a Granada estaba lloviendo.* When we got to Granada it was raining.
◆ **¿A qué hora llegaste a casa?** What time did you get home?
2 to arrive

> *Cuando no se menciona dónde se llega, se usa* **arrive**.

◊ *Carmen no ha llegado todavía.* Carmen hasn't arrived yet.
◆ **No llegues tarde.** Don't be late.
◆ **Con 200 pesetas no me llega.** 200 pesetas isn't enough.
3 to reach (*alcanzar*) ◊ *No llego al estante de arriba.* I can't reach the top shelf.
◆ **El agua me llegaba hasta las rodillas.** The water came up to my knees.
◆ **llegar a ser** to become

llenar VERBO
to fill ◊ *Llena la jarra de agua.* Fill the jug with water.

lleno ADJETIVO
full ◊ *Todos los hoteles están llenos.* All the hotels are full. ◊ *El restaurante estaba lleno de gente.* The restaurant was full of people.

llevar VERBO
1 to take ◊ *¿Llevas los vasos a la cocina?* Can you take the glasses to the kitchen? ◊ *No llevará mucho tiempo.* It won't take long.
2 to wear ◊ *María llevaba un abrigo muy bonito.* María was wearing a nice coat.
3 to give a lift (*en coche*) ◊ *Sofía nos llevó a casa.* Sofía gave us a lift home.
4 to carry ◊ *Yo te llevo la maleta.* I'll carry your case.
◆ **Sólo llevo mil pesetas.** I've only got one thousand pesetas on me.
◆ **¿Cuánto tiempo llevas aquí?** How long have you been here?
◆ **Llevo horas esperando aquí.** I've been waiting here for hours.
◆ **Mi hermana mayor me lleva ocho años.** My elder sister is eight years older than me.
◆ **llevarse algo** to take something ◊ *Llévatelo.* Take it with you. ◊ *¿Le gusta? – Sí, me lo llevo.* Do you like it? – Yes, I'll take it!
◆ **Me llevo bien con mi hermano.** I get on well with my brother.

☞

◆ **Nos llevamos muy mal.** We get on very badly.

llorar VERBO
to cry

llover* VERBO
to rain
◆ **llover a cántaros** to pour down

la **llovizna** SUSTANTIVO
drizzle

llueve VERBO *ver* **llover**

la **lluvia** SUSTANTIVO
rain ◇ *bajo la lluvia* in the rain
◆ **la lluvia ácida** acid rain

lluvioso ADJETIVO
rainy

lo (1) ARTÍCULO
◆ **Lo peor fue que no pudimos entrar.** The worst thing was we couldn't get in.
◆ **No me gusta lo picante.** I don't like spicy things.
◆ **Pon en mi habitación lo de Pedro.** Put Pedro's things in my room.
◆ **Lo mío son las matemáticas.** Maths is my thing.
◆ **Lo de vender la casa no me parece bien.** I don't like this idea of selling the house.
◆ **Olvida lo de ayer.** Forget what happened yesterday.

Cuando se hace hincapié en una cualidad, a menudo se usa ***how.***

◆ **¡No sabes lo aburrido que es!** You don't know how boring he is!
◆ **lo que (1)** what ◇ *Lo que más me gusta es nadar.* What I like most is swimming.
◆ **lo que (2)** whatever ◇ *Ponte lo que quieras.* Wear whatever you like.
◆ **más de lo que** more than ◇ *Cuesta más de lo que crees.* It costs more than you think.

lo (2) PRONOMBRE
1 him

Cuando nos referimos a "él".

◇ *No lo conozco.* I don't know him.
◆ **Lo han despedido.** He's been sacked.
2 you

Cuando nos referimos a "usted".

◇ *Yo a usted lo conozco.* I know you.
3 it

Cuando nos referimos a "una cosa".

◇ *No lo veo.* I can't see it. ◇ *Voy a pensarlo.* I'll think about it.
◆ **No lo sabía.** I didn't know.
◆ **No parece lista pero lo es.** She doesn't seem clever but she is.

el **lobo** SUSTANTIVO
wolf (PL wolves)

la **loca** SUSTANTIVO
madwoman (PL madwomen)

local ADJETIVO
local ◇ *un producto local* a local product

el **local** SUSTANTIVO
premises PL ◇ *Lo echaron del local.* They threw him off the premises.
◆ **Ensayan en un local cerca de aquí.** They rehearse in a place near here.

la **localidad** SUSTANTIVO
1 town (*población*) ◇ *una localidad al sur de Madrid* a town south of Madrid
2 seat (*asiento*) ◇ *Reserve sus localidades con antelación.* Book your seats in advance.

localizar* VERBO
1 to reach ◇ *Me puedes localizar en este teléfono.* You can reach me at this number.
2 to locate ◇ *No han conseguido localizar a las víctimas.* They have been unable to locate the victims.

la **loción** SUSTANTIVO (PL las **lociones**)
lotion

loco ADJETIVO
1 mad ◇ *volverse loco* to go mad
◆ **volver loco a alguien** to drive somebody mad
2 crazy ◇ *¿Estás loco?* Are you crazy? ◇ *Está loco con su moto nueva.* He's crazy about his new motorbike.
◆ **volver loco a alguien** to drive somebody mad
◆ **Me vuelve loco el marisco.** I'm crazy about seafood.

el **loco** SUSTANTIVO
madman (PL madmen)

la **locura** SUSTANTIVO
madness ◇ *Es una locura ir solo.* It's madness to go on your own.

el **locutor**, la **locutora** SUSTANTIVO
newsreader

lógico ADJETIVO
1 logical ◇ *No es un razonamiento lógico.* It's not logical reasoning.
2 natural ◇ *Es una reacción lógica.* It's a natural reaction.
◆ **Es lógico que no quiera venir.** It's only natural he doesn't want to come.

lograr VERBO
1 to get ◇ *Lograron lo que se proponían.* They got what they wanted.
2 to manage ◇ *Logré que me concediera una entrevista.* I managed to get an interview with him.

la **lombriz** SUSTANTIVO (PL las **lombrices**)
worm

el **lomo** SUSTANTIVO
1 back (*de animal*)
2 loin (*para comer*)
3 spine (*de un libro*)

la **lona** SUSTANTIVO
canvas (PL canvases)

la **loncha** SUSTANTIVO
slice

* Verbs marked with this symbol are irregular. See pages 380-382 for further details

Londres SUSTANTIVO MASC
London

la **longitud** SUSTANTIVO
length
◆ **Tiene tres metros de longitud.** It's three metres long.

el **loro** SUSTANTIVO
parrot

los (1) ARTÍCULO
the ◇ *los barcos* the boats
◆ **los de las bufandas rojas** the people in the red scarves

El artículo se traduce por el posesivo cuando se refiere a una parte del cuerpo, a una prenda que se lleva puesta o a algo que se posee.

◆ **Se lavaron los pies en el río.** They washed their feet in the river.
◆ **Abrochaos los abrigos.** Button your coats.
◆ **Me gustan sus cuadros, pero prefiero los de Ana.** I like his paintings, but I prefer Ana's.

El artículo a veces no se traduce; por ejemplo cuando se refiere a algo en general o con algunas expresiones de tiempo.

◆ **No me gustan los melocotones.** I don't like peaches.
◆ **Sólo vienen los lunes.** They only come on Mondays.

los (2) PRONOMBRE
1 them

Cuando nos referimos a "ellos".

◇ *Los vi por la calle.* I saw them in the street.
◆ **Los han despedido.** They've been sacked.
2 you

Cuando nos referimos a "ustedes".

◇ *Los acompaño hasta la puerta, señores.* I'll see you to the door, gentlemen.

la **lotería** SUSTANTIVO
lottery (PL lotteries) ◇ *Le tocó la lotería.* He won the lottery.

la **lucha** SUSTANTIVO
fight
◆ **lucha libre** wrestling

luchar VERBO
to fight

lucir* VERBO
to shine ◇ *Lucían las estrellas.* The stars were shining.
◆ **Fernando se lució en el examen.** Fernando performed brilliantly in the exam.

luego (1) ADVERBIO
1 then (*después*) ◇ *Primero se puso de pie y luego habló.* First he stood up and then he spoke.
2 later (*más tarde*) ◇ *Mi mujer viene luego.* My wife's coming later.
◆ **desde luego** of course ◇ *¡Desde luego que me gusta!* Of course I like it!
◆ **¡Hasta luego!** See you!
3 soon Chile, Mexico
◇ *Vuelvo luego.* I'll be back soon.

luego (2) CONJUNCIÓN
therefore ◇ *Yo he pagado, luego tengo derecho a verlo.* I have paid, therefore I have a right to see it.

el **lugar** SUSTANTIVO
place ◇ *Este lugar es muy bonito.* This is a lovely place.
◆ **Llegó en último lugar.** He came last.
◆ **en lugar de** instead of
◆ **tener lugar** to take place

el **lujo** SUSTANTIVO
luxury (PL luxuries)
◆ **un coche de lujo** a luxury car

lujoso ADJETIVO
luxurious

la **luna** SUSTANTIVO
1 moon (*satélite*)
2 window pane (*de un escaparate*)
3 window (*de un coche*)
◆ **la luna de miel** honeymoon

el **lunar** SUSTANTIVO
mole (*en la piel*)
◆ **una corbata de lunares** a spotted tie

el **lunes** SUSTANTIVO (PL los **lunes**)

Los días de la semana se escriben con mayúscula.

Monday ◇ *La vi el lunes.* I saw her on Monday. ◇ *todos los lunes* every Monday ◇ *el lunes pasado* last Monday ◇ *el lunes que viene* next Monday ◇ *Jugamos los lunes.* We play on Mondays.

la **lupa** SUSTANTIVO
magnifying glass

el **luto** SUSTANTIVO
◆ **estar de luto por alguien** to be in mourning for somebody

Luxemburgo SUSTANTIVO MASC
Luxembourg

la **luz** SUSTANTIVO (PL las **luces**)
1 light ◇ *Enciende la luz, por favor.* Put on the light please.
2 electricity ◇ *No hay luz en todo el edificio.* There's no electricity in the whole building.
◆ **dar a luz** to give birth

M

los **macarrones** SUSTANTIVO
macaroni SING ◊ *Los macarrones no engordan.* Macaroni isn't fattening.

la **macedonia** SUSTANTIVO
fruit salad (*de fruta*)

la **maceta** SUSTANTIVO
flowerpot

machacar* VERBO
1 to crush ◊ *Machacó los ajos en el mortero.* He crushed the garlic in the mortar.
2 to thrash ◊ *El equipo visitante los machacó.* The visiting team thrashed them.

el **macho** ADJETIVO, SUSTANTIVO
male ◊ *un conejo macho* a male rabbit

la **madera** SUSTANTIVO
wood ◊ *Está hecho de madera.* It's made of wood.
◆ **un juguete de madera** a wooden toy
◆ **Dame esa madera.** Give me that piece of wood.
◆ **Tiene madera de profesor.** He's got the makings of a teacher.

la **madrastra** SUSTANTIVO
stepmother

la **madre** SUSTANTIVO
mother
◆ **¡Madre mía!** Goodness!

Madrid SUSTANTIVO MASC
Madrid

la **madrina** SUSTANTIVO
1 (*en bautizo*)
godmother
2 (*en boda*)
matron of honour (PL matrons of honour)

la **madrugada** SUSTANTIVO
early morning
◆ **levantarse de madrugada (1)** (*temprano*) to get up early
◆ **levantarse de madrugada (2)** (*al amanecer*) to get up at daybreak
◆ **a las 4 de la madrugada** at 4 o'clock in the morning

madrugar* VERBO
to get up early

maduro ADJETIVO
1 mature (*persona*)
2 ripe (*fruta*)

el **maestro,** la **maestra** SUSTANTIVO
teacher ◊ *Mi tía es maestra.* My aunt's a teacher.
◆ **un maestro de escuela** a schoolteacher

la **magia** SUSTANTIVO
magic

mágico ADJETIVO
magic ◊ *una varita mágica* a magic wand

el **magisterio** SUSTANTIVO
◆ **Estudia magisterio.** He's training to be a teacher.

magnífico ADJETIVO
splendid

el **mago,** la **maga** SUSTANTIVO
magician
◆ **los Reyes Magos** the Three Wise Men

el **maíz** SUSTANTIVO (PL los **maíces**)
1 maize (*planta*)
2 sweetcorn (*desgranado*)
◆ **una mazorca de maíz** a corn cob

la **majestad** SUSTANTIVO
◆ **Su Majestad (1)** (*rey*) His Majesty
◆ **Su Majestad (2)** (*reina*) Her Majesty

majo ADJETIVO
1 nice (*simpático*)
2 pretty (*bonito*)

mal (1) ADJETIVO = **malo**

mal (2) ADVERBIO
1 badly ◊ *Toca la guitarra muy mal.* He plays the guitar very badly. ◊ *un trabajo mal pagado* a badly paid job
◆ **Esta habitación huele mal.** This room smells bad.
◆ **Lo pasé muy mal.** I had a very bad time.
◆ **Me entendió mal.** He misunderstood me.
◆ **hablar mal de alguien** to speak ill of someone
2 wrong ◊ *Han escrito mal mi apellido.* They've spelt my surname wrong. ◊ *Está mal mentir.* It's wrong to tell lies.

el **mal** SUSTANTIVO
evil ◊ *el bien y el mal* good and evil

la **mala** SUSTANTIVO
◆ **la mala de la película** the villain in the film

malcriado ADJETIVO
badly brought up

maldito ADJETIVO
damned (*coloquial*) ◊ *¡Malditos vecinos!* Damned neighbours!
◆ **¡Malditas las ganas que tengo de verle!** I really don't feel like seeing him!
◆ **¡Maldita sea!** Damn it!

maleducado ADJETIVO
bad-mannered

el **malentendido** SUSTANTIVO
misunderstanding

el **malestar** SUSTANTIVO
discomfort

la **maleta** SUSTANTIVO
suitcase

* Verbs marked with this symbol are irregular. See pages 380-382 for further details

◆**hacer la maleta** to pack

el **maletero** SUSTANTIVO
boot

el **maletín** SUSTANTIVO (PL los **maletines**)
briefcase

malgastar VERBO
to waste

malhumorado ADJETIVO
bad-tempered (*por naturaleza*)
◆**Hoy parece malhumorado.** He appears to be in a bad mood today.

la **malicia** SUSTANTIVO
1 malice (*mala intención*)
2 mischief (*picardía*)

malicioso ADJETIVO
malicious

la **malla** SUSTANTIVO
1 mesh (*tejido*)
2 leotard (*de gimnasia*)
◆**una malla de baño** River Plate a swimsuit
◆**mallas (1)** (*con pie*) tights
◆**mallas (2)** (*hasta el tobillo*) leggings

Mallorca SUSTANTIVO FEM
Majorca

el **malo** SUSTANTIVO
◆**el malo de la película** the villain in the film

malo ADJETIVO
*Use **mal** before a masculine noun.*
1 bad ◇ *un mal día* a bad day ◇ *Este programa es muy malo.* This is a very bad programme. ◇ *Soy muy mala para las matemáticas.* I'm very bad at maths.
◆**Hace malo.** The weather's bad.
◆**Lo malo es que ...** the trouble is that ...
2 naughty ◇ *¿Por qué eres tan malo?* Why are you so naughty?
3 off ◇ *Esta carne está mala.* This meat's off.
4 ill ◇ *Mi hija está mala.* My daughter's ill. ◇ *Se puso malo después de comer.* He started to feel ill after lunch.

maltratar VERBO
to ill-treat ◇ *Maltrata a su perro.* He ill-treats his dog.
◆**los niños maltratados** abused children

malvado ADJETIVO
evil

la **mama** SUSTANTIVO
1 breast (*pecho*)
2 mum (*coloquial: madre*)

la **mamá** SUSTANTIVO (PL las **mamás**)
mum (*coloquial*) ◇ *tu mamá* your mum ◇ *¡Hola mamá!* Hi Mum!

mamar VERBO
to suckle (*animal*) ◇ *El cordero aún mama.* The lamb is still suckling.
◆**El bebé mama cada cuatro horas.** The baby has a feed every four hours.
◆**dar de mamar** to breastfeed

el **mamífero** SUSTANTIVO
mammal

el **manantial** SUSTANTIVO
spring

la **mancha** SUSTANTIVO
stain

manchar VERBO
to stain ◇ *La cerveza no mancha.* Beer doesn't stain.
◆**mancharse** to get dirty ◇ *No te manches la camisa.* Don't get your shirt dirty.
◆**Me he manchado el vestido de tinta.** I've got ink stains on my dress.

mandar VERBO
1 to order ◇ *El sargento le mandó barrer el patio.* The sergeant ordered him to sweep the yard.
◆**Nos mandó callar.** He told us to be quiet.
◆**Aquí mando yo.** I'm the boss here.
2 to send ◇ *Se lo mandaremos por correo.* We'll send it to you by post. ◇ *Me mandaron a hacer un recado.* They sent me on an errand.
◆**mandar llamar a alguien** Latin America to send for someone
◆**mandar a arreglar algo** Latin America to have something repaired
◆**¿Mande?** Mexico Pardon?
◆**El médico me mandó un jarabe.** The doctor gave me a prescription for syrup.

la **mandarina** SUSTANTIVO
tangerine

la **mandíbula** SUSTANTIVO
jaw

el **mando** SUSTANTIVO
◆**un alto mando** a high-ranking officer
◆**Está al mando del proyecto.** He's in charge of the project.
◆**el mando a distancia** the remote control
◆**los mandos** (*en avión*) the controls

la **manecilla** SUSTANTIVO
hand ◇ *las manecillas del reloj* the hands of the clock

manejable ADJETIVO
1 manoeuvrable ◇ *un coche muy manejable* a very manoeuvrable car
2 easy to use ◇ *Este taladro es muy manejable.* This drill is very easy to use.

manejar VERBO
1 to operate (*máquina*)
2 to manage (*casa, negocio*)
3 to drive (*coche*) Latin America
◆**un examen de manejar** a driving test Latin America

la **manera** SUSTANTIVO
way ◇ *Lo hice a mi manera.* I did it my way.
◆**de todas maneras** anyway
◆**No hay manera de convencerla.** There's nothing one can do to convince her.
◆**de manera que (1)** so ◇ *No has hecho los deberes, de manera que no hay tele.* You

haven't done your homework so there's no TV.

♦ **de manera que (2)** so that ◊ *Lo puse de manera que pudieran verlo.* I put it so that they could see it.

♦ **¡De ninguna manera!** Certainly not!

la **manga** SUSTANTIVO
sleeve ◊ *Súbete las mangas.* Roll your sleeves up.
♦ **de manga corta** short-sleeved
♦ **de manga larga** long-sleeved

el **mango** SUSTANTIVO
1 handle (*asa*)
2 mango (*fruta*)

la **manguera** SUSTANTIVO
hose

la **manía** SUSTANTIVO
♦ **Tiene la manía de repetir todo lo que digo.** He has an irritating habit of repeating everything I say.
♦ **El profesor me tiene manía.** (*coloquial*) The teacher has it in for me.

maniático ADJETIVO
♦ **Es muy maniático para comer.** He's very fussy about eating.
♦ **Es una maniática del orden.** She's obsessed with keeping things tidy.

la **manifestación** SUSTANTIVO (PL las **manifestaciones**)
demonstration ◊ *Hicieron una manifestación contra el terrorismo.* They held a demonstration against terrorism.

el/la **manifestante** SUSTANTIVO
demonstrator

manifestarse* VERBO
to demonstrate

el **manillar** SUSTANTIVO
handlebars PL

la **maniobra** SUSTANTIVO
manoeuvre ◊ *una maniobra política* a political manoeuvre
♦ **hacer maniobras** to manoeuvre

manipular VERBO
1 to handle ◊ *La higiene es imprescindible para manipular alimentos.* Hygiene is essential when handling food.
2 to manipulate ◊ *La publicidad manipula a la opinión pública.* Advertising manipulates public opinion.

el/la **maniquí** SUSTANTIVO (PL los/las **maniquíes**)
model (*persona*)

el **maniquí** SUSTANTIVO (PL los **maniquíes**) (*de escaparate*)
dummy (PL dummies)

la **manivela** SUSTANTIVO
crank

la **mano** SUSTANTIVO
hand ◊ *Dame la mano.* Give me your hand.
♦ **tener algo a mano** to have something to hand
♦ **hecho a mano** handmade
♦ **de segunda mano** secondhand
♦ **echar una mano** to lend a hand
♦ **estrechar la mano a alguien** to shake somebody's hand
♦ **la mano de obra** labour
♦ **una mano de pintura** a coat of paint

el **manojo** SUSTANTIVO
bunch (PL bunches) ◊ *un manojo de llaves* a bunch of keys

la **manopla** SUSTANTIVO
mitten ◊ *El niño llevaba manoplas.* The child was wearing mittens.
♦ **una manopla de cocina** an oven-glove

manso ADJETIVO
tame

la **manta** SUSTANTIVO
blanket

la **manteca** SUSTANTIVO
butter [River Plate]
♦ **manteca de cerdo** lard

el **mantel** SUSTANTIVO
tablecloth

mantener* VERBO
1 to keep ◊ *Les mantendremos informados.* We'll keep you informed. ◊ *mantener la calma* to keep calm
2 to support ◊ *Mantiene a su familia.* He supports his family.
♦ **mantener una conversación** to have a conversation
♦ **mantenerse** (*económicamente*) to support oneself
♦ **mantenerse en forma** to keep fit
♦ **mantenerse en pie** to remain standing

el **mantenimiento** SUSTANTIVO
maintenance ◊ *el encargado de mantenimiento* the person in charge of maintenance
♦ **ejercicios de mantenimiento** keep-fit exercises

la **mantequilla** SUSTANTIVO
butter

mantuve VERBO *ver* **mantener**

el **manual** ADJETIVO, SUSTANTIVO
manual

el **manubrio** SUSTANTIVO [Latin America]
handlebars PL

el **manuscrito** SUSTANTIVO
manuscript

la **manzana** SUSTANTIVO
1 apple (*fruta*)
2 block (*de edificios*)

la **maña** SUSTANTIVO
♦ **Tiene mucha maña para hacer arreglos caseros.** She's a dab hand at mending things around the house.

la **mañana** SUSTANTIVO

morning ◊ *Llegó a las nueve de la mañana.* He arrived at nine o'clock in the morning.
◆**a media mañana** mid-morning
mañana ADVERBIO
tomorrow ◊ *¡Hasta mañana!* See you tomorrow!
◆**pasado mañana** the day after tomorrow
◆**Por la mañana voy al gimnasio.** In the mornings I go to the gym.
◆**mañana por la mañana** tomorrow morning
◆**mañana por la noche** tomorrow night
el **mapa** SUSTANTIVO
map ◊ *El pueblo no está en el mapa.* The village isn't on the map. ◊ *un mapa de carreteras* a road map
la **maqueta** SUSTANTIVO
model
el **maquillaje** SUSTANTIVO
make-up SING
maquillarse VERBO
to put one's make-up on
la **máquina** SUSTANTIVO
machine ◊ *una máquina de coser* a sewing machine ◊ *una máquina expendedora* a vending machine ◊ *una máquina tragaperras* a fruit machine
◆**una máquina de escribir** a typewriter
◆**escrito a máquina** typed
la **maquinilla** SUSTANTIVO
razor ◊ *una maquinilla eléctrica* an electric razor
el **mar** SUSTANTIVO
sea
◆**por mar** by sea
Note that in certain idiomatic phrases, mar is feminine.
◆**en alta mar** on the high seas
◆**Lo hizo la mar de bien.** He did it really well.
el **maratón** SUSTANTIVO (PL los **maratones**)
marathon
la **maravilla** SUSTANTIVO
◆**¡Qué maravilla de casa!** What a wonderful house!
◆**ser una maravilla** to be wonderful
◆**Se llevan de maravilla.** They get on wonderfully well together.
maravilloso ADJETIVO
marvellous
la **marca** SUSTANTIVO
1 mark ◊ *Había marcas de neumático en la arena.* There were tyre marks in the sand.
2 make (*de máquina, coche*) ◊ *¿De qué marca es tu coche?* What make's your car?
3 brand (*de detergente, café*) ◊ *una conocida marca de cigarrillos* a well-known brand of cigarettes
◆**la ropa de marca** designer clothes
el **marcador** SUSTANTIVO
scoreboard
el **marcador** SUSTANTIVO
bookmark (*informática*)
marcar* VERBO
1 to mark (*ropa, objetos personales*)
2 to brand (*ganado*)
3 to dial (*número de teléfono*)
4 to score (*gol*)
5 to set (*en peluquería*)
◆**Mi reloj marca las 2.** It's 2 o'clock according to my watch.
◆**marcar algo con una equis** to put a cross on something
la **marcha** SUSTANTIVO
1 departure ◊ *Su marcha les dejó muy tristes.* His departure left them feeling very sad.
2 gear ◊ *cambiar de marcha* to change gear
◆**salir de marcha** (*coloquial*) to go out on the town
◆**a toda marcha** at full speed
◆**estar en marcha (1)** (*motor*) to be running
◆**estar en marcha (2)** (*proyecto*) to be underway
◆**dar marcha atrás** to reverse
◆**No te subas nunca a un tren en marcha.** Never get onto a moving train.
marcharse VERBO
to leave
el **marco** SUSTANTIVO
1 frame (*de fotografía*)
2 mark (*moneda alemana*)
la **marea** SUSTANTIVO
tide
◆**una marea negra** an oil slick
marear VERBO
to make...feel sick ◊ *El olor a alquitrán me marea.* The smell of tar makes me feel sick.
◆**marearse (1)** to get dizzy ◊ *Te marearás si das tantas vueltas.* You'll get dizzy going round and round like that.
◆**marearse (2)** to get seasick ◊ *¿Te mareas cuando vas en barco?* Do you get seasick when you travel by boat?
◆**marearse (3)** to get carsick ◊ *Siempre me mareo en coche.* I always get carsick.
◆**¡No me marees!** Stop going on at me!
el **mareo** SUSTANTIVO
1 sea sickness (*en barco*)
2 car sickness (*en coche*)
◆**Le dio un mareo a causa del calor.** The heat made her feel ill.
el **marfil** SUSTANTIVO
ivory
la **margarina** SUSTANTIVO
margarine
la **margarita** SUSTANTIVO
daisy (PL daisies)
el **margen** SUSTANTIVO (PL los **márgenes**)
margin (*de página*) ◊ *Escribe las notas al margen.* Write your notes in the margin.

M

el **marido** SUSTANTIVO
husband

el **marinero** SUSTANTIVO
sailor

la **mariposa** SUSTANTIVO
butterfly (PL butterflies)

el **marisco** SUSTANTIVO
shellfish (PL shellfish) ◇ *No me gusta el marisco.* I don't like shellfish.

el **mármol** SUSTANTIVO
marble

marrón ADJETIVO (FEM **marrón**, PL **marrones**)
brown ◇ *un traje marrón* a brown suit

el **martes** SUSTANTIVO (PL los **martes**)
Los días de la semana se escriben con mayúscula.
Tuesday ◇ *La vi el martes.* I saw her on Tuesday. ◇ *todos los martes* every Tuesday ◇ *el martes pasado* last Tuesday ◇ *el martes que viene* next Tuesday ◇ *Jugamos los martes.* We play on Tuesdays.

el **martillo** SUSTANTIVO
hammer

marzo SUSTANTIVO MASC
Los meses se escriben con mayúscula.
March ◇ *en marzo* in March ◇ *Nací el 17 de marzo.* I was born on 17 March.

más ADVERBIO
more ◇ *Ahora salgo más.* I go out more these days.
- **Últimamente nos vemos más.** We've been seeing more of each other lately.
- **¿Quieres más?** Would you like some more?
- **No tengo más dinero.** I haven't any more money.

La mayoría de los adjetivos y adverbios de una sílaba, o de dos sílabas con terminación en 'y', forman el comparativo añadiendo la terminación -er. A veces se produce un cambio ortográfico.
◇ *barato – más barato* cheap – cheaper ◇ *joven – más joven* young – younger ◇ *largo – más largo* long – longer ◇ *grande – más grande* big – bigger ◇ *contento – más contento* happy – happier ◇ *rápido – más rápido* fast – faster ◇ *temprano – más temprano* early – earlier
- **lejos – más lejos** far – further

*El resto de los adjetivos y adverbios forman el comparativo con **more**.*
◇ *hermoso – más hermoso* beautiful – more beautiful ◇ *guapo – más guapo* handsome – more handsome

*Independientemente del número de sílabas, los adverbios de modo que acaban en **-ly** forman el comparativo con **more**.*
◇ *deprisa – más deprisa* quickly – more quickly

*Para decir **más...que**, se añade **than** a la forma comparativa.*
◇ *Es más grande que el tuyo.* It's bigger than yours. ◇ *Corre más rápido que yo.* He runs faster than I do.
- **Trabaja más que yo.** He works harder than I do.
- **más de mil libros** more than a thousand books
- **No tiene más de dieciséis años.** He isn't more than sixteen.
- **más de lo que yo creía** more than I thought

*Siguiendo las mismas normas del comparativo, el superlativo se forma añadiendo **the ...-est** o **the most ...**.*
◇ *el bolígrafo más barato* the cheapest pen ◇ *el niño más joven* the youngest child ◇ *el coche más grande* the biggest car ◇ *la persona más feliz* the happiest person ◇ *el más inteligente de todos* the most intelligent of all of them
- **su película más innovadora** his most innovative film
- **Paco es el que come más.** Paco's the one who eats the most.
- **Fue el que más trabajó.** He was the one who worked the hardest.
- **el punto más lejano** the furthest point
- **¿Qué más?** What else?
- **¡Qué perro más sucio!** What a filthy dog!
- **Tenemos uno de más.** We have one too many.
- **Por más que estudio no apruebo.** However hard I study I don't pass.
- **más o menos** more or less
- **2 más 2 son 4** 2 and 2 are 4
- **14 más 20 menos 12 es igual a 22** 14 plus 20 minus 12 equals 22

la **masa** SUSTANTIVO
1 dough ◇ *la masa de pan* bread dough
2 (*en física*)
mass (PL masses)
- **las masas** the masses
- **en masa (1)** mass

mass en este caso va siempre delante del sustantivo.
◇ *la producción en masa* mass production
- **en masa (2)** en masse ◇ *Fueron en masa a recibir al futbolista.* They went en masse to greet the footballer.

el **masaje** SUSTANTIVO
massage

la **máscara** SUSTANTIVO
mask

masculino ADJETIVO
1 male (*hormona, sexo*) ◇ *el sexo masculino* the male sex

[2] men's (*moda, deporte*) ◊ *la ropa masculina* men's clothing
[3] masculine (*voz*) ◊ *el pronombre masculino "él"* the masculine pronoun "él"

masticar* VERBO
to chew

matar VERBO
to kill ◊ *El jefe me va a matar.* The boss will kill me.
◆ **matarse** to be killed ◊ *Se mataron en un accidente de coche.* They were killed in a car accident.

el **matasellos** SUSTANTIVO (PL los **matasellos**)
postmark

mate ADJETIVO
matt

el **mate** SUSTANTIVO
[1] checkmate (*en ajedrez*)
[2] maté (*infusión*)

las **matemáticas** SUSTANTIVO
mathematics SING

la **materia** SUSTANTIVO
[1] matter ◊ *materia orgánica* organic matter
[2] material ◊ *la materia prima* raw material
[3] subject ◊ *Es un experto en la materia.* He's an expert on the subject.
◆ **entrar en materia** to get to the point

el **material** ADJETIVO, SUSTANTIVO
material

materno ADJETIVO
maternal ◊ *mi abuela materna* my maternal grandmother
◆ **mi lengua materna** my mother tongue

el **matiz** SUSTANTIVO (PL los **matices**)
shade (*de color*)

el **matorral** SUSTANTIVO
bushes PL

la **matrícula** SUSTANTIVO
registration (*de colegio, universidad*)
◆ **la matrícula del coche (1)** (*número*) the registration number of the car
◆ **la matrícula del coche (2)** (*placa*) the number plate of the car

matricular VERBO
to register (*coche*)
◆ **matricularse** to enrol (*alumno*)

el **matrimonio** SUSTANTIVO
[1] marriage ◊ *El matrimonio se celebró en la iglesia del pueblo.* The marriage took place in the village church.
[2] couple ◊ *Eran un matrimonio feliz.* They were a happy couple.

maullar VERBO
to miaow

máximo ADJETIVO
maximum ◊ *la velocidad máxima* the maximum speed

el **máximo** SUSTANTIVO
maximum ◊ *un máximo de 10.000 pesetas* a maximum of 10,000 pesetas
◆ **como máximo (1)** at the most ◊ *Te costará 5.000 como máximo.* It'll cost you 5,000 at the most.
◆ **como máximo (2)** at the latest ◊ *Llegaré a las diez como máximo.* I'll be there by ten o'clock at the latest.

mayo SUSTANTIVO MASC
Los meses se escriben con mayúscula.
May ◊ *en mayo* in May ◊ *Nací el 28 de mayo.* I was born on 28 May.

la **mayonesa** SUSTANTIVO
mayonnaise

mayor ADJETIVO, PRONOMBRE (FEM **mayor**)
[1] older ◊ *Paco es mayor que Nacho.* Paco is older than Nacho. ◊ *Es tres años mayor que yo.* He is three years older than me.
◆ **el hermano mayor (1)** (*de dos hermanos*) the older brother
◆ **el hermano mayor (2)** (*de más de dos hermanos*) the oldest brother
◆ **Soy el mayor. (1)** (*de dos*) I'm the older.
◆ **Soy el mayor. (2)** (*de más de dos*) I'm the oldest.
◆ **Nuestros hijos ya son mayores.** Our children are grown-up now.
◆ **la gente mayor** the elderly
[2] bigger ◊ *Necesitamos una casa mayor.* We need a bigger house.
◆ **la mayor iglesia del mundo.** the biggest church in the world

el/la **mayor** SUSTANTIVO
◆ **un mayor de edad** an adult
◆ **los mayores** grown-ups

la **mayoría** SUSTANTIVO
majority (PL majorities)
◆ **Somos mayoría.** We are in the majority.
◆ **La mayoría de los estudiantes son pobres.** Most students are poor.
◆ **la mayoría de nosotros** most of us

la **mayúscula** SUSTANTIVO
capital letter ◊ *Empieza cada frase con una mayúscula.* Start each sentence with a capital letter.
◆ **Escríbelo con mayúsculas.** Write it in capitals.
◆ **una M mayúscula** a capital M

el **mazapán** SUSTANTIVO (PL los **mazapanes**)
marzipan

me PRONOMBRE
[1] me ◊ *Me quiere.* He loves me. ◊ *Me regaló una pulsera.* He gave me a bracelet.
◆ **Me lo dio.** He gave it to me.
◆ **¿Me echas esta carta?** Will you post this letter for me?
[2] myself ◊ *No me hice daño.* I didn't hurt myself.
◆ **me dije a mí mismo** I said to myself

Con partes del cuerpo o con prendas que se llevan puestas se usa el adjetivo posesivo.
◊ *Me duelen los pies.* My feet hurt. ◊ *Me puse el abrigo.* I put my coat on.

mear VERBO
to piss (*vulgar*)
♦ **mearse** to wet oneself
♦ **mearse de risa** (*vulgar*) to piss oneself laughing

la **mecánica** SUSTANTIVO
[1] mechanic (*persona*) ◊ *Quiere ser mecánica.* She wants to be a mechanic.
[2] mechanics SING (*técnica*)

mecánico ADJETIVO
mechanical

el **mecánico** SUSTANTIVO
mechanic ◊ *Es mecánico.* He's a mechanic.

el **mecanismo** SUSTANTIVO
mechanism

la **mecanografía** SUSTANTIVO
typing

la **mecha** SUSTANTIVO
[1] wick (*de vela*)
[2] fuse (*de explosivo*)

el **mechero** SUSTANTIVO
cigarette lighter

la **medalla** SUSTANTIVO
medal

la **media** SUSTANTIVO
[1] average ◊ *Trabajo una media de seis horas diarias.* I work an average of six hours a day.
[2] sock (*calcetín*) [Latin America]
♦ **medias (1)** (*hasta el muslo*) stockings
♦ **medias (2)** (*hasta la cintura*) tights
♦ **medias bombachas** [River Plate] tights
♦ **a las cuatro y media** at half past four

mediados SUSTANTIVO PLURAL
♦ **a mediados de** around the middle of

mediano ADJETIVO
medium ◊ *de mediana estatura* of medium height
♦ **de tamaño mediano** medium-sized
♦ **el hijo mediano** the middle son

la **medianoche** SUSTANTIVO
midnight ◊ *a medianoche* at midnight

mediante PREPOSICIÓN
♦ **Izaron las cajas mediante una polea.** They lifted the crates using a pulley.

mediático ADJETIVO
media (*campaña, cultura, estrella*)

***media** en este caso va siempre delante del sustantivo.*

el **medicamento** SUSTANTIVO
medicine

la **medicina** SUSTANTIVO
medicine ◊ *Estudia medicina en la universidad.* He's studying medicine at university. ◊ *¿Te has tomado ya la medicina?* Have you taken your medicine yet?

el **médico**, la **médica** SUSTANTIVO
doctor ◊ *Quiere ser médica.* She wants to be a doctor. ◊ *el médico de cabecera* the family doctor
♦ **ir al médico** to go to the doctor's

la **medida** SUSTANTIVO
measure ◊ *medidas de seguridad* security measures ◊ *tomar medidas contra la inflación* to take measures against inflation
♦ **El sastre le tomó las medidas.** The tailor took his measurements.
♦ **un traje a medida** a made-to-measure suit
♦ **a medida que ...** as ... ◊ *Saludaba a los invitados a medida que iban llegando.* He greeted the guests as they arrived.

medio (1) ADJETIVO
[1] half ◊ *medio litro* half a litre ◊ *Nos queda media botella de leche.* We've got half a bottle of milk left. ◊ *media hora* half an hour ◊ *una hora y media* an hour and a half
♦ **Son las ocho y media.** It's half past eight.
[2] average ◊ *la temperatura media* the average temperature

medio (2) ADVERBIO
half ◊ *Estaba medio dormido.* He was half asleep. ◊ *una manzana a medio comer* a half eaten apple

el **medio** SUSTANTIVO
[1] middle (*centro*) ◊ *Está en el medio.* It's in the middle.
♦ **en medio de** in the middle of
[2] means (*recurso*) ◊ *un medio de transporte* a means of transport
♦ **por medio de** by means of
♦ **medios** means ◊ *por medios pacíficos* by peaceful means
♦ **los medios de comunicación** the media
♦ **el medio ambiente** the environment

el **mediodía** SUSTANTIVO
♦ **al mediodía (1)** (*a las 12 de la mañana*) at midday
♦ **al mediodía (2)** (*a la hora de comer*) at lunchtime

medir* VERBO
to measure ◊ *¿Has medido la ventana?* Have you measured the window?
♦ **¿Cuánto mides? – Mido 1.50 m.** How tall are you? – I'm 1.5 m tall.
♦ **¿Cuánto mide esta habitación? – Mide 3 m por 4.** How big is this room? – It measures 3 m by 4.

el **Mediterráneo** SUSTANTIVO
the Mediterranean

* Verbs marked with this symbol are irregular. See pages 380-382 for further details

mediterráneo ADJETIVO
Mediterranean

la **medusa** SUSTANTIVO
jellyfish (PL jellyfish)

el **mejicano**, la **mejicana** ADJETIVO, SUSTANTIVO
Mexican

Méjico SUSTANTIVO MASC
Mexico

la **mejilla** SUSTANTIVO
cheek

el **mejillón** SUSTANTIVO (PL los **mejillones**)
mussel

mejor ADJETIVO (FEM **mejor**)
1 better ◊ *Éste es mejor que el otro.* This one is better than the other one.
♦ **Es el mejor de los dos.** He's the better of the two.
2 best ◊ *mi mejor amiga* my best friend ◊ *el mejor de la clase* the best in the class ◊ *Es el mejor de todos.* He's the best of the lot.

mejor ADVERBIO
1 better ◊ *La conozco mejor que tú.* I know her better than you do.
2 best ◊ *¿Quién lo hace mejor?* Who does it best?
♦ **a lo mejor** probably
♦ **Mejor nos vamos.** We had better go.

la **mejora** SUSTANTIVO
improvement

mejorar VERBO
to improve ◊ *El tiempo está mejorando.* The weather's improving. ◊ *Han mejorado el servicio.* They have improved the service.
♦ **¡Que te mejores!** Get well soon!

la **mejoría** SUSTANTIVO
improvement

la **melena** SUSTANTIVO
1 long hair (*de persona*) ◊ *Lleva una melena rubia.* She has long blond hair.
2 mane (*de león*)

el **mellizo**, la **melliza** ADJETIVO, SUSTANTIVO
twin ◊ *Son mellizos.* They're twins.

el **melocotón** SUSTANTIVO (PL los **melocotones**)
peach (PL peaches)

la **melodía** SUSTANTIVO
tune ◊ *tararear una melodía* to hum a tune

el **melón** SUSTANTIVO (PL los **melones**)
melon

la **memoria** SUSTANTIVO
memory (PL memories) ◊ *tener mala memoria* to have a bad memory
♦ **aprender algo de memoria** to learn something by heart

memorizar* VERBO
to memorize

mencionar VERBO
to mention

el **mendigo**, la **mendiga** SUSTANTIVO
beggar

menor ADJETIVO, PRONOMBRE (FEM **menor**)
1 younger ◊ *Es tres años menor que yo.* He's three years younger than me. ◊ *Juanito es menor que Pepe.* Juanito is younger than Pepe.
♦ **el hermano menor (1)** (*de dos hermanos*) the younger brother
♦ **el hermano menor (2)** (*de más de dos hermanos*) the youngest brother
♦ **Yo soy el menor. (1)** (*de dos*) I'm the younger.
♦ **Yo soy el menor. (2)** (*de más de dos*) I'm the youngest.
2 smaller ◊ *una talla menor* a smaller size

el/la **menor** SUSTANTIVO
♦ **un menor de edad** a minor
♦ **los menores** the under-18s

Menorca SUSTANTIVO FEM
Minorca

menos (1) ADJETIVO, ADVERBIO
1 less ◊ *Fernando está menos deprimido.* Fernando is less depressed. ◊ *Ahora salgo menos.* I go out less these days.
♦ **Últimamente nos vemos menos.** We've been seeing less of each other recently.

Para formar el comparativo con sustantivos, se utiliza ***less*** *si son incontables y* ***fewer*** *si son contables.*

◊ *menos harina* less flour ◊ *menos gatos* fewer cats ◊ *menos gente* fewer people
♦ **menos...que** less...than ◊ *Me gusta menos que el otro.* I like it less than the other one. ◊ *Lo hizo menos cuidadosamente que ayer.* He did it less carefully than yesterday.
♦ **Trabaja menos que yo.** He doesn't work as hard as I do.
♦ **menos de 50 cajas** fewer than 50 boxes
♦ **Tiene menos de dieciocho años.** He's under eighteen.
2 least ◊ *el chico menos desobediente de la clase* the least disobedient boy in the class
♦ **Fue el que menos trabajó.** He was the one who worked the least hard.

Para formar el superlativo con sustantivos, se utiliza ***least*** *si son incontables y* ***fewest*** *si son contables.*

◊ *el método que lleva menos tiempo* the method which takes the least time ◊ *el examen con menos errores* the exam paper with the fewest mistakes
♦ **No quiero verle y menos visitarle.** I don't want to see him, let alone visit him.
♦ **¡Menos mal!** Thank goodness!
♦ **al menos** at least
♦ **5 menos 2 son 3** 5 minus 2 is 3

menos (2) PREPOSICIÓN
except
♦ **todos menos él** everyone except him

M

♦ **a menos que** unless

el **mensaje** SUSTANTIVO
message

el **mensajero,** la **mensajera** SUSTANTIVO
messenger

mensual ADJETIVO
monthly (*pago, revista*)
♦ **50 dólares mensuales** 50 dollars a month

la **menta** SUSTANTIVO
mint ◊ *un caramelo de menta* a mint sweet

la **mentalidad** SUSTANTIVO
mentality (PL mentalities) ◊ *Tiene mentalidad de burócrata.* He has a bureaucratic mentality.
♦ **Tiene una mentalidad muy abierta.** He has a very open mind.

la **mente** SUSTANTIVO
mind ◊ *No me lo puedo quitar de la mente.* I can't get it out of my mind.
♦ **tener en mente hacer algo** to be thinking of doing something ◊ *Tiene en mente cambiar de empleo.* He's thinking of changing jobs.

mentir* VERBO
to lie ◊ *No me mientas.* Don't lie to me.

la **mentira** SUSTANTIVO
lie ◊ *No digas mentiras.* Don't tell lies.
♦ **Parece mentira que aún no te haya pagado.** It's incredible that he still hasn't paid you.
♦ **una pistola de mentira** a toy pistol

el **mentiroso,** la **mentirosa** SUSTANTIVO
liar

el **menú** SUSTANTIVO (PL los **menús**)
menu (*carta*)
♦ **el menú del día** the set meal

menudo ADJETIVO
slight ◊ *Es una chica muy menuda.* She's a very slight girl.
♦ **¡Menudo lío!** What a mess!
♦ **a menudo** often

el **meñique** SUSTANTIVO
little finger

el **mercado** SUSTANTIVO
market

la **mercancía** SUSTANTIVO
commodity (PL commodities)

la **mercería** SUSTANTIVO
haberdasher's (PL haberdashers' shops)

merecer* VERBO
to deserve ◊ *Mereces que te castiguen.* You deserve to be punished.
♦ **merece la pena** it's worthwhile

merendar* VERBO
to have tea

el **merengue** SUSTANTIVO
meringue

la **merienda** SUSTANTIVO
tea

el **mérito** SUSTANTIVO
merit ◊ *una obra de gran mérito artístico* a work of great artistic merit
♦ **Eso tiene mucho mérito.** That's very commendable.
♦ **El mérito es todo suyo.** The credit is all his.

la **merluza** SUSTANTIVO
hake

la **mermelada** SUSTANTIVO
jam

mero ADVERBIO Mexico
almost ◊ *Ya mero no vengo.* I almost didn't come.

el **mes** SUSTANTIVO (PL los **meses**)
month ◊ *el mes que viene* next month ◊ *a final de mes* at the end of the month

la **mesa** SUSTANTIVO
table
♦ **poner la mesa** to lay the table
♦ **quitar la mesa** to clear the table

la **mesera** SUSTANTIVO Latin America
waitress (PL waitresses)

el **mesero** SUSTANTIVO Latin America
waiter

la **mesilla** SUSTANTIVO
♦ **una mesilla de noche** a bedside table

la **meta** SUSTANTIVO
1 aim (*objetivo*)
2 finishing line (*en atletismo*)
3 goal (*en fútbol*)

el **metal** SUSTANTIVO
metal

metálico ADJETIVO
metal
***metal** en este caso va siempre delante del sustantivo.*
◊ *un objeto metálico* a metal object
♦ **en metálico** in cash

meter VERBO
to put ◊ *¿Dónde has metido las llaves?* Where have you put the keys?
♦ **meterse** to go into ◊ *Se metió en la cueva.* He went into the cave.
♦ **meterse en política** to go into politics
♦ **No te metas donde no te llaman.** Don't poke your nose in where it doesn't belong.
♦ **meterse con alguien** to pick on somebody

el **método** SUSTANTIVO
method

el **metro** SUSTANTIVO
1 underground ◊ *coger el metro* to take the underground
2 metre ◊ *Mide tres metros de largo.* It's three metres long.

México SUSTANTIVO MASC
Mexico

la **mezcla** SUSTANTIVO

* Verbs marked with this symbol are irregular. See pages 380-382 for further details

mixture

mezclar VERBO
to mix ◊ *Hay que mezclar el azúcar y la harina.* You need to mix the sugar and the flour.
◆ **mezclarse en algo** to get mixed up in something

mezquino ADJETIVO
mean

la **mezquita** SUSTANTIVO
mosque

mi ADJETIVO (PL **mis**)
my ◊ *mis hermanas* my sisters

mí PRONOMBRE
me ◊ *para mí* for me
◆ **Para mí que ...** I think that ...
◆ **Por mí no hay problema.** There's no problem as far as I'm concerned.

el **microbio** SUSTANTIVO
microbe

el **micrófono** SUSTANTIVO
microphone

el **microondas** SUSTANTIVO (PL los **microondas**)
microwave ◊ *un horno microondas* a microwave oven

el **microscopio** SUSTANTIVO
microscope

midiendo VERBO *ver* **medir**

el **miedo** SUSTANTIVO
fear ◊ *el miedo a la oscuridad* fear of the dark
◆ **tener miedo** to be afraid ◊ *Le tenía miedo a su padre.* He was afraid of his father. ◊ *Tengo miedo a morir.* I'm afraid of dying. ◊ *Tenemos miedo de que nos ataquen.* We're afraid that they may attack us.
◆ **dar miedo a** to scare ◊ *Me daba miedo hacerlo.* I was scared of doing it.
◆ **pasarlo de miedo** to have a fantastic time (*coloquial*)

miedoso ADJETIVO
◆ **¡No seas tan miedoso!** Don't be such a coward!
◆ **Mi hijo es muy miedoso.** My son gets frightened very easily.

la **miel** SUSTANTIVO
honey

el/la **miembro** SUSTANTIVO
1 member (*de organización, de familia*)
2 limb (*del cuerpo*)

mientras ADVERBIO, CONJUNCIÓN
while ◊ *Lava tú mientras yo seco.* You wash while I dry.
◆ **Seguiré conduciendo mientras pueda.** I'll carry on driving for as long as I can.
◆ **mientras que** while
◆ **mientras tanto** meanwhile

el **miércoles** SUSTANTIVO (PL los **miércoles**)

Los días de la semana se escriben con mayúscula.

Wednesday ◊ *La vi el miércoles.* I saw her on Wednesday. ◊ *todos los miércoles* every Wednesday ◊ *el miércoles pasado* last Wednesday ◊ *el miércoles que viene* next Wednesday ◊ *Jugamos los miércoles.* We play on Wednesdays.

la **mierda** SUSTANTIVO
shit (*vulgar: excremento*)
◆ **Esta película es una mierda.** (*vulgar*) This film's a load of crap.
◆ **¡Vete a la mierda!** (*coloquial*) Go to hell!

la **miga** SUSTANTIVO
crumb
◆ **hacer buenas migas** (*coloquial*) to hit it off

mil ADJETIVO, PRONOMBRE
thousand ◊ *miles de personas* thousands of people ◊ *dos mil pesetas* two thousand pesetas
◆ **miles de veces** hundreds of times

el **milagro** SUSTANTIVO
miracle ◊ *No nos hemos matado de milagro.* It was a miracle we didn't get killed.

la **mili** SUSTANTIVO
military service ◊ *hacer la mili* to do one's military service

el **milímetro** SUSTANTIVO
millimetre

el/la **militar** SUSTANTIVO
soldier
◆ **los militares** the military

militar VERBO
◆ **militar en un partido** to be an active member of a party

la **milla** SUSTANTIVO
mile

el **millón** SUSTANTIVO (PL los **millones**)
million ◊ *millones de personas* millions of people
◆ **mil millones** a billion

el **millonario**, la **millonaria** SUSTANTIVO
millionaire

mimado ADJETIVO
spoiled

la **mina** SUSTANTIVO
mine

el **mineral** ADJETIVO, SUSTANTIVO
mineral

la **miniatura** SUSTANTIVO
miniature
◆ **una casa en miniatura** a miniature house

el **minidisco** SUSTANTIVO
Minidisc ®

la **minifalda** SUSTANTIVO
miniskirt

mínimo ADJETIVO
minimum ◊ *el salario mínimo* the minimum wage
◆ **No tienes ni la más mínima idea.** You haven't the faintest idea.

el **mínimo** SUSTANTIVO

M

minimum ◊ *un mínimo de 2.000 pesetas* a minimum of 2,000 pesetas
♦ **lo mínimo que puede hacer** the least he can do
♦ **Como mínimo podrías haber llamado.** You could at least have called.

el **ministerio** SUSTANTIVO
ministry (PL ministries)

el **ministro,** la **ministra** SUSTANTIVO
minister

la **minoría** SUSTANTIVO
minority (PL minorities) ◊ *las minorías étnicas* ethnic minorities

minucioso ADJETIVO
thorough

la **minúscula** SUSTANTIVO
small letter

la **minusválida** SUSTANTIVO
disabled woman (PL disabled women)

el **minusválido** SUSTANTIVO
disabled man (PL disabled men)
♦ **los minusválidos** the disabled

el **minuto** SUSTANTIVO
minute ◊ *Espera un minuto.* Wait a minute.

mío ADJETIVO, PRONOMBRE (FEM **mía**)
mine ◊ *Estos caballos son míos.* Those horses are mine. ◊ *¿De quién es esta bufanda? – Es mía.* Whose scarf is this? – It's mine. ◊ *El mío está en el armario.* Mine's in the cupboard. ◊ *Éste es el mío.* This one's mine.
♦ **un amigo mío** a friend of mine

miope ADJETIVO
short-sighted

la **mirada** SUSTANTIVO
look ◊ *con una mirada de odio* with a look of hatred
♦ **echar una mirada a algo** to have a look at something ◊ *¿Has tenido tiempo de echarle una mirada a mi informe?* Have you had time to have a look at my report?

mirar VERBO
to look ◊ *¡Mira! Un ratón.* Look! A mouse. ◊ *Mira a ver si está ahí.* Look and see if he is there.
♦ **mirar algo** to look at something ◊ *Mira esta foto.* Look at this photo.
♦ **mirar por la ventana** to look out of the window
♦ **mirar algo fijamente** to stare at something
♦ **¡Mira que es tonto!** What an idiot!
♦ **mirarse al espejo** to look at oneself in the mirror
♦ **Se miraron asombrados.** They looked at each other in amazement.

la **misa** SUSTANTIVO
mass (PL masses) ◊ *la misa del gallo* midnight mass ◊ *ir a misa* to go to mass

la **miseria** SUSTANTIVO
1 poverty ◊ *estar en la miseria* to be living in poverty
2 pittance ◊ *Gano una miseria.* I earn a pittance.

la **misión** SUSTANTIVO (PL las **misiones**)
mission

el **misionero,** la **misionera** SUSTANTIVO
missionary (PL missionaries)

mismo (1) ADJETIVO
same ◊ *Nos gustan los mismos libros.* We like the same books. ◊ *Vivo en su misma calle.* I live in the same street as him.
♦ **yo mismo** myself ◊ *Lo hice yo mismo.* I did it myself.

mismo (2) ADVERBIO
♦ **Hoy mismo le escribiré.** I'll write to him today.
♦ **Nos podemos encontrar aquí mismo.** We can meet right here.
♦ **enfrente mismo del colegio** right opposite the school

mismo (3) PRONOMBRE
♦ **lo mismo** the same ◊ *Yo tomaré lo mismo.* I'll have the same.
♦ **Da lo mismo.** It doesn't matter.
♦ **No ha llamado pero lo mismo viene.** He hasn't phoned but he may well come.

el **misterio** SUSTANTIVO
mystery (PL mysteries)

misterioso ADJETIVO
mysterious

la **mitad** SUSTANTIVO
half (PL halves) ◊ *Se comió la mitad del pastel.* He ate half the cake. ◊ *más de la mitad de los trabajadores* more than half the workers
♦ **La mitad son chicas.** Half of them are girls.
♦ **a mitad de precio** half-price
♦ **a mitad de camino** halfway there
♦ **Corta el pan por la mitad.** Cut the loaf in half.

el **mito** SUSTANTIVO
myth

mixto ADJETIVO
mixed ◊ *una escuela mixta* a mixed school

el **mobiliario** SUSTANTIVO
furniture

la **mochila** SUSTANTIVO
rucksack

el **moco** SUSTANTIVO
♦ **Límpiate los mocos.** Wipe your nose.
♦ **tener mocos** to have a runny nose

la **moda** SUSTANTIVO
fashion
♦ **estar de moda** to be in fashion
♦ **pasado de moda** old-fashioned

los **modales** SUSTANTIVO
manners ◊ *buenos modales* good manners

el/la **modelo** ADJETIVO, SUSTANTIVO
model ◊ *una niña modelo* a model child ◊ *Quiero ser modelo.* I want to be a model.

moderado ADJETIVO
moderate

modernizar* VERBO
to modernize (*fábrica*)
♦**modernizarse** (*persona*) to get up to date

moderno ADJETIVO
modern

la **modestia** SUSTANTIVO
modesty

modesto ADJETIVO
modest

modificar* VERBO
to modify

el **modisto**, la **modista** SUSTANTIVO
dressmaker ◊ *Es modista.* She's a dressmaker.

el **modo** SUSTANTIVO
way ◊ *Le gusta hacerlo todo a su modo.* She likes to do everything her own way.
♦**de todos modos** anyway
♦**de modo que (1)** so ◊ *No has hecho los deberes, de modo que no puedes salir.* You haven't done your homework so you can't go out.
♦**de modo que (2)** so that ◊ *Mueve la tele de modo que todos la podamos ver.* Move the TV so that we can all see it.
♦**los buenos modos** good manners
♦**los malos modos** bad manners
♦**"modo de empleo"** "instructions for use"

el **moho** SUSTANTIVO
1 mould (*en pan, fruta*)
2 rust (*en metal*)

mojado ADJETIVO
wet

mojar VERBO
to get...wet ◊ *¡No mojes la alfombra!* Don't get the carpet wet! ◊ *Me he mojado las mangas.* I got my sleeves wet.
♦**Moja el pan en la salsa.** Dip the bread into the sauce.
♦**mojarse** to get wet

el **molde** SUSTANTIVO
mould

moler* VERBO
to grind (*café, pimienta*)
♦**Estoy molido.** (*coloquial*) I'm knackered.

molestar VERBO
1 to bother ◊ *¿Te molesta la radio?* Is the radio bothering you? ◊ *Siento molestarle.* I'm sorry to bother you.
2 to disturb ◊ *No me molestes, que estoy trabajando.* Don't disturb me, I'm working.
♦**molestarse** to get upset ◊ *Se molestó por algo que dije.* She got upset because of something I said.
♦**molestarse en hacer algo** to bother to do something

la **molestia** SUSTANTIVO
♦**tomarse la molestia de hacer algo** to take the trouble to do something
♦**"perdonen las molestias"** "we apologize for any inconvenience"
♦**Aún tengo molestias en el hombro.** My shoulder still bothers me.

molesto ADJETIVO
annoying (*ruido*)
♦**estar molesto** (*enfadado*) to be annoyed

el **molinillo** SUSTANTIVO
♦**un molinillo de café** a coffee grinder

el **molino** SUSTANTIVO
mill ◊ *un molino de viento* a windmill

el **momento** SUSTANTIVO
moment ◊ *Espera un momento.* Wait a moment. ◊ *en un momento* in a moment
♦**en este momento** at the moment ◊ *Tenemos mucho trabajo en este momento.* We've got a lot of work at the moment.
♦**de un momento a otro** any moment now ◊ *Llegarán de un momento a otro.* They'll be here any moment now.
♦**por el momento** for the moment
♦**Llegó el momento de irnos.** The time came for us to go.

la **momia** SUSTANTIVO
mummy (PL mummies)

el/la **monarca** SUSTANTIVO
monarch

la **monarquía** SUSTANTIVO
monarchy (PL monarchies)

el **monasterio** SUSTANTIVO
monastery (PL monasteries)

la **moneda** SUSTANTIVO
coin ◊ *una moneda de 5 pesetas* a 5-peseta coin
♦**la moneda extranjera** foreign currency

el **monedero** SUSTANTIVO
purse

el **monitor**, la **monitora** SUSTANTIVO
instructor ◊ *un monitor de esquí* a skiing instructor

el **monitor** SUSTANTIVO
monitor (*pantalla*)

la **monja** SUSTANTIVO
nun

el **monje** SUSTANTIVO
monk

mono ADJETIVO
pretty ◊ *¡Qué piso tan mono!* What a pretty flat!
♦**¡Qué niña tan mona!** What a sweet little girl!

el **mono** SUSTANTIVO
1 monkey (*animal*)

M

☞

[2] overalls PL (*prenda entera*)
[3] dungarees PL (*prenda con peto*)

el **monopatín** SUSTANTIVO (PL los **monopatines**)
skateboard

monótono ADJETIVO
monotonous

el **monstruo** SUSTANTIVO
monster

la **montaña** SUSTANTIVO
mountain ◊ *Todos los años pasamos un mes en la montaña.* We spend a month in the mountains every year.
♦ **la montaña rusa** the roller coaster

montañoso ADJETIVO
mountainous

montar VERBO
[1] to assemble (*máquina, armario*)
[2] to set up (*negocio*)
♦ **montar una tienda** to put up a tent
♦ **montar a caballo** to ride a horse
♦ **montar en bici** to ride a bike
♦ **montarse** to get on ◊ *Llegó corriendo y se montó en el autobús.* He came running up and got on the bus.

el **monte** SUSTANTIVO
mountain

el **montón** SUSTANTIVO (PL los **montones**)
pile (*pila*) ◊ *Puso el montón de libros sobre la mesa.* He put the pile of books on the table.
♦ **un montón de ...** loads of ... (*coloquial: muchos*) ◊ *un montón de gente* loads of people ◊ *un montón de dinero* loads of money

el **monumento** SUSTANTIVO
monument

el **moño** SUSTANTIVO
bun ◊ *Mi abuela siempre lleva moño.* My grandmother always wears her hair in a bun.

la **moqueta** SUSTANTIVO
carpet

la **mora** SUSTANTIVO
[1] (*de la zarzamora*)
blackberry (PL blackberries)
[2] (*del moral*)
mulberry (PL mulberries)

morado ADJETIVO
purple ◊ *un vestido morado* a purple dress

moral ADJETIVO
moral

la **moral** SUSTANTIVO
[1] morale (*ánimo*)
♦ **levantar la moral a alguien** to cheer somebody up
♦ **estar bajo de moral** to be down
[2] morals PL (*moralidad*) ◊ *No tienen moral.* They have no morals.

la **moraleja** SUSTANTIVO
moral

la **morcilla** SUSTANTIVO
black pudding

morder* VERBO
to bite
♦ **morderse las uñas** to bite one's nails

el **mordisco** SUSTANTIVO
bite ◊ *Dame un mordisco de tu bocadillo.* Let me have a bite of your sandwich.
♦ **dar un mordisco** to bite ◊ *Me dio un mordisco.* He bit me.

moreno ADJETIVO
[1] dark (*pelo, piel*)
♦ **Es moreno. (1)** (*de pelo moreno*) He has dark hair.
♦ **Es moreno. (2)** (*de tez morena*) He is dark-skinned.
♦ **ponerse moreno** to get brown
[2] brown (*pan, azúcar*)

morir* VERBO
to die ◊ *Murió de cáncer.* He died of cancer.
♦ **morirse de hambre** to starve ◊ *¡Me muero de hambre!* I'm starving!
♦ **morirse de vergüenza** to die of shame
♦ **Me muero de ganas de ir a nadar.** I'm dying to go for a swim.

la **mortadela** SUSTANTIVO
mortadella

mortal ADJETIVO
[1] fatal (*herida, accidente*)
[2] mortal (*enemigo*)

la **mosca** SUSTANTIVO
fly (PL flies)
♦ **por si las moscas** just in case

el **mosquito** SUSTANTIVO
mosquito (PL mosquitoes)

la **mostaza** SUSTANTIVO
mustard

el **mostrador** SUSTANTIVO
counter

mostrar* VERBO
to show ◊ *Nos mostró el camino.* He showed us the way.
♦ **mostrarse amable** to be kind

el **mote** SUSTANTIVO
nickname

el **motivo** SUSTANTIVO
[1] reason ◊ *Dejó el trabajo por motivos personales.* He left the job for personal reasons.
♦ **sin motivo** for no reason
[2] motive ◊ *¿Cuál fue el motivo del crimen?* What was the motive for the crime?

la **moto** SUSTANTIVO
motorbike

la **motocicleta** SUSTANTIVO

motorbike

el **motor** SUSTANTIVO
motor

el/la **motorista** SUSTANTIVO
motorcyclist

mover* VERBO
to move ◊ *Mueve un poco las cajas para que podamos pasar.* Move the boxes a bit so that we can get past.
♦ **moverse** to move ◊ *¡No te muevas!* Don't move!

móvil ADJETIVO
mobile

el **móvil** SUSTANTIVO
1 mobile (*teléfono*)
2 motive (*de un crimen*)

el **movimiento** SUSTANTIVO
movement

la **muchacha** SUSTANTIVO
1 girl (*chica*)
2 maid (*criada*)

el **muchacho** SUSTANTIVO
boy

la **muchedumbre** SUSTANTIVO
crowd

mucho (1) ADJETIVO
1 a lot of
***a lot of** se usa en oraciones afirmativas, sobre todo en medio de la oración.*
◊ *Había mucha gente.* There were a lot of people. ◊ *Tiene muchas plantas.* He has got a lot of plants.
2 much (PL many)
***much** y **many** se usan en oraciones negativas e interrogativas. También se usan al principio de oraciones afirmativas.*
◊ *No tenemos mucho tiempo.* We haven't got much time. ◊ *¿Conoces a mucha gente?* Do you know many people? ◊ *Muchas personas creen que ...* Many people think that ...
♦ **no hace mucho tiempo** not long ago
♦ **Hace mucho calor.** It's very hot.
♦ **Tengo mucho frío.** I'm very cold.
♦ **Tengo mucha hambre.** I'm very hungry.
♦ **Tengo mucha sed.** I'm very thirsty.

mucho (2) PRONOMBRE
1 a lot
***a lot** se usa en oraciones afirmativas, sobre todo en medio de la oración.*
◊ *Tengo mucho que hacer.* I've got a lot to do. ◊ *¿Cuántos había? – Muchos.* How many were there? – A lot.
***much** y **many** se usan en oraciones negativas e interrogativas. También se usan al principio de oraciones afirmativas.*
2 much (PL many) ◊ *No tengo mucho que hacer.* I haven't got much to do. ◊ *¿Hay manzanas? – Sí pero no muchas.* Are there any apples? – Yes, but not many.
♦ **¿Vinieron muchos?** Did many people come?
♦ **Muchos dicen que ...** Many people say that ...

mucho (3) ADVERBIO
1 very much ◊ *Te quiero mucho.* I love you very much. ◊ *No me gusta mucho la carne.* I don't like meat very much.
*También se usa **really** con el mismo significado.*
◊ *Me gusta mucho el jazz.* I really like jazz.
2 a lot ◊ *Come mucho.* He eats a lot.
♦ **mucho más** a lot more
♦ **mucho antes** long before
♦ **No tardes mucho.** Don't be long.
♦ **Como mucho leo un libro al mes.** At most I read one book a month.
♦ **Fue, con mucho, el mejor.** He was by far the best.
♦ **Por mucho que lo quieras no debes mimarlo.** No matter how much you love him, you shouldn't spoil him.

la **mudanza** SUSTANTIVO
move

mudarse VERBO
to move
♦ **mudarse de casa** to move house

mudo ADJETIVO
dumb
♦ **quedarse mudo de asombro** to be dumbfounded

el **mueble** SUSTANTIVO
♦ **un mueble** a piece of furniture
♦ **los muebles** furniture SING
♦ **seis muebles** six pieces of furniture

la **muela** SUSTANTIVO
tooth (PL teeth)
♦ **una muela del juicio** a wisdom tooth

el **muelle** SUSTANTIVO
1 spring (*de colchón*)
2 quay (*de puerto*)

muelo VERBO *ver* **moler**

muerdo VERBO *ver* **morder**

la **muerta** SUSTANTIVO
dead woman (PL dead women)

la **muerte** SUSTANTIVO
death ◊ *Lo condenaron a muerte.* He was sentenced to death.
♦ **Nos dio un susto de muerte.** (*coloquial*) He nearly frightened us to death.
♦ **un hotel de mala muerte** (*coloquial*) a grotty hotel

muerto VERBO *ver* **morir**

muerto ADJETIVO
dead
♦ **Está muerto de cansancio.** (*coloquial*) He's dead tired.

el **muerto** SUSTANTIVO
dead man (PL dead men)
♦ **los muertos** the dead

M

◆ **Hubo tres muertos.** Three people were killed.
◆ **hacer el muerto** to float

la **muestra** SUSTANTIVO
1 sample ◊ *una muestra gratuita* a free sample
2 sign ◊ *dar muestras de* to show signs of
3 token ◊ *Me lo regaló como muestra de afecto.* She gave it to me as a token of affection.

muestro VERBO *ver* **mostrar**

muevo VERBO *ver* **mover**

la **mujer** SUSTANTIVO
1 woman (PL women) ◊ *Vino a verte una mujer.* A woman came to see you.
2 wife (PL wives) ◊ *la mujer del médico* the doctor's wife

la **muleta** SUSTANTIVO
(*para andar*)
crutch (PL crutches)

> *In bullfighting, the **muleta** is a special stick with a red cloth attached to it that the matador uses.*

la **multa** SUSTANTIVO
fine ◊ *una multa de 5.000 pesetas* a 5,000-peseta fine
◆ **poner una multa a alguien** to fine somebody

multiplicar* VERBO
to multiply ◊ *Hay que multiplicarlo por cinco.* You have to multiply it by five.
◆ **la tabla de multiplicar** the multiplication tables PL

la **multitud** SUSTANTIVO
crowd
◆ **multitud de** lots of

mundial ADJETIVO
1 world (*política, historia, guerra*)
***world** en este caso va siempre delante del sustantivo.*
2 worldwide (*problema, reconocimiento*)

el **mundial** SUSTANTIVO
world championship

el **mundo** SUSTANTIVO
world
◆ **todo el mundo** everybody ◊ *Se lo ha dicho a todo el mundo.* He has told everybody.
◆ **No lo cambiaría por nada del mundo.** I wouldn't change it for anything in the world.

municipal ADJETIVO
1 council (*empleado, oficina*)
***council** en este caso va siempre delante del sustantivo.*
2 local (*impuesto*)
3 public (*piscina*)

el **municipio** SUSTANTIVO
1 (*territorio*)
municipality (PL municipalities)
2 (*organismo*)
town council

la **muñeca** SUSTANTIVO
1 wrist (*del brazo*)
2 doll (*juguete*)

el **muñeco** SUSTANTIVO
1 doll (*con forma humana*)
◆ **un muñeco de peluche** a soft toy
2 figure (*dibujo*)

la **muralla** SUSTANTIVO
city wall

el **murciélago** SUSTANTIVO
bat

el **murmullo** SUSTANTIVO
murmur

la **murmuración** SUSTANTIVO (PL las **murmuraciones**)
gossip SING

el **muro** SUSTANTIVO
wall

el **músculo** SUSTANTIVO
muscle

el **museo** SUSTANTIVO
museum
◆ **un mueso de arte** an art gallery

la **música** SUSTANTIVO
1 music (*arte*)
2 musician (*persona*)

el **músico** SUSTANTIVO
musician

el **muslo** SUSTANTIVO
thigh

el **musulmán**, la **musulmana** ADJETIVO, SUSTANTIVO (MASC PL los **musulmanes**)
Moslem

mutuo ADJETIVO
mutual ◊ *de mutuo acuerdo* by mutual agreement ◊ *El sentimiento es mutuo.* The feeling is mutual.

muy ADVERBIO
very ◊ *Mi pueblo es muy bonito.* My village is very pretty.
◆ **Eso es muy español.** That's typically Spanish.
◆ **No me gusta por muy guapa que sea.** No matter how pretty she is, I don't like her.

N

el **nabo** SUSTANTIVO
turnip
nacer* VERBO
to be born ◊ *Nació en 1964.* He was born in 1964.
el **nacimiento** SUSTANTIVO
[1] birth (*de persona*)
[2] crib (*pesebre*)
la **nación** SUSTANTIVO (PL las **naciones**)
nation
nacional ADJETIVO
[1] national (*himno, frontera*)
[2] home (*mercado*)
***home** en este caso va siempre delante del sustantivo.*
◆**vuelos nacionales** domestic flights
la **nacionalidad** SUSTANTIVO
nationality (PL nationalities)
el **nacionalismo** SUSTANTIVO
nationalism
el/la **nacionalista** ADJETIVO, SUSTANTIVO
nationalist
nada (1) PRONOMBRE
[1] nothing
*Se usa **nothing** cuando el verbo está en la forma afirmativa.*
◊ *¿Qué has comprado? – Nada.* What have you bought? – Nothing. ◊ *No dijo nada.* He said nothing.
[2] anything
*Se usa **anything** cuando el verbo está en la forma negativa.*
◊ *No quiero nada.* I don't want anything.
◆**No dijo nada más.** He didn't say anything else.
◆**Quiero uno nada más.** I only want one, that's all.
◆**Encendió la tele nada más llegar.** He turned on the TV as soon as he came in.
◆**¡Gracias! – De nada.** Thanks! – Don't mention it.
◆**Se lo advertí, pero como si nada.** I warned him but he paid no attention.
◆**No sabe nada de español.** He knows no Spanish at all.
◆**No me dio nada de nada.** He gave me absolutely nothing.
nada (2) ADVERBIO
at all ◊ *Esto no me gusta nada.* I don't like this at all. ◊ *No está nada triste.* He isn't sad at all.
nadar VERBO
to swim
nadie PRONOMBRE
[1] nobody
*Se usa **nobody** cuando el verbo está en la forma afirmativa.*
◊ *Nadie habló.* Nobody spoke. ◊ *No había nadie.* There was nobody there.
[2] anybody
*Se usa **anybody** cuando el verbo está en la forma negativa.*
◊ *No quiere ver a nadie.* He doesn't want to see anybody.
la **nafta** SUSTANTIVO [River Plate]
petrol
el **naipe** SUSTANTIVO
playing card
las **nalgas** SUSTANTIVO
buttocks
la **nana** SUSTANTIVO
lullaby (PL lullabies)
naranja ADJETIVO
orange ◊ *un anorak naranja* an orange anorak
el **naranja** SUSTANTIVO
orange (*color*)
la **naranja** SUSTANTIVO
orange (*fruta*)
el **narcotráfico** SUSTANTIVO
drug trafficking
la **nariz** SUSTANTIVO (PL las **narices**)
nose
◆**No metas las narices en mis asuntos.** Don't poke your nose into my business.
◆**estar hasta las narices de algo** to be totally fed up with something
la **narración** SUSTANTIVO (PL las **narraciones**)
story (PL stories)
narrar VERBO
to tell
la **narrativa** SUSTANTIVO
fiction
la **nata** SUSTANTIVO
[1] cream (*crema*)
[2] skin (*de la leche*)
◆**la nata líquida** single cream
◆**la nata montada** whipped cream
la **natación** SUSTANTIVO
swimming
natal ADJETIVO
home
***home** en este caso va siempre delante del sustantivo.*
◊ *su pueblo natal* his home town
las **natillas** SUSTANTIVO
custard SING
nato ADJETIVO
◆**un actor nato** a born actor
natural ADJETIVO
natural ◊ *con ingredientes naturales* with natural ingredients ◊ *Comes mucho y es natural que estés gordo.* You eat a lot, so it's only natural you're fat.

☞

◆ **Es natural de Alicante.** He's from Alicante.

la **naturaleza** SUSTANTIVO
nature
◆ **Es despistado por naturaleza.** He's naturally absent-minded.

el **naufragio** SUSTANTIVO
shipwreck

las **náuseas** SUSTANTIVO
◆ **tener náuseas** to feel sick

náutico ADJETIVO
◆ **club náutico** yacht club

la **navaja** SUSTANTIVO
clasp knife (PL clasp knives)
◆ **una navaja de afeitar** a razor

Navarra SUSTANTIVO FEM
Navarre

la **nave** SUSTANTIVO
ship (*barco*)
◆ **una nave espacial** a spaceship

el **navegador** SUSTANTIVO
browser
◆ **un navegador de Web** a web browser (*informática*)

navegar* VERBO
to sail

la **Navidad** SUSTANTIVO
Christmas
◆ **¡Feliz Navidad!** Happy Christmas!

la **neblina** SUSTANTIVO
mist

necesario ADJETIVO
necessary ◊ *No estudié más de lo necesario.* I didn't study any more than necessary.
◆ **Ya tengo el dinero necesario para el billete.** I've now got the money I need for the ticket.
◆ **Llamaré al médico si es necesario.** I'll call the doctor if need be.
◆ **No es necesario que vengas.** You don't have to come.

la **necesidad** SUSTANTIVO
1 need ◊ *No hay necesidad de hacerlo.* There is no need to do it.
2 (*cosa esencial*)
necessity (PL necessities) ◊ *Comer bien es una necesidad, no un lujo.* Eating well is a necessity, not a luxury.
◆ **Hizo sus necesidades.** He did his business.

necesitar VERBO
to need ◊ *Necesito mil pesetas.* I need a thousand pesetas. ◊ *Necesito sacar un notable en el examen.* I need to get a good mark in the exam. ◊ *Necesito que me ayudes.* I need you to help me.
◆ **"Se necesita camarero"** "Waiter wanted"

negar* VERBO
1 to deny ◊ *Decían que era el ladrón, pero él lo negaba.* They said that he was the thief, but he denied it.
◆ **negar con la cabeza** to shake one's head
2 to refuse ◊ *Me negaron el permiso para entrar en el bar.* They refused me permission to go into the bar.
◆ **Se negó a pagar la multa.** He refused to pay the fine.

negativo ADJETIVO
negative

el **negativo** SUSTANTIVO
negative (*de foto*)

la **negociación** SUSTANTIVO
negotiation

negociar VERBO
◆ **Su empresa negocia con armas.** His company deals in arms.
◆ **Los dos gobiernos están negociando un acuerdo.** The two governments are negotiating an agreement.

el **negocio** SUSTANTIVO
(*empresa*)
business (PL businesses) ◊ *Hemos montado un negocio de videojuegos.* We set up a video games business.
◆ **el mundo de los negocios** the business world

la **negra** SUSTANTIVO
(*persona*)
black woman (PL black women)
◆ **tener la negra** to be out of luck

negro ADJETIVO
black

el **negro** SUSTANTIVO
1 (*color*)
black
2 (*persona*)
black man (PL black men)
◆ **los negros** Blacks

el **nervio** SUSTANTIVO
nerve
◆ **Me pone de los nervios.** He gets on my nerves.

el **nerviosismo** SUSTANTIVO
◆ **Me entra nerviosismo cuando la veo.** I get nervous when I see her.

nervioso ADJETIVO
nervous ◊ *Me pongo muy nervioso en los exámenes.* I get very nervous during exams.
◆ **¡Me pone nervioso!** He gets on my nerves!

el **neumático** SUSTANTIVO
tyre

neutral ADJETIVO
neutral

la **nevada** SUSTANTIVO
snowfall

nevar* VERBO

* Verbs marked with this symbol are irregular. See pages 380-382 for further details

to snow

la **nevera** SUSTANTIVO
refrigerator

ni CONJUNCIÓN
[1] or ◊ *No bebe ni fuma.* He doesn't drink or smoke.
[2] neither ◊ *Ella no fue, ni yo tampoco.* She didn't go and neither did I.
♦ **ni ... ni** neither ... nor ◊ *No vinieron ni Carlos ni Sofía.* Neither Carlos nor Sofía came.
♦ **No me gustan ni el bacalao ni el hígado.** I don't like either cod or liver.
♦ **No compré ni uno ni otro.** I didn't buy either of them.
♦ **Ni siquiera me saludó.** He didn't even say hello.

Nicaragua SUSTANTIVO FEM
Nicaragua

el/la **nicaragüense** ADJETIVO, SUSTANTIVO
Nicaraguan

la **nicotina** SUSTANTIVO
nicotine

el **nido** SUSTANTIVO
nest

la **niebla** SUSTANTIVO
fog
♦ **Hay niebla.** It's foggy.

niego VERBO *ver* **negar**

la **nieta** SUSTANTIVO
granddaughter

el **nieto** SUSTANTIVO
grandson
♦ **los nietos** grandchildren

nieva VERBO *ver* **nevar**

la **nieve** SUSTANTIVO
snow

NIF ABREVIATURA (= *número de identificación fiscal*)

> *This is an ID number used for tax purposes in Spain.*

ningún PRONOMBRE *ver* **ninguno**

ninguno ADJETIVO, PRONOMBRE (FEM **ninguna**)
[1] no

*Se usa **no** cuando el verbo está en la forma afirmativa.*

◊ *No tengo ningún interés en ir.* I have no interest in going.
[2] any

*Se usa **any** cuando el verbo está en la forma negativa.*

◊ *No vimos ninguna serpiente en el río.* We didn't see any snakes in the river.
[3] none ◊ *¿Cuál eliges? – Ninguno.* Which do you want? – None of them.
◊ *No me queda ninguno.* I have none left. ◊ *Ninguno de nosotros va a ir a la fiesta.* None of us are going to the party.
♦ **No lo encuentro por ningún sitio.** I can't find it anywhere.
♦ **ninguno de los dos (1)** neither of them ◊ *A ninguna de las dos les gusta el café.* Neither of them likes coffee.
♦ **ninguno de los dos (2)** either of them ◊ *No me gusta ninguno de los dos.* I don't like either of them.

la **niña** SUSTANTIVO
girl

la **niñera** SUSTANTIVO
nursemaid

la **niñez** SUSTANTIVO
childhood

niño ADJETIVO
young ◊ *Es todavía muy niño.* He's still very young.

el **niño** SUSTANTIVO
boy
♦ **de niño** as a child
♦ **los niños** the children

el **nitrógeno** SUSTANTIVO
nitrogen

el **nivel** SUSTANTIVO
[1] level ◊ *el nivel del agua* the water level
[2] standard ◊ *Pretenden aumentar el nivel educativo.* They are trying to raise the standard of education.
♦ **el nivel de vida** the standard of living

no ADVERBIO
no ◊ *¿Quieres venir? – No.* Do you want to come? – No.
♦ **¿Te gusta? – No mucho.** Do you like it? – Not really.

En inglés la mayoría de los verbos necesitan auxiliares para formar la negación.

◊ *No me gusta.* I don't like it. ◊ *María no habla inglés.* María doesn't speak English.

*Los verbos modales y el verbo **to be** no necesitan auxiliar.*

◊ *No puedo venir esta noche.* I can't come tonight. ◊ *No tengo tiempo.* I haven't got time. ◊ *No debes preocuparte.* You mustn't worry. ◊ *No hace frío.* It isn't cold.

En inglés no se usa la doble negación.

◊ *No conozco a nadie.* I don't know anyone.

Cuando se usa al final para confirmar, en inglés se usa un verbo auxiliar.

◊ *Esto es tuyo, ¿no?* This is yours, isn't it? ◊ *Fueron al cine, ¿no?* They went to the cinema, didn't they?
♦ **¿Puedo salir esta noche? – ¡Que no!** Can I go out tonight? – I said no!
♦ **los no fumadores** non-smokers

noble ADJETIVO
noble

la **noche** SUSTANTIVO
night ◊ *Pasó la noche sin dormir.* He had a sleepless night. ◊ *¡Buenas noches! (1)*

☞

N

(saludo) Good evening! ◊ *¡Buenas noches!* *(2)* *(al acostarse)* Goodnight!
♦ **esta noche** tonight
♦ **hoy por la noche** tonight
♦ **por la noche** at night ◊ *Estudia por la noche.* He studies at night. ◊ *el sábado por la noche* on Saturday night
♦ **Era de noche cuando llegamos a casa.** It was night time when we got back home.
♦ **No me gusta conducir de noche.** I don't like driving at night.

la **Nochebuena** SUSTANTIVO
Christmas Eve

> *En los países anglosajones no se celebra la cena de Nochebuena. La celebración familiar es el día de Navidad.*

la **Nochevieja** SUSTANTIVO
New Year's Eve

las **nociones** SUSTANTIVO
♦ **Tengo nociones de informática.** I know a little about computers.

nocturno ADJETIVO
[1] night *(club)*
> ***night*** *en este caso va siempre delante del sustantivo.*

[2] evening *(clases)*
> ***evening*** *en este caso va siempre delante del sustantivo.*

nomás ADVERBIO [Latin America]
just ◊ *Está ahí nomás.* It's just there.
♦ **así nomás** just like that

nombrar VERBO
[1] to appoint ◊ *Lo han nombrado director del colegio.* He was appointed Head of the school.
[2] to mention ◊ *Me nombró en su discurso.* He mentioned me in his speech.

el **nombre** SUSTANTIVO
[1] name *(de persona)*
♦ **nombre de pila** first name
♦ **nombre y apellidos** full name
[2] noun *(en gramática)*

la **nómina** SUSTANTIVO
pay slip *(hoja de pago)*
♦ **estar en nómina** to be on the payroll

el **nordeste** SUSTANTIVO
northeast

el **noreste** SUSTANTIVO
northeast

la **noria** SUSTANTIVO
big wheel *(atracción)*

la **norma** SUSTANTIVO
rule *(regla)*

normal ADJETIVO
[1] normal ◊ *una persona normal* a normal person
[2] ordinary ◊ *¿Es guapo? – No, normal.* Is he handsome? – No, just ordinary. ◊ *Es normal que quiera divertirse.* It's only normal that he wants to enjoy himself.

normalmente ADVERBIO
normally

el **noroeste** SUSTANTIVO
northwest

el **norte** SUSTANTIVO
north

el **norteamericano,** la **norteamericana** ADJETIVO, SUSTANTIVO
American

Noruega SUSTANTIVO FEM
Norway

el **noruego,** la **noruega** ADJETIVO, SUSTANTIVO
Norwegian

el **noruego** SUSTANTIVO
Norwegian *(idioma)*

nos PRONOMBRE
[1] us ◊ *Nos vinieron a ver.* They came to see us. ◊ *Nos dio un consejo.* He gave us some advice.
♦ **Nos lo dio.** He gave it to us.
♦ **Nos tienen que arreglar el ordenador.** They have to fix the computer for us.
[2] ourselves ◊ *Tenemos que defendernos.* We must defend ourselves.
♦ **Nos levantamos a las ocho.** We got up at eight o'clock.
[3] each other ◊ *No nos hablamos desde hace tiempo.* We haven't spoken to each other for a long time.
> *Con partes del cuerpo o con prendas que se llevan puestas se usa el adjetivo posesivo.*

◊ *Nos dolían los pies.* Our feet were hurting. ◊ *Nos pusimos los abrigos.* We put our coats on.

nosotros PRONOMBRE (FEM **nosotras**)
[1] we ◊ *Nosotros no somos italianos.* We are not Italian.
[2] us ◊ *¿Quién es? – Somos nosotros.* Who is it? – It's us. ◊ *Tu hermano vino con nosotros.* Your brother came with us. ◊ *Llegaron antes que nosotros.* They arrived before us.
♦ **nosotros mismos** ourselves

la **nota** SUSTANTIVO
[1] mark ◊ *Saca muy malas notas.* He gets very bad marks.
[2] note ◊ *Tomó muchas notas en la conferencia.* He took a lot of notes during the lecture. ◊ *Te he dejado una nota encima de la mesa.* I've left you a note on the table.

notar VERBO
[1] to notice ◊ *Notó que le seguían.* He noticed they were following him.

2 to feel ◊ *Con este abrigo no noto el frío.* I don't feel the cold with this coat on.
◆ **Se nota que has estudiado mucho este trimestre.** You can tell that you've studied a lot this term.

el **notario,** la **notaria** SUSTANTIVO
notary (PL notaries)

la **noticia** SUSTANTIVO
news SING ◊ *Tengo una buena noticia que darte.* I've got some good news for you.
◆ **Fue una noticia excelente para la economía.** It was an excellent piece of news for the economy.
◆ **Vi las noticias de las nueve.** I watched the nine o'clock news.
◆ **No tengo noticias de Juan.** I haven't heard from Juan.
*No confundir **noticia** con **notice**.*

notificar* VERBO
to notify

el **novato,** la **novata** SUSTANTIVO
beginner

novecientos ADJETIVO, PRONOMBRE (FEM **novecientas**)
nine hundred

la **novedad** SUSTANTIVO
◆ **Las últimas novedades en moda infantil.** The latest in children's fashions.
◆ **¿Cómo sigue tu hijo? – Sin novedad.** How's your son? – There's no change.

la **novela** SUSTANTIVO
novel
◆ **una novela policíaca** a detective story

noveno ADJETIVO, PRONOMBRE (FEM **novena**)
ninth
◆ **Vivo en el noveno.** I live on the ninth floor.

noventa ADJETIVO, PRONOMBRE
ninety
◆ **el noventa aniversario** the ninetieth anniversary

la **novia** SUSTANTIVO
1 girlfriend (*amiga íntima*)
2 fiancée (*prometida*)
3 bride (*en la boda*)

noviembre SUSTANTIVO MASC
Los meses se escriben con mayúscula.
November ◊ *en noviembre* in November ◊ *Llegará el 30 de noviembre.* He'll arrive on 30 November.

los **novillos** SUSTANTIVO
◆ **hacer novillos** to play truant

el **novio** SUSTANTIVO
1 boyfriend (*amigo íntimo*)
2 fiancé (*prometido*)
3 bridegroom (*en boda*)
◆ **los novios** (*en la boda*) the bride and groom

la **nube** SUSTANTIVO
cloud

nublado ADJETIVO
cloudy

nublarse VERBO
to cloud over (*cielo*)

nuboso ADJETIVO
cloudy

la **nuca** SUSTANTIVO
nape

nuclear ADJETIVO
nuclear
◆ **una central nuclear** a nuclear power station

el **núcleo** SUSTANTIVO
◆ **el núcleo urbano** the city centre

el **nudo** SUSTANTIVO
knot
◆ **atar con un nudo** to tie in a knot

la **nuera** SUSTANTIVO
daughter-in-law (PL daughters-in-law)

nuestro ADJETIVO, PRONOMBRE (FEM **nuestra**)
1 our ◊ *nuestro perro* our dog ◊ *nuestras bicicletas* our bicycles
2 ours ◊ *¿De quién es esto? – Es nuestro.* Whose is this? – It's ours. ◊ *Esta casa es la nuestra.* This house is ours.
◆ **un amigo nuestro** a friend of ours

nueve ADJETIVO, PRONOMBRE
nine
◆ **Son las nueve.** It's nine o'clock.
◆ **el nueve de marzo** the ninth of March

nuevo ADJETIVO
new ◊ *Necesito un ordenador nuevo.* I need a new computer. ◊ *Soy nuevo en el colegio.* I'm new at the school.
◆ **El mecánico me dejó el coche como nuevo.** The mechanic left my car like new.
◆ **Tuve que leer el libro de nuevo.** I had to read the book again.

la **nuez** SUSTANTIVO (PL las **nueces**)
1 nut
◆ **la nuez moscada** nutmeg
2 Adam's apple (*en el cuello*)

el **número** SUSTANTIVO
1 number (*cifra*)
2 size (*de zapato*)
3 issue (*de publicación*)
◆ **Calle Aribau, sin número.** Aribau street, no number.
◆ **número de teléfono** telephone number
◆ **montar un número** to make a scene

nunca ADVERBIO
1 never ◊ *No viene nunca.* He never comes.
◆ **No le veré nunca más.** I'll never see him again.
2 ever ◊ *Ninguno de nosotros había esquiado nunca.* Neither of us had ever skied before. ◊ *Casi nunca me escribe.* He hardly ever writes to me.

la **nutria** SUSTANTIVO
otter

el **nylon** SUSTANTIVO
nylon

ñoño ADJETIVO
soppy (*película, novela*)

el **ñu** SUSTANTIVO
gnu (PL gnus)

O

o CONJUNCIÓN
or ◇ *¿Quieres té o café?* Would you like tea or coffee? ◇ *¿Vas a ayudarme o no?* Are you going to help me or not?
◆**o ... o ...** either ... or ... ◇ *O ha salido o no coge el teléfono.* Either he's out or he's not answering the phone.
◆**O te callas o no sigo hablando.** If you're not quiet I won't go on.

obedecer* VERBO
to obey
◆**obedecer a alguien** to obey someone

obediente ADJETIVO
obedient

obeso ADJETIVO
obese

el **obispo** SUSTANTIVO
bishop

la **objeción** SUSTANTIVO (PL las **objeciones**)
objection
◆**No puso ninguna objeción.** He didn't object.

el **objetivo** SUSTANTIVO
objective ◇ *un objetivo militar* a military objective
◆**Nuestro principal objetivo es ganar las elecciones.** Our main aim is to win the elections.

el **objeto** SUSTANTIVO
object ◇ *un objeto metálico* a metal object
◆**¿Cuál es el objeto de su visita?** What's the reason for your visit?
◆**con objeto de hacer algo** in order to do something
◆**los objetos de valor** valuables

la **obligación** SUSTANTIVO (PL **obligaciones**)
obligation
◆**Obedecer a tus padres es tu obligación.** It's your duty to obey your parents.

obligado ADJETIVO
◆**verse obligado a hacer algo** to be forced to do something ◇ *Se vieron obligados a vender su casa.* They were forced to sell their house.
◆**No estás obligado a venir si no quieres.** You don't have to come if you don't want to.

obligar* VERBO
[1] to force ◇ *Nadie te obliga a aceptar este empleo.* Nobody's forcing you to accept this job.
[2] to make ◇ *No puedes obligarme a ir.* You can't make me go.

obligatorio ADJETIVO
compulsory

la **obra** SUSTANTIVO
[1] work
◆**una obra de arte** a work of art
◆**la obra completa de Neruda** the complete works of Neruda
◆**una obra de teatro** a play
◆**una obra maestra** a masterpiece
[2] building site (*edificio en construcción*)
◆**"obras"** "roadworks" (*en carretera*)

el **obrero**, la **obrera** SUSTANTIVO
worker ◇ *Mi primo es obrero de la construcción.* My cousin works on a building site.

el **obsequio** SUSTANTIVO
gift ◇ *como obsequio* as a gift

la **observación** SUSTANTIVO (PL las **observaciones**)
[1] observation ◇ *El paciente está en observación.* The patient is under observation.
[2] comment ◇ *hacer una observación* to make a comment

observador ADJETIVO (FEM **observadora**)
observant

observar VERBO
[1] to observe (*mirar*)
[2] to remark (*comentar*)

la **obsesión** SUSTANTIVO (PL las **obsesiones**)
obsession ◇ *su obsesión por la limpieza* his obsession with cleanliness

obsesionar VERBO
◆**Es un tema que le obsesiona.** He's obsessed by the subject.

el **obstáculo** SUSTANTIVO
obstacle ◇ *Nos puso muchos obstáculos.* He put many obstacles in our way.

obstante ADVERBIO
◆**no obstante** nevertheless

obstinado ADJETIVO
obstinate

* Verbs marked with this symbol are irregular. See pages 380-382 for further details

obstinarse VERBO
to insist ◊ *¿Por qué te obstinas en hacerlo?* Why do you insist on doing it?

obtener* VERBO
to obtain

obvio ADJETIVO
obvious

la **oca** SUSTANTIVO
goose (PL geese)

la **ocasión** SUSTANTIVO (PL las **ocasiones**)
1 opportunity (PL opportunities) ◊ *Ésta es la ocasión que esperábamos.* This is the opportunity we've been waiting for.
2 occasion ◊ *en varias ocasiones* on several occasions
♦ **un libro de ocasión** a secondhand book

ocasionar VERBO
to cause

occidental ADJETIVO
western
♦ **los países occidentales** the West

el **occidente** SUSTANTIVO
♦ **el Occidente** the West

el **océano** SUSTANTIVO
ocean ◊ *el océano Atlantico* the Atlantic Ocean

ochenta ADJETIVO, PRONOMBRE
eighty ◊ *Tiene ochenta años.* He's eighty.
♦ **el ochenta aniversario** the eightieth anniversary

ocho ADJETIVO, PRONOMBRE
eight
♦ **Son las ocho.** It's eight o'clock.
♦ **el ocho de agosto** the eighth of August

ochocientos ADJETIVO, PRONOMBRE (FEM **ochocientas**)
eight hundred

el **ocio** SUSTANTIVO
♦ **en mis ratos de ocio** in my spare time

octavo ADJETIVO, PRONOMBRE (FEM **octava**)
eighth
♦ **Vivo en el octavo.** I live on the eighth floor.

octubre SUSTANTIVO MASC
Los meses se escriben con mayúscula.
October ◊ *en octubre* in October ◊ *Llegaré el 3 de octubre.* I'll arrive on 3 October.

el/la **oculista** SUSTANTIVO
eye specialist ◊ *Es oculista.* He's an eye specialist.

ocultar VERBO
to conceal ◊ *Nos ocultó su edad.* He concealed his age from us.
♦ **No nos ocultes la verdad.** Don't try to hide the truth from us.
♦ **ocultarse** to hide

la **ocupación** SUSTANTIVO (PL las **ocupaciones**)
1 activity (PL activities) ◊ *Tiene muchas ocupaciones.* He's involved in many activities.
2 occupation ◊ *¿Qué ocupación tiene?* What's his occupation? ◊ *la ocupación de la embajada por parte de los guerrilleros* the occupation of the embassy by the guerrillas

ocupado ADJETIVO
1 busy ◊ *Estoy muy ocupado.* I'm very busy.
2 engaged ◊ *Si la línea está ocupada vuelva a llamar.* If the line's engaged please call back later.
♦ **"ocupado"** "engaged"
♦ **¿Está ocupado este asiento?** Is this seat taken?

ocupar VERBO
1 to occupy ◊ *Los obreros han ocupado la fábrica.* The workers have occupied the factory. ◊ *El edifico ocupa todo el solar.* The building occupies the whole site.
2 to take up ◊ *Ocupa casi todo mi tiempo.* It takes up almost all my time.
♦ **Los espectadores ocuparon sus asientos.** The spectators took their seats.
♦ **ocuparse de algo** to look after something
♦ **Yo me ocuparé de decírselo.** I'll tell him.

la **ocurrencia** SUSTANTIVO
♦ **Juan tuvo la ocurrencia de decírselo a la cara.** Juan had the bright idea to tell her to her face.
♦ **¡Qué ocurrencia!** Him and his crazy ideas!

ocurrir VERBO
to happen ◊ *Lo que ocurrió podría haberse evitado.* What happened could have been avoided.
♦ **¿Qué te ocurre?** What's the matter?
♦ **Se nos ocurrió una idea brillante.** We had a brilliant idea.

odiar VERBO
to hate ◊ *Odio tener que levantarme pronto.* I hate having to get up early.

el **odio** SUSTANTIVO
hate

el **oeste** SUSTANTIVO, ADJETIVO
west ◊ *el oeste del país* the west of the country ◊ *en la costa oeste* on the west coast
♦ **al oeste de la ciudad** west of the city
♦ **Viajábamos hacia el oeste.** We were travelling west.
♦ **una película del oeste** a western
♦ **vientos del oeste** westerly winds

ofender VERBO
offend
♦ **ofenderse** to take offence

la **ofensa** SUSTANTIVO
insult

la **oferta** SUSTANTIVO
offer
♦ **una oferta especial** a special offer
♦ **estar de oferta** to be on special offer
♦ **"ofertas de trabajo"** "situations vacant"

O

oficial ADJETIVO
official

el/la **oficial** SUSTANTIVO
officer ◇ *Es oficial de marina.* He's an officer in the navy.

la **oficina** SUSTANTIVO
office
- **la oficina de turismo** the tourist office
- **la oficina de empleo** the job centre
- **la oficina de correos** the post office
- **la oficina de objetos perdidos** the lost property office

el **oficio** SUSTANTIVO
trade ◇ *Es carpintero de oficio.* He's a carpenter by trade.

ofrecer* VERBO
to offer ◇ *Nos ofrecieron tabaco.* They offered us cigarettes.
- **ofrecerse para hacer algo** to offer to do something
- **¿Qué se le ofrece?** What can I get you?

el **ofrecimiento** SUSTANTIVO
offer

el **oído** SUSTANTIVO
1 hearing (*sentido*)
2 ear (*órgano*)
- **tener buen oído** to have a good ear

oír* VERBO
1 to hear ◇ *He oído un ruido.* I heard a noise. ◇ *¿Me oyes bien desde la habitación?* Can you hear me all right from your room?
2 to listen to ◇ *Óyeme bien, no vuelvas a hacerlo.* Now listen to what I'm telling you, don't do it again.
- **oír la radio** to listen to the radio
- **¡Oye!** Hey! (*coloquial*)
- **¡Oiga, por favor!** Excuse me!

el **ojal** SUSTANTIVO
buttonhole

ojalá EXCLAMACIÓN
1 I hope ◇ *¡Ojalá Toni venga hoy!* I hope Toni comes today!
2 if only
- **¡Ojalá pudiera!** If only I could!

las **ojeras** SUSTANTIVO
- **tener ojeras** to have bags under one's eyes

el **ojo** SUSTANTIVO
eye ◇ *Tengo algo en el ojo.* I've got something in my eye.
- **ir con ojo** to keep one's eyes open for trouble
- **costar un ojo de la cara** to cost an arm and a leg (*coloquial*)
- **¡Ojo! Es muy mentiroso.** Be careful! He's an awful liar.

la **ola** SUSTANTIVO
wave

oler* VERBO
to smell ◇ *Me gusta oler las flores.* I like smelling the flowers.
- **Huele a tabaco.** It smells of cigarette smoke.
- **oler bien** to smell nice ◇ *Esta salsa huele muy bien.* This sauce smells very good.
- **oler mal** to smell awful ◇ *¡Qué mal huelen estos zapatos!* These shoes smell awful!

el **olfato** SUSTANTIVO
sense of smell

las **Olimpiadas** SUSTANTIVO
the Olympics

olímpico ADJETIVO
Olympic
- **los Juegos Olímpicos** the Olympic Games

la **oliva** SUSTANTIVO
olive
- **el aceite de oliva** olive oil

el **olivo** SUSTANTIVO
olive tree

la **olla** SUSTANTIVO
pot
- **una olla a presión** a pressure cooker

el **olor** SUSTANTIVO
smell ◇ *un olor a tabaco* a smell of cigarette smoke
- **¡Qué mal olor!** What a horrible smell!

olvidar VERBO
1 to forget ◇ *No olvides comprar el pan.* Don't forget to buy the bread.
- **olvidarse de hacer algo** to forget to do something
- **Se me olvidó por completo.** I completely forgot.

2 to leave ◇ *Olvidé las llaves encima de la mesa.* I left the keys on top of the table.

el **olvido** SUSTANTIVO
- **Ha sido un olvido imperdonable.** It was an unforgivable oversight.

el **ombligo** SUSTANTIVO
navel

omitir VERBO
to leave out ◇ *Han omitido varios nombres de la lista.* They've left several names out of the list.

once ADJETIVO, PRONOMBRE
eleven ◇ *Tengo once años.* I'm eleven.
- **Son las once.** It's eleven o'clock.
- **el once de agosto** the eleventh of August

la **onda** SUSTANTIVO
wave
- **onda corta** short wave

ondear VERBO
to fly (*bandera*)

ondulado ADJETIVO
wavy ◇ *un chico con el pelo ondulado* a boy with wavy hair

ONG ABREVIATURA (= *Organización no gubernamental*)
ONG

la **ONU** SUSTANTIVO (= *Organización de las Naciones Unidas*)
UN (= United Nations)

opaco ADJETIVO
1 opaque (*no transparente*)
2 dull (*sin brillo*)

la **opción** SUSTANTIVO (PL las **opciones**)
option ◊ *No tienes otra opción.* You have no option.

la **ópera** SUSTANTIVO
opera

la **operación** SUSTANTIVO (PL **operaciones**)
operation ◊ *una operación de cataratas* a cataract operation

operar VERBO
to operate on ◊ *Lo tienen que operar.* They have to operate on him.
◆ **Me van a operar del corazón.** I'm going to have a heart operation.
◆ **operarse** to have an operation ◊ *Me tengo que operar de la rodilla.* I have to have a knee operation.

opinar VERBO
to think ◊ *¿Y tú qué opinas de la propuesta?* So what do you think about the proposal?

la **opinión** SUSTANTIVO (PL las **opiniones**)
opinion
◆ **en mi opinión** in my opinion

oponerse* VERBO
to oppose ◊ *Se opuso al proyecto.* He opposed the project.
◆ **No me opongo.** I don't object.

la **oportunidad** SUSTANTIVO
chance ◊ *No tuvo la oportunidad de hacerlo.* He didn't have a chance to do it.
◆ **dar otra oportunidad a alguien** to give someone another chance

oportuno ADJETIVO
◆ **en el momento oportuno** at the right time

la **oposición** SUSTANTIVO (PL las **oposiciones**)
opposition
◆ **las oposiciones** public examinations

> ***Oposiciones** are exams held periodically for posts in the public sector, state education and the judiciary. Such posts are permanent, so the number of candidates is high and the exams very hard.*

optar VERBO
◆ **optar por hacer algo** to choose to do something ◊ *Al final, optó por ir.* In the end, she chose to go.

optativo ADJETIVO
optional ◊ *las asignaturas optativas* optional subjects

la **óptica** SUSTANTIVO
optician's ◊ *En la óptica de mi barrio hay una oferta de monturas.* There's a special offer on frames at my local optician's.

el **optimismo** SUSTANTIVO
optimism

optimista ADJETIVO
optimistic

el/la **optimista** SUSTANTIVO
optimist

óptimo ADJETIVO
optimum

opuesto ADJETIVO
1 conflicting (*opinión, punto de vista*)
2 opposite (*extremos, direcciones*)

opuse VERBO *ver* **oponer**

la **oración** SUSTANTIVO (PL las **oraciones**)
1 prayer (*rezo*)
2 sentence (*frase*)

el **orador,** la **oradora** SUSTANTIVO
speaker

oral ADJETIVO
oral
◆ **por vía oral** orally
◆ **un examen oral** an oral exam

la **órbita** SUSTANTIVO
1 orbit (*de satélite*)
2 eye socket (*de ojo*)

el **orden** SUSTANTIVO
order
◆ **por orden alfabético** in alphabetical order
◆ **La casa está en orden.** The house is tidy.

la **orden** SUSTANTIVO (PL las **órdenes**)
order
◆ **¡Deja de darme órdenes!** Stop bossing me about!

ordenado ADJETIVO
tidy ◊ *Siempre tiene la habitación muy ordenada.* He always keeps his room very tidy.

el **ordenador** SUSTANTIVO
computer
◆ **un ordenador portátil** a laptop

ordenar VERBO
1 to tidy up ◊ *¿Por qué no ordenas tu habitación?* Why don't you tidy your room up?
2 to order ◊ *El policía nos ordenó que saliéramos del edificio.* The policeman ordered us to get out of the building.

ordeñar VERBO
to milk

ordinario ADJETIVO
1 common (*vulgar*) ◊ *Es una mujer muy ordinaria.* She's a very common woman.
2 ordinary (*corriente*) ◊ *los acontecimientos ordinarios* ordinary events
◆ **de ordinario** usually ◊ *De ordinario coge el autobús para ir a trabajar.* He usually takes the bus to work.

la **oreja** SUSTANTIVO

☞

ear

orgánico ADJETIVO
organic

el **organismo** SUSTANTIVO
organization ◊ *un organismo internacional* an international organization

la **organización** SUSTANTIVO (PL las **organizaciones**)
organization

organizar* VERBO
to organize
◆ **organizarse** to organize oneself ◊ *Te tienes que organizar mejor.* You need to organize yourself better.

el **órgano** SUSTANTIVO
organ

el **orgullo** SUSTANTIVO
pride

orgulloso ADJETIVO
proud

la **orientación** SUSTANTIVO (PL las **orientaciones**)
◆ **tener sentido de la orientación** to have a good sense of direction
◆ **la orientación profesional** careers advice

el **oriente** SUSTANTIVO
◆ **el Oriente** the East

el **origen** SUSTANTIVO (PL los **orígenes**)
origin

original ADJETIVO
original

la **originalidad** SUSTANTIVO
originality

la **orilla** SUSTANTIVO
[1] shore (*del mar, de un lago*)
[2] bank (*de un río*)
◆ **a orillas de (1)** on the shores of (*del mar, de un lago*)
◆ **a orillas de (2)** on the banks of (*de un río*)
◆ **un paseo a la orilla del mar** a walk along the seashore

la **orina** SUSTANTIVO
urine

orinar VERBO
to urinate

el **oro** SUSTANTIVO
gold ◊ *un collar de oro* a gold necklace
◆ **oros**

> *Oros are "golden coins", one of the suits in the Spanish card deck.*

la **orquesta** SUSTANTIVO
orchestra
◆ **una orquesta de jazz** a jazz band

ortodoxo ADJETIVO
orthodox

la **ortografía** SUSTANTIVO
spelling

la **oruga** SUSTANTIVO
caterpillar

os PRONOMBRE
[1] you ◊ *No os oigo.* I can't hear you. ◊ *Os he comprado un libro a cada uno.* I've bought each of you a book.
◆ **Os lo doy.** I'll give it to you.
◆ **¿Os han arreglado ya el ordenador?** Have they fixed the computer for you yet?
[2] yourselves ◊ *¿Os habéis hecho daño?* Did you hurt yourselves?
◆ **Os tenéis que levantar antes de las ocho.** You have to get up before eight.
[3] each other ◊ *Quiero que os pidáis perdón.* I want you to say sorry to each other.

> *Con partes del cuerpo o con prendas que se llevan puestas se usa el adjetivo posesivo.*

◊ *No hace falta que os quitéis el abrigo.* You don't need to take your coats off. ◊ *Lavaos las manos.* Wash your hands.

oscilar VERBO
to range ◊ *Las máximas han oscilado entre los 15 y los 20 grados.* Maximum temperatures have ranged from 15 to 20 degrees.

oscurecer* VERBO
to get dark

la **oscuridad** SUSTANTIVO
darkness
◆ **Estaban hablando en la oscuridad.** They were talking in the dark.

oscuro ADJETIVO
dark ◊ *una habitación muy oscura* a very dark room
◆ **azul oscuro** dark blue
◆ **a oscuras** in darkness

el **oso**, la **osa** SUSTANTIVO
bear
◆ **un oso de peluche** a teddy bear

el **ostión** SUSTANTIVO (PL los **ostiones**) Mexico
oyster

la **ostra** SUSTANTIVO
oyster
◆ **¡Ostras!** (*sorpresa*) Good grief!

la **OTAN** SUSTANTIVO (= *Organización del Tratado del Atlántico Norte*)
NATO

el **otoño** SUSTANTIVO
autumn ◊ *en otoño* in autumn ◊ *el otoño pasado* last autumn

otro ADJETIVO, PRONOMBRE
[1] another (*singular*) ◊ *otro coche* another car ◊ *¿Me das otra manzana, por favor?* Can you give me another apple, please?
◆ **¿Has perdido el lápiz? – No importa, tengo otro.** Have you lost your pencil? – It doesn't matter, I've got another one.

* Verbs marked with this symbol are irregular. See pages 380-382 for further details

- **¿Hay alguna otra manera de hacerlo?** Is there any other way of doing it?
- **No quiero éste, quiero el otro.** I don't want this one, I want the other one.

[2] other (*plural*) ◊ *Tengo otros planes.* I have other plans.

- **Quiero otra cosa.** I want something else.
- **otra vez** again
- **otros tres libros** another three books
- **Que lo haga otro.** Let someone else do it.
- **Están enamorados el uno del otro.** They're in love with each other.

ovalado ADJETIVO
oval

la **oveja** SUSTANTIVO
sheep (PL sheep)

el **ovillo** SUSTANTIVO
ball ◊ *un ovillo de lana* a ball of wool

el **OVNI** SUSTANTIVO (= *objeto volador no identificado*)
UFO (= unidentified flying object)

oxidado ADJETIVO
rusty

oxidarse VERBO
to rust ◊ *Se ha oxidado la barandilla.* The rail has rusted.

el **oxígeno** SUSTANTIVO
oxygen

oyendo VERBO *ver* **oír**

el/la **oyente** SUSTANTIVO
[1] listener (*de programa de radio*)
[2] occasional student (*en instituto, universidad*)

O

P

la **paciencia** SUSTANTIVO
patience ◊ *No tengo paciencia.* I have very little patience. ◊ *Perdí la paciencia.* I lost my patience.
♦ **¡Ten paciencia!** Be patient!

el/la **paciente** ADJETIVO, SUSTANTIVO
patient

el **Pacífico** SUSTANTIVO
the Pacific

pacífico ADJETIVO
peaceful

el/la **pacifista** ADJETIVO, SUSTANTIVO
pacifist
♦ **el movimiento pacifista** the peace movement

el **pacto** SUSTANTIVO
agreement ◊ *hacer un pacto* to make an agreement

padecer* VERBO
1 to suffer from ◊ *Padece reúma.* He suffers from rheumatism.
♦ **Padece del corazón.** He has heart trouble.
2 to suffer ◊ *El pobrecito ha padecido mucho.* The poor man has suffered a lot.

el **padrastro** SUSTANTIVO
stepfather

el **padre** SUSTANTIVO
father
♦ **Es padre de familia.** He's a family man.
♦ **mis padres** my parents
♦ **rezar el Padre Nuestro** to say the Lord's Prayer

el **padrino** SUSTANTIVO
godfather
♦ **mis padrinos** my godparents

> *At a wedding, the **padrino** is the person who escorts the bride down the aisle and gives her away, usually her father.*

la **paella** SUSTANTIVO
paella

la **paga** SUSTANTIVO
1 pocket money ◊ *Me dan la paga los domingos.* I get my pocket money on Sundays.
2 pay (*sueldo*)
♦ **la paga extra**

> *In Spain, most employees receive two extra payments **pagas extras** a year, each equivalent to a month's salary.*

pagar* VERBO
1 to pay (*facturas, impuestos, deuda*) ◊ *No han pagado el alquiler.* They haven't paid the rent. ◊ *Me pagan muy poco.* I get paid very little.
♦ **Se puede pagar con tarjeta de crédito.** You can pay by credit card.
2 to pay for (*producto, compra*) ◊ *Tengo que pagar las entradas.* I have to pay for the tickets.

la **página** SUSTANTIVO
page ◊ *Está en la página 17.* It's on page 17.
♦ **una página web** a Web page
♦ **las páginas amarillas** the yellow pages ®

el **pago** SUSTANTIVO
payment

el **país** SUSTANTIVO (PL los **países**)
country (PL countries)
♦ **el País Vasco** the Basque Country
♦ **los Países Bajos** the Netherlands

el **paisaje** SUSTANTIVO
1 landscape ◊ *el paisaje de Castilla* the Castilian landscape ◊ *pintar un paisaje to paint a landscape*
2 scenery

> *Se utiliza **scenery** cuando se habla de la belleza del paisaje.*

◊ *Estaba contemplando el paisaje.* I was looking at the scenery.

la **paja** SUSTANTIVO
1 straw ◊ *un sombrero de paja* a straw hat
2 padding ◊ *El resto del texto es sólo paja.* The rest of the text is just padding.

la **pajarita** SUSTANTIVO
bow tie

el **pájaro** SUSTANTIVO
bird

la **pajita** SUSTANTIVO
drinking straw

la **pala** SUSTANTIVO
1 spade (*para cavar, de niño*)
2 shovel (*para mover tierra, nieve*)
3 bat (*de ping pong*)
4 blade (*de remo*)

la **palabra** SUSTANTIVO
word ◊ *un título de dos palabras* a two-word title ◊ *Cumplió su palabra.* He was true to his word. ◊ *sin decir palabra* without a word
♦ **No me dirige la palabra.** He doesn't speak to me.

la **palabrota** SUSTANTIVO

* Verbs marked with this symbol are irregular. See pages 380-382 for further details

swearword
◆ **soltar palabrotas** to swear

el **palacio** SUSTANTIVO
palace

el **paladar** SUSTANTIVO
palate

la **palanca** SUSTANTIVO
lever
◆ **la palanca de cambio** gear lever

la **palangana** SUSTANTIVO
washbasin

el **palco** SUSTANTIVO
box (PL boxes)

Palestina SUSTANTIVO FEM
Palestine

el **palestino,** la **palestina** ADJETIVO, SUSTANTIVO
Palestinian

la **paleta** SUSTANTIVO
1 trowel (*de albañil*)
2 palette (*de pintor*)

pálido ADJETIVO
pale ◊ *Se puso pálida.* She turned pale.

el **palillo** SUSTANTIVO
1 toothpick (*para los dientes*)
2 chopstick (*para la comida oriental*)

la **paliza** SUSTANTIVO
1 beating ◊ *Los ladrones le dieron una paliza.* The burglars gave him a beating.
2 thrashing ◊ *Si mi padre se entera me va a dar una paliza.* If my father finds out he'll give me a thrashing.
◆ **Sus clases son una paliza.** (*coloquial*) His classes are a real pain.
◆ **¡No me des la paliza!** (*coloquial*) Don't be such a pain!

la **palma** SUSTANTIVO
palm
◆ **dar palmas** to clap

la **palmera** SUSTANTIVO
palm tree

el **palmo** SUSTANTIVO
◆ **Mide un palmo.** It's several inches long.
◆ **Se conoce el lugar de palmo a palmo.** He knows every inch of the place.

el **palo** SUSTANTIVO
1 stick ◊ *Le pegó con un palo.* He hit him with a stick.
2 club (*de golf*)
3 suit (*de baraja*)
◆ **una cuchara de palo** a wooden spoon

la **paloma** SUSTANTIVO
pigeon ◊ *una paloma mensajera* a carrier pigeon ◊ *la paloma de la paz* the dove of peace

las **palomitas** SUSTANTIVO
◆ **las palomitas de maíz** popcorn SING

palpar VERBO
to feel

la **palpitación** SUSTANTIVO (PL las **palpitaciones**)
palpitation

palpitar VERBO
1 to pound ◊ *El corazón me palpitaba de miedo.* My heart was pounding with fear.
2 to beat ◊ *El corazón del enfermo dejó de palpitar.* The patient's heart stopped beating.

la **palta** SUSTANTIVO Chile, River Plate
avocado (PL avocados)

el **pan** SUSTANTIVO
1 bread ◊ *pan con mantequilla* bread and butter ◊ *pan integral* wholemeal bread ◊ *pan de molde* sliced bread ◊ *una barra de pan* a loaf of bread
◆ **pan rallado** breadcrumbs PL
◆ **pan tostado** toast
2 loaf (PL loaves) ◊ *Compré dos panes.* I bought two loaves.

la **pana** SUSTANTIVO
corduroy

la **panadera** SUSTANTIVO
baker ◊ *Es panadera.* She's a baker.

la **panadería** SUSTANTIVO
bakery (PL bakeries)

el **panadero** SUSTANTIVO
baker ◊ *Es panadero.* He's a baker.

Panamá SUSTANTIVO MASC
Panama

el **panameño,** la **panameña** ADJETIVO, SUSTANTIVO
Panamanian

la **pancarta** SUSTANTIVO
banner

el **pancito** SUSTANTIVO Latin America
bread roll

el **panda** SUSTANTIVO
panda (PL pandas)

la **pandereta** SUSTANTIVO
tambourine

la **pandilla** SUSTANTIVO
gang

el **panfleto** SUSTANTIVO
pamphlet

el **pánico** SUSTANTIVO
panic ◊ *en un momento de pánico* in a moment of panic
◆ **Me entró pánico.** I panicked.
◆ **Les tengo pánico a las arañas.** I'm terrified of spiders.

las **pantaletas** SUSTANTIVO Mexico
panties ◊ *unas pantaletas* a pair of panties

la **pantalla** SUSTANTIVO
1 screen (*de cine, televisión, ordenador*)
2 lampshade (*de lámpara*)

los **pantalones** SUSTANTIVO
trousers PL
◆ **unos pantalones** a pair of trousers
◆ **pantalones cortos** shorts
◆ **pantalones vaqueros** jeans

el **pantano** SUSTANTIVO
reservoir

P

la **pantera** SUSTANTIVO
panther

las **pantimedias** SUSTANTIVO Mexico
tights ◊ *unas pantimedias* a pair of tights

los **pantis** SUSTANTIVO
tights ◊ *unos pantis* a pair of tights

la **pantorrilla** SUSTANTIVO
calf (PL calves)

los **pants** SUSTANTIVO Mexico
tracksuit SING

el **pañal** SUSTANTIVO
nappy (PL nappies)

el **paño** SUSTANTIVO
cloth
- **un paño de cocina** a dishcloth

el **pañuelo** SUSTANTIVO
1 (*para la nariz*)
handkerchief (PL handkerchieves)
2 (*para el cuello*)
scarf (PL scarves)
3 (*para la cabeza*)
headscarf (PL headscarves)

el **papa** SUSTANTIVO
pope
- **el Papa** the Pope

la **papa** SUSTANTIVO Latin America
potato (PL potatoes)
- **pescado frito con papas fritas** fish and chips
- **un paquete de papas fritas** a packet of crisps

el **papá** SUSTANTIVO (PL los **papás**)
dad
- **mis papás** my mum and dad
- **Papá Noel** Father Christmas

el **papalote** SUSTANTIVO Mexico
kite ◊ *volar un papalote* to fly a kite

el **papel** SUSTANTIVO
1 paper ◊ *una bolsa de papel* a paper bag
2 piece of paper ◊ *Lo escribí en un papel.* I wrote it on a piece of paper.
- **papel de aluminio** tinfoil
- **papel higiénico** toilet paper
- **papel pintado** wallpaper

3 role ◊ *la actriz que tiene el papel principal* the actress who has the leading role ◊ *Jugó un papel muy importante en las negociaciones.* He played a very important part in the negotiations.
- **¿Qué papeles te piden para sacar el pasaporte?** What documents do you need to get a passport?

el **papeleo** SUSTANTIVO
paperwork

la **papelera** SUSTANTIVO
1 wastepaper bin (*en la oficina, en casa*)
2 litter bin (*en la calle*)

la **papelería** SUSTANTIVO
stationer's (PL stationers' shops)

la **papeleta** SUSTANTIVO
1 results slip (*de examen*)
2 ballot paper (*de votación*)
3 raffle ticket (*de rifa*)

las **paperas** SUSTANTIVO
mumps ◊ *tener paperas* to have the mumps

la **papilla** SUSTANTIVO
1 baby food (*para bebé*)
2 pap (*para enfermos*)

el **paquete** SUSTANTIVO
1 packet (*de galletas, cigarrillos*)
2 parcel ◊ *Me mandaron un paquete por correo.* I got a parcel in the post.

Paquistán SUSTANTIVO MASC
Pakistan

el/la **paquistaní** ADJETIVO, SUSTANTIVO (PL los **paquistaníes**)
Pakistani

par ADJETIVO (FEM **par**)
- **número par** even number

el **par** SUSTANTIVO
1 couple ◊ *un par de horas al día* a couple of hours a day
2 pair ◊ *un par de calcetines* a pair of socks
- **Abrió la ventana de par en par.** He opened the window wide.

para PREPOSICIÓN
1 for ◊ *Es para ti.* It's for you. ◊ *Tengo muchos deberes para mañana.* I have a lot of homework to do for tomorrow. ◊ *el autobús para Marbella* the bus for Marbella
- **¿Para qué lo quieres?** What do you want it for?
- **¿Para qué sirve?** What's it for?
- **para siempre** forever
- **Para entonces ya era tarde.** It was already too late by then.

2 to ◊ *Estoy ahorrando para comprarme una moto.* I'm saving up to buy a motorbike. ◊ *Tengo bastante para vivir.* I have enough to live on. ◊ *Son cinco para las ocho.* Latin America It's five to eight.
- **Entré despacito para no despertarla.** I went in slowly so as not to wake her.
- **para que te acuerdes de mí** so that you remember me

la **parabólica** SUSTANTIVO
satellite dish

el **parabrisas** SUSTANTIVO (PL los **parabrisas**)
windscreen

el **paracaídas** SUSTANTIVO (PL los **paracaídas**)
parachute

el/la **paracaidista** SUSTANTIVO
1 paratrooper (*soldado*)
2 parachutist (*civil*)

el **parachoques** SUSTANTIVO (PL los **parachoques**)

bumper

la **parada** SUSTANTIVO

stop ◊ *Hicimos una parada corta para descansar.* We made a short stop to rest.

♦ **una parada de autobús** a bus stop

♦ **una parada de taxis** a taxi rank

el **paradero** SUSTANTIVO Latin America

bus stop

parado ADJETIVO

unemployed ◊ *Hace seis meses que está parada.* She's been unemployed for six months.

♦ **No te quedes ahí parado.** Don't just stand there.

♦ **Estuve toda la mañana parado.** Latin America I was standing all morning.

el **parador** SUSTANTIVO

> *The **paradores** are a group of luxury Spanish hotels occupying castles, monasteries and other historical buildings and sited in scenic areas.*

el **paraguas** SUSTANTIVO (PL los **paraguas**)

umbrella

Paraguay SUSTANTIVO MASC

Paraguay

el **paraguayo,** la **paraguaya** ADJETIVO, SUSTANTIVO

Paraguayan

el **paraíso** SUSTANTIVO

paradise

el **paralelo** ADJETIVO, SUSTANTIVO

parallel

la **parálisis** SUSTANTIVO (PL las **parálisis**)

paralysis (PL paralyses)

♦ **parálisis cerebral** cerebral palsy

paralítico ADJETIVO

♦ **Está paralítico.** He's paralyzed.

el **parapente** SUSTANTIVO

1 paragliding (*deporte*)

2 paraglider (*aparato*)

parar VERBO

to stop ◊ *Paramos a poner gasolina.* We stopped to get some petrol. ◊ *No paró de llover en toda la noche.* It didn't stop raining all night.

♦ **Nos equivocamos de tren y fuimos a parar a Manchester.** We got on the wrong train and ended up in Manchester.

♦ **pararse (1)** to stop ◊ *El reloj se ha parado.* The clock has stopped.

♦ **pararse (2)** (*ponerse de pie*) Latin America to stand up

♦ **hablar sin parar** to talk non-stop

el **pararrayos** SUSTANTIVO (PL los **pararrayos**)

lightning conductor

la **parcela** SUSTANTIVO

plot of land

el **parche** SUSTANTIVO

patch (PL patches)

el **parchís** SUSTANTIVO

> ***parchís** is a Spanish version of **ludo**.*

parcial ADJETIVO

1 partial (*retirada, victoria*) ◊ *un eclipse parcial* a partial eclipse

♦ **a tiempo parcial** part time

2 biased (*árbitro, juicio*)

el **parcial** SUSTANTIVO

mid-term exam

parecer* VERBO

1 to seem ◊ *Parece muy simpática.* She seems very nice. ◊ *Todo parecía indicar que estaba muy interesado.* It all seemed to indicate that he was very interested.

♦ **Parece mentira que ya haya pasado tanto tiempo.** I can't believe it has been so long.

2 to look ◊ *Parece más joven.* He looks younger.

♦ **Parece una modelo.** She looks like a model.

♦ **Parece que va a llover.** It looks as if it's going to rain.

3 to think

♦ **¿Qué te pareció la película?** What did you think of the film? ◊ *Me parece bien que los multen.* I think it's right that they should be fined.

♦ **Me parece que sí.** I think so.

♦ **Me parece que no.** I don't think so.

♦ **si te parece bien** if that's all right with you

♦ **parecerse** to look alike ◊ *María y Ana se parecen mucho.* María and Ana look very much alike.

♦ **parecerse a** to look like ◊ *Te pareces mucho a tu madre.* You look very much like your mother.

parecido ADJETIVO

similar ◊ *Las casas son todas parecidas.* The houses are all similar. ◊ *Tu blusa es parecida a la mía.* Your blouse is similar to mine.

♦ **o algo parecido** or something like that

la **pared** SUSTANTIVO

wall

la **pareja** SUSTANTIVO

1 couple (*hombre y mujer*) ◊ *Había varias parejas bailando.* There were several couples dancing.

2 pair ◊ *En este juego hay que formar parejas.* For this game you have to get into pairs.

3 partner (*compañero*) ◊ *Vino con su pareja.* He came with his partner.

parejo ADJETIVO Latin America

even (*superficie, color*)

el **paréntesis** SUSTANTIVO (PL los **paréntesis**)

bracket ◊ *entre paréntesis* in brackets

el/la **pariente** SUSTANTIVO

☞

relative ◊ *Es pariente mío.* He's a relative of mine.

No confundir ***pariente*** *con* ***parent****.*

París SUSTANTIVO MASC
Paris

el/la **parisiense** ADJETIVO, SUSTANTIVO
Parisian

el **parisino,** la **parisina** ADJETIVO, SUSTANTIVO
Parisian

el **parking** SUSTANTIVO (PL los **parkings**)
car park

el **parlamento** SUSTANTIVO
parliament

parlanchín ADJETIVO (FEM **parlanchina,** MASC PL **parlanchines**)
chatty

el **parlante** SUSTANTIVO Latin America
loudspeaker

el **paro** SUSTANTIVO
1 unemployment (*desempleo*) ◊ *Ha bajado el paro.* Unemployment has come down.
◆ **Mi hermano está en paro.** My brother is on the dole.
◆ **cobrar el paro** to get the dole
2 strike (*huelga*) ◊ *un paro de tres días* a three-day strike

parpadear VERBO
to blink

el **párpado** SUSTANTIVO
eyelid

el **parque** SUSTANTIVO
park ◊ *un parque nacional* a national park
◆ **un parque de atracciones** an amusement park
◆ **un parque infantil** a children's playground

el **parquímetro** SUSTANTIVO
parking meter

la **parra** SUSTANTIVO
vine

el **párrafo** SUSTANTIVO
paragraph

la **parrilla** SUSTANTIVO
grill
◆ **carne a la parrilla** grilled meat

la **parrillada** SUSTANTIVO
grill

el **párroco** SUSTANTIVO
parish priest

la **parroquia** SUSTANTIVO
parish (PL parishes)

la **parte** SUSTANTIVO
1 part ◊ *El examen está compuesto de dos partes.* The exam consists of two parts. ◊ *¿De qué parte de Inglaterra eres?* What part of England are you from?
2 share ◊ *mi parte de la herencia* my share of the inheritance

También se traduce por ***-where*** *en palabras compuestas.*

◊ *Tengo que haberlo dejado en alguna parte.* I must have left it somewhere.
◊ *por todas partes* everywhere
◆ **en parte** partly ◊ *Se debe en parte a su falta de experiencia.* It's partly due to his lack of experience.
◆ **la mayor parte de los españoles** most Spanish people
◆ **la parte delantera** the front
◆ **la parte de atrás** the back
◆ **la parte de arriba** the top
◆ **la parte de abajo** the bottom
◆ **por una parte ..., por otra ...** on the one hand ..., on the other hand ...
◆ **Llamo de parte de Juan.** I'm calling on behalf of Juan.
◆ **¿De parte de quién?** (*al teléfono*) Who's calling please?
◆ **Estoy de tu parte.** I'm on your side.

participar VERBO
to take part
◆ **participar en un concurso** to take part in a competition

el **participio** SUSTANTIVO
participle

particular ADJETIVO
private ◊ *clases particulares* private classes
◆ **El vestido no tiene nada de particular.** The dress is nothing special.
◆ **en particular** in particular

la **partida** SUSTANTIVO
1 game ◊ *echar una partida de cartas* to have a game of cards
2 certificate ◊ *partida de nacimiento* birth certificate

partidario ADJETIVO
◆ **ser partidario de algo** to be in favour of something

el **partidario,** la **partidaria** SUSTANTIVO
supporter

el **partido** SUSTANTIVO
1 (*político*)
party (PL parties)
2 (*de fútbol, tenis*)
match (PL matches)
3 game Latin America ◊ *un partido de ajedrez* a game of chess
◆ **Sabe sacarle partido a todo.** He knows how to make the most out of everything.

partir VERBO
1 to cut (*tarta, sandía*)
2 to crack (*nuez, almendra*)
3 to break off (*rama, tableta de chocolate*)
4 to leave ◊ *La expedición partirá mañana de París.* The expedition is to leave from Paris tomorrow.
◆ **a partir de enero** from January ◊ *a partir de ahora* from now on

◆**partirse** to break ◇ *El remo se partió en dos.* The oar broke in two.

◆**partirse de risa** to split one's sides laughing

la **partitura** SUSTANTIVO
score

el **parto** SUSTANTIVO
birth

◆**estar de parto** to be in labour

la **pasa** SUSTANTIVO
raisin

la **pasada** SUSTANTIVO

◆**¡Ese coche es una pasada!** This car is amazing!

◆**¿Has visto cómo ha saltado? ¡Qué pasada!** Did you see him jump? Amazing!

pasado ADJETIVO

[1] last ◇ *el verano pasado* last summer

[2] after ◇ *Pasado el semáforo verás un cine.* After the traffic lights you'll see a cinema. ◇ *Volvió pasadas las tres de la mañana.* He returned after three in the morning.

◆**pasado mañana** the day after tomorrow

◆**un sombrero pasado de moda** an old-fashioned hat

el **pasado** SUSTANTIVO
past ◇ *en el pasado* in the past

el **pasador** SUSTANTIVO

[1] hair slide (*de pelo*)

[2] tiepin (*de corbata*)

el **pasaje** SUSTANTIVO

[1] ticket (*de barco, avión*)

[2] passage (*de un texto*)

pasajero ADJETIVO

[1] temporary (*dolor, molestia*)

[2] passing (*moda, fase*)

el **pasajero**, la **pasajera** SUSTANTIVO
passenger

el **pasamanos** SUSTANTIVO (PL los **pasamanos**)
banister

el **pasaporte** SUSTANTIVO
passport

pasar VERBO

[1] to pass ◇ *¿Me pasas la sal, por favor?* Can you pass me the salt, please?

◆**Cuando termines pásasela a Isabel.** When you've finished pass it on to Isabel.

◆**La foto fue pasando de mano en mano.** The photo was passed around.

◆**Cuando muera la empresa pasará al hijo.** When he dies the company will go to his son.

◆**Un momento, te paso con Pedro.** Just a moment, I'll put you on to Pedro.

[2] to go past ◇ *Pasaron varios coches.* A number of cars went past. ◇ *El autobús nos pasó de largo.* The bus went straight past us.

◆**¡Pase, por favor!** Please come in.

◆**El tiempo pasa deprisa.** Time goes so quickly.

◆**Pasaron cinco años.** Five years went by.

◆**Ya ha pasado una hora.** It's been an hour already.

[3] to spend ◇ *Voy a pasar el fin de semana con ella.* I'm going to spend the weekend with her. ◇ *Me pasé el fin de semana estudiando.* I spent the weekend studying.

[4] to happen ◇ *Por suerte no le pasó nada.* Luckily nothing happened to him. ◇ *pase lo que pase* whatever happens

◆**¿Qué pasa? (1)** (*¿cuál es el problema?*) What's the matter?

◆**¿Qué pasa? (2)** (*¿qué está ocurriendo?*) What's happening?

◆**¿Qué le pasa a Juan?** What's the matter with Juan?

◆**pasar la aspiradora** to do the vacuuming

◆**pasarlo bien** to have a good time

◆**pasarlo mal** to have a bad time

◆**Hemos pasado mucho frío.** We were very cold.

◆**Están pasando hambre.** They are starving.

◆**pasar algo a máquina** to type something

◆**¡Paso de todo!** (*coloquial*) I couldn't care less!

◆**pasar por (1)** to go though ◇ *Pasamos por un túnel muy largo.* We went through a very long tunnel. ◇ *No creo que el sofá pase por esa puerta.* I don't think the settee will go through the door. ◇ *pasar por la aduana* to go through customs ◇ *Está pasando por un mal momento.* He's going through a bad patch.

◆**No pasamos por la ciudad.** We don't go through the city.

◆**Podrían perfectamente pasar por gemelos.** They could easily pass for twins.

◆**pasar por (2)** to go past ◇ *Ese autobús pasa por mi colegio.* That bus goes past my school.

◆**No puedo pasar sin teléfono.** I can't get by without a telephone.

◆**Está bien hacer ejercicio pero no hay que pasarse.** It's OK to exercise but there's no point in overdoing it.

◆**pasarse de moda** to go out of fashion

el **pasatiempo** SUSTANTIVO
hobby (PL hobbies)

la **Pascua** SUSTANTIVO
Easter (*Semana Santa*)

◆**¡Felices Pascuas!** Happy Christmas!

el **pase** SUSTANTIVO
pass (PL passes) ◇ *un pase gratis* a free pass

◆**un pase de modelos** a fashion show

pasear VERBO
to walk

P

◆ **ir a pasear** to go for a walk

el **paseo** SUSTANTIVO
walk ◇ *Salimos a dar un paseo.* We went out for a walk.
◆ **ir de paseo** to go for a walk
◆ **el paseo marítimo** the promenade

el **pasillo** SUSTANTIVO
1 corridor (*de casa, oficina*)
2 aisle (*de cine, avión*)

la **pasión** SUSTANTIVO (PL las **pasiones**)
passion

pasivo ADJETIVO
passive

pasmado ADJETIVO
amazed ◇ *Cuando me enteré me quedé pasmado.* I was amazed when I found out.

el **paso** SUSTANTIVO
1 step ◇ *Dio un paso hacia atrás.* He took a step backwards. ◇ *paso a paso* step by step
◆ **He oído pasos.** I heard footsteps.
◆ **Vive a un paso de aquí.** He lives right near here.
◆ **A ese paso no terminarán nunca.** At this rate they'll never finish.
2 way ◇ *Han cerrado el paso.* They've blocked the way. ◇ *La policía le abría paso.* The police made way for him.
◆ **"Ceda el paso"** "Give way"
◆ **"Prohibido el paso"** "No entry"
◆ **El banco me pilla de paso.** The bank is on my way.
◆ **Están de paso por Barcelona.** They're just passing through Barcelona.
◆ **un paso de peatones** a pedestrian crossing
◆ **un paso de cebra** a zebra crossing
◆ **un paso a nivel** a level crossing

la **pasta** SUSTANTIVO
1 pasta (*macarrones, fideos*)
2 dosh (*coloquial: dinero*)
◆ **pastas de té** biscuits
◆ **pasta de dientes** toothpaste

pastar VERBO
to graze

el **pastel** SUSTANTIVO
cake

la **pastelería** SUSTANTIVO
patisserie

la **pastilla** SUSTANTIVO
1 pill (*medicina*)
◆ **pastillas para la tos** cough sweets
2 bar (*de jabón*)
3 piece (*de chocolate*)
◆ **pastillas de caldo** stock cubes

el **pasto** SUSTANTIVO Latin America
grass

el **pastor** SUSTANTIVO
shepherd
◆ **un pastor alemán** an Alsatian
◆ **un perro pastor** a sheepdog

la **pastora** SUSTANTIVO
shepherdess

la **pata** SUSTANTIVO
leg (*de animal, mueble*) ◇ *las patas de la silla* the chair legs
◆ **saltar a la pata coja** to hop
◆ **Encontramos la casa patas arriba.** We found the house in a right mess.
◆ **¡He vuelto a meter la pata!** I've gone and put my foot in it again!
◆ **Me parece que he metido la pata en el examen de física.** I think I messed up my physics exam.

la **patada** SUSTANTIVO
◆ **Me dio una patada.** He kicked me.

Patagonia SUSTANTIVO FEM
Patagonia

la **patata** SUSTANTIVO
potato (PL potatoes)
◆ **un filete con patatas fritas** steak and chips
◆ **una bolsa de patatas fritas** a bag of crisps

el **paté** SUSTANTIVO (PL los **patés**)
paté

la **patera** SUSTANTIVO
small boat

paterno ADJETIVO
paternal

la **patilla** SUSTANTIVO
1 sideburn ◇ *dejarse patillas* to grow sideburns
2 arm (*de gafas*)

el **patín** SUSTANTIVO (PL los **patines**)
1 roller skate (*con ruedas*)
2 skate (*de hielo*)
3 pedal boat (*de playa*)

el **patinaje** SUSTANTIVO
1 roller skating (*sobre ruedas*)
2 ice skating (*sobre hielo*)
◆ **patinaje artístico** figure skating

patinar VERBO
1 to roller-skate (*sobre ruedas*)
2 to skate (*sobre hielo*)
3 to skid (*vehículo*)

el **patinete** SUSTANTIVO
scooter

el **patio** SUSTANTIVO
1 playground (*de colegio*)
2 courtyard (*de convento, bloque de pisos*)
◆ **el patio de butacas** the stalls PL

el **pato** SUSTANTIVO
duck

patoso ADJETIVO
clumsy

la **patria** SUSTANTIVO
homeland

patriota ADJETIVO
patriotic

el **patrocinador**, la **patrocinadora** SUSTANTIVO
sponsor

patrocinar VERBO
to sponsor

el **patrón** SUSTANTIVO (PL los **patrones**)
1 (*santo*)
patron saint
2 (*en trabajo*)
boss (PL bosses)

la **patrona** SUSTANTIVO
1 (*santa*)
patron saint
2 (*de pensión*)
landlady (PL landladies)

la **patrulla** SUSTANTIVO
patrol ◊ *estar de patrulla* to be on patrol

la **pausa** SUSTANTIVO
1 pause (*al hablar, leer*)
2 break (*en medio de programa, reunión*)

el **pavimento** SUSTANTIVO
1 paving (*de calle*)
2 surface (*de carretera*)

el **pavo** SUSTANTIVO
turkey
♦ **un pavo real** a peacock

el **payaso**, la **payasa** SUSTANTIVO
clown
♦ **Deja de hacer el payaso.** Stop clowning around.

la **paz** SUSTANTIVO (PL las **paces**)
peace
♦ **¡Déjame en paz!** Leave me alone!
♦ **Ha hecho las paces con su novio.** She's made it up with her boyfriend.

el **PC** ABREVIATURA
PC (PL PCs)

P.D. ABREVIATURA (= *posdata*)
P.S.

el **peaje** SUSTANTIVO
toll

el **peatón** SUSTANTIVO (PL los **peatones**)
pedestrian

la **peca** SUSTANTIVO
freckle

el **pecado** SUSTANTIVO
sin

pecar* VERBO
to sin

el **pecho** SUSTANTIVO
1 chest (*tórax*)
2 breast (*de mujer*)
♦ **dar el pecho a un niño** to breastfeed a baby
♦ **¡No te lo tomes a pecho! Era una broma.** Don't take it to heart. I was only joking.

la **pechuga** SUSTANTIVO
breast

el **pedal** SUSTANTIVO
pedal ◊ *el pedal del freno* the brake pedal

pedalear VERBO
to pedal

pedante ADJETIVO
pedantic

el **pedazo** SUSTANTIVO
piece ◊ *un pedazo de pan* a piece of bread
♦ **hacer pedazos (1)** (*jarrón*) to smash
♦ **hacer pedazos (2)** (*carta*) to tear up

el/la **pediatra** SUSTANTIVO
paediatrician

el **pedido** SUSTANTIVO
order ◊ *hacer un pedido* to place an order

pedir* VERBO
1 to ask for ◊ *Le pedí dinero a mi padre.* I asked my father for some money. ◊ *He pedido hora para el médico.* I've asked for a doctor's appointment.
2 to ask ◊ *¿Te puedo pedir un favor?* Can I ask you a favour? ◊ *¿Cuánto pide por el coche?* How much is he asking for the car?
♦ **Pedí que me enviaran la información por correo.** I asked them to mail me the information.
3 to order ◊ *Yo pedí paella.* I ordered paella.
♦ **Le pedí disculpas.** I apologized to him.
♦ **Tuve que pedir dinero prestado.** I had to borrow some money.

el **pedo** SUSTANTIVO
fart (*vulgar*)
♦ **tirarse un pedo** (*vulgar*) to fart

la **pega** SUSTANTIVO
snag ◊ *La única pega es que la oficina me queda lejos.* The only snag is that the office is a long way away.
♦ **Me pusieron muchas pegas.** They made things very difficult for me.

pegadizo ADJETIVO
catchy

pegajoso ADJETIVO
1 sticky (*sustancia, calor*)
2 catchy (*canción*) Latin America

el **pegamento** SUSTANTIVO
glue

pegar* VERBO
1 to hit ◊ *Andrés me ha pegado.* Andrés hit me. ◊ *La pelota pegó en el árbol.* The ball hit the tree.
2 to stick ◊ *Lo puedes pegar con celo.* You can stick it on with sellotape. ◊ *Tengo que pegar las fotos en el álbum.* I have to stick the photos in the album.
♦ **Se te va a pegar el arroz.** Be careful or the rice will stick.
3 to give ◊ *Le pegaron un tremendo empujón.* They gave him a great push. ◊ *Le pegó una bofetada.* He gave him a slap. ◊ *Me has pegado la gripe.* You've given me the flu. ◊ *¡Qué susto me has pegado!* What a fright you gave me!
♦ **Pegó un grito.** He shouted.
♦ **Le pegaron un tiro.** They shot him.

☞

[4] to look right ◊ *Ese jarrón no pega aquí.* That vase doesn't look right here.
◆**Esta camisa no pega con el traje.** This shirt doesn't look right with the suit.
◆**El niño se pegó a su madre.** The boy clung to his mother.

la **pegatina** SUSTANTIVO
sticker

el **peinado** SUSTANTIVO
hairstyle

peinar VERBO
[1] to comb (*con peine*) ◊ *Péinate antes de salir.* Comb your hair before you go out.
[2] to brush (*con cepillo*) ◊ *Su madre la estaba peinando.* Her mother was brushing her hair.
◆**Mañana voy a peinarme.** I'm going to have my hair done tomorrow.

el **peine** SUSTANTIVO
comb

p.ej. ABREVIATURA (= *por ejemplo*)
e.g.

pelar VERBO
[1] to peel (*patatas, naranjas*)
[2] to shell (*nueces*)
◆**Se me está pelando la espalda.** My back is peeling.
◆**Hace un frío que pela.** It's bitterly cold.

el **peldaño** SUSTANTIVO
[1] step (*de escalera*)
[2] rung (*de escalera de mano*)

la **pelea** SUSTANTIVO
[1] fight (*lucha*) ◊ *Hubo una pelea en la discoteca.* There was a fight at the disco.
[2] argument (*discusión*) ◊ *Tuvo una pelea con su novio.* She had an argument with her boyfriend.

peleado ADJETIVO
◆**Están peleados.** They've fallen out.

pelear VERBO
[1] to fight (*luchar*) ◊ *¡Deja de pelear con tu hermano!* Stop fighting with your brother! ◊ *Dos niños se estaban peleando en el patio.* There were two children fighting in the playground.
[2] to argue (*discutir*) ◊ *Pelean por cualquier tontería.* They argue over the slightest thing.

el **pelícano** SUSTANTIVO
pelican

la **película** SUSTANTIVO
film ◊ *A las ocho ponen una película.* There's a film on at eight.
◆**una película de dibujos animados** a cartoon
◆**una película del oeste** a western
◆**una película de suspense** a thriller

el **peligro** SUSTANTIVO
danger ◊ *Está fuera de peligro.* He's out of danger.

peligroso ADJETIVO
dangerous

pelirrojo ADJETIVO
◆**es pelirrojo** he has red hair

el **pellejo** SUSTANTIVO
skin
◆**No me gustaría estar en su pellejo.** I wouldn't like to be in his shoes.
◆**arriesgar el pellejo** (*coloquial*) to risk one's neck

pellizcar* VERBO
to pinch ◊ *Me pellizcó el brazo.* He pinched my arm.

el **pellizco** SUSTANTIVO
pinch ◊ *un pellizco de sal* a pinch of salt

el **pelmazo**, la **pelmaza** SUSTANTIVO
bore (*coloquial*)

el **pelo** SUSTANTIVO
hair ◊ *pelo rizado* curly hair
◆**No perdí el avión por un pelo.** I only just caught the plane.
◆**Se me pusieron los pelos de punta.** It made my hair stand on end.
◆**Me estás tomando el pelo.** You're pulling my leg.

la **pelota** SUSTANTIVO
ball ◊ *jugar a la pelota* to play ball
◆**hacer la pelota a alguien** (*coloquial*) to suck up to someone

el/la **pelota** SUSTANTIVO
creep (*coloquial*)

la **peluca** SUSTANTIVO
wig

peludo ADJETIVO
hairy

la **peluquera** SUSTANTIVO
hairdresser

la **peluquería** SUSTANTIVO
hairdresser's

el **peluquero** SUSTANTIVO
hairdresser

la **pena** SUSTANTIVO
shame ◊ *Es una pena que no puedas venir.* It's a shame you can't come. ◊ *¡Qué pena!* What a shame!
◆**Me dio tanta pena el pobre animal.** I felt so sorry for the poor animal.
◆**Me da pena tener que marcharme.** I'm so sad to have to go away.
◆**No tengas pena.** [Latin America] Don't be embarrassed.
◆**Vale la pena.** It's worth it.
◆**No vale la pena gastarse tanto dinero.** It's not worth spending so much money.
◆**la pena de muerte** the death penalty

el **penalty** SUSTANTIVO (PL los **penaltys**)
penalty (PL penalties) ◊ *pitar penalty* to award a penalty

el **pendejo**, la **pendeja** SUSTANTIVO
[Latin America]
nerd (*coloquial*)

* Verbs marked with this symbol are irregular. See pages 380-382 for further details

pendiente ADJETIVO
- **Tenemos un par de asuntos pendientes.** We have a couple of matters to sort out.
- **Tiene una asignatura pendiente.** He has to resit one subject.
- **Estaban pendientes de ella.** They were watching her intently.

el **pendiente** SUSTANTIVO
earring

la **pendiente** SUSTANTIVO
slope

el **pene** SUSTANTIVO
penis (PL penises)

penetrar VERBO
- **penetrar en** to find one's way into ◊ *Ocho hombres armados penetraron en la embajada.* Eight gunmen found their way into the embassy. ◊ *La luz apenas penetra en la cueva.* The light hardly finds its way into the cave.

la **penicilina** SUSTANTIVO
penicillin

la **península** SUSTANTIVO
peninsula
- **la Península Ibérica** the Iberian Peninsula

el **penique** SUSTANTIVO
penny (PL pence)

el **pensamiento** SUSTANTIVO
1 (*mental*)
thought
2 (*flor*)
pansy (PL pansies)

pensar* VERBO
1 to think ◊ *Piénsalo bien antes de responder.* Think carefully before you answer. ◊ *¿Piensas que vale la pena?* Do you think it's worth it? ◊ *¿Qué piensas de Manolo?* What do you think of Manolo?
- **¿Qué piensas del aborto?** What do you think about abortion?

2 to think about ◊ *Tengo que pensarlo.* I'll have to think about it.
- **Sólo piensa en pasarlo bien.** All he thinks about is having a good time.
- **Estaba pensando en ir al cine esta tarde.** I was thinking of going to the cinema this evening.
- **¡Ni pensarlo!** (*coloquial*) No way!
- **pensándolo bien ...** on second thoughts ...
- **Piénsatelo.** Think it over.

pensativo ADJETIVO
pensive

la **pensión** SUSTANTIVO (PL las **pensiones**)
1 pension (*de jubilación, viudedad*)
2 guest house (*casa de huéspedes*)
- **pensión completa** full board
- **media pensión** half board

el/la **pensionista** SUSTANTIVO
pensioner

penúltimo ADJETIVO
- **la penúltima estación** the last station but one

el **penúltimo**, la **penúltima** SUSTANTIVO
- **Soy el penúltimo.** I'm second to last.

el **peñón** SUSTANTIVO (PL los **peñones**)
- **el Peñón de Gibraltar** the Rock of Gibraltar

el **peón** SUSTANTIVO (PL los **peones**)
1 labourer (*albañil*)
2 pawn (*en ajedrez*)

la **peonza** SUSTANTIVO
spinning top

peor ADJETIVO, ADVERBIO (FEM **peor**)
1 worse (*comparativo*) ◊ *Su caso es peor que el nuestro.* His case is worse than ours. ◊ *Hoy me siento peor.* I feel worse today.
2 worst (*superlativo*) ◊ *el peor día de mi vida* the worst day of my life ◊ *Sacó la peor nota de toda la clase.* He got the worst mark in the whole class.
- **el restaurante donde peor se come** the restaurant with the worst food
- **y lo peor es que ...** and the worst thing is that ...
- **Si no viene, peor para ella.** If she doesn't come, too bad for her.

el **pepinillo** SUSTANTIVO
gherkin

el **pepino** SUSTANTIVO
cucumber
- **Me importa un pepino lo que piense.** (*coloquial*) I couldn't care less what he thinks.

la **pepita** SUSTANTIVO
1 pip (*de fruta*)
2 nugget (*de oro*)

pequeño ADJETIVO
small ◊ *Prefiero los coches pequeños.* I prefer small cars. ◊ *Estos zapatos me quedan pequeños.* These shoes are too small for me.
- **¿Cuál prefieres? – El pequeño.** Which one do you prefer? – The small one.
- **mi hermana pequeña** my younger sister
- **La pequeña estudia medicina.** The youngest is studying medicine.
- **Tuvimos un pequeño problema.** We had a slight problem.

el **pequinés** SUSTANTIVO
Pekinese

la **pera** SUSTANTIVO
pear

percatarse VERBO
- **percatarse de algo** to notice something

la **percha** SUSTANTIVO
1 coat hanger (*en un armario*)
2 coat hook (*en la pared*)

el **perchero** SUSTANTIVO
1 coat rack (*en la pared*)
2 coat stand (*de pie*)

la **percusión** SUSTANTIVO
percussion

perdedor ADJETIVO (FEM **perdedora**)

☞

P

losing ◊ *la pareja perdedora* the losing pair

el **perdedor,** la **perdedora** SUSTANTIVO
loser ◊ *Eres mal perdedor.* You're a bad loser.

perder* VERBO
1 to lose ◊ *He perdido el monedero.* I've lost my purse. ◊ *Está intentando perder peso.* He's trying to lose weight. ◊ *perder el conocimiento* to lose consciousness ◊ *Perdimos dos a cero.* We lost two nil.
♦ **Se le perdieron las llaves.** He lost his keys.
2 to miss (*autobús, avión*) ◊ *Date prisa o perderás el tren.* Hurry up or you'll miss the train. ◊ *No quiero perder esta oportunidad.* I don't want to miss this opportunity.
♦ **¡No te lo pierdas!** Don't miss it!
♦ **¡Me estás haciendo perder el tiempo!** You're wasting my time!
♦ **Has echado a perder la sorpresa.** You've ruined the surprise.
♦ **Ana es la que saldrá perdiendo.** Ana is the one who will lose out.
♦ **Tenía miedo de perderme.** I was afraid of getting lost.

la **perdición** SUSTANTIVO
ruin

la **pérdida** SUSTANTIVO
1 (*de calor, peso*)
loss (PL losses)
2 (*escape de líquido, gas*)
leak
♦ **Fue una pérdida de tiempo.** It was a waste of time.

perdido ADJETIVO
1 lost ◊ *la oficina de objetos perdidos* the lost property office
2 remote ◊ *un pueblecito perdido en la montaña* a remote little village in the mountains
♦ **Es tonto perdido.** He's a complete idiot.

el **perdigón** SUSTANTIVO (PL los **perdigones**)
pellet

la **perdiz** SUSTANTIVO (PL las **perdices**)
partridge

el **perdón** SUSTANTIVO
♦ **Le pedí perdón.** I apologized to him.
♦ **¡Perdón! (1)** (*para disculparse*) Sorry!
♦ **¡Perdón! (2)** (*para llamar la atención*) Excuse me!

perdonar VERBO
to forgive ◊ *¿Me perdonas?* Do you forgive me? ◊ *No perdona que me haya olvidado de su cumpleaños.* He hasn't forgiven me for forgetting his birthday.
♦ **¡Perdona! ¿Tienes hora?** Excuse me, do you have the time?
♦ **¡Perdona! ¿Te he hecho daño?** I'm so sorry. Did I hurt you?

el **peregrino,** la **peregrina** SUSTANTIVO
pilgrim

el **perejil** SUSTANTIVO
parsley

la **pereza** SUSTANTIVO
laziness
♦ **¡Qué pereza tengo!** I feel so lazy!
♦ **Me da pereza levantarme.** I can't be bothered to get up.

perezoso ADJETIVO
lazy

perfeccionar VERBO
to improve (*mejorar*) ◊ *Fue a Inglaterra para perfeccionar el inglés.* He went to England to improve his English.

perfectamente ADVERBIO
perfectly

perfecto ADJETIVO
perfect

el **perfil** SUSTANTIVO
profile ◊ *un retrato de perfil* a profile portrait
♦ **ponerse de perfil** to stand side on

el **perfume** SUSTANTIVO
perfume

la **perfumería** SUSTANTIVO
perfume shop

periódico ADJETIVO
periodic

el **periódico** SUSTANTIVO
newspaper

el **periodismo** SUSTANTIVO
journalism

el/la **periodista** SUSTANTIVO
journalist ◊ *Mi tío es periodista.* My uncle is a journalist.

el **periodo** SUSTANTIVO
period ◊ *un periodo de tres meses* a three-month period
♦ **Tiene el periodo.** She has her period.

el **periquito** SUSTANTIVO
budgerigar

perjudicar* VERBO
1 to damage (*salud, reputación*)
2 to be harmful to (*intereses, desarrollo, economía*) ◊ *Esta nueva ley puede perjudicarnos.* This new law could be harmful to our interests.
♦ **El cambio ha perjudicado sus estudios.** The change has had an adverse effect on his studies.

perjudicial ADJETIVO
damaging
♦ **El tabaco es perjudicial para la salud.** Smoking damages your health.

la **perla** SUSTANTIVO
pearl

permanecer* VERBO
to remain

permanente ADJETIVO

* Verbs marked with this symbol are irregular. See pages 380-382 for further details

permanent

la **permanente** SUSTANTIVO
perm
♦ **hacerse la permanente** to have a perm

el **permiso** SUSTANTIVO
1 permission ◊ *Tengo que pedirles permiso a mis padres.* I have to ask my parents' permission.
2 leave ◊ *Pidió cinco días de permiso.* He requested five days' leave. ◊ *Mi hermano está de permiso.* My brother is on leave.
3 permit (*documento*) ◊ *Necesitas un permiso de trabajo.* You need a work permit.
♦ **¡Con permiso!** (*para abrirse paso*) Excuse me.

permitir VERBO
to allow ◊ *No nos permiten fumar en la oficina.* We're not allowed to smoke in the office.
♦ **No me lo puedo permitir.** I can't afford it.
♦ **¿Me permite?** May I?

pero CONJUNCIÓN
but ◊ *Me gustaría, pero no puedo.* I'd like to, but I can't.

perpendicular ADJETIVO
at right angles ◊ *una pared perpendicular a otra* one wall at right angles to another

perplejo ADJETIVO
puzzled

la **perra** SUSTANTIVO
dog ◊ *Es una perra muy buena.* She's a very good dog.
♦ **¿Es perra o perro?** Is it a bitch or a dog?

la **perrera** SUSTANTIVO
dog's home

el **perrito** SUSTANTIVO
♦ **un perrito caliente** a hot dog

el **perro** SUSTANTIVO
dog
♦ **un perro callejero** a stray dog
♦ **un perro guardián** a guard dog
♦ **un perro pastor** a sheepdog
♦ **un perro policía** a police dog
♦ **un perro salchicha** a dachshund

el/la **persa** ADJETIVO, SUSTANTIVO
Persian

perseguir* VERBO
1 to chase (*delincuente*) ◊ *Me persigue la policía.* The police are chasing me.
2 to persecute (*por ideología, raza*) ◊ *Se siente perseguido por su ideología.* He feels persecuted for his ideology.

la **persiana** SUSTANTIVO
blind

persiguiendo VERBO *ver* **perseguir**

la **persona** SUSTANTIVO
person ◊ *Es una persona encantadora.* He's a charming person.
♦ **en persona** in person
♦ **personas** people ◊ *Había unas diez personas en la sala.* There were about ten people in the hall.

el **personaje** SUSTANTIVO
1 character ◊ *los personajes de la novela* the characters in the novel
2 figure ◊ *un personaje público* a public figure

personal ADJETIVO
personal

el **personal** SUSTANTIVO
staff

la **personalidad** SUSTANTIVO
personality (PL personalities)

personalmente ADVERBIO
personally

la **perspectiva** SUSTANTIVO
perspective (*espacial*) ◊ *en perspectiva* in perspective
♦ **perspectivas** prospects ◊ *buenas perspectivas económicas* good economic prospects

persuadir VERBO
to persuade ◊ *Me persuadió para que la acompañara.* She persuaded me to go with her.

pertenecer* VERBO
♦ **pertenecer a** to belong to ◊ *Este reloj perteneció a su abuelo.* This watch belonged to his grandfather. ◊ *No pertenezco a ningún partido político.* I don't belong to any political party.

las **pertenencias** SUSTANTIVO
belongings

la **pértiga** SUSTANTIVO
pole
♦ **el salto con pértiga** the pole vault

Perú SUSTANTIVO MASC
Peru

el **peruano**, la **peruana** ADJETIVO, SUSTANTIVO
Peruvian

perverso ADJETIVO
wicked

el **pervertido**, la **pervertida** SUSTANTIVO
pervert

la **pesa** SUSTANTIVO
weight
♦ **hacer pesas** to do weight training

la **pesadez** SUSTANTIVO
♦ **Es una pesadez tener que madrugar.** (*coloquial*) It's such a pain having to get up early.
♦ **¡Qué pesadez de película!** What a boring film!

la **pesadilla** SUSTANTIVO
nightmare

pesado ADJETIVO
1 heavy (*paquete, comida*)
2 tiring (*trabajo, viaje*)
3 boring (*película, novela*)
♦ **¡No seas pesado!** (*coloquial*) Don't be a pain in the neck!

el **pesado,** la **pesada** SUSTANTIVO
◆**Mi primo es un pesado.** (*coloquial*) My cousin is a pain in the neck.

el **pésame** SUSTANTIVO
condolences PL ◊ *Fuimos a darle el pésame.* We went to offer our condolences.

pesar VERBO
[1] to weigh ◊ *El paquete pesaba 2 kilos.* The package weighed 2 kilos. ◊ *¿Cuánto pesas?* How much do you weigh? ◊ *Tengo que pesarme.* I must weigh myself.
[2] to be heavy ◊ *Esta maleta pesa mucho.* This suitcase is very heavy. ◊ *¡No pesa nada!* It's not heavy at all!
◆**pesar poco** to be very light
◆**Me pesa haberlo hecho.** I regret having done it.
◆**a pesar del mal tiempo** in spite of the bad weather
◆**a pesar de que la quiero** even though I love her

la **pesca** SUSTANTIVO
fishing ◊ *ir de pesca* to go fishing

la **pescadería** SUSTANTIVO
fishmonger's (PL fishmongers' shops)

la **pescadilla** SUSTANTIVO
whiting (PL whiting)

el **pescado** SUSTANTIVO
fish (PL fish) ◊ *Quiero comprar pescado.* I want to buy some fish.

el **pescador** SUSTANTIVO
fisherman (PL fishermen) ◊ *Mi tío es pescador.* My uncle is a fisherman.

pescar* VERBO
[1] to fish ◊ *Los domingos íbamos a pescar.* On Sundays we used to go fishing.
[2] to catch ◊ *Pescamos varias truchas.* We caught several trout. ◊ *Me pescaron fumando.* I got caught smoking.

el **pesero** SUSTANTIVO Mexico
minibus (PL minibuses)

la **peseta** SUSTANTIVO
peseta

pesimista ADJETIVO
pessimistic ◊ *una visión pesimista* a pessimistic view
◆**No seas pesimista.** Don't be a pessimist.

el/la **pesimista** SUSTANTIVO
pessimist

pésimo ADJETIVO
terrible ◊ *La comida era pésima.* The food was terrible.

el **peso** SUSTANTIVO
[1] weight ◊ *ganar peso* to gain weight ◊ *Ha perdido mucho peso.* He's lost a lot of weight.
◆**La fruta se vende a peso.** Fruit is sold by weight.
[2] scales PL (*en la cocina*)
[3] peso (*moneda*)

pesquero ADJETIVO
fishing

***fishing* en este caso va siempre delante del sustantivo.**

◊ *un pueblecito pesquero* a fishing village

la **pestaña** SUSTANTIVO
eyelash (PL eyelashes)

pestañear VERBO
to blink

la **peste** SUSTANTIVO
[1] plague (*enfermedad*)
[2] stink (*mal olor*) ◊ *¡Qué peste hay aquí!* There's a real stink in here!

el **pesticida** SUSTANTIVO
pesticide

el **pestillo** SUSTANTIVO
[1] (*de puerta, ventana*)
bolt
[2] (*de cerradura*)
latch (PL latches)

la **petaca** SUSTANTIVO
hip flask (*botella*)

el **pétalo** SUSTANTIVO
petal

el **petardo** SUSTANTIVO
firecracker

la **petición** SUSTANTIVO (PL las **peticiones**)
[1] request (*ruego*) ◊ *Hicieron una petición al gobierno.* They made a request to the government. ◊ *a petición de la pareja* at the request of the couple
[2] petition (*escrito*) ◊ *firmar una petición* to sign a petition

el **petirrojo** SUSTANTIVO
robin

el **petróleo** SUSTANTIVO
oil

el **petrolero** SUSTANTIVO
oil tanker

el **pez** SUSTANTIVO (PL los **peces**)
fish (PL fish) ◊ *Cogimos tres peces.* We caught three fish.
◆**un pez de colores** a goldfish
◆**Se sentía como el pez en el agua.** He felt in his element.

la **pezuña** SUSTANTIVO
hoof (PL hooves)

el/la **pianista** SUSTANTIVO
pianist ◊ *Soy pianista.* I'm a pianist.

el **piano** SUSTANTIVO
piano
◆**un piano de cola** a grand piano

piar* VERBO
to chirp

el **pibe,** la **piba** SUSTANTIVO River Plate
kid (*coloquial*)

la **picada** SUSTANTIVO Latin America

* Verbs marked with this symbol are irregular. See pages 380-382 for further details

◆**El avión cayó en picada.** The plane nose-dived.

picado ADJETIVO
1 bad (*diente*)
2 choppy (*mar*)
◆**El avión cayó en picado.** The plane nose-dived.

la **picadura** SUSTANTIVO
1 bite (*de mosquito, serpiente*)
2 sting (*de avispa, abeja*)

picante ADJETIVO
hot (*comida, salsa*)

el **picaporte** SUSTANTIVO
door handle

picar* VERBO
1 to bite (*mosquito, serpiente*) ◊ *Me han picado los mosquitos.* I've been bitten by mosquitoes.
2 to sting (*avispa, abeja*)
3 to chop up (*cebolla, pimiento*) ◊ *Luego picas un poquito de jamón.* Then you chop up a bit of ham.
4 to mince (*carne*)
◆**La salsa pica bastante.** The sauce is quite hot.
◆**Saqué algunas cosas para picar.** I put out some nibbles.
◆**Me pica la espalda.** I've got an itchy back.
◆**Me pica la garganta.** My throat tickles.

el **pichi** SUSTANTIVO
pinafore

el **picnic** SUSTANTIVO (PL los **picnics**)
picnic

el **pico** SUSTANTIVO
1 beak (*de ave*)
2 peak (*de montaña*)
3 pick (*herramienta*)
◆**Eran las tres y pico.** It was after three.
◆**tres mil pesetas y pico** over three thousand pesetas
◆**cuello de pico** V-neck
◆**la hora pico** Latin America the rush hour

picoso ADJETIVO Mexico
hot (*comida*)

pidiendo VERBO *ver* **pedir**

el **pie** SUSTANTIVO
foot (PL feet) ◊ *Fuimos a pie.* We went on foot. ◊ *Al pie de la página hay una explicación.* There's an explanation at the foot of the page.
◆**Estaba de pie junto a mi cama.** He was standing next to my bed.
◆**ponerse de pie** to stand up
◆**de pies a cabeza** from head to foot

la **piedad** SUSTANTIVO
mercy ◊ *tener piedad de alguien* to have mercy on someone

la **piedra** SUSTANTIVO
stone ◊ *Nos tiraban piedras.* They were throwing stones at us.
◆**una piedra preciosa** a precious stone
◆**Cuando me lo dijeron me quedé de piedra.** I was stunned when they told me.

la **piel** SUSTANTIVO
1 skin ◊ *Tengo la piel grasa.* I have greasy skin.
2 fur ◊ *un abrigo de pieles* a fur coat
3 leather ◊ *un bolso de piel* a leather bag
4 peel (*de naranja, patata, manzana*)

pienso VERBO *ver* **pensar**

pierdo VERBO *ver* **perder**

la **pierna** SUSTANTIVO
leg
◆**una pierna de cordero** a leg of lamb

la **pieza** SUSTANTIVO
piece ◊ *una pieza del rompecabezas* a piece of the jigsaw puzzle ◊ *una pieza de recambio* a spare part

el **pijama** SUSTANTIVO
pyjamas PL

pijo ADJETIVO
posh (*coloquial*)

la **pila** SUSTANTIVO
1 battery (PL batteries) ◊ *Funciona con pilas.* It goes on batteries.
2 pile ◊ *una pila de revistas* a pile of magazines
3 (*en la cocina*)
sink

el **pilar** SUSTANTIVO
pillar

la **píldora** SUSTANTIVO
pill ◊ *¿Tomas la píldora?* Are you on the pill?

la **pileta** SUSTANTIVO River Plate
sink

pillar VERBO
1 to catch ◊ *pillar a un ladrón* to catch a thief ◊ *¡Vaya catarro que has pillado!* That's a nasty cold you've caught. ◊ *Lo pillé fumando .* I caught him smoking.
◆**Se pilló los dedos en la puerta.** He caught his fingers in the door.
2 to hit ◊ *La pilló una moto.* She was hit by a motorbike.
◆**La estación nos pilla cerca de casa.** The station is pretty close to our house.

pillo ADJETIVO
1 crafty (*astuto*)
2 naughty (*travieso*)

el/la **piloto** SUSTANTIVO
1 pilot (*de avión*)
2 driver (*de coche*)
◆**piloto de carreras** racing driver

el **pimentón** SUSTANTIVO
paprika

la **pimienta** SUSTANTIVO
pepper ◊ *pimienta negra* black pepper

el **pimiento** SUSTANTIVO
pepper ◊ *un pimiento morrón* a red pepper

el **pin** SUSTANTIVO (PL los **pins**)

P

☞

badge

el **pincel** SUSTANTIVO
paintbrush (PL paintbrushes)

el/la **pinchadiscos** SUSTANTIVO (PL los/las **pinchadiscos**)
disk jockey (PL disk jockeys)

pinchar VERBO
1 to prick ◊ *Me pinché con un alfiler.* I pricked myself on a pin.
2 to burst ◊ *El clavo pinchó la pelota.* The nail burst the ball.
♦ **Me pincharon en el brazo.** They gave me an injection in the arm.
♦ **Se me pinchó una rueda.** I had a puncture.
♦ **Los cactus pinchan.** Cactuses are prickly.

el **pinchazo** SUSTANTIVO
1 puncture ◊ *Tuve un pinchazo en la autopista.* I got a puncture on the motorway.
2 sharp pain (*de dolor*)

el **pincho** SUSTANTIVO
1 thorn (*de rosal, cactus*)
2 snack ◊ *Tomamos unos pinchos en el bar.* We had some snacks in the bar.
♦ **un pincho moruno** a kebab

el **ping-pong** SUSTANTIVO
table tennis ◊ *jugar al ping-pong* to play table tennis

el **pingüino** SUSTANTIVO
penguin

el **pino** SUSTANTIVO
pine tree
♦ **hacer el pino** to do a headstand

la **pinta** SUSTANTIVO
♦ **tener buena pinta** to look good ◊ *La paella tiene muy buena pinta.* The paella looks delicious.
♦ **Con esas gafas tienes pinta de maestra.** You look like a teacher with those glasses on.

las **pintadas** SUSTANTIVO
graffiti

pintar VERBO
1 to paint (*con pintura*) ◊ *Quiero pintar la habitación de azul.* I want to paint the room blue.
2 to colour in (*con lápices de colores*) ◊ *Dibujó un árbol y lo pintó.* He drew a tree and coloured it in.
♦ **Nunca me pinto.** I never wear makeup.
♦ **pintarse los labios** to put on lipstick
♦ **pintarse las uñas** to paint one's nails

el **pintor**, la **pintora** SUSTANTIVO
painter ◊ *Soy pintor.* I'm a painter.

pintoresco ADJETIVO
picturesque

la **pintura** SUSTANTIVO
1 paint ◊ *Tengo que comprar más pintura.* I've got to buy some more paint.
2 painting ◊ *Me gusta la pintura abstracta.* I like abstract painting. ◊ *varias pinturas al óleo* several oil paintings

la **pinza** SUSTANTIVO
1 clothes peg (*para la ropa*)
2 hairgrip (*para el pelo*)
3 pincer (*de cangrejo*)
♦ **unas pinzas** (*para depilar*) a pair of tweezers

la **piña** SUSTANTIVO
1 pine cone (*de pino*)
2 pineapple (*fruta tropical*)

el **piñón** SUSTANTIVO (PL los **piñones**)
1 pine nut (*del pino*)
2 sprocket (*de bicicleta*)

el **piojo** SUSTANTIVO
louse (PL lice)

la **pipa** SUSTANTIVO
1 pipe ◊ *Fuma en pipa.* He smokes a pipe.
2 seed (*de girasol, calabaza*)
♦ **comer pipas** to eat sunflower seeds

el **pipí** SUSTANTIVO
wee (*coloquial*) ◊ *hacer pipí* to have a wee

la **piragua** SUSTANTIVO
canoe (PL canoes)

el **piragüismo** SUSTANTIVO
canoeing

la **pirámide** SUSTANTIVO
pyramid

pirata ADJETIVO
pirate (*barco, vídeo*)

> ***pirate** en este caso va siempre delante del sustantivo.*

el/la **pirata** SUSTANTIVO
pirate
♦ **un/una pirata informático/a** a hacker

piratear VERBO
to hack into a system (*informática*)

los **Pirineos** SUSTANTIVO
the Pyrenees

el **piropo** SUSTANTIVO
compliment ◊ *echar piropos a alguien* to make compliments to someone

el **pirulí** SUSTANTIVO (PL los **pirulís**)
lollipop

la **pisada** SUSTANTIVO
1 footprint (*huella*)
2 footstep (*sonido*)

el **pisapapeles** SUSTANTIVO (PL los **pisapapeles**)
paperweight

pisar VERBO
1 to walk on
♦ **¿Se puede pisar el suelo de la cocina?** Can I walk on the kitchen floor?
2 to tread on ◊ *Perdona, te he pisado.* Sorry, I trod on your foot.
♦ **Pisé el acelerador a fondo.** I put my foot down.

la **piscina** SUSTANTIVO
swimming pool

Piscis SUSTANTIVO MASC
Pisces ◊ *Soy Piscis.* I'm Pisces.

el **piso** SUSTANTIVO
1 flat (*apartamento*) ◊ *Vivimos en un piso céntrico.* We live in a flat in the town centre.
2 floor (*planta, suelo*) ◊ *Su oficina está en el segundo piso.* His office is on the second floor. ◊ *El piso estaba lleno de papeles.* The floor was covered in pieces of paper.

la **pista** SUSTANTIVO
1 clue (*dato*) ◊ *¿Te doy una pista?* Shall I give you a clue?
2 track (*huella*) ◊ *Los cazadores siguen las pistas del animal.* The hunters follow the animal's tracks.
3 court (*de deportes*)
♦ **la pista de aterrizaje** the runway
♦ **la pista de baile** the dance floor
♦ **la pista de carreras** the racetrack
♦ **la pista de esquí** the ski slope
♦ **la pista de patinaje** the ice rink

la **pistola** SUSTANTIVO
pistol

pitar VERBO
1 to blow one's whistle (*con silbato*) ◊ *El policía nos pitó.* The policeman blew his whistle at us.
2 to hoot (*con claxon*) ◊ *No sé por qué me pita.* I don't know why he's hooting at me.
♦ **Salió pitando.** He was off like a shot.

pitear VERBO Latin America
to whistle

el **pito** SUSTANTIVO
whistle
♦ **Me importa un pito.** (*coloquial*) I don't care a hoot.

el **piyama** SUSTANTIVO Latin America
pyjamas PL

la **pizarra** SUSTANTIVO
1 blackboard (*encerado*)
2 slate (*mineral*)

la **pizca** SUSTANTIVO
pinch ◊ *una pizca de sal* a pinch of salt

la **pizza** SUSTANTIVO
pizza

la **placa** SUSTANTIVO
1 plaque (*letrero*) ◊ *una placa conmemorativa* a commemorative plaque
2 badge (*de policía*)
3 hotplate (*de una cocina eléctrica*)
♦ **una placa de matrícula** a number plate

el **placer** SUSTANTIVO
pleasure

la **plaga** SUSTANTIVO
1 pest ◊ *una plaga que estropea los cultivos* a pest that damages the crops
2 plague ◊ *las plagas de Egipto* the plagues of Egypt
♦ **la plaga del terrorismo** the scourge of terrorism

el **plan** SUSTANTIVO
plan ◊ *¿Qué planes tienes para este verano?* What are your plans for the summer?
♦ **viajar en plan económico** to travel cheap
♦ **Lo dije en plan de broma.** I said it as a joke.
♦ **el plan de estudios** the syllabus

la **plancha** SUSTANTIVO
iron (*aparato*)
♦ **pescado a la plancha** grilled fish

planchar VERBO
1 to iron ◊ *Tengo que planchar esta camisa.* I've got to iron this shirt.
2 to do the ironing ◊ *¿Quieres que planche?* Do you want me to do the ironing?

el **planeador** SUSTANTIVO
glider

planear VERBO
1 to plan (*organizar*)
2 to glide (*avión*)

el **planeta** SUSTANTIVO
planet

la **planificación** SUSTANTIVO
planning
♦ **planificación familiar** family planning

planificar* VERBO
to plan

plano ADJETIVO
flat (*superficie, zapato*)

el **plano** SUSTANTIVO
1 street plan (*de la ciudad, el metro*)
2 plan (*de edificio*)
♦ **en primer plano** in close-up

la **planta** SUSTANTIVO
1 plant ◊ *regar las plantas* to water the plants
2 floor ◊ *El edificio tiene tres plantas.* The building has three floors. ◊ *la planta baja* the ground floor
♦ **la planta del pie** the sole of the foot

plantado ADJETIVO
♦ **dejar a alguien plantado** to stand someone up

plantar VERBO
to plant

plantear VERBO
to bring up ◊ *Se lo plantearé al jefe.* I'll bring it up with the boss.
♦ **Incluso me planteé dejar los estudios.** I even thought of giving up my studies.

la **plantilla** SUSTANTIVO
1 insole (*de zapato*)
2 staff (*de empresa*)

el **plástico** SUSTANTIVO
plastic ◊ *cubiertos de plástico* plastic cutlery

P

la **plastilina** ® SUSTANTIVO
plasticine

la **plata** SUSTANTIVO
1 silver (*metal*)
2 money (*dinero*) Latin America

la **plataforma** SUSTANTIVO
platform ◊ *zapatos de plataforma* platform shoes
♦ **una plataforma petrolífera** an oil rig

el **plátano** SUSTANTIVO
banana

platicar* VERBO Mexico
1 to talk (*hablar*) ◊ *Estuve platicando con Manuel.* I was talking to Manuel.
2 to tell (*decir*) ◊ *¿Qué te platicaron?* What did they tell you?

el **platillo** SUSTANTIVO
♦ **un platillo volante** a flying saucer
♦ **los platillos** (*instrumento musical*) the cymbals

el **platino** SUSTANTIVO
platinum

el **plato** SUSTANTIVO
1 plate ◊ *¿Me pasas un plato?* Could you pass me a plate?
2 dish (PL dishes) ◊ *un plato típico de Galicia* a typical Galician dish
3 course ◊ *¿Qué hay de segundo plato?* What's for the main course?
4 (*para la taza*)
saucer

la **playa** SUSTANTIVO
1 beach (PL beaches) ◊ *Los niños jugaban en la playa.* The children were playing on the beach.
2 (*costa*)
seaside ◊ *Prefiero la playa a la montaña.* I prefer the seaside to the mountains.

la **playera** SUSTANTIVO
1 canvas shoe (*zapatilla*)
2 T-shirt (*camiseta*) Mexico

la **plaza** SUSTANTIVO
1 square ◊ *la plaza del pueblo* the town square
♦ **la plaza mayor** the main square
2 market ◊ *No había pescado en la plaza.* There was no fish at the market.
3 place (*en colegio, sala*) ◊ *Todavía quedan plazas.* There are still some places left.
♦ **una plaza de toros** a bullring

el **plazo** SUSTANTIVO
1 period ◊ *en un plazo de diez días* within a period of ten days
♦ **El viernes se cumple el plazo.** Friday is the deadline.
2 instalment ◊ *pagar a plazos* to pay in instalments ◊ *comprar a plazos* to buy on instalments
♦ **una solución a corto plazo** a short-term solution

plegable ADJETIVO
folding

plegar* VERBO
to fold

pleno ADJETIVO
♦ **en pleno verano** in the middle of summer
♦ **a plena luz del día** in broad daylight

la **pletina** SUSTANTIVO
tape deck

pliegue VERBO *ver* **plegar**

el **pliegue** SUSTANTIVO
1 fold (*en papel, tela*)
2 pleat (*de falda*)

el **plomero,** la **plomera** SUSTANTIVO
Latin America
plumber

el **plomo** SUSTANTIVO
lead
♦ **gasolina sin plomo** unleaded petrol
♦ **Se han fundido los plomos.** The fuses have blown.

la **pluma** SUSTANTIVO
1 feather (*de ave*)
2 pen (*para escribir*)
♦ **una pluma atómica** Latin America a ballpoint pen
♦ **una pluma estilográfica** a fountain pen

el **plural** ADJETIVO, SUSTANTIVO
plural

la **población** SUSTANTIVO (PL las **poblaciones**)
1 population (*habitantes*)
2 town (*ciudad*)

pobre ADJETIVO
poor ◊ *Somos pobres.* We're poor.
♦ **¡Pobre Pedro!** Poor Pedro!
♦ **los pobres** the poor

la **pobreza** SUSTANTIVO
poverty

poco ADJETIVO, ADVERBIO, PRONOMBRE
not much ◊ *Hay poca leche.* There isn't much milk. ◊ *Tenemos muy poco tiempo.* We have very little time.
♦ **Sus libros son poco conocidos aquí.** His books are not very well known here.
♦ **un poco** a bit ◊ *¿Tienes frío? – Un poco.* Are you cold? – A bit. ◊ *¿Me das un poco?* Can I have a bit? ◊ *He bebido un poco, pero no estoy borracho.* I had a bit to drink, but I'm not drunk.
♦ **Tomé un poco de vino.** I had a little wine.
♦ **pocos** not many ◊ *Tiene pocos amigos.* He hasn't got many friends.
♦ **unos pocos** a few ◊ *Me llevé unos pocos.* I took a few with me.
♦ **poco a poco** little by little
♦ **poco después** shortly after
♦ **dentro de poco** in a short time
♦ **hace poco** not long ago
♦ **por poco** nearly ◊ *Por poco me caigo.* I nearly fell.

* Verbs marked with this symbol are irregular. See pages 380-382 for further details

podar VERBO
to prune

el **poder** SUSTANTIVO
power ◊ *estar en el poder* to be in power

poder* VERBO
[1] can

*El verbo **can** no tiene forma de infinitivo ni futuro. La forma del pasado es **could**.*

◊ *Yo puedo ayudarte.* I can help you.
◊ *¡No puede ser!* That can't be true!
◊ *¿Puedo usar tu teléfono?* Can I use your phone? ◊ *Pudiste haberte hecho daño.* You could have hurt yourself.
◊ *¡Me lo podías haber dicho!* You could have told me! ◊ *Aquí no se puede fumar.* You can't smoke here.
[2] to be able to

*Para formar el futuro se utiliza **to be able to**.*

◊ *Creo que mañana no voy a poder ir.* I don't think I'll be able to come tomorrow.
♦ **¿Se puede?** May I?
♦ **Puede que llegue mañana.** He might arrive tomorrow.
♦ **Puede ser.** It's possible.
♦ **No puedo con tanto trabajo.** I can't cope with so much work.

poderoso ADJETIVO
powerful

el **podólogo,** la **podóloga** SUSTANTIVO
chiropodist

podrido ADJETIVO
rotten

podrirse VERBO = **pudrirse**

el **poema** SUSTANTIVO
poem

la **poesía** SUSTANTIVO
[1] poetry ◊ *Me gusta la poesía.* I like poetry.
[2] poem ◊ *una poesía de Machado* a poem by Machado

el/la **poeta** SUSTANTIVO
poet

el **póker** SUSTANTIVO
poker

polaco ADJETIVO
Polish

el **polaco,** la **polaca** SUSTANTIVO
Pole
♦ **los polacos** the Poles

el **polaco** SUSTANTIVO
Polish (*idioma*)

la **polémica** SUSTANTIVO
controversy (PL controversies)

polémico ADJETIVO
controversial

el **polen** SUSTANTIVO
pollen
♦ **alergia al polen** hay fever

el **policía** SUSTANTIVO
policeman (PL policemen) ◊ *Es policía.* He's a policeman.

la **policía** SUSTANTIVO
[1] police ◊ *Llamamos a la policía.* We called the police.
[2] (*mujer policía*)
policewoman (PL policewomen) ◊ *Soy policía.* I'm a policewoman.

el **polideportivo** SUSTANTIVO
sports centre

la **polilla** SUSTANTIVO
moth (PL moths)

la **polio** SUSTANTIVO
polio

la **política** SUSTANTIVO
[1] politics SING ◊ *Hablaban de política.* They were talking about politics.
[2] policy (PL policies) ◊ *política exterior* foreign policy
[3] (*mujer*)
politician ◊ *Soy política.* I'm a politician.

político ADJETIVO
political

el **político** SUSTANTIVO
politician

el **pollo** SUSTANTIVO
chicken
♦ **pollo asado** roast chicken

el **polluelo** SUSTANTIVO
chick

el **polo** SUSTANTIVO
[1] (*helado*)
ice lolly (PL ice lollies)
[2] (*camisa*)
polo shirt
♦ **el Polo Norte** the North Pole
♦ **el Polo Sur** the South Pole

Polonia SUSTANTIVO FEM
Poland

el **polvo** SUSTANTIVO
dust
♦ **limpiar el polvo** to dust
♦ **quitar el polvo** to do the dusting
♦ **quitar el polvo a algo** to dust something
♦ **en polvo** powdered ◊ *leche en polvo* powdered milk
♦ **polvos de talco** talcum powder
♦ **Estoy hecho polvo.** (*coloquial*) I'm shattered.
♦ **echar un polvo** (*vulgar*) to have a shag

la **pólvora** SUSTANTIVO
gunpowder

la **pomada** SUSTANTIVO
ointment

el **pomelo** SUSTANTIVO
grapefruit (PL grapefruit)

el **pomo** SUSTANTIVO
handle

la **pompa** SUSTANTIVO
[1] bubble (*burbuja*) ◊ *pompas de jabón* soap bubbles
[2] pomp (*ostentación*)

P

☞

el **pómulo** SUSTANTIVO
cheekbone

ponchar VERBO Mexico
◆ **Se nos ponchó una llanta.** We had a puncture.

el **ponche** SUSTANTIVO
punch (PL punches)

el **poncho** SUSTANTIVO
poncho (PL ponchos)

pondrá VERBO *ver* **poner**

poner* VERBO
1 to put (*colocar*) ◇ *¿Dónde pongo mis cosas?* Where shall I put my things?
2 to put on (*prenda, televisión, obra teatral*) ◇ *Me puse el abrigo.* I put on my coat. ◇ *Voy a poner las patatas.* I'm going to put the potatoes on. ◇ *¿Pongo música?* Shall I put some music on? ◇ *Pon el radiador.* Put the heater on.
◆ **No sé que ponerme.** I don't know what to wear.
◆ **Ponlo más alto.** Turn it up.
◆ **¿Ponen alguna película esta noche?** Is there a film on tonight?
3 to set (*deberes, despertador*) ◇ *La maestra nos puso un examen.* Our teacher set us an exam. ◇ *Puse el despertador para las siete.* I set the alarm for seven o'clock. ◇ *poner la mesa* to set the table
4 to put in (*instalar*) ◇ *Queremos poner calefacción.* We want to put in central heating.
◆ **¿Me pone con el Sr. García, por favor?** Could you put me through to Mr. Garcia, please?
◆ **Le pusieron Mónica.** They called her Monica.
◆ **¿Qué te pongo?** What can I get you?
◆ **Cuando se lo dije se puso muy triste.** He was very sad when I told him.
◆ **¡Qué guapa te has puesto!** You look beautiful!
◆ **Se puso a mi lado en clase.** He sat down beside me in class.
◆ **ponerse a hacer algo** to start doing something

el **poney** SUSTANTIVO (PL los **poneys**)
pony (PL ponies)

pongo VERBO *ver* **poner**

pop ADJETIVO (FEM **pop,** PL **pop**)
pop ◇ *música pop* pop music

el **popote** SUSTANTIVO Mexico
straw

popular ADJETIVO
popular

por PREPOSICIÓN
1 for ◇ *Lo hice por mis padres.* I did it for my parents. ◇ *Lo vendió por dos mil pesetas.* He sold it for two thousand pesetas. ◇ *Me castigaron por mentir.* I was punished for lying.
2 through ◇ *La conozco por mi hermano.* I know her through my brother. ◇ *por la ventana* through the window ◇ *Pasamos por Valencia.* We went through Valencia.
3 by ◇ *Fueron apresados por la policía.* They were captured by the police. ◇ *por correo* by post ◇ *Me agarró por el brazo.* He grabbed me by the arm.
4 along ◇ *Paseábamos por la playa.* We were walking along the beach.
5 around ◇ *viajar por el mundo* to travel around the world ◇ *Viven por esta zona.* They live around this area.
6 because of ◇ *Tuvo que suspenderse por el mal tiempo.* It had to be cancelled because of bad weather.
7 per ◇ *100 kilómetros por hora* 100 kilometres per hour ◇ *mil pesetas por persona* a thousand pesetas per person
◆ **por aquí cerca** near here
◆ **por escrito** in writing
◆ **por la mañana** in the morning
◆ **por la noche** at night
◆ **por mí ...** as far as I'm concerned ...
◆ **¿Por qué?** Why?

la **porcelana** SUSTANTIVO
porcelain

el **porcentaje** SUSTANTIVO
percentage

el **porche** SUSTANTIVO
(*de casa*)
porch (PL porches)

la **porción** SUSTANTIVO (PL las **porciones**)
portion

porno ADJETIVO (FEM **porno,** PL **porno**)
porn
***porn** en este caso va siempre delante del sustantivo.*
◇ *una película porno* a porn film

la **pornografía** SUSTANTIVO
pornography

pornográfico ADJETIVO
pornographic

el **poro** SUSTANTIVO
1 pore (*en la piel*)
2 leek (*vegetal*) Mexico

el **poroto** SUSTANTIVO Chile, River Plate
bean

porque CONJUNCIÓN
because ◇ *No fuimos porque llovía.* We didn't go because it was raining.

la **porquería** SUSTANTIVO
◆ **Este CD es una porquería.** This CD's rubbish.

la **porra** SUSTANTIVO
truncheon (*de policía*)
◆ **mandar a alguien a la porra** (*coloquial*) to send someone packing

* Verbs marked with this symbol are irregular. See pages 380-382 for further details

el **porrazo** SUSTANTIVO
♦**Me di un porrazo en la rodilla.** I banged my knee.
♦**Daba porrazos en la puerta.** He was banging on the door.

el **porro** SUSTANTIVO
joint (*coloquial*)

la **portada** SUSTANTIVO
1 front page (*de periódico*)
2 cover (*de revista*)

el **portal** SUSTANTIVO
1 hallway ◊ *Los buzones están en el portal.* The letterboxes are in the hallway.
2 portal (*Internet*)
♦**el portal de Belén** the nativity scene

portarse VERBO
♦**portarse bien** to behave well
♦**portarse mal** to behave badly
♦**Se portó muy bien conmigo.** He treated me very well.

portátil ADJETIVO
portable

el **portavoz** SUSTANTIVO (PL los **portavoces**)
spokesman (PL spokesmen)

la **portavoz** SUSTANTIVO (PL las **portavoces**)
spokeswoman (PL spokeswomen)

el **portazo** SUSTANTIVO
♦**Dio un portazo.** He slammed the door.

la **portera** SUSTANTIVO
1 caretaker (*de bloque de pisos*)
2 goalkeeper (*de equipo*)

la **portería** SUSTANTIVO
goal ◊ *El balón entró en la portería.* The ball went into the goal.

el **portero** SUSTANTIVO
1 caretaker (*de bloque de pisos*)
2 goalkeeper (*de equipo*)
♦**un portero automático** an entryphone

el **portorriqueño,** la **portorriqueña** ADJETIVO, SUSTANTIVO
Puerto Rican

Portugal SUSTANTIVO MASC
Portugal

el **portugués,** la **portuguesa** ADJETIVO, SUSTANTIVO (MASC PL los **portugueses**)
Portuguese

el **portugués** SUSTANTIVO
Portuguese (*idioma*)

el **porvenir** SUSTANTIVO
future

posar VERBO
to pose ◊ *Posó para los fotógrafos.* He posed for photographs.
♦**posarse** to land ◊ *El pájaro se posó en la rama.* The bird landed on the branch.

la **posdata** SUSTANTIVO
postscript

poseer* VERBO
to possess

la **posguerra** SUSTANTIVO
♦**durante la posguerra** during the postwar period
♦**los años de posguerra** the years after the war

la **posibilidad** SUSTANTIVO
1 possibility (PL possibilities) ◊ *Es una posibilidad.* It's a possibility.
2 chance ◊ *Tendrás la posibilidad de viajar.* You'll have the chance to travel.
♦**Tiene muchas posibilidades de ganar.** He has a good chance of winning.

posible ADJETIVO
possible ◊ *Es posible.* It's possible.
♦**hacer todo lo posible** to do everything possible
♦**Es posible que ganen.** They might win.

la **posición** SUSTANTIVO (PL las **posiciones**)
position ◊ *una posición estratégica* a strategic position
♦**Está en primera posición.** He's in first place.

positivo ADJETIVO
positive
♦**El test dio positivo.** The test was positive.

posponer* VERBO
to postpone

posta
♦**a posta** ADVERBIO
on purpose

la **postal** SUSTANTIVO
postcard

el **poste** SUSTANTIVO
1 post (*de valla, portería*)
2 pole (*de teléfono, telégrafo*)

el **póster** SUSTANTIVO (PL los **pósters**)
poster

posterior ADJETIVO (FEM **posterior**)
rear ◊ *los asientos posteriores* the rear seats
♦**la parte posterior** the rear

postizo ADJETIVO
false

el **postizo** SUSTANTIVO
hairpiece

el **postre** SUSTANTIVO
dessert ◊ *De postre tomé un helado.* I had ice cream for dessert. ◊ *¿Qué hay de postre?* What's for dessert?

la **postura** SUSTANTIVO
position

potable ADJETIVO
♦**agua potable** drinking water

el **potaje** SUSTANTIVO
stew ◊ *potaje de garbanzos* chickpea stew

la **potencia** SUSTANTIVO
power ◊ *la potencia del motor* the power of the engine
♦**Es un artista en potencia.** He has the makings of an artist.

potencial ADJETIVO

☞

potential

potente ADJETIVO

powerful

el **potro** SUSTANTIVO

1 colt (*animal*)

2 horse (*para saltar*)

el **pozo** SUSTANTIVO

well

la **práctica** SUSTANTIVO

practice ◇ *No tengo mucha práctica.* I haven't had much practice.

◆ **en la práctica** in practice

◆ **poner algo en práctica** to put something into practice

prácticamente ADVERBIO

practically

practicante ADJETIVO

practising ◇ *Es una católica practicante.* She is a practising Catholic.

el/la **practicante** SUSTANTIVO

nurse

practicar* VERBO

to practise (*idioma, profesión, instrumento*) ◇ *Tengo que practicar un poco más.* I need to practise a bit more.

◆ **No practico ningún deporte.** I don't do any sports.

práctico ADJETIVO

practical ◇ *Es una mujer muy práctica.* She is a very practical woman.

el **prado** SUSTANTIVO

meadow

la **precaución** SUSTANTIVO (PL las **precauciones**)

precaution ◇ *tomar precauciones* to take precautions

◆ **con precaución** with caution

precavido ADJETIVO

◆ **Es muy precavida.** She's always very well-prepared.

el **precinto** SUSTANTIVO

seal

el **precio** SUSTANTIVO

price ◇ *Han subido los precios.* Prices have gone up.

◆ **¿Qué precio tiene?** How much is it?

la **preciosidad** SUSTANTIVO

◆ **La casa es una preciosidad.** The house is beautiful.

precioso ADJETIVO

beautiful ◇ *¡Es precioso!* It's beautiful!

el **precipicio** SUSTANTIVO

precipice

precipitarse VERBO

◆ **No hay que precipitarse.** There's no need to rush into anything.

◆ **Reconozco que me precipité al tomar esa decisión.** I admit I rushed into the decision.

precisamente ADVERBIO

precisely

precisar VERBO

◆ **¿Puedes precisar un poco más?** Can you be a little more specific?

◆ **Precisó que no se trataba de un virus.** He said specifically that it was not a virus.

preciso ADJETIVO

1 precise ◇ *Recibió instrucciones precisas.* He received precise instructions. ◇ *en ese preciso momento* at that precise moment

2 accurate ◇ *un reloj muy preciso* a very accurate watch

◆ **si es preciso** if necessary

◆ **No es preciso que vengas.** There's no need for you to come.

precoz ADJETIVO (FEM **precoz**, PL **precoces**)

precocious

predecir* VERBO

to predict

predicar* VERBO

to preach

la **predicción** SUSTANTIVO (PL las **predicciones**)

prediction

predicho VERBO *ver* **predecir**

preescolar ADJETIVO

pre-school

> ***pre-school** en este caso va siempre delante del sustantivo.*

prefabricado ADJETIVO

prefabricated

la **preferencia** SUSTANTIVO

1 preference ◇ *No tengo ninguna preferencia.* I have no preference.

2 priority ◇ *Tienen preferencia los coches que vienen por la derecha.* Cars coming from the right have priority.

preferir* VERBO

to prefer ◇ *Prefiero un buen libro a una película.* I prefer a good book to a film.

◆ **Prefiero ir mañana.** I'd rather go tomorrow.

prefiero VERBO *ver* **preferir**

el **prefijo** SUSTANTIVO

code ◇ *¿Cuál es el prefijo de Andorra?* What is the code for Andorra?

la **pregunta** SUSTANTIVO

question ◇ *hacer una pregunta* to ask a question

preguntar VERBO

to ask ◇ *Siempre me preguntas lo mismo.* You're always asking me the same question.

◆ **Me preguntó por ti.** He asked after you.

◆ **Me pregunto si estará enterado.** I wonder if he's heard yet.

prehistórico ADJETIVO

prehistoric

el **prejuicio** SUSTANTIVO

prejudice

◆**Yo no tengo prejuicios.** I'm not prejudiced.

prematuro ADJETIVO
premature

premiar VERBO
1 to award a prize to ◇ *Han premiado su película.* His film has been awarded a prize.
◆**el director premiado** the award-winning director
2 to reward ◇ *premiar los esfuerzos de un niño* to reward a child's efforts

el **premio** SUSTANTIVO
1 prize ◇ *llevarse un premio* to get a prize
2 reward ◇ *como premio a tu sacrificio* as a reward for your sacrifice
◆**el premio gordo** the jackpot

la **prenda** SUSTANTIVO
garment (*de vestir*)

prender VERBO
1 to light (*cerilla, cigarro*)
2 to switch on (*luz, gas, radio*) Latin America
◆**prender fuego a algo** to set fire to something

la **prensa** SUSTANTIVO
press ◇ *una conferencia de prensa* a press conference

la **preocupación** SUSTANTIVO (PL las **preocupaciones**)
worry (PL worries)

preocupado ADJETIVO
worried
◆**estar preocupado por algo** to be worried about something

preocupar VERBO
to worry ◇ *No te preocupes.* Don't worry. ◇ *Me preocupa su salud.* I'm worried about his health.
◆**preocuparse por algo** to worry about something
◆**Si llego un poco tarde se preocupa.** If I arrive a bit late he gets worried.
◆**Yo me preocupo de comprar las entradas.** I'll see to buying the tickets.

preparar VERBO
1 to prepare ◇ *No he preparado el discurso.* I haven't prepared my speech.
2 to prepare for ◇ *¿Te has preparado el examen?* Have you prepared for the exam?
3 to cook (*comida*) ◇ *Mi madre estaba preparando la cena.* My mother was cooking dinner.
◆**Me estaba preparando para salir.** I was getting ready to go out.

los **preparativos** SUSTANTIVO
preparations

la **presa** SUSTANTIVO
1 dam (*de agua*)
2 prey (*de animal*)
3 prisoner (*en la cárcel*)

prescindir VERBO
◆**prescindir de** to do without ◇ *No puede prescindir de su secretaria.* He can't do without his secretary.

la **presencia** SUSTANTIVO
presence ◇ *en presencia de un sacerdote* in the presence of a priest
◆**El puesto requiere buena presencia.** A smart appearance is required for the position.

presenciar VERBO
to witness

el **presentador**, la **presentadora** SUSTANTIVO
1 presenter (*de programa*)
2 newsreader (*de noticias*)

presentar VERBO
1 to introduce ◇ *Me presentó a sus padres.* He introduced me to his parents.
2 to hand in ◇ *Mañana tengo que presentar un trabajo.* I have to hand in an essay tomorrow. ◇ *Presentó la dimisión.* He handed in his resignation.
3 to present ◇ *J. Pérez presenta el programa.* The programme is presented by J. Pérez.
◆**presentarse (1)** to turn up ◇ *Se presentó en mi casa a las doce de la noche.* He turned up at my house at twelve o'clock at night.
◆**presentarse (2)** to introduce oneself ◇ *Antes de nada, me voy a presentar.* First of all, let me introduce myself.
◆**presentarse a un examen** to sit an exam

el **presente** ADJETIVO, SUSTANTIVO
present ◇ *Juan no estaba presente en la reunión.* Juan was not present at the meeting.
◆**el presente** the present
◆**los presentes** those present
◆**¡Presente!** Present!

el **presentimiento** SUSTANTIVO
premonition

el **preservativo** SUSTANTIVO
condom

la **presidenta** SUSTANTIVO
1 president (*de país*)
2 chairperson (*de comité, jurado, empresa*)

el **presidente** SUSTANTIVO
1 (*de país*)
president
2 (*de comité, jurado, empresa*)
chairman (PL chairmen)

la **presión** SUSTANTIVO (PL las **presiones**)
pressure
◆**la presión sanguínea** blood pressure

presionar VERBO
1 to put pressure on ◇ *Sus amigos lo están presionando para que se compre otro coche.* His friends are putting pressure on him to buy a new car.
2 to press (*botón, timbre*)

P

preso ADJETIVO

- **Estuvo tres años preso.** He was in prison for three years.
- **llevarse a alguien preso** to take someone prisoner

el **preso** SUSTANTIVO

prisoner

prestado ADJETIVO

- **La cinta no es mía, es prestada.** It's not my tape, someone lent it to me.
- **Le pedí prestada la bicicleta.** I asked if I could borrow his bicycle.
- **Me dejó el coche prestado.** He lent me his car.

el **préstamo** SUSTANTIVO

loan ◇ *Pidieron un préstamo al banco.* They asked the bank for a loan.

prestar VERBO

to lend (*dinero, coche*) ◇ *Un amigo me prestó el traje.* A friend lent me the suit.

- **¿Me prestas el boli?** Can I borrow your pen?
- **Tienes que prestar atención.** You must pay attention.
- **Se negó a prestar ayuda.** He refused to help.

el **prestigio** SUSTANTIVO

prestige

- **una marca de prestigio** a prestigious brand

presumido ADJETIVO

vain

presumir VERBO

to show off ◇ *Lleva ropa cara para presumir.* He dresses expensively just to show off.

- **Luis presume de guapo.** Luis thinks he's really handsome.

el **presupuesto** SUSTANTIVO

1 budget ◇ *No puedo salirme del presupuesto.* I can't go over the budget.

2 estimate ◇ *Le he pedido un presupuesto al carpintero.* I've asked the joiner for an estimate.

pretender VERBO

1 to intend ◇ *Pretendo sacar al menos un notable.* I intend to get at least a B.

- **¿Qué pretendes decir con eso?** What do you mean by that?

2 to expect ◇ *¡No pretenderás que te pague la comida!* You're not expecting me to pay for your meal, are you?

No confundir ***pretender*** *con* ***to pretend.***

el **pretexto** SUSTANTIVO

excuse ◇ *Era sólo un pretexto.* It was only an excuse.

- **Vino con el pretexto de ver al abuelo.** He came in order to see Granddad, or so he said.

la **prevención** SUSTANTIVO

prevention ◇ *prevención de incendios* fire prevention

- **las medidas de prevención** preventive measures

prevenir* VERBO

1 to prevent ◇ *prevenir un accidente* to prevent an accident

2 to warn ◇ *Mi madre ya me había prevenido.* My mother had already warned me.

prever* VERBO

1 to foresee (*anticipar*) ◇ *Nadie había previsto esta tragedia.* Nobody had foreseen this tragedy.

- **Han previsto nevadas en el norte.** Snow is forecast for the north.

2 plan (*planear*)

- **Tienen previsto acabar el metro para el 2003.** They plan to finish the metro by the year 2003.

previo ADJETIVO

previous ◇ *No tengo experiencia previa en ese campo.* I have no previous experience in the field.

previsible ADJETIVO

foreseeable

previsto (1) VERBO *ver* **prever**

previsto (2) ADJETIVO

- **Tengo previsto volver mañana.** I plan to return tomorrow.
- **El avión tiene prevista su llegada a las dos.** The plane is due in at two o'clock.
- **Como estaba previsto, ganó él.** As expected, he was the winner.

la **prima** SUSTANTIVO

1 cousin (*pariente*)

2 bonus (*pago extra*)

la **primavera** SUSTANTIVO

spring ◇ *en primavera* in spring

primer *ver* **primero**

primero ADJETIVO, PRONOMBRE (FEM **primera**)

first ◇ *el primer día* the first day ◇ *Primer plato: sopa.* First course: soup. ◇ *Primero vamos a comer.* Let's eat first.

- **en primera fila** in the front row
- **En primer lugar, veamos los datos.** Firstly, let's look at the facts.
- **primer ministro** prime minister
- **Vivo en el primero.** I live on the first floor.
- **Fui la primera en llegar.** I was the first to arrive.
- **Juan es el primero de la clase.** Juan is top of the class.
- **Lo primero es la salud.** The most important thing is your health.
- **El examen será a primeros de mayo.** The exam will be at the beginning of May.

primitivo ADJETIVO

primitive

el **primo** SUSTANTIVO

cousin
♦ **primo segundo** second cousin

la **princesa** SUSTANTIVO
princess (PL princesses)

principal ADJETIVO
main ◊ *el personaje principal* the main character
♦ **Lo principal es estar sano.** The main thing is to stay healthy.

principalmente ADVERBIO
mainly

el **príncipe** SUSTANTIVO
prince

el/la **principiante** SUSTANTIVO
beginner

el **principio** SUSTANTIVO
1 beginning ◊ *El principio del libro es muy interesante.* The beginning of the book is very interesting.
♦ **Al principio parecía fácil.** It seemed easy at first.
♦ **a principios de año** at the beginning of the year
2 principle ◊ *No tiene principios.* He has no principles.
♦ **En principio me parece una buena idea.** On the face of it, it's a good idea.

la **prioridad** SUSTANTIVO
priority (PL priorities)

la **prisa** SUSTANTIVO
rush
♦ **Con las prisas me olvidé el paraguas.** In the rush I forgot my umbrella.
♦ **¡Date prisa!** Hurry up!
♦ **Tengo prisa.** I'm in a hurry.

la **prisión** SUSTANTIVO (PL las **prisiones**)
prison ◊ *Lo condenaron a seis años de prisión.* He was sentenced to six years in prison.

el **prisionero**, la **prisionera** SUSTANTIVO
prisoner

los **prismáticos** SUSTANTIVO
binoculars

privado ADJETIVO
private ◊ *un colegio privado* a private school

privarse VERBO
♦ **En vacaciones no me privo de nada.** When I'm on holiday I really spoil myself.

privatizar* VERBO
to privatize

el **privilegio** SUSTANTIVO
privilege

el **pro** SUSTANTIVO
♦ **los pros y contras** the pros and cons

las **probabilidades** SUSTANTIVO
♦ **Tiene muchas probabilidades de ganar.** He has a very good chance of winning.
♦ **No tengo muchas probabilidades de aprobar.** I don't have much chance of passing.

probable ADJETIVO
likely ◊ *Es muy probable.* It's very likely.
♦ **Es probable que llegue tarde.** He'll probably arrive late.

probablemente ADVERBIO
probably

el **probador** SUSTANTIVO
changing room

probar* VERBO
1 to prove ◊ *La policía no pudo probarlo.* The police could not prove it.
2 to taste ◊ *Probé la sopa para ver si le faltaba sal.* I tasted the soup to see if it needed more salt.
3 to try ◊ *Prueba estas patatas a ver si te gustan.* Try these potatoes and see if you like them. ◊ *Pruébalo antes para ver si funciona bien.* Try it first and see if it works properly.
♦ **Me probé un vestido.** I tried on a dress.

la **probeta** SUSTANTIVO
test tube
♦ **un niño probeta** a test-tube baby

el **problema** SUSTANTIVO
problem ◊ *Tengo que resolver este problema.* I have to solve this problem.
♦ **Este coche nunca me ha dado problemas.** This car has never given me any trouble.
♦ **tener problemas de estómago** to have stomach trouble

procedente ADJETIVO
♦ **procedente de** from ◊ *el tren procedente de Barcelona* the train from Barcelona

el **procesador** SUSTANTIVO
processor
♦ **un procesador de textos** a word processor

el **procesamiento** SUSTANTIVO
♦ **el procesamiento de textos** word processing

la **procesión** SUSTANTIVO (PL las **procesiones**)
procession

el **proceso** SUSTANTIVO
process (PL processes) ◊ *Será un proceso muy largo.* It will be a long process.
♦ **el proceso de datos** data processing

proclamar VERBO
to proclaim

procurar VERBO
to try
♦ **Procura terminarlo mañana.** Try to finish it tomorrow.

la **producción** SUSTANTIVO (PL las **producciones**)
production
♦ **la producción en serie** mass production

producir* VERBO
1 to produce ◊ *La película fue producida por Juan Pérez.* The film was produced by Juan Pérez. ◊ *No producimos lo suficiente.* We are not producing enough.

☞

[2] to cause ◊ *Puede producir efectos secundarios.* It can cause side-effects.
♦ **¿Cómo se produjo el accidente?** How did the accident happen?

productivo ADJETIVO
productive

el **producto** SUSTANTIVO
product ◊ *productos de limpieza* cleaning products ◊ *productos lácteos* dairy products
♦ **los productos del campo** farm produce

el **productor,** la **productora** SUSTANTIVO
producer

la **profesión** SUSTANTIVO (PL las **profesiones**)
profession

el/la **profesional** ADJETIVO, SUSTANTIVO
professional

el **profesor,** la **profesora** SUSTANTIVO
teacher ◊ *Amelia es profesora de inglés.* Amelia is an English teacher.
♦ **mi profesor particular** my private tutor
♦ **un profesor universitario** a university lecturer

No confundir ***profesor*** *con la palabra inglesa* ***professor.***

profundamente ADVERBIO
[1] deeply (*respirar*)
[2] soundly (*dormir*)

la **profundidad** SUSTANTIVO
depth (PL depths) ◊ *la profundidad de la piscina* the depth of the pool ◊ *analizar un texto en profundidad* to analyze a text in depth
♦ **Tiene dos metros de profundidad.** It's two metres deep.

profundo ADJETIVO
deep (*pozo, voz, sueño*)
♦ **una piscina poco profunda** a shallow pool

el **programa** SUSTANTIVO
[1] programme ◊ *un programa de televisión* a television programme
♦ **un programa-concurso** a quiz show
♦ **el programa de estudios** the syllabus
[2] program (*informática*)

la **programación** SUSTANTIVO
[1] programmes PL (*de televisión*)
[2] programming (*en informática*)

el **programador,** la **programadora** SUSTANTIVO
programmer ◊ *Balbino es programador.* Balbino is a programmer.

programar VERBO
to programme ◊ *Programé el vídeo para grabar el partido.* I programmed the video to tape the match.

progresar VERBO
to progress

el **progreso** SUSTANTIVO
progress ◊ *progreso tecnológico* technological progress
♦ **Carmen ha hecho muchos progresos este trimestre.** Carmen has made great progress this term.

prohibir* VERBO
to ban ◊ *Le prohibieron la entrada en el edificio.* He was banned from entering the building. ◊ *Han prohibido las armas de fuego.* Firearms have been banned.
♦ **queda terminantemente prohibido** it is strictly forbidden
♦ **Te prohíbo que toques mi ordenador.** I won't allow you to touch my computer.
♦ **"prohibido fumar"** "no smoking"

prolijo ADJETIVO River Plate
neat

el **prólogo** SUSTANTIVO
prologue

prolongar* VERBO
to extend

el **promedio** SUSTANTIVO
average

la **promesa** SUSTANTIVO
promise

prometer VERBO
to promise ◊ *Prometió llevarnos al cine.* He promised to take us to the cinema.
♦ **¡Te lo prometo!** I promise!

el **pronombre** SUSTANTIVO
pronoun

pronosticar* VERBO
to forecast

el **pronóstico** SUSTANTIVO
♦ **el pronóstico del tiempo** the weather forecast

pronto ADVERBIO
[1] soon (*dentro de poco*) ◊ *Los invitados llegarán pronto.* The guests will be here soon.
♦ **lo más pronto posible** as soon as possible
♦ **¡Hasta pronto!** See you soon!
[2] early (*temprano*) ◊ *¿Por qué has llegado tan pronto?* Why have you arrived so early? ◊ *Hoy me he levantado muy pronto.* I got up very early today.
♦ **De pronto, empezó a nevar.** All of a sudden it began to snow.

pronunciar VERBO
to pronounce ◊ *¿Cómo se pronuncia esta palabra?* How do you pronounce that word?

la **propaganda** SUSTANTIVO
[1] advertising ◊ *Las revistas están llenas de propaganda.* Magazines are full of advertising.
♦ **Han hecho mucha propaganda del concierto.** The concert has been well-advertised.
[2] junk mail ◊ *Los buzones están llenos de propaganda.* The letterboxes are full of junk mail.

* Verbs marked with this symbol are irregular. See pages 380-382 for further details

propagarse* VERBO
to spread

la **propiedad** SUSTANTIVO
property (PL properties)

el **propietario**, la **propietaria** SUSTANTIVO
owner

la **propina** SUSTANTIVO
tip ◊ *¿Vamos a dejar propina?* Shall we leave a tip?
♦ **Siempre doy propina a los camareros.** I always tip waiters.

propio ADJETIVO
1 own ◊ *Tengo mi propia habitación.* I have my own room.
2 himself (FEM herself) ◊ *Lo anunció el propio ministro.* It was announced by the minister himself.
3 typical ◊ *Eso es muy propio de los países mediterráneos.* That's very typical of the Mediterranean countries.
♦ **un nombre propio** a proper noun

proponer* VERBO
1 to suggest ◊ *Nos propuso pagar la cena a medias.* He suggested that we should share the cost of the meal.
♦ **Me propuso un trato.** He made me a proposition.
2 to nominate ◊ *Propusieron a Manuel para alcalde.* Manuel was nominated for mayor.
♦ **Se ha propuesto adelgazar.** He's decided to lose some weight.

la **proporción** SUSTANTIVO (PL las **proporciones**)
proportion

proporcional ADJETIVO
proportional

proporcionar VERBO
to provide ◊ *Ellos me proporcionaron la información.* They provided me with the information.

el **propósito** SUSTANTIVO
purpose ◊ *¿Cuál es el propósito de su visita?* What is the purpose of your visit?
♦ **A propósito, ya tengo los billetes.** By the way, I've got the tickets.
♦ **Lo hizo a propósito.** He did it deliberately.

la **propuesta** SUSTANTIVO
proposal

propuesto VERBO *ver* **proponer**

la **prórroga** SUSTANTIVO
1 extension (*de plazo*)
2 extra time (*de partido*)

el **prospecto** SUSTANTIVO
leaflet

prosperar VERBO
to do well

próspero ADJETIVO
♦ **¡Próspero Año Nuevo!** A prosperous New Year!

la **prostituta** SUSTANTIVO
prostitute

el/la **protagonista** SUSTANTIVO
main character ◊ *El protagonista no muere en la película.* The main character doesn't die in the film.
♦ **El protagonista es Tom Cruise.** Tom Cruise plays the lead.

la **protección** SUSTANTIVO
protection

protector ADJETIVO (FEM **protectora**)
protective ◊ *una funda protectora* a protective cover

proteger* VERBO
to protect ◊ *El muro le protegió de las balas.* The wall protected him from the bullets.
♦ **Nos protegimos de la lluvia en la cabaña.** We sheltered from the rain in the hut.

la **proteína** SUSTANTIVO
protein

la **protesta** SUSTANTIVO
protest ◊ *como protesta por los despidos* as a protest against redundancies

el/la **protestante** ADJETIVO, SUSTANTIVO
Protestant

protestar VERBO
1 to protest ◊ *Protestaron contra la subida de la gasolina.* They protested against the rise in the price of petrol.
2 to complain ◊ *Cómete la verdura y no protestes.* Eat your vegetables and don't complain.

el **provecho** SUSTANTIVO
♦ **¡Buen provecho!** Enjoy your meal!
♦ **Sacó mucho provecho del curso.** He got a lot out of the course.

el **proverbio** SUSTANTIVO
proverb

la **provincia** SUSTANTIVO
province

provisional ADJETIVO
provisional

las **provisiones** SUSTANTIVO
provisions

provocar* VERBO
1 to provoke ◊ *No quería pegarle pero me provocó.* I didn't mean to hit him but he provoked me.
2 to cause ◊ *La lluvia ha provocado graves inundaciones.* The rain caused serious flooding.
♦ **El incendio fue provocado.** The fire was started deliberately.

provocativo ADJETIVO
provocative

próximo ADJETIVO
next ◊ *Lo haremos la próxima semana.* We'll do it next week. ◊ *la próxima vez* next time ◊ *la próxima calle a la izquierda* the next street on the left

P

proyectar VERBO
1 to show (*diapositivas, película*)
2 to cast (*sombra*)
◆ **la imagen que un país proyecta al extranjero** the image a country projects abroad

el **proyectil** SUSTANTIVO
missile

el **proyecto** SUSTANTIVO
1 plan ◇ *¿Tienes algún proyecto para este verano?* Have you got any plans for the summer?
2 project ◇ *el proyecto en el que estamos trabajando* the project we are working on
◆ **un proyecto de ley** a bill

el **proyector** SUSTANTIVO
projector

prudente ADJETIVO
wise ◇ *Lo más prudente sería esperar.* It would be wisest to wait.
◆ **Debería ser más prudente.** He should be more careful.

prueba VERBO *ver* **probar**

la **prueba** SUSTANTIVO
1 test ◇ *El médico me hizo más pruebas.* The doctor did some more tests.
◆ **pruebas nucleares** nuclear tests
2 proof ◇ *Eso es la prueba de que lo hizo él.* This is the proof that he did it.
◆ **El fiscal presentó nuevas pruebas.** The prosecutor presented new evidence.
3 heat ◇ *la prueba de los cien metros valla* the hundred metres hurdles heat
◆ **a prueba de balas** bullet-proof

pruebo VERBO *ver* **probar**

la **psicóloga** SUSTANTIVO
psychologist

la **psicología** SUSTANTIVO
psychology

psicológico ADJETIVO
psychological

el **psicólogo** SUSTANTIVO
psychologist

el/la **psiquiatra** SUSTANTIVO
psychiatrist

psiquiátrico ADJETIVO
psychiatric

ptas. ABREVIATURA (= *pesetas*)
pesetas

la **púa** SUSTANTIVO
1 (*para guitarra*)
plectrum
2 (*de peine*)
tooth (PL teeth)

el **pub** SUSTANTIVO (PL los **pubs**)
bar

publicar* VERBO
to publish

la **publicidad** SUSTANTIVO
1 advertising (*de producto*) ◇ *una campaña de publicidad* an advertising campaign
2 publicity (*de suceso, persona*) ◇ *La conferencia tuvo poca publicidad.* The conference received little publicity.

público ADJETIVO
public

el **público** SUSTANTIVO
1 public ◇ *cerrado al público* closed to the public
2 audience (*en teatro, concierto*)
3 spectators PL (*en campo de deporte*)

pude VERBO *ver* **poder**

pudrirse VERBO
to rot

el **pueblo** SUSTANTIVO
1 village (*pequeño*)
2 town (*más grande*)
3 people PL ◇ *El pueblo está a favor de la democracia.* The people are in favour of democracy.

puedo VERBO *ver* **poder**

el **puente** SUSTANTIVO
bridge
◆ **el puente aéreo** the shuttle service
◆ **hacer puente** to make a long weekend of it

> *When a public holiday falls on a Tuesday or Thursday people often take off Monday or Friday as well to give themselves a long weekend.*

el **puerco** SUSTANTIVO
1 pig (*animal*)
2 pork (*carne*) Mexico

el **puerro** SUSTANTIVO
leek

la **puerta** SUSTANTIVO
1 door
◆ **un coche de 4 puertas** a 4-door car
2 gate (*de jardín*)
◆ **Llaman a la puerta.** Somebody's at the door.
◆ **Susana me acompañó a la puerta.** Susana saw me out.
◆ **la puerta de embarque** boarding gate

el **puerto** SUSTANTIVO
port ◇ *un puerto pesquero* a fishing port
◆ **un puerto deportivo** a marina
◆ **un puerto de montaña** a mountain pass

Puerto Rico SUSTANTIVO MASC
Puerto Rico

el **puertorriqueño**, la **puertorriqueña** ADJETIVO, SUSTANTIVO
Puerto Rican

pues CONJUNCIÓN
1 then ◇ *Tengo sueño. – ¡Pues vete a la cama!* I'm tired. – Then go to bed!

* Verbs marked with this symbol are irregular. See pages 380-382 for further details

[2] well ◊ *Pues, como te iba contando ...* Well, as I was saying ... ◊ *¡Pues no lo sabía!* Well I didn't know!
♦ **¡Pues claro!** Yes, of course!

la **puesta** SUSTANTIVO
♦ **la puesta de sol** sunset
♦ **la puesta en libertad de dos presos** the release of two prisoners

puesto VERBO *ver* **poner**

el **puesto** SUSTANTIVO
[1] place ◊ *Acabé la carrera en primer puesto.* I finished in first place.
[2] stall ◊ *un puesto de verduras* a vegetable stall
♦ **un puesto de trabajo** a job
♦ **un puesto de socorro** a first aid station
♦ **puesto que** since ◊ *Puesto que no lo querías, se lo di a Pedro.* Since you didn't want it, I gave it to Pedro.

la **pulga** SUSTANTIVO
flea

la **pulgada** SUSTANTIVO
inch (PL inches)

el **pulgar** SUSTANTIVO
thumb

pulir VERBO
to polish

el **pulmón** SUSTANTIVO (PL los **pulmones**)
lung

la **pulpería** SUSTANTIVO Latin America
shop

el **púlpito** SUSTANTIVO
pulpit

el **pulpo** SUSTANTIVO
octopus (PL octopuses) ◊ *Me gusta el pulpo.* I like octopus.

pulsar VERBO
to press

la **pulsera** SUSTANTIVO
bracelet
♦ **un reloj de pulsera** a wrist watch

el **pulso** SUSTANTIVO
pulse ◊ *El doctor le tomó el pulso.* The doctor took his pulse.
♦ **Tengo muy mal pulso.** My hand is very unsteady.
♦ **Echamos un pulso y le gané.** We had an arm-wrestling match and I won.
♦ **Lo levantó a pulso.** He lifted it with his bare hands.

el **pulverizador** SUSTANTIVO
spray

el/la **punk** ADJETIVO, SUSTANTIVO
punk

la **punta** SUSTANTIVO
[1] nail (*clavo*)
[2] tip (*de dedo, lengua*)
[3] point (*de bolígrafo, cuchillo*)
♦ **Sácale punta al lápiz.** Sharpen your pencil.
♦ **Vivo en la otra punta del pueblo.** I live at the other end of the town.
♦ **la hora punta** the rush hour

el **puntapié** SUSTANTIVO (PL los **puntapiés**)
♦ **Le dio un puntapié a la piedra.** He kicked the stone.

la **puntería** SUSTANTIVO
♦ **tener buena puntería** to be a good shot

puntiagudo ADJETIVO
pointed

la **puntilla** SUSTANTIVO
lace edging
♦ **andar de puntillas** to tiptoe
♦ **ponerse de puntillas** to stand on tiptoe

el **punto** SUSTANTIVO
[1] point ◊ *Perdieron por tres puntos.* They lost by three points. ◊ *Ése es un punto importante.* That's an important point. ◊ *desde ese punto de vista* from that point of view
[2] (*en costura, cirugía*)
stitch (PL stitches)
[3] (*sobre la "i"*)
dot
[4] (*al final de una frase*)
full stop
♦ **punto y seguido** full stop, new sentence
♦ **punto y aparte** full stop, new paragraph
♦ **punto y coma** semi-colon
♦ **dos puntos** colon
♦ **puntos suspensivos** dot, dot, dot
♦ **Estábamos a punto de salir cuando llamaste.** We were about to go out when you phoned.
♦ **Mila estaba a punto de llorar.** Mila was on the verge of tears.
♦ **Estuve a punto de perder el tren.** I very nearly missed the train.
♦ **a la una en punto** at one o'clock sharp
♦ **Me gusta hacer punto.** I like knitting.

la **puntuación** SUSTANTIVO (PL las **puntuaciones**)
[1] punctuation ◊ *los signos de puntuación* punctuation marks
[2] score ◊ *Recibió una alta puntuación.* He got a high score.

puntual ADJETIVO
[1] punctual ◊ *Sé puntual.* Be punctual.
♦ **Jamás llega puntual.** He never arrives on time.
[2] specific ◊ *Sólo trató aspectos puntuales del tema.* He only dealt with specific aspects of the subject.

la **puntualidad** SUSTANTIVO
punctuality

puntuar* VERBO
♦ **Este trabajo no puntúa para la nota final.** This essay doesn't count towards the final mark.
♦ **un profesor que puntúa muy bajo** a teacher who gives very low marks

el **puñado** SUSTANTIVO
handful ◊ *un puñado de arena* a handful of sand

el **puñal** SUSTANTIVO

P

☞

dagger

la **puñalada** SUSTANTIVO
◆ **Le dieron una puñalada.** He was stabbed.

el **puñetazo** SUSTANTIVO
punch (PL punches) ◊ *un puñetazo en la cara* a punch in the face
◆ **Le pegó un puñetazo.** He punched him.

el **puño** SUSTANTIVO
1 fist (*mano cerrada*)
2 cuff (*de una camisa*)

la **pupa** SUSTANTIVO
◆ **¿Te has hecho pupa?** Did you hurt yourself?

el **pupitre** SUSTANTIVO
desk

el **puré** SUSTANTIVO (PL los **purés**)
◆ **puré de verduras** puréed vegetables
◆ **puré de patatas** mashed potato

puro ADJETIVO
pure ◊ *pura lana* pure wool ◊ *por pura casualidad* by pure chance
◆ **Es la pura verdad.** That's the absolute truth.
◆ **Son puras mentiras.** Latin America It's all lies.

el **puro** SUSTANTIVO
cigar

el **pus** SUSTANTIVO
pus

puse VERBO *ver* **poner**

Q

que (1) CONJUNCIÓN

[1] than (*en comparaciones*) ◊ *Es más alto que tú.* He's taller than you.

◆ **Yo que tú, iría.** I'd go if I were you.

[2] that (*en oraciones subordinadas*) ◊ *José sabe que estás aquí.* José knows that you're here.

*Es frecuente omitir **that** en el habla normal.*

◊ *Dijo que vendría.* He said he'd come.

◆ **Dile a Rosa que me llame.** Ask Rosa to call me.

Cuando introduce frases exclamativas no se traduce.

◆ **¡Que te mejores!** Get well soon!

◆ **¿De verdad que te gusta? – ¡Que sí!** Do you really like it? – Of course I do!

que (2) PRONOMBRE

[1] which ◊ *la película que ganó el premio* the film which won the award

Es frecuente omitir el pronombre en el habla normal cuando no funciona como sujeto.

◊ *el sombrero que te compraste* the hat you bought ◊ *el libro del que te hablé* the book I spoke to you about

[2] who ◊ *el hombre que vino ayer* the man who came yesterday

Es frecuente omitir el pronombre en el habla normal cuando no funciona como sujeto.

◊ *la chica que conocí* the girl I met

qué ADJETIVO, ADVERBIO, PRONOMBRE

[1] what

En preguntas en general.

◊ *¿Qué fecha es hoy?* What's today's date? ◊ *No sabe qué es.* He doesn't know what it is. ◊ *No sé qué hacer.* I don't know what to do.

◆ **¿qué?** what?

[2] which

Cuando se pregunta cuál en concreto.

◊ *¿Qué película quieres ver?* Which film do you want to see?

◆ **¡Qué asco!** How revolting!

◆ **¡Qué día más bonito!** What a glorious day!

◆ **¿Qué tal?** (*saludo*) How are things?

◆ **¿Qué tal está tu madre?** How's your mother?

◆ **No lo he hecho. ¿Y qué?** (*coloquial*) I haven't done it. So what?

el **quebrado** SUSTANTIVO

fraction

quebrar* VERBO

to go bankrupt (*un negocio*)

◆ **quebrarse** [Latin America] to break ◊ *Alberto se quebró una pierna.* Alberto broke his leg.

quedar VERBO

[1] to be left ◊ *No queda ninguno.* There are none left.

◆ **Me quedan 1.000 pesetas.** I've got 1,000 pesetas left.

[2] to be ◊ *Eso queda muy lejos de aquí.* That's a long way from here.

[3] to arrange to meet ◊ *He quedado con ella en el cine.* I've arranged to meet her at the cinema.

◆ **¿Quedamos en la parada?** Shall we meet at the bus stop?

[4] to suit ◊ *No te queda bien ese vestido.* That dress doesn't suit you.

◆ **quedarse** to stay ◊ *Ve tú, yo me quedo.* You go, I'll stay.

◆ **quedarse atrás** to fall behind

◆ **quedarse sordo** to go deaf

◆ **quedarse con algo** to keep something ◊ *Quédate con el cambio.* Keep the change.

los **quehaceres** SUSTANTIVO

◆ **los quehaceres de la casa** the household chores

la **queja** SUSTANTIVO

complaint

quejarse VERBO

to complain

◆ **quejarse de algo** to complain about something

◆ **quejarse de que ...** to complain that ... ◊ *Pablo se quejó de que nadie lo escuchaba.* Pablo complained that nobody listened to him.

el **quejido** SUSTANTIVO

[1] moan (*de persona*)

[2] whine (*de animal*)

quemado ADJETIVO

burnt

la **quemadura** SUSTANTIVO

burn

◆ **quemaduras de sol** sunburn SING

quemar VERBO

[1] to burn ◊ *Un incendio quemó todo el bosque.* A fire burned the entire forest.

[2] to be burning hot ◊ *Esta sopa quema.* This soup's burning hot.

◆ **quemarse** to burn oneself ◊ *Me quemé con una cerilla.* I burned myself with a match.

quepa VERBO *ver* **caber**

querer* VERBO

[1] to want ◊ *No quiero ir.* I don't want to go.

◆ **Quiero que vayas.** I want you to go.

☞

◆**¿Quieres un café?** Would you like some coffee?
2 to love ◊ *Ana quiere mucho a sus hijos.* Ana loves her children dearly.
3 to mean ◊ *No quería hacerte daño.* I didn't mean to hurt you. ◊ *Lo hice sin querer.* I didn't mean to do it.
◆**querer decir** to mean ◊ *¿Qué quieres decir?* What do you mean?

querido ADJETIVO
dear

querré VERBO *ver* **querer**

el **queso** SUSTANTIVO
cheese

el **quicio** SUSTANTIVO
◆**sacar a alguien de quicio** to drive somebody up the wall

la **quiebra** SUSTANTIVO
◆**ir a la quiebra** to go bankrupt

quien PRONOMBRE
who ◊ *Fue Juan quien nos lo dijo.* It was Juan who told us.

***Quien** generalmente no se traduce cuando no funciona como sujeto.*

◊ *Vi al chico con quien sales.* I saw the boy you're going out with.

quién PRONOMBRE
who ◊ *¿Quién es ésa?* Who's that? ◊ *¿A quién viste?* Who did you see? ◊ *No sé quién es.* I don't know who he is.
◆**¿De quién es ...?** Whose is ...? ◊ *¿De quién es este libro?* Whose is this book?
◆**¿Quién es? (1)** (*en la puerta*) Who's there?
◆**¿Quién es? (2)** (*al teléfono*) Who's calling?

quiero VERBO *ver* **querer**

quieto ADJETIVO
still
◆**¡Estáte quieto!** Keep still!

la **química** SUSTANTIVO
1 chemistry (*ciencia*) ◊ *clase de química* chemistry class
2 chemist (*persona*) ◊ *Es química.* She's a chemist.

el **químico** SUSTANTIVO
chemist ◊ *Es químico.* He's a chemist.

quince ADJETIVO, PRONOMBRE
fifteen
◆**el quince de enero** the fifteenth of January
◆**quince días** a fortnight

el **quinceañero**, la **quinceañera** SUSTANTIVO
teenager

la **quincena** SUSTANTIVO
fortnight

quincenal ADJETIVO
fortnightly

la **quiniela** SUSTANTIVO
football pools PL

quinientos ADJETIVO, PRONOMBRE (FEM **quinientas**)
five hundred

quinto ADJETIVO, PRONOMBRE (FEM **quinta**)
fifth
◆**Vivo en el quinto.** I live on the fifth floor.

el **quiosco** SUSTANTIVO
1 news stand (*de periódicos*)
2 drinks stand (*de refrescos*)
3 flower stall (*de flores*)
4 bandstand (*de banda de música*)

el **quirófano** SUSTANTIVO
operating theatre

quirúrgico ADJETIVO
surgical
◆**una intervención quirúrgica** an operation

quise VERBO *ver* **querer**

quisquilloso ADJETIVO
1 fussy ◊ *No soy quisquillosa con la comida.* I'm not fussy about what I eat.
2 touchy ◊ *Está muy quisquilloso últimamente.* He's been very touchy lately.

el **quitaesmalte** SUSTANTIVO
nail polish remover

el **quitamanchas** SUSTANTIVO (PL los **quitamanchas**)
stain remover

la **quitanieves** SUSTANTIVO (PL las **quitanieves**)
snowplough

quitar VERBO
1 to remove ◊ *Tardaron dos días en quitar los escombros.* It took two days to remove the rubble. ◊ *Este producto quita todo tipo de manchas.* This product removes all types of stain.
2 to take away ◊ *Su hermana le quitó la pelota.* His sister took the ball away from him.
◆**Me han quitado la cartera.** I've had my wallet stolen.
◆**Esto te quitará el dolor.** This will relieve the pain.
◆**quitarse** to take off ◊ *Juan se quitó la chaqueta.* Juan took his jacket off.
◆**¡Quítate de en medio!** Get out of the way!

quizá ADVERBIO = **quizás**

quizás ADVERBIO
perhaps

R

el **rábano** SUSTANTIVO
radish (PL radishes)
♦ **¡Me importa un rábano!** I don't give a monkey's!

la **rabia** SUSTANTIVO
1 rage ◊ *Lo hizo por rabia.* He did it out of rage.
♦ **Me da mucha rabia.** It's really annoying.
2 rabies SING ◊ *Vacunamos al perro contra la rabia.* We had the dog vaccinated against rabies.

la **rabieta** SUSTANTIVO
tantrum
♦ **agarrarse una rabieta** to throw a tantrum

el **rabo** SUSTANTIVO
tail

la **racha** SUSTANTIVO
♦ **una racha de buen tiempo** a spell of good weather
♦ **una racha de viento** a gust of wind
♦ **pasar una mala racha** to go through a bad patch

racial ADJETIVO
racial

el **racimo** SUSTANTIVO
bunch (PL bunches)

la **ración** SUSTANTIVO (PL las **raciones**)
portion

el **racismo** SUSTANTIVO
racism

el/la **racista** ADJETIVO, SUSTANTIVO
racist

el **radar** SUSTANTIVO
radar
♦ **"velocidad controlada por radar"** "radar speed checks in operation"

la **radiación** SUSTANTIVO
radiation

la **radiactividad** SUSTANTIVO
radioactivity

radiactivo ADJETIVO
radioactive

el **radiador** SUSTANTIVO
radiator

la **radio** SUSTANTIVO
radio ◊ *Por la mañana escucho la radio.* In the morning I listen to the radio.
♦ **Lo oí por la radio.** I heard it on the radio.

el **radio** SUSTANTIVO
1 (*de círculo*)
radius (PL radii *o* radiuses) ◊ *La explosión se oyó en un radio de 50 kilómetros.* The explosion could be heard within a 50-kilometre radius.
2 (*medio de comunicación*)
radio Latin America
3 (*de rueda*)
spoke

el **radiocasete** SUSTANTIVO
radio cassette player

la **radiografía** SUSTANTIVO
X-ray
♦ **Tengo que hacerme una radiografía.** I've got to have an X-ray.

el **radiotaxi** SUSTANTIVO
radio taxi

el **raíl** SUSTANTIVO
rail

la **raíz** SUSTANTIVO (PL las **raíces**)
root
♦ **La planta está echando raíces.** The plant's taking root.
♦ **a raíz de** as a result of

la **raja** SUSTANTIVO
1 crack (*grieta*)
2 tear (*rotura en tela*)
3 slice (*de melón, limón*)

rajarse VERBO
1 to crack (*pared, espejo*)
2 to split (*falda, tapicería*)

rallar VERBO
to grate

el **rally** SUSTANTIVO (PL los **rallys**)
rally (PL rallies)

la **rama** SUSTANTIVO
branch (PL branches)

el **ramo** SUSTANTIVO
bunch (PL bunches) ◊ *un ramo de claveles* a bunch of carnations
♦ **el ramo textil** the textile industry

la **rampa** SUSTANTIVO
ramp

la **rana** SUSTANTIVO
frog

la **ranchera** SUSTANTIVO
1 Mexican folk song (*canción*)
2 estate car (*automóvil*)

el **rancho** SUSTANTIVO
(*hacienda*)
ranch (PL ranches)

rancio ADJETIVO
rancid (*mantequilla, queso*)

el **rango** SUSTANTIVO
rank
♦ **políticos de alto rango** high-ranking politicians

la **ranura** SUSTANTIVO
slot ◊ *Introduzca la moneda en la ranura.* Put the coin in the slot.

rapar VERBO
1 to crop (*pelo*)
2 to shave (*cabeza*)

el **rape** SUSTANTIVO
(*pescado*)
monkfish (PL monkfish)

rápidamente ADVERBIO

☞

quickly

la **rapidez** SUSTANTIVO
speed
◆ **con rapidez** quickly

rápido (1) ADJETIVO
1 fast (*veloz*) ◊ *un coche muy rápido* a very fast car
2 quick (*de poca duración*) ◊ *Fue una visita muy rápida.* It was a very quick visit.

rápido (2) ADVERBIO
fast ◊ *Conduces demasiado rápido.* You drive too fast.
◆ **Lo hice tan rápido como pude.** I did it as quickly as I could.
◆ **¡Rápido!** Hurry up!

raptar VERBO
to kidnap

el **rapto** SUSTANTIVO
kidnapping

la **raqueta** SUSTANTIVO
1 racket (*de tenis, bádminton*)
2 bat (*de ping-pong*)

raramente ADVERBIO
rarely

raro ADJETIVO
1 strange (*extraño*) ◊ *Tiene unas costumbres muy raras.* He has some very strange habits.
◆ **¡Qué raro!** How strange!
◆ **Sabe un poco raro.** It tastes a bit funny.
2 rare (*poco frecuente*) ◊ *una especie muy rara* a very rare species
◆ **Es raro que haga tan buen tiempo.** It's unusual to have such good weather.
◆ **rara vez** seldom

el **rascacielos** SUSTANTIVO (PL los **rascacielos**)
skyscraper

rascar* VERBO
1 to scratch (*con las uñas*) ◊ *¿Me rascas la espalda?* Could you scratch my back for me?
2 to scrape (*con cuchillo, espátula*) ◊ *Tuvimos que rascar la pintura de la puerta.* We had to scrape the paint off the door.
◆ **rascarse** to scratch ◊ *No deja de rascarse.* He can't stop scratching.

rasgar* VERBO
to rip

el **rasgo** SUSTANTIVO
feature ◊ *Tiene unos rasgos muy delicados.* He has very fine features.

el **rasguño** SUSTANTIVO
scratch (PL scratches)
◆ **Me he hecho un rasguño.** I've scratched myself.

el **rastrillo** SUSTANTIVO
1 rake (*herramienta*)
2 razor (*de afeitar*) Mexico

el **rastro** SUSTANTIVO
1 trail (*pista, huellas*) ◊ *seguir el rastro de alguien* to follow somebody's trail
2 trace ◊ *Desaparecieron sin dejar rastro.* They vanished without trace.
3 fleamarket (*mercadillo*)

rasurarse VERBO Latin America
to shave

la **rata** SUSTANTIVO
rat

el **rato** SUSTANTIVO
while ◊ *después de un rato* after a while
◆ **Estaba aquí hace un rato.** He was here a few minutes ago.
◆ **al poco rato** shortly after
◆ **pasar el rato** to while away the time
◆ **pasar un buen rato** to have a good time
◆ **Pasamos un mal rato.** We had a dreadful time.
◆ **en mis ratos libres** in my free time
◆ **Tengo para rato con esta redacción.** I've got a way to go yet with this essay.
◆ **Tenemos para rato; el avión tiene retraso.** We'll be here for a while yet; the plane has been delayed.

el **ratón** SUSTANTIVO (PL los **ratones**)
(*también informática*)
mouse (PL mice)

la **raya** SUSTANTIVO
1 line ◊ *trazar una raya* to draw a line
◆ **pasarse de la raya** to overstep the mark
2 stripe
◆ **un jersey a rayas** a striped jumper
3 parting ◊ *Me hago la raya en medio.* I have my parting in the middle.
4 (*del pantalón*)
crease (PL creases)
5 (*guión largo*)
dash (PL dashes)

rayar VERBO
to scratch

el **rayo** SUSTANTIVO
1 lightning ◊ *Cayó un rayo en la torre de la iglesia.* The church tower was struck by lightning.
2 ray ◊ *un rayo de luz* a ray of light ◊ *los rayos del sol* the sun's rays
◆ **los rayos X** X-rays
◆ **los rayos láser** laser beams

la **raza** SUSTANTIVO
1 race ◊ *la raza humana* the human race
2 breed (*de animal*) ◊ *¿De qué raza es tu gato?* What breed's your cat?
◆ **un perro de raza** a pedigree dog

la **razón** SUSTANTIVO (PL las **razones**)
reason ◊ *¿Cuál era la razón de su visita?* What was the reason for his visit?
◆ **tener razón** to be right
◆ **dar la razón a alguien** to agree that somebody is right
◆ **no tener razón** to be wrong

razonable ADJETIVO

* Verbs marked with this symbol are irregular. See pages 380-382 for further details

reasonable

la **reacción** SUSTANTIVO (PL las **reacciones**)
reaction

reaccionar VERBO
to react

el **reactor** SUSTANTIVO
1 jet plane (*avión*)
2 jet engine (*motor*)
◆ **un reactor nuclear** a nuclear reactor

real ADJETIVO
1 real ◇ *Esta vez el dolor era real.* This time the pain was real.
◆ **La película está basada en hechos reales.** The film is based on actual events.
2 royal ◇ *la familia real* the royal family

la **realidad** SUSTANTIVO
reality (PL realities)
◆ **en la realidad** in real life
◆ **en realidad** actually ◇ *Parece mayor, pero en realidad es más joven que yo.* He looks older but actually he's younger than I am.
◆ **Mi sueño se hizo realidad.** My dream came true.
◆ **realidad virtual** virtual reality

realista ADJETIVO
realistic

realizar* VERBO
1 to carry out (*proyecto, encuesta*) ◇ *realizar una investigación* to carry out an investigation
◆ **Has realizado un buen trabajo.** You've done a good job.
2 to realize (*ilusión, ambición*) ◇ *Nunca realizó su sueño de dar la vuelta al mundo.* He never realized his dream of going round the world.
◆ **realizarse** to come true ◇ *Su sueño nunca llegó a realizarse.* His dream never came true.

realmente ADVERBIO
1 really ◇ *Fue una época realmente difícil.* It was a really difficult period.
2 actually ◇ *No creí que realmente ganara.* I didn't think he would actually win.

la **rebaja** SUSTANTIVO
1 discount ◇ *Me hizo una rebaja por pagar al contado.* He gave me a discount for paying cash.
2 reduction ◇ *La blusa tenía una mancha y pedí una rebaja.* There was a mark on the blouse so I asked for a reduction.
◆ **las rebajas** the sales ◇ *las rebajas de enero* the January sales
◆ **Todos los grandes almacenes están de rebajas.** There are sales on in all the department stores.

rebajar VERBO
to reduce (*artículo, precio*) ◇ *Han rebajado los abrigos.* Coats have been reduced. ◇ *Cada fin de temporada rebajan los precios.* Prices are reduced at the end of every season.
◆ **rebajarse** to demean oneself ◇ *No quiere rebajarse a pedirme perdón.* He won't demean himself by apologizing to me.

la **rebanada** SUSTANTIVO
slice ◇ *Cortó el pan en rebanadas.* He cut the bread into slices.

el **rebaño** SUSTANTIVO
flock ◇ *un rebaño de ovejas* a flock of sheep

la **rebeca** SUSTANTIVO
cardigan

rebelarse VERBO
to rebel ◇ *rebelarse contra alguien* to rebel against somebody

rebelde ADJETIVO
rebellious (*muchacho, carácter*)

el/la **rebelde** SUSTANTIVO
rebel

la **rebelión** SUSTANTIVO (PL las **rebeliones**)
rebellion

rebobinar VERBO
to rewind

rebotar VERBO
to bounce
◆ **La pelota rebotó en el poste.** The ball bounced off the post.

rebozado ADJETIVO
1 breaded (*empanado*)
2 battered (*con huevo y harina*)

el **recado** SUSTANTIVO
1 message ◇ *Dejé recado de que me llamara.* I left a message for him to call me.
2 errand ◇ *Fui a hacer unos recados.* I went to do some errands.

la **recaída** SUSTANTIVO
relapse ◇ *sufrir una recaída* to have a relapse

recalcar* VERBO
to stress ◇ *Me gustaría recalcar que ...* I'd like to stress that ...

la **recámara** SUSTANTIVO Mexico
bedroom

el **recambio** SUSTANTIVO
1 spare ◇ *la rueda de recambio* the spare wheel
◆ **una pieza de recambio** a spare part
2 refill (*de bolígrafo, pluma*)

recargar* VERBO
1 to recharge (*pila*)
2 to fill up (*encendedor, bolígrafo*)

el **recargo** SUSTANTIVO
◆ **El taxista me cobró un recargo por el equipaje.** The taxi driver charged me extra for my luggage.

recaudar VERBO
to collect ◇ *Recaudó dinero para una obra benéfica.* He collected money for a charity.

R

la **recepción** SUSTANTIVO (PL las **recepciones**)
reception

el/la **recepcionista** SUSTANTIVO
receptionist

el **receptor** SUSTANTIVO
receiver (*de teléfono, radio*)

la **recesión** SUSTANTIVO (PL las **recesiones**)
recession

la **receta** SUSTANTIVO
1 recipe ◊ *Me dio la receta de los raviolis.* He gave me the recipe for the ravioli.
2 prescription ◊ *Los antibióticos sólo se venden con receta.* Antibiotics are only available on prescription.

*No confundir **receta** con **receipt**.*

recetar VERBO
to prescribe ◊ *Las enfermeras no pueden recetar medicamentos.* Nurses can't prescribe drugs.
◆ **El médico me recetó un jarabe.** The doctor gave me a prescription for cough syrup.

rechazar* VERBO
1 to reject (*sugerencia, idea*) ◊ *El director rechazó mi propuesta.* The manager rejected my proposal.
2 to turn down (*oferta, candidato*) ◊ *Tuve que rechazar su oferta.* I had to turn down his offer.

rechoncho ADJETIVO
stocky

el **recibidor** SUSTANTIVO
entrance hall

recibir VERBO
1 to receive ◊ *No he recibido tu carta.* I haven't received your letter.
◆ **Recibí muchos regalos.** (*coloquial*) I got a lot of presents.
2 to meet ◊ *Vinieron a recibirnos al aeropuerto.* They came and met us at the airport.
◆ **El director me recibió en su despacho.** The manager saw me in his office.

el **recibo** SUSTANTIVO
1 receipt ◊ *No se admiten devoluciones sin recibo.* No refunds will be given without a receipt.
2 bill ◊ *pagar el recibo del teléfono* to pay the telephone bill

el **reciclaje** SUSTANTIVO
recycling

reciclar VERBO
to recycle

recién ADVERBIO
just ◊ *El comedor está recién pintado.* The dining room has just been painted.
◆ **Recién se fueron.** Latin America They've just left.
◆ **los recién casados** the newly-weds
◆ **un recién nacido** a newborn baby
◆ **"recién pintado"** "wet paint"

reciente ADJETIVO
recent
◆ **pan reciente** fresh bread

recientemente ADVERBIO
recently

el **recipiente** SUSTANTIVO
container

el **recital** SUSTANTIVO
recital (*de música*) ◊ *dar un recital de piano* to give a piano recital

recitar VERBO
to recite

la **reclamación** SUSTANTIVO (PL las **reclamaciones**)
complaint ◊ *presentar una reclamación* to make a complaint
◆ **el libro de reclamaciones** the complaints' book

reclamar VERBO
1 to complain (*protestar*) ◊ *Fui a reclamar al director.* I went and complained to the manager.
2 to demand ◊ *Reclaman mejores condiciones de trabajo.* They're demanding better working conditions.

el **reclamo** SUSTANTIVO Latin America
complaint (*queja*)

el/la **recluta** SUSTANTIVO
recruit

el **recogedor** SUSTANTIVO
dustpan

recoger* VERBO
1 to pick up (*objeto, persona*) ◊ *Se agachó para recoger la cuchara.* He bent down to pick up the spoon. ◊ *Recogí el papel del suelo.* I picked the paper up off the floor. ◊ *Me recogieron en la estación.* They picked me up at the station.
◆ **recoger fruta** to pick fruit
2 to collect (*recolectar*) ◊ *A las diez recogen la basura.* The rubbish gets collected at ten o'clock.
3 to clear up (*ordenar*) ◊ *Recógelo todo antes de marcharte.* Clear up everything before you leave.
◆ **Recogí los platos y los puse en el fregadero.** I cleared away the plates and put them in the sink.
◆ **recoger la mesa** to clear the table

la **recogida** SUSTANTIVO
collection ◊ *la recogida de basura* the refuse collection ◊ *el horario de recogida del correo* the mail collection times
◆ **recogida de equipajes** baggage reclaim

la **recomendación** SUSTANTIVO (PL las **recomendaciones**)
1 recommendation (*sugerencia*) ◊ *Fuimos a ese restaurante por recomendación de un amigo.* We went to

that restaurant on the recommendation of a friend.

◆ **una carta de recomendación** a letter of recommendation

[2] advice (*consejo*) ◊ *Hago régimen por recomendación del médico.* I'm on a diet on my doctor's advice.

recomendar* VERBO
to recommend

la **recompensa** SUSTANTIVO
reward ◊ *Ofrecen una recompensa de 10.000 pesetas.* They're offering a 10,000-peseta reward.

reconciliarse VERBO
◆ **reconciliarse con alguien** to make it up with somebody ◊ *Riñeron, pero se han vuelto a reconciliar.* They had a row but they've made it up again.

reconocer* VERBO
[1] to recognize ◊ *No te he reconocido con ese sombrero.* I didn't recognize you in that hat.
[2] to admit ◊ *Reconócelo, ha sido culpa tuya.* Admit it, it was your fault.

el **reconocimiento** SUSTANTIVO
checkup ◊ *hacerse un reconocimiento médico* to have a checkup

la **reconquista** SUSTANTIVO
reconquest

reconstruir* VERBO
to rebuild

el **récord** SUSTANTIVO (PL los **récords**)
record ◊ *Posee el récord mundial de salto de altura.* He holds the world record in the high jump.

◆ **batir el récord** to break the record

◆ **establecer un récord** to set a record

recordar* VERBO
[1] to remember ◊ *No recuerdo dónde lo puse.* I can't remember where I put it.
[2] to remind ◊ *Recuérdame que hable con Daniel.* Remind me to speak to Daniel. ◊ *Me recuerda a su padre.* He reminds me of his father.

*No confundir **recordar** con **to record.***

recorrer VERBO
[1] to travel around ◊ *Recorrimos Francia en moto.* We travelled around France on a motorbike.
[2] to do ◊ *Ese día recorrimos 100 kilómetros.* We did 100 kilometres that day.

el **recorrido** SUSTANTIVO
◆ **¿Qué recorrido hace este autobús?** Which route does this bus take?

◆ **un recorrido turístico** a tour

◆ **un tren de largo recorrido** an inter-city train

recortar VERBO
to cut out ◊ *Recorté el artículo para enseñárselo a Pedro.* I cut the article out to show it to Pedro.

◆ **recortar gastos** to cut costs

el **recorte** SUSTANTIVO
◆ **recortes de prensa** press cuttings

◆ **recortes de personal** staff cutbacks

recostarse* VERBO
to lie down ◊ *Se recostó en el sofá.* He lay down on the settee.

el **recreo** SUSTANTIVO
break ◊ *Tenemos 20 minutos de recreo.* We have a 20-minute break.

◆ **Salimos al recreo a las 11.** We have a break at 11 o'clock.

◆ **la hora del recreo** playtime

la **recta** SUSTANTIVO
straight line

◆ **la recta final** the home straight (*en carrera*)

rectangular ADJETIVO
rectangular

el **rectángulo** SUSTANTIVO
rectangle

recto ADJETIVO, ADVERBIO
straight ◊ *una línea recta* a straight line ◊ *Mantén la espalda recta.* Keep your back straight.

◆ **todo recto** straight on ◊ *Siga todo recto.* Go straight on.

el **recuadro** SUSTANTIVO
box (PL boxes)

recuerdo VERBO *ver* **recordar**

el **recuerdo** SUSTANTIVO
[1] memory (PL memories) ◊ *Me trae buenos recuerdos.* It brings back happy memories.
[2] souvenir ◊ *una tienda de recuerdos* a souvenir shop

◆ **un recuerdo de familia** a family heirloom

◆ **¡Recuerdos a tu madre!** Give my regards to your mother!

◆ **Dale recuerdos de mi parte.** Give him my regards.

la **recuperación** SUSTANTIVO (PL las **recuperaciones**)
[1] recovery (*de un enfermo*)
[2] resit (*examen*)

recuperar VERBO
to get back ◊ *Tardé unos minutos en recuperar el aliento.* It took me a few minutes to get my breath back.

◆ **recuperar fuerzas** to get one's strength back

◆ **recuperarse de (1)** (*gripe, resfriado*) to get over ◊ *Tardé una semana en recuperarme de la gripe.* It took me a week to get over my flu.

◆ **recuperarse de (2)** (*operación, infarto*) to recover from ◊ *Se está recuperando de la operación.* He's recovering from the operation.

◆ **recuperar el tiempo perdido** to make up for lost time

recurrir VERBO

☞

◆**recurrir a algo** to resort to something ◊ *Hay que evitar recurrir a la violencia.* We must avoid resorting to violence.
◆**recurrir a alguien** to turn to somebody ◊ *¿A quién puedo recurrir?* Who can I turn to?

el **recurso** SUSTANTIVO
◆**como último recurso** as a last resort
◆**recursos** resources ◊ *recursos naturales* natural resources

la **red** SUSTANTIVO
1 net ◊ *una red de pesca* a fishing net ◊ *La pelota dio contra la red.* The ball went into the net.
2 network (*de carreteras, ferrocarriles*) ◊ *una red informática* a computer network
◆**la Red** the Net (*Internet*)
◆**una red de tiendas** a chain of shops

la **redacción** SUSTANTIVO (PL las **redacciones**)
essay (PL essays)
◆**hacer una redacción sobre algo** to do an essay on something
◆**el equipo de redacción** the editorial staff

redactar VERBO
to write ◊ *redactar un artículo de periódico* to write a newspaper article

el **redactor**, la **redactora** SUSTANTIVO
editor ◊ *el redactor deportivo* the sports editor ◊ *la redactora jefe* the editor in chief

la **redada** SUSTANTIVO
raid ◊ *Fue detenido en una redada policial.* He was arrested during a police raid.
◆**La policía hizo una redada en el club.** The police raided the club.

redondo ADJETIVO
round ◊ *una mesa redonda* a round table
◆**Todo salió redondo.** Everything worked out perfectly.

la **reducción** SUSTANTIVO (PL las **reducciones**)
reduction

reducir* VERBO
1 to reduce (*producción, condena, fotografía*) ◊ *Reduzca la velocidad.* Reduce speed.
2 to cut (*gastos, impuestos*) ◊ *Van a reducir personal.* They're going to cut staff.

reembolsar VERBO
to refund

el **reembolso** SUSTANTIVO
refund ◊ *Cancelaron la excursión y nos hicieron un reembolso.* They cancelled the trip and gave us a refund.
◆**enviar algo contra reembolso** to send something cash on delivery

reemplazar* VERBO
to replace

la **referencia** SUSTANTIVO
reference ◊ *un punto de referencia* a point of reference
◆**con referencia a** with reference to
◆**hacer referencia a** to refer to
◆**referencias** references ◊ *La niñera traía muy buenas referencias.* The nanny had very good references.

el **referéndum** SUSTANTIVO (PL los **referéndums**)
referendum (PL referenda *o* referendums)

referente ADJETIVO
◆**referente a** concerning ◊ *el párrafo referente al uniforme escolar* the paragraph concerning school uniform

referirse* VERBO
◆**referirse a** to refer to ◊ *¿Te refieres a mí?* Are you referring to me?
◆**¿A qué te refieres? (1)** (*¿qué quieres decir?*) What exactly do you mean?
◆**¿A qué te refieres? (2)** (*más en concreto*) What are you referring to?

la **refinería** SUSTANTIVO
refinery (PL refineries)

refiriendo VERBO *ver* **referir**

reflejar VERBO
to reflect

el **reflejo** SUSTANTIVO
reflection ◊ *el reflejo de la luna en el lago* the reflection of the moon in the lake
◆**reflejos** reflexes ◊ *Estás bien de reflejos.* You have good reflexes.

la **reflexión** SUSTANTIVO (PL las **reflexiones**)
reflection

reflexionar VERBO
to think ◊ *Hace las cosas sin reflexionar.* He does things without thinking. ◊ *reflexionar sobre algo* to think about something
◆**Reflexiona bien antes de tomar una decisión.** Think it over carefully before taking a decision.

reflexivo ADJETIVO
reflexive (*verbo*)

la **reforma** SUSTANTIVO
1 reform (*de ley*) ◊ *la reforma educativa* the education reforms PL
2 alteration (*de edificio, casa*) ◊ *Estamos haciendo reformas en el piso.* We're having alterations made to the flat.
◆**"Cerrado por reformas"** "Closed for refurbishment"

reformar VERBO
1 to reform (*ley*)
2 to do up (*edificio, casa*)

el **refrán** SUSTANTIVO (PL los **refranes**)
saying

refrescante ADJETIVO
refreshing

refrescar* VERBO
to get cooler
♦ **refrescarse** to freshen up

el **refresco** SUSTANTIVO
soft drink

el **refrigerador** SUSTANTIVO
fridge

el **refugiado**, la **refugiada** SUSTANTIVO
refugee

refugiarse VERBO
1 to shelter (*de la lluvia*) ◊ *Nos refugiamos de la lluvia en un portal.* We sheltered from the rain in a doorway.
2 to take refuge (*de peligro, enemigo*) ◊ *La gente se refugiaba en los sótanos.* People took refuge in the cellars.

el **refugio** SUSTANTIVO
refuge ◊ *un refugio de montaña* a mountain refuge
♦ **Los montañeros buscaron refugio en una cueva.** The climbers sheltered in a cave.
♦ **un refugio antiaéreo** an air-raid shelter

la **regadera** SUSTANTIVO
1 watering can (*para las plantas*)
2 shower (*ducha*) Mexico
♦ **estar como una regadera** (*coloquial*) to be as mad as a hatter

regalar VERBO
1 to give ◊ *¿Y si le regalamos un libro?* What about giving him a book?
♦ **Ayer fue mi cumpleaños. – ¿Qué te regalaron?** It was my birthday yesterday. – What did you get?
2 to give away (*objeto usado*) ◊ *La tele vieja la vamos a regalar.* We're going to give the old TV away.

el **regaliz** SUSTANTIVO
liquorice

el **regalo** SUSTANTIVO
present ◊ *hacer un regalo a alguien* to give somebody a present
♦ **una tienda de regalos** a gift shop
♦ **papel de regalo** wrapping paper
♦ **de regalo** free ◊ *un CD de regalo con la compra del radiocasete* a free CD when you buy the radio cassette

regañadientes
♦ **a regañadientes** ADVERBIO
reluctantly

regañar VERBO
to tell off ◊ *La maestra me regañó por llegar tarde.* The teacher told me off for being late.

regar* VERBO
to water

la **regata** SUSTANTIVO
yacht race

regatear VERBO
1 to haggle ◊ *Regateaban por el precio de la alfombra.* They were haggling over the price of the carpet.
2 to dodge past (*esquivar*) ◊ *Regateó a varios defensas.* He dodged past several defenders.

el **régimen** SUSTANTIVO (PL los **regímenes**)
1 diet
♦ **estar a régimen** to be on a diet
♦ **ponerse a régimen** to go on a diet
2 regime ◊ *un régimen comunista* a communist regime

el **regimiento** SUSTANTIVO
regiment

la **región** SUSTANTIVO (PL las **regiones**)
region

regional ADJETIVO
regional

registrar VERBO
1 to search (*inspeccionar*) ◊ *Estuvieron registrando la casa.* They were searching the house. ◊ *Me registraron.* They searched me.
2 to register (*inscribir*) ◊ *Tienes que registrarte en el consulado.* You have to register at the consulate.
3 to check in ◊ *Fui a recepción a registrarme.* I went to reception to check in.
♦ **Me registré en el hotel.** I checked into the hotel.

el **registro** SUSTANTIVO
1 (*inspección*)
search (PL searches)
♦ **realizar un registro en un lugar** to carry out a search of a place
2 (*libro*)
register
♦ **el registro civil** the registry office

la **regla** SUSTANTIVO
1 rule ◊ *saltarse las reglas* to break the rules
2 period ◊ *Estoy con la regla.* I've got my period.
3 ruler ◊ *Trazó la línea con una regla.* He drew the line with a ruler.
♦ **por regla general** generally
♦ **tener todo en regla** to have everything in order

el **reglamento** SUSTANTIVO
regulations PL ◊ *El reglamento no lo permite.* The regulations don't allow it.

regresar VERBO
1 to go back (*a donde se estaba*) ◊ *Paco regresó a casa a coger el paraguas.* Paco went back home to pick up his umbrella.
2 to come back (*a donde se está*) ◊ *Regresaré sobre las ocho.* I'll come back at about eight.
♦ **Regresamos tarde.** We got back late.
3 to give back (*devolver*) Latin America
♦ **regresarse (1)** (*a donde se estaba*) Latin America to go back
♦ **regresarse (2)** (*a donde se está*) Latin America to come back

R

el **regreso** SUSTANTIVO
return
◆**a nuestro regreso** on our return
◆**de regreso** on the way back ◇ *De regreso paramos a comer en Ávila.* On the way back we stopped to have lunch in Ávila.
regulable ADJETIVO
adjustable
regular (1) ADJETIVO
regular ◇ *un verbo regular* a regular verb ◇ *a intervalos regulares* at regular intervals
◆**La obra estuvo regular.** The play was pretty ordinary.
regular (2) ADVERBIO
◆**El examen me fue regular.** My exam didn't go brilliantly.
◆**¿Cómo te encuentras? – Regular.** How are you? – Not too bad.
rehacer* VERBO
to redo
el/la **rehén** SUSTANTIVO (PL los/las **rehenes**)
hostage
la **reina** SUSTANTIVO
queen
el **reinado** SUSTANTIVO
reign
el **reino** SUSTANTIVO
kingdom
el **Reino Unido** SUSTANTIVO
the United Kingdom
reír* VERBO
to laugh ◇ *No te rías.* Don't laugh.
◆**echarse a reír** to burst out laughing
◆**Siempre nos reímos con él.** We always have a good laugh with him.
◆**reírse** to laugh
◆**reírse de** to laugh at ◇ *¿De qué te ríes?* What are you laughing at?
la **reivindicación** SUSTANTIVO (PL las **reivindicaciones**)
claim ◇ *reivindicaciones salariales* wage claims
la **reja** SUSTANTIVO
grille ◇ *La puerta de la joyería está protegida con una reja.* The door to the jeweller's is protected with a grille.
◆**estar entre rejas** to be behind bars
relación SUSTANTIVO (PL las **relaciones**)
1 link ◇ *la relación entre el tabaco y el cáncer* the link between smoking and cancer
2 relationship ◇ *Tenemos una relación de amistad.* We have a friendly relationship.
las relaciones entre empresarios y trabajadores the relationship between employers and workers
con relación a in relation to
relaciones públicas public relations
◆**relaciones sexuales** sexual relations
relacionar VERBO
to link ◇ *Los expertos relacionan el tabaco con el cáncer.* The experts link smoking with cancer.
◆**Le gusta relacionarse con niños mayores que él.** He likes mixing with older children.
◆**No se relaciona mucho con la gente.** He doesn't mix much.
relajado ADJETIVO
1 relaxed (*músculo, cuerpo*) ◇ *¿Estás relajado?* Are you feeling relaxed?
2 laid-back (*despreocupado*) ◇ *Es un tipo muy relajado.* He's a very laid-back guy.
relajante ADJETIVO
relaxing
relajar VERBO
to relax ◇ *Relaja los músculos.* Relax your muscles. ◇ *¡Relájate!* Relax!
◆**La música clásica me relaja mucho.** I find classical music really relaxing.
el **relámpago** SUSTANTIVO
flash of lightning (PL flashes of lightning) ◇ *Vimos varios relámpagos.* We saw several flashes of lightning.
◆**No me gustan los relámpagos.** I don't like lightning.
relativamente ADVERBIO
relatively
relativo ADJETIVO
relative ◇ *un pronombre relativo* a relative pronoun ◇ *Eso es muy relativo.* That's all relative.
◆**en lo relativo a** concerning
el **relato** SUSTANTIVO
story
el **relevo** SUSTANTIVO
◆**una carrera de relevos** a relay race
◆**tomar el relevo a alguien** to take over from somebody
la **religión** SUSTANTIVO (PL las **religiones**)
religion
religioso ADJETIVO
religious
el **rellano** SUSTANTIVO
landing (*de escalera*)
rellenar VERBO
1 to stuff (*tomates, pollo, muñeco*) ◇ *Rellene los pimientos con el arroz.* Stuff the peppers with the rice.
2 to fill in (*agujero, formulario*) ◇ *Rellene este impreso, por favor.* Can you fill in this form please.
el **reloj** SUSTANTIVO
1 (*grande, de pared*)
clock ◇ *El reloj de la cocina va atrasado.* The kitchen clock's slow.
◆**un reloj despertador** an alarm clock
◆**un reloj de cuco** a cuckoo clock
◆**contra reloj** against the clock

[2] (*de pulsera*)
watch (PL watches) ◊ *Se me ha parado el reloj.* My watch has stopped.
♦**un reloj digital** a digital watch
♦**un reloj sumergible** a waterproof watch
♦**El horno tiene un reloj automático.** The cooker has an automatic timer.
♦**un reloj de sol** a sundial

la **relojera** SUSTANTIVO
watchmaker

la **relojería** SUSTANTIVO
watchmaker's (PL watchmakers' shops)

el **relojero** SUSTANTIVO
watchmaker

relucir* VERBO
to shine

remar VERBO
[1] to paddle (*con pala*)
[2] to row (*con remos*)

remediar VERBO
to solve (*problema*) ◊ *Con llorar no vas a remediar nada.* You're not going to solve anything by crying.
♦**Me eché a reír, no lo pude remediar.** I began to laugh, I couldn't help it.

el **remedio** SUSTANTIVO
remedy (PL remedies) ◊ *un remedio contra la tos* a cough remedy ◊ *un remedio casero* a household remedy
♦**No tuve más remedio que hacerlo.** I had no choice but to do it.

el **remite** SUSTANTIVO
name and address of sender

el/la **remitente** SUSTANTIVO
sender

el **remo** SUSTANTIVO
[1] oar (*objeto*)
[2] rowing (*deporte*)

remojar VERBO
to soak

el **remojo** SUSTANTIVO
♦**poner algo en remojo** to leave something to soak

la **remolacha** SUSTANTIVO
beetroot

remolcar* VERBO
to tow

el **remolque** SUSTANTIVO
trailer (*vehículo*)

el **remordimiento** SUSTANTIVO
remorse SING ◊ *No siente remordimientos por lo que ha hecho.* He feels no remorse for what he has done.

remoto ADJETIVO
remote

remover* VERBO
[1] to stir (*café, guiso*)
[2] to toss (*ensalada*)
[3] to turn over (*tierra*)

el **renacuajo** SUSTANTIVO
tadpole

el **rencor** SUSTANTIVO
ill-feeling ◊ *Existe mucho rencor entre ella y su ex-marido.* There's a lot of ill-feeling between her and her ex-husband.
♦**guardar rencor a alguien** to bear a grudge against somebody ◊ *No le guardo rencor.* I don't bear him a grudge.

rencoroso ADJETIVO
♦**No soy rencoroso.** I don't bear grudges.

rendido ADJETIVO
worn out ◊ *Estaba rendido de tanto andar.* I was worn out after so much walking.

la **rendija** SUSTANTIVO
[1] crack (*grieta*)
[2] gap (*hueco*)

el **rendimiento** SUSTANTIVO
performance (*de máquina, empleado*)

rendir* VERBO
♦**Este negocio no rinde.** This business doesn't pay.
♦**El dinero rinde poco en una cuenta corriente.** You don't get much interest on your money in a current account.
♦**rendirse (1)** to give up ◊ *No sé la respuesta; me rindo.* I don't know the answer; I give up.
♦**rendirse (2)** to surrender ◊ *El enemigo se rindió.* The enemy surrendered.

el **renglón** SUSTANTIVO (PL los **renglones**)
line

el **reno** SUSTANTIVO
reindeer (PL reindeer *o* reindeers)

renovable ADJETIVO
renewable

renovar* VERBO
[1] to renew (*contrato, carnet*) ◊ *Tengo que renovarme el pasaporte.* I must renew my passport.
[2] to renovate (*edificio, casa*) ◊ *Van a renovar la fachada del edificio.* They're going to renovate the front of the building.
[3] to change (*muebles*) ◊ *Han renovado el mobiliario de la casa.* They've changed the furniture in the house.

la **renta** SUSTANTIVO
[1] income (*ingresos*)
[2] rent (*alquiler*)

rentable ADJETIVO
profitable (*inversión, compañía*) ◊ *No es rentable organizar cursos para tan pocos alumnos.* It isn't profitable to put on courses for so few students.
♦**una fábrica poco rentable** an uneconomic factory

rentar VERBO Mexico
to rent

reñido ADJETIVO
hard-fought (*partido*)

reñir* VERBO
[1] to tell somebody off (*regañar*) ◊ *No la riñas, la culpa no es suya.* Don't tell her off, it's not her fault.

☞

2 to quarrel (*discutir*) ◊ *Mi hermana y yo siempre estábamos riñendo.* My sister and I were always quarrelling.
3 to fall out (*enemistarse*) ◊ *Ángeles y Manolo han reñido.* Ángeles and Manolo have fallen out. ◊ *Ha reñido con su novio.* She has fallen out with her boyfriend.

la **reparación** SUSTANTIVO (PL las **reparaciones**)
repair
◆ **"reparaciones en el acto"** "repairs while you wait"

reparar VERBO
to repair

repartir VERBO
1 to hand out (*propaganda, fotocopias*) ◊ *El profesor repartió los exámenes.* The teacher handed out the examination papers.
2 to share out (*beneficios, trabajo, pastel*) ◊ *Nos repartimos el dinero.* We shared out the money.
3 to deliver (*periódicos*) ◊ *Repartimos pizzas a domicilio.* We deliver pizzas.
4 to deal (*barajas*)

el **reparto** SUSTANTIVO
1 (*de mercancías*)
delivery (PL deliveries)
◆ **reparto a domicilio** home delivery service
2 (*de película*)
cast ◊ *un reparto estelar* a star cast

repasar VERBO
1 to check (*suma, texto*) ◊ *Repasé la carta antes de firmarla.* I checked the letter before signing it.
2 to revise (*lección*)
◆ **repasar para un examen** to revise for an exam

el **repaso** SUSTANTIVO
revision (*para un examen*)
◆ **Tengo que darles un repaso a los apuntes.** I must revise my notes.

el **repelente** SUSTANTIVO
repellent (*para insectos*)

repelente SUSTANTIVO
know-all (*niño, persona*)

repente ADVERBIO
◆ **de repente** suddenly

repentino ADJETIVO
sudden

epertorio SUSTANTIVO
repertoire

epetición SUSTANTIVO (PL las **repeticiones**)
repetition

petidamente ADVERBIO
epeatedly

petir* VERBO
] to repeat (*palabra, experimento*)
¿Podría repetirlo, por favor? Could you peat that, please?
2 to have a second helping ◊ *El arroz está tan bueno que voy a repetir.* The rice is so good that I'm going to have a second helping.

repetitivo ADJETIVO
repetitive

la **repisa** SUSTANTIVO
shelf (PL shelves)
◆ **la repisa de la chimenea** the mantlepiece

repitiendo VERBO *ver* **repetir**

el **repollo** SUSTANTIVO
cabbage

el **reportaje** SUSTANTIVO
1 (*en televisión*)
documentary (PL documentaries)
2 (*en periódico*)
article

el **reposacabezas** SUSTANTIVO (PL los **reposacabezas**)
headrest

la **reposición** SUSTANTIVO (PL las **reposiciones**)
1 repeat (*en televisión*)
2 revival (*en teatro*)

repostar VERBO
to refuel (*avión*)

la **repostería** SUSTANTIVO
confectionery (*dulces*)

la **representación** SUSTANTIVO (PL las **representaciones**)
performance (*de teatro*)

el/la **representante** SUSTANTIVO
1 representative (*de organización, empresa*)
2 agent (*de artista*)

representar VERBO
1 to represent (*país, organización*) ◊ *La representaba su abogado.* Her lawyer was representing her.
2 to put on (*obra teatral*) ◊ *Los niños van a representar una obra de teatro.* The children are going to put on a play.
3 to play (*papel*) ◊ *Representa el papel de Don Juan.* He's playing the part of Don Juan.
◆ **Tiene cuarenta años pero no los representa.** He's forty but he doesn't look it.

representativo ADJETIVO
representative

el **reprimido**, la **reprimida** ADJETIVO, SUSTANTIVO
◆ **Es una reprimida.** She's repressed.

reprobar* VERBO Latin America
to fail ◊ *Le reprobaron en matemáticas.* He failed maths.

reprochar VERBO
◆ **Me reprochó que no la hubiera invitado.** He reproached me for not having invited her.

rbs marked with this symbol are irregular. See pages 380-382 for further details

la **reproducción** SUSTANTIVO (PL las **reproducciones**)
reproduction

reproducirse* VERBO
to reproduce

el **reproductor** SUSTANTIVO
◆ **un reproductor de CD** a CD player

el **reptil** SUSTANTIVO
reptile

la **república** SUSTANTIVO
republic

la **República Dominicana** SUSTANTIVO
the Dominican Republic

el **republicano**, la **republicana** ADJETIVO, SUSTANTIVO
republican

el **repuesto** SUSTANTIVO
spare part (*pieza*)
◆ **de repuesto** spare ◇ *la rueda de repuesto* the spare wheel

repugnante ADJETIVO
revolting

la **reputación** SUSTANTIVO (PL las **reputaciones**)
reputation
◆ **tener buena reputación** to have a good reputation

el **requesón** SUSTANTIVO
cottage cheese

el **requisito** SUSTANTIVO
requirement ◇ *Cumple todos los requisitos para el puesto.* He satisfies all the requirements for the job.

la **resaca** SUSTANTIVO
hangover
◆ **tener resaca** to have a hangover

resaltar VERBO
1 to stand out ◇ *Lo escribí en mayúsculas para que resaltara.* I wrote it in capitals to make it stand out.
2 to highlight ◇ *El conferenciante resaltó el problema del paro.* The speaker highlighted the problem of unemployment.

resbaladizo ADJETIVO
slippery

resbalar VERBO
1 to be slippery (*superficie*) ◇ *Ten cuidado que este suelo resbala.* Be careful, this floor's slippery.
2 to skid (*vehículo*) ◇ *El coche resbaló y casi nos estrellamos.* The car skidded and we almost crashed.
◆ **resbalarse** to slip ◇ *Me resbalé con el hielo de la acera.* I slipped on the icy pavement.

rescatar VERBO
to rescue

el **rescate** SUSTANTIVO
1 rescue (*salvamento*) ◇ *un equipo de rescate* a rescue team
2 ransom (*dinero*)
◆ **pedir un rescate por alguien** to hold somebody to ransom

el/la **reserva** SUSTANTIVO
reserve (*jugador*)

la **reserva** SUSTANTIVO
1 reservation ◇ *He hecho una reserva en el Hilton para dos noches.* I've made a reservation at the Hilton for two nights.
◆ **Tengo mis reservas al respecto.** I've got reservations about it.
2 reserve ◇ *una reserva natural* a nature reserve ◇ *El país tiene abundantes reservas de trigo.* The country has got plentiful reserves of wheat.

reservado ADJETIVO
reserved (*persona*)

reservar VERBO
to reserve (*mesa, entradas*)

resfriado ADJETIVO
◆ **estar resfriado** to have a cold ◇ *No fui porque estaba muy resfriado.* I didn't go because I had a bad cold.

el **resfriado** SUSTANTIVO
cold
◆ **agarrarse un resfriado** to catch a cold

resfriarse* VERBO
to catch a cold

el **resguardo** SUSTANTIVO
1 ticket (*de tintorería, relojería*)
2 receipt (*recibo de compra*)

la **residencia** SUSTANTIVO
residence ◇ *un permiso de residencia* a residence permit ◇ *La reunión tuvo lugar en la residencia del primer ministro.* The meeting took place at the prime minister's residence.
◆ **una residencia de ancianos** an old people's home
◆ **una residencia de estudiantes** a hall of residence
◆ **una residencia sanitaria** a hospital

residencial ADJETIVO
residential ◇ *una zona residencial* a residential area

los **residuos** SUSTANTIVO
waste SING ◇ *residuos radiactivos* radioactive waste

la **resistencia** SUSTANTIVO
resistance ◇ *Los manifestantes no ofrecieron resistencia.* The demonstrators didn't offer any resistance.
◆ **resistencia física** stamina

resistente ADJETIVO
tough ◇ *El diamante es una piedra muy resistente.* Diamond is a very tough stone.
◆ **resistente al calor** heat-resistant

resistir VERBO
1 to resist (*tentación*) ◇ *No pude resistir las ganas de decírselo.* I couldn't resist the urge to tell him.

R

[2] to take (*peso, presión*) ◊ *Esta caja no va a resistir tanto peso.* This box won't take so much weight.
[3] to stand (*dolor*) ◊ *No puedo resistir este frío.* I can't stand this cold.
♦ **Se resisten a cooperar.** They are refusing to cooperate.

resolver* VERBO
to solve (*problema, caso*)

respaldar VERBO
to back up ◊ *Mis hermanos me respaldaron.* My brothers and sisters backed me up.

el **respaldo** SUSTANTIVO
back (*de asiento*)

respectivamente ADVERBIO
respectively

respecto SUSTANTIVO
♦ **con respecto a** with regard to

respetable ADJETIVO
respectable

respetar VERBO
[1] to respect (*persona, opinión*)
[2] to obey (*código, norma*) ◊ *No se respetan las normas de seguridad.* The safety regulations aren't being obeyed.

el **respeto** SUSTANTIVO
respect ◊ *el respeto a los animales* respect for animals
♦ **tener respeto a alguien** to respect somebody
♦ **No le faltes al respeto.** Don't be disrespectful to him.

la **respiración** SUSTANTIVO
breathing ◊ *Tenía la respiración irregular.* His breathing was irregular.
♦ **quedarse sin respiración** to be out of breath
♦ **la respiración boca a boca** the kiss of life ◊ *Le hicieron la respiración boca a boca.* They gave him the kiss of life.
♦ **la respiración artificial** artificial respiration

respirar VERBO
to breathe

responder VERBO
[1] to answer (*pregunta*) ◊ *Eso no responde a mi pregunta.* That doesn't answer my question.
[2] to reply ◊ *No han respondido a mi carta.* They haven't replied to my letter. ◊ *Respondió que habían salido con unos amigos.* He replied that they had gone out with some friends.
[3] to respond (*reaccionar*) ◊ *No responde al tratamiento.* He's not responding to the treatment.

la **responsabilidad** SUSTANTIVO
responsibility (PL responsibilities)

responsable ADJETIVO
responsible ◊ *Cada cual es responsable de sus acciones.* Everybody is responsible for their own actions.

el/la **responsable** SUSTANTIVO
♦ **Tú eres la responsable de lo ocurrido.** You're responsible for what happened.
♦ **Los responsables serán castigados.** Those responsible will be punished.
♦ **Juan es el responsable de la cocina.** Juan is in charge of the kitchen.

la **respuesta** SUSTANTIVO
answer

resquebrajarse VERBO
to crack

la **resta** SUSTANTIVO
subtraction

restante ADJETIVO
remaining

restar VERBO
to subtract ◊ *Está aprendiendo a restar.* He's learning to subtract.
♦ **Tienes que restar 16 de 36.** You have to take 16 away from 36.

la **restauración** SUSTANTIVO (PL las **restauraciones**)
restoration

el **restaurante** SUSTANTIVO
restaurant

restaurar VERBO
to restore

el **resto** SUSTANTIVO
rest ◊ *Yo haré el resto.* I'll do the rest.
♦ **los restos (1)** (*de comida*) the leftovers
♦ **los restos (2)** (*de avión, naufragio*) the wreckage SING

restregar* VERBO
to rub ◊ *Cuando tiene sueño se restriega los ojos.* He rubs his eyes when he's sleepy.

la **restricción** SUSTANTIVO (PL las **restricciones**)
restriction

resuelto VERBO *ver* **resolver**

resuelvo VERBO *ver* **resolver**

el **resultado** SUSTANTIVO
[1] result (*de examen, experimento*)
[2] score (*de encuentro deportivo*)
♦ **dar resultado** to work ◊ *Nuestro plan no dio resultado.* Our plan didn't work.

resultar VERBO
to turn out ◊ *Al final resultó que él tenía razón.* In the end it turned out that he was right.
♦ **Me resultó violento decírselo.** I found it embarrassing to tell him.

el **resumen** SUSTANTIVO (PL los **resúmenes**)
summary (PL summaries) ◊ *un resumen de las noticias* a news summary
♦ **hacer un resumen de algo** to summarize something
♦ **en resumen** in short

resumir VERBO
to summarize (*artículo, libro*)
♦ **Dijo, resumiendo, que el viaje había sido un desastre.** He said, in short, that the trip had been a disaster.

retar VERBO
1 to challenge (*desafiar*)
2 to tell off (*regañar*) Chile, River Plate

retirar VERBO
1 to take away ◊ *La camarera retiró las copas.* The waitress took the glasses away. ◊ *Le han retirado el permiso de conducir.* He's had his driving licence taken away.
2 to withdraw ◊ *Fui a retirar dinero de la cuenta.* I went to withdraw some money from my account. ◊ *Se retiraron del torneo.* They withdrew from the tournament.
♦ **retirarse** to retire ◊ *Mi padre se retira el año que viene.* My father will be retiring next year.

el **reto** SUSTANTIVO
challenge

retorcer* VERBO
to twist ◊ *Me retorció el brazo.* He twisted my arm.
♦ **retorcerse de risa** to double up with laughter

la **retransmisión** SUSTANTIVO (PL las **retransmisiones**)
broadcast ◊ *una retransmisión en directo* a live broadcast

retransmitir VERBO
to broadcast

retrasado ADJETIVO
1 behind (*en una actividad*) ◊ *Voy retrasado con este trabajo.* I'm behind with this work.
2 slow (*reloj*) ◊ *Este reloj va retrasado veinte minutos.* This clock is twenty minutes slow.
♦ **Tienen un hijo un poco retrasado.** They've got a son with learning difficulties.

retrasar VERBO
1 to postpone (*reunión, viaje*) ◊ *Retrasaron la boda al quince.* They postponed the wedding until the fifteenth.
2 to delay (*salida*) ◊ *El mal tiempo retrasó nuestro vuelo.* Our flight was delayed due to bad weather.
3 to put back (*reloj*) ◊ *A las doce hay que retrasar los relojes una hora.* At twelve o'clock the clocks have to be put back one hour.
♦ **retrasarse** (*persona, tren*) to be late ◊ *El tren de las nueve se retrasó.* The nine o'clock train was late.
♦ **Tu reloj se retrasa.** Your watch is slow.

el **retraso** SUSTANTIVO
delay (PL delays) ◊ *La niebla causó algunos retrasos.* The fog caused some delays.
♦ **Perdonad por el retraso.** Sorry I'm late.
♦ **ir con retraso** to be running late
♦ **llegar con retraso** to be late ◊ *El vuelo llegó con una hora de retraso.* The flight was an hour late.

el **retrato** SUSTANTIVO
portrait (*cuadro*)
♦ **hacer un retrato a alguien** to paint somebody's portrait

el **retrete** SUSTANTIVO
toilet

retroceder VERBO
to go back

el **retrovisor** SUSTANTIVO
rear-view mirror

retuerzo VERBO *ver* **retorcer**

el **reúma** SUSTANTIVO
rheumatism

la **reunión** SUSTANTIVO (PL las **reuniones**)
1 meeting (*de trabajo*) ◊ *Mañana tenemos una reunión.* We've got a meeting tomorrow.
2 gathering (*social*) ◊ *una reunión familiar* a family gathering

reunir* VERBO
1 to gather together (*personas*) ◊ *La maestra reunió a los niños en el patio.* The teacher gathered the children together in the playground.
2 to satisfy (*requisitos*) ◊ *Paula reúne los requisitos para el puesto.* Paula satisfies all the requirements for the job.
3 to raise (*fondos*) ◊ *Estamos reuniendo dinero para el viaje de fin de curso.* We're raising money for the end-of-year trip.
♦ **reunirse (1)** to gather ◊ *Miles de personas se reunieron en la plaza.* Thousands of people gathered in the square.
♦ **reunirse (2)** to get together ◊ *En Navidad nos reunimos toda la familia.* The whole family gets together at Christmas.
♦ **reunirse (3)** to meet ◊ *El comité se reúne una vez al mes.* The committee meets once a month.

revelar VERBO
1 to develop ◊ *Luis revela sus propias fotos.* Luis develops his own photos.
♦ **Todavía no hemos revelado las fotos.** We haven't had the photos developed yet.
♦ **Llevé los carretes a revelar.** I took the films to be developed.
2 to reveal (*secreto*) ◊ *No quería revelar su identidad.* He didn't want to reveal his identity.

reventar* VERBO
to burst (*globo, rueda*)

R ☞

◆ **Me revienta tener que ponerme corbata.** I hate having to wear a tie.

el **revés** SUSTANTIVO (PL los **reveses**)
backhand (*en tenis*)
◆ **al revés (1)** the other way round ◊ *¿Tres, tres, dos? – No, al revés: dos, dos, tres.* Three, three, two? – No, the other way round: two, two, three.
◆ **al revés (2)** inside out ◊ *Te has puesto los calcetines al revés.* You've put your socks on inside out.
◆ **al revés (3)** back to front ◊ *Miré el cuello y vi que llevaba el jersey al revés.* I looked at the collar and realized that I had my jumper on back to front.
◆ **al revés (4)** upside down ◊ *El dibujo está al revés.* The picture's upside down.

reviento VERBO *ver* **reventar**

revisar VERBO
[1] to check ◊ *Un electricista me revisó la instalación.* An electrician checked the wiring for me.
◆ **Tengo que ir a que me revisen el coche.** I must take my car for a service.
[2] to search (*maleta, bolsillos*) Latin America

la **revisión** SUSTANTIVO (PL las **revisiones**)
service ◊ *He llevado el coche a revisión.* I've taken the car for a service.
◆ **una revisión médica** a checkup

el **revisor,** la **revisora** SUSTANTIVO
ticket inspector

la **revista** SUSTANTIVO
magazine
◆ **una revista electrónica** a webzine

revoltoso ADJETIVO
naughty

la **revolución** SUSTANTIVO (PL las **revoluciones**)
revolution

el **revolucionario,** la **revolucionaria** SUSTANTIVO
revolutionary (PL revolutionaries)

revolver* VERBO
[1] to mess up (*desordenar*) ◊ *Los niños han revuelto la habitación otra vez.* The children have messed the room up again.
◆ **No revuelvas mis papeles.** Don't muddle my papers up.
[2] to turn upside down ◊ *Los ladrones revolvieron toda la casa.* The burglars turned the whole house upside down.
[3] to rummage in (*fisgar*) ◊ *No me gusta que me revuelvas el bolso.* I don't like you rummaging in my bag.

el **revólver** SUSTANTIVO (PL los **revólveres**)
revolver

revuelto (1) VERBO *ver* **revolver**

revuelto (2) ADJETIVO
in a mess (*desordenado*) ◊ *Todo estaba revuelto.* Everything was in a mess.
◆ **Las fotos están revueltas.** The photos are muddled up.
◆ **El tiempo está muy revuelto.** The weather's very unsettled.
◆ **Tengo el estómago revuelto.** I've got an upset stomach.

el **rey** SUSTANTIVO (PL los **reyes**)
king
◆ **Los reyes visitaron China.** The King and Queen visited China.
◆ **los Reyes Magos** the Three Wise Men

> *As part of the Christmas festivities, the Spanish celebrate **el día de Reyes** (Epiphany) on 6th of January, when the Three Wise Men bring presents to children.*

rezar* VERBO
to pray ◊ *rezar por algo* to pray for something
◆ **rezar el Padrenuestro** to say the Lord's Prayer

la **ría** SUSTANTIVO
estuary (PL estuaries)

el **riachuelo** SUSTANTIVO
stream

la **ribera** SUSTANTIVO
bank (*del río*)

la **rica** SUSTANTIVO
rich woman (PL rich women)

el **rico** SUSTANTIVO
rich man (PL rich men)
◆ **los ricos** the rich

rico ADJETIVO
[1] rich (*persona, barrio*) ◊ *Son muy ricos.* They're very rich.
[2] delicious (*comida*) ◊ *¡Qué rico!* How delicious!

ridiculizar* VERBO
to ridicule

ridículo ADJETIVO
ridiculous ◊ *¿A que suena ridículo?* Doesn't it sound ridiculous?
◆ **hacer el ridículo** to make a fool of oneself
◆ **poner a alguien en ridículo** to make a fool of somebody

el **riel** SUSTANTIVO
rail

las **riendas** SUSTANTIVO
reins

riendo VERBO *ver* **reír**

el **riesgo** SUSTANTIVO
risk
◆ **correr riesgos** to take risks ◊ *No quiero correr ese riesgo.* I'd rather not take that risk.
◆ **Corres el riesgo de que te despidan.** You run the risk of being dismissed.

◆ **un seguro a todo riesgo** a fully comprehensive insurance policy

la **rifa** SUSTANTIVO
raffle

el **rifle** SUSTANTIVO
rifle

rígido ADJETIVO
1 stiff (*tieso*)
2 strict (*estricto*)

riguroso ADJETIVO
1 strict (*control, dieta, disciplina*)
2 severe (*castigo*)

la **rima** SUSTANTIVO
rhyme

el **rímel** SUSTANTIVO
mascara ◊ *No me he puesto rímel.* I haven't put any mascara on.

el **rincón** SUSTANTIVO (PL los **rincones**)
corner

el **rinoceronte** SUSTANTIVO
rhinoceros (PL rhinoceroses *o* rhinoceros)

la **riña** SUSTANTIVO
1 row (*discusión*)
2 brawl (*pelea*)

riñendo VERBO *ver* **reñir**

el **riñón** SUSTANTIVO (PL los **riñones**)
kidney (PL kidneys) ◊ *un transplante de riñón* a kidney transplant

◆ **Me duelen los riñones.** I've got a pain in my lower back.

la **riñonera** SUSTANTIVO
bum bag

río VERBO *ver* **reír**

el **río** SUSTANTIVO
river ◊ *el río Támesis* the River Thames

la **riqueza** SUSTANTIVO
1 wealth (*posesiones*) ◊ *la distribución de la riqueza* the distribution of wealth
2 richness (*abundancia*) ◊ *la riqueza de su lenguaje* the richness of his language

la **risa** SUSTANTIVO
laugh ◊ *una risa contagiosa* an infectious laugh

◆ **Me da risa.** It makes me laugh.
◆ **Daba risa la manera en que lo explicaba.** It was so funny the way he told it.
◆ **¡Qué risa!** What a laugh!
◆ **partirse de risa** to split one's sides laughing

el **ritmo** SUSTANTIVO
1 rhythm ◊ *No tiene sentido del ritmo.* He has no sense of rhythm.

◆ **Daban palmas al ritmo de la música.** They were clapping in time to the music.

2 pace ◊ *el ritmo de vida* the pace of life

el **ritual** SUSTANTIVO
ritual

el/la **rival** ADJETIVO, SUSTANTIVO
rival

la **rivalidad** SUSTANTIVO
rivalry (PL rivalries)

rizado ADJETIVO
curly ◊ *Tiene el pelo rizado.* He has curly hair.

rizar* VERBO
1 to curl (*con rulos, rizador*) ◊ *Me rizo las pestañas.* I curl my eyelashes.
2 to perm (*con permanente*)

◆ **Se ha rizado el pelo.** She has had her hair permed.

el **rizo** SUSTANTIVO
curl

robar VERBO
1 to steal (*objeto, dinero*) ◊ *Me han robado la cartera.* My wallet has been stolen. ◊ *Les robaba dinero a sus compañeros de clase.* He was stealing money from his classmates.
2 to rob (*banco, persona*) ◊ *¡Nos han robado!* We've been robbed!
3 to break into (*en una casa, oficina*) ◊ *Entraron a robar en mi casa.* They broke into my house.

el **roble** SUSTANTIVO
oak

el **robo** SUSTANTIVO
1 (*de dinero, objetos*)
theft
2 (*a una persona, tienda, banco*)
robbery (PL robberies)
3 (*en una casa*)
burglary (PL burglaries)

◆ **¡Estos precios son un robo!** This is daylight robbery!

el **robot** SUSTANTIVO (PL los **robots**)
robot

◆ **el robot de cocina** the food processor

la **roca** SUSTANTIVO
rock

rociar* VERBO
to spray

el **rocío** SUSTANTIVO
dew

la **rodaja** SUSTANTIVO
slice ◊ *cortar algo en rodajas* to cut something into slices

el **rodaje** SUSTANTIVO
shooting (*de película*)

◆ **El coche está en rodaje.** The car's running in.

rodar* VERBO
1 to roll ◊ *La pelota bajó rodando por la cuesta.* The ball rolled down the slope.
2 to shoot ◊ *rodar una película* to shoot a film

rodear VERBO
to surround ◊ *el bosque que rodea el palacio* the forest that surrounds the palace

◆ **rodeado de** surrounded by

la **rodilla** SUSTANTIVO
knee

◆ **ponerse de rodillas** to kneel down

el **rodillo** SUSTANTIVO
[1] rolling pin (*para amasar*)
[2] roller (*para pintar*)

rogar* VERBO
[1] to beg ◊ *Me rogó que le perdonara.* He begged me to forgive him.
[2] to pray (*rezar*) ◊ *Le rogué a Dios que se curara.* I prayed to God to make him better.
◆ **"Se ruega no fumar"** "Please do not smoke"

el **rojo** ADJETIVO, SUSTANTIVO
red ◊ *Va vestida de rojo.* She's wearing red.
◆ **ponerse rojo** to go red ◊ *Se puso rojo de vergüenza.* He went red with embarrassment.

el **rollo** SUSTANTIVO
roll (*de película, papel, tela*) ◊ *un rollo de papel higiénico* a roll of toilet paper
◆ **La conferencia fue un rollo.** The lecture was really boring.
◆ **¡Qué rollo de película!** What a boring film.
◆ **Nos soltó el rollo de siempre.** He gave us the same old lecture.

Roma SUSTANTIVO FEM
Rome

el **romano,** la **romana** ADJETIVO, SUSTANTIVO
Roman ◊ *los números romanos* Roman numerals
◆ **Es romano.** He's from Rome.
◆ **los romanos (1)** (*de la antigua Roma*) the Romans
◆ **los romanos (2)** (*actualmente*) Romans

el **romántico,** la **romántica** ADJETIVO, SUSTANTIVO
romantic

el **rombo** SUSTANTIVO
rhombus (PL rhombuses *o* rhombi)

el **rompecabezas** SUSTANTIVO (PL los **rompecabezas**)
[1] jigsaw (*de piezas*)
[2] puzzle (*problema*)

romper* VERBO
[1] to break (*cristal, objeto, pierna*) ◊ *Me rompí el brazo.* I broke my arm. ◊ *Se ha roto una taza.* A cup has got broken. ◊ *romper una promesa* to break a promise
[2] to tear up (*papel*) ◊ *Rompí la foto de mi novia.* I tore up the photo of my girlfriend. ◊ *Rompió la carta a pedazos.* He tore the letter up.
◆ **Se ha roto una sábana.** A sheet has got torn.
◆ **Se me han roto los pantalones.** I've torn my trousers.
◆ **romper con alguien** to finish with somebody ◊ *Ha roto con el novio.* She has finished with her boyfriend.

el **ron** SUSTANTIVO
rum

roncar* VERBO
to snore

ronco ADJETIVO
hoarse
◆ **quedarse ronco** to go hoarse

la **ronda** SUSTANTIVO
round ◊ *Esta ronda la pago yo.* I'll get this round.
◆ **hacer la ronda** (*guarda, soldado*) to be on patrol

el **ronquido** SUSTANTIVO
snore

ronronear VERBO
to purr

la **ropa** SUSTANTIVO
clothes PL ◊ *Voy a cambiarme de ropa.* I'm going to change my clothes.
◆ **la ropa interior** underwear
◆ **ropa de deporte** sportswear
◆ **la ropa de cama** bed linen
◆ **la ropa lavada** the washing
◆ **la ropa sucia** the dirty washing

el **rosa** ADJETIVO, SUSTANTIVO
pink ◊ *Va vestida de rosa.* She's wearing pink.
◆ **Llevaba unos calcetines rosa.** He was wearing pink socks.

la **rosa** SUSTANTIVO
rose

rosado ADJETIVO
rosé (*vino*)

el **rosal** SUSTANTIVO
rosebush (PL rosebushes)

el **rostro** SUSTANTIVO
face

roto VERBO *ver* **romper**

roto ADJETIVO
[1] broken (*cristal, objeto, brazo*)
[2] torn (*papel, tela*)
[3] worn out (*zapatos*)

el **roto** SUSTANTIVO
hole (*en prenda*)

la **rotonda** SUSTANTIVO
roundabout

el **rotulador** SUSTANTIVO
[1] felt-tip pen (*para escribir, dibujar*)
[2] highlighter pen (*fluorescente*)

el **rótulo** SUSTANTIVO
sign (*letrero*)

rozar* VERBO
to rub against ◊ *Los sofás rozan la pared.* The sofas are rubbing against the wall. ◊ *Las botas me rozan el tobillo.* My boots are rubbing against my ankle.
◆ **La rocé al pasar.** I brushed past her.

rubio ADJETIVO
fair ◊ *Luis tiene el pelo rubio.* Luis has got fair hair. ◊ *Yo soy morena pero mi*

* Verbs marked with this symbol are irregular. See pages 380-382 for further details

hermana es rubia. I'm dark but my sister is fair.
♦ **Es rubia con los ojos azules.** She has got fair hair and blue eyes.

*Si nos referimos a un rubio tipo nórdico (rubio platino), o bien a un rubio teñido, se usa **blond** (FEM: **blonde**) en lugar de **fair**.*

◊ *Quiero teñirme el pelo de rubio.* I want to dye my hair blond.

ruborizarse* VERBO
to blush

rudimentario ADJETIVO
basic

la **rueda** SUSTANTIVO
wheel ◊ *la rueda delantera* the front wheel ◊ *la rueda trasera* the back wheel
♦ **Se te ha pinchado la rueda.** You've got a puncture.
♦ **una rueda de prensa** a press conference

ruedo VERBO *ver* **rodar**

ruego VERBO *ver* **rogar**

el **rugby** SUSTANTIVO
rugby ◊ *jugar al rugby* to play rugby

rugir* VERBO
to roar

el **ruido** SUSTANTIVO
noise ◊ *¿Has oído ese ruido?* Did you hear that noise? ◊ *No hagáis tanto ruido.* Don't make so much noise.

ruidoso ADJETIVO
noisy

la **ruina** SUSTANTIVO
♦ **Su socio lo llevó a la ruina.** His business partner ruined him financially.
♦ **las ruinas** (*de edificio, ciudad*) the ruins ◊ *El castillo está en ruinas.* The castle is in ruins.

el **rulo** SUSTANTIVO
roller

la **rulot** SUSTANTIVO (PL las **rulots**)
caravan

la **rumana** SUSTANTIVO
Romanian

Rumanía SUSTANTIVO FEM
Romania

el **rumano** ADJETIVO, SUSTANTIVO
Romanian (*persona, idioma*)

la **rumba** SUSTANTIVO
rumba

el **rumor** SUSTANTIVO
1 rumour ◊ *Corre el rumor de que se retira.* There's a rumour going round that he's retiring.
2 murmur ◊ *el rumor de las olas* the murmur of the waves

rural ADJETIVO
rural

la **rusa** SUSTANTIVO
Russian

Rusia SUSTANTIVO FEM
Russia

el **ruso** ADJETIVO, SUSTANTIVO
Russian (*persona, idioma*)

la **ruta** SUSTANTIVO
route

la **rutina** SUSTANTIVO
routine
♦ **un chequeo de rutina** a routine check-up ◊ *la rutina diaria* the daily routine

R

S

el **sábado** SUSTANTIVO

Los días de la semana se escriben con mayúscula.

Saturday ◊ *La vi el sábado.* I saw her on Saturday. ◊ *todos los sábados* every Saturday ◊ *el sábado pasado* last Saturday ◊ *el sábado que viene* next Saturday ◊ *Jugamos los sábados.* We play on Saturdays.

la **sábana** SUSTANTIVO

sheet

saber* VERBO

[1] to know ◊ *No lo sé.* I don't know. ◊ *Sabe mucho de ordenadores.* He knows a lot about computers.

♦ **Lo dudo, pero nunca se sabe.** I doubt it, but you never know. ◊ *¡Y yo que sé!* How should I know?

[2] to find out ◊ *En cuanto lo supimos fuimos a ayudarle.* As soon as we found out, we went to help him.

♦ **No sé nada de ella.** I haven't heard from her.

♦ **que yo sepa** as far as I know

[3] can ◊ *No sabe nadar.* She can't swim. ◊ *¿Sabes inglés?* Can you speak English?

[4] to taste ◊ *Sabe a pescado.* It tastes of fish.

♦ **saberse** to know ◊ *Se sabe la lista de memoria.* He knows the list off by heart.

sabio ADJETIVO

wise

el **sabor** SUSTANTIVO

[1] taste ◊ *Tiene un sabor muy raro.* It's got a very strange taste.

[2] flavour ◊ *¿De qué sabor lo quieres?* What flavour do you want?

el **sabotaje** SUSTANTIVO

sabotage

sabré VERBO *ver* **saber**

sabroso ADJETIVO

tasty

el **sacacorchos** SUSTANTIVO (PL los **sacacorchos**)

corkscrew

el **sacapuntas** SUSTANTIVO (PL los **sacapuntas**)

pencil sharpener

sacar* VERBO

[1] to take out ◊ *Voy a sacar dinero del cajero.* I'm going to take some money out of the machine. ◊ *Se sacó las llaves del bolsillo.* He took the keys out of his pocket. ◊ *sacar la basura* to take the rubbish out

♦ **Me han sacado una muela.** I've had a tooth taken out.

♦ **sacar a pasear al perro** to take the dog out for a walk

♦ **sacar a alguien a bailar** to get somebody up for a dance

[2] to get ◊ *Yo sacaré las entradas.* I'll get the tickets. ◊ *sacar buenas notas* to get good marks

[3] to release ◊ *Han sacado un nuevo disco.* They've released a new record.

♦ **sacar algo adelante** (*proyecto, negocio*) to conclude

♦ **sacar una foto a alguien** to take a photo of somebody

♦ **sacar la lengua a alguien** to stick your tongue out at somebody

♦ **sacarse el carnet de conducir** to pass one's driving test

♦ **sacarse el título de abogado** to qualify as a lawyer

♦ **sacarse las botas** to take off one's boots

la **sacarina** SUSTANTIVO

saccharin

el **sacerdote** SUSTANTIVO

priest

el **saco** SUSTANTIVO

[1] sack ◊ *un saco de harina* a sack of flour

♦ **un saco de dormir** a sleeping bag

[2] jacket (*chaqueta*) Latin America

el **sacrificio** SUSTANTIVO

sacrifice

sacudir VERBO

to shake ◊ *Hay que sacudir la alfombra.* The carpet needs shaking. ◊ *Un terremoto sacudió la ciudad.* An earthquake shook the city.

Sagitario SUSTANTIVO MASC

Sagittarius ◊ *Soy Sagitario.* I'm a Sagittarius.

sagrado ADJETIVO

[1] sacred (*lugar*)

[2] holy (*escrituras, altar*)

la **sal** SUSTANTIVO

salt

la **sala** SUSTANTIVO

[1] room (*habitación*)

[2] ward (*en hospital*)

[3] hall (*de conferencias, conciertos*)

♦ **sala de embarque** departure lounge

♦ **sala de espera** waiting room

♦ **sala de estar** living room

♦ **sala de fiestas** nightclub

♦ **sala de juegos recreativos** amusement arcade

♦ **sala de profesores** staffroom

salado ADJETIVO

* Verbs marked with this symbol are irregular. See pages 380-382 for further details

1 salty ◊ *La carne está muy salada.* The meat's very salty.
2 savoury ◊ *¿Es dulce o salado?* Is it sweet or savoury?

el **salario** SUSTANTIVO
pay
♦ **el salario mínimo** the minimum wage

la **salchicha** SUSTANTIVO
sausage

el **salchichón** SUSTANTIVO (PL los **salchichones**)
spiced salami sausage

el **saldo** SUSTANTIVO
balance (*de cuenta*)
♦ **saldos** (*rebajas*) sales

saldré VERBO *ver* **salir**

el **salero** SUSTANTIVO
salt cellar

salgo VERBO *ver* **salir**

la **salida** SUSTANTIVO
1 exit ◊ *salida de emergencia* emergency exit ◊ *salida de incendios* fire exit
♦ **a la salida del teatro** on the way out of the theatre
2 departure ◊ *la terminal de salidas nacionales* the domestic departures terminal
♦ **El tren de Londres efectuará su salida por el andén número dos.** The London train will depart from platform two.
3 start (*de una carrera*)
♦ **El juez dio la salida a la carrera.** The referee started the race.
♦ **la salida del sol** sunrise

salir* VERBO
1 to come out ◊ *cuando salimos del cine* when we came out of the cinema ◊ *Acaba de salir un disco suyo.* A record of his has just come out. ◊ *Nos levantamos antes de que saliera el sol.* We got up before the sun came out.
2 to go out ◊ *¿Vas a salir esta noche?* Are you going out tonight?
♦ **Ha salido.** She's out.
♦ **salir con alguien** to go out with somebody ◊ *Está saliendo con un compañero de clase.* She's going out with one of her classmates.
3 to get out ◊ *¡Sal de ahí ahora mismo!* Get out of here right now!
4 to leave ◊ *El autocar sale a las ocho.* The coach leaves at eight. ◊ *Quiere salir del país.* She wants to leave the country.
5 to appear ◊ *Su foto salió en todos los periódicos.* Her picture appeared in all the newspapers.
♦ **Sale a 2.000 pesetas por persona.** It works out at 2,000 pesetas each.
♦ **Me está saliendo una muela del juicio.** One of my wisdom teeth is coming through.
♦ **No sé cómo vamos a salir adelante.** I don't know how we're going to go on.
♦ **salir bien** to work out well ◊ *El plan salió bien.* The plan worked out well.
♦ **Espero que todo salga bien.** I hope everything works out all right.
♦ **Les salió mal el proyecto.** Their plan didn't work out.
♦ **¡Qué mal me ha salido el dibujo!** My drawing hasn't come out very well, has it!
♦ **salirse (1)** (*rebosar*) to boil over ◊ *Se ha salido la leche.* The milk's boiled over.
♦ **salirse (2)** (*filtrarse*) to leak ◊ *Se salía el aceite del motor.* Oil was leaking out of the engine.
♦ **salirse (3)** (*desviarse*) to come off ◊ *Nos salimos de la carretera.* We came off the road.
♦ **salirse (4)** to come out ◊ *Se ha salido el enchufe.* The plug has come out.

la **saliva** SUSTANTIVO
saliva

el **salmón** SUSTANTIVO (PL los **salmones**)
salmon
♦ **rosa salmón** salmon pink

el **salón** SUSTANTIVO (PL los **salones**)
1 living room (*de una casa*)
♦ **salón de actos** meeting hall
♦ **salón de belleza** beauty salon
♦ **salón de juegos recreativos** amusement arcade
2 classroom (*aula*) Mexico

la **salpicadera** SUSTANTIVO Mexico
mudguard

el **salpicadero** SUSTANTIVO
dashboard

salpicar* VERBO
to splash

la **salsa** SUSTANTIVO
1 sauce ◊ *salsa de tomate* tomato sauce
2 salsa (*música*)

el **saltamontes** SUSTANTIVO (PL los **saltamontes**)
grasshopper

saltar VERBO
to jump ◊ *El caballo saltó la valla.* The horse jumped over the wall. ◊ *saltar por la ventana* to jump out of the window
♦ **hacer saltar algo por los aires** to blow something up
♦ **saltarse** to skip ◊ *Te has saltado una página.* You've skipped a page.
♦ **saltarse un semáforo en rojo** to go through a red light

el **salto** SUSTANTIVO
1 jump (*hacia arriba*)
2 dive (*en el agua*)
♦ **dar un salto** to jump
♦ **salto de altura** high jump
♦ **salto de longitud** long jump
♦ **salto mortal** somersault
♦ **salto con pértiga** pole vault

☞

◆ **salto de trampolín** springboard diving

la **salud** SUSTANTIVO
health

salud EXCLAMACIÓN
1 cheers! (*al brindar*)
2 bless you! (*al estornudar*)

saludable ADJETIVO
healthy

saludar VERBO
1 to say hello ◊ *Entré a saludarla.* I went in to say hello to her.
2 to greet ◊ *Me saludó dándome un beso.* He greeted me with a kiss.
◆ **Lo saludé desde la otra acera.** I waved to him from the other side of the street.
3 to salute (*en el ejército*)

el **saludo** SUSTANTIVO
1 greeting ◊ *No contestó a mi saludo.* He didn't respond to my greeting.
2 regards ◊ *Carolina te manda un saludo.* Carolina sends her regards. ◊ *Saludos cordiales.* Kind regards.
◆ **¡Saludos a Teresa de mi parte!** Say hello to Teresa for me!

salvaje ADJETIVO
wild

el **salvapantallas** SUSTANTIVO
screensaver

salvar VERBO
to save ◊ *Pocos se salvaron del naufragio.* Few were saved from the shipwreck.

el **salvavidas** SUSTANTIVO (PL los **salvavidas**)
lifebelt

salvo PREPOSICIÓN
except ◊ *todos salvo yo* everyone except me
◆ **salvo que** unless
◆ **estar a salvo** to be safe
◆ **Consiguieron ponerse a salvo.** They managed to reach safety.

San ADJETIVO
Saint ◊ *San Pedro* Saint Peter

la **sandalia** SUSTANTIVO
sandal
◆ **unas sandalias** a pair of sandals

la **sandía** SUSTANTIVO
watermelon

el **sandwich** SUSTANTIVO (PL los **sandwiches**)
1 (*emparedado*)
sandwich (PL sandwiches)
2 (*caliente*)
toasted sandwich

sangrar VERBO
to bleed ◊ *Me sangra la nariz.* My nose is bleeding.

la **sangre** SUSTANTIVO
blood

la **sangría** SUSTANTIVO
sangria (*bebida*)

la **sanidad** SUSTANTIVO
public health ◊ *una reforma de la sanidad pública* a reform in public health

sano ADJETIVO
healthy (*con salud*) ◊ *una dieta sana* a healthy diet
◆ **sano y salvo** safe and sound

*No confundir **sano** con **sane**.*

la **santa** SUSTANTIVO
saint ◊ *Santa Clara* Saint Clara

santo ADJETIVO
holy

el **santo** SUSTANTIVO
1 saint ◊ *Santo Domingo* Saint Dominic
2 name day

> *Besides birthdays, some Spaniards also celebrate the feast day of the saint they are named after.*

el **sapo** SUSTANTIVO
toad

el **saque** SUSTANTIVO
service (*en tenis*)
◆ **saque de esquina** corner
◆ **saque inicial** kick-off

el **sarampión** SUSTANTIVO (PL los **sarampiones**)
measles SING

sarcástico ADJETIVO
sarcastic

la **sardina** SUSTANTIVO
sardine

el/la **sargento** SUSTANTIVO
sergeant

el **sarpullido** SUSTANTIVO
rash (PL rashes) ◊ *Le ha salido un sarpullido en la cara.* His face has come out in a rash.

el **sarro** SUSTANTIVO
tartar

la **sarta** SUSTANTIVO
◆ **Nos contó una sarta de mentiras.** He told us a pack of lies.

la **sartén** SUSTANTIVO (PL las **sartenes**)
frying pan

el **sartén** SUSTANTIVO (PL los **sartenes**)
Latin America
frying pan

el **sastre** SUSTANTIVO
tailor

el **satélite** SUSTANTIVO
satellite ◊ *la televisión vía satélite* satellite television

la **satisfacción** SUSTANTIVO (PL las **satisfacciones**)
satisfaction ◊ *Expresó su satisfacción por la victoria.* She expressed her satisfaction at the victory.

◆ **Recibió la noticia con satisfacción.** He was pleased to hear the news.

satisfacer* VERBO
to satisfy

satisfactorio ADJETIVO
satisfactory

satisfecho ADJETIVO
satisfied ◊ *No estoy satisfecho con el resultado.* I'm not satisfied with the result.

la **sauna** SUSTANTIVO
sauna

el **saxofón** SUSTANTIVO (PL los **saxofones**)
saxophone

sazonar VERBO
to season

se PRONOMBRE

*Cuando **se** funciona como complemento indirecto, junto a otro pronombre, se traduce por **him, her, them** o **you,** según nos refiramos a "él", "ella", "ellos" o "ellas" y "usted" o "ustedes".*

◊ *Pedro necesitaba la calculadora y se la dejé.* Pedro needed the calculator and I lent it to him. ◊ *No quiero que Rosa lo sepa. No se lo digas.* I don't want Rosa to know. Don't tell her. ◊ *He hablado con mis padres y se lo he explicado.* I've talked to my parents and explained it to them. ◊ *Aquí tiene las flores. ¿Se las envuelvo, señor?* Here are your flowers. Shall I wrap them for you, sir?

Pero cuando se repite el complemento, no se traduce.

◊ *Dáselo a Enrique.* Give it to Enrique. ◊ *No se lo digas a Susana.* Don't tell Susana. ◊ *¿Se lo has preguntado a tus padres?* Have you asked your parents about it?

*Cuando **se** tiene un valor reflexivo se traduce por **himself, herself, itself, themselves, yourself** o **yourselves** según nos refiramos a "él", "ella", "ellos" o "ellas", "usted" o "ustedes".*

◊ *Marcos se ha cortado con un cristal.* Marcos cut himself on a piece of broken glass. ◊ *Margarita se estaba preparando para salir.* Margarita was getting herself ready to go out. ◊ *La calefacción se apaga sola.* The heating turns itself off automatically. ◊ *¿Se ha hecho usted daño?* Have you hurt yourself?

◆ **Se está afeitando.** He's shaving.

◆ **Mi hermana nunca se queja.** My sister never complains.

Con partes del cuerpo o con prendas que se llevan puestas se usa el adjetivo posesivo.

◊ *Pablo se lavó los dientes.* Pablo brushed his teeth. ◊ *Carmen no podía abrocharse el vestido.* Carmen couldn't do up her dress.

*Cuando **se** tiene un valor recíproco se traduce por **each other.***

◊ *Se dieron un beso.* They gave each other a kiss.

*Cuando **se** tiene un valor impersonal suele traducirse por **it** o **you.***

◊ *Se cree que el tabaco produce cáncer.* It is believed that smoking causes cancer. ◊ *Es lo que pasa cuando se come tan deprisa.* That's what happens when you eat so fast.

◆ **"se vende"** "for sale"

sé VERBO *ver* **saber**

sea VERBO *ver* **ser**

el **secador** SUSTANTIVO
hair dryer *

la **secadora** SUSTANTIVO
1 tumble dryer (*de ropa*)
2 hair dryer (*de pelo*) Mexico

secar* VERBO
to dry (*pelo, platos*) ◊ *Voy a secarme el pelo.* I'm going to dry my hair.

◆ **secarse** to dry ◊ *Sécate con la toalla.* Dry yourself with the towel.

◆ **¿Se ha secado ya la ropa?** Is the washing dry yet?

◆ **Se han secado las plantas.** The plants have dried up.

la **sección** SUSTANTIVO (PL las **secciones**)
1 section (*división*) ◊ *la sección de deportes del periódico* the sports section of the newspaper
2 department (*en grandes almacenes*) ◊ *la sección de perfumería* the perfumery department

seco ADJETIVO
1 dry ◊ *El suelo ya está seco.* The floor's dry now. ◊ *Tiene una tos muy seca.* He's got a very dry cough.
2 dried ◊ *flores secas* dried flowers

el **secretario**
la **secretaria** SUSTANTIVO
secretary (PL secretaries)

◆ **una secretaria de dirección** a PA (= personal assistant)

el **secreto** SUSTANTIVO
secret ◊ *Te voy a contar un secreto.* I'm going to tell you a secret.

◆ **en secreto** in secret

secreto ADJETIVO
secret

la **secta** SUSTANTIVO
sect

el **sector** SUSTANTIVO
sector ◊ *el sector de la minería* the mining sector

la **secuencia** SUSTANTIVO
sequence (*de una película*)

el **secuestrador,** la **secuestradora** SUSTANTIVO
1 kidnapper (*de persona*)
2 hijacker (*de avión*)

S

secuestrar VERBO
1 to kidnap (*persona*)
2 to hijack (*avión*)

el **secuestro** SUSTANTIVO
1 kidnapping (*de persona*)
2 hijack (*de avión*)

secundario ADJETIVO
secondary

la **sed** SUSTANTIVO
thirst
◆ **tener sed** to be thirsty

la **seda** SUSTANTIVO
silk ◇ *una camisa de seda* a silk shirt

el **sedal** SUSTANTIVO
fishing line

el **sedante** SUSTANTIVO
sedative

la **sede** SUSTANTIVO
1 headquarters PL ◇ *la sede de la ONU en Zagreb* the UN headquarters in Zagreb
2 venue ◇ *Barcelona fue la sede de los Juegos Olímpicos del 92.* Barcelona was the venue for the 1992 Olympics.

sediento ADJETIVO
thirsty

segar* VERBO
1 to reap (*trigo*)
2 to mow (*hierba*)

seguido ADJETIVO
in a row ◇ *La he visto tres días seguidos.* I've seen her three days in a row.
◆ **en seguida** straight away ◇ *En seguida estoy con usted.* I'll be with you straight away.
◆ **En seguida termino.** I'm just about to finish.
◆ **todo seguido** straight on ◇ *Vaya todo seguido hasta la plaza y luego ...* Go straight on until the square and then ...

seguir* VERBO
1 to carry on (*acción, movimiento*) ◇ *¡Sigue, por favor!* Carry on, please! ◇ *El ordenador seguía funcionando pese al apagón.* The computer carried on working despite the black out.

*Cuando el verbo **seguir** indica la continuidad de una situación, se traduce muchas veces por el adverbio "still".*

◆ **El ascensor sigue estropeado.** The lift's still not working.
◆ **Sigo sin comprender.** I still don't understand.
◆ **Sigue lloviendo.** It's still raining.
2 to follow (*ir detrás*) ◇ *Tú ve primero que yo te sigo.* You go first and I'll follow you.
◆ **seguir adelante** to go ahead ◇ *Los Juegos Olímpicos siguieron adelante a pesar del atentado.* The Olympics went ahead despite the attack.

según PREPOSICIÓN
1 according to ◇ *Según tú, no habrá problemas de entradas.* According to you there won't be any problems with the tickets.
2 depending on ◇ *Iremos o no, según esté el tiempo.* We might go, depending on the weather.

segundo ADJETIVO, PRONOMBRE (FEM **segunda**)
second
◆ **el segundo plato** the second course
◆ **Vive en el segundo.** He lives on the second floor.

el **segundo** SUSTANTIVO
second ◇ *Es un segundo nada más.* It'll only take a second.

seguramente ADVERBIO
probably ◇ *Seguramente llegarán mañana.* They'll probably arrive tomorrow.
◆ **¿Lo va a comprar? – Seguramente.** Are you going to buy it? – Almost certainly.

la **seguridad** SUSTANTIVO
1 safety (*falta de peligro*) ◇ *Hay que mejorar la seguridad en los autocares.* Safety on coaches must be improved.
2 security (*prevención*) ◇ *Las medidas de seguridad son muy estrictas.* The security measures are very strict.
3 certainty (*certeza*) ◇ *con toda seguridad* with complete certainty
◆ **seguridad en uno mismo** self-confidence ◇ *Le falta seguridad en sí mismo.* He lacks self-confidence.
◆ **la seguridad social** social security

seguro ADJETIVO
1 safe ◇ *Este avión es muy seguro.* This plane is very safe. ◇ *Aquí estaremos seguros.* We'll be safe here.
2 sure ◇ *Estoy segura de que ganaremos.* I'm sure we'll win. ◇ *Está muy seguro de sí mismo.* He's very sure of himself.
3 certain ◇ *No es seguro que vayan a venir.* It's not certain that they're going to come.

el **seguro** SUSTANTIVO
insurance ◇ *el seguro del coche* car insurance
◆ **seguro de vida** life assurance

seis ADJETIVO, PRONOMBRE
six
◆ **Son las seis.** It's six o'clock.
◆ **el seis de enero** the sixth of January

seiscientos ADJETIVO, PRONOMBRE (FEM **seiscientas**)
six hundred

la **selección** SUSTANTIVO (PL las **selecciones**)
1 selection ◇ *una selección de los mejores vídeos* a selection of the finest videos

[2] team ◇ *la selección nacional* the national team

seleccionar VERBO
to pick ◇ *Lo seleccionaron para jugar en la Ryder Cup.* He was picked to play in the Ryder Cup.

la **selectividad** SUSTANTIVO
university entrance exam

sellar VERBO
[1] to seal (*carta, paquete*)
[2] to stamp (*pasaporte*)
[3] to sign on (*en el paro*)

el **sello** SUSTANTIVO
[1] stamp ◇ *Colecciona sellos.* He collects stamps.
[2] seal ◇ *El producto lleva un sello de calidad.* The product bears a seal of quality.

la **selva** SUSTANTIVO
jungle
♦ **la selva tropical** the rainforest

el **semáforo** SUSTANTIVO
traffic lights PL
♦ **un semáforo en rojo** a red light

la **semana** SUSTANTIVO
week ◇ *dentro de una semana* in a week's time ◇ *una vez a la semana* once a week
♦ **entre semana** during the week
♦ **Semana Santa** Holy Week

semanal ADJETIVO
weekly

sembrar* VERBO
[1] to plant (*flor, patata*)
[2] to sow (*semillas*)

semejante ADJETIVO
[1] similar (*parecido*) ◇ *Tenemos los rasgos muy semejantes.* We have very similar features.
[2] such ◇ *Nunca he dicho semejante cosa.* I've never said such a thing.

el **semicírculo** SUSTANTIVO
semicircle

la **semifinal** SUSTANTIVO
semi-final

la **semilla** SUSTANTIVO
seed

el **senado** SUSTANTIVO
senate

el **senador**, la **senadora** SUSTANTIVO
senator

sencillamente ADVERBIO
simply ◇ *Es sencillamente imposible.* It's simply impossible.

sencillo ADJETIVO
[1] simple ◇ *Es muy sencillo.* It's really simple. ◇ *un vestido sencillo* a simple dress
[2] modest ◇ *Es muy sencillo en el trato.* He has a very modest manner.

el **sencillo** SUSTANTIVO
[1] single (*disco*)
[2] small change (*dinero*) Latin America

el **senderismo** SUSTANTIVO
trekking

el **sendero** SUSTANTIVO
path

la **sensación** SUSTANTIVO (PL las **sensaciones**)
feeling ◇ *Tengo la sensación de que mienten sobre Pilar.* I get the feeling they're lying about Pilar. ◇ *una sensación de picor* an itchy feeling

sensacional ADJETIVO
sensational

sensato ADJETIVO
sensible ◇ *Lo sensato sería no moverse de aquí.* The sensible thing would be not to move from here.

sensible ADJETIVO
sensitive ◇ *Es un chico muy sensible.* He's a very sensitive boy. ◇ *Tengo los ojos muy sensibles.* My eyes are very sensitive.

*No confundir **sensible** con la palabra inglesa **sensible**.*

sensual ADJETIVO
sensuous

sentado ADJETIVO
♦ **estar sentado** to be sitting down

sentar* VERBO
[1] to suit ◇ *Ese vestido te sienta muy bien.* That dress really suits you.
[2] to agree with ◇ *No me sienta bien cenar tanto.* Having so much dinner doesn't agree with me.
♦ **Le ha sentado mal que no lo invitaras a la boda.** He was put out that you didn't invite him to the wedding.
♦ **sentarse** to sit down ◇ *Por favor, siéntese.* Please sit down.

la **sentencia** SUSTANTIVO
sentence

el **sentido** SUSTANTIVO
[1] sense ◇ *No tiene sentido.* It doesn't make sense.
[2] meaning (*significado*) ◇ *palabras con doble sentido* words with a double meaning
♦ **sentido común** common sense
♦ **sentido del humor** sense of humour
♦ **una calle de sentido único** a one-way street
♦ **en algún sentido** in some respects
♦ **en cierto sentido** in a certain sense

sentimental ADJETIVO
sentimental

el **sentimiento** SUSTANTIVO
feeling

sentir* VERBO
[1] to feel ◇ *Sentí un dolor en la pierna.* I felt a pain in my leg.
♦ **De pronto sentí un poco de frío.** Suddenly I felt a bit cold.
[2] to hear ◇ *No la sentí entrar.* I didn't hear her come in.

S

☞

3 to be sorry ◊ *Lo siento mucho.* I'm very sorry. ◊ *Siento llegar tarde.* I'm sorry I'm late.
◆ **sentirse** to feel ◊ *No me siento nada bien.* I don't feel at all well.

la **seña** SUSTANTIVO
sign ◊ *Les hice una seña.* I made a sign to them. ◊ *Nos comunicábamos por señas.* We communicated by signs.
◆ **señas** (*domicilio*) address

la **señal** SUSTANTIVO
1 sign
◆ **señal de tráfico** road sign
◆ **señal indicadora** signpost
◆ **señal de llamada** (*al teléfono*) dialling tone
2 signal ◊ *Yo daré la señal.* I'll give the signal.
◆ **Les hice una señal para que se fueran.** I signalled to them to go.
3 deposit ◊ *Dimos una señal de 5.000 pesetas.* We paid a deposit of 5,000 pesetas.

señalar VERBO
to mark ◊ *Señálalo con un bolígrafo rojo.* Mark it with a red pen.
◆ **señalar con el dedo** to point

señalizar* VERBO
1 to indicate (*con la mano*)
2 to signpost (*camino, carretera*)

el **señor** SUSTANTIVO
1 man (PL men) ◊ *Este señor ha llegado antes que yo.* This man was before me.
◆ **¿Le ocurre algo, señor?** Is there something the matter?
◆ **¿Qué le pongo, señor?** What would you like, sir?
2 Mr ◊ *el señor Delgado* Mr Delgado
3 lord ◊ *un señor feudal* a feudal lord
◆ **Muy señor mío ...** Dear Sir ...
◆ **el señor alcalde** the mayor

la **señora** SUSTANTIVO
1 lady (PL ladies) ◊ *Deja pasar a esta señora.* Let the lady past.
◆ **¿Le ocurre algo, señora?** Is there something the matter?
◆ **¿Qué le pongo, señora?** What would you like, madam?
2 Mrs ◊ *la señora Delgado* Mrs Delgado

*La forma abreviada **Mrs** se usa en inglés cuando queremos especificar que la mujer está casada, pero cuando no queremos dar importancia a este hecho, se prefiere el uso de **Ms**.*

3 wife ◊ *Vino con su señora.* He came with his wife.

la **señorita** SUSTANTIVO
young lady ◊ *Deja pasar a esta señorita.* Let the young lady past. ◊ *la señorita Delgado* Miss Delgado

*La forma abreviada **Miss** se usa en inglés cuando queremos especificar que la mujer es soltera, pero cuando no queremos dar importancia a este hecho, se prefiere el uso de **Ms**.*

sepa VERBO *ver* **saber**

la **separación** SUSTANTIVO (PL las **separaciones**)
1 separation (*entre personas, de matrimonio*)
2 gap (*entre objetos*) ◊ *Había una gran separación entre el andén y la vía.* There was a large gap between the platform and the rails.

separado ADJETIVO
1 separate ◊ *Duermen en camas separadas.* They sleep in separate beds.
◆ **por separado** separately
2 separated ◊ *Está separado de su mujer.* He's separated from his wife.

separar VERBO
to separate
◆ **separarse (1)** (*matrimonio*) to separate
◆ **separarse (2)** (*novios, grupo*) to split up

septiembre SUSTANTIVO MASC

Los meses se escriben con mayúscula.

September ◊ *en septiembre* in September ◊ *Ella nació el 11 de septiembre.* She was born on 11 September.

séptimo ADJETIVO, PRONOMBRE (FEM **séptima**)
seventh
◆ **Vivo en el séptimo.** I live on the seventh floor.

la **sequía** SUSTANTIVO
drought

ser* VERBO
to be ◊ *Es muy alto.* He's very tall. ◊ *Es médico.* He's a doctor. ◊ *La fiesta va a ser en su casa.* The party's going to be in her house. ◊ *Fue construido en 1960.* It was built in 1960. ◊ *Era de noche.* It was night.
◆ **Soy Lucía.** (*al teléfono*) It's Lucía.
◆ **Son las seis y media.** It's half past six.
◆ **Éramos cinco en el coche.** There were five of us in the car.

*Cuando en español decimos **somos tres**, **son ocho**, esta estructura se traduce al inglés por **there are** + el número + **of us**, **of them**, etc.*

◆ **¡Es cierto!** That's right!
◆ **Me es imposible asistir.** It's impossible for me to attend.
◆ **ser de (1)** (*pertenecer a*)
◆ **Es de Joaquín.** It's Joaquín's.
◆ **ser de (2)** (*venir de*) to be from ◊ *¿De dónde eres?* Where are you from?
◆ **ser de (3)** (*estar hecho de*) to be made of ◊ *Es de piedra.* It's made of stone.

- ◆**a no ser que ...** unless ... ◇ *a no ser que salgamos mañana* unless we leave tomorrow
- ◆**O sea, que no vienes.** So you're not coming.
- ◆**mis hijos, o sea, Juan y Pedro** my children, that is, Juan and Pedro

el **ser** SUSTANTIVO
being
- ◆**un ser humano** a human being
- ◆**un ser vivo** a living being

la **serie** SUSTANTIVO
series ◇ *Tuvimos una serie de reuniones.* We had a series of meetings. ◇ *una serie policíaca* a police series

serio ADJETIVO
serious
- ◆**en serio** seriously ◇ *No hablaba en serio.* I wasn't speaking seriously.
- ◆**¿Lo dices en serio?** Do you really mean it?

el **sermón** SUSTANTIVO (PL los **sermones**)
sermon

la **serpiente** SUSTANTIVO
snake
- ◆**una serpiente de cascabel** a rattlesnake

serrar* VERBO
to saw

el **serrucho** SUSTANTIVO
saw

servicial ADJETIVO
helpful

el **servicio** SUSTANTIVO
[1] service ◇ *el servicio militar* national service ◇ *El servicio no va incluido.* Service is not included.
- ◆**Tenemos servicio a domicilio.** We have a home delivery service.
- ◆**estar de servicio** to be on duty
- ◆**estar fuera de servicio (1)** (*máquina*) to be out of service
- ◆**estar fuera de servicio (2)** (*persona*) to be off duty

[2] toilet ◇ *Está en el servicio.* He's in the toilet.
- ◆**el servicio de caballeros** the gents'
- ◆**el servicio de señoras** the ladies'
- ◆**Al servicio, Costa.** (*en tenis*) Costa to serve.

el **servidor** SUSTANTIVO
server (*informática*)

la **servilleta** SUSTANTIVO
napkin

servir* VERBO
[1] to be useful for ◇ *Estas bolsas sirven para guardar alimentos.* These bags are useful for storing food.
- ◆**¿Para qué sirve esto?** What's this for?
- ◆**Esta radio aún sirve.** This radio still works.

[2] to serve ◇ *Yo serviré la cena.* I'll serve supper.
- ◆**Sírveme un poco más de vino.** Give me a little bit more wine.
- ◆**Trabaja sirviendo mesas.** She works as a waitress.
- ◆**no servir para nada** to be useless
- ◆**¿En qué puedo servirlo?** How can I help you?

sesenta ADJETIVO, PRONOMBRE
sixty ◇ *Tiene sesenta años.* He's sixty.
- ◆**el sesenta aniversario** the sixtieth anniversary

la **sesión** SUSTANTIVO (PL las **sesiones**)
[1] session ◇ *una sesión parlamentaria* a parliamentary session
[2] showing ◇ *Fuimos a la última sesión del sábado.* We went to the last showing on Saturday night.

la **seta** SUSTANTIVO
mushroom
- ◆**seta venenosa** toadstool

setecientos ADJETIVO, PRONOMBRE (FEM **setecientas**)
seven hundred

setenta ADJETIVO, PRONOMBRE
seventy ◇ *Tiene setenta años.* He's seventy.
- ◆**el setenta aniversario** the seventieth anniversary

el **seto** SUSTANTIVO
hedge

el **seudónimo** SUSTANTIVO
pseudonym

severo ADJETIVO
[1] strict (*profesor*)
[2] harsh (*críticas, castigo, invierno*)

Sevilla SUSTANTIVO FEM
Seville

el/la **sexista** ADJETIVO, SUSTANTIVO
sexist

el **sexo** SUSTANTIVO
sex

sexto ADJETIVO, PRONOMBRE (FEM **sexta**)
sixth
- ◆**Vivo en el sexto.** I live on the sixth floor.

sexual ADJETIVO
sexual ◇ *acoso sexual* sexual harassment
- ◆**educación sexual** sex education

la **sexualidad** SUSTANTIVO
sexuality

si CONJUNCIÓN
[1] if ◇ *Si quieres, te dejo el coche.* I'll lend you the car if you like. ◇ *¿Sabes si hemos cobrado ya?* Do you know if we've been paid yet?
- ◆**¿Y si llueve?** And what if it rains?
- ◆**Si me hubiera tocado la lotería ...** If only I had won the lottery ...

[2] whether ◇ *No sé si ir o no.* I don't know whether to go or not.

♦**si no (1)** otherwise ◊ *Ponte crema. Si no, te quemarás.* Put some cream on, otherwise you'll get sunburned.

♦**si no (2)** if...not ◊ *Avisadme si no podéis venir.* Let me know if you can't come.

sí (1) ADVERBIO
yes ◊ *¿Te apetece un café? – Sí, gracias.* Do you fancy a coffee? – Yes, please.

♦**¿Te gusta? – Sí.** Do you like it? – Yes, I do.

♦**Creo que sí.** I think so.

♦**Él no quiere pero yo sí.** He doesn't want to but I do.

sí (2) PRONOMBRE

Cuando tiene un valor reflexivo, ***sí*** *se traduce por* ***himself, herself, itself*** *o* ***themselves****, o por el pronombre* ***yourself*** *o* ***yourselves*** *cuando nos referimos a "usted", "ustedes".*

◊ *Sólo habla de sí mismo.* He only talks about himself. ◊ *Se perjudica a sí misma.* She's harming herself. ◊ *Pregúntese a sí mismo el motivo.* Ask yourself the reason. ◊ *La pregunta en sí no era difícil.* The question itself wasn't difficult. ◊ *Hablaban entre sí.* They were talking among themselves.

♦**La Tierra gira sobre sí misma.** The Earth turns on its own axis.

Cuando se usa con valor impersonal se traduce por ***yourself****.*

◊ *Es mejor aprender las cosas por sí mismo.* It's better to learn things by yourself.

Sicilia SUSTANTIVO FEM
Sicily

el **sida** SUSTANTIVO
AIDS

la **sidra** SUSTANTIVO
cider

siego VERBO *ver* **segar**

siembro VERBO *ver* **sembrar**

siempre ADVERBIO
always ◊ *Siempre llega tarde.* She always arrives late.

♦**como siempre** as usual

♦**para siempre** forever

♦**siempre y cuando** provided ◊ *siempre y cuando acepte nuestras condiciones* provided he accepts our conditions

siendo VERBO *ver* **ser**

siento VERBO *ver* **sentir**

la **sierra** SUSTANTIVO
1 saw (*herramienta*)
2 mountain range (*cordillera*)

♦**Tenemos una casa en la sierra.** We have a house in the mountains.

la **siesta** SUSTANTIVO
nap

♦**echarse la siesta** to have a nap

♦**la hora de la siesta** siesta time

siete ADJETIVO, PRONOMBRE
seven

♦**Son las siete.** It's seven o'clock.

♦**el siete de marzo** the seventh of March

las **siglas** SUSTANTIVO
abbreviation SING

el **siglo** SUSTANTIVO
century (PL centuries) ◊ *el siglo 20* the 20th century

el **significado** SUSTANTIVO
meaning

significar* VERBO
1 to mean ◊ *¿Qué significa "wild"?* What does "wild" mean? ◊ *No sé lo que significa.* I don't know what it means.
2 to stand for (*con siglas*) ◊ *"B.C." significa "before Christ".* "B.C." stands for "before Christ".

significativo ADJETIVO
significant

el **signo** SUSTANTIVO
sign ◊ *Ese apetito es signo de buena salud.* Such an appetite is a sign of good health.

♦**¿De qué signo del zodíaco eres?** What star sign are you?

♦**signo de admiración** exclamation mark

♦**signo de interrogación** question mark

siguiendo VERBO *ver* **seguir**

siguiente ADJETIVO
next ◊ *el siguiente vuelo* the next flight ◊ *Al día siguiente visitamos Toledo.* The next day we visited Toledo.

♦**¡Que pase el siguiente, por favor!** Next please!

la **sílaba** SUSTANTIVO
syllable

silbar VERBO
to whistle

el **silbato** SUSTANTIVO
whistle

el **silbido** SUSTANTIVO
whistle

el **silencio** SUSTANTIVO
silence

♦**guardar silencio** to keep quiet

♦**¡Silencio!** Quiet!

silencioso ADJETIVO
silent

la **silla** SUSTANTIVO
chair

♦**silla de montar** saddle

♦**silla de paseo** (*de bebé*) pushchair

♦**silla de ruedas** wheelchair

el **sillín** SUSTANTIVO (PL los **sillines**)
saddle

el **sillón** SUSTANTIVO (PL los **sillones**)
armchair

la **silueta** SUSTANTIVO
outline

* Verbs marked with this symbol are irregular. See pages 380-382 for further details

♦ **Tiene una silueta perfecta.** She has a perfect figure.

el **símbolo** SUSTANTIVO
symbol

simpático ADJETIVO
nice ◊ *Estuvo muy simpática con todos.* She was very nice to everybody. ◊ *Los cubanos son muy simpáticos.* Cubans are very nice people.
♦ **Me cae simpático.** I think he's really nice.
*No confundir **simpático** con **sympathetic**.*

simple ADJETIVO
simple

simplemente ADVERBIO
simply

simultáneo ADJETIVO
simultaneous

sin PREPOSICIÓN
without ◊ *Es peligroso ir en moto sin casco.* It's dangerous to ride a motorbike without a helmet. ◊ *Salió sin hacer ruido.* She went out without making a noise. ◊ *sin que él se diera cuenta* without him realising
♦ **He dejado el crucigrama sin terminar.** I left the crossword unfinished.
♦ **Me quedé sin habla.** I was speechless.
♦ **la gente sin hogar** the homeless

sincero ADJETIVO
honest ◊ *Fui sincera con él.* I was honest with him.

el/la **sindicalista** SUSTANTIVO
trade unionist

el **sindicato** SUSTANTIVO
trade union

la **sinfonía** SUSTANTIVO
symphony (PL symphonies)

el **singular** ADJETIVO, SUSTANTIVO
singular
♦ **en singular** in the singular

siniestro ADJETIVO
sinister

sino CONJUNCIÓN
but ◊ *No son ingleses sino galeses.* They're not English, but Welsh.
♦ **No hace sino pedirnos dinero.** All he does is ask us for money.
♦ **No solo nos ayudó, sino que también nos invitó a cenar.** He didn't just help us, he also bought us dinner.

sintético ADJETIVO
synthetic

sintiendo VERBO *ver* **sentir**

el **síntoma** SUSTANTIVO
symptom

el/la **sinvergüenza** SUSTANTIVO
crook (*canalla*)
♦ **Es una sinvergüenza.** She's shameless.

siquiera ADVERBIO
♦ **ni siquiera** not even ◊ *Ni siquiera me dirigió la palabra.* She didn't even acknowledge me.

la **sirena** SUSTANTIVO
[1] siren (*de alarma*)
[2] mermaid (*personaje mitológico*)

sirviendo VERBO *ver* **servir**

la **sirvienta** SUSTANTIVO
maid

el **sirviente** SUSTANTIVO
servant

el **sistema** SUSTANTIVO
system

el **sitio** SUSTANTIVO
[1] place ◊ *un sitio tranquilo* a peaceful place
♦ **cambiar algo de sitio** to move something around
♦ **en cualquier sitio** anywhere
♦ **en algún sitio** somewhere
♦ **en ningún sitio** nowhere
[2] room ◊ *Hay sitio de sobra.* There's room to spare.
♦ **Hemos hecho sitio para ti en el coche.** We've made room for you in the car.
♦ **un sitio web** website

la **situación** SUSTANTIVO (PL las **situaciones**)
situation

situado ADJETIVO
♦ **está situado en ...** it's situated in ...

el **sobaco** SUSTANTIVO
armpit

el **soborno** SUSTANTIVO
[1] bribery (*delito*)
[2] bribe (*cantidad de dinero*)
♦ **Denunció un intento de soborno.** He reported an attempted bribe.

sobra SUSTANTIVO FEM
♦ **Tenemos comida de sobra.** We've got more than enough food.
♦ **Sabes de sobra que yo no he sido.** You know full well that it wasn't me.
♦ **las sobras** (*de comida*) the leftovers

sobrar VERBO
[1] to be left over ◊ *Ha sobrado mucha comida.* There's plenty of food left over.
[2] to be spare ◊ *Esta pieza sobra.* This piece is spare.
♦ **Este ejemplo sobra.** This example is unnecessary.
♦ **Con este dinero sobrará.** This money will be more than enough.

sobre PREPOSICIÓN
[1] on ◊ *Dejó el dinero sobre la mesa.* He left the money on the table.
[2] about ◊ *información sobre vuelos* information about flights
♦ **sobre las seis** at about six o'clock
♦ **sobre todo** above all

el **sobre** SUSTANTIVO
envelope

la **sobredosis** SUSTANTIVO (PL las **sobredosis**)

S ☞

overdose

sobrenatural ADJETIVO
supernatural

el **sobresaliente** SUSTANTIVO
distinction

sobrevivir VERBO
to survive

la **sobrina** SUSTANTIVO
niece

el **sobrino** SUSTANTIVO
nephew
◆ **mis sobrinos (1)** (*varones*) my nephews
◆ **mis sobrinos (2)** (*varones y mujeres*) my nieces and nephews

sobrio ADJETIVO
sober

la **socia** SUSTANTIVO
1 partner (*en negocio*)
2 member (*de club, organización*)

social ADJETIVO
social

el **socialismo** SUSTANTIVO
socialism

el/la **socialista** ADJETIVO, SUSTANTIVO
socialist

la **sociedad** SUSTANTIVO
society (PL societies)
◆ **una sociedad anónima** a limited company

el **socio** SUSTANTIVO
1 partner (*en negocio*)
2 member (*de club, organización*)

la **sociología** SUSTANTIVO
sociology

el/la **socorrista** SUSTANTIVO
lifeguard

el **socorro** SUSTANTIVO
help
◆ **pedir socorro** to ask for help
◆ **Acudió en su socorro.** She went to his aid.

socorro EXCLAMACIÓN
help!

la **soda** SUSTANTIVO
soda

el **sofá** SUSTANTIVO (PL los **sofás**)
sofa
◆ **un sofá-cama** a sofa bed

sofisticado ADJETIVO
sophisticated

el **software** SUSTANTIVO
software

sois VERBO *ver* **ser**

la **soja** SUSTANTIVO
soya

el **sol** SUSTANTIVO
sun
◆ **estar al sol** to be in the sun
◆ **Hace sol.** It's sunny.
◆ **tomar el sol** to sunbathe

solamente ADVERBIO
only

el **soldado** SUSTANTIVO
soldier

soleado ADJETIVO
sunny

la **soledad** SUSTANTIVO
loneliness

soler* VERBO
En presente, ***soler*** *se traduce por el adverbio* ***usually.***
◇ *Suele salir a las ocho.* He usually leaves at eight.
En pasado, ***soler*** *se traduce por la construcción* ***used to.***
◇ *Solíamos ir todos los años a la playa.* We used to go to the beach every year.

solicitar VERBO
1 to ask for (*ayuda, información*)
2 to apply for (*empleo, puesto*)

la **solicitud** SUSTANTIVO
1 application (*de trabajo*)
◆ **presentar una solicitud** to submit an application
2 request (*de ayuda, información*)

sólido ADJETIVO
solid

solitario ADJETIVO
solitary

sollozar* VERBO
to sob

solo ADJETIVO
1 alone ◇ *¡Déjame solo!* Leave me alone! ◇ *Me quedé solo.* I was left alone.
◆ **¿Estás solo?** Are you on your own?
◆ **Lo hice solo.** I did it on my own.
2 lonely ◇ *A veces me siento solo.* Sometimes I feel lonely.
3 single (*uso enfático*) ◇ *No hubo una sola queja.* There wasn't a single complaint.
◆ **Había un solo problema.** There was just one problem.
◆ **Habla solo.** He talks to himself.
◆ **un café solo** a black coffee

el **solo** SUSTANTIVO
solo ◇ *un solo de guitarra* a guitar solo

sólo ADVERBIO
only ◇ *Sólo cuesta diez libras.* It only costs ten pounds. ◇ *Era sólo una idea.* It was only an idea. ◇ *Yo también fumo, sólo que en pipa.* I smoke as well, only a pipe.
◆ **no sólo ... sino ...** not only ... but ... ◇ *No sólo es barato sino también de buena calidad.* It's not only cheap, but it's good quality too.

el **solomillo** SUSTANTIVO
sirloin

soltar* VERBO

* Verbs marked with this symbol are irregular. See pages 380-382 for further details

1 to let go of ◊ *No sueltes la cuerda.* Don't let go of the rope.
♦ **¡Suéltame!** Let me go!
2 to put down ◊ *Soltó la bolsa de la compra en un banco.* She put her shopping bag down on a bench.
3 to release ◊ *Han soltado a los rehenes.* They've released the hostages.
4 to let out (*suspiro, grito*) ◊ *Solté un suspiro de alivio.* I let out a sigh of relief.

la **soltera** SUSTANTIVO
single woman

soltero ADJETIVO
single ◊ *Es soltero.* He's single.

el **soltero** SUSTANTIVO
bachelor

la **solución** SUSTANTIVO (PL las **soluciones**)
1 solution (*de problema*)
2 answer (*de crucigrama, preguntas*)

solucionar VERBO
to solve
♦ **un problema sin solucionar** an unsolved problem

la **sombra** SUSTANTIVO
1 shade ◊ *Prefiero quedarme a la sombra.* I prefer to stay in the shade.
2 shadow ◊ *Sólo vi una sombra.* I only saw a shadow.
♦ **sombra de ojos** eye shadow

el **sombrero** SUSTANTIVO
hat

la **sombrilla** SUSTANTIVO
1 parasol (*de mano*)
2 sunshade (*de playa*)

el **somier** SUSTANTIVO
mattress base

el **somnífero** SUSTANTIVO
sleeping pill

el **sonajero** SUSTANTIVO
rattle

sonar* VERBO
1 to sound ◊ *Sonabas un poco triste por teléfono.* You sounded a bit sad on the phone.
♦ **Escríbelo tal y como suena.** Write it down just the way it sounds.
2 to play (*música*) ◊ *Sonaba una canción de Madonna por la radio.* They were playing a Madonna song on the radio.
3 to ring (*timbre, teléfono*)
4 to go off (*despertador*)
♦ **Me suena esa cara.** That face rings a bell.
♦ **sonarse la nariz** to blow one's nose

el **sondeo** SUSTANTIVO
♦ **un sondeo de opinión** an opinion poll

el **sonido** SUSTANTIVO
sound

sonreír* VERBO
to smile ◊ *Me sonrió.* She smiled at me.

la **sonrisa** SUSTANTIVO
smile

sonrojarse VERBO
to blush

soñar* VERBO
to dream ◊ *Ayer soñé con él.* I dreamed about him yesterday.

la **sopa** SUSTANTIVO
soup ◊ *sopa de pescado* fish soup

soplar VERBO
to blow ◊ *¡Sopla con fuerza!* Blow hard! ◊ *Soplaba un viento fuerte.* A strong wind was blowing.

soportar VERBO
to stand ◊ *No lo soporto.* I can't stand him. ◊ *No soporta que la critiquen.* She can't stand being criticised.

No confundir ***soportar*** *con* ***to support.***

la **soprano** SUSTANTIVO
soprano

sorber VERBO
to sip

sordo ADJETIVO
deaf
♦ **quedarse sordo** to go deaf

sordomudo ADJETIVO
deaf and dumb

sorprendente ADJETIVO
surprising

sorprender VERBO
to surprise ◊ *No me sorprende.* It doesn't surprise me.
♦ **Me sorprendí al verlo allí.** I was surprised to see him there.

la **sorpresa** SUSTANTIVO
surprise ◊ *¡Qué sorpresa!* What a surprise!
♦ **coger a alguien de sorpresa** to take somebody by surprise

el **sorteo** SUSTANTIVO
draw

la **sortija** SUSTANTIVO
ring

soso ADJETIVO
1 dull (*persona*)
2 bland (*sin sabor*)
♦ **Estas patatas fritas están sosas.** (*sin sal*) These chips need more salt.

la **sospecha** SUSTANTIVO
suspicion

sospechar VERBO
to suspect
♦ **Sospechan de él.** They suspect him.

el **sospechoso**, la **sospechosa** SUSTANTIVO
suspect

sospechoso ADJETIVO
suspicious

el **sostén** SUSTANTIVO (PL los **sostenes**)
bra

sostener* VERBO
1 to support ◊ *Está sostenido por cuatro columnas.* It is supported by four columns.

☞

[2] to hold ◊ *Sostuvieron la caja entre los dos.* They held the box between the two of them.

♦ **¿Puedes sostener la puerta un momento?** Can you hold the door open for a moment?

♦ **La sombrilla no se sostiene con el viento.** The sunshade won't stay up in the wind.

la **sota** SUSTANTIVO
jack

el **sótano** SUSTANTIVO
[1] basement (*habitable*)
[2] cellar (*para almacenar cosas*)

soy VERBO *ver* **ser**

el **spot** SUSTANTIVO
♦ **un spot publicitario** a commercial

Sr. ABREVIATURA
Mr

Sra. ABREVIATURA
Mrs

La forma abreviada **Mrs** *se usa en inglés cuando queremos especificar que la mujer está casada, pero cuando no queremos dar importancia a este hecho, se prefiere el uso de* **Ms.**

Srta. ABREVIATURA
Miss

La forma abreviada **Miss** *se usa en inglés cuando queremos especificar que la mujer es soltera, pero cuando no queremos dar importancia a este hecho, se prefiere el uso de* **Ms.**

su ADJETIVO
[1] his (*de él*) ◊ *su máquina de afeitar* his razor ◊ *sus padres* his parents
[2] her (*de ella*) ◊ *su falda* her skirt ◊ *sus amigas* her friends
[3] its (*de cosa, animal*) ◊ *un oso y su cachorro* a bear and its cub ◊ *el coche y sus accesorios* the car and its fittings
[4] their (*de ellos, ellas*) ◊ *su equipo favorito* their favourite team ◊ *sus amigos* their friends
[5] your (*de usted, ustedes*) ◊ *Su abrigo, señora.* Your coat, madam. ◊ *No olviden sus paraguas.* Don't forget your umbrellas.

suave ADJETIVO
[1] smooth (*piel, superficie*)
[2] soft (*pelo*)
[3] gentle (*brisa, caricia, voz*)
[4] mild (*clima, temperaturas*)

el **suavizante** SUSTANTIVO
[1] conditioner (*de pelo*)
[2] fabric conditioner (*de ropa*)

la **subasta** SUSTANTIVO
auction

el **subcampeón**, la **subcampeona** SUSTANTIVO (MASC PL los **subcampeones**)
runner-up (PL runners-up)

subdesarrollado ADJETIVO
underdeveloped

el **subdirector**, la **subdirectora** SUSTANTIVO
[1] (*de colegio*)
deputy head
[2] (*de organización*)
deputy director
[3] (*de empresa*)
deputy manager deputy manageress

la **subida** SUSTANTIVO
[1] rise ◊ *una subida de los precios* a rise in prices
[2] ascent ◊ *una subida muy empinada* a very steep ascent

subir VERBO
[1] to go up ◊ *Subimos la cuesta.* We went up the hill. ◊ *La gasolina ha vuelto a subir.* Petrol's gone up again.
[2] to come up ◊ *Sube, que te voy a enseñar unos discos.* Come up, I've got some records to show you.
[3] to climb (*montaña*) ◊ *subir una montaña* to climb a mountain
[4] to take up ◊ *¿Me puedes ayudar a subir las maletas?* Can you help me to take up the cases?
[5] to put up ◊ *Los taxistas han subido sus tarifas.* Taxi drivers have put their fares up.
[6] to raise ◊ *Sube los brazos.* Raise your arms.
[7] to turn up ◊ *Sube la radio, que no se oye.* Turn the radio up, I can't hear it.

♦ **subirse a (1)** (*coche*) to get into
♦ **subirse a (2)** (*bici*) to get onto
♦ **subirse a (3)** (*autobús, tren, avión*) to get on
♦ **subirse a un árbol** to climb a tree

el **subjuntivo** SUSTANTIVO
subjunctive

el **submarino** SUSTANTIVO
submarine

subrayar VERBO
to underline

el **subsidio** SUSTANTIVO
subsidy (PL subsidies) ◊ *subsidio de paro* unemployment benefit

el **subte** SUSTANTIVO [River Plate]
underground

subterráneo ADJETIVO
underground

subtitulado ADJETIVO
subtitled

los **subtítulos** SUSTANTIVO
subtitles

el **suburbio** SUSTANTIVO
slum area (*barrio pobre*)

la **subvención** SUSTANTIVO (PL las **subvenciones**)
subsidy (PL subsidies)

subvencionar VERBO
to subsidize

suceder VERBO
to happen (*ocurrir*) ◊ *¿Les ha sucedido algo?* Has something happened to them?

el **suceso** SUSTANTIVO
1 event ◊ *los sucesos de la última decada* the events of the last decade ◊ *sucesos históricos* historical events
2 incident ◊ *El suceso ocurrió sobre las tres de la tarde.* The incident happened at around three in the afternoon.
♦ **Acudieron rápidamente al lugar del suceso.** They rushed to the scene.
*No confundir **suceso** con **success**.*

la **suciedad** SUSTANTIVO
dirt

sucio ADJETIVO
dirty ◊ *Tienes las manos sucias.* You've got dirty hands.

la **sucursal** SUSTANTIVO
branch (PL branches)

la **sudadera** SUSTANTIVO
sweatshirt

Sudáfrica SUSTANTIVO FEM
South Africa

Sudamérica SUSTANTIVO FEM
South America

el **sudamericano,** la **sudamericana** ADJETIVO, SUSTANTIVO
South American

sudar VERBO
to sweat

el **sudeste** SUSTANTIVO
southeast

el **sudoeste** SUSTANTIVO
southwest

el **sudor** SUSTANTIVO
sweat

sudoroso ADJETIVO
sweaty

la **sueca** SUSTANTIVO
Swede

Suecia SUSTANTIVO FEM
Sweden

sueco ADJETIVO
Swedish

el **sueco** SUSTANTIVO
1 Swede (*persona*)
2 Swedish (*idioma*)

la **suegra** SUSTANTIVO
mother-in-law (PL mothers-in-law)

el **suegro** SUSTANTIVO
father-in-law (PL fathers-in-law)

los **suegros** SUSTANTIVO
in-laws

la **suela** SUSTANTIVO
sole (*de zapato*)

el **sueldo** SUSTANTIVO
1 (*mensual*)
salary (PL salaries)
2 (*semanal*)
wages PL

el **suelo** SUSTANTIVO
1 floor (*en casa, edificio*) ◊ *un suelo de mármol* a marble floor
2 ground (*de la calle, del exterior*)
♦ **Me caí al suelo.** I fell over.

suelo VERBO *ver* **soler**

suelto VERBO *ver* **soltar**

suelto ADJETIVO
loose ◊ *Tiene varias hojas sueltas.* Some of the pages are loose. ◊ *Lleva el pelo suelto.* She wears her hair loose. ◊ *No dejes al perro suelto.* Don't let the dog loose.

el **suelto** SUSTANTIVO
change (*dinero*)

sueno VERBO *ver* **sonar**

sueño VERBO *ver* **soñar**

el **sueño** SUSTANTIVO
1 dream ◊ *Anoche tuve un mal sueño.* I had a bad dream last night.
2 sleep ◊ *un sueño profundo* a deep sleep
♦ **Tengo sueño.** I'm sleepy.

la **suerte** SUSTANTIVO
luck ◊ *No ha tenido mucha suerte.* She hasn't had much luck.
♦ **por suerte** luckily
♦ **Tuvo suerte.** She was lucky.
♦ **¡Qué suerte!** How lucky!
♦ **¡Qué mala suerte!** What bad luck!

el **suéter** SUSTANTIVO
sweater

suficiente ADJETIVO
enough ◊ *No tenía dinero suficiente.* I didn't have enough money.

suficientemente ADVERBIO
sufficiently

sufrir VERBO
1 to have ◊ *Sufrió un ataque al corazón.* He had a heart attack.
2 to suffer ◊ *Sufre de artritis.* He suffers from arthritis.
♦ **sufrir un colapso** to collapse

la **sugerencia** SUSTANTIVO
suggestion
♦ **hacer una sugerencia** to make a suggestion

sugerir* VERBO
to suggest ◊ *Sugirió que saliéramos a tomar una pizza.* She suggested going out for a pizza.

sugiero VERBO *ver* **sugerir**

el **suicidio** SUSTANTIVO
suicide

Suiza SUSTANTIVO FEM
Switzerland

el **suizo,** la **suiza** ADJETIVO, SUSTANTIVO
Swiss
♦ **los suizos** the Swiss

el **sujetador** SUSTANTIVO
bra

S

sujetar VERBO
[1] to hold ◊ *Sujétame estos libros un momento.* Hold these books for me a moment.
[2] to fasten ◊ *Lo sujetó con un clip.* He fastened it with a paper clip.
♦ **Sujeta al perro, que no se escape.** Hold on to the dog so it doesn't get away.

el **sujeto** SUSTANTIVO
subject

la **suma** SUSTANTIVO
sum ◊ *una suma de dinero* a sum of money
♦ **¿Cuánto es la suma de todos los gastos?** What are the total expenses?
♦ **hacer una suma** to do a sum

sumar VERBO
to add up

suministrar VERBO
to supply

el **suministro** SUSTANTIVO
supply (PL supplies)

supe VERBO *ver* **saber**

súper ADJETIVO
♦ **gasolina súper** four-star petrol

superar VERBO
[1] to get over (*enfermedad, crisis*)
[2] to beat (*récord*)
[3] to pass (*prueba*)
♦ **Las ventas han superado nuestras expectativas.** Sales have exceeded our expectations.

la **superficie** SUSTANTIVO
[1] surface ◊ *en la superficie terrestre* on the Earth's surface
[2] area ◊ *una superficie de 100 metros cuadrados* an area of 100 square metres

superior ADJETIVO (FEM **superior**)
[1] upper (*directamente encima*)
♦ **el labio superior** the upper lip
[2] top (*en lo más alto*) ◊ *el piso superior* the top floor
♦ **superior a** (*mejor que*) superior to
♦ **Su inteligencia es superior a la media.** He has above-average intelligence.
♦ **un curso de inglés de nivel superior** an advanced level English course

el **supermercado** SUSTANTIVO
supermarket

el/la **superviviente** SUSTANTIVO
survivor

el **suplemento** SUSTANTIVO
supplement ◊ *el suplemento dominical* the Sunday supplement

el/la **suplente** SUSTANTIVO
[1] reserve (*jugador, deportista*)
[2] supply teacher (*profesor*)
[3] locum (*médico*)

suplicar* VERBO
to beg

suponer* VERBO
[1] to suppose (*indicando expectación*) ◊ *Supongo que vendrá.* I suppose she'll come.
♦ **Supongo que sí.** I suppose so.
[2] to think (*indicando decepción*) ◊ *Te suponía más alto.* I thought you'd be taller. ◊ *Supusimos que no vendrías.* We didn't think you would be coming.
[3] to involve ◊ *Tener un coche supone más gastos.* Having a car involves more expenses.

el **supositorio** SUSTANTIVO
suppository

suprimir VERBO
to delete (*borrar*)

supuesto VERBO *ver* **suponer**

el **supuesto** SUSTANTIVO
♦ **¿Y en el supuesto de que no venga?** And supposing he doesn't come?
♦ **por supuesto** of course
♦ **¡Por supuesto que no!** Of course not!

supuse VERBO *ver* **suponer**

el **sur** SUSTANTIVO, ADJETIVO
south ◊ *el sur del país* the south of the country ◊ *en la costa sur* on the south coast
♦ **vientos del sur** southerly winds

sureño ADJETIVO
southern

el **sureste** SUSTANTIVO
southeast

el **surf** SUSTANTIVO
surfing
♦ **surf a vela** windsurfing
♦ **practicar el surf** to surf

surgir* VERBO
to come up ◊ *Ha surgido un problema.* A problem has come up.

el **suroeste** SUSTANTIVO
southwest

surtido ADJETIVO
assorted ◊ *pasteles surtidos* assorted cakes
♦ **estar bien surtido** to have a good selection

el **surtido** SUSTANTIVO
selection

el **surtidor** SUSTANTIVO
petrol pump (*de gasolina*)

susceptible ADJETIVO
touchy (*persona*)

la **suscripción** SUSTANTIVO (PL las **suscripciones**)
subscription

suspender VERBO
[1] to call off (*definitivamente*) ◊ *Han suspendido la boda.* They've called the wedding off.

[2] to postpone (*temporalmente*) ◊ *Ha suspendido su visita hasta la semana que viene.* He's postponed his visit until next week.
♦ **El partido se suspendió a causa de la lluvia.** The game was rained off.
[3] to fail ◊ *He suspendido las matemáticas.* I've failed maths.

el **suspense** SUSTANTIVO
suspense ◊ *una película de suspense* a thriller

el **suspenso** SUSTANTIVO
suspense (*misterio*) Latin America ◊ *una película de suspenso* a thriller
♦ **Tengo un suspenso en inglés.** I failed English.

suspicaz ADJETIVO (PL **suspicaces**)
suspicious

suspirar VERBO
to sigh

el **suspiro** SUSTANTIVO
sigh

la **sustancia** SUSTANTIVO
substance
♦ **una sustancia química** a chemical

el **sustantivo** SUSTANTIVO
noun

sustituir* VERBO
[1] to replace (*para siempre*) ◊ *Lo sustituí como secretario de la asociación.* I replaced him as club secretary.
[2] to stand in for (*temporalmente*) ◊ *¿Me puedes sustituir un par de semanas?* Can you stand in for me for a couple of weeks?

el **sustituto**, la **sustituta** SUSTANTIVO
[1] replacement (*para siempre*)
[2] substitute (*temporal*)
♦ **Soy el sustituto del profesor de inglés.** I'm standing in for the English teacher.

sustituyendo VERBO *ver* **sustituir**

el **susto** SUSTANTIVO
fright ◊ *¡Qué susto!* What a fright!
♦ **dar un susto a alguien** to give somebody a fright

susurrar VERBO
to whisper ◊ *Me susurró su nombre al oído.* He whispered his name in my ear.

sutil ADJETIVO
subtle

suyo PRONOMBRE, ADJETIVO (FEM **suya**)
[1] his
Cuando nos referimos a "él".
◊ *Todas estas tierras son suyas.* All this land is his. ◊ *¿Es éste su cuarto? – No, el suyo está abajo.* Is this his room? – No, his is downstairs.
♦ **un amigo suyo** a friend of his
[2] hers
Cuando nos referimos a "ella".
◊ *Es suyo.* It's hers. ◊ *¿Es éste su abrigo? – No, el suyo es marrón.* Is this her coat? – No, hers is brown.
♦ **un amigo suyo** a friend of hers
[3] theirs
Cuando nos referimos a "ellos" o "ellas".
◊ *Es suyo.* It's theirs. ◊ *¿Es ésta su casa? – No, la suya está más adelante.* Is this their house? – No, theirs is further on.
♦ **un amigo suyo** a friend of theirs
[4] yours
Cuando nos referimos a "usted" o "ustedes".
◊ *Todos estos libros son suyos.* All these books are yours. ◊ *¿Es ésta nuestra habitación? – No, la suya está arriba.* Is this our room? – No, yours is upstairs.
♦ **un amigo suyo** a friend of yours

T

el **tabaco** SUSTANTIVO
1 tobacco
◆ **tabaco negro** dark tobacco
◆ **tabaco rubio** Virginia tobacco
2 cigarettes PL

la **taberna** SUSTANTIVO
bar

el **tabique** SUSTANTIVO
partition

la **tabla** SUSTANTIVO
plank ◊ *El agujero estaba cubierto con tablas.* The hole was covered with planks.
◆ **la tabla de multiplicar** the multiplication table
◆ **una tabla de cocina** a chopping board
◆ **la tabla de planchar** the ironing board
◆ **la tabla de surf** the surfboard
◆ **quedar en tablas** to draw

el **tablero** SUSTANTIVO
board
◆ **el tablero de ajedrez** the chessboard
◆ **el tablero de mandos** the dashboard

la **tableta** SUSTANTIVO
1 bar (*de chocolate*)
2 tablet (*medicamento*)

el **tablón** SUSTANTIVO (PL los **tablones**)
plank ◊ *los tablones del andamio* the scaffolding planks
◆ **el tablón de anuncios** the notice board

el **tabú** SUSTANTIVO (PL los **tabúes**)
taboo (PL taboos)

el **taburete** SUSTANTIVO
stool

tacaño ADJETIVO
mean

el **tacaño**, la **tacaña** SUSTANTIVO
skinflint

tachar VERBO
to cross out ◊ *No lo taches, bórralo.* Don't cross it out, erase it.
◆ **La tacharon de mentirosa.** They accused her of being a liar.

el **taco** SUSTANTIVO
1 rawlplug (*para tornillo*)
2 stud (*de botas de fútbol*)
3 cube (*de jamón, queso*)
4 cue (*en billar*)
5 swearword (*palabrota*)
◆ **soltar tacos** to swear
6 heel (*de zapato*) Chile, River Plate

el **tacón** SUSTANTIVO (PL los **tacones**)
heel
◆ **zapatos de tacón** high-heeled shoes

la **táctica** SUSTANTIVO
tactics PL ◊ *El equipo cambió de táctica.* The team changed tactics.

el **tacto** SUSTANTIVO
1 touch (*sentido*) ◊ *suave al tacto* smooth to the touch
2 tact (*delicadeza*)
◆ **Lo dijo con mucho tacto.** He said it very tactfully.

la **tajada** SUSTANTIVO
slice (*de melón, sandía*)

tajante ADJETIVO
1 emphatic (*actitud*)
2 sharp (*tono*) ◊ *Lo dijo de manera tajante.* He said it sharply.

tal ADJETIVO, PRONOMBRE
such ◊ *En tales casos es mejor consultar con un médico.* In such cases it's better to see a doctor. ◊ *¡En el aeropuerto había tal confusión!* There was such confusion at the airport!
◆ **Lo dejé tal como estaba.** I left it just as it was.
◆ **con tal de que** as long as ◊ *con tal de que regreséis antes de las once* as long as you get back before eleven
◆ **¿Qué tal?** How are things?
◆ **¿Qué tal has dormido?** How did you sleep?
◆ **tal vez** perhaps

la **taladradora** SUSTANTIVO
1 (*para obras*)
pneumatic drill
2 (*para papel*)
punch (PL punches)

taladrar VERBO
to drill

el **taladro** SUSTANTIVO
drill

el **talento** SUSTANTIVO
talent ◊ *Sus hijos tienen talento para la música.* Their children have a talent for music.

la **talla** SUSTANTIVO
size ◊ *¿Tienen esta camisa en la talla cuatro?* Do you have this shirt in a size four?

tallar VERBO
1 to carve (*madera*)
2 to sculpt (*piedra, mármol*)
3 to scrub (*suelo, cazuela*)
Chile, River Plate

los **tallarines** SUSTANTIVO
noodles

el **taller** SUSTANTIVO
1 garage (*de mecánico*) ◊ *Tengo el coche en el taller.* My car is in the garage.

2 workshop (*de carpintero, electricista*)
◆ **un taller de teatro** a theatre workshop

el **tallo** SUSTANTIVO
stem

el **talón** SUSTANTIVO (PL los **talones**)
1 heel (*de pie, zapato*)
2 cheque (*cheque*) ◇ *cobrar un talón* to cash a cheque

el **talonario** SUSTANTIVO
1 chequebook (*de cheques*)
2 book of tickets (*de entradas*)
3 receipt book (*de recibos*)

el **tamaño** SUSTANTIVO
size
◆ **¿Qué tamaño tiene?** What size is it?

tambalearse VERBO
1 to wobble (*silla*)
2 to stagger (*persona*)

también ADVERBIO
also ◇ *Canta flamenco y también baila.* He sings flamenco and also dances.
◆ **Tengo hambre. – Yo también.** I'm hungry. – So am I.
◆ **Yo estoy de acuerdo. – Nosotros también.** I agree. – So do we.

el **tambor** SUSTANTIVO
drum

el **Támesis** SUSTANTIVO
the Thames

el **tamiz** SUSTANTIVO (PL los **tamices**)
sieve

tampoco ADVERBIO
1 either ◇ *Yo tampoco lo compré.* I didn't buy it either.
2 neither ◇ *Yo no la vi. – Yo tampoco.* I didn't see her. – Neither did I. ◇ *Nunca he estado en París. – Yo tampoco.* I've never been to Paris. – Neither have I.

el **tampón** SUSTANTIVO (PL los **tampones**)
tampon

tan ADVERBIO
1 so ◇ *No creía que vendrías tan pronto.* I didn't think you'd come so soon. ◇ *¡No es tan difícil!* It's not so difficult!
◆ **¡Qué hombre tan amable!** What a kind man!
◆ **tan ... que ...** so ... that ...

*A menudo se omite **that** en esta construcción.*

◇ *Habla tan deprisa que no la entiendo.* She talks so fast that I can't understand her.
2 such ◇ *No era una idea tan buena.* It wasn't such a good idea. ◇ *¡Tiene unos amigos tan simpáticos!* He has such nice friends!
◆ **tan...como** as...as ◇ *No es tan guapa como su madre.* She's not as pretty as her mother. ◇ *Vine tan pronto como pude.* I came as soon as I could.

el **tanque** SUSTANTIVO
tank

tantear VERBO
to weigh up (*situación*)

tanto ADJETIVO, ADVERBIO, PRONOMBRE (FEM **tanta**)
1 so much (PL so many) ◇ *Ahora no bebo tanta leche.* I don't drink so much milk now. ◇ *Se preocupa tanto que no puede dormir.* He worries so much that he can't sleep. ◇ *¡Tengo tantas cosas que hacer hoy!* I have so many things to do today! ◇ *No necesitamos tantas.* We don't need so many.
◆ **Vinieron tantos que no cabían en la sala.** So many people came that they couldn't fit into the room.
◆ **No recibe tantas llamadas como yo.** He doesn't get as many calls as I do.
◆ **Gano tanto como tú.** I earn as much as you.
2 so often ◇ *Ahora no la veo tanto.* Now I don't see her so often.
◆ **¡No corras tanto!** Don't run so fast!
◆ **tanto tú como yo** both you and I
◆ **tanto si viene como si no** whether he comes or not
◆ **¡Tanto gusto!** How do you do?
◆ **entre tanto** meanwhile
◆ **por lo tanto** therefore

el **tanto** SUSTANTIVO
1 goal ◇ *Juárez marcó el segundo tanto.* Juárez scored the second goal.
2 amount ◇ *Me paga un tanto fijo cada semana.* He pays me a fixed amount each week.
◆ **un tanto por ciento** a percentage
◆ **Había cuarenta y tantos invitados.** There were forty-odd guests.
◆ **Manténme al tanto.** Keep me informed.

la **tapa** SUSTANTIVO
1 lid (*de cazuela, caja*)
2 top (*de botella, tarro*)
3 cover (*de revista, libro*)
4 tapa (*con bebida*) ◇ *Pedimos unas tapas en el bar.* We ordered some tapas in the bar.

la **tapadera** SUSTANTIVO
lid

el **tapado** SUSTANTIVO River Plate
coat

tapar VERBO
to cover ◇ *La tapé con una manta.* I covered her with a blanket.
◆ **Tapa la olla.** Put the lid on the pan.
◆ **Me estás tapando el sol.** You're keeping the sun off me.
◆ **Tápate bien que hace frío.** Wrap up well as it's cold.

el **tapete** SUSTANTIVO
1 embroidered tablecloth (*mantel*)
2 rug (*alfombra*) Mexico

la **tapia** SUSTANTIVO
wall ◇ *la tapia del jardín* the garden wall

la **tapicería** SUSTANTIVO
1 upholstery (*de coche, mueble*)

☞

[2] upholsterer's (*taller*)

el **tapiz** SUSTANTIVO (PL los **tapices**)
tapestry (PL tapestries)

tapizar* VERBO
to upholster (*sillón*)

el **tapón** SUSTANTIVO (PL los **tapones**)
[1] plug (*de bañera, lavabo*)
[2] top (*de botella, dentífrico*)
[3] cork (*de corcho*)
♦ **tapón de rosca** screw top

la **taquigrafía** SUSTANTIVO
shorthand

la **taquilla** SUSTANTIVO
[1] box office (*de teatro*)
[2] ticket office (*de estadio, estación*)
[3] locker (*armario*)

tararear VERBO
to hum

tardar VERBO
to be late (*retrasarse*) ◊ *Te espero a las ocho. No tardes.* I expect you at eight. Don't be late.
♦ **Tardaron una semana en contestar.** They took a week to reply. ◊ *El arroz tarda media hora en hacerse.* Rice takes half an hour to cook.
♦ **En avión se tarda dos horas.** The plane takes two hours.

la **tarde** SUSTANTIVO
[1] afternoon (*antes de anochecer*) ◊ *a las tres de la tarde* at three in the afternoon ◊ *¡Buenas tardes!* Good afternoon! ◊ *por la tarde* in the afternoon ◊ *hoy por la tarde* this afternoon
[2] evening (*después de anochecer*) ◊ *a las ocho de la tarde* at eight in the evening ◊ *¡Buenas tardes!* Good evening! ◊ *por la tarde* in the evening ◊ *hoy por la tarde* this evening

tarde ADVERBIO
late ◊ *Se está haciendo tarde.* It's getting late.
♦ **más tarde** later
♦ **tarde o temprano** sooner or later
♦ **Llegaré a las nueve como muy tarde.** I'll arrive at nine at the latest.

la **tarea** SUSTANTIVO
task ◊ *Una de sus tareas es repartir la correspondencia.* One of his tasks is to hand out the mail.
♦ **las tareas domésticas** the chores
♦ **las tareas** Latin America
homework (*deberes escolares*)

la **tarifa** SUSTANTIVO
[1] rate (*eléctrica, bancaria*)
[2] fare (*de transportes*)
♦ **tarifa de precios** price list

la **tarima** SUSTANTIVO
platform

la **tarjeta** SUSTANTIVO
card ◊ *Me mandó una tarjeta de Navidad.* He sent me a Christmas card.
♦ **una tarjeta de cajero automático** a cash card
♦ **una tarjeta de crédito** a credit card
♦ **una tarjeta de visita** a visiting card
♦ **una tarjeta telefónica** a phonecard
♦ **una tarjeta de embarque** a boarding pass

el **tarro** SUSTANTIVO
[1] jar (*frasco*)
[2] mug (*taza*) Mexico

la **tarta** SUSTANTIVO
[1] cake (*pastel*) ◊ *una tarta de cumpleaños* a birthday cake
[2] tart (*de hojaldre*)

tartamudear VERBO
to stammer

tartamudo ADJETIVO
♦ **ser tartamudo** to stutter

la **tasa** SUSTANTIVO
rate ◊ *la tasa de natalidad* the birthrate

tasar VERBO
to value

la **tasca** SUSTANTIVO
tavern

el **tata** SUSTANTIVO Latin America
[1] daddy (*padre*)
[2] grandpa (*abuelo*)

el **tatuaje** SUSTANTIVO
tattoo (PL tattoos)

tatuar* VERBO
to tattoo

Tauro SUSTANTIVO MASC
Taurus ◊ *Soy Tauro.* I'm Taurus.

el **taxi** SUSTANTIVO
taxi ◊ *tomar un taxi* to take a taxi

el **taxímetro** SUSTANTIVO
taximeter

el/la **taxista** SUSTANTIVO
taxi driver

la **taza** SUSTANTIVO
[1] cup ◊ *Tomamos una taza de café.* We had a cup of coffee.
[2] cupful (*cantidad*) ◊ *una taza de arroz* a cupful of rice
[3] bowl (*de retrete*)

el **tazón** SUSTANTIVO (PL los **tazones**)
bowl

te PRONOMBRE
[1] you ◊ *Te quiero.* I love you. ◊ *Te voy a dar un consejo.* I'm going to give you some advice.
♦ **Me gustaría comprártelo.** I'd like to buy it for you.
[2] yourself ◊ *¿Te has hecho daño?* Have you hurt yourself?

Con partes del cuerpo o con prendas que se llevan puestas se usa el adjetivo posesivo.

* Verbs marked with this symbol are irregular. See pages 380-382 for further details

◊ *¿Te duelen los pies?* Do your feet hurt? ◊ *Te tienes que poner el abrigo.* You should put your coat on.

el **té** SUSTANTIVO (PL los **tés**)
tea
♦ **Me hice un té.** I made myself a cup of tea.

el **teatro** SUSTANTIVO
theatre ◊ *Por la noche fuimos al teatro.* At night we went to the theatre.
♦ **una obra de teatro** a play

el **tebeo** SUSTANTIVO
comic

el **techo** SUSTANTIVO
1 ceiling ◊ *El techo está pintado de blanco.* The ceiling is painted white.
2 roof (*tejado*) Latin America

la **tecla** SUSTANTIVO
key (PL keys)
♦ **pulsar una tecla** to press a key

el **teclado** SUSTANTIVO
keyboard (*de ordenador, de máquina de escribir*)

teclear VERBO
to type

la **técnica** SUSTANTIVO
1 (*método*)
technique
2 (*tecnología*)
technology (PL technologies)
3 (*persona*)
technician ◊ *Mi hermana es técnica de laboratorio.* My sister is a laboratory technician.

técnico ADJETIVO
technical

el **técnico** SUSTANTIVO
1 technician ◊ *un técnico de laboratorio* a laboratory technician
2 repairman (PL repairmen) ◊ *El técnico me arregló la lavadora.* The repairman fixed my washing machine.

el **tecno** SUSTANTIVO
techno

la **tecnología** SUSTANTIVO
technology (PL technologies)
♦ **tecnología punta** state-of-the-art technology

tecnológico ADJETIVO
technological

la **teja** SUSTANTIVO
tile

el **tejado** SUSTANTIVO
roof (PL roofs)

tejer VERBO
1 to weave (*en telar*)
2 to knit (*hacer punto*)

el **tejido** SUSTANTIVO
1 fabric (*tela*)
2 tissue (*corporal*)

tel. ABREVIATURA (= *teléfono*)
tel.

la **tela** SUSTANTIVO
fabric
♦ **tela metálica** wire netting

la **telaraña** SUSTANTIVO
cobweb

la **tele** SUSTANTIVO
TV ◊ *Estábamos viendo la tele.* We were watching TV.

las **telecomunicaciones** SUSTANTIVO
telecommunications

el **telediario** SUSTANTIVO
news SING ◊ *el telediario de las nueve* the nine o'clock news

teledirigido ADJETIVO
remote-controlled (*coche*)

el **teleférico** SUSTANTIVO
cable car

telefonear VERBO
to phone ◊ *Tengo que telefonear a mis padres.* I have to phone my parents.

telefónico ADJETIVO
telephone

***telephone* en este caso va siempre delante del sustantivo.**

♦ **la guía telefónica** the telephone directory

el/la **telefonista** SUSTANTIVO
telephonist

el **teléfono** SUSTANTIVO
telephone
♦ **No tengo teléfono.** I don't have a phone.
♦ **Hablamos por teléfono.** We spoke on the phone.
♦ **Está hablando por teléfono.** He's on the phone.
♦ **colgar el teléfono a alguien** to hang up the phone on somebody
♦ **un teléfono de tarjeta** a card phone
♦ **el teléfono móvil** the mobile phone

el **telegrama** SUSTANTIVO
telegram

la **telenovela** SUSTANTIVO
soap opera (PL soap operas)

la **telepatía** SUSTANTIVO
telepathy

el **telescopio** SUSTANTIVO
telescope

el **telesilla** SUSTANTIVO
chairlift

el **telespectador**, la **telespectadora** SUSTANTIVO
viewer

el **telesquí** SUSTANTIVO (PL los **telesquís**)
ski-lift

el **teletexto** SUSTANTIVO
Teletext ®

las **televentas** SUSTANTIVO
telesales

televisar VERBO
to televise

la **televisión** SUSTANTIVO (PL las **televisiones**)
television

☞

◆ **Dieron la noticia por la televisión.** They gave the news on the television.
◆ **¿Qué ponen en la televisión esta noche?** What's on the television tonight?
◆ **la televisión por cable** cable television
◆ **la televisión digital** digital TV

el **televisor** SUSTANTIVO
television set

el **telón** SUSTANTIVO (PL los **telones**)
curtain ◇ *Subió el telón.* The curtain rose.

el **tema** SUSTANTIVO
[1] topic (*de conferencia, redacción*) ◇ *El tema de la composición era "Las vacaciones".* The topic of the essay was "The holidays".
[2] subject (*asunto*) ◇ *Luego hablaremos de ese tema.* We'll talk about that subject later.
◆ **cambiar de tema** to change the subject
◆ **temas de actualidad** current affairs
◆ **el tema de conversación** the talking point

temblar* VERBO
to tremble ◇ *Me temblaban las manos.* My hands were trembling.
◆ **temblar de miedo** to tremble with fear
◆ **temblar de frío** to shiver

el **temblor de tierra** SUSTANTIVO
earthquake

tembloroso ADJETIVO
trembling (*manos, voz*)

temer VERBO
[1] to be afraid ◇ *No temas.* Don't be afraid.
[2] to be afraid of ◇ *Le teme al profesor.* He's afraid of the teacher. ◇ *Temo ofenderles.* I'm afraid of offending them.

temible ADJETIVO
fearsome

el **temor** SUSTANTIVO
fear ◇ *el temor a la oscuridad* fear of the dark ◇ *por temor a equivocarme* for fear of making a mistake

temperamental ADJETIVO
temperamental

el **temperamento** SUSTANTIVO
temperament

la **temperatura** SUSTANTIVO
temperature ◇ *El médico le tomó la temperatura.* The doctor took his temperature.

la **tempestad** SUSTANTIVO
storm

templado ADJETIVO
[1] lukewarm (*agua, comida*)
[2] mild (*clima*)

el **templo** SUSTANTIVO
temple

la **temporada** SUSTANTIVO
season ◇ *la temporada de esquí* the ski season ◇ *la temporada alta* the high season ◇ *la temporada baja* the low season

temporal ADJETIVO
temporary

el **temporal** SUSTANTIVO
storm

temporario ADJETIVO Latin America
temporary

temprano ADVERBIO
early
◆ **por la mañana temprano** early in the morning

ten VERBO *ver* **tener**

tenaz ADJETIVO (PL **tenaces**)
tenacious

las **tenazas** SUSTANTIVO
pliers

el **tendedero** SUSTANTIVO
[1] clothes line (*con cuerda*)
[2] clothes horse (*extensible*)

la **tendencia** SUSTANTIVO
tendency (PL tendencies)
◆ **Tengo tendencia a engordar.** I tend to put on weight.

tender* VERBO
[1] to hang out (*ropa*) ◇ *Marta estaba tendiendo la ropa.* Martha was hanging out the washing.
[2] to lay out (*sobre una superficie*) ◇ *Tendí la toalla sobre la arena.* I laid the towel out on the sand.
◆ **Me tendió la mano.** He stretched out his hand to me.
◆ **tender a hacer algo** to tend to do something
◆ **tender una trampa** to set a trap
◆ **tenderse en el sofá** to lie down on the sofa
◆ **tender la cama** Latin America to make the bed
◆ **tender la mesa** Latin America to lay the table

el **tendero,** la **tendera** SUSTANTIVO
shopkeeper

tendido ADJETIVO
◆ **La ropa estaba tendida.** The washing was hanging out.
◆ **Lo encontré tendido en el suelo.** I found him lying on the floor.

el **tendón** SUSTANTIVO (PL los **tendones**)
tendon

tendrá VERBO *ver* **tener**

el **tenedor** SUSTANTIVO
fork

tener* VERBO
[1] to have ◇ *Tengo dos hermanas.* I have two sisters. ◇ *¿Tienes dinero?* Do you have any money? ◇ *Tiene el pelo rubio.*

He has blond hair. ◊ *Va a tener un niño.* She's going to have a baby. ◊ *Luis tiene la gripe.* Luis has the flu.
♦ **¿Cuántos años tienes?** How old are you?
♦ **Tiene cinco metros de largo.** It's five metres long.
♦ **Ten cuidado.** Be careful.
♦ **No tengas miedo.** Don't be afraid.
♦ **Tenía el pelo mojado.** His hair was wet.
[2] to hold ◊ *Tenía el pasaporte en la mano.* He was holding his passport in his hand.
♦ **tener que hacer algo** to have to do something
♦ **Tendrías que comer más.** You should eat more.
♦ **No tienes por qué ir.** There's no reason why you should go.
♦ **Eso no tiene nada que ver.** That's got nothing to do with it.
♦ **¡Tenga!** Here you are!
♦ **tenerse en pie** to stand

tenga VERBO *ver* **tener**

el/la **teniente** SUSTANTIVO
lieutenant

el **tenis** SUSTANTIVO
tennis
♦ **¿Juegas al tenis?** Do you play tennis?
♦ **tenis de mesa** table tennis

el/la **tenista** SUSTANTIVO
tennis player

el **tenor** SUSTANTIVO
tenor

tensar VERBO
to tighten (*cuerda, cable*)

la **tensión** SUSTANTIVO (PL las **tensiones**)
[1] tension ◊ *Hubo mucha tensión durante la reunión.* There was a lot of tension during the meeting.
[2] blood pressure ◊ *El médico me tomó la tensión.* The doctor took my blood pressure.
♦ **un cable de alta tensión** a high-voltage cable

tenso ADJETIVO
[1] tense (*persona, situación*)
[2] taut (*cuerda*)

la **tentación** SUSTANTIVO (PL las **tentaciones**)
temptation
♦ **caer en la tentación** to give in to temptation

tentador ADJETIVO (FEM **tentadora**)
tempting

tentar* VERBO
to tempt ◊ *Estuve tentado de marcharme.* I was tempted to leave.
♦ **No me tienta la idea.** The idea isn't very tempting.

la **tentativa** SUSTANTIVO
attempt

el **tentempié** SUSTANTIVO (PL los **tentempiés**)
snack

tenue ADJETIVO
faint (*luz, voz*)

teñir* VERBO
to dye ◊ *Se ha teñido el pelo.* He's dyed his hair.

la **teología** SUSTANTIVO
theology

la **teoría** SUSTANTIVO
theory (PL theories) ◊ *En teoría es fácil.* In theory it's easy.

teórico ADJETIVO
theoretical ◊ *Ése es un caso teórico.* It's a theoretical case.
♦ **un examen teórico** a theory exam

terapéutico ADJETIVO
therapeutic

la **terapia** SUSTANTIVO
therapy (PL therapies)

tercer ADJETIVO *ver* **tercero**

tercero ADJETIVO, PRONOMBRE (FEM **tercera**)
third ◊ *la tercera vez* the third time ◊ *Llegué el tercero.* I arrived third.
♦ **una tercera parte de la población** a third of the population
♦ **Vivo en el tercero.** I live on the third floor.
♦ **el Tercer Mundo** the Third World

el **tercio** SUSTANTIVO
third

el **terciopelo** SUSTANTIVO
velvet

terco ADJETIVO
obstinate

tergiversar VERBO
to distort

el **terminal** SUSTANTIVO
terminal (*ordenador*)

la **terminal** SUSTANTIVO
terminal (*en aeropuerto*)

terminante ADJETIVO
[1] categorical (*respuesta*)
[2] strict (*orden*)

terminantemente ADVERBIO
strictly

terminar VERBO
[1] to finish ◊ *He terminado el libro.* I've finished the book.
♦ **cuando terminó de hablar** when he finished talking
[2] to end (*reunión, película*) ◊ *¿A qué hora termina la clase?* At what time does the class end?
♦ **Terminé rendido.** I ended up exhausted.
♦ **Terminaron peleándose.** They ended up fighting.
♦ **Se nos ha terminado el café.** We've run out of coffee.
♦ **He terminado con Andrés.** I've broken up with Andrés.

el **término** SUSTANTIVO
term ◊ *un término médico* a medical term
♦ **por término medio** on average

T

la **termita** SUSTANTIVO
termite
el **termo** ® SUSTANTIVO
Thermos flask ®
el **termómetro** SUSTANTIVO
thermometer
◆ **Le puse el termómetro.** I took his temperature.
el **termostato** SUSTANTIVO
thermostat
la **ternera** SUSTANTIVO
veal (*carne*)
el **ternero,** la **ternera** SUSTANTIVO
(*animal*)
calf (PL calves)
la **ternura** SUSTANTIVO
tenderness
◆ **con ternura** tenderly
el/la **terrateniente** SUSTANTIVO
landowner
la **terraza** SUSTANTIVO
1 (*balcón*)
balcony (PL balconies)
2 (*azotea*)
roof terrace
◆ **Salimos a la terraza del bar a tomar algo.** We went out to the beer garden for a drink.
el **terremoto** SUSTANTIVO
earthquake
el **terreno** SUSTANTIVO
1 land ◇ *una granja con mucho terreno* a farm with a lot of land
◆ **un terreno** a piece of land ◇ *Hemos comprado un terreno.* We've bought a piece of land.
2 field ◇ *terrenos plantados de naranjos* fields planted with orange trees ◇ *en el terreno de la informática* in the field of computing science
◆ **el terreno de juego** the pitch
◆ **Lo decidiremos sobre el terreno.** We'll decide as we go along.
terrestre ADJETIVO
land (*animal, transporte*)
land *en este caso va siempre delante del sustantivo.*
terrible ADJETIVO
terrible ◇ *Fue una experiencia terrible.* It was a terrible experience.
◆ **Tenía un cansancio terrible.** I was awfully tired.
el/la **terrier** SUSTANTIVO (PL los/las **terriers**)
terrier
el **territorio** SUSTANTIVO
territory (PL territories)
el **terrón** SUSTANTIVO (PL los **terrones**)
lump (*de azúcar*)
el **terror** SUSTANTIVO
terror ◇ *Fuimos víctimas de una campaña de terror.* We were the victims of a terror campaign.
◆ **Les tiene terror a los perros.** He's terrified of dogs.
◆ **una película de terror** a horror film
el **terrorismo** SUSTANTIVO
terrorism
el/la **terrorista** ADJETIVO, SUSTANTIVO
terrorist
la **tesis** SUSTANTIVO (PL las **tesis**)
thesis (PL theses)
el **tesón** SUSTANTIVO
determination
el **tesorero,** la **tesorera** SUSTANTIVO
treasurer
el **tesoro** SUSTANTIVO
treasure
◆ **Ven aquí, tesoro.** Come here, darling.
el **test** SUSTANTIVO (PL los **tests**)
test ◇ *Hoy nos han hecho un test.* We had a test today.
el **testamento** SUSTANTIVO
will
◆ **hacer testamento** to make one's will
◆ **el Antiguo Testamento** the Old Testament
◆ **el Nuevo Testamento** the New Testament
testarudo ADJETIVO
stubborn
el/la **testigo** SUSTANTIVO
witness (PL witnesses)
◆ **un Testigo de Jehová** a Jehovah's Witness
◆ **Fui testigo del accidente.** I witnessed the accident.
el **tétanos** SUSTANTIVO
tetanus
la **tetera** SUSTANTIVO
1 teapot (*para el té*)
2 kettle (*para hervir agua*) Chile, Mexico
3 baby's bottle (*para el bebé*) Mexico
la **tetina** SUSTANTIVO
teat
el **textil** ADJETIVO, SUSTANTIVO
textile
el **texto** SUSTANTIVO
text
◆ **un libro de texto** a textbook
la **textura** SUSTANTIVO
texture
la **tez** SUSTANTIVO
complexion
ti PRONOMBRE
you ◇ *una llamada para ti* a call for you
◆ **Sólo piensas en ti mismo.** You only think of yourself.
la **tía** SUSTANTIVO
1 aunt (*pariente*) ◇ *mi tía* my aunt

2 girl (*chica*) ◊ *Es una tía majísima.* She's a really nice girl.

tibio ADJETIVO
lukewarm

el **tiburón** SUSTANTIVO (PL los **tiburones**)
shark

el **tic** SUSTANTIVO
tic ◊ *un tic nervioso* a nervous tic

el **tictac** SUSTANTIVO
tick-tock

tiemblo VERBO *ver* **temblar**

el **tiempo** SUSTANTIVO
1 time ◊ *No tengo tiempo.* I don't have time. ◊ *¿Qué haces en tu tiempo libre?* What do you do in your spare time? ◊ *Me llevó bastante tiempo.* It took me quite a long time.
◆ **¿Cuánto tiempo hace que vives aquí?** How long have you been living here?
◆ **Hace mucho tiempo que no la veo.** I haven't seen her for a long time.
◆ **al mismo tiempo** at the same time
◆ **perder el tiempo** to waste time
◆ **al poco tiempo** soon after
◆ **a tiempo** in time ◊ *Llegamos a tiempo de ver la película.* We got there in time to see the film.
◆ **¿Qué tiempo tiene el niño?** How old is the baby?
2 weather
◆ **¿Qué tiempo hace ahí?** What's the weather like there?
◆ **hizo buen tiempo** the weather was fine
◆ **Hace mal tiempo.** The weather's bad.
3 half (*en partido*)
◆ **Metieron el gol durante el segundo tiempo.** They scored the goal during the second half.

la **tienda** SUSTANTIVO
shop
◆ **una tienda de comestibles** a grocer's shop (PL grocers' shops)
◆ **una tienda de discos** a record shop
◆ **ir de tiendas** to go shopping
◆ **una tienda de campaña** a tent

tiendo VERBO *ver* **tender**

tiene VERBO *ver* **tener**

tiento VERBO *ver* **tentar**

tierno ADJETIVO
1 tender (*carne, mirada*)
2 fresh (*pan*)

la **tierra** SUSTANTIVO
1 land ◊ *Trabajan la tierra.* They work the land.
◆ **la Tierra Santa** the Holy Land
◆ **tierra adentro** inland
2 soil (*para macetas, plantas*)
◆ **echar algo por tierra** to ruin something ◊ *Echó por tierra todos nuestros planes.* It ruined all our plans.
◆ **la Tierra** the Earth

tieso ADJETIVO
1 stiff (*rígido*)
◆ **quedarse tieso de frío** to be frozen stiff
2 straight (*derecho*) ◊ *Ponte tiesa.* Stand up straight.

el **tiesto** SUSTANTIVO
flowerpot

el **tigre** SUSTANTIVO
tiger

las **tijeras** SUSTANTIVO
scissors ◊ *Es más fácil cortarlo con las tijeras.* It's easier to cut with scissors.
◆ **¿Tienes unas tijeras?** Do you have a pair of scissors?
◆ **unas tijeras de podar** a pair of secateurs

timar VERBO
1 to con (*engañar*)
2 to rip off (*cobrar demasiado*) ◊ *Te han timado con ese coche.* They've ripped you off with that car.

el **timbrazo** SUSTANTIVO
ring

el **timbre** SUSTANTIVO
1 bell (*de puerta, alarma, colegio*) ◊ *Ya ha sonado el timbre.* The bell has already gone.
◆ **llamar al timbre** to ring the bell
2 stamp (*para cartas*) Mexico

la **timidez** SUSTANTIVO
shyness

tímido ADJETIVO
shy

el **timo** SUSTANTIVO
1 con (*engaño*)
2 rip off (*pago excesivo*)
◆ **¡Vaya timo!** What a rip-off!

la **tinaja** SUSTANTIVO
large earthenware vat

tiñendo VERBO *ver* **teñir**

la **tinta** SUSTANTIVO
ink ◊ *escrito con tinta* written in ink
◆ **tinta China** Indian ink
◆ **sudar tinta** to sweat blood

el **tinte** SUSTANTIVO
dye (*sustancia*)

el **tintero** SUSTANTIVO
inkwell

el **tinto** SUSTANTIVO
red wine (*vino*)

la **tintorería** SUSTANTIVO
dry cleaner's

el **tío** SUSTANTIVO
1 uncle (*pariente*)
◆ **mis tíos** my uncle and aunt (*tío y tía*)
2 guy (*coloquial: hombre*) ◊ *Es un tío muy simpático.* He's a really nice guy.
◆ **Oye, tío, me alegro de verte.** Hey, man, nice to see you.

el **tiovivo** SUSTANTIVO
merry-go-round (PL merry-go-rounds)

típicamente ADVERBIO
typically

típico ADJETIVO
typical

T

☞

◆ **Eso es muy típico de ella.** That's very typical of her.

el **tipo** SUSTANTIVO
1 kind ◇ *No me gusta este tipo de fiestas.* I don't like this kind of party.
◆ **todo tipo de ...** all sorts of ...
2 figure ◇ *Marisa tiene un tipo muy bonito.* Marisa has a lovely figure.
3 bloke (*coloquial*) ◇ *un tipo de aspecto sospechoso* a suspicious-looking bloke

el **tíquet** SUSTANTIVO (PL los **tíquets**)
1 ticket (*de autobús, tren*)
2 receipt (*recibo de compra*)

la **tira** SUSTANTIVO
strip ◇ *una tira de papel* a strip of paper ◇ *una tira cómica* a comic strip
◆ **Tiene la tira de libros.** He has lots of books.
◆ **Hace la tira de tiempo que no la veo.** I haven't seen her for ages.

la **tirada** SUSTANTIVO
1 print run ◇ *La tirada inicial fue de 50.000 ejemplares.* The initial print run was 50,000 copies.
2 circulation ◇ *La revista tiene una tirada semanal de 200.000 ejemplares.* The magazine has a weekly circulation of 200,000 copies.
◆ **de una tirada** in one go

tirado ADJETIVO
1 dirt-cheap (*coloquial: barato*)
2 dead easy (*coloquial: fácil*)

el **tirador** SUSTANTIVO
handle (*de cajón, puerta*)

la **tirana** SUSTANTIVO
tyrant

tiránico ADJETIVO
tyrannical

el **tirano** SUSTANTIVO
tyrant

tirante ADJETIVO
1 tight (*cuerda*)
2 tense (*situación, relación*)

el **tirante** SUSTANTIVO
strap (*de vestido*)
◆ **tirantes** braces (*para pantalones*)

tirar VERBO
1 to throw ◇ *Tírame la pelota.* Throw me the ball. ◇ *Les tiraban piedras a los soldados.* They were throwing stones at the soldiers. ◇ *Se tiró al suelo.* He threw himself to the ground.
2 to throw away (*desechar*) ◇ *No tires la comida.* Don't throw away the food.
◆ **tirar algo a la basura** to throw something out
◆ **tirar al suelo** to knock over ◇ *La moto la tiró al suelo.* The motorbike knocked her over.
◆ **Tropezó con la maceta y la tiró al suelo.** He tripped on the flowerpot and knocked it to the ground.
3 to knock down (*derribar*) ◇ *Queremos tirar esta pared.* We want to knock this wall down.
4 to drop (*bomba*)
◆ **tirar a la derecha** to turn right
◆ **tirar de algo** to pull something
◆ **tirar la cadena** (*de váter*) Latin America to pull the chain
◆ **Vamos tirando.** We're getting by.
◆ **tirarse al agua** to plunge into the water
◆ **tirarse de cabeza** to dive in head first
◆ **tirarse en el sofá** Latin America to lie down on the sofa
◆ **Se tiró toda la mañana estudiando.** He spent the whole morning studying.

la **tirita** SUSTANTIVO
plaster

tiritar VERBO
to shiver
◆ **tiritar de frío** to shiver with cold

el **tiro** SUSTANTIVO
shot ◇ *Oímos un tiro.* We heard a shot.
◆ **Lo mataron de un tiro.** They shot him dead.
◆ **Me salió el tiro por la culata.** It backfired on me.
◆ **tiro al blanco** target practice
◆ **un tiro libre** (*en fútbol*) a free kick

el **tiroteo** SUSTANTIVO
shoot-out

el **títere** SUSTANTIVO
puppet

titubear VERBO
to hesitate (*vacilar*) ◇ *Respondí sin titubear.* I answered without hesitating.

titulado ADJETIVO
qualified ◇ *una enfermera titulada* a qualified nurse

el **titular** SUSTANTIVO
headline (*de periódico*)

el/la **titular** SUSTANTIVO
1 holder (*de pasaporte*)
2 owner (*de vivienda*)

titular VERBO
to call ◇ *La novela se titula "Marcianos".* The novel is called "Marcianos".
◆ **¿Cómo vas a titular el trabajo?** What title are you going to give the essay?

el **título** SUSTANTIVO
1 title ◇ *Tengo que pensar en un título para el poema.* I have to think of a title for the poem.
2 qualification (*carrera*) ◇ *Tiene el título de enfermera.* She has a nursing qualification.
3 certificate (*diploma*) ◇ *Hay varios títulos colgados en la pared.* There are several certificates hanging on the wall.

* Verbs marked with this symbol are irregular. See pages 380-382 for further details

la **tiza** SUSTANTIVO
chalk (*material*)
◆**una tiza** a piece of chalk

la **toalla** SUSTANTIVO
towel ◊ *una toalla de baño* a bath towel

el **tobillo** SUSTANTIVO
ankle ◊ *Me he torcido el tobillo.* I've twisted my ankle.

el **tobogán** SUSTANTIVO (PL los **toboganes**)
1 slide (*en parque, piscina*)
2 toboggan (*trineo*)

el **tocadiscos** SUSTANTIVO (PL los **tocadiscos**)
record player

el **tocador** SUSTANTIVO
dressing table

tocar* VERBO
1 to touch ◊ *Si lo tocas te quemarás.* If you touch it you'll burn yourself.
2 to play (*instrumento, vals*) ◊ *Toca el violín.* He plays the violin.
3 to ring (*campana, timbre*)
4 to blow (*bocina*)
◆**tocar a la puerta** Latin America to knock on the door
◆**Te toca fregar los platos.** It's your turn to do the dishes.
◆**Le tocó la lotería.** He won the lottery.

el **tocino** SUSTANTIVO
pork fat

todavía ADVERBIO
1 still ◊ *¿Todavía estás en la cama?* Are you still in bed? ◊ *¡Y todavía se queja!* And he still complains!
2 yet (*en oraciones negativas*) ◊ *Todavía no han llegado.* They haven't arrived yet. ◊ *¿Todavía no has comido?* Have you not eaten yet? ◊ *Todavía no.* Not yet.

todo ADJETIVO, PRONOMBRE (FEM **toda**)
1 all ◊ *todos los niños* all the children ◊ *Todos son caros.* They're all expensive. ◊ *el más bonito de todos* the prettiest of all
◆**toda la noche** all night
◆**todos vosotros** all of you
◆**todos los que quieran venir** all those who want to come
2 every (*cada*) ◊ *todos los días* every day
3 the whole ◊ *He limpiado toda la casa.* I've cleaned the whole house.
◆**Ha viajado por todo el mundo.** He has travelled throughout the world.
◆**Todo el mundo lo sabe.** Everybody knows.
4 everything ◊ *Lo sabemos todo.* We know everything. ◊ *todo lo que me dijeron* everything they told me
5 everybody ◊ *Todos estaban de acuerdo.* Everybody agreed.
◆**Vaya todo seguido.** Keep straight on.
◆**todo lo contrario** quite the opposite

el **toldo** SUSTANTIVO
1 sun blind (*de ventana*)
2 awning (*de tienda*)
3 sunshade (*en la playa*)

tolerante ADJETIVO
tolerant

tolerar VERBO
to tolerate ◊ *No voy a tolerar ese comportamiento.* I won't tolerate that behaviour.
◆**Sus padres le toleran demasiado.** His parents let him get away with too much.

tomar VERBO
1 to take (*tren, foto, decisión*) ◊ *En clase tomamos apuntes.* We take notes in class. ◊ *Se lo ha tomado muy en serio.* He's taken it very seriously. ◊ *Se tomó la molestia de acompañarnos.* He took the trouble to accompany us.
◆**tomar a alguien de la mano** to take somebody by the hand
◆**tomarse algo a mal** to take something badly
2 to have (*café, bocadillo*) ◊ *¿Qué quieres tomar?* What are you going to have? ◊ *De postre tomé un helado.* I had an ice cream for dessert.
◆**Toma, esto es tuyo.** Here, this is yours.
◆**tomar cariño a alguien** to become fond of somebody
◆**tomar el pelo a alguien** to pull somebody's leg
◆**tomar el aire** to get some fresh air
◆**tomar el sol** to sunbathe
◆**tomar nota de algo** to note something down

el **tomate** SUSTANTIVO
tomato (PL tomatoes)
◆**ponerse como un tomate** to turn as red as a beetroot

el **tomillo** SUSTANTIVO
thyme

el **tomo** SUSTANTIVO
volume

el **tonel** SUSTANTIVO
barrel

la **tonelada** SUSTANTIVO
ton

la **tónica** SUSTANTIVO
tonic

el **tono** SUSTANTIVO
1 tone (*de voz*) ◊ *Lo dijo en tono cariñoso.* He said it in an affectionate tone.
2 shade (*de color*) ◊ *un tono un poco más oscuro* a slightly darker shade

la **tonta** SUSTANTIVO
fool
◆**hacerse la tonta** to act dumb

la **tontería** SUSTANTIVO
silly thing (*cosa sin importancia*) ◊ *Se pelearon por una tontería.* They fell out over a silly thing.
◆**tonterías** nonsense ◊ *¡Eso son tonterías!* That's nonsense! ◊ *¡No digas tonterías!* Don't talk nonsense!

T

tonto ADJETIVO
silly ◊ *¡Qué error más tonto!* What a silly mistake!

el **tonto** SUSTANTIVO
fool
◆**hacer el tonto** (*hacer payasadas*) to act the fool
◆**hacerse el tonto** to act dumb

toparse VERBO
◆**toparse con alguien** to bump into somebody

los **topes** SUSTANTIVO
◆**El autobús iba hasta los topes.** The bus was packed.

el **tópico** SUSTANTIVO
cliché (PL clichés)

topless ADJETIVO (FEM + PL **topless**)
topless

el **topo** SUSTANTIVO
mole

el **toque** SUSTANTIVO
◆**dar los últimos toques a algo** to put the finishing touches to something
◆**el toque de queda** the curfew

el **tórax** SUSTANTIVO
thorax

la **torcedura** SUSTANTIVO
◆**una torcedura de tobillo** a sprained ankle

torcer* VERBO
1 to twist ◊ *¡Me estás torciendo el brazo!* You're twisting my arm!
◆**torcerse el tobillo** to sprain one's ankle
2 to turn (*cambiar de dirección*) ◊ *torcer a la derecha* to turn right ◊ *torcer la esquina* to turn the corner

torcido ADJETIVO
1 crooked (*nariz, línea*) ◊ *Tiene la boca un poco torcida.* His mouth's a bit crooked.
2 bent (*doblado*) ◊ *El tronco está torcido.* The trunk is bent.
◆**Ese cuadro está torcido.** That picture isn't straight.

torear VERBO
to fight ◊ *No volverá a torear.* He will never fight again.

el **toreo** SUSTANTIVO
bullfighting

el **torero,** la **torera** SUSTANTIVO
bullfighter

la **tormenta** SUSTANTIVO
storm
◆**Hubo tormenta.** There was a storm.
◆**un día de tormenta** a stormy day

el **torneo** SUSTANTIVO
tournament

el **tornillo** SUSTANTIVO
1 screw
◆**A tu hermana le falta un tornillo.** (*coloquial*) Your sister's got a screw loose.
2 bolt (*para tuerca*)

el **toro** SUSTANTIVO
bull
◆**los toros** bullfighting
◆**ir a los toros** to go to a bullfight

la **toronja** SUSTANTIVO Latin America
grapefruit (PL grapefruit)

torpe ADJETIVO
1 clumsy (*manazas*)
2 dim (*zoquete*)

la **torre** SUSTANTIVO
1 tower (*de castillo, iglesia*) ◊ *la torre de control* the control tower
2 pylon (*de alta tensión*)
3 rook (*en ajedrez*)

la **torta** SUSTANTIVO
1 small flat cake (*dulce*)
2 pie (*de verduras*) Latin America
3 filled roll (*bocadillo*) Mexico
◆**pegar una torta a alguien** to give somebody a slap
◆**No entiendo ni torta.** I don't understand a thing.
◆**No ve ni torta.** (*coloquial*) He's as blind as a bat.

la **tortilla** SUSTANTIVO
1 omelette (*de huevos*)
◆**una tortilla de patatas** a Spanish omelette
2 tortilla (*de maíz*)

la **tortuga** SUSTANTIVO
1 tortoise (*de tierra*)
2 turtle (*de mar*)

la **tortura** SUSTANTIVO
torture

torturar VERBO
to torture

la **tos** SUSTANTIVO (PL las **toses**)
cough (PL coughs)
◆**Tengo mucha tos.** I have a bad cough.

toser VERBO
to cough

la **tostada** SUSTANTIVO
1 piece of toast ◊ *¿Quieres una tostada?* Do you want a piece of toast?
◆**tostadas** toast ◊ *Tomé café con tostadas.* I had coffee and toast.
2 fried corn tortilla Mexico

tostado ADJETIVO
1 toasted (*pan, avellanas*)
2 roasted (*café*)
3 tanned (*bronceado*)

el **tostador** SUSTANTIVO
toaster

tostar* VERBO
1 to toast (*pan, avellanas*)
2 to roast (*café*)

el **total** ADJETIVO, SUSTANTIVO

* Verbs marked with this symbol are irregular. See pages 380-382 for further details

total ◊ *Fue un fracaso total.* It was a total failure. ◊ *El total son 2.321 ptas.* The total is 2,321 pesetas.
♦ **un cambio total** a complete change
♦ **En total éramos catorce.** There were fourteen of us altogether.

total ADVERBIO
♦ **Total, que perdí mi trabajo.** So, in the end, I lost my job.

totalitario ADJETIVO
totalitarian

totalmente ADVERBIO
[1] totally ◊ *Mario es totalmente distinto a Luis.* Mario is totally different from Luis.
[2] completely ◊ *Estoy totalmente de acuerdo.* I completely agree.
♦ **¿Estás seguro? – Totalmente.** Are you sure? – Absolutely.

tóxico ADJETIVO
toxic

el **toxicómano**, la **toxicómana** SUSTANTIVO
drug addict (PL drug addicts)

la **toxina** SUSTANTIVO
toxin

tozudo ADJETIVO
obstinate

trabajador ADJETIVO (FEM **trabajador**)
hard-working ◊ *un chico muy trabajador* a very hard-working boy

el **trabajador**, la **trabajadora** SUSTANTIVO
worker ◊ *trabajadores no cualificados* unskilled workers

trabajar VERBO
to work ◊ *No trabajes tanto.* Don't work so hard.
♦ **¿En qué trabajas?** What's your job?
♦ **Trabajo de camarero.** I work as a waiter.
♦ **trabajar jornada completa** to work full-time
♦ **trabajar media jornada** to work part-time

el **trabajo** SUSTANTIVO
[1] work ◊ *Tengo mucho trabajo.* I have a lot of work. ◊ *Me puedes llamar al trabajo.* You can call me at work.
♦ **estar sin trabajo** to be unemployed
♦ **trabajo en equipo** teamwork
♦ **el trabajo de la casa** the housework
♦ **trabajos manuales** handicrafts
[2] (*empleo*)
job ◊ *Le han ofrecido un trabajo en el banco.* He's been offered a job in the bank. ◊ *No encuentro trabajo.* I can't find a job.
♦ **quedarse sin trabajo** to find oneself out of work
[3] (*escolar*)
essay (PL essays) ◊ *Tengo que entregar dos trabajos mañana.* I have to hand in two essays tomorrow.

el **tractor** SUSTANTIVO
tractor

la **tradición** SUSTANTIVO (PL las **tradiciones**)
tradition

tradicional ADJETIVO
traditional

la **traducción** SUSTANTIVO (PL las **traducciones**)
translation ◊ *Una traducción del italiano al inglés.* A translation from Italian into English.

traducir* VERBO
to translate ◊ *traducir del inglés al francés* to translate from English into French

el **traductor**, la **traductora** SUSTANTIVO
translator

traer* VERBO
[1] to bring ◊ *He traído el paraguas por si acaso.* I've brought the umbrella just in case.
[2] to carry ◊ *El periódico trae un artículo sobre la Reina.* The newspaper carries an article on the Queen.
[3] to wear ◊ *Traía un vestido nuevo.* She was wearing a new dress.

el/la **traficante** SUSTANTIVO
dealer ◊ *traficantes de armas* arms dealers

el **tráfico** SUSTANTIVO
traffic
♦ **un accidente de tráfico** a road accident
♦ **tráfico de drogas** drug-trafficking

tragar* VERBO
to swallow (*comida, pastilla*)
♦ **Nadie se va a tragar esa historia.** Nobody is going to swallow that story.
♦ **No la trago.** (*coloquial*) I can't stand her.

la **tragedia** SUSTANTIVO
tragedy (PL tragedies)

trágico ADJETIVO
tragic

el **trago** SUSTANTIVO
drink ◊ *¿Te apetece un trago?* Do you fancy a drink?
♦ **de un trago** in one gulp

la **traición** SUSTANTIVO (PL las **traiciones**)
[1] betrayal (*engaño*)
[2] treason (*contra el Estado*)

traicionar VERBO
to betray

traicionero ADJETIVO
treacherous

el **traidor**, la **traidora** SUSTANTIVO
traitor

traigo VERBO *ver* **traer**

el **tráiler** SUSTANTIVO (PL los **tráilers**)
[1] trailer (*de película, de vehículo*)
[2] articulated lorry (*camión*)

el **traje** SUSTANTIVO
[1] (*de hombre*)
suit ◊ *Luis llevaba un traje negro.* Luis was wearing a black suit.
♦ **un traje de chaqueta** a suit
♦ **un traje de buzo** a diving suit
[2] (*vestido de mujer*)

T

dress (PL dresses) ◊ *un traje de noche* an evening dress
◆ **el traje de novia** the bridal gown
◆ **un traje de baño (1)** (*de hombre*) a pair of swimming trunks
◆ **un traje de baño (2)** (*de mujer*) a swimsuit

la **trama** SUSTANTIVO
plot (*de obra*)

tramitar VERBO
◆ **Estoy tramitando un préstamo con el banco.** I'm negotiating a loan with the bank.
◆ **Estamos tramitando el divorcio.** We are going through the divorce proceedings.

el **tramo** SUSTANTIVO
1 section (*de carretera*)
2 flight (*de escalera*)

la **trampa** SUSTANTIVO
trap ◊ *caer en la trampa* to fall into the trap
◆ **Les tendió una trampa.** He set a trap for them.
◆ **hacer trampa** to cheat

el **trampolín** SUSTANTIVO (PL los **trampolines**)
1 diving board (*en piscina*) ◊ *Se tiró desde el trampolín.* He plunged from the diving board.
2 trampoline (*en gimnasia*)

el **tramposo**, la **tramposa** SUSTANTIVO
cheat

tranquilamente ADVERBIO
calmly ◊ *Háblale tranquilamente.* Speak to him calmly.
◆ **Yo estaba sentado tranquilamente viendo la tele.** I was sitting peacefully watching TV.

la **tranquilidad** SUSTANTIVO
peace and quiet ◊ *Necesito un poco de tranquilidad.* I need a little peace and quiet.
◆ **Respondió con tranquilidad.** He answered calmly.
◆ **Llévatelo a casa y léelo con tranquilidad.** Take it home with you and read it at your leisure.
◆ **¡Qué tranquilidad! ¡Ya se han acabado los exámenes!** What a relief! The exams are over at last!

tranquilizar* VERBO
to calm down ◊ *¡Tranquilízate!* Calm down!
◆ **Las palabras del médico me tranquilizaron.** The doctor's words reassured me.

tranquilo ADJETIVO
1 calm ◊ *El día del examen estaba bastante tranquilo.* On the day of the exam I was quite calm.
2 peaceful (*pueblo, lugar*)

el **transatlántico** SUSTANTIVO
ocean liner

el **transbordador** SUSTANTIVO
ferry (PL ferries)
◆ **el transbordador espacial** the space shuttle

el **transbordo** SUSTANTIVO
◆ **Hay que hacer transbordo en París.** You have to change trains in Paris.

transcurrir VERBO
to pass ◊ *Transcurrieron dos años.* Two years passed.

el/la **transeúnte** SUSTANTIVO
passer-by (PL passers-by)

la **transferencia** SUSTANTIVO
transfer ◊ *transferencia bancaria* bank transfer

la **transformación** SUSTANTIVO (PL las **transformaciones**)
transformation

transformar VERBO
to transform (*lugar, país*) ◊ *La cirugía estética le ha transformado completamente.* Plastic surgery has completely transformed him.
◆ **Hemos transformado el garaje en sala de estar.** We've converted the garage into a living room.
◆ **El príncipe se transformó en un monstruo.** The prince turned into a monster.

la **transfusión** SUSTANTIVO (PL las **transfusiones**)
◆ **Me hicieron una transfusión de sangre.** They gave me a blood transfusion.

transgénico ADJETIVO
genetically modified

la **transición** SUSTANTIVO
transition

el **transistor** SUSTANTIVO
transistor

transitivo ADJETIVO
transitive

el **tránsito** SUSTANTIVO
traffic
◆ **los pasajeros en tránsito para Moscú** transfer passengers to Moscow

la **transmisión** SUSTANTIVO (PL las **transmisiones**)
broadcast ◊ *una transmisión en directo* a live broadcast

transmitir VERBO
1 to transmit (*señal, sonido*)
2 to broadcast (*programa*)

transparente ADJETIVO
transparent

la **transpiración** SUSTANTIVO
perspiration

transportar VERBO
to carry ◊ *El camión transportaba medicamentos.* The lorry was carrying medicines.

* Verbs marked with this symbol are irregular. See pages 380-382 for further details

el **transporte** SUSTANTIVO
transport
♦ **el transporte público** public transport

el/la **transportista** SUSTANTIVO
carrier

el **tranvía** SUSTANTIVO
tram

el **trapo** SUSTANTIVO
cloth ◊ *Lo limpié con un trapo.* I wiped it with a cloth.
♦ **un trapo de cocina** a dishcloth
♦ **Pásale un trapo al espejo.** Give the mirror a wipe over.
♦ **el trapo del polvo** the duster

la **tráquea** SUSTANTIVO
windpipe

tras PREPOSICIÓN
after ◊ *Salimos corriendo tras ella.* We ran out after her. ◊ *semana tras semana* week after week

trasero ADJETIVO
back ◊ *la rueda trasera de la bici* the back wheel of the bike

el **trasero** SUSTANTIVO
bottom

trasladar VERBO
1 to move (*oficina, tienda*) ◊ *Mañana nos trasladamos al piso.* We're moving to the flat tomorrow.
2 to transfer (*empleado, preso*) ◊ *Me quieren trasladar a otra sucursal.* They want to transfer me to another branch.

el **traslado** SUSTANTIVO
move (*mudanza*)
♦ **He pedido traslado a Barcelona.** I've asked for a transfer to Barcelona.
♦ **los gastos de traslado de la oficina** the office's relocation expenses

el **trasluz** SUSTANTIVO
♦ **al trasluz** against the light

trasnochar VERBO
to stay up late

traspapelarse VERBO
to get mislaid

traspasar VERBO
1 to go through ◊ *La bala traspasó el sofá.* The bullet went through the sofa.
2 to transfer (*empleado, jugador, dinero*)
3 to sell (*tienda*)

el **traspié** SUSTANTIVO (PL los **traspiés**)
♦ **dar un traspié** to trip

trasplantar VERBO
to transplant

el **trasplante** SUSTANTIVO
transplant

el **trastero** SUSTANTIVO
storage room

los **trastes** SUSTANTIVO Mexico
pots and pans
♦ **lavar los trastes** to do the dishes

el **trasto** SUSTANTIVO
piece of junk ◊ *El coche que se ha comprado es un trasto.* The car he's bought is a piece of junk.
♦ **El desván está lleno de trastos.** The loft is full of junk.

trastornado ADJETIVO
disturbed (*mentalmente*)

el **trastorno** SUSTANTIVO
disruption ◊ *La huelga ha causado muchos trastornos.* The strike has caused a lot of disruption.
♦ **trastornos mentales** mental disorders

el **tratado** SUSTANTIVO
treaty (PL treaties)

el **tratamiento** SUSTANTIVO
treatment
♦ **Está en tratamiento médico.** He's having medical treatment.
♦ **tratamiento de datos** data processing
♦ **tratamiento de textos** word processing

tratar VERBO
1 to treat ◊ *Su novio la trata muy mal.* Her boyfriend treats her very badly.
2 to deal with ◊ *Trataremos este tema en la reunión.* We'll deal with this subject in the meeting.
♦ **Trato con todo tipo de gente.** I deal with all sorts of people.
♦ **tratar de hacer algo** to try to do something
♦ **¿De qué se trata?** What's it about?
♦ **La película trata de un adolescente en Nueva York.** The film is about a teenager in New York.

el **trato** SUSTANTIVO
deal ◊ *hacer un trato* to make a deal
♦ **¡Trato hecho!** It's a deal!
♦ **No tengo mucho trato con él.** I don't have much to do with him.
♦ **recibir malos tratos de alguien** to be treated badly by somebody

el **trauma** SUSTANTIVO
trauma

través PREPOSICIÓN
♦ **a través de (1)** (*de lado a lado*) across ◊ *Nadó a través del río.* He swam across the river.
♦ **a través de (2)** through (*por medio de*) ◊ *Se enteraron a través de un amigo.* They found out through a friend.

la **travesía** SUSTANTIVO
1 crossing (*viaje en barco*)
2 side-street (*calle*)

la **travesura** SUSTANTIVO
prank
♦ **hacer travesuras** to get up to mischief

travieso ADJETIVO
naughty

el **trayecto** SUSTANTIVO
1 (*viaje*)
journey (PL journeys)
2 (*ruta*)
way (PL ways)

T

☞

◆ **¿Qué trayecto hace el 34?** What way does the 34 go?

trazar* VERBO
1 to draw (*línea, mapa*)
2 to draw up (*plan*)

el **trébol** SUSTANTIVO
clover
◆ **tréboles** (*en la baraja*) clubs

trece ADJETIVO, PRONOMBRE
thirteen ◊ *Tengo trece años.* I'm thirteen.
◆ **el trece de enero** the thirteenth of January

treinta ADJETIVO, PRONOMBRE
thirty ◊ *Tiene treinta años.* He's thirty.
◆ **el treinta aniversario** the thirtieth anniversary

tremendo ADJETIVO
1 terrible (*dolor, ruido, fracaso*) ◊ *Tenía un tremendo dolor de cabeza.* I had a terrible headache.
◆ **Hacía un frío tremendo.** It was terribly cold.
2 tremendous (*diferencia, velocidad, éxito*) ◊ *La película tuvo un éxito tremendo.* The film was a tremendous success.

el **tren** SUSTANTIVO
train
◆ **viajar en tren** to travel by train
◆ **Tomé un tren directo.** I took a through train.
◆ **con este tren de vida** with such a hectic life

la **trenza** SUSTANTIVO
plait
◆ **Le hice una trenza.** I plaited her hair.

la **trepadora** SUSTANTIVO
climber (*planta*)

trepar VERBO
to climb
◆ **trepar a un árbol** to climb a tree

tres ADJETIVO, PRONOMBRE
three
◆ **Son las tres.** It's three o'clock.
◆ **el tres de febrero** the third of February

trescientos ADJETIVO, PRONOMBRE (FEM **trescientas**)
three hundred

el **tresillo** SUSTANTIVO
three-seater sofa (*sofá*)

el **triángulo** SUSTANTIVO
triangle

la **tribu** SUSTANTIVO
tribe

la **tribuna** SUSTANTIVO
1 platform (*para orador*)
2 stand (*para espectadores*)

el **tribunal** SUSTANTIVO
1 court (*de justicia*)
2 board of examiners (*de examen*)

el **triciclo** SUSTANTIVO
tricycle

tridimensional ADJETIVO
three-dimensional

el **trigo** SUSTANTIVO
wheat

trillar VERBO
to thresh

los **trillizos**, las **trillizas** SUSTANTIVO
triplets

trimestral ADJETIVO
quarterly (*revista*)
◆ **los exámenes trimestrales** the end-of-term exams

el **trimestre** SUSTANTIVO
term (*escolar*)

trinchar VERBO
to carve

la **trinchera** SUSTANTIVO
trench

el **trineo** SUSTANTIVO
1 sledge (*para niños*)
2 sleigh (*tirado por perros*)

la **Trinidad** SUSTANTIVO
the Trinity (*deidad*)

el **trío** SUSTANTIVO
trio

la **tripa** SUSTANTIVO
gut (*intestino*)

el **triple** SUSTANTIVO
◆ **Esta habitación es el triple de grande.** This room is three times as big.
◆ **Gastan el triple que nosotros.** They spend three times as much as we do.

triplicar* VERBO
to treble

la **tripulación** SUSTANTIVO (PL las **tripulaciones**)
crew

triste ADJETIVO
1 sad ◊ *Me puse muy triste cuando me enteré de la noticia.* I was very sad when I heard the news.
◆ **El invierno me pone triste.** Winter makes me miserable.
2 gloomy (*color, paisaje*)

la **tristeza** SUSTANTIVO
sadness

triturar VERBO
1 to crush (*ajos*)
2 to grind (*nueces*)

triunfar VERBO
to triumph ◊ *Los socialistas triunfaron en las elecciones.* The socialists triumphed in the elections.
◆ **triunfar en la vida** to succeed in life

el **triunfo** SUSTANTIVO
triumph (*victoria*)

trivial ADJETIVO
trivial

* Verbs marked with this symbol are irregular. See pages 380-382 for further details

las **trizas** SUSTANTIVO
◆ **hacer algo trizas** (*documento, tela*) to tear something to shreds

trocear VERBO
to cut up ◊ *trocear las zanahorias* to cut up the carrots

el **trofeo** SUSTANTIVO
trophy (PL trophies)

el **trombón** SUSTANTIVO (PL los **trombones**)
trombone

la **trompa** SUSTANTIVO
[1] trunk (*de elefante*)
[2] horn (*instrumento musical*)
◆ **coger una trompa** (*coloquial*) to get plastered

la **trompeta** SUSTANTIVO
trumpet

tronar* VERBO
to thunder ◊ *Ha estado tronando toda la noche.* It has been thundering all night.

troncharse VERBO
◆ **Yo me tronchaba de risa.** I was killing myself laughing.

el **tronco** SUSTANTIVO
[1] trunk (*de árbol*)
[2] log (*leño*)
◆ **dormir como un tronco** to sleep like a log

el **trono** SUSTANTIVO
throne

las **tropas** SUSTANTIVO
troops

tropezar* VERBO
to trip ◊ *Tropecé y me caí.* I tripped and fell.
◆ **tropezar con una piedra** to trip on a stone
◆ **tropezar contra un árbol** to bump into a tree
◆ **Me tropecé con Juan en el banco.** I bumped into Juan in the bank.

el **tropezón** SUSTANTIVO (PL los **tropezones**)
trip
◆ **dar un tropezón** to trip

tropical ADJETIVO
tropical

el **trópico** SUSTANTIVO
tropic

tropiece VERBO *ver* **tropezar**

trotar VERBO
to trot

el **trote** SUSTANTIVO
◆ **El abuelo ya no está para estos trotes.** Grandad is not up to that sort of thing any more.

el **trozo** SUSTANTIVO
piece ◊ *un trozo de madera* a piece of wood ◊ *Dame un trocito sólo.* Just give me a small piece.
◆ **Vi la película a trozos.** I saw bits of the film.

la **trucha** SUSTANTIVO
trout

el **truco** SUSTANTIVO
trick
◆ **Ya le he cogido el truco.** I've got the hang of it already.

truena VERBO *ver* **tronar**

el **trueno** SUSTANTIVO
◆ **Oímos un trueno.** We heard a clap of thunder.
◆ **Me despertaron los truenos.** The thunder woke me up.

la **trufa** SUSTANTIVO
truffle

tu ADJETIVO
your ◊ *tu coche* your car ◊ *tus familiares* your relations

tú PRONOMBRE
you ◊ *Cuando tú quieras.* Whenever you like. ◊ *Llegamos antes que tú.* We arrived before you.

la **tuberculosis** SUSTANTIVO
tuberculosis

la **tubería** SUSTANTIVO
pipe ◊ *Ha reventado una tubería.* A pipe has burst.

el **tubo** SUSTANTIVO
[1] pipe ◊ *el tubo de escape* the exhaust pipe
◆ **el tubo de desagüe** the drainpipe
[2] tube ◊ *un tubo de crema para las manos* a tube of hand cream

la **tuerca** SUSTANTIVO
nut

tuerto ADJETIVO
◆ **Es tuerto.** He's blind in one eye.

tuerzo VERBO *ver* **torcer**

el **tuétano** SUSTANTIVO
marrow

el **tufo** SUSTANTIVO
stench

el **tulipán** SUSTANTIVO (PL los **tulipanes**)
tulip

la **tumba** SUSTANTIVO
[1] grave (*en la tierra*)
[2] tomb ◊ *una tumba egipcia* an Egyptian tomb

tumbar VERBO
to knock down ◊ *El perro me tumbó.* The dog knocked me down.
◆ **tumbarse** to lie down ◊ *Me tumbé en el sofá.* I lay down on the sofa.

el **tumbo** SUSTANTIVO
◆ **El borracho iba dando tumbos.** The drunk staggered along.

la **tumbona** SUSTANTIVO
deck chair

el **tumor** SUSTANTIVO
tumour

el **túnel** SUSTANTIVO
tunnel
◆ **un túnel de lavado** a car wash

Túnez SUSTANTIVO MASC

[1] Tunisia (*país*)
[2] Tunis (*ciudad*)

tupido ADJETIVO
[1] dense (*bosque, vegetación*)
[2] close-woven (*tela*)
[3] bushy (*cejas*)

el **turbante** SUSTANTIVO
turban

la **turbina** SUSTANTIVO
turbine

turbio ADJETIVO
cloudy (*agua*)

turbulento ADJETIVO
turbulent

turco ADJETIVO
Turkish

el **turco,** la **turca** SUSTANTIVO
Turk (*persona*)

el **turco** SUSTANTIVO
Turkish (*idioma*)

el **turismo** SUSTANTIVO
[1] tourism (*industria*) ◊ *El turismo es importante para nuestra economía.* Tourism is important for our economy.
◆ **turismo rural** tourism in rural areas
◆ **casas de turismo rural** holiday cottages
[2] tourists PL (*turistas*) ◊ *En verano hay mucho turismo.* In summer there are a lot of tourists.
[3] car (*coche*)
◆ **la oficina de turismo** the tourist office

el/la **turista** SUSTANTIVO
tourist

turístico ADJETIVO
tourist (*lugar, folleto*)

turnarse VERBO
to take it in turns ◊ *Nos turnamos para fregar los platos.* We take it in turns to do the washing-up.

el **turno** SUSTANTIVO
[1] turn ◊ *cuando me tocó el turno* when it was my turn
[2] shift ◊ *Hago el turno de tarde.* I do the afternoon shift.

la **turquesa** ADJETIVO, SUSTANTIVO
turquoise ◊ *un anorak turquesa* a turquoise anorak

Turquía SUSTANTIVO FEM
Turkey

el **turrón** SUSTANTIVO (PL los **turrones**)

> ❶ ***Turrón** is a kind of nougat traditionally eaten at Christmas.*

tutear VERBO

> ❶ *to address somebody using the familiar **tú** form rather than the more formal **usted** form.*

◊ *Se tutean con el jefe.* They address the boss in familiar terms.

el **tutor,** la **tutora** SUSTANTIVO
[1] tutor (*profesor*)
[2] guardian (*de un menor de edad*)

tuve VERBO *ver* **tener**

tuyo ADJETIVO, PRONOMBRE (FEM **tuya**)
yours ◊ *¿Es tuyo este abrigo?* Is this coat yours? ◊ *La tuya está en el armario.* Yours is in the cupboard. ◊ *mis amigos y los tuyos* my friends and yours
◆ **un amigo tuyo** a friend of yours

U

u CONJUNCIÓN
or
***u* is used instead of *o* before words starting with *o-* or *ho-*.**
◊ *¿Minutos u horas?* Minutes or hours?
Ud. ABREVIATURA = **usted**
Uds. ABREVIATURA = **ustedes**
la **UE** ABREVIATURA (= *Unión Europea*)
EU
uf INTERJECCIÓN
1 phew! (*expresión de cansancio*)
2 ugh! (*expresión de asco*)
la **úlcera** SUSTANTIVO
ulcer
últimamente ADVERBIO
recently
el **ultimátum** SUSTANTIVO (PL los **ultimátums**)
ultimatum (PL ultimatums)
último ADJETIVO
1 last (*en el tiempo*) ◊ *la última vez que hablé con ella* the last time I spoke to her
2 top (*más alto*) ◊ *No llego al último estante.* I can't reach the top shelf.
3 back (*más al fondo*) ◊ *Nos sentamos en la última fila.* We sat in the back row.
♦ **la última moda** the latest fashion
♦ **a última hora** at the last minute ◊ *A última hora decidió acompañarme.* He decided to come with me at the last minute.
♦ **llegar en último lugar** to arrive last
el **último,** la **última** SUSTANTIVO
the last one
♦ **a últimos de mes** towards the end of the month
♦ **por último** lastly
el/la **ultra** SUSTANTIVO
right-wing extremist
ultrasónico ADJETIVO
ultrasonic
ultravioleta ADJETIVO
ultraviolet
un, una ARTÍCULO
1 a ◊ *una silla* a chair
2 an ◊ *un paraguas* an umbrella
3 some (*en plural*) ◊ *Fui con unos amigos.* I went with some friends.
♦ **Tiene unas uñas muy largas.** He has very long nails.
♦ **Había unas 20 personas.** There were about 20 people.
♦ **Me he comprado unos zapatos de tacón.** I have bought a pair of high-heels.
unánime ADJETIVO
unanimous
undécimo, undécima ADJETIVO, PRONOMBRE
eleventh ◊ *Vivo en el undécimo piso.* I live on the eleventh floor.

únicamente ADVERBIO
only ◊ *Me encargo únicamente de cuidar a los niños.* I'm only in charge of looking after the children.
el **único,** la **única** ADJETIVO, SUSTANTIVO
only ◊ *El miércoles es el único día que tengo libre.* Wednesday is the only day I have free.
♦ **Soy hija única.** I'm an only child.
♦ **el único que me queda** the only one I've got left
♦ **Lo único que no me gusta ...** The only thing I don't like ...
♦ **una colección de sellos única** a unique stamp collection
la **unidad** SUSTANTIVO
1 unit ◊ *una unidad de peso* a unit of weight
♦ **unidad de cuidados intensivos** intensive care unit
2 unity (*armonía*) ◊ *falta de unidad en la familia* lack of family unity
unido ADJETIVO
close (*familia, grupo*) ◊ *una familia muy unida* a very close family
uniforme ADJETIVO
even ◊ *una superficie uniforme* an even surface
el **uniforme** SUSTANTIVO
uniform ◊ *Llevaba el uniforme del colegio.* He was wearing his school uniform.
la **unión** SUSTANTIVO (PL las **uniones**)
union
♦ **la Unión Europea** the European Union
unir VERBO
1 to link ◊ *Este pasaje une los dos edificios.* This passage links the two buildings.
2 to join ◊ *Unió los dos extremos con una cuerda.* He joined the two ends with some string.
3 to unite ◊ *Los unió en matrimonio.* He united them in marriage.
4 to bring together ◊ *La enfermedad de la madre ha unido a los hijos.* The mother's illness has brought the children together.
♦ **unirse a algo** to join something ◊ *Andrés se unió a la expedición.* Andrés joined the expedition.
♦ **Más adelante los dos caminos se unen.** The two paths join further on.
♦ **Los dos bancos se han unido.** The two banks have merged.
universal ADJETIVO
universal
la **universidad** SUSTANTIVO

☞

university (PL universities) ◊ *El año que viene voy a la universidad.* I'm going to university next year.

◆ **Universidad a Distancia** Open University

> *La **Open University** imparte cursos a distancia con el apoyo de programas de radio y televisión emitidos por la BBC.*

universitario ADJETIVO
university

> ***university** en este caso va siempre delante del sustantivo.*

◊ *estudiantes universitarios* university students

el **universitario**, la **universitaria** SUSTANTIVO
1 university student (*estudiante*)
2 graduate (*licenciado*)

el **universo** SUSTANTIVO
universe

uno, una ADJETIVO, PRONOMBRE
one ◊ *Vivo en el número uno.* I live at number one. ◊ *Uno de ellos era mío.* One of them was mine.

◆ **unos pocos** a few
◆ **uno mismo** oneself
◆ **Entraron uno a uno.** They came in one by one.
◆ **unas diez personas** about ten people
◆ **el uno de abril** the first of April
◆ **Es la una.** It's one o'clock.
◆ **Unos querían ir, otros no.** Some of them wanted to go, others didn't.
◆ **Se miraron uno al otro.** They looked at each other.

untar VERBO
◆ **untar algo con algo** to spread something on something ◊ *Primero hay que untar el pan con mantequilla.* First you have to spread the butter on the bread.
◆ **Te has untado las manos de chocolate.** You've got chocolate all over your hands.
◆ **Unta el molde con aceite.** Grease the baking dish with oil.

la **uña** SUSTANTIVO
1 nail (*de dedo*)
2 claw (*de gato*)

el **uranio** SUSTANTIVO
uranium

la **urbanización** SUSTANTIVO (PL las **urbanizaciones**)
housing estate (*zona residencial*)

la **urgencia** SUSTANTIVO
(*emergencia*)
emergency (PL emergencies) ◊ *en caso de urgencia* in an emergency ◊ *los servicios de urgencia* the emergency services

◆ **urgencias** (*en hospital*) accident and emergency
◆ **Tuvimos que ir a urgencias.** We had to go to casualty.
◆ **con urgencia** urgently

urgente ADJETIVO
urgent (*mensaje, trabajo*)
◆ **Lo mandé por correo urgente.** I sent it express.

la **urna** SUSTANTIVO
ballot box (*para votar*)

Uruguay SUSTANTIVO MASC
Uruguay

el **uruguayo**, la **uruguaya** ADJETIVO, SUSTANTIVO
Uruguayan

usado ADJETIVO
1 secondhand (*de segunda mano*) ◊ *una tienda de ropa usada* a secondhand clothes shop
2 worn (*viejo*) ◊ *Estas zapatillas están muy usadas.* These slippers are very worn.

usar VERBO
1 to use ◊ *Uso una afeitadora eléctrica.* I use an electric razor.
2 to wear (*perfume, zapatillas*) ◊ *¿Qué número de zapato usas?* What size shoe do you take?

el **uso** SUSTANTIVO
use ◊ *instrucciones de uso* instructions for use

usted PRONOMBRE
you ◊ *Quisiera hablar con usted en privado.* I'd like to speak to you in private.

ustedes PRONOMBRE PL
you ◊ *Quisiera hablar con ustedes en privado.* I'd like to speak to you in private.

usual ADJETIVO
usual

el **usuario**, la **usuaria** SUSTANTIVO
user

el **utensilio** SUSTANTIVO
utensil ◊ *utensilios de cocina* kitchen utensils

el **útero** SUSTANTIVO
uterus

útil ADJETIVO
useful

utilizar* VERBO
to use

la **uva** SUSTANTIVO
grape
◆ **estar de mala uva** to be in a bad mood

V

va VERBO *ver* **ir**

la **vaca** SUSTANTIVO
[1] cow (*animal*)
[2] beef (*carne*) ◊ *No como carne de vaca.* I don't eat beef.

las **vacaciones** SUSTANTIVO
holidays
♦ **las vacaciones de Navidad** the Christmas holidays
♦ **La secretaria está de vacaciones.** The secretary is on holiday.
♦ **En agosto me voy de vacaciones.** I'm going on holiday in August.

vacante ADJETIVO
[1] vacant (*puesto*)
[2] unoccupied (*piso, habitación*)

la **vacante** SUSTANTIVO
vacancy (PL vacancies)

vaciar* VERBO
to empty ◊ *Vacié la nevera para limpiarla.* I emptied the fridge to clean it.

vacilar VERBO
to hesitate ◊ *Vaciló unos instantes antes de responder.* He hesitated for a moment or two before answering.
♦ **sin vacilar** without hesitating

vacío ADJETIVO
empty

el **vacío** SUSTANTIVO
void (*precipicio*) ◊ *Se arrojó al vacío.* He hurled himself into the void.
♦ **envasado al vacío** vacuum-packed

la **vacuna** SUSTANTIVO
vaccine ◊ *la vacuna de la hepatitis* the hepatitis vaccine
♦ **¿Te has puesto la vacuna?** Have they given you the vaccination?

vacunar VERBO
to vaccinate
♦ **Mi abuelo se vacuna contra la gripe.** My grandfather has flu vaccinations.

el **vado** SUSTANTIVO
♦ **"vado permanente"** "no parking – in constant use"

la **vaga** SUSTANTIVO
layabout

la **vagabunda** SUSTANTIVO
tramp

vagabundo ADJETIVO
stray (*perro*)

el **vagabundo** SUSTANTIVO
tramp

vagar* VERBO
to wander

la **vagina** SUSTANTIVO
vagina

vago ADJETIVO
[1] lazy (*persona*)
[2] vague (*recuerdo, explicación*)

el **vago** SUSTANTIVO
layabout
♦ **hacer el vago** to laze around

el **vagón** SUSTANTIVO (PL los **vagones**)
carriage
♦ **vagón cama** sleeper
♦ **vagón restaurante** restaurant car

el **vaho** SUSTANTIVO
steam (*vapor*)

la **vainilla** SUSTANTIVO
vanilla ◊ *un helado de vainilla* a vanilla ice cream

la **vajilla** SUSTANTIVO
dishes PL ◊ *La vajilla está en el lavaplatos.* The dishes are in the dishwasher.
♦ **Me regaló una vajilla de porcelana.** She gave me a china dinner service.

el **vale** SUSTANTIVO
[1] voucher ◊ *un vale-regalo* a gift voucher
♦ **un vale de descuento** a money-off coupon
[2] credit note (*de compra*)

el **valenciano,** la **valenciana** ADJETIVO, SUSTANTIVO
Valencian
♦ **Hablan valenciano.** They speak Valencian.

la **valentía** SUSTANTIVO
bravery
♦ **con valentía** bravely

valer* VERBO
[1] to cost ◊ *¿Cuánto vale?* How much does it cost?
[2] to be worth ◊ *El terreno vale más que la casa.* The land is worth more than the house.
♦ **No vale mirar.** You're not allowed to look.
♦ **¡Eso no vale!** That's not fair!
♦ **vale la pena** it's worth it
♦ **Vale la pena hacer el esfuerzo.** It's worth the effort.
♦ **no vale la pena** it's not worth it
♦ **No vale la pena gastar tanto dinero.** It's not worth spending that much money.
♦ **Este cuchillo no vale para nada.** This knife is useless.
♦ **Yo no valdría para enfermera.** I'd make a hopeless nurse.
♦ **¿Vale?** OK?
♦ **¿Vamos a tomar algo? – ¡Vale!** Shall we go for a drink? – OK!
♦ **Más vale que te lleves el abrigo.** You'd better take your coat.
♦ **No puede valerse por sí mismo.** He can't look after himself.

válido ADJETIVO
valid

valiente ADJETIVO
brave

la **valija** SUSTANTIVO
suitcase River Plate
◆ **valija diplomática** diplomatic bag

valioso ADJETIVO
valuable

la **valla** SUSTANTIVO
fence
◆ **valla publicitaria** hoarding
◆ **los cien metros vallas** the hundred metre hurdles

el **valle** SUSTANTIVO
valley (PL valleys)

el **valor** SUSTANTIVO
1 value ◊ *valor sentimental* sentimental value
◆ **una pulsera de gran valor** an extremely valuable bracelet
2 courage (*valentía*) ◊ *armarse de valor* to pluck up courage
◆ **objetos de valor** valuables
◆ **valor adquisitivo** purchasing power

valorar VERBO
to value (*joya, amistad*)

el **vals** SUSTANTIVO
waltz
◆ **bailar un vals** to waltz

la **válvula** SUSTANTIVO
valve

el **vampiro**, la **vampira** SUSTANTIVO
vampire

el **vandalismo** SUSTANTIVO
vandalism

la **vanguardia** SUSTANTIVO
avant-garde
◆ **de vanguardia** avant-garde

la **vanidad** SUSTANTIVO
vanity

vanidoso ADJETIVO
vain

vano ADJETIVO
vain ◊ *un intento vano* a vain attempt
◆ **en vano** in vain

el **vapor** SUSTANTIVO
steam
◆ **plancha de vapor** steam iron
◆ **al vapor** steamed

vaquero ADJETIVO
denim

denim en este caso va siempre delante del sustantivo.

◊ *una falda vaquera* a denim skirt

el **vaquero** SUSTANTIVO
cowboy (PL cowboys)
◆ **una película de vaqueros** a western
◆ **vaqueros** jeans ◊ *Llevaba unos vaqueros negros.* He was wearing black jeans.

variable ADJETIVO
variable (*velocidad, ánimo*)
◆ **El tiempo es muy variable.** The weather is very changeable.

variado ADJETIVO
varied ◊ *Prefiero un trabajo más variado.* I prefer a more varied job.

variar* VERBO
to vary ◊ *Los precios varían según las tallas.* Prices vary according to size.
◆ **Decidí ir en tren, para variar.** I decided to go by train for a change.

la **varicela** SUSTANTIVO
chicken pox ◊ *Yo no he pasado la varicela.* I've never had chicken pox.

la **variedad** SUSTANTIVO
variety (PL varieties) ◊ *una nueva variedad de clavel* a new variety of carnation

la **varilla** SUSTANTIVO
rod
◆ **la varilla del aceite** the dipstick

varios ADJETIVO, PRONOMBRE (FEM **varias**)
several ◊ *Estuve enfermo varios días.* I was ill for several days. ◊ *Le hicimos un regalo entre varios.* Several of us clubbed together to get him a present.

la **variz** SUSTANTIVO (PL las **varices**)
varicose vein

varón ADJETIVO (PL **varones**)
male ◊ *los herederos varones* the male heirs

el **varón** SUSTANTIVO (PL los **varones**)
◊ *Tiene dos hembras y un varón.* She has two girls and a boy.
◆ **Sexo: varón.** Sex: male.

Varsovia SUSTANTIVO FEM
Warsaw

el **vasco**, la **vasca** ADJETIVO, SUSTANTIVO
Basque
◆ **Hablamos vasco.** We speak Basque.
◆ **el País Vasco** the Basque Country

la **vasija** SUSTANTIVO
vessel (*cacharro*) ◊ *una vasija fenicia* a Phoenician vessel

el **vaso** SUSTANTIVO
glass (PL glasses) ◊ *Bebí un vaso de leche.* I drank a glass of milk.
◆ **un vaso de plástico** a plastic cup
◆ **un vaso sanguíneo** a blood vessel

el **váter** SUSTANTIVO
loo (*coloquial*)

el **Vaticano** SUSTANTIVO
Vatican

el **vatio** SUSTANTIVO
watt

vaya VERBO *ver* **ir**

Vd. ABREVIATURA = **usted**

Vds. ABREVIATURA = **ustedes**

ve VERBO *ver* **ir, ver**

* Verbs marked with this symbol are irregular. See pages 380-382 for further details

la **vecina** SUSTANTIVO
[1] neighbour (*de la misma calle*)
[2] inhabitant (*habitante*)
el **vecindario** SUSTANTIVO
neighbourhood (*barrio*)
vecino ADJETIVO
neighbouring ◊ *las ciudades vecinas* the neighbouring towns
el **vecino** SUSTANTIVO
[1] neighbour (*de la misma calle*) ◊ *los vecinos de al lado* the next door neighbours
[2] inhabitant (*habitante*) ◊ *todos los vecinos de Torrevieja* all the inhabitants of Torrevieja
la **vegetación** SUSTANTIVO (PL las **vegetaciones**)
vegetation (*de plantas*)
♦ **vegetaciones** (*en la nariz*) adenoids
el **vegetal** ADJETIVO, SUSTANTIVO
vegetable ◊ *aceite vegetal* vegetable oil
el **vegetariano,** la **vegetariana** ADJETIVO, SUSTANTIVO
vegetarian ◊ *Es vegetariano.* He's vegetarian.
el **vehículo** SUSTANTIVO
vehicle
veinte ADJETIVO, PRONOMBRE
twenty ◊ *Tiene veinte años.* He's twenty.
♦ **el veinte de enero** the twentieth of January
♦ **el siglo veinte** the twentieth century
la **vejez** SUSTANTIVO
old age
la **vejiga** SUSTANTIVO
bladder
la **vela** SUSTANTIVO
[1] candle ◊ *Encendimos una vela.* We lit a candle.
[2] sail (*de barco*)
[3] sailing (*deporte*)
♦ **un barco de vela** a yacht
♦ **Pasé la noche en vela.** I had a sleepless night.
♦ **estar a dos velas** (*coloquial*) to be broke
velarse VERBO
♦ **Se han velado las fotos.** The photos got exposed by accident.
el **velero** SUSTANTIVO
yacht
el **vello** SUSTANTIVO
[1] hair (*en el cuerpo*) ◊ *Tiene mucho vello.* He's very hairy.
[2] down (*en la cara*)
el **velo** SUSTANTIVO
veil
la **velocidad** SUSTANTIVO
[1] speed ◊ *Pasó una moto a toda velocidad.* A motorbike went past at full speed.
♦ **¿A qué velocidad ibas?** How fast were you going?
[2] gear (*marcha*) ◊ *cambiar de velocidad* to change gear
el **velocímetro** SUSTANTIVO
speedometer
el/la **velocista** SUSTANTIVO
sprinter
el **velódromo** SUSTANTIVO
cycle track
veloz ADJETIVO (PL **veloces**)
swift
ven VERBO *ver* **ir, ver**
la **vena** SUSTANTIVO
vein
vencedor ADJETIVO (FEM **vencedora**)
winning ◊ *el equipo vencedor* the winning team
el **vencedor,** la **vencedora** SUSTANTIVO
the winner
vencer* VERBO
[1] to defeat (*derrotar*)
[2] to overcome (*miedo, obstáculo*)
[3] to expire (*expirar*) ◊ *El pasaporte me vence mañana.* My passport expires tomorrow.
vencido ADJETIVO
♦ **darse por vencido** to give up
la **venda** SUSTANTIVO
[1] bandage (*para herida, lesión*)
♦ **Me pusieron una venda en el brazo.** They bandaged my arm.
[2] blindfold (*para los ojos*)
♦ **poner una venda en los ojos a alguien** to blindfold someone
vendar VERBO
to bandage ◊ *Me vendaron el codo.* They bandaged my elbow.
♦ **vendar los ojos a alguien** to blindfold someone
el **vendedor** SUSTANTIVO
salesman (PL salesmen)
♦ **vendedor ambulante** pedlar
♦ **vendedor de periódicos** newspaper seller
la **vendedora** SUSTANTIVO
saleswoman (PL saleswomen)
vender VERBO
to sell ◊ *He vendido el coche.* I've sold the car.
♦ **Venden la oficina de arriba.** The office upstairs is for sale.
♦ **"se vende"** "for sale"
♦ **venderse por** to sell for ◊ *El cuadro se vendió por cuatro millones de pesetas.* The painting sold for four million pesetas.
la **vendimia** SUSTANTIVO
grape harvest
vendré VERBO *ver* **venir**
el **veneno** SUSTANTIVO
[1] poison (*tóxico*)
[2] venom (*de serpiente*)
venenoso ADJETIVO

☞

poisonous

el **venezolano**, la **venezolana** ADJETIVO, SUSTANTIVO
Venezuelan

Venezuela SUSTANTIVO FEM
Venezuela

la **venganza** SUSTANTIVO
revenge

vengarse* VERBO
to take revenge
- **vengarse de alguien** to take revenge on someone
- **vengarse de algo** to avenge something

vengo VERBO *ver* **venir**

la **venida** SUSTANTIVO
arrival (*llegada*)
- **La venida la hicimos en autobús.** We came by bus on the way here.

venir* VERBO
[1] to come ◊ *Vino en taxi.* He came by taxi. ◊ *Vinieron a verme al hospital.* They came to see me in hospital. ◊ *Viene en varios colores.* It comes in several colours. ◊ *¡Ven aquí!* Come here! ◊ *Enseguida vengo.* I'll be back in a minute.
[2] to be ◊ *La noticia venía en el periódico.* The news was in the paper.
- **¡Venga, vámonos!** Come on, let's go!
- **La casa se está viniendo abajo.** The house is falling apart.
- **Mañana me viene mal.** Tomorrow isn't good for me.
- **¿Te viene bien el sábado?** Is Saturday alright for you?
- **el año que viene** next year
- **¡Venga ya!** (*coloquial*) Come off it!

la **venta** SUSTANTIVO
sale
- **estar en venta** to be for sale

la **ventaja** SUSTANTIVO
advantage ◊ *Tiene la ventaja de que está cerca de casa.* It has the advantage of being close to home.
- **llevar ventaja a alguien** to have an advantage over someone
- **jugar con ventaja** to be at an advantage

la **ventana** SUSTANTIVO
window

la **ventanilla** SUSTANTIVO
[1] window (*de coche, banco*) ◊ *Baja la ventanilla.* Open the window.
[2] box office (*en cine, teatro*)

la **ventilación** SUSTANTIVO
ventilation
- **El sótano tiene poca ventilación.** The basement is poorly ventilated.

ventilar VERBO
to air (*habitación, ropa*)

la **ventisca** SUSTANTIVO
[1] gale force winds (*viento fuerte*)
[2] blizzard (*con nieve*)

ver* VERBO
[1] to see ◊ *Te vi en el parque.* I saw you in the park. ◊ *¡Cuánto tiempo sin verte!* I haven't seen you for ages! ◊ *No he visto esa película.* I haven't seen that film. ◊ *El médico todavía no la ha visto.* The doctor hasn't seen her yet. ◊ *¿Ves? Ya te lo dije.* See? I told you so.
- **Voy a ver si está en su despacho.** I'll see if he's in his office.
- **Quedamos en vernos en la estación.** We arranged to meet at the station.
- **¡Luego nos vemos!** See you later!
- **Eso no tiene nada que ver.** That has nothing to do with it.
- **¡No la puede ver!** He can't stand her!
- **A ver ...** Let's see ...
- **Se ve que no tiene idea de informática.** It's clear he's got no idea about computers.

[2] to watch (*televisión*)

veranear VERBO
to spend the summer holidays
◊ *Veraneamos en Calpe.* We spend our summer holidays in Calpe.

el **veraneo** SUSTANTIVO
- **lugar de veraneo** summer resort
- **No pudimos ir de veraneo el año pasado.** We couldn't go on holiday last summer.

el **verano** SUSTANTIVO
summer ◊ *En verano hace mucho calor.* It's very hot in summer. ◊ *las vacaciones de verano* the summer holidays

veraz ADJETIVO (PL **veraces**)
truthful

la **verbena** SUSTANTIVO
open-air dance (*baile*)
- **la verbena de San Roque** the festival of San Roque

el **verbo** SUSTANTIVO
verb

la **verdad** SUSTANTIVO
truth ◊ *Les dije la verdad.* I told them the truth.
- **¡Es verdad!** It's true!
- **La verdad es que no tengo ganas.** I don't really feel like it.
- **¿De verdad?** Really?
- **De verdad que yo no dije eso.** I didn't say that, honestly.
- **No era un policía de verdad.** He wasn't a real policeman.
- **Es bonito, ¿verdad?** It's pretty, isn't it?
- **No te gusta, ¿verdad?** You don't like it, do you?

verdadero ADJETIVO
real ◊ *Su apellido verdadero es Rodríguez.* His real surname is

Rodríguez. ◊ *Es un verdadero caballero.* He's a real gentleman.

el **verde** ADJETIVO, SUSTANTIVO
1 green ◊ *Tiene los ojos verdes.* She has green eyes. ◊ *Estos plátanos están todavía verdes.* These bananas are still green.
2 dirty (*coloquial: obsceno*) ◊ *un chiste verde* a dirty joke
♦ **los verdes** (*grupo político*) the Green Party

el **verdugo** SUSTANTIVO
1 executioner (*en la guillotina*)
2 hangman (*en la horca*)

la **verdulería** SUSTANTIVO
greengrocer's (PL greengrocers' shops)

la **verdura** SUSTANTIVO
vegetables PL ◊ *Comemos mucha verdura.* We eat a lot of vegetables.

la **vereda** SUSTANTIVO
1 path (*camino*)
2 pavement (*acera*) Chile, River Plate

vergonzoso ADJETIVO
1 shy ◊ *Es muy vergonzosa.* She is very shy.
2 disgraceful ◊ *Es vergonzoso cómo los trataron.* It's disgraceful the way they were treated.

la **vergüenza** SUSTANTIVO
1 embarrassment ◊ *Casi me muero de vergüenza.* I almost died of embarrassment.
2 shame (*decencia*) ◊ *No tienen vergüenza.* They have no shame.
♦ **¡Qué vergüenza!** How embarrassing!
♦ **Le da vergüenza pedírselo.** He's embarrassed to ask her.
♦ **¡Es una vergüenza!** It's disgraceful!

verídico ADJETIVO
true

verificar* VERBO
to check

la **verja** SUSTANTIVO
1 railings PL (*cerca*)
2 gate (*puerta*)

el **vermut** SUSTANTIVO
vermouth

la **verruga** SUSTANTIVO
1 wart (*en manos, cara*)
2 verruca (*en pies*)

la **versión** SUSTANTIVO (PL las **versiones**)
version
♦ **una película francesa en versión original** a film in the original French version

el **verso** SUSTANTIVO
1 line (*línea de poema*)
2 verse (*estilo poético*)

la **vértebra** SUSTANTIVO
vertebra (PL vertebrae)

el **vertedero** SUSTANTIVO
rubbish tip

verter* VERBO
1 to pour ◊ *Vertió un poco de leche en el cazo.* He poured a little milk into the saucepan.
2 to dump (*basura, residuos radiactivos*)

vertical ADJETIVO
vertical
♦ **Ponlo vertical.** Put it upright.

el **vértigo** SUSTANTIVO
vertigo
♦ **Me da vértigo.** It makes me dizzy.

la **Vespa** ® SUSTANTIVO
scooter

vespertino ADJETIVO
evening

***evening** en este caso va siempre delante del sustantivo.*

◊ *un diario vespertino* an evening paper

el **vestíbulo** SUSTANTIVO
1 hall (*de casa*)
2 foyer (*de teatro*)

vestido ADJETIVO
♦ **Iba vestida de negro.** She was dressed in black.
♦ **Yo iba vestido de payaso.** I was dressed as a clown.
♦ **un hombre bien vestido** a well-dressed man

el **vestido** SUSTANTIVO
dress (PL dresses) (*de mujer*)
♦ **el vestido de novia** the bridal gown

vestir* VERBO
to wear (*llevar puesto*) ◊ *Vestía pantalones vaqueros y una camiseta azul.* He was wearing jeans and a blue T-shirt.
♦ **vestir a alguien** to dress someone ◊ *Estaba vistiendo a los niños.* I was dressing the children.
♦ **vestir bien** to dress well
♦ **vestirse** to get dressed ◊ *Se está vistiendo.* He's getting dressed.
♦ **Se vistió de princesa.** She dressed up as a princess.
♦ **ropa de vestir** smart clothes PL

el **vestón** SUSTANTIVO (PL los **vestones**)
jacket (*para hombres*) Chile, River Plate

el **vestuario** SUSTANTIVO
1 changing room (*en piscina, gimnasio*)
2 wardrobe (*de película, obra teatral*)

el **veterinario**, la **veterinaria** SUSTANTIVO
vet

la **vez** SUSTANTIVO (PL las **veces**)
time ◊ *la próxima vez* next time ◊ *¿Cuántas veces al año?* How many times a year?
♦ **a la vez** at the same time
♦ **a veces** sometimes
♦ **algunas veces** sometimes
♦ **cada vez más** more and more
♦ **cada vez menos** less and less
♦ **de una vez** once and for all
♦ **de vez en cuando** from time to time
♦ **en vez de** instead of

☞

◆ **¿La has visto alguna vez?** Have you ever seen her?
◆ **otra vez** again
◆ **tal vez** maybe
◆ **una vez** once ◇ *La veo una vez a la semana.* I see her once a week.
◆ **dos veces** twice
◆ **una y otra vez** again and again

vi VERBO *ver* **ver**

la **vía** SUSTANTIVO
[1] track (*raíl*)
[2] platform (*andén*) ◇ *Nuestro tren sale por la vía dos.* Our train leaves from platform two.
◆ **por vía aérea** by airmail
◆ **Madrid-Berlín vía París** Madrid-Berlin via Paris

viajar VERBO
to travel ◇ *viajar en autocar* to travel by coach

el **viaje** SUSTANTIVO
[1] trip
◆ **¡Buen viaje!** Have a good trip!
◆ **un viaje de negocios** a business trip
[2] journey (*trayecto*) ◇ *Es un viaje muy largo.* It's a very long journey.
◆ **estar de viaje** to be away
◆ **salir de viaje** to go away
◆ **una agencia de viajes** a travel agency
◆ **el viaje de novios** honeymoon

el **viajero,** la **viajera** SUSTANTIVO
passenger

la **víbora** SUSTANTIVO
viper

la **vibración** SUSTANTIVO (PL las **vibraciones**)
vibration

vibrar VERBO
to vibrate

la **vicepresidenta** SUSTANTIVO
[1] (*de gobierno*)
vice president
[2] (*de empresa, comité*)
chairwoman (PL chairwomen)

el **vicepresidente** SUSTANTIVO
[1] (*de gobierno*)
vice president
[2] (*de empresa, comité*)
chairman (PL chairmen)

viceversa ADVERBIO
vice versa

viciarse VERBO
to deteriorate (*estilo, lenguaje*)
◆ **viciarse con las drogas** to become addicted to drugs

el **vicio** SUSTANTIVO
vice ◇ *El tabaco es mi único vicio.* Smoking is my only vice.
◆ **Tengo el vicio de morderme las uñas.** I bite my nails; I know it's a bad habit.

la **víctima** SUSTANTIVO
victim

la **victoria** SUSTANTIVO
victory (PL victories) ◇ *la victoria del partido conservador* the conservative party victory
◆ **su primera victoria fuera de casa** their first away win

la **vid** SUSTANTIVO
vine

la **vida** SUSTANTIVO
life (PL lives) ◇ *He vivido aquí toda mi vida.* I've lived here all my life. ◇ *Llevan una vida muy tranquila.* They lead a very quiet life. ◇ *¡Esto sí que es vida!* This is the life!
◆ **la media de vida de un televisor** the average life span of a television set
◆ **vida nocturna** nightlife
◆ **estar con vida** to be alive
◆ **salir con vida** to escape alive
◆ **Se gana la vida haciendo traducciones.** He earns his living by translating.
◆ **¡Vida mía!** My darling!

el **video** SUSTANTIVO Latin America
video

el **vídeo** SUSTANTIVO
video ◇ *Tengo la película en vídeo.* I've got the film on video.
◆ **cinta de vídeo** videotape

la **videocámara** SUSTANTIVO
video camera

el **videojuego** SUSTANTIVO
video game

la **vidriera** SUSTANTIVO
[1] stained glass window (*en iglesia*)
[2] shop window (*escaparate*) Latin America

el **vidrio** SUSTANTIVO
[1] glass (*material*) ◇ *botellas de vidrio* glass bottles
◆ **Me corté el dedo con un vidrio.** I cut my finger on a piece of glass.
[2] windowpane (*de ventana*)

la **vieja** SUSTANTIVO
old woman (PL old women) ◇ *Había una viejecita sentada a mi lado.* There was an old woman sitting next to me.

viejo ADJETIVO
old ◇ *un viejo amigo mío* an old friend of mine ◇ *Estos zapatos ya están muy viejos.* These shoes are very old now.
◆ **hacerse viejo** to get old

el **viejo** SUSTANTIVO
old man (PL old men)
◆ **los viejos** old people
◆ **llegar a viejo** to reach old age

viene VERBO *ver* **venir**

el **viento** SUSTANTIVO
wind

◆ **Hace mucho viento.** It's very windy.

el **vientre** SUSTANTIVO
stomach
◆ **hacer de vientre** to go to the toilet

el **viernes** SUSTANTIVO (PL los **viernes**)
Los días de la semana se escriben con mayúscula.
Friday ◊ *La vi el viernes.* I saw her on Friday. ◊ *todos los viernes* every Friday ◊ *el viernes pasado* last Friday ◊ *el viernes que viene* next Friday
◆ **Viernes Santo** Good Friday

vierta VERBO *ver* **verter**

el/la **vietnamita** ADJETIVO, SUSTANTIVO
Vietnamese
◆ **los vietnamitas** the Vietnamese

la **viga** SUSTANTIVO
1 beam (*de madera*)
2 girder (*de acero*)

la **vigilancia** SUSTANTIVO
1 surveillance ◊ *bajo vigilancia policial* under police surveillance
2 vigilance (*cuidado*) ◊ *El paciente necesita vigilancia constante.* The patient needs constant vigilance.
◆ **patrulla de vigilancia** security patrol

el/la **vigilante** SUSTANTIVO
1 (*en banco, edificio público*)
security guard
2 (*en tienda*)
store detective
◆ **vigilante jurado** security guard
◆ **vigilante nocturno** night watchman (PL night watchmen)

vigilar VERBO
1 to guard (*frontera, tienda, cuadro*) ◊ *Un policía vigilaba al preso.* A policeman was guarding the prisoner.
2 to watch (*persona*) ◊ *Nos vigilan.* They're watching us.
3 to keep an eye on (*cuidar*) ◊ *¿Me vigilas el bolso un momento?* Can you keep an eye on my bag for a minute?

VIH ABREVIATURA (= *virus de inmunodeficiencia humana*)
HIV

la **villa** SUSTANTIVO
1 town (*población*)
2 villa (*chalé*)

el **villancico** SUSTANTIVO
carol

el **vinagre** SUSTANTIVO
vinegar

el **vínculo** SUSTANTIVO
bond

vine VERBO *ver* **venir**

viniendo VERBO *ver* **venir**

el **vino** SUSTANTIVO
wine
◆ **vino blanco** white wine
◆ **vino tinto** red wine
◆ **vino de la casa** house wine

la **viña** SUSTANTIVO
vineyard

el **viñedo** SUSTANTIVO
vineyard

la **violación** SUSTANTIVO (PL las **violaciones**)
1 rape (*de persona*)
2 violation (*de ley, acuerdo*)

el **violador**, la **violadora** SUSTANTIVO
rapist

violar VERBO
1 to rape (*persona*)
2 to violate (*ley, acuerdo*)

la **violencia** SUSTANTIVO
violence

violento ADJETIVO
1 violent ◊ *La película contiene algunas escenas violentas.* The film contains some violent scenes.
2 embarrassing ◊ *Era una situación violenta.* It was an embarrassing situation.
◆ **Me resulta violento decírselo.** I'm embarrassed to tell him.

el **violeta** ADJETIVO, SUSTANTIVO
purple (*color*) ◊ *unas cortinas violeta* some purple curtains

la **violeta** SUSTANTIVO
violet (*flor*)

el **violín** SUSTANTIVO (PL los **violines**)
violin

el/la **violinista** SUSTANTIVO
violinist

el **violón** SUSTANTIVO (PL los **violones**)
double bass (PL double basses)

el/la **violonchelista** SUSTANTIVO
cellist

el **violonchelo** SUSTANTIVO
cello (PL cellos)

virgen ADJETIVO (PL **vírgenes**)
1 virgin (*persona, selva*)
◆ **ser virgen** to be a virgin
2 blank (*cinta*)

la **virgen** SUSTANTIVO (PL las **vírgenes**)
virgin
◆ **la Virgen** the Virgin

Virgo SUSTANTIVO MASC
Virgo
◆ **Soy Virgo.** I'm Virgo.

viril ADJETIVO
virile

la **virilidad** SUSTANTIVO
virility

la **virtud** SUSTANTIVO
virtue

la **viruela** SUSTANTIVO
smallpox ◊ *Tiene la viruela.* He has smallpox.

el **virus** SUSTANTIVO (PL los **virus**)
(*también informática*)
virus (PL viruses)

la **visa** SUSTANTIVO Latin America
visa

el **visado** SUSTANTIVO
visa

la **visera** SUSTANTIVO
1 peak (*en gorra*)
2 visor (*transparente*)

la **visibilidad** SUSTANTIVO
visibility ◊ *Había muy poca visibilidad.* Visibility was very poor.

visible ADJETIVO
visible

el **visillo** SUSTANTIVO
net curtain

la **visión** SUSTANTIVO (PL las **visiones**)
1 vision ◊ *la visión nocturna* night vision
2 view (*enfoque*) ◊ *una visión pesimista de la vida* a pessimistic view of life
♦ **Tú estás viendo visiones.** You're seeing things.

la **visita** SUSTANTIVO
1 visit
♦ **hacer una visita a alguien** to visit someone
2 visitor (*visitante*) ◊ *Tienes visita.* You've got visitors.
♦ **horario de visita** visiting hours PL
♦ **tarjeta de visita** business card

el/la **visitante** SUSTANTIVO
visitor

visitar VERBO
to visit ◊ *5.000 personas han visitado ya la exposición.* 5,000 people have already visited the exhibition.

el **viso** SUSTANTIVO
slip (*prenda*)
♦ **visos** signs ◊ *La situación no tiene visos de mejorar.* The situation shows no signs of improving.
♦ **esta tela hace visos** this material is two-tone

el **visón** SUSTANTIVO (PL los **visones**)
mink
♦ **un abrigo de visón** a mink coat

la **víspera** SUSTANTIVO
the day before ◊ *la víspera de la boda* the day before the wedding
♦ **la víspera de Navidad** Christmas Eve

la **vista** SUSTANTIVO
1 sight (*sentido*)
2 view (*panorama*) ◊ *una habitación con vistas al mar* a room with a sea view
♦ **a primera vista** at first glance
♦ **alzar la vista** to look up
♦ **bajar la vista** to look down
♦ **perder la vista** to lose one's sight
♦ **volver la vista** to look back
♦ **conocer a alguien de vista** to know someone by sight
♦ **hacer la vista gorda** to turn a blind eye
♦ **¡Hasta la vista!** See you!

el **vistazo** SUSTANTIVO
♦ **echar un vistazo a algo** to have a look at something

vistiendo VERBO *ver* **vestir**

visto (1) VERBO *ver* **ver**

visto (2) ADJETIVO
♦ **Está visto que ...** It's clear that ...
♦ **Hurgarse la nariz está mal visto.** Picking your nose is frowned upon.
♦ **por lo visto** apparently
♦ **dar el visto bueno a algo** to give something one's approval

vistoso ADJETIVO
showy

vital ADJETIVO
vital

la **vitalidad** SUSTANTIVO
vitality

la **vitamina** SUSTANTIVO
vitamin

vitorear VERBO
to cheer

la **vitrina** SUSTANTIVO
1 glass cabinet (*en casa*)
2 shop window (*escaparate*)
Latin America

viuda ADJETIVO
♦ **Es viuda.** She's a widow.
♦ **quedarse viuda** to be widowed

la **viuda** SUSTANTIVO
widow

viudo ADJETIVO
♦ **Es viudo.** He's a widower.
♦ **Se quedó viudo a los 50 años.** He was widowed at 50.

el **viudo** SUSTANTIVO
widower

vivaracho ADJETIVO
lively (*persona*)

los **víveres** SUSTANTIVO
provisions PL

el **vivero** SUSTANTIVO
(*de plantas*)
nursery (PL nurseries)

la **vivienda** SUSTANTIVO
1 house (*casa*)
2 flat (*piso*)
3 housing (*alojamiento*) ◊ *la escasez de la vivienda* the housing shortage

vivir VERBO
1 to live ◊ *¿Dónde vives?* Where do you live?
2 to be alive ◊ *¿Todavía vive?* Is he still alive?
♦ **vivir de algo** to live on something ◊ *Viven de su pensión.* They live on his pension.
♦ **¡Viva!** Hurray!

vivo ADJETIVO
1 alive (*con vida*) ◊ *Estaba vivo.* He was alive.

2 bright (*color, ojos*)
◆ **en vivo** live ◇ *una retransmisión en vivo* a live broadcast

el **vocabulario** SUSTANTIVO
vocabulary

la **vocación** SUSTANTIVO (PL las **vocaciones**)
vocation

la **vocal** SUSTANTIVO
vowel

el **vodka** SUSTANTIVO
vodka

el **volante** SUSTANTIVO
1 steering wheel (*de coche*)
2 shuttlecock (*de bádminton*)
3 referral note (*para médico*)
◆ **volantes** flounce SING (*de vestido, colcha*)

volar* VERBO
1 to fly ◇ *El helicóptero volaba muy bajo.* The helicopter was flying very low. ◇ *Se me pasó la semana volando.* The week just flew by.
2 to blow up ◇ *Volaron el puente.* They blew up the bridge.
◆ **Tuvimos que ir volando al hospital.** We had to rush to the hospital.

el **volcán** SUSTANTIVO (PL los **volcanes**)
volcano (PL volcanoes)

volcar* VERBO
1 to knock over (*tumbar*) ◇ *El perro volcó el cubo de la basura.* The dog knocked the dustbin over.
2 to capsize (*barco*)
3 to overturn (*coche*)

el **voleibol** SUSTANTIVO
volleyball

el **voltaje** SUSTANTIVO
voltage

la **voltereta** SUSTANTIVO
1 forward roll (*sobre el suelo*)
◆ **dar una voltereta** to do a forward roll
2 somersault (*en el aire*)

el **voltio** SUSTANTIVO
volt

el **volumen** SUSTANTIVO (PL los **volúmenes**)
volume
◆ **bajar el volumen** to turn the volume down
◆ **subir el volumen** to turn the volume up

la **voluntad** SUSTANTIVO
1 will (*deseo*) ◇ *Lo hizo contra mi voluntad.* He did it against my will.
2 willpower (*fuerza de voluntad*) ◇ *Le cuesta, pero tiene mucha voluntad.* It's difficult for him, but he has a lot of willpower.

la **voluntaria** SUSTANTIVO
volunteer

voluntario ADJETIVO
voluntary
◆ **ofrecerse voluntario para algo** to volunteer for something

el **voluntario** SUSTANTIVO
volunteer

volver* VERBO
1 to come back (*a donde se está*)
2 to go back (*a donde se estaba*)
3 to turn (*colcha, cabeza, esquina*) ◇ *Me volvió la espalda.* He turned away from me.
◆ **Me volví para ver quién era.** I turned round to see who it was.
4 to become (*convertirse*)
◆ **Se ha vuelto muy cariñoso.** He's become very affectionate.
◆ **volver a hacer algo** to do something again
◆ **volver en sí** to come round

vomitar VERBO
to be sick ◇ *Ha vomitado dos veces.* He's been sick twice.
◆ **Vomitó todo lo que había comido.** He threw up everything he'd eaten.

vos PRONOMBRE River Plate
you

vosotros PRONOMBRE PL (FEM **vosotras**)
you ◇ *Vosotros vendréis conmigo.* You'll come with me.
◆ **Hacedlo vosotros mismos.** Do it yourselves.

la **votación** SUSTANTIVO (PL las **votaciones**)
◆ **Hicimos una votación.** We took a vote.
◆ **Salió elegida por votación.** She was voted in.

votar VERBO
to vote ◇ *Voté por Alcántara.* I voted for Alcántara.
◆ **Votaron a los socialistas.** They voted for the Socialists.

voy VERBO *ver* **ir**

la **voz** SUSTANTIVO (PL las **voces**)
voice ◇ *No tengo buena voz.* I don't have a very good voice.
◆ **hablar en voz alta** to speak loudly
◆ **dar voces** to shout

vuelco VERBO *ver* **volcar**

el **vuelco** SUSTANTIVO
◆ **dar un vuelco (1)** (*coche*) to overturn
◆ **dar un vuelco (2)** (*barco*) to capsize
◆ **Me dio un vuelco el corazón.** My heart missed a beat.

vuelo VERBO *ver* **volar**

el **vuelo** SUSTANTIVO
flight
◆ **vuelo chárter** charter flight
◆ **vuelo regular** scheduled flight
◆ **Las gaviotas levantaron el vuelo.** The seagulls flew away.

la **vuelta** SUSTANTIVO
1 return (*regreso*) ◇ *un billete de ida y vuelta* a return ticket
2 lap (*en circuito*) ◇ *Di tres vueltas a la pista.* I did three laps of the track.
3 change (*cambio*) ◇ *Quédese con la vuelta.* Keep the change.
◆ **a vuelta de correo** by return of post

☞

- **Vive a la vuelta de la esquina.** He lives round the corner.
- **El coche dio la vuelta.** The car turned round.
- **Dimos una vuelta de campana.** We overturned completely.
- **dar la vuelta a la página** to turn the page
- **dar la vuelta al mundo** to go round the world
- **No le des más vueltas a lo que dijo.** Stop worrying about what he said.
- **dar una vuelta (1)** (*a pie*) to go for a walk
- **dar una vuelta (2)** (*en coche*) to go for a drive
- **dar media vuelta** to turn round
- **estar de vuelta** to be back
- **vuelta ciclista** cycle race

vuelto VERBO *ver* **volver**

el **vuelto** SUSTANTIVO Latin America
change

vuelvo VERBO *ver* **volver**

vuestro ADJETIVO, PRONOMBRE (FEM **vuestra**)
1 your ◊ *vuestra casa* your house ◊ *vuestros amigos* your friends
- **un amigo vuestro** a friend of yours

2 yours ◊ *¿Son vuestros?* Are they yours?
- **¿Es ésta la vuestra?** Is this one yours?
- **¿Y los bocadillos? – Los vuestros están aquí.** Where are the sandwiches? – Yours are over here.

vulgar ADJETIVO
vulgar (*no refinado*)

W

el **walkie-talkie** SUSTANTIVO (PL los **walkie-talkies**)
walkie-talkie

el **walkman** ® SUSTANTIVO (PL los **walkmans**)
Walkman ®

el **wáter** SUSTANTIVO
loo (*coloquial*)

la **web** SUSTANTIVO
1 website (*página*)
2 (World Wide) Web (*red*)

el **western** SUSTANTIVO (PL los **westerns**)
western

el **whisky** SUSTANTIVO (PL los **whiskys**)
whisky (PL whiskies)

el **windsurf** SUSTANTIVO
1 windsurfing (*deporte*)
2 windsurf (*tabla*)

xenófobo ADJETIVO
xenophobic

el **xilófono** SUSTANTIVO
xylophone

y CONJUNCIÓN
and ◊ *Andrés y su novia.* Andrés and his girlfriend.
◆ **Yo quiero una ensalada. ¿Y tú?** I'd like a salad. What about you?
◆ **¡Y yo!** Me too!
◆ **¿Y qué?** So what?
◆ **Son las tres y cinco.** It's five minutes past three.

ya ADVERBIO
already ◊ *Ya se han ido.* They've already left. ◊ *¿Ya has terminado?* Have you finished already?
◆ **ya no** any more ◊ *Ya no salimos juntos.* We're not going out any more.
◆ **Estos zapatos ya me están pequeños.** These shoes are too small for me now.
◆ **ya que** since
◆ **Ya lo sé.** I know.
◆ **Ya veremos.** We'll see.
◆ **Rellena el impreso y ya está.** Fill in the form and that's it.
◆ **¡Ya voy!** I'm coming!

el **yacimiento** SUSTANTIVO
site (*arqueológico*)
◆ **un yacimiento petrolífero** an oilfield

el/la **yanqui** ADJETIVO, SUSTANTIVO (MASC PL los **yanquis**)
Yank (*coloquial*)

el **yate** SUSTANTIVO
1 pleasure cruiser (*con motor*)
2 yacht (*de vela*)

la **yedra** SUSTANTIVO
ivy

la **yegua** SUSTANTIVO
mare

la **yema** SUSTANTIVO
1 yolk (*de huevo*)
2 fingertip (*del dedo*)

yendo VERBO *ver* **ir**

el **yerno** SUSTANTIVO
son-in-law (PL sons-in-law)

el **yeso** SUSTANTIVO
plaster

yo PRONOMBRE
1 I ◊ *Carlos y yo no fuimos.* Carlos and I didn't go.
2 me ◊ *¿Quién ha visto la película? – Ana y yo.* Who's seen the film? – Ana and me. ◊ *Es más alta que yo.* She's taller than me. ◊ *Soy yo, María.* It's me, María.
◆ **¡Yo también!** Me too!
◆ **yo mismo** myself ◊ *Lo hice yo misma.* I did it myself.
◆ **yo que tú** if I were you

el **yoga** SUSTANTIVO
yoga

el **yogur** SUSTANTIVO
yoghurt

el **yudo** SUSTANTIVO
judo

Yugoslavia SUSTANTIVO FEM
Yugoslavia ◊ *en la antigua Yugoslavia* in the former Yugoslavia

Z

el **zafiro** SUSTANTIVO
sapphire
zambullirse* VERBO
to dive underwater (*sumergirse*)
zamparse VERBO
to wolf down (*coloquial*) ◊ *Se zampó todo un paquete de galletas.* He wolfed down a whole packet of biscuits.
la **zanahoria** SUSTANTIVO
carrot
la **zancadilla** SUSTANTIVO
◆ **poner la zancadilla a alguien** to trip someone up
el **zancudo** SUSTANTIVO Latin America
mosquito (PL mosquitos)
la **zanja** SUSTANTIVO
ditch (PL ditches)
zanjar VERBO
to settle (*deuda, diferencias*)
la **zapatera** SUSTANTIVO
shoemaker
la **zapatería** SUSTANTIVO
1 shoe shop (*tienda*)
2 shoe repairer's (*para reparaciones*)
el **zapatero** SUSTANTIVO
shoemaker
la **zapatilla** SUSTANTIVO
slipper (*pantufla*)
◆ **zapatillas de ballet** ballet shoes
◆ **zapatillas de deporte** training shoes
el **zapato** SUSTANTIVO
shoe
◆ **zapatos de tacón** high-heeled shoes
◆ **zapatos planos** flat shoes
la **zarpa** SUSTANTIVO
paw
zarpar VERBO
to set sail
la **zarza** SUSTANTIVO
bramble
la **zarzamora** SUSTANTIVO
blackberry bush
el **zigzag** SUSTANTIVO
zigzag
◆ **una carretera en zigzag** a winding road
Zimbabue SUSTANTIVO MASC
Zimbabwe
el **zinc** SUSTANTIVO
zinc
el **zíper** SUSTANTIVO (PL los **zípers**)
Latin America
zip
el **zócalo** SUSTANTIVO
1 skirting board (*rodapié*)
2 main square Latin America
el **zodíaco** SUSTANTIVO
zodiac ◊ *los signos del zodíaco* the signs of the zodiac
la **zona** SUSTANTIVO
area ◊ *Viven en una zona muy tranquila.* They live in a very quiet area.
◆ **Fue declarada zona neutral.** It was declared a neutral zone.
◆ **zona verde** green space
◆ **zona industrial** industrial park
el **zoo** SUSTANTIVO
zoo
la **zoóloga** SUSTANTIVO
zoologist
la **zoología** SUSTANTIVO
zoology
el **zoológico** SUSTANTIVO
zoo
el **zoólogo** SUSTANTIVO
zoologist
el **zoom** SUSTANTIVO (PL los **zooms**)
zoom lens (PL zoom lenses)
zoquete ADJETIVO
dim (*coloquial*)
el/la **zoquete** SUSTANTIVO
blockhead (*coloquial*)
el **zorro** SUSTANTIVO
fox (PL foxes) ◊ *piel de zorro* fox fur
el **zueco** SUSTANTIVO
clog
zumbar VERBO
to buzz (*abeja, oídos*) ◊ *Me zumban los oídos.* My ears are buzzing.
◆ **salir zumbando** (*coloquial*) to whizz off
el **zumo** SUSTANTIVO
juice ◊ *zumo de naranja* orange juice
zurcir* VERBO
to darn
zurdo ADJETIVO
1 left-handed (*de la mano*)
2 left-footed (*del pie*)
zurrar VERBO
to thrash

INGLÉS ACTIVO — SPANISH IN ACTION

JUEGOS

Los pasatiempos de las páginas siguientes están pensados para ayudarte a manejar tu diccionario de una forma práctica. Para ello te conviene leer la sección "Cómo usar este diccionario" del principio antes de empezar y, aunque es mejor que intentes resolverlos sin mirar la solución, si te quedas atascado puedes mirar al final de la sección.

GAMES

The wordgames on the followin pages have been designed to giv you practice in using your dictionar Make sure you read the "Dictionar Skills" section at the front of this boo before you start. Don't worry, ther are answers at the end of th wordgames in case you get real stuck!

JUEGO 1

▶ ARTÍCULOS DEL DICCIONARIO ◀

ompleta este crucigrama con las traducciones en inglés de la lista de palabras spañolas. Hay un pequeño inconveniente: todas estas palabras españolas tienen ás de un significado en inglés y sólo una de las traducciones encaja en las asillas del crucigrama. Por lo tanto tienes que fijarte en todos los distintos gnificados y elegir el que encaje en las casillas.

ecuerda que, si tienes que insertar un verbo en infinitivo no es necesario que scribas 'to', como en 'to go', que sería sólo 'go'.)

ÚLTIMO
TODAVÍA
MAÑANA
PICADURA
COPA
CLARO
7. DISCO
8. CURVA
9. ROBO
10. REPORTAJE
11. ARTE
12. ABURRIDO

JUEGO 2

▶ PARTES DE LA ORACIÓN ◀

Indica con una cruz la función gramatical que tienen las palabras señaladas e
cada una de las siguientes oraciones.

ORACIÓN	SUST	ADJ	ADV	VERBO
1. Are you going to wash your car?				
2. Hand me the hammer, please.				
3. Your dress is not very clean.				
4. Shall we go for a drive?				
5. We arrived just in time.				
6. The garage serviced my car last week.				
7. My foot is very sore.				
8. Are we having stew for dinner?				
9. They live in Manchester.				
10. He switched off the light.				

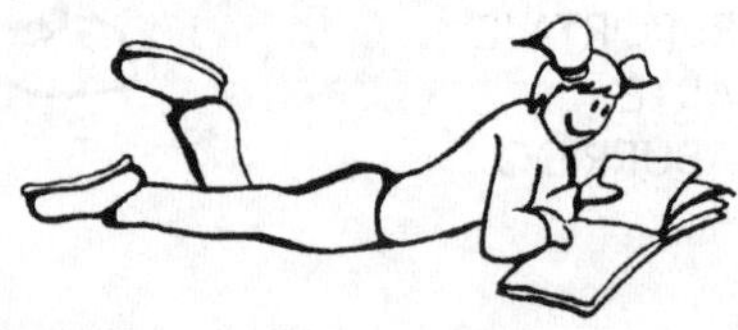

JUEGO 3

▶ DAMERO ◀

En las siguientes casillas las letras de diez palabras inglesas han sido sustituidas por números. Cada dígito representa siempre la misma letra.

Intenta descifrar el código para encontrar las diez palabras. Puedes recurrir a tu diccionario si necesitas ayuda.

Aquí tienes una pista: Todas las palabras están relacionadas con EL TRANSPORTE.

1. A(1) E(2) R(3) 4 5 6 1 7 2
2. 8 9 10
3. 11 3 1 12 7
4. 13 4 14 2 3 15 3 1 16 11
5. 15 4 1 15 13
6. 8 12 15 17 15 6 2
7. 15 1 3
8. 15 1 3 1 14 1 7
9. 10 9 8 18 1 17
10. 16 2 3 3 17

WORDGAME 4

▶ ANTONYMS ◀

Complete the crossword by supplying ANTONYMS (i.e. opposites) in Spanish of the words below. Use your dictionary to help.

1. FEO
2. ABRIR
3. LIGERO
4. RIQUEZA
5. SALIR
6. ENGORDAR
7. INQUIETO
8. PONER
9. TODO
10. OSCURO

WORDGAME 5

▶ VERB TENSES ◀

Use your dictionary to help you fill in the blanks in the table below.

INFINITIVE	PRESENT SUBJUNCTIVE	PRETERITE	FUTURE
tener		yo	
hacer			yo
poder			yo
decir		yo	
agradecer	yo		
saber			yo
reír	yo		
querer		yo	
caber	yo		
ir	yo		
salir			yo
ser		yo	

WORDGAME 6

Here is a list of Spanish words for things you will find in the kitchen. Unfortunately, they have all been jumbled up. Try to work out what each word is and put the word in the boxes on the right. You will see that there are seven shaded boxes below. With the seven letters in the shaded boxes make up another Spanish word for an object you can find in the kitchen.

1. azta — **¿Quieres una ______ de café?**

2. eanevr — **¡Meta la mantequilla en la ______ !**

3. asme — **¡La comida está en la ______!**

4. zoac — **Su madre está calentando la leche en el ______.**

5. roegcanldo — **¡No saques el helado del ______ todavía!**

6. uclclohi — **¿Dónde has puesto el ______ del queso?**

7. rgoif — **¿Puedes cerrar ya el ______ del agua caliente?**

The word you are looking for is:

JUEGO 1

1. last
2. still
3. morning
4. sting
5. top
6. clear
7. record
8. bend
9. robbery
10. documentary
11. art
12. bored

JUEGO 2

1. Verbo
2. Verbo
3. Adjetivo
4. Sustantivo
5. Adverbio
6. Verbo
7. Adjetivo
8. Sustantivo
9. Verbo
10. Sustantivo

JUEGO 3

1. aeroplane
2. bus
3. train
4. hovercraft
5. coach
6. bicycle
7. car
8. caravan
9. subway
10. ferry

WORDGAME 4

1. bonito
2. cerrar
3. pesado
4. pobreza
5. entrar
6. adelgazar
7. tranquilo
8. quitar
9. nada
10. claro

WORDGAME 5

tuve
haré
podré
dije
agradezca
sabré

ría
quise
quepa
vaya
saldré
fui

WORDGAME 6

1. taza
2. nevera
3. mesa
4. cazo
5. congelador
6. cuchillo
7. grifo

Missing word – ARMARIO

CORRESPONDENCIA

▶ LA CARTA PERSONAL

Dirección del remitente

18 Slateford Ave
Leeds
L24 3PR

Fecha

14 February 2001

Dear Gran and Grandad,

Thank you both very much for the CDs which you sent me for my birthday. They are two of my favourite groups and I'll really enjoy listening to them.

There's not much news here. I seem to be spending most of my time studying for my exams which start in two weeks. I'm hoping to pass all of them but I'm not looking forward to the maths exam as that's my worst subject.

Mum says that you're off to Crete on holiday next week, so I hope that you have a great time and come back with a good tan.

With love from

Kerry

O:
With best wishes
Yours ever
Lots of love from

EL SALUDO EN UNA CARTA PERSONAL

Thank you for your letter.	*Gracias por tu carta.*
It was lovely to hear from you.	*Me alegró mucho tener noticias tuyas.*
I'm sorry I didn't write earlier.	*Perdona que no te haya escrito antes.*

LA DESPEDIDA EN UNA CARTA PERSONAL

Write soon!	*¡Escríbeme pronto!*
Give my love to Vanessa.	*Dale un beso a Vanessa de mi parte.*
Samuel sends his best wishes.	*Samuel te manda recuerdos.*

CORRESPONDENCE

▶ LETTER

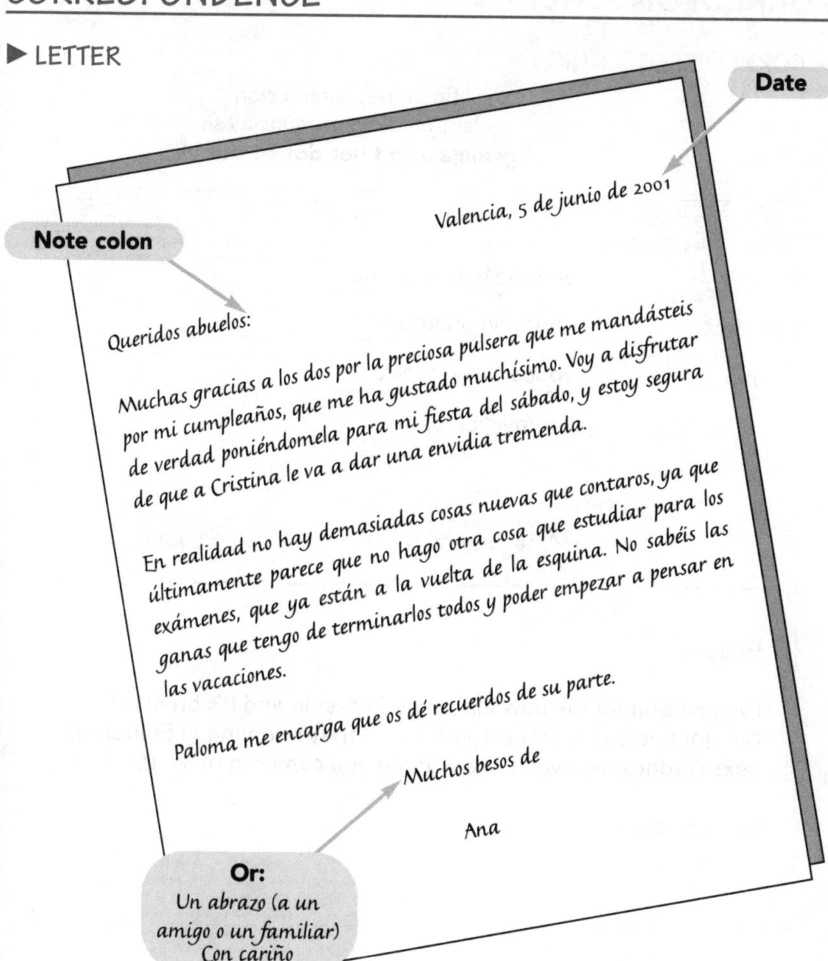

Date
Note colon
Valencia, 5 de junio de 2001
Queridos abuelos:
Muchas gracias a los dos por la preciosa pulsera que me mandásteis por mi cumpleaños, que me ha gustado muchísimo. Voy a disfrutar de verdad poniéndomela para mi fiesta del sábado, y estoy segura de que a Cristina le va a dar una envidia tremenda.
En realidad no hay demasiadas cosas nuevas que contaros, ya que últimamente parece que no hago otra cosa que estudiar para los exámenes, que ya están a la vuelta de la esquina. No sabéis las ganas que tengo de terminarlos todos y poder empezar a pensar en las vacaciones.
Paloma me encarga que os dé recuerdos de su parte.
Muchos besos de
Ana
Or:
Un abrazo (a un amigo o un familiar)
Con cariño

STARTING A PERSONAL LETTER

Gracias por tu carta.	*Thank you for your letter.*
Me alegró mucho tener noticias tuyas.	*It was lovely to hear from you.*
Perdona que no te haya escrito antes.	*I'm sorry I didn't write earlier.*

ENDING A PERSONAL LETTER

¡Escríbeme pronto!	*Write soon!*
Dale un beso a Vanesa de mi parte.	*Give my love to Vanesa.*
Samuel te manda recuerdos.	*Samuel sends his best wishes.*

CORRESPONDENCIA

▶ CORREO ELECTRÓNICO

En inglés, la dirección electrónica se pronuncia así: **"gemma at n t net dot co dot uk"**

New Message

To: gemma@ntnet.co.uk

From: gordon@onemo.net

Subject: concert next week

cc: jeremy@blt.com

bcc:

Attachment | Send

Hi guys

I've just bought the new album by Rockstar, and it's brilliant! I've got two spare tickets to a concert they're giving in Edinburgh next Wednesday evening, so I hope you can both make it.

See you soon!

New message	Nuevo mensaje
To	A
From	De
Subject	Asunto
cc	cc
bcc	Copia oculta
Attachment	Archivo adjunto
Send	Enviar

▶ EMAIL

To give your email address to someone in Spanish, say:
"belen punto huertas arroba globanet punto es"

Nuevo Message

a:	belen.huertas@globanet.es
de:	teresa@onemo.es
asunto:	concierto
cc:	pedro@infotec.es
bcc:	

Archivo adjunto   Enviar

Hola, ¿qué tal el fin de semana?

Me sobran dos entradas para el concierto de mañana, de unos amigos que no pueden venir. Si te interesa, o conoces a alguien que quiera ir, avísame en cuanto puedas.

Saludos

Nuevo mensaje	New message
A	To
De	From
Asunto	Subject
cc	cc
Copia oculta	bcc
Archivo adjunto	Attachment
Enviar	Send

▶ CUANDO OTROS CONTESTAN

– Hola, ¿está Susana?

– Le puede decir que me llame, por favor?

– Le vuelvo a llamar dentro de media hora.

▶ WHEN YOUR NUMBER ANSWERS

– Hello! Could I speak to Susana, please?

– Would you ask him/her to call me back, please?

– I'll call back in half an hour.

▶ PARA CONTESTAR AL TELÉFONO

– ¿Diga? Soy Marcos.

– Sí, soy yo.

– ¿Con quién hablo?

▶ ANSWERING THE TELEPHONE

– Hello! It's Marcos speaking.

– Speaking.

– Who's speaking?

▶ HABLA EL TELEFONISTA

– ¿De parte de quién?

– Le paso.

– No cuelgue.

– ¿Quiere dejar un mensaje?

▶ WHEN THE SWITCHBOARD ANSWERS

– Who shall I say is calling?

– I'm putting you through.

– Please hold.

– Would you like to leave a message?

▶ DIFICULTADES

– No hay línea.

– Perdone, me he equivocado de número.

– Se oye muy mal.

– No les funciona el teléfono.

▶ DIFFICULTIES

– I can't get through.

– I'm sorry, I've got the wrong number.

– This is a very bad line.

– Their phone is out of order.

LOS NÚMEROS

1	**uno**
2	**dos**
3	**tres**
4	**cuatro**
5	**cinco**
6	**seis**
7	**siete**
8	**ocho**
9	**nueve**
10	**diez**
11	**once**
12	**doce**
13	**trece**
14	**catorce**
15	**quince**
16	**dieciséis**
17	**diecisiete**
18	**dieciocho**
19	**diecinueve**
20	**veinte**
21	**veintiuno**
30	**treinta**
31	**treinta y uno**
40	**cuarenta**
41	**cuarenta y uno**
50	**cincuenta**
60	**sesenta**
70	**setenta**
80	**ochenta**
90	**noventa**
100	**cien**
101	**ciento uno**
200	**doscientos**
201	**doscientos uno**
1000	**mil**
1001	**mil uno**
1,000,000	**un millón**

▶ EJEMPLOS

en la página diecinueve
en el capítulo siete
en una escala del uno al quince

NUMBERS

1	**one**
2	**two**
3	**three**
4	**four**
5	**five**
6	**six**
7	**seven**
8	**eight**
9	**nine**
10	**ten**
11	**eleven**
12	**twelve**
13	**thirteen**
14	**fourteen**
15	**fifteen**
16	**sixteen**
17	**seventeen**
18	**eighteen**
19	**nineteen**
20	**twenty**
21	**twenty-one**
30	**thirty**
31	**thirty-one**
40	**forty**
41	**forty-one**
50	**fifty**
60	**sixty**
70	**seventy**
80	**eighty**
90	**ninety**
100	**a hundred**
101	**a hundred and one**
200	**two hundred**
201	**two hundred and one**
1000	**a thousand**
1001	**a thousand and one**
1,000,000	**a million**

▶ EXAMPLES

on page nineteen
in chapter seven
on a scale of one to fifteen

1º	**primero**	1st	**first**
2º	**segundo**	2nd	**second**
3º	**tercero**	3rd	**third**
4º	**cuarto**	4th	**fourth**
5º	**quinto**	5th	**fifth**
6º	**sexto**	6th	**sixth**
7º	**séptimo**	7th	**seventh**
8º	**octavo**	8th	**eighth**
9º	**noveno**	9th	**ninth**
10º	**décimo**	10th	**tenth**
11º	**decimoprimero**	11th	**eleventh**
12º	**decimosegundo**	12th	**twelfth**
13º	**decimotercero**	13th	**thirteenth**
14º	**decimocuarto**	14th	**fourteenth**
15º	**decimoquinto**	15th	**fifteenth**
16º	**decimosexto**	16th	**sixteenth**
17º	**decimoséptimo**	17th	**seventeenth**
18º	**decimoctavo**	18th	**eighteenth**
19º	**decimonoveno**	19th	**nineteenth**
20º	**vigésimo**	20th	**twentieth**
21º	**vigésimo primero**	21st	**twenty-first**
30º	**trigésimo**	30th	**thirtieth**
100º	**centésimo**	100th	**hundredth**
101º	**centésimo primero**	101st	**hundred-and-first**
1000º	**milésimo**	1000th	**thousandth**

▶ LAS FRACCIONES *etc.* / ▶ FRACTIONS *etc.*

1/2	**un medio**	1/2	**a half**
1/3	**un tercio**	1/3	**a third**
1/4	**un cuarto**	1/4	**a quarter**
1/5	**un quinto**	1/5	**a fifth**
0,5	**cero coma cinco**	0.5	**(nought) point five**
3,4	**tres coma cuatro**	3.4	**three point four**
6,89	**seis coma ochenta y nueve**	6.89	**six point eight nine**
10%	**diez por ciento**	10%	**ten per cent**
100%	**cien por cien**	100%	**a hundred per cent**

▶ EJEMPLOS / ▶ EXAMPLES

vive en el quinto piso	he lives on the fifth floor
llegó el tercero	he came in third
un cuarto del pastel	a quarter of the cake

LA FECHA — DATE

▶ DÍAS DE LA SEMANA — ▶ DAYS OF THE WEEK

lunes	Monday
martes	Tuesday
miércoles	Wednesday
jueves	Thursday
viernes	Friday
sábado	Saturday
domingo	Sunday
¿Cuándo?	**When?**
el lunes	on Monday
los lunes	on Mondays
todos los lunes	every Monday
el martes pasado	last Tuesday
el próximo viernes	next Friday
el sábado de la semana que viene	a week on Saturday
el sábado de dentro de dos semanas	two weeks on Saturday

▶ MONTHS OF THE YEAR — ▶ MESES DE AÑO

enero	January
febrero	February
marzo	March
abril	April
mayo	May
junio	June
julio	July
agosto	August
septiembre	September
octubre	October
noviembre	November
diciembre	December
¿Cuándo?	**When?**
en febrero	in February
el uno de diciembre de 2001	on December 1st *or* first 2001
en dos mil dos	in two thousand and two
¿Qué día es hoy?	**What day is it?**
Es ...	**It's ...**
lunes, vientiséis de mayo	Monday, the 26th May *o* Monday, the twenty-sixth of May

¿Qué hora es? — What time is it? What's the time?

Es la una — **It's one o'clock**

Es la una y diez — **It's ten past one**

Es la una y cuarto — **It's quarter past one**

Es la una y media — **It's half past one**

Son las dos menos veinte — **It's twenty to two**

Son las dos menos cuarto — **It's quarter to two**

¿A qué hora? — What time?

a medianoche — **at midnight**

al mediodía — **at midday**

a la una (de la tarde) — **at one o'clock (in the afternoon)**

a las once (de la noche) — **at eleven o'clock (in the evening)**

las 11:15 *or* **las once quince** — **11:15** *o* **eleven fifteen**

las 20:45 *or* **las veinte cuarenta y cinco** — **8:45** *o* **eight forty-five**

en veinte minutos — **in twenty minutes**
hace diez minutos — **ten minutes ago**

español ≠ English

actual ≠ actual

La situación **actual** del país. → The country's **present** situation.

The film is based on **actual** events. → La película está basada en hechos **reales**.

agenda ≠ agenda

Perdí mi **agenda**. → I lost my **diary**.

on the **agenda** → en el **orden del día**

apuntar ≠ appoint

Apúntalo o se te olvidará. → **Write it down** or you'll forget.

They **appointed** him chairman. → Lo **nombraron** presidente.

constipado ≠ constipated

Estoy **constipado**. → I have **a cold**.

I'm **constipated**. → Estoy **estreñido**.

decepción ≠ deception

Me he llevado una gran **decepción** con él. → I was really **disappointed** in him.

Katie continued to keep up the **deception**. → Katie siguió manteniendo el **engaño**.

disgustado ≠ disgusted

Está **disgustado** porque suspendió el examen. → He's **upset** because he failed the exam.

I was completely **disgusted** at his behaviour. → Estaba **indignado** con su comportamiento.

diversión ≠ diversion

Necesita un poco de **diversión.**	⟶	He needs to have some **fun.**
"**Diversion**" (road sign)	⟶	"**Desvío**" (señal)

embarazada ≠ embarrassed

Estaba **embarazada** de cuatro meses.	⟶	She was four months **pregnant.**
I was really **embarrassed.**	⟶	Me dio mucha **vergüenza.**

espada ≠ spade

Una **espada** de hierro	⟶	An iron **sword**
He dug a hole with his **spade.**	⟶	Cavó un hoyo con la **pala.**

éxito ≠ exit

Esa novela será un gran **éxito.**	⟶	That novel will be a great **success.**
"**Exit**" (sign)	⟶	"**Salida**" (letrero)

fábrica ≠ fabric

Trabaja en una **fábrica.**	⟶	He works in a **factory.**
400 metres of **fabric**	⟶	400 metros de **tela**

largo ≠ large

Fue una conferencia muy **larga.**	⟶	It was a very **long** conference.
a **large** house	⟶	una casa **grande**

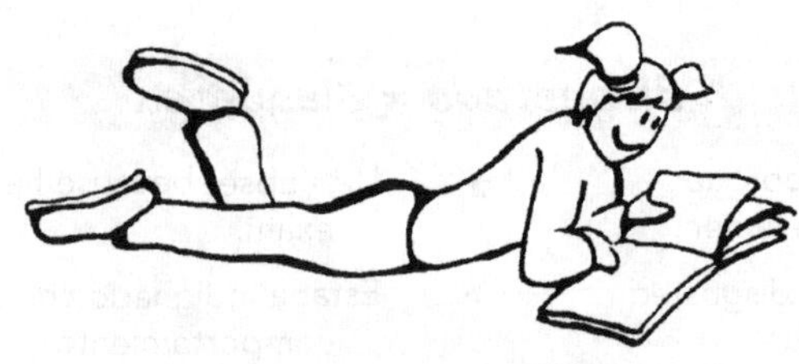

librería ≠ *library*

una **librería** de ocasión → a second-hand **bookshop**

the public **library** → la **biblioteca** pública

noticia ≠ *notice*

Tengo una buena **noticia** que darte. → I've got some good **news** for you.

There's a **notice** on the board about the trip. → Hay un **aviso** en el tablón sobre el viaje.

pariente ≠ *parent*

Es **pariente** mío. → He's a **relative** of mine.

My **parents** are Irish. → Mis **padres** son irlandeses.

pretender ≠ *pretend*

Pretendo sacar al menos un notable. → I **intend** to get at least a B.

He's not really ill, he's just **pretending**. → No está enfermo, sólo está **fingiendo**.

profesor ≠ *professor*

Amelia es **profesora** de inglés. → Amelia is an English **teacher**.

He is the **professor** of Spanish at Glasgow University. → Es **catedrático** de español en la Universidad de Glasgow.

receta ≠ *receipt*

Me dio la **receta** de los raviolis. → He gave me the **recipe** for the ravioli.

Do you have a **receipt** for the dress? → ¿Tiene el **ticket de compra** del vestido?

*recordar** ≠ *record*

No **recuerdo** dónde lo puse. → I can't **remember** where I put it.

They've just **recorded** their new album. → Acaban de **grabar** su nuevo álbum.

sano ≠ sane

una dieta **sana** → a **healthy** diet

She is as **sane** as you or me. → Está tan **cuerda** como tú o como yo.

sensible ≠ sensible

Es un chico muy **sensible**. → He's a very **sensitive** boy.

Be **sensible**! → ¡Sé **sensato**!

simpático ≠ sympathetic

Estuvo muy **simpática** con todos. → She was very **nice** to everybody.

She is a **sympathetic** listener. → Es una persona **comprensiva** que sabe escuchar.

soportar ≠ support

No lo **suporto**. → I can't **stand** him.

My mum has always **supported** me. → Mi madre siempre me ha **apoyado**.

suceso ≠ success

Los **sucesos** de la última decada. → The **events** of the last decade.

He was a great **success** as a writer. → Tuvo gran **éxito** como escritor.

LA CONJUGACIÓN INGLESA

▶ ÍNDICE

LA CONJUGACIÓN INGLESA

Las tablas de verbos que siguen a esta breve introducción del verbo en inglés muestran la conjugación de un modelo de verbo regular (**to work**), de los verbos irregulares o auxiliares **to do**, **to have** y **to be** y del auxiliar modal **can**.

En la parte superior de cada modelo aparecen las formas básicas de infinitivo, gerundio y participio, así como algunos ejemplos del uso de cada verbo, además de la forma de pretérito perfecto y el futuro simple y continuo, de cuya conjugación se puede deducir el resto de las formas correspondientes a cada una de las personas verbales.

Al final de esta sección encontraremos las formas afirmativas del PRESENTE, del PASADO y del PARTICIPIO de los verbos irregulares.

▶ VERBOS REGULARES E IRREGULARES – PRESENTE SIMPLE

La forma del PRESENTE SIMPLE AFIRMATIVO de la mayoría de los verbos ingleses es la misma que en infinitivo para todas las personas verbales, salvo para la tercera persona del singular, que añade normalmente una **-s**:

to say – I say, he say**s**
to speak – I speak, he speak**s**

Pero si un verbo acaba en **s**, **-sh**, **-ch**, o en **x**, se le añade **-es**.

Y si un verbo acaba en CONSONATE + **-y**, se cambia la **y** por **i** y se le añade **-es**:

to pass – he pass**es**
to try – he tr**ies**

La negación se forma con **don't** o **do not** delante del INFINITIVO sin *to* para todas las personas, excepto para la tercera persona singular, que utiliza **doesn't** o **does not**, también con el INFINITIVO sin *to*:

to say – I **don't** *o* **do not** say, he **doesn't** *o* **does not** say, etc.
to try – I **don't** *o* **do not** try, he **doesn't** *o* **does not** try, etc.

La interrogación se forma con **do** y el INFINITIVO sin *to* para todas las personas, excepto para la tercera persona del singular, que utiliza **does** con el INFINITIVO sin *to*:

to speak – **do** you speak English? **does** he speak English? etc.

▶ PASADO SIMPLE

En inglés, el PASADO SIMPLE AFIRMATIVO de los verbos regulares se suele formar, para todas las personas, añadiendo la terminación **-ed** a la forma de INFINITIVO:

to scream – I scream**ed**, he scream**ed**, etc.

Si un verbo acaba en **-e**, se añada solamente **-d**:

to love – we love**d**, etc.

Si un verbo acaba en una sola VOCAL+CONSONANTE y además consta de una sola sílaba o acaba en sílaba tónica, la consonante se duplica antes de añadir **-ed**:

to shop – they shop**ped**, etc **PERO** to shout – they shout**ed**, etc.
to sob – she sob**bed**, etc **PERO** to seem – it seem**ed**, etc.
to refer – they refer**red**, etc **PERO** to fear – they fear**ed**, etc.

Si un verbo acaba en una sola vocal + -l, en inglés británico se duplica la **l** antes de añadirle **-ed**:

to travel – he travel**led**, etc **PERO** to peel – they peel**ed**, etc.

La terminación CONSONANTE + -y se transforma en **-ied**:

to cry – she cr**ied**, etc.
to worry – we worr**ied**, etc.

En el caso de los verbos irregulares ver la lista de la página 353-355 en la que se dan las tres formas de cada verbo. La segunda forma es la del PASADO AFIRMATIVO, que sirve para todas las personas.

to swim, **swam**, swum – he **swam**, they **swam**, etc.

Las formas irregulares también aparecen en las entradas correspondientes a verbos en la parte inglés-español del diccionario.

Para la forma negativa se emplea, para todas las personas, **didn't** o **did not** seguido del INFINITIVO sin *to*, tanto si el verbo es regular como irregular:

to say – I **didn't** o **did not** say, etc.
to go – I **didn't** o **did not** go, etc.

Para la forma interrogativa se emplea **did** seguido del INFINITIVO sin *to* con todas las personas tanto si el verbo es regular como irregular:

to scream – **did** she scream? etc.
to swim – **did** they swim? etc.

▶ *OTROS TIEMPOS, VERBOS AUXILIARES*

Hay otros tiempos verbales que se forman con los verbos auxiliares como **have**, **will** y **be**, que normalmente se contraen en inglés hablado.

El PRETÉRITO PERFECTO se forma con la forma conjugada del verbo **to have** (ver el modelo de la página 349), seguida del PARTICIPIO del verbo principal:

to work

AFIRMATIVO: **I've** *o* I **have** work**ed**, he**'s** *o* he **has** work**ed**, etc.
NEGATIVO: I **haven't** *o* I **have not** work**ed**, he **hasn't** *o* he **has not** work**ed**, etc.
INTERROGATIVO: **have** you work**ed**? **has** he work**ed**? etc.

to swim

AFIRMATIVO: **I've** *o* I **have swum**, he**'s** *o* he **has swum**, etc.
NEGATIVO: I **haven't** *o* I **have not swum**, he **hasn't** *o* he **has not swum**, etc.
INTERROGATIVO: **have** you **swum**? **has** he **swum**? etc.

Hay que tener en cuenta que los PARTICIPIOS de los verbos regulares acaban en **-ed** y se corresponden con las formas del PASADO SIMPLE. Ver el PARTICIPIO de los verbos irregulares en la tercera columna de las listas de página 353-355.

Para formar el FUTURO, hay que usar el VERBO AUXILIAR **will** delante de la forma de INFINITIVO sin *to* del verbo que queremos conjugar:

to work

AFIRMATIVO: I'**ll** *o* I **will** work, they'**ll** *o* they **will** work, etc.
NEGATIVO: I **won't** *o* I **will not** work, he **won't** *o* he **will not** work, etc.
INTERROGATIVO: **will** you work? **will** he work? etc.

Para formar los tiempos CONTINUOS, se utiliza la forma conjugada del verbo **to be** (habitualmente contraída) seguida del GERUNDIO:

to work

PRESENTE AFIRMATIVO: I'**m** *o* I **am** work**ing**, he'**s** *o* he **is** work**ing**, etc.
PRESENTE NEGATIVO: I'**m not** *o* I **am not** work**ing**, he'**s not** *o* he **is not** work**ing**, etc.
PRESENTE INTERROGATIVO: **are** you work**ing**? **is** he work**ing**? etc.

PASADO AFIRMATIVO: I **was** work**ing**, you **were** work**ing**, etc.
PASADO NEGATIVO: I **wasn't** *o* I **was not** work**ing**, he **wasn't** *o* he **was not** work**ing**, etc.
PASADO INTERROGATIVO: **were** you work**ing**? **was** he work**ing**? etc.

Tal como se ha visto anteriormente, la forma negativa de los AUXILIARES y del verbo **to be** se forma colocando **not** o su forma contraída entre el AUXILIAR y el verbo PRINCIPAL. La forma INTERROGATIVA se forma invirtiendo el orden del AUXILIAR y el SUJETO.

▶ FORMACIÓN DEL GERUNDIO

En inglés, el GERUNDIO de todos los verbos, tanto si son regulares como si no, se forma habitualmente añadiendo la terminación **-ing** a la forma de INFINITIVO:

to scream – scream**ing**

Si el verbo acaba en una sola **-e**, ésta desaparece al añadir en sola **-ing**:

to love – lov**ing**

Si el verbo acaba en una sola VOCAL+CONSONANTE y consta de una sola sílaba o acaba en sílaba tónica, la consonante final se duplica antes de añadir **-ing**:

to shop – shop**ping** **PERO** to shout – shout**ing**
to sob – sob**bing** **PERO** to seem – seem**ing**
to refer – refer**ring** **PERO** to fear – fear**ing**

Si un verbo acaba en una sola VOCAL+-l, en inglés británico se duplica antes de añadirle **-ing**:

to travel – travel**ling** **PERO** to feel – feel**ing**

▶ USO DE LAS FORMAS SIMPLES Y CONTINUAS

En general, las formas continuas se utilizan para describir una acción que transcurre o transcurría en un momento concreto:

Don't distract him, he **is preparing** for his exam.
This time tomorrow, she **will be travelling** up north.
When he came into the room, I **was watching** TV.

Las formas continuas también sirven para mostrar que una acción todavía no ha terminado o que se trata de una situación temporal:

The doorbell rang while I **was having** a shower.
I **am working** with Jim and Craig at the moment.

Las formas simples se utilizan para referirse a acciones habituales y a hechos ocurridos en un momento concreto, en el caso del pasado:

I **visited** my grandmother regularly.
I **get up** at seven every morning.
He **cut** his knee when he fell.

Comparar las oraciones siguientes fijándose en el uso de las formas verbales simples y continuas:

I **was speaking** to my friend when the phone rang.
I **spoke** to my friend and then rang my mother.

John **reads** the paper at the breakfast table every morning.
John **is** just **reading** the paper.

▶ to work

trabajar

GERUNDIO

working

EJEMPLOS

She **works** *in a shop.*
Trabaja en una tienda.
Don't **work** *so hard.*
No trabajes tanto.
He **worked** *hard last month.*
Trabajó mucho el mes pasado.

PARTICIPIO

worked

PRETÉRITO PERFECTO

have/has worked

FUTURO

will work

FUTURO CONTINUO

will be working

PRESENTE SIMPLE

I work
you work
he works
we work
you work
they work

PASADO SIMPLE

I worked
you worked
he worked
we worked
you worked
they worked

PRESENTE CONTINUO

I am working
you are working
he is working
we are working
you are working
they are working

PASADO CONTINUO

I was working
you were working
he was working
we were working
you were working
they were working

▶ to do

hacer

GERUNDIO

doing

EJEMPLOS

What shall we **do** *now?*
¿Ahora qué hacemos?
How **do** *you* **do**?
¡Encantado de conocerlo!
*He***'s doing** *his homework.*
Está haciendo los deberes.

PARTICIPIO

done

PRETÉRITO PERFECTO

have/has done

FUTURO SIMPLE

will do

FUTURO CONTINUO

will be doing

PRESENTE SIMPLE

I	do
you	do
he	does
we	do
you	do
they	do

PASADO SIMPLE

I	did
you	did
he	did
we	did
you	did
they	did

PRESENTE CONTINUO

I	am doing
you	are doing
he	is doing
we	are doing
you	are doing
they	are doing

PASADO CONTINUO

I	was doing
you	were doing
he	was doing
we	were doing
you	were doing
they	were doing

▶ to have

tener

GERUNDIO

having

EJEMPLOS

She **has** *brown hair.*
Tiene el pelo castaño.
I **had** *sandwiches for lunch.*
He tomado unos sandwiches para comer.
*We'***re having** *a party tonight.*
Esta noche vamos a celebrar una fiesta.

PARTICIPIO

had

PRETÉRITO PERFECTO

have/has had

FUTURO SIMPLE

will have

FUTURO CONTINUO

will be having

PRESENTE SIMPLE

I	have
you	have
he	has
we	have
you	have
they	have

PRESENTE CONTINUO

I	am having
you	are having
he	is having
we	are having
you	are having
they	are having

PASADO SIMPLE

I	had
you	had
he	had
we	had
you	had
they	had

PASADO CONTINUO

I	was having
you	were having
he	was having
we	were having
you	were having
they	were having

▶ to be

ser

GERUNDIO

being

EJEMPLOS

How **are** *you?* ¿Cómo estás?
She **is** *thirteen years old.*
Tiene trece años.
*It'***s** *cold today.* Hace frío hoy.
*I'***m** *hungry.* Tengo hambre.

PARTICIPIO

been

PRETÉRITO PERFECTO

have/has been

FUTURO SIMPLE

will be

FUTURO CONTINUO

will be being

PRESENTE SIMPLE

I am
you are
he is
we are
you are
they are

PRESENTE CONTINUO

I am being
you are being
he is being
we are being
you are being
they are being

PASADO SIMPLE

I was
you were
he was
we were
you were
they were

PASADO CONTINUO

I was being
you were being
he was being
we were being
you were being
they were being

▶ *can*

poder, saber

EJEMPLOS

She **can** *swim well.* Sabe nadar bien.
I **can***'t speak French.* No sé hablar francés.
We **could***n't get tickets.* No pudimos conseguir entradas.

PRESENTE SIMPLE		*CONDICIONAL/PASADO SIMPLE*	
I	can	I	could
you	can	you	could
he	can	he	could
we	can	we	could
you	can	you	could
they	can	they	could

VERBOS IRREGULARES EN INGLÉS

PRESENTE	PRETÉRITO	PARTICIPIO DE PASADO
awake	awoke	awoken
be (am, is, are; being)	was, were	been
bear	bore	born(e)
beat	beat	beaten
become	became	become
begin	began	begun
bend	bent	bent
bet	bet, betted	bet, betted
bite	bit	bitten
bleed	bled	bled
blow	blew	blown
break	broke	broken
breed	bred	bred
bring	brought	brought
build	built	built
burn	burnt, burned	burnt, burned
burst	burst	burst
buy	bought	bought
can	could	(been able)
catch	caught	caught
choose	chose	chosen
come	came	come
cost	cost	cost
creep	crept	crept
cut	cut	cut
deal	dealt	dealt
dig	dug	dug
do (does)	did	done
draw	drew	drawn
dream	dreamed, dreamt	dreamed, dreamt
drink	drank	drunk
drive	drove	driven
eat	ate	eaten
fall	fell	fallen
feed	fed	fed
feel	felt	felt
fight	fought	fought
find	found	found
fling	flung	flung
fly	flew	flown
forbid	forbad(e)	forbidden
forget	forgot	forgotten
forgive	forgave	forgiven
freeze	froze	frozen

PRESENTE	PRETÉRITO	PARTICIPIO DE PASADO
get	got	got, (*US*) gotten
give	gave	given
go (goes)	went	gone
grind	ground	ground
grow	grew	grown
hang	hung	hung
hang (*execute*)	hanged	hanged
have	had	had
hear	heard	heard
hide	hid	hidden
hit	hit	hit
hold	held	held
hurt	hurt	hurt
keep	kept	kept
kneel	knelt, kneeled	knelt, kneeled
know	knew	known
lay	laid	laid
lead	led	led
lean	leant, leaned	leant, leaned
leap	leapt, leaped	leapt, leaped
learn	learnt, learned	learnt, learned
leave	left	left
lend	lent	lent
let	let	let
lie (lying)	lay	lain
light	lit, lighted	lit, lighted
lose	lost	lost
make	made	made
may	might	—
mean	meant	meant
meet	met	met
mistake	mistook	mistaken
mow	mowed	mown, mowed
must	(had to)	(had to)
pay	paid	paid
put	put	put
quit	quit, quitted	quit, quitted
read	read	read
rid	rid	rid
ride	rode	ridden
ring	rang	rung
rise	rose	risen
run	ran	run
say	said	said
see	saw	seen
sell	sold	sold
send	sent	sent

PRESENTE	PRETÉRITO	PARTICIPIO DE PASADO
set	set	set
sew	sewed	sewn
shake	shook	shaken
shine	shone	shone
shoot	shot	shot
show	showed	shown
shrink	shrank	shrunk
shut	shut	shut
sing	sang	sung
sink	sank	sunk
sit	sat	sat
sleep	slept	slept
slide	slid	slid
smell	smelt, smelled	smelt, smelled
speak	spoke	spoken
speed	sped, speeded	sped, speeded
spell	spelt, spelled	spelt, spelled
spend	spent	spent
spill	spilt, spilled	spilt, spilled
spit	spat	spat
spoil	spoiled, spoilt	spoiled, spoilt
spread	spread	spread
stand	stood	stood
steal	stole	stolen
stick	stuck	stuck
sting	stung	stung
stink	stank	stunk
strike	struck	struck
swear	swore	sworn
sweep	swept	swept
swim	swam	swum
swing	swung	swung
take	took	taken
teach	taught	taught
tear	tore	torn
tell	told	told
think	thought	thought
throw	threw	thrown
tread	trod	trodden
wake	woke, waked	woken, waked
wear	wore	worn
weep	wept	wept
win	won	won
wind	wound	wound
write	wrote	written

▶ CONTENTS

SPANISH VERB TABLES

This section contains 16 tables of very important Spanish verbs that you need to learn and 3 pages of other types of irregular verbs.

Spanish verbs fall into two main categories – **regular** and **irregular** – and it is important to learn which verbs fall into which category.

The tables are arranged in the following order:

1. Regular verbs – **hablar**, **comer**, **vivir** and **lavarse**
2. The most basic irregular verbs
3. Other types of irregular verb

At the top of each full-page table you will find the infinitive, the imperative, the past participle, and the gerund. The lower section of the table shows you how to form six tenses of the verb:

PRESENT
IMPERFECT
PRETERITE
PRESENT SUBJUNCTIVE
FUTURE
CONDITIONAL

▶ REGULAR VERBS

There are three groups of regular verbs:

1. "-AR" verbs = verbs that end in **-ar** like **hablar** and **lavarse** on p360 and p363.
2. "-ER" verbs = verbs that end in **-er** like **comer** on p361.
3. "-IR" verbs = verbs that end in **-ir** like **vivir** on p362.

They are called regular verbs because they follow one of three set patterns. When you have learnt these patterns, you will be able to form any regular verb.

The subject pronouns like *yo*, *tú*, *él* will appear in brackets because they are not always necessary in Spanish when **I**, **you**, **he** are in English.

HOW TO FORM A REGULAR VERB

i. a) To form the present, imperfect, preterite, present subjunctive and past subjunctive tenses, take the infinitive minus the last two letters. This is called the **stem** e.g. *hablar* → **habl-**, *comer* → **com-**, and *vivir* → **viv-**.

b) To form the future or conditional tense, the stem is the whole **infinitive** for all three verb types e.g. *hablar* → **hablar**, *comer* → **comer** and *vivir* → **vivir**.

ii. Next add the appropriate ending. You need to ask yourself three questions:

a) **What sort of** verb am I using (-AR, -ER, -IR)?
b) **Who** is doing the verb? (yo, tú, él *etc*)?
c) **When** are they doing it (in the present, the past or the future)?

Look at the verb tables for **hablar**, **comer** and **vivir**. The verb endings are in colour. These endings can be added onto the stem of any regular verb.

▶ THE MOST COMMON IRREGULAR VERBS

Many Spanish verbs are irregular and this means you have to learn them individually. There are full-page tables of the most important irregular verbs such as **tener**, **ser** and **estar** in this section. When you are translating from Spanish and meet an unfamiliar verb form, you may be able to guess from the context that it comes from one of these verbs, and you can use the verb tables to check. Irregular verb parts are listed on the Spanish side of the dictionary, so you could also look there.

HOW TO USE THE VERB TABLES

You will find some useful examples at the top of each verb table, but if you can't find what you need to say or write in Spanish there, use the verb table itself to help you. Imagine that you want to find the Spanish for "he wants". Here's how to do it:

a) Look up **want** on the English-Spanish side of the dictionary to find the Spanish translation
b) Spanish translation = **querer**
c) Turn to the verb tables section of your dictionary and find **querer**
d) When does he want it? He wants it **now**, so look for the heading *PRESENT*
e) Who wants it? **He** does. The Spanish for "he" is **él** so look for **él** under the *PRESENT* heading
f) The Spanish for "he wants" is "**quiere**"

▶ OTHER IRREGULAR VERBS

On pages 380 and 382 there is an alphabetical list of all irregular verbs, each of which is followed by a number. These numbers refer to the pattern which these verbs follow, and if you look on pages 376-379 you will see these patterns shown in summary form.

▶ hablar

to speak

IMPERATIVE

habla
hablad

EXAMPLE PHRASES

*No **hablo** francés.* I don't speak French
*Ayer **hablé** con tu hermano.* I spoke to your brother yesterday.
*Esta tarde **hablaré** con ella por teléfono.* I'll speak to her on the phone tonight.

PAST PARTICIPLE

hablado

GERUND

hablando

PRESENT

(yo)	hablo
(tú)	hablas
(él)	habla
(nosotros)	hablamos
(vosotros)	habláis
(ellos)	hablan

PRESENT SUBJUNCTIVE

(yo)	hable
(tú)	hables
(él)	hable
(nosotros)	hablemos
(vosotros)	habléis
(ellos)	hablen

PRETERITE

(yo)	hablé
(tú)	hablaste
(él)	habló
(nosotros)	hablamos
(vosotros)	hablasteis
(ellos)	hablaron

IMPERFECT

(yo)	hablaba
(tú)	hablabas
(él)	hablaba
(nosotros)	hablábamos
(vosotros)	hablabais
(ellos)	hablaban

FUTURE

(yo)	hablaré
(tú)	hablarás
(él)	hablará
(nosotros)	hablaremos
(vosotros)	hablaréis
(ellos)	hablarán

CONDITIONAL

(yo)	hablaría
(tú)	hablarías
(él)	hablaría
(nosotros)	hablaríamos
(vosotros)	hablarías
(ellos)	hablarían

▸ comer

to eat

IMPERATIVE

come
comed

EXAMPLE PHRASES

No ***como*** *carne.* I don't eat meat.
Aún no ***hemos comido****.*
We haven't eaten yet.
Ayer ***comimos*** *en un restaurante.*
Yesterday we ate in a restaurant.

PAST PARTICIPLE

comido

GERUND

comiendo

PRESENT

(yo)	como
(tú)	comes
(él)	come
(nosotros)	comemos
(vosotros)	coméis
(ellos)	comen

PRETERITE

(yo)	comí
(tú)	comiste
(él)	comió
(nosotros)	comimos
(vosotros)	comisteis
(ellos)	comieron

FUTURE

(yo)	comeré
(tú)	comerás
(él)	comerá
(nosotros)	comeremos
(vosotros)	comeréis
(ellos)	comerán

PRESENT SUBJUNCTIVE

(yo)	coma
(tú)	comas
(él)	coma
(nosotros)	comamos
(vosotros)	comáis
(ellos)	coman

IMPERFECT

(yo)	comía
(tú)	comías
(él)	comía
(nosotros)	comíamos
(vosotros)	comíais
(ellos)	comían

CONDITIONAL

(yo)	comería
(tú)	comerías
(él)	comería
(nosotros)	comeríamos
(vosotros)	comeríais
(ellos)	comerían

▶ vivir

to live

IMPERATIVE

vive
vivid

EXAMPLE PHRASES

***Vive** en esta calle.* He lives in this street.
*Antes **vivía** en Madrid.*
He used to live in Madrid.
*En verano **viviremos** en el piso nuevo.*
In the summer we'll be living in the new flat.

PAST PARTICIPLE

vivido

GERUND

viviendo

PRESENT

(yo)	vivo
(tú)	vives
(él)	vive
(nosotros)	vivimos
(vosotros)	vivís
(ellos)	viven

PRETERITE

(yo)	viví
(tú)	viviste
(él)	vivió
(nosotros)	vivimos
(vosotros)	vivisteis
(ellos)	vivieron

FUTURE

(yo)	viviré
(tú)	vivirás
(él)	vivirá
(nosotros)	viviremos
(vosotros)	viviréis
(ellos)	vivirán

PRESENT SUBJUNCTIVE

(yo)	viva
(tú)	vivas
(él)	viva
(nosotros)	vivamos
(vosotros)	viváis
(ellos)	vivan

IMPERFECT

(yo)	vivía
(tú)	vivías
(él)	vivía
(nosotros)	vivíamos
(vosotros)	vivíais
(ellos)	vivían

CONDITIONAL

(yo)	viviría
(tú)	vivirías
(él)	viviría
(nosotros)	viviríamos
(vosotros)	viviríais
(ellos)	vivirían

▶ lavarse

to wash (oneself)

IMPERATIVE

lávate

lavaos

EXAMPLE PHRASES

Se lava *todos los días.*
He washes every day.
Ayer ***me lavé*** *el pelo.*
I washed my hair yesterday.
Nos lavaremos *con agua fría.*
We'll wash in cold water.

PAST PARTICIPLE

lavado

GERUND

lavándose

PRESENT

(yo)	me lavo
(tú)	te lavas
(él)	se lava
(nosotros)	nos lavamos
(vosotros)	os laváis
(ellos)	se lavan

PRETERITE

(yo)	me lavé
(tú)	te lavaste
(él)	se lavó
(nosotros)	nos lavamos
(vosotros)	os lavasteis
(ellos)	se lavaron

FUTURE

(yo)	me lavaré
(tú)	te lavarás
(él)	se lavará
(nosotros)	nos lavaremos
(vosotros)	os lavaréis
(ellos)	se lavarán

PRESENT SUBJUNCTIVE

(yo)	me lave
(tú)	te laves
(él)	se lave
(nosotros)	nos lavemos
(vosotros)	os lavéis
(ellos)	se laven

IMPERFECT

(yo)	me lavaba
(tú)	te lavabas
(él)	se lavaba
(nosotros)	nos lavábamos
(vosotros)	os lavabais
(ellos)	se lavaban

CONDITIONAL

(yo)	me lavaría
(tú)	te lavarías
(él)	se lavaría
(nosotros)	nos lavaríamos
(vosotros)	os lavaríais
(ellos)	se lavarían

▶ dar

to give

IMPERATIVE

da

dad

EXAMPLE PHRASES

Mi tía siempre nos ***da*** *caramelos.* My aunt always gives us sweets.
Me ***dio*** *un libro.* He gave me a book.
El lunes me ***darán*** *las notas.* They will give me my marks on Monday

PAST PARTICIPLE

dado

GERUND

dando

PRESENT

(yo)	doy
(tú)	das
(él)	da
(nosotros)	damos
(vosotros)	dais
(ellos)	dan

PRETERITE

(yo)	di
(tú)	diste
(él)	dio
(nosotros)	dimos
(vosotros)	disteis
(ellos)	dieron

FUTURE

(yo)	daré
(tú)	darás
(él)	dará
(nosotros)	daremos
(vosotros)	daréis
(ellos)	darán

PRESENT SUBJUNCTIVE

(yo)	dé
(tú)	des
(él)	dé
(nosotros)	demos
(vosotros)	deis
(ellos)	den

IMPERFECT

(yo)	daba
(tú)	dabas
(él)	daba
(nosotros)	dábamos
(vosotros)	dabais
(ellos)	daban

CONDITIONAL

(yo)	daría
(tú)	darías
(él)	daría
(nosotros)	daríamos
(vosotros)	daríais
(ellos)	darían

▶ *decir*

to say

IMPERATIVE

di

decid

EXAMPLE PHRASES

Siempre ***dice*** *lo que piensa.*
He always says what he thinks.
Me ***dijo*** *una mentira.* He told me a lie.
Se lo ***diré*** *a todo el mundo.*
I'll tell everyone about it.

PAST PARTICIPLE

dicho

GERUND

diciendo

PRESENT

(yo)	digo
(tú)	dices
(él)	dice
(nosotros)	decimos
(vosotros)	decís
(ellos)	dicen

PRETERITE

(yo)	dije
(tú)	dijiste
(él)	dijo
(nosotros)	dijimos
(vosotros)	dijisteis
(ellos)	dijeron

FUTURE

(yo)	diré
(tú)	dirás
(él)	dirá
(nosotros)	diremos
(vosotros)	diréis
(ellos)	dirán

PRESENT SUBJUNCTIVE

(yo)	diga
(tú)	digas
(él)	diga
(nosotros)	digamos
(vosotros)	digáis
(ellos)	digan

IMPERFECT

(yo)	decía
(tú)	decías
(él)	decía
(nosotros)	decíamos
(vosotros)	decíais
(ellos)	decían

CONDITIONAL

(yo)	diría
(tú)	dirías
(él)	diría
(nosotros)	diríamos
(vosotros)	diríais
(ellos)	dirían

▶ estar

to be

IMPERATIVE

está
estad

EXAMPLE PHRASES

Estoy *enfermo.* I'm ill.
Estaba *muy enfadada contigo.*
She was very angry with you.
Mañana ***estaré*** *en casa todo el día.*
I'll be at home all day tomorrow.

PAST PARTICIPLE

estado

GERUND

estando

PRESENT

(yo)	estoy
(tú)	estás
(él)	está
(nosotros)	estamos
(vosotros)	estáis
(ellos)	están

PRESENT SUBJUNCTIVE

(yo)	esté
(tú)	estés
(él)	esté
(nosotros)	estemos
(vosotros)	estéis
(ellos)	estén

PRETERITE

(yo)	estuve
(tú)	estuviste
(él)	estuvo
(nosotros)	estuvimos
(vosotros)	estuvisteis
(ellos)	estuvieron

IMPERFECT

(yo)	estaba
(tú)	estabas
(él)	estaba
(nosotros)	estábamos
(vosotros)	estabais
(ellos)	estaban

FUTURE

(yo)	estaré
(tú)	estarás
(él)	estará
(nosotros)	estaremos
(vosotros)	estaréis
(ellos)	estarán

CONDITIONAL

(yo)	estaría
(tú)	estarías
(él)	estaría
(nosotros)	estaríamos
(vosotros)	estaríais
(ellos)	estarían

▸ haber

to have (*auxiliary*)

IMPERATIVE

not used

EXAMPLE PHRASES

*¿**Hay** alguien en la oficina?*
Is there anyone in the office?
***Había** mucha gente en la fiesta.*
There were a lot of people at the party.
*El domingo **habrá** una manifestación.*
There will be a demonstration on Sunday.

PAST PARTICIPLE

habido

GERUND

habiendo

PRESENT

(yo)	he
(tú)	has
(él)	ha
(nosotros)	hemos
(vosotros)	habéis
(ellos)	han

PRESENT SUBJUNCTIVE

(yo)	haya
(tú)	hayas
(él)	haya
(nosotros)	hayamos
(vosotros)	hayáis
(ellos)	hayan

PRETERITE

(yo)	hube
(tú)	hubiste
(él)	hubo
(nosotros)	hubimos
(vosotros)	hubisteis
(ellos)	hubieron

IMPERFECT

(yo)	había
(tú)	habías
(él)	había
(nosotros)	habíamos
(vosotros)	habíais
(ellos)	habían

FUTURE

(yo)	habré
(tú)	habrás
(él)	habrá
(nosotros)	habremos
(vosotros)	habréis
(ellos)	habrán

CONDITIONAL

(yo)	habría
(tú)	habrías
(él)	habría
(nosotros)	habríamos
(vosotros)	habríais
(ellos)	habrían

▸ hacer

to do, to make

IMPERATIVE

haz
haced

EXAMPLE PHRASES

¿*Qué* ***haces***? What are you doing?
He hecho *las camas.*
I've made the beds.
Ayer no ***hicimos*** *nada.*
We didn't do anything yesterday.

PAST PARTICIPLE

hecho

GERUND

haciendo

PRESENT

(yo)	hago
(tú)	haces
(él)	hace
(nosotros)	hacemos
(vosotros)	hacéis
(ellos)	hacen

PRETERITE

(yo)	hice
(tú)	hiciste
(él)	hizo
(nosotros)	hicimos
(vosotros)	hicisteis
(ellos)	hicieron

FUTURE

(yo)	haré
(tú)	harás
(él)	hará
(nosotros)	haremos
(vosotros)	haréis
(ellos)	harán

PRESENT SUBJUNCTIVE

(yo)	haga
(tú)	hagas
(él)	haga
(nosotros)	hagamos
(vosotros)	hagáis
(ellos)	hagan

IMPERFECT

(yo)	hacía
(tú)	hacías
(él)	hacía
(nosotros)	hacíamos
(vosotros)	hacíais
(ellos)	hacían

CONDITIONAL

(yo)	haría
(tú)	harías
(él)	haría
(nosotros)	haríamos
(vosotros)	haríais
(ellos)	harían

▶ ir

to go

IMPERATIVE

ve

id

EXAMPLE PHRASES

Van *al colegio en autobús.*
They go to school by bus.
Fui *a España con mi familia.*
I went to Spain with my family.
Mañana no ***iré*** *a trabajar.*
I'm not going to work tomorrow.

PAST PARTICIPLE

ido

GERUND

yendo

PRESENT

(yo)	voy
(tú)	vas
(él)	va
(nosotros)	vamos
(vosotros)	vais
(ellos)	van

PRESENT SUBJUNCTIVE

(yo)	vaya
(tú)	vayas
(él)	vaya
(nosotros)	vayamos
(vosotros)	vayáis
(ellos)	vayan

PRETERITE

(yo)	fui
(tú)	fuiste
(él)	fue
(nosotros)	fuimos
(vosotros)	fuisteis
(ellos)	fueron

IMPERFECT

(yo)	iba
(tú)	ibas
(él)	iba
(nosotros)	íbamos
(vosotros)	ibais
(ellos)	iban

FUTURE

(yo)	iré
(tú)	irás
(él)	irá
(nosotros)	iremos
(vosotros)	iréis
(ellos)	irán

CONDITIONAL

(yo)	iría
(tú)	irías
(él)	iría
(nosotros)	iríamos
(vosotros)	iríais
(ellos)	irían

▶ poner

to put

IMPERATIVE

pon

poned

EXAMPLE PHRASES

Cada día ***pongo*** *la mesa.*
I set the table every day.
Puse *el despertador para las cinco.*
I set the alarm clock for five o'clock.
Pondremos *la tele después de cenar.*
We'll put the TV on after dinner.

PAST PARTICIPLE

puesto

GERUND

poniendo

PRESENT

(yo)	pongo
(tú)	pones
(él)	pone
(nosotros)	ponemos
(vosotros)	ponéis
(ellos)	ponen

PRETERITE

(yo)	puse
(tú)	pusiste
(él)	puso
(nosotros)	pusimos
(vosotros)	pusisteis
(ellos)	pusieron

FUTURE

(yo)	pondré
(tú)	pondrás
(él)	pondrá
(nosotros)	pondremos
(vosotros)	pondréis
(ellos)	pondrán

PRESENT SUBJUNCTIVE

(yo)	ponga
(tú)	pongas
(él)	ponga
(nosotros)	pongamos
(vosotros)	pongáis
(ellos)	pongan

IMPERFECT

(yo)	ponía
(tú)	ponías
(él)	ponía
(nosotros)	poníamos
(vosotros)	poníais
(ellos)	ponían

CONDITIONAL

(yo)	pondría
(tú)	pondrías
(él)	pondría
(nosotros)	pondríamos
(vosotros)	pondríais
(ellos)	pondrían

▶ querer

to want

IMPERATIVE

quiere
quered

EXAMPLE PHRASES

*¿**Quieres** beber algo?*
Do you want something to drink?
*No **querían** irse a dormir.*
They didn't want to go to sleep.
*¿**Querrás** venir al cine?*
Would you like to come to the cinema?

PAST PARTICIPLE

querido

GERUND

queriendo

PRESENT

(yo)	quiero
(tú)	quieres
(él)	quiere
(nosotros)	queremos
(vosotros)	queréis
(ellos)	quieren

PRETERITE

(yo)	quise
(tú)	quisiste
(él)	quiso
(nosotros)	quisimos
(vosotros)	quisisteis
(ellos)	quisieron

FUTURE

(yo)	querré
(tú)	querrás
(él)	querrá
(nosotros)	querremos
(vosotros)	querréis
(ellos)	querrán

PRESENT SUBJUNCTIVE

(yo)	quiera
(tú)	quieras
(él)	quiera
(nosotros)	queramos
(vosotros)	queráis
(ellos)	quieran

IMPERFECT

(yo)	quería
(tú)	querías
(él)	quería
(nosotros)	queríamos
(vosotros)	queríais
(ellos)	querían

CONDITIONAL

(yo)	querría
(tú)	querrías
(él)	querría
(nosotros)	querríamos
(vosotros)	querríais
(ellos)	querrían

▶ saber

to know

IMPERATIVE

sabe
sabed

EXAMPLE PHRASES

No lo ***sé****.* I don't know.
No ***sabía*** *nada.* I didn't know anything.
El martes ***sabremos*** *los resultados.* We'll know the results on Tuesday.

PAST PARTICIPLE

sabido

GERUND

sabiendo

PRESENT

(yo)	sé
(tú)	sabes
(él)	sabe
(nosotros)	sabemos
(vosotros)	sabéis
(ellos)	saben

PRETERITE

(yo)	supe
(tú)	supiste
(él)	supo
(nosotros)	supimos
(vosotros)	supisteis
(ellos)	supieron

FUTURE

(yo)	sabré
(tú)	sabrás
(él)	sabrá
(nosotros)	sabremos
(vosotros)	sabréis
(ellos)	sabrán

PRESENT SUBJUNCTIVE

(yo)	sepa
(tú)	sepas
(él)	sepa
(nosotros)	sepamos
(vosotros)	sepáis
(ellos)	sepan

IMPERFECT

(yo)	sabía
(tú)	sabías
(él)	sabía
(nosotros)	sabíamos
(vosotros)	sabíais
(ellos)	sabían

CONDITIONAL

(yo)	sabría
(tú)	sabrías
(él)	sabría
(nosotros)	sabríamos
(vosotros)	sabríais
(ellos)	sabrían

ser

to be

IMPERATIVE

sé
sed

EXAMPLE PHRASES

Es *inglesa.* She's English.
La película ***era*** *malísima.*
The film was awful.
Seremos *más de cuarenta en la fiesta.*
There will be more than forty of us at the party.

PAST PARTICIPLE

sido

GERUND

siendo

PRESENT

(yo)	soy
(tú)	eres
(él)	es
(nosotros)	somos
(vosotros)	sois
(ellos)	son

PRESENT SUBJUNCTIVE

(yo)	sea
(tú)	seas
(él)	sea
(nosotros)	seamos
(vosotros)	seáis
(ellos)	sean

PRETERITE

(yo)	fui
(tú)	fuiste
(él)	fue
(nosotros)	fuimos
(vosotros)	fuisteis
(ellos)	fueron

IMPERFECT

(yo)	era
(tú)	eras
(él)	era
(nosotros)	éramos
(vosotros)	erais
(ellos)	eran

FUTURE

(yo)	seré
(tú)	serás
(el)	será
(nosotros)	seremos
(vosotros)	seréis
(ellos)	serán

CONDITIONAL

(yo)	sería
(tú)	serías
(él)	sería
(nosotros)	seríamos
(vosotros)	seríais
(ellos)	serían

▸ tener

to have

IMPERATIVE

ten
tened

EXAMPLE PHRASES

¿***Tienes*** *hambre?* Are you hungry?
El niño **tenía** *diez años.*
The boy was ten years old.
Mañana **tendremos** *mucho trabajo.*
We'll have a lot of work tomorrow.

PAST PARTICIPLE

tenido

GERUND

teniendo

PRESENT

(yo)	tengo
(tú)	tienes
(él)	tiene
(nosotros)	tenemos
(vosotros)	tenéis
(ellos)	tienen

PRETERITE

(yo)	tuve
(tú)	tuviste
(él)	tuvo
(nosotros)	tuvimos
(vosotros)	tuvisteis
(ellos)	tuvieron

FUTURE

(yo)	tendré
(tú)	tendrás
(él)	tendrá
(nosotros)	tendremos
(vosotros)	tendréis
(ellos)	tendrán

PRESENT SUBJUNCTIVE

(yo)	tenga
(tú)	tengas
(él)	tenga
(nosotros)	tengamos
(vosotros)	tengáis
(ellos)	tengan

IMPERFECT

(yo)	tenía
(tú)	tenías
(él)	tenía
(nosotros)	teníamos
(vosotros)	teníais
(ellos)	tenían

CONDITIONAL

(yo)	tendría
(tú)	tendrías
(él)	tendría
(nosotros)	tendríamos
(vosotros)	tendríais
(ellos)	tendrían

▶ venir

to come

IMPERATIVE

ven

venid

EXAMPLE PHRASES

*¿De dónde **vienes**?*
Where do you come from?
***Vino** en tren.* He came by train.
*Mi padre **vendrá** a las cuatro.*
My father is coming at four.

PAST PARTICIPLE

venido

GERUND

viniendo

PRESENT

(yo)	vengo
(tú)	vienes
(él)	viene
(nosotros)	venimos
(vosotros)	venís
(ellos)	vienen

PRETERITE

(yo)	vine
(tú)	viniste
(él)	vino
(nosotros)	vinimos
(vosotros)	vinisteis
(ellos)	vinieron

FUTURE

(yo)	vendré
(tú)	vendrás
(él)	vendrá
(nosotros)	vendremos
(vosotros)	vendréis
(ellos)	vendrán

PRESENT SUBJUNCTIVE

(yo)	venga
(tú)	vengas
(él)	venga
(nosotros)	vengamos
(vosotros)	vengáis
(ellos)	vengan

IMPERFECT

(yo)	venía
(tú)	venías
(él)	venía
(nosotros)	veníamos
(vosotros)	veníais
(ellos)	venían

CONDITIONAL

(yo)	vendría
(tú)	vendrías
(él)	vendría
(nosotros)	vendríamos
(vosotros)	vendríais
(ellos)	vendrían

SPANISH IRREGULAR VERB FORMS

The following list is a summary of the main forms of other irregular verbs that you are likely to come across.

1 *marcar*

PRETERITE	marqué, marcaste, marcó, marcamos, marcasteis, marcaron
PRESENT SUBJUNCTIVE	marque, marques, marque marquemos, marquéis, marquen

2 *pagar*

PRETERITE	pagué, pagaste, pagó, pagamos, pagasteis, pagaron
PRESENT SUBJUNCTIVE	pague, pagues, pague, paguemos, paguéis, paguen

3 *abrazar*

PRETERITE	abracé, abrazaste, abrazó, abrazamos, abrazasteis, abrazaron
PRESENT SUBJUNCTIVE	abrace, abraces, abrace, abracemos, abracéis, abracen

4 *empezar*

PRESENT	empiezo, empiezas, empieza, empezamos, empezáis, empiezan
PRETERITE	empecé, empezaste, empezó, empezamos, empezasteis, empezaron
PRESENT SUBJUNCTIVE	empiece, empieces, empiece, empecemos, empecéis, empiecen

5 *encontrar*

PRESENT	encuentro, encuentras, encuentra, encontramos, encontráis, encuentran
PRESENT SUBJUNCTIVE	encuentre, encuentres, encuentre, encontremos, encontréis, encuentren

6 *pensar*

PRESENT	pienso, piensas, piensa, pensamos, pensáis, piensan
PRESENT SUBJUNCTIVE	piense, pienses, piense, pensemos, penséis, piensen

7 *negar*

PRESENT	niego, niegas, niega, negamos, negáis niegan
PRETERITE	negué, negaste, negó, negamos, negasteis, negaron
PRESENT SUBJUNCTIVE	niegue, niegues, niegue, neguemos, neguéis, nieguen

8 *colgar*

PRESENT	cuelgo, cuelgas, cuelga, colgamos, colgáis, cuelgan
PRETERITE	colgué, colgaste, colgó, colgamos, colgasteis, colgaron
PRESENT SUBJUNCTIVE	cuelgue, cuelgues, cuelgue, colguemos, colguéis, cuelguen

9 *almorzar*

PRESENT	almuerzo, almuerzas, almuerza, almorzamos, almorzáis, almuerzan
PRETERITE	almorcé, almorzaste, almorzó, almorzamos, almorzasteis, almorzaron
PRESENT SUBJUNCTIVE	almuerce, almuerces, almuerce, almorcemos, almorcéis, almuercen

10 *continuar*

PRESENT	continúo, continúas, continúa, continuamos, continuáis, continúan
PRESENT SUBJUNCTIVE	continúe, continúes, continúe, continuemos, continuéis, continúen

11 *jugar*

PRESENT	juego, juegas, juega, jugamos, jugáis, juegan
PRETERITE	jugué, jugaste, jugó, jugamos, jugasteis, jugaron
PRESENT SUBJUNCTIVE	juegue, juegues, juegue, juguemos, juguéis, jueguen

12 *enviar*

PRESENT	envío, envías, envía, enviamos, enviáis, envían
PRESENT SUBJUNCTIVE	envíe, envíes, envíe, enviemos, enviéis, envíen

13 *andar*

PRETERITE	anduve, anduviste, anduvo, anduvimos, anduvisteis, anduvieron

14 *vencer*

PRESENT	venzo, vences, vence, vencemos, vencéis, vencen
PRESENT SUBJUNCTIVE	venza, venzas, venza, venzamos, venzáis, venzan

15 *conocer*

PRESENT	conozco, conoces, conoce, conocemos, conocéis, conocen
PRESENT SUBJUNCTIVE	conozca, conozcas, conozca, conozcamos, conozcáis, conozcan

16 *coger*

PRESENT	cojo, coges, coge, cogemos, cogéis, cogen
PRESENT SUBJUNCTIVE	coja, cojas, coja, cojamos, cojáis, cojan

17 *entender*

PRESENT	entiendo, entiendes, entiende, entendemos, entendéis, entienden
PRESENT SUBJUNCTIVE	entienda, entiendas, entienda, entendamos, entendáis, entiendan

18 *mover*

PRESENT	muevo, mueves, mueve, movemos, movéis, mueven
PRESENT SUBJUNCTIVE	mueva, muevas, mueva, movamos, mováis, muevan

19 *torcer*

PRESENT	tuerzo, tuerces, tuerce, torcemos, torcéis, tuercen
PRESENT SUBJUNCTIVE	tuerza, tuerzas, tuerza, torzamos, torzáis, tuerzan

20 *volver*

PRESENT	vuelvo, vuelves, vuelve, volvemos, volvéis, vuelven
PAST PARTICIPLE	vuelto
PRESENT SUBJUNCTIVE	vuelva, vuelvas, vuelva, volvamos, volváis, vuelvan

21 *oler*

PRESENT	huelo, hueles, huele, olemos, oléis, huelen
PRESENT SUBJUNCTIVE	huela, huelas, huela, olamos, oláis, huelan

22 *creer*

PRESENT	creí, creíste, creyó, creímos, creísteis, creyeron
PAST PARTICIPLE	creído
GERUND	creyendo

23 *caber*

PRESENT	quepo, cabes, cabe, cabemos, cabéis, caben
PRETERITE	cupe, cupiste, cupo, cupimos, cupisteis, cupieron
FUTURE	cabré, cabrás, cabrá, cabremos, cabréis, cabrán
PRESENT SUBJUNCTIVE	quepa, quepas, quepa, quepamos, quepáis, quepan

24 *caer*

PRESENT	caigo, caes, cae, caemos, caéis, caen
PAST PARTICIPLE	caído
PRETERITE	caí, caíste, cayó, caímos, caísteis, cayeron
PRESENT SUBJUNCTIVE	caiga, caigas, caiga, caigamos, caigáis, caigan
GERUND	cayendo

25 *poder*

PRESENT	puedo, puedes, puede, podemos, podéis, pueden
PRETERITE	pude, pudiste, pudo, pudimos, pudisteis, pudieron
FUTURE	podré, podrás, podrá, podremos, podréis, podrán
PRESENT SUBJUNCTIVE	pueda, puedas, pueda, podamos, podáis, puedan

26 *traer*

PRESENT	traigo, traes, trae, traemos, traéis, traen
PAST PARTICIPLE	traído
PRETERITE	traje, trajiste, trajo, trajimos, trajisteis, trajeron
PRESENT SUBJUNCTIVE	traiga, traigas, traiga, traigamos, traigáis, traigan
GERUND	trayendo

27 *valer*

PRESENT	valgo, vales, vale, valemos, valéis, valen
FUTURE	valdré, valdrás, valdrá, valdremos, valdréis, valdrán
PRESENT SUBJUNCTIVE	valga, valgas, valga, valgamos, valgáis, valgan

28 ver

PRESENT	veo, ves, ve, vemos, veis, ven
PAST PARTICIPLE	visto
PRETERITE	vi, viste, vio, vimos, visteis, vieron
PRESENT SUBJUNCTIVE	vea, veas, vea, veamos, veáis, vean
GERUND	viendo

29 romper

PAST PARTICIPLE	roto

30 extinguir

PRESENT	extingo, extingues, extingue, extinguimos, extinguís, extinguen
PRESENT SUBJUNCTIVE	extinga, extingas, extinga, extingamos, extingáis, extingan

31 producir

PRESENT	produzco, produces, produce, producimos, producís, producen
PRETERITE	produje, produjiste, produjo, produjimos, produjisteis, produjeron
PRESENT SUBJUNCTIVE	produzca, produzcas, produzca, produzcamos, produzcáis, produzcan

32 dirigir

PRESENT	dirijo, diriges, dirige, dirigimos, dirigís, dirigen
PRESENT SUBJUNCTIVE	dirija, dirijas, dirija, dirijamos, dirijáis, dirijan

33 corregir

PRESENT	corrijo, corriges, corrige, corregimos, corregís, corrigen
PRETERITE	corregí, corregiste, corrigió, corregimos, corregisteis, corrigieron
PRESENT SUBJUNCTIVE	corrija, corrijas, corrija, corrijamos, corrijáis, corrijan

34 sentir

PRESENT	siento, sientes, siente, sentimos, sentís, sienten
PRETERITE	sentí, sentiste, sintió, sentimos, sentisteis, sintieron
PRESENT SUBJUNCTIVE	sienta, sientas, sienta, sintamos, sintáis, sientan
GERUND	sintiendo

35 adquirir

PRESENT	adquiero, adquieres, adquiere, adquirimos, adquirís, adquieren
PRESENT SUBJUNCTIVE	adquiera, adquieras, adquiera, adquiramos, adquiráis, adquieran

36 pedir

PRESENT	pido, pides, pide, pedimos, pedís, piden
PRETERITE	pedí, pediste, pidió, pedimos, pedisteis, pidieron
PRESENT SUBJUNCTIVE	pida, pidas, pida, pidamos, pidáis, pidan

37 dormir

PRESENT	duermo, duermes, duerme, dormimos, dormís, duermen
PRETERITE	dormí, dormiste, durmió, dormimos, dormisteis, durmieron
PRESENT SUBJUNCTIVE	duerma, duermas, duerma, durmamos, durmáis, duerman
GERUND	durmiendo

38 reír

PRESENT	río, ríes, ríe, reímos, reís, ríen
PAST PARTICIPLE	reído
PRETERITE	reí, reíste, rió, reímos, reísteis, rieron
FUTURE	reiré, reirás, reirá, reiremos, reiréis, reirán
PRESENT SUBJUNCTIVE	ría, rías, ría, riamos, riáis, rían
GERUND	riendo

39 construir

PRESENT	construyo, construyes, construye, construimos, construís, construyen
PAST PARTICIPLE	construido
PRETERITE	construí, construiste, construyó, construimos, construisteis, construyeron
PRESENT SUBJUNCTIVE	construya, construyas, construya, construyamos, construyáis, construyan
GERUND	construyendo

40 prohibir

PRESENT	prohíbo, prohíbes, prohíbe, prohibimos, prohibís, prohíben
PRESENT SUBJUNCTIVE	prohíba, prohíbas, prohíba, prohibamos, prohibáis, prohíban

41 *oír*

PRESENT oigo, oyes, oye, oímos, oís, oyen
PAST PARTICIPLE oído
PRETERITE oí, oíste, oyó, oímos, oísteis, oyeron
PRESENT SUBJUNCTIVE oiga, oigas, oiga, oigamos, oigáis, oigan
GERUND oyendo

42 salir

PRESENT salgo, sales, sale, salimos, salís, salen
PRETERITE salí, saliste, salió, salimos, salisteis, salieron
FUTURE saldré, saldrás, saldrá, saldremos, saldréis, saldrán
PRESENT SUBJUNCTIVE salga, salgas, salga, salgamos, salgáis, salgan

43 *seguir*

PRESENT sigo, sigues, sigue, seguimos, seguís, siguen
PRETERITE seguí, seguiste, siguió, seguimos, seguisteis, siguieron
PRESENT SUBJUNCTIVE siga, sigas, siga, sigamos, sigáis, sigan
GERUND siguiendo

44 *abrir*

FUTURE abierto

45 *escribir*

FUTURE escrito

46 freír

PRESENT frío, fríes, fríe, freímos, freís, fríen
PAST PARTICIPLE frito
PRETERITE freí, freíste, frió, freímos, freísteis, frieron
FUTURE freiré, freirás, freirá, freiremos, freiréis, freirán
PRESENT SUBJUNCTIVE fría, frías, fría, friamos, friáis, frían
GERUND friendo

47 *morir*

PRESENT muero, mueres, muere, morimos, morís, mueren
PAST PARTICIPLE muerto
PRETERITE morí, moriste, murió, morimos, moristeis, murieron
PRESENT SUBJUNCTIVE muera, mueras, muera, muramos, muráis, mueran
GERUND muriendo

48 reunir

PRESENT reúno, reúnes, reúne, reunimos, reunís, reúnen
PRESENT SUBJUNCTIVE reúna, reúnas, reúna, reunamos, reunáis, reúnan

49 reñir

PRESENT riño, riñes, riñe, reñimos, reñís, riñen
PRETERITE reñí, reñiste, riñó, reñimos, reñisteis, riñeron
PRESENT SUBJUNCTIVE riña, riñas, riña, riñamos, riñáis, riñan
GERUND riñendo

50 gruñir

PRETERITE gruñí, gruñiste, gruñó, gruñimos, gruñisteis, gruñeron
GERUND gruñendo

51 lucir

PRESENT luzco, luces, luce, lucimos, lucís, lucen
PRESENT SUBJUNCTIVE luzca, luzcas, luzca, luzcamos, luzcáis, luzcan

52 imprimir

PAST PARTICIPLE impreso

NB

averiguar, amortiguar: like **hablar** except **u** of the stem is written **ü** before **e**:
1st person preterite **averigüe**, and all the present subjunctive **averigüe, averigües, averigüe, averigüemos, averigüéis, averigüen**

zurcir, fruncir: like **vivir** except stem consonant **c** is written **z** before **a** and **o**: 1st person present **zurzo**,

OTHER IRREGULAR VERBS

The numbers on this list refer to model numbers shown on pages 376-379. Verbs described as FULL PAGE are treated in detail on pages 360-375.

Verb	Model
abastecer	15
abrazar	3
abrigar	2
abrir	44
abstenerse	see TENER
acentuarse	10
acercar	1
acertar	6
acoger	16
acordar	5
acostarse	5
actuar	10
acurrucarse	1
adelgazar	3
adquirir	35
advertir	34
agradecer	15
ahogarse	2
ahorcar	1
alargar	2
alcanzar	3
aliarse	12
almorzar	9
alzar	3
amanecer	15
amargar	2
amenazar	3
amortiguar	see NB
ampliar	12
analizar	3
andar	13
anochecer	15
apagar	2
aparcar	1
aparecer	15
apetecer	15
aplazar	3
aplicar	1
apostar	5
apretar	6
aprobar	5
arrancar	1
arrepentirse	34
arriesgarse	2
arrugarse	2
ascender	17
atacar	1
atardecer	15
atender	17
aterrizar	3
atracar	1
atraer	26
atravesar	6
autorizar	3
avanzar	3
aventar	6
avergonzar	3+5
averiarse	12
averiguar	See NB
barnizar	3
bendecir	see DECIR
bostezar	3
brincar	1
buscar	1
caber	23
caducar	1
caer	24
cagar	2
calcar	1
calentar	6
calificar	1
cargar	2
cascar	1
castigar	2
cazar	3
cerrar	6
checar	1
chirriar	12
chocar	1
clasificar	1
cocer	19
coger	16
colgar	8
colocar	1
colonizar	3
compenzar	17
compadecer	15
competir	36
complacer	15
complicar	1
componer	see PONER
comprobar	5
comunicar	1
concertar	6
conducir	31
confesar	6
confiar	12
conmover	18
conocer	15
conseguir	43
consentir	34
consolar	5
construir	39
contar	5
contener	see TENER
continuar	10
contradecir	see DECIR
contraer	26
contribuir	39
convencer	14
convenir	see VENIR
convertir	34
convocar	1
corregir	33
costar	5
crecer	15
creer	22
criar	12
criticar	1
cruzar	3
cubrir	44
dar	FULL PAGE
decir	FULL PAGE
dedicar	1
deducir	31
defender	17
demostrar	5
derretir	36
desafiar	12
desahogarse	2
desaparecer	15
descalzarse	3
descargar	2
descender	17
descolgar	8
descomponerse	see PONER
desconcertar	6
desconfiar	12
descontar	5
describir	45
descubrir	44
desembarcar	1
desembocar	1
desempacar	1
desenroscar	1
desenvolver	20
deshacer	see HACER
deslizarse	3
desobedecer	15
despedir	36
despegar	2
desperezarse	3
despertar	6
desplegar	7
destacar	1
desteñir	49
destrozar	3
destruir	39
desviar	12
detener	see TENER
devolver	20
dialogar	2
digerir	34

a [eɪ, ə] INDEFINITE ARTICLE

*Use **un** for masculine nouns, **una** for feminine nouns.*

[1] un MASC ◊ *a book* un libro

[2] una FEM ◊ *an apple* una manzana

*Sometimes **a** is not translated, particularly if referring to professions.*

◊ *He's a butcher.* Es carnicero. ◊ *I haven't got a car.* No tengo coche. ◊ *a year ago* hace un año

♦ **a hundred pounds** cien libras

♦ **once a week** una vez a la semana

♦ **70 kilometres an hour** 70 kilómetros por hora

♦ **30 pence a kilo** 30 peniques el kilo

to **abandon** [ə'bændən] VERB
abandonar

abbey ['æbɪ] NOUN
la abadía

abbreviation [əbriːvɪ'eɪʃən] NOUN
la abreviatura

ability [ə'bɪlɪtɪ] NOUN (PL **abilities**)
la capacidad

♦ **to have the ability to do something** tener* la capacidad de hacer algo

able ['eɪbl] ADJECTIVE

♦ **to be able to do something** poder* hacer algo ◊ *Will you be able to come on Saturday?* ¿Puedes venir el sábado?

to **abolish** [ə'bɒlɪʃ] VERB
abolir*

abortion [ə'bɔːʃən] NOUN
el aborto

♦ **to have an abortion** abortar

about [ə'baut] PREPOSITION, ADVERB

[1] sobre ◊ *a book about London* un libro sobre Londres ◊ *I don't know anything about it.* No sé nada sobre eso.

♦ **I'm phoning you about tomorrow's meeting.** Te llamo por lo de la reunión de mañana.

♦ **What's it about?** ¿De qué trata?

[2] (*approximately*)
unos MASC
unas FEM
◊ *It takes about 10 hours.* Se tarda unas 10 horas.

♦ **at about 11 o'clock** sobre las 11

[3] por ◊ *to walk about the town* caminar por la ciudad

♦ **What about me?** ¿Y yo?

♦ **to be about to do something** estar* a punto de hacer algo ◊ *I was about to go out.* Estaba a punto de salir*.

♦ **How about going to the cinema?** ¿Qué tal si vamos al cine?

above [ə'bʌv] PREPOSITION, ADVERB

*When something is located above something, use **encima de**. When there is movement involved, use **por encima de**.*

[1] encima de ◊ *There was a picture above the fireplace.* Había un cuadro encima de la chimenea.

[2] por encima de ◊ *He put his hands above his head.* Puso las manos por encima de la cabeza.

♦ **the flat above** el piso de arriba

♦ **above all** sobre todo

[3] más de (*more than*) ◊ *above 40 degrees* más de 40 grados

abroad [ə'brɔːd] ADVERB

♦ **to go abroad** ir* al extranjero

♦ **to live abroad** vivir en el extranjero

abrupt [ə'brʌpt] ADJECTIVE

[1] brusco ◊ *He was a bit abrupt with me.* Fue un poco brusco conmigo.

[2] repentino ◊ *His abrupt departure aroused suspicion.* Su repentina marcha levantó sospechas.

abruptly [ə'brʌptlɪ] ADVERB
de repente ◊ *He got up abruptly.* Se levantó de repente.

absence ['æbsəns] NOUN

[1] la ausencia (*of people*)

[2] la falta (*of things*)

♦ **absence from school** la falta de asistencia a clase

absent ['æbsənt] ADJECTIVE
ausente

absent-minded ['æbsənt'maɪndɪd] ADJECTIVE
distraído

absolutely [æbsə'luːtlɪ] ADVERB
totalmente ◊ *I absolutely refuse to do it.* Me niego totalmente a hacerlo.

♦ **Jill's absolutely right.** Jill tiene toda la razón.

♦ **It's absolutely delicious!** ¡Está riquísimo!

♦ **They did absolutely nothing to help him.** No hicieron absolutamente nada para ayudarle.

♦ **Do you think it's a good idea? – Absolutely!** ¿Te parece una buena idea? – ¡Desde luego!

absorbed [əb'zɔːbd] ADJECTIVE

♦ **to be absorbed in something** estar* absorto en algo

absurd [əb'səːd] ADJECTIVE
absurdo

abuse [ə'bjuːs] NOUN

see also **abuse** VERB

el abuso (*of power*)

♦ **to shout abuse at somebody** insultar a alguien

to **abuse** [ə'bjuːz] VERB

☞

see also **abuse** NOUN
maltratar ◊ *abused children* niños maltratados

abusive [ə'bju:sɪv] ADJECTIVE
♦**He became abusive.** Se puso a insultar.

academic [ækə'dɛmɪk] ADJECTIVE
académico ◊ *the academic year* el año académico

academy [ə'kædəmɪ] NOUN (PL **academies**)
la academia ◊ *a military academy* una academia militar
♦**an academy of music** un conservatorio

to **accelerate** [æk'sɛləreɪt] VERB
acelerar

accelerator [æk'sɛləreɪtə^r] NOUN
el acelerador

accent ['æksɛnt] NOUN
el acento ◊ *He's got a Spanish accent.* Tiene acento español.

to **accept** [ək'sɛpt] VERB
aceptar ◊ *She accepted the offer.* Aceptó la oferta.
♦**to accept responsibility for something** asumir la responsabilidad de algo
♦**This telephone accepts 10 pence coins only.** Este teléfono sólo admite monedas de 10 peniques.

acceptable [ək'sɛptəbl] ADJECTIVE
aceptable

access ['æksɛs] NOUN
el acceso ◊ *He has access to confidential information.* Tiene acceso a información reservada.
♦**Her ex-husband has access to the children.** Su ex marido puede ver a los niños.

accessible [æk'sɛsəbl] ADJECTIVE
accesible

accessory [æk'sɛsərɪ] NOUN (PL **accessories**)
el accesorio ◊ *fashion accessories* los accesorios de moda

accident ['æksɪdənt] NOUN
el accidente ◊ *to have an accident* sufrir un accidente
♦**by accident (1)** por casualidad ◊ *They made the discovery by accident.* Lo descubrieron por casualidad.
♦**by accident (2)** sin querer* ◊ *The burglar killed him by accident.* El ladrón lo mató sin querer.

accidental [æksɪ'dɛntl] ADJECTIVE
♦**I didn't do it deliberately, it was accidental.** No lo hice adrede, fue sin querer*.
♦**accidental death** la muerte por accidente

to **accommodate** [ə'kɔmədeɪt] VERB
alojar

accommodation [əkɔmə'deɪʃən] NOUN
el alojamiento

to **accompany** [ə'kʌmpənɪ] VERB
(**accompanied, accompanied**)
acompañar

accord [ə'kɔ:d] NOUN
♦**of his own accord** por su cuenta

accordingly [ə'kɔ:dɪŋlɪ] ADVERB
en consecuencia (*consequently*)

according to [ə'kɔ:dɪŋtu:] PREPOSITION
según ◊ *According to him, everyone had gone.* Según él, todos se habían ido.

account [ə'kaunt] NOUN
1 la cuenta ◊ *a bank account* una cuenta bancaria
♦**to do the accounts** llevar la contabilidad
2 el informe ◊ *He gave a detailed account of what happened.* Dio un informe detallado de lo ocurrido.
♦**to take something into account** tener* algo en cuenta
♦**by all accounts** a decir* de todos
♦**on account of** a causa de ◊ *We couldn't go out on account of the bad weather.* No pudimos salir* a causa del mal tiempo.

to **account for** [ə'kauntfɔ:^r] VERB
explicar* ◊ *If she was ill, that would account for her poor results.* Si estuviera enferma, se explicarían sus malos resultados.

accountable [ə'kauntəbl] ADJECTIVE
♦**to be accountable to someone** responder ante alguien

accountancy [ə'kauntənsɪ] NOUN
la contabilidad

accountant [ə'kauntənt] NOUN
el/la contable (el contador, la contadora *LatAm*) ◊ *She's an accountant.* Es contable.

accuracy ['ækjurəsɪ] NOUN
la exactitud

accurate ['ækjurɪt] ADJECTIVE
exacto

accurately ['ækjurɪtlɪ] ADVERB
con exactitud

accusation [ækju'zeɪʃən] NOUN
la acusación (PL las acusaciones)

to **accuse** [ə'kju:z] VERB
♦**to accuse somebody of something** acusar a alguien de algo ◊ *The police are accusing her of murder.* La policía la acusa de asesinato.

ace [eɪs] NOUN
el as ◊ *the ace of hearts* el as de corazones

ache [eɪk] NOUN
see also **ache** VERB
el dolor ◊ *stomach ache* dolor de estómago

to **ache** [eɪk] VERB
see also **ache** NOUN
♦**My leg's aching.** Me duele la pierna.

* Verbs marked with this symbol are irregular. See pages 380-382 for further details

to **achieve** [ə'tʃiːv] VERB
conseguir*

achievement [ə'tʃiːvmənt] NOUN
el logro ◊ *That was quite an achievement.* Aquello fue todo un logro.

acid ['æsɪd] NOUN
el ácido

acid rain ['æsɪdreɪn] NOUN
la lluvia ácida

acne ['æknɪ] NOUN
el acné

to **acquit** [ə'kwɪt] VERB
absolver*

acre ['eɪkəʳ] NOUN
el acre
Equivale a 4.047 metros cuadrados.

acrobat ['ækrəbæt] NOUN
el/la acróbata

across [ə'krɔs] PREPOSITION, ADVERB
1 al otro lado de ◊ *He lives across the river.* Vive al otro lado del río.
2 a través de ◊ *an expedition across the Sahara* una expedición a través del Sahara
◆ **the shop across the road** la tienda en la acera de enfrente
◆ **to run across the road** cruzar* la calle corriendo
◆ **across from** frente a ◊ *He sat down across from her.* Se sentó frente a ella.

to **act** [ækt] VERB
see also **act** NOUN
actuar* ◊ *The police acted quickly.* La policía actuó con rapidez. ◊ *He acts really well.* Actúa muy bien.
◆ **She's acting the part of Juliet.** Interpreta el papel de Julieta.
◆ **She acts as his interpreter.** Ella le hace de intérprete.

act [ækt] NOUN
see also **act** VERB
el acto ◊ *in the first act* en el primer acto
◆ **It was all an act.** Era todo un cuento.
◆ **an Act of Parliament** una ley parlamentaria

action ['ækʃən] NOUN
la acción (PL las acciones) ◊ *The film was full of action.* Era una película con mucha acción.
◆ **to take firm action against** tomar severas medidas contra

active ['æktɪv] ADJECTIVE
activo ◊ *He's a very active person.* Es una persona muy activa.
◆ **an active volcano** un volcán en actividad

activity [æk'tɪvɪtɪ] NOUN (PL **activities**)
la actividad ◊ *outdoor activities* actividades al aire libre

actor ['æktəʳ] NOUN
el actor

actress ['æktrɪs] NOUN (PL **actresses**)
la actriz (PL las actrices)

actual ['æktjuəl] ADJECTIVE
real ◊ *The film is based on actual events.* La película está basada en hechos reales.
Be careful not to translate ***actual*** *by the Spanish word* ***actual****.*

actually ['æktjuəlɪ] ADVERB
1 realmente ◊ *Did it actually happen?* ¿Ocurrió realmente?
◆ **You only pay for the electricity you actually use.** Sólo pagas la electricidad que consumes.
2 de hecho ◊ *I was so bored I actually fell asleep!* ¡Me aburría tanto que de hecho me quedé dormido!
◆ **Fiona's awful, isn't she? – Actually, I quite like her.** Fiona es una antipática, ¿verdad? – Pues a mí me cae bien.
◆ **Actually, I don't know him at all.** La verdad es que no lo conozco de nada.

acupuncture ['ækjupʌŋktʃəʳ] NOUN
la acupuntura

AD [eɪ'diː] ABBREVIATION (= *Anno Domini*)
d.C. (= después de Cristo) ◊ *in 800 AD* en el año 800 d.C.

ad [æd] NOUN
el anuncio

to **adapt** [ə'dæpt] VERB
adaptar ◊ *His novel was adapted for television.* Su novela fue adaptada para la televisión.
◆ **to adapt to something** adaptarse a algo ◊ *He adapted to his new school very quickly.* Se adaptó a su nuevo colegio muy rápidamente.

adaptor [ə'dæptəʳ] NOUN
1 (*for several plugs*)
el ladrón (PL los ladrones)
2 (*for different types of plugs*)
el adaptador

to **add** [æd] VERB
añadir ◊ *Add more flour to the dough.* Añada más harina a la masa.

to **add up** [ædʌp] VERB
sumar ◊ *Add up the figures.* Suma las cifras.

addict ['ædɪkt] NOUN
el adicto
la adicta
◆ **a drug addict** un drogadicto ◊ *She's a drug addict.* Es drogadicta.
◆ **Martin's a football addict.** Martin es un fanático del fútbol.

addicted [ə'dɪktɪd] ADJECTIVE
◆ **to be addicted to drugs** ser* drogadicto
◆ **She's addicted to heroin.** Es heroinómana.
◆ **She's addicted to soaps.** Es una apasionada de las telenovelas.

addition [ə'dɪʃən] NOUN
◆ **in addition** además ◊ *He's bought a new car and, in addition, a motorbike.* Se ha comprado un coche nuevo y además una moto.

☞

◆ **in addition to** además de ◊ *In addition to the price of the cassette, there's a charge for postage.* Además del precio del casete, hay un recargo por los gastos de envío.

address [ə'drɛs] NOUN (PL **addresses**)
la dirección (PL las direcciones)

adjective ['ædʒɛktɪv] NOUN
el adjetivo

to **adjust** [ə'dʒʌst] VERB
1 regular (*temperature, height*) ◊ *You can adjust the height of the chair.* Se puede regular la altura de la silla.
2 ajustar (*mechanism*) ◊ *It can be easily adjusted using a screwdriver.* Se ajusta fácilmente con un destornillador.
◆ **to adjust to something** adaptarse a algo ◊ *He adjusted to his new school very quickly.* Se adaptó a su nuevo colegio muy rápidamente.

adjustable [ə'dʒʌstəbl] ADJECTIVE
regulable

administration [ədmɪnɪs'treɪʃən] NOUN
la administración

admiral ['ædmərəl] NOUN
el almirante

to **admire** [əd'maɪə[r]] VERB
admirar

admission [əd'mɪʃən] NOUN
la entrada ◊ *"admission free"* "entrada gratuita"

to **admit** [əd'mɪt] VERB
reconocer* ◊ *I must admit that I've never heard of him.* Tengo que reconocer que nunca he oído hablar de él. ◊ *He admitted that he'd done it.* Reconoció que lo había hecho.

adolescent [ædəu'lɛsnt] NOUN
el/la adolescente

to **adopt** [ə'dɔpt] VERB
adoptar

adopted [ə'dɔptɪd] ADJECTIVE
adoptivo

adoption [ə'dɔpʃən] NOUN
la adopción (PL las adopciones)

to **adore** [ə'dɔː[r]] VERB
adorar

adult ['ædʌlt] NOUN
el adulto
la adulta
◆ **adult education** la educación de adultos

to **advance** [əd'vɑːns] VERB
see also **advance** NOUN
avanzar* ◊ *The troops are advancing.* Las tropas avanzan. ◊ *Technology has advanced a lot.* La tecnología ha avanzado mucho.

advance [əd'vɑːns] NOUN
see also **advance** VERB
◆ **in advance** con antelación ◊ *They bought the tickets a month in advance.* Compraron los billetes con un mes de antelación.

advance booking [əd'vɑːns'bukɪŋ] NOUN
◆ **Advance booking is essential.** Es indispensable reservar con antelación.

advanced [əd'vɑːnst] ADJECTIVE
avanzado

advantage [əd'vɑːntɪdʒ] NOUN
la ventaja ◊ *Going to university has many advantages.* Ir* a la universidad tiene muchas ventajas.
◆ **to take advantage of something** aprovechar algo ◊ *He took advantage of his day off to have a rest.* Aprovechó su día libre para descansar.
◆ **to take advantage of somebody** aprovecharse de alguien ◊ *The company was taking advantage of its employees.* La compañía se aprovechaba de sus empleados.

adventure [əd'vɛntʃə[r]] NOUN
la aventura

adverb ['ædvəːb] NOUN
el adverbio

advert ['ædvəːt] NOUN
el anuncio

to **advertise** ['ædvətaɪz] VERB
anunciar ◊ *Jobs are advertised in the papers.* Las ofertas de empleo se anuncian en los periódicos.

advertisement [əd'vəːtɪsmənt] NOUN
el anuncio

advertising ['ædvətaɪzɪŋ] NOUN
la publicidad

advice [əd'vaɪs] NOUN
el consejo ◊ *to ask for advice* pedir* consejo ◊ *I'd like to ask your advice.* Quería pedirte consejo.
◆ **to give somebody advice** aconsejar a alguien
◆ **a piece of advice** un consejo ◊ *He gave me a good piece of advice.* Me ha dado un buen consejo.

to **advise** [əd'vaɪz] VERB
aconsejar ◊ *He advised me to wait.* Me aconsejó que esperara. ◊ *He advised me not to go there.* Me aconsejó que no fuera.

> ***aconsejar que** has to be followed by a verb in the subjunctive.*

aerial ['ɛərɪəl] NOUN
la antena

aerobics [ɛə'rəubɪks] NOUN
aerobic MASC ◊ *I do aerobics.* Hago aerobic.

aeroplane ['ɛərəpleɪn] NOUN
el avión (PL los aviones)

aerosol ['ɛərəsɔl] NOUN
el aerosol

* Verbs marked with this symbol are irregular. See pages 380-382 for further details

affair [ə'fɛəʳ] NOUN
1 la aventura ◊ *to have an affair with somebody* tener* una aventura con alguien
2 el asunto ◊ *The government has mishandled the affair.* El gobierno ha llevado mal el asunto.

to **affect** [ə'fɛkt] VERB
afectar

affectionate [ə'fɛkʃənɪt] ADJECTIVE
cariñoso

to **afford** [ə'fɔːd] VERB
permitirse ◊ *I can't afford a new pair of jeans.* No puedo permitirme comprar otros vaqueros.
◆ **We can't afford to go on holiday.** No podemos permitirnos el lujo de ir de vacaciones.

afraid [ə'freɪd] ADJECTIVE
◆ **to be afraid of something** tener* miedo de algo ◊ *I'm afraid of spiders.* Tengo miedo de las arañas.
◆ **I'm afraid I can't come.** Me temo que no puedo ir.
◆ **I'm afraid so.** Me temo que sí.
◆ **I'm afraid not.** Me temo que no.

Africa ['æfrɪkə] NOUN
África FEM

African ['æfrɪkən] ADJECTIVE
see also **African** NOUN
africano

African ['æfrɪkən] NOUN
see also **African** ADJECTIVE
el africano
la africana

after ['ɑːftəʳ] PREPOSITION, CONJUNCTION, ADVERB
1 después de ◊ *after the match* después del partido ◊ *After watching the television I went to bed.* Después de ver* la televisión me fui a la cama. ◊ *After I'd had a rest I went for a walk.* Después de descansar me fui a dar un paseo.
2 después de que

*When there's a change of subject in an **after** clause, use **después de que** with a verb in an appropriate tense instead of **después de** + infinitive.*

◊ *I met her after she had left the company.* La conocí después de que dejó la empresa.

***después de que** has to be followed by a verb in the subjunctive when referring to an event in the future.*

◊ *I'll help you after we've finished this.* Te ayudaré después de que terminemos esto. ◊ *She said she'd phone after her mother had gone out.* Dijo que me llamaría después de que se marchara su madre.
◆ **after dinner** después de cenar
◆ **He ran after me.** Corrió detrás de mí.
◆ **after all** después de todo
◆ **soon after** poco después

afternoon ['ɑːftə'nuːn] NOUN
la tarde ◊ *in the afternoon* por la tarde ◊ *3 o'clock in the afternoon* las 3 de la tarde ◊ *on Saturday afternoon* el sábado por la tarde

afters ['ɑːftəz] NOUN
el postre ◊ *What's for afters?* ¿Qué hay de postre?

aftershave ['ɑːftəʃeɪv] NOUN
el after shave

afterwards ['ɑːftəwədz] ADVERB
después ◊ *She left not long afterwards.* Se marchó poco después.

again [ə'gɛn] ADVERB
otra vez ◊ *They're friends again.* Ya son amigos otra vez. ◊ *I'd like to hear it again.* Me gustaría escucharlo otra vez.

*In Spanish you often use the verb **volver a** and an infinitive to talk about doing something **again**.*

◊ *I'd like to hear it again.* Me gustaría volver* a escucharlo. ◊ *I won't tell you again!* ¡No te lo vuelvo a repetir!
◆ **Can you tell me again?** ¿Me lo puedes repetir?
◆ **not...again** no...más ◊ *I won't go there again.* No volveré más por allí.
◆ **Do it again!** ¡Vuelve a hacerlo!
◆ **again and again** una y otra vez

against [ə'gɛnst] PREPOSITION
1 contra ◊ *He leant against the wall.* Se apoyó contra la pared.
2 en contra de ◊ *I'm against nuclear testing.* Estoy en contra de las pruebas nucleares.

age [eɪdʒ] NOUN
la edad ◊ *an age limit* un límite de edad
◆ **at the age of sixteen** a los dieciséis años
◆ **I haven't been to the cinema for ages.** Hace siglos que no voy al cine.

aged [eɪdʒd] ADJECTIVE
◆ **aged 10** de 10 años

agenda [ə'dʒɛndə] NOUN
el orden del día

*Be careful not to translate **agenda** by the Spanish word **agenda**.*

agent ['eɪdʒənt] NOUN
el/la agente ◊ *an estate agent* un agente inmobiliario
◆ **She's a travel agent.** Es empleada de una agencia de viajes.

aggressive [ə'grɛsɪv] ADJECTIVE
agresivo

ago [ə'gəu] ADVERB
◆ **two days ago** hace dos días
◆ **not long ago** no hace mucho
◆ **How long ago did it happen?** ¿Cuánto hace que ocurrió?

agony ['ægənɪ] NOUN (PL **agonies**)
◆ **to be in agony** sufrir mucho dolor
◆ **It was agony!** ¡Fue un suplicio!

to **agree** [ə'griː] VERB

☞

estar* de acuerdo ◊ *I don't agree!* ¡No estoy de acuerdo! ◊ *I agree with Carol.* Estoy de acuerdo con Carol.
◆ **to agree to do something (1)** (*when someone requests*) aceptar hacer algo ◊ *He agreed to go with her.* Aceptó acompañarla.
◆ **to agree to do something (2)** (*arrange*) acordar* hacer algo ◊ *They agreed to meet again next week.* Acordaron volver a reunirse la semana próxima.
◆ **to agree that...** reconocer* que... ◊ *I agree it's difficult.* Reconozco que es difícil.
◆ **Garlic doesn't agree with me.** El ajo no me sienta bien.

agreed [ə'griːd] ADJECTIVE
acordado ◊ *at the agreed time* a la hora acordada

agreement [ə'griːmənt] NOUN
el acuerdo
◆ **to be in agreement** estar* de acuerdo

agricultural [ægrɪ'kʌltʃərəl] ADJECTIVE
agrícola

agriculture ['ægrɪkʌltʃər] NOUN
la agricultura

ahead [ə'hɛd] ADVERB
delante ◊ *She looked straight ahead.* Miró hacia delante.
◆ **ahead of time** con antelación
◆ **to plan ahead** hacer* planes con antelación
◆ **The Spanish are five points ahead.** Los españoles llevan cinco puntos de ventaja.
◆ **Go ahead! Help yourself!** ¡Venga! ¡Sírvete!

aid [eɪd] NOUN
la ayuda
◆ **in aid of children** a beneficio de la infancia

AIDS [eɪdz] NOUN
el sida

to **aim** [eɪm] VERB
see also **aim** NOUN
◆ **to aim at** apuntar a ◊ *He aimed a gun at me.* Me apuntó con una pistola.
◆ **The film is aimed at children.** La película está dirigida a los niños.
◆ **to aim to do something** pretender hacer algo

aim [eɪm] NOUN
see also **aim** VERB
el propósito

air [ɛər] NOUN
el aire ◊ *to get some fresh air* tomar un poco el aire
◆ **by air** en avión

air-conditioned ['ɛəkən'dɪʃənd] ADJECTIVE
con aire acondicionado

air conditioning ['ɛəkən'dɪʃənɪŋ] NOUN
el aire acondicionado

Air Force ['ɛəfɔːs] NOUN
el ejército del aire

air hostess ['ɛəhəʊstɪs] NOUN (PL **air hostesses**)
la azafata ◊ *She's an air hostess.* Es azafata.

airline ['ɛəlaɪn] NOUN
la línea aérea

airmail ['ɛəmeɪl] NOUN
◆ **by airmail** por correo aéreo

airplane ['ɛəpleɪn] NOUN US
el avión (PL los aviones)

airport ['ɛəpɔːt] NOUN
el aeropuerto

aisle [aɪl] NOUN
el pasillo (*in plane, cinema*)

alarm [ə'lɑːm] NOUN
la alarma
◆ **a fire alarm** una alarma contra incendios

alarm clock [ə'lɑːmklɔk] NOUN
el despertador

album ['ælbəm] NOUN
el álbum

alcohol ['ælkəhɔl] NOUN
el alcohol

alcoholic [ælkə'hɔlɪk] NOUN
see also **alcoholic** ADJECTIVE
el alcohólico
la alcohólica

alcoholic [ælkə'hɔlɪk] ADJECTIVE
see also **alcoholic** NOUN
alcohólico ◊ *alcoholic drinks* bebidas alcohólicas

alert [ə'ləːt] ADJECTIVE
1 despierto ◊ *He's a very alert baby.* Es un bebé muy despierto.
2 atento ◊ *We must stay alert.* Hay que estar* atentos.

A levels ['eɪlɛvlz] PL NOUN

> *Under the reformed Spanish Educational System, if students stay on at school after the age of 16, they can do a two-year course -* ***bachillerato****. In order to get in to university, they sit an entrance exam -* ***la selectividad*** *- in the subjects they have been studying for the* ***bachillerato****.*

Algeria [æl'dʒɪərɪə] NOUN
Argelia FEM

alike [ə'laɪk] ADVERB
◆ **to look alike** parecerse* ◊ *The two sisters look alike.* Las dos hermanas se parecen.

alive [ə'laɪv] ADJECTIVE
vivo

all [ɔːl] ADJECTIVE, PRONOUN, ADVERB

todo ◊ *That's all I can remember.* Eso es todo lo que recuerdo. ◊ *I ate all of it.* Me lo comí todo. ◊ *all day* todo el día ◊ *all the apples* todas las manzanas
◆**All of us went.** Fuimos todos.
◆**all alone** completamente solo
◆**not at all** en absoluto ◊ *I'm not at all tired.* No estoy en absoluto cansado.
◆**Thank you. – Not at all.** Gracias. – De nada.
◆**She talks all the time.** No para de hablar.
◆**The score is five all.** El marcador es de empate a cinco.

allergic [ə'lə:dʒɪk] ADJECTIVE
alérgico ◊ *to be allergic to something* ser* alérgico a algo

allergy ['ælədʒɪ] NOUN
la alergia

alley ['ælɪ] NOUN
la callejuela

to **allow** [ə'lau] VERB
◆**to allow somebody to do something** dejar a alguien hacer* algo ◊ *His mum allowed him to go out.* Su madre le dejó salir*. ◊ *He's not allowed to go out at night.* No le dejan salir por la noche.
◆**Smoking is not allowed.** Está prohibido fumar.

all right [ɔ:lraɪt] ADVERB, ADJECTIVE
bien ◊ *Everything turned out all right.* Todo salió bien. ◊ *Are you all right?* ¿Estás bien?
◆**Is that all right with you?** ¿Te parece bien?
◆**The film was all right.** La película no estuvo mal.
◆**We'll talk about it later. — All right.** Lo hablamos después. – Vale.

almond ['ɑ:mənd] NOUN
la almendra

almost ['ɔ:lməust] ADVERB
casi ◊ *I've almost finished.* Ya casi he terminado.

alone [ə'ləun] ADJECTIVE, ADVERB
solo ◊ *She lives alone.* Vive sola.
◆**to leave somebody alone** dejar en paz a alguien ◊ *Leave her alone!* ¡Déjala en paz!
◆**to leave something alone** no tocar* algo ◊ *Leave my things alone!* ¡No toques mis cosas!

along [ə'lɔŋ] PREPOSITION, ADVERB
por ◊ *Chris was walking along the beach.* Chris paseaba por la playa.
◆**all along (1)** a lo largo de ◊ *There were bars all along the street.* Había bares a lo largo de toda la calle.
◆**all along (2)** desde el principio ◊ *He was lying to me all along.* Me había mentido desde el principio.

aloud [ə'laud] ADVERB
en voz alta

alphabet ['ælfəbɛt] NOUN
el alfabeto

Alps [ælps] PL NOUN
los Alpes

already [ɔ:l'rɛdɪ] ADVERB
ya ◊ *Liz had already gone.* Liz ya se había ido.

also ['ɔ:lsəu] ADVERB
también

altar ['ɔltə^r] NOUN
el altar

to **alter** ['ɔltə^r] VERB
cambiar

alternate [ɔl'tə:nɪt] ADJECTIVE
◆**on alternate days** en días alternos

alternative [ɔl'tə:nətɪv] NOUN
see also **alternative** ADJECTIVE
la alternativa ◊ *You have no alternative.* No tienes otra alternativa.
◆**Fruit is a healthy alternative to chocolate.** La fruta es una opción más sana que el chocolate.
◆**There are several alternatives.** Hay varias posibilidades.

alternative [ɔl'tə:nətɪv] ADJECTIVE
see also **alternative** NOUN
otro ◊ *They made alternative plans.* Hicieron otros planes.
◆**an alternative solution** otra solución
◆**alternative medicine** la medicina alternativa

alternatively [ɔl'tə:nətɪvlɪ] ADVERB
◆**Alternatively, we could just stay at home.** Si no, podemos simplemente quedarnos en casa.

although [ɔ:l'ðəu] CONJUNCTION
aunque ◊ *Although she was tired, she stayed up late.* Aunque estaba cansada, se quedó levantada hasta tarde.

altogether [ɔ:ltə'gɛðə^r] ADVERB
1 en total (*in total*) ◊ *You owe me £20 altogether.* En total me debes 20 libras.
2 del todo (*completely*) ◊ *I'm not altogether happy with your work.* No estoy del todo satisfecho con tu trabajo.

aluminium [ælju'mɪnɪəm] NOUN (US **aluminum**)
el aluminio

always ['ɔ:lweɪz] ADVERB
siempre ◊ *He's always moaning.* Siempre está quejándose.

am [æm] VERB *see* **be**

a.m. [eɪ'ɛm] ABBREVIATION
de la mañana ◊ *at 4 a.m.* a las 4 de la mañana

amateur ['æmətə^r] NOUN
el/la amateur (PL los/las amateurs)

amazed [ə'meɪzd] ADJECTIVE
asombrado ◊ *I was amazed that I managed to do it.* Estaba asombrado de haberlo conseguido.

amazing [ə'meɪzɪŋ] ADJECTIVE

☞

1 asombroso ◇ *That's amazing news!* ¡Es una noticia asombrosa!
2 extraordinario ◇ *Vivian's an amazing cook.* Vivian es una cocinera extraordinaria.

ambassador [æm'bæsədə^r] NOUN
el embajador
la embajadora

amber ['æmbə^r] ADJECTIVE
◆ **an amber light** (*when driving*) un semáforo en ámbar

ambition [æm'bɪʃən] NOUN
la ambición (PL las ambiciones)

ambitious [æm'bɪʃəs] ADJECTIVE
ambicioso

ambulance ['æmbjuləns] NOUN
la ambulancia

amenities [ə'mi:nɪtɪz] PL NOUN
◆ **The hotel has very good amenities.** El hotel tiene excelentes servicios e instalaciones.
◆ **The town has many amenities.** La ciudad ofrece gran variedad de servicios.

America [ə'mɛrɪkə] NOUN
1 los Estados Unidos MASC PL (*United States*)
2 América FEM (*continent*)

American [ə'mɛrɪkən] ADJECTIVE
see also **American** NOUN
norteamericano

American [ə'mɛrɪkən] NOUN
see also **American** ADJECTIVE
el norteamericano
la norteamericana
◇ *the Americans* los norteamericanos

among [ə'mʌŋ] PREPOSITION
entre

amount [ə'maunt] NOUN
la cantidad ◇ *a huge amount of rice* una cantidad enorme de arroz
◆ **a large amount of money** una alta suma de dinero

amp [æmp] NOUN
1 el amplificador (*amplifier*)
2 el amperio (*ampere*)

amplifier ['æmplɪfaɪə^r] NOUN
el amplificador

to **amuse** [ə'mju:z] VERB
1 divertir* ◇ *The thought seemed to amuse him.* La idea parecía divertirle.
2 entretener* ◇ *He was most amused by the story.* El cuento le entretuvo mucho.

amusement arcade [ə'mju:zməntɑ:'keɪd] NOUN
el salón de juegos

an [æn, ən] INDEFINITE ARTICLE *see* **a**

to **analyse** ['ænəlaɪz] VERB
analizar*

analysis [ə'næləsɪs] NOUN (PL **analyses**)
el análisis (PL los análisis)

to **analyze** ['ænəlaɪz] VERB US
analizar*

ancestor ['ænsɪstə^r] NOUN
el antepasado

anchor ['æŋkə^r] NOUN
el ancla FEM
Although it's a feminine noun, remember that you use ***el*** *and* ***un*** *with* ***ancla.***

ancient ['eɪnʃənt] ADJECTIVE
antiguo ◇ *ancient Greece* la antigua Grecia
◆ **an ancient monument** un monumento histórico

and [ænd] CONJUNCTION
y ◇ *Mary and Jane.* Mary y Jane.
Use ***e*** *to translate* ***and*** *before words beginning with "i" or "hi" but not "hie".*
◇ *Miguel and Ignacio.* Miguel e Ignacio.
and *is not translated when linking numbers.*
◇ *two hundred and fifty* doscientos cincuenta
◆ **Please try and come!** ¡Procura venir*!
◆ **He talked and talked.** No paraba de hablar.
◆ **better and better** cada vez mejor

angel ['eɪndʒəl] NOUN
el ángel

anger ['æŋgə^r] NOUN
el enfado (el enojo *LatAm*)

angle ['æŋgl] NOUN
el ángulo

angler ['æŋglə^r] NOUN
el pescador
la pescadora

angling ['æŋglɪŋ] NOUN
◆ **His hobby is angling.** Su hobby es la pesca.

angry ['æŋgrɪ] ADJECTIVE
enfadado (enojado *LatAm*) ◇ *to be angry with somebody* estar* enfadado con alguien ◇ *Your father looks very angry.* Tu padre parece estar muy enfadado.
◆ **to get angry** enfadarse (enojarse *LatAm*)

animal ['ænɪməl] NOUN
el animal

ankle ['æŋkl] NOUN
el tobillo ◇ *I've twisted my ankle.* Me he torcido el tobillo.

anniversary [ænɪ'və:sərɪ] NOUN (PL **anniversaries**)
el aniversario ◇ *wedding anniversary* aniversario de bodas

to **announce** [ə'nauns] VERB
anunciar

announcement [ə'naunsmənt] NOUN
el anuncio

to **annoy** [ə'nɔɪ] VERB
molestar ◇ *Make a note of the things that annoy you.* Haz una lista de las cosas que te molestan.
◆ **He's really annoying me.** Me está fastidiando de verdad.
◆ **to be annoyed with somebody** estar* molesto con alguien
◆ **to get annoyed** enfadarse (enojarse LatAm) ◇ *Don't get annoyed!* ¡No te enfades!

annoying [ə'nɔɪɪŋ] ADJECTIVE
molesto ◇ *the most annoying problem* el problema más molesto
◆ **I find it very annoying.** Me molesta mucho.

annual ['ænjuəl] ADJECTIVE
anual

anonymous [ə'nɔnɪməs] ADJECTIVE
anónimo

anorak ['ænəræk] NOUN
el anorak (PL los anoraks)

another [ə'nʌðəʳ] ADJECTIVE, PRONOUN
otro ◇ *Have you got another skirt?* ¿Tienes otra falda?
◆ **Another two kilometres.** Dos kilómetros más.

to **answer** ['ɑːnsəʳ] VERB
see also **answer** NOUN
responder ◇ *Can you answer my question?* ¿Puedes contestar a mi pregunta?
◆ **to answer the phone** contestar al teléfono
◆ **to answer the door** abrir* la puerta ◇ *Can you answer the door please?* ¿Puedes ir a abrir la puerta?

answer ['ɑːnsəʳ] NOUN
see also **answer** VERB
1 (*to question*)
la respuesta
2 (*to problem*)
la solución (PL las soluciones)

answering machine ['ɑːnsərɪŋmə'ʃiːn] NOUN
el contestador automático

ant [ænt] NOUN
la hormiga

Antarctic [ænt'ɑːktɪk] NOUN
◆ **the Antarctic** el Antártico

anthem ['ænθəm] NOUN
◆ **the national anthem** el himno nacional

antibiotic ['æntɪbaɪ'ɔtɪk] NOUN
el antibiótico

antidepressant [æntɪdɪ'presnt] NOUN
el antidepresivo

antique [æn'tiːk] NOUN
la antigüedad

antique shop [æn'tiːkʃɔp] NOUN
la tienda de antigüedades

antiseptic [æntɪ'sɛptɪk] NOUN
el antiséptico

any ['ɛnɪ] ADJECTIVE, ADVERB
see also **any** PRONOUN

In questions and negative sentences ***any*** *is usually not translated.*

◇ *Have you got any change?* ¿Tienes cambio? ◇ *Are there any beans left?* ¿Quedan alubias? ◇ *He hasn't got any friends.* No tiene amigos.

Use ***algún/alguna*** *+ singular noun in questions and* ***ningún/ninguna*** *+ singular noun in negatives where* ***any*** *is used with plural nouns and the number of items is important.*

◇ *Do you speak any foreign languages?* ¿Hablas algún idioma extranjero? ◇ *I haven't got any books by Cervantes.* No tengo ningún libro de Cervantes.

Use ***cualquier*** *in affirmative sentences.*

◇ *Any teacher will tell you.* Cualquier profesor te lo dirá.
◆ **Come any time you like.** Ven cuando quieras.
◆ **Would you like any more coffee?** ¿Quieres más café?
◆ **I don't love him any more.** Ya no le quiero.

any ['ɛnɪ] PRONOUN
see also **any** ADJECTIVE, ADVERB
1 (*in questions*)
alguno MASC
alguna FEM
◇ *I need a stamp. Have you got any left?* Necesito un sello. ¿Te queda alguno?

Only use ***alguno/alguna*** *if* ***any*** *refers to a countable noun. Otherwise don't translate it.*

◇ *I fancy some soup. Have we got any?* Me apetece sopa. ¿Tenemos?
2 (*in negatives*)
ninguno MASC
ninguna FEM
◇ *I don't like any of them.* No me gusta ninguno.

Only use ***ninguno/ninguna*** *if* ***any*** *refers to a countable noun. Otherwise don't translate it.*

◇ *Did you buy the oranges? – No, there weren't any.* ¿Compraste las naranjas? – No, no había.

anybody ['ɛnɪbɔdɪ] PRONOUN
1 alguien

Use ***alguien*** *in questions.*

◇ *Has anybody got a pen?* ¿Tiene alguien un bolígrafo?
2 nadie

Use ***nadie*** *in negative sentences.*

◇ *I can't see anybody.* No veo a nadie.
3 cualquiera

Use ***cualquiera*** *in affirmative sentences.*

◇ *Anybody can learn to swim.* Cualquiera puede aprender a nadar.

anyhow ['ɛnɪhau] ADVERB

☞

de todas maneras ◊ *He doesn't want to go out and anyhow he's not allowed.* No quiere salir* y de todas maneras no le dejan.

anyone ['ɛnɪwʌn] PRONOUN
1 alguien
*Use **alguien** in questions.*
◊ *Has anyone got a pen?* ¿Tiene alguien un bolígrafo?
2 nadie
*Use **nadie** in negative sentences.*
◊ *I can't see anyone.* No veo a nadie.
3 cualquiera
*Use **cualquiera** in affirmative sentences.*
◊ *Anyone can learn to swim.* Cualquiera puede aprender a nadar.

anything ['ɛnɪθɪŋ] PRONOUN
1 algo
*Use **algo** in questions.*
◊ *Do you need anything?* ¿Necesitas algo? ◊ *Would you like anything to eat?* ¿Quieres algo de comer?
2 nada
*Use **nada** in negative sentences.*
◊ *I can't hear anything.* No oigo nada.
3 cualquier cosa
*Use **cualquier cosa** in affirmative sentences.*
◊ *Anything could happen.* Puede pasar cualquier cosa.

anyway ['ɛnɪweɪ] ADVERB
de todas maneras ◊ *He doesn't want to go out and anyway he's not allowed.* No quiere salir* y de todas maneras no le dejan.

anywhere ['ɛnɪwɛəʳ] ADVERB
1 en algún sitio
*Use **en** or **a algún sitio** in questions.*
◊ *Have you seen my coat anywhere?* ¿Has visto mi abrigo en algún sitio? ◊ *Are we going anywhere?* ¿Vamos a algún sitio?
2 en ningún sitio
*Use **en** or **a ningún sitio** in negative sentences.*
◊ *I can't find it anywhere.* No lo encuentro en ningún sitio. ◊ *I can't go anywhere.* No puedo ir* a ningún sitio.
3 en cualquier sitio
*Use **en cualquier sitio** in affirmative sentences.*
◊ *You can buy stamps almost anywhere.* Se pueden comprar sellos casi en cualquier sitio.
♦ **You can sit anywhere you like.** Siéntate donde quieras.

apart [ə'pɑːt] ADVERB
♦ **The two towns are 10 kilometres apart.** Los dos pueblos están a 10 kilómetros el uno del otro.
♦ **It was the first time we had been apart.** Era la primera vez que estábamos separados.
♦ **apart from** aparte de ◊ *Apart from that, everything's fine.* Aparte de eso, todo va bien.

apartment [ə'pɑːtmənt] NOUN
el piso (el apartamento *LatAm*)

to **apologize** [ə'pɒlədʒaɪz] VERB
disculparse ◊ *He apologized for being late.* Se disculpó por llegar* tarde.
♦ **I apologize!** ¡Lo siento!

apology [ə'pɒlədʒɪ] NOUN (PL **apologies**)
la disculpa ◊ *I owe you an apology.* Te debo una disculpa.

apostrophe [ə'pɒstrəfɪ] NOUN
el apóstrofo

apparatus [æpə'reɪtəs] NOUN (PL **apparatus** *or* **apparatuses**)
los aparatos

apparent [ə'pærənt] ADJECTIVE
1 aparente ◊ *for no apparent reason* sin razón aparente
2 claro ◊ *It was apparent that he disliked me.* Estaba claro que no le caigo bien.

apparently [ə'pærəntlɪ] ADVERB
por lo visto (dizque *LatAm*)
♦ **Apparently he was abroad when it happened.** Por lo visto estaba en el extranjero cuando ocurrió.

to **appeal** [ə'piːl] VERB
see also **appeal** NOUN
1 hacer* un llamamiento ◊ *They appealed for help.* Hicieron un llamamiento de ayuda.
2 atraer* ◊ *Greece doesn't appeal to me.* Grecia no me atrae.

appeal [ə'piːl] NOUN
see also **appeal** VERB
el llamamiento ◊ *They have launched an appeal for unity.* Han hecho un llamamiento a la unidad.

to **appear** [ə'pɪəʳ] VERB
1 aparecer* ◊ *The bus appeared around the corner.* El autobús apareció por la esquina.
♦ **to appear on TV** salir* en la tele
2 parecer* ◊ *She appeared to be asleep.* Parecía estar dormida.

appearance [ə'pɪərəns] NOUN
el aspecto ◊ *She takes great care over her appearance.* Cuida mucho su aspecto.
♦ **to make an appearance** aparecer*

appendicitis [əpendɪ'saɪtɪs] NOUN
la apendicitis ◊ *She's got appendicitis.* Tiene apendicitis.

appetite ['æpɪtaɪt] NOUN
el apetito

to **applaud** [ə'plɔːd] VERB

aplaudir
applause [ə'plɔːz] NOUN
los aplausos
apple ['æpl] NOUN
la manzana
♦ **an apple tree** un manzano
applicant ['æplɪkənt] NOUN
el candidato
la candidata
application [æplɪ'keɪʃən] NOUN
♦ **a job application** una solicitud de empleo
application form [æplɪ'keɪʃənfɔːm] NOUN
el impreso de solicitud
to **apply** [ə'plaɪ] VERB **(applied, applied)**
♦ **to apply for a job** solicitar un empleo
♦ **to apply to** afectar a ◊ *This rule doesn't apply to us.* Esta norma no nos afecta.
to **appoint** [ə'pɔɪnt] VERB
nombrar ◊ *They appointed him chairman.* Le nombraron presidente.
Be careful not to translate ***to appoint*** *by* ***apuntar****.*
appointment [ə'pɔɪntmənt] NOUN
la cita ◊ *to make an appointment with someone* concertar* una cita con alguien
♦ **I've got a dental appointment.** Tengo hora con el dentista.
to **appreciate** [ə'priːʃɪeɪt] VERB
agradecer* ◊ *I really appreciate your help.* Agradezco de veras tu ayuda.
apprentice [ə'prentɪs] NOUN
el aprendiz (PL los aprendices)
la aprendiza
to **approach** [ə'prəutʃ] VERB
1 acercarse* a ◊ *He approached the house.* Se acercó a la casa.
2 abordar ◊ *to approach a problem* abordar un problema
appropriate [ə'prəuprɪɪt] ADJECTIVE
apropiado ◊ *That dress isn't very appropriate for an interview.* Ese vestido no es muy apropiado para una entrevista.
♦ **Tick the appropriate box.** Marque la casilla que corresponda.
approval [ə'pruːvəl] NOUN
la aprobación
to **approve** [ə'pruːv] VERB
♦ **I don't approve of his choice.** No me parece bien su elección.
♦ **They didn't approve of his girlfriend.** No veían con buenos ojos a su novia.
approximate [ə'prɔksɪmɪt] ADJECTIVE
aproximado
apricot ['eɪprɪkɔt] NOUN
el albaricoque
April ['eɪprəl] NOUN
abril MASC ◊ *in April* en abril ◊ *on 4 April* el 4 de abril
♦ **April Fool's Day** el día de los Santos Inocentes (*1 de abril*)

ⓘ *In Spanish-speaking countries* ***el día de los Santos Inocentes*** *falls on the 28th of December. People play practical jokes in the same way as they do on April Fool's Day.*

apron ['eɪprən] NOUN
el delantal
Aquarius [ə'kwɛərɪəs] NOUN
el Acuario (*sign*) ◊ *I'm Aquarius.* Soy Acuario.
♦ **an Aquarius** un/una Acuario
Arab ['ærəb] ADJECTIVE
see also **Arab** NOUN
árabe
Arab ['ærəb] NOUN
see also **Arab** ADJECTIVE
el/la árabe ◊ *the Arabs* los árabes
Arabic ['ærəbɪk] ADJECTIVE
árabe
arch [ɑːtʃ] NOUN (PL **arches**)
el arco
archaeologist [ɑːkɪ'ɔlədʒɪst] NOUN
el arqueólogo
la arqueóloga
◊ *He's an archaeologist.* Es arqueólogo.
archaeology [ɑːkɪ'ɔlədʒɪ] NOUN
la arqueología
archbishop [ɑːtʃ'bɪʃəp] NOUN
el arzobispo
archeologist [ɑːkɪ'ɔlədʒɪst] NOUN US
el arqueólogo
la arqueóloga
archeology [ɑːkɪ'ɔlədʒɪ] NOUN US
la arqueología
architect ['ɑːkɪtɛkt] NOUN
el arquitecto
la arquitecta
◊ *She's an architect.* Es arquitecta.
architecture ['ɑːkɪtɛktʃəʳ] NOUN
la arquitectura
Arctic ['ɑːktɪk] NOUN
♦ **the Arctic** el Ártico
are [ɑːʳ] VERB *see* **be**
area ['ɛərɪə] NOUN
1 la zona ◊ *a mountainous area of Spain* una zona montañosa de España
2 la superficie ◊ *The field has an area of 1500 m2.* El terreno tiene una superficie de 1500 m2.
3 el área FEM (*in football*)
Although it's a feminine noun, remember that you use ***el*** *and* ***un*** *with* ***área****.*
Argentina [ɑːdʒən'tiːnə] NOUN
Argentina FEM
Argentinian [ɑːdʒən'tɪnɪən] ADJECTIVE
see also **Argentinian** NOUN
argentino
Argentinian [ɑːdʒən'tɪnɪən] NOUN
see also **Argentinian** ADJECTIVE

☞

el argentino
la argentina

to **argue** ['ɑ:gju:] VERB
discutir ◊ *They never stop arguing.* Siempre están discutiendo.

argument ['ɑ:gjumənt] NOUN
la discusión (PL las discusiones) ◊ *to have an argument* discutir

Aries ['ɛərɪz] NOUN
el Aries (*sign*) ◊ *I'm Aries.* Soy Aries.
◆ **an Aries** un/una Aries

arm [ɑ:m] NOUN
el brazo ◊ *I burnt my arm.* Me quemé el brazo.

armchair ['ɑ:mtʃɛəʳ] NOUN
el sillón (PL los sillones)

armour ['ɑ:məʳ] NOUN (US **armor**)
la armadura

army ['ɑ:mɪ] NOUN (PL **armies**)
el ejército

around [ə'raund] PREPOSITION, ADVERB
1 alrededor de ◊ *She wore a scarf around her neck.* Llevaba una bufanda alrededor del cuello. ◊ *It costs around £100.* Cuesta alrededor de 100 libras.
◆ **She ignored the people around her.** Ignoró a la gente que estaba a su alrededor.
◆ **Shall we meet at around 8 o'clock?** ¿Quedamos sobre las 8?
2 por ◊ *I've been walking around the town.* He estado paseando por la ciudad.
◆ **We walked around for a while.** Paseamos por ahí durante un rato.
◆ **around here** por aquí ◊ *Is there a chemist's around here?* ¿Hay alguna farmacia por aquí?

to **arrange** [ə'reɪndʒ] VERB
organizar* ◊ *to arrange a party* organizar una fiesta
◆ **to arrange to do something** quedar en hacer* algo ◊ *They arranged to go out together on Friday.* Quedaron en salir* juntos el viernes.

arrangement [ə'reɪndʒmənt] NOUN
◆ **to make an arrangement to do something** quedar en hacer* algo
◆ **a flower arrangement** un arreglo floral
◆ **arrangements** los preparativos ◊ *Pamela is in charge of the travel arrangements.* Pamela se encarga de los preparativos para el viaje.
◆ **They made arrangements to go out on Friday night.** Hicieron planes de salir* el viernes por la noche.

to **arrest** [ə'rɛst] VERB
see also **arrest** NOUN
detener*

arrest [ə'rɛst] NOUN
see also **arrest** VERB
la detención (PL las detenciones)
◆ **You're under arrest!** ¡Queda detenido!

arrival [ə'raɪvl] NOUN
la llegada ◊ *the airport arrivals hall* la sala de llegadas del aeropuerto

to **arrive** [ə'raɪv] VERB
llegar* ◊ *I arrived at 5 o'clock.* Llegué a las 5.

arrogant ['ærəgənt] ADJECTIVE
arrogante

arrow ['ærəu] NOUN
la flecha

art [ɑ:t] NOUN
el arte
◆ **works of art** las obras de arte
◆ **art school** la escuela de Bellas Artes

artery ['ɑ:tərɪ] NOUN (PL **arteries**)
la arteria

art gallery [ɑ:t'gælərɪ] NOUN (PL **art galleries**)
1 el museo (*state-owned*)
2 la galería de arte (*private*)

article ['ɑ:tɪkl] NOUN
el artículo

artificial [ɑ:tɪ'fɪʃəl] ADJECTIVE
artificial

artist ['ɑ:tɪst] NOUN
el/la artista ◊ *She's an artist.* Es artista.

artistic [ɑ:'tɪstɪk] ADJECTIVE
artístico

as [æz, əz] CONJUNCTION, ADVERB
1 cuando ◊ *He came in as I was leaving.* Entró cuando yo me iba.
2 mientras ◊ *All the jury's eyes were on him as he continued.* Todo el jurado le observaba mientras él proseguía.
3 como ◊ *As it's Sunday, you can have a lie-in.* Como es domingo, puedes quedarte en la cama hasta tarde.
4 de ◊ *He works as a waiter in the holidays.* En vacaciones trabaja de camarero.
◆ **as...as** tan...como ◊ *Peter's as tall as Michael.* Peter es tan alto como Michael.
◆ **as much...as** tanto...como ◊ *I haven't got as much energy as you.* No tengo tanta energía como tú. ◊ *Her coat cost twice as much as mine.* Su abrigo costó el doble que el mío.
◆ **as soon as possible** cuanto antes
◆ **as from tomorrow** a partir de mañana
◆ **as if** como si

> ***como si** has to be followed by a verb in the subjunctive.*

◊ *She acted as if she hadn't seen me.* Hizo como si no me hubiese visto.
◆ **as though** como si ◊ *She acted as though she hadn't seen me.* Hizo como si no me hubiese visto.

asap [eɪeseɪ'pi:] ABBREVIATION (= *as soon as possible*)
cuanto antes

ash [æʃ] NOUN

* Verbs marked with this symbol are irregular. See pages 380-382 for further details

1 la ceniza (*from fire, cigarette*)
2 el fresno (*tree, wood*)

ashamed [ə'ʃeɪmd] ADJECTIVE
- **to be ashamed** estar* avergonzado ◊ *I'm ashamed of myself for shouting at you.* Estoy avergonzado de gritarte.
- **You should be ashamed of yourself!** ¡Debería darte vergüenza!

ashtray ['æʃtreɪ] NOUN
el cenicero

Asia ['eɪʃə] NOUN
Ásia FEM

Asian ['eɪʃən] ADJECTIVE
see also **Asian** NOUN
asiático

Asian ['eɪʃən] NOUN
see also **Asian** ADJECTIVE
el asiático
la asiática

to **ask** [ɑːsk] VERB
1 preguntar ◊ *"Have you finished?" she asked.* "¿Has terminado?" preguntó.
- **to ask somebody something** preguntar algo a alguien
- **to ask about something** preguntar por algo ◊ *I asked about train times to Leeds.* Pregunté por el horario de trenes a Leeds.
- **to ask somebody a question** hacer* una pregunta a alguien

2 pedir* ◊ *She asked him to do the shopping.* Le pidió que hiciera la compra.

__pedir que__ has to be followed by a verb in the subjunctive.

- **to ask for something** pedir algo ◊ *He asked for a cup of tea.* Pidió una taza de té.
- **Peter asked her out.** Peter le pidió que saliera con él.

3 invitar ◊ *Have you asked Matthew to the party?* ¿Has invitado a Matthew a la fiesta?

asleep [ə'sliːp] ADJECTIVE
- **to be asleep** estar* dormido
- **to fall asleep** quedarse dormido

asparagus [əs'pærəgəs] NOUN
los espárragos

aspect ['æspɛkt] NOUN
el aspecto

aspirin ['æsprɪn] NOUN
la aspirina

asset ['æsɛt] NOUN
la ventaja ◊ *Her experience will be an asset to the firm.* Su experiencia supondrá una ventaja para la empresa.

assignment [ə'saɪnmənt] NOUN
la tarea (*at school*)

assistance [ə'sɪstəns] NOUN
la ayuda

assistant [ə'sɪstənt] NOUN
1 (*in shop*)
el dependiente
la dependienta
2 (*helper*)
el/la ayudante

association [əsəusɪ'eɪʃən] NOUN
la asociación (PL las asociaciones)

assortment [ə'sɔːtmənt] NOUN
el surtido

to **assume** [ə'sjuːm] VERB
suponer* ◊ *I assume she won't be coming.* Supongo que no vendrá.

to **assure** [ə'ʃuəʳ] VERB
asegurar ◊ *He assured me he was coming.* Me aseguró que venía.

asthma ['æsmə] NOUN
el asma FEM

Although it's a feminine noun, remember that you use __el__ with __asma__.

◊ *He's got asthma.* Tiene asma.

to **astonish** [ə'stɔnɪʃ] VERB
pasmar

astrology [əs'trɔlədʒɪ] NOUN
la astrología

astronaut ['æstrənɔːt] NOUN
el/la astronauta

astronomy [əs'trɔnəmɪ] NOUN
la astronomía

asylum seeker [ə'saɪləmsiːkəʳ] NOUN
el/la solicitante de asilo

at [æt] PREPOSITION
1 en ◊ *at home* en casa ◊ *at school* en la escuela ◊ *at the office* en la oficina
2 a ◊ *at 50 km/h* a 50 km/h
- **two at a time** de dos en dos
- **at 4 o'clock** a las 4
- **at night** por la noche
- **at Christmas** en Navidad
- **What are you doing at the weekend?** ¿Qué haces este fin de semana?

ate [eɪt] VERB *see* **eat**

Athens ['æθɪnz] NOUN
Atenas FEM

athlete ['æθliːt] NOUN
el/la atleta

athletic [æθ'lɛtɪk] ADJECTIVE
atlético

athletics [æθ'lɛtɪks] NOUN
el atletismo ◊ *I enjoy watching the athletics on television.* Me gusta ver* el atletismo en la televisión.

Atlantic [ət'læntɪk] NOUN
el Atlántico

atlas ['ætləs] NOUN (PL **atlases**)
el atlas (PL los atlas)

atmosphere ['ætməsfɪəʳ] NOUN
la atmósfera

atom ['ætəm] NOUN
el átomo

atomic [ə'tɔmɪk] ADJECTIVE
atómico

to **attach** [ə'tætʃ] VERB
atar ◊ *They attached a rope to the car.* Ataron una cuerda al coche.

◆ **Please find attached a cheque for £10.** Se adjunta cheque de 10 libras.

attached [ə'tætʃt] ADJECTIVE
◆ **to be attached to somebody** tener* cariño a alguien

to **attack** [ə'tæk] VERB
see also **attack** NOUN
atacar*

attack [ə'tæk] NOUN
see also **attack** VERB
el ataque
◆ **to be under attack** ser* atacado

attempt [ə'tɛmpt] NOUN
see also **attempt** VERB
el intento

to **attempt** [ə'tɛmpt] VERB
see also **attempt** NOUN
◆ **to attempt to do something** intentar hacer algo ◊ *I attempted to write a song.* Intenté escribir una canción.

to **attend** [ə'tɛnd] VERB
asistir a ◊ *to attend a meeting* asistir a una reunión

attention [ə'tɛnʃən] NOUN
la atención
◆ **to pay attention to** prestar atención a ◊ *He didn't pay attention to what I was saying.* No prestó atención a lo que estaba diciendo.
◆ **Don't pay any attention to him!** ¡No le hagas caso!

attic ['ætɪk] NOUN
el desván (PL los desvanes)
(el altillo *LatAm*)

attitude ['ætɪtju:d] NOUN
la actitud

attorney [ə'tə:nɪ] NOUN US
el abogado
la abogada

to **attract** [ə'trækt] VERB
atraer* ◊ *The Lake District attracts lots of tourists.* La Región de los Lagos atrae a muchos turistas.

attraction [ə'trækʃən] NOUN
la atracción (PL las atracciones) ◊ *a tourist attraction* una atracción turística

attractive [ə'træktɪv] ADJECTIVE
atractivo

aubergine ['əubəʒi:n] NOUN
la berenjena

auction ['ɔ:kʃən] NOUN
la subasta

audience ['ɔ:dɪəns] NOUN
el público

audition [ɔ:'dɪʃən] NOUN
la prueba

August ['ɔ:gəst] NOUN
agosto MASC ◊ *in August* en agosto ◊ *on 13 August* el 13 agosto

aunt [ɑ:nt] NOUN
la tía
◆ **my aunt and uncle** mis tíos

aunty ['ɑ:ntɪ] NOUN (PL **aunties**)
la tía

au pair ['əu'pɛə^r] NOUN
la au pair (PL las au pairs)

Australia [ɔs'treɪlɪə] NOUN
Australia FEM

Australian [ɔs'treɪlɪən] ADJECTIVE
see also **Australian** NOUN
australiano

Australian [ɔs'treɪlɪən] NOUN
see also **Australian** ADJECTIVE
el australiano
la australiana
◊ *the Australians* los australianos

Austria ['ɔstrɪə] NOUN
Austria FEM

Austrian ['ɔstrɪən] ADJECTIVE
see also **Austrian** NOUN
austríaco

Austrian ['ɔstrɪən] NOUN
see also **Austrian** ADJECTIVE
el austríaco
la austríaca
◊ *the Austrians* los austríacos

author ['ɔ:θə^r] NOUN
el autor
la autora
◊ *the author of the book* el autor del libro
◊ *a famous author* un escritor famoso

autobiography [ɔ:təbaɪ'ɔgrəfɪ] NOUN (PL **autobiographies**)
la autobiografía

autograph ['ɔ:təgrɑ:f] NOUN
el autógrafo

automatic [ɔ:tə'mætɪk] ADJECTIVE
automático

automatically [ɔ:tə'mætɪklɪ] ADVERB
automáticamente

autumn ['ɔ:təm] NOUN
el otoño ◊ *in autumn* en el otoño

availability [əveɪlə'bɪlɪtɪ] NOUN
la disponibilidad

available [ə'veɪləbl] ADJECTIVE
disponible ◊ *According to the available information, it can't be done.* De acuerdo con la información disponible, no se puede hacer*.
◆ **Free brochures are available on request.** Disponemos de folletos gratuitos para quien los solicite.
◆ **Is Mr Cooke available today?** ¿Está libre el señor Cooke hoy?

avalanche ['ævəlɑ:nʃ] NOUN
el alud

avenue ['ævənju:] NOUN
la avenida

average ['ævərɪdʒ] NOUN
see also **average** ADJECTIVE

la media ◊ *on average* de media

average ['ævərɪdʒ] ADJECTIVE

see also **average** NOUN

medio ◊ *the average price* el precio medio

avocado [ævə'kɑːdəu] NOUN (PL **avocados**)

el aguacate

to **avoid** [ə'vɔɪd] VERB

evitar ◊ *Avoid going out on your own at night.* Evite salir* solo por la noche.

awake [ə'weɪk] ADJECTIVE

♦ **to be awake** estar* despierto

award [ə'wɔːd] NOUN

el premio ◊ *the award for the best actor* el premio al mejor actor

aware [ə'wɛəʳ] ADJECTIVE

♦ **to be aware that** saber que

♦ **to be aware of something** ser consciente de algo ◊ *We are aware of what is happening.* Somos conscientes de lo que ocurre.

♦ **not that I am aware of** que yo sepa, no

away [ə'weɪ] ADJECTIVE, ADVERB

♦ **It's two kilometres away.** Está a dos kilómetros de distancia.

♦ **The coast is two hours away by car.** La costa está a dos horas en coche.

♦ **The holiday was two weeks away.** Faltaban dos semanas para las vacaciones.

♦ **to be away** estar* fuera ◊ *Jason was away on a business trip.* Jason estaba fuera en viaje de negocios.

♦ **He's away for a week.** Se ha ido una semana.

♦ **Go away!** ¡Vete!

♦ **away from** lejos de ◊ *away from family and friends* lejos de la familia y los amigos

♦ **It's 30 miles away from town.** Está a 30 millas de la ciudad.

away *se emplea a veces para recalcar la continuidad o reiteración de la acción del verbo.*

◊ *He was still working away in the library.* Seguía trabajando sin parar en la biblioteca.

away match [ə'weɪ mætʃ] NOUN (PL **away matches**)

♦ **It is their last away match.** Es el último partido que juegan fuera.

awful ['ɔːfəl] ADJECTIVE

horrible ◊ *The weather's awful.* Hace un tiempo horrible.

♦ **I feel awful.** Me siento fatal.

♦ **We met and I thought he was awful.** Nos conocimos y me cayó fatal.

♦ **an awful lot of work** un montón de trabajo

awfully ['ɔːfəlɪ] ADVERB

♦ **I'm awfully sorry.** Lo siento muchísimo.

awkward ['ɔːkwəd] ADJECTIVE

1 incómodo ◊ *It was awkward to carry.* Era incómodo de llevar. ◊ *an awkward situation* una situación incómoda

♦ **Mike's being awkward about letting me have the car.** Mike no hace más que ponerme pegas para dejarme el coche.

♦ **It's a bit awkward for me to come and see you.** Me viene un poco mal pasar a verte.

2 torpe ◊ *an awkward gesture* un gesto torpe

axe [æks] NOUN

el hacha FEM

Although it's a feminine noun, remember that you use ***el*** *and* ***un*** *with* ***hacha****.*

B

BA [biːˈeɪ] ABBREVIATION (= *Bachelor of Arts*)
la licenciatura en Letras
◆ **a BA in French** una licenciatura en Filología Francesa
◆ **She's got a BA in History.** Es licenciada en Historia.

baby [ˈbeɪbɪ] NOUN (PL **babies**)
el/la bebé (PL los/las bebés)

baby carriage [beɪbɪkærɪdʒ] NOUN US
el cochecito de niño

to **babysit** [ˈbeɪbɪsɪt] VERB (**babysat, babysat**)
hacer* de canguro

babysitter [ˈbeɪbɪsɪtəʳ] NOUN
el/la canguro

babysitting [ˈbeɪbɪsɪtɪŋ] NOUN
◆ **I don't like babysitting.** No me gusta hacer* de canguro.

bachelor [ˈbætʃələʳ] NOUN
el soltero

back [bæk] NOUN
see also **back** ADJECTIVE, ADVERB, VERB
1 la espalda (*of person*) ◊ *He's got a bad back.* Tiene problemas de espalda.
2 el lomo (*of animal*)
◆ **the back of a chair** el respaldo de una silla
◆ **on the back of the cheque** al dorso del cheque
◆ **at the back of the house** en la parte de atrás de la casa
◆ **in the back of the car** en la parte trasera del coche
◆ **at the back of the class** al fondo de la clase

back [bæk] ADJECTIVE, ADVERB
see also **back** NOUN, VERB
trasero ◊ *the back seat* el asiento trasero
◆ **the back door** la puerta de atrás
◆ **He's not back yet.** Todavía no ha vuelto.
◆ **to get back** volver* ◊ *What time did you get back?* ¿A qué hora volviste? ◊ *We went there by bus and walked back.* Fuimos allí en autobús y volvimos a pie.
◆ **to call somebody back** volver* a llamar a alguien
◆ **I'll call back later.** Volveré a llamar más tarde.

to **back** [bæk] VERB
see also **back** NOUN, ADJECTIVE
respaldar ◊ *The union is backing his claim for compensation.* El sindicato respalda su demanda de compensación.
◆ **to back a horse** apostar* por un caballo
◆ **She backed into the parking space.** Aparcó dando marcha atrás.

to **back out** [bækˈaut] VERB
echarse para atrás ◊ *They promised to help us and then backed out.* Prometieron ayudarnos y luego se echaron para atrás.

to **back up** [bækˈʌp] VERB
respaldar ◊ *She complained, and her colleagues backed her up.* Presentó una queja y sus colegas la respaldaron.

backache [ˈbækeɪk] NOUN
el dolor de espalda ◊ *to have backache* tener* dolor de espalda

backbone [ˈbækbəun] NOUN
la columna vertebral

to **backfire** [bækˈfaɪəʳ] VERB
tener* el efecto contrario (*go wrong*)

background [ˈbækgraund] NOUN
el fondo (*of picture*) ◊ *a house in the background* una casa en el fondo
◆ **background noise** ruido de fondo
◆ **his family background** su historial familiar

backhand [ˈbækhænd] NOUN
el revés (PL los reveses)

backing [ˈbækɪŋ] NOUN
el apoyo ◊ *They promised their backing.* Prometieron su apoyo.

backpack [ˈbækpæk] NOUN
la mochila

backpacker [ˈbækpækəʳ] NOUN
el mochilero
la mochilera

backside [ˈbæksaɪd] NOUN
el trasero

backstroke [ˈbækstrəuk] NOUN
la espalda

backup [ˈbækʌp] NOUN
el apoyo ◊ *We have extensive computer backup.* Tenemos amplio apoyo informático.
◆ **They've got a generator as an emergency backup.** Tienen un generador de reserva para emergencias.
◆ **a backup file** una copia de seguridad

backwards [ˈbækwədz] ADVERB
hacia atrás ◊ *to take a step backwards* dar* un paso hacia atrás
◆ **to fall backwards** caerse* de espaldas

back yard [bækˈjɑːd] NOUN
el patio trasero

bacon [ˈbeɪkən] NOUN
el bacon (el tocino *LatAm*) ◊ *bacon and eggs* los huevos fritos con bacon

bad [bæd] ADJECTIVE
1 malo ◊ *You bad boy!* ¡Malo!

* Verbs marked with this symbol are irregular. See pages 380-382 for further details

*Use **mal** before a masculine singular noun.*
◊ *bad weather* mal tiempo
♦ **to be in a bad mood** estar* de mal humor
♦ **to be bad at something** ser* malo para algo ◊ *I'm really bad at maths.* Soy muy malo para las matemáticas.
2 grave (*serious*) ◊ *a bad accident* un accidente grave
♦ **to go bad** (*food*) echarse a perder
♦ **I feel bad about it.** (*guilty*) Me siento un poco culpable.
♦ **How are you? – Not bad.** ¿Cómo estás? – Bien
♦ **That's not bad at all.** No está nada mal.
♦ **bad language** las palabrotas

badge [bædʒ] NOUN
1 la chapa (*metal, plastic*)
2 el escudo (*cloth*)

badly ['bædlɪ] ADVERB
mal ◊ *badly paid* mal pagado
♦ **badly wounded** gravemente herido
♦ **He badly needs a rest.** Le hace muchísima falta un descanso.

badminton ['bædmɪntən] NOUN
el bádminton ◊ *to play badminton* jugar* al bádminton

bad-tempered ['bæd'tɛmpəd] ADJECTIVE
♦ **to be bad-tempered (1)** (*by nature*) tener* mal genio ◊ *He's a really bad-tempered person.* Es una persona con muy mal genio.
♦ **to be bad-tempered (2)** (*temporarily*) estar* de mal humor ◊ *He was really bad-tempered yesterday.* Ayer estaba de muy mal humor.

to **baffle** ['bæfl] VERB
desconcertar*

bag [bæg] NOUN
la bolsa

baggage ['bægɪdʒ] NOUN
el equipaje

baggage reclaim ['bægɪdʒrɪkleɪm] NOUN
la recogida de equipajes

baggy ['bægɪ] ADJECTIVE
ancho (*trousers*)

bagpipes ['bægpaɪps] PL NOUN
la gaita SING

to **bake** [beɪk] VERB
♦ **to bake bread** hacer* pan
♦ **She loves to bake.** Le gusta cocinar al horno.

baked beans [beɪkt'biːnz] PL NOUN
las alubias blancas en salsa de tomate

baker ['beɪkəʳ] NOUN
el panadero
la panadera
◊ *He's a baker.* Es panadero. ◊ *at the baker's* en la panadería

bakery ['beɪkərɪ] NOUN (PL **bakeries**)
la panadería

baking ['beɪkɪŋ] ADJECTIVE
♦ **It's baking in here!** ¡Aquí hace un calor insoportable!

balance ['bæləns] NOUN
see also **balance** VERB
el equilibrio ◊ *to lose one's balance* perder* el equilibrio

to **balance** ['bæləns] VERB
see also **balance** NOUN
mantener* el equilibrio ◊ *I balanced on the window ledge.* Mantenía el equilibrio en el poyo de la ventana.
♦ **She balanced on one leg.** Se mantenía a la pata coja.
♦ **The boxes were carefully balanced.** Las cajas estaban cuidadosamente contrapesadas.

balanced ['bælənst] ADJECTIVE
equilibrado

balcony ['bælkənɪ] NOUN (PL **balconies**)
el balcón (PL los balcones)

bald [bɔːld] ADJECTIVE
calvo

ball [bɔːl] NOUN
1 (*for tennis, basketball, rugby*)
la pelota
2 (*for football*)
el balón (PL los balones) ◊ *a golf ball* una pelota de golf

ballet ['bæleɪ] NOUN
el ballet (PL los ballets) ◊ *We went to a ballet.* Fuimos a ver un ballet.
♦ **ballet lessons** las clases de ballet

ballet dancer ['bæleɪ'dɑːnsəʳ] NOUN
el bailarín (PL los bailarines)
la bailarina

ballet shoes ['bæleɪʃuːz] PL NOUN
las zapatillas de ballet

balloon [bə'luːn] NOUN
el globo
♦ **a hot-air balloon** un globo aerostático

ballpoint pen ['bɔːlpɔɪnt'pɛn] NOUN
el bolígrafo

ballroom dancing ['bɔːlrum'dɑːnsɪŋ] NOUN
el baile de salón

ban [bæn] NOUN
see also **ban** VERB
la prohibición (PL las prohibiciones)

to **ban** [bæn] VERB
see also **ban** NOUN
prohibir*

banana [bə'nɑːnə] NOUN
el plátano ◊ *a banana skin* una piel de plátano

band [bænd] NOUN
1 el grupo (*pop, rock*)
2 la banda (*military*)
3 la orquesta (*at a dance*)

bandage ['bændɪdʒ] NOUN
see also **bandage** VERB
la venda

to **bandage** ['bændɪdʒ] VERB
see also **bandage** NOUN
vendar ◊ *The nurse bandaged his arm.* La enfermera le vendó el brazo.

Band-Aid® ['bændeɪd] NOUN US la tirita

bandit ['bændɪt] NOUN
el bandido

bang [bæŋ] NOUN
see also **bang** VERB
1 el estallido (*noise*) ◊ *I heard a loud bang.* Oí un fuerte estallido.
2 el golpe (*blow*) ◊ *a bang on the head* un golpe en la cabeza

to **bang** [bæŋ] VERB
see also **bang** NOUN
golpear ◊ *I banged my head.* Me golpeé la cabeza.
◆ **to bang on the door** aporrear la puerta
◆ **to bang the door** dar* un portazo

banger ['bæŋəʳ] NOUN
la salchicha (*informal*) ◊ *bangers and mash* las salchichas con puré de patatas

bank [bæŋk] NOUN
1 el banco (*financial*)
2 la orilla (*of river, lake*)

bank account [bæŋkə'kaunt] NOUN
la cuenta bancaria

banker ['bæŋkəʳ] NOUN
el banquero
la banquera
◊ *He's a banker.* Es banquero.

bank holiday [bæŋk'hɔlɪdeɪ] NOUN
el día festivo

banknote ['bæŋknəut] NOUN
el billete de banco

to **bank on** ['bæŋkɔn] VERB
contar* con ◊ *I was banking on your coming today.* Contaba con que vendrías hoy.
◆ **I wouldn't bank on it.** Yo no me confiaría demasiado.

bankrupt ['bæŋkrʌpt] ADJECTIVE
en quiebra ◊ *to be bankrupt* estar en quiebra
◆ **to go bankrupt** ir a la quiebra

bar [bɑːʳ] NOUN
1 el bar (*pub*)
2 la barra (*counter*)
◆ **a bar of chocolate (1)** (*large*) una tableta de chocolate
◆ **a bar of chocolate (2)** (*small*) una chocolatina
◆ **a bar of soap** una pastilla de jabón

barbaric [bɑː'bærɪk] ADJECTIVE
bárbaro

barbecue ['bɑːbɪkjuː] NOUN
la barbacoa ◊ *to have a barbecue* hacer* una barbacoa

barber ['bɑːbəʳ] NOUN
el barbero ◊ *He's a barber.* Es barbero.
◊ *at the barber's* en la barbería

bare [beəʳ] ADJECTIVE
desnudo

barefoot ['beəfut] ADJECTIVE, ADVERB
descalzo ◊ *The children go around barefoot.* Los niños van descalzos.

barely ['beəlɪ] ADVERB
apenas ◊ *I could barely hear what she was saying.* Apenas oía lo que estaba diciendo.

bargain ['bɑːgɪn] NOUN
la ganga ◊ *It was a bargain!* ¡Era una ganga!

barge [bɑːdʒ] NOUN
la barcaza

to **bark** [bɑːk] VERB
ladrar

barmaid ['bɑːmeɪd] NOUN
la camarera ◊ *She's a barmaid.* Es camarera.

barman ['bɑːmən] NOUN (PL **barmen**)
el barman (PL los barmans)
◊ *He's a barman.* Es barman.

barn [bɑːn] NOUN
el granero

barrel ['bærəl] NOUN
1 (*container*)
el barril
2 (*of gun*)
el cañón (PL los cañones)

barrier ['bærɪəʳ] NOUN
la barrera

bartender ['bɑːtendəʳ] NOUN US
el barman (PL los barmans)
◊ *He's a bartender.* Es barman.

base [beɪs] NOUN
la base

baseball ['beɪsbɔːl] NOUN
el béisbol ◊ *to play baseball* jugar* al béisbol
◆ **a baseball cap** una gorra de béisbol

based [beɪst] ADJECTIVE
◆ **based on** basado en

basement ['beɪsmənt] NOUN
el sótano ◊ *a basement flat* un apartamento en el sótano

to **bash** [bæʃ] VERB
see also **bash** NOUN
golpear con fuerza

bash [bæʃ] NOUN
see also **bash** VERB
◆ **I'll have a bash at it.** Lo intentaré.

basic ['beɪsɪk] ADJECTIVE
básico ◊ *It's a basic model.* Es un modelo básico.
◆ **The accommodation was pretty basic.** El alojamiento tenía sólo lo imprescindible.

basically ['beɪsɪklɪ] ADVERB

básicamente ◊ *They are basically the same thing.* Son básicamente lo mismo.
◆ **Basically, Simon just doesn't like Michael.** Simplemente, que a Simon no le gusta Michael.

basics ['beɪsɪks] PL NOUN
los principios básicos

basil ['bæzl] NOUN
la albahaca

basin ['beɪsn] NOUN
1 el lavabo (*washbasin*)
2 el cuenco (*for cooking, mixing food*)

basis ['beɪsɪs] NOUN
la base ◊ *on the basis of what you've said* en base a lo que has dicho
◆ **on a daily basis** diariamente
◆ **on a regular basis** regularmente

basket ['bɑːskɪt] NOUN
el cesto

basketball ['bɑːskɪtbɔːl] NOUN
el baloncesto ◊ *John plays basketball every day.* John juega al baloncesto todos los días.

bass [beɪs] NOUN (PL **basses**)
el bajo (*voice*)
◆ **a bass guitar** un bajo
◆ **a double bass** un contrabajo

bass drum [beɪs'drʌm] NOUN
el bombo

bassoon [bə'suːn] NOUN
el fagot (PL los fagots)

bastard ['bɑːstəd] NOUN (*rude*)
el cabrón (PL los cabrones) ◊ *You bastard!* ¡Cabrón!

bat [bæt] NOUN
1 el bate (*for baseball, cricket*)
2 la raqueta (*for table tennis*)
3 el murciélago (*animal*)

bath [bɑːθ] NOUN
1 el baño
◆ **a hot bath** un baño caliente
◆ **to have a bath** bañarse
2 la bañera (*bathtub*)

to **bathe** [beɪð] VERB
bañarse

bathing suit ['beɪðɪŋsut] NOUN US
el traje de baño

bathroom ['bɑːθrum] NOUN
el cuarto de baño

baths [bɑːðz] PL NOUN
◆ **swimming baths** la piscina
◆ **Turkish baths** los baños turcos

bath towel ['bɑːθtauəl] NOUN
la toalla de baño

batter ['bætə^r] NOUN
la masa para rebozar

battery ['bætərɪ] NOUN (PL **batteries**)
1 la pila (*for torch, toy*)
2 la batería (*for car*)

battle ['bætl] NOUN
la batalla ◊ *the Battle of Hastings* la batalla de Hastings
◆ **It was a battle, but we managed in the end.** Fue muy difícil, pero al final lo conseguimos.

battleship ['bætlʃɪp] NOUN
el acorazado

bay [beɪ] NOUN
la bahía

BC [biː'siː] ABBREVIATION (= *before Christ*)
a.C. (= antes de Cristo)

to **be** [biː] VERB (**is, was, been**)

*There are two basic verbs to translate **be** into Spanish: **estar** and **ser**. **estar** is used to form continuous tenses; to talk about where something is; and with adjectives describing a temporary state. It is also used with past participles used adjectivally even if these describe a permanent state.*

1 estar* ◊ *What are you doing?* ¿Qué estás haciendo? ◊ *Edinburgh is in Scotland.* Edimburgo está en Escocia. ◊ *I've never been to Madrid.* No he estado nunca en Madrid. ◊ *I'm very happy.* Estoy muy contento. ◊ *The window is broken.* La ventana está rota. ◊ *Is he hurt?* ¿Está herido? ◊ *He's dead.* Está muerto.
◆ **You're late.** Llegas tarde.

***ser** is used to talk about the time and date; with adjectives describing permanent or inherent states such as nationality and colour; with nouns to say what somebody or something is; and to form the passive.*

2 ser* ◊ *It's four o'clock.* Son las cuatro. ◊ *It's the 28th of October today.* Hoy es 28 de octubre. ◊ *She's English.* Es inglesa. ◊ *He's a doctor.* Es médico. ◊ *Paris is the capital of France.* París es la capital de Francia. ◊ *He's very tall.* Es muy alto. ◊ *The house was destroyed by an earthquake.* La casa fue destruida por un terremoto.

Passive constructions are not as common in Spanish as in English. Either the active or a reflexive construction are preferred.

◊ *He was killed by a terrorist.* Lo mató un terrorista. ◊ *These cars are produced in Spain.* Estos coches se fabrican en España.

*When referring to the weather, use **hacer**.*

◆ **It's a nice day, isn't it?** Hace buen día, ¿verdad?
◆ **It's cold.** Hace frío.
◆ **It's too hot.** Hace demasiado calor.

*With certain adjectives, such as **cold**, **hot**, **hungry**, and **thirsty**, use **tener*** with a noun.*

◆ **I'm cold.** Tengo frío.
◆ **I'm hungry.** Tengo hambre.

☞

*When saying how old somebody is, use **tener**.*

◆**I'm fourteen.** Tengo catorce años.
◆**How old are you?** ¿Cuántos años tienes?

beach [biːtʃ] NOUN (PL **beaches**)
la playa

bead [biːd] NOUN
la cuenta

beak [biːk] NOUN
el pico

beam [biːm] NOUN
el rayo (*of light*)

beans [biːnz] PL NOUN
las alubias
◆**beans on toast** las alubias blancas en salsa de tomate sobre una tostada
◆**green beans** las judías verdes

bean sprouts ['biːnsprauts] PL NOUN
los brotes de soja

bear [bɛəʳ] NOUN
see also **bear** VERB
el oso

to **bear** [bɛəʳ] VERB (**bore, borne**)
see also **bear** NOUN
aguantar ◇ *I can't bear it!* ¡No lo aguanto!

to **bear with** [bɛə'wɪð] VERB
◆**If you would bear with me for a moment...** Tenga la bondad de esperar un momento...

beard [bɪəd] NOUN
la barba
◆**He's got a beard.** Lleva barba.
◆**a man with a beard** un hombre con barba

bearded ['bɪədɪd] ADJECTIVE
con barba

beat [biːt] NOUN
see also **beat** VERB
el ritmo

to **beat** [biːt] VERB (**beat, beaten**)
see also **beat** NOUN
1 ganar ◇ *We beat them three-nil.* Les ganamos tres a cero.
2 batir (*eggs*)
◆**Beat it!** ¡Lárgate! (*informal*)

to **beat up** [biːt'ʌp] VERB
dar* una paliza a

beautiful ['bjuːtɪful] ADJECTIVE
precioso

beauty ['bjuːtɪ] NOUN (PL **beauties**)
la belleza

beauty spot ['bjuːtɪspɔt] NOUN
el lugar pintoresco (*place*)

became [bɪ'keɪm] VERB *see* **become**

because [bɪ'kɔz] CONJUNCTION
porque
◆**because of** a causa de

to **become** [bɪ'kʌm] VERB (**became, become**)
llegar* a ser

bed [bɛd] NOUN
la cama
◆**to go to bed** acostarse*
◆**to go to bed with somebody** irse* a la cama con alguien

bed and breakfast [bɛdən'brɛkfəst] NOUN
la pensión (PL las pensiones) ◇ *We stayed in a bed and breakfast.* Nos quedamos en una pensión.
◆**How much is it for bed and breakfast?** ¿Cuánto es la habitación con desayuno?

bedclothes ['bɛdkləuðz] PL NOUN
la ropa de cama

bedding ['bɛdɪŋ] NOUN
la ropa de cama

bedroom ['bɛdrum] NOUN
el dormitorio
◆**a three-bedroom house** una casa de tres dormitorios

bedsit ['bɛdsɪt] NOUN

> ℹ *Un **bedsit** es una habitación amueblada, cuyo alquiler incluye cocina y baño comunes. Este sistema de alojamiento es muy común en Gran Bretaña entre estudiantes, jóvenes profesionales, etc.*

bedspread ['bɛdsprɛd] NOUN
la colcha

bedtime ['bɛdtaɪm] NOUN
◆**Ten o'clock is my usual bedtime.** Normalmente me voy a la cama a las diez.
◆**Bedtime!** ¡A la cama!

bee [biː] NOUN
la abeja

beef [biːf] NOUN
la carne de vaca
◆**roast beef** el rosbif

beefburger ['biːfbəːgəʳ] NOUN
la hamburguesa

been [biːn] VERB *see* **be**

beer [bɪəʳ] NOUN
la cerveza

beetle ['biːtl] NOUN
el escarabajo

beetroot ['biːtruːt] NOUN
la remolacha

before [bɪ'fɔːʳ] PREPOSITION, CONJUNCTION, ADVERB
1 antes de ◇ *before Tuesday* antes del martes ◇ *Before opening the packet, read the instructions.* Antes de abrir el paquete, lea las instrucciones. ◇ *I'll phone before I leave.* Llamaré antes de salir.
2 antes de que

antes de que *has to be followed by a verb in the subjunctive.*

◊ *I'll call her before she leaves.* La llamaré antes de que se vaya.

♦ **I've seen this film before.** Esta película ya la he visto.

♦ **the week before** la semana anterior

beforehand [bɪ'fɔːhænd] ADVERB
con antelación

to **beg** [bɛg] VERB
1 mendigar* (*for money, food*)
2 suplicar*

suplicar que *has to be followed by a verb in the subjunctive.*

◊ *He begged me to stop.* Me suplicó que parara.

began [bɪ'gæn] VERB *see* **begin**

beggar ['bɛgəʳ] NOUN
el mendigo
la mendiga

to **begin** [bɪ'gɪn] VERB (**began, begun**)
empezar*

♦ **to begin doing something** empezar a hacer algo

beginner [bɪ'gɪnəʳ] NOUN
el/la principiante

beginning [bɪ'gɪnɪŋ] NOUN
el comienzo

♦ **in the beginning** al principio

begun [bɪ'gʌn] VERB *see* **begin**

behalf [bɪ'hɑːf] NOUN

♦ **on behalf of somebody** de parte de alguien

to **behave** [bɪ'heɪv] VERB
comportarse ◊ *He behaved like an idiot.* Se comportó como un idiota.

♦ **to behave oneself** portarse bien ◊ *Did the children behave themselves?* ¿Se portaron bien los niños?

♦ **Behave!** ¡Compórtate!

behaviour [bɪ'heɪvjəʳ] NOUN (US **behavior**)
el comportamiento

behind [bɪ'haɪnd] PREPOSITION, ADVERB
see also **behind** NOUN
detrás de ◊ *behind the television* detrás de la televisión

♦ **to be behind** (*late*) ir* atrasado ◊ *I'm behind with my work.* Voy atrasado con mi trabajo.

behind [bɪ'haɪnd] NOUN
see also **behind** PREPOSITION, ADVERB
el trasero

beige [beɪʒ] ADJECTIVE
beige MASC, FEM, PL

Pronounce this word like the English word ***base***.

Belgian ['bɛldʒən] ADJECTIVE
see also **Belgian** NOUN
belga ◊ *He's Belgian.* Es belga.

Belgian ['bɛldʒən] NOUN
see also **Belgian** ADJECTIVE
el/la belga ◊ *the Belgians* los belgas

Belgium ['bɛldʒəm] NOUN
Bélgica FEM

to **believe** [bɪ'liːv] VERB
creer* ◊ *I don't believe you.* No te creo.

♦ **I don't believe it!** ¡No me lo creo!

♦ **to believe in something** creer* en algo ◊ *Do you believe in ghosts?* ¿Crees en los fantasmas?

bell [bɛl] NOUN
1 el timbre (*of door, in school*) ◊ *The bell goes at half past three.* El timbre suena a las tres y media.
2 la campana (*of church*) ◊ *the church bell* la campana de la iglesia
3 el cascabel (*of toy, on animal*) ◊ *Our cat has a bell on its collar.* Nuestro gato lleva un cascabel en el collar.

belly ['bɛlɪ] NOUN (PL **bellies**)
la barriga

to **belong** [bɪ'lɔŋ] VERB

♦ **to belong to somebody** pertenecer* a alguien ◊ *This ring belonged to my grandmother.* Este anillo pertenecía a mi abuela.

♦ **Who does it belong to?** ¿De quién es?

♦ **That belongs to me.** Eso es mío.

♦ **Do you belong to any clubs?** ¿Eres miembro de algún club?

♦ **Where does this belong?** ¿Dónde va esto?

belongings [bɪ'lɔŋɪŋz] PL NOUN

♦ **I collected my belongings and left the flat.** Recogí mis cosas y me marché del piso.

♦ **personal belongings** los efectos personales

below [bɪ'ləu] PREPOSITION, ADVERB
1 debajo de ◊ *the apartment directly below ours* el apartamento que está justo debajo del nuestro
2 abajo ◊ *seen from below* visto desde abajo ◊ *on the floor below* en el piso de abajo

♦ **ten degrees below freezing** diez grados bajo cero

belt [bɛlt] NOUN
el cinturón (PL los cinturones)

beltway ['bɛltweɪ] NOUN US
la carretera de circunvalación

bench [bɛntʃ] NOUN (PL **benches**)
el banco

bend [bɛnd] NOUN
see also **bend** VERB
la curva

to **bend** [bɛnd] VERB (**bent, bent**)
see also **bend** NOUN
1 doblar ◊ *I can't bend my arm.* No puedo doblar el brazo.
2 torcerse*

♦ **It bends easily.** Se tuerce fácilmente.

to **bend down** [bɛnd'daun] VERB
agacharse

to **bend over** [bɛnd'əuvəʳ] VERB
inclinarse

beneath [bɪ'niːθ] PREPOSITION
bajo

benefit ['bɛnɪfɪt] NOUN
see also **benefit** VERB
el beneficio
♦ **unemployment benefit** el subsidio de desempleo
♦ **state benefits** los subsidios estatales

to **benefit** ['bɛnɪfɪt] VERB
see also **benefit** NOUN
beneficiar ◊ *This will benefit us all.* Esto nos beneficiará a todos.
♦ **He'll benefit from the change.** Se beneficiará con el cambio.

bent [bɛnt] VERB *see* **bend**

bent [bɛnt] ADJECTIVE
torcido ◊ *a bent fork* un tenedor torcido
♦ **to be bent on doing something** estar* empeñado en hacer algo

beret ['bɛreɪ] NOUN
la boina

berserk [bə'səːk] ADJECTIVE
♦ **to go berserk** ponerse* hecho una fiera

berth [bəːθ] NOUN
la litera (*bunk*)

beside [bɪ'saɪd] PREPOSITION
al lado de ◊ *beside the television* al lado de la televisión
♦ **He was beside himself.** Estaba fuera de sí.
♦ **That's beside the point.** Eso no viene al caso.

besides [bɪ'saɪdz] ADVERB
además ◊ *Besides, it's too expensive.* Además, es demasiado caro.
♦ **... and much more besides.** ... y mucho más todavía.

best [bɛst] ADJECTIVE, ADVERB
mejor ◊ *He's the best player in the team.* Es el mejor jugador del equipo. ◊ *Janet's the best at maths.* Janet es la mejor en matemáticas. ◊ *Emma sings best.* Emma es la que canta mejor.
♦ **That's the best I can do.** No puedo hacer* más.
♦ **to do one's best** hacer* todo lo posible ◊ *It's not perfect, but I did my best.* No es perfecto, pero he hecho todo lo posible.
♦ **You'll just have to make the best of it.** Tendrás que arreglártelas con lo que hay.

best man [bɛst'mæn] NOUN
el padrino de boda

bet [bɛt] NOUN
see also **bet** VERB
la apuesta

to **bet** [bɛt] VERB **(bet, bet)**
see also **bet** NOUN
apostar* ◊ *I bet you he won't come.* Te apuesto a que no viene.

to **betray** [bɪ'treɪ] VERB
traicionar

better ['bɛtəʳ] ADJECTIVE, ADVERB
mejor ◊ *This one's better than that one.* Éste es mejor que aquél. ◊ *Are you feeling better now?* ¿Te sientes mejor ahora?
♦ **That's better!** ¡Así está mejor!
♦ **better still** mejor todavía
♦ **to get better (1)** mejorar (*improve*) ◊ *I hope the weather gets better soon.* Espero que el tiempo mejore pronto.
♦ **to get better (2)** mejorarse (*from illness*) ◊ *I hope you get better soon.* Espero que te mejores pronto.
♦ **You'd better do it straight away.** Más vale hacerlo enseguida.
♦ **I'd better go home.** Tengo que irme a casa.

betting shop ['bɛtɪŋʃɔp] NOUN
la casa de apuestas

between [bɪ'twiːn] PREPOSITION
entre ◊ *between 15 and 20 minutes* entre 15 y 20 minutos

to **beware** [bɪ'wɛəʳ] VERB
♦ **Beware of the dog!** ¡Cuidado con el perro!

bewildered [bɪ'wɪldəd] ADJECTIVE
desconcertado

beyond [bɪ'jɔnd] PREPOSITION, ADVERB
al otro lado de ◊ *There is a lake beyond the mountains.* Hay un lago al otro lado de las montañas.
♦ **We have no plans beyond the year 2005.** No tenemos planes para después del año 2005.
♦ **the wheat fields and the mountains beyond** los campos de trigo y las montañas al fondo
♦ **it's beyond me** no lo entiendo
♦ **beyond belief** increíble
♦ **beyond repair** irreparable

biased ['baɪəst] ADJECTIVE
parcial

Bible ['baɪbl] NOUN
la Biblia

bicycle ['baɪsɪkl] NOUN
la bicicleta

bifocals [baɪ'fəuklz] PL NOUN
las gafas bifocales

big [bɪg] ADJECTIVE
grande ◊ *a big house* una casa grande ◊ *a big car* un coche grande
Use ***gran*** *before a singular noun.*
◊ *it's a big business* es un gran negocio
♦ **my big brother** mi hermano mayor
♦ **He's a big guy.** Es un tipo grandote.
♦ **Big deal!** ¡Vaya cosa!

bigheaded ['bɪg'hɛdɪd] ADJECTIVE

◆**to be bigheaded** ser* engreído

bike [baɪk] NOUN

1 la bici (*bicycle*) ◊ *by bike* en bici

2 la moto (*motorbike*)

*Although **moto** ends in **-o**, it is actually a feminine noun.*

bikini [bɪ'kiːnɪ] NOUN

el bikini

bilingual [baɪ'lɪŋgwəl] ADJECTIVE

bilingüe

bill [bɪl] NOUN

1 la cuenta (*in restaurant*) ◊ *Can we have the bill, please?* ¿Nos trae la cuenta, por favor?

2 la factura (*for gas, electricity, telephone*) ◊ *the gas bill* la factura del gas

3 el billete US ◊ *a five-dollar bill* un billete de cinco dólares

billiards ['bɪljədz] NOUN

el billar ◊ *to play billiards* jugar* al billar

billion ['bɪljən] NOUN

los mil millones ◊ *two billion dollars* dos mil millones de dólares

bin [bɪn] NOUN

1 el cubo de la basura (*in kitchen*)

2 la papelera (*for paper*)

bingo ['bɪŋgəu] NOUN

el bingo

binoculars [bɪ'nɔkjuləz] PL NOUN

los prismáticos

◆**a pair of binoculars** unos prismáticos

biochemistry [baɪə'kɛmɪstrɪ] NOUN

la bioquímica

biography [baɪ'ɔgrəfɪ] NOUN (PL **biographies**)

la biografía

biology [baɪ'ɔlədʒɪ] NOUN

la biología

bird [bəːd] NOUN

el pájaro

birdwatching ['bəːdwɔtʃɪŋ] NOUN

◆**He likes to go birdwatching on Sundays.** Los domingos le gusta ir a ver pájaros.

Biro ® ['baɪərəu] NOUN

el bolígrafo

birth [bəːθ] NOUN

el nacimiento ◊ *date of birth* la fecha de nacimiento

birth certificate ['bəːθsətɪfɪkɪt] NOUN

la partida de nacimiento

birth control ['bəːθkəntrəul] NOUN

el control de natalidad

birthday ['bəːθdeɪ] NOUN

el cumpleaños (PL los cumpleaños) ◊ *a birthday cake* un pastel de cumpleaños ◊ *a birthday party* una fiesta de cumpleaños ◊ *When's your birthday?* ¿Cuándo es tu cumpleaños?

biscuit ['bɪskɪt] NOUN

la galleta

bishop ['bɪʃəp] NOUN

el obispo

bit [bɪt] VERB *see* **bite**

bit [bɪt] NOUN

el trozo ◊ *Would you like another bit?* ¿Quieres otro trozo?

◆**a bit** un poco ◊ *He's a bit mad.* Está un poco loco. ◊ *Wait a bit!* ¡Espera un poco!

◆**a bit of (1)** un trozo de ◊ *a bit of cake* un trozo de pastel

◆**a bit of (2)** un poco de ◊ *a bit of music* un poco de música

◆**It's a bit of a nuisance.** Es un poco fastidioso.

◆**to fall to bits** caerse* a pedazos

◆**to take something to bits** desmontar algo

◆**bit by bit** poco a poco

bitch [bɪtʃ] NOUN (PL **bitches**)

1 la perra (*female dog*)

2 la bruja (*rude: woman*)

to **bite** [baɪt] VERB (**bit, bitten**)

see also **bite** NOUN

1 morder* (*person, dog*) ◊ *My dog's never bitten anyone.* Mi perro nunca ha mordido a nadie.

2 picar* (*insect*) ◊ *I got bitten by mosquitoes.* Me picaron los mosquitos.

◆**to bite one's nails** morderse* las uñas

bite [baɪt] NOUN

see also **bite** VERB

1 la picadura (*insect bite*)

2 el mordisco (*animal bite*)

◆**to have a bite to eat** comer alguna cosa

bitter ['bɪtə^r] ADJECTIVE

see also **bitter** NOUN

1 amargo ◊ *It tastes bitter.* Sabe amargo.

2 glacial ◊ *It's bitter today.* Hoy hace un frío glacial.

bitter ['bɪtə^r] NOUN

see also **bitter** ADJECTIVE

ℹ *La cerveza británica a base de lúpulos.*

black [blæk] ADJECTIVE

negro ◊ *a black jacket* una chaqueta negra ◊ *She's black.* Es negra.

◆**black and white** blanco y negro

blackberry ['blækbərɪ] NOUN (PL **blackberries**)

la mora

blackbird ['blækbəːd] NOUN

el mirlo

blackboard ['blækbɔːd] NOUN

la pizarra

black coffee [blæk'kɔfɪ] NOUN

el café solo

blackcurrant ['blæk'kʌrənt] NOUN

la grosella negra

blackmail ['blækmeɪl] NOUN

see also **blackmail** VERB

el chantaje

to **blackmail** ['blækmeɪl] VERB

see also **blackmail** NOUN

chantajear

blackout ['blækaut] NOUN

(*power cut*)

el apagón (PL los apagones)

◆ **to have a blackout** (*faint*) sufrir un desvanecimiento

black pudding [blæk'pudɪŋ] NOUN

la morcilla

blacksmith ['blæksmɪθ] NOUN

el herrero ◇ *He's a blacksmith.* Es herrero.

blade [bleɪd] NOUN

la hoja

to **blame** [bleɪm] VERB

echar la culpa a ◇ *Don't blame me!* ¡No me eches la culpa a mí!

◆ **He blamed it on my sister.** Le echó la culpa a mi hermana.

blank [blæŋk] ADJECTIVE

see also **blank** NOUN

1 (*sheet of paper*)

en blanco

2 (*cassette*)

virgen (PL vírgenes)

◆ **My mind went blank.** Me quedé en blanco.

blank [blæŋk] NOUN

see also **blank** ADJECTIVE

el espacio en blanco ◇ *Fill in the blanks.* Rellene los espacios en blanco.

blank cheque [blæŋk'tʃɛk] NOUN

el cheque en blanco

blanket ['blæŋkɪt] NOUN

la manta

blast [blɑːst] NOUN

◆ **a bomb blast** una explosión

blatant ['bleɪtənt] ADJECTIVE

flagrante

blaze [bleɪz] NOUN

el incendio

blazer ['bleɪzəʳ] NOUN

el blazer (PL los blazers)

bleach [bliːtʃ] NOUN (PL **bleaches**)

la lejía

bleached hair ['bliːtʃthɛəʳ] NOUN

el cabello decolorado

bleak [bliːk] ADJECTIVE

poco prometedor ◇ *The future looks bleak.* Se presenta un futuro poco prometedor.

to **bleed** [bliːd] VERB (**bled, bled**)

sangrar

◆ **to bleed to death** morir* desangrado

◆ **My nose is bleeding.** Me sangra la nariz.

bleeper ['bliːpəʳ] NOUN

el busca

*Although **busca** ends in **-a**, it is actually a masculine noun.*

blender ['blɛndəʳ] NOUN

la licuadora

to **bless** [blɛs] VERB

bendecir*

◆ **Bless you!** ¡Jesús! (¡Salud! *LatAm*) (*after sneezing*)

blew [bluː] VERB *see* **blow**

blind [blaɪnd] ADJECTIVE

see also **blind** NOUN

ciego

blind [blaɪnd] NOUN

see also **blind** ADJECTIVE

la persiana (*for window*)

blindfold ['blaɪndfəuld] NOUN

see also **blindfold** VERB

la venda

to **blindfold** ['blaɪndfəuld] VERB

see also **blindfold** NOUN

◆ **to blindfold somebody** vendar los ojos a alguien

to **blink** [blɪŋk] VERB

parpadear

bliss [blɪs] NOUN

◆ **It was bliss!** ¡Era la gloria!

blister ['blɪstəʳ] NOUN

la ampolla

blizzard ['blɪzəd] NOUN

la ventisca de nieve

blob [blɔb] NOUN

la gota ◇ *a blob of glue* una gota de pegamento

block [blɔk] NOUN

see also **block** VERB

el bloque ◇ *He lives in our block.* Vive en nuestro bloque. ◇ *a block of flats* un bloque de apartamentos

to **block** [blɔk] VERB

see also **block** NOUN

bloquear

blockage ['blɔkɪdʒ] NOUN

la obstrucción (PL las obstrucciones)

bloke [bləuk] NOUN

el tío (*informal*)

blonde [blɔnd] ADJECTIVE

rubio ◇ *She's got blonde hair.* Tiene el pelo rubio.

blood [blʌd] NOUN

la sangre

blood pressure ['blʌdprɛʃəʳ] NOUN

la presión sanguínea ◇ *to have high blood pressure* tener* la tensión alta

blood sports ['blʌdspɔːts] PL NOUN

los deportes sangrientos

blood test ['blʌdtɛst] NOUN

el análisis de sangre (PL los análisis de sangre)

bloody ['blʌdɪ] ADJECTIVE

◆ **that bloody television** esa maldita televisión

◆ **Bloody hell!** ¡Me cago en la mar!
◆ **The exam was bloody difficult.** El examen fue difícil con ganas.

blouse [blauz] NOUN
la blusa

blow [bləu] NOUN
see also **blow** VERB
el golpe

to **blow** [bləu] VERB (**blew, blown**)
see also **blow** NOUN
soplar ◊ *A cold wind was blowing.* Soplaba un viento frío. ◊ *He blew on his fingers.* Se sopló los dedos.
◆ **They were one-all when the whistle blew.** Iban uno a uno cuando sonó el pito.
◆ **to blow one's nose** sonarse* la nariz

to **blow out** [bləu'aut] VERB
apagar* ◊ *Blow out the candles!* ¡Apaga las velas!

to **blow up** [bləu'ʌp] VERB
1 volar* ◊ *They blew up a plane.* Volaron un avión.
2 inflar ◊ *We've blown up the balloons.* Hemos inflado los globos.
3 saltar por los aires ◊ *The house blew up.* La casa saltó por los aires.

blow-dry ['bləudraɪ] NOUN
el secado con secador de mano
◆ **Cut and blow-dry.** Corte y secado a mano.

blue [blu:] ADJECTIVE
azul ◊ *a blue dress* un vestido azul
◆ **a blue movie** una película porno
◆ **out of the blue** en el momento menos pensado

blues [blu:z] PL NOUN
(*music*)
el blues (PL los blues)

to **bluff** [blʌf] VERB
see also **bluff** NOUN
farolear

bluff [blʌf] NOUN
see also **bluff** VERB
el farol

blunder ['blʌndəʳ] NOUN
la metedura de pata

blunt [blʌnt] ADJECTIVE
1 directo (*person*)
2 desafilado (*knife*)

to **blush** [blʌʃ] VERB
ruborizarse*

board [bɔ:d] NOUN
1 (*plank*)
la tabla
2 (*blackboard*)
la pizarra
3 (*noticeboard*)
el tablón de anuncios (PL los tablones de anuncios)
4 (*for diving*)
el trampolín (PL los trampolines)
5 (*for games*)
el tablero
◆ **a chopping board** una tabla de picar
◆ **on board** a bordo
◆ **"full board"** "pensión completa"

boarder ['bɔ:dəʳ] NOUN
el interno
la interna

board game ['bɔ:dgeɪm] NOUN
el juego de mesa

boarding card ['bɔ:dɪŋkɑ:d] NOUN
la tarjeta de embarque

boarding school ['bɔ:dɪŋsku:l] NOUN
el internado

to **boast** [bəust] VERB
alardear
◆ **to boast about something** alardear de algo
◆ **Stop boasting!** ¡Deja ya de presumir!

boat [bəut] NOUN
el barco

body ['bɔdɪ] NOUN (PL **bodies**)
1 el cuerpo ◊ *the human body* el cuerpo humano
2 el cadáver (*corpse*)

bodybuilding ['bɔdɪ'bɪldɪŋ] NOUN
el culturismo

bodyguard ['bɔdɪgɑ:d] NOUN
el guardaespaldas (PL los guardaespaldas) ◊ *He's a bodyguard.* Es guardaespaldas.

bog [bɔg] NOUN
la ciénaga (*marsh*)

boil [bɔɪl] NOUN
see also **boil** VERB
el furúnculo

to **boil** [bɔɪl] VERB
see also **boil** NOUN
hervir* ◊ *to boil some water* hervir* un poco de agua ◊ *The water's boiling.* El agua está hirviendo.
◆ **to boil an egg** cocer* un huevo

to **boil over** [bɔɪl'əuvəʳ] VERB
salirse*

boiled [bɔɪld] ADJECTIVE
hervido
◆ **a boiled egg** un huevo pasado por agua

boiling ['bɔɪlɪŋ] ADJECTIVE
◆ **It's boiling in here!** ¡Aquí dentro se asa uno!
◆ **a boiling hot day** un día asfixiante de calor

bolt [bəult] NOUN
1 el cerrojo (*on door, window*)
2 el tornillo (*type of screw*)

bomb [bɔm] NOUN
see also **bomb** VERB
la bomba

to **bomb** [bɔm] VERB
see also **bomb** NOUN
bombardear

bomber ['bɔmər] NOUN
el bombardero (*plane*)
bombing ['bɔmɪŋ] NOUN
el bombardeo
bond [bɔnd] NOUN
el vínculo ◊ *the bond between mother and child* el vínculo entre la madre y el hijo
bone [bəun] NOUN
1 el hueso (*of human, animal*)
2 la espina (*of fish*)
bone dry [bəun'draɪ] ADJECTIVE
completamente seco
bonfire ['bɔnfaɪər] NOUN
la hoguera
bonnet ['bɔnɪt] NOUN
el capó (*of car*)
bonus ['bəunəs] NOUN
1 el plus (*extra payment*)
2 la ventaja (*added advantage*)
book [buk] NOUN
see also **book** VERB
el libro
to **book** [buk] VERB
see also **book** NOUN
reservar
♦ **We haven't booked.** No hemos hecho reserva.
bookcase ['bukkeɪs] NOUN
la librería
booklet ['buklɪt] NOUN
el folleto
bookmark ['bʊkmɑ:k] NOUN
el marcador (*book, computer*)
bookshelf ['bukʃelf] NOUN (PL **bookshelves**)
la estantería
bookshop ['bukʃɔp] NOUN
la librería
to **boost** [bu:st] VERB
♦ **The win boosted the team's morale.** La victoria levantó la moral del equipo.
♦ **They're trying to boost the economy.** Intentan dar un empuje a la economía.
boot [bu:t] NOUN
1 (*of car*)
el maletero
2 (*fashion boots*)
la bota
3 (*for hiking*)
el borceguí (PL los borceguíes)
♦ **football boots** las botas de fútbol
booze [bu:z] NOUN
la bebida
border ['bɔ:dər] NOUN
la frontera
bore [bɔ:r] VERB *see* **bear**
bored [bɔ:d] ADJECTIVE
aburrido ◊ *to be bored* estar* aburrido
♦ **to get bored** aburrirse
boredom ['bɔ:dəm] NOUN
el aburrimiento
boring ['bɔ:rɪŋ] ADJECTIVE
aburrido ◊ *It's boring.* Es aburrido.
born [bɔ:n] ADJECTIVE
♦ **to be born** nacer* ◊ *I was born in 1992.* Nací en 1992.
borne [bɔ:n] VERB *see* **bear**
to **borrow** ['bɔrəu] VERB
pedir* prestado
♦ **to borrow something from somebody** pedir* algo prestado a alguien ◊ *I borrowed some money from a friend.* Le pedí dinero prestado a un amigo.
♦ **Can I borrow your pen?** ¿Me prestas el bolígrafo?
Bosnia ['bɔznɪə] NOUN
la Bosnia
Bosnian ['bɔznɪən] ADJECTIVE
bosnio
boss [bɔs] NOUN (PL **bosses**)
el jefe
la jefa
to **boss around** [bɔsə'raund] VERB
♦ **to boss somebody around** mandonear a alguien
bossy ['bɔsɪ] ADJECTIVE
mandón MASC (PL mandones)
mandona FEM
both [bəuθ] ADJECTIVE, PRONOUN, ADVERB
los dos ◊ *We both went.* Fuimos los dos. ◊ *Both of your answers are wrong.* Tus respuestas están las dos mal. ◊ *Both of them play the piano.* Los dos tocan el piano.
♦ **Both Emma and Jane went.** Fueron Emma y Jane.
♦ **He has houses in both France and in Spain.** Tiene casas tanto en Francia como en España.
to **bother** ['bɔðər] VERB
see also **bother** NOUN
1 preocupar (*worry*) ◊ *What's bothering you?* ¿Qué es lo que te preocupa?
2 molestar (*disturb*) ◊ *I'm sorry to bother you.* Siento molestarle.
♦ **Don't bother!** ¡No te preocupes!
♦ **to bother to do something** tomarse la molestia de hacer algo ◊ *He didn't bother to tell me about it.* Ni se tomó la molestia de decírmelo.
bother ['bɔðər] NOUN
see also **bother** VERB
la molestia ◊ *no bother* no es ninguna molestia
bottle ['bɔtl] NOUN
la botella
bottle bank ['bɔtlbæŋk] NOUN
el contenedor del vidrio
bottle-opener ['bɔtləupnər] NOUN

* Verbs marked with this symbol are irregular. See pages 380-382 for further details

el abrebotellas (PL los abrebotellas)

bottom ['bɔtəm] NOUN

see also **bottom** ADJECTIVE

1 el fondo (*of container, bag, sea*)

◆ **at the bottom of the page** al final de la página

◆ **He was always bottom of the class.** Siempre era el último de la clase.

2 el trasero (*buttocks*)

bottom ['bɔtəm] ADJECTIVE

see also **bottom** NOUN

de abajo ◇ *the bottom shelf* el estante de abajo

bought [bɔːt] VERB *see* **buy**

to **bounce** [bauns] VERB

rebotar

bouncer ['baunsəʳ] NOUN

el gorila

Although **gorila** *ends in* **-a**, *it is actually a masculine noun in this case.*

bound [baund] ADJECTIVE

◆ **He's bound to fail.** Seguro que suspende.

◆ **She's bound to come.** Es seguro que vendrá.

boundary ['baundrɪ] NOUN (PL **boundaries**)

el límite

bow [bəu] NOUN

see also **bow** VERB

1 el lazo (*knot*) ◇ *to tie a bow* hacer* un lazo

2 el arco ◇ *a bow and arrow* un arco y flecha

to **bow** [bau] VERB

see also **bow** NOUN

hacer* una reverencia

bowels ['bauəlz] PL NOUN

los intestinos

bowl [bəul] NOUN

see also **bowl** VERB

1 (*for soup, cereals*)

el tazón (PL los tazones)

2 (*for cooking, mixing food*)

el cuenco

to **bowl** [bəul] VERB

see also **bowl** NOUN

lanzar* la pelota

bowler ['bəuləʳ] NOUN

el lanzador

la lanzadora

bowling ['bəulɪŋ] NOUN

los bolos

◆ **to go bowling** jugar* a los bolos

◆ **a bowling alley** una bolera

bowls [bəulz] PL NOUN

ℹ *Juego parecido a la petanca que se juega en césped.*

bow tie [bəu'taɪ] NOUN

la pajarita

box [bɔks] NOUN (PL **boxes**)

1 la caja ◇ *a box of matches* una caja de cerillas

◆ **a cardboard box** una caja de cartón

2 la casilla (*on form*)

boxer ['bɔksəʳ] NOUN

el boxeador

boxer shorts ['bɔksəʃɔːts] PL NOUN

los bóxers

◆ **a pair of boxer shorts** unos bóxers

boxing ['bɔksɪŋ] NOUN

el boxeo

Boxing Day ['bɔksɪŋdeɪ] NOUN

el 26 de diciembre

boy [bɔɪ] NOUN

1 el muchacho (*young man*) ◇ *a boy of fifteen* un muchacho de quince años

2 el niño (*child*) ◇ *a boy of seven* un niño de siete años

◆ **She has two boys and a girl.** Tiene dos niños y una niña.

◆ **a baby boy** un niño

boyfriend ['bɔɪfrɛnd] NOUN

el novio ◇ *Have you got a boyfriend?* ¿Tienes novio?

bra [brɑː] NOUN

el sostén (PL los sostenes)

brace [breɪs] NOUN

el aparato (*on teeth*) ◇ *Richard wears a brace.* Richard lleva un aparato.

bracelet ['breɪslɪt] NOUN

la pulsera

brackets ['brækɪts] PL NOUN

◆ **in brackets** entre paréntesis

brain [breɪn] NOUN

el cerebro

brainy ['breɪnɪ] ADJECTIVE

inteligente

brake [breɪk] NOUN

see also **brake** VERB

el freno

to **brake** [breɪk] VERB

see also **brake** NOUN

frenar

branch [brɑːntʃ] NOUN (PL **branches**)

1 la rama (*of tree*)

2 la sucursal (*of bank*)

brand [brænd] NOUN

la marca ◇ *a well-known brand of coffee* una marca de café muy conocida

brand name ['brændneɪm] NOUN

la marca

brand-new ['brænd'njuː] ADJECTIVE

flamante

brandy ['brændɪ] NOUN (PL **brandies**)

el coñac (PL los coñacs)

brass [brɑːs] NOUN

el latón (*metal*)

◆ **the brass section** los bronces

brass band [brɑːs'bænd] NOUN

la banda de música

brat [bræt] NOUN

☞

el mocoso
la mocosa
◊ *He's a spoiled brat.* Es un mocoso consentido.

brave [breɪv] ADJECTIVE
valiente

Brazil [brə'zɪl] NOUN
el Brasil

bread [brɛd] NOUN
el pan
◆ **bread and butter** el pan con mantequilla

break [breɪk] NOUN
see also **break** VERB
1 la pausa (*rest*) ◊ *to take a break* hacer* una pausa
2 el recreo (*at school*)
◆ **the Christmas break** las vacaciones de Navidad
◆ **Give me a break!** ¡Déjame en paz!

to **break** [breɪk] VERB (**broke, broken**)
see also **break** NOUN
1 romper* ◊ *Careful, you'll break something!* ¡Cuidado, que vas a romper algo!
◆ **I broke my leg.** Me rompí la pierna.
2 romperse* ◊ *Careful, it'll break!* ¡Ten cuidado, que se va a romper!
◆ **to break a promise** faltar a una promesa
◆ **to break a record** batir un récord

to **break down** [breɪk'daun] VERB
averiarse*
◆ **the car broke down** el coche se averió

to **break in** [breɪk'ɪn] VERB
◆ **The thief had broken in through a window.** El ladrón había entrado por una ventana.

to **break into** [breɪk'ɪntu] VERB
entrar en ◊ *Thieves broke into the house.* Los ladrones entraron en la casa.

to **break off** [breɪk'ɔf] VERB
desprenderse (*come free*)

to **break out** [breɪk'aut] VERB
1 estallar (*war*)
2 desencadenarse (*fire, fighting*)
3 escaparse (*prisoner*)
◆ **He broke out in a rash.** Le salió un sarpullido.

to **break up** [breɪk'ʌp] VERB
1 disolver* ◊ *Police broke up the demonstration.* La policía disolvió la demostración.
2 dispersarse ◊ *The crowd broke up.* La muchedumbre se dispersió.
3 fracasar (*marriage*) ◊ *More and more marriages break up.* Cada día fracasan más matrimonios.
4 romper* (*two lovers*) ◊ *Richard and Marie have broken up.* Richard y Marie han roto.
◆ **to break up a fight** poner* fin a una pelea
◆ **We break up next Wednesday.** El miércoles que viene empezamos las vacaciones.

breakdown ['breɪkdaun] NOUN
1 la crisis nerviosa (PL las crisis nerviosas) ◊ *He had a breakdown because of the stress.* Sufrió una crisis nerviosa debida al estrés.
2 (*in vehicle*)
la avería ◊ *to have a breakdown* tener* una avería

breakdown van ['breɪkdaunvæn] NOUN
la grúa

breakfast ['brɛkfəst] NOUN
el desayuno
◆ **to have breakfast** desayunar

break-in ['breɪkɪn] NOUN
◆ **There have been a lot of break-ins in my area.** Han entrado a robar en muchas casas de mi barrio.

breast [brɛst] NOUN
el pecho
◆ **chicken breast** la pechuga de pollo

to **breast-feed** ['brɛstfi:d] VERB (**breast-fed, breast-fed**)
amamantar

breaststroke ['brɛststrəuk] NOUN
la braza

breath [brɛθ] NOUN
el aliento ◊ *He's got bad breath.* Tiene mal aliento.
◆ **I'm out of breath.** Estoy sin aliento.
◆ **to get one's breath back** recobrar el aliento

to **breathe** [bri:ð] VERB
respirar

to **breathe in** [bri:ð'ɪn] VERB
aspirar

to **breathe out** [bri:ð'aut] VERB
espirar

to **breed** [bri:d] VERB (**bred, bred**)
see also **breed** NOUN
reproducirse* (*reproduce*)
◆ **to breed dogs** criar* perros

breed [bri:d] NOUN
see also **breed** VERB
la raza

breeze [bri:z] NOUN
la brisa

brewery ['bru:ərɪ] NOUN (PL **breweries**)
la fábrica de cerveza

bribe [braɪb] NOUN
see also **bribe** VERB
el soborno

to **bribe** [braɪb] VERB
see also **bribe** NOUN
sobornar

brick [brɪk] NOUN

el ladrillo
bricklayer ['brɪkleɪə'] NOUN
el albañil ◊ *he's a bricklayer* es albañil
bride [braɪd] NOUN
la novia
bridegroom ['braɪdgru:m] NOUN
el novio
bridesmaid ['braɪdzmeɪd] NOUN
la dama de honor
bridge [brɪdʒ] NOUN
1 el puente ◊ *a suspension bridge* un puente colgante
2 el bridge (*card game*) ◊ *to play bridge* jugar* al bridge
brief [bri:f] ADJECTIVE
breve
briefcase ['bri:fkeɪs] NOUN
el maletín (PL los maletines)
briefly ['bri:flɪ] ADVERB
brevemente
briefs [bri:fs] PL NOUN
los calzoncillos
◆ **a pair of briefs** unos calzoncillos
bright [braɪt] ADJECTIVE
1 vivo ◊ *a bright colour* un color vivo
◆ **bright red** rojo vivo
2 brillante (*light*)
3 listo ◊ *He's not very bright.* No es muy listo.
brilliant ['brɪljənt] ADJECTIVE
1 estupendo
◆ **We had a brilliant time!** ¡Lo pasamos estupendo!
2 genial ◊ *Sean Connery is a brilliant actor.* Sean Connery es un genial actor.
to **bring** [brɪŋ] VERB (**brought, brought**)
traer* ◊ *Bring warm clothes.* Trae ropa de abrigo. ◊ *Can I bring a friend?* ¿Puedo traer a un amigo?
to **bring about** [brɪŋə'baut] VERB
provocar*
to **bring back** [brɪŋ'bæk] VERB
devolver* (*book*)
◆ **That song brings back memories.** Esa canción me trae recuerdos.
to **bring forward** [brɪŋ'fɔ:wəd] VERB
adelantar ◊ *The meeting was brought forward.* La reunión se adelantó.
to **bring up** [brɪŋ'ʌp] VERB
criar*
◆ **She brought up five children on her own.** Crió a cinco hijos ella sola.
Britain ['brɪtən] NOUN
la Gran Bretaña
British ['brɪtɪʃ] ADJECTIVE
británico
◆ **the British** los británicos
◆ **the British Isles** las Islas Británicas
◆ **She's British.** Es británica.
broad [brɔ:d] ADJECTIVE
ancho
◆ **in broad daylight** a plena luz del día
broad bean [brɔ:d'bi:n] NOUN
el haba FEM

Although it's a feminine noun, remember that you use ***el*** *and* ***un*** *with* ***haba.***

broadcast ['brɔ:dkɑ:st] NOUN
see also **broadcast** VERB
la emisión (PL las emisiones)
to **broadcast** ['brɔ:dkɑ:st] VERB (**broadcast, broadcast**)
see also **broadcast** NOUN
emitir ◊ *The interview was broadcast all over the world.* La entrevista se emitió a todo el mundo.
emitirse ◊ *The show broadcasts live every Saturday.* El programa se emite todos los sábados.
broad-minded ['brɔ:d'maɪndɪd] ADJECTIVE
◆ **He's very broad-minded.** Tiene una mentalidad muy abierta.
broccoli ['brɔkəlɪ] NOUN
el brécol
brochure ['brəuʃjuə'] NOUN
el folleto
to **broil** [brɔɪl] VERB US
1 hacer* al grill (*in cooker*)
2 asar a la parrilla (*barbecue*)
broke [brəuk] VERB *see* **break**
broke [brəuk] ADJECTIVE
◆ **to be broke** estar* sin blanca (*informal*)
broken ['brəukn] VERB *see* **break**
broken ['brəukn] ADJECTIVE
roto ◊ *It's broken.* Está roto.
◆ **He's got a broken arm.** Tiene un brazo roto.
bronchitis [brɔŋ'kaɪtɪs] NOUN
la bronquitis
bronze [brɔnz] NOUN
el bronce ◊ *the bronze medal* la medalla de bronce
brooch [brəutʃ] NOUN (PL **brooches**)
el broche
broom [brum] NOUN
la escoba
brother ['brʌðə'] NOUN
el hermano
brother-in-law ['brʌðərɪnlɔ:] NOUN (PL **brothers-in-law**)
el cuñado
brought [brɔ:t] VERB *see* **bring**
brown [braun] ADJECTIVE
1 (*clothes*)
marrón MASC (PL marrones)
marrón FEM
2 (*hair, eyes*)
castaño
3 (*tanned*)
moreno
◆ **brown bread** el pan integral
Brownie ['braunɪ] NOUN
la guía

☞

*Un miembro joven de las **Girl Guides** - la versión femenina de los **Boy Scouts**.*

to **browse** [braʊz] VERB
echar una ojeada (a) (*on internet*)
browser ['braʊzəʳ] NOUN
el navegador
bruise [bru:z] NOUN
el moretón (PL los moretones)
brush [brʌʃ] NOUN (PL **brushes**)
see also **brush** VERB
1 el cepillo (*for hair, teeth*)
2 el pincel (*paintbrush*)
to **brush** [brʌʃ] VERB
see also **brush** NOUN
cepillar
♦ **to brush one's hair** cepillarse el pelo
♦ **to brush one's teeth** cepillarse los dientes ◊ *I brush my teeth every night.* Me cepillo los dientes todas las noches.
Brussels ['brʌslz] NOUN
la Bruselas
Brussels sprouts [brʌslz'sprauts] PL NOUN
las coles de Bruselas
brutal ['bru:tl] ADJECTIVE
brutal
BSc [bi:ɛs'si:] ABBREVIATION (= *Bachelor of Science*)
la licenciatura en Ciencias
♦ **a BSc in Mathematics** una licenciatura en Matemáticas
♦ **She's got a BSc in Chemistry.** Es licenciada en Química.
bubble ['bʌbl] NOUN
1 la pompa (*of soap*)
2 la burbuja (*of air, gas*)
bubble bath ['bʌblbɑ:θ] NOUN
el baño de espuma
bubble gum ['bʌblgʌm] NOUN
el chicle
bucket ['bʌkɪt] NOUN
el cubo
buckle ['bʌkl] NOUN
la hebilla (*on belt, watch, shoe*)
Buddhism ['budɪzəm] NOUN
el budismo
Buddhist ['budɪst] ADJECTIVE
budista
buddy ['bʌdɪ] NOUN (PL **buddies**) US
el amiguete
la amigueta
budget ['bʌdʒɪt] NOUN
see also **budget** VERB
el presupuesto
to **budget** ['bʌdʒɪt] VERB
see also **budget** NOUN
♦ **I'm learning how to budget.** Estoy aprendiendo a administrar el dinero.
♦ **They budgeted $10 million for advertising.** Asignaron 10 millones de dólares para la publicidad.
budgie ['bʌdʒɪ] NOUN
el periquito
buffet ['bufeɪ] NOUN
el buffet
buffet car ['bufeɪkɑ:ʳ] NOUN
el coche restaurante
bug [bʌg] NOUN
1 (*insect*)
el insecto
2 (*illness, in computer*)
el virus (PL los virus)
◊ *There's a bug going round.* Hay un virus en el ambiente.
♦ **a stomach bug** una gastroenteritis
bugged [bʌgd] ADJECTIVE
♦ **The phone at the office was bugged.** El teléfono de la oficina estaba pinchado.
to **build** [bɪld] VERB (**built, built**)
construir* ◊ *They're going to build houses here.* Van a construir viviendas aquí.
to **build up** [bɪld'ʌp] VERB
1 acumular ◊ *He has built up a huge collection of stamps.* Ha ido acumulando una gran colección de sellos.
2 acumularse ◊ *Our debts are building up.* Nuestras deudas se están acumulando.
builder ['bɪldəʳ] NOUN
1 el/la contratista (*contractor*)
2 el albañil (*worker*)
building ['bɪldɪŋ] NOUN
el edificio
built [bɪlt] VERB *see* **build**
bulb [bʌlb] NOUN
1 la bombilla (*electric*)
2 el bulbo (*of flower*)
bull [bul] NOUN
el toro
bullet ['bulɪt] NOUN
la bala
bulletin board ['bʊlɪtɪnbɔ:d] NOUN
el tablón de noticias
bullfighting ['bulfaɪtɪŋ] NOUN
♦ **Do you like bullfighting?** ¿Te gustan los toros?
bullring ['bulrɪŋ] NOUN
la plaza de toros
bully ['bulɪ] NOUN (PL **bullies**)
see also **bully** VERB
el matón (PL los matones) ◊ *Marcus is a big bully.* Marcus es un matón.
to **bully** ['bulɪ] VERB (**bullied, bullied**)
see also **bully** NOUN
intimidar

bum [bʌm] NOUN
el culo (*informal*)
bum bag ['bʌmbæg] NOUN
la riñonera
bump [bʌmp] NOUN
see also **bump** VERB
1 (*on head*)
el chichón (PL los chichones)
2 (*on surface*)
el bulto
3 (*on road*)
el bache
4 (*minor accident*)
el golpe
◆**We had a bump.** Nos dimos un golpe.
to **bump** [bʌmp] VERB
see also **bump** NOUN
◆**I bumped my head on the wall.** Me di con la cabeza en la pared.
to **bump into** [bʌmp'ɪntu] VERB
1 tropezarse* con ◇ *I bumped into Paul yesterday.* Me tropecé con Paul ayer.
2 darse* contra ◇ *We bumped into a tree.* Nos dimos contra un árbol.
bumper ['bʌmpəʳ] NOUN
el parachoques (PL los parachoques)
bumpy ['bʌmpɪ] ADJECTIVE
lleno de baches (*road*)
bun [bʌn] NOUN
el bollo (*bread*)
bunch [bʌntʃ] NOUN (PL **bunches**)
◆**a bunch of flowers** un ramo de flores
◆**a bunch of grapes** un racimo de uvas
◆**a bunch of keys** un manojo de llaves
bunches ['bʌntʃəz] PL NOUN
las coletas ◇ *She has her hair in bunches.* Lleva coletas.
bungalow ['bʌŋgələu] NOUN
el bungalow
bunk [bʌŋk] NOUN
la litera
burger ['bə:gəʳ] NOUN
la hamburguesa
burglar ['bə:gləʳ] NOUN
el ladrón (PL los ladrones)
la ladrona
to **burglarize** ['bə:gləraɪz] VERB US
entrar a robar en
burglary ['bə:glərɪ] NOUN (PL **burglaries**)
el robo (*con allanamiento de morada*)
to **burgle** ['bə:gl] VERB
entrar a robar en ◇ *Her house was burgled.* Le entraron a robar en casa.
burn [bə:n] NOUN
see also **burn** VERB
la quemadura
to **burn** [bə:n] VERB (**burned** *or* **burnt, burned** *or* **burnt**)
see also **burn** NOUN
quemar (*rubbish, documents*) ◇ *I burned the rubbish.* Quemé la basura.
◆**I burned the cake.** Se me quemó el pastel.
◆**to burn oneself** quemarse
◆**I've burned my hand.** Me quemé la mano.
to **burn down** [bə:n'daun] VERB
quedar reducido a cenizas ◇ *The factory burned down.* La fábrica quedó reducida a cenizas.
to **burst** [bə:st] VERB (**burst, burst**)
reventarse* ◇ *The balloon burst.* El globo se reventó.
◆**to burst a balloon** reventar* un globo
◆**to burst out laughing** echarse a reír
◆**to burst into tears** romper* a llorar
◆**to burst into flames** incendiarse
to **bury** ['bɛrɪ] VERB (**buried, buried**)
enterrar*
bus [bʌs] NOUN (PL **buses**)
el autobús (PL los autobuses) ◇ *by bus* en autobús
◆**the school bus** el autocar escolar
◆**a bus ticket** un billete de autobús
bush [buʃ] NOUN (PL **bushes**)
el arbusto
business ['bɪznɪs] NOUN (PL **businesses**)
1 el negocio (*firm*) ◇ *He's got his own business.* Tiene su propio negocio.
2 los negocios ◇ *He's away on business.* Está en un viaje de negocios.
◆**a business trip** un viaje de negocios
◆**It's none of my business.** No es asunto mío.
businessman ['bɪznɪsmən] NOUN (PL **businessmen**)
el hombre de negocios
businesswoman ['bɪznɪswumən] NOUN (PL **businesswomen**)
la mujer de negocios
busker ['bʌskəʳ] NOUN
el músico callejero
la música callejera
bus pass ['bʌspɑ:s] NOUN
el bonobús (PL los bonobuses)
bus station ['bʌssteɪʃən] NOUN
la estación de autobuses (PL las estaciones de autobuses)
bus stop ['bʌsstɔp] NOUN
la parada de autobús
bust [bʌst] NOUN
el busto
busy ['bɪzɪ] ADJECTIVE
1 ocupado (*person, telephone line*) ◇ *She's a very busy woman.* Es una mujer muy ocupada.
2 ajetreado (*day, week*) ◇ *It's been a very busy day.* Ha sido un día muy ajetreado.
3 concurrido (*street, shop*)
busy signal ['bɪzɪsɪgnl] NOUN US
la señal de comunicando
but [bʌt] PREPOSITION, CONJUNCTION

☞

1 pero
♦ **I'd like to come, but I'm busy.** Me gustaría venir*, pero tengo trabajo.
2 sino
*Use **sino** when you want to correct a previous negative statement.*
◊ *He's not English but French.* No es inglés sino francés.
3 menos ◊ *They won all but two of their matches.* Ganaron todos los partidos menos dos.
♦ **the last but one** el penúltimo

butcher ['butʃər] NOUN
el carnicero
la carnicera
♦ **He's a butcher.** Es carnicero. ◊ *at the butcher's* en la carnicería

butter ['bʌtər] NOUN
la mantequilla

butterfly ['bʌtəflaɪ] NOUN (PL **butterflies**)
la mariposa (*insect, swimming*) ◊ *Her favourite stroke is the butterfly.* Su estilo favorito es mariposa.

buttocks ['bʌtəks] PL NOUN
las nalgas

button ['bʌtn] NOUN
1 el botón (PL los botones)
2 (*metal, plastic*)
la chapa US

to **buy** [baɪ] VERB (**bought, bought**)
see also **buy** NOUN
comprar
♦ **He bought me an ice cream.** Me compró un helado.
♦ **to buy something from somebody** comprar algo a alguien ◊ *I bought a watch from him.* Le compré un reloj.

buy [baɪ] NOUN
see also **buy** VERB
♦ **It was a good buy.** Fue una buena compra.

by [baɪ] PREPOSITION
1 por ◊ *The thieves were caught by the police.* Los ladrones fueron capturados por la policía.
2 de ◊ *a painting by Picasso* un cuadro de Picasso
3 en ◊ *by car* en coche
♦ **by train** en tren
♦ **by bus** en autobús
4 junto a ◊ *Where's the bank? – It's by the post office.* ¿Dónde está el banco? – Está junto a la oficina de correos.
5 para ◊ *We have to be there by 4 o'clock.* Tenemos que estar* allí para las cuatro.
♦ **by the time...** cuando ◊ *By the time I got there it was too late.* Cuando llegué allí ya era demasiado tarde. ◊ *It'll be ready by the time you get back.* Estará listo para cuando regreses.
♦ **That's fine by me.** Por mí no hay problema.
♦ **all by himself** él solo
♦ **I did it all by myself.** Lo hice yo solo.
♦ **by the way** a propósito

bye [baɪ] EXCLAMATION
¡adiós!

bypass ['baɪpɑːs] NOUN (PL **bypasses**)
la carretera de circunvalación (*road*)

* Verbs marked with this symbol are irregular. See pages 380-382 for further details

C

cab [kæb] NOUN
el taxi ◇ *I'll go by cab.* Iré en taxi.
cabbage ['kæbɪdʒ] NOUN
la berza
cabin ['kæbɪn] NOUN
1 el camarote (*on ship*)
2 la cabina (*on aeroplane*)
cabinet ['kæbɪnɪt] NOUN
◆**a bathroom cabinet** un armario de cuarto de baño
◆**a drinks cabinet** un mueble-bar
cable ['keɪbl] NOUN
el cable
cable car ['keɪblkɑːʳ] NOUN
el teleférico
cable television ['keɪbl'tɛlɪvɪʒən] NOUN
la televisión por cable
cadet [kə'dɛt] NOUN
el/la cadete ◇ *a police cadet* un cadete de policía
café ['kæfeɪ] NOUN
la cafetería
cage [keɪdʒ] NOUN
la jaula
cagoule [kə'guːl] NOUN
el canguro (*chubasquero*)
cake [keɪk] NOUN
el pastel
to **calculate** ['kælkjuleɪt] VERB
calcular
calculation [kælkju'leɪʃən] NOUN
el cálculo
calculator ['kælkjuleɪtəʳ] NOUN
la calculadora
calendar ['kæləndəʳ] NOUN
el calendario
calf [kɑːf] NOUN (PL **calves**)
1 el ternero (*of cow*)
2 la pantorrilla (*of leg*)
call [kɔːl] NOUN
see also **call** VERB
la llamada ◇ *Thanks for your call.* Gracias por su llamada. ◇ *a phone call* una llamada telefónica
◆**to be on call** (*doctor*) estar* de guardia
to **call** [kɔːl] VERB
see also **call** NOUN
llamar ◇ *We called the police.* Llamamos a la policía. ◇ *I'll tell him you called.* Le diré que has llamado.
◆**to be called** llamarse ◇ *He's called Fluffy.* Se llama Fluffy. ◇ *What's she called?* ¿Cómo se llama?
to **call back** [kɔːl'bæk] VERB
volver* a llamar ◇ *I'll call back later.* Volveré a llamar más tarde.
◆**Can I call you back?** ¿Puedo llamarte más tarde?
to **call for** ['kɔːlfɔːʳ] VERB
1 pasar a recoger ◇ *Shall I call for you at seven thirty?* ¿Paso a recogerte a las siete y media?
2 requerir* ◇ *This job calls for strong nerves.* Este trabajo requiere nervios de acero.
◆**This calls for a drink!** ¡Esto hay que celebrarlo!
to **call off** [kɔːl'ɔf] VERB
suspender ◇ *The match was called off.* El partido se suspendió.
call box ['kɔːlbɔks] NOUN (PL **call boxes**)
la cabina telefónica
call centre [kɔːl 'sɛntəʳ] NOUN
el centro de atención al cliente
calm [kɑːm] ADJECTIVE
tranquilo
to **calm down** [kɑːm'daun] VERB
calmarse ◇ *Calm down!* ¡Cálmate!
Calor gas ® ['kæləgæs] NOUN
el butano
calorie ['kælərɪ] NOUN
la caloría
calves [kɑːvz] PL NOUN *see* **calf**
camcorder ['kæmkɔːdəʳ] NOUN
la videocámara
came [keɪm] VERB *see* **come**
camel ['kæməl] NOUN
el camello
camera ['kæmərə] NOUN
la cámara
cameraman ['kæmərəmæn] NOUN (PL **cameramen**)
el cámara
to **camp** [kæmp] VERB
see also **camp** NOUN
acampar
camp [kæmp] NOUN
see also **camp** VERB
el campamento ◇ *a summer camp* un campamento de verano
◆**a refugee camp** un campo de refugiados
campaign [kæm'peɪn] NOUN
see also **campaign** VERB
la campaña
to **campaign** [kæm'peɪn] VERB
see also **campaign** NOUN
hacer* campaña ◇ *They are campaigning for a change in the law.* Están haciendo campaña a favor de un cambio legislativo.
camp bed ['kæmpbɛd] NOUN
la cama plegable
camper ['kæmpəʳ] NOUN
el/la campista

☞

◆ **a camper van** una autocaravana

camping ['kæmpɪŋ] NOUN

◆ **to go camping** ir* de camping

camping gas ® ['kæmpɪŋgæs] NOUN

el camping gas ®

campsite ['kæmpsaɪt] NOUN

el camping (PL los campings)

campus ['kæmpəs] NOUN (PL **campuses**)

el campus (PL los campus)

can [kæn] NOUN

see also **can** VERB

la lata ◊ *a can of peas* una lata de guisantes ◊ *a can of beer* una lata de cerveza

◆ **a can of petrol** un bidón de gasolina

can [kæn] VERB (**could**)

see also **can** NOUN

1 poder* (*be able to, be allowed to*) ◊ *Can I use your phone?* ¿Puedo usar el teléfono? ◊ *I can't do that.* No puedo hacer eso. ◊ *I'll do it as soon as I can.* Lo haré tan pronto como pueda. ◊ *That can't be true!* ¡No puede ser cierto! ◊ *You could hire a bike.* Podrías alquilar una bici. ◊ *He couldn't concentrate because of the noise.* No se podía concentrar a causa del ruido.

2 saber* (*know how to*) ◊ *I can swim.* Sé nadar. ◊ *He can't drive.* No sabe conducir.

can is sometimes not translated.

◊ *I can't hear you.* No te oigo. ◊ *I can't remember.* No me acuerdo. ◊ *Can you speak French?* ¿Hablas francés?

◆ **You could be right.** Es posible que tengas razón.

Canada ['kænədə] NOUN

el Canadá

Canadian [kə'neɪdɪən] ADJECTIVE

see also **Canadian** NOUN

canadiense

Canadian [kə'neɪdɪən] NOUN

see also **Canadian** ADJECTIVE

el/la canadiense

canal [kə'næl] NOUN

el canal

Canaries [kə'nɛərɪz] NOUN

◆ **the Canaries** las Canarias

canary [kə'nɛərɪ] NOUN (PL **canaries**)

el canario

◆ **the Canary Islands** las islas Canarias

to **cancel** ['kænsəl] VERB

cancelar ◊ *I had to cancel my appointment.* Tuve que cancelar la cita. ◊ *Our flight was cancelled.* Cancelaron nuestro vuelo.

cancellation [kænsə'leɪʃən] NOUN

la cancelación (PL las cancelaciones)

cancer ['kænsə^r] NOUN

el cáncer ◊ *He's got cancer.* Tiene cáncer.

◆ **I'm Cancer.** Soy Cáncer.

◆ **a Cancer** un/una Cáncer

candidate ['kændɪdeɪt] NOUN

el candidato

la candidata

candle ['kændl] NOUN

1 la vela

2 el cirio (*in church*)

candy ['kændɪ] NOUN (PL **candies**) US

los dulces ◊ *I love candy.* Me encantan los dulces.

◆ **a candy** un caramelo

candyfloss ['kændɪflɔs] NOUN

el algodón de azúcar

cannabis ['kænəbɪs] NOUN

el canabis

canned [kænd] ADJECTIVE

(*food*)

en lata MASC, FEM, PL

cannot ['kænɔt] VERB = **can not**

canoe [kə'nu:] NOUN

la canoa

canoeing [kə'nu:ɪŋ] NOUN

◆ **We went canoeing with the school.** Fuimos a hacer piragüismo con el colegio.

◆ **I like canoeing.** Me gusta el piragüismo.

can-opener ['kænəupnə^r] NOUN

el abrelatas (PL los abrelatas)

can't [kænt] VERB = **can not**

canteen [kæn'ti:n] NOUN

la cantina

canvas ['kænvəs] NOUN (PL **canvases**)

la lona

cap [kæp] NOUN

1 (*of bottle, tube*)

el tapón (PL los tapones)

2 (*hat*)

la gorra

capable ['keɪpəbl] ADJECTIVE

capaz

◆ **to be capable of doing something** ser* capaz de hacer algo ◊ *She's capable of doing much more.* Es capaz de hacer mucho más.

capacity [kə'pæsɪtɪ] NOUN (PL **capacities**)

la capacidad ◊ *The tank has a 40-litre capacity.* El depósito tiene una capacidad de 40 litros. ◊ *He has a capacity for hard work.* Tiene mucha capacidad de trabajo.

capital ['kæpɪtl] NOUN

1 la capital ◊ *Cardiff is the capital of Wales.* Cardiff es la capital del país de Gales.

2 la mayúscula (*letter*) ◊ *in capitals* en mayúsculas

capitalism ['kæpɪtəlɪzəm] NOUN

* Verbs marked with this symbol are irregular. See pages 380-382 for further details

el capitalismo

capital punishment [ˈkæpɪtlˈpʌnɪʃmənt] NOUN
la pena capital

Capricorn [ˈkæprɪkɔːn] NOUN
el Capricornio (*sign*) ◊ *I'm Capricorn.* Soy Capricornio.
♦ **a Capricorn** un/una Capricornio

to **capsize** [kæpˈsaɪz] VERB
volcar*

captain [ˈkæptɪn] NOUN
el capitán (PL los capitanes)
la capitana

caption [ˈkæpʃən] NOUN
la leyenda

to **capture** [ˈkæptʃəʳ] VERB
capturar

car [kɑːʳ] NOUN
el coche
♦ **to go by car** ir* en coche ◊ *We went by car.* Fuimos en coche.
♦ **a car crash** un accidente de coche

caramel [ˈkærəməl] NOUN
el caramelo ◊ *a box of caramels* una caja de caramelos

caravan [ˈkærəvæn] NOUN
la caravana ◊ *a caravan site* un cámping de caravanas

card [kɑːd] NOUN
1 la tarjeta ◊ *I got lots of cards and presents on my birthday.* Recibí muchas tarjetas y regalos para mi cumpleaños.
2 la carta
♦ **a card game** un juego de cartas

cardboard [ˈkɑːdbɔːd] NOUN
el cartón ◊ *a cardboard box* una caja de cartón

cardigan [ˈkɑːdɪgən] NOUN
la chaqueta de punto

cardphone [ˈkɑːdfəun] NOUN
el teléfono de tarjeta

care [kɛəʳ] NOUN
see also **care** VERB
el cuidado ◊ *with care* con cuidado
♦ **to take care of** cuidar a ◊ *I take care of the children on Saturdays.* Yo cuido a los niños los sábados.
♦ **Take care! (1)** (*be careful!*) ¡Ten cuidado!
♦ **Take care! (2)** (*look after yourself!*) ¡Cuídate!

to **care** [kɛəʳ] VERB
see also **care** NOUN
♦ **to care about** preocuparse por ◊ *a company that cares about the environment* una empresa que se preocupa por el medio ambiente ◊ *They don't care about their image.* No se preocupan por su imagen.
♦ **I don't care!** ¡No me importa!
♦ **Who cares?** ¿Y a quién le importa?

to **care for** [ˈkɛəfɔːʳ] VERB
1 preocuparse por ◊ *He wanted me to know he still cared for me.* Quería que supiera que todavía se preocupaba por mí.
2 cuidar ◊ *They employed a nurse to care for her.* Emplearon a una enfermera para cuidarla.

career [kəˈrɪəʳ] NOUN
la carrera

careful [ˈkɛəful] ADJECTIVE
♦ **Be careful!** ¡Ten cuidado!

carefully [ˈkɛəfəlɪ] ADVERB
con cuidado (*cautiously*) ◊ *Drive carefully!* ¡Conduce con cuidado!
♦ **Think carefully!** ¡Piénsalo bien!
♦ **She carefully avoided talking about it.** Tuvo mucho cuidado de no hablar del tema.

careless [ˈkɛəlɪs] ADJECTIVE
1 poco cuidado (*work*)
♦ **a careless mistake** un error de descuido
2 poco cuidadoso (*person*) ◊ *She's very careless.* Es muy poco cuidadosa.
♦ **a careless driver** un conductor imprudente

caretaker [ˈkɛəteɪkəʳ] NOUN
el/la conserje
♦ **school caretaker** el bedel

car ferry [ˈkɑːferɪ] NOUN (PL **car ferries**)
el ferry (PL los ferrys)

cargo [ˈkɑːgəu] NOUN (PL **cargoes**)
el cargamento

car hire [ˈkɑːhaɪəʳ] NOUN
el alquiler de coches

Caribbean [kærɪˈbiːən] ADJECTIVE
see also **Caribbean** NOUN
caribeño

Caribbean [kærɪˈbiːən] NOUN
see also **Caribbean** ADJECTIVE
♦ **We're going to the Caribbean.** Vamos al Caribe.
♦ **the Caribbean** (*sea*) el mar Caribe

caring [ˈkɛərɪŋ] ADJECTIVE
bondadoso
♦ **the caring professions** las profesiones de vocación social

carnation [kɑːˈneɪʃən] NOUN
el clavel

carnival [ˈkɑːnɪvl] NOUN
el carnaval

carol [ˈkærəl] NOUN
♦ **a Christmas carol** un villancico

car park [ˈkɑːpɑːk] NOUN
el aparcamiento

carpenter [ˈkɑːpɪntəʳ] NOUN
el carpintero
la carpintera
◊ *He's a carpenter.* Es carpintero.

carpet [ˈkɑːpɪt] NOUN
1 la moqueta (*fitted*)
2 la alfombra ◊ *a Persian carpet* una alfombra persa

C

car phone [ˈkɑːfəun] NOUN
el teléfono de coche

car rental [ˈkɑːrɛntl] NOUN US
el alquiler de coches

carriage [ˈkærɪdʒ] NOUN
(*of train*)
el vagón (PL los vagones)

carrier bag [ˈkærɪəbæg] NOUN
la bolsa de plástico

carrot [ˈkærət] NOUN
la zanahoria

to **carry** [ˈkærɪ] VERB (**carried, carried**)
1 llevar ◇ *I'll carry your bag.* Te llevo la bolsa.
2 transportar ◇ *a plane carrying 100 passengers* un avión que transporta 100 pasajeros

to **carry on** [kærɪˈɔn] VERB
seguir* ◇ *She carried on talking.* Siguió hablando.
♦ **Carry on!** ¡Sigue! ◇ *Am I boring you? – No, carry on!* ¿Te estoy aburriendo? – ¡No, sigue!

to **carry out** [kærɪˈaut] VERB
1 cumplir (*orders*)
2 llevar a cabo (*threat, task, instructions*)

carrycot [ˈkærɪkɔt] NOUN
el moisés (PL los moisés)

cart [kɑːt] NOUN
el carro

carton [ˈkɑːtən] NOUN
(*of milk, fruit juice*)
el cartón (PL los cartones)

cartoon [kɑːˈtuːn] NOUN
1 los dibujos animados (*film*)
2 el chiste (*in newspaper*)
♦ **a strip cartoon** una tira cómica

cartridge [ˈkɑːtrɪdʒ] NOUN
el cartucho

to **carve** [kɑːv] VERB
trinchar ◇ *Dad carved the roast.* Papá trinchó el asado.
♦ **a carved oak chair** una silla de roble tallado

case [keɪs] NOUN
1 la maleta ◇ *I've packed my case.* He hecho mi maleta.
2 el caso ◇ *in some cases* en algunos casos ◇ *The police are investigating the case.* La policía está investigando el caso.
♦ **in case it rains** por si llueve
♦ **just in case** por si acaso ◇ *Take some money with you, just in case.* Llévate algo de dinero por si acaso.

cash [kæʃ] NOUN
see also **cash** VERB
el dinero ◇ *I'm a bit short of cash.* Ando un poco justo de dinero.
♦ **in cash** en efectivo ◇ *£200 in cash* 200 libras esterlinas en efectivo
♦ **to pay cash** pagar* al contado

to **cash** [kæʃ] VERB
see also **cash** NOUN
♦ **to cash a cheque** cobrar un cheque

cash card [ˈkæʃkɑːd] NOUN
la tarjeta de cajero automático

cash desk [ˈkæʃdɛsk] NOUN
la caja

cash dispenser [ˈkæʃdɪsˈpensəʳ] NOUN
el cajero automático

cashew nut [kæˈʃuːnʌt] NOUN
el anacardo

cashier [kæˈʃɪəʳ] NOUN
el cajero
la cajera

cashmere [ˈkæʃmɪəʳ] NOUN
el cachemir ◇ *a cashmere sweater* un suéter de cachemir

cash register [ˈkæʃrɛdʒɪstəʳ] NOUN
la caja registradora

casino [kəˈsiːnəu] NOUN (PL **casinos**)
el casino

casserole [ˈkæsərəul] NOUN
el guiso ◇ *to make a casserole* hacer* un guiso
♦ **a casserole dish** una cazuela

cassette [kæˈsɛt] NOUN
el casete
♦ **a cassette player** un casete
♦ **a cassette recorder** un casete

cast [kɑːst] NOUN
el reparto ◇ *The cast of the film includes many famous actors.* El reparto de la película incluye a muchos actores famosos.
♦ **After the play, we met the cast.** Cuando terminó la obra charlamos con los actores.

castle [ˈkɑːsl] NOUN
el castillo

casual [ˈkæʒjul] ADJECTIVE
1 informal ◇ *I prefer casual clothes.* Prefiero la ropa informal.
2 despreocupado ◇ *a casual attitude* una actitud despreocupada
3 eventual ◇ *It's just a casual job.* Es sólo un trabajo eventual.
♦ **a casual remark** un comentario hecho de pasada

casually [ˈkæʒjulɪ] ADVERB
♦ **to dress casually** vestir* informal

casualty [ˈkæʒjultɪ] NOUN (PL **casualties**)
1 urgencias FEM PL (*hospital department*) ◇ *He was taken to casualty after the accident.* Lo llevaron a urgencias después del accidente.

2 la víctima ◊ *The casualties include a young boy.* Entre las víctimas se encuentra un niño.

cat [kæt] NOUN
el gato
la gata

catalogue ['kætəlɔg] NOUN
el catálogo

catalytic converter [kætə'lɪtɪkkən'vəːtəʳ] NOUN
el catalizador

catarrh [kə'tɑːʳ] NOUN
el catarro

catastrophe [kə'tæstrəfɪ] NOUN
la catástrofe

to **catch** [kætʃ] VERB (**caught, caught**)
1 coger* (agarrar *LatAm*)

Be very careful with the verb ***coger****: in most of Latin America this is an extremely rude word that should be avoided. Use* ***tomar*** *in Latin America instead if catching train, bus etc. However, in Spain this verb is common and not rude at all.*

◊ *They caught the thief.* Cogieron al ladrón. ◊ *We caught the last train.* Cogimos el último tren.

♦ **My cat catches birds.** Mi gato caza pájaros.

2 agarrar ◊ *He caught her arm.* La agarró del brazo.

♦ **to catch a cold** resfriarse*

♦ **I didn't catch his name.** No me enteré de su nombre.

♦ **He caught her stealing.** La pilló robando.

♦ **If they catch you smoking you'll be in trouble.** Si te pillan fumando te la vas a cargar.

to **catch up** [kætʃ'ʌp] VERB
1 ponerse* al día ◊ *I've got to catch up on my work.* Tengo que ponerme al día con el trabajo.
2 alcanzar* ◊ *She caught me up.* Me alcanzó.

catching ['kætʃɪŋ] ADJECTIVE
contagioso ◊ *Don't worry, it's not catching!* ¡No te preocupes, no es contagioso!

catering ['keɪtərɪŋ] NOUN
♦ **The hotel did all the catering for the wedding.** El hotel se encargó de organizar el banquete de bodas.

cathedral [kə'θiːdrəl] NOUN
la catedral

Catholic ['kæθəlɪk] ADJECTIVE
see also **Catholic** NOUN
católico

Catholic ['kæθəlɪk] NOUN
see also **Catholic** ADJECTIVE
el católico
la católica
◊ *I'm a Catholic.* Soy católico.

cattle ['kætl] PL NOUN
el ganado

caught [kɔːt] VERB *see* **catch**

cauliflower ['kɔlɪflauəʳ] NOUN
la coliflor

cause [kɔːz] NOUN
see also **cause** VERB
la causa

to **cause** [kɔːz] VERB
see also **cause** NOUN
causar

cautious ['kɔːʃəs] ADJECTIVE
prudente

cautiously ['kɔːʃəslɪ] ADVERB
con cautela

cave [keɪv] NOUN
la cueva

caviar ['kævɪɑːʳ] NOUN
el caviar

CCTV [siːsiːtiː'viː] NOUN (= *closed-circuit television*)
el circuito cerrado de televisión

CD [siː'diː] NOUN
el CD (PL los CDs)

CD player [siː'diːpleɪəʳ] NOUN
el reproductor de CD

CD-ROM [siːdiː'rɔm] NOUN
el CD-ROM

ceasefire ['siːsfaɪəʳ] NOUN
el alto el fuego

ceiling ['siːlɪŋ] NOUN
el techo

to **celebrate** ['sɛlɪbreɪt] VERB
celebrar

celebration [sɛlɪ'breɪʃən] NOUN
la celebración

celebrity [sɪ'lɛbrɪtɪ] NOUN (PL **celebrities**)
la celebridad

celery ['sɛlərɪ] NOUN
el apio

cell [sɛl] NOUN
1 la celda ◊ *Prisoners spend many hours in their cells.* Los prisioneros pasan muchas horas en sus celdas.
2 la célula (*in biology*)

cellar ['sɛləʳ] NOUN
el sótano

♦ **a wine cellar** una bodega

cello ['tʃɛləu] NOUN (PL **cellos**)
el violonchelo

cement [sə'mɛnt] NOUN
el cemento

cemetery ['sɛmɪtrɪ] NOUN (PL **cemeteries**)
el cementerio

cent [sɛnt] NOUN
el centavo

centenary [sɛn'tiːnərɪ] NOUN (PL **centenaries**)
el centenario

center ['sɛntəʳ] NOUN US
el centro

centigrade ['sɛntɪgreɪd] ADJECTIVE

☞

centígrado ◊ *20 degrees centigrade* 20 grados centígrados

centimetre ['sɛntɪmiːtəʳ] NOUN (US **centimeter**)
el centímetro

central ['sɛntrəl] ADJECTIVE
central

central heating ['sɛntrəl'hiːtɪŋ] NOUN
la calefacción central

central reservation ['sɛntrəlrɛzə'veɪʃən] NOUN
la mediana

centre ['sɛntəʳ] NOUN
el centro

century ['sɛntjurɪ] NOUN (PL **centuries**)
el siglo ◊ *the twentieth century* el siglo veinte

cereal ['siːrɪəl] NOUN
los cereales ◊ *I have cereal for breakfast.* Desayuno cereales.

ceremony ['sɛrɪmənɪ] NOUN (PL **ceremonies**)
la ceremonia

certain ['səːtən] ADJECTIVE
1 cierto (*particular*) ◊ *a certain person* cierta persona
2 seguro (*definite*) ◊ *I am certain he's not coming.* Estoy seguro de que no viene.
◆ **for certain** con certeza
◆ **to make certain** cerciorarse ◊ *I made certain the door was locked.* Me cercioré de que la puerta estaba cerrada con llave.

certainly ['səːtənlɪ] ADVERB
por supuesto ◊ *I shall certainly be there.* Por supuesto que estaré allí. ◊ *Certainly not!* ¡Por supuesto que no!
◆ **So it was a surprise? – It certainly was!** ¿Así que fue una sorpresa? – ¡Ya lo creo!

certificate [sə'tɪfɪkɪt] NOUN
el certificado

chain [tʃeɪn] NOUN
la cadena ◊ *a gold chain* una cadena de oro

chair [tʃɛəʳ] NOUN
1 la silla ◊ *a table and four chairs* una mesa y cuatro sillas
2 (*armchair*)
el sillón (PL los sillones)

chairlift ['tʃɛəlɪft] NOUN
el telesilla

Although ***telesilla*** *ends in* ***-a****, it is actually a masculine noun.*

chairman ['tʃɛəmən] NOUN (PL **chairmen**)
el presidente
la presidenta

chalet ['ʃæleɪ] NOUN
el chalet (PL los chalets)

chalk [tʃɔːk] NOUN
la tiza
◆ **a piece of chalk** una tiza

challenge ['tʃælɪndʒ] NOUN
see also **challenge** VERB
el reto

to **challenge** ['tʃælɪndʒ] VERB
see also **challenge** NOUN
retar ◊ *She challenged me to a race.* Me retó a echar una carrera.

challenging ['tʃælɪndʒɪŋ] ADJECTIVE
estimulante ◊ *a challenging job* un trabajo estimulante

chambermaid ['tʃeɪmbəʳmeɪd] NOUN
la camarera

champagne [ʃæm'peɪn] NOUN
el champán

champion ['tʃæmpɪən] NOUN
el campeón (PL los campeones)
la campeona

championship ['tʃæmpɪənʃɪp] NOUN
el campeonato

chance [tʃɑːns] NOUN
1 la posibilidad ◊ *The team's chances of winning are very good.* El equipo tiene muchas posibilidades de ganar.
2 la oportunidad ◊ *I had the chance of working in Brazil.* Tuve la oportunidad de trabajar en Brasil.
◆ **I'll write when I get the chance.** Te escribiré cuando tenga un momento.
◆ **by chance** por casualidad
◆ **No chance!** ¡Ni en broma!
◆ **to take a chance** arriesgarse* ◊ *I'm taking no chances!* ¡No me quiero arriesgar!

Chancellor of the Exchequer ['tʃɑːnslər-əvðɪks'tʃɛkəʳ] NOUN
el Ministro de Economía y Hacienda
la Ministra de Economía y Hacienda

to **change** [tʃeɪndʒ] VERB
see also **change** NOUN
1 cambiar ◊ *The town has changed a lot.* La ciudad ha cambiado mucho. ◊ *I'd like to change £50.* Quisiera cambiar 50 libras esterlinas. ◊ *I'd like to change this jumper, it's too small.* Me gustaría cambiar este jersey, es demasiado pequeño.
2 cambiar de ◊ *He wants to change his job.* Quiere cambiar de trabajo. ◊ *I'm going to change my shoes.* Voy a cambiarme de zapatos.
◆ **to get changed** cambiarse
◆ **to change one's mind** cambiar de idea

change [tʃeɪndʒ] NOUN
see also **change** VERB
1 el cambio ◊ *There's been a change of plan.* Ha habido un cambio de planes.
◆ **a change of clothes** una muda
◆ **for a change** para variar
2 el dinero suelto ◊ *I haven't got any change.* No tengo dinero suelto.

♦ **Can you give me change for a pound?** ¿Me puede cambiar una libra?
♦ **There's your change.** Aquí tiene el cambio.

changeable ['tʃeɪndʒəbl] ADJECTIVE
variable

changing room ['tʃeɪndʒɪŋrum] NOUN
1 el probador (*in shop*)
2 el vestuario (*for sport*)

channel ['tʃænl] NOUN
el canal (*TV*)
♦ **the English Channel** el Canal de la Mancha
♦ **the Channel Islands** las islas del Canal de la Mancha
♦ **the Channel Tunnel** el túnel del Canal de la Mancha

chaos ['keɪɔs] NOUN
el caos

chap [tʃæp] NOUN
el tipo (*informal*)

chapel ['tʃæpl] NOUN
la capilla

chapter ['tʃæptəʳ] NOUN
el capítulo

character ['kærɪktəʳ] NOUN
1 el carácter ◊ *Can you give me some idea of his character?* ¿Puede describirme un poco su carácter?
2 el personaje (*in film, book*)
♦ **She's quite a character.** Es todo un personaje.

characteristic [kærɪktə'rɪstɪk] NOUN
la característica

charcoal ['tʃɑːkəul] NOUN
1 el carbón vegetal (*for barbecue*)
2 el carboncillo (*for drawing*)

charge [tʃɑːdʒ] NOUN
see also **charge** VERB
♦ **Is there a charge for delivery?** ¿Cobran por el envío?
♦ **an extra charge** un suplemento
♦ **free of charge** gratuito
♦ **I'd like to reverse the charges.** Quisiera llamar a cobro revertido.
♦ **to be in charge** ser* el responsable ◊ *She was in charge of the group.* Ella era la responsable del grupo.

to **charge** [tʃɑːdʒ] VERB
see also **charge** NOUN
1 cobrar ◊ *How much did he charge you?* ¿Cuánto te cobró?
2 acusar (*with crime*) ◊ *The police have charged him with murder.* La policía lo ha acusado de asesinato.

charity ['tʃærɪtɪ] NOUN (PL **charities**) (*organization*)
la organización benéfica (PL las organizaciones benéficas) ◊ *He gave the money to charity.* Donó el dinero a una organización benéfica.
♦ **to collect for charity** recaudar dinero para obras benéficas
♦ **charity shop**

> ℹ ***Charity shops*** *son tiendas de artículos de segunda mano baratos. Los beneficios de las ventas se destinan enteramente a obras benéficas.*

charm [tʃɑːm] NOUN
el encanto

charming ['tʃɑːmɪŋ] ADJECTIVE
encantador MASC
encantadora FEM

chart [tʃɑːt] NOUN
el gráfico ◊ *The chart shows the rise of unemployment.* El gráfico muestra el aumento del desempleo.
♦ **the charts** la lista de éxitos ◊ *His record has been in the charts for 10 weeks.* Su disco ha estado en la lista de éxitos durante 10 semanas.

charter flight ['tʃɑːtəflaɪt] NOUN
el vuelo chárter

to **chase** [tʃeɪs] VERB
see also **chase** NOUN
1 perseguir* ◊ *The policeman chased the thief along the road.* El policía persiguió al ladrón a lo largo de la calle.
2 ir* detrás de ◊ *He's always chasing the girls.* Siempre va detrás de las chicas.

chase [tʃeɪs] NOUN
see also **chase** VERB
la persecución (PL las persecuciones) ◊ *a car chase* una persecución en coche

chat [tʃæt] NOUN
la charla
♦ **to have a chat** charlar

chatroom ['tʃætrum] NOUN
el chat

chat show ['tʃætʃəu] NOUN
el programa de entrevistas

> *Although **programa** ends in **-a**, it is actually a masculine noun.*

to **chat up** [tʃæt'ʌp] VERB
intentar ligarse a ◊ *Jake was chatting up one of the girls.* Jake estaba intentando ligarse a una de las chicas.

cheap [tʃiːp] ADJECTIVE
barato ◊ *a cheap T-shirt* una camiseta barata ◊ *It's cheaper by bus.* Es más barato en autobús.
♦ **a cheap flight** un vuelo económico

to **cheat** [tʃiːt] VERB
see also **cheat** NOUN
1 hacer* trampa (*at cards*) ◊ *You're cheating!* ¡Estás haciendo trampa!
2 copiar (*in exam*)

cheat [tʃiːt] NOUN
see also **cheat** VERB
el tramposo
la tramposa

check [tʃɛk] NOUN

see also **check** VERB

1 el control ◊ *a security check* un control de seguridad

2 el cheque US

◊ *to write a check* extender* un cheque

3 la cuenta US

◊ *The waiter brought us the check.* El camarero nos trajo la cuenta.

to **check** [tʃɛk] VERB

see also **check** NOUN

comprobar* ◊ *Could you check the oil, please?* ¿Podría comprobar el aceite, por favor?

◆ **to check with somebody** preguntarle a alguien ◊ *I'll check with the driver what time the bus leaves.* Le preguntaré al conductor a qué hora sale el autobús.

to **check in** [tʃɛk'ɪn] VERB

1 facturar (*at airport*)

2 registrarse (*in hotel*)

to **check out** [tʃɛk'aut] VERB

dejar el hotel

checked [tʃɛkt] ADJECTIVE

a cuadros MASC, FEM, PL

checkers ['tʃɛkəz] NOUN US

las damas ◊ *to play checkers* jugar* a las damas

check-in ['tʃɛkɪn] NOUN (PL **check-ins**)

la facturación de equipajes

checking account ['tʃɛkɪŋəkaunt] NOUN US

la cuenta corriente

checkout ['tʃɛkaut] NOUN

la caja

check-up ['tʃɛkʌp] NOUN (PL **check-ups**)

el reconocimiento

cheek [tʃi:k] NOUN

la mejilla ◊ *He kissed her on the cheek.* La besó en la mejilla.

◆ **What a cheek!** ¡Qué cara!

cheeky ['tʃi:kɪ] ADJECTIVE

descarado ◊ *Don't be cheeky!* ¡No seas descarado!

◆ **a cheeky smile** una sonrisilla maliciosa

cheer [tʃɪəʳ] NOUN

see also **cheer** VERB

◆ **Three cheers for the winner!** ¡Viva el ganador!

◆ **Cheers! (1)** (*when drinking*) ¡Salud!

◆ **Cheers! (2)** (*thank you*) ¡Gracias!

to **cheer** [tʃɪəʳ] VERB

see also **cheer** NOUN

vitorear

◆ **to cheer somebody up** levantar el ánimo a alguien ◊ *I was trying to cheer him up.* Estaba intentando levantarle el ánimo.

◆ **Cheer up!** ¡Anímate!

cheerful ['tʃɪəful] ADJECTIVE

alegre

cheerio [tʃɪərɪ'əu] EXCLAMATION

¡hasta luego!

cheese [tʃi:z] NOUN

el queso

chef [ʃɛf] NOUN

el/la chef (PL los/las chefs)

chemical ['kɛmɪkl] NOUN

la sustancia química

chemist ['kɛmɪst] NOUN

1 (*dispenser*)

el farmacéutico

la farmacéutica

2 (*shop*)

la farmacia ◊ *You get it from the chemist.* Se compra en la farmacia.

> *Chemist's shops in Spain are identified by a special green cross outside the shop.*

3 (*scientist*)

el químico

la química

chemistry ['kɛmɪstrɪ] NOUN

la química ◊ *the chemistry lab* el laboratorio de química

cheque [tʃɛk] NOUN

el cheque ◊ *to write a cheque* extender* un cheque ◊ *to pay by cheque* pagar* con cheque

chequebook ['tʃɛkbuk] NOUN

el talonario de cheques

cherry ['tʃɛrɪ] NOUN (PL **cherries**)

la cereza

chess [tʃɛs] NOUN

el ajedrez ◊ *He likes playing chess.* Le gusta jugar al ajedrez.

chessboard ['tʃɛsbɔ:d] NOUN

el tablero de ajedrez

chest [tʃɛst] NOUN

el pecho ◊ *I've got a pain in my chest.* Tengo un dolor en el pecho.

chestnut ['tʃɛsnʌt] NOUN

la castaña

chest of drawers [tʃɛstəv'drɔ:z] NOUN

la cómoda

to **chew** [tʃu:] VERB

masticar*

chewing gum ['tʃu:ɪŋgʌm] NOUN

el chicle

◆ **a piece of chewing gum** un chicle

chick [tʃɪk] NOUN

el polluelo ◊ *a hen and her chicks* una gallina y sus polluelos

chicken ['tʃɪkɪn] NOUN

1 la gallina (*animal*)

2 el pollo (*food*)

chickenpox ['tʃɪkɪnpɔks] NOUN

la varicela ◊ *I've got chickenpox.* Tengo la varicela.

chickpeas ['tʃɪkpi:z] PL NOUN

los garbanzos
chief [tʃiːf] NOUN
see also **chief** ADJECTIVE
el jefe
la jefa
◊ *the chief of security* el jefe de seguridad
chief [tʃiːf] ADJECTIVE
see also **chief** NOUN
principal ◊ *His chief reason for resigning was the low pay.* El motivo principal de su dimisión fue el sueldo bajo.
child [tʃaɪld] NOUN (PL **children**)
1 el niño
la niña
◊ *a child of six* un niño de seis años
2 el hijo
la hija
◊ *Susan is our eldest child.* Susan es nuestra hija mayor. ◊ *They've got three children.* Tienen tres hijos.
childish ['tʃaɪldɪʃ] ADJECTIVE
infantil
child minder ['tʃaɪldmaɪndə^r] NOUN
la niñera
children ['tʃɪldrən] PL NOUN see **child**
Chile ['tʃɪlɪ] NOUN
Chile MASC
to **chill** [tʃɪl] VERB
see also **chill** NOUN
poner* a enfriar (*drink, food*)
♦**Serve chilled.** Sírvase bien frío.
chill [tʃɪl] NOUN
see also **chill** VERB
♦**to catch a chill** resfriarse*
chilli ['tʃɪlɪ] NOUN
el chile
♦**chilli con carne** el chile con carne
chilly ['tʃɪlɪ] ADJECTIVE
frío
chimney ['tʃɪmnɪ] NOUN
la chimenea
chin [tʃɪn] NOUN
la barbilla
♦**Keep your chin up!** ¡No pierdas el ánimo!
china ['tʃaɪnə] NOUN
la porcelana ◊ *a china plate* un plato de porcelana
China ['tʃaɪnə] NOUN
China FEM
Chinese [tʃaɪ'niːz] ADJECTIVE
see also **Chinese** NOUN
chino
♦**a Chinese man** un chino
♦**a Chinese woman** una china
Chinese [tʃaɪ'niːz] NOUN
see also **Chinese** ADJECTIVE
el chino (*language*)
♦**the Chinese** los chinos
chip [tʃɪp] NOUN
1 (*food*)
la patata frita (la papa frita *LatAm*)
2 (*in computer*)
el chip (PL los chips)
chiropodist [kɪ'rɔpədɪst] NOUN
el podólogo
la podóloga
◊ *He's a chiropodist.* Es podólogo.
chives [tʃaɪvz] PL NOUN
los cebollinos
chocolate ['tʃɔklɪt] NOUN
1 el chocolate ◊ *a chocolate cake* un pastel de chocolate ◊ *a cup of hot chocolate* una taza de chocolate
2 el bombón (PL los bombones) ◊ *a box of chocolates* una caja de bombones
choice [tʃɔɪs] NOUN
la elección (PL las elecciones)
♦**I had no choice.** No tenía otro remedio.
choir ['kwaɪə^r] NOUN
el coro
to **choke** [tʃəuk] VERB
atragantarse (*on food*)
to **choose** [tʃuːz] VERB (**chose, chosen**)
elegir*
to **chop** [tʃɔp] VERB
see also **chop** NOUN
1 picar* (*onion, herbs*)
2 cortar en trozos pequeños (*meat*)
chop [tʃɔp] NOUN
see also **chop** VERB
la chuleta ◊ *a pork chop* una chuleta de cerdo
chopsticks ['tʃɔpstɪks] PL NOUN
los palillos
chose, chosen [tʃəuz, 'tʃəuzn] VERB see **choose**
Christ [kraɪst] NOUN
Cristo MASC
christening ['krɪsnɪŋ] NOUN
el bautismo
Christian ['krɪstɪən] NOUN
see also **Christian** ADJECTIVE
el cristiano
la cristiana
Christian ['krɪstɪən] ADJECTIVE
see also **Christian** NOUN
cristiano
Christian name ['krɪstɪənneɪm] NOUN
el nombre de pila
Christmas ['krɪsməs] NOUN
la Navidad ◊ *Happy Christmas!* ¡Feliz Navidad!
♦**Christmas Day** el día de Navidad
♦**on Christmas Day** el día de Navidad
♦**Christmas Eve** Nochebuena
♦**a Christmas tree** un árbol de Navidad
♦**Christmas dinner** la comida de Navidad

i As well as lunch on Christmas Day, Spaniards also have a special supper on Christmas Eve.

◆**a Christmas present** un regalo de Navidad

> *In Spain Christmas presents are traditionally given on 6th January although more and more people are exchanging gifts on Christmas Eve.*

◆**Christmas pudding**

> ***Christmas pudding** es un pudding de frutas confitadas que se come el día de Navidad. Antes de servir, se riega con coñac y se flamea.*

◆**Christmas card** la tarjeta de Navidad
◆**at Christmas** en Navidad

to **chuck out** ['tʃʌk'aut] VERB
tirar a la basura ◊ *You'll need to chuck out some of these books.* Tendrás que tirar a la basura alguno de estos libros.

chunk [tʃʌŋk] NOUN
el pedazo ◊ *Cut the meat into chunks.* Córtese la carne en pedazos.

church [tʃəːtʃ] NOUN (PL **churches**)
la iglesia
◆**the Church of England** la Iglesia Anglicana

cider ['saɪdəʳ] NOUN
la sidra

cigar [sɪ'gɑːʳ] NOUN
el puro

cigarette [sɪgə'rɛt] NOUN
el cigarrillo

cigarette lighter [sɪgə'rɛtlaɪtəʳ] NOUN
el mechero

cinema ['sɪnəmə] NOUN
el cine

cinnamon ['sɪnəmən] NOUN
la canela

circle ['səːkl] NOUN
el círculo

circular ['səːkjuləʳ] ADJECTIVE
circular

circulation [səːkju'leɪʃən] NOUN
1 la circulación ◊ *She has poor circulation.* Tiene mala circulación.
2 la tirada ◊ *The newspaper has a circulation of around 8000.* El periódico tiene una tirada de unos 8.000 ejemplares.

circumstances ['səːkəmstənsɪz] PL NOUN
las circunstancias ◊ *in the circumstances* dadas las circunstancias
◆**under no circumstances** bajo ningún concepto

circus ['səːkəs] NOUN (PL **circuses**)
el circo

citizen ['sɪtɪzn] NOUN
el ciudadano
la ciudadana

City ['sɪtɪ] NOUN
◆**the City** la City de Londres

city ['sɪtɪ] NOUN (PL **cities**)
la ciudad ◊ *the city centre* el centro de la ciudad

city technology college ['sɪtɪtɛk'nɔlədʒɪkɔlɪdʒ] NOUN
el centro de formación profesional

> *En Gran Bretaña los **city technology colleges** son centros de enseñanza secundaria que dan especial importancia a la ciencia y tecnología.*

civilization [sɪvɪlaɪ'zeɪʃən] NOUN
la civilización (PL las civilizaciones)

civil servant [sɪvɪl'səːvənt] NOUN
el funcionario
la funcionaria
◊ *He's a civil servant.* Es funcionario.

civil war [sɪvɪl'wɔːʳ] NOUN
la guerra civil

to **claim** [kleɪm] VERB
see also **claim** NOUN
1 asegurar ◊ *He claims he found the money.* Asegura haber encontrado el dinero.
2 reclamar ◊ *He's claiming compensation from the company.* Reclama una indemnización por parte de la empresa.
3 cobrar ◊ *She's claiming unemployment benefit.* Cobra subsidio de desempleo.
◆**We claimed on our insurance.** Reclamamos al seguro.

claim [kleɪm] NOUN
see also **claim** VERB
1 (*on insurance policy*)
la reclamación (PL las reclamaciones)
◆**to make a claim** reclamar al seguro
2 la afirmación (PL las afirmaciones) ◊ *The manufacturer's claims are obviously untrue.* Las afirmaciones del fabricante son obviamente falsas.

to **clap** [klæp] VERB
aplaudir
◆**to clap one's hands** dar* palmadas

clarinet [klærɪ'nɛt] NOUN
el clarinete

to **clash** [klæʃ] VERB
1 desentonar (*colours*) ◊ *Red clashes with orange.* El rojo desentona con el naranja.
2 coincidir (*events*) ◊ *The party clashes with the meeting.* La fiesta coincide con la reunión.

clasp [klɑːsp] NOUN

el cierre (*of necklace, handbag*)

class [klɑːs] NOUN (PL **classes**)
la clase ◊ *We're in the same class.* Estamos en la misma clase. ◊ *I go to dancing classes.* Voy a clases de baile.

classic ['klæsɪk] ADJECTIVE
see also **classic** NOUN
clásico ◊ *a classic example* un ejemplo clásico

classic ['klæsɪk] NOUN
see also **classic** ADJECTIVE
el clásico

classical ['klæsɪkl] ADJECTIVE
clásico ◊ *classical music* la música clásica

classmate ['klɑːsmeɪt] NOUN
el compañero de clase
la compañera de clase

classroom ['klɑːsrum] NOUN
la clase

clause [klɔːz] NOUN
1 (*in legal document*)
la cláusula
2 (*in grammar*)
la oración (PL las oraciones)

claw [klɔː] NOUN
1 la garra (*of lion, eagle*)
2 la uña (*of cat, parrot*)
3 la pinza (*of crab, lobster*)

clean [kliːn] ADJECTIVE
see also **clean** VERB
limpio

to **clean** [kliːn] VERB
see also **clean** ADJECTIVE
limpiar
♦ **I clean my teeth after every meal.** Me lavo los dientes después de cada comida.

cleaner ['kliːnəʳ] NOUN
1 (*person*)
el hombre de la limpieza
la mujer de la limpieza
2 (*substance*)
el producto de limpieza

cleaner's ['kliːnəz] NOUN
la tintorería ◊ *He took his coat to the cleaner's.* Llevó el abrigo a la tintorería.

cleaning lady ['kliːnɪŋleɪdɪ] NOUN
la mujer de la limpieza

cleansing lotion ['klɛnzɪŋ'ləuʃən] NOUN
la leche limpiadora

clear [klɪəʳ] ADJECTIVE
see also **clear** VERB
1 claro ◊ *a clear explanation* una explicación clara ◊ *It's clear you don't believe me.* Está claro que no me crees.
♦ **Have I made myself clear?** ¿Me explico?
2 despejado ◊ *Wait till the road is clear.* Espera hasta que la carretera esté despejada. ◊ *a clear day* un día despejado
3 transparente ◊ *It comes in a clear plastic bottle.* Viene en una botella de plástico transparente.

to **clear** [klɪəʳ] VERB
see also **clear** ADJECTIVE
1 despejar ◊ *They are clearing the road.* Están despejando la carretera.
2 despejarse (*fog, mist*)
♦ **She was cleared of murder.** La absolvieron del cargo de asesinato.
♦ **to clear the table** quitar la mesa

to **clear off** [klɪər'ɔf] VERB
largarse* ◊ *Clear off and leave me alone!* ¡Lárgate y déjame en paz!

to **clear up** [klɪər'ʌp] VERB
1 ordenar ◊ *Who's going to clear all this up?* ¿Quién va a ordenar todo esto?
2 resolver* ◊ *I'm sure we can clear up this problem right away.* Estoy seguro de que podemos resolver este problema enseguida.
♦ **I think it's going to clear up.** (*weather*) Creo que va a despejar.

clearly ['klɪəlɪ] ADVERB
claramente ◊ *to speak clearly* hablar claramente
♦ **Clearly this project will cost money.** Evidentemente este proyecto costará dinero.

clementine ['klɛməntaɪn] NOUN
la clementina

to **clench** [klɛntʃ] VERB
apretar* ◊ *She clenched her fists.* Apretó los puños.

clerk [klɑːk] NOUN
el empleado
la empleada
◊ *She's a clerk.* Es empleada.

clever ['klɛvəʳ] ADJECTIVE
1 listo ◊ *She's very clever.* Es muy lista.
2 ingenioso ◊ *a clever system* un sistema ingenioso
♦ **What a clever idea!** ¡Qué idea más genial!

to **click on** [klɪk] VERB
hacer* clic en (*computing*)
♦ **to click on the mouse** hacer clic con el ratón
♦ **to click on an icon** hacer clic en un icono

client ['klaɪənt] NOUN
el cliente
la clienta

cliff [klɪf] NOUN
el acantilado

climate ['klaɪmɪt] NOUN
el clima

*Although **clima** ends in **-a**, it is actually a masculine noun.*

to **climb** [klaɪm] VERB
1 escalar ◊ *Her ambition is to climb Mount Everest.* Su ambición es escalar el Monte Everest.

☞

[2] trepar a ◊ *They climbed a tree.* Treparon a un árbol.
◆**to climb the stairs** subir las escaleras
climber [ˈklaɪməʳ] NOUN
el escalador
la escaladora
climbing [ˈklaɪmɪŋ] NOUN
el montañismo
◆**to go climbing** hacer* montañismo ◊ *We're going climbing in Scotland.* Vamos a hacer montañismo en Escocia.
cling film [ˈklɪŋfɪlm] NOUN
el plástico para envolver alimentos
clinic [ˈklɪnɪk] NOUN
[1] el consultorio (*in NHS hospital*)
[2] la clínica (*private hospital*)
clip [klɪp] NOUN
[1] la horquilla (*for hair*)
[2] la secuencia ◊ *some clips from Kevin Costner's latest film* unas secuencias de la última película de Kevin Costner
clippers [ˈklɪpəz] PL NOUN
◆**nail clippers** el cortauñas (PL los cortauñas)
cloakroom [ˈkləukrum] NOUN
[1] el guardarropa (*for coats*)
*Although **guardarropa** ends in -a, it is actually a masculine noun.*
[2] los servicios (*toilet*)
clock [klɔk] NOUN
el reloj
◆**an alarm clock** un despertador
◆**a clock radio** un radio-despertador
clockwork [ˈklɔkwəːk] NOUN
◆**to go like clockwork** ir* sobre ruedas
clone [kləun] NOUN
see also **clone** VERB
el clon
to **clone** [kləun] VERB
see also **clone** NOUN
clonar ◊ *to clone a sheep* clonar una oveja
◆**a cloned sheep** una oveja clónica
close [kləus] ADJECTIVE, ADVERB
see also **close** VERB
[1] cerca ◊ *The shops are very close.* Las tiendas están muy cerca. ◊ *The hotel is close to the station.* El hotel está cerca de la estación.
◆**Come closer.** Acércate más.
◆**She was close to tears.** Estaba a punto de llorar.
[2] cercano ◊ *We have only invited close relations.* Sólo hemos invitado a parientes cercanos.
[3] íntimo ◊ *She's a close friend of mine.* Es amiga íntima mía.
◆**I'm very close to my sister.** Estoy muy unida a mi hermana.
[4] reñido ◊ *It was a very close contest.* Fue un concurso muy reñido.
◆**It's close this afternoon.** Hace bochorno esta tarde.
to **close** [kləuz] VERB
see also **close** ADJECTIVE
[1] cerrar* ◊ *The shops close at five thirty.* Las tiendas cierran a las cinco y media. ◊ *Please close the door.* Cierra la puerta, por favor.
[2] cerrarse* ◊ *The doors close automatically.* Las puertas se cierran automáticamente.
closed [kləuzd] ADJECTIVE
cerrado
closely [ˈkləuslɪ] ADVERB
de cerca (*look, examine*)
◆**This will be a closely fought race.** Será una carrera muy reñida.
cloth [klɔθ] NOUN
la tela ◊ *I would like five metres of this cloth, please.* Quisiera cinco metros de esta tela, por favor.
◆**a cloth** un trapo ◊ *Wipe it with a damp cloth.* Límpialo con un trapo húmedo.
clothes [kləuðz] PL NOUN
la ropa
◆**clothes horse** el tendedero plegable
◆**clothes line** la cuerda de tender
◆**clothes peg** la pinza para tender la ropa
cloud [klaud] NOUN
la nube
cloudy [ˈklaudɪ] ADJECTIVE
nublado
clove [kləuv] NOUN
◆**a clove of garlic** un diente de ajo
clown [klaun] NOUN
el payaso
club [klʌb] NOUN
[1] el club ◊ *a golf club* un club de golf ◊ *the youth club* el club juvenil
[2] la discoteca ◊ *We had dinner and went on to a club.* Cenamos y fuimos a una discoteca.
◆**clubs** (*at cards*) los tréboles ◊ *the ace of clubs* el as de tréboles
clubbing [ˈklʌbɪŋ] NOUN
◆**to go clubbing** ir* de discotecas
to **club together** [klʌbtəˈgɛðəʳ] VERB
hacer* una colecta ◊ *We clubbed together to buy her a present.* Hicimos una colecta para comprarle un regalo.
clue [kluː] NOUN
la pista ◊ *an important clue* una pista clave
◆**I haven't a clue.** No tengo ni idea.
clumsy [ˈklʌmzɪ] ADJECTIVE
torpe
clutch [klʌtʃ] NOUN
see also **clutch** VERB
el embrague (*of car*)
to **clutch** [klʌtʃ] VERB

* Verbs marked with this symbol are irregular. See pages 380-382 for further details

see also **clutch** NOUN
agarrar ◊ *She clutched my arm and begged me not to go.* Me agarró el brazo y me suplicó que no me marchara.

coach [kəutʃ] NOUN (PL **coaches**)
1 el autobús ◊ *by coach* en autobús ◊ *the coach station* la estación de autobuses ◊ *a coach trip* una excursión en autobús
2 (*trainer*)
el entrenador
la entrenadora
♦ **the Spanish coach** el entrenador del equipo español

coal [kəul] NOUN
el carbón
♦ **a coal mine** una mina de carbón
♦ **a coal miner** un minero de carbón

coarse [kɔːs] ADJECTIVE
1 basto ◊ *The bag was made of coarse black cloth.* La bolsa estaba hecha de una tela basta de color negro.
2 grueso ◊ *The sand is very coarse on that beach.* La arena es muy gruesa en esa playa.

coast [kəust] NOUN
la costa ◊ *It's on the west coast of Scotland.* Está en la costa oeste de Escocia.

coastguard ['kəustgɑːd] NOUN
el guardacostas (PL los guardacostas)

coat [kəut] NOUN
el abrigo ◊ *a woollen coat* un abrigo de lana
♦ **a coat of paint** una mano de pintura

coat hanger ['kəuthæŋəʳ] NOUN
la percha

cobweb ['kɔbwɛb] NOUN
la telaraña

cocaine [kə'keɪn] NOUN
la cocaína

cockerel ['kɔkərl] NOUN
el gallo

cocoa ['kəukəu] NOUN
el cacao
♦ **a cup of cocoa** una taza de chocolate

coconut ['kəukənʌt] NOUN
el coco

cod [kɔd] NOUN
el bacalao

code [kəud] NOUN
1 la clave ◊ *It's written in code.* Está escrito en clave.
2 el prefijo (*for telephone*) ◊ *What is the code for London?* ¿Cuál es el prefijo de Londres?

coffee ['kɔfɪ] NOUN
el café (PL los cafés)
◊ *a cup of coffee* una taza de café
♦ **A cup of coffee, please.** Un café, por favor.

coffeepot ['kɔfɪpɔt] NOUN
la cafetera

coffee table ['kɔfɪteɪbl] NOUN
la mesa de centro

coffin ['kɔfɪn] NOUN
el ataúd

coin [kɔɪn] NOUN
la moneda ◊ *a 20p coin* una moneda de 20 peniques

coincidence [kəu'ɪnsɪdəns] NOUN
la coincidencia

Coke ® [kəuk] NOUN
la Coca-Cola ®

colander ['kɔləndəʳ] NOUN
el colador

cold [kəuld] ADJECTIVE
see also **cold** NOUN
frío ◊ *The water's cold.* El agua está fría. ◊ *It's cold.* Hace frío. ◊ *Are you cold?* ¿Tienes frío?

cold [kəuld] NOUN
see also **cold** ADJECTIVE
1 el frío ◊ *I can't stand the cold.* No soporto el frío.
2 el resfriado (*illness*)
♦ **to catch a cold** resfriarse*
♦ **to have a cold** estar* resfriado

cold sore ['kəuldsɔːʳ] NOUN
la calentura

coleslaw ['kəulslɔː] NOUN

> *Ensalada de col, zanahoria, cebolla y mayonesa.*

to **collapse** [kə'læps] VERB
1 venirse* abajo
♦ **The bridge collapsed during the storm.** El puente se vino abajo en medio de la tormenta.
2 sufrir un colapso ◊ *He collapsed while playing tennis.* Sufrió un colapso mientras jugaba al tenis.

collar ['kɔləʳ] NOUN
1 el cuello (*of coat, shirt*)
2 el collar (*for animal*)

collarbone ['kɔləbəun] NOUN
la clavícula

colleague ['kɔliːg] NOUN
el/la colega

to **collect** [kə'lɛkt] VERB
1 recoger* ◊ *The teacher collected the exercise books.* El maestro recogió los cuadernos. ◊ *Their mother collects them from school.* Su madre los recoge del colegio.
2 coleccionar ◊ *He collects stamps.* Colecciona sellos.
3 hacer* una colecta ◊ *I'm collecting for UNICEF.* Estoy haciendo una colecta para la UNICEF.

collect call [kə'lɛktkɔːl] NOUN US
la llamada a cobro revertido

collection [kə'lɛkʃən] NOUN

[1] la colección (PL las colecciones) ◊ *my CD collection* mi colección de CDs
[2] la colecta ◊ *a collection for charity* una colecta para obras benéficas

collector [kə'lɛktər] NOUN
el/la coleccionista

college ['kɔlɪdʒ] NOUN
la universidad (*university*)

> ℹ *Aparte de significar "universidad", **college** se refiere también a un centro de educación superior para jóvenes que han terminado la educación obligatoria, **secondary school**. Algunos ofrecen cursos de especialización en materias técnicas, artísticas o comerciales. Otros ofrecen carreras universitarias.*

to **collide** [kə'laɪd] VERB
chocar*

collision [kə'lɪʒən] NOUN
la colisión (PL las colisiones)

colon ['kəulən] NOUN
dos puntos (*punctuation mark*)

colonel ['kə:nl] NOUN
el/la coronel

colour ['kʌlər] NOUN (US **color**)
el color ◊ *What colour is it?* ¿De qué color es?
♦ **a colour TV** una televisión en color

colourful ['kʌləful] ADJECTIVE (US **colorful**)
de colores muy vistosos

colouring ['kʌlərɪŋ] NOUN (US **coloring**)
el colorante (*for food*)

comb [kəum] NOUN
see also **comb** VERB
el peine

to **comb** [kəum] VERB
see also **comb** NOUN
♦ **You haven't combed your hair.** No te has peinado.

combination [kɔmbɪ'neɪʃən] NOUN
la combinación (PL las combinaciones)

to **combine** [kəm'baɪn] VERB
[1] combinar ◊ *The film combines humour with suspense.* La película combina el humor con el suspense.
[2] compaginar ◊ *It's difficult to combine a career with a family.* Es difícil compaginar la profesión con la vida familiar.

to **come** [kʌm] VERB (**came, come**)
[1] venir* ◊ *Helen came with me.* Helen vino conmigo. ◊ *Come home.* Ven a casa. ◊ *Come and see us soon.* Ven a vernos pronto.
♦ **Where do you come from?** ¿De dónde eres?
[2] llegar* ◊ *They came late.* Llegaron tarde. ◊ *The letter came this morning.* La carta llegó esta mañana.
♦ **I'm coming!** ¡Ya voy!

to **come across (1)** [kʌmə'krɔs] VERB
encontrarse* ◊ *I came across a dress that I hadn't worn for years.* Me encontré un vestido que hacía años que no me ponía.

to **come across (2)** [kʌmə'krɔs] VERB
♦ **She comes across as a nice girl.** Da la impresión de ser una chica simpática.

to **come back** [kʌm'bæk] VERB
volver* ◊ *My brother is coming back tomorrow.* Mi hermano vuelve mañana.

to **come down** [kʌm'daun] VERB
bajar

to **come in** [kʌm'ɪn] VERB
entrar ◊ *Come in!* ¡Entra!

to **come on** [kʌm'ɔn] VERB
♦ **Come on! (1)** (*expressing encouragement, urging haste*) ¡Venga!
♦ **Come on! (2)** (*expressing disbelief*) ¡Venga ya!

to **come out** [kʌm'aut] VERB
[1] salir* ◊ *We came out of the cinema at 10.* Salimos del cine a las 10. ◊ *Her book comes out in May.* Su libro sale en mayo.
♦ **None of my photos came out.** No salió ninguna de mis fotos.
[2] irse* ◊ *I don't think this stain will come out.* No creo que esta mancha se vaya a quitar.

to **come round** [kʌm'raund] VERB
volver* en sí (*after faint, operation*) ◊ *He came round after about 10 minutes.* Volvió en sí después de unos 10 minutos.

to **come up** [kʌm'ʌp] VERB
[1] subir ◊ *Come up here!* ¡Sube aquí!
[2] surgir* ◊ *Something's come up so I'll be late home.* Ha surgido algo, así es que llegaré tarde a casa.
♦ **to come up to somebody** acercarse a alguien ◊ *She came up to me and kissed me.* Se me acercó y me besó.

comedian [kə'mi:dɪən] NOUN
el cómico
la cómica

comedy ['kɔmɪdɪ] NOUN (PL **comedies**)
la comedia

comfortable ['kʌmfətəbl] ADJECTIVE
[1] cómodo ◊ *comfortable shoes* zapatos cómodos ◊ *Make yourself comfortable!* ¡Ponte cómodo!
[2] confortable (*house, room*) ◊ *Their house is small but comfortable.* Su casa es pequeña pero confortable.

comic ['kɔmɪk] NOUN
el comic (PL los comics)

comic strip ['kɔmɪkstrɪp] NOUN

la tira cómica
coming ['kʌmɪŋ] ADJECTIVE
próximo ◊ *In the coming weeks, we will all have to work hard.* En las próximas semanas todos tendremos que trabajar duro.
comma ['kɔmə] NOUN
la coma
command [kə'mɑːnd] NOUN
la orden (PL las órdenes)
comment ['kɔmɛnt] NOUN
see also **comment** VERB
el comentario ◊ *He made no comment.* No hizo ningún comentario.
♦ **No comment!** ¡Sin comentarios!
to **comment** ['kɔmɛnt] VERB
see also **comment** NOUN
hacer* comentarios ◊ *The police have not commented on these rumours.* La policía no ha hecho comentarios sobre estos rumores.
commentary ['kɔməntərɪ] NOUN (PL **commentaries**)
la crónica
commentator ['kɔmənteɪtəʳ] NOUN
el/la comentarista
commercial [kə'məːʃəl] NOUN
see also **commercial** ADJECTIVE
el spot publicitario (PL los spots publicitarios)
commercial [kə'məːʃəl] ADJECTIVE
see also **commercial** NOUN
comercial
commission [kə'mɪʃən] NOUN
la comisión (PL las comisiones) ◊ *The bank charges 1% commission.* El banco cobra un 1% de comisión. ◊ *to work on commission* trabajar a comisión
to **commit** [kə'mɪt] VERB
♦ **to commit a crime** cometer un crimen
♦ **to commit suicide** suicidarse
♦ **I don't want to commit myself.** No quiero comprometerme.
committee [kə'mɪtɪ] NOUN
el comité
common ['kɔmən] ADJECTIVE
see also **common** NOUN
común (PL comunes) ◊ *"Smith" is a very common surname.* "Smith" es un apellido muy común.
♦ **in common** en común ◊ *We've got a lot in common.* Tenemos mucho en común.
common ['kɔmən] NOUN
see also **common** ADJECTIVE
el campo comunal ◊ *We went for a walk on the common.* un paseo por el campo comunal
Commons ['kɒmənz] PL NOUN
♦ **the House of Commons** la Cámara de los Comunes
common sense ['kɔmənsɛns] NOUN
el sentido común

to **communicate** [kə'mjuːnɪkeɪt] VERB
comunicar*
communication [kəmjuːnɪ'keɪʃən] NOUN
la comunicación (PL las comunicaciones)
communion [kə'mjuːnɪən] NOUN
la comunión (PL las comuniones)
communism ['kɔmjunɪzəm] NOUN
el comunismo
communist ['kɔmjunɪst] NOUN
see also **communist** ADJECTIVE
el/la comunista
communist ['kɔmjunɪst] ADJECTIVE
see also **communist** NOUN
comunista
community [kə'mjuːnɪtɪ] NOUN (PL **communities**)
la comunidad ◊ *the local community* el vecindario
♦ **community service**

> ℹ *El* ***community service*** *es un trabajo comunitario prestado en lugar de cumplir una pena de prisión.*

to **commute** [kə'mjuːt] VERB
♦ **She commutes between Oxford and London.** Para ir al trabajo se desplaza diariamente de Oxford a Londres.
compact disc [kɔmpækt'dɪsk] NOUN
el disco compacto
♦ **compact disc player** el lector de discos compactos
companion [kəm'pænjən] NOUN
el compañero
la compañera
company ['kʌmpənɪ] NOUN (PL **companies**)
1 la empresa ◊ *He works for a big company.* Trabaja para una empresa grande.
2 la compañía ◊ *an insurance company* una compañía de seguros ◊ *a theatre company* una compañía de teatro
♦ **to keep somebody company** hacerle* compañía a alguien
comparatively [kəm'pærətɪvlɪ] ADVERB
relativamente
to **compare** [kəm'pɛəʳ] VERB
comparar ◊ *They compared his work to that of Joyce.* Compararon su obra a la de Joyce. ◊ *People always compare him with his brother.* La gente siempre lo compara con su hermano.
♦ **compared with** en comparación a ◊ *Oxford is small compared with London.* Oxford es pequeño en comparación a Londres.
comparison [kəm'pærɪsn] NOUN
la comparación (PL las comparaciones)
compartment [kəm'pɑːtmənt] NOUN
el compartimento
compass ['kʌmpəs] NOUN (PL **compasses**)
la brújula
compensation [kɔmpən'seɪʃən] NOUN

la indemnización ◊ *They got £2000 compensation.* Recibieron 2.000 libras esterlinas de indemnización.

compere ['kɔmpɛəʳ] NOUN
el presentador
la presentadora

to **compete** [kəm'pi:t] VERB
◆ **to compete in** competir* en ◊ *I'm competing in the marathon.* Compito en el maratón.
◆ **to compete for something** competir* por algo ◊ *There are 50 students competing for 6 places.* Hay 50 estudiantes compitiendo por 6 puestos.

competent ['kɔmpɪtənt] ADJECTIVE
competente

competition [kɔmpɪ'tɪʃən] NOUN
1 el concurso ◊ *a singing competition* un concurso de canto
2 la competencia ◊ *Competition in the computer sector is fierce.* La competencia en el sector de la informática es muy intensa.

competitive [kəm'pɛtɪtɪv] ADJECTIVE
competitivo

competitor [kəm'pɛtɪtəʳ] NOUN
el/la concursante

to **complain** [kəm'pleɪn] VERB
1 reclamar ◊ *We're going to complain to the manager.* Vamos a reclamar al director.
2 quejarse ◊ *She's always complaining about her husband.* Siempre se está quejando de su marido.

complaint [kəm'pleɪnt] NOUN
la queja

complete [kəm'pli:t] ADJECTIVE
completo

completely [kəm'pli:tlɪ] ADVERB
completamente

complexion [kəm'plɛkʃən] NOUN
el cutis (PL los cutis)

complicated ['kɔmplɪkeɪtɪd] ADJECTIVE
complicado

compliment ['kɔmplɪmənt] NOUN
see also **compliment** VERB
el cumplido
◆ **to pay somebody a compliment** hacerle* un cumplido a alguien

to **compliment** ['kɔmplɪmɛnt] VERB
see also **compliment** NOUN
felicitar
◆ **They complimented me on my Spanish.** Me felicitaron por mi español.

complimentary [kɔmplɪ'mentərɪ] ADJECTIVE
◆ **complimentary ticket** entrada de regalo

to **compose** [kəm'pəuz] VERB
componer* (*music*)
◆ **to be composed of** componerse* de

composer [kəm'pəuzəʳ] NOUN
el compositor
la compositora

comprehension [,kɔmprɪ'henʃən] NOUN
el ejercicio de comprensión (*school exercise*)

comprehensive school [kɔmprɪ'hensɪvsku:l] NOUN
el instituto

compromise ['kɔmprəmaɪz] NOUN
see also **compromise** VERB
el arreglo ◊ *We reached a compromise.* Llegamos a un arreglo.

to **compromise** ['kɔmprəmaɪz] VERB
see also **compromise** NOUN
llegar* a un acuerdo

compulsory [kəm'pʌlsərɪ] ADJECTIVE
obligatorio

computer [kəm'pju:təʳ] NOUN
el ordenador (la computadora *LatAm*)

computer game [kəm'pju:təgeɪm] NOUN
el juego de ordenador

computer programmer [kəm'pju:tə'prəugræməʳ] NOUN
el programador
la programadora

computer science [kəm'pju:tə'saɪəns] NOUN
la informática

computing [kəm'pju:tɪŋ] NOUN
la informática

to **concentrate** ['kɔnsəntreɪt] VERB
concentrarse ◊ *I couldn't concentrate.* No me podía concentrar. ◊ *I was concentrating on my homework.* Me estaba concentrando en los deberes.

concentration [kɔnsən'treɪʃən] NOUN
la concentración

concerned [kən'sə:nd] ADJECTIVE
preocupado ◊ *His mother is concerned about him.* Su madre está preocupada por él.
◆ **as far as the new project is concerned ...** en lo que respecta al nuevo proyecto ...
◆ **As far as I'm concerned, you can come any time you like.** Por mí, puedes venir cuando quieras.
◆ **It's a stressful situation for everyone concerned.** Es una situación estresante para todos los involucrados.

concert ['kɔnsət] NOUN
el concierto

concrete ['kɔŋkri:t] NOUN
el hormigón

to **condemn** [kən'dem] VERB
condenar

condition [kən'dɪʃən] NOUN
la condición (PL las condiciones) ◊ *I'll do it, on one condition.* Lo haré, con una condición.

◆ **in good condition** en buen estado

conditional [kən'dɪʃənl] NOUN
el condicional

conditioner [kən'dɪʃənəʳ] NOUN
el suavizante (el enjuague *LatAm*) (*for hair*)

condom ['kɔndəm] NOUN
el preservativo

to **conduct** [kən'dʌkt] VERB
dirigir* (*orchestra*)

conductor [kən'dʌktəʳ] NOUN
1 (*of orchestra*)
el director de orquesta
la directora de orquesta
2 (*on bus*)
el cobrador
la cobradora

cone [kəun] NOUN
1 el cucurucho ◊ *an ice cream cone* un cucurucho
2 el cono (*geometric shape*)
◆ **a traffic cone** un cono para señalizar el tráfico

conference ['kɔnfərəns] NOUN
la conferencia

to **confess** [kən'fɛs] VERB
confesar* ◊ *He confessed to the murder.* Confesó haber cometido el asesinato.

confession [kən'fɛʃən] NOUN
la confesión (PL las confesiones)

confidence ['kɔnfɪdns] NOUN
1 la confianza ◊ *I've got a lot of confidence in him.* Tengo mucha confianza en él.
2 la confianza en sí mismo ◊ *She lacks confidence.* Le falta confianza en sí misma.
◆ **I told you that story in confidence.** Te conté esa historia de manera confidencial.

confident ['kɔnfɪdənt] ADJECTIVE
1 seguro (*sure of something*) ◊ *I'm confident everything will be okay.* Estoy seguro de que todo saldrá bien.
2 seguro de sí mismo (*self-assured*) ◊ *She seems quite confident.* Parece muy segura de sí misma.

confidential [kɔnfɪ'dɛnʃəl] ADJECTIVE
confidencial

to **confirm** [kən'fə:m] VERB
confirmar

confirmation [kɔnfə'meɪʃən] NOUN
la confirmación (PL las confirmaciones)

conflict ['kɔnflɪkt] NOUN
el conflicto

to **confuse** [kən'fju:z] VERB
confundir

confused [kən'fju:zd] ADJECTIVE
confuso (*person*)

confusing [kən'fju:zɪŋ] ADJECTIVE
poco claro ◊ *The traffic signs are confusing.* Las señales de tráfico están poco claras.

confusion [kən'fju:ʒən] NOUN
la confusión

to **congratulate** [kən'grætjuleɪt] VERB
felicitar ◊ *My friends congratulated me on passing my test.* Mis amigos me felicitaron por aprobar el examen.

congratulations [kəngrætju'leɪʃənz] PL NOUN
la enhorabuena ◊ *Congratulations on your new job!* ¡Enhorabuena por tu nuevo empleo!

conjunction [kən'dʒʌŋkʃən] NOUN
la conjunción

conjurer ['kʌndʒərəʳ] NOUN
el prestidigitador
la prestidigitadora

connection [kə'nɛkʃən] NOUN
1 la conexión (PL las conexiones) ◊ *There's no connection between the two events.* No hay ninguna conexión entre los dos sucesos.
2 el enlace ◊ *We missed our connection.* Perdimos el enlace.
◆ **There's a loose connection.** Hay un hilo suelto.

to **conquer** ['kɔŋkəʳ] VERB
1 conquistar (*country*)
2 vencer* (*enemy, fear*)

conscience ['kɔnʃəns] NOUN
la conciencia
◆ **to have a guilty conscience** tener* remordimientos de conciencia

conscious ['kɔnʃəs] ADJECTIVE
consciente ◊ *He was still conscious when the doctor arrived.* Estaba todavía consciente cuando llegó el médico. ◊ *She was conscious of Max looking at her.* Era consciente de que Max la miraba.
◆ **He made a conscious decision to tell nobody.** Tomó la firme decisión de no decírselo a nadie.

consciousness ['kɔnʃəsnɪs] NOUN
el conocimiento ◊ *I lost consciousness.* Perdí el conocimiento.

consequence ['kɒnsɪkwəns] NOUN
la consecuencia

consequently ['kɔnsɪkwəntlɪ] ADVERB
por consiguiente

conservation [kɔnsə'veɪʃən] NOUN
la conservación
◆ **energy conservation** la conservación de la energía

conservative [kən'sə:vətɪv] ADJECTIVE
see also **Conservative** NOUN
conservador MASC
conservadora FEM
◆ **the Conservative Party** el partido Conservador

Conservative [kən'sə:vətɪv] NOUN

see also **conservative** ADJECTIVE
el conservador
la conservadora
♦ **to vote Conservative** votar a favor del partido Conservador

conservatory [kən'sə:vətrɪ] NOUN (PL **conservatories**)
el invernadero

to **consider** [kən'sɪdə^r] VERB
[1] considerar ◊ *He considers it a waste of time.* Lo considera una pérdida de tiempo.
[2] pensar* en ◊ *We considered cancelling our holiday.* Pensamos en cancelar nuestras vacaciones.

considerate [kən'sɪdərɪt] ADJECTIVE
considerado

considering [kən'sɪdərɪŋ] PREPOSITION
[1] teniendo en cuenta ◊ *Considering we were there for a month we did not spend too much money.* Teniendo en cuenta que estuvimos allí durante un mes no nos gastamos mucho dinero.
[2] después de todo ◊ *I got a good mark, considering.* Saqué buena nota, después de todo.

to **consist** [kən'sɪst] VERB
♦ **to consist of** consistir en

consonant ['kɔnsənənt] NOUN
la consonante

constant ['kɔnstənt] ADJECTIVE
constante

constantly ['kɔnstəntlɪ] ADVERB
constantemente

constipated ['kɔnstɪpeɪtɪd] ADJECTIVE
estreñido ◊ *I'm constipated.* Estoy estreñido.

*Be careful not to translate **constipated** by **constipado**.*

to **construct** [kən'strʌkt] VERB
construir*

construction [kən'strʌkʃən] NOUN
la construcción (PL las construcciones)

to **consult** [kən'sʌlt] VERB
consultar

consumer [kən'sju:mə^r] NOUN
el consumidor
la consumidora

contact ['kɔntækt] NOUN
see also **contact** VERB
el contacto ◊ *I'm in contact with her.* Estoy en contacto con ella.

to **contact** ['kɔntækt] VERB
see also **contact** NOUN
ponerse* en contacto con ◊ *Where can we contact you?* ¿Dónde podemos ponernos en contacto contigo?

contact lenses ['kɔntæktlenzɪz] PL NOUN
las lentillas (los lentes de contacto *LatAm*)

to **contain** [kən'teɪn] VERB
contener*

container [kən'teɪnə^r] NOUN
el recipiente

contempt [kən'tempt] NOUN
el desprecio

contents ['kɔntents] PL NOUN
el contenido

contest ['kɔntest] NOUN
la competición (PL las competiciones) ◊ *a fishing contest* una competición de pesca
♦ **a beauty contest** un concurso de belleza

contestant [kən'testənt] NOUN
el/la concursante

context ['kɔntekst] NOUN
el contexto

continent ['kɔntɪnənt] NOUN
el continente
♦ **the Continent** el continente europeo

continental breakfast [kɔntɪnentl-'brekfəst] NOUN
el desayuno continental

continental quilt [kɔntɪnentl'kwɪlt] NOUN
el edredón (PL los edredones)

to **continue** [kən'tɪnju:] VERB
continuar* ◊ *She continued talking to her friend.* Continuó hablando con su amiga. ◊ *We continued working after lunch.* Continuamos trabajando después de la comida.

continuous [kən'tɪnjuəs] ADJECTIVE
continuo
♦ **continuous assessment** la evaluación continua

contraceptive [kɔntrə'septɪv] NOUN
el anticonceptivo

contract ['kɔntrækt] NOUN
el contrato

to **contradict** [kɔntrə'dɪkt] VERB
contradecir*

contrary ['kɔntrərɪ] NOUN
♦ **on the contrary** al contrario

contrast ['kɔntrɑ:st] NOUN
el contraste

to **contribute** [kən'trɪbju:t] VERB
♦ **to contribute to** contribuir* a ◊ *Everyone contributed to the success of the play.* Todos contribuyeron al éxito de la obra. ◊ *She contributed £10 to the collection.* Contribuyó 10 libras esterlinas a la colecta.

contribution [kɔntrɪ'bju:ʃən] NOUN
la contribución (PL las contribuciones)

control [kən'trəul] NOUN
see also **control** VERB
el control
♦ **to lose control** perder* el control (*of vehicle*)
♦ **the controls** los mandos (*of machine*)

- **He always seems to be in control.** Parece que siempre está en control de la situación.
- **She can't keep control of the class.** No sabe controlar a la clase.
- **out of control** fuera de control ◊ *That boy is out of control.* Ese muchacho está fuera de control.

to **control** [kən'trəul] VERB
see also **control** NOUN
controlar ◊ *He can't control the class.* No sabe controlar a la clase. ◊ *I couldn't control the horse.* No pude controlar al caballo. ◊ *Please control yourself, everyone's looking at us.* Por favor contrólate, todos nos están mirando.

controversial [kɔntrə'vəːʃl] ADJECTIVE
polémico ◊ *Euthanasia is a controversial subject.* La eutanasia es un tema polémico.

convenient [kən'viːnɪənt] ADJECTIVE
bien situado (*place*) ◊ *The hotel's convenient for the airport.* El hotel está bien situado con respecto al aeropuerto.
- **It's not a convenient time for me.** A esa hora no me va bien.
- **Would Monday be convenient for you?** ¿Te iría bien el lunes?

conventional [kən'vɛnʃənl] ADJECTIVE
convencional

convent school ['kɔnvəntskuːl] NOUN
el colegio de monjas

conversation [kɔnvə'seɪʃən] NOUN
la conversación (PL las conversaciones) ◊ *We had a long conversation.* Tuvimos una larga conversación.

to **convert** [kən'vəːt] VERB
convertir* ◊ *We've converted the loft into a bedroom.* Hemos convertido el desván en un dormitorio.

to **convict** [kən'vɪkt] VERB
see also **convict** NOUN
declarar culpable ◊ *He was convicted of the murder.* Fue declarado culpable del asesinato.

convict [kən'vɪkt] NOUN
see also **convict** VERB
el presidiario
la presidiaria

to **convince** [kən'vɪns] VERB
convencer*
- **I'm not convinced.** No me convence.

to **cook** [kuk] VERB
see also **cook** NOUN
1 cocinar ◊ *I can't cook.* No sé cocinar.
- **The chicken isn't cooked.** El pollo no está hecho.

2 preparar ◊ *She's cooking lunch.* Está preparando el almuerzo.

cook [kuk] NOUN
see also **cook** VERB
el cocinero
la cocinera
◊ *She is a cook in a hotel.* Es cocinera en un hotel.
- **Maria's an excellent cook.** María es una cocinera excelente.

cookbook ['kukbuk] NOUN
el libro de cocina

cooker ['kukəʳ] NOUN
la cocina (*aparato*) ◊ *a gas cooker* una cocina de gas

cookery ['kukərɪ] NOUN
la cocina (*gastronomía*)

cookie ['kukɪ] NOUN US
la galleta

cooking ['kukɪŋ] NOUN
la cocina (*gastronomía*) ◊ *French cooking* la cocina francesa
- **I like cooking.** Me gusta cocinar.

cool [kuːl] ADJECTIVE
fresco ◊ *a cool place* un lugar fresco
- **to stay cool** mantenerse en calma (*keep calm*) ◊ *He stayed cool throughout the crisis.* Se mantuvo en calma durante toda la crisis.

cooperation [kəuɔpə'reɪʃən] NOUN
la cooperación

cop [kɔp] NOUN
el/la poli (*informal*)

to **cope** [kəup] VERB
arreglárselas ◊ *It was hard, but we coped.* Fue difícil, pero nos las arreglamos.
- **She's got a lot of problems to cope with.** Tiene muchos problemas a los que hacer frente.

copper ['kɔpəʳ] NOUN
1 el cobre ◊ *a copper bracelet* un brazalete de cobre
2 el/la poli (*informal*) (*policeman*)

copy ['kɔpɪ] NOUN (PL **copies**)
see also **copy** VERB
1 la copia (*of letter, document*)
2 el ejemplar (*of book*)

to **copy** ['kɔpɪ] VERB (**copied, copied**)
see also **copy** NOUN
copiar
- **to copy and paste** copiar y pegar (*computing*)

core [kɔːʳ] NOUN
(*of fruit*)
el corazón (PL los corazones)

cork [kɔːk] NOUN
el corcho

corkscrew ['kɔːkskruː] NOUN
el sacacorchos (PL los sacacorchos)

corn [kɔːn] NOUN
1 el trigo (*wheat*)
2 el maíz (*sweetcorn*)
- **corn on the cob** la mazorca de maíz

corner ['kɔːnəʳ] NOUN

☞

1 la esquina ◊ *the shop on the corner* la tienda de la esquina ◊ *He lives just round the corner.* Vive a la vuelta de la esquina.
2 el rincón (PL los rincones) ◊ *in a corner of the room* en un rincón de la habitación
3 (*in football*)
el saque de esquina

cornet ['kɔːnɪt] NOUN
1 la corneta (*instrument*)
2 el cucurucho (*ice cream*)

cornflakes ['kɔːnfleɪks] PL NOUN
los copos de maíz

cornstarch ['kɔːnstɑːtʃ] NOUN US
la harina de maíz

Cornwall ['kɔːnwəl] NOUN
el Cornualles

corporal ['kɔːpərl] NOUN
el cabo

corporal punishment ['kɔːpərl'pʌnɪʃmənt] NOUN
el castigo corporal

corpse [kɔːps] NOUN
el cadáver

correct [kə'rɛkt] ADJECTIVE
see also **correct** VERB
correcto ◊ *That's correct!* ¡Correcto!
♦ **the correct answer** la respuesta correcta
♦ **You're absolutely correct.** Tienes toda la razón.

to **correct** [kə'rɛkt] VERB
see also **correct** ADJECTIVE
corregir*

correction [kə'rɛkʃən] NOUN
la corrección (PL las correcciones)

correctly [kə'rɛktlɪ] ADVERB
correctamente

correspondent [kɒrɪs'pɒndənt] NOUN
el/la corresponsal

corridor ['kɒrɪdɔːʳ] NOUN
el pasillo

corruption [kə'rʌpʃən] NOUN
la corrupción

cosmetics [kɔz'mɛtɪks] PL NOUN
los productos de belleza

to **cost** [kɔst] VERB (**cost, cost**)
see also **cost** NOUN
costar* ◊ *The meal cost £20.* La comida costó 20 libras esterlinas. ◊ *How much does it cost?* ¿Cuánto cuesta?

cost [kɔst] NOUN
see also **cost** VERB
el coste (el costo *LatAm*) ◊ *the cost of living* el coste de vida
♦ **at all costs** a toda costa

costume ['kɔstjuːm] NOUN
el traje

cosy ['kəuzɪ] ADJECTIVE
acogedor MASC
acogedora FEM
◊ *a cosy room* una habitación acogedora

cot [kɔt] NOUN
la cuna

cottage ['kɔtɪdʒ] NOUN
el chalet (PL los chalets)

cottage cheese [kɔtɪdʒ'tʃiːz] NOUN
el requesón

cotton ['kɔtn] NOUN
el algodón ◊ *a cotton shirt* una camisa de algodón

cotton wool [kɔtn'wul] NOUN
el algodón

couch [kautʃ] NOUN (PL **couches**)
el sofá (PL los sofás)

couchette [kuː'ʃɛt] NOUN
la litera

to **cough** [kɔf] VERB
see also **cough** NOUN
toser

cough [kɔf] NOUN
see also **cough** VERB
la tos ◊ *I've got a cough.* Tengo tos.
♦ **cough mixture** el jarabe para la tos

could [kud] VERB *see* **can**

council ['kaunsl] NOUN
el ayuntamiento (*in town*) ◊ *He's on the council.* Es concejal del ayuntamiento.
♦ **a council estate** un barrio de viviendas de protección oficial
♦ **a council house** una casa de protección oficial

councillor ['kaunslәʳ] NOUN
el concejal
la concejala

to **count** [kaunt] VERB
contar*

to **count on** ['kauntɔn] VERB
contar* con ◊ *You can count on me.* Puedes contar conmigo.

counter ['kauntәʳ] NOUN
1 el mostrador (*in shop*)
2 la ventanilla (*in bank, post office*)
3 la ficha (*in game*)

country ['kʌntrɪ] NOUN (PL **countries**)
1 el país ◊ *the border between the two countries* la frontera entre los dos países
2 el campo ◊ *I live in the country.* Vivo en el campo.
♦ **country dancing** la danza folklórica

countryside ['kʌntrɪsaɪd] NOUN
el campo

county ['kauntɪ] NOUN (PL **counties**)
el condado

> *The nearest Spanish equivalent of a county would be a* ***provincia.***

♦ **county council** una corporación administrativa que gobierna un condado

> The nearest Spanish equivalent of a county council would be a **diputación provincial**.

couple ['kʌpl] NOUN
1 la pareja ◊ *the couple who live next door* la pareja que vive al lado
2 el par ◊ *a couple of hours* un par de horas

courage ['kʌrɪdʒ] NOUN
el valor

courgette [kuə'ʒɛt] NOUN
el calabacín (PL los calabacines)

courier ['kurɪəʳ] NOUN
1 el/la guía (*for tourists*)
2 el servicio de mensajero (*delivery service*) ◊ *They sent it by courier.* Lo enviaron por servicio de mensajero.

course [kɔːs] NOUN
1 el curso ◊ *a Spanish course* un curso de español ◊ *to go on a course* hacer* un curso
2 el plato ◊ *the main course* el segundo plato ◊ *the first course* el primer plato
3 el campo ◊ *a golf course* un campo de golf
◆ **of course** por supuesto ◊ *Do you love me? – Of course I do!* ¿Me quieres? – ¡Por supuesto que te quiero!

court [kɔːt] NOUN
el tribunal (*of law*)
◆ **a tennis court** una pista de tenis (una cancha de tenis LatAm)

courtyard ['kɔːtjɑːd] NOUN
el patio

cousin ['kʌzn] NOUN
el primo
la prima

cover ['kʌvəʳ] NOUN
see also **cover** VERB
1 la tapa (*of book*)
2 la funda (*of duvet*)

to **cover** ['kʌvəʳ] VERB
see also **cover** NOUN
cubrir* ◊ *My face was covered with mosquito bites.* Tenía la cara cubierta de picaduras de mosquito. ◊ *Our insurance didn't cover it.* Nuestro seguro no lo cubría.

to **cover up** [kʌvər'ʌp] VERB
ocultar ◊ *The government tried to cover up the details of the accident.* El gobierno trató de ocultar los detalles del accidente.

cow [kau] NOUN
la vaca

coward ['kauəd] NOUN
el/la cobarde

cowardly ['kauədlɪ] ADJECTIVE
cobarde

cowboy ['kaubɔɪ] NOUN
el vaquero

crab [kræb] NOUN
el cangrejo

crack [kræk] NOUN
see also **crack** VERB
1 la grieta (*in wall*)
2 la raja (*in cup, window*)
3 el crack (*drug*)
◆ **He opened the door a crack.** Abrió la puerta un poquito.
◆ **I'll have a crack at it.** Lo intentaré.

to **crack** [kræk] VERB
see also **crack** NOUN
cascar* (*nut, egg*)
◆ **He cracked his head on the pavement.** Se dio con la cabeza en la acera.
◆ **I think we've cracked it!** ¡Creo que lo hemos resuelto!
◆ **to crack a joke** contar* un chiste

to **crack down on** [kræk'daunɔn] VERB
tomar medidas severas contra ◊ *The police are cracking down on motorists who drive too fast.* La policía está tomando medidas severas contra los automovilistas que exceden el límite de velocidad.

cracked [krækt] ADJECTIVE
1 rajado (*cup, window*)
2 resquebrajado (*wall*)

cracker ['krækəʳ] NOUN
la galleta salada (*biscuit*)
◆ **Christmas cracker**

> *Es un cilindro de cartón que al abrirlo hace estallar un pequeño petardo. Contiene un regalo sorpresa y una corona de papel que cada comensal se pone durante la comida de Navidad.*

cradle ['kreɪdl] NOUN
la cuna

craft [krɑːft] NOUN
la artesanía
◆ **a craft shop** una tienda de objetos de artesanía

craftsman ['krɑːftsmən] NOUN (PL **craftsmen**)
el artesano

to **cram** [kræm] VERB
◆ **We crammed our stuff into the boot.** Apretamos nuestras cosas dentro del maletero.
◆ **She crammed her bag with books.** Abarrotó su bolso de libros.
◆ **to cram for an exam** empollar a última hora para un examen (*informal*)

crane [kreɪn] NOUN
la grúa (*machine*)

to **crash** [kræʃ] VERB
see also **crash** NOUN
chocar* ◊ *The two cars crashed.* Los dos coches chocaron.
◆ **to crash into something** chocar con algo

♦ **He's crashed his car.** Ha tenido un accidente con el coche.
♦ **The plane crashed.** El avión se estrelló.

crash [kræʃ] NOUN (PL **crashes**)
see also **crash** VERB
el accidente
♦ **a crash helmet** un casco protector
♦ **a crash course** un curso intensivo

to **crawl** [krɔːl] VERB
see also **crawl** NOUN
gatear (*baby*)

crawl [krɔːl] NOUN
see also **crawl** VERB
el crol
♦ **to do the crawl** nadar estilo crol

crazy ['kreɪzɪ] ADJECTIVE
loco

cream [kriːm] ADJECTIVE
see also **cream** NOUN
de color crema MASC, FEM, PL
◇ *a cream silk blouse* una blusa de seda de color crema

cream [kriːm] NOUN
see also **cream** ADJECTIVE
1 la nata (la crema de leche *LatAm*)
◇ *strawberries and cream* fresas con nata
◇ *a cream cake* un pastel de nata
♦ **cream cheese** el queso cremoso
2 la crema (*for skin*) ◇ *sun cream* la crema solar

crease [kriːs] NOUN
1 la arruga (*in clothes, paper*)
2 la raya (*in trousers*)

creased [kriːst] ADJECTIVE
arrugado

to **create** [kriː'eɪt] VERB
crear

creation [kriː'eɪʃən] NOUN
la creación (PL las creaciones)

creative [kriː'eɪtɪv] ADJECTIVE
creativo

creature ['kriːtʃəʳ] NOUN
la criatura

crèche [krɛʃ] NOUN
la guardería infantil

credit ['krɛdɪt] NOUN
el crédito ◇ *on credit* a crédito
♦ **He's a credit to his family.** Hace honor a su familia.

credit card ['krɛdɪtkɑːd] NOUN
la tarjeta de crédito

to **creep up** [kriːp'ʌp] VERB (**crept, crept**)
♦ **to creep up on somebody** acercarse sigilosamente a alguien

crept [krɛpt] VERB *see* **creep up**

cress [krɛs] NOUN
el berro

crew [kruː] NOUN
(*of plane, boat*)
la tripulación (PL las tripulaciones)
♦ **a film crew** un equipo de rodaje

crew cut ['kruːkʌt] NOUN
el pelo cortado al rape

cricket ['krɪkɪt] NOUN
1 el críquet ◇ *I play cricket.* Juego al críquet.
2 el grillo (*insect*)

crime [kraɪm] NOUN
1 (*offence*)
el delito ◇ *He committed a crime.* Cometió un delito. ◇ *the scene of the crime* el lugar del delito
2 (*very serious*)
el crimen (PL los crímenes)
◇ *a crime against humanity* un crimen contra la humanidad
3 (*activity*)
la delincuencia ◇ *Crime is rising.* La delincuencia va en aumento.

criminal ['krɪmɪnl] NOUN
see also **criminal** ADJECTIVE
el/la delincuente

criminal ['krɪmɪnl] ADJECTIVE
see also **criminal** NOUN
♦ **It's a criminal offence.** Constituye un delito.
♦ **to have a criminal record** tener* antecedentes penales

crippled ['krɪpld] ADJECTIVE
♦ **He was crippled in an accident.** Quedó lisiado en un accidente.
♦ **He was crippled with arthritis.** La artritis lo tenía paralizado.

crisis ['kraɪsɪs] NOUN (PL **crises**)
la crisis (PL las crisis)

crisp [krɪsp] ADJECTIVE
crujiente (*food*)

crisps [krɪsps] PL NOUN
las patatas fritas (las papas fritas *LatAm*) ◇ *a bag of crisps* una bolsa de patatas fritas

criterion [kraɪ'tɪərɪən] NOUN (PL **criteria**)
el criterio ◇ *the selection criteria* los criterios de selección
♦ **Only one candidate met all the criteria.** Sólo uno de los candidatos cumplía todos los requisitos.

critic ['krɪtɪk] NOUN
el crítico
la crítica

critical ['krɪtɪkl] ADJECTIVE
crítico

criticism ['krɪtɪsɪzəm] NOUN
la crítica

to **criticize** ['krɪtɪsaɪz] VERB
criticar*

Croatia [krəu'eɪʃə] NOUN
Croacia FEM

to **crochet** ['krəuʃeɪ] VERB

hacer* ganchillo ◊ *She enjoys crocheting.* Le gusta hacer ganchillo.

crocodile ['krɔkədaɪl] NOUN
el cocodrilo

crook [kruk] NOUN
el/la sinvergüenza

crop [krɔp] NOUN
la cosecha ◊ *a good crop of apples* una buena cosecha de manzanas

cross [krɔs] NOUN (PL **crosses**)
see also **cross** ADJECTIVE, VERB
la cruz (PL las cruces)

cross [krɔs] ADJECTIVE
see also **cross** NOUN, VERB
enfadado (enojado *LatAm*) ◊ *He was cross about something.* Estaba enojado por algo.

to **cross** [krɔs] VERB
see also **cross** NOUN, ADJECTIVE
cruzar* (*road, river*)

to **cross out** [krɔs'aut] VERB
tachar

cross-country [krɔs'kʌntrɪ] NOUN
♦ **a cross-country race** un cross (PL unos cross)
♦ **cross-country skiing** el esquí de fondo

crossing ['krɔsɪŋ] NOUN
1 la travesía ◊ *a 10-hour crossing* una travesía de 10 horas
2 el paso de peatones (*for pedestrians*)

crossroads ['krɔsrəudz] NOUN
el cruce

crossword ['krɔswəːd] NOUN
el crucigrama

*Although **crucigrama** ends in **-a**, it is actually a masculine noun.*

to **crouch down** [krautʃ'daun] VERB
agacharse

crow [krəu] NOUN
el cuervo

crowd [kraud] NOUN
1 la muchedumbre
2 el público (*at sports match*)

crowded ['kraudɪd] ADJECTIVE
abarrotado de gente

crown [kraun] NOUN
la corona

crucifix ['kruːsɪfɪks] NOUN (PL **crucifixes**)
el crucifijo

crude [kruːd] ADJECTIVE
vulgar ◊ *crude language* lenguaje vulgar
♦ **crude oil** el petróleo en crudo

cruel ['kruəl] ADJECTIVE
cruel

cruise [kruːz] NOUN
el crucero

crumb [krʌm] NOUN
la miga

to **crush** [krʌʃ] VERB
1 aplastar (*box, fingers*)
2 machacar* ◊ *Crush two cloves of garlic.* Machacar dos dientes de ajo.

crutch [krʌtʃ] NOUN (PL **crutches**)
la muleta

cry [kraɪ] NOUN
see also **cry** VERB
el grito ◊ *He gave a cry of pain.* Dio un grito de dolor.
♦ **She had a good cry.** Se dio una buena de llorar.

to **cry** [kraɪ] VERB (**cried, cried**)
see also **cry** NOUN
1 llorar ◊ *The baby's crying.* El bebé está llorando.
2 gritar ◊ *"You're wrong", he cried.* "No es cierto", gritó.

crystal ['krɪstl] NOUN
el cristal

CTC [siːtiː'siː] NOUN (= *city technology college*)
el centro de formación profesional

*En Gran Bretaña los **CTC** son centros de enseñanza secundaria que dan especial importancia a la ciencia y la tecnología.*

cub [kʌb] NOUN
1 el cachorro (*animal*)
2 el lobato (*scout*)

cube [kjuːb] NOUN
1 (*geometric shape*)
el cubo
2 el dado ◊ *Cut the meat into cubes.* Cortar la carne en dados.
3 (*of sugar*)
el terrón (PL los terrones)

cubic ['kjuːbɪk] ADJECTIVE
♦ **a cubic metre** un metro cúbico

cucumber ['kjuːkʌmbər] NOUN
el pepino

to **cuddle** ['kʌdl] VERB
abrazar*

cue [kjuː] NOUN
el taco (*for snooker, pool*)

culottes [kjuː'lɔts] PL NOUN
la falda pantalón (PL las faldas pantalón)

culture ['kʌltʃər] NOUN
la cultura

cunning ['kʌnɪŋ] ADJECTIVE
1 astuto (*person*)
2 ingenioso ◊ *a cunning plan* un plan ingenioso

cup [kʌp] NOUN
1 la taza ◊ *a china cup* una taza de porcelana
2 la copa (*trophy*)

cupboard ['kʌbəd] NOUN
el armario

to **cure** [kjuər] VERB
see also **cure** NOUN

curar
cure [kjuəʳ] NOUN
see also **cure** VERB
la cura ◊ *There is no simple cure for the common cold.* No hay una cura sencilla para el catarro común.
curious ['kjuərɪəs] ADJECTIVE
curioso
♦ **to be curious about something** sentir* curiosidad por algo
curl [kəːl] NOUN
el rizo
curly ['kəːlɪ] ADJECTIVE
rizado
currant ['kʌrnt] NOUN
la pasa
currency ['kʌrnsɪ] NOUN (PL **currencies**)
la moneda ◊ *foreign currency* la moneda extranjera
current ['kʌrnt] NOUN
see also **current** ADJECTIVE
la corriente ◊ *The current is very strong.* La corriente es muy fuerte.
current ['kʌrnt] ADJECTIVE
see also **current** NOUN
1 actual ◊ *the current situation* la situación actual
2 presente ◊ *the current financial year* el presente año financiero
current account ['kʌrntə'kaunt] NOUN
la cuenta corriente
current affairs [kʌrntə'fɛəz] PL NOUN
los temas de actualidad
curriculum [kə'rɪkjuləm] NOUN (PL **curricula**)
el plan de estudios
curriculum vitae [kərɪkjuləm'viːtaɪ] NOUN (PL **curriculum vitaes**)
el currículum vitae
curry ['kʌrɪ] NOUN (PL **curries**)
el curry (PL los curries)
curse [kəːs] NOUN
la maldición (PL las maldiciones)
curtain ['kəːtn] NOUN
la cortina
cushion ['kuʃən] NOUN
el cojín (PL los cojines)
custard ['kʌstəd] NOUN
las natillas
custody ['kʌstədɪ] NOUN
la custodia ◊ *The mother has custody of the children.* La madre tiene la custodia de los hijos.
♦ **to be remanded in custody** estar* detenido
custom ['kʌstəm] NOUN
la costumbre ◊ *It's an old custom.* Es una vieja costumbre.
customer ['kʌstəməʳ] NOUN
el cliente
la clienta
customs ['kʌstəmz] PL NOUN
la aduana
♦ **to go through customs** pasar por la aduana
customs officer ['kʌstəmz'ɔfɪsəʳ] NOUN
el oficial de aduanas
la oficial de aduanas
cut [kʌt] NOUN
see also **cut** VERB
1 el corte ◊ *He's got a cut on his forehead.* Tiene un corte en la frente.
2 (*in price, spending*)
la reducción (PL las reducciones)
to **cut** [kʌt] VERB (**cut, cut**)
see also **cut** NOUN
1 cortar ◊ *I'll cut some bread.* Voy a cortar pan. ◊ *I cut my foot on a piece of glass.* Me corté el pie con un cristal.
♦ **to cut oneself** cortarse
2 reducir* (*price, spending*)
to **cut down (1)** [kʌt'daun] VERB
cortar (*tree*)
to **cut down (2)** [kʌt'daun] VERB
♦ **I'm cutting down on coffee and cigarettes.** Estoy intentando tomar menos café y fumar menos.
to **cut off** [kʌt'ɔf] VERB
cortar ◊ *The electricity has been cut off.* Han cortado la electricidad. ◊ *We've been cut off.* Se ha cortado la comunicación.
to **cut up** [kʌt'ʌp] VERB
picar* (*vegetables, meat*)
cutback ['kʌtbæk] NOUN
el recorte ◊ *Over the past year there have been large cutbacks in public services.* En este último año ha habido grandes recortes en los servicios públicos.
cute [kjuːt] ADJECTIVE
mono (*baby, pet*) ◊ *Isn't he cute!* ¡Qué mono es!
cutlery ['kʌtlərɪ] NOUN
la cubertería
CV [siː'viː] NOUN
el currículum vitae
cybercafé ['saɪbəkæfeɪ] NOUN
el cibercafé
to **cycle** ['saɪkl] VERB
see also **cycle** NOUN
ir* en bicicleta ◊ *I cycle to school.* Voy al colegio en bicicleta.
cycle ['saɪkl] NOUN
see also **cycle** VERB
la bicicleta ◊ *a cycle ride* un paseo en bicicleta
cycle lane ['saɪkl leɪn] NOUN
el carril-bici
cycling ['saɪklɪŋ] NOUN

el ciclismo
- **The roads round here are ideal for cycling.** Las carreteras de por aquí son ideales para ir en bicicleta.

cyclist ['saɪklɪst] NOUN
el/la ciclista

cylinder ['sɪlɪndəʳ] NOUN
el cilindro

Cyprus ['saɪprəs] NOUN
Chipre FEM

Czech [tʃɛk] NOUN
see also **Czech** ADJECTIVE
1 (*person*)
el checo
la checa
◊ *the Czechs* los checos
2 (*language*)
el checo

Czech [tʃɛk] ADJECTIVE
see also **Czech** NOUN
checo
- **the Czech Republic** la República Checa

D

dad [dæd] NOUN
1 el padre ◇ *my dad* mi padre
2 papá ◇ *I'll ask Dad.* Se lo preguntaré a papá.

daddy ['dædɪ] NOUN
papá

daffodil ['dæfədɪl] NOUN
el narciso

daft [dɑːft] ADJECTIVE
estúpido

daily ['deɪlɪ] ADJECTIVE, ADVERB
1 diario ◇ *daily life* la vida diaria
◆ **It's part of my daily routine.** Forma parte de mi rutina diaria.
◆ **a daily paper** un periódico
2 todos los días ◇ *The pool is open daily.* La piscina abre todos los días.

dairy ['dɛərɪ] NOUN (PL **dairies**)
la lechería

dairy products ['dɛərɪprɔdʌkts] PL NOUN
los productos lácteos

daisy ['deɪzɪ] NOUN (PL **daisies**)
la margarita

dam [dæm] NOUN
la presa

damage ['dæmɪdʒ] NOUN
see also **damage** VERB
los daños ◇ *The storm did a lot of damage.* La tormenta provocó muchos daños.

to **damage** ['dæmɪdʒ] VERB
see also **damage** NOUN
dañar

damn [dæm] NOUN
see also **damn** ADJECTIVE
◆ **I don't give a damn!** ¡Me importa un rábano! (*informal*)
◆ **Damn!** ¡Maldita sea! (*informal*)

damn [dæm] ADJECTIVE
see also **damn** NOUN
◆ **It's a damn nuisance!** ¡Es una verdadera lata! (*informal*)

damp [dæmp] ADJECTIVE
húmedo

dance [dɑːns] NOUN
see also **dance** VERB
el baile

to **dance** [dɑːns] VERB
see also **dance** NOUN
bailar

dancer ['dɑːnsəʳ] NOUN
1 el bailador
la bailadora
◆ **He is not a very good dancer.** No baila muy bien.
2 (*professional*)
el bailarín (PL los bailarines)
la bailarina

dancing ['dɑːnsɪŋ] NOUN
◆ **to go dancing** ir* a bailar

dandruff ['dændrəf] NOUN
la caspa

Dane [deɪn] NOUN
el danés (PL los daneses)
la danesa
◆ **the Danes** los daneses

danger ['deɪndʒəʳ] NOUN
el peligro
◆ **in danger** en peligro
◆ **We were in danger of missing the plane.** Corríamos el riesgo de perder el avión.

dangerous ['deɪndʒrəs] ADJECTIVE
peligroso

Danish ['deɪnɪʃ] ADJECTIVE
see also **Danish** NOUN
danés MASC
danesa FEM

Danish ['deɪnɪʃ] NOUN
see also **Danish** ADJECTIVE
el danés (*language*)

to **dare** [dɛəʳ] VERB
atreverse ◇ *I didn't dare to tell my parents.* No me atrevía a decírselo a mis padres.
◆ **I dare say it'll be okay.** Yo diría que va a salir bien.
◆ **Don't you dare!** ¡Ni se te ocurra!
◆ **I dare you!** ¡A que no te atreves!

daring ['dɛərɪŋ] ADJECTIVE
atrevido

dark [dɑːk] ADJECTIVE
see also **dark** NOUN
oscuro ◇ *a dark green sweater* un jersey verde oscuro ◇ *It's dark in here.* Está oscuro aquí dentro.
◆ **She's got dark hair.** Tiene el pelo oscuro.
◆ **He's got dark skin.** Tiene la piel morena.
◆ **It's getting dark.** Está oscureciendo.

dark [dɑːk] NOUN
see also **dark** ADJECTIVE
la oscuridad ◇ *I'm afraid of the dark.* Me da miedo la oscuridad.
◆ **after dark** después del anochecer

darkness ['dɑːknɪs] NOUN
la oscuridad ◇ *in the darkness* en la oscuridad
◆ **The room was in darkness.** La habitación estaba a oscuras.

darling ['dɑːlɪŋ] NOUN
cariño ◇ *Thank you, darling.* Gracias, cariño.

dart [dɑːt] NOUN

el dardo ◊ *to play darts* jugar* a los dardos

to **dash** [dæʃ] VERB

see also **dash** NOUN

ir* corriendo ◊ *Everyone dashed to the window.* Todos fueron corriendo a la ventana.

♦**I've got to dash!** ¡Tengo que salir pitando!

dash [dæʃ] NOUN

see also **dash** VERB

1 el chorrito ◊ *a dash of vinegar* un chorrito de vinagre

2 la raya (*punctuation mark*)

dashboard ['dæʃbɔːd] NOUN

el salpicadero

data ['deɪtə] PL NOUN

los datos

database ['deɪtəbeɪs] NOUN

la base de datos

date [deɪt] NOUN

1 la fecha ◊ *my date of birth* mi fecha de nacimiento

♦**What's the date today?** ¿A qué estamos hoy?

♦**He's got a date with his girlfriend.** Ha quedado con su novia.

♦**out of date (1)** (*document*) caducado ◊ *My passport's out of date.* Tengo el pasaporte caducado.

♦**out of date (2)** (*technology, idea*) anticuado

2 el dátil (*fruit*)

daughter ['dɔːtəʳ] NOUN

la hija

daughter-in-law ['dɔːtərɪnlɔː] NOUN (PL **daughters-in-law**)

la nuera

dawn [dɔːn] NOUN

el amanecer ◊ *at dawn* al amanecer

day [deɪ] NOUN

el día

*Although **día** ends in **-a**, it is actually a masculine noun.*

◊ *during the day* por el día ◊ *It's a lovely day.* Hace un día precioso. ◊ *every day* todos los días

♦**the day after tomorrow** pasado mañana

♦**the day before yesterday** anteayer

♦**a day off** un día libre

♦**a day return** un billete de ida y vuelta para el día

dead [dɛd] ADJECTIVE

see also **dead** ADVERB

muerto ◊ *He was dead.* Estaba muerto.

♦**He was shot dead.** Lo mataron de un tiro.

dead [dɛd] ADVERB

see also **dead** ADJECTIVE

♦**You're dead right!** ¡Tienes toda la razón!

♦**It was dead easy.** Fue facilísimo.

♦**dead centre** justo en el centro

♦**dead on time** a la hora exacta

dead end [dɛd'ɛnd] NOUN

el callejón sin salida

deadline ['dɛdlaɪn] NOUN

♦**October is the deadline for applications.** El plazo para presentar las solicitudes se acaba en octubre.

♦**We're going to miss the deadline.** No vamos a poder cumplir con el plazo.

deaf [dɛf] ADJECTIVE

sordo

deafening ['dɛfnɪŋ] ADJECTIVE

ensordecedor MASC

ensordecedora FEM

deal [diːl] NOUN

see also **deal** VERB

el trato ◊ *It's a good deal.* Es un buen trato. ◊ *He made a deal with the kidnappers.* Hizo un trato con los secuestradores.

♦**It's a deal!** ¡Trato hecho!

♦**Big deal!** ¡Vaya cosa!

♦**It's no big deal.** No pasa nada.

♦**a great deal** mucho ◊ *a great deal of money* mucho dinero

to **deal** [diːl] VERB (**dealt, dealt**)

see also **deal** NOUN

dar* cartas ◊ *It's your turn to deal.* Te toca dar cartas.

to **deal with** ['diːlwɪð] VERB

ocuparse de ◊ *He promised to deal with it immediately.* Prometió ocuparse de ello enseguida.

dealer ['diːləʳ] NOUN

♦**a drug dealer** un traficante de drogas (FEM una traficante de drogas)

♦**an antique dealer** un anticuario (FEM una anticuaria)

dealt [dɛlt] VERB *see* **deal**

dear [dɪəʳ] ADJECTIVE

1 querido ◊ *Dear Paul* Querido Paul

♦**Dear Mrs Smith** Estimada señora Smith

♦**Dear Sir** Muy señor mío

♦**Dear Madam** Estimada señora

♦**Dear Sir/Madam** (*in a circular*) Estimados Sres.

♦**Oh dear! I've spilled my coffee.** ¡Oh, no! He derramado el café.

2 caro (*expensive*) ◊ *These shoes are too dear.* Estos zapatos son demasiado caros.

death [dɛθ] NOUN

la muerte ◊ *after his death* después de su muerte

♦**I was bored to death.** Estaba aburrido como una ostra.

debate [dɪ'beɪt] NOUN

see also **debate** VERB

el debate

to **debate** [dɪ'beɪt] VERB

see also **debate** NOUN

discutir

debt [dɛt] NOUN
la deuda ◊ *heavy debts* grandes deudas
◆ **to be in debt** estar* endeudado

decade ['dɛkeɪd] NOUN
la década

decaffeinated [dɪ'kæfɪneɪtɪd] ADJECTIVE
descafeinado

decay [dɪ'keɪ] NOUN
◆ **tooth decay** la caries

to **deceive** [dɪ'siːv] VERB
engañar

deception [dɪ'sɛpʃən] NOUN
el engaño ◊ *Katie continued to keep up the deception.* Katie siguió manteniendo el engaño.

*Be careful not to translate **deception** by **decepción**.*

December [dɪ'sɛmbəʳ] NOUN
diciembre MASC
◆ **in December** en diciembre
◆ **on 22 December** el 22 de diciembre

decent ['diːsənt] ADJECTIVE
decente

to **decide** [dɪ'saɪd] VERB
1 decidir ◊ *I decided to write to her.* Decidí escribirle. ◊ *I decided not to go.* Decidí no ir.
2 decidirse ◊ *Haven't you decided yet?* ¿Aún no te has decidido?

to **decide on** [dɪ'saɪdɔn] VERB
decidirse por

decimal ['dɛsɪməl] ADJECTIVE
decimal ◊ *the decimal system* el sistema decimal
◆ **decimal point** la coma decimal

decision [dɪ'sɪʒən] NOUN
la decisión (PL las decisiones)
◆ **to make a decision** tomar una decisión

decisive [dɪ'saɪsɪv] ADJECTIVE
decidido (*person*)

deck [dɛk] NOUN
1 la cubierta (*of ship*)
◆ **on deck** en cubierta
2 el piso (*of bus*)
◆ **a deck of cards** una baraja

deckchair ['dɛktʃɛəʳ] NOUN
la tumbona

to **declare** [dɪ'klɛəʳ] VERB
declarar

to **decline** [dɪ'klaɪn] VERB
disminuir* ◊ *The birth rate has declined by five per cent.* La tasa de natalidad ha disminuido un cinco por ciento.

to **decorate** ['dɛkəreɪt] VERB
1 decorar ◊ *I decorated the cake with glacé cherries.* Decoré el pastel con guindas confitadas.
2 pintar (*paint*)
3 empapelar (*wallpaper*)

decorations [dɛkə'reɪʃənz] PL NOUN
los adornos ◊ *Christmas decorations* adornos de Navidad

decrease ['diːkriːs] NOUN
see also **decrease** VERB
la disminución (PL las disminuciones) ◊ *There has been a decrease in the number of unemployed people.* Ha habido una disminución del número de desempleados.

to **decrease** [diː'kriːs] VERB
see also **decrease** NOUN
disminuir*

dedicated ['dɛdɪkeɪtɪd] ADJECTIVE
◆ **a very dedicated teacher** un maestro totalmente entregado a su trabajo
◆ **dedicated followers of classical music** devotos seguidores de la música clásica

to **deduct** [dɪ'dʌkt] VERB
descontar*

deep [diːp] ADJECTIVE
1 profundo
◆ **a hole four metres deep** un agujero de cuatro metros de profundidad
◆ **How deep is the lake?** ¿Qué profundidad tiene el lago?
2 espeso ◊ *a deep layer of snow* una espesa capa de nieve
3 grave ◊ *He's got a deep voice.* Tiene la voz grave.
◆ **to take a deep breath** respirar hondo
◆ **to be deep in debt** estar* hasta el cuello de deudas

deeply ['diːplɪ] ADVERB
profundamente ◊ *deeply grateful* profundamente agradecido

deer [dɪəʳ] NOUN (PL **deer**)
el ciervo

defeat [dɪ'fiːt] NOUN
see also **defeat** VERB
la derrota

to **defeat** [dɪ'fiːt] VERB
see also **defeat** NOUN
derrotar

defect ['diːfɛkt] NOUN
el defecto

defence [dɪ'fɛns] NOUN
la defensa

to **defend** [dɪ'fɛnd] VERB
defender*

defender [dɪ'fɛndəʳ] NOUN
1 (*of person, ideas*)
el defensor
la defensora
2 (*in sports*)
el/la defensa

defense [dɪ'fɛns] NOUN US
la defensa

to **define** [dɪ'faɪn] VERB
definir

definite ['dɛfɪnɪt] ADJECTIVE

1 concreto ◊ *I haven't got any definite plans.* No tengo planes concretos.
2 definitivo ◊ *It's too soon to give a definite answer.* Es pronto aún para dar una respuesta definitiva.
3 seguro ◊ *Maybe we'll go to Spain, but it's not definite.* Quizá vayamos a España, pero no es seguro.
♦ **He was definite about it.** Fue rotundo acerca de esto.
4 claro ◊ *It's a definite improvement.* Es una clara mejoría.

definitely ['dɛfɪnɪtlɪ] ADVERB
sin duda ◊ *He's definitely the best player.* Es sin duda el mejor jugador.
♦ **He's the best player. – Definitely!** Es el mejor jugador. – ¡Desde luego!
♦ **Are you going out with him? – Definitely not!** ¿Vas a salir con él? – ¡En absoluto!

definition [dɛfɪ'nɪʃən] NOUN
la definición (PL las definiciones)

degree [dɪ'gri:] NOUN
1 el grado ◊ *a temperature of 30 degrees* una temperatura de 30 grados
2 la licenciatura ◊ *a degree in English* una licenciatura en filología inglesa
♦ **She's got a degree in English.** Es licenciada en filología inglesa.

to **delay** [dɪ'leɪ] VERB
see also **delay** NOUN
retrasar ◊ *We decided to delay our departure.* Decidimos retrasar la salida.
♦ **Don't delay!** ¡No pierdas tiempo!
♦ **to be delayed** retrasarse ◊ *Our flight was delayed.* Nuestro vuelo se retrasó.

delay [dɪ'leɪ] NOUN
see also **delay** VERB
el retraso ◊ *The tests have caused some delay.* Las pruebas han ocasionado algún retraso.
♦ **without delay** enseguida

to **delete** [dɪ'li:t] VERB
suprimir

deliberate [dɪ'lɪbərɪt] ADJECTIVE
intencionado

deliberately [dɪ'lɪbərɪtlɪ] ADVERB
a propósito

delicate ['dɛlɪkɪt] ADJECTIVE
delicado

delicatessen [dɛlɪkə'tɛsn] NOUN
la charcutería

> ℹ *En un **delicatessen** se venden productos de charcutería, mantequería, etc., de alta calidad.*

delicious [dɪ'lɪʃəs] ADJECTIVE
delicioso

delight [dɪ'laɪt] NOUN
el placer

delighted [dɪ'laɪtɪd] ADJECTIVE
encantado ◊ *He'll be delighted to see you.* Estará encantado de verte.

delightful [dɪ'laɪtful] ADJECTIVE
encantador MASC
encantadora FEM

to **deliver** [dɪ'lɪvər] VERB
1 repartir ◊ *I deliver newspapers.* Reparto periódicos.
2 entregar* ◊ *The package was delivered in the morning.* Entregaron el paquete por la mañana.
♦ **Doctor Hamilton delivered the twins.** El Doctor Hamilton asistió en el parto de los gemelos.

delivery [dɪ'lɪvərɪ] NOUN (PL **deliveries**)
1 la entrega ◊ *Allow 28 days for delivery.* La entrega se realizará en un plazo de 28 días.
2 el parto (*of baby*)

to **demand** [dɪ'mɑ:nd] VERB
see also **demand** NOUN
exigir* ◊ *I demand an explanation.* Exijo una explicación.

demand [dɪ'mɑ:nd] NOUN
see also **demand** VERB
1 (*firm request*)
la petición (PL las peticiones)
◊ *His demand for compensation was rejected.* Rechazaron su petición de indemnización.
2 (*of trade union*)
la reivindicación (PL las reivindicaciones)
◊ *They met to discuss the union's demands.* Se reunieron para discutir las reivindicaciones del sindicato.
3 la demanda ◊ *Demand for coal is down.* Ha bajado la demanda de carbón.

demanding [dɪ'mɑ:ndɪŋ] ADJECTIVE
♦ **It's a very demanding job.** Es un trabajo que exige mucho.
♦ **a demanding child** un niño exigente

demo ['dɛməu] NOUN (PL **demos**)
la manifestación (PL las manifestaciones)

democracy [dɪ'mɔkrəsɪ] NOUN
la democracia

democratic [dɛmə'krætɪk] ADJECTIVE
democrático

to **demolish** [dɪ'mɔlɪʃ] VERB
derribar

to **demonstrate** ['dɛmənstreɪt] VERB
1 demostrar* ◊ *You have to demonstrate that you are reliable.* Tienes que demostrar que se puede confiar en ti.
♦ **She demonstrated the technique.** Hizo una demostración de la técnica.
2 manifestarse* ◊ *They demonstrated outside the court.* Se manifestaron a las puertas del tribunal.

demonstration [dɛmən'streɪʃən] NOUN
1 (*of method, product*)
la demostración (PL las demostraciones)
2 (*protest*)
la manifestación (PL las manifestaciones)

demonstrator ['dɛmənstreɪtər] NOUN

el/la manifestante

denial [dɪ'naɪəl] NOUN
♦ **an official denial** un desmentido oficial

denim ['dɛnɪm] NOUN
♦ **a denim jacket** una cazadora vaquera

denims ['dɛnɪmz] PL NOUN
los vaqueros

Denmark ['dɛnmɑːk] NOUN
Dinamarca FEM

dense [dɛns] ADJECTIVE
1 denso (*smoke, fog*)
2 espeso (*vegetation*)
♦ **He's so dense!** ¡Mira que es corto! (*informal*)

dent [dɛnt] NOUN
see also **dent** VERB
la abolladura

to **dent** [dɛnt] VERB
see also **dent** NOUN
abollar

dental ['dɛntl] ADJECTIVE
dental ◊ *dental treatment* el tratamiento dental
♦ **a dental appointment** una cita con el dentista
♦ **dental floss** la seda dental

dentist ['dɛntɪst] NOUN
el/la dentista ◊ *Catherine is a dentist.* Catherine es dentista. ◊ *at the dentist's* en el dentista

to **deny** [dɪ'naɪ] VERB (**denied, denied**)
negar* ◊ *She denied everything.* Lo negó todo.

deodorant [diː'əudərənt] NOUN
el desodorante

to **depart** [dɪ'pɑːt] VERB
1 partir* (*person*) ◊ *He departed at three o'clock precisely.* Partió a las tres en punto.
2 salir* ◊ *Trains depart for the airport every half hour.* Los trenes salen para el aeropuerto cada media hora.

department [dɪ'pɑːtmənt] NOUN
1 la sección (PL las secciones) ◊ *the toy department* la sección de juguetes
2 el departamento ◊ *the English department* el departamento de inglés

department store [dɪ'pɑːtməntstɔːʳ] NOUN
los grandes almacenes

departure [dɪ'pɑːtʃəʳ] NOUN
la salida ◊ *The departure of this flight has been delayed.* Se ha retrasado la salida de este vuelo.
♦ **His sudden departure worried us.** Su marcha repentina nos dejó preocupados.

departure lounge [dɪ'pɑːtʃəlaundʒ] NOUN
la sala de embarque

to **depend** [dɪ'pɛnd] VERB
♦ **to depend on** depender de ◊ *The price depends on the quality.* El precio depende de la calidad.
♦ **You can depend on him.** Puedes confiar* en él.
♦ **depending on** según
***según** has to be followed by a verb in the subjunctive.*
◊ *depending on the weather* según el tiempo que haga
♦ **It depends.** Depende.

to **deport** [dɪ'pɔːt] VERB
deportar

deposit [dɪ'pɔzɪt] NOUN
1 el depósito (*on hired goods*) ◊ *You get the deposit back when you return the bike.* Al devolver la bici te devuelven el depósito.
2 la señal (*advance payment*) ◊ *You have to pay a deposit when you book.* Se paga una señal al hacer la reserva.
3 la entrada (*in house buying*) ◊ *He paid a £2000 deposit on the house.* Dio una entrada de 2.000 libras para la casa.

depressed [dɪ'prɛst] ADJECTIVE
deprimido ◊ *I'm feeling depressed.* Estoy deprimido.

depressing [dɪ'prɛsɪŋ] ADJECTIVE
deprimente

depth [dɛpθ] NOUN
la profundidad ◊ *14 feet in depth* 14 pies de profundidad
♦ **to deal with a subject in depth** tratar un tema a fondo

deputy head [dɛpjutɪ'hɛd] NOUN
el subdirector
la subdirectora

to **descend** [dɪ'sɛnd] VERB
descender* ◊ *They descended from the roof slowly.* Descendieron con cuidado del tejado.

to **describe** [dɪs'kraɪb] VERB
describir*

description [dɪs'krɪpʃən] NOUN
la descripción (PL las descripciones)

desert ['dɛzət] NOUN
el desierto

desert island [dɛzət'aɪlənd] NOUN
la isla desierta

to **deserve** [dɪ'zəːv] VERB
merecer*

design [dɪ'zaɪn] NOUN
see also **design** VERB
1 el diseño ◊ *The design of the plane makes it safer.* El diseño del avión lo hace más seguro. ◊ *a design fault* un fallo en el diseño
2 el motivo ◊ *a geometric design* un motivo geométrico
♦ **fashion design** diseño de modas

to **design** [dɪ'zaɪn] VERB

see also **design** NOUN

1 diseñar ◊ *She designed the dress herself.* Ella misma diseñó el vestido.

2 elaborar ◊ *We will design an exercise plan specially for you.* Elaboraremos un programa de ejercicios especial para ti.

designer [dɪ'zaɪnəʳ] NOUN

el/la modista (*of clothes*)

♦ **designer clothes** la ropa de diseño

desire [dɪ'zaɪəʳ] NOUN

see also **desire** VERB

el deseo

to **desire** [dɪ'zaɪəʳ] VERB

see also **desire** NOUN

desear

desk [dɛsk] NOUN

1 el escritorio (*in office*)

2 el pupitre (*for pupil*)

3 el mostrador (*in hotel, at airport*)

despair [dɪs'pɛəʳ] NOUN

la desesperación ◊ *a feeling of despair* un sentimiento de desesperación

♦ **to be in despair** estar* desesperado

desperate ['dɛspərɪt] ADJECTIVE

desesperado ◊ *a desperate situation* una situación desesperada

♦ **I was starting to get desperate.** Estaba empezando a desesperarme.

desperately ['dɛspərɪtlɪ] ADVERB

1 tremendamente ◊ *We're desperately worried.* Estamos tremendamente preocupados.

2 desesperadamente ◊ *He was desperately trying to persuade her.* Intentaba desesperadamente convencerla.

to **despise** [dɪs'paɪz] VERB

despreciar

despite [dɪs'paɪt] PREPOSITION

a pesar de

dessert [dɪ'zəːt] NOUN

el postre ◊ *for dessert* de postre

destination [dɛstɪ'neɪʃən] NOUN

el destino

to **destroy** [dɪs'trɔɪ] VERB

destruir*

destruction [dɪs'trʌkʃən] NOUN

la destrucción

detached house [dɪtætʃt'haus] NOUN

la casa no adosada

detail ['diːteɪl] NOUN

el detalle ◊ *I can't remember the details.* No recuerdo los detalles.

♦ **in detail** detalladamente

detailed ['diːteɪld] ADJECTIVE

detallado

detective [dɪ'tɛktɪv] NOUN

el/la detective ◊ *He's a detective.* Es detective. ◊ *a private detective* un detective privado

♦ **a detective story** una novela policíaca

detention [dɪ'tɛnʃən] NOUN

♦ **to get a detention** quedarse castigado después de clase

detergent [dɪ'təːdʒənt] NOUN

el detergente

determined [dɪ'təːmɪnd] ADJECTIVE

decidido ◊ *She's determined to succeed.* Está decidida a triunfar.

detour ['diːtuəʳ] NOUN

el desvío

devaluation [dɪvælju'eɪʃən] NOUN

la devaluación

devastated ['dɛvəsteɪtɪd] ADJECTIVE

deshecho ◊ *I was devastated when they told me.* Cuando me lo dijeron me quedé deshecho.

devastating ['dɛvəsteɪtɪŋ] ADJECTIVE

(*flood, storm*)

devastador MASC

devastadora FEM

◊ *Unemployment has a devastating effect on people.* El desempleo tiene efectos devastadores en la gente.

♦ **She received some devastating news.** Recibió unas noticias desoladoras.

to **develop** [dɪ'vɛləp] VERB

1 desarrollar (*idea, quality*) ◊ *I developed his original idea.* Yo desarrollé su idea original.

2 desarrollarse ◊ *Girls develop faster than boys.* Las chicas se desarrollan más rápido que los chicos.

3 revelar ◊ *to get a film developed* revelar un carrete

♦ **to develop into** convertirse* en ◊ *The argument developed into a fight.* La discusión se convirtió en una pelea.

developing [dɪ'vɛləpɪŋ] ADJECTIVE

♦ **a developing country** un país en vías de desarrollo

development [dɪ'vɛləpmənt] NOUN

el desarrollo ◊ *Economic development in Pakistan.* El desarrollo económico de Pakistán.

♦ **the latest developments** los últimos acontecimientos

device [dɪ'vaɪs] NOUN

el dispositivo

devil ['dɛvl] NOUN

el diablo

to **devise** [dɪ'vaɪz] VERB

idear

devoted [dɪ'vəutɪd] ADJECTIVE

leal (*friend*)

♦ **a devoted wife** una abnegada esposa

♦ **He's completely devoted to her.** Está totalmente entregado a ella.

diabetes [daɪə'biːtiːz] NOUN

la diabetes

diabetic [daɪə'bɛtɪk] ADJECTIVE

diabético ◊ *I'm diabetic.* Soy diabético.

♦ **diabetic chocolate** el chocolate para diabéticos

D

diagonal [daɪ'ægənl] ADJECTIVE
diagonal
diagram ['daɪəgræm] NOUN
el diagrama
*Although **diagrama** ends in -**a**, it is actually a masculine noun.*
to **dial** ['daɪəl] VERB
marcar* (discar* *LatAm*)
dialling tone ['daɪəlɪŋtəun] NOUN
la señal de marcar
dialogue ['daɪəlɔg] NOUN
el diálogo
diamond ['daɪəmənd] NOUN
el diamante ◇ *a diamond ring* un anillo de diamantes
◆ **diamonds** (*at cards*) los diamantes ◇ *the ace of diamonds* el as de diamantes
diaper ['daɪəpəʳ] NOUN US
el pañal
diarrhoea [daɪə'riːə] NOUN
la diarrea ◇ *to have diarrhoea* tener* diarrea
diary ['daɪərɪ] NOUN (PL **diaries**)
1 la agenda ◇ *I've got her phone number in my diary.* Tengo su número de teléfono en la agenda.
2 el diario ◇ *I keep a diary.* Estoy escribiendo un diario.
dice [daɪs] NOUN (PL **dice**)
el dado
dictation [dɪk'teɪʃən] NOUN
el dictado
dictator [dɪk'teɪtəʳ] NOUN
el dictador
dictionary ['dɪkʃənrɪ] NOUN (PL **dictionaries**)
el diccionario
did [dɪd] VERB *see* **do**
didn't ['dɪdnt] = **did not**
to **die** [daɪ] VERB
morir* ◇ *He died last year.* Murió el año pasado. ◇ *She's dying.* Se está muriendo.
◆ **to be dying to do something** morirse* de ganas de hacer algo
to **die down** [daɪ'daun] VERB
amainar ◇ *The wind is dying down.* El viento está amainando.
diesel ['diːzl] NOUN
1 el gasoil (*fuel*)
2 el coche diesel (*car*)
diet ['daɪət] NOUN
see also **diet** VERB
1 la dieta ◇ *a healthy diet* una dieta sana
2 el régimen (PL los regímenes) ◇ *I'm on a diet.* Estoy a régimen.
◆ **a diet Coke** ® una Coca-Cola light ®
to **diet** ['daɪət] VERB
see also **diet** NOUN
hacer* régimen ◇ *I've been dieting for two months.* Llevo dos meses haciendo régimen.
difference ['dɪfrəns] NOUN
la diferencia ◇ *There's not much difference in age between us.* No hay mucha diferencia de edad entre nosotros.
◆ **Good weather makes all the difference.** Con buen tiempo la cosa cambia mucho.
◆ **It makes no difference.** Da lo mismo.
different ['dɪfrənt] ADJECTIVE
distinto
difficult ['dɪfɪkəlt] ADJECTIVE
difícil ◇ *It was difficult to choose.* Era difícil escoger. ◇ *It was a difficult decision to make.* Era una decisión difícil de tomar.
difficulty ['dɪfɪkəltɪ] NOUN (PL **difficulties**)
la dificultad ◇ *What's the difficulty?* ¿Cuál es la dificultad?
◆ **to have difficulty doing something** tener* dificultades para hacer algo
to **dig** [dɪg] VERB (**dug, dug**)
1 cavar ◇ *They're digging a hole in the road.* Están cavando un hoyo en la calle. ◇ *Dad's out digging the garden.* Papá está fuera cavando en el jardín.
2 escarbar ◇ *The dog dug a hole in the sand.* El perro escarbó un agujero en la arena.
to **dig up** [dɪg'ʌp] VERB
1 arrancar* ◇ *The cat's dug up my plants.* El gato me ha arrancado las plantas.
2 desenterrar* ◇ *The police have dug up a body.* La policía ha desenterrado un cadáver.
digestion [dɪ'dʒɛstʃən] NOUN
la digestión
digger ['dɪgəʳ] NOUN
la excavadora
digital television [dɪdʒɪtl'tɛlɪvɪʒən] NOUN
la televisión digital
digital watch [dɪdʒɪtl'wɔtʃ] NOUN (PL **digital watches**)
el reloj digital (PL los relojes digitales)
dim [dɪm] ADJECTIVE
1 tenue (*light*)
2 lerdo (*person*)
dimension [daɪ'mɛnʃən] NOUN
la dimensión (PL las dimensiones)
to **diminish** [dɪ'mɪnɪʃ] VERB
disminuir*
din [dɪn] NOUN
1 el estruendo (*of traffic, machinery*)
2 el jaleo (*of crowd, voices*)
diner ['daɪnəʳ] NOUN US
el restaurante barato
dinghy ['dɪŋgɪ] NOUN (PL **dinghies**)

D

◆ **a rubber dinghy** una lancha neumática
◆ **a sailing dinghy** una embarcación de vela ligera

dining car ['daɪnɪŋkɑːʳ] NOUN
el vagón restaurante (PL los vagones restaurante)

dining room ['daɪnɪŋrum] NOUN
el comedor

dinner ['dɪnəʳ] NOUN
1 la comida (*at midday*)
2 la cena (la comida *LatAm*) (*in the evening*)
◆ **The children have dinner at school.** Los niños comen en la escuela.

dinner jacket ['dɪnədʒækɪt] NOUN
el esmoquin (PL los esmóquines)

dinner party ['dɪnəpɑːtɪ] NOUN (PL **dinner parties**)
la cena

dinner time ['dɪnətaɪm] NOUN
1 la hora de la comida (*at midday*)
2 la hora de la cena (*in the evening*)

dinosaur ['daɪnəsɔːʳ] NOUN
el dinosaurio

dip [dɪp] NOUN
see also **dip** VERB
la salsa ◊ *a spicy dip* una salsa picante
◆ **to go for a dip** ir* a darse un chapuzón

to **dip** [dɪp] VERB
see also **dip** NOUN
mojar ◊ *He dipped a biscuit into his tea.* Mojó una galleta en el té.

diploma [dɪ'pləumə] NOUN
el diploma
*Although **diploma** ends in **-a**, it is actually a masculine noun.*

diplomat ['dɪpləmæt] NOUN
el diplomático
la diplomática

diplomatic [dɪplə'mætɪk] ADJECTIVE
diplomático

direct [daɪ'rɛkt] ADJECTIVE, ADVERB
see also **direct** VERB
directo ◊ *the most direct route* el camino más directo
◆ **You can't fly to Manchester direct from Seville.** No hay vuelos directos a Manchester desde Sevilla.

to **direct** [daɪ'rɛkt] VERB
see also **direct** ADJECTIVE
dirigir*

direction [dɪ'rɛkʃən] NOUN
la dirección (PL las direcciones) ◊ *We're going in the wrong direction.* Vamos en la dirección equivocada.
◆ **to ask somebody for directions** preguntar el camino a alguien

director [dɪ'rɛktəʳ] NOUN
el director
la directora

directory [dɪ'rɛktərɪ] NOUN (PL **directories**)
1 la guía telefónica (*telephone*)
◆ **directory enquiries** información telefónica
2 el directorio (*in computing*)

dirt [dəːt] NOUN
la suciedad

dirty ['dəːtɪ] ADJECTIVE
sucio ◊ *It's dirty.* Está sucio.
◆ **to get dirty** ensuciarse
◆ **to get something dirty** ensuciarse algo ◊ *He got his hands dirty.* Se ensució las manos.
◆ **a dirty joke** un chiste verde (un chiste colorado *LatAm*)

disabled [dɪs'eɪbld] ADJECTIVE, NOUN
minusválido
◆ **disabled people** los minusválidos

disadvantage [dɪsəd'vɑːntɪdʒ] NOUN
la desventaja
◆ **to be at a disadvantage** estar* en desventaja

to **disagree** [dɪsə'griː] VERB
◆ **We always disagree.** Nunca estamos de acuerdo.
◆ **He disagrees with me.** No está de acuerdo conmigo.

disagreement [dɪsə'griːmənt] NOUN
el desacuerdo

to **disappear** [dɪsə'pɪəʳ] VERB
desaparecer*

disappearance [dɪsə'pɪərəns] NOUN
la desaparición (PL las desapariciones)

disappointed [dɪsə'pɔɪntɪd] ADJECTIVE
decepcionado ◊ *I'm disappointed.* Estoy decepcionado.

disappointing [dɪsə'pɔɪntɪŋ] ADJECTIVE
decepcionante ◊ *It's disappointing.* Es decepcionante.

disappointment [dɪsə'pɔɪntmənt] NOUN
la decepción (PL las decepciones)

disaster [dɪ'zɑːstəʳ] NOUN
el desastre

disastrous [dɪ'zɑːstrəs] ADJECTIVE
desastroso

disc [dɪsk] NOUN
el disco

discipline ['dɪsɪplɪn] NOUN
la disciplina

disc jockey ['dɪskdʒɔkɪ] NOUN
el/la discjockey (PL los/las discjockeys) ◊ *he's a disc jockey* es discjockey

disco ['dɪskəu] NOUN (PL **discos**)
1 la discoteca (*place*)
2 el baile ◊ *There's a disco at school tonight.* Esta noche hay baile en la escuela.

to **disconnect** [dɪskə'nɛkt] VERB
desconectar (*appliance*)
◆ **to disconnect the water supply** cortar el agua

discount ['dɪskaunt] NOUN
el descuento ◊ *a 20% discount* un descuento del 20 por ciento

to **discourage** [dɪs'kʌrɪdʒ] VERB
desanimar
♦ **to get discouraged** desanimarse

to **discover** [dɪs'kʌvəʳ] VERB
descubrir*

discovery [dɪs'kʌvərɪ] NOUN
el descubrimiento

discrimination [dɪskrɪmɪ'neɪʃən] NOUN
la discriminación ◊ *racial discrimination* la discriminación racial

to **discuss** [dɪs'kʌs] VERB
1 discutir ◊ *I'll discuss it with my parents.* Lo discutiré con mis padres.
2 discutir sobre (*topic*) ◊ *We discussed the topic at length.* Discutimos sobre el tema largo y tendido.

discussion [dɪs'kʌʃən] NOUN
la discusión (PL las discusiones)

disease [dɪ'zi:z] NOUN
la enfermedad

disgraceful [dɪs'greɪsful] ADJECTIVE
vergonzoso

disguise [dɪs'gaɪz] NOUN
el disfraz (PL los disfraces)
♦ **in disguise** disfrazado

disguised [dɪs'gaɪzd] ADJECTIVE
♦ **He was disguised as a policeman.** Iba disfrazado de policía.

disgusted [dɪs'gʌstɪd] ADJECTIVE
indignado
♦ **I was completely disgusted.** Estaba totalmente indignado.

*Be careful not to translate **disgusted** by **disgustado**.*

disgusting [dɪs'gʌstɪŋ] ADJECTIVE
1 asqueroso (*food, smell*) ◊ *It looks disgusting.* Tiene un aspecto asqueroso.
2 indignante (*disgraceful*) ◊ *That's disgusting!* ¡Es indignante!

dish [dɪʃ] NOUN (PL **dishes**)
el plato ◊ *a china dish* un plato de porcelana ◊ *a vegetarian dish* un plato vegetariano
♦ **to do the dishes** fregar* los platos
♦ **a satellite dish** una antena parabólica

dishonest [dɪs'ɔnɪst] ADJECTIVE
poco honrado

dish soap ['dɪʃsəup] NOUN US
el lavavajillas (PL los lavavajillas)

dish towel ['dɪʃtauəl] NOUN US
el paño de cocina

dishwasher ['dɪʃwɔʃəʳ] NOUN
el lavaplatos (PL los lavaplatos)

disinfectant [dɪsɪn'fɛktənt] NOUN
el desinfectante

disk [dɪsk] NOUN
el disco
♦ **the hard disk** el disco duro

diskette [dɪs'kɛt] NOUN
el disquete

to **dislike** [dɪs'laɪk] VERB
see also **dislike** NOUN
♦ **I dislike it.** No me gusta.

dislike [dɪs'laɪk] NOUN
see also **dislike** VERB
♦ **to take a dislike to somebody** coger* antipatía a alguien (agarrar antipatía a alguien *LatAm*)

*Be very careful with the verb **coger**: in most of Latin America this is an extremely rude word that should be avoided. However, in Spain this verb is common and not rude at all.*

♦ **my likes and dislikes** lo que me gusta y lo que no

to **dismiss** [dɪs'mɪs] VERB
despedir* (*employee*)

disobedient [dɪsə'bi:dɪənt] ADJECTIVE
desobediente

display [dɪs'pleɪ] NOUN
see also **display** VERB
♦ **The assistant took the watch out of the display.** El dependiente sacó el reloj de la vitrina.
♦ **There was a lovely display of fruit in the window.** Había un estupendo surtido de fruta en el escaparate.
♦ **to be on display** estar* expuesto
♦ **a firework display** fuegos artificiales

to **display** [dɪs'pleɪ] VERB
see also **display** NOUN
1 mostrar* ◊ *She proudly displayed her medal.* Mostró con orgullo su medalla.
2 exponer* (*in shop window*)

disposable [dɪs'pəuzəbl] ADJECTIVE
desechable
◊ *a disposable razor* una maquinilla desechable

to **disqualify** [dɪs'kwɔlɪfaɪ] VERB (**disqualified, disqualified**)
descalificar*
♦ **to be disqualified** ser* descalificado ◊ *They were disqualified from the competition.* Fueron descalificados del campeonato.
♦ **He was disqualified from driving.** Le retiraron el carnet de conducir.

to **disrupt** [dɪs'rʌpt] VERB
interrumpir ◊ *The meeting was disrupted by protesters.* La reunión fue interrumpida por unos manifestantes.
♦ **Train services are being disrupted by the strike.** El servicio ferroviario se está viendo alterado por la huelga.

dissatisfied [dɪs'sætɪsfaɪd] ADJECTIVE
insatisfecho
♦ **We were dissatisfied with the service.** Estábamos insatisfechos con el servicio.

to **dissolve** [dɪ'zɔlv] VERB
disolver*

distance ['dɪstns] NOUN

la distancia ◊ *a distance of forty kilometres* una distancia de cuarenta kilómetros
♦ **It's within walking distance.** Se puede ir* andando.
♦ **in the distance** a lo lejos

distant ['dɪstnt] ADJECTIVE
lejano ◊ *in the distant future* en un futuro lejano

distinction [dɪs'tɪŋkʃən] NOUN
1 la distinción (PL las distinciones) ◊ *to make a distinction between two things* hacer* una distinción entre dos cosas
2 la matrícula de honor ◊ *I got a distinction in Spanish.* Saqué una matrícula de honor en lengua española.

distinctive [dɪs'tɪŋktɪv] ADJECTIVE
característico

to **distract** [dɪs'trækt] VERB
distraer*

to **distribute** [dɪs'trɪbju:t] VERB
distribuir*

district ['dɪstrɪkt] NOUN
1 *(of town)*
el barrio
2 *(of country)*
la región (PL las regiones)

to **disturb** [dɪs'tə:b] VERB
molestar ◊ *I'm sorry to disturb you.* Siento molestarte.

ditch [dɪtʃ] NOUN (PL **ditches**)
see also **ditch** VERB
la zanja

to **ditch** [dɪtʃ] VERB
see also **ditch** NOUN
dejar ◊ *She's just ditched her boyfriend.* Acaba de dejar al novio.

dive [daɪv] NOUN
see also **dive** VERB
1 el salto de cabeza *(into water)*
2 el buceo *(under water)*

to **dive** [daɪv] VERB
see also **dive** NOUN
1 tirarse de cabeza *(into water)*
2 bucear *(under water)*

diver ['daɪvər] NOUN
el/la buzo

diversion [daɪ'və:ʃən] NOUN
el desvío *(for traffic)*
*Be careful not to translate **diversion** by **diversión**.*

to **divide** [dɪ'vaɪd] VERB
1 dividir ◊ *Divide the pastry in half.* Divide la masa en dos.
♦ **12 divided by 3 is 4.** 12 dividido entre 3 es 4.
2 dividirse ◊ *We divided into two groups.* Nos dividimos en dos grupos.

diving ['daɪvɪŋ] NOUN
1 el buceo ◊ *diving equipment* equipo de buceo
2 el salto de trampolín ◊ *a diving competition* una competición de saltos de trampolín

diving board ['daɪvɪŋbɔ:d] NOUN
el trampolín (PL los trampolines)

division [dɪ'vɪʒən] NOUN
la división (PL las divisiones)

divorce [dɪ'vɔ:s] NOUN
el divorcio

divorced [dɪ'vɔ:st] ADJECTIVE
divorciado ◊ *My parents are divorced.* Mis padres están divorciados.
♦ **to get divorced** divorciarse

DIY [di:aɪ'waɪ] NOUN
el bricolaje ◊ *to do DIY* hacer* bricolaje ◊ *a DIY shop* una tienda de bricolaje

dizzy ['dɪzɪ] ADJECTIVE
♦ **I feel dizzy.** Estoy mareado.

DJ [di:'dʒeɪ] NOUN
el/la discjockey (PL los/las discjockeys) ◊ *he's a DJ* es discjockey

to **do** [du:] VERB (**does, did, done**)
1 hacer* ◊ *What are you doing this evening?* ¿Qué vas a hacer esta noche? ◊ *She did it by herself.* Lo hizo ella sola. ◊ *I'll do my best.* Haré todo lo que pueda. ◊ *I want to do physics at university.* Quiero hacer física en la universidad.
♦ **What does your father do?** ¿A qué se dedica tu padre?
2 ir* ◊ *She's doing well at school.* Va bien en el colegio.
♦ **How are you doing?** ¿Qué tal?
♦ **How do you do?** Mucho gusto.
3 valer* ◊ *It's not very good, but it'll do.* No es muy bueno, pero valdrá. ◊ *Will £10 do?* ¿Valdrá con diez libras?
♦ **That'll do, thanks.** Así está bien, gracias.
***Do** is not translated when used to form questions.*
◊ *Do you speak English?* ¿Hablas inglés? ◊ *Do you like reading?* ¿Te gusta leer*? ◊ *Where does he live?* ¿Dónde vive? ◊ *Where did you go for your holidays?* ¿Dónde te fuiste de vacaciones?
*Use **no** in negative sentences for **don't**.*
◊ *I don't understand.* No entiendo. ◊ *You didn't tell me anything.* No me dijiste nada. ◊ *He didn't come.* No vino. ◊ *Why didn't you come?* ¿Por qué no viniste?
***Do** is not translated when it is used in place of another verb.*
◊ *I hate maths. – So do I.* Odio las matemáticas. – Yo también. ◊ *I didn't like the film. – Neither did I.* No me gustó la película. – A mí tampoco. ◊ *Do you speak English? – Yes, I do.* ¿Hablas inglés? – Sí. ◊ *Do you like horses? – No, I don't.* ¿Te gustan los caballos? – No.
*Use **¿no?** or **¿verdad?** to check information.*

☞

◊ *You go swimming on Fridays, don't you?* Los viernes vas a nadar, ¿no? ◊ *It doesn't matter, does it?* No importa, ¿verdad?

to **do up** [du:'ʌp] VERB
1 atarse (*shoes*) ◊ *Do up your shoes!* ¡Átate los zapatos!
2 abrocharse (*shirt, cardigan, coat*) ◊ *Do your coat up.* Abróchate el abrigo.
♦ **Do up your zip!** ¡Súbete la cremallera!
3 reformar (*house, room*)

to **do with** ['du:wɪð] VERB
♦ **I could do with a holiday.** Me vendrían bien unas vacaciones.

to **do without** ['du:wɪð'aut] VERB
pasar sin ◊ *I can't do without my computer.* Yo no puedo pasar sin el ordenador.

dock [dɔk] NOUN
el muelle

doctor ['dɔktə^r] NOUN
el médico
la médica
◊ *He's a doctor.* Es médico. ◊ *at the doctor's* en el médico

document ['dɔkjumənt] NOUN
el documento

documentary [dɔkju'mɛntərɪ] NOUN (PL **documentaries**)
el documental

to **dodge** [dɔdʒ] VERB
esquivar (*attacker, blow*)

dodgems ['dɔdʒəmz] PL NOUN
los coches de choque

does [dʌz] VERB *see* **do**

doesn't ['dʌznt] = **does not**

dog [dɔg] NOUN
el perro ◊ *Have you got a dog?* ¿Tienes perro?

do-it-yourself ['du:ɪtjɔ:'sɛlf] NOUN
el bricolaje

dole [dəul] NOUN
el subsidio de paro
♦ **He's on the dole.** Está parado.
♦ **to go on the dole** quedarse parado

doll [dɔl] NOUN
la muñeca

dollar ['dɔlə^r] NOUN
el dólar

dolphin ['dɔlfɪn] NOUN
el delfín (PL los delfines)

domestic [də'mɛstɪk] ADJECTIVE
♦ **a domestic flight** un vuelo nacional

dominoes ['dɔmɪnəuz] PL NOUN
♦ **to have a game of dominoes** echar una partida al dominó

to **donate** [də'neɪt] VERB
donar

done [dʌn] VERB *see* **do**

done [dʌn] ADJECTIVE
listo ◊ *Is the pasta done?* ¿Está lista la pasta?
♦ **How do you like your steak? – Well done.** ¿Cómo quieres el filete? – Muy hecho.

donkey ['dɔŋkɪ] NOUN
el burro

donor ['dəunə^r] NOUN
el/la donante

don't [dəunt] = **do not**

door [dɔ:^r] NOUN
la puerta

doorbell ['dɔ:bɛl] NOUN
el timbre

doorman ['dɔ:mən] NOUN (PL **doormen**)
el portero

doorstep ['dɔ:stɛp] NOUN
el peldaño de la puerta
♦ **on my doorstep** en mi puerta

dormitory ['dɔ:mɪtrɪ] NOUN (PL **dormitories**)
el dormitorio

dose [dəus] NOUN
la dosis (PL las dosis)

dosh [dɔʃ] NOUN
la pasta (la lana *LatAm*) (*informal*)

dot [dɔt] NOUN
el punto
♦ **on the dot** en punto ◊ *He arrived at nine on the dot.* Llegó a las nueve en punto.

to **double** ['dʌbl] VERB
see also **double** ADJECTIVE, ADVERB
1 doblar ◊ *They doubled their prices.* Doblaron los precios.
2 doblarse ◊ *The number of attacks has doubled.* El número de agresiones se ha doblado.

double ['dʌbl] ADJECTIVE, ADVERB
see also **double** VERB
doble ◊ *a double helping* una ración doble ◊ *to cost double* costar* el doble
♦ **double bed** la cama de matrimonio
♦ **a double room** una habitación doble

double bass [dʌbl'beɪs] NOUN (PL **double basses**)
el contrabajo

to **double-click** [dʌbl'klɪk] VERB
hacer* doble clic ◊ *to double-click on an icon* hacer doble clic en un icono

double-decker bus ['dʌbldɛkəbʌs] NOUN
el autobús de dos pisos

double glazing [dʌbl'gleɪzɪŋ] NOUN
el doble acristalamiento

doubles ['dʌblz] PL NOUN
dobles MASC PL (*in tennis*) ◊ *to play mixed doubles* jugar* un partido de dobles mixtos

doubt [daut] NOUN
see also **doubt** VERB

* Verbs marked with this symbol are irregular. See pages 380-382 for further details

la duda ◊ *I have my doubts.* Tengo mis dudas.

♦ **no doubt** sin duda ◊ *as you no doubt know* como sin duda sabrá

to **doubt** [daut] VERB

see also **doubt** NOUN

dudar ◊ *I doubt it.* Lo dudo.

*Use the subjunctive after **dudar que**.*

◊ *I doubt that he'll agree.* Dudo que vaya a estar de acuerdo.

doubtful ['dautful] ADJECTIVE

dudoso ◊ *It's doubtful.* Es dudoso.

♦ **to be doubtful about doing something** no estar* seguro de hacer algo ◊ *I'm doubtful about going by myself.* No estoy seguro de ir solo.

♦ **You sound doubtful.** No pareces muy convencido.

dough [dəu] NOUN

la masa

doughnut ['dəunʌt] NOUN

el buñuelo ◊ *a jam doughnut* un buñuelo de mermelada

down [daun] ADJECTIVE, ADVERB, PREPOSITION

1 abajo ◊ *His office is down on the first floor.* Su despacho está abajo en el primer piso. ◊ *It's down there.* Está allí abajo.

2 al suelo ◊ *He threw down his racket.* Tiró la raqueta al suelo.

♦ **They live just down the road.** Viven más adelante en esta calle.

♦ **to feel down** estar* desanimado

♦ **The computer's down.** El ordenador no funciona.

to **download** ['daunləud] VERB

descargar ◊ *to download a file* descargar un fichero

downpour ['daunpɔːʳ] NOUN

el chaparrón (PL los chaparrones)

downstairs ['daun'stɛəz] ADVERB, ADJECTIVE

1 abajo ◊ *The bathroom's downstairs.* El baño está abajo.

♦ **to go downstairs** bajar

2 de abajo ◊ *the downstairs bathroom* el baño de abajo

♦ **the neighbours downstairs** los vecinos de abajo

downtown ['daun'taun] ADVERB US

1 al centro de la ciudad (*go, come*)

2 en el centro de la ciudad (*live, be*)

to **doze** [dəuz] VERB

dormitar

to **doze off** [dəuz'ɔf] VERB

quedarse dormido

dozen ['dʌzn] NOUN

la docena ◊ *a dozen eggs* una docena de huevos ◊ *two dozen* dos docenas

♦ **I've told you that dozens of times.** Te lo he dicho cientos de veces.

drab [dræb] ADJECTIVE

triste (*clothes*)

draft [drɑːft] NOUN US

la corriente de aire

to **drag** [dræg] VERB

see also **drag** NOUN

arrastrar (*thing, person*)

drag [dræg] NOUN

see also **drag** VERB

♦ **It's a real drag!** ¡Es una verdadera lata! (*informal*)

dragon ['drægn] NOUN

el dragón (PL los dragones)

drain [dreɪn] NOUN

see also **drain** VERB

1 el desagüe (*of house*)

2 la alcantarilla (*in street*)

to **drain** [dreɪn] VERB

see also **drain** NOUN

escurrir (*vegetables, pasta*)

draining board ['dreɪnɪŋbɔːd] NOUN

el escurridero

drainpipe ['dreɪnpaɪp] NOUN

el tubo de desagüe

drama ['drɑːmə] NOUN

1 el drama

*Although **drama** ends in **-a**, it is actually a masculine noun.*

◊ *a TV drama* un drama para televisión

2 el teatro ◊ *Greek drama* el teatro griego ◊ *Drama is my favourite subject.* Mi asignatura favorita es teatro.

♦ **drama school** la escuela de arte dramático

dramatic [drə'mætɪk] ADJECTIVE

espectacular ◊ *a dramatic improvement* una espectacular mejoría

♦ **dramatic news** noticias sensacionales

drank [dræŋk] VERB *see* **drink**

drapes [dreɪps] PL NOUN US

las cortinas

drastic ['dræstɪk] ADJECTIVE

drástico ◊ *to take drastic action* tomar medidas drásticas

draught [drɑːft] NOUN

la corriente de aire ◊ *There's a draught from the window.* Entra corriente por la ventana.

♦ **draught beer** la cerveza de barril

draughts [drɑːfts] NOUN

las damas ◊ *to play draughts* jugar* a las damas

draw [drɔː] NOUN

see also **draw** VERB

1 el empate ◊ *The game ended in a draw.* El partido terminó en empate.

2 el sorteo ◊ *The draw takes place on Saturday.* El sorteo es el sábado.

to **draw** [drɔː] VERB (**drew, drawn**)

see also **draw** NOUN

1 dibujar (*a scene, a person*)

♦ **to draw a picture** hacer* un dibujo

♦ **to draw a picture of somebody** hacer* un retrato de alguien

♦ **to draw a line** trazar* una línea

☞

2 empatar ◊ *We drew two all.* Empatamos a dos.

◆ **to draw the curtains (1)** (*open*) descorrer las cortinas

◆ **to draw the curtains (2)** (*close*) correr las cortinas

to **draw on** ['drɔ:ɔn] VERB
recurrir a ◊ *He drew on his own experience to write the book.* Recurrió a su propia experiencia para escribir el libro.

to **draw up** [drɔ:'ʌp] VERB
pararse ◊ *The car drew up in front of the house.* El coche se paró delante de la casa.

drawback ['drɔ:bæk] NOUN
el inconveniente

drawer [drɔ:ʳ] NOUN
el cajón (PL los cajones)

drawing ['drɔ:ɪŋ] NOUN
el dibujo
◆ **He's good at drawing.** Se le da bien dibujar.

drawing pin ['drɔ:ɪŋpɪn] NOUN
la chincheta

drawn [drɔ:n] VERB *see* **draw**

dreadful ['drɛdful] ADJECTIVE
1 terrible ◊ *a dreadful mistake* un terrible error
2 horrible ◊ *The weather was dreadful.* Hizo un tiempo horrible.
◆ **You look dreadful.** Tienes muy mal aspecto.
◆ **I feel dreadful about not having phoned.** Me siento muy mal por no haber llamado.

to **dream** [dri:m] VERB (**dreamt, dreamt**)
see also **dream** NOUN
soñar* ◊ *Do you dream every night?* ¿Sueñas todas las noches?
◆ **She dreamt about her baby.** Soñó con su bebé.

dream [dri:m] NOUN
see also **dream** VERB
el sueño

to **drench** [drɛntʃ] VERB
◆ **I got drenched.** Me puse empapado.

dress [drɛs] NOUN (PL **dresses**)
see also **dress** VERB
el vestido

to **dress** [drɛs] VERB
see also **dress** NOUN
vestirse* ◊ *I got up, dressed, and went downstairs.* Me levanté, me vestí y bajé.
◆ **to dress somebody** vestir* a alguien
◆ **to get dressed** vestirse*

to **dress up** [drɛs'ʌp] VERB
disfrazarse* ◊ *I dressed up as a ghost.* Me disfracé de fantasma.

dressed [drɛst] ADJECTIVE
vestido ◊ *I'm not dressed yet.* Aún no estoy vestido. ◊ *How was she dressed?* ¿Cómo iba vestida? ◊ *She was dressed in white.* Iba vestida de blanco.
◆ **She was dressed in a green sweater and jeans.** Llevaba un jersey verde y vaqueros.

dresser ['drɛsəʳ] NOUN
el aparador (*furniture*)

dressing ['drɛsɪŋ] NOUN
el aliño (*for salad*)

dressing gown ['drɛsɪŋgaun] NOUN
la bata

dressing table ['drɛsɪŋteɪbl] NOUN
el tocador

drew [dru:] VERB *see* **draw**

dried [draɪd] ADJECTIVE
seco
◆ **dried milk** la leche en polvo
◆ **dried fruits** las frutas pasas

drier ['draɪəʳ] = **dryer**

drift [drɪft] NOUN
see also **drift** VERB
◆ **a snow drift** el ventisquero

to **drift** [drɪft] VERB
see also **drift** NOUN
1 ir* a la deriva (*boat*)
2 amontonarse (*snow*)

drill [drɪl] NOUN
see also **drill** VERB
la taladradora

to **drill** [drɪl] VERB
see also **drill** NOUN
taladrar
◆ **He drilled a hole in the wall.** Hizo un agujero en la pared.

to **drink** [drɪŋk] VERB (**drank, drunk**)
see also **drink** NOUN
beber (tomar *LatAm*) ◊ *What would you like to drink?* ¿Qué te apetece beber? ◊ *She drank three cups of tea.* Se bebió tres tazas de té. ◊ *He had been drinking.* Había bebido.

drink [drɪŋk] NOUN
see also **drink** VERB
1 la bebida ◊ *a cold drink* una bebida fría
2 la copa (*alcoholic*) ◊ *They've gone out for a drink.* Han salido a tomar una copa.
◆ **to have a drink** tomar algo ◊ *Would you like a drink?* ¿Quieres tomar algo?

drinking water ['drɪŋkɪŋ'wɔ:təʳ] NOUN
el agua potable FEM
Although it's a feminine noun, remember that you use **el** *with* **agua**.

drive [draɪv] NOUN
see also **drive** VERB
1 el paseo en coche ◊ *to go for a drive* ir* a dar un paseo en coche

* Verbs marked with this symbol are irregular. See pages 380-382 for further details

♦ **We've got a long drive tomorrow.** Mañana nos espera un largo viaje en coche.
2 el camino de entrada a la casa ◊ *He parked his car in the drive.* Aparcó el coche en el camino de entrada a la casa.
♦ **disk drive** la unidad de disco

to **drive** [draɪv] VERB (**drove, driven**)
see also **drive** NOUN
1 conducir* (manejar *LatAm*) (*a car*) ◊ *Can you drive?* ¿Sabes conducir?
2 ir* en coche (*go by car*) ◊ *We never drive into the town centre.* Nunca vamos en coche al centro.
3 llevar en coche (*transport*) ◊ *My mother drives me to school.* Mi madre me lleva al colegio en coche.
♦ **to drive somebody home** acercar* a alguien a su casa en coche
♦ **to drive somebody mad** volver* loco a alguien ◊ *He drives her mad.* La vuelve loca.

driver ['draɪvəʳ] NOUN
el conductor
la conductora
◊ *He's a bus driver.* Es conductor de autobús.
♦ **She's an excellent driver.** Conduce muy bien.

driver's license ['draɪvəzlaɪsns] NOUN US
el permiso de conducir

driving instructor ['draɪvɪŋɪn'strʌktəʳ] NOUN
el profesor de autoescuela
la profesora de autoescuela
◊ *He's a driving instructor.* Es profesor de autoescuela.

driving lesson ['draɪvɪŋlɛsn] NOUN
la clase de conducir

driving licence ['draɪvɪŋlaɪsns] NOUN
el permiso de conducir

driving test ['draɪvɪŋtɛst] NOUN
♦ **to take one's driving test** hacer* el examen de conducir
♦ **She's just passed her driving test.** Acaba de sacarse el carnet de conducir.

drizzle ['drɪzl] NOUN
la llovizna

drop [drɔp] NOUN
see also **drop** VERB
1 la gota (*of liquid*) ◊ *Would you like some milk? – Just a drop.* ¿Quieres leche? – Una gota nada más.
2 la bajada ◊ *a drop in temperature* una bajada de las temperaturas

to **drop** [drɔp] VERB
see also **drop** NOUN
1 bajar ◊ *The temperature will drop tonight.* La temperatura bajará esta noche.
2 soltar* ◊ *The cat dropped the mouse at my feet.* El gato soltó al ratón junto a mis pies.
♦ **I dropped the glass.** Se me cayó el vaso.
3 dejar ◊ *Could you drop me at the station?* ¿Me puedes dejar en la estación?
♦ **I'm going to drop chemistry.** No voy a dar más química.

drought [draut] NOUN
la sequía

drove [drəuv] VERB *see* **drive**

to **drown** [draun] VERB
ahogarse* ◊ *A boy drowned here yesterday.* Un chico se ahogó ayer aquí.

drug [drʌg] NOUN
1 el medicamento ◊ *They need food and drugs.* Necesitan comida y medicamentos.
2 la droga ◊ *hard drugs* drogas duras ◊ *soft drugs* drogas blandas
♦ **to take drugs** drogarse*
♦ **a drug addict** un drogadicto
♦ **a drug pusher** un camello (*informal*)
♦ **a drug smuggler** un narcotraficante
♦ **the drugs squad** la brigada antidroga

drugstore ['drʌgstɔːʳ] NOUN US

> *Tienda donde se venden artículos muy variados como medicinas, prensa, cosméticos y comida rápida.*

drum [drʌm] NOUN
el tambor ◊ *an African drum* un tambor africano
♦ **a drum kit** una batería
♦ **to play the drums** tocar* la batería

drummer ['drʌməʳ] NOUN
el/la batería (*in rock group*)

drunk [drʌŋk] VERB *see* **drink**

drunk [drʌŋk] ADJECTIVE
see also **drunk** NOUN
borracho ◊ *He was drunk.* Estaba borracho.
♦ **to get drunk** emborracharse

drunk [drʌŋk] NOUN
see also **drunk** ADJECTIVE
el borracho
la borracha

dry [draɪ] ADJECTIVE
see also **dry** VERB
seco ◊ *The paint isn't dry yet.* Aún no está seca la pintura. ◊ *It's been exceptionally dry this spring.* Esta primavera ha sido extraordinariamente seca.
♦ **a long dry period** un largo periodo sin lluvia

to **dry** [draɪ] VERB (**dried, dried**)
see also **dry** ADJECTIVE
1 secar* ◊ *to dry the dishes* secar los platos ◊ *There's nowhere to dry clothes here.* Aquí no hay un sitio para poner a secar la ropa.

☞

2 secarse* ◊ *The washing will dry quickly in the sun.* La colada se secará rápido al sol.
◆**to dry one's hair** secarse* el pelo
dry-cleaner's ['draɪ'kli:nəz] NOUN
la tintorería
dryer ['draɪəʳ] NOUN
◆**a tumble dryer** una secadora
◆**a hair dryer** un secador
DTP ['desktɒp pʌblɪʃɪŋ] NOUN (= *desktop publishing*)
la autoedición
dubbed [dʌbd] ADJECTIVE
doblado ◊ *The film was dubbed into Spanish.* La película estaba doblada al español.
dubious ['dju:bɪəs] ADJECTIVE
◆**My parents were a bit dubious about it.** Mis padres tenían sus dudas sobre el tema.
duck [dʌk] NOUN
el pato
due [dju:] ADJECTIVE, ADVERB
◆**He's due to arrive tomorrow.** Debe llegar mañana.
◆**The plane's due in half an hour.** El avión llegará en media hora.
◆**When's the baby due?** ¿Para cuándo nacerá el niño?
◆**due to** debido a ◊ *The trip was cancelled due to bad weather.* El viaje se suspendió debido al mal tiempo.
dug [dʌg] VERB *see* **dig**
dull [dʌl] ADJECTIVE
1 soso ◊ *He's nice, but a bit dull.* Es simpático, pero un poco soso.
2 gris ◊ *It's always dull and wet.* El tiempo está siempre gris y lluvioso.
dumb [dʌm] ADJECTIVE
1 mudo
◆**She's deaf and dumb.** Es sordomuda.
2 bobo ◊ *Don't be so dumb!* ¡No seas bobo!
◆**That was a really dumb thing I did!** ¡Lo que hice fue una verdadera bobada!
dummy ['dʌmɪ] NOUN (PL **dummies**)
el chupete (*for baby*)
dump [dʌmp] NOUN
see also **dump** VERB
◆**It's a real dump!** ¡Es una auténtica pocilga!
◆**a rubbish dump** un vertedero
to **dump** [dʌmp] VERB
see also **dump** NOUN
verter* (*waste*) ◊ *"No dumping."* "Prohibido verter basuras."
dungarees [dʌŋgə'ri:z] PL NOUN
el mono (el overol *LatAm*)
dungeon ['dʌndʒən] NOUN
la mazmorra

duration [djuə'reɪʃən] NOUN
la duración ◊ *Courses are of two years' duration.* Los cursos tienen una duración de dos años.
◆**for the duration of the trial** durante todo el juicio
during ['djuərɪŋ] PREPOSITION
durante
dusk [dʌsk] NOUN
el anochecer
◆**at dusk** al anochecer
dust [dʌst] NOUN
see also **dust** VERB
el polvo
to **dust** [dʌst] VERB
see also **dust** NOUN
limpiar el polvo de ◊ *I dusted the shelves.* Limpié el polvo de las estanterías.
dustbin ['dʌstbɪn] NOUN
el cubo de la basura (el balde *LatAm*)
dustman ['dʌstmən] NOUN (PL **dustmen**)
el basurero
dusty ['dʌstɪ] ADJECTIVE
polvoriento
Dutch [dʌtʃ] ADJECTIVE
see also **Dutch** NOUN
holandés MASC
holandesa FEM
◊ *She's Dutch.* Es holandesa.
Dutch [dʌtʃ] NOUN
see also **Dutch** ADJECTIVE
el holandés (*language*)
◆**the Dutch** los holandeses
Dutchman ['dʌtʃmən] NOUN (PL **Dutchmen**)
el holandés
Dutchwoman ['dʌtʃwumən] NOUN (PL **Dutchwomen**)
la holandesa
duty ['dju:tɪ] NOUN (PL **duties**)
el deber ◊ *It was his duty to tell the police.* Su deber era decírselo a la policía.
◆**to be on duty (1)** (*policeman*) estar* de servicio
◆**to be on duty (2)** (*doctor, nurse*) estar* de guardia
duty-free ['dju:tɪ'fri:] ADJECTIVE
libre de impuestos
duvet ['du:veɪ] NOUN
el edredón (PL los edredones)
DVD [di:vi:'di:] NOUN
el DVD
dwarf [dwɔ:f] NOUN (PL **dwarves**)
el enano
la enana
dye [daɪ] NOUN
see also **dye** VERB
el tinte ◊ *hair dye* el tinte para el pelo
to **dye** [daɪ] VERB

* Verbs marked with this symbol are irregular. See pages 380-382 for further details

see also **dye** NOUN

teñir

- **to dye sth red** teñir algo de rojo
- **She has dyed her hair blonde.** Se ha teñido el pelo de rubio.

dying ['daɪɪŋ] VERB *see* **die**

dynamic [daɪ'næmɪk] ADJECTIVE

dinámico

dyslexia [dɪs'lɛksɪə] NOUN

la dislexia

E

each [iːtʃ] ADJECTIVE, PRONOUN
1 cada MASC
cada FEM
◊ *each day* cada día
♦ **Each house has its own garden.** Todas las casas tienen jardín.
2 cada uno MASC
cada una FEM
◊ *They have 10 points each.* Tienen 10 puntos cada uno. ◊ *The plates cost £5 each.* Los platos cuestan 5 libras cada uno. ◊ *He gave each of us £10.* Nos dio 10 libras a cada uno.
Use a reflexive verb to translate ***each other.***
◊ *Rachel and Julie hate each other.* Rachel y Julie se odian. ◊ *We write to each other.* Nos escribimos. ◊ *They don't know each other.* No se conocen.

eager ['iːgəʳ] ADJECTIVE
♦ **He was eager to tell us about his experiences.** Estaba impaciente por contarnos sus experiencias.

eagle ['iːgl] NOUN
el águila FEM
Although it's a feminine noun, remember that you use ***el*** *and* ***un*** *with* ***águila.***

ear [ɪəʳ] NOUN
la oreja

earache ['ɪəreɪk] NOUN
♦ **to have earache** tener* dolor de oídos

earlier ['əːlɪəʳ] ADVERB
1 antes ◊ *I saw him earlier.* Lo vi antes.
2 más temprano (*in the morning*) ◊ *I ought to get up earlier.* Debería levantarme más temprano.

early ['əːlɪ] ADVERB, ADJECTIVE
1 temprano ◊ *I have to get up early.* Tengo que levantarme temprano.
♦ **to have an early night** irse* a la cama temprano
2 pronto (*ahead of time*) ◊ *I came early to avoid the heavy traffic.* Vine pronto para evitar el tráfico denso.

to **earn** [əːn] VERB
ganar ◊ *She earns £5 an hour.* Gana 5 libras esterlinas a la hora.

earnings ['əːnɪŋz] PL NOUN
los ingresos ◊ *Average earnings rose two percent last year.* Los ingresos medios aumentaron un dos por ciento el año pasado.

earring ['ɪərɪŋ] NOUN
el pendiente (el arete *LatAm*)

earth [əːθ] NOUN
la tierra
♦ **What on earth are you doing here?** ¿Qué diablos haces aquí?

earthquake ['əːθkweɪk] NOUN
el terremoto

easily ['iːzɪlɪ] ADVERB
fácilmente

east [iːst] ADJECTIVE, ADVERB
see also **east** NOUN
hacia el este ◊ *We were travelling east.* Viajábamos hacia el este.
♦ **an east wind** un viento del este
♦ **the east coast** la costa oriental
♦ **east of** al este de ◊ *It's east of London.* Está al este de Londres.

east [iːst] NOUN
see also **east** ADJECTIVE, ADVERB
el este (*direction, region*) ◊ *in the east of the country* al este del país

Easter ['iːstəʳ] NOUN
la Pascua
♦ **Easter egg** el huevo de Pascua
♦ **the Easter holidays** las vacaciones de Semana Santa

eastern ['iːstən] ADJECTIVE
oriental ◊ *The eastern part of the island is the most beautiful.* La parte oriental de la isla es la más bonita.
♦ **Eastern Europe** la Europa del Este

easy ['iːzɪ] ADJECTIVE
fácil

easy chair ['iːzɪtʃɛəʳ] NOUN
el sillón (PL los sillones)

easy-going ['iːzɪ'gəuɪŋ] ADJECTIVE
♦ **to be easy-going** ser* una persona de trato fácil ◊ *She's very easy-going and gets on well with everybody.* Es una persona de trato fácil y se lleva bien con todos.

to **eat** [iːt] VERB (**ate, eaten**)
comer ◊ *Would you like something to eat?* ¿Quieres comer algo?

EC [iː'siː] NOUN (= *European Community*)
la CE (= la Comunidad Europea)

eccentric [ɪk'sɛntrɪk] ADJECTIVE
excéntrico

echo ['ɛkəu] NOUN (PL **echoes**)
el eco

ecology [ɪ'kɔlədʒɪ] NOUN
la ecología

e-commerce ['ikɒmɜːs] NOUN
el comercio electrónico

economic [iːkə'nɔmɪk] ADJECTIVE
1 económico (*growth, development, policy*)
2 rentable (*profitable*)

* Verbs marked with this symbol are irregular. See pages 380-382 for further details

economical [iːkəˈnɔmɪkl] ADJECTIVE
económico ◊ *My car is very economical to run.* Mi coche me sale muy económico.
economics [iːkəˈnɔmɪks] NOUN
la economía ◊ *the economics of the third world countries* la economía de los países tercermundistas
♦ **He's doing economics at university.** Estudia económicas en la universidad.
to **economize** [ɪˈkɔnəmaɪz] VERB
economizar*
♦ **to economize on something** economizar en algo
economy [ɪˈkɔnəmɪ] NOUN (PL **economies**)
la economía
ecstasy [ˈɛkstəsɪ] NOUN
el éxtasis (*drug*)
♦ **to be in ecstasy** estar* en éxtasis
ecu [ˈeɪkjuː] NOUN (= *European Currency Unit*)
el ecu
eczema [ˈɛksɪmə] NOUN
el eczema
*Although **eczema** ends in **-a**, it is actually a masculine noun.*
◊ *She's got eczema.* Tiene eczema.
edge [ɛdʒ] NOUN
1 el borde ◊ *on the edge of the desk* en el borde del escritorio
♦ **They live on the edge of the town.** Viven en los límites de la ciudad.
2 la orilla (*of lake*)
♦ **to be on the edge of tears** estar* a punto de llorar
edgy [ˈɛdʒɪ] ADJECTIVE
nervioso
Edinburgh [ˈɛdɪnbərə] NOUN
Edimburgo MASC
editor [ˈɛdɪtə^r] NOUN
1 (*of newspaper, magazine*)
el director
la directora
2 el redactor
la redactora
◊ *the sports editor* el redactor de la sección de deportes
educated [ˈɛdjukeɪtɪd] ADJECTIVE
culto
education [ɛdjuˈkeɪʃən] NOUN
1 la educación ◊ *There should be more investment in education.* Debería invertirse más dinero en educación.
2 la enseñanza (*teaching*) ◊ *She works in education.* Trabaja en la enseñanza.
educational [ɛdjuˈkeɪʃənl] ADJECTIVE
1 educativo (*toy*)
2 instructivo (*experience, film*)
effect [ɪˈfɛkt] NOUN
el efecto ◊ *special effects* los efectos especiales
effective [ɪˈfɛktɪv] ADJECTIVE
eficaz (PL eficaces)
efficient [ɪˈfɪʃənt] ADJECTIVE
1 eficiente ◊ *His secretary is very efficient.* Su secretaria es muy eficiente.
2 eficaz (PL eficaces) ◊ *It's a very efficient system.* Es un sistema muy eficaz.
effort [ˈɛfət] NOUN
el esfuerzo
♦ **to make an effort to do something** esforzarse* en hacer algo
e.g. [iːˈdʒiː] ABBREVIATION
p.ej.
egg [ɛg] NOUN
el huevo ◊ *a hard-boiled egg* un huevo duro ◊ *a soft-boiled egg* un huevo pasado por agua ◊ *a fried egg* un huevo frito ◊ *scrambled eggs* los huevos revueltos
egg cup [ˈɛgkʌp] NOUN
la huevera
eggplant [ˈɛgplɑːnt] NOUN US
la berenjena
Egypt [ˈiːdʒɪpt] NOUN
Egipto MASC
eight [eɪt] NUMERAL
ocho ◊ *She's eight.* Tiene ocho años.
eighteen [eɪˈtiːn] NUMERAL
dieciocho ◊ *She's eighteen.* Tiene dieciocho años.
eighteenth [eɪˈtiːnθ] ADJECTIVE
decimoctavo
♦ **the eighteenth floor** la planta dieciocho
♦ **the eighteenth of August** el dieciocho de agosto
eighth [eɪtθ] ADJECTIVE
octavo ◊ *the eighth floor* el octavo piso
♦ **the eighth of August** el ocho de agosto
eighty [ˈeɪtɪ] NUMERAL
ochenta ◊ *He's eighty.* Tiene ochenta años.
Eire [ˈɛərə] NOUN
Eire MASC
either [ˈaɪðə^r] ADJECTIVE, CONJUNCTION, PRONOUN, ADVERB
tampoco ◊ *I don't like milk, and I don't like eggs either.* No me gusta la leche, y tampoco me gustan los huevos. ◊ *I've never been to Spain. – I haven't either.* No he estado nunca en España. – Yo tampoco.
♦ **either...or...** o...o... ◊ *You can have either ice cream or yoghurt.* Puedes tomar o helado o yogur.
♦ **either of them** uno u otro ◊ *I don't like either of them.* No me gusta cualquiera de los dos.
♦ **Choose either of them.** elige cualquiera de los dos
♦ **on either side of the road** a ambos lados de la carretera
elastic [ɪˈlæstɪk] NOUN
el elástico

elastic band [ɪlæstɪk'bænd] NOUN
la goma elástica
elbow ['ɛlbəu] NOUN
el codo
elder ['ɛldəʳ] ADJECTIVE
mayor ◊ *my elder sister* mi hermana mayor
elderly ['ɛldəlɪ] ADJECTIVE
anciano
- **an elderly man** un anciano
- **the elderly** los ancianos

eldest ['ɛldɪst] ADJECTIVE, NOUN
mayor ◊ *my eldest sister* mi hermana mayor
- **He's the eldest.** Él es el mayor.

to **elect** [ɪ'lɛkt] VERB
elegir*
election [ɪ'lɛkʃən] NOUN
la elección (PL las elecciones)
electric [ɪ'lɛktrɪk] ADJECTIVE
eléctrico ◊ *an electric fire* una estufa eléctrica ◊ *an electric guitar* una guitarra eléctrica ◊ *an electric blanket* una manta eléctrica
electrical [ɪ'lɛktrɪkl] ADJECTIVE
eléctrico ◊ *electrical engineering* la ingeniería eléctrica
- **an electrical engineer** un ingeniero en electrónica

electrician [ɪlɛk'trɪʃən] NOUN
el/la electricista ◊ *He's an electrician.* Es electricista.
electricity [ɪlɛk'trɪsɪtɪ] NOUN
la electricidad
electronic [ɪlɛk'trɔnɪk] ADJECTIVE
electrónico
electronics [ɪlɛk'trɔnɪks] NOUN
la electrónica
elegant ['ɛlɪgənt] ADJECTIVE
elegante
elementary school [ɛlɪ'mɛntərɪsku:l] NOUN US
la escuela primaria
elephant ['ɛlɪfənt] NOUN
el elefante
elevator ['ɛlɪveɪtəʳ] NOUN US
el ascensor
eleven [ɪ'lɛvn] NUMERAL
once ◊ *She's eleven.* Tiene once años.
eleventh [ɪ'lɛvnθ] ADJECTIVE
undécimo
- **the eleventh floor** el piso once
- **the eleventh of August** el once de agosto

else [ɛls] ADVERB
- **somebody else** otra persona
- **nobody else** nadie más
- **something else** otra cosa
- **nothing else** nada más
- **somewhere else** en algún otro sitio
- **Did you look anywhere else?** ¿Miraste en otro sitio?
- **I would be happy anywhere else.** Estaría contento en cualquier otro sitio.
- **I didn't look anywhere else.** No miré en ningún otro sitio.
- **Would you like anything else?** ¿Desea alguna otra cosa?
- **I don't want anything else.** No quiero nada más.
- **Arrive on time or else!** ¡Llega a tiempo o si no...!

email ['i:meɪl] NOUN
see also **email** VERB
el correo electrónico
to **email** ['i:meɪl] VERB
see also **email** NOUN
- **to email somebody** enviar* un mensaje a alguien por correo electrónico
- **I'll email you the details.** Te mandaré la información por correo electrónico.

email address ['i:meɪlə'drɛs] NOUN
la dirección de correo electrónico ◊ *my email address is jones at collins dot com* mi dirección de correo electrónico es jones arroba collins punto com
embankment [ɪm'bæŋkmənt] NOUN
(*of railway*)
el terraplén (PL los terraplenes)
embarrassed [ɪm'bærəst] ADJECTIVE
- **I was really embarrassed.** Me dio mucha vergüenza.

*Be careful not to translate **embarrassed** by **embarazada**.*

embarrassing [ɪm'bærəsɪŋ] ADJECTIVE
embarazoso (*mistake, situation*)
- **It was so embarrassing.** Fue una situación muy violenta.
- **How embarrassing!** ¡Qué vergüenza!

embassy ['ɛmbəsɪ] NOUN (PL **embassies**)
la embajada
to **embroider** [ɪm'brɔɪdəʳ] VERB
bordar
embroidery [ɪm'brɔɪdərɪ] NOUN
el bordado
- **I do embroidery in the afternoon.** Bordo por las tardes.

emergency [ɪ'mə:dʒənsɪ] NOUN (PL **emergencies**)
la emergencia ◊ *This is an emergency!* ¡Es una emergencia!
- **in an emergency** en caso de emergencia
- **an emergency exit** una salida de emergencia
- **an emergency landing** un aterrizaje forzoso
- **the emergency services** los servicios de urgencia

to **emigrate** ['ɛmɪgreɪt] VERB
emigrar
emotion [ɪ'məuʃən] NOUN

* Verbs marked with this symbol are irregular. See pages 380-382 for further details

la emoción (PL las emociones)
emotional [ɪ'məuʃənl] ADJECTIVE
emotivo ◊ *She's very emotional.* Es una persona muy emotiva.
♦ **He got very emotional at the farewell party.** Se emocionó mucho en la fiesta de despedida.
emperor ['ɛmpərəʳ] NOUN
el emperador
to **emphasize** ['ɛmfəsaɪz] VERB
recalcar* ◊ *He emphasized the importance of the issue.* Recalcó la importancia de la cuestión.
♦ **to emphasize that** subrayar que
empire ['ɛmpaɪəʳ] NOUN
el imperio
to **employ** [ɪm'plɔɪ] VERB
emplear ◊ *The factory employs 600 people.* La fábrica emplea a 600 trabajadores.
♦ **Thousands of people are employed in tourism.** Miles de personas trabajan en el sector de turismo.
employee [ɪmplɔɪ'iː] NOUN
el empleado
la empleada
employer [ɪm'plɔɪəʳ] NOUN
el empresario
la empresaria
employment [ɪm'plɔɪmənt] NOUN
el empleo
empty ['ɛmptɪ] ADJECTIVE
see also **empty** VERB
vacío
to **empty** ['ɛmptɪ] VERB (**emptied, emptied**)
see also **empty** ADJECTIVE
vaciar*
♦ **to empty something out** vaciar algo
to **encourage** [ɪn'kʌrɪdʒ] VERB
animar ◊ *to encourage somebody to do something* animar a alguien a hacer algo
encouragement [ɪn'kʌrɪdʒmənt] NOUN
el estímulo
encyclopedia [ɛnsaɪkləu'piːdɪə] NOUN
la enciclopedia
end [ɛnd] NOUN
see also **end** VERB
1 el final ◊ *the end of the film* el final de la película ◊ *the end of the holidays* el final de las vacaciones
♦ **in the end** al final ◊ *In the end I decided to stay at home.* Al final decidí quedarme en casa. ◊ *It turned out all right in the end.* Al final resultó bien.
2 el extremo ◊ *at the other end of the table* al otro extremo de la mesa
♦ **at the end of the street** al final de la calle
♦ **for hours on end** durante horas enteras
to **end** [ɛnd] VERB
see also **end** NOUN
terminar ◊ *What time does the film end?* ¿A qué hora termina la película?
♦ **to end up doing something** terminar haciendo algo ◊ *I ended up walking home.* Terminé yendo a casa andando.
ending ['ɛndɪŋ] NOUN
el final ◊ *a happy ending* un final feliz
endless ['ɛndlɪs] ADJECTIVE
interminable ◊ *The journey seemed endless.* El viaje parecía interminable.
enemy ['ɛnəmɪ] NOUN (PL **enemies**)
el enemigo
la enemiga
energetic [ɛnə'dʒɛtɪk] ADJECTIVE
activo ◊ *She's very energetic.* Es muy activa.
energy ['ɛnədʒɪ] NOUN
la energía
engaged [ɪn'geɪdʒd] ADJECTIVE
1 ocupado (*telephone, toilet*)
2 prometido ◊ *Brian and Mary are engaged.* Brian y Mary están prometidos.
♦ **to get engaged** prometerse
engaged tone [ɪn'geɪdʒdtəun] NOUN
la señal de comunicando
engagement [ɪn'geɪdʒmənt] NOUN
compromiso ◊ *They announced their engagement yesterday.* Anunciaron su compromiso ayer.
♦ **The engagement lasted 10 months.** El noviazgo duró 10 meses.
♦ **engagement ring** anillo de compromiso
engine ['ɛndʒɪn] NOUN
1 el motor (*of vehicle*)
2 la locomotora (*of train*)
engineer [ɛndʒɪ'nɪəʳ] NOUN
el ingeniero
la ingeniera
◊ *He's an engineer.* Es ingeniero.
♦ **service engineer** el técnico
engineering [ɛndʒɪ'nɪərɪŋ] NOUN
la ingeniería
England ['ɪŋglənd] NOUN
Inglaterra FEM
English ['ɪŋglɪʃ] ADJECTIVE
see also **English** NOUN
inglés MASC (PL ingleses)
inglesa FEM
English ['ɪŋglɪʃ] NOUN
see also **English** ADJECTIVE
el inglés (*language*) ◊ *the English teacher* el profesor de inglés
♦ **the English** (*people*) los ingleses
Englishman ['ɪŋglɪʃmən] NOUN (PL **Englishmen**)
el inglés (PL los ingleses)
Englishwoman ['ɪŋglɪʃwumən] NOUN (PL **Englishwomen**)
la inglesa
to **enjoy** [ɪn'dʒɔɪ] VERB
♦ **Did you enjoy the film?** ¿Te gustó la película?

☞

♦ **to enjoy oneself** divertirse* ◊ *Did you enjoy yourselves at the party?* ¿Os divertisteis en la fiesta?

enjoyable [ɪn'dʒɔɪəbl] ADJECTIVE
agradable

enlargement [ɪn'lɑːdʒmənt] NOUN
(*of photo*)
la ampliación (PL las ampliaciones)

enormous [ɪ'nɔːməs] ADJECTIVE
enorme

enough [ɪ'nʌf] ADJECTIVE, PRONOUN, ADVERB
bastante ◊ *I didn't have enough money.* No tenía bastante dinero. ◊ *Have you got enough?* ¿Tienes bastante?
♦ **big enough** suficientemente grande
♦ **I've had enough!** ¡Ya estoy harto!
♦ **That's enough!** ¡Ya basta!

to **enquire** [ɪn'kwaɪəʳ] VERB
♦ **to enquire about something** informarse acerca de algo

enquiry [ɪn'kwaɪərɪ] NOUN (PL **enquiries**)
(*official investigation*)
la investigación (PL las investigaciones)

to **enter** ['ɛntəʳ] VERB
entrar en ◊ *He entered the room and sat down.* Entró en la habitación y se sentó.
♦ **to enter a competition** presentarse a un concurso

to **entertain** [ɛntə'teɪn] VERB
recibir (*guests*)

entertainer [ɛntə'teɪnəʳ] NOUN
el animador
la animadora

entertaining [ɛntə'teɪnɪŋ] ADJECTIVE
entretenido (*book, movie*)

enthusiasm [ɪn'θuːzɪæzəm] NOUN
el entusiasmo

enthusiast [ɪn'θuːzɪæst] NOUN
el/la entusiasta ◊ *She's a DIY enthusiast.* Es una entusiasta del bricolaje.

enthusiastic [ɪnθuːzɪ'æstɪk] ADJECTIVE
entusiasta (*response, welcome*)
♦ **She didn't seem very enthusiastic about your idea.** No pareció muy entusiasmada con tu idea.

entire [ɪn'taɪəʳ] ADJECTIVE
entero ◊ *the entire world* el mundo entero

entirely [ɪn'taɪəlɪ] ADVERB
completamente ◊ *an entirely new approach* un enfoque completamente nuevo
♦ **I agree entirely.** Estoy totalmente de acuerdo.

entrance ['ɛntrns] NOUN
la entrada
♦ **an entrance exam** un examen de ingreso
♦ **entrance fee** la cuota de entrada

entry ['ɛntrɪ] NOUN (PL **entries**)
la entrada
♦ **"no entry" (1)** (*on door*) "prohibido el paso"
♦ **"no entry" (2)** (*on road sign*) "dirección prohibida"
♦ **an entry form** un impreso de inscripción

entry phone ['ɛntrɪfəun] NOUN
el portero automático

envelope ['ɛnvələup] NOUN
el sobre

envious ['ɛnvɪəs] ADJECTIVE
envidioso

environment [ɪn'vaɪərnmənt] NOUN
el entorno (*surroundings*) ◊ *She adjusted to the changes in her environment.* Se adaptó a los cambios de su nuevo entorno.
♦ **the environment** el medio ambiente ◊ *We are fighting pollution to protect the environment.* Estamos combatiendo la contaminación para proteger el medio ambiente.

environmental [ɪnvaɪərn'mɛntl] ADJECTIVE
medioambiental ◊ *environmental pollution* contaminación ambiental
♦ **environmental groups** grupos ecologistas

environment-friendly [ɪn'vaɪərnmənt'frɛndlɪ] ADJECTIVE
ecológico

envy ['ɛnvɪ] NOUN
see also **envy** VERB
la envidia

to **envy** ['ɛnvɪ] VERB (**envied, envied**)
see also **envy** NOUN
envidiar

epileptic [ɛpɪ'lɛptɪk] NOUN
el epiléptico
la epiléptica

episode ['ɛpɪsəud] NOUN
el episodio

equal ['iːkwl] ADJECTIVE
igual ◊ *The cake was divided into 12 equal parts.* El pastel se dividió en 12 partes iguales.
♦ **Women demand equal rights at work.** Las mujeres exigen igualdad de derechos en el trabajo.

equality [iː'kwɔlɪtɪ] NOUN
la igualdad

to **equalize** ['iːkwəlaɪz] VERB
empatar (*in sport*)

equator [ɪ'kweɪtəʳ] NOUN
el ecuador

equipment [ɪ'kwɪpmənt] NOUN
el equipo ◊ *skiing equipment* el equipo de esquí

equipped [ɪ'kwɪpt] ADJECTIVE

* Verbs marked with this symbol are irregular. See pages 380-382 for further details

equipado ◊ *This caravan is equipped for four people.* Esta caravana está equipada para cuatro personas.

♦ **equipped with** provisto de ◊ *All rooms are equipped with computers and faxes.* Todas las habitaciones están provistas de ordenadores y fax.

♦ **He was well equipped for the job.** Estaba bien preparado para el puesto.

equivalent [ɪ'kwɪvələnt] ADJECTIVE

see also **equivalent** NOUN

equivalente

♦ **to be equivalent to something** equivaler* a algo

equivalent [ɪ'kwɪvələnt] NOUN

see also **equivalent** ADJECTIVE

el equivalente

error ['ɛrəʳ] NOUN

el error

escalator ['ɛskəleɪtəʳ] NOUN

la escalera mecánica

escape [ɪs'keɪp] NOUN

see also **escape** VERB

la fuga (*from prison*)

♦ **We had a narrow escape.** Nos salvamos por muy poco.

to **escape** [ɪs'keɪp] VERB

see also **escape** NOUN

escaparse ◊ *A lion has escaped.* Se ha escapado un león.

♦ **The passengers escaped unhurt.** Los pasajeros salieron ilesos.

♦ **to escape from prison** fugarse* de la cárcel

escort ['ɛskɔːt] NOUN

la escolta ◊ *a police escort* una escolta policial

Eskimo ['ɛskɪməu] NOUN (PL **Eskimos**)

el/la esquimal

especially [ɪs'pɛʃlɪ] ADVERB

especialmente ◊ *It's very hot there, especially in the summer.* Allí hace mucho calor, especialmente en verano.

essay ['ɛseɪ] NOUN

el trabajo ◊ *a history essay* un trabajo de historia

essential [ɪ'sɛnʃl] ADJECTIVE

esencial ◊ *It's essential to bring warm clothes.* Es esencial traer ropa de abrigo.

estate [ɪs'teɪt] NOUN

1 la urbanización (PL las urbanizaciones) ◊ *I live on an estate.* Vivo en una urbanización.

2 la finca ◊ *He's got a large estate in the country.* Tiene una finca grande en el campo.

estate agent [ɪs'teɪteɪdʒənt] NOUN

el agente inmobiliario

la agente inmobiliaria

◊ *She's an estate agent.* Es agente inmobiliaria.

estate car [ɪs'teɪtkɑːʳ] NOUN

la ranchera

to **estimate** ['ɛstɪmeɪt] VERB

calcular ◊ *They estimated it would take 3 weeks.* Calcularon que llevaría 3 semanas.

etc [ɪt'setrə] ABBREVIATION (= *et cetera*)

etc.

Ethiopia [iːθɪ'əupɪə] NOUN

Etiopía FEM

ethnic ['ɛθnɪk] ADJECTIVE

1 étnico ◊ *an ethnic minority* una minoría étnica

♦ **ethnic cleansing** la limpieza étnica

2 exótico (*restaurant, food*)

EU [iː'juː] NOUN (= *European Union*)

la UE

euro ['juərəu] NOUN (PL **euros**)

el euro

Eurocheque ['juərəutʃɛk] NOUN

el eurocheque

Europe ['juərəp] NOUN

Europa FEM

European [juərə'piːən] ADJECTIVE

see also **European** NOUN

europeo

European [juərə'piːən] NOUN

see also **European** ADJECTIVE

el europeo

la europea

to **evacuate** [ɪ'vækjueɪt] VERB

evacuar*

eve [iːv] NOUN

♦ **Christmas Eve** la Nochebuena

♦ **New Year's Eve** la Nochevieja

even ['iːvn] ADVERB

see also **even** ADJECTIVE

incluso ◊ *I like all animals, even snakes.* Me gustan todos los animales, incluso las serpientes.

♦ **not even** ni siquiera ◊ *He didn't even say hello.* Ni siquiera saludó.

♦ **even if** aunque

Use the subjunctive after ***aunque*** *when translating* ***even if***.

◊ *I'd never do that, even if you asked me.* Nunca haría eso, aunque me lo pidieras.

♦ **even though** aunque ◊ *He's never got any money, even though his parents are quite rich.* Nunca tiene dinero aunque sus padres son bastante ricos.

♦ **even more** aún más ◊ *I liked Granada even more than Seville.* Me gustó Granada aún más que Sevilla.

even ['iːvn] ADJECTIVE

see also **even** ADVERB

uniforme ◊ *an even layer of snow* una capa de nieve uniforme

♦ **an even surface** una superficie lisa

♦ **an even number** un número par

♦ **to get even with somebody** vengarse en alguien

evening ['iːvnɪŋ] NOUN

☞

1 la tarde (*before dark*)
2 la noche (*after dark*) ◇ *in the evening* por la tarde/noche
◆**Good evening!** ¡Buenas tardes/noches!
◆**evening class** la clase nocturna

event [ɪ'vɛnt] NOUN
1 el acontecimiento ◇ *It was one of the most important events in his life.* Fue uno de los acontecimientos más importantes de su vida.
◆**a sporting event** un acontecimiento deportivo
2 la prueba ◇ *She took part in two events at the last Olympic Games.* Participó en dos pruebas en los últimos Juegos Olímpicos.
◆**in the event of** en caso de ◇ *in the event of an accident* en caso de accidente

eventful [ɪ'vɛntful] ADJECTIVE
lleno de incidentes (*race, journey*)

eventually [ɪ'vɛntʃuəlɪ] ADVERB
finalmente

ever ['ɛvəʳ] ADVERB
◆**Have you ever been to Portugal?** ¿Has estado alguna vez en Portugal?
◆**Have you ever seen her?** ¿La has visto alguna vez?
◆**the best I've ever seen** el mejor que he visto
◆**I haven't ever done that.** Jamás he hecho eso.
◆**It will become ever more complex.** Irá siendo cada vez más complicado.
◆**for the first time ever** por primera vez
◆**ever since** desde que ◇ *ever since I met him* desde que lo conozco
◆**ever since then** desde entonces
◆**It's ever so kind of you.** Es muy amable de su parte.

every ['ɛvrɪ] ADJECTIVE
cada MASC
cada FEM
◇ *every pupil* cada alumno ◇ *every time* cada vez
◆**every day** todos los días
◆**every now and then** de vez en cuando

everybody ['ɛvrɪbɔdɪ] PRONOUN
todo el mundo ◇ *Everybody makes mistakes.* Todo el mundo se equivoca.
◆**Everybody had a good time.** Todos se lo pasaron bien.

everyone ['ɛvrɪwʌn] PRONOUN
todo el mundo ◇ *Everyone makes mistakes.* Todo el mundo se equivoca.
◆**Everyone had a good time.** Todos se lo pasaron bien.

everything ['ɛvrɪθɪŋ] PRONOUN
todo ◇ *You've thought of everything!* ¡Has pensado en todo! ◇ *Money isn't everything.* El dinero no lo es todo.

everywhere ['ɛvrɪwɛəʳ] ADVERB
en todas partes ◇ *I looked everywhere, but I couldn't find it.* Miré en todas partes, pero no lo encontré.
◆**I see him everywhere I go.** Lo veo dondequiera que vaya.

***dondequiera** has to be followed by a verb in the subjunctive.*

evil ['i:vl] ADJECTIVE
1 malvado (*person*)
2 maligno (*plan, spirit*)

ex- [ɛks] PREFIX
ex- ◇ *his ex-wife* su ex-esposa

exact [ɪg'zækt] ADJECTIVE
exacto

exactly [ɪg'zæktlɪ] ADVERB
exactamente ◇ *exactly the same* exactamente igual
◆**It's exactly 10 o'clock.** Son las 10 en punto.

to **exaggerate** [ɪg'zædʒəreɪt] VERB
exagerar

exaggeration [ɪgzædʒə'reɪʃən] NOUN
la exageración (PL las exageraciones)

exam [ɪg'zæm] NOUN
el examen (PL los exámenes) ◇ *a French exam* un examen de francés ◇ *the exam results* los resultados de los exámenes

examination [ɪgzæmɪ'neɪʃən] NOUN
el examen (PL los exámenes)

to **examine** [ɪg'zæmɪn] VERB
examinar ◇ *He examined her passport.* Le examinó el pasaporte. ◇ *The doctor examined him.* El médico lo examinó.

examiner [ɪg'zæmɪnəʳ] NOUN
el examinador
la examinadora

example [ɪg'zɑ:mpl] NOUN
el ejemplo ◇ *for example* por ejemplo

excellent ['ɛksələnt] ADJECTIVE
excelente

except [ɪk'sɛpt] PREPOSITION
excepto ◇ *everyone except me* todos excepto yo
◆**except for** excepto
◆**except that** salvo que ◇ *The weather was great, except that it was a bit cold.* El tiempo fue estupendo, salvo que hizo un poco de frío.

***salvo que** may be followed by a verb in subjunctive.*

exception [ɪk'sɛpʃən] NOUN
la excepción (PL las excepciones)
◇ *to make an exception* hacer* una excepción

exceptional [ɪk'sɛpʃənl] ADJECTIVE
excepcional

excess baggage [ɛksɛs'bægɪdʒ] NOUN
el exceso de equipaje

to **exchange** [ɪks'tʃeɪndʒ] VERB
see also **exchange** NOUN

* Verbs marked with this symbol are irregular. See pages 380-382 for further details

cambiar ◊ *I exchanged the book for a CD.* Cambié el libro por un CD.

exchange [ɪks'tʃeɪndʒ] NOUN
see also **exchange** VERB
el intercambio ◊ *I'd like to do an exchange with an English student.* Me gustaría hacer un intercambio con un estudiante inglés.
♦**in exchange for** a cambio de

exchange rate [ɪks'tʃeɪndʒreɪt] NOUN
el tipo de cambio

excited [ɪk'saɪtɪd] ADJECTIVE
entusiasmado

exciting [ɪk'saɪtɪŋ] ADJECTIVE
emocionante

exclamation mark [ekskləˈmeɪʃənmɑːk] NOUN
el signo de admiración

excuse [ɪks'kjuːs] NOUN
see also **excuse** VERB
la excusa

to **excuse** [ɪks'kjuːz] VERB
see also **excuse** NOUN
♦**Excuse me! (1)** (*to attract attention, apologize*) ¡Perdón!
♦**Excuse me! (2)** (*when you want to get past*) ¡Con permiso!

ex-directory ['ɛksdɪ'rɛktərɪ] ADJECTIVE
♦**She's ex-directory.** Su nombre no aparece en la guía.

to **execute** ['ɛksɪkjuːt] VERB
ejecutar

execution [ɛksɪ'kjuːʃən] NOUN
la ejecución (PL las ejecuciones)

executive [ɪg'zɛkjutɪv] NOUN
el ejecutivo
la ejecutiva
◊ *He's an executive.* Es ejecutivo.

exercise ['ɛksəsaɪz] NOUN
el ejercicio ◊ *page ten, exercise three* página diez, ejercicio tres ◊ *to take some exercise* hacer* un poco de ejercicio
♦**exercise book** el cuaderno
♦**an exercise bike** una bicicleta estática

exhaust [ɪg'zɔːst] NOUN
el tubo de escape

exhausted [ɪg'zɔːstɪd] ADJECTIVE
agotado

exhaust fumes [ɪg'zɔːstfjuːmz] PL NOUN
los gases de escape

exhaust pipe [ɪg'zɔːstpaɪp] NOUN
el tubo de escape

exhibition [ɛksɪ'bɪʃən] NOUN
la exposición (PL las exposiciones)

to **exist** [ɪg'zɪst] VERB
existir

exit ['ɛksɪt] NOUN
la salida
*Be careful not to translate **exit** by **éxito**.*

exotic [ɪg'zɔtɪk] ADJECTIVE
exótico

to **expect** [ɪks'pɛkt] VERB
1 esperar ◊ *I'm expecting him for dinner.* Lo espero para cenar. ◊ *She's expecting a baby.* Está esperando un bebé. ◊ *I didn't expect that from him.* No me esperaba eso de él.
2 imaginarse ◊ *I expect he'll be late.* Me imagino que llegará tarde.
♦**I expect so.** Me imagino que sí.

expedition [ɛkspə'dɪʃən] NOUN
la expedición (PL las expediciones)

to **expel** [ɪks'pɛl] VERB
♦**to get expelled** ser* expulsado (*from school*)

expenses [ɪks'pɛnsəs] PL NOUN
los gastos

expensive [ɪks'pɛnsɪv] ADJECTIVE
caro

experience [ɪks'pɪərɪəns] NOUN
la experiencia

experienced [ɪks'pɪərɪənst] ADJECTIVE
♦**an experienced teacher** un maestro con experiencia
♦**She's very experienced in looking after children.** Tiene mucha experiencia en cuidar niños.

experiment [ɪks'pɛrɪmənt] NOUN
el experimento

expert ['ɛkspəːt] NOUN
see also **expert** ADJECTIVE
el experto
la experta
◊ *He's a computer expert.* Es un experto en informática.

expert ['ɛkspəːt] ADJECTIVE
see also **expert** NOUN
experto
♦**He's an expert cook.** Es un experto cocinero.

to **expire** [ɪks'paɪəʳ] VERB
caducar ◊ *My passport has expired.* Mi pasaporte ha caducado.

to **explain** [ɪks'pleɪn] VERB
explicar*

explanation [ɛksplə'neɪʃən] NOUN
la explicación (PL las explicaciones)

to **explode** [ɪks'pləud] VERB
estallar

to **exploit** [ɪks'plɔɪt] VERB
explotar

exploitation [ɛksplɔɪ'teɪʃən] NOUN
la explotación

to **explore** [ɪks'plɔːʳ] VERB
explorar (*place*)

explorer [ɪks'plɔːrəʳ] NOUN
el explorador
la exploradora

explosion [ɪks'pləuʒən] NOUN
la explosión (PL las explosiones)

explosive [ɪks'pləusɪv] ADJECTIVE
see also **explosive** NOUN
explosivo

explosive [ɪks'pləusɪv] NOUN

see also **explosive** ADJECTIVE
el explosivo
to **export** [ɪk'spɔːt] VERB
see also **export** NOUN
exportar
to **express** [ɪks'pres] VERB
expresar
♦ **to express oneself** expresarse ◊ *It's not easy to express oneself in a foreign language.* No es fácil expresarse en un idioma extranjero.
expression [ɪks'prɛʃən] NOUN
la expresión (PL las expresiones) ◊ *It's an English expression.* Es una expresión inglesa.
expressway [ɪks'prɛsweɪ] NOUN US
la autopista
extension [ɪks'tɛnʃən] NOUN
1 (*of building*)
la ampliación (PL las ampliaciones)
2 (*telephone*)
la extensión (PL las extensiones)
◊ *Extension three one three seven, please.* Con la extensión tres uno tres siete, por favor.
extensive [ɪks'tɛnsɪv] ADJECTIVE
1 extenso ◊ *The hotel is situated in extensive grounds.* El hotel está situado en medio de extensos jardines.
2 amplio ◊ *My brother has an extensive knowledge of this subject.* Mi hermano tiene amplio conocimiento sobre esta materia.
♦ **extensive damage** daños de consideración
extent [ɪks'tɛnt] NOUN
♦ **to some extent** hasta cierto punto
exterior [ɛks'tɪərɪəʳ] ADJECTIVE
exterior
extinct [ɪks'tɪŋkt] ADJECTIVE
extinto ◊ *to be extinct* estar* extinto
◊ *Dinosaurs are extinct.* Los dinosaurios están extintos.
♦ **to become extinct** extinguirse*
extinguisher [ɪks'tɪŋgwɪʃəʳ] NOUN
el extintor (el extinguidor *LatAm*)
extortionate [ɪks'tɔːʃnɪt] ADJECTIVE
exorbitante
extra ['ɛkstrə] ADJECTIVE, ADVERB
♦ **He gave me an extra blanket.** Me dio una manta más.
♦ **to pay extra** pagar* un suplemento
♦ **Breakfast is extra.** El desayuno no está incluido.
♦ **Be extra careful!** ¡Ten muchísimo cuidado!
extraordinary [ɪks'trɔːdnrɪ] ADJECTIVE
extraordinario
extravagant [ɪks'trævəgənt] ADJECTIVE
(*person*)
derrochador MASC
derrochadora FEM
extreme [ɪks'triːm] ADJECTIVE
extremo
♦ **with extreme caution** con sumo cuidado
extremely [ɪks'triːmlɪ] ADVERB
sumamente
extremist [ɪks'triːmɪst] NOUN
el/la extremista
eye [aɪ] NOUN
el ojo ◊ *I've got green eyes.* Tengo los ojos verdes.
♦ **to keep an eye on something** vigilar algo
eyebrow ['aɪbrau] NOUN
la ceja
eyelash ['aɪlæʃ] NOUN (PL **eyelashes**)
la pestaña
eyelid ['aɪlɪd] NOUN
el párpado
eyeliner ['aɪlaɪnəʳ] NOUN
el lápiz de ojos (PL los lápices de ojos)
eye shadow ['aɪʃædəu] NOUN
la sombra de ojos
eyesight ['aɪsaɪt] NOUN
la vista ◊ *to have good eyesight* tener* buena vista

F

fabric ['fæbrɪk] NOUN
la tela
*Be careful not to translate **fabric** by **fábrica**.*
fabulous ['fæbjuləs] ADJECTIVE
fabuloso
face [feɪs] NOUN
see also **face** VERB
1 la cara ◊ *He was red in the face.* Tenía la cara colorada. ◊ *the north face of the mountain* la cara norte de la montaña
2 la esfera (*of clock*)
◆ **on the face of it** a primera vista
◆ **in the face of these difficulties** en vista de estas dificultades
◆ **face to face** cara a cara
to **face** [feɪs] VERB
see also **face** NOUN
1 estar* frente a ◊ *They stood facing each other.* Estaban de pie el uno frente al otro.
◆ **The garden faces south.** El jardín da al sur.
2 enfrentarse a ◊ *They face serious problems.* Se enfrentan a graves problemas.
◆ **Let's face it, we're lost.** Tenemos que admitirlo, estamos perdidos.
to **face up to** [feɪs'ʌptu:] VERB
afrontar ◊ *He refuses to face up to his responsibilities.* Se niega a afrontar sus responsabilidades.
face cloth ['feɪsklɔθ] NOUN
la toallita para lavarse
facilities [fə'sɪlɪtɪz] PL NOUN
las instalaciones ◊ *This school has excellent facilities.* Esta escuela tiene unas instalaciones magníficas.
◆ **The youth hostel has cooking facilities.** El albergue juvenil dispone de cocina.
fact [fækt] NOUN
◆ **the fact that ...** el hecho de que ...
*Use the subjunctive after **el hecho de que**.*
◊ *The fact that you are very busy is of no interest to me.* El hecho de que estés muy ocupado no me interesa.
◆ **facts and figures** datos y cifras
◆ **in fact** de hecho
factory ['fæktərɪ] NOUN (PL **factories**)
la fábrica
to **fade** [feɪd] VERB
1 desteñirse* ◊ *My jeans have faded.* Se me han desteñido los vaqueros.
2 apagarse* ◊ *The light was fading fast.* La luz se apagaba con rapidez. ◊ *The noise gradually faded.* El ruido se fue apagando.

fag [fæg] NOUN
el cigarro
to **fail** [feɪl] VERB
see also **fail** NOUN
1 suspender ◊ *He failed his driving test.* Suspendió el examen de conducir.
2 fallar ◊ *The lorry's brakes failed.* Al camión le fallaron los frenos.
3 fracasar ◊ *The plan failed.* El plan fracasó.
◆ **to fail to do something** no lograr hacer algo ◊ *They failed to reach the quarter finals.* No lograron llegar a los cuartos de final.
◆ **The bomb failed to explode.** La bomba no llegó a estallar.
fail [feɪl] NOUN
see also **fail** VERB
el suspenso ◊ *D is a pass, E is a fail.* D es un aprobado, E es un suspenso.
◆ **without fail** sin falta
failure ['feɪljəʳ] NOUN
1 el fracaso ◊ *The attempt was a complete failure.* El intento fue un completo fracaso.
2 el fallo ◊ *a mechanical failure* un fallo mecánico
◆ **I feel a failure.** Me siento un fracasado.
faint [feɪnt] ADJECTIVE
see also **faint** VERB
débil ◊ *His voice was very faint.* Tenía la voz muy débil.
◆ **to feel faint** sentirse* mareado
to **faint** [feɪnt] VERB
see also **faint** ADJECTIVE
desmayarse
fair [fɛəʳ] ADJECTIVE
see also **fair** NOUN
1 justo ◊ *That's not fair.* Eso no es justo.
◆ **I paid more than my fair share.** Pagué más de lo que me correspondía.
2 rubio ◊ *He's got fair hair.* Tiene el pelo rubio.
3 blanco ◊ *people with fair skin* la gente con la piel blanca
◆ **I have a fair chance of winning.** Tengo bastantes posibilidades de ganar.
4 considerable ◊ *That's a fair distance.* Esa es una distancia considerable.
5 bueno (*weather*) ◊ *The weather was fair.* El tiempo era bueno.
*Use **buen** before a masculine singular noun.*
fair [fɛəʳ] NOUN
see also **fair** ADJECTIVE
1 la feria (*travelling funfair*)
2 el parque de atracciones (*on permanent site*)

☞

♦ **a trade fair** una feria de muestras

fair-haired [fɛə'hɛəd] ADJECTIVE
rubio

fairly ['fɛəlɪ] ADVERB
1 equitativamente ◇ *The cake was divided fairly.* La tarta se repartió equitativamente.
2 bastante ◇ *My car is fairly new.* Mi coche es bastante nuevo. ◇ *The weather was fairly good.* El tiempo fue bastante bueno.

fairy ['fɛərɪ] NOUN (PL **fairies**)
el hada FEM

fairy tale ['fɛərɪteɪl] NOUN
el cuento de hadas

faith [feɪθ] NOUN
1 la confianza ◇ *People have lost faith in the government.* La gente ha perdido la confianza en el gobierno.
2 la fe ◇ *the Catholic faith* la fe católica

faithful ['feɪθful] ADJECTIVE
fiel

faithfully ['feɪθfəlɪ] ADVERB
♦ **Yours faithfully...** (*in letter*) Le saluda atentamente...

fake [feɪk] NOUN
see also **fake** ADJECTIVE
la falsificación (PL las falsificaciones) ◇ *The painting was a fake.* El cuadro era una falsificación.

fake [feɪk] ADJECTIVE
see also **fake** NOUN
falso ◇ *a fake banknote* un billete falso
♦ **a fake fur coat** un abrigo de piel sintética

fall [fɔːl] NOUN
see also **fall** VERB
1 la caída ◇ *She had a nasty fall.* Tuvo una mala caída.
♦ **a fall of snow** una nevada
♦ **Niagara Falls** las cataratas del Niágara
2 el otoño (*autumn*) US

to **fall** [fɔːl] VERB (**fell, fallen**)
see also **fall** NOUN
1 caer* ◇ *Bombs fell on the town.* Las bombas caían sobre la ciudad.
When the action of falling is not deliberate, use ***caerse***.
◇ *He tripped and fell.* Tropezó y se cayó. ◇ *The book fell off the shelf.* El libro se cayó de la estantería.
♦ **to fall in love with someone** enamorarse de alguien
2 bajar ◇ *Prices are falling.* Están bajando los precios.

to **fall apart** [fɔːlə'pɑːt] VERB
romperse* ◇ *The book fell apart when he opened it.* El libro se rompió cuando lo abrió.

to **fall down** [fɔːl'daun] VERB
caerse* ◇ *She's fallen down.* Se ha caído. ◇ *The house is slowly falling down.* La casa se está cayendo poco a poco.

to **fall for** ['fɔːlfɔːʳ] VERB
1 tragarse* ◇ *They fell for it!* ¡Se lo tragaron!
2 enamorarse de ◇ *She fell for him immediately.* Se enamoró de él en el acto.

to **fall out** [fɔːl'aut] VERB
reñir* ◇ *Sarah's fallen out with her boyfriend.* Sarah ha reñido con su novio.

to **fall through** [fɔːl'θruː] VERB
fracasar ◇ *Our plans have fallen through.* Nuestros planes han fracasado.

false [fɔːls] ADJECTIVE
falso
♦ **a false alarm** una falsa alarma
♦ **false teeth** la dentadura postiza

fame [feɪm] NOUN
la fama

familiar [fə'mɪlɪəʳ] ADJECTIVE
familiar ◇ *The name sounded familiar to me.* El nombre me sonaba familiar.
♦ **a familiar face** un rostro conocido
♦ **to be familiar with something** conocer* bien algo ◇ *I'm familiar with his work.* Conozco bien su obra.

family ['fæmɪlɪ] NOUN (PL **families**)
la familia ◇ *the Cooke family* la familia Cooke

famine ['fæmɪn] NOUN
la hambruna

famous ['feɪməs] ADJECTIVE
famoso

fan [fæn] NOUN
1 el/la hincha ◇ *the England fans* los hinchas ingleses
2 el/la fan (PL los/las fans) ◇ *the Oasis fan club* el club de fans de Oasis
♦ **I'm one of his greatest fans.** Soy uno de sus mayores admiradores.
3 el aficionado
la aficionada
◇ *a rap music fan* un aficionado al rap
4 el abanico ◇ *a silk fan* un abanico de seda
♦ **an electric fan** un ventilador

fanatic [fə'nætɪk] NOUN
el fanático
la fanática

to **fancy** ['fænsɪ] VERB (**fancied, fancied**)
apetecer* ◇ *I fancy an ice cream.* Me apetece un helado. ◇ *What do you fancy doing?* ¿Qué te apetece hacer?
apetecer que *has to be followed by a verb in the subjunctive.*
◇ *Do you fancy going to the cinema sometime?* ¿Te apetece que vayamos al cine algún día?

* Verbs marked with this symbol are irregular. See pages 380-382 for further details

♦**He fancies her.** Le gusta ella.

fancy dress [fænsɪ'drɛs] NOUN
el disfraz (PL los disfraces)
♦**a fancy dress ball** un baile de disfraces

fantastic [fæn'tæstɪk] ADJECTIVE
fantástico

far [fɑːʳ] ADJECTIVE, ADVERB
lejos ◊ *Is it far?* ¿Está lejos? ◊ *It's not far from London.* No está lejos de Londres.
♦**How far is it to Madrid?** ¿A qué distancia está Madrid?
♦**It's far from easy.** No es nada fácil.
♦**How far have you got?** ¿Hasta dónde has llegado?
♦**at the far end of the swimming pool** al otro extremo de la piscina
♦**far better** mucho mejor
♦**as far as I know** por lo que yo sé
♦**so far** hasta ahora

fare [fɛəʳ] NOUN
la tarifa ◊ *Rail fares are very high in Britain.* Las tarifas de tren son muy altas en Gran Bretaña. ◊ *The air fare was very reasonable.* La tarifa del vuelo fue bastante razonable.
♦**He didn't have the bus fare, so he had to walk.** No tenía dinero para el autobús, así que tuvo que ir andando.
♦**full fare** el precio del billete completo
♦**Children pay half fare on the bus.** Los niños pagan la mitad en el autobús.

Far East [fɑːr'iːst] NOUN
♦**the Far East** el Extremo Oriente

farm [fɑːm] NOUN
la granja (la estancia LatAm)

farmer ['fɑːməʳ] NOUN
el granjero (el estanciero LatAm)
la granjera (la estanciera LatAm)
◊ *He's a farmer.* Es granjero.

farmhouse ['fɑːmhaus] NOUN
el caserío

farming ['fɑːmɪŋ] NOUN
la agricultura ◊ *organic farming* agricultura biológica
♦**dairy farming** la ganadería (*especializada en la producción de leche*)

fascinating ['fæsɪneɪtɪŋ] ADJECTIVE
fascinante

fashion ['fæʃən] NOUN
la moda
♦**to be in fashion** estar* de moda
♦**to go out of fashion** pasar de moda

fashionable ['fæʃnəbl] ADJECTIVE
de moda MASC, FEM, PL
◊ *That colour is very fashionable.* Ese color está muy de moda.
♦**Jane wears fashionable clothes.** Jane viste a la moda.

fast [fɑːst] ADJECTIVE, ADVERB
rápido ◊ *a fast car* un coche rápido
◊ *They work very fast.* Trabajan muy rápido.
♦**That clock's fast.** Ese reloj va adelantado.
♦**He's fast asleep.** Está profundamente dormido.

fat [fæt] ADJECTIVE
see also **fat** NOUN
gordo ◊ *She thinks she's too fat.* Piensa que está demasiado gorda.

fat [fæt] NOUN
see also **fat** ADJECTIVE
1 la grasa (*on meat, in food*) ◊ *It's very high in fat.* Es muy rico en grasas.
2 la manteca (*used for cooking*)

fatal ['feɪtl] ADJECTIVE
1 mortal ◊ *a fatal accident* un accidente mortal
2 fatal ◊ *a fatal mistake* un error fatal

father ['fɑːðəʳ] NOUN
el padre
♦**my father and mother** mis padres
♦**Father Christmas** Papá Noel

father-in-law ['fɑːðərənlɔː] NOUN (PL **fathers-in-law**)
el suegro

faucet ['fɔːsɪt] NOUN US
el grifo

fault [fɔːlt] NOUN
1 la culpa ◊ *It wasn't my fault.* No fue culpa mía.
2 el defecto ◊ *He has his faults, but I still like him.* Tiene sus defectos, pero aun así me gusta.
♦**a mechanical fault** un fallo mecánico

faulty ['fɔːltɪ] ADJECTIVE
defectuoso

favour ['feɪvəʳ] NOUN (US **favor**)
el favor (PL los favores) ◊ *Could you do me a favour?* ¿Me harías un favor?
♦**to be in favour of something** estar* a favor de algo

favourite ['feɪvrɪt] ADJECTIVE (US **favorite**)
see also **favourite** NOUN
favorito ◊ *Blue's my favourite colour.* El azul es mi color favorito.

favourite ['feɪvrɪt] NOUN (US **favorite**)
see also **favourite** ADJECTIVE
el favorito
la favorita
◊ *Liverpool are favourites to win the Cup.* El Liverpool es el favorito para ganar la Copa.

fawn [fɔːn] ADJECTIVE
beige MASC, FEM, PL
Pronounce this word like the English word ***base***.

fax [fæks] NOUN
see also **fax** VERB
el fax (PL los faxes)

to **fax** [fæks] VERB
see also **fax** NOUN

mandar por fax ◊ *I'll fax you the details.* Te mandaré la información por fax.

fear [fɪəʳ] NOUN
see also **fear** VERB
el miedo

to **fear** [fɪəʳ] VERB
see also **fear** NOUN
temer ◊ *You have nothing to fear.* No tienes nada que temer.

feather ['fɛðəʳ] NOUN
la pluma

feature ['fi:tʃəʳ] NOUN
la característica ◊ *an important feature* una característica importante

February ['fɛbruərɪ] NOUN
febrero MASC ◊ *in February* en febrero ◊ *on 18 February* el 18 de febrero

fed [fɛd] VERB *see* **feed**

fed up [fɛd'ʌp] ADJECTIVE
◆**to be fed up with something** estar* harto de algo

to **feed** [fi:d] VERB **(fed, fed)**
dar* de comer a ◊ *Have you fed the cat?* ¿Le has dado de comer al gato? ◊ *He worked hard to feed his family.* Trabajaba mucho para dar de comer a su familia.

to **feel** [fi:l] VERB **(felt, felt)**
1 sentir* ◊ *I didn't feel much pain.* No sentí mucho dolor.
2 sentirse* ◊ *I don't feel well.* No me siento bien. ◊ *I felt lonely.* Me sentía solo.
◆**I was feeling hungry.** Tenía hambre.
◆**I was feeling cold, so I went inside.** Tenía frío, así que entré.
3 tocar* ◊ *The doctor felt his forehead.* El médico le tocó la frente.
◆**to feel like doing something** tener* ganas de hacer algo ◊ *I don't feel like going out tonight.* No tengo ganas de salir esta noche.
◆**Do you feel like an ice cream?** ¿Te apetece un helado?

feeling ['fi:lɪŋ] NOUN
1 la sensación (PL las sensaciones) ◊ *a burning feeling* una sensación de escozor
2 el sentimiento ◊ *He was afraid of hurting my feelings.* Tenía miedo de herir mis sentimientos.
◆**What are your feelings about it?** ¿Tú qué opinas de ello?

feet [fi:t] PL NOUN *see* **foot**

fell [fɛl] VERB *see* **fall**

fellow ['fɛləu] ADJECTIVE
◆**fellow students** los compañeros de clase
◆**fellow workers** los compañeros de trabajo

felt [fɛlt] VERB *see* **feel**

felt-tip pen [fɛlttɪp'pɛn] NOUN
el rotulador

female ['fi:meɪl] ADJECTIVE
see also **female** NOUN
1 hembra MASC, FEM, PL ◊ *a female bat* un murciélago hembra
2 femenino ◊ *the female sex* el sexo femenino

female ['fi:meɪl] NOUN
see also **female** ADJECTIVE
la hembra (*animal*)

feminine ['fɛmɪnɪn] ADJECTIVE
femenino

feminist ['fɛmɪnɪst] NOUN
el/la feminista

fence [fɛns] NOUN
la valla

fern [fə:n] NOUN
el helecho

ferocious [fə'rəuʃəs] ADJECTIVE
feroz (PL feroces)

ferry ['fɛrɪ] NOUN (PL **ferries**)
el ferry

fertile ['fə:taɪl] ADJECTIVE
fértil

fertilizer ['fə:tɪlaɪzəʳ] NOUN
el abono

festival ['fɛstɪvəl] NOUN
el festival ◊ *a jazz festival* un festival de jazz

to **fetch** [fɛtʃ] VERB
1 ir* a por ◊ *Fetch the bucket.* Ve a por el cubo.
◆**to fetch something for someone** traer* algo a alguien ◊ *Fetch me a glass of water.* Tráeme un vaso de agua.
2 venderse por ◊ *His painting fetched £5000.* Su cuadro se vendió por 5.000 libras esterlinas.

fever ['fi:vəʳ] NOUN
la fiebre

few [fju:] ADJECTIVE, PRONOUN
1 pocos ◊ *He has few friends.* Tiene pocos amigos.
◆**a few** unos ◊ *She was silent for a few seconds.* Se quedó callada unos segundos.
2 algunos ◊ *a few of them* algunos de ellos
◆**quite a few people** bastante gente

fewer ['fju:əʳ] ADJECTIVE
menos ◊ *There were fewer people than yesterday.* Había menos gente que ayer.

fiancé [fɪ'ɑ̃:seɪ] NOUN
el novio (*prometido*)

fiancée [fɪ'ɑ̃:seɪ] NOUN
la novia (*prometida*)

fiction ['fɪkʃən] NOUN
la narrativa (*novels*)

field [fi:ld] NOUN

* Verbs marked with this symbol are irregular. See pages 380-382 for further details

el campo ◊ *a field of wheat* un campo de trigo ◊ *a football field* un campo de fútbol (una cancha de fútbol *LatAm*) ◊ *He's an expert in his field.* Es un experto en su campo.

fierce [fɪəs] ADJECTIVE
1 feroz (PL feroces) ◊ *a fierce Alsatian* un pastor alemán feroz
2 encarnizado ◊ *There's fierce competition between the companies.* Existe una encarnizada competencia entre las empresas.
3 violento ◊ *a fierce attack* un violento ataque

fifteen [fɪf'tiːn] NUMERAL
quince ◊ *I'm fifteen.* Tengo quince años.

fifteenth [fɪf'tiːnθ] ADJECTIVE
decimoquinto
♦ **the fifteenth floor** la planta quince
♦ **the fifteenth of August** el quince de agosto

fifth [fɪfθ] ADJECTIVE
quinto ◊ *the fifth floor* el quinto piso
♦ **the fifth of August** el cinco de agosto

fifty ['fɪftɪ] NUMERAL
cincuenta ◊ *He's fifty.* Tiene cincuenta años.

fifty-fifty ['fɪftɪ'fɪftɪ] ADJECTIVE, ADVERB
a medias ◊ *They split the prize money fifty-fifty.* Se repartieron a medias el dinero del premio.
♦ **a fifty-fifty chance** un cincuenta por ciento de posibilidades

fight [faɪt] NOUN
see also **fight** VERB
1 la pelea ◊ *There was a fight in the pub.* Hubo una pelea en el pub.
♦ **She had a fight with her best friend.** Se peleó con su mejor amiga.
2 la lucha ◊ *the fight against cancer* la lucha contra el cáncer

to **fight** [faɪt] VERB **(fought, fought)**
see also **fight** NOUN
1 pelearse ◊ *The fans started fighting.* Los hinchas empezaron a pelearse.
2 luchar ◊ *She has fought against racism all her life.* Ha luchado toda su vida contra el racismo. ◊ *The demonstrators fought with the police.* Los manifestantes lucharon con la policía.
♦ **The doctors tried to fight the disease.** Los médicos intentaron combatir la enfermedad.

to **fight back** [faɪt'bæk] VERB
defenderse*

fighting ['faɪtɪŋ] NOUN
1 la pelea ◊ *Fighting broke out outside the pub.* Se desató una pelea a las puertas del pub.
2 los combates ◊ *Many people have died in the fighting.* Ha muerto mucha gente en los combates.

figure ['fɪgəʳ] NOUN
1 la cifra ◊ *Can you give me the exact figures?* ¿Me puedes dar las cifras exactas?
2 la silueta ◊ *Helen saw the figure of a man on the bridge.* Helen vio la silueta de un hombre en el puente.
♦ **She's got a good figure.** Tiene buen tipo.
♦ **I have to watch my figure.** Tengo que mantener la línea.
3 la figura ◊ *She's an important political figure.* Es una importante figura política.

to **figure out** [fɪgər'aut] VERB
1 calcular ◊ *I'll try to figure out how much it'll cost.* Intentaré calcular lo que va a costar.
2 llegar* a comprender ◊ *I couldn't figure out what it meant.* No llegué a comprender lo que significaba.

file [faɪl] NOUN
see also **file** VERB
1 el expediente ◊ *There was stuff in that file that was private.* Había cosas privadas en ese expediente.
♦ **The police have a file on him.** Está fichado por la policía.
2 la carpeta ◊ *She put the photocopy into her file.* Metió la fotocopia en su carpeta.
3 la lima ◊ *a nail file* una lima de uñas
4 el fichero (*on computer*)

to **file** [faɪl] VERB
see also **file** NOUN
1 archivar ◊ *You have to file all these documents.* Tienes que archivar todos estos documentos.
2 limarse ◊ *She was filing her nails.* Se estaba limando las uñas.

to **fill** [fɪl] VERB
llenar ◊ *She filled the glass with water.* Llenó el vaso de agua.

to **fill in** [fɪl'ɪn] VERB
1 rellenar ◊ *Can you fill in this form, please?* Rellene este impreso, por favor.
2 llenar ◊ *He filled the hole in with soil.* Llenó el agujero de tierra.

to **fill up** [fɪl'ʌp] VERB
llenar ◊ *He filled the cup up to the brim.* Llenó la taza hasta el borde.
♦ **Fill it up, please.** (*at petrol station*) Lleno, por favor.

film [fɪlm] NOUN
1 la película (*movie*)
2 el carrete ◊ *I need a 36 exposure film.* Quería un carrete de 36.

film star ['fɪlmstɑːʳ] NOUN
la estrella de cine

filthy ['fɪlθɪ] ADJECTIVE
mugriento

final ['faɪnl] ADJECTIVE
see also **final** NOUN
1 <u>último</u> ◊ *a final attempt* un último intento
2 <u>definitivo</u> ◊ *a final decision* una decisión definitiva
♦ **I'm not going and that's final.** He dicho que no voy y se acabó.

final ['faɪnl] NOUN
see also **final** ADJECTIVE
la <u>final</u> ◊ *Boris Becker is in the final.* Boris Becker ha llegado a la final.

finally ['faɪnəlɪ] ADVERB
1 <u>por último</u> ◊ *Finally, I would like to say thank you to all of you.* Por último me gustaría darles las gracias a todos.
2 <u>al final</u> ◊ *They finally decided to leave on Saturday.* Al final decidieron salir* el sábado.

to **find** [faɪnd] VERB (**found, found**)
<u>encontrar*</u> ◊ *I can't find the exit.* No encuentro la salida.

to **find out** [faɪnd'aut] VERB
<u>averiguar*</u> ◊ *I found out what happened.* Averigüé lo que ocurrió.
♦ **to find out about** enterarse de ◊ *Try to find out about the cost of a hotel.* Intenta enterarte de lo que costaría un hotel. ◊ *Find out as much as possible about the town.* Entérate de todo lo que puedas sobre la ciudad.

fine [faɪn] ADJECTIVE, ADVERB
see also **fine** NOUN
1 <u>estupendo</u> ◊ *He's a fine musician.* Es un músico estupendo.
♦ **How are you? – I'm fine.** ¿Qué tal estás? – Bien.
♦ **I feel fine.** Me siento bien.
♦ **It'll be ready tomorrow. – That's fine, thanks.** Mañana estará listo. – Muy bien, gracias.
♦ **The weather is fine today.** Hoy hace muy buen tiempo.
2 <u>fino</u> ◊ *She's got very fine hair.* Tiene el pelo muy fino.

fine [faɪn] NOUN
see also **fine** ADJECTIVE
la <u>multa</u> ◊ *I got a fine for driving through a red light.* Me pusieron una multa por saltarme un semáforo en rojo.

finger ['fɪŋgəʳ] NOUN
el <u>dedo</u>
♦ **my little finger** el meñique ◊ *I hurt my little finger.* Me hice daño en el meñique.

fingernail ['fɪŋgəneɪl] NOUN
la <u>uña</u>

finish ['fɪnɪʃ] NOUN
see also **finish** VERB
1 el <u>fin</u> ◊ *from start to finish* de principio a fin
2 la <u>llegada</u> ◊ *We saw the finish of the London Marathon.* Vimos la llegada del maratón de Londres.

to **finish** ['fɪnɪʃ] VERB
see also **finish** NOUN
<u>terminar</u> ◊ *I've finished!* ¡Ya he terminado! ◊ *to finish doing something* terminar de hacer algo ◊ *Have you finished eating?* ¿Has terminado de comer?

Finland ['fɪnlənd] NOUN
<u>Finlandia</u> FEM

Finn [fɪn] NOUN
el <u>finlandés</u> (PL los finlandeses)
la <u>finlandesa</u>
◊ *the Finns* los finlandeses

Finnish ['fɪnɪʃ] ADJECTIVE
see also **Finnish** NOUN
<u>finlandés</u> MASC (PL finlandeses)
<u>finlandesa</u> FEM

Finnish ['fɪnɪʃ] NOUN
see also **Finnish** ADJECTIVE
el <u>finlandés</u> (*language*)

fir [fəːʳ] NOUN
el <u>abeto</u>

fire ['faɪəʳ] NOUN
see also **fire** VERB
1 el <u>fuego</u> (*flames*) ◊ *The fire spread quickly.* El fuego se extendió rápidamente.
2 el <u>incendio</u> (*blaze*) ◊ *The house was destroyed by a fire.* La casa fue destruida por un incendio.
3 la <u>hoguera</u> ◊ *He made a fire to warm himself up.* Encendió una hoguera para calentarse.
4 la <u>estufa</u> ◊ *an electric fire* una estufa eléctrica
♦ **to be on fire** estar* ardiendo

to **fire** ['faɪəʳ] VERB
see also **fire** NOUN
<u>disparar</u> ◊ *She fired at him.* Le disparó.
♦ **to fire a gun** disparar
♦ **to fire somebody** despedir* a alguien ◊ *He was fired from his job.* Le despidieron del trabajo.

fire alarm ['faɪərə'lɑːm] NOUN
la <u>alarma contra incendios</u>

fire brigade ['faɪəbrɪ'geɪd] NOUN
el <u>cuerpo de bomberos</u>

fire engine ['faɪərendʒɪn] NOUN
el <u>coche de bomberos</u>

fire escape ['faɪərɪskeɪp] NOUN
la <u>escalera de incendios</u>

fire extinguisher ['faɪərɪkstɪŋgwɪʃəʳ] NOUN
el <u>extintor</u>

fireman ['faɪəmən] NOUN (PL **firemen**)
el <u>bombero</u> ◊ *He's a fireman.* Es bombero.

fireplace ['faɪəpleɪs] NOUN

la chimenea

fire station ['faɪəsteɪʃən] NOUN
el parque de bomberos

fireworks ['faɪəwəːks] PL NOUN
los fuegos artificiales

firm [fəːm] ADJECTIVE
see also **firm** NOUN
1 firme ◊ *to be firm with somebody* mostrarse* firme con alguien
2 duro ◊ *a firm mattress* un colchón duro

firm [fəːm] NOUN
see also **firm** ADJECTIVE
la empresa

first [fəːst] ADJECTIVE, NOUN, ADVERB
1 primero ◊ *for the first time* por primera vez
Use **primer** *before a masculine singular noun.*
◊ *my first job* mi primer trabajo ◊ *Rachel came first in the race.* Rachel quedó primera en la carrera. ◊ *She was the first to arrive.* Fue la primera en llegar.
♦ **the first of September** el uno de septiembre
♦ **at first** al principio
2 antes ◊ *I want to get a job, but first I have to pass my exams.* Quiero conseguir* un trabajo, pero antes tengo que aprobar los exámenes.
♦ **first of all** ante todo

first aid [fəːst'eɪd] NOUN
los primeros auxilios
♦ **a first aid kit** un botiquín

first-class [fəːst'klɑːs] ADJECTIVE
1 de primera clase MASC, FEM, PL
◊ *a first-class ticket* un billete de primera clase
2 de primera MASC, FEM, PL
◊ *a first-class meal* una comida de primera
♦ **a first-class stamp** un sello para correo urgente

> *In Spain there is no first-class or second-class postage. If you want your mail to arrive fast, you must have it sent express -* ***urgente*** *- from a post office.*

firstly ['fəːstlɪ] ADVERB
en primer lugar

fish [fɪʃ] NOUN (PL **fish**)
see also **fish** VERB
1 (*animal*)
el pez (PL los peces) ◊ *I caught three fish.* Pesqué tres peces.
2 (*food*)
el pescado ◊ *I don't like fish.* No me gusta el pescado. ◊ *fish and chips* pescado rebozado con patatas fritas

> *Es el plato por excelencia de la comida rápida británica; se compra en las* ***chip shops*** *o* ***fish and chip shops****, servido en envases de plástico o cartón.*

to **fish** [fɪʃ] VERB
see also **fish** NOUN
pescar*
♦ **to go fishing** ir* a pescar

fisherman ['fɪʃəmən] NOUN (PL **fishermen**)
el pescador ◊ *He's a fisherman.* Es pescador.

fish fingers [fɪʃ'fɪŋgəz] PL NOUN
los palitos de pescado

fishing ['fɪʃɪŋ] NOUN
la pesca ◊ *I enjoy fishing.* Me gusta la pesca.
♦ **a fishing boat** un barco pesquero
♦ **fishing rod** la caña de pescar

fishing tackle ['fɪʃɪŋtækl] NOUN
los aparejos de pesca

fishmonger's ['fɪʃmʌŋgəz] NOUN
la pescadería

fish sticks ['fɪʃstɪks] PL NOUN US
los palitos de pescado

fist [fɪst] NOUN
el puño

fit [fɪt] ADJECTIVE
see also **fit** VERB, NOUN
en forma ◊ *He felt relaxed and fit after his holiday.* Se sentía relajado y en forma tras las vacaciones.
♦ **Will he be fit to play next Saturday?** ¿Estará en condiciones de jugar el próximo sábado?

fit [fɪt] NOUN
see also **fit** ADJECTIVE, VERB
♦ **to have a fit (1)** sufrir un ataque de epilepsia (*epileptic*)
♦ **to have a fit (2)** (*be angry*) ponerse* hecho una furia ◊ *My Mum will have a fit when she sees the carpet!* ¡Mi madre se va a poner hecha una furia cuando vea la moqueta!

to **fit** [fɪt] VERB
see also **fit** ADJECTIVE, NOUN
1 caber* (*go into a space*) ◊ *It's small enough to fit into your pocket.* Es lo bastante pequeño como para que caber en el bolsillo.
2 encajar ◊ *Make sure the cork fits well into the bottle.* Asegúrese de que el corcho encaja bien en la botella.
3 instalar (*install*) ◊ *He fitted an alarm in his car.* Instaló una alarma en el coche.
4 poner* (*attach*) ◊ *She fitted a plug to the hair dryer.* Le puso un enchufe al secador.
♦ **to fit somebody** estar* bien a alguien ◊ *These trousers don't fit me.* Estos pantalones no me están bien.

☞

◆ **Does it fit?** ¿Te está bien?

to **fit in** [fɪt'ɪn] VERB

1 encajar ◇ *That story doesn't fit in with what he told us.* Esa historia no encaja con lo que él nos contó.

2 adaptarse ◇ *She fitted in well at her new school.* Se adaptó bien al nuevo colegio.

fitted carpet [fɪtɪd'kɑːpɪt] NOUN

la moqueta

fitted kitchen [fɪtɪd'kɪtʃɪn] NOUN

la cocina amueblada

fitting room ['fɪtɪŋrum] NOUN

el probador (PL los probadores)

five [faɪv] NUMERAL

cinco ◇ *He's five.* Tiene cinco años.

to **fix** [fɪks] VERB

1 arreglar ◇ *Can you fix my bike?* ¿Me puedes arreglar la bici?

2 fijar ◇ *Let's fix a date for the party.* Vamos a fijar una fecha para la fiesta.

fixed [fɪkst] ADJECTIVE

fijo ◇ *at a fixed time* a una hora fija

◆ **My parents have very fixed ideas.** Mis padres son de ideas fijas.

fizzy ['fɪzɪ] ADJECTIVE

gaseoso

flabby ['flæbɪ] ADJECTIVE

fofo

flag [flæg] NOUN

la bandera

flame [fleɪm] NOUN

la llama

flamingo [flə'mɪŋgəu] NOUN (PL **flamingos** *or* **flamingoes**)

el flamenco (*pájaro*)

flan [flæn] NOUN

1 la tarta (*sweet*) ◇ *a raspberry flan* una tarta de frambuesa

2 el pastel (*savoury*) ◇ *a cheese and onion flan* un pastel de queso y cebolla

flannel ['flænl] NOUN

la toallita para lavarse (*for face*)

to **flap** [flæp] VERB

◆ **The bird flapped its wings.** El pájaro batió las alas.

flash [flæʃ] NOUN (PL **flashes**)

see also **flash** VERB

el flash (*of camera*)

◆ **a flash of lightning** un relámpago

◆ **in a flash** en un abrir y cerrar de ojos

to **flash** [flæʃ] VERB

see also **flash** NOUN

◆ **A lorry driver flashed him.** Un camionero le hizo señales con los faros.

◆ **They flashed a torch in his face.** Le enfocaron con una linterna en la cara.

flask [flɑːsk] NOUN

el termo (*vacuum flask*)

flat [flæt] ADJECTIVE

see also **flat** NOUN

llano ◇ *a flat surface* una superficie llana

◆ **flat shoes** zapatos bajos

◆ **I've got a flat tyre.** Tengo una rueda desinflada.

flat [flæt] NOUN

see also **flat** ADJECTIVE

el piso (el apartamento *LatAm*)

flattered ['flætəd] ADJECTIVE

halagado

flavour ['fleɪvə^r] NOUN

el sabor (PL los sabores) ◇ *a very strong flavour* un sabor muy fuerte ◇ *Which flavour of ice cream would you like?* ¿De qué sabor quieres el helado?

flavouring ['fleɪvərɪŋ] NOUN

el condimento

flew [fluː] VERB *see* **fly**

flexible ['flɛksəbl] ADJECTIVE

flexible ◇ *flexible working hours* un horario de trabajo flexible

to **flick** [flɪk] VERB

◆ **She flicked the switch to turn the light on.** Le dio al interruptor para encender* la luz.

◆ **to flick through a book** hojear* un libro

to **flicker** ['flɪkə^r] VERB

parpadear (*light*)

flight [flaɪt] NOUN

el vuelo ◇ *What time is the flight to Paris?* ¿A qué hora es el vuelo para París?

◆ **a flight of stairs** un tramo de escaleras

flight attendant ['flaɪtə'tɛndənt] NOUN

el/la auxiliar de vuelo

to **fling** [flɪŋ] VERB (**flung, flung**)

arrojar ◇ *He flung the dictionary onto the floor.* Arrojó el diccionario al suelo.

to **float** [fləut] VERB

flotar

flock [flɔk] NOUN

◆ **a flock of sheep** un rebaño de ovejas

◆ **a flock of birds** una bandada de pájaros

flood [flʌd] NOUN

see also **flood** VERB

la inundación (PL las inundaciones) ◇ *The rain has caused many floods.* La lluvia ha provocado muchas inundaciones.

◆ **He received a flood of letters.** Recibió un aluvión de cartas.

to **flood** [flʌd] VERB

see also **flood** NOUN

inundar ◇ *The river has flooded the village.* El río ha inundado el pueblo.

flooding ['flʌdɪŋ] NOUN

la inundación

floor [flɔː^r] NOUN

1 el suelo (el piso *LatAm*) ◊ *a tiled floor* un suelo embaldosado
♦ **the dance floor** la pista de baile
2 el piso ◊ *the first floor* el primer piso ◊ *on the first floor* en el primer piso

flop [flɔp] NOUN
el fracaso ◊ *The film was a flop.* La película fue un fracaso.

floppy disk [flɔpɪ'dɪsk] NOUN
el disquete

florist ['flɔrɪst] NOUN
el/la florista

flour ['flauəʳ] NOUN
la harina

to **flow** [fləu] VERB
fluir* ◊ *The river flows through the valley.* El río fluye por el valle.
♦ **Traffic is now flowing normally.** El tráfico ya fluye con normalidad.
♦ **Water was flowing from the pipe.** El agua brotaba de la tubería.

flower ['flauəʳ] NOUN
see also **flower** VERB
la flor (PL las flores)

to **flower** ['flauəʳ] VERB
see also **flower** NOUN
florecer*

flown [fləun] VERB *see* **fly**

flu [flu:] NOUN
la gripe ◊ *I've got flu.* Tengo gripe.

fluent ['flu:ənt] ADJECTIVE
♦ **He speaks fluent Spanish.** Habla español con fluidez.

flung [flʌŋ] VERB *see* **fling**

to **flush** [flʌʃ] VERB
♦ **to flush the toilet** tirar de la cadena

flute [flu:t] NOUN
la flauta

fly [flaɪ] NOUN (PL **flies**)
see also **fly** VERB
la mosca

to **fly** [flaɪ] VERB (**flew, flown**)
see also **fly** NOUN
volar* ◊ *He flew from London to Glasgow.* Voló de Londres a Glasgow. ◊ *The bird flew away.* El pájaro salió volando.

foal [fəul] NOUN
el potro

focus ['fəukəs] NOUN (PL **focuses**)
see also **focus** VERB
el centro ◊ *He was the focus of attention.* Era el centro de atención.
♦ **to be out of focus** estar* desenfocado

to **focus** ['fəukəs] VERB
see also **focus** NOUN
enfocar* ◊ *Try to focus the binoculars.* Intenta enfocar los prismáticos.
♦ **to focus on something (1)** enfocar* algo (*with camera, telescope*) ◊ *The cameraman focused on the bird.* El cámara enfocó al pájaro.
♦ **to focus on something (2)** centrarse en algo (*concentrate on*)

fog [fɔg] NOUN
la niebla

foggy ['fɔgɪ] ADJECTIVE
♦ **It's foggy.** Hay niebla.
♦ **a foggy day** un día de niebla

foil [fɔɪl] NOUN
el papel de aluminio (*kitchen foil*)

fold [fəuld] NOUN
see also **fold** VERB
el pliegue

to **fold** [fəuld] VERB
see also **fold** NOUN
doblar ◊ *He folded the newspaper in half.* Dobló el periódico por la mitad.
♦ **to fold one's arms** cruzarse* de brazos

to **fold up** [fəuld'ʌp] VERB
plegar* ◊ *She folded the chair up and walked off.* Plegó la silla y se marchó.

folder ['fəuldəʳ] NOUN
la carpeta

folding ['fəuldɪŋ] ADJECTIVE
plegable (*bed, chair*)

to **follow** ['fɔləu] VERB
seguir* ◊ *You go first and I'll follow.* Ve tú primero y yo te sigo. ◊ *He followed my advice.* Siguió mi consejo.

following ['fɔləuɪŋ] ADJECTIVE
siguiente ◊ *the following day* al día siguiente

fond [fɔnd] ADJECTIVE
♦ **to be fond of somebody** tener* cariño a alguien ◊ *I'm very fond of her.* Le tengo mucho cariño.

food [fu:d] NOUN
la comida ◊ *cat food* comida para gatos ◊ *We need to buy some food.* Hay que comprar comida.

food processor ['fu:dprəusesəʳ] NOUN
el robot de cocina (PL los robots de cocina)

fool [fu:l] NOUN
el/la idiota

foot [fut] NOUN (PL **feet**)
1 el pie (*of person*) ◊ *My feet are aching.* Me duelen los pies.
♦ **on foot** a pie

> *In Spain measurements are in metres and centimetres rather than feet and inches. A foot is about 30 centimetres.*

◊ *Dave is six foot tall.* Dave mide un metro ochenta.
2 la pata (*of animal*)

football ['futbɔ:l] NOUN
1 el fútbol ◊ *I like playing football.* Me gusta jugar* al fútbol.

2 el balón (PL los balones) ◊ *Paul threw the football over the fence.* Paul lanzó el balón por encima de la valla.

footballer ['futbɔːləʳ] NOUN
el/la futbolista

football player ['futbɔːlpleɪəʳ] NOUN
el/la futbolista

footpath ['futpɑːθ] NOUN
el sendero

footprint ['futprɪnt] NOUN
la pisada ◊ *He saw some footprints in the sand.* Vio algunas pisadas en la arena.

footstep ['futstɛp] NOUN
el paso ◊ *I can hear footsteps on the stairs.* Oigo pasos en la escalera.

for [fɔːʳ] PREPOSITION

*There are three basic ways of translating **for** into Spanish: **para**, **por** and **durante**. Check the boxes at the beginning of each translation to find the meaning or example you need. If you can't find it look at the phrases at the end of the entry.*

1 para

***para** is used to indicate destination, employment, intention and purpose.*

◊ *a present for me* un regalo para mí ◊ *the train for London* el tren para Londres ◊ *He works for the government.* Trabaja para el gobierno. ◊ *What for?* ¿Para qué? ◊ *What's it for?* ¿Para qué es?

2 por

***por** is used to indicate reason or cause. Use it also when talking about amounts of money.*

◊ *for fear of being criticized* por temor a ser* criticado ◊ *Oxford is famous for its university.* Oxford es famoso por su universidad. ◊ *I'll do it for you.* Lo haré por ti. ◊ *I'm sorry for Steve, but it's his own fault.* Lo siento por Steve, pero es culpa suya. ◊ *I sold it for £5.* Lo vendí por 5 libras. ◊ *What did he do that for?* ¿Por qué ha hecho eso?

3 durante

*When referring to periods of time, use **durante** to refer to the future and completed actions in the past. Note that it can often be omitted, as in the next two examples.*

◊ *She will be away for a month.* Estará fuera (durante) un mes. ◊ *He worked in Spain for two years.* Trabajó (durante) dos años en España.

*Use **hace...que** and the present to describe actions and states that started in the past and are still going on. Alternatively use the present and **desde hace**. Another option is **llevar** and an **-ando/-iendo** form.*

◊ *He has been learning French for two years.* Hace dos años que estudia francés. ◊ *I haven't seen her for two years.* No la veo desde hace dos años. ◊ *She's been learning German for four years.* Lleva cuatro años estudiando alemán.

*See how the tenses change when talking about something that **had** happened or **had been** happening **for** a time.*

◊ *He had been learning French for two years.* Hacía dos años que estudiaba francés. ◊ *I hadn't seen her for two years.* No la veía desde hacía dos años. ◊ *She had been learning German for four years.* Llevaba cuatro años estudiando alemán.

◆ **There are road works for three kilometres.** Hay obras en tres kilómetros.
◆ **What's the English for "león"?** ¿Cómo se dice "león" en inglés?
◆ **It's time for lunch.** Es la hora de comer.
◆ **Can you do it for tomorrow?** ¿Puedes hacerlo para mañana?
◆ **Are you for or against the idea?** ¿Estás a favor o en contra de la idea?

to **forbid** [fə'bɪd] VERB (**forbade, forbidden**)
prohibir*
◆ **to forbid somebody to do something** prohibir a alguien que haga algo

force [fɔːs] NOUN
see also **force** VERB
la fuerza ◊ *the force of the explosion* la fuerza de la explosión
◆ **UN forces** las fuerzas de la ONU
◆ **in force** (*law, rules*) en vigor

to **force** [fɔːs] VERB
see also **force** NOUN
obligar* ◊ *They forced him to open the safe.* Le obligaron a abrir la caja fuerte.

forecast ['fɔːkɑːst] NOUN
◆ **the weather forecast** el pronóstico del tiempo

foreground ['fɔːgraund] NOUN
el primer plano ◊ *in the foreground* en primer plano

forehead ['fɔrɪd] NOUN
la frente

foreign ['fɔrɪn] ADJECTIVE
1 extranjero ◊ *a foreign language* una lengua extranjera
2 exterior ◊ *US foreign policy* la política exterior estadounidense

foreigner ['fɔrɪnəʳ] NOUN
el extranjero
la extranjera

to **foresee** [fɔː'siː] VERB
(**foresaw, foreseen**)
prever*

forest ['fɔrɪst] NOUN
el bosque
forever [fə'rɛvəʳ] ADVERB
1 para siempre ◊ *He's gone forever.* Se ha ido para siempre.
2 siempre ◊ *She's forever complaining.* Siempre se está quejando.
forgave [fə'geɪv] VERB *see* **forgive**
to **forge** [fɔːdʒ] VERB
falsificar* ◊ *She forged his signature.* Falsificó su firma.
to **forget** [fə'gɛt] VERB (**forgot, forgotten**)
olvidar ◊ *I've forgotten his name.* He olvidado su nombre.
♦ **to forget to do something** olvidarse de hacer algo ◊ *I forgot to close the window.* Me olvidé de cerrar la ventana.
♦ **I'm sorry, I had completely forgotten!** ¡Lo siento, se me había olvidado por completo!
♦ **Forget it!** ¡No importa!
to **forgive** [fə'gɪv] VERB (**forgave, forgiven**)
perdonar ◊ *I forgive you.* Te perdono.
♦ **to forgive somebody for doing something** perdonar a alguien que haya hecho algo
forgot, forgotten [fə'gɔt, fə'gɔtn] VERB *see* **forget**
fork [fɔːk] NOUN
1 (*for eating*)
el tenedor
2 la horca ◊ *The farmer was piling up hay with a fork.* El granjero á heno con una horca.
3 (*in road*)
la bifurcación (PL las bifurcaciones)
form [fɔːm] NOUN
1 el impreso (la planilla *LatAm*)
♦ **to fill in a form** rellenar un impreso
2 la forma ◊ *I'm against hunting in any form.* Estoy en contra de cualquier forma de caza.
♦ **in top form** en plena forma
♦ **She's in the first form.** Está haciendo primero de secundaria.
formal ['fɔːməl] ADJECTIVE
1 oficial ◊ *a formal occasion* un acto oficial
♦ **a formal dinner** una cena de gala
♦ **formal clothes** la ropa de etiqueta
2 formal ◊ *In English, "residence" is a formal term.* En inglés, "residence" es un término formal.
♦ **He's got no formal education.** No tiene formación académica.
former ['fɔːməʳ] ADJECTIVE
antiguo
Put **antiguo** *before the noun when translating* **former**.
◊ *a former pupil* un antiguo alumno
formerly ['fɔːməlɪ] ADVERB
antiguamente

fort [fɔːt] NOUN
el fuerte
forth [fɔːθ] ADVERB
♦ **to go back and forth** ir* de acá para allá
♦ **and so forth** y demás
fortnight ['fɔːtnaɪt] NOUN
♦ **a fortnight** quince días ◊ *I'm going on holiday for a fortnight.* Me voy quince días de vacaciones.
fortunate ['fɔːtʃənɪt] ADJECTIVE
♦ **He was extremely fortunate to survive.** Tuvo la gran suerte de salir vivo.
♦ **It's fortunate that I remembered the map.** Menos mal que me acordé de traer el mapa.
fortunately ['fɔːtʃənɪtlɪ] ADVERB
afortunadamente
fortune ['fɔːtʃən] NOUN
la fortuna ◊ *He made his fortune in car sales.* Consiguió su fortuna con la venta de coches.
♦ **Kate earns a fortune!** ¡Kate gana un dineral!
♦ **to tell somebody's fortune** decir* la buenaventura a alguien
forty ['fɔːtɪ] NUMERAL
cuarenta ◊ *He's forty.* Tiene cuarenta años.
forward ['fɔːwəd] ADVERB
see also **forward** VERB
hacia delante ◊ *to look forward* mirar hacia delante
♦ **to move forward** avanzar*
to **forward** ['fɔːwəd] VERB
see also **forward** ADVERB
remitir (*letter*)
to **foster** ['fɔstəʳ] VERB
acoger* ◊ *She has fostered more than fifteen children.* Ha acogido a más de quince niños.
foster child ['fɔstətʃaɪld] NOUN (PL **foster children**)
el niño acogido en una familia
fought [fɔːt] VERB *see* **fight**
foul [faul] ADJECTIVE
see also **foul** NOUN
1 horrible ◊ *The weather was foul.* El tiempo era horrible.
2 asqueroso ◊ *It smells foul.* Huele asqueroso.
♦ **Brenda is in a foul mood.** Brenda está de muy mal humor.
foul [faul] NOUN
see also **foul** ADJECTIVE
la falta (*in sports*)
found [faund] VERB *see* **find**
to **found** [faund] VERB
fundar
foundations [faun'deɪʃənz] PL NOUN
los cimientos
fountain ['fauntɪn] NOUN
la fuente

fountain pen ['fauntɪnpɛn] NOUN
la pluma estilográfica (la plumafuente LatAm)

four [fɔːʳ] NUMERAL
cuatro ◊ *She's four.* Tiene cuatro años.

fourteen ['fɔː'tiːn] NUMERAL
catorce ◊ *I'm fourteen.* Tengo catorce años.

fourteenth ['fɔː'tiːnθ] ADJECTIVE
decimocuarto
♦ **the fourteenth floor** la planta catorce
♦ **the fourteenth of July** el catorce de julio

fourth ['fɔːθ] ADJECTIVE
cuarto ◊ *the fourth floor* el cuarto piso
♦ **the fourth of July** el cuatro de julio

fox [fɔks] NOUN (PL **foxes**)
el zorro

fragile ['frædʒaɪl] ADJECTIVE
frágil

frame [freɪm] NOUN
el marco ◊ *a silver frame* un marco de plata
♦ **glasses with plastic frames** gafas con montura de plástico

France [frɑːns] NOUN
Francia FEM

frantic ['fræntɪk] ADJECTIVE
frenético ◊ *There was frantic activity backstage on the opening night.* Había una actividad frenética entre bastidores la noche del estreno. ◊ *I was going frantic.* Me estaba poniendo frenético.
♦ **to be frantic with worry** estar* muerto de preocupación

fraud [frɔːd] NOUN
1 el fraude ◊ *He was jailed for fraud.* Lo encarcelaron por fraude.
2 el impostor
la impostora
◊ *You're a fraud!* ¡Eres un impostor!

freckles ['frɛklz] PL NOUN
las pecas

free [friː] ADJECTIVE
see also **free** VERB
1 gratuito ◊ *a free brochure* un folleto gratuito
♦ **You can get it for free.** Se puede conseguir* gratis.
2 libre ◊ *Is this seat free?* ¿Está libre este asiento? ◊ *Are you free after school?* ¿Estás libre después de clase?

to **free** [friː] VERB
see also **free** ADJECTIVE
liberar

freedom ['friːdəm] NOUN
la libertad

freeway ['friːweɪ] NOUN US
la autopista

to **freeze** [friːz] VERB (**froze, frozen**)
1 congelar ◊ *She froze the rest of the raspberries.* Congeló el resto de las frambuesas.
2 helarse*
♦ **The water had frozen.** El agua se había helado.

freezer ['friːzəʳ] NOUN
el congelador

freezing ['friːzɪŋ] ADJECTIVE
♦ **It's freezing!** ¡Hace un frío que pela! (*informal*)
♦ **I'm freezing!** ¡Me estoy congelando!
♦ **three degrees below freezing** tres grados bajo cero

freight [freɪt] NOUN
las mercancías (*goods*)
♦ **a freight train** un tren de mercancías

French [frɛntʃ] ADJECTIVE
see also **French** NOUN
francés MASC (PL franceses)
francesa FEM

French [frɛntʃ] NOUN
see also **French** ADJECTIVE
el francés (*language*) ◊ *the French teacher* el profesor de francés
♦ **the French** los franceses

French beans [frɛntʃ'biːnz] PL NOUN
las judías verdes

French fries [frɛntʃ'fraɪz] PL NOUN
las patatas fritas (las papas fritas LatAm)

French horn [frɛntʃ'hɔːn] NOUN
la trompa de llaves

French loaf [frɛntʃ'ləuf] NOUN (PL **French loaves**)
la barra de pan

Frenchman ['frɛntʃmən] NOUN (PL **Frenchmen**)
el francés (PL los franceses)

French windows [frɛntʃ'wɪndəuz] PL NOUN
la puerta ventana

Frenchwoman ['frɛntʃwumən] NOUN (PL **Frenchwomen**)
la francesa

frequent ['friːkwənt] ADJECTIVE
frecuente

fresh [frɛʃ] ADJECTIVE
fresco ◊ *I always buy fresh fish.* Siempre compro pescado fresco.
♦ **I need some fresh air.** Necesito tomar el aire.

to **freshen up** [frɛʃən'ʌp] VERB
refrescarse*

to **fret** [frɛt] VERB
preocuparse

Friday ['fraɪdɪ] NOUN
el viernes (PL los viernes) ◊ *I saw her on Friday.* La vi el viernes. ◊ *every Friday* todos los viernes ◊ *last Friday* el viernes

* Verbs marked with this symbol are irregular. See pages 380-382 for further details

pasado ◊ *next Friday* el viernes que viene ◊ *on Fridays* los viernes

fridge [frɪdʒ] NOUN
la nevera (la refrigeradora LatAm)

fried [fraɪd] ADJECTIVE
frito ◊ *a fried egg* un huevo frito

friend [frɛnd] NOUN
el amigo
la amiga

friendly ['frɛndlɪ] ADJECTIVE
simpático ◊ *She's really friendly.* Es muy simpática.
♦ **Liverpool is a friendly city.** Liverpool es una ciudad acogedora.
♦ **a friendly match** un partido amistoso

friendship ['frɛndʃɪp] NOUN
la amistad

fright [fraɪt] NOUN
el susto ◊ *She gave us a fright.* Nos dio un susto. ◊ *to get a fright* llevarse un susto

to **frighten** ['fraɪtn] VERB
asustar ◊ *She was trying to frighten him.* Intentaba asustarlo.
♦ **Horror films frighten him.** Le dan miedo las películas de terror.

frightened ['fraɪtnd] ADJECTIVE
♦ **to be frightened** tener* miedo ◊ *I'm frightened!* ¡Tengo miedo!
♦ **Anna's frightened of spiders.** A Anna le dan miedo las arañas.

frightening ['fraɪtnɪŋ] ADJECTIVE
aterrador MASC
aterradora FEM

fringe [frɪndʒ] NOUN
el flequillo ◊ *She's got a fringe.* Lleva flequillo.

Frisbee ® ['frɪzbɪ] NOUN
el disco volador

fro [frəu] ADVERB
♦ **to go to and fro** ir* de acá para allá

frog [frɔg] NOUN
la rana

from [frɔm] PREPOSITION
1 de ◊ *Where do you come from?* ¿De dónde eres? ◊ *a letter from my sister* una carta de mi hermana ◊ *The hotel is one kilometre from the beach.* El hotel está a un kilómetro de la playa. ◊ *The price was reduced from £10 to £5.* Rebajaron el precio de 10 a 5 libras esterlinas.
2 desde ◊ *Breakfast is available from 6 a.m.* Se puede desayunar desde las 6 de la mañana. ◊ *I can't see anything from here.* Desde aquí no veo nada.

In the following phrases **de** *and* **desde** *are interchangeable. Use* **a** *to translate* **to** *if you have chosen* **de** *and* **hasta** *if you have opted for* **desde.**

♦ **He flew from London to Bilbao.** Voló de Londres a Bilbao.
♦ **from one o'clock to three** desde la una hasta las tres
♦ **She works from nine to five.** Trabaja de nueve a cinco.
♦ **from...onwards** a partir de... ◊ *We'll be at home from seven o'clock onwards.* Estaremos en casa a partir de las siete.

front [frʌnt] NOUN
see also **front** ADJECTIVE
la parte delantera ◊ *The switch is at the front of the vacuum cleaner.* El interruptor está en la parte delantera de la aspiradora.
♦ **the front of the dress** el delantero del vestido
♦ **the front of the house** la fachada de la casa
♦ **I was sitting in the front.** (*of car*) Yo iba sentado delante.
♦ **at the front of the train** al principio del tren
♦ **in front** delante ◊ *the car in front* el coche de delante
♦ **in front of** delante de ◊ *Irene sits in front of me in class.* Irene se sienta delante de mí en clase.

front [frʌnt] ADJECTIVE
see also **front** NOUN
1 primero ◊ *the front row* la primera fila

Use **primer** *before a masculine singular noun.*

2 delantero ◊ *the front seats of the car* los asientos delanteros del coche
♦ **the front door** la puerta principal

frontier ['frʌntɪə'] NOUN
la frontera

frost [frɔst] NOUN
la helada ◊ *There was a frost last night.* Anoche cayó una helada.

frosting ['frɔstɪŋ] NOUN US
el glaseado (*on cake*)

frosty ['frɔstɪ] ADJECTIVE
♦ **It's frosty today.** Hoy ha helado.

to **frown** [fraun] VERB
fruncir* el ceño

froze, frozen [frəuz, 'frəuzn] VERB *see* **freeze**

frozen ['frəuzn] ADJECTIVE
congelado

fruit [fru:t] NOUN
la fruta
♦ **fruit juice** el zumo de fruta (el jugo de fruta LatAm)
♦ **fruit salad** la macedonia (la ensalada de frutas LatAm)

fruit machine ['fru:tmə'ʃi:n] NOUN
la máquina tragaperras (PL las máquinas tragaperras)

frustrated [frʌs'treɪtɪd] ADJECTIVE
frustrado

to **fry** [fraɪ] VERB (**fried, fried**)
freír*

frying pan ['fraɪɪŋpæn] NOUN
la sartén (PL las sartenes)

fuel ['fjuəl] NOUN
el combustible ◊ *We've run out of fuel.* Nos hemos quedado sin combustible.

to **fulfil** [ful'fɪl] VERB
realizar* ◊ *He fulfilled his dream to visit China.* Realizó su sueño de viajar a China.
♦ **to fulfil a promise** cumplir una promesa

full [ful] ADJECTIVE
1 lleno ◊ *The tank's full.* El depósito está lleno.
♦ **I'm full.** Estoy lleno.
♦ **There was a full moon.** Había luna llena.
2 completo ◊ *He asked for full information on the job.* Solicitó información completa sobre el trabajo.
♦ **My full name is Ian John Marr.** Mi nombre completo es Ian John Marr.
♦ **full board** la pensión completa
♦ **at full speed** a toda velocidad

full stop [ful'stɔp] NOUN
el punto (*signo de puntuación*)

full-time ['ful'taɪm] ADJECTIVE, ADVERB
♦ **She's got a full-time job.** Tiene un trabajo de jornada completa.
♦ **She works full-time.** Trabaja la jornada completa.

fully ['fulɪ] ADVERB
completamente ◊ *He hasn't fully recovered from his illness.* No se ha recuperado completamente de su enfermedad.

fumes [fju:mz] PL NOUN
el humo ◊ *exhaust fumes* el humo de los tubos de escape

fun [fʌn] ADJECTIVE
see also **fun** NOUN
divertido ◊ *She's a fun person.* Es una persona divertida.

fun [fʌn] NOUN
see also **fun** ADJECTIVE
♦ **to have fun** divertirse*
♦ **It's fun!** ¡Es divertido!
♦ **Have fun!** ¡Que te diviertas!
♦ **for fun** por gusto
♦ **to make fun of somebody** reírse* de alguien

funds [fʌndz] PL NOUN
los fondos ◊ *to raise funds* recaudar fondos

funeral ['fju:nərəl] NOUN
el funeral

funfair ['fʌnfɛəʳ] NOUN
1 la feria (*travelling fair*)
2 el parque de atracciones (*fair on permanent site*)

funny ['fʌnɪ] ADJECTIVE
1 gracioso ◊ *a funny joke* un chiste gracioso
2 raro ◊ *There's something funny about him.* Hay algo raro en él.

fur [fə:ʳ] NOUN
1 la piel
♦ **a fur coat** un abrigo de pieles
2 el pelaje ◊ *the cat's fur* el pelaje del gato

furious ['fjuərɪəs] ADJECTIVE
furioso

furniture ['fə:nɪtʃəʳ] NOUN
los muebles
♦ **a piece of furniture** un mueble

further ['fə:ðəʳ] ADVERB, ADJECTIVE
1 más lejos ◊ *London is further from here than Paris.* Londres está más lejos de aquí que París.
♦ **I can't walk any further.** No puedo andar* más.
♦ **How much further is it?** ¿Cuánto queda todavía?
2 más ◊ *Please write to us if you need any further information.* No dude en escribirnos si necesita más información.

further education ['fə:ðəredju'keɪʃən] NOUN

> *Son cursos de formación no universitaria que se ofrecen después de la etapa de educación obligatoria.*

fuse [fju:z] NOUN
el fusible ◊ *The fuse has blown.* Se ha fundido el fusible.

fuss [fʌs] NOUN
el jaleo ◊ *What's all the fuss about?* ¿A qué viene tanto jaleo?
♦ **He's always making a fuss about nothing.** Siempre monta el número por cualquier tontería. (*informal*)

fussy ['fʌsɪ] ADJECTIVE
quisquilloso ◊ *She is very fussy about her food.* Es muy quisquillosa con la comida.

future ['fju:tʃəʳ] NOUN
el futuro ◊ *What are your plans for the future?* ¿Qué planes tienes para el futuro?
♦ **in future** de ahora en adelante ◊ *Be more careful in future.* De ahora en adelante ten más cuidado.

G

to **gain** [geɪn] VERB
ganar ◊ *What do you hope to gain from this?* ¿Qué esperas ganar con esto?
◆ **to gain speed** adquirir* velocidad
◆ **to gain weight** engordar

gallery ['gælərɪ] NOUN (PL **galleries**)
1 el museo de arte (*state-owned*)
2 una galería de arte (*private*)

to **gamble** ['gæmbl] VERB
jugarse* ◊ *He gambled £100 at the casino.* Se jugó 100 libras en el casino.

gambler ['gæmbləʳ] NOUN
el jugador
la jugadora

gambling ['gæmblɪŋ] NOUN
el juego (*de azar*)

game [geɪm] NOUN
1 el juego ◊ *The children were playing a game.* Los niños jugaban a un juego.
2 el partido ◊ *a game of football* un partido de fútbol
◆ **a game of cards** una partida de cartas
◆ **We have games on Thursdays.** Tenemos deporte los jueves.

gang [gæŋ] NOUN
1 la banda (*of thieves, troublemakers*)
2 la pandilla (*of friends*)

gangster ['gæŋstəʳ] NOUN
el gángster

gap [gæp] NOUN
1 el hueco ◊ *There's a gap in the hedge.* Hay un hueco en el seto.
2 el intervalo ◊ *a gap of four years* un intervalo de cuatro años

garage ['gærɑːʒ] NOUN
1 el garaje (*for keeping the car*)
2 el taller (*for car repairs*)

garbage ['gɑːbɪdʒ] NOUN
la basura ◊ *the garbage can* el cubo de la basura
◆ **That's garbage!** ¡Eso son tonterías!

garden ['gɑːdn] NOUN
el jardín (PL los jardines)

gardener ['gɑːdnəʳ] NOUN
el jardinero
la jardinera
◊ *He's a gardener.* Es jardinero.

gardening ['gɑːdnɪŋ] NOUN
la jardinería ◊ *Margaret loves gardening.* A Margaret le encanta la jardinería.

gardens ['gɑːdnz] PL NOUN
el parque

garlic ['gɑːlɪk] NOUN
el ajo

garment ['gɑːmənt] NOUN
la prenda de vestir

gas [gæs] NOUN
1 el gas
◆ **a gas cooker** una cocina de gas
◆ **a gas cylinder** una bombona de gas
◆ **a gas fire** una estufa de gas
◆ **a gas leak** un escape de gas
2 la gasolina (*petrol*) US

gasoline ['gæsəliːn] NOUN US
la gasolina

gate [geɪt] NOUN
1 la puerta (*made of wood*)
2 la verja (*made of metal*)
◆ **Please go to gate seven.** Diríjanse a la puerta siete.

gateau ['gætəu] NOUN (PL **gateaux**)
la tarta

to **gather** ['gæðəʳ] VERB
1 reunirse* ◊ *We gathered around the fireplace.* Nos reunimos en torno a la chimenea.
2 reunir* ◊ *We gathered enough firewood to last the night.* Reunimos leña suficiente para toda la noche. ◊ *to gather information* reunir información
◆ **to gather speed** adquirir* velocidad ◊ *The train gathered speed.* El tren adquirió velocidad.

gave [geɪv] VERB *see* **give**

gay [geɪ] ADJECTIVE
gay

to **gaze** [geɪz] VERB
◆ **to gaze at** mirar fijamente ◊ *He was gazing at her.* La miraba fijamente.

GCSE [dʒiːsiːɛs'iː] NOUN (= *General Certificate of Secondary Education*)

> *El **GCSE** es el certificado que obtienen los estudiantes británicos a los dieciséis años para cada asignatura al hacer los examenes de la educación secundaria obligatoria.*

gear [gɪəʳ] NOUN
1 la marcha ◊ *to change gear* cambiar de marcha ◊ *He left the car in gear.* Dejó el coche con una marcha metida.
◆ **in first gear** en primera
2 el equipo ◊ *camping gear* el equipo de acampada
◆ **sports gear** la ropa de deporte

gear lever ['gɪəliːvəʳ] NOUN
la palanca de cambio

gearshift ['gɪəʃɪft] NOUN US
la palanca de cambio

geese [giːs] PL NOUN *see* **goose**

gel [dʒɛl] NOUN
el gel
◆ **hair gel** el fijador

gem [dʒɛm] NOUN

la gema
Gemini ['dʒɛmɪnaɪ] NOUN
el Géminis (*sign*) ◊ *I'm Gemini.* Soy Géminis.
◆ **a Gemini** un/una Géminis
gender ['dʒɛndəʳ] NOUN
el género (*of noun*)
general ['dʒɛnərl] NOUN
see also **general** ADJECTIVE
el general
general ['dʒɛnərl] ADJECTIVE
see also **general** NOUN
general
◆ **in general** en general
general election ['dʒɛnərlɪ'lɛkʃən] NOUN
las elecciones generales
general knowledge ['dʒɛnərl'nɔlɪdʒ] NOUN
la cultura general
generally ['dʒɛnrəlɪ] ADVERB
generalmente ◊ *I generally go shopping on Saturdays.* Generalmente voy de compras los sábados.
generation [dʒɛnə'reɪʃən] NOUN
la generación (PL las generaciones)
◊ *the younger generation* la nueva generación
generator ['dʒɛnəreɪtəʳ] NOUN
el generador
generous ['dʒɛnərəs] ADJECTIVE
generoso ◊ *That's very generous of you.* Es muy generoso de tu parte.
Geneva [dʒɪ'ni:və] NOUN
Ginebra FEM
genius ['dʒi:nɪəs] NOUN (PL **geniuses**)
el genio ◊ *She's a genius.* Es un genio.
gentle ['dʒɛntl] ADJECTIVE
1 dulce (*person, voice*)
2 suave (*wind, touch*)
gentleman ['dʒɛntlmən] NOUN (PL **gentlemen**)
el caballero
gently ['dʒɛntlɪ] ADVERB
1 dulcemente (*to say, smile*)
2 suavemente (*to touch*)
gents [dʒɛnts] NOUN
el servicio de caballeros ◊ *Can you tell me where the gents is, please?* ¿El servicio de caballeros, por favor?
◆ **"gents"** (*on sign*) "caballeros"
genuine ['dʒɛnjuɪn] ADJECTIVE
1 auténtico ◊ *These are genuine diamonds.* Estos son diamantes auténticos.
2 sincero ◊ *She's a very genuine person.* Es una persona muy sincera.
geography [dʒɪ'ɔgrəfɪ] NOUN
la geografía
germ [dʒə:m] NOUN
el microbio
German ['dʒə:mən] ADJECTIVE
see also **German** NOUN
alemán MASC (PL alemanes)
alemana FEM
German ['dʒə:mən] NOUN
see also **German** ADJECTIVE
1 (*person*)
el alemán (PL los alemanes)
la alemana
◊ *the Germans* los alemanes
2 (*language*)
el alemán ◊ *our German teacher* nuestro profesor de alemán
German measles ['dʒə:mən'mi:zlz] NOUN
la rubéola ◊ *to have German measles* tener* rubéola
Germany ['dʒə:mənɪ] NOUN
Alemania FEM
gesture ['dʒɛstjəʳ] NOUN
el gesto
to **get** [gɛt] VERB (**got, got**)
There are several ways of translating ***get****. Scan the examples to find one that is similar to what you want to say.*
1 recibir (*have, receive*) ◊ *I got a letter from him.* Recibí una carta de él.
◆ **I got lots of presents.** Me hicieron muchos regalos.
2 conseguir* (*obtain*) ◊ *He had trouble getting a hotel room.* Tuvo dificultades para conseguir una habitación de hotel.
◆ **to get something for somebody** conseguir algo a alguien ◊ *The librarian got the book for me.* El bibliotecario me consiguió el libro.
◆ **Jackie got good exam results.** Jackie sacó buenas notas en los exámenes.
3 ir* a buscar (*fetch*) ◊ *Quick, get help!* ¡Rápido, ve a buscar ayuda!
4 coger* (*catch, take*)
Be very careful with the verb ***coger****: in most of Latin America this is an extremely rude word that should be avoided. However, in Spain this verb is common and not rude at all.*
◊ *They've got the thief.* Han cogido al ladrón. (Han atrapado al ladrón. LatAm)
◊ *I'm getting the bus into town.* Voy a coger el autobús al centro. (Voy a tomar el autobús al centro. LatAm)
5 entender* (*understand*) ◊ *I don't get the joke.* No entiendo el chiste.
6 llegar* (*arrive*) ◊ *He should get here soon.* Debería llegar pronto. ◊ *How do you get to the cinema?* ¿Cómo se llega al cine?
◆ **to get angry** enfadarse (enojarse LatAm)
◆ **to get tired** cansarse
For other phrases with ***get*** *and an adjective, such as "to get old, to get drunk", you should look under the word* ***old, drunk****, etc.*

◆**to get something done** mandar hacer algo ◇ *I'm getting my car fixed.* He mandado arreglar el coche.
◆**I got my hair cut.** Me corté el pelo.
◆**I'll get it! (1)** (*telephone*) ¡Yo contesto!
◆**I'll get it! (2)** (*door*) ¡Ya voy yo!

to **get away** [gɛtə'weɪ] VERB
escapar ◇ *One of the burglars got away.* Uno de los ladrones escapó.

to **get away with** [gɛtə'weɪwɪð] VERB
◆**You'll never get away with it.** Esto no te lo van a consentir*.

to **get back** [gɛt'bæk] VERB
1 volver* ◇ *What time did you get back?* ¿A qué hora volvisteis?
2 recuperar ◇ *He got his money back.* Recuperó su dinero.

to **get down** [gɛt'daun] VERB
bajar ◇ *Get down from there!* ¡Baja de ahí!

to **get in** [gɛt'ɪn] VERB
llegar* ◇ *What time did you get in last night?* ¿A qué hora llegaste anoche?

to **get into** [gɛt'ɪntu] VERB
entrar en ◇ *How did you get into the house?* ¿Cómo entraste en la casa?
◆**Sharon got into the car.** Sharon subió al coche.
◆**Get into bed!** ¡Métete en la cama!

to **get off** [gɛt'ɔf] VERB
1 bajarse de ◇ *Isobel got off the train.* Isobel se bajó del tren.
2 salir* ◇ *He managed to get off early from work yesterday.* Logró salir de trabajar pronto ayer.

to **get on** [gɛt'ɔn] VERB
1 subirse a ◇ *Phyllis got on the bus.* Phyllis se subió al autobús.
2 llevarse bien ◇ *We got on really well.* Nos llevábamos muy bien. ◇ *He doesn't get on with his parents.* No se lleva bien con sus padres.
◆**How are you getting on?** ¿Cómo te va?

to **get out** [gɛt'aut] VERB
1 salir* ◇ *Get out!* ¡Sal!
◆**She got out of the car.** Se bajó del coche.
2 sacar* ◇ *She got the map out.* Sacó el mapa.

to **get over** [gɛt'əuvəʳ] VERB
1 recuperarse de ◇ *It took her a long time to get over the illness.* Tardó mucho tiempo en recuperarse de la enfermedad.
2 superar ◇ *He managed to get over the problem.* Logró superar el problema.

to **get round to** [gɛt'raundtu:] VERB
encontrar* tiempo para ◇ *I'll get round to it eventually.* Ya encontraré tiempo para hacerlo.

to **get together** [gɛttə'gɛðəʳ] VERB
reunirse* ◇ *Could we get together this evening?* ¿Podemos reunirnos esta tarde?

to **get up** [gɛt'ʌp] VERB
levantarse ◇ *What time do you get up?* ¿A qué hora te levantas?

ghetto blaster ['gɛtəublɑ:stəʳ] NOUN
el radiocasete portátil (*muy grande*)

ghost [gəust] NOUN
el fantasma
*Although **fantasma** ends in **-a**, it is actually a masculine noun.*

giant ['dʒaɪənt] ADJECTIVE
see also **giant** NOUN
enorme

giant ['dʒaɪənt] NOUN
see also **giant** ADJECTIVE
1 el gigante
2 la giganta

gift [gɪft] NOUN
el regalo
◆**to have a gift for something** tener* dotes para algo ◇ *Dave's got a gift for painting.* Dave tiene dotes para la pintura.

gifted ['gɪftɪd] ADJECTIVE
de talento ◇ *Janice is a gifted dancer.* Janice es una bailarina de talento.
◆**He's one of this country's most gifted artists.** Es uno de los artistas con más dotes de este país.

gift shop ['gɪftʃɔp] NOUN
la tienda de regalos

gift token ['gɪfttəukən] NOUN
el vale-regalo

gigantic [dʒaɪ'gæntɪk] ADJECTIVE
gigantesco

to **giggle** ['gɪgl] VERB
soltar* una risilla tonta

gin [dʒɪn] NOUN
la ginebra

ginger ['dʒɪndʒəʳ] NOUN
see also **ginger** ADJECTIVE
el jengibre

ginger ['dʒɪndʒəʳ] ADJECTIVE
see also **ginger** NOUN
◆**She's got ginger hair.** Es pelirroja.

gipsy ['dʒɪpsɪ] NOUN (PL **gipsies**)
el gitano
la gitana

giraffe [dʒɪ'rɑ:f] NOUN
la jirafa

girl [gə:l] NOUN
1 la niña (*young*) ◇ *a five-year old girl* una niña de cinco años ◇ *They've got a girl and two boys.* Tienen una niña y dos niños.
2 la chica (*older*) ◇ *a sixteen-year old girl* una chica de dieciséis años

girlfriend ['gə:lfrɛnd] NOUN
1 la novia ◇ *Paul's girlfriend is called Janice.* La novia de Paul se llama

Janice.
[2] la amiga ◊ *She often went out with her girlfriends.* Solía salir* con sus amigas.

to **give** [gɪv] VERB (**gave, given**)
dar*
♦ **to give something to somebody** dar algo a alguien ◊ *He gave me £10.* Me dio 10 libras.
♦ **to give somebody a present** hacer* un regalo a alguien
♦ **to give way** (*in car*) ceder el paso

to **give away** [gɪvə'weɪ] VERB
regalar
♦ **She gave away all her money.** Dió todo su dinero.

to **give back** [gɪv'bæk] VERB
devolver* ◊ *I gave the book back to him.* Le devolví el libro.

to **give in** [gɪv'ɪn] VERB
rendirse* ◊ *I give in!* ¡Me rindo!

to **give out** [gɪv'aut] VERB
repartir ◊ *He gave out the exam papers.* Repartió las hojas de examen.

to **give up** [gɪv'ʌp] VERB
darse* por vencido ◊ *I couldn't do it, so I gave up.* No podía hacerlo, así que me di por vencido.
♦ **to give oneself up** entregarse* ◊ *She gave herself up.* Se entregó.
♦ **to give up doing something** dejar de hacer algo ◊ *He gave up smoking.* Dejó de fumar.

glad [glæd] ADJECTIVE
contento ◊ *She's glad she's done it.* Está contenta de haberlo hecho.
♦ **I'm glad you're here.** Me alegro de que estés aquí.

***alegrarse de que** has to be followed by a verb in the subjunctive.*

glamorous ['glæmərəs] ADJECTIVE
atractivo

to **glance** [glɑːns] VERB
see also **glance** NOUN
♦ **to glance at something** echar una mirada a algo ◊ *Peter glanced at his watch.* Peter echó una mirada al reloj.

glance [glɑːns] NOUN
see also **glance** VERB
la mirada ◊ *We exchanged a glance.* Intercambiamos una mirada.
♦ **at first glance** a primera vista

to **glare** [glɛəʳ] VERB
♦ **to glare at somebody** lanzar* una mirada de odio a alguien ◊ *She glared at him.* Le lanzó una mirada de odio.

glaring ['glɛərɪŋ] ADJECTIVE
♦ **a glaring mistake** un error patente

glass [glɑːs] NOUN (PL **glasses**)
[1] el vaso (*without stem*) ◊ *a glass of milk* un vaso de leche
[2] la copa (*with stem*) ◊ *a glass of champagne* una copa de champán
[3] el vidrio (*substance*) ◊ *a glass door* una puerta de vidrio

glasses ['glɑːsəs] PL NOUN
las gafas (los anteojos *LatAm*)

to **gleam** [gliːm] VERB
brillar ◊ *Her eyes gleamed with excitement.* Los ojos le brillaban de emoción.

glider ['glaɪdəʳ] NOUN
el planeador

to **glitter** ['glɪtəʳ] VERB
relucir*

global ['gləubl] ADJECTIVE
mundial ◊ *on a global scale* a escala mundial
♦ **a global view** una visión global

global warming ['gləubl'wɔːmɪŋ] NOUN
el calentamiento del planeta

globe [gləub] NOUN
el globo terráqueo

gloomy ['gluːmɪ] ADJECTIVE
oscuro ◊ *He lives in a small gloomy flat.* Vive en un piso pequeño y oscuro.
♦ **She's been feeling very gloomy recently.** Últimamente está muy desanimada.

glorious ['glɔːrɪəs] ADJECTIVE
espléndido

glove [glʌv] NOUN
el guante

glove compartment ['glʌvkəmpɑːtmənt] NOUN
la guantera

to **glow** [gləu] VERB
brillar ◊ *He bought a watch which glows in the dark.* Se compró un reloj que brilla en la oscuridad.

glue [gluː] NOUN
see also **glue** VERB
el pegamento

to **glue** [gluː] VERB
see also **glue** NOUN
pegar*
♦ **to glue something together** pegar algo

GM [dʒiː'em] ADJECTIVE (= *genetically-modified*)
♦ **GM foods** los alimentos transgénicos

GMO [dʒiːem'əu] NOUN (= *genetically-modified organism*)
el organismo transgénico

go [gəu] NOUN
see also **go** VERB
♦ **to have a go at doing something** probar* a hacer algo ◊ *He had a go at making a cake.* Probó a hacer una tarta.
♦ **Whose go is it?** ¿A quién le toca?
♦ **It's your go.** Te toca a ti.

to **go** [gəu] VERB **(went, gone)**
see also **go** NOUN
1 ir* ◇ *Where are you going?* ¿Adónde vas? ◇ *I'm going to the cinema tonight.* Voy al cine esta noche.
2 irse* (*leave, go away*) ◇ *Where's Judy? – She's gone.* ¿Dónde está Judy? – Se ha ido. ◇ *I'm going now.* Yo me voy ya. ◇ *We went home.* Nos fuimos a casa.
3 funcionar (*work*) ◇ *My car won't go.* El coche no funciona.
◆**to go home** irse a casa
◆**to go into** entrar en ◇ *She went into the kitchen.* Entró en la cocina.
◆**to go for a walk** ir a dar un paseo
◆**How did the exam go?** ¿Cómo te fue en el examen?
◆**I'm going to do it tomorrow.** Lo voy a hacer mañana.
◆**It's going to be difficult.** Va a ser difícil.

to **go after** [gəu'ɑːftəʳ] VERB
perseguir* ◇ *Quick, go after them!* ¡Rápido, persíguelos!

to **go ahead** [gəuə'hɛd] VERB
seguir* adelante ◇ *We'll go ahead with your suggestion.* Seguiremos adelante con su propuesta.

to **go around** [gəuə'raund] VERB
correr ◇ *There's a rumour going around that they're getting married.* Corre el rumor de que se van a casar.

to **go away** [gəuə'weɪ] VERB
irse* ◇ *Go away!* ¡Vete!

to **go back** [gəu'bæk] VERB
volver* ◇ *We went back to the same place.* Volvimos al mismo sitio. ◇ *He's gone back home.* Ha vuelto a casa.

to **go by** [gəu'baɪ] VERB
pasar ◇ *Two policemen went by.* Pasaron dos policías.

to **go down** [gəu'daun] VERB
1 bajar ◇ *He went down the stairs.* Bajó las escaleras. ◇ *The price of computers has gone down.* Ha bajado el precio de los ordenadores.
2 desinflarse ◇ *My airbed's gone down.* Mi colchoneta se ha desinflado.
◆**My brother's gone down with flu.** Mi hermano ha pillado la gripe.

to **go for** ['gəufɔːʳ] VERB
ir* a por ◇ *Suddenly the dog went for me.* De pronto el perro fue a por mí.
◆**Go for it!** ¡Adelante!
◆**I don't go for it much.** No me gusta mucho.

to **go in** [gəu'ɪn] VERB
entrar ◇ *He knocked on the door and went in.* Llamó a la puerta y entró.

to **go off** [gəu'ɔf] VERB
1 marcharse ◇ *They went off after lunch.* Se marcharon después de comer.
2 estallar ◇ *The bomb went off at 10 o'clock.* La bomba estalló a las 10.
◆**The gun went off by accident.** El arma se disparó accidentalmente.
3 sonar* ◇ *My alarm goes off at seven.* Mi despertador suena a las siete.
4 echarse a perder* ◇ *This milk has gone off.* Esta leche se ha echado a perder.
5 apagarse* ◇ *All the lights went off.* Se apagaron todas las luces.
◆**I've gone off that idea.** Ya no me gusta la idea.

to **go on** [gəu'ɔn] VERB
1 pasar ◇ *What's going on?* ¿Qué pasa?
2 seguir*
◆**to go on doing** seguir* haciendo ◇ *He went on reading.* Siguió leyendo.
3 durar ◇ *The concert went on until 11 o'clock at night.* El concierto duró hasta las 11 de la noche.
◆**to go on at somebody** dar* la lata a alguien ◇ *They're always going on at me.* Están siempre dándome la lata.
◆**Go on!** ¡Venga! ◇ *Go on, tell me what the problem is!* ¡Venga, dime cuál es el problema!

to **go out** [gəu'aut] VERB
1 salir* ◇ *Are you going out tonight?* ¿Vas a salir esta noche? ◇ *I went out with Steven last night.* Ayer por la noche salí con Steven. ◇ *They went out for a meal.* Salieron a comer.
◆**Are you going out with him?** ¿Estás saliendo con él?
2 apagarse* ◇ *Suddenly the lights went out.* De pronto se apagaron las luces.

to **go past** [gəu'pɑːst] VERB
◆**to go past something** pasar por delante de algo ◇ *He went past the shop.* Pasó por delante de la tienda.

to **go round** [gəu'raund] VERB
visitar ◇ *We want to go round the museum today.* Hoy queremos visitar el museo.
◆**I love going round the shops.** Me encanta ir de tiendas.
◆**to go round to somebody's house** ir* a casa de alguien ◇ *We're all going round to Linda's house tonight.* Esta noche vamos todos a casa de Linda.
◆**There's a bug going round.** Hay un virus por ahí rondando.
◆**Is there enough food to go round?** ¿Hay comida suficiente para todos?

to **go through** [gəu'θruː] VERB
1 atravesar* ◇ *We went through London to get to Brighton.* Atravesamos Londres para llegar a Brighton.
2 pasar por ◇ *I know what you're going through.* Sé por lo que estás pasando.
3 repasar ◇ *They went through the plan again.* Repasaron de nuevo el plan.

G

4 registrar ◊ *Someone had gone through her things.* Alguien había registrado sus cosas.

to **go up** [gəu'ʌp] VERB
subir ◊ *She went up the stairs.* Subió las escaleras. ◊ *The price has gone up.* El precio ha subido.
♦ **to go up in flames** arder en llamas

to **go with** ['gəuwɪð] VERB
pegar* con ◊ *Does this blouse go with that skirt?* ¿Pega esta blusa con la falda?

goal [gəul] NOUN
1 el gol ◊ *He scored the first goal.* Él metió el primer gol.
2 el objetivo ◊ *His goal is to become the world champion.* Su objetivo es ser* campeón del mundo.

goalkeeper ['gəulki:pəʳ] NOUN
el portero

goat [gəut] NOUN
la cabra
♦ **goat's cheese** el queso de cabra

god [gɔd] NOUN
el dios ◊ *I believe in God.* Creo en Dios.

goddaughter ['gɔddɔ:təʳ] NOUN
la ahijada

godfather ['gɔdfɑ:ðəʳ] NOUN
el padrino

godmother ['gɔdmʌðəʳ] NOUN
la madrina

godson ['gɔdsʌn] NOUN
el ahijado

goggles ['gɔglz] PL NOUN
las gafas protectoras (los anteojos protectores *LatAm*)

gold [gəuld] NOUN
el oro ◊ *a gold necklace* un collar de oro ◊ *the gold medal* la medalla de oro

goldfish ['gəuldfɪʃ] NOUN (PL **goldfish**)
el pez de colores (PL los peces de colores)

gold-plated ['gəuld'pleɪtɪd] ADJECTIVE
chapado en oro

golf [gɔlf] NOUN
el golf
♦ **a golf club (1)** (*stick*) un palo de golf
♦ **a golf club (2)** (*place*) un club de golf
♦ **a golf course** un campo de golf

gone [gɔn] VERB *see* **go**

good [gud] ADJECTIVE
1 bueno

*Use **buen** before a masculine singular noun.*

◊ *It's a very good film.* Es una película muy buena. ◊ *a good day* un buen día ◊ *Be good!* ¡Sé bueno! ◊ *The soup is very good here.* Aquí la sopa es muy buena.
2 amable (*kind*) ◊ *That's very good of you.* Es muy amable de tu parte.
♦ **They were very good to me.** Se portaron muy bien conmigo.
♦ **Have a good journey!** ¡Buen viaje!
♦ **Good!** ¡Bien!
♦ **Good morning!** ¡Buenos días!
♦ **Good afternoon!** ¡Buenas tardes!
♦ **Good evening!** ¡Buenas noches!
♦ **Good night!** ¡Buenas noches!
♦ **I'm feeling really good today.** Hoy me siento realmente bien.
♦ **to be good for somebody** hacer* bien a alguien ◊ *Vegetables are good for you.* La verdura te hace bien.
♦ **Jane's very good at maths.** A Jane se le dan muy bien las matemáticas.
♦ **for good** definitivamente ◊ *One day he left for good.* Un día se marchó definitivamente.
♦ **It's no good complaining.** De nada sirve quejarse.

goodbye [gud'baɪ] EXCLAMATION
¡adiós!

Good Friday [gud'fraɪdɪ] NOUN
el Viernes Santo

good-looking ['gud'lukɪŋ] ADJECTIVE
guapo

good-natured ['gud'neɪtʃəd] ADJECTIVE
bueno

*Use **buen** before a masculine singular noun.*

goods ['gudz] PL NOUN
los productos ◊ *They sell a wide range of goods.* Venden una amplia gama de productos.
♦ **a goods train** un tren de mercancías

goose [gu:s] NOUN (PL **geese**)
la oca

gooseberry ['guzbərɪ] NOUN (PL **gooseberries**)
la grosella espinosa

gorgeous ['gɔ:dʒəs] ADJECTIVE
1 guapísimo ◊ *She's gorgeous!* ¡Es guapísima!
2 estupendo ◊ *The weather was gorgeous.* El tiempo fue estupendo.

gorilla [gə'rɪlə] NOUN
el gorila

*Although **gorila** ends in **-a**, it is actually a masculine noun.*

gospel ['gɔspl] NOUN
el evangelio

gossip ['gɔsɪp] NOUN
see also **gossip** VERB
1 el cotilleo ◊ *Tell me the gossip!* ¡Cuéntame el cotilleo!
2 el/la cotilla ◊ *What a gossip!* ¡Menudo cotilla!

to **gossip** ['gɔsɪp] VERB
see also **gossip** NOUN

* Verbs marked with this symbol are irregular. See pages 380-382 for further details

cotillear (comadrear *LatAm*) ◊ *They were always gossiping.* Siempre estaban cotilleando.

got [gɒt] VERB

♦**to have got** tener* (*own*) ◊ *How many have you got?* ¿Cuántos tienes?

♦**to have got to do something** tener que hacer algo ◊ *I've got to tell him.* Tengo que decírselo.

government ['gʌvnmənt] NOUN
el gobierno

GP [dʒiː'piː] NOUN (= *General Practitioner*)
el médico de cabecera
la médica de cabecera

to **grab** [græb] VERB
agarrar ◊ *He grabbed my arm.* Me agarró el brazo.

graceful ['greɪsful] ADJECTIVE
elegante

grade [greɪd] NOUN
la nota ◊ *He got good grades in his exams.* Sacó buenas notas en los exámenes.

grade school ['greɪdskuːl] NOUN US
la escuela primaria

gradual ['grædjuəl] ADJECTIVE
gradual

gradually ['grædjuəlɪ] ADVERB
gradualmente

graduate ['grædjuɪt] NOUN
see also **graduate** VERB
1 (*from university*)
el licenciado (el egresado *LatAm*)
la licenciada (la egresada *LatAm*)
2 (*from US high school*)
el/la bachiller

to **graduate** ['grædjuɪt] VERB
see also **graduate** NOUN
licenciarse (recibirse *LatAm*)

graffiti [grə'fiːtɪ] PL NOUN
las pintadas

grain [greɪn] NOUN
1 el grano ◊ *a grain of rice* un grano de arroz
2 los cereales ◊ *She only eats grain and pulses.* Sólo come cereales y legumbres.

gram [græm] NOUN
el gramo

grammar ['græmə^r] NOUN
la gramática

♦**a grammar exercise** un ejercicio de gramática

grammar school ['græməskuːl] NOUN

> ℹ *En Gran Bretaña* **grammar school** *es un colegio selectivo, estatal o privado, de enseñanza secundaria para alumnos de 11 a 18 años.*

grammatical [grə'mætɪkl] ADJECTIVE
gramatical

gramme [græm] NOUN
el gramo

grand [grænd] ADJECTIVE
grandioso ◊ *Her house is very grand.* Su casa es grandiosa.

grandchildren ['græntʃɪldrən] PL NOUN
los nietos

granddad ['grændæd] NOUN
el abuelo

granddaughter ['grændɔːtə[r]] NOUN
la nieta

grandfather ['grændfɑːðə[r]] NOUN
el abuelo

grandma ['grænmɑː] NOUN
la abuela

grandmother ['grænmʌðə[r]] NOUN
la abuela

grandpa ['grænpɑː] NOUN
el abuelo

grandparents ['grændpɛərənts] PL NOUN
los abuelos

grandson ['grænsʌn] NOUN
el nieto

granny ['grænɪ] NOUN (PL **grannies**)
la abuelita

grant [grɑːnt] NOUN
1 (*for study*)
la beca
2 (*for industry, organization*)
la subvención (PL las subvenciones)

grape [greɪp] NOUN
la uva

grapefruit ['greɪpfruːt] NOUN
el pomelo

graph [grɑːf] NOUN
el gráfico

to **grasp** [grɑːsp] VERB
agarrar

grass [grɑːs] NOUN
1 la hierba ◊ *The grass is long.* La hierba está alta.
2 el césped (*lawn*) ◊ *"Keep off the grass"* "Prohibido pisar el césped"

♦**to cut the grass** cortar el césped

grasshopper ['grɑːshɒpə[r]] NOUN
el saltamontes (PL los saltamontes)

to **grate** [greɪt] VERB
rallar ◊ *grated cheese* el queso rallado

grateful ['greɪtful] ADJECTIVE
agradecido

grave [greɪv] NOUN
la tumba

gravel ['grævl] NOUN
la grava

graveyard ['greɪvjɑːd] NOUN
el cementerio

gravy ['greɪvɪ] NOUN
el jugo de carne

grease [griːs] NOUN
1 la grasa (*in hair, on skin*)
2 el aceite (*for cars, machines*)

greasy ['griːsɪ] ADJECTIVE

G

1 aceitoso ◊ *The food was very greasy.* La comida estaba muy aceitosa.
2 graso ◊ *He has greasy hair.* Tiene el pelo graso.

great [greɪt] ADJECTIVE
1 estupendo (chévere *LatAm*) ◊ *That's great!* ¡Estupendo!
2 grande
*Use **gran** before a singular noun.*
◊ *a great oak tree* un gran roble ◊ *a greatest hits album* un disco de grandes éxitos

Great Britain [greɪt'brɪtən] NOUN
Gran Bretaña FEM

great-grandfather [greɪt'grænfɑːðəʳ] NOUN
el bisabuelo

great-grandmother [greɪt'grænmʌðəʳ] NOUN
la bisabuela

Greece [griːs] NOUN
Grecia FEM

greedy ['griːdɪ] ADJECTIVE
1 glotón MASC (PL glotones)
glotona FEM
◊ *Don't be greedy, you've already had three doughnuts.* No seas glotón, ya te has comido tres donuts.
2 codicioso ◊ *She is greedy and selfish.* Es codiciosa y egoísta.

Greek [griːk] ADJECTIVE
see also **Greek** NOUN
griego

Greek [griːk] NOUN
see also **Greek** ADJECTIVE
1 (*person*)
el griego
la griega
◊ *the Greeks* los griegos
2 (*language*)
el griego ◊ *our Greek teacher* nuestro profesor de griego

green [griːn] ADJECTIVE
see also **green** NOUN
verde ◊ *a green car* un coche verde ◊ *a green light* un semáforo en verde (*at traffic lights*)
◆ **the Green Party** el Partido Verde

green [griːn] NOUN
see also **green** ADJECTIVE
el verde ◊ *a dark green* un verde oscuro
◆ **greens** (*vegetables*) la verdura
◆ **the Greens** (*party*) los verdes

greengrocer's ['griːngrəusəz] NOUN
la verdulería

greenhouse ['griːnhaus] NOUN
el invernadero
◆ **the greenhouse effect** el efecto invernadero

to **greet** [griːt] VERB
saludar ◊ *He greeted me with a kiss.* Me saludó con un beso.

greetings ['griːtɪŋz] PL NOUN
◆ **Greetings from London!** ¡Saludos desde Londres!
◆ **Season's greetings** Felices Fiestas

greetings card ['griːtɪŋzkɑːd] NOUN
la tarjeta de felicitación

grew [gruː] VERB *see* **grow**

grey [greɪ] ADJECTIVE
gris ◊ *They wore grey suits.* Llevaban trajes grises.
◆ **He's going grey.** Le están saliendo canas.
◆ **grey hair** las canas

grey-haired [greɪ'hɛəd] ADJECTIVE
canoso

grid [grɪd] NOUN
1 la cuadrícula (*in road, on map*)
2 la red (*of electricity*)

grief [griːf] NOUN
la pena

grill [grɪl] NOUN
see also **grill** VERB
1 el grill (*of cooker*)

> *In Spain the grill is always inside the oven, if there is one at all. They are not as common as they are in Britain.*

2 la parrilla (*for barbecue*)
◆ **a mixed grill** una parrillada mixta

to **grill** [grɪl] VERB
see also **grill** NOUN
1 hacer* al grill (*in cooker*)
2 asar a la parrilla (*barbecue*)

grim [grɪm] ADJECTIVE
deprimente ◊ *The outskirts of the city are very grim.* Las afueras de la ciudad son muy deprimentes.

to **grin** [grɪn] VERB
see also **grin** NOUN
sonreír* ampliamente ◊ *Mr. McMahon grinned at me.* Mr. McMahon me sonrió ampliamente.

grin [grɪn] NOUN
see also **grin** VERB
la amplia sonrisa

to **grind** [graɪnd] VERB (**ground, ground**)
1 moler* (*coffee, pepper*)
2 picar (*meat*) US

to **grip** [grɪp] VERB
agarrar

gripping ['grɪpɪŋ] ADJECTIVE
emocionante

grit [grɪt] NOUN
la gravilla

to **groan** [grəun] VERB
see also **groan** NOUN

gemir* ◊ *He groaned with pain.* Gimió de dolor.

groan [grəun] NOUN
see also **groan** VERB
el gemido

grocer ['grəusəʳ] NOUN
1 el tendero
2 la tendera

groceries ['grəusərɪz] PL NOUN
los comestibles
◆ **I'll get some groceries.** Traeré algunas provisiones.

grocer's ['grəusəz] NOUN
la tienda de ultramarinos

grocery store ['grəusərɪstɔːʳ] NOUN US
la tienda de ultramarinos

groom [gruːm] NOUN
el novio ◊ *the groom and his best man* el novio y su padrino de boda

to **grope** [grəup] VERB
◆ **to grope for something** buscar* algo a tientas ◊ *He groped for the light switch.* Buscó a tientas el interruptor.

gross [grəus] ADJECTIVE
1 horrible (*revolting*)
◆ **That's gross!** ¡Qué asco!
2 bruto ◊ *gross income* ingresos brutos

grossly ['grəuslɪ] ADVERB
enormemente ◊ *It's grossly unfair.* Es enormemente injusto.
◆ **We're grossly underpaid.** Estamos tremendamente mal pagados.

ground [graund] NOUN
see also **ground** VERB
1 el suelo ◊ *The ground's wet.* El suelo está húmedo.
2 el campo (la cancha LatAm) ◊ *a football ground* un campo de fútbol
3 el motivo ◊ *We've got grounds for complaint.* Tenemos motivos para quejarnos.
◆ **on the ground** en el suelo ◊ *We sat on the ground.* Nos sentamos en el suelo.

ground [graund] VERB *see* **grind**
see also **ground** NOUN

ground coffee [graund'kɔfɪ] NOUN
el café molido

ground floor [graund'flɔːʳ] NOUN
la planta baja

group [gruːp] NOUN
el grupo

to **grow** [grəu] VERB (**grew, grown**)
1 crecer* ◊ *Haven't you grown!* ¡Cómo has crecido!
2 aumentar ◊ *The number of unemployed has grown.* Ha aumentado el número de desempleados.
3 cultivar ◊ *He grew vegetables in his garden.* Cultivaba hortalizas en su jardín.
◆ **He's grown out of his jacket.** La chaqueta se le ha quedado pequeña.
◆ **to grow a beard** dejarse barba ◊ *I'm growing a beard.* Me estoy dejando barba.
◆ **He grew a moustache.** Se dejó bigote.

to **grow up** [grəu'ʌp] VERB
criarse* ◊ *I grew up in Rome.* Me crié en Roma.
◆ **Oh, grow up!** ¡No seas crío!

to **growl** [graul] VERB
gruñir*

grown [grəun] VERB *see* **grow**

growth [grəuθ] NOUN
el crecimiento ◊ *economic growth* crecimiento económico

grub [grʌb] NOUN
la manduca (*informal*)

grudge [grʌdʒ] NOUN
◊ *to bear a grudge against somebody* guardar rencor a alguien ◊ *He's always had a grudge against me.* Siempre me ha guardado rencor.

gruesome ['gruːsəm] ADJECTIVE
horroroso

guarantee [gærən'tiː] NOUN
see also **guarantee** VERB
la garantía ◊ *a five-year guarantee* una garantía de cinco años ◊ *It's still under guarantee.* Todavía tiene garantía.

to **guarantee** [gærən'tiː] VERB
see also **guarantee** NOUN
garantizar* ◊ *I can't guarantee he'll come.* No puedo garantizar que venga.

to **guard** [gɑːd] VERB
see also **guard** NOUN
vigilar ◊ *The police were guarding the entrance.* La policía vigilaba la entrada.

guard [gɑːd] NOUN
see also **guard** VERB
1 el/la guardia (*person*)
2 el jefe de tren (*on train*)
◆ **a security guard** un guarda jurado

guard dog ['gɑːddɔg] NOUN
el perro guardián

to **guess** [gɛs] VERB
see also **guess** NOUN
adivinar ◊ *Can you guess what it is?* A ver si adivinas qué es.
◆ **to guess wrong** equivocarse*
◆ **Guess what!** ¿Sabes qué?

guess [gɛs] NOUN (PL **guesses**)
see also **guess** VERB
la suposición (PL las suposiciones)
◊ *It's just a guess.* Sólo es una suposición.
◆ **Have a guess!** ¡Adivina!

guest [gɛst] NOUN
1 el invitado
la invitada
◊ *We have guests staying with us.* Tenemos invitados en casa.
2 (*in hotel*)
el/la huésped

G

guesthouse ['gɛsthaus] NOUN
la pensión (PL las pensiones)
guide [gaɪd] NOUN
1 la guía ◊ *We bought a guide to Granada.* Compramos una guía de Granada.
2 el/la guía ◊ *The guide showed us around the castle.* El guía nos enseñó el castillo.
3 la exploradora (*girl guide*)
guidebook ['gaɪdbuk] NOUN
la guía
guide dog ['gaɪddɔg] NOUN
el perro lazarillo
guilty ['gɪltɪ] ADJECTIVE
culpable ◊ *She was found guilty.* Fue declarada culpable. ◊ *He felt guilty about lying to her.* Se sentía culpable por haberle mentido.
♦ **He has a guilty conscience.** Tiene remordimientos de conciencia.
guinea pig ['gɪnɪpɪg] NOUN
el cobayo ◊ *She's got a guinea pig.* Tiene un cobayo.
guitar [gɪ'tɑːʳ] NOUN
la guitarra
gum [gʌm] NOUN
el chicle (*chewing gum*)
♦ **a piece of gum** un chicle
♦ **gums** (*in mouth*) las encías
gun [gʌn] NOUN
1 la pistola (*small*)
2 el fusil (*rifle*)
gunpoint ['gʌnpɔɪnt] NOUN
♦ **at gunpoint** a punta de pistola
gust [gʌst] NOUN
♦ **a gust of wind** una ráfaga de viento
guts [gʌts] PL NOUN
♦ **He's certainly got guts.** Desde luego tiene agallas.
♦ **I hate his guts.** Lo odio con toda mi alma.
guy [gaɪ] NOUN
1 el tío (*informal*)
*The word **tío** in this sense is confined to Spain. In Latin America, the equivalent is **tipo**.*
2 el tipo ◊ *Who's that guy?* ¿Quién es ese tío? ◊ *He's a nice guy.* Es un tío simpático.
gym [dʒɪm] NOUN
el gimnasio ◊ *I go to the gym every day.* Voy al gimnasio todos los días.
♦ **gym classes** las clases de gimnasia
gymnast ['dʒɪmnæst] NOUN
el/la gimnasta
gymnastics [dʒɪm'næstɪks] NOUN
la gimnasia
gypsy ['dʒɪpsɪ] NOUN (PL **gypsies**)
el gitano
la gitana

H

habit ['hæbɪt] NOUN
la costumbre

to **hack** VERB
♦ **to hack into a system** piratear un sistema

hacker NOUN
el pirata informático
la pirata informática

had [hæd] VERB *see* **have**

haddock ['hædək] NOUN (PL **haddock**)
el abadejo

hadn't ['hædnt] = **had not**

hail [heɪl] NOUN
see also **hail** VERB
el granizo

to **hail** [heɪl] VERB
see also **hail** NOUN
granizar*

hair [hɛəʳ] NOUN
el pelo ◊ *She's got long hair.* Tiene el pelo largo. ◊ *I'm allergic to cat hair.* Soy alérgico al pelo de los gatos.
♦ **to have one's hair cut** cortarse el pelo
♦ **grey hair** las canas
♦ **to brush one's hair** cepillarse el pelo
♦ **to wash one's hair** lavarse la cabeza

hairbrush ['hɛəbrʌʃ] NOUN (PL **hairbrushes**)
el cepillo (*para el pelo*)

haircut ['hɛəkʌt] NOUN
el corte de pelo ◊ *You need a haircut.* Necesitas un corte de pelo.
♦ **to have a haircut** cortarse el pelo

hairdresser ['hɛədrɛsəʳ] NOUN
el peluquero
la peluquera
◊ *He's a hairdresser.* Es peluquero.
♦ **at the hairdresser's** en la peluquería

hair dryer ['hɛədraɪəʳ] NOUN
el secador de pelo

hair gel ['hɛədʒɛl] NOUN
el fijador

hairgrip ['hɛəgrɪp] NOUN
la horquilla

hair spray ['hɛəspreɪ] NOUN
la laca

hairstyle ['hɛəstaɪl] NOUN
el peinado

hairy ['hɛərɪ] ADJECTIVE
peludo ◊ *He's very hairy.* Es muy peludo.
♦ **He's got hairy legs.** Tiene mucho pelo en las piernas.

half [hɑːf] NOUN (PL **halves**)
see also **half** ADJECTIVE
1 la mitad ◊ *half of the cake* la mitad de la tarta
♦ **to cut something in half** cortar algo por la mitad
2 el billete para niños (*ticket*) ◊ *One and two halves, please.* Un billete normal y dos para niños, por favor.
♦ **two and a half** dos y medio
♦ **half a kilo** medio kilo
♦ **half an hour** media hora
♦ **half past ten** las diez y media

half [hɑːf] ADJECTIVE, ADVERB
see also **half** NOUN
medio ◊ *a half chicken* medio pollo
When you use ***medio*** *before an adjective, it does not change.*
◊ *She was half asleep.* Estaba medio dormida. ◊ *They were half drunk.* Estaban medio borrachos.

half-price ['hɑːf'praɪs] ADJECTIVE, ADVERB
a mitad de precio ◊ *I bought it half-price.* Lo compré a mitad de precio.

half-term [hɑːf'tɜːm] NOUN
las vacaciones de mitad de trimestre

> ℹ *En Gran Bretaña los colegios dan unos días de vacaciones hacia la mitad de cada trimestre.*

half-time [hɑːf'taɪm] NOUN
el descanso (*del partido*)

halfway ['hɑːf'weɪ] ADVERB
1 a medio camino ◊ *Reading is halfway between Oxford and London.* Reading está a medio camino entre Oxford y Londres.
2 a la mitad ◊ *halfway through the film* a la mitad de la película

hall [hɔːl] NOUN
1 el vestíbulo (*in house*)
2 la sala ◊ *a lecture hall* una sala de conferencias
♦ **a concert hall** un auditorio
♦ **a sports hall** un gimnasio
♦ **village hall** el salón de actos municipal

hall of residence [hɔːləv'rɛzɪdəns] NOUN
el colegio mayor

Hallowe'en ['hæləu'iːn] NOUN
la víspera de Todos los Santos

> ℹ *La tradición dice que* ***Hallowe'en****, la noche del 31 de octubre, es la noche de las brujas. Los niños, disfrazados de fantasmas y portando faroles hechos con calabazas vacías, van de casa en casa pidiendo golosinas o un aguinaldo.*

hallway ['hɔːlweɪ] NOUN
el vestíbulo

halt [hɔːlt] NOUN
♦ **to come to a halt** pararse

halves [hɑːvz] PL NOUN *see* **half**

ham [hæm] NOUN
el jamón (PL los jamones)

> *In Spain there are two basic kinds of ham in the shops:* ***jamón serrano****, which is cured and similar to Parma ham, and* ***jamón de York*** *or* ***jamón dulce****, which is boiled and similar to British ham.*

hamburger ['hæmbəːgəʳ] NOUN
la hamburguesa

hammer ['hæməʳ] NOUN
el martillo

hamster ['hæmstəʳ] NOUN
el hámster

hand [hænd] NOUN
see also **hand** VERB
1 la mano (*of person*)
Although ***mano*** *ends in* ***-o*** *it is actually a feminine noun.*
2 la manecilla (*of clock*)
◆ **to give someone a hand** echar una mano a alguien ◊ *Can you give me a hand?* ¿Me echas una mano?
◆ **on the one hand ..., on the other hand ...** por un lado ..., por otro ...

to **hand** [hænd] VERB
see also **hand** NOUN
pasar ◊ *He handed me the book.* Me pasó el libro.

to **hand in** [hænd'ɪn] VERB
entregar* ◊ *Martin handed in his exam paper.* Martin entregó su examen.

to **hand out** [hænd'aut] VERB
repartir ◊ *The teacher handed out the books.* El profesor repartió los libros.

to **hand over** [hænd'əuvəʳ] VERB
entregar* ◊ *She handed the keys over to me.* Me entregó las llaves.

handbag ['hændbæg] NOUN
el bolso (la cartera *LatAm*)

handball ['hændbɔːl] NOUN
el balonmano

handbook ['hændbuk] NOUN
el manual

handcuffs ['hændkʌfs] PL NOUN
las esposas

handkerchief ['hæŋkətʃɪf] NOUN (PL **handkerchieves**)
el pañuelo

handle ['hændl] NOUN
see also **handle** VERB
1 el picaporte (*of door*)
2 la asa (*of cup, briefcase*)
3 el mango (*of knife, saucepan*)

to **handle** ['hændl] VERB
see also **handle** NOUN
1 encargarse* de ◊ *Kath handled the travel arrangements.* Kath se encargó de organizar el viaje.
2 manejar ◊ *It was a difficult situation, but he handled it well.* Era una situación difícil, pero él supo manejarla bien.
3 tratar ◊ *She's good at handling children.* Sabe tratar a los niños.
◆ **"handle with care"** "frágil"

handlebars ['hændlbɑːz] PL NOUN
el manillar

handmade ['hænd'meɪd] ADJECTIVE
hecho a mano MASC
hecha a mano FEM

handsome ['hænsəm] ADJECTIVE
guapo ◊ *My father's very handsome.* Mi padre es muy guapo.

handwriting ['hændraɪtɪŋ] NOUN
la letra ◊ *His handwriting is terrible.* Tiene una letra horrible.

handy ['hændɪ] ADJECTIVE
1 práctico ◊ *This knife's very handy.* Este cuchillo es muy práctico.
2 a mano ◊ *Have you got a pen handy?* ¿Tienes un bolígrafo a mano?

to **hang** [hæŋ] VERB (**hung, hung**)
1 colgar* ◊ *Mike hung the painting on the wall.* Mike colgó el cuadro en la pared. ◊ *There was a bulb hanging from the ceiling.* Una bombilla colgaba del techo.
2 ahorcar*
Se usa ***hanged*** *para el pasado y participio pasado de este sentido de* ***to hang****.*
◊ *In the past criminals were hanged.* Antiguamente se ahorcaba a los criminales.

to **hang around** [hæŋə'raund] VERB
pasar el rato ◊ *On Saturdays we hang around in the park.* Los sábados pasamos el rato en el parque.

to **hang on** [hæŋ'ɔn] VERB
esperar ◊ *Hang on a minute please.* Espera un momento, por favor.

to **hang up** [hæŋ'ʌp] VERB
colgar* (*clothes, phone*) ◊ *Don't hang up!* ¡No cuelgues! ◊ *He hung up on me.* Me colgó.

hanger ['hæŋəʳ] NOUN
la percha

hang-gliding ['hæŋglaɪdɪŋ] NOUN
el ala delta
Although it's a feminine noun, remember that you use ***el*** *and* ***un*** *with* ***ala****.*
◊ *to go hang-gliding* hacer* ala delta

hangover ['hæŋəuvəʳ] NOUN
la resaca ◊ *I woke up with a hangover.* Me desperté con resaca.

to **happen** ['hæpən] VERB

pasar ◇ *What happened?* ¿Qué pasó?
◆**As it happens, I do know him.** Da la casualidad de que lo conozco.
◆**Do you happen to know if she's at home?** ¿Por casualidad sabes si está en casa?

happily [ˈhæpɪlɪ] ADVERB
1 alegremente ◇ *"Don't worry!", he said happily.* "¡No te preocupes!" dijo alegremente.
2 felizmente ◇ *He's happily married.* Está felizmente casado.
◆**And they lived happily ever after.** Y vivieron felices y comieron perdices.
3 afortunadamente ◇ *Happily, everything went well.* Afortunadamente todo fue bien.

happiness [ˈhæpɪnɪs] NOUN
la felicidad

happy [ˈhæpɪ] ADJECTIVE
feliz (PL felices) ◇ *Janet looks happy.* Janet parece feliz.
◆**to be happy with something** estar* contento con algo ◇ *I'm very happy with your work.* Estoy muy contento con tu trabajo.
◆**Happy birthday!** ¡Feliz cumpleaños!
◆**a happy ending** un final feliz

harbour [ˈhɑːbəʳ] NOUN (US **harbor**)
el puerto

hard [hɑːd] ADJECTIVE, ADVERB
1 duro ◇ *This cheese is very hard.* Este queso está muy duro. ◇ *to work hard* trabajar duro
2 difícil ◇ *The geography exam was very hard.* El examen de geografía fue muy difícil.

hard disk [ˈhɑːddɪsk] NOUN
el disco duro

hardly [ˈhɑːdlɪ] ADVERB
apenas ◇ *I hardly know you.* Apenas te conozco.
◆**I've got hardly any money.** Casi no tengo dinero.
◆**hardly ever** casi nunca
◆**hardly anything** casi nada

hard up [hɑːdˈʌp] ADJECTIVE
◆**to be hard up** estar* sin un duro (estar* sin plata LatAm) (*informal*)

hardware [ˈhɑːdwɛəʳ] SUSTANTIVO
el hardware

hare [hɛəʳ] NOUN
la liebre

to **harm** [hɑːm] VERB
◆**to harm somebody** hacer* daño a alguien ◇ *I didn't mean to harm you.* No quería hacerte daño.
◆**to harm something** dañar algo ◇ *Chemicals harm the environment.* Los productos químicos dañan el medio ambiente.

harmful [ˈhɑːmful] ADJECTIVE
perjudicial ◇ *Global warming is harmful to the environment.* El calentamiento global es perjudicial para el medio ambiente.

harmless [ˈhɑːmlɪs] ADJECTIVE
inofensivo

harsh [hɑːʃ] ADJECTIVE
1 severo ◇ *He deserves a harsh punishment for what he did.* Merece un severo castigo por lo que ha hecho.
2 áspero ◇ *She's got a very harsh voice.* Tiene una voz muy áspera.

harvest [ˈhɑːvɪst] NOUN
la cosecha (*of fruit, vegetables, cereals*)
◆**the grape harvest** la vendimia

has [hæz] VERB *see* **have**

hasn't [ˈhæznt] = **has not**

hat [hæt] NOUN
el sombrero

to **hate** [heɪt] VERB
odiar

hatred [ˈheɪtrɪd] NOUN
el odio

haunted [ˈhɔːntɪd] ADJECTIVE
◆**a haunted house** una casa embrujada

to **have** [hæv] VERB (**had, had**)

*Use the verb **haber** to form the perfect tenses.*

1 haber* ◇ *I've already seen that film.* Ya he visto esa película. ◇ *Has he gone?* ¿Se ha ido? ◇ *If you had phoned me I would have come around.* Si me hubieras llamado habría venido.

*If you are using **have** in question tags to confirm a statement use **¿no?** or **¿verdad?**.*

◇ *You've done it, haven't you?* Lo has hecho, ¿verdad? ◇ *They've arrived, haven't they?* Ya han llegado, ¿no?

***Have** is not translated when giving simple negative or positive answers to questions.*

◇ *Have you read that book? – Yes, I have.* ¿Has leído el libro? – Sí. ◇ *Has he told you? – No, he hasn't.* ¿Te lo ha dicho? – No.
2 tener* ◇ *I have a terrible cold.* Tengo un resfriado horrible. ◇ *She had a baby last year.* Tuvo un niño el año pasado. ◇ *Do you have any brothers or sisters?* ¿Tienes hermanos?
◆**to have to do something.** tener que hacer algo.
3 tomar ◇ *I'll have a coffee.* Tomaré un café. ◇ *Shall we have a drink?* ¿Tomamos algo de beber?
◆**to have a shower** ducharse
◆**to have one's hair cut** cortarse el pelo

haven't [ˈhævnt] = **have not**

hay [heɪ] NOUN
el heno

hay fever [ˈheɪfiːvəʳ] NOUN
la alergia al polen

hazelnut ['heɪzlnʌt] NOUN
la avellana

he [hiː] PRONOUN
él

***he** generally isn't translated unless it is emphatic.*

◊ *He is very tall.* Es muy alto.

*Use **él** for emphasis.*

◊ *He did it but she didn't.* Él lo hizo, pero ella no.

head [hɛd] NOUN
see also **head** VERB

1 la cabeza ◊ *Mind your head!* ¡Cuidado con la cabeza! ◊ *The wine went to my head.* El vino se me subió a la cabeza. ◊ *He lost his head and started screaming.* Perdió la cabeza y empezó a gritar.

2 (*of school*)
el director
la directora

3 (*leader*)
el jefe
la jefa
◊ *a head of state* un jefe de Estado

♦ **I've got no head for figures.** No se me dan bien los números.

♦ **Heads or tails? – Heads.** ¿Cara o cruz? – Cara.

to **head** [hɛd] VERB
see also **head** NOUN

♦ **to head for** dirigirse* a ◊ *They headed for the church.* Se dirigieron a la iglesia.

headache ['hɛdeɪk] NOUN
el dolor de cabeza ◊ *I've got a headache.* Tengo dolor de cabeza.

headlight ['hɛdlaɪt] NOUN
el faro (*de coche*)

headline ['hɛdlaɪn] NOUN
el titular

headmaster [hɛd'mɑːstəʳ] NOUN
el director

headmistress [hɛd'mɪstrɪs] NOUN (PL **headmistresses**)
la directora

headphones ['hɛdfəunz] PL NOUN
los auriculares

headquarters ['hɛdkwɔːtəz] PL NOUN
el cuartel general (*of army*)

♦ **The bank's headquarters are in London.** La oficina central del banco está en Londres.

headteacher [hɛd'tiːtʃəʳ] NOUN
el director
la directora

to **heal** [hiːl] VERB
curar

health [hɛlθ] NOUN
la salud ◊ *She's in good health.* Tiene buena salud.

healthy ['hɛlθɪ] ADJECTIVE
sano ◊ *She's very healthy.* Es muy sana. ◊ *a healthy diet* una dieta sana

heap [hiːp] NOUN
el montón (PL los montones)

to **hear** [hɪəʳ] VERB (**heard, heard**)
oír* ◊ *We heard the dog bark.* Oímos ladrar al perro. ◊ *She can't hear very well.* No oye bien.

♦ **I heard she was ill.** Me han dicho que estaba enferma.

♦ **to hear about something** enterarse de algo ◊ *I've heard about your new job.* Me he enterado de que tienes un nuevo trabajo. ◊ *Did you hear the good news?* ¿Te has enterado de la buena noticia?

♦ **to hear from somebody** tener* noticias de alguien ◊ *I haven't heard from him recently.* Últimamente no tengo noticias de él.

heart [hɑːt] NOUN
el corazón (PL los corazones)

♦ **hearts** (*at cards*) los corazones ◊ *the ace of hearts* el as de corazones

♦ **to learn something by heart** aprenderse algo de memoria

heart attack ['hɑːtətæk] NOUN
el infarto

heartbroken ['hɑːtbrəukən] ADJECTIVE

♦ **to be heartbroken** tener* el corazón partido

heat [hiːt] NOUN
see also **heat** VERB
el calor

to **heat** [hiːt] VERB
see also **heat** NOUN
calentar* ◊ *Heat gently for five minutes.* Caliente a fuego lento durante cinco minutos.

to **heat up** [hiːt'ʌp] VERB

1 calentar* ◊ *He heated the soup up.* Calentó la sopa.

2 calentarse* (*water, oven*) ◊ *The water is heating up.* El agua se está calentando.

heater ['hiːtəʳ] NOUN
el calentador ◊ *a water heater* un calentador de agua

♦ **an electric heater** una estufa eléctrica

♦ **Could you put on the heater?** (*in car*) ¿Puedes poner la calefacción?

heather ['hɛðəʳ] NOUN
el brezo

heating ['hiːtɪŋ] NOUN
la calefacción

heaven ['hɛvn] NOUN
el cielo

♦ **to go to heaven** ir* al cielo

heavily ['hɛvɪlɪ] ADVERB

♦ **It rained heavily in the night.** Llovió con fuerza por la noche.

♦ **He's a heavily built man.** Es un hombre corpulento.

◆ **He drinks heavily.** Bebe demasiado.

heavy [ˈhɛvɪ] ADJECTIVE
pesado ◊ *a heavy load* una carga pesada
◆ **This bag's very heavy.** Esta bolsa pesa mucho.
◆ **heavy rain** fuerte lluvia
◆ **he's a heavy drinker** es un bebedor empedernido

he'd [hiːd] = **he would**, = **he had**

hedge [hɛdʒ] NOUN
el seto

hedgehog [ˈhɛdʒhɔg] NOUN
el erizo

heel [hiːl] NOUN
1 (*of shoe*)
el tacón (PL los tacones)
2 (*of foot*)
el talón (PL los talones)

height [haɪt] NOUN
1 la estatura (*of person*)
2 la altura (*of object, mountain*)

heir [ɛəʳ] NOUN
el heredero

heiress [ˈɛərɛs] NOUN (PL **heiresses**)
la heredera

held [hɛld] VERB *see* **hold**

helicopter [ˈhɛlɪkɔptəʳ] NOUN
el helicóptero

hell [hɛl] NOUN
el infierno
◆ **Hell!** ¡Maldita sea!

he'll [hiːl] = **he will**, = **he shall**

hello [həˈləu] EXCLAMATION
1 ¡hola! (*when you see somebody*)
2 ¡dígame! (¡aló! LatAm) (*on the phone*)

helmet [ˈhɛlmɪt] NOUN
el casco

to **help** [hɛlp] VERB
see also **help** NOUN
ayudar ◊ *Can you help me?* ¿Puedes ayudarme?
◆ **Help!** ¡Socorro!
◆ **Help yourself!** ¡Sírvete!
◆ **I couldn't help laughing.** No pude evitar reírme.

help [hɛlp] NOUN
see also **help** VERB
la ayuda ◊ *Do you need any help?* ¿Necesitas ayuda?

helpful [ˈhɛlpful] ADJECTIVE
útil ◊ *He gave me some helpful advice.* Me dio algunos consejos útiles.
◆ **You've been very helpful!** ¡Muchas gracias por su ayuda!

hen [hɛn] NOUN
la gallina

her [həːʳ] ADJECTIVE
see also **her** PRONOUN
su (PL sus)
◊ *her father* su padre ◊ *her house* su casa ◊ *her two best friends* sus dos mejores amigos ◊ *her sisters* sus hermanas

***her** is usually translated by the definite article **el/los** or **la/las** when it's clear from the sentence who the possessor is or when referring to clothing or parts of the body.*

◊ *They stole her car.* Le robaron el coche. ◊ *She took off her coat.* Se quitó el abrigo. ◊ *She's washing her hair.* Se está lavando la cabeza.

her [həːʳ] PRONOUN
see also **her** ADJECTIVE
1 la
*Use **la** when **her** is the direct object of the verb in the sentence.*
◊ *I saw her.* La vi. ◊ *Look at her!* ¡Mírala!
2 le
*Use **le** when **her** means **to her**.*
◊ *I gave her a book.* Le di un libro. ◊ *You have to tell her the truth.* Tienes* que decirle la verdad.
3 se
*Use **se** not **le** when **her** is used in combination with a direct-object pronoun.*
◊ *Give it to her.* Dáselo.
4 ella
*Use **ella** after prepositions, in comparisons, and with the verb **to be**.*
◊ *I'm going with her.* Voy con ella. ◊ *I'm older than her.* Soy mayor que ella. ◊ *It must be her.* Debe de ser ella.
◆ **She was carrying it on her.** Lo llevaba consigo.

herb [həːb] NOUN
la hierba (*medicinal o aromática*)

here [hɪəʳ] ADVERB
aquí ◊ *I live here.* Vivo aquí. ◊ *Here he is!* ¡Aquí está! ◊ *Here are the books.* Aquí están los libros.
◆ **Here's your coffee.** Aquí tienes el café.
◆ **Have you got my pen? – Here you are.** ¿Tienes mi boli? – Aquí tienes.
◆ **Here are the papers you asked for.** Aquí tienes los papeles que pediste.

hero [ˈhɪərəu] NOUN (PL **heroes**)
el héroe

heroin [ˈhɛrəuɪn] NOUN
la heroína
◆ **a heroin addict** un heroinómano

heroine [ˈhɛrəuɪn] NOUN
la heroína

hers [həːz] PRONOUN
1 el suyo MASC (PL los suyos) ◊ *Is this her coat? – No, hers is black.* ¿Es éste su abrigo? – No, el suyo es negro. ◊ *my parents and hers* mis padres y los suyos
2 la suya FEM (PL las suyas) ◊ *Is this her scarf? – No, hers is red.* ¿Es ésta su bufanda? – No, la suya es roja. ◊ *my sisters and hers* mis hermanas y las suyas
3 suyo MASC (PL suyos)

☞

◊ *Is that car hers?* ¿Es suyo ese coche?
[4] suya FEM (PL suyas)
◊ *Is that wallet hers?* ¿Es suya esa cartera?
♦ **Isobel is a friend of hers.** Isobel es amiga suya.

*Use **de ella** instead of **suyo** if you want to avoid confusion with "his", "theirs", etc.*

◊ *Whose is this? – It's hers.* ¿De quién es esto? – Es de ella.

herself [hə:'sɛlf] PRONOUN
[1] se (*reflexive*) ◊ *She's hurt herself.* Se ha hecho daño.
[2] sí misma (*after preposition*) ◊ *She talked mainly about herself.* Habló principalmente de sí misma.
[3] ella misma (*for emphasis*) ◊ *She did it herself.* Lo hizo ella misma.
♦ **by herself** (*alone*) sola ◊ *She came by herself.* Vino sola.

he's [hi:z] = **he is,**= **he has**

to **hesitate** ['hɛzɪteɪt] VERB
dudar ◊ *Don't hesitate to ask.* No dudes en preguntar.

heterosexual ['hɛtərəu'sɛksjuəl] ADJECTIVE
heterosexual

hi [haɪ] EXCLAMATION
¡hola!

hiccup ['hɪkʌp] NOUN
el hipo ◊ *The baby's got hiccups.* El bebé tiene hipo.

to **hide** [haɪd] VERB (**hid, hidden**)
[1] esconder ◊ *Paula hid the present.* Paula escondió el regalo.
[2] esconderse ◊ *He hid behind a bush.* Se escondió detrás de un arbusto.

hide-and-seek ['haɪdən'si:k] NOUN
♦ **to play hide-and-seek** jugar* al escondite

hideous ['hɪdɪəs] ADJECTIVE
horroroso

hi-fi ['haɪfaɪ] NOUN
el equipo de alta fidelidad

high [haɪ] ADJECTIVE, ADVERB
[1] alto ◊ *The gate's too high.* La verja es demasiado alta. ◊ *Prices are higher in Germany.* Los precios están más altos en Alemania. ◊ *It's very high in fat.* Tiene un alto contenido en grasas. ◊ *The plane flew high over the mountains.* El avión volaba alto sobre las montañas.
♦ **How high is the wall?** ¿Cómo es de alto el muro?
♦ **The wall's two metres high.** El muro tiene dos metros de altura.
[2] agudo ◊ *She's got a very high voice.* Tiene la voz muy aguda.
♦ **at high speed** a gran velocidad
♦ **to be high** (*on drugs*) estar* colocado (*informal*)
♦ **to get high** (*on drugs*) colocarse* (*informal*)

higher education ['haɪərɛdju'keɪʃən] NOUN
la enseñanza superior

high-heeled [haɪ'hi:ld] ADJECTIVE
♦ **high-heeled shoes** los zapatos de tacón alto

high jump ['haɪdʒʌmp] NOUN
el salto de altura

highlight ['haɪlaɪt] NOUN
see also **highlight** VERB
el punto culminante ◊ *the highlight of the evening* el punto culminante de la velada

to **highlight** ['haɪlaɪt] VERB
see also **highlight** NOUN
poner* de relieve

highlighter ['haɪlaɪtəʳ] NOUN
el rotulador

high-rise ['haɪraɪz] NOUN
la torre de pisos

high school ['haɪsku:l] NOUN
el instituto (el liceo *LatAm*)

to **hijack** ['haɪdʒæk] VERB
secuestrar

hijacker ['haɪdʒækəʳ] NOUN
el secuestrador
la secuestradora

hike [haɪk] NOUN
la caminata (*por el campo*)

hiking ['haɪkɪŋ] NOUN
♦ **to go hiking** ir* de excursión al campo

hilarious [hɪ'lɛərɪəs] ADJECTIVE
graciosísimo

hill [hɪl] NOUN
[1] la colina ◊ *a house at the top of a hill* una casa en lo alto de una colina
[2] la cuesta ◊ *I climbed the hill up to the office.* Subí la cuesta hasta la oficina.

hill-walking ['hɪlwɔ:kɪŋ] NOUN
el senderismo ◊ *to go hill-walking* hacer* senderismo

him [hɪm] PRONOUN
[1] lo

*Use **lo** when **him** is the direct object of the verb in the sentence.*

◊ *I saw him.* Lo vi. ◊ *Look at him!* ¡Míralo!
[2] le

*Use **le** when **him** means **to him**.*

◊ *I gave him a book.* Le di un libro. ◊ *You have to tell him the truth.* Tienes* que decirle la verdad.
[3] se

*Use **se** not **le** when **him** is used in combination with a direct-object pronoun.*

◊ *Give it to him.* Dáselo.
[4] él

*Use **él** after prepositions, in comparisons and with the verb **to be**.*

◊ *I'm going with him.* Voy con él. ◊ *I'm older than him.* Soy mayor que él. ◊ *It must be him.* Debe de ser él.
♦ **He was carrying it on him.** Lo llevaba consigo.

himself [hɪm'sɛlf] PRONOUN
1 se (*reflexive*) ◊ *He's hurt himself.* Se ha hecho daño.
2 sí mismo (*after preposition*) ◊ *He talked mainly about himself.* Habló principalmente de sí mismo.
3 él mismo (*for emphasis*) ◊ *He did it himself.* Lo hizo él mismo.
♦ **by himself** (*alone*) solo ◊ *He came by himself.* Vino solo.

Hindu ['hɪndu:] ADJECTIVE
hindú (PL hindúes)

hint [hɪnt] NOUN
see also **hint** VERB
la indirecta
♦ **to drop a hint** soltar* una indirecta
♦ **to take a hint** captar una indirecta

to **hint** [hɪnt] VERB
see also **hint** NOUN
insinuar* ◊ *He hinted that I had a good chance of getting the job.* Insinuó que tenía muchas posibilidades de conseguir el trabajo.

hip [hɪp] NOUN
la cadera ◊ *She put her hands on her hips.* Se puso las manos en las caderas.

hippie ['hɪpɪ] NOUN
el/la hippy (PL los hippies)

hippo ['hɪpəu] NOUN (PL **hippos**)
el hipopótamo

to **hire** ['haɪəʳ] VERB
see also **hire** NOUN
1 alquilar ◊ *We hired a car.* Alquilamos un coche.
2 contratar ◊ *They hired a lawyer.* Contrataron a un abogado.

hire ['haɪəʳ] NOUN
see also **hire** VERB
el alquiler ◊ *car hire* el alquiler de coches
♦ **"for hire"** "se alquila"

hire car ['haɪəkɑ:ʳ] NOUN
el coche de alquiler

his [hɪz] ADJECTIVE
see also **his** PRONOUN
su (PL sus) ◊ *his father* su padre ◊ *his house* su casa ◊ *his two best friends* sus dos mejores amigos ◊ *his sisters* sus hermanas

__his__ is usually translated by the definite article __el/los__ or __la/las__ when it's clear from the sentence who the possessor is or when referring to clothing or parts of the body.

◊ *They stole his car.* Le robaron el coche. ◊ *He took off his coat.* Se quitó el abrigo. ◊ *He's washing his hair.* Se está lavando la cabeza.

his [hɪz] PRONOUN
see also **his** ADJECTIVE
1 el suyo MASC (PL los suyos) ◊ *Is this his coat? – No, his is black.* ¿Es éste su abrigo? – No, el suyo es negro. ◊ *my parents and his* mis padres y los suyos
2 la suya FEM (PL las suyas) ◊ *Is this his scarf? – No, his is red.* ¿Es ésta su bufanda? – No, la suya es roja. ◊ *my sisters and his* mis hermanas y las suyas
3 suyo MASC (PL suyos) ◊ *Is that car his?* ¿Es suyo ese coche?
4 suya FEM (PL suyas) ◊ *Is that wallet his?* ¿Es suya esa cartera?
♦ **Isobel is a friend of his.** Isobel es amiga suya.

Use __de él__ instead of __suyo__ if you want to avoid confusion with "hers", "theirs", etc.

◊ *Whose is this? – It's his.* ¿De quién es esto? – Es de él.

H

history ['hɪstərɪ] NOUN
la historia

to **hit** [hɪt] VERB (**hit, hit**)
see also **hit** NOUN
1 pegar* ◊ *He hit the ball.* Le pegó a la bola. ◊ *Andrew hit him.* Andrew le pegó.
2 chocar* con ◊ *The car hit a road sign.* El coche chocó con una señal de tráfico.
♦ **He was hit by a car.** Le pilló un coche.
♦ **to hit the target** dar* en el blanco
♦ **to hit it off with somebody** hacer* buenas migas con alguien

hit [hɪt] NOUN
see also **hit** VERB
el éxito ◊ *Sting's latest hit.* El último éxito de Sting. ◊ *The film was a massive hit.* La película fue un éxito enorme.

hitch [hɪtʃ] NOUN (PL **hitches**)
el contratiempo ◊ *There's been a slight hitch.* Ha habido un pequeño contratiempo.

to **hitchhike** ['hɪtʃhaɪk] VERB
hacer* autoestop

hitchhiker ['hɪtʃhaɪkəʳ] NOUN
el/la autoestopista

hitchhiking ['hɪtʃhaɪkɪŋ] NOUN
el autoestop

hit man ['hɪtmæn] NOUN (PL **hit men**)
el asesino a sueldo

HIV [eɪtʃaɪ'vi:] NOUN (= *human immunodeficiency virus*)
el VIH

HIV-positive [eɪtʃaɪvi:'pɔsɪtɪv] ADJECTIVE
seropositivo

hobby ['hɔbɪ] NOUN (PL **hobbies**)
la afición (PL las aficiones)

hockey ['hɔkɪ] NOUN
el hockey ◊ *I like playing hockey.* Me gusta jugar* al hockey.

to **hold** [həuld] VERB (**held, held**)

☞

1 tener* ◊ *He was holding her in his arms.* La tenía entre sus brazos.
2 sujetar ◊ *Hold the ladder.* Sujeta la escalera.
3 contener* ◊ *This bottle holds one litre.* Esta botella contiene un litro.
◆**to hold a meeting** celebrar una reunión
◆**Hold the line!** (*on telephone*) ¡No cuelgue!
◆**Hold it!** ¡Espera!
◆**to get hold of something** hacerse* con algo

to **hold on** [həuld'ɔn] VERB
1 agarrar (*keep hold*) ◊ *The cliff was slippery but he managed to hold on.* El acantilado se escurría, pero logró agarrarse.
◆**to hold on to something** agarrarse a algo
2 esperar (*wait*) ◊ *Hold on, I'm coming!* ¡Espera que ya voy!
◆**Hold on!** (*on telephone*) ¡No cuelgue!

to **hold up** [həuld'ʌp] VERB
1 levantar ◊ *Peter held up his hand.* Peter levantó la mano.
2 retrasar ◊ *We were held up by the traffic.* Nos retrasamos por culpa del tráfico.
3 atracar* ◊ *to hold up a bank* atracar un banco
◆**I was held up at the office.** Me entretuvieron en la oficina.

hold-up ['həuldʌp] NOUN
1 el atraco ◊ *A bank clerk was injured in the hold-up.* Un empleado del banco resultó herido en el atraco.
2 el retraso ◊ *No-one explained the reason for the hold-up.* Nadie explicó el motivo del retraso.
3 el embotellamiento ◊ *a hold-up on the motorway* un embotellamiento en la autopista

hole [həul] NOUN
1 el agujero (*in general*) ◊ *a hole in the wall* un agujero en la pared
2 el hoyo (*in the ground, in golf*)
◆**to dig a hole** cavar un hoyo

holiday ['hɔlɪdeɪ] NOUN
1 las vacaciones ◊ *the school holidays* las vacaciones escolares ◊ *on holiday* de vacaciones ◊ *to go on holiday* irse* de vacaciones ◊ *to be on holiday* estar* de vacaciones
2 el día festivo (el día feriado *LatAm*) ◊ *Next Monday is a holiday.* El lunes que viene es día festivo.
◆**He took a day's holiday.** Se tomó un día libre.

holiday camp ['hɔlɪdeɪkæmp] NOUN
la colonia de veraneo

Holland ['hɔlənd] NOUN
Holanda FEM

hollow ['hɔləu] ADJECTIVE
hueco

holly ['hɔlɪ] NOUN
el acebo

holy ['həulɪ] ADJECTIVE
1 santo ◊ *the Holy Spirit* el Espíritu Santo
2 sagrado ◊ *a holy place* un lugar sagrado

home [həum] NOUN
see also **home** ADVERB
la casa ◊ *at home* en casa
◆**Make yourself at home.** Estás* en tu casa.
◆**an old people's home** una residencia de ancianos

home [həum] ADVERB
see also **home** NOUN
1 en casa ◊ *I'll be home at five o'clock.* Estaré* en casa a las cinco.
2 a casa
◆**to get home** llegar* a casa

home address [həumə'drɛs] NOUN
el domicilio

homeless ['həumlɪs] ADJECTIVE, NOUN
sin hogar
◆**homeless people** los sin techo

home match ['həummætʃ] NOUN
el partido en casa

homeopathy [həumɪ'ɔpəθɪ] NOUN
la homeopatía

home page ['həumpeɪdʒ] NOUN
la página principal

homesick ['həumsɪk] ADJECTIVE
◆**to be homesick** tener* morriña

homework ['həumwəːk] NOUN
los deberes ◊ *Have you done your homework?* ¿Has hecho los deberes? ◊ *my geography homework* mis deberes de geografía

homosexual [hɔməu'sɛksjuəl] ADJECTIVE
homosexual

honest ['ɔnɪst] ADJECTIVE
1 honrado ◊ *She's a very honest person.* Es una persona muy honrada.
2 sincero ◊ *Tell me your honest opinion.* Dame tu sincera opinión.
◆**To be honest, I don't like the idea.** La verdad es que no me gusta la idea.

honestly ['ɔnɪstlɪ] ADVERB
francamente ◊ *I honestly don't know.* Francamente no lo sé.

honesty ['ɔnɪstɪ] NOUN
la honradez

honey ['hʌnɪ] NOUN
la miel

honeymoon ['hʌnɪmuːn] NOUN
la luna de miel
◆**to go on honeymoon** irse* de luna de miel

honour ['ɔnər] NOUN (US **honor**)
el honor
hood [hud] NOUN
1 la capucha (*on coat*)
2 el capó (*bonnet of car*) US
hook [huk] NOUN
1 el gancho ◇ *The jacket hung from a hook.* La chaqueta estaba colgada de un gancho.
2 la alcayata ◇ *He hung the painting on the hook.* Colgó el cuadro de la alcayata.
3 el anzuelo ◇ *He felt a fish pull at his hook.* Notó que un pez tiraba del anzuelo.
♦ **to take the phone off the hook** descolgar* el teléfono
hooligan ['huːlɪgən] NOUN
el gamberro
la gamberra
hooray [huː'reɪ] EXCLAMATION
¡hurra!
Hoover ® ['huːvər] NOUN
la aspiradora
to **hoover** ['huːvər] VERB
pasar la aspiradora por ◇ *He hoovered the lounge.* Pasó la aspiradora por el salón.
to **hop** [hɔp] VERB
1 brincar* (*animal*)
2 ir* a pata coja (*person*)
to **hope** [həup] VERB
see also **hope** NOUN
esperar
Use the subjunctive after ***esperar que.***
◇ *I hope he comes.* Espero que venga.
♦ **I hope so.** Espero que sí.
♦ **I hope not.** Espero que no.
hope [həup] NOUN
see also **hope** VERB
la esperanza
♦ **to give up hope** perder* la esperanza
hopeful ['həupful] ADJECTIVE
prometedor MASC
prometedora FEM
◇ *The prospects look hopeful.* Las perspectivas parecen prometedoras.
♦ **He's hopeful of winning.** Tiene esperanzas de ganar.
♦ **How did the interview go? – I'm hopeful.** ¿Cómo fue la entrevista? – Tengo esperanzas.
♦ **We're hopeful everything will go okay.** Confiamos en que todo irá bien.
hopefully ['həupfulɪ] ADVERB
♦ **Hopefully, he'll make it in time.** Esperemos que llegue a tiempo.
Use the subjunctive after ***esperar que.***
hopeless ['həuplɪs] ADJECTIVE
♦ **She's hopeless at maths.** Es una negada para las matemáticas.
horizon [hə'raɪzn] NOUN
el horizonte
horizontal [hɔrɪ'zɔntl] ADJECTIVE
horizontal
horn [hɔːn] NOUN
1 el claxon ◇ *He sounded the horn.* Tocó el claxon.
2 la trompa ◇ *He plays the horn.* Toca la trompa.
3 el cuerno (el cacho *LatAm*) ◇ *a bull's horns* los cuernos de un toro
horoscope ['hɔrəskəup] NOUN
el horóscopo
horrible ['hɔrɪbl] ADJECTIVE
horrible ◇ *What a horrible dress!* ¡Qué vestido tan horrible!
to **horrify** ['hɔrɪfaɪ] VERB
horrorizar*
horror ['hɔrər] NOUN
el horror ◇ *To my horror I discovered I was locked out.* Descubrí con horror que me había dejado las llaves dentro.
horror film ['hɔrəfɪlm] NOUN
la película de terror
horse [hɔːs] NOUN
el caballo
horse-racing ['hɔːsreɪsɪŋ] NOUN
las carreras de caballos
horseshoe ['hɔːsʃuː] NOUN
la herradura
hose [həuz] NOUN
la manguera
hosepipe ['həuzpaɪp] NOUN
la manguera
hospital ['hɔspɪtl] NOUN
el hospital ◇ *to go into hospital* ingresar en el hospital
hospitality [hɔspɪ'tælɪtɪ] NOUN
la hospitalidad
host [həust] NOUN
el anfitrión (PL los anfitriones)
la anfitriona
hostage ['hɔstɪdʒ] NOUN
el rehén (PL los rehenes)
♦ **to take somebody hostage** tomar como rehén a alguien
hostile ['hɔstaɪl] ADJECTIVE
hostil
hot [hɔt] ADJECTIVE
1 caliente ◇ *a hot bath* un baño caliente
2 caluroso ◇ *a hot country* un país caluroso
When you are talking about a person being hot, you use ***tener* calor.***
◇ *I'm hot.* Tengo calor.
When you talk about the weather being hot, you use ***hacer* calor.***
◇ *It's hot today.* Hoy hace calor.
3 picante ◇ *Mexican food's too hot.* La comida mejicana es demasiado picante.
hot dog ['hɔtdɔg] NOUN
el perrito caliente
hotel [həu'tɛl] NOUN
el hotel
hour ['auər] NOUN

☞

la hora ◊ *She always takes hours to get ready.* Siempre se tira horas para arreglarse.
◆ **a quarter of an hour** un cuarto de hora
◆ **two and a half hours** dos horas y media
◆ **half an hour** media hora

hourly ['auəlɪ] ADJECTIVE, ADVERB
◆ **There are hourly buses.** Hay autobuses cada hora.
◆ **She's paid hourly.** Le pagan por horas.

house [haus] NOUN
la casa ◊ *at his house* en su casa

housewife ['hauswaɪf] NOUN (PL **housewives**)
el ama de casa (PL las amas de casa)
◊ *She's a housewife.* Es ama de casa.

housework ['hauswəːk] NOUN
las tareas de la casa

hovercraft ['hɔvəkrɑːft] NOUN
el aerodeslizador

how [hau] ADVERB
1 cómo ◊ *How are you?* ¿Cómo estás?
2 qué ◊ *How strange!* ¡Qué raro!
◆ **He told them how happy he was.** Les dijo lo feliz que era.
◆ **How many?** ¿Cuántos?
◆ **How much?** ¿Cuánto? ◊ *How much is it?* ¿Cuánto es? ◊ *How much sugar do you want?* ¿Cuánto azúcar quieres?
◆ **How old are you?** ¿Cuántos años tienes?
◆ **How far is it to Edinburgh?** ¿Qué distancia hay de aquí a Edimburgo?
◆ **How long have you been here?** ¿Cuánto tiempo llevas aquí?
◆ **How long does it take?** ¿Cuánto se tarda?

*Remember the accents on question and exclamation words **cómo, qué** and **cuánto**.*

however [hau'ɛvəʳ] CONJUNCTION
sin embargo ◊ *This, however, isn't true.* Esto, sin embargo, no es cierto.

to **howl** [haul] VERB
aullar* ◊ *The dog howled all night.* El perro estuvo aullando toda la noche.
◊ *He howled with pain.* Aullaba de dolor.

HTML [eɪtʃtiːem'el] NOUN
el HTML

to **hug** [hʌg] VERB
see also **hug** NOUN
abrazar* ◊ *They hugged each other.* Se abrazaron.

hug [hʌg] NOUN
see also **hug** VERB
el abrazo ◊ *to give somebody a hug* dar* un abrazo a alguien

huge [hjuːdʒ] ADJECTIVE
enorme

to **hum** [hʌm] VERB
tararear

human ['hjuːmən] ADJECTIVE
humano ◊ *the human body* el cuerpo humano

human being [hjuːmən'biːɪŋ] NOUN
el ser humano

humble ['hʌmbl] ADJECTIVE
humilde

humour ['hjuːməʳ] NOUN (US **humor**)
el humor
◆ **to have a sense of humour** tener* sentido del humor

hundred ['hʌndrəd] NUMERAL

*Use **cien** before nouns or before another number that is being multiplied by a hundred.*

◆ **a hundred** cien ◊ *a hundred people* cien personas ◊ *a hundred thousand* cien mil

*Use **ciento** before a number that is not multiplied but simply added to a hundred.*

◊ *a hundred and one* ciento uno

*When **hundred** follows another number, use the compound forms, which must agreee with the noun.*

◊ *three hundred* trescientos ◊ *five hundred people* quinientas personas
◊ *five hundred and one* quinientos uno
◆ **hundreds of people** cientos de personas

hung [hʌŋ] VERB *see* **hang**

Hungary ['hʌŋgərɪ] NOUN
Hungría FEM

hunger ['hʌŋgəʳ] NOUN
el hambre FEM

*Although it's a feminine noun, remember that you use **el** and **un** with **hambre**.*

hungry ['hʌŋgrɪ] ADJECTIVE
◆ **to be hungry** tener* hambre ◊ *I'm very hungry.* Tengo mucha hambre.

to **hunt** [hʌnt] VERB
1 cazar* ◊ *They hunt foxes.* Cazan zorros.
2 buscar* ◊ *The police are hunting the killer.* La policía está buscando al asesino.
◆ **to go hunting** ir* de caza
◆ **to hunt for something** buscar* algo
◊ *I've hunted everywhere for that book.* He buscado ese libro por todas partes.

hunting ['hʌntɪŋ] NOUN
la caza ◊ *fox-hunting* la caza del zorro

hurricane ['hʌrɪkən] NOUN
el huracán (PL los huracanes)

to **hurry** ['hʌrɪ] VERB (**hurried, hurried**)
see also **hurry** NOUN
darse* prisa (apurarse *LatAm*) ◊ *Hurry up!* ¡Date prisa!
◆ **Sharon hurried back home.** Sharon volvió a casa a toda prisa.

hurry ['hʌrɪ] NOUN

see also **hurry** VERB

♦ **to be in a hurry** tener* prisa (tener* apuro *LatAm*)

♦ **to do something in a hurry** hacer* algo a toda prisa

♦ **There's no hurry.** No hay prisa.

to **hurt** [hə:t] VERB (**hurt, hurt**)

see also **hurt** ADJECTIVE

1 hacer* daño a ◊ *You're hurting me!* ¡Me haces daño! ◊ *Have you hurt yourself?* ¿Te has hecho daño?

2 doler* ◊ *My leg hurts.* Me duele la pierna.

♦ **Hey! That hurts!** ¡Hey! ¡Que me haces daño!

3 herir* ◊ *His remarks really hurt me.* Sus comentarios me hirieron mucho.

hurt [hə:t] ADJECTIVE

see also **hurt** VERB

herido ◊ *Is he badly hurt?* ¿Está herido de gravedad? ◊ *Luckily, nobody got hurt.* Por suerte, nadie salió herido.

♦ **I was hurt by what he said.** Me hirió lo que dijo.

husband ['hʌzbənd] NOUN
el marido

hut [hʌt] NOUN
la cabaña

hymn [hɪm] NOUN
el himno (*religioso*)

hypermarket ['haɪpəmɑ:kɪt] NOUN
el hipermercado

hyphen ['haɪfn] NOUN
el guión (PL los guiones)

H

I

I [aɪ] PRONOUN
yo ◊ *Ann and I.* Ann y yo.
***I** generally isn't translated unless it is emphatic.*
◊ *I speak Spanish.* Hablo español.
*Use **yo** for emphasis.*
◊ *Cristina was frightened but I wasn't.* Cristina estaba asustado, pero yo no.

ice [aɪs] NOUN
el hielo

iceberg ['aɪsbəːg] NOUN
el iceberg (PL los icebergs)

icebox ['aɪsbɔks] NOUN (PL **iceboxes**) US
la nevera

ice cream ['aɪskriːm] NOUN
el helado ◊ *vanilla ice cream* el helado de vainilla

ice cube ['aɪskjuːb] NOUN
el cubito de hielo

ice hockey ['aɪshɔkɪ] NOUN
el hockey sobre hielo ◊ *I like playing ice hockey.* Me gusta jugar* al hockey sobre hielo.

Iceland ['aɪslənd] NOUN
Islandia FEM

ice lolly ['aɪslɔlɪ] NOUN (PL **ice lollies**)
el polo

ice rink ['aɪsrɪŋk] NOUN
la pista de patinaje sobre hielo

ice-skating ['aɪsskeɪtɪŋ] NOUN
el patinaje sobre hielo
♦ **Yesterday we went ice-skating.** Ayer fuimos a patinar sobre hielo.

icing ['aɪsɪŋ] NOUN
el glaseado (*on cake*)
♦ **icing sugar** el azúcar glas

icon ['aɪkɔn] NOUN
el icono

icy ['aɪsɪ] ADJECTIVE
helado ◊ *an icy wind* un viento helado
◊ *The roads are icy.* Las carreteras están heladas.

I'd [aɪd] = **I had**, = **I would**

idea [aɪ'dɪə] NOUN
la idea ◊ *Good idea!* ¡Buena idea!

ideal [aɪ'dɪəl] ADJECTIVE
ideal

identical [aɪ'dɛntɪkl] ADJECTIVE
idéntico

identification [aɪdɛntɪfɪ'keɪʃən] NOUN
la identificación (PL las identificaciones)

to **identify** [aɪ'dɛntɪfaɪ] VERB (**identified, identified**)
identificar*

identity card [aɪ'dɛntɪtɪ'kɑːd] NOUN
el carnet de identidad

idiom ['ɪdɪəm] NOUN
el modismo

idiot ['ɪdɪət] NOUN
el/la idiota

idiotic [ɪdɪ'ɔtɪk] ADJECTIVE
idiota

idle ['aɪdl] ADJECTIVE
♦ **It's just idle gossip.** No es más que cotilleo.
♦ **I asked out of idle curiosity.** Lo pregunté por pura curiosidad.
♦ **to be idle** (*worker*) estar* sin trabajo

i.e. [aɪ'iː] ABBREVIATION
es decir

if [ɪf] CONJUNCTION
si ◊ *You can go if you like.* Puedes ir si quieres. ◊ *He asked me if I had eaten.* Me preguntó si había comido. ◊ *If it's fine we'll go swimming.* Si hace bueno, iremos a nadar.
*Use **si** with a past subjunctive to translate **if** followed by a past tense when talking about conditions.*
◊ *If you studied harder you would pass your exams.* Si estudiaras más aprobarías los exámenes.
♦ **if only** ojalá
***ojalá** has to be followed by a verb in the subjunctive.*
◊ *If only I had more money!* ¡Ojalá tuviera más dinero!
♦ **if not** si no ◊ *Are you coming? If not, I'll go with Mark.* ¿Vienes? Si no, iré con Mark.
♦ **if so** si es así ◊ *Are you coming? If so, I'll wait.* ¿Vienes? Si es así te espero.
♦ **If I were you I would go to Spain.** Yo que tú iría a España.

ignorant ['ɪgnərənt] ADJECTIVE
ignorante

to **ignore** [ɪg'nɔːr] VERB
♦ **to ignore something** hacer* caso omiso de algo ◊ *She ignored my advice.* Hizo caso omiso de mi consejo.
♦ **to ignore somebody** ignorar a alguien
◊ *She saw me, but she ignored me.* Me vió, pero me ignoró completamente.
♦ **Just ignore him!** ¡No le hagas caso!

ill [ɪl] ADJECTIVE
enfermo ◊ *She was taken ill.* Se puso enferma.

I'll [aɪl] = **I will**

illegal [ɪ'liːgl] ADJECTIVE
ilegal

illegible [ɪ'lɛdʒɪbl] ADJECTIVE

ilegible

illness [ˈɪlnɪs] NOUN (PL **illnesses**)
la enfermedad

illusion [ɪˈluːʒən] NOUN
la ilusión (PL las ilusiones) ◊ *an optical illusion* una ilusión óptica
♦ **He was under the illusion that he would win.** Se creía que iba a ganar.

illustration [ɪləˈstreɪʃən] NOUN
la ilustración (PL las ilustraciones)

I'm [aɪm] = **I am**

image [ˈɪmɪdʒ] NOUN
la imagen (PL las imágenes) ◊ *The company has changed its image.* La empresa ha cambiado de imagen.

imagination [ɪmædʒɪˈneɪʃən] NOUN
la imaginación (PL las imaginaciones) ◊ *She lets her imagination run away with her.* Se deja llevar por su imaginación. ◊ *It's only your imagination.* Son imaginaciones tuyas.

to **imagine** [ɪˈmædʒɪn] VERB
imaginarse ◊ *You can imagine how I felt!* ¡Imagínate cómo me sentí! ◊ *Is he angry? – I imagine so!* ¿Está enfadado? – ¡Me imagino que sí!

to **imitate** [ˈɪmɪteɪt] VERB
imitar

imitation [ɪmɪˈteɪʃən] NOUN
la imitación (PL las imitaciones)
♦ **imitation leather** el cuero de imitación

immediate [ɪˈmiːdɪət] ADJECTIVE
inmediato ◊ *We need an immediate answer.* Necesitamos una respuesta inmediata.

immediately [ɪˈmiːdɪətlɪ] ADVERB
inmediatamente

immigrant [ˈɪmɪgrənt] NOUN
el/la inmigrante

immigration [ɪmɪˈgreɪʃən] NOUN
la inmigración (PL las inmigraciones)

immoral [ɪˈmɔrl] ADJECTIVE
inmoral

immune [ɪˈmjuːn] ADJECTIVE
♦ **to be immune to something** ser* inmune a algo ◊ *She is immune to measles.* Es inmune al sarampión.

impartial [ɪmˈpɑːʃl] ADJECTIVE
imparcial

impatience [ɪmˈpeɪʃəns] NOUN
la impaciencia

impatient [ɪmˈpeɪʃənt] ADJECTIVE
impaciente
♦ **to get impatient** impacientarse ◊ *People are getting impatient.* La gente se está impacientando.

impatiently [ɪmˈpeɪʃəntlɪ] ADVERB
con impaciencia

impersonal [ɪmˈpəːsənl] ADJECTIVE
impersonal

to **implement** [ˈɪmplɪmɛnt] VERB
llevar a cabo ◊ *It'll take a few months to implement the plan.* Se tardarán unos cuantos meses en llevar a cabo el plan.

to **imply** [ɪmˈplaɪ] VERB
insinuar* ◊ *Are you implying I did it on purpose?* ¿Insinúas que lo hice adrede?

import [ˈɪmpɔːt] NOUN
see also **import** VERB
importación
♦ **imports** los productos de importación

to **import** [ɪmˈpɔːt] VERB
see also **import** NOUN
importar

importance [ɪmˈpɔːtns] NOUN
la importancia

important [ɪmˈpɔːtənt] ADJECTIVE
importante

impossible [ɪmˈpɔsɪbl] ADJECTIVE
imposible

to **impress** [ɪmˈprɛs] VERB
impresionar ◊ *She's trying to impress you.* Está tratando de impresionarte.

impressed [ɪmˈprɛst] ADJECTIVE
impresionado
♦ **I'm very impressed!** ¡Estoy impresionado!

impression [ɪmˈprɛʃən] NOUN
la impresión (PL las impresiones) ◊ *I was under the impression that you were going out.* Tenía la impresión de que te ibas.

impressive [ɪmˈprɛsɪv] ADJECTIVE
impresionante

to **improve** [ɪmˈpruːv] VERB
mejorar ◊ *They have improved the service.* Han mejorado el servicio. ◊ *The weather is improving.* El tiempo está mejorando.

improvement [ɪmˈpruːvmənt] NOUN
1 la mejora (*in situation, design*)
♦ **There's been an improvement in his French.** Su francés ha mejorado.
2 la mejoría (*in health*)

in [ɪn] PREPOSITION, ADVERB

*There are several ways of translating **in**. Scan the examples to find one that is similar to what you want to say. For other expressions with **in**, see the verbs **go, come, get, give**, etc.*

1 en ◊ *in the house* en casa ◊ *in my bag* en mi bolsa ◊ *in the country* en el campo ◊ *in town* en la ciudad ◊ *in Spain* en España ◊ *in school* en el colegio ◊ *in hospital* en el hospital ◊ *in London* en Londres ◊ *in spring* en primavera ◊ *in May* en Mayo ◊ *in 1996* en mil novecientos noventa y seis ◊ *I did it in three hours.* Lo hice en tres horas. ◊ *in French* en francés ◊ *in a loud voice* en voz alta ◊ *in good condition* en buen estado

☞

2 de ◊ *the best pupil in the class* el mejor alumno de la clase ◊ *at two o'clock in the afternoon* a las dos de la tarde ◊ *at six in the morning* a las seis de la mañana ◊ *the boy in the blue shirt* el muchacho de la camisa azul
3 dentro de ◊ *I'll see you in three weeks.* Te veré dentro de tres semanas. ◊ *I'll be back in one hour.* Volveré dentro de una hora.
4 por ◊ *I've got an exam in the morning.* Tengo un examen por la mañana. ◊ *I always feel sleepy in the afternoon.* Siempre tengo sueño por la tarde.
♦ **in the sun** al sol
♦ **in the rain** bajo la lluvia
♦ **It was written in pencil.** Estaba escrito a lápiz.
♦ **in here** aquí dentro ◊ *It's hot in here.* Aquí dentro hace calor.
♦ **one person in ten** una persona de cada diez
♦ **to be in** (*at home, work*) estar* ◊ *He wasn't in.* No estaba.
♦ **in writing** por escrito

inaccurate [ɪn'ækjurət] ADJECTIVE
inexacto

incentive [ɪn'sɛntɪv] NOUN
el incentivo ◊ *There's no incentive to work.* No hay incentivo para trabajar.

inch [ɪntʃ] NOUN (PL **inches**)
la pulgada

> *In Spain measurements are in metres and centimetres rather than feet and inches. An inch is about 2.5 centimetres.*

◊ *6 inches* 15 centímetros

incident ['ɪnsɪdnt] NOUN
el incidente

inclined [ɪn'klaɪnd] ADJECTIVE
♦ **to be inclined to do something** tener* tendencia a hacer algo ◊ *He's inclined to arrive late.* Tiene tendencia a llegar tarde.

to **include** [ɪn'klu:d] VERB
incluir* ◊ *Service is not included.* El servicio no está incluido.

including [ɪn'klu:dɪŋ] PREPOSITION
♦ **It will be two hundred pounds, including tax.** Son doscientas libras esterlinas con impuestos incluidos.

inclusive [ɪn'klu:sɪv] ADJECTIVE
♦ **The inclusive price is two hundred pounds.** Son doscientas libras esterlinas con todo incluido.
♦ **inclusive of VAT** con el IVA incluido

income ['ɪnkʌm] NOUN
los ingresos ◊ *his main source of income* su principal fuente de ingresos

income tax ['ɪnkʌmtæks] NOUN
el impuesto sobre la renta

incompetent [ɪn'kɔmpɪtnt] ADJECTIVE
incompetente

incomplete [ɪnkəm'pli:t] ADJECTIVE
incompleto

inconvenience [ɪnkən'vi:njəns] NOUN
la molestia ◊ *I don't want to cause any inconvenience.* No quiero causar molestia.

inconvenient [ɪnkən'vi:njənt] ADJECTIVE
♦ **It's a bit inconvenient at the moment.** Me viene un poco mal en este momento.

incorrect [ɪnkə'rɛkt] ADJECTIVE
incorrecto

increase ['ɪnkri:s] NOUN
see also **increase** VERB
el aumento ◊ *an increase in road accidents* un aumento de accidentes de tráfico

to **increase** [ɪn'kri:s] VERB
see also **increase** NOUN
aumentar ◊ *Traffic on motorways has increased.* El tráfico en las autopistas ha aumentado. ◊ *They have increased his salary.* Le han aumentado el sueldo.
♦ **to increase in size** aumentar de tamaño

incredible [ɪn'krɛdɪbl] ADJECTIVE
increíble

indecisive [ɪndɪ'saɪsɪv] ADJECTIVE
indeciso (*person*)

indeed [ɪn'di:d] ADVERB
realmente ◊ *It's very hard indeed.* Es realmente difícil.
♦ **Know what I mean? – Indeed I do.** ¿Me comprendes? – Por supuesto que sí.
♦ **Thank you very much indeed!** ¡Muchísimas gracias!

independence [ɪndɪ'pɛndns] NOUN
la independencia

independent [ɪndɪ'pɛndnt] ADJECTIVE
independiente
♦ **an independent school** un colegio privado

index ['ɪndɛks] NOUN (PL **indexes**)
el índice alfabético (*in book*)

index finger ['ɪndɛksfɪŋgə^r] NOUN
el dedo índice

India ['ɪndɪə] NOUN
la India

Indian ['ɪndɪən] ADJECTIVE
see also **Indian** NOUN
indio

Indian ['ɪndɪən] NOUN
see also **Indian** ADJECTIVE
el indio
la india
◊ *the Indians* los indios
♦ **American Indian** el indio americano (FEM la india americana)

to **indicate** ['ɪndɪkeɪt] VERB

1 indicar* ◊ *The report indicates that changes are needed.* El informe indica que se necesitan cambios.
2 señalizar* (*when driving*) ◊ *He indicated right and turned into the Gran Vía.* Señalizó hacia la derecha y torció a la Gran Vía.

indicator ['ɪndɪkeɪtə^r] NOUN
el intermitente (*in car*)

indigestion [ɪndɪ'dʒɛstʃən] NOUN
la indigestión (PL las indigestiones) ◊ *I've got indigestion.* Tengo indigestión.

individual [ɪndɪ'vɪdjuəl] ADJECTIVE
see also **individual** NOUN
individual

individual [ɪndɪ'vɪdjuəl] NOUN
see also **individual** ADJECTIVE
el individuo

indoor ['ɪndɔː^r] ADJECTIVE
♦ **an indoor swimming pool** una piscina cubierta

indoors [ɪn'dɔːz] ADVERB
dentro ◊ *They're indoors.* Están dentro.
♦ **We'd better go indoors.** Es mejor que entremos.

industrial [ɪn'dʌstrɪəl] ADJECTIVE
industrial

industrial estate [ɪn'dʌstrɪəlɪs'teɪt] NOUN
la zona industrial

industry ['ɪndəstrɪ] NOUN (PL **industries**)
la industria ◊ *the oil industry* la industria petrolífera ◊ *I'd like to work in industry.* Me gustaría trabajar en la industria.
♦ **the tourist industry** el turismo

inefficient [ɪnɪ'fɪʃənt] ADJECTIVE
ineficiente

inevitable [ɪn'ɛvɪtəbl] ADJECTIVE
inevitable

inexpensive [ɪnɪk'spɛnsɪv] ADJECTIVE
económico

inexperienced [ɪnɪk'spɪərɪənst] ADJECTIVE
inexperto

infant school ['ɪnfəntskuːl] NOUN
el colegio

infection [ɪn'fɛkʃən] NOUN
la infección (PL las infecciones) ◊ *an ear infection* una infección de oído

infectious [ɪn'fɛkʃəs] ADJECTIVE
contagioso

infinitive [ɪn'fɪnɪtɪv] NOUN
el infinitivo

infirmary [ɪn'fəːmərɪ] NOUN (PL **infirmaries**)
el hospital

inflatable [ɪn'fleɪtəbl] ADJECTIVE
inflable (*mattress, dinghy*)

inflation [ɪn'fleɪʃən] NOUN
la inflación las inflaciones

influence ['ɪnfluəns] NOUN
see also **influence** VERB
la influencia ◊ *He's a bad influence on her.* Ejerce mala influencia sobre ella.

to **influence** ['ɪnfluəns] VERB
see also **influence** NOUN
influenciar

influenza [ɪnflu'ɛnzə] NOUN
la gripe ◊ *to have influenza* tener* gripe

to **inform** [ɪn'fɔːm] VERB
informar ◊ *Nobody informed me of the change of plan.* Nadie me informó del cambio de planes.

informal [ɪn'fɔːml] ADJECTIVE
♦ **informal language** el lenguaje coloquial
♦ **an informal visit** una visita informal
♦ **"informal dress"** "no se requiere traje de etiqueta"

information [ɪnfə'meɪʃən] NOUN
la información (PL las informaciones) ◊ *Could you give me some information about trains to Barcelona?* ¿Podría darme información sobre trenes a Barcelona?
♦ **a piece of information** un dato

information office [ɪnfə'meɪʃənɔfɪs] NOUN
la oficina de información

information technology [ɪnfəmeɪʃəntek'nɔlədʒɪ] NOUN
la informática

infuriating [ɪn'fjuərɪeɪtɪŋ] ADJECTIVE
exasperante

ingredient [ɪn'griːdɪənt] NOUN
el ingrediente

inhabitant [ɪn'hæbɪtnt] NOUN
el/la habitante

to **inherit** [ɪn'hɛrɪt] VERB
heredar ◊ *She inherited her father's house.* Heredó la casa de su padre.

initials [ɪ'nɪʃlz] PL NOUN
las iniciales ◊ *Her initials are CDT.* Sus iniciales son CDT.

initiative [ɪ'nɪʃətɪv] NOUN
la iniciativa

to **inject** [ɪn'dʒɛkt] VERB
inyectar ◊ *They injected me with antibiotics.* Me inyectaron antibióticos.

injection [ɪn'dʒɛkʃən] NOUN
la inyección (PL las inyecciones) ◊ *The doctor gave me an injection.* El médico me puso una inyección.

to **injure** ['ɪndʒə^r] VERB
herir* ◊ *He injured his leg.* Se hirió la pierna.

injured ['ɪndʒəd] ADJECTIVE
herido

injury ['ɪndʒərɪ] NOUN (PL **injuries**)
la lesión (PL las lesiones)

injury time ['ɪndʒərɪtaɪm] NOUN
el tiempo de descuento

injustice [ɪn'dʒʌstɪs] NOUN
la injusticia

ink [ɪŋk] NOUN
la tinta

in-laws ['ɪnlɔːz] PL NOUN
los suegros

inn [ɪn] NOUN
el hostal

I

inner ['ɪnəʳ] ADJECTIVE
interior
◆**the inner city** los núcleos urbanos deprimidos
inner tube ['ɪnətju:b] NOUN
la cámara de aire
innocent ['ɪnəsnt] ADJECTIVE
inocente
inquest ['ɪnkwɛst] NOUN
la investigación judicial (PL las investigaciones judiciales)
to **inquire** [ɪn'kwaɪəʳ] VERB
◆**to inquire about something** informarse acerca de algo
inquiry [ɪn'kwaɪərɪ] NOUN (PL **inquiries**)
(*official investigation*)
la investigación (PL las investigaciones)
inquisitive [ɪn'kwɪzɪtɪv] ADJECTIVE
curioso
insane [ɪn'seɪn] ADJECTIVE
loco
inscription [ɪn'skrɪpʃən] NOUN
la inscripción (PL las inscripciones)
insect ['ɪnsɛkt] NOUN
el insecto
insect repellent ['ɪnsɛktrɪ'pɛlənt] NOUN
la loción anti-insectos (PL las lociones anti-insectos)
insensitive [ɪn'sɛnsɪtɪv] ADJECTIVE
insensible
to **insert** [ɪn'sə:t] VERB
introducir* ◊ *I inserted the coin into the slot.* Introducí la moneda en la ranura.
inside ['ɪn'saɪd] NOUN
see also **inside** PREPOSITION, ADVERB
el interior
inside ['ɪn'saɪd] PREPOSITION, ADVERB
see also **inside** NOUN
dentro ◊ *inside the house* dentro de la casa ◊ *He opened the envelope and read what was inside.* Abrió el sobre y leyó lo que había dentro.
◆**Come inside!** ¡Entra!
◆**Let's go inside, it's starting to rain.** Entremos, está empezando a llover.
◆**inside out** al revés ◊ *He put his jumper on inside out.* Se puso el jersey al revés.
insincere [ɪnsɪn'sɪəʳ] ADJECTIVE
falso
to **insist** [ɪn'sɪst] VERB
insistir ◊ *I didn't want to, but he insisted.* Yo no quería, pero él insistió. ◊ *He insisted he was innocent.* Insistía en que era inocente.
◆**to insist on doing something** insistir en hacer algo ◊ *She insisted on paying.* Insistió en pagar.
to **inspect** [ɪn'spɛkt] VERB
inspeccionar
inspector [ɪn'spɛktəʳ] NOUN
el inspector
la inspectora
to **install** [ɪn'stɔ:l] VERB
instalar
instalment [ɪn'stɔ:lmənt] NOUN
1 el plazo (*of payment*) ◊ *to pay in instalments* pagar* a plazos
2 el episodio (*of TV, radio serial*)
3 el fascículo (*of publication*)
instance ['ɪnstəns] NOUN
◆**for instance** por ejemplo
instant ['ɪnstənt] ADJECTIVE
see also **instant** NOUN
inmediato ◊ *It was an instant success.* Fue un éxito inmediato.
◆**instant coffee** el café instantáneo
instant ['ɪnstənt] NOUN
see also **instant** ADJECTIVE
el instante
instantly ['ɪnstəntlɪ] ADVERB
al instante
instead [ɪn'stɛd] PREPOSITION, ADVERB
◆**instead of** en lugar de ◊ *We played tennis instead of going swimming.* Jugamos al tenis en lugar de ir a nadar. ◊ *She went instead of Peter.* En lugar de ir Peter, fue ella.
◆**The pool was closed, so we played tennis instead.** La piscina estaba cerrada, así que jugamos al tenis.
instinct ['ɪnstɪŋkt] NOUN
el instinto
institute ['ɪnstɪtju:t] NOUN
el instituto
institution [ɪnstɪ'tju:ʃən] NOUN
la institución (PL las instituciones)
to **instruct** [ɪn'strʌkt] VERB
◆**to instruct somebody to do something** ordenar a alguien que haga algo
***ordenar que** has to be followed by a verb in the subjunctive.*
◊ *She instructed us to wait outside.* Nos ordenó que esperáramos fuera.
instructions [ɪn'strʌkʃənz] PL NOUN
las instrucciones
instructor [ɪn'strʌktəʳ] NOUN
el instructor
la instructora
◊ *skiing instructor* el instructor de esquí
◊ *driving instructor* el instructor de autoescuela
instrument ['ɪnstrumənt] NOUN
el instrumento ◊ *Do you play an instrument?* ¿Tocas algún instrumento?
insufficient [ɪnsə'fɪʃənt] ADJECTIVE
insuficiente
insulin ['ɪnsjulɪn] NOUN
la insulina
insult ['ɪnsʌlt] NOUN
see also **insult** VERB

el insulto

to **insult** [ɪn'sʌlt] VERB
see also **insult** NOUN
insultar

insurance [ɪn'ʃuərəns] NOUN
el seguro ◊ *his car insurance* su seguro de automóvil
♦ **an insurance policy** una póliza de seguros

intelligent [ɪn'tɛlɪdʒənt] ADJECTIVE
inteligente

to **intend** [ɪn'tɛnd] VERB
♦ **to intend to do something** tener* la intención de hacer algo ◊ *I intend to do languages at university.* Tengo la intención de estudiar idiomas en la universidad.

intense [ɪn'tɛns] ADJECTIVE
intenso

intensive [ɪn'tɛnsɪv] ADJECTIVE
intensivo

intention [ɪn'tɛnʃən] NOUN
la intención (PL las intenciones)

intercom ['ɪntəkɔm] NOUN
el interfono

interest ['ɪntrɪst] NOUN
see also **interest** VERB
1 el interés (PL los intereses) ◊ *to show an interest in something* mostrar* interés en algo
2 la afición (PL las aficiones) ◊ *My main interest is music.* Mi mayor afición es la música.
♦ **It's in your own interest to study hard.** Te conviene estudiar mucho.

to **interest** ['ɪntrɪst] VERB
see also **interest** NOUN
interesar ◊ *It doesn't interest me.* No me interesa.
♦ **to be interested in something** estar* interesado en algo ◊ *I'm very interested in what you're telling me.* Estoy muy interesado en lo que me dices.
♦ **Are you interested in politics?** ¿Te interesa la política?

interesting ['ɪntrɪstɪŋ] ADJECTIVE
interesante

interior [ɪn'tɪərɪə[r]] NOUN
el interior

interior designer [ɪn'tɪərɪədɪ'zaɪnə[r]] NOUN
el diseñador de interiores
la diseñadora de interiores

intermediate [ɪntə'mi:dɪət] ADJECTIVE
intermedio

internal [ɪn'tə:nl] ADJECTIVE
interno

international [ɪntə'næʃənl] ADJECTIVE
internacional

internet ['ɪntənɛt] NOUN
el/la Internet ◊ *on the internet* en Internet

internet café ['ɪntənɛtkæfeɪ] NOUN
el cibercafé

internet user ['ɪntənɛt] NOUN
el/la internauta

to **interpret** [ɪn'tə:prɪt'ju:zə[r]] VERB
hacer* de intérprete ◊ *Steve couldn't speak Spanish so his friend interpreted.* Steve no hablaba español, así que su amigo hizo de intérprete.

interpreter [ɪn'tə:prɪtə[r]] NOUN
el/la intérprete

to **interrupt** [ɪntə'rʌpt] VERB
interrumpir

interruption [ɪntə'rʌpʃən] NOUN
la interrupción (PL las interrupciones)

interval ['ɪntəvl] NOUN
el intervalo

interview ['ɪntəvju:] NOUN
see also **interview** VERB
la entrevista

to **interview** ['ɪntəvju:] VERB
see also **interview** NOUN
entrevistar ◊ *I was interviewed on the radio.* Me entrevistaron en la radio.

interviewer ['ɪntəvjuə[r]] NOUN
el entrevistador
la entrevistadora

intimate ['ɪntɪmət] ADJECTIVE
íntimo

into ['ɪntu] PREPOSITION
1 a ◊ *I'm going into town.* Voy a la ciudad. ◊ *Translate it into Spanish.* Tradúcelo al español. ◊ *He got into the car.* Subió al coche.
2 en ◊ *to get into bed* meterse en la cama ◊ *I poured the milk into a cup.* Vertí la leche en una taza. ◊ *They divided into two groups.* Se dividieron en dos grupos.
♦ **to walk into a lamppost** tropezar* con una farola

intranet ['ɪntrənɛt] NOUN
la intranet

to **introduce** [ɪntrə'dju:s] VERB
presentar ◊ *He introduced me to his parents.* Me presentó a sus padres.

introduction [ɪntrə'dʌkʃən] NOUN
(*in book*)
la introducción (PL las introducciones)

intruder [ɪn'tru:də[r]] NOUN
el intruso
la intrusa

intuition [ɪntju:'ɪʃən] NOUN
la intuición (PL las intuiciones)

to **invade** [ɪn'veɪd] VERB
invadir

invalid ['ɪnvəlɪd] NOUN
el inválido
la inválida

to **invent** [ɪn'vɛnt] VERB
inventar

invention [ɪn'vɛnʃən] NOUN
el invento

inventor [ɪn'vɛntə[r]] NOUN
el inventor

la inventora

to **invest** [ɪn'vɛst] VERB
invertir

investigation [ɪnvɛstɪ'geɪʃən] NOUN
la investigación (PL las investigaciones)

investment [ɪn'vɛstmənt] NOUN
la inversión (PL las inversiones)

invisible [ɪn'vɪzɪbl] ADJECTIVE
invisible

invitation [ɪnvɪ'teɪʃən] NOUN
la invitación (PL las invitaciones)

to **invite** [ɪn'vaɪt] VERB
invitar ◊ *Michael's not invited.* Michael no está invitado. ◊ *You're invited to a party at Claire's house.* Estás invitado a una fiesta en casa de Claire.

to **involve** [ɪn'vɔlv] VERB
suponer* ◊ *It involves a lot of work.* Supone mucho trabajo.
♦ **He wasn't involved in the robbery.** No estuvo implicado en el robo.
♦ **She was involved in politics.** Estaba metida en política.
♦ **to be involved with somebody** tener una relación con alguien ◊ *She was involved with a married man.* Tenía una relación con un hombre casado.
♦ **I don't want to get involved in the argument.** No quiero meterme en la discusión.

IQ [aɪ'kjuː] ABBREVIATION (= *intelligence quotient*)
el CI (= el coeficiente intelectual)

Iran [ɪ'rɑːn] NOUN
Irán MASC

Iraq [ɪ'rɑːk] NOUN
Iraq MASC

Ireland ['aɪələnd] NOUN
Irlanda FEM

Irish ['aɪrɪʃ] NOUN
see also **Irish** ADJECTIVE
el irlandés (*language*)
♦ **the Irish** (*people*) los irlandeses

Irish ['aɪrɪʃ] ADJECTIVE
see also **Irish** NOUN
irlandés MASC (PL irlandeses)
irlandesa FEM

Irishman ['aɪrɪʃmən] NOUN (PL **Irishmen**)
el irlandés (PL los irlandeses)

Irishwoman ['aɪrɪʃwumən] NOUN (PL **Irishwomen**)
la irlandesa

iron ['aɪən] NOUN
see also **iron** VERB
1 la plancha (*for clothes*)
2 el hierro (*metal*)

to **iron** ['aɪən] VERB
see also **iron** NOUN
planchar

ironic [aɪ'rɔnɪk] ADJECTIVE
irónico

ironing ['aɪənɪŋ] NOUN
♦ **to do the ironing** planchar
♦ **I hate ironing.** No me gusta nada planchar.

ironing board ['aɪənɪŋbɔːd] NOUN
la tabla de planchar

ironmonger's ['aɪənmʌŋgəz] NOUN
la ferretería

irrelevant [ɪ'rɛləvənt] ADJECTIVE
irrelevante ◊ *That's irrelevant.* Eso es irrelevante.

irresponsible [ɪrɪ'spɔnsɪbl] ADJECTIVE
irresponsable ◊ *That was irresponsible of him.* Eso fue irresponsable por su parte.

irritating ['ɪrɪteɪtɪŋ] ADJECTIVE
irritante

is [ɪz] VERB *see* **be**

Islam ['ɪzlɑːm] NOUN
el Islam

Islamic [ɪz'læmɪk] ADJECTIVE
islámico ◊ *Islamic law* la ley islámica

island ['aɪlənd] NOUN
la isla

isle [aɪl] NOUN
♦ **the Isle of Man** la Isla de Man
♦ **the Isle of Wight** la Isla de Wight

isn't ['ɪznt] = **is not**

isolated ['aɪsəleɪtɪd] ADJECTIVE
aislado

ISP [aɪes'piː] NOUN (= *internet Service Provider*)
el proveedor de servicios de internet

Israel ['ɪzreɪl] NOUN
Israel MASC

issue ['ɪʃjuː] NOUN
see also **issue** VERB
1 el tema
*Although **tema** ends in **-a**, it is actually a masculine noun.*
◊ *a controversial issue* un tema polémico
2 el número (*magazine*) ◊ *a back issue* un número atrasado

to **issue** ['ɪʃjuː] VERB
see also **issue** NOUN
1 hacer* público ◊ *The minister issued a statement yesterday.* El ministro hizo pública una declaración ayer.
2 proporcionar (*equipment, supplies*)

it [ɪt] PRONOUN
*When **it** is the subject of a sentence it is practically never translated.*
◊ *Where's my book? – It's on the table.* ¿Dónde está mi libro? – Está sobre la mesa. ◊ *It's raining.* Está lloviendo. ◊ *It's six o'clock.* Son las seis. ◊ *It's Friday tomorrow.* Mañana es viernes. ◊ *It's expensive.* Es caro. ◊ *Who is it? – It's me.* ¿Quién es? – Soy yo.

* Verbs marked with this symbol are irregular. See pages 380-382 for further details

*When **it** is the direct object of the verb in a sentence, use **lo** if it stands for a masculine noun or **la** if it stands for a feminine noun.*

◊ *There's a croissant left. Do you want it?* Queda un croissant. ¿Lo quieres? ◊ *I doubt it.* Lo dudo. ◊ *It's a good film. Have you seen it?* Es una buena película. ¿La has visto?

*Use **le** when **it** is the indirect object of the verb in the sentence.*

◊ *Give it another coat of paint.* Dale otra mano de pintura.

*For general concepts use the word **ello**.*

◊ *I spoke to him about it.* Hablé con él sobre ello. ◊ *I'm against it.* Estoy en contra de ello.

Italian [ɪ'tæljən] ADJECTIVE
see also **Italian** NOUN
italiano

Italian [ɪ'tæljən] NOUN
see also **Italian** ADJECTIVE
1 (*person*)
el italiano
la italiana
◊ *the Italians* los italianos
2 (*language*)
el italiano

italics [ɪ'tælɪks] PL NOUN
la cursiva ◊ *in italics* en cursiva

Italy ['ɪtəlɪ] NOUN
Italia FEM

to **itch** [ɪtʃ] VERB
picar* ◊ *It itches.* Me pica. ◊ *My head is itching.* Me pica la cabeza.

itchy ['ɪtʃɪ] ADJECTIVE
♦ **My head's itchy.** Me pica la cabeza.
♦ **I've got an itchy nose.** Me pica la nariz.

it'd ['ɪtd] = **it had**, = **it would**

item ['aɪtəm] NOUN
1 la pieza ◊ *a collector's item* una pieza de colección
2 el artículo ◊ *The first item he bought was an alarm clock.* El primer artículo que compró fue un despertador.
3 la partida ◊ *He checked the items on his bill.* Comprobó las partidas de su factura.
4 el punto ◊ *The next item on the agenda is...* El siguiente punto del orden del día es...
♦ **an item of news** una noticia

itinerary [aɪ'tɪnərərɪ] NOUN (PL **itineraries**)
el itinerario

it'll ['ɪtl] = **it will**

its [ɪts] ADJECTIVE
su (PL sus) ◊ *Everything in its place.* Cada cosa en su sitio. ◊ *It has its advantages.* Tiene sus ventajas.

***Its** is usually translated by the definite article **el/los** or **la/las** when it's clear from the sentence who the possessor is or when referring to clothing or parts of the body.*

◊ *The dog is losing its hair.* El perro está perdiendo el pelo. ◊ *The bird was in its cage.* El pájaro estaba en la jaula.

it's [ɪts] = **it is**, = **it has**

itself [ɪt'sɛlf] PRONOUN
se (*reflexive*) ◊ *The heating switches itself off.* La calefacción se apaga sola. ◊ *The dog scratched itself.* El perro se rascó.
♦ **The lesson itself was easy but the homework was very difficult.** la clase en sí fue fácil, pero les deberes eran difíciles.

I've [aɪv] = **I have**

I

J

jab [dʒæb] NOUN
la <u>inyección</u> (PL las inyecciones)

jack [dʒæk] NOUN
[1] el <u>gato</u> ◊ *The jack's in the boot.* El gato está en el maletero.
[2] la <u>jota</u> (*in ordinary pack of cards*)
[3] la <u>sota</u> (*in Spanish pack of cards*)

jacket ['dʒækɪt] NOUN
la <u>chaqueta</u>
♦ **jacket potatoes** las patatas asadas con piel (las papas asadas con cáscara *LatAm*)

jackpot ['dʒækpɔt] NOUN
el <u>premio gordo</u> ◊ *to win the jackpot* sacarse* el premio gordo

jail [dʒeɪl] NOUN
see also **jail** VERB
la <u>cárcel</u> ◊ *to go to jail* ir* a la cárcel

to **jail** [dʒeɪl] VERB
see also **jail** NOUN
♦ **He was jailed for ten years.** Lo condenaron a diez años de cárcel.

jam [dʒæm] NOUN
la <u>mermelada</u> ◊ *strawberry jam* la mermelada de fresas
♦ **a traffic jam** un atasco

jammed [dʒæmd] ADJECTIVE
<u>atascado</u> ◊ *The window's jammed.* La ventana está atascada.

jam-packed [dʒæm'pækt] ADJECTIVE
<u>atestado</u> ◊ *The room was jam-packed.* La habitación estaba atestada.

janitor ['dʒænɪtə^r] NOUN
el/la <u>conserje</u> ◊ *He's a janitor.* Es conserje.

January ['dʒænjuərɪ] NOUN
<u>enero</u> MASC ◊ *in January* en enero ◊ *the January sales* las rebajas de enero

Japan [dʒə'pæn] NOUN
el <u>Japón</u> MASC

Japanese [dʒæpə'ni:z] ADJECTIVE
see also **Japanese** NOUN
<u>japonés</u> MASC (PL japoneses)
<u>japonesa</u> FEM

Japanese [dʒæpə'ni:z] NOUN (PL **Japanese**)
see also **Japanese** ADJECTIVE
[1] (*person*)
el <u>japonés</u>
la <u>japonesa</u>
◊ *the Japanese* los japoneses
[2] (*language*)
el <u>japonés</u>

jar [dʒɑ:^r] NOUN
el <u>tarro</u> ◊ *a jar of honey* un tarro de miel

jaundice ['dʒɔ:ndɪs] NOUN
la <u>ictericia</u> ◊ *He's got jaundice.* Tiene ictericia.

javelin ['dʒævlɪn] NOUN
la <u>jabalina</u>

jaw [dʒɔ:] NOUN
la <u>mandíbula</u>

jazz [dʒæz] NOUN
el <u>jazz</u>

jealous ['dʒɛləs] ADJECTIVE
<u>celoso</u> ◊ *to be jealous* estar* celoso

jeans [dʒi:nz] PL NOUN
los <u>vaqueros</u> ◊ *a pair of jeans* unos vaqueros

Jehovah's Witness [dʒɪhəuvəz'wɪtnɪs] NOUN (PL **Jehovah's Witnesses**)
el/la <u>testigo de Jehová</u> ◊ *She's a Jehovah's Witness.* Es testigo de Jehová.

Jello ® ['dʒɛləu] NOUN US
la <u>gelatina</u>

jelly ['dʒɛlɪ] NOUN (PL **jellies**)
la <u>gelatina</u>

jellyfish ['dʒɛlɪfɪʃ] NOUN (PL **jellyfish**)
la <u>medusa</u>

jersey ['dʒə:zɪ] NOUN
el <u>jersey</u> (PL los jerseys)

Jesus ['dʒi:zəs] NOUN
<u>Jesús</u> MASC

jet [dʒɛt] NOUN
el <u>reactor</u>

jet lag ['dʒɛtlæg] NOUN
♦ **to be suffering from jet lag** tener* jet lag

jetty ['dʒɛtɪ] NOUN (PL **jetties**)
el <u>embarcadero</u>

Jew [dʒu:] NOUN
el <u>judío</u>
la <u>judía</u>

jewel ['dʒu:əl] NOUN
la <u>joya</u>

jeweller ['dʒu:ələ^r] NOUN (US **jeweler**)
el <u>joyero</u>
la <u>joyera</u>
◊ *She's a jeweller.* Es joyera.

jeweller's shop ['dʒu:ələzʃɔp] NOUN (US **jeweler's shop**)
la <u>joyería</u>

jewellery ['dʒu:əlrɪ] NOUN (US **jewelry**)
las <u>joyas</u>

Jewish ['dʒu:ɪʃ] ADJECTIVE
<u>judío</u>

jigsaw ['dʒɪgsɔ:] NOUN
el <u>rompecabezas</u> (PL los rompecabezas)

job [dʒɔb] NOUN
el <u>trabajo</u> ◊ *a part-time job* un trabajo de media jornada

♦ **You've done a good job.** Lo has hecho muy bien.

job centre ['dʒɔbsɛntəʳ] NOUN
la oficina de empleo

jobless ['dʒɔblɪs] ADJECTIVE
desempleado

jockey ['dʒɔkɪ] NOUN
el/la jockey (PL los/las jockeys)

to **jog** [dʒɔg] VERB
hacer* footing

jogging ['dʒɔgɪŋ] NOUN
el footing ◇ *to go jogging* hacer* footing

john [dʒɔn] NOUN US
el wáter

to **join** [dʒɔɪn] VERB
hacerse* socio de ◇ *I'm going to join the ski club.* Voy a hacerme socio del club de esquí.
♦ **I'll join you later if I can.** Yo iré luego si puedo.
♦ **If you're going for a walk, do you mind if I join you?** Si vais a dar un paseo, ¿os importa que os acompañe?

to **join in** [dʒɔɪn'ɪn] VERB
♦ **He doesn't join in with what we do.** No participa en lo que hacemos.
♦ **She started singing, and the audience joined in.** Empezó a cantar, y el público se unió a ella.

joiner ['dʒɔɪnəʳ] NOUN
el carpintero
la carpintera
◇ *He's a joiner.* Es carpintero.

joint [dʒɔɪnt] NOUN
1 la articulación (PL las articulaciones) ◇ *I've got pains in my joints.* Me duelen las articulaciones.
2 (*informal*) (*drugs*)
el porro
♦ **We had a joint of lamb for lunch.** Comimos asado de cordero.

joke [dʒəuk] NOUN
see also **joke** VERB
1 la broma ◇ *Don't get upset, it was only a joke.* No te enfades, era sólo una broma.
♦ **to play a joke on somebody** gastarle una broma a alguien
2 el chiste
♦ **to tell a joke** contar* un chiste

to **joke** [dʒəuk] VERB
see also **joke** NOUN
bromear
♦ **You must be joking!** ¡Estás de broma!

jolly ['dʒɔlɪ] ADJECTIVE
alegre

Jordan ['dʒɔ:dən] NOUN
Jordania FEM

to **jot down** [dʒɔt'daun] VERB
apuntar

jotter ['dʒɔtəʳ] NOUN
el bloc (PL los blocs)

journalism ['dʒə:nəlɪzəm] NOUN
el periodismo

journalist ['dʒə:nəlɪst] NOUN
el/la periodista ◇ *I'm a journalist.* Soy periodista.

journey ['dʒə:nɪ] NOUN
el viaje ◇ *to go on a journey* hacer* un viaje
♦ **The journey to school takes about half an hour.** Se tarda una media hora en ir al colegio.

joy [dʒɔɪ] NOUN
la alegría

joystick ['dʒɔɪstɪk] NOUN
el mando (*for computer games*)

judge [dʒʌdʒ] NOUN
see also **judge** VERB
el/la juez (PL los/las jueces)

to **judge** [dʒʌdʒ] VERB
see also **judge** NOUN
juzgar*

judo ['dʒu:dəu] NOUN
el judo ◇ *My favourite sport is judo.* Mi deporte favorito es el judo.

jug [dʒʌg] NOUN
la jarra

juggler ['dʒʌgləʳ] NOUN
el/la malabarista

juice [dʒu:s] NOUN
el zumo ◇ *orange juice* el zumo de naranja

July [dʒu:'laɪ] NOUN
julio MASC ◇ *in July* en julio

jumble sale ['dʒʌmblseɪl] NOUN

> ℹ *Un **jumble sale** es un mercadillo con fines benéficos donde se venden objetos de segunda mano a precios baratos.*

to **jump** [dʒʌmp] VERB
saltar ◇ *They jumped over the wall.* Saltaron el muro. ◇ *He jumped out of the window.* Saltó por la ventana. ◇ *He jumped off the roof.* Saltó del tejado.
♦ **You made me jump!** ¡Qué susto me has dado!

jumper ['dʒʌmpəʳ] NOUN
el jersey (PL los jerseys)

junction ['dʒʌŋkʃən] NOUN
el cruce (*of roads*)

June [dʒu:n] NOUN
junio MASC ◇ *in June* en junio

jungle ['dʒʌŋgl] NOUN
la selva

junior school ['dʒu:nɪəsku:l] NOUN
el colegio

junk [dʒʌŋk] NOUN
los trastos viejos ◇ *The attic's full of junk.* El desván está lleno de trastos viejos.

J

☞

♦**to eat junk food** comer porquerías
♦**junk shop** la tienda de objetos usados

jury ['dʒuərɪ] NOUN (PL **juries**)
el jurado

just [dʒʌst] ADVERB
1 justo ◊ *just in time* justo a tiempo ◊ *just after Christmas* justo después de Navidad ◊ *We had just enough money.* Teníamos el dinero justo.
♦**He's just arrived.** Acaba de llegar.
♦**I did it just now.** Lo acabo de hacer.
♦**I'm rather busy just now.** Ahora mismo estoy bastante ocupada.
♦**I'm just coming!** ¡Ya voy!
♦**just here** aquí mismo
2 sólo ◊ *It's just a suggestion.* Es sólo una sugerencia.
♦**I just thought that you would like it.** Yo pensé que te gustaría.
♦**Just a minute!** ¡Un momento!
♦**just about** casi ◊ *It's just about finished.* Está casi terminado.

justice ['dʒʌstɪs] NOUN
la justicia

to **justify** ['dʒʌstɪfaɪ] VERB (**justified, justified**)
justificar*

* Verbs marked with this symbol are irregular. See pages 380-382 for further details

K

kangaroo [kæŋgəˈruː] NOUN
el canguro
karate [kəˈrɑːtɪ] NOUN
el kárate ◊ *My favourite sport is karate.* Mi deporte favorito es el kárate.
kebab [kəˈbæb] NOUN
el pincho moruno
keen [kiːn] ADJECTIVE
entusiasta ◊ *a keen supporter* un hincha entusiasta
♦ **He doesn't seem very keen.** No parece muy entusiasmado.
♦ **She's a keen student.** Es una alumna aplicada.
♦ **I'm not very keen on maths.** No me gustan mucho las matemáticas.
♦ **He's keen on her.** Ella le gusta.
♦ **to be keen on doing something** tener* ganas de hacer algo ◊ *I'm not very keen on going.* No tengo muchas ganas de ir.
to **keep** [kiːp] VERB (**kept, kept**)
1 quedarse con ◊ *You can keep the watch.* Puedes quedarte con el reloj.
♦ **You can keep it.** Puedes quedártelo.
2 mantenerse* (*remain*) ◊ *to keep fit* mantenerse en forma
♦ **Keep still!** ¡Estáte quieto!
♦ **Keep quiet!** ¡Cállate!
3 seguir* ◊ *Keep straight on.* Siga recto.
♦ **I keep forgetting my keys.** Siempre me olvido las llaves.
♦ **"keep out"** "prohibida la entrada"
♦ **"keep off the grass"** "prohibido pisar el césped"
to **keep on** [kiːpˈɔn] VERB
continuar* ◊ *He kept on reading.* Continuó leyendo.
♦ **The car keeps on breaking down.** El coche no deja de averiarse.
to **keep up** [kiːpˈʌp] VERB
♦ **Matthew walks so fast I can't keep up.** Matthew camina tan rápido que no puedo seguirle el ritmo.
keep-fit [kiːpˈfɪt] NOUN
la gimnasia ◊ *I go to keep-fit classes.* Voy a clases de gimnasia.
kennel [ˈkɛnl] NOUN
la caseta del perro (*in garden*)
♦ **a kennels** una residencia canina
kept [kɛpt] VERB *see* **keep**
kerosene [ˈkɛrəsiːn] NOUN US
el queroseno
kettle [ˈkɛtl] NOUN
el hervidor
key [kiː] NOUN
la llave
keyboard [ˈkiːbɔːd] NOUN
el teclado
keyring [ˈkiːrɪŋ] NOUN
el llavero
kick [kɪk] NOUN
see also **kick** VERB
la patada
to **kick** [kɪk] VERB
see also **kick** NOUN
♦ **to kick somebody** dar* una patada a alguien ◊ *He kicked me.* Me dio una patada.
♦ **He kicked the ball hard.** Le dio un puntapié fuerte al balón.
♦ **to kick off** hacer* el saque inicial (*in football*)
kick-off [ˈkɪkɔf] NOUN
el saque inicial
♦ **The kick-off is at 10 o'clock.** El partido empieza a las diez.
kid [kɪd] NOUN (*informal*)
see also **kid** VERB
el crío
la cría
♦ **the kids** los críos
to **kid** [kɪd] VERB
see also **kid** NOUN
bromear ◊ *I'm not kidding, it's snowing.* No estoy bromeando, está nevando.
♦ **I'm just kidding.** Es una broma.
to **kidnap** [ˈkɪdnæp] VERB
secuestrar
kidney [ˈkɪdnɪ] NOUN
el riñón (PL los riñones) ◊ *He's got kidney trouble.* Tiene problemas de riñón. ◊ *I don't like kidneys.* No me gustan los riñones.
to **kill** [kɪl] VERB
matar ◊ *She killed her husband.* Mató a su marido.
♦ **to be killed** morir* ◊ *He was killed in a car accident.* Murió en un accidente de coche.
♦ **to kill oneself** suicidarse ◊ *He killed himself.* Se suicidó.
killer [ˈkɪləʳ] NOUN
1 (*murderer*)
el asesino
la asesina
◊ *The police are searching for the killer.* La policía está buscando al asesino.
2 (*hired killer*)
el asesino a sueldo
la asesina a sueldo
♦ **Meningitis can be a killer.** La meningitis puede ser mortal.
kilo [ˈkiːləu] NOUN (PL **kilos**)
el kilo ◊ *at £5 a kilo* a 5 libras esterlinas el kilo

kilometre ['kɪləmiːtə^r] NOUN (US **kilometer**)
el kilómetro

kilt [kɪlt] NOUN
la falda escocesa

kind [kaɪnd] ADJECTIVE
see also **kind** NOUN
amable ◊ *to be kind to somebody* ser* amable con alguien
♦ **Thank you for being so kind.** Gracias por su amabilidad.

kind [kaɪnd] NOUN
see also **kind** ADJECTIVE
el tipo ◊ *It's a kind of sausage.* Es un tipo de salchicha.

kindergarten ['kɪndəgɑːtn] NOUN
el jardín de infancia (PL los jardines de infancia)

kindly ['kaɪndlɪ] ADVERB
amablemente

kindness ['kaɪndnɪs] NOUN
la amabilidad

king [kɪŋ] NOUN
el rey
♦ **the King and Queen** los reyes

kingdom ['kɪŋdəm] NOUN
el reino

kiosk ['kiːɔsk] NOUN
el quiosco (*stall*)
♦ **a telephone kiosk** una cabina telefónica

kipper ['kɪpə^r] NOUN
el arenque ahumado

kiss [kɪs] NOUN (PL **kisses**)
see also **kiss** VERB
el beso

to **kiss** [kɪs] VERB
see also **kiss** NOUN
1 besar ◊ *He kissed her passionately.* La besó apasionadamente.
2 besarse ◊ *Adam and Rachel kissed.* Adam y Rachel se besaron.

kit [kɪt] NOUN
el equipo ◊ *I've forgotten my gym kit again.* Me he olvidado el equipo de gimnasia otra vez.
♦ **a tool kit** un juego de herramientas
♦ **a sewing kit** un costurero
♦ **a first-aid kit** un botiquín
♦ **a puncture repair kit** un juego de reparación de pinchazos
♦ **a drum kit** una batería

kitchen ['kɪtʃɪn] NOUN
la cocina ◊ *a fitted kitchen* una cocina amueblada
♦ **the kitchen units** los armarios de cocina
♦ **a kitchen knife** un cuchillo de cocina

kite [kaɪt] NOUN
la cometa

kitten ['kɪtn] NOUN
el gatito
la gatita

knee [niː] NOUN
la rodilla ◊ *to be on one's knees* estar* de rodillas

to **kneel** [niːl] VERB (**knelt** *o* **kneeled, knelt** *o* **kneeled**)
arrodillarse

to **kneel down** [niːl'daun] VERB
arrodillarse

knew [njuː] VERB *see* **know**

knickers ['nɪkəz] PL NOUN
las bragas (los calzones *LatAm*)
♦ **a pair of knickers** unas bragas

knife [naɪf] NOUN (PL **knives**)
el cuchillo
♦ **a kitchen knife** un cuchillo de cocina
♦ **a sheath knife** un cuchillo de monte
♦ **a penknife** una navaja

to **knit** [nɪt] VERB
hacer* punto (tejer *LatAm*) ◊ *I like knitting.* Me gusta hacer punto.
♦ **She is knitting a jumper.** Está haciendo un jersey a punto.

knives [naɪvz] PL NOUN *see* **knife**

knob [nɔb] NOUN
1 el pomo (*on door*)
2 el dial (*on radio, TV*)

to **knock** [nɔk] VERB
see also **knock** NOUN
llamar ◊ *Someone's knocking at the door.* Alguien llama a la puerta.
♦ **to knock somebody down** atropellar a alguien ◊ *She was knocked down by a car.* La atropelló un coche.
♦ **to knock somebody out (1)** (*defeat*) eliminar a alguien ◊ *They were knocked out early in the tournament.* Fueron eliminados al poco de iniciarse el torneo.
♦ **to knock somebody out (2)** (*stun*) dejar sin sentido a alguien ◊ *They knocked out the watchman.* Dejaron al vigilante sin sentido.

knock [nɔk] NOUN
see also **knock** VERB
el golpe

knot [nɔt] NOUN
el nudo ◊ *to tie a knot in something* hacer* un nudo en algo

to **know** [nəu] VERB (**knew, known**)
Use ***saber*** *for knowing facts,* ***conocer*** *for knowing people and places.*
1 saber* ◊ *Yes, I know.* Sí, ya lo sé. ◊ *I don't know.* No sé. ◊ *I don't know any German.* No sé nada de alemán.
♦ **to know that** saber* que ◊ *I didn't know that your Dad was a policeman.* No sabía que tu padre era policía.
2 conocer* ◊ *I know her.* La conozco. ◊ *I know Paris well.* Conozco bien París.
♦ **to know about something (1)** (*be aware of*) estar* enterado de algo ◊ *Do you*

* Verbs marked with this symbol are irregular. See pages 380-382 for further details

know about the meeting this afternoon? ¿Estás enterado de la reunión de esta tarde?

♦ to know about something (2) (*be knowledgeable about*) saber* de algo ◊ *He knows a lot about cars.* Sabe mucho de coches. ◊ *I don't know much about computers.* No sé mucho de ordenadores.

♦ to get to know somebody llegar* a conocer a alguien

♦ How should I know? ¿Y yo qué sé?

♦ You never know! ¡Nunca se sabe!

know-all ['nəuɔːl] NOUN
el/la sabelotodo ◊ *He's such a know-all!* ¡Es un sabelotodo!

know-how ['nəuhau] NOUN
la pericia

knowledge ['nɔlɪdʒ] NOUN
el conocimiento ◊ *scientific knowledge* el conocimiento científico

♦ my knowledge of French mis conocimientos de francés

knowledgeable ['nɔlɪdʒəbl] ADJECTIVE

♦ to be knowledgeable about something saber* mucho de algo

known [nəun] VERB *see* **know**

Koran [kɔ'rɑːn] NOUN
el Corán

Korea [kə'rɪə] NOUN
Corea FEM

kosher ['kəuʃər] ADJECTIVE
kosher

K

L

lab [læb] NOUN
el laboratorio ◊ *a lab technician* un técnico de laboratorio
label ['leɪbl] NOUN
la etiqueta
labor ['leɪbəʳ] NOUN US
♦ **to be in labor** estar* de parto
♦ **the labor market** el mercado de trabajo
♦ **labor union** el sindicato
laboratory [lə'bɔrətərɪ] NOUN (PL **laboratories**)
el laboratorio
Labour ['leɪbəʳ] NOUN
los laboristas ◊ *My parents vote Labour.* Mis padres votan a los laboristas.
♦ **the Labour Party** el Partido Laborista
labour ['leɪbəʳ] NOUN
♦ **to be in labour** estar* de parto
♦ **the labour market** el mercado de trabajo
labourer ['leɪbərəʳ] NOUN
el peón (PL los peones)
♦ **farm labourer** el jornalero
lace [leɪs] NOUN
1 (*of shoe*)
el cordón (PL los cordones)
2 el encaje ◊ *a lace collar* un cuello de encaje
lack [læk] NOUN
la falta ◊ *He got the job, despite his lack of experience.* Consiguió el empleo, a pesar de su falta de experiencia.
lacquer ['lækəʳ] NOUN
la laca
lad [læd] NOUN
el muchacho
ladder ['lædəʳ] NOUN
la escalera (*de mano*)
lady ['leɪdɪ] NOUN (PL **ladies**)
la señora
♦ **Ladies and gentlemen...** Damas y caballeros...
♦ **the ladies'** los servicios de señoras
♦ **a young lady** una señorita
ladybird ['leɪdɪbɜːd] NOUN
la mariquita
to **lag behind** [lægbɪ'haɪnd] VERB
quedarse atrás
lager ['lɑːgəʳ] NOUN
la cerveza rubia
laid [leɪd] VERB *see* **lay**
laid-back [leɪd'bæk] ADJECTIVE
relajado (*informal*)
lain [leɪn] VERB *see* **lie**
lake [leɪk] NOUN
el lago ◊ *Lake Michigan* el Lago Michigan

lamb [læm] NOUN
el cordero ◊ *a lamb chop* una chuleta de cordero
lame [leɪm] ADJECTIVE
cojo ◊ *to be lame* estar* cojo ◊ *The accident left her lame.* Se quedó coja después del accidente.
♦ **My pony is lame.** Mi pony cojea.
lamp [læmp] NOUN
la lámpara
lamppost ['læmppəust] NOUN
la farola
lampshade ['læmpʃeɪd] NOUN
la pantalla
land [lænd] NOUN
see also **land** VERB
la tierra ◊ *We have a lot of land.* Tenemos mucha tierra.
♦ **to work on the land** trabajar la tierra
♦ **a piece of land** un terreno
to **land** [lænd] VERB
see also **land** NOUN
aterrizar* ◊ *The plane landed at five o'clock.* El avión aterrizó a las cinco.
landing ['lændɪŋ] NOUN
1 el aterrizaje (*of plane*)
2 el rellano (*of staircase*)
landlady ['lændleɪdɪ] NOUN (PL **landladies**)
1 la casera (*of rented property*)
2 la patrona (*of pub*)
landlord ['lændlɔːd] NOUN
1 el casero (*of rented property*)
2 el patrón (PL los patrones) (*of pub*)
landmark ['lændmɑːk] NOUN
el punto de referencia ◊ *Big Ben is one of London's landmarks.* El Big Ben es uno de los puntos de referencia de Londres.
landowner ['lændəunəʳ] NOUN
el/la terrateniente
landscape ['lændskeɪp] NOUN
el paisaje
lane [leɪn] NOUN
1 el camino ◊ *a country lane* un camino rural
2 el carril ◊ *the outside lane* (*in the UK*) el carril de la derecha ◊ *the outside lane* (*on the Continent*) el carril de la izquierda
language ['læŋgwɪdʒ] NOUN
el idioma
*Although **idioma** ends in **-a**, it is actually a masculine noun.*
◊ *Greek is a difficult language.* El griego es un idioma difícil.

♦ **to use bad language** decir* palabrotas

language laboratory ['læŋgwɪdʒlə'bɔrətərɪ] NOUN (PL **language laboratories**)
el laboratorio de idiomas

lap [læp] NOUN
la vuelta ◊ *I ran 10 laps.* Corrí 10 vueltas.
♦ **Andrew was sitting on his mother's lap.** Andrew estaba sentado en el regazo de su madre.

laptop ['læptɔp] NOUN
el ordenador portátil (el computador portátil *LatAm*)

larder ['lɑːdəʳ] NOUN
la despensa

large [lɑːdʒ] ADJECTIVE
grande ◊ *a large house* una casa grande ◊ *a large dog* un perro grande
Use **gran** *before a singular noun.*
◊ *a large number of people* un gran número de personas
Be careful not to translate **large** *by* **largo**.

largely ['lɑːdʒlɪ] ADVERB
en gran parte

laser ['leɪzəʳ] NOUN
el láser

lass [læs] NOUN (PL **lasses**)
la muchacha

last [lɑːst] ADJECTIVE, ADVERB
see also **last** VERB
1 pasado ◊ *last Friday* el viernes pasado
2 último ◊ *the last time* la última vez
3 por última vez ◊ *I've lost my bag. – When did you last see it?* He perdido el bolso. – ¿Cuándo lo viste por última vez?
4 en último lugar ◊ *the team which finished last* el equipo que quedó en último lugar
♦ **He arrived last.** Llegó el último.
♦ **last night** anoche ◊ *I got home at midnight last night.* Anoche llegué a casa a medianoche. ◊ *I couldn't sleep last night.* Anoche no pude dormir.
♦ **at last** por fin

to **last** [lɑːst] VERB
see also **last** ADJECTIVE, ADVERB
durar ◊ *The concert lasts two hours.* El concierto dura dos horas.

lastly ['lɑːstlɪ] ADVERB
por último

late [leɪt] ADJECTIVE, ADVERB
tarde ◊ *Hurry up or you'll be late!* ¡Date prisa o llegarás tarde! ◊ *I'm often late for school.* A menudo llego tarde al colegio. ◊ *I went to bed late.* Me fui a la cama tarde. ◊ *to arrive late* llegar* tarde
♦ **The flight will be one hour late.** El vuelo llegará con una hora de retraso.
♦ **in the late afternoon** al final de la tarde
♦ **in late May** a finales de mayo
♦ **the late Mr Philips** el difunto Sr. Philips

lately ['leɪtlɪ] ADVERB
últimamente ◊ *I haven't seen him lately.* No lo he visto últimamente.

later ['leɪtəʳ] ADVERB
más tarde ◊ *I'll do it later.* Lo haré más tarde.
♦ **See you later!** ¡Hasta luego!

latest ['leɪtɪst] ADJECTIVE
último ◊ *their latest album* su último álbum
♦ **at the latest** como muy tarde ◊ *by 10 o'clock at the latest* a las 10 como muy tarde

Latin ['lætɪn] NOUN
el latín ◊ *I do Latin.* Estudio latín.

Latin America ['lætɪnə'mɛrɪkə] NOUN
América Latina FEM

Latin American ['lætɪnə'mɛrɪkən] ADJECTIVE
see also **Latin American** NOUN
latinoamericano

Latin American ['lætɪnə'mɛrɪkən] NOUN
see also **Latin American** ADJECTIVE
el latinoamericano
la latinoamericana

laugh [lɑːf] NOUN
see also **laugh** VERB
la risa
♦ **It was a good laugh.** Fue muy divertido.

to **laugh** [lɑːf] VERB
see also **laugh** NOUN
reírse*
♦ **to laugh at something** reírse de algo ◊ *He laughed at my accent.* Se rió de mi acento.
♦ **to laugh at somebody** reírse de alguien ◊ *They laughed at her.* Se rieron de ella.

to **launch** [lɔːntʃ] VERB
lanzar* (*product, rocket*)

Launderette ® [lɔːn'drɛt] NOUN
la lavandería automática

Laundromat ® ['lɔːndrəmæt] NOUN US
la lavandería automática

laundry ['lɔːndrɪ] NOUN
la colada ◊ *She does my laundry.* Me hace la colada.

lavatory ['lævətərɪ] NOUN (PL **lavatories**)
el servicio

lavender ['lævəndəʳ] NOUN
la lavanda

law [lɔː] NOUN
1 la ley ◊ *strict laws* leyes severas
♦ **It's against the law.** Es ilegal.
2 el derecho ◊ *My sister's studying law.* Mi hermana estudia derecho.

lawn [lɔːn] NOUN
el césped

lawnmower ['lɔːnməuəʳ] NOUN
el cortacésped

law school ['lɔːskuːl] NOUN US
la facultad de derecho

lawyer ['lɔːjəʳ] NOUN
el abogado
la abogada

◊ *My mother's a lawyer.* Mi madre es abogada.

to **lay** [leɪ] VERB **(laid, laid)**
poner* ◊ *She laid the baby in his cot.* Puso al bebé en la cuna. ◊ *to lay the table* poner* la mesa

to **lay off** [leɪ'ɔf] VERB
despedir* ◊ *My father's been laid off.* Han despedido a mi padre.

to **lay on** [leɪ'ɔn] VERB
1 proporcionar (*provide*) ◊ *They laid on extra buses.* Proporcionaron más autobuses.
2 preparar (*prepare*) ◊ *They laid on a special meal.* Prepararon una comida especial.

lay-by ['leɪbaɪ] NOUN
el área de descanso
Although it's a feminine noun, remember that you use ***el*** *and* ***un*** *with* ***área.***

layer ['leɪəʳ] NOUN
la capa

lazy ['leɪzɪ] ADJECTIVE
perezoso

lead (1) [lɛd] NOUN
el plomo (*metal*) ◊ *a lead pipe* una tubería de plomo

lead (2) [li:d] NOUN
see also **lead** VERB
1 el cable (*cable*)
2 la correa ◊ *Dogs must be kept on a lead.* Los perros deben llevarse siempre sujetos con una correa.
♦ **to be in the lead** ir* en cabeza

to **lead** [li:d] VERB **(led, led)**
see also **lead (2)** NOUN
llevar ◊ *the street that leads to the station* la calle que lleva a la estación ◊ *It could lead to a civil war.* Podría llevar a una guerra civil.
♦ **to lead the way** ir* delante

to **lead away** [li:də'weɪ] VERB
llevarse ◊ *The police led the man away.* La policía se llevó al hombre.

leaded petrol [lɛdɪd'pɛtrəl] NOUN
la gasolina con plomo

leader ['li:dəʳ] NOUN
el/la líder

lead-free petrol [lɛdfri:'pɛtrəl] NOUN
la gasolina sin plomo

lead singer [li:d'sɪŋəʳ] NOUN
el/la cantante principal

leaf [li:f] NOUN (PL **leaves**)
la hoja

leaflet ['li:flɪt] NOUN
el folleto

league [li:g] NOUN
la liga ◊ *They are at the top of the league.* Están a la cabeza de la liga.
♦ **the Premier League** la primera división

leak [li:k] NOUN
see also **leak** VERB
1 el escape ◊ *a gas leak* un escape de gas ◊ *a leak in the pipe* un escape en la tubería
2 la gotera ◊ *a leak in the roof* una gotera en el tejado

to **leak** [li:k] VERB
see also **leak** NOUN
1 tener* un agujero (*bucket, pipe*)
2 tener* goteras (*roof*)
3 salirse* (*water, gas*)

to **lean** [li:n] VERB **(leaned** *or* **leant, leaned** *or* **leant)**
apoyar ◊ *to lean something against the wall* apoyar algo contra la pared
♦ **to lean on something** apoyarse en algo ◊ *He leant on the table.* Se apoyó en la mesa.
♦ **to be leaning against something** estar* apoyado contra algo ◊ *The ladder was leaning against the wall.* La escalera estaba apoyada contra la pared.

to **lean forward** [li:n'fɔ:wəd] VERB
inclinarse hacia adelante

to **lean out** [li:n'aut] VERB
asomarse ◊ *She leant out of the window.* Se asomó a la ventana.

to **lean over** [li:n'əuvəʳ] VERB
inclinarse ◊ *Don't lean over too far.* No te inclines demasiado.

to **leap** [li:p] VERB **(leaped** *or* **leapt, leaped** *or* **leapt)**
saltar
♦ **He leapt out of his chair when his team scored.** Dio un salto de la silla cuando su equipo marcó.

leap year ['li:pjɪəʳ] NOUN
el año bisiesto

to **learn** [lə:n] VERB **(learned** *or* **learnt, learned** *or* **learnt)**
aprender ◊ *I'm learning to ski.* Estoy aprendiendo a esquiar.

learner ['lə:nəʳ] NOUN
♦ **She's a quick learner.** Aprende con mucha rapidez.
♦ **Spanish learners** los estudiantes de español

learner driver [lə:nə'draɪvəʳ] NOUN
el conductor en prácticas
la conductora en prácticas

learnt [lə:nt] VERB *see* **learn**

least [li:st] ADJECTIVE, PRONOUN, ADVERB
1 menor ◊ *I haven't the least idea.* No tengo la menor idea.
2 menos ◊ *Go for the ones with least fat.* Escoge los que tengan menos grasa. ◊ *the least expensive hotel* el hotel

* Verbs marked with this symbol are irregular. See pages 380-382 for further details

menos caro ◊ *It takes the least time.* Es lo que menos tiempo lleva. ◊ *It's the least I can do.* Es lo menos que puedo hacer. ◊ *Maths is the subject I like the least.* Las matemáticas es la asignatura que menos me gusta. ◊ *That's the least of my worries.* Eso es lo que menos me preocupa.

♦ **at least** por lo menos ◊ *It'll cost at least £200.* Costará por lo menos 200 libras esterlinas.

♦ **There was a lot of damage but at least nobody was hurt.** Hubo muchos daños pero al menos nadie resultó herido.

♦ **It's very unfair, at least that's my opinion.** Es muy injusto, al menos eso pienso yo.

leather ['lɛðəʳ] NOUN
el cuero ◊ *a black leather jacket* una chaqueta de cuero negra

leave [li:v] NOUN
see also **leave** VERB
el permiso (*from job, army*) ◊ *My brother is on leave for a week.* Mi hermano está de permiso durante una semana.

to **leave** [li:v] VERB (**left, left**)
see also **leave** NOUN
1 dejar ◊ *Don't leave your camera in the car.* No dejes la cámara en el coche.
2 salir* ◊ *The bus leaves at eight.* El autobús sale a las ocho.
3 salir* de ◊ *We leave London at six o'clock.* Salimos de Londres a las seis.
4 irse* ◊ *They left yesterday.* Se fueron ayer. ◊ *She left home when she was sixteen.* Se fue de casa a los dieciséis años.

♦ **to leave somebody alone** dejar a alguien en paz ◊ *Leave me alone!* ¡Déjame en paz!

to **leave behind** [li:vbɪ'haɪnd] VERB
dejarse ◊ *I left my umbrella behind in the shop.* Me dejé el paraguas en la tienda.

to **leave out** [li:v'aut] VERB
excluir* ◊ *Not knowing the language I felt really left out.* Al no saber el idioma me sentía muy excluido.

leaves [li:vz] PL NOUN *see* **leaf**

Lebanon ['lɛbənən] NOUN
Líbano MASC

lecture ['lɛktʃəʳ] NOUN
see also **lecture** VERB
1 la clase (*at university*)
2 la conferencia (*public*)

to **lecture** ['lɛktʃəʳ] VERB
see also **lecture** NOUN
1 dar* clases ◊ *She lectures at the technical college.* Da clases en la escuela politécnica.
2 sermonear ◊ *He's always lecturing us.* Siempre nos está sermoneando.

lecturer ['lɛktʃərəʳ] NOUN
el profesor universitario
la profesora universitaria

♦ **She's a lecturer in German.** Es profesora de alemán en la universidad.

led [lɛd] VERB *see* **lead**

leek [li:k] NOUN
el puerro

left [lɛft] VERB *see* **leave**

left [lɛft] ADJECTIVE, ADVERB
see also **left** NOUN
1 izquierdo ◊ *my left hand* mi mano izquierda
2 a la izquierda ◊ *Turn left at the traffic lights.* Doble a la izquierda al llegar al semáforo.

♦ **I haven't got any money left.** No me queda nada de dinero.

♦ **Is there any ice cream left?** ¿Queda algo de helado?

left [lɛft] NOUN
see also **left** ADJECTIVE
la izquierda ◊ *on the left* a la izquierda

left-hand ['lɛfthænd] ADJECTIVE

♦ **the left-hand side** la izquierda ◊ *It's on the left-hand side.* Está a la izquierda.

left-handed [lɛft'hændɪd] ADJECTIVE
zurdo

left-luggage office [lɛft'lʌgɪdʒɔfɪs] NOUN
la consigna

leg [lɛg] NOUN
la pierna ◊ *She's broken her leg.* Se ha roto la pierna.

♦ **a chicken leg** un muslo de pollo

♦ **a leg of lamb** una pierna de cordero

legal ['li:gl] ADJECTIVE
legal

leggings ['lɛgɪŋz] NOUN
las mallas

leisure ['lɛʒəʳ] NOUN
el tiempo libre ◊ *What do you do in your leisure time?* ¿Qué haces en tu tiempo libre?

leisure centre ['lɛʒəsɛntəʳ] NOUN
el centro recreativo

lemon ['lɛmən] NOUN
el limón (PL los limones)

lemonade [lɛmə'neɪd] NOUN
la gaseosa

to **lend** [lɛnd] VERB (**lent, lent**)
prestar ◊ *I can lend you some money.* Te puedo prestar algo de dinero.

length [lɛŋθ] NOUN
la longitud

♦ **It's about a metre in length.** Mide aproximadamente un metro de largo.

lens [lɛnz] NOUN (PL **lenses**)
1 la lentilla (el lente de contacto *LatAm*) (*contact lens*)
2 el cristal (*of spectacles*)
3 el objetivo (*of camera*)

L

Lent [lɛnt] NOUN
la Cuaresma
lent [lɛnt] VERB *see* **lend**
lentil ['lɛntɪl] NOUN
la lenteja
Leo ['liːəu] NOUN
el Leo (*sign*) ◇ *I'm Leo.* Soy Leo.
♦ **a Leo** un/una Leo
leotard ['liːətɑːd] NOUN
el leotardo
lesbian ['lɛzbɪən] NOUN
la lesbiana
less [lɛs] ADJECTIVE, PRONOUN, ADVERB
menos ◇ *A bit less, please.* Un poco menos, por favor. ◇ *It's less than a kilometre from here.* Está a menos de un kilómetro de aquí. ◇ *less than half* menos de la mitad ◇ *I've got less than you.* Tengo menos que tú. ◇ *It cost less than we thought.* Costó menos de lo que pensábamos.
♦ **less and less** cada vez menos
lesson ['lɛsn] NOUN
1 la clase ◇ *an English lesson* una clase de inglés ◇ *The lessons last forty minutes.* Las clases duran cuarenta minutos.
2 (*in textbook*)
la lección (PL las lecciones)
to **let** [lɛt] VERB **(let, let)**
1 dejar
♦ **to let somebody do something** dejar a alguien hacer algo ◇ *Let me have a look.* Déjame ver.
♦ **Let me go!** ¡Suéltame!
♦ **to let somebody know something** informar a alguien de algo ◇ *We must let him know that we are coming to stay.* Tenemos que informarle de que venimos a quedarnos.
♦ **When can you come to dinner? – I'll let you know.** ¿Cuándo puedes venir a cenar? – Ya te lo diré.
♦ **to let in** dejar entrar ◇ *They wouldn't let me in because I was under 18.* No me dejaron entrar porque tenía menos de 18 años.

*To make suggestions using **let's**, you can ask questions using **por qué no**.*

◇ *Let's go to the cinema!* ¿Por qué no vamos al cine?
♦ **Let's have a break! – Yes, let's.** Vamos a descansar un poco. – ¡Buena idea!
2 alquilar ◇ *"to let"* "se alquila"
to **let down** [lɛt'daun] VERB
defraudar ◇ *I won't let you down.* No te defraudaré.
letter ['lɛtəʳ] NOUN
1 la carta ◇ *She wrote me a long letter.* Me escribió una carta larga.
2 la letra ◇ *A is the first letter of the alphabet.* La "a" es la primera letra del alfabeto.
letterbox ['lɛtəbɔks] NOUN (PL **letterboxes**)
el buzón (PL los buzones)
lettuce ['lɛtɪs] NOUN
la lechuga
leukaemia [luː'kiːmɪə] NOUN
la leucemia ◇ *He suffers from leukaemia.* Tiene leucemia.
level ['lɛvl] ADJECTIVE
see also **level** NOUN
llano ◇ *a level surface* una superficie llana
level ['lɛvl] NOUN
see also **level** ADJECTIVE
el nivel ◇ *The level of the river is rising.* El nivel del río está subiendo.
♦ **"A" levels**

> ℹ *Los **A-levels** son las calificaciones obtenidas en los exámenes que hacen los estudiantes británicos para las dos o tres asignaturas que se preparan en dos años al terminar la educación secundaria obligatoria.*

level crossing [lɛvl'krɔsɪŋ] NOUN
el paso a nivel
lever ['liːvəʳ] NOUN
la palanca
liable ['laɪəbl] ADJECTIVE
♦ **He's liable to panic.** Tiene tendencia a dejarse llevar por el pánico.
liar ['laɪəʳ] NOUN
el mentiroso
la mentirosa
liberal ['lɪbərl] ADJECTIVE
liberal (*view, system*)
♦ **the Liberal Democrats** los demócratas liberales
liberation [lɪbə'reɪʃən] NOUN
la liberación
Libra ['liːbrə] NOUN
la Libra (*sign*) ◇ *I'm Libra.* Soy Libra.
♦ **a Libra** un/una Libra
librarian [laɪ'brɛərɪən] NOUN
el bibliotecario
la bibliotecaria
◇ *I'm a librarian.* Soy bibliotecaria.
library ['laɪbrərɪ] NOUN (PL **libraries**)
la biblioteca

*Be careful not to translate **library** by **librería**.*

Libya ['lɪbɪə] NOUN
Libia FEM
licence ['laɪsns] NOUN (US **license**)
el permiso
♦ **a driving licence** un carnet de

conducir
◆ **a television licence**

> ⓘ *En el Reino Unido, para tener un aparato de televisión es necesario poseer una licencia. El dinero recaudado va a parar a los fondos de la BBC.*

to **lick** [lɪk] VERB
lamer
lid [lɪd] NOUN
la tapa
lie [laɪ] NOUN
see also **lie** VERB
la mentira
◆ **to tell a lie** mentir*
to **lie** [laɪ] VERB
see also **lie** NOUN
1 mentir* ◊ *I know she's lying.* Sé que está mintiendo. ◊ *You lied to me!* ¡Me mentiste!
2 tumbarse
Se usa **lay** *para el pasado y* **lain** *para el participio pasado de este sentido de* **lie.**
◊ *I lay on the floor.* Me tumbé en el suelo.
◆ **He was lying on the sofa.** Estaba tumbado en el sofá.
to **lie down** [laɪ'daun] VERB
acostarse* ◊ *Why not go and lie down for a bit?* ¿Por qué no vas a acostarte un rato?
◆ **to be lying down** estar* tendido
lie-in ['laɪɪn] NOUN
◆ **to have a lie-in** quedarse en la cama hasta tarde
lieutenant [lɛf'tɛnənt] NOUN
el/la teniente
life [laɪf] NOUN (PL **lives**)
la vida
lifebelt ['laɪfbɛlt] NOUN
el salvavidas (PL los salvavidas)
lifeboat ['laɪfbəut] NOUN
el bote salvavidas (PL los botes salvavidas)
lifeguard ['laɪfgɑːd] NOUN
el/la socorrista
life jacket ['laɪfdʒækɪt] NOUN
el chaleco salvavidas (PL los chalecos salvavidas)
life-saving ['laɪfseɪvɪŋ] NOUN
el socorrismo ◊ *I've done a course in life-saving.* He hecho un curso de socorrismo.
lifestyle ['laɪfstaɪl] NOUN
el estilo de vida
to **lift** [lɪft] VERB
see also **lift** NOUN
levantar ◊ *The box is too heavy, I can't lift it.* La caja pesa mucho, no la puedo levantar.
lift [lɪft] NOUN
see also **lift** VERB
el ascensor ◊ *The lift isn't working.* El ascensor no funciona.
◆ **He gave me a lift to the cinema last night.** Me llevó al cine en coche ayer por la noche.
◆ **Would you like a lift?** ¿Quieres que te lleve en coche?
light [laɪt] ADJECTIVE
see also **light** NOUN, VERB
1 ligero (*not heavy*) ◊ *a light jacket* una chaqueta ligera ◊ *a light meal* una comida ligera
2 claro (*colour*) ◊ *a light blue sweater* un jersey azul claro
light [laɪt] NOUN
see also **light** ADJECTIVE, VERB
la luz (PL las luces) ◊ *He switched on the light.* Encendió la luz. ◊ *He switched off the light.* Apagó la luz.
◆ **the traffic lights** el semáforo
◆ **Have you got a light?** ¿Tienes fuego?
to **light** [laɪt] VERB (**lit, lit**)
see also **light** ADJECTIVE, NOUN
encender*
light bulb ['laɪtbʌlb] NOUN
la bombilla
lighter ['laɪtəʳ] NOUN
el mechero
lighthouse ['laɪthaus] NOUN
el faro
lightning ['laɪtnɪŋ] NOUN
el relámpago ◊ *thunder and lightning* truenos y relámpagos ◊ *a flash of lightning* un relámpago
to **like** [laɪk] VERB
see also **like** PREPOSITION
The most common translation for **to like** *when talking about things and activities is* **gustar***. Remember that the construction is the opposite of English, with the thing you like being the subject of the sentence.*
◊ *I don't like mustard.* No me gusta la mostaza. ◊ *Do you like apples?* ¿Te gustan las manzanas? ◊ *I like riding.* Me gusta montar a caballo.
◆ **I like him.** Me cae bien.
◆ **I'd like...** quería... ◊ *I'd like this blouse in size 10, please.* Quería esta blusa en la talla 10, por favor.
◆ **I'd like an orange juice, please.** Un zumo de naranja, por favor.
◆ **I'd like to...** Me gustaría... ◊ *I'd like to go to China.* Me gustaría ir a China.
To ask someone if they would like something, or like to do something, use **querer***.*
◊ *Would you like some coffee?* ¿Quieres café? ◊ *Would you like to go for a walk?* ¿Quieres ir a dar un paseo?
◆ **... if you like ...** si quieres
like [laɪk] PREPOSITION

☞

see also **like** VERB

como ◊ *a city like Paris* una ciudad como París

*When asking questions, use **cómo** instead of **como**.*

◊ *What was his house like?* ¿Cómo era su casa?

♦ **What's the weather like?** ¿Qué tiempo hace?

♦ **It's a bit like salmon.** Se parece un poco al salmón.

♦ **It's fine like that.** Así está bien.

♦ **Do it like this.** Hazlo así.

♦ **something like that** algo así

likely ['laɪklɪ] ADJECTIVE

probable ◊ *That's not very likely.* Es poco probable.

***es probable que** has to be followed by a verb in the subjunctive.*

◊ *She's likely to come.* Es probable que venga. ◊ *She's not likely to come.* Es probable que no venga.

lilo ® ['laɪləu] NOUN (PL **lilos**)

la colchoneta inflable

lime [laɪm] NOUN

la lima (*fruit*)

limit ['lɪmɪt] NOUN

el límite ◊ *the speed limit* el límite de velocidad

limousine ['lɪməzi:n] NOUN

la limusina

to **limp** [lɪmp] VERB

cojear

line [laɪn] NOUN

1 la línea ◊ *a straight line* una línea recta ◊ *He wrote a few lines.* Escribió unas cuantas líneas. ◊ *to draw a line* trazar* una línea

2 la fila ◊ *a line of people* una fila de gente

♦ **railway line** la vía férrea

♦ **Hold the line, please.** No cuelgue, por favor.

♦ **It's a very bad line.** Se oye muy mal.

linen ['lɪnɪn] NOUN

el lino ◊ *a linen jacket* una chaqueta de lino

liner ['laɪnəʳ] NOUN

el transatlántico

link [lɪŋk] NOUN

see also **link** VERB

1 la relación (PL las relaciones) ◊ *the link between smoking and cancer* la relación entre el tabaco y el cáncer

♦ **cultural links** los lazos culturales

2 (*computing*)

el enlace

to **link** [lɪŋk] VERB

see also **link** NOUN

1 asociar (*facts*)

2 conectar (*towns, terminals*)

lino ['laɪnəu] NOUN

el linóleo

lion ['laɪən] NOUN

el león (PL los leones)

lioness ['laɪənɪs] NOUN (PL **lionesses**)

la leona

lip [lɪp] NOUN

el labio

to **lip-read** ['lɪpri:d] VERB (**lip-read, lip-read**)

leer* los labios

lip salve ['lɪpsælv] NOUN

la crema protectora para los labios

lipstick ['lɪpstɪk] NOUN

el lápiz de labios (PL los lápices de labios)

liqueur [lɪ'kjuəʳ] NOUN

el licor

liquid ['lɪkwɪd] NOUN

el líquido

liquidizer ['lɪkwɪdaɪzəʳ] NOUN

la licuadora

Lisbon ['lɪzbən] NOUN

Lisboa FEM

list [lɪst] NOUN

see also **list** VERB

la lista

to **list** [lɪst] VERB

see also **list** NOUN

1 hacer* una lista de (*in writing*)

2 enumerar (*verbally*)

to **listen** ['lɪsn] VERB

escuchar ◊ *Listen to this!* ¡Escucha esto! ◊ *Listen to me!* ¡Escúchame!

listener ['lɪsnəʳ] NOUN

el/la oyente

lit [lɪt] VERB *see* **light**

liter ['li:təʳ] NOUN US

el litro

literally ['lɪtrəlɪ] ADVERB

literalmente ◊ *It was literally impossible to find a seat.* Era literalmente imposible encontrar un asiento. ◊ *to translate literally* traducir* literalmente

literature ['lɪtrɪtʃəʳ] NOUN

la literatura

litre ['li:təʳ] NOUN

el litro

litter ['lɪtəʳ] NOUN

la basura

litter bin ['lɪtəbɪn] NOUN

el cubo de la basura

little ['lɪtl] ADJECTIVE, PRONOUN

pequeño ◊ *a little girl* una niña pequeña

♦ **a little** un poco ◊ *How much would you like? – Just a little.* ¿Cuánto quiere? – Sólo un poco.

♦ **very little** muy poco ◊ *We've got very little time.* Tenemos muy poco tiempo.

♦ **little by little** poco a poco

live [laɪv] ADJECTIVE
see also **live** VERB
vivo ◇ *I'm against tests on live animals.* Estoy en contra de los experimentos en animales vivos.
◆ **a live broadcast** una emisión en directo
◆ **a live concert** un concierto en vivo

to **live** [lɪv] VERB
see also **live** ADJECTIVE
vivir ◇ *Where do you live?* ¿Dónde vives? ◇ *I live in Edinburgh.* Vivo en Edimburgo.

to **live together** ['lɪvtəgɛðəʳ] VERB
vivir juntos

lively ['laɪvlɪ] ADJECTIVE
animado (*place*)
◆ **She's got a lively personality.** Tiene un carácter muy alegre.

liver ['lɪvəʳ] NOUN
el hígado

lives [laɪvz] PL NOUN *see* **life**

living ['lɪvɪŋ] NOUN
◆ **to make a living** ganarse la vida
◆ **What does she do for a living?** ¿A qué se dedica?

living room ['lɪvɪŋruːm] NOUN
la sala de estar

lizard ['lɪzəd] NOUN
1 la lagartija (*small*)
2 el lagarto (*big*)

load [ləud] NOUN
see also **load** VERB
◆ **loads of** un montón de (*informal*) ◇ *They've got loads of money.* Tienen un montón de dinero.
◆ **You're talking a load of rubbish!** ¡Lo que dices es una estupidez!

to **load** [ləud] VERB
see also **load** NOUN
cargar* ◇ *a trolley loaded with luggage* un carrito cargado de equipaje

loaf [ləuf] NOUN (PL **loaves**)
el pan
◆ **a loaf of bread (1)** (*French bread*) una barra de pan
◆ **a loaf of bread (2)** (*baked in tin*) un pan de molde

loan [ləun] NOUN
see also **loan** VERB
el préstamo

to **loan** [ləun] VERB
see also **loan** NOUN
prestar

to **loathe** [ləuð] VERB
detestar ◇ *I loathe her.* La detesto.

loaves [ləuvz] PL NOUN *see* **loaf**

lobster ['lɔbstəʳ] NOUN
la langosta

local ['ləukl] ADJECTIVE
local ◇ *the local paper* el periódico local
◆ **a local call** una llamada urbana

loch [lɔx] NOUN
el lago

lock [lɔk] NOUN
see also **lock** VERB
la cerradura

to **lock** [lɔk] VERB
see also **lock** NOUN
cerrar* con llave ◇ *Make sure you lock your door.* No te olvides de cerrar tu puerta con llave.

to **lock out** [lɔk'aut] VERB
◆ **The door slammed and I was locked out.** La puerta se cerró de golpe y me quedé fuera sin llaves.

locker ['lɔkəʳ] NOUN
la taquilla ◇ *left-luggage lockers* las taquillas de consigna
◆ **locker room** el vestuario

locket ['lɔkɪt] NOUN
el relicario

lodger ['lɔdʒəʳ] NOUN
el inquilino
la inquilina

loft [lɔft] NOUN
el desván (PL los desvanes)

log [lɔg] NOUN
el leño

logical ['lɔdʒɪkl] ADJECTIVE
lógico

to **log in** [lɔg'ɪn] VERB
entrar en el sistema

to **log off** [lɔg'ɔf] VERB
salir* del sistema

to **log on** [lɔg'ɔn] VERB
entrar en el sistema
◆ **to log on to the Net** conectarse a la Red

to **log out** [lɔg'aut] (*Comput*) VERB
salir* del sistema

lollipop ['lɔlɪpɔp] NOUN
el pirulí (PL los pirulís)

lolly ['lɔlɪ] NOUN (PL **lollies**)
◆ **ice lolly** el polo (la paleta helada *LatAm*)

London ['lʌndən] NOUN
Londres MASC

Londoner ['lʌndənəʳ] NOUN
el/la londinense

loneliness ['ləunlɪnɪs] NOUN
la soledad

lonely ['ləunlɪ] ADJECTIVE
solo ◇ *I sometimes feel lonely.* A veces me siento solo.
◆ **a lonely cottage** una casita aislada

long [lɔŋ] ADJECTIVE, ADVERB
see also **long** VERB
largo ◇ *She's got long hair.* Tiene el pelo largo. ◇ *The room is six metres long.* La habitación tiene seis metros de largo.
◆ **a long time** mucho tiempo ◇ *It takes a long time.* Lleva mucho tiempo. ◇ *I've been waiting a long time.* Llevo esperando mucho tiempo.
◆ **How long?** (*time*) ¿Cuánto tiempo? ◇ *How long have you been here?*

☞

¿Cuánto tiempo llevas aquí? ◊ *How long will it take?* ¿Cuánto tiempo llevará?

♦ **How long is the flight?** ¿Cuánto dura el vuelo?

♦ **as long as** siempre que

siempre que *has to be followed by a verb in the subjunctive.*

◊ *I'll come as long as it's not too expensive.* Iré siempre que no sea demasiado caro.

to **long** [lɔŋ] VERB

see also **long** ADJECTIVE

♦ **to long to do something** estar* deseando hacer algo

long-distance [lɔŋ'dɪstəns] ADJECTIVE

♦ **a long-distance call** una llamada de larga distancia

longer ['lɔŋgəʳ] ADVERB

see also **long** ADJECTIVE

♦ **They're no longer going out together.** Ya no salen juntos.

♦ **I can't stand it any longer.** Ya no lo aguanto más.

long jump ['lɔŋdʒʌmp] NOUN

el salto de longitud

loo [luː] NOUN

el wáter (el baño *LatAm*)

look [luk] NOUN

see also **look** VERB

♦ **Have a look at this!** ¡Echale una ojeada a esto!

♦ **I don't like the look of it.** No me gusta nada.

to **look** [luk] VERB

see also **look** NOUN

1 mirar ◊ *Look!* ¡Mira!

♦ **to look at something** mirar algo ◊ *Look at the picture.* Mira la foto.

♦ **Look out!** ¡Cuidado!

2 parecer* ◊ *She looks surprised.* Parece sorprendida.

♦ **That cake looks nice.** Ese pastel tiene buena pinta.

♦ **to look like somebody** parecerse* a alguien ◊ *He looks like his brother.* Se parece a su hermano.

♦ **What does she look like?** ¿Cómo es físicamente?

to **look after** [luk'ɑːftəʳ] VERB

cuidar ◊ *I look after my little sister.* Cuido a mi hermana pequeña.

to **look for** ['lukfɔːʳ] VERB

buscar* ◊ *I'm looking for my passport.* Estoy buscando mi pasaporte.

to **look forward to** [luk'fɔːwədtuː] VERB

tener* muchas ganas de ◊ *to look forward to doing something* tener muchas ganas de hacer algo ◊ *I'm looking forward to meeting you.* Tengo muchas ganas de conocerte.

♦ **I'm really looking forward to the holidays.** Estoy deseando que lleguen las vacaciones.

♦ **Looking forward to hearing from you...** A la espera de sus noticias...

to **look round** [luk'raund] VERB

1 volverse* ◊ *I called him and he looked round.* Lo llamé y se volvió.

2 mirar ◊ *I'm just looking round.* Sólo estoy mirando.

♦ **to look round an exhibition** visitar una exposición

♦ **I like looking round the shops.** Me gusta ir a ver tiendas.

to **look up** [luk'ʌp] VERB

buscar* ◊ *If you don't know a word, look it up in the dictionary.* Si no conoces una palabra, búscala en el diccionario.

loose [luːs] ADJECTIVE

holgado ◊ *a loose shirt* una camisa holgada

♦ **a loose screw** un tornillo flojo

♦ **loose change** dinero suelto

lord [lɔːd] NOUN

el señor (*feudal*)

♦ **the House of Lords** la Cámara de los Lores

♦ **the Lord** el Señor (*God*)

♦ **Good Lord!** ¡Dios mío!

lorry ['lɔrɪ] NOUN (PL **lorries**)

el camión (PL los camiones)

lorry driver ['lɔrɪdraɪvəʳ] NOUN

el camionero

la camionera

◊ *He's a lorry driver.* Es camionero.

to **lose** [luːz] VERB **(lost, lost)**

perder* ◊ *I've lost my purse.* He perdido el monedero.

♦ **to get lost** perderse* ◊ *I was afraid of getting lost.* Tenía miedo de perderme.

loss [lɔs] NOUN (PL **losses**)

la pérdida

lost [lɔst] VERB *see* **lose**

lost [lɔst] ADJECTIVE

perdido

lost-and-found [lɔstən'faund] NOUN US

la oficina de objetos perdidos

lost property office [lɔst'prɔpətɪɔfɪs] NOUN

la oficina de objetos perdidos

lot [lɔt] NOUN

♦ **a lot** mucho ◊ *She talks a lot.* Habla mucho. ◊ *Do you like football? – Not a lot.* ¿Te gusta el fútbol? – No mucho.

♦ **a lot of** mucho ◊ *I drink a lot of coffee.* Bebo mucho café. ◊ *We saw a lot of interesting things.* Vimos muchas cosas interesantes. ◊ *He's got lots of friends.* Tiene muchos amigos. ◊ *She's got lots of self-confidence.* Tiene mucha confianza en sí misma.

◆**That's the lot.** Eso es todo.

lottery ['lɔtərɪ] NOUN (PL **lotteries**)
la lotería ◇ *to win the lottery* ganar la lotería

loud [laud] ADJECTIVE
fuerte ◇ *The television is too loud.* La televisión está muy fuerte.

loudly ['laudlɪ] ADVERB
fuerte

loudspeaker [laud'spiːkəʳ] NOUN
el altavoz (PL los altavoces)

lounge [laundʒ] NOUN
la sala de estar

lousy ['lauzɪ] ADJECTIVE
asqueroso (*informal*) ◇ *It was a lousy meal.* Fue una comida asquerosa.
◆**I feel lousy.** Me siento fatal.

love [lʌv] NOUN
see also **love** VERB
el amor
◆**to be in love** estar* enamorado ◇ *She's in love with Paul.* Está enamorada de Paul.
◆**to make love** hacer* el amor
◆**Give Gloria my love.** Dale recuerdos a Gloria de mi parte.
◆**Love, Rosemary.** Un abrazo, Rosemary.

to **love** [lʌv] VERB
see also **love** NOUN
querer* ◇ *Everybody loves her.* Todos la quieren. ◇ *I love you.* Te quiero.
◆**I love chocolate.** Me encanta el chocolate.
◆**Would you like to come? – Yes, I'd love to.** ¿Te gustaría venir? – Sí, me encantaría.

lovely ['lʌvlɪ] ADJECTIVE
1 (*person*)
encantador MASC
encantadora FEM
◇ *She's a lovely person.* Es una persona encantadora.
2 precioso ◇ *They've got a lovely house.* Tienen una casa preciosa.
◆**What a lovely surprise!** ¡Qué sorpresa tan agradable!
◆**It's a lovely day.** Hace un tiempo estupendo.
◆**Is your meal okay? – Yes, it's lovely.** ¿Está bueno? – Sí, buenísimo.
◆**Have a lovely time!** ¡Que lo paséis bien!

lover ['lʌvəʳ] NOUN
el/la amante

low [ləu] ADJECTIVE, ADVERB
bajo ◇ *low prices* los bajos precios ◇ *That plane is flying very low.* Ese avión vuela muy bajo. ◇ *in the low season* en temporada baja

to **lower** ['ləuəʳ] VERB
see also **lower** ADJECTIVE
bajar ◇ *He was so tall that the dentist had to lower the chair.* Era tan alto que el dentista tuvo que bajar la silla.

lower ['ləuəʳ] ADJECTIVE
see also **lower** VERB
inferior

low-fat ['ləu'fæt] ADJECTIVE
1 de bajo contenido graso (*margarine, cheese*)
2 desnatado (*milk, yoghurt*)

loyalty ['lɔɪəltɪ] NOUN (PL **loyalties**)
la lealtad

loyalty card ['lɔɪəltɪkɑːd] NOUN
la tarjeta de cliente

L-plate ['ɛlpleɪt] NOUN
la L

> *En el Reino Unido, la L roja indica que el conductor está aprendiendo a conducir. Una vez aprobado el examen, la L verde, que es opcional, se lleva durante un año.*

luck [lʌk] NOUN
la suerte ◇ *She hasn't had much luck.* No ha tenido mucha suerte.
◆**Bad luck!** ¡Mala suerte!
◆**Good luck!** ¡Suerte!

luckily ['lʌkɪlɪ] ADVERB
afortunadamente

lucky ['lʌkɪ] ADJECTIVE
afortunado ◇ *I consider myself lucky.* Me considero afortunado.
◆**to be lucky** tener* suerte (*fortunate*) ◇ *He's lucky, he's got a job.* Tiene suerte de tener trabajo.
◆**That was lucky!** ¡Qué suerte!
◆**Black cats are lucky in Britain.** En Gran Bretaña los gatos negros traen buena suerte.
◆**a lucky horseshoe** una herradura de la suerte

luggage ['lʌgɪdʒ] NOUN
el equipaje

lukewarm ['luːkwɔːm] ADJECTIVE
tibio

lump [lʌmp] NOUN
1 el trozo ◇ *a lump of butter* un trozo de mantequilla
2 (*swelling*)
el chichón (PL los chichones) ◇ *He's got a lump on his forehead.* Tiene un chichón en la frente.

lunatic ['luːnətɪk] NOUN
el loco
la loca
◇ *He's an absolute lunatic.* Está loco perdido.

lunch [lʌntʃ] NOUN (PL **lunches**)
el almuerzo
◆**to have lunch** almorzar* ◇ *We have lunch at half past twelve.* Almorzamos a las doce y media.

luncheon voucher ['lʌntʃənvautʃəʳ] NOUN
el tíquet restaurante (PL los tíquets restaurante)

L

lung [lʌŋ] NOUN
el pulmón (PL los pulmones) ◊ *lung cancer* el cáncer de pulmón

luscious ['lʌʃəs] ADJECTIVE
exquisito

lush [lʌʃ] ADJECTIVE
exuberante

lust [lʌst] NOUN
la lujuria

Luxembourg ['lʌksəmbəːg] NOUN
Luxemburgo MASC

luxurious [lʌg'zjuərɪəs] ADJECTIVE
lujoso

luxury ['lʌkʃərɪ] NOUN (PL **luxuries**)
el lujo ◊ *It was luxury!* ¡Era un lujo! ◊ *a luxury hotel* un hotel de lujo

lying ['laɪɪŋ] VERB *see* **lie**

lyrics ['lɪrɪks] PL NOUN
la letra

M

mac [mæk] NOUN
el impermeable
macaroni [mækə'rəunɪ] NOUN
los macarrones
machine [mə'ʃiːn] NOUN
la máquina ◊ *It's a complicated machine.* Es una máquina complicada.
♦ **I put my clothes in the machine.** Puse mi ropa en la lavadora.
machine gun [mə'ʃiːngʌn] NOUN
la ametralladora
machinery [mə'ʃiːnərɪ] NOUN
la maquinaria
mackerel ['mækrl] NOUN (PL **mackerel**)
la caballa
mad [mæd] ADJECTIVE
[1] loco ◊ *You're mad!* ¡Estás loco! ◊ *Have you gone mad?* ¿Te has vuelto loco?
[2] furioso ◊ *She'll be mad when she finds out.* Se pondrá furiosa cuando se entere.
♦ **He's mad about football.** Está loco por el fútbol.
♦ **She's mad about horses.** Le encantan los caballos.
madam ['mædəm] NOUN
la señora ◊ *How may I help you, Madam?* ¿Qué desea la señora?
made [meɪd] VERB *see* **make**
madly ['mædlɪ] ADVERB
♦ **They're madly in love.** Están locamente enamorados.
madman ['mædmən] NOUN (PL **madmen**)
el loco
madness ['mædnɪs] NOUN
la locura ◊ *It's absolute madness.* Es una locura.
magazine [mægə'ziːn] NOUN
la revista
maggot ['mægət] NOUN
el gusano
magic ['mædʒɪk] NOUN
see also **magic** ADJECTIVE
la magia ◊ *My hobby is magic.* Mi hobby es la magia.
magic ['mædʒɪk] ADJECTIVE
see also **magic** NOUN
mágico ◊ *a magic wand* una varita mágica
♦ **It was magic!** ¡Fue fantástico! (*brilliant*)
magician [mə'dʒɪʃən] NOUN
el mago
la maga
◊ *There was a magician at the party.* Había un mago en la fiesta.
magnet ['mægnɪt] NOUN
el imán (PL los imanes)
magnificent [mæg'nɪfɪsnt] ADJECTIVE
espléndido ◊ *a magnificent view* una vista espléndida
♦ **It was a magnificent effort on their part.** Fue un esfuerzo extraordinario por su parte.
magnifying glass ['mægnɪfaɪɪŋ'glɑːs] NOUN
la lupa
maid [meɪd] NOUN
[1] la sirvienta (*servant*)
[2] la camarera (*in hotel*)
♦ **an old maid** una solterona (*spinster*)
maiden name ['meɪdnneɪm] NOUN
el apellido de soltera

> *When women marry in Spain they don't usually take the name of their husband but keep their own instead. If the couple have children they take both their father's and mother's surnames.*

mail [meɪl] NOUN
[1] el correo
♦ **by mail** por correo
[2] la correspondencia (*letters*) ◊ *We receive a lot of mail.* Recibimos mucha correspondencia.
mailbox ['meɪlbɔks] NOUN (PL **mailboxes**)
US
el buzón (PL los buzones)
mailing list ['meɪlɪŋ lɪst] NOUN
la lista de correo
mailman ['meɪlmæn] NOUN (PL **mailmen**)
US
el cartero
main [meɪn] ADJECTIVE
principal ◊ *the main suspect* el principal sospechoso ◊ *The main thing is to get it finished.* Lo principal es terminarlo.
mainly ['meɪnlɪ] ADVERB
principalmente
main road [meɪn'rəud] NOUN
la carretera principal
to **maintain** [meɪn'teɪn] VERB
mantener* ◊ *Teachers try hard to maintain standards.* Los maestros se esfuerzan por mantener el nivel educativo. ◊ *Old houses are expensive to maintain.* Las casas viejas son costosas de mantener.
maintenance ['meɪntənəns] NOUN
[1] el mantenimiento ◊ *car maintenance* el mantenimiento del coche
[2] la pensión alimenticia ◊ *£30 a week in maintenance* 30 libras esterlinas a la semana en concepto de pensión alimenticia
maize [meɪz] NOUN

el maíz

majesty ['mædʒɪstɪ] NOUN (PL **majesties**)
la majestad
♦ **Your Majesty** su Majestad

major ['meɪdʒəʳ] ADJECTIVE
muy importante ◊ *a major factor* un factor muy importante
♦ **Drugs are a major problem.** La droga es un grave problema.
♦ **in C major** en do mayor

Majorca [mə'jɔːkə] NOUN
Mallorca FEM

majority [mə'dʒɔrɪtɪ] NOUN (PL **majorities**)
la mayoría

make [meɪk] NOUN
see also **make** VERB
la marca ◊ *What make is it?* ¿De qué marca es?

to **make** [meɪk] VERB (**made, made**)
see also **make** NOUN
1 hacer* ◊ *I'm going to make a cake.* Voy a hacer un pastel. ◊ *I'd like to make a phone call.* Quisiera hacer una llamada. ◊ *I make my bed every morning.* Me hago la cama cada mañana. ◊ *It's well made.* Está bien hecho.
♦ **She's making lunch.** Está preparando el almuerzo.
♦ **Two and two make four.** Dos y dos son cuatro.
2 fabricar* ◊ *"made in Spain"* "fabricado en España"
3 ganar ◊ *He makes a lot of money.* Gana mucho dinero.
♦ **to make somebody do something** hacer* a alguien hacer algo ◊ *My mother makes me eat vegetables.* Mi madre me hace comer verduras.
♦ **You'll have to make do with a cheaper car.** Tendrás que conformarte con un coche más barato.
♦ **What time do you make it?** ¿Qué hora tienes?

to **make out** [meɪk'aut] VERB
1 descifrar ◊ *I can't make out the address on the label.* No consigo descifrar la dirección que viene en la etiqueta.
2 comprender ◊ *I can't make her out at all.* No la comprendo en absoluto.
3 dar* a entender ◊ *They're making out it was my fault.* Están dando a entender que fue culpa mía.
♦ **to make a cheque out to somebody** hacer* un cheque a favor de alguien

to **make up** [meɪk'ʌp] VERB
1 componer* ◊ *Women make up thirty per cent of the police force.* Las mujeres componen el treinta por ciento del cuerpo de policía.
2 inventarse ◊ *He made up the whole story.* Se inventó toda la historia.
3 hacer* las paces ◊ *They had a quarrel, but soon made up.* Riñeron, pero poco después hicieron las paces.
4 maquillarse ◊ *She spends hours making herself up.* Pasa horas maquillándose.

maker ['meɪkəʳ] NOUN
el/la fabricante ◊ *Spain's biggest car maker.* El mayor fabricante de automóviles de España.

make-up ['meɪkʌp] NOUN
el maquillaje
♦ **She put on her make-up.** Se maquilló.

male [meɪl] ADJECTIVE
see also **male** NOUN
1 (*animal, plant*)
macho ◊ *a male kitten* un gatito macho
2 (*person*)
varón (PL varones)
◊ *Sex: Male* Sexo: Varón
♦ **Most football players are male.** La mayoría de los futbolistas son hombres.
♦ **a male nurse** un enfermero
♦ **a male chauvinist** un machista

male [meɪl] NOUN
see also **male** ADJECTIVE
el macho (*animal*)

mall [mɔːl] NOUN
el centro comercial

Malta ['mɔːltə] NOUN
Malta FEM

mammoth ['mæməθ] NOUN
see also **mammoth** ADJECTIVE
el mamut

mammoth ['mæməθ] ADJECTIVE
see also **mammoth** NOUN
colosal (*project, building*)
♦ **a mammoth task** una obra de titanes

man [mæn] NOUN (PL **men**)
el hombre

to **manage** ['mænɪdʒ] VERB
1 arreglárselas ◊ *We haven't got much money, but we manage.* No tenemos mucho dinero, pero nos las arreglamos.
2 dirigir* ◊ *She manages a big store.* Dirige una tienda grande. ◊ *He manages our football team.* Dirige nuestro equipo de fútbol.
♦ **to manage to do something** conseguir* hacer algo ◊ *Luckily I managed to pass the exam.* Por suerte, conseguí aprobar el examen.
♦ **Can you manage a bit more?** ¿Te pongo un poco más? (*food*)
♦ **Can you manage with that suitcase?** ¿Puedes con la maleta?

manageable ['mænɪdʒəbl] ADJECTIVE
factible (*task, goal*)

management ['mænɪdʒmənt] NOUN

la dirección ◇ *He's responsible for the management of the project.* Es responsable de la dirección del proyecto. ◇ *management and workers* la dirección y los trabajadores

manager ['mænɪdʒəʳ] NOUN
1 (*of company, department, performer*)
el director
la directora
◇ *I complained to the manager.* Fui a reclamar al director.
2 (*of restaurant, store*)
el/la gerente
3 (*of team*)
el entrenador
la entrenadora
◇ *the England manager* el entrenador de la selección inglesa

manageress [mænɪdʒə'rɛs] NOUN (PL **manageresses**)
la gerente (*of restaurant, store*)

mandarin ['mændərɪn] NOUN
la mandarina

mango ['mæŋgəu] NOUN (PL **mangos** *or* **mangoes**)
el mango

maniac ['meɪnɪæk] NOUN
el maníaco
la maníaca
◆ **He drives like a maniac.** Conduce como un loco.

to **manipulate** [mə'nɪpjuleɪt] VERB
manipular

man-made ['mæn'meɪd] ADJECTIVE
sintético (*fibre*)

manner ['mænəʳ] NOUN
la manera ◇ *She was behaving in an odd manner.* Se comportaba de una manera extraña.
◆ **He has a confident manner.** Se muestra seguro de sí mismo.

manners ['mænəz] PL NOUN
los modales ◇ *Victoria's manners are appalling.* Victoria tiene muy malos modales.
◆ **good manners** la buena educación
◆ **It's bad manners to speak with your mouth full.** Es de mala educación hablar con la boca llena.

manpower ['mænpauəʳ] NOUN
la mano de obra

> *Although **mano** ends in **-o**, **mano de obra** is actually a feminine noun.*

mansion ['mænʃən] NOUN
la mansión (PL las mansiones)

mantelpiece ['mæntlpi:s] NOUN
la repisa de la chimenea

manual ['mænjuəl] NOUN
el manual
◆ **manual labour** el trabajo manual

to **manufacture** [mænju'fæktʃəʳ] VERB
fabricar*

manufacturer [mænju'fæktʃərəʳ] NOUN
el/la fabricante

manure [mə'njuəʳ] NOUN
el estiércol

manuscript ['mænjuskrɪpt] NOUN
el manuscrito

many ['mɛnɪ] ADJECTIVE, PRONOUN
muchos MASC
muchas FEM
◇ *He hasn't got many friends.* No tiene muchos amigos. ◇ *Were there many people at the concert? – Not many.* ¿Había mucha gente en el concierto? – No mucha.
◆ **very many** muchos (FEM muchas) ◇ *I haven't got very many CDs.* No tengo muchos CDs.
◆ **how many?** ¿cuántos? (FEM ¿cuántas?) ◇ *How many hours a week do you work?* ¿Cuántas horas trabajas a la semana?
◆ **too many** demasiados (FEM demasiadas) ◇ *Sixteen people? That's too many.* ¿Dieciséis personas? Son demasiadas.
◆ **so many** tantos (FEM tantas) ◇ *He told so many lies!* ¡Dijo tantas mentiras!

map [mæp] NOUN
1 el mapa (*of country, region*)

> *Although **mapa** ends in **-a**, it is actually a masculine noun.*

2 el plano (*of town, city*)

marathon ['mærəθən] NOUN
el maratón (PL los maratones)

marble ['mɑ:bl] NOUN
el mármol ◇ *a marble statue* una estatua de mármol
◆ **a marble** una canica

March [mɑ:tʃ] NOUN
marzo MASC ◇ *in March* en marzo ◇ *on 9 March* el 9 de marzo

to **march** [mɑ:tʃ] VERB
see also **march** NOUN
desfilar ◇ *The troops marched past the King.* Las tropas desfilaron delante del Rey.

march [mɑ:tʃ] NOUN (PL **marches**)
see also **march** VERB
la marcha ◇ *a peace march* una marcha por la paz

mare [mɛəʳ] NOUN
la yegua

margarine [mɑ:dʒə'ri:n] NOUN
la margarina

margin ['mɑ:dʒɪn] NOUN
el margen (PL los márgenes) ◇ *Daphne wrote a note in the margin.* Daphne escribió una nota al margen.

marijuana [mærɪ'wɑ:nə] NOUN
la marihuana

marital status [mærɪtl'steɪtəs] NOUN
el estado civil

mark [mɑ:k] NOUN

M

☞

see also **mark** VERB
1 la nota ◊ *I get good marks for French.* Saco buenas notas en francés.
2 la mancha ◊ *There were red marks all over his back.* Tenía manchas rojas por toda la espalda. ◊ *You've got a mark on your shirt.* Tienes una mancha en la camisa.
3 el marco (*German currency*) ◊ *30 million marks* 30 millones de marcos

to **mark** [mɑ:k] VERB
see also **mark** NOUN
1 corregir* ◊ *The teacher hasn't marked my homework yet.* El maestro no me ha corregido los deberes todavía.
2 señalar ◊ *Mark its position on the map.* Señala su posición en el mapa.

market ['mɑ:kɪt] NOUN
el mercado

marketing ['mɑ:kɪtɪŋ] NOUN
el márketing

marmalade ['mɑ:məleɪd] NOUN
la mermelada de naranja

maroon [mə'ru:n] ADJECTIVE
granate MASC, FEM, PL

marriage ['mærɪdʒ] NOUN
el matrimonio

married ['mærɪd] ADJECTIVE
casado ◊ *They are not married.* No están casados.
♦ **a married couple** un matrimonio
♦ **to get married** casarse

marrow ['mærəu] NOUN
(*vegetable*)
el calabacín grande (PL los calabacines grandes)
♦ **bone marrow** la médula

to **marry** ['mærɪ] VERB (**married, married**)
1 casarse ◊ *They married in June.* Se casaron en junio.
2 casarse con ◊ *He wants to marry her.* Quiere casarse con ella.
♦ **to get married** casarse ◊ *My brother's getting married in March.* Mi hermano se casa en marzo.

marvellous ['mɑ:vləs] ADJECTIVE (US **marvelous**)
estupendo ◊ *The weather was marvellous.* Hacía un tiempo estupendo. ◊ *That's a marvellous idea!* ¡Es una idea estupenda!

marzipan ['mɑ:zɪpæn] NOUN
el mazapán

mascara [mæs'kɑ:rə] NOUN
el rímel

masculine ['mæskjulɪn] ADJECTIVE
masculino

mashed potatoes [mæʃtpə'teɪtəuz] PL NOUN
el puré de patatas (el puré de papas *LatAm*)

mask [mɑ:sk] NOUN
la máscara

masked [mɑ:skt] ADJECTIVE
encapuchado (*terrorist, attacker*)

mass [mæs] NOUN (PL **masses**)
1 el montón (PL los montones) ◊ *a mass of books and papers* un montón de libros y papeles
2 la misa ◊ *We go to mass on Sunday.* Vamos a misa los domingos.
♦ **the mass media** los medios de comunicación de masas

massage ['mæsɑ:ʒ] NOUN
el masaje

massive ['mæsɪv] ADJECTIVE
enorme

master ['mɑ:stə'] NOUN
see also **master** VERB
1 el maestro (*at primary school*)
2 el profesor (*at secondary school*)

to **master** ['mɑ:stə'] VERB
see also **master** NOUN
dominar ◊ *Students need to master a second language.* Los estudiantes tienen que dominar un segundo idioma.

masterpiece ['mɑ:stəpi:s] NOUN
la obra maestra (PL las obras maestras)

mat [mæt] NOUN
el felpudo (*doormat*)
♦ **a table mat** un mantel individual

match [mætʃ] NOUN (PL **matches**)
see also **match** VERB
1 el partido ◊ *a football match* un partido de fútbol
2 la cerilla ◊ *a box of matches* una caja de cerillas

to **match** [mætʃ] VERB
see also **match** NOUN
1 hacer* juego con ◊ *The jacket matches the trousers.* La chaqueta hace juego con los pantalones.
2 hacer* juego ◊ *These colours don't match.* Estos colores no hacen juego.

matching ['mætʃɪŋ] ADJECTIVE
a juego ◊ *My bedroom has matching wallpaper and curtains.* Mi habitación tiene el papel y las cortinas a juego.

mate [meɪt] NOUN
el amigo
la amiga
◊ *He always goes on holiday with his mates.* Siempre va de vacaciones con sus amigos.

material [mə'tɪərɪəl] NOUN
1 el tejido ◊ *The curtains are made of a thin material.* Las cortinas están hechas de un tejido fino.
2 el material ◊ *I'm collecting material for my project.* Estoy recogiendo material para mi proyecto.

* Verbs marked with this symbol are irregular. See pages 380-382 for further details

mathematics [mæθə'mætɪks] NOUN
las matemáticas
maths [mæθs] NOUN
las matemáticas
matron ['meɪtrən] NOUN
la enfermera jefe (*in hospital*)
matter ['mætə^r] NOUN
see also **matter** VERB
el asunto ◊ *It's a matter of life and death.* Es un asunto de vida o muerte.
♦ **What's the matter?** ¿Qué pasa?
♦ **as a matter of fact** de hecho
to **matter** ['mætə^r] VERB
see also **matter** NOUN
importar ◊ *I can't give you the money today. – It doesn't matter.* No te puedo dar el dinero hoy. – No importa.
♦ **Shall I phone today or tomorrow? – Whenever, it doesn't matter.** ¿Telefoneo hoy o mañana? – Cuando quieras, da igual.
♦ **It matters a lot to me.** Significa mucho para mí.
mattress ['mætrɪs] NOUN (PL **mattresses**)
el colchón (PL los colchones)
mature [mə'tjuə^r] ADJECTIVE
maduro
maximum ['mæksɪməm] NOUN
see also **maximum** ADJECTIVE
el máximo ◊ *a maximum of two years in prison* un máximo de dos años de cárcel
maximum ['mæksɪməm] ADJECTIVE
see also **maximum** NOUN
máximo ◊ *The maximum speed is 100 km/h.* La velocidad máxima permitida es 100km/h.
May [meɪ] NOUN
mayo MASC ◊ *in May* en mayo ◊ *on 7 May* el 7 de mayo
♦ **May Day** el Primero de Mayo
may [meɪ] VERB
poder* ◊ *The police may come and catch us here.* La policía puede venir y pillarnos aquí. ◊ *May I smoke?* ¿Puedo fumar?
Puede que *has to be followed by a verb in the subjunctive.*
◊ *I may go.* Puede que vaya. ◊ *It may rain.* Puede que llueva.
A lo mejor *can also be used but it is a more colloquial alternative.*
◊ *Are you going to the party? – I don't know, I may.* ¿Vas a ir a la fiesta? – No sé, a lo mejor.
maybe ['meɪbi:] ADVERB
a lo mejor ◊ *Maybe she's at home.* A lo mejor está en casa.
♦ **Maybe he'll change his mind.** A lo mejor cambia de idea.
mayonnaise [meɪə'neɪz] NOUN
la mayonesa
mayor [mɛə^r] NOUN
el alcalde
la alcaldesa
maze [meɪz] NOUN
el laberinto
me [mi:] PRONOUN
Use ***me*** *to translate* ***me*** *when it is the direct object of the verb in the sentence, or when it means* ***to me.***
me ◊ *Look at me!* ¡Mírame! ◊ *Could you lend me your pen?* ¿Me prestas tu bolígrafo?
Use ***yo*** *after the verb* ***to be*** *and in comparisons.*
◊ *It's me.* Soy yo. ◊ *He's older than me.* Es mayor que yo.
Use ***mí*** *after prepositions.*
◊ *without me* sin mí
Remember that ***with me*** *translates as* ***conmigo.***
◊ *He was with me.* Estaba conmigo.
meal [mi:l] NOUN
la comida
♦ **Enjoy your meal!** ¡Que aproveche!
mealtime ['mi:ltaɪm] NOUN
♦ **at mealtimes** a las horas de comer
to **mean** [mi:n] VERB (**meant, meant**)
see also **mean** ADJECTIVE
1 significar* ◊ *What does "alcalde" mean?* ¿Qué significa "alcalde"? ◊ *I don't know what it means.* No sé lo que significa.
2 querer* decir ◊ *That's not what I meant.* Eso no es lo que quería decir.
3 referirse* a ◊ *Which one did he mean?* ¿A cuál se refería? ◊ *Do you mean me?* ¿Te refieres a mí?
♦ **to mean to do something** querer* hacer algo ◊ *I didn't mean to hurt you.* No quería hacerte daño.
♦ **Do you really mean it?** ¿Lo dices en serio?
♦ **He means what he says.** Habla en serio.
mean [mi:n] ADJECTIVE
see also **mean** VERB
1 tacaño ◊ *He's too mean to buy presents.* Es demasiado tacaño para comprar regalos.
2 mezquino ◊ *You're being mean to me.* Estás siendo mezquino conmigo.
♦ **That's a really mean thing to say!** ¡Parece mentira que digas eso!
meaning ['mi:nɪŋ] NOUN
el significado
means [mi:nz] NOUN
el medio ◊ *a means of transport* un medio de transporte ◊ *He'll do it by any possible means.* Lo hará por todos los medios.
♦ **by means of** por medio de ◊ *They reached agreement by means of secret negotiations.* Llegaron a un acuerdo por medio de negociaciones secretas.

M

☞

♦**Can I come in? – By all means!** ¿Puedo entrar? – ¡Claro que sí!

meant [mɛnt] VERB *see* **mean**

meanwhile ['mi:nwaɪl] ADVERB
mientras tanto

measles ['mi:zlz] NOUN
el sarampión ◊ *I've got measles.* Tengo el sarampión.

to **measure** ['mɛʒəʳ] VERB
medir*

measurement ['mɛʒəmənt] NOUN
la medida ◊ *What are the measurements of the room?* ¿Cuáles son las medidas de la habitación? ◊ *Are you sure the measurements are correct?* ¿Estás seguro de que las medidas son correctas?
♦**What's your waist measurement?** ¿Cuánto mides de cintura?

meat [mi:t] NOUN
la carne

Mecca ['mɛkə] NOUN
La Meca

mechanic [mɪ'kænɪk] NOUN
el mecánico
la mecánica
◊ *He's a mechanic.* Es mecánico.

mechanical [mɪ'kænɪkl] ADJECTIVE
mecánico

medal ['mɛdl] NOUN
la medalla

media ['mi:dɪə] PL NOUN
♦**the media** los medios de comunicación

median strip [mi:dɪən'strɪp] NOUN US
la mediana

medical ['mɛdɪkl] ADJECTIVE
see also **medical** NOUN
médico ◊ *medical treatment* el tratamiento médico
♦**medical insurance** el seguro médico
♦**to have medical problems** tener* problemas de salud
♦**She's a medical student.** Es una estudiante de medicina.

medical ['mɛdɪkl] NOUN
see also **medical** ADJECTIVE
♦**He had a medical last week.** Se hizo un chequeo la semana pasada.

medicine ['mɛdsɪn] NOUN
1 la medicina (*science*) ◊ *Martin wants to study medicine.* Martin quiere estudiar medicina.
♦**alternative medicine** la medicina alternativa
2 el medicamento (*medication*) ◊ *I need some medicine.* Necesito un medicamento.

Mediterranean [mɛdɪtə'reɪnɪən] ADJECTIVE
see also **Mediterranean** NOUN
mediterráneo

Mediterranean [mɛdɪtə'reɪnɪən] NOUN
see also **Mediterranean** ADJECTIVE
♦**the Mediterranean** el Mediterráneo

medium ['mi:dɪəm] ADJECTIVE
mediano ◊ *a man of medium height* un hombre de estatura mediana

medium-sized ['mi:dɪəm'saɪzd] ADJECTIVE
♦**a medium-sized town** una ciudad de tamaño mediano

to **meet** [mi:t] VERB (**met, met**)
1 encontrarse* con (*by chance*) ◊ *I met Paul in town.* Me encontré con Paul en el centro.
♦**We met by chance in the supermarket.** Nos encontramos por casualidad en el supermercado.
2 reunirse* (*by arrangement*) ◊ *The committee met at two o'clock.* El comité se reunió a las dos.
♦**Where shall we meet?** ¿Dónde quedamos?
♦**I'm going to meet my friends at the swimming pool.** He quedado con mis amigos en la piscina.
♦**I'll meet you at the station.** Te voy a buscar a la estación.
3 conocer* (*get to know*) ◊ *He met Tim at a party.* Conoció a Tim en una fiesta.
♦**Have you met her before?** ¿La conoces?

meeting ['mi:tɪŋ] NOUN
1 (*socially*)
el encuentro ◊ *their first meeting* su primer encuentro
2 (*for work*)
la reunión (PL las reuniones) ◊ *a business meeting* una reunión de trabajo

mega ['mɛgə] ADJECTIVE
♦**Richard's mega rich.** Richard es super rico. (*informal*)

melody ['mɛlədɪ] NOUN (PL **melodies**)
la melodía

melon ['mɛlən] NOUN
el melón (PL los melones)

to **melt** [mɛlt] VERB
1 derretir* ◊ *Melt 100 grams of butter in a saucepan.* Derrita 100 gramos de mantequilla en una sartén.
2 derretirse* ◊ *The snow is melting.* La nieve se está derritiendo.

member ['mɛmbəʳ] NOUN
el/la miembro
♦**"members only"** "reservado para los socios"
♦**a Member of Parliament** un diputado (FEM una diputada)

membership ['mɛmbəʃɪp] NOUN
(*of party, union*)
la afiliación (PL las afiliaciones)

◆ **I'm going to apply for membership of the club.** Voy a solicitar el ingreso al club.

membership card [ˈmɛmbəʃɪpkɑːd] NOUN
el carnet de socio (PL los carnets de socio)

memento [məˈmɛntəu] NOUN (PL **mementos** *or* **mementoes**)
el recuerdo

memorial [mɪˈmɔːrɪəl] NOUN
◆ **a war memorial** un monumento a los caídos

to **memorize** [ˈmɛməraɪz] VERB
memorizar*

memory [ˈmɛmərɪ] NOUN (PL **memories**)
1 la memoria (*also for computer*) ◊ *I've got a terrible memory.* Tengo una memoria espantosa.
2 el recuerdo ◊ *happy memories* los recuerdos felices

men [mɛn] PL NOUN *see* **man**

to **mend** [mɛnd] VERB
arreglar

meningitis [mɛnɪnˈdʒaɪtɪs] NOUN
la meningitis ◊ *Her daughter's got meningitis.* Su hija tiene meningitis.

mental [ˈmɛntl] ADJECTIVE
mental ◊ *mental illness* la enfermedad mental
◆ **mental hospital** el hospital psiquiátrico

to **mention** [ˈmɛnʃən] VERB
mencionar ◊ *He didn't mention it to me.* No me lo mencionó.
◆ **I mentioned she might come later.** Dije que a lo mejor vendría más tarde.
◆ **Thank you! – Don't mention it!** ¡Gracias! – ¡No hay de qué!

menu [ˈmɛnjuː] NOUN
1 la carta ◊ *Could I have the menu please?* ¿Me trae la carta por favor?
2 (*on computer*)
el menú (PL los menús)

merchant [ˈməːtʃənt] NOUN
el/la comerciante
◆ **a wine merchant** un vinatero

mercy [ˈməːsɪ] NOUN
la compasión

mere [mɪəʳ] ADJECTIVE
◆ **a mere five percent** sólo un cinco por ciento
◆ **It's a mere formality.** No es más que una formalidad.

meringue [məˈræŋ] NOUN
el merengue

merry [ˈmɛrɪ] ADJECTIVE
◆ **Merry Christmas!** ¡Feliz Navidad!

merry-go-round [ˈmɛrɪgəuraund] NOUN
el tiovivo

mess [mɛs] NOUN
el desorden
◆ **My hair's a mess, it needs cutting.** Tengo el pelo hecho un desastre; tengo que cortármelo.
◆ **I'll be in a mess if I fail the exam.** Voy a tener problemas si suspendo el examen.

to **mess about** [mɛsəˈbaut] VERB
◆ **I didn't do much at the weekend, just messed about with some friends.** No hice mucho el fin de semana; estuve ganduleando con unos amigos.
◆ **Stop messing about with my computer!** ¡Deja de toquetear mi ordenador!

message [ˈmɛsɪdʒ] NOUN
el mensaje ◊ *a secret message* un mensaje secreto
◆ **Would you like to leave him a message?** ¿Quiere dejarle un recado?

to **mess up** [mɛsˈʌp] VERB
estropear ◊ *You've messed up my cassettes!* ¡Me has estropeado los casetes!
◆ **I messed up my chemistry exam.** Metí la pata en el examen de química.

messenger [ˈmɛsɪndʒəʳ] NOUN
el mensajero
la mensajera

messy [ˈmɛsɪ] ADJECTIVE
desordenado ◊ *Your room is really messy.* Tu habitación está muy desordenada. ◊ *She's so messy!* ¡Es más desordenada!
◆ **a really messy job** un trabajo muy sucio
◆ **Her writing is very messy.** Tiene muy mala letra.

met [mɛt] VERB *see* **meet**

metal [ˈmɛtl] NOUN
el metal

meter [ˈmiːtəʳ] NOUN
1 el contador (*for gas, electricity*)
2 el taxímetro (*for taxi*)
3 el parquímetro (*parking meter*)
4 el metro (*unit of measurement*) US

method [ˈmɛθəd] NOUN
el método

Methodist [ˈmɛθədɪst] NOUN
el/la metodista ◊ *He's a Methodist.* Es metodista.

metre [ˈmiːtəʳ] NOUN
el metro

metric [ˈmɛtrɪk] ADJECTIVE
métrico

Mexico [ˈmɛksɪkəu] NOUN
Méjico MASC

to **miaow** [miːˈau] VERB
maullar*

mice [maɪs] PL NOUN *see* **mouse**

microchip [ˈmaɪkrəutʃɪp] NOUN
el microchip (PL los microchips)

microphone [ˈmaɪkrəfəun] NOUN
el micrófono

microscope [ˈmaɪkrəskəup] NOUN
el microscopio

M

microwave ['maɪkrəuweɪv] NOUN
el microondas (PL los microondas)

mid [mɪd] ADJECTIVE
♦ **in mid May** a mediados de mayo
♦ **He's in his mid twenties.** Tiene unos veinticinco años.

midday [mɪd'deɪ] NOUN
el mediodía ◊ *at midday* al mediodía

middle ['mɪdl] NOUN
see also **middle** ADJECTIVE
el medio ◊ *The car was in the middle of the road.* El coche estaba en medio de la carretera.
♦ **in the middle of May** a mediados de mayo
♦ **I woke up in the middle of the morning.** Me desperté a media mañana.
♦ **She was in the middle of her exams.** Estaba en plenos exámenes.

middle ['mɪdl] ADJECTIVE
see also **middle** NOUN
del medio MASC, FEM, PL
◊ *the middle seat* el asiento del medio

middle-aged [mɪdl'eɪdʒd] ADJECTIVE
de mediana edad

Middle Ages [mɪdl'eɪdʒəz] PL NOUN
♦ **the Middle Ages** la Edad Media

middle-class [mɪdl'klɑːs] ADJECTIVE
de clase media MASC, FEM, PL

Middle East [mɪdl'iːst] NOUN
♦ **the Middle East** el Oriente Medio

middle name ['mɪdlneɪm] NOUN
el segundo nombre

midge [mɪdʒ] NOUN
el mosquito

midnight ['mɪdnaɪt] NOUN
la medianoche ◊ *at midnight* a medianoche

midwife ['mɪdwaɪf] NOUN (PL **midwives**)
la comadrona ◊ *She's a midwife.* Es comadrona.

might [maɪt] VERB
poder* ◊ *The teacher might come at any moment.* El profesor podría venir en cualquier momento.

***Puede que** has to be followed by a verb in the subjunctive.*

◊ *He might come later.* Puede que venga más tarde. ◊ *She might not have understood.* Puede que no haya entendido.

***A lo mejor** can also be used but it is a more colloquial alternative.*

◊ *We might go to Spain next year.* A lo mejor vamos a España el año que viene.

migraine ['miːgreɪn] NOUN
la jaqueca ◊ *I've got a migraine.* Tengo jaqueca.

mike [maɪk] NOUN
el micro

mild [maɪld] ADJECTIVE
suave ◊ *a mild flavour* un sabor suave
♦ **The winters are quite mild.** Los inviernos son bastante suaves.
♦ **mild soap** el jabón suave

mile [maɪl] NOUN
la milla

> *In Spain distances are expressed in kilometres. A mile is about 1.6 kilometres.*

◊ *It's five miles from here.* Está a unas cinco millas de aquí. ◊ *at 50 miles per hour* a 50 millas por hora
♦ **We walked for miles!** ¡Caminamos kilómetros y kilómetros!

military ['mɪlɪtərɪ] ADJECTIVE
militar

milk [mɪlk] NOUN
see also **milk** VERB
la leche

to **milk** [mɪlk] VERB
see also **milk** NOUN
ordeñar

milk chocolate [mɪlk'tʃɔklɪt] NOUN
el chocolate con leche

milkman ['mɪlkmən] NOUN (PL **milkmen**)
el lechero

> *In Spain milk is not delivered to people's homes.*

milk shake ['mɪlkʃeɪk] NOUN
el batido

mill [mɪl] NOUN
el molino (*for grain*)

millennium [mɪ'lenɪəm] NOUN
el milenio

millimetre ['mɪlɪmiːtə^r] NOUN (US **millimeter**)
el milímetro

million ['mɪljən] NOUN
el millón (PL los millones) ◊ *two million pounds* dos millones de libras esterlinas

millionaire [mɪljə'nɛə^r] NOUN
el millonario
la millonaria

to **mimic** ['mɪmɪk] VERB (**mimicked, mimicked**)
imitar

mince [mɪns] NOUN
la carne picada (la carne molida *LatAm*)

mince pie [mɪns'paɪ] NOUN

> *En Navidad es tradicional comer **mince pies**, que son pequeños pastelitos de fruta confitada.*

* Verbs marked with this symbol are irregular. See pages 380-382 for further details

to **mind** [maɪnd] VERB
see also **mind** NOUN
1 cuidar (*look after*) ◇ *Could you mind the baby this afternoon?* ¿Podrías cuidar al niño esta tarde? ◇ *Could you mind my bags for a few minutes?* ¿Me cuidas las bolsas un momento?
2 importar (*matter*) ◇ *Do you mind if I open the window? – No, I don't mind.* ¿Le importa que abra la ventana? – No, no me importa.
◆**I don't mind the noise.** No me molesta el ruido.
◆**Never mind! (1)** (*don't worry*) ¡No te preocupes!
◆**Never mind! (2)** (*it's not important*) ¡No importa!
◆**Mind you don't fall.** Ten cuidado, no te vayas a caer.
◆**Mind the step!** ¡Cuidado con el escalón!

mind [maɪnd] NOUN
see also **mind** VERB
la mente ◇ *What have you got in mind?* ¿Qué tienes en mente?
◆**I haven't made up my mind yet.** No me he decidido todavía.
◆**He's changed his mind.** Ha cambiado de idea.
◆**Are you out of your mind?** ¿Estás loco?

mine [maɪn] PRONOUN
see also **mine** NOUN
1 el mío MASC (PL los míos) ◇ *Is this your coat? – No, mine is black.* ¿Es éste tu abrigo? – No, el mío es negro. ◇ *your parents and mine* tus padres y los míos
2 la mía FEM (PL las mías) ◇ *Is this your scarf? – No, mine is red.* ¿Es ésta tu bufanda? – No, la mía es roja. ◇ *her sisters and mine* sus hermanas y las mías
3 mío MASC (PL míos) ◇ *That car is mine.* Ese coche es mío.
4 mía FEM (PL mías) ◇ *Sorry, that beer is mine.* Disculpa, esa cerveza es mía. ◇ *Isabel is a friend of mine.* Isabel es amiga mía.

mine [maɪn] NOUN
see also **mine** PRONOUN
la mina ◇ *a coal mine* una mina de carbón ◇ *a land mine* una mina

miner ['maɪnəʳ] NOUN
el minero
la minera
◇ *My father was a miner.* Mi padre era minero.

mineral water ['mɪnərəlwɔːtəʳ] NOUN
el agua mineral FEM

*Although it's a feminine noun, remember that you use **el** and **un** with **agua mineral**.*

miniature ['mɪnətʃəʳ] ADJECTIVE
en miniatura

minibus ['mɪnɪbʌs] NOUN (PL **minibuses**)
el microbús (PL los microbuses)

minicab ['mɪnɪkæb] NOUN
el taxi

> *El **minicab** es un taxi que se pide por teléfono y que no se puede parar por la calle.*

Minidisc® ['mɪnɪdɪsk] NOUN
el minidisco

minimum ['mɪnɪməm] NOUN
see also **minimum** ADJECTIVE
el mínimo

minimum ['mɪnɪməm] ADJECTIVE
see also **minimum** NOUN
mínimo ◇ *The minimum age for driving is 17.* La edad mínima para poder conducir es 17 años. ◇ *minimum wage* salario mínimo

miniskirt ['mɪnɪskəːt] NOUN
la minifalda

minister ['mɪnɪstəʳ] NOUN
1 el ministro
la ministra
◇ *the Minister for Education* el Ministro de Educación
2 (*of church*)
el pastor
la pastora

ministry ['mɪnɪstrɪ] NOUN (PL **ministries**)
el ministerio (*in politics*)

minor ['maɪnəʳ] ADJECTIVE
secundario ◇ *a minor problem* un problema secundario
◆**a minor operation** una operación de poca importancia
◆**in D minor** en re menor

minority [maɪ'nɔrɪtɪ] NOUN (PL **minorities**)
la minoría

mint [mɪnt] NOUN
1 el caramelo de menta (*sweet*)
2 la menta (*plant*) ◇ *mint sauce* salsa de menta

minus ['maɪnəs] PREPOSITION
menos ◇ *sixteen minus three* dieciséis menos tres ◇ *I got a B minus for my French.* Me pusieron un notable bajo en francés.
◆**minus two degrees** dos grados bajo cero

minute ['mɪnɪt] NOUN
see also **minute** ADJECTIVE
el minuto ◇ *Wait a minute!* ¡Espera un minuto!

minute [maɪ'njuːt] ADJECTIVE
see also **minute** NOUN
minúsculo ◇ *Charlotte's flat is minute.* El apartamento de Charlotte es minúsculo.

miracle ['mɪrəkl] NOUN
el milagro

M

mirror ['mɪrəʳ] NOUN
1 el espejo ◊ *She looked at herself in the mirror.* Se miró en el espejo.
2 el retrovisor ◊ *She got in the car and adjusted the mirror.* Entró en el coche y ajustó el retrovisor.

to **misbehave** [mɪsbɪ'heɪv] VERB
portarse mal

mischief ['mɪstʃɪf] NOUN
♦ **She's always up to mischief.** Siempre está haciendo travesuras.
♦ **full of mischief** travieso

mischievous ['mɪstʃɪvəs] ADJECTIVE
travieso

miser ['maɪzəʳ] NOUN
el avaro
la avara

miserable ['mɪzərəbl] ADJECTIVE
infeliz (PL infelices) ◊ *a miserable life* una vida infeliz
♦ **I'm feeling miserable.** Me siento deprimido.
♦ **miserable weather** un tiempo deprimente

misfortune [mɪs'fɔːtʃən] NOUN
la desgracia

mishap ['mɪshæp] NOUN
el contratiempo ◊ *without mishap* sin contratiempos

to **misjudge** [mɪs'dʒʌdʒ] VERB
juzgar* mal ◊ *I may have misjudged him.* A lo mejor lo juzgué mal.
♦ **The driver misjudged the bend.** El conductor no calculó bien la curva.

to **mislay** [mɪs'leɪ] VERB (**mislaid, mislaid**)
♦ **I've mislaid my glasses.** No sé dónde he puesto las gafas.

misleading [mɪs'liːdɪŋ] ADJECTIVE
engañoso

misprint ['mɪsprɪnt] NOUN
el error de imprenta

Miss [mɪs] NOUN
1 señorita FEM ◊ *Miss Peters wants to see you.* La señorita Peters quiere verte.
2 Srta. (*in address*)

to **miss** [mɪs] VERB
perder* ◊ *Hurry or you'll miss the bus.* Date prisa o perderás el autobús.
♦ **It's too good an opportunity to miss.** Es una oportunidad demasiado buena para dejarla pasar.
♦ **He missed the target.** No dio en el blanco.
♦ **I miss my family.** Echo de menos a mi familia.
♦ **You've missed a page.** Te has saltado una página.

missing ['mɪsɪŋ] ADJECTIVE
perdido ◊ *the missing link* el eslabón perdido
♦ **to be missing** faltar ◊ *Two members of the group are missing.* Faltan dos miembros del grupo.
♦ **a missing person** una persona desaparecida

missionary ['mɪʃənrɪ] NOUN (PL **missionaries**)
el misionero
la misionera

mist [mɪst] NOUN
la neblina

mistake [mɪs'teɪk] NOUN
see also **mistake** VERB
el error ◊ *There must be some mistake.* Debe de haber algún error.
♦ **a spelling mistake** una falta de ortografía
♦ **to make a mistake (1)** (*in speaking*) cometer un error ◊ *He makes a lot of mistakes when he speaks English.* Comete muchos errores cuando habla inglés.
♦ **to make a mistake (2)** (*get mixed up*) equivocarse* ◊ *I'm sorry, I made a mistake.* Lo siento, me equivoqué.
♦ **by mistake** por error

to **mistake** [mɪs'teɪk] VERB (**mistook, mistaken**)
see also **mistake** NOUN
confundir ◊ *He mistook me for my sister.* Me confundió con mi hermana.

mistaken [mɪs'teɪkən] ADJECTIVE
♦ **to be mistaken** estar* equivocado ◊ *If you think I'm going to pay, you're mistaken.* Estás equivocado si piensas que voy a pagar.

mistletoe ['mɪsltəu] NOUN
el muérdago

mistook [mɪs'tuk] VERB *see* **mistake**

mistress ['mɪstrɪs] NOUN (PL **mistresses**)
1 la maestra (*in primary school*)
2 la profesora (*in secondary school*) ◊ *our English mistress* nuestra profesora de inglés
3 la amante ◊ *He's got a mistress.* Tiene una amante.

to **mistrust** [mɪs'trʌst] VERB
desconfiar* de

misty ['mɪstɪ] ADJECTIVE
neblinoso ◊ *a misty morning* una mañana neblinosa

to **misunderstand** [mɪsʌndə'stænd] VERB (**misunderstood, misunderstood**)
entender* mal ◊ *Sorry, I misunderstood you.* Lo siento, te entendí mal.

misunderstanding ['mɪsʌndə'stændɪŋ] NOUN
el malentendido

misunderstood [mɪsʌndə'stud] VERB *see* **misunderstand**

mix [mɪks] NOUN (PL **mixes**)
see also **mix** VERB
la mezcla ◊ *The film is a mix of science fiction and comedy.* La película es una mezcla de ciencia ficción y comedia.
♦ **a cake mix** un preparado para pastel

to **mix** [mɪks] VERB
see also **mix** NOUN
mezclar ◊ *Mix the flour with the sugar.* Mezcle la harina con el azúcar. ◊ *He's mixing business with pleasure.* Está mezclando los negocios con el placer.
♦ **I like mixing with all sorts of people.** Me gusta tratar con todo tipo de gente.
♦ **He doesn't mix much.** No se relaciona mucho.

to **mix up** [mɪks'ʌp] VERB
confundir ◊ *He mixed up their names.* Confundió sus nombres. ◊ *The travel agent mixed up the bookings.* La agencia de viajes confundió las reservas.
♦ **I'm getting mixed up.** Me estoy confundiendo.

mixed [mɪkst] ADJECTIVE
mixto ◊ *a mixed salad* una ensalada mixta ◊ *a mixed school* un colegio mixto
♦ **I've got mixed feelings about it.** No sé qué pensar de ello.

mixer ['mɪksəʳ] NOUN
la batidora (*for food*)

mixture ['mɪkstʃəʳ] NOUN
la mezcla ◊ *a mixture of spices* una mezcla de especias

mix-up ['mɪksʌp] NOUN
la confusión (PL las confusiones)

to **moan** [məun] VERB
quejarse ◊ *She's always moaning about something.* Siempre se está quejando de algo.

mobile home [məubaɪl'həum] NOUN
la caravana fija (el trailer *LatAm*)

mobile phone [məubaɪl'fəun] NOUN
el teléfono portátil

to **mock** [mɔk] VERB
see also **mock** ADJECTIVE
ridiculizar*

mock [mɔk] ADJECTIVE
see also **mock** VERB
♦ **a mock exam** un examen de práctica

mod cons ['mɔd'kɔnz] PL NOUN
♦ **with all mod cons** con todas las comodidades

model ['mɔdl] NOUN
see also **model** ADJECTIVE
1 el modelo ◊ *His car is the latest model.* Su coche es el último modelo.
2 la maqueta ◊ *a model of the castle* una maqueta del castillo
3 el/la modelo ◊ *She's a famous model.* Es una modelo famosa.

model ['mɔdl] ADJECTIVE
see also **model** NOUN
♦ **a model railway** una vía férrea en miniatura
♦ **a model plane** una maqueta de avión
♦ **He's a model pupil.** Es un alumno modelo.

modem ['məudɛm] NOUN
el módem (PL los módems)

moderate ['mɔdərət] ADJECTIVE
moderado ◊ *His views are quite moderate.* Tiene opiniones bastante moderadas.
♦ **I do a moderate amount of exercise.** Hago un poco de gimnasia.

modern ['mɔdən] ADJECTIVE
moderno

to **modernize** ['mɔdənaɪz] VERB
modernizar*

modest ['mɔdɪst] ADJECTIVE
modesto

to **modify** ['mɔdɪfaɪ] VERB (**modified, modified**)
modificar*

moist [mɔɪst] ADJECTIVE
húmedo ◊ *Sow the seeds in moist compost.* Plantar las semillas en abono húmedo.

moisture ['mɔɪstʃəʳ] NOUN
la humedad

moisturizer ['mɔɪstʃəraɪzəʳ] NOUN
la crema hidratante

moldy ['məuldɪ] ADJECTIVE US
mohoso

mole [məul] NOUN
1 el lunar ◊ *I've got a mole on my back.* Tengo un lunar en la espalda.
2 el topo (*animal*)

moment ['məumənt] NOUN
el momento ◊ *Just a moment!* ¡Un momento! ◊ *at the moment* en este momento ◊ *any moment now* de un momento a otro

monarch ['mɔnək] NOUN
el/la monarca

monarchy ['mɔnəkɪ] NOUN (PL **monarchies**)
la monarquía

monastery ['mɔnəstərɪ] NOUN (PL **monasteries**)
el monasterio

Monday ['mʌndɪ] NOUN
el lunes (PL los lunes) ◊ *I saw her on Monday.* La vi el lunes. ◊ *every Monday* todos los lunes ◊ *last Monday* el lunes pasado ◊ *next Monday* el lunes que viene ◊ *on Mondays* los lunes

money ['mʌnɪ] NOUN
el dinero ◊ *I need to change some money.* Tengo que cambiar dinero. ◊ *to make money* ganar dinero

mongrel ['mʌŋgrəl] NOUN
el perro mestizo

M

♦ **My dog's a mongrel.** Mi perro es mestizo.

monitor ['mɔnɪtəʳ] NOUN
el monitor (*on computer*)

monk [mʌŋk] NOUN
el monje

monkey ['mʌŋkɪ] NOUN
el mono
la mona

monster ['mɔnstəʳ] NOUN
el monstruo

month [mʌnθ] NOUN
el mes ◊ *this month* este mes ◊ *next month* el mes que viene ◊ *last month* el mes pasado ◊ *at the end of the month* a fin de mes

monthly ['mʌnθlɪ] ADJECTIVE
mensual

monument ['mɔnjumənt] NOUN
el monumento

mood [mu:d] NOUN
el humor ◊ *to be in a good mood* estar* de buen humor ◊ *to be in a bad mood* estar* de mal humor

moody ['mu:dɪ] ADJECTIVE
malhumorado (*in a bad mood*)
♦ **to be moody** tener* un humor cambiante (*temperamental*)

moon [mu:n] NOUN
la luna ◊ *There's a full moon tonight.* Esta noche hay luna llena.
♦ **She's over the moon about it.** Está en el séptimo cielo de contenta.

moor [muəʳ] NOUN
see also **moor** VERB
el páramo

to **moor** [muəʳ] VERB
see also **moor** NOUN
amarrar

mop [mɔp] NOUN
la fregona (el trapeador *LatAm*)

moped ['məupɛd] NOUN
el ciclomotor

moral ['mɔrl] NOUN
la moraleja ◊ *the moral of the story is...* la moraleja de la historia es...
♦ **morals** la moral

morale [mɔ'rɑ:l] NOUN
la moral ◊ *Morale was at an all-time low.* La moral estaba más baja que nunca.

more [mɔ:ʳ] ADJECTIVE, PRONOUN, ADVERB
más ◊ *It costs a lot more.* Cuesta mucho más. ◊ *There isn't any more.* Ya no hay más. ◊ *A bit more?* ¿Un poco más? ◊ *Is there any more?* ¿Hay más? ◊ *It'll take a few more days.* Llevará unos cuantos días más.
♦ **more than** más que

*Use **más que** when comparing two things or people and **más de** when talking about quantities.*

◊ *He's more intelligent than me.* Es más inteligente que yo. ◊ *I spent more than £10.* Yo gasté más de 10 libras esterlinas. ◊ *more than 20 people* más de 20 personas
♦ **more or less** más o menos
♦ **more than ever** más que nunca
♦ **more and more** cada vez más

moreover [mɔ:'rəuvəʳ] ADVERB
además

morning ['mɔ:nɪŋ] NOUN
la mañana ◊ *in the morning* por la mañana ◊ *at 7 o'clock in the morning* a las 7 de la mañana ◊ *on Saturday morning* el sábado por la mañana ◊ *tomorrow morning* mañana por la mañana
♦ **the morning papers** los periódicos de la mañana

Morocco [mə'rɔkəu] NOUN
Marruecos MASC

mortgage ['mɔ:gɪdʒ] NOUN
la hipoteca

Moscow ['mɔskəu] NOUN
Moscú MASC

Moslem ['mɔzləm] NOUN
el musulmán (PL los musulmanes)
la musulmana
◊ *He's a Moslem.* Es musulmán.

mosque [mɔsk] NOUN
la mezquita

mosquito [mɔs'ki:təu] NOUN (PL **mosquitoes**)
el mosquito
♦ **a mosquito bite** una picadura de mosquito

most [məust] ADJECTIVE, PRONOUN, ADVERB
más ◊ *the thing she feared most* lo que más temía ◊ *He's the one who talks the most.* Es el que más habla. ◊ *the most expensive restaurant* el restaurante más caro
♦ **most of** la mayor parte de ◊ *most of the time* la mayor parte del tiempo ◊ *I did most of the work alone.* Hice la mayor parte del trabajo solo.
♦ **most of them** la mayoría ◊ *Most of them have cars.* La mayoría tienen coches. ◊ *Most people go out on Friday nights.* La mayoría de la gente sale los viernes por la noche.
♦ **He won the most votes.** Fue el que sacó más votos.
♦ **at the most** como mucho ◊ *two hours at the most* dos horas como mucho
♦ **to make the most of something** aprovechar algo al máximo ◊ *He made*

the most of his holiday. Aprovechó sus vacaciones al máximo.

mostly ['məustlɪ] ADVERB
♦ **The teachers are mostly quite nice.** La mayoría de los profesores son bastante simpáticos.

MOT [ɛməu'tiː] NOUN
la ITV ◊ *My car has failed its MOT.* El coche no me ha pasado la ITV.

motel [məu'tɛl] NOUN
el motel

moth [mɔθ] NOUN
1 la mariposa nocturna
2 la polilla (*clothes moth*)

mother ['mʌðər] NOUN
la madre
♦ **my mother and father** mis padres
♦ **mother tongue** la lengua materna

mother-in-law ['mʌðərɪnlɔː] NOUN (PL **mothers-in-law**)
la suegra

Mother's Day ['mʌðəzdeɪ] NOUN
el Día de la Madre

motionless ['məuʃənlɪs] ADJECTIVE
inmóvil

motivated ['məutɪveɪtɪd] ADJECTIVE
♦ **He is highly motivated.** Está muy motivado.

motivation [məutɪ'veɪʃən] NOUN
la motivación (PL las motivaciones)

motive ['məutɪv] NOUN
1 el motivo ◊ *the motive for the killing* el motivo del homicidio
2 la intención (PL las intenciones) ◊ *for the best of motives* con la mejor de las intenciones

motor ['məutər] NOUN
el motor

motorbike ['məutəbaɪk] NOUN
la moto

> *Although **moto** ends in **-o**, it is actually a feminine noun.*

motorboat ['məutəbəut] NOUN
la lancha motora

motorcycle ['məutəsaɪkl] NOUN
la motocicleta

motorcyclist ['məutəsaɪklɪst] NOUN
el/la motociclista

motorist ['məutərɪst] NOUN
el conductor
la conductora

motor mechanic ['məutəmɪ'kænɪk] NOUN
el mecánico
la mecánica

motor racing ['məutəreɪsɪŋ] NOUN
las carreras de coches

motorway ['məutəweɪ] NOUN
la autopista ◊ *I had an accident on the motorway.* Tuve un accidente en la autopista.

mouldy ['məuldɪ] ADJECTIVE
mohoso

mountain ['mauntɪn] NOUN
la montaña ◊ *in the mountains* en la montaña
♦ **a mountain bike** una bicicleta de montaña

mountaineer [mauntɪ'nɪər] NOUN
el/la alpinista

mountaineering [mauntɪ'nɪərɪŋ] NOUN
el alpinismo ◊ *I go mountaineering.* Hago alpinismo.

mountainous ['mauntɪnəs] ADJECTIVE
montañoso

mouse [maus] NOUN (PL **mice**)
(*also for computer*)
el ratón (PL los ratones)

mouse mat ['mausmæt] NOUN
la alfombrilla del ratón

mousse [muːs] NOUN
1 la mousse ◊ *chocolate mousse* la mousse de chocolate
2 la espuma (*for hair*)

moustache [məs'tɑːʃ] NOUN
el bigote ◊ *He's got a moustache.* Tiene bigote.

mouth [mauθ] NOUN
la boca

mouthful ['mauθful] NOUN
1 el bocado (*of food*)
2 el trago (*of drink*)

mouth organ ['mauθɔːgən] NOUN
la armónica

mouthwash ['mauθwɔʃ] NOUN
el elixir bucal

move [muːv] NOUN
see also **move** VERB
1 el paso ◊ *That was a good move!* ¡Ese fue un paso bien dado!
♦ **It's your move.** Te toca jugar.
2 la mudanza ◊ *our move from Oxford to Luton* nuestra mudanza de Oxford a Luton
♦ **Get a move on!** ¡Date prisa!

to **move** [muːv] VERB
see also **move** NOUN
1 moverse* ◊ *Don't move!* ¡No te muevas!
2 mover* ◊ *He can't move his arm.* No puede mover el brazo.
♦ **Could you move your stuff please?** ¿Podrías quitar tus cosas de aquí, por favor?
3 avanzar* ◊ *The car was moving very slowly.* El coche avanzaba muy lentamente.
4 conmover* ◊ *I was very moved by the film.* La película me conmovió mucho.
♦ **to move house** mudarse de casa ◊ *We're moving in July.* Nos mudamos en julio.

to **move forward** [muːv'fɔːwəd] VERB
avanzar*

to **move in** [muːv'ɪn] VERB

♦When are the new tenants moving in? ¿Cuándo vienen los nuevos inquilinos?

to **move over** [muːv'əuvəʳ] VERB
correrse ◊ *Could you move over a bit, please?* ¿Te podrías correr un poco, por favor?

movement ['muːvmənt] NOUN
el movimiento

movie ['muːvɪ] NOUN
la película
♦the movies el cine

moving ['muːvɪŋ] ADJECTIVE
1 en movimiento ◊ *a moving bus* un autobús en movimiento
2 conmovedor MASC
conmovedora FEM
◊ *a moving story* una historia conmovedora

to **mow** [məu] VERB (**mowed, mowed** *or* **mown**)
cortar ◊ *I sometimes mow the lawn.* A veces corto el césped.

mower ['məuəʳ] NOUN
el cortacésped

mown [məun] VERB *see* **mow**

MP [ɛm'piː] ABBREVIATION
el diputado
la diputada

Mr ['mɪstəʳ] ABBREVIATION
1 señor MASC ◊ *Mr Jones wants to see you.* El señor Jones quiere verte.
2 Sr. (*in address*)

Mrs ['mɪsɪz] ABBREVIATION
1 señora FEM ◊ *Mrs Philips wants to see you.* La señora Philips quiere verte.
2 Sra. (*in address*)

Ms [mɪz] ABBREVIATION
1 señora FEM ◊ *Ms Brown wants to see you.* La señora Brown quiere verte.
2 Sra. (*in address*)

> *There isn't a direct equivalent of* ***Ms*** *in Spanish. If you are writing to a woman and don't know whether she is married, use* ***Señora.***

much [mʌtʃ] ADJECTIVE, PRONOUN, ADVERB
mucho ◊ *I feel much better now.* Ahora me siento mucho mejor. ◊ *I haven't got much money.* No tengo mucho dinero. ◊ *Have you got a lot of luggage? – No, not much.* ¿Tienes mucho equipaje? – No, no mucho.
♦very much mucho ◊ *I enjoyed myself very much.* Me divertí mucho.
♦Thank you very much. Muchas gracias.
♦how much? ¿cuánto? ◊ *How much time have you got?* ¿Cuánto tiempo tienes? ◊ *How much is it?* ¿Cuánto es?
♦too much demasiado ◊ *That's too much!* ¡Eso es demasiado! ◊ *They give us too much homework.* Nos ponen* demasiados deberes.
♦so much tanto ◊ *I didn't think it would cost so much.* No pensé* que costaría tanto. ◊ *I've never seen so much rain.* Nunca había visto tanta lluvia.
♦What's on TV? – Not much. ¿Qué ponen* en la tele? – Nada especial.

mud [mʌd] NOUN
el barro

muddle ['mʌdl] NOUN
♦to be in a muddle estar* todo revuelto ◊ *The photos are in a muddle.* Las fotos están* todas revueltas.

to **muddle up** [mʌdl'ʌp] VERB
confundir ◊ *He muddles me up with my sister.* Me confunde con mi hermana.
♦to get muddled up hacerse* un lío (*informal*) ◊ *I'm getting muddled up.* Me estoy haciendo un lío.

muddy ['mʌdɪ] ADJECTIVE
lleno de barro

muesli ['mjuːzlɪ] NOUN
el muesli

muffler ['mʌfləʳ] NOUN US
el silenciador

mug [mʌg] NOUN
see also **mug** VERB
la taza alta ◊ *Do you want a cup or a mug?* ¿Quieres una taza normal o una taza alta?
♦a beer mug una jarra de cerveza

to **mug** [mʌg] VERB
see also **mug** NOUN
atracar* ◊ *He was mugged in the city centre.* Lo atracaron en el centro de la ciudad.

mugger ['mʌgəʳ] NOUN
el atracador
la atracadora

mugging ['mʌgɪŋ] NOUN
el atraco

muggy ['mʌgɪ] ADJECTIVE
♦It's muggy today. Hoy hace bochorno.

multiple choice test [mʌltɪpl'tʃɔɪstest] NOUN
el examen tipo test

multiple sclerosis ['mʌltɪplsklɪ'rəusɪs] NOUN
la esclerosis múltiple ◊ *She's got multiple sclerosis.* Tiene esclerosis múltiple.

multiplication [mʌltɪplɪ'keɪʃən] NOUN
la multiplicación

to **multiply** ['mʌltɪplaɪ] VERB (**multiplied, multiplied**)
multiplicar* ◊ *to multiply six by three* multiplicar seis por tres

multi-storey car park [mʌltɪstɔːrɪ'kɑːpɑːk] NOUN
el aparcamiento de varias plantas

mum [mʌm] NOUN
mamá FEM ◊ *I'll ask Mum.* Le preguntaré a mamá. ◊ *my mum* mi mamá

mummy ['mʌmɪ] NOUN (PL **mummies**)
1 mamá FEM ◊ *Mummy says I can go.* Mamá dice que puedo ir.
2 la momia (*Egyptian*)

mumps [mʌmps] NOUN
las paperas ◊ *My brother's got mumps.* Mi hermano tiene paperas.

murder ['məːdəʳ] NOUN
see also **murder** VERB
el asesinato

to **murder** ['məːdəʳ] VERB
see also **murder** NOUN
asesinar ◊ *He was murdered.* Fue asesinado.

murderer ['məːdərəʳ] NOUN
el asesino
la asesina

muscle ['mʌsl] NOUN
el músculo

muscular ['mʌskjuləʳ] ADJECTIVE
musculoso ◊ *He's got muscular legs.* Tiene piernas musculosas.

museum [mjuː'zɪəm] NOUN
el museo

mushroom ['mʌʃrum] NOUN
el champiñón (PL los champiñones)

music ['mjuːzɪk] NOUN
la música

musical ['mjuːzɪkl] ADJECTIVE
see also **musical** NOUN
musical
♦ **I'm not musical.** No tengo aptitudes para la música.

musical ['mjuːzɪkl] NOUN
see also **musical** ADJECTIVE
el musical

music centre ['mjuːzɪksentəʳ] NOUN
el equipo de música

musician [mjuː'zɪʃən] NOUN
el músico
la música
◊ *He's a musician.* Es músico.

Muslim ['mʌzlɪm] NOUN
el musulmán (PL musulmanes)
la musulmana
◊ *She's a Muslim.* Es musulmana.

mussel ['mʌsl] NOUN
el mejillón (PL los mejillones)

must [mʌst] VERB
1 tener* que (*it's necessary*) ◊ *I must do it.* Tengo que hacerlo. ◊ *I must buy some presents.* Tengo que comprar unos regalos. ◊ *I really must go now.* De verdad que me tengo que ir ya. ◊ *You must come again next year.* Tienes que volver el año que viene.
♦ **You mustn't forget to send her a card.** No te vayas a olvidar de mandarle una tarjeta.
2 deber de (*I suppose*) ◊ *There must be some problem.* Debe de haber algún problema. ◊ *You must be tired.* Debes de estar cansada.

mustard ['mʌstəd] NOUN
la mostaza

mustn't ['mʌsnt] VERB = **must not**

to **mutter** ['mʌtəʳ] VERB
mascullar

mutton ['mʌtn] NOUN
la carne de cordero

mutual ['mjuːtʃuəl] ADJECTIVE
mutuo ◊ *The feeling was mutual.* El sentimiento era mutuo.
♦ **a mutual friend** un amigo común

my [maɪ] ADJECTIVE
mi (PL mis) ◊ *my father* mi padre ◊ *my house* mi casa ◊ *my two best friends* mis dos mejores amigos ◊ *my sisters* mis hermanas

> ***My** is usually translated by the definite article **el/los** or **la/las** when it's clear from the sentence who the possessor is or when referring to clothing or parts of the body.*

◊ *They stole my car.* Me robaron el coche. ◊ *I took off my coat.* Me quité el abrigo. ◊ *I'm washing my hair.* Me estoy lavando la cabeza.

myself [maɪ'sɛlf] PRONOUN
1 (*reflexive*)
me ◊ *I've hurt myself.* Me he hecho daño.
2 (*after preposition*)
mí mismo MASC
mí misma FEM
◊ *I talked mainly about myself.* Hablé principalmente de mí mismo.
♦ **a beginner like myself** un principiante como yo
3 (*for emphasis*)
yo mismo MASC
yo misma FEM
◊ *I made it myself.* Lo hice yo misma.
♦ **by myself** solo (FEM sola) ◊ *I don't like travelling by myself.* No me gusta viajar solo.

mysterious [mɪs'tɪərɪəs] ADJECTIVE
misterioso

mystery ['mɪstərɪ] NOUN (PL **mysteries**)
el misterio
♦ **a murder mystery** una novela policíaca

myth [mɪθ] NOUN
el mito ◊ *a Greek myth* un mito griego ◊ *That's a myth.* Eso es un mito. (*untrue story*)

mythology [mɪ'θɔlədʒɪ] NOUN
la mitología

M

N

naff [næf] ADJECTIVE
hortera
to **nag** [næg] VERB
dar* la lata ◊ *She's always nagging me.* Siempre me está dando la lata.
nail [neɪl] NOUN
1 la uña ◊ *She bites her nails.* Se muerde las uñas.
2 el clavo (*made of metal*)
nailbrush ['neɪlbrʌʃ] NOUN (PL **nailbrushes**)
el cepillo de uñas
nailfile ['neɪlfaɪl] NOUN
la lima para las uñas
nail scissors ['neɪlsɪzəz] PL NOUN
las tijeras para las uñas
nail varnish ['neɪlvɑːnɪʃ] NOUN (PL **nail varnishes**)
el esmalte de uñas
♦ **nail varnish remover** el quitaesmaltes
naked ['neɪkɪd] ADJECTIVE
desnudo
name [neɪm] NOUN
el nombre
♦ **What's your name?** ¿Cómo te llamas?
nanny ['nænɪ] NOUN (PL **nannies**)
la niñera (*nursemaid*)
nap [næp] NOUN
la siesta ◊ *She likes to have a nap in the afternoon.* Le gusta echarse una siesta por la tarde.
napkin ['næpkɪn] NOUN
la servilleta
nappy ['næpɪ] NOUN (PL **nappies**)
el pañal
narrow ['nærəu] ADJECTIVE
estrecho
narrow-minded [nærəu'maɪndɪd] ADJECTIVE
estrecho de miras
nasty ['nɑːstɪ] ADJECTIVE
1 malo
*Use **mal** before a masculine singular noun.*
◊ *Don't be nasty.* No seas malo. ◊ *What nasty weather!* ¡Qué tiempo más malo!
2 desagradable ◊ *a nasty smell* un olor desagradable
♦ **He gave me a nasty look.** Me miró de mala manera.
nation ['neɪʃən] NOUN
la nación (PL las naciones)
national ['næʃənl] ADJECTIVE
nacional
national anthem [næʃənl'ænθəm] NOUN
el himno nacional
National Health Service [næʃənl'hɛlθsəːvɪs] NOUN
el servicio sanitario de la Seguridad Social
nationalism ['næʃnəlɪzəm] NOUN
el nacionalismo
nationalist ['næʃnəlɪst] NOUN
el/la nacionalista
nationality [næʃə'nælɪtɪ] NOUN (PL **nationalities**)
la nacionalidad
national park [næʃənl'pɑːk] NOUN
el parque nacional
native ['neɪtɪv] ADJECTIVE
natal ◊ *my native country* mi país natal
♦ **his native language** su lengua materna
natural ['nætʃrəl] ADJECTIVE
natural ◊ *Helping him seemed the natural thing to do.* Ayudarlo parecía lo más natural.
naturalist ['nætʃrəlɪst] NOUN
el/la naturalista
naturally ['nætʃrəlɪ] ADVERB
naturalmente ◊ *Naturally, we were very disappointed.* Naturalmente, estábamos muy decepcionados.
nature ['neɪtʃəʳ] NOUN
la naturaleza ◊ *the wonders of nature* las maravillas de la naturaleza
♦ **It's not in his nature to behave like that.** Comportarse así no es propio de él.
naughty ['nɔːtɪ] ADJECTIVE
travieso ◊ *Naughty girl!* ¡Qué traviesa!
navy ['neɪvɪ] NOUN (PL **navies**)
la armada ◊ *He's in the navy.* Está en la armada.
navy-blue [neɪvɪ'bluː] ADJECTIVE
azul marino MASC, FEM, PL
◊ *a navy-blue skirt* una falda azul marino
near [nɪəʳ] ADJECTIVE
see also **near** PREPOSITION, ADVERB
1 cerca ◊ *It's fairly near.* Está bastante cerca. ◊ *My house is near enough to walk.* Mi casa está muy cerca, se puede ir andando.
2 cercano ◊ *Where's the nearest service station?* ¿Dónde está la gasolinera más cercana?
♦ **in the near future** en un futuro cercano
near [nɪəʳ] PREPOSITION, ADVERB
see also **near** ADJECTIVE
1 cerca ◊ *Is there a bank near here?* ¿Hay algún banco por aquí cerca?
2 cerca de ◊ *I live near Liverpool.* Vivo cerca de Liverpool.
♦ **near to** cerca de ◊ *It's very near to the school.* Está muy cerca del colegio.
nearby [nɪə'baɪ] ADJECTIVE

* Verbs marked with this symbol are irregular. See pages 380-382 for further details

see also **nearby** ADVERB
cercano ◊ *a nearby village* un pueblo cercano

nearby [nɪə'baɪ] ADVERB
see also **nearby** ADJECTIVE
cerca ◊ *There's a supermarket nearby.* Hay un supermercado cerca.

nearly ['nɪəlɪ] ADVERB
casi ◊ *Dinner's nearly ready.* La cena está casi lista. ◊ *I'm nearly fifteen.* Tengo casi quince años.
♦ **I nearly missed the train.** Por poco pierdo el tren.

neat [ni:t] ADJECTIVE
ordenado ◊ *My flatmate's not very neat.* Mi compañero de piso no es muy ordenado.
♦ **He always looks very neat.** Siempre está muy pulcro.

neatly ['ni:tlɪ] ADVERB
♦ **neatly folded** cuidadosamente doblado
♦ **neatly dressed** bien vestido

necessarily ['nɛsɪsrɪlɪ] ADVERB
♦ **not necessarily** no necesariamente

necessary ['nɛsɪsrɪ] ADJECTIVE
necesario

necessity [nɪ'sɛsɪtɪ] NOUN (PL **necessities**)
la necesidad ◊ *A car is a necessity, not a luxury.* Un coche es una necesidad, no un lujo.

neck [nɛk] NOUN
el cuello ◊ *a V-neck sweater* un jersey de cuello en pico
♦ **She had a stiff neck.** Tenía tortícolis.
♦ **the back of your neck** la nuca

necklace ['nɛklɪs] NOUN
el collar

to **need** [ni:d] VERB
see also **need** NOUN
necesitar ◊ *I need a bigger size.* Necesito una talla más grande. ◊ *I need to change some money.* Necesito cambiar dinero.
♦ **You don't need to go.** No tienes por qué ir.

need [ni:d] NOUN
see also **need** VERB
♦ **There's no need to book.** No hace falta hacer reserva.

***hace falta que** has to be followed by a verb in the subjunctive.*

◊ *There's no need for you to do that.* No hace falta que hagas eso.

needle ['ni:dl] NOUN
la aguja

needlework ['ni:dlwə:k] NOUN
la costura ◊ *We have needlework lessons at school.* En el colegio tenemos clase de costura.

negative ['nɛgətɪv] NOUN
see also **negative** ADJECTIVE
el negativo (*photo*)

negative ['nɛgətɪv] ADJECTIVE
see also **negative** NOUN
negativo ◊ *He's got a very negative attitude.* Tiene una actitud muy negativa.

neglected [nɪ'glɛktɪd] ADJECTIVE
abandonado ◊ *The garden is neglected.* El jardín está abandonado.

to **negotiate** [nɪ'gəuʃɪeɪt] VERB
negociar

negotiations [nɪˌgəuʃɪ'eɪʃənz] PL NOUN
las negociaciones

neighbour ['neɪbə^r] NOUN (US **neighbor**)
el vecino
la vecina

neighbourhood ['neɪbəhud] NOUN (US **neighborhood**)
el barrio

neither ['naɪðə^r] ADJECTIVE, CONJUNCTION, PRONOUN
1 ninguno de los dos MASC
ninguna de las dos FEM
◊ *Carrots or peas? – Neither, thanks.* ¿Zanahorias o guisantes? – Ninguno de los dos, gracias. ◊ *Neither of them is coming.* No viene ninguno de los dos. ◊ *Neither woman looked happy.* Ninguna de las dos parecía contenta.
2 tampoco ◊ *I don't like him. – Neither do I!* No me cae bien. – ¡A mí tampoco! ◊ *I've never been to Spain. – Neither have we.* No he estado nunca en España. – Nosotros tampoco.
♦ **neither...nor...** ni...ni... ◊ *Neither Sarah nor Tamsin is coming to the party.* No vienen ni Sarah ni Tamsin a la fiesta.

neon ['ni:ɔn] NOUN
el neón ◊ *a neon light* una lámpara de neón

nephew ['nɛvju:] NOUN
el sobrino

nerve [nə:v] NOUN
el nervio ◊ *That noise really gets on my nerves.* Ese ruido me pone los nervios de punta.
♦ **He's got a nerve!** ¡Qué cara tiene!
♦ **I wouldn't have the nerve to do that!** ¡Yo no me atrevería a hacer eso!

nerve-racking ['nə:vrækɪŋ] ADJECTIVE
angustioso

nervous ['nə:vəs] ADJECTIVE
nervioso ◊ *I bite my nails when I'm nervous.* Cuando estoy nervioso me muerdo las uñas. ◊ *I'm a bit nervous about the exams.* Estoy un poco nervioso por los exámenes.

nest [nɛst] NOUN
el nido

net [nɛt] NOUN
la red ◊ *a fishing net* una red de pesca

Net [nɛt] NOUN
la Red
♦ **to surf the Net** navegar* por la Red

netball ['nɛtbɔ:l] NOUN

☞

> ℹ **Netball** *es un deporte parecido al baloncesto, que juegan especialmente las niñas en los colegios.*

Netherlands ['nɛðələndz] PL NOUN
♦**the Netherlands** los Países Bajos
network ['nɛtwəːk] NOUN
la red
neurotic [njuə'rɔtɪk] ADJECTIVE
neurótico
never ['nɛvəʳ] ADVERB
nunca ◊ *Have you ever been to Argentina? – No, never.* ¿Has estado alguna vez en Argentina? – No, nunca. ◊ *Never leave valuables in your car.* No dejen nunca objetos de valor en el coche.

> *When **nunca** comes before the verb in Spanish it is not necessary to use **no** as well.*

◊ *I never believed him.* Yo nunca le creí.
♦**Never again!** ¡Nunca más!
♦**Never, ever do that again!** ¡No vuelvas a hacer eso nunca jamás!
♦**Never mind.** No importa.
new [njuː] ADJECTIVE
nuevo ◊ *her new boyfriend* su nuevo novio
newborn ['njuːbɔːn] ADJECTIVE
♦**a newborn baby** un bebé recién nacido
newcomer ['njuːkʌməʳ] NOUN
♦**They were newcomers to the area.** Eran nuevos en la zona.
news [njuːz] NOUN
1 las noticias ◊ *good news* buenas noticias ◊ *I watch the news every evening.* Veo las noticias todas las noches.
♦**It was nice to have your news.** Me dio alegría saber de ti.
2 la noticia ◊ *That's wonderful news!* ¡Qué buena noticia!
♦**an interesting piece of news** una noticia interesante
newsagent ['njuːzeɪdʒənt] NOUN
la tienda de periódicos

> ℹ *En Gran Bretaña, los* ***newsagents*** *son tiendas en las que se venden periódicos y revistas; y también dulces, cigarrillos y productos de papelería.*

news dealer ['njuːzdiːləʳ] NOUN US
el vendedor de periódicos
la vendedora de periódicos
newspaper ['njuːzpeɪpəʳ] NOUN
el periódico
newsreader ['njuːzriːdəʳ] NOUN
1 (*on TV*)
el presentador
la presentadora
2 (*on radio*)
el locutor
la locutora
New Year [njuː'jɪəʳ] NOUN
el Año Nuevo ◊ *to celebrate New Year* celebrar el Año Nuevo
♦**Happy New Year!** ¡Feliz Año Nuevo!
♦**New Year's Day** el día de Año Nuevo
♦**New Year's Eve** Nochevieja (la noche de Fin de Año *LatAm*)
♦**a New Year's Eve party** una fiesta de Nochevieja
New Zealand [njuː'ziːlənd] NOUN
Nueva Zelanda FEM
New Zealander [njuː'ziːləndəʳ] NOUN
el neozelandés (PL los neozelandeses)
la neozelandesa
next [nɛkst] ADJECTIVE, ADVERB, PREPOSITION
1 próximo ◊ *next Saturday* el próximo sábado ◊ *the next time I see you* la próxima vez que te vea
2 siguiente ◊ *Next please!* ¡El siguiente, por favor! ◊ *The next day we visited Gerona.* Al día siguiente visitamos Gerona.
3 luego ◊ *What did you do next?* ¿Qué hiciste luego?
♦**next to** al lado de ◊ *next to the bank* al lado del banco
♦**next door** al lado ◊ *They live next door.* Viven al lado.
♦**the next-door neighbours** los vecinos de al lado
♦**the next room** la habitación de al lado
NHS [ɛneɪtʃ'ɛs] ABBREVIATION (= *National Health Service*)
el servicio sanitario de la Seguridad Social
nice [naɪs] ADJECTIVE
1 simpático (*friendly*) ◊ *Your parents are very nice.* Tus padres son muy simpáticos.
2 amable (*kind*) ◊ *She was always very nice to me.* Siempre fue muy amable conmigo. ◊ *It was nice of you to remember my birthday.* Fue muy amable de tu parte que te acordaras de mi cumpleaños.
3 bonito (*pretty*) ◊ *That's a nice dress!* ¡Qué vestido más bonito! ◊ *Segovia is a nice town.* Segovia es una ciudad bonita.
4 bueno (*good*)

> *Use **buen** before a masculine singular noun.*

◊ *nice weather* buen tiempo ◊ *It's a nice day.* Hace buen día. ◊ *This paella is very nice.* Esta paella está muy buena. ◊ *a nice cup of coffee* una buena taza de café
♦**Have a nice time!** ¡Que te diviertas!
nickname ['nɪkneɪm] NOUN
el apodo

niece [niːs] NOUN
la sobrina

night [naɪt] NOUN
la noche ◊ *I want a single room for two nights.* Quiero una habitación individual para dos noches.
♦ **at night** por la noche
♦ **Good night!** ¡Buenas noches!
♦ **last night** anoche ◊ *We went to a party last night.* Anoche fuimos a una fiesta.

night club ['naɪtklʌb] NOUN
la sala de fiestas

nightdress ['naɪtdrɛs] NOUN
el camisón (PL los camisones)

nightie ['naɪtɪ] NOUN
el camisón (PL los camisones)

nightlife ['naɪtlaɪf] NOUN
la vida nocturna ◊ *There's plenty of nightlife in Madrid.* Hay mucha vida nocturna en Madrid.

nightmare ['naɪtmɛəʳ] NOUN
la pesadilla ◊ *to have nightmares* tener* pesadillas ◊ *The whole trip was a nightmare.* El viaje entero fue una pesadilla.

nightshift ['naɪtʃɪft] NOUN
el turno de noche

nil [nɪl] NOUN
el cero ◊ *We won one-nil.* Ganamos uno a cero.

nine [naɪn] NUMERAL
nueve
♦ **She's nine.** Tiene nueve años.

nineteen ['naɪn'tiːn] NUMERAL
diecinueve
♦ **She's nineteen.** Tiene diecinueve años.

nineteenth [naɪn'tiːnθ] ADJECTIVE
decimonoveno
♦ **the nineteenth floor** la planta diecinueve
♦ **the nineteenth of March** el diecinueve de marzo

ninety ['naɪntɪ] NUMERAL
noventa ◊ *He's ninety.* Tiene noventa años.

ninth [naɪnθ] ADJECTIVE
noveno ◊ *on the ninth floor* en el noveno piso
♦ **on ninth of August** el nueve de agosto

no [nəu] ADVERB, ADJECTIVE
no ◊ *Are you coming? – No.* ¿Vienes? – No. ◊ *Would you like some more? – No thank you.* ¿Quieres un poco más? – No, gracias. ◊ *There's no hot water.* No hay agua caliente.
♦ **I've got no idea.** No tengo ni idea.
♦ **I have no questions.** No tengo ninguna pregunta.
♦ **No way!** ¡Ni hablar!
♦ **"no smoking"** "prohibido fumar"

nobody ['nəubədɪ] PRONOUN
nadie ◊ *Who's going with you? – Nobody.* ¿Quién va contigo? – Nadie. ◊ *There was nobody in the office.* No había nadie en la oficina.
♦ **I've got nobody to play with.** No tengo a nadie con quien jugar.

> *When **nobody** goes before a verb in English it can be translated by either **nadie ...** or **no ... nadie**.*

◊ *Nobody likes him.* No le cae bien a nadie. ◊ *Nobody saw me.* Nadie me vio.

to **nod** [nɔd] VERB
1 asentir* con la cabeza (*in agreement*)
2 saludar con la cabeza (*as greeting*)

noise [nɔɪz] NOUN
el ruido
♦ **to make a noise** hacer* ruido

noisy ['nɔɪzɪ] ADJECTIVE
ruidoso ◊ *the noisiest city in the world* la ciudad más ruidosa del mundo
♦ **It's very noisy here.** Hay mucho ruido aquí.

to **nominate** ['nɔmɪneɪt] VERB
nombrar* ◊ *She was nominated for the post.* La nombraron para el cargo.
♦ **He was nominated for an Oscar.** Le nominaron para un Oscar.

none [nʌn] PRONOUN

> *When **none** refers to something you can count, such as sisters or friends, Spanish uses **ninguno** with a singular verb. When it refers to something you cannot count, such as wine, Spanish uses **nada**.*

1 ninguno MASC
ninguna FEM
◊ *How many sisters have you got? – None.* ¿Cuántas hermanas tienes? – Ninguna. ◊ *None of my friends wanted to come.* Ninguno de mis amigos quiso venir. ◊ *There are none left.* No queda ninguno.
2 nada ◊ *There's none left.* No queda nada.

nonsense ['nɔnsəns] NOUN
las tonterías PL ◊ *She talks a lot of nonsense.* Dice muchas tonterías.
♦ **Nonsense!** ¡Tonterías!

non-smoker ['nɔn'sməukəʳ] NOUN
el no fumador
la no fumadora
♦ **He's a non-smoker.** No fuma.

non-smoking ['nɔn'sməukɪŋ] ADJECTIVE
♦ **a non-smoking area** un área reservada para no fumadores

> *Although it's a feminine noun, remember that you use **el** and **un** with **área**.*

♦ **a non-smoking carriage** un vagón para no fumadores

non-stop ['nɔn'stɔp] ADJECTIVE, ADVERB
1 directo ◊ *a non-stop flight* un vuelo directo
♦ **We flew non-stop.** Tomamos un vuelo directo.

☞

2 sin parar ◇ *He talks non-stop.* Habla sin parar.

noodles ['nu:dlz] PL NOUN
los fideos

noon [nu:n] NOUN
las doce del mediodía
♦ **at noon** a las doce del mediodía

no one ['nəuwʌn] PRONOUN
nadie ◇ *Who's going with you? – No one.* ¿Quién va contigo? – Nadie. ◇ *There was no one in the office.* No había nadie en la oficina.
♦ **I've got no one to play with.** No tengo a nadie con quien jugar.

*When **nobody** goes before a verb in English it can be translated by either **nadie ... or no ... nadie.***

◇ *No one likes him.* No le cae bien a nadie. ◇ *No one saw me.* Nadie me vio.

nor [nɔ:ʳ] CONJUNCTION
tampoco ◇ *I didn't like the film. – Nor did I.* No me gustó la película. – A mí tampoco. ◇ *We haven't seen him. – Nor have we.* No lo hemos visto. – Nosotros tampoco.
♦ **neither...nor** ni...ni ◇ *neither the cinema nor the swimming pool* ni el cine ni la piscina

normal ['nɔ:məl] ADJECTIVE
normal

normally ['nɔ:məlɪ] ADVERB
1 normalmente (*usually*) ◇ *I normally arrive at nine o'clock.* Normalmente llego a las nueve.
2 con normalidad (*as normal*) ◇ *In spite of the strike, airports are working normally.* A pesar de la huelga, los aeropuertos funcionan con normalidad.

north [nɔ:θ] NOUN
see also **north** ADJECTIVE, ADVERB
el norte ◇ *in the north of Spain* en el norte de España

north [nɔ:θ] ADJECTIVE, ADVERB
see also **north** NOUN
1 el norte ◇ *North London* el norte de Londres
2 hacia el norte ◇ *We were travelling north.* Viajábamos hacia el norte.
♦ **north of** al norte de ◇ *It's north of London.* Está al norte de Londres.
♦ **the north coast** la costa septentrional

North America [nɔ:θə'mɛrɪkə] NOUN
América del Norte FEM

northbound ['nɔ:θbaund] ADJECTIVE
♦ **Northbound traffic is moving very slowly.** El tráfico que se dirige hacia el norte avanza muy despacio.

northeast [nɔ:θ'i:st] NOUN
el noreste
♦ **in the northeast** al noreste

northern ['nɔ:ðən] ADJECTIVE
del norte ◇ *Northern Europe* Europa del Norte
♦ **the northern part of the island** la zona norte de la isla

Northern Ireland [nɔ:ðən'aɪələnd] NOUN
Irlanda del Norte FEM

North Pole [nɔ:θ'pəul] NOUN
♦ **the North Pole** el Polo Norte

North Sea [nɔ:θ'si:] NOUN
♦ **the North Sea** el Mar del Norte

northwest [nɔ:θ'wɛst] NOUN
el noroeste
♦ **in the northwest** al noroeste

Norway ['nɔ:weɪ] NOUN
Noruega FEM

Norwegian [nɔ:'wi:dʒən] ADJECTIVE
see also **Norwegian** NOUN
noruego

Norwegian [nɔ:'wi:dʒən] NOUN
see also **Norwegian** ADJECTIVE
1 (*person*)
el noruego
la noruega
◇ *the Norwegians* los noruegos
2 (*language*)
el noruego

nose [nəuz] NOUN
la nariz (PL las narices)

nosebleed ['nəuzbli:d] NOUN
♦ **I often get nosebleeds.** Me sangra la nariz a menudo.

nosy ['nəuzɪ] ADJECTIVE
fisgón MASC
fisgona FEM

not [nɔt] ADVERB
no ◇ *I'm not sure.* No estoy seguro. ◇ *Are you coming or not?* ¿Vienes o no? ◇ *Did you like it? – Not really.* ¿Te gustó? – No mucho.
♦ **Thank you very much. – Not at all.** Muchas gracias. – De nada.
♦ **not yet** todavía no ◇ *They haven't arrived yet.* Todavía no han llegado.

note [nəut] NOUN
1 la nota ◇ *I'll drop her a note.* Le dejaré una nota.
♦ **Remember to take notes.** Acuérdate de tomar apuntes.
♦ **to make a note of something** tomar nota de algo
2 el billete ◇ *a five pound note* un billete de cinco libras

to **note down** [nəut'daun] VERB
anotar

notebook ['nəutbuk] NOUN
el cuaderno

notepad ['nəutpæd] NOUN
el bloc de notas (PL los blocs de notas)

notepaper ['nəutpeɪpəʳ] NOUN
el papel de cartas

nothing ['nʌθɪŋ] NOUN
nada ◊ *What's wrong? – Nothing.* ¿Qué pasa? – Nada. ◊ *What are you doing tonight? – Nothing special.* ¿Qué haces esta noche? – Nada especial. ◊ *He does nothing.* No hace nada.
♦ **He does nothing but sleep.** No hace nada más que dormir.
♦ **There's nothing to do.** No hay nada que hacer.
When ***nothing*** *goes before a verb in English it can be translated by either* ***nada ...*** *or* ***no ... nada.***
◊ *Nothing frightens him.* Nada lo asusta. ◊ *Nothing will happen.* No pasará nada.

notice ['nəutɪs] NOUN
see also **notice** VERB
1 el letrero (*physical object*) ◊ *There was a notice outside the house.* Había un letrero fuera de la casa.
2 el aviso (*information*) ◊ *There's a notice on the board about the trip.* Hay un aviso en el tablón sobre el viaje.
♦ **a warning notice** un aviso
♦ **He was transferred without notice.** Lo trasladaron sin previo aviso.
♦ **until further notice** hasta nuevo aviso
♦ **Don't take any notice of him!** ¡No le hagas caso!
Be careful not to translate ***notice*** *by* ***noticia.***

to **notice** ['nəutɪs] VERB
see also **notice** NOUN
♦ **to notice something** darse* cuenta de algo ◊ *Don't worry. He won't notice the mistake.* No te preocupes. No se dará cuenta del error.

notice board ['nəutɪsbɔ:d] NOUN
el tablón de anuncios (PL los tablones de anuncios)

nought [nɔ:t] NOUN
cero MASC

noun [naun] NOUN
el nombre

novel ['nɔvl] NOUN
la novela

novelist ['nɔvəlɪst] NOUN
el/la novelista

November [nəu'vɛmbəʳ] NOUN
noviembre MASC ◊ *in November* en noviembre ◊ *on 7th November* el 7 de noviembre

now [nau] ADVERB
ahora ◊ *What are you doing now?* ¿Qué haces ahora?
♦ **just now** en este momento ◊ *I'm rather busy just now.* En este momento estoy muy ocupado.
♦ **I did it just now.** Lo acabo de hacer*.
♦ **It should be ready by now.** Ya debería estar listo.
♦ **from now on** de ahora en adelante
♦ **now and then** de vez en cuando

nowhere ['nəuwɛəʳ] ADVERB
a ninguna parte ◊ *Where are you going for your holidays? – Nowhere.* ¿Adónde vas en vacaciones? – A ninguna parte.
♦ **nowhere else** a ninguna otra parte ◊ *You can go to the shops but nowhere else.* Puedes ir a las tiendas pero a ninguna otra parte.
♦ **The children were nowhere to be seen.** No se podía ver a los niños por ninguna parte.
♦ **There was nowhere to play.** No se podía jugar en ninguna parte.

nuclear ['nju:klɪəʳ] ADJECTIVE
nuclear ◊ *nuclear power* la energía nuclear

nude [nju:d] NOUN
see also **nude** ADJECTIVE
♦ **in the nude** desnudo

nude [nju:d] ADJECTIVE
see also **nude** NOUN
desnudo

nudist ['nju:dɪst] NOUN
el/la nudista

nuisance ['nju:sns] NOUN
fastidio ◊ *It's a nuisance having to clean the car.* Es un fastidio tener que limpiar el coche.
♦ **Sorry to be a nuisance.** Siento molestarle.
♦ **You're a nuisance!** ¡Eres un pesado!

numb [nʌm] ADJECTIVE
♦ **numb with cold** helado de frío

number ['nʌmbəʳ] NOUN
el número ◊ *I can't read the second number.* No puedo leer el segundo número. ◊ *They live at number five.* Viven en el número cinco. ◊ *You've got the wrong number.* Se ha equivocado de número.
♦ **a large number of people** un gran número de gente
♦ **What's your number?** (*telephone*) ¿Cuál es tu teléfono?

number plate ['nʌmbəpleɪt] NOUN
la matrícula (la placa *LatAm*)

nun [nʌn] NOUN
la monja

nurse [nə:s] NOUN
el enfermero
la enfermera
♦ **She's a nurse.** Es enfermera.

nursery ['nə:sərɪ] NOUN (PL **nurseries**)
1 la guardería infantil (*for children*)
2 el vivero (*for plants*)

nursery school ['nə:sərɪsku:l] NOUN
el preescolar (guardería *LatAm*)

nursery slope ['nə:sərɪsləup] NOUN
la pista para principiantes

nut [nʌt] NOUN

N

☞

1 (*almond*)
la almendra
2 (*peanut*)
el cacahuete
3 (*hazelnut*)
la avellana
4 (*walnut*)
la nuez (PL las nueces)
◆**I don't like nuts.** No me gustan los frutos secos.
5 (*made of metal*)
la tuerca

nutmeg ['nʌtmɛg] NOUN
la nuez moscada

nutritious [nju:'trɪʃəs] ADJECTIVE
nutritivo

nuts [nʌts] ADJECTIVE
◆**He's nuts.** Está chiflado. (*informal*)

nutter ['nʌtə^r] NOUN
◆**He's a nutter.** Es un chiflado. (*informal*)

nylon ['naɪlɔn] NOUN
nylon

O

oak [əuk] NOUN
el <u>roble</u> ◊ *an oak barrel* un barril de roble

oar [ɔːʳ] NOUN
el <u>remo</u>

oats [əuts] PL NOUN
la <u>avena</u>

obedient [əˈbiːdɪənt] ADJECTIVE
<u>obediente</u>

to **obey** [əˈbeɪ] VERB
<u>obedecer*</u>
♦ **to obey the rules** (*in game*) atenerse a las reglas del juego

object [ˈɔbdʒɪkt] NOUN
el <u>objeto</u>

objection [əbˈdʒɛkʃən] NOUN
la <u>objeción</u> (PL las objeciones) ◊ *There were no objections to the plan.* No hubo objeciones al plan.

objective [əbˈdʒɛktɪv] NOUN
see also **objective** ADJECTIVE
el <u>objetivo</u>

objective [əbˈdʒɛktɪv] ADJECTIVE
see also **objective** NOUN
<u>objetivo</u>

oblong [ˈɔblɔŋ] ADJECTIVE
<u>rectangular</u>

oboe [ˈəubəu] NOUN
el <u>oboe</u>

obscene [əbˈsiːn] ADJECTIVE
<u>obsceno</u>

observant [əbˈzəːvənt] ADJECTIVE
<u>observador</u> MASC
<u>observadora</u> FEM

to **observe** [əbˈzəːv] VERB
<u>observar</u>

obsessed [əbˈsɛst] ADJECTIVE
<u>obsesionado</u> ◊ *He's obsessed with trains.* Está obsesionado con los trenes.

obsession [əbˈsɛʃən] NOUN
la <u>obsesión</u> (PL las obsesiones) ◊ *Football's an obsession of mine.* El fútbol es una obsesión mía.

obsolete [ˈɔbsəliːt] ADJECTIVE
<u>obsoleto</u>

obstacle [ˈɔbstəkl] NOUN
el <u>obstáculo</u>

obstinate [ˈɔbstɪnɪt] ADJECTIVE
<u>terco</u>

to **obstruct** [əbˈstrʌkt] VERB
<u>bloquear</u> ◊ *A lorry was obstructing the traffic.* Un camión bloqueaba el tráfico.

to **obtain** [əbˈteɪn] VERB
<u>obtener*</u>

obvious [ˈɔbvɪəs] ADJECTIVE
<u>obvio</u>

obviously [ˈɔbvɪəslɪ] ADVERB
<u>claro</u> ◊ *Do you want to pass the exam? – Obviously!* ¿Quieres aprobar el examen? – ¡Claro! ◊ *It was obviously impossible.* Estaba claro que era imposible.
♦ **Obviously not!** ¡Claro que no!

occasion [əˈkeɪʒən] NOUN
la <u>ocasión</u> (PL las ocasiones) ◊ *a special occasion* una ocasión especial
♦ **on several occasions** en varias ocasiones

occasionally [əˈkeɪʒənəlɪ] ADVERB
<u>de vez en cuando</u>

occupation [ɔkjuˈpeɪʃən] NOUN
el <u>empleo</u>

to **occupy** [ˈɔkjupaɪ] VERB (**occupied, occupied**)
<u>ocupar</u> ◊ *The toilet was occupied.* El lavabo estaba ocupado.

to **occur** [əˈkəːʳ] VERB
<u>ocurrir</u> ◊ *The accident occurred yesterday.* El accidente ocurrió ayer.
♦ **It suddenly occurred to me that...** De repente se me ocurrió que...

ocean [ˈəuʃən] NOUN
el <u>océano</u>

o'clock [əˈklɔk] ADVERB
♦ **at four o'clock** a las cuatro
♦ **It's one o'clock.** Es la una.
♦ **It's five o'clock.** Son las cinco.

October [ɔkˈtəubəʳ] NOUN
<u>octubre</u> MASC ◊ *in October* en octubre ◊ *on 12 October* el 12 de octubre

octopus [ˈɔktəpəs] NOUN (PL **octopuses**)
el <u>pulpo</u>

odd [ɔd] ADJECTIVE
1 <u>raro</u> ◊ *That's odd!* ¡Qué raro!
2 <u>impar</u> ◊ *an odd number* un número impar
♦ **odd socks** calcetines desparejados

of [ɔv, əv] PREPOSITION
<u>de</u> ◊ *a boy of 10* un niño de 10 años ◊ *a kilo of oranges* un kilo de naranjas ◊ *It's made of wood.* Es de madera. ◊ *a glass of wine* un vaso de vino

***de + el** changes to **del**.*

◊ *the wheels of the car* las ruedas del coche
♦ **There were three of us.** Éramos tres.
♦ **a friend of mine** un amigo mío
♦ **That's very kind of you.** Es muy amable de su parte.

off [ɔf] ADJECTIVE, ADVERB, PREPOSITION

*For other expressions with **off**, see the verbs **get, take, turn** etc.*

1 <u>apagado</u> (*heater, light, TV*) ◊ *All the lights are off.* Todas las luces están apagadas.
2 <u>cerrado</u> (*tap, gas*) ◊ *Are you sure the tap is off?* ¿Seguro que el grifo está cerrado?
3 <u>cortado</u> (*milk*)

☞

4 estropeado (*meat*)
♦ **to be off sick** estar* ausente por enfermedad
♦ **a day off** un día libre ◊ *She took a day off work to go to the wedding.* Se tomó un día libre para ir* a la boda.
♦ **I've got tomorrow off.** Mañana tengo el día libre.
♦ **She's off school today.** Hoy no ha ido al colegio.
♦ **I must be off now.** Me tengo que ir ahora.
♦ **I'm off.** Me voy.
♦ **The match is off.** El partido se ha suspendido.

offence [ə'fɛns] NOUN (US **offense**)
el delito (*crime*)

offensive [ə'fɛnsɪv] ADJECTIVE
ofensivo

offer ['ɔfəʳ] NOUN
see also **offer** VERB
1 la oferta (*of money, job*)
2 el ofrecimiento (*of help*)
♦ **There was a special offer on tapes.** Las cintas estaban de oferta.

to **offer** ['ɔfəʳ] VERB
see also **offer** NOUN
ofrecer* ◊ *He offered me a cigarette.* Me ofreció un cigarrillo.
♦ **He offered to help me.** Se ofreció a ayudarme.

office ['ɔfɪs] NOUN
la oficina
♦ **during office hours** en horas de oficina

officer ['ɔfɪsəʳ] NOUN
el/la oficial (*in the army*)
♦ **police officer** el/la agente de policía

official [ə'fɪʃl] ADJECTIVE
oficial

off-licence ['ɔflaɪsns] NOUN
la tienda de bebidas alcohólicas

off-peak ['ɔf'pi:k] ADJECTIVE
♦ **off-peak calls** llamadas de tarifa reducida

offside ['ɔf'saɪd] ADJECTIVE
fuera de juego

often ['ɔfn] ADVERB
a menudo ◊ *It often rains.* Llueve a menudo.
♦ **How often do you go to the gym?** ¿Cada cuánto vas al gimnasio?

oil [ɔɪl] NOUN
see also **oil** VERB
1 el aceite (*for lubrication, cooking*)
2 el petróleo (*crude oil*)
♦ **an oil painting** una pintura al óleo

to **oil** [ɔɪl] VERB
see also **oil** NOUN
engrasar

oil rig ['ɔɪlrɪg] NOUN
la plataforma petrolífera

oil slick ['ɔɪlslɪk] NOUN
la marea negra

oil well ['ɔɪlwɛl] NOUN
el pozo de petróleo

ointment ['ɔɪntmənt] NOUN
la pomada

okay ['əu'keɪ] EXCLAMATION, ADVERB
1 de acuerdo (*more formally*) ◊ *Your appointment's at six o'clock. – Okay.* Su cita es a las seis. – De acuerdo.
2 vale (*less formally*) ◊ *I'll meet you at six o'clock, okay?* Te veré a las seis, ¿vale?
♦ **Are you okay?** ¿Estás bien?
♦ **I'll do it tomorrow, if that's okay with you.** Lo haré mañana, si te parece bien.
♦ **The film was okay.** La película no estuvo mal.

old [əuld] ADJECTIVE
1 viejo ◊ *an old house* una casa vieja ◊ *an old man* un viejo
When talking about people it is more polite to use **anciano** *instead of* **viejo.**
◊ *old people* los ancianos
2 antiguo (*former*) ◊ *my old English teacher* mi antiguo profesor de inglés
♦ **How old are you?** ¿Cuántos años tienes?
♦ **How old is the baby?** ¿Cuánto tiempo tiene el bebé?
♦ **a twenty-year-old woman** una mujer de veinte años
♦ **He's ten years old.** Tiene diez años.
♦ **older** mayor ◊ *my older brother* mi hermano mayor ◊ *my older sister* mi hermana mayor ◊ *She's two years older than me.* Es dos años mayor que yo.
♦ **I'm the oldest in the family.** Soy el mayor de la familia.

old age pensioner [əuldeɪdʒ'pɛnʃənəʳ] NOUN
el/la pensionista

old-fashioned ['əuld'fæʃnd] ADJECTIVE
anticuado ◊ *My parents are rather old-fashioned.* Mis padres son bastante anticuados.

olive ['ɔlɪv] NOUN
la aceituna

olive oil ['ɔlɪvɔɪl] NOUN
el aceite de oliva

olive tree ['ɔlɪvtri:] NOUN
el olivo

Olympic [əu'lɪmpɪk] ADJECTIVE
olímpico
♦ **the Olympics** las Olimpiadas

omelette ['ɔmlɪt] NOUN
la tortilla francesa

on [ɔn] PREPOSITION, ADVERB
see also **on** ADJECTIVE
There are several ways of translating **on.** *Scan the examples to find one that is similar to what you want to say. For other expressions with* **on,** *see the verbs* **go, put, turn** *etc.*

1 en ◇ *on an island* en una isla ◇ *on the wall* en la pared ◇ *It's on Channel Four.* Lo dan en el Canal cuatro. ◇ *on TV* en la tele ◇ *on the 2nd floor* en el segundo piso ◇ *I go to school on my bike.* Voy al colegio en bicicleta. ◇ *We went on the train.* Fuimos en tren.
2 sobre (*on top of, about*) ◇ *on the table* sobre la mesa ◇ *a book on Gandhi* un libro sobre Gandhi

*With days and dates, the definite article - **el, los** - is used in Spanish instead of a preposition.*

◇ *on Friday* el viernes ◇ *on Fridays* los viernes ◇ *on 20 September* el 20 de septiembre

◆ **on the left** a la izquierda
◆ **on holiday** de vacaciones
◆ **It's about 10 minutes on foot.** Está a unos 10 minutos andando.
◆ **She was on antibiotics for a week.** Estuvo una semana tomando antibióticos.
◆ **The coffee is on the house.** Al café invita la casa.
◆ **The drinks are on me.** Invito yo.
◆ **What is he on about?** ¿De qué está hablando?

on [ɔn] ADJECTIVE
see also **on** PREPOSITION, ADVERB
1 encendido (*heater, light, TV*) ◇ *I think I left the light on.* Me parece que he dejado la luz encendida.
2 abierto (*tap, gas*) ◇ *Leave the tap on.* Deja el grifo abierto.
3 en marcha ◇ *Is the dishwasher on?* ¿Está en marcha el lavavajillas?
◆ **What's on at the cinema?** ¿Qué echan en el cine?
◆ **Is the party still on?** ¿Todavía se va a hacer* la fiesta?
◆ **I've got a lot on this weekend.** Tengo mucho que hacer este fin de semana.

once [wʌns] ADVERB
una vez ◇ *once a week* una vez a la semana ◇ *once more* una vez más ◇ *I've been to Italy once before.* Ya he estado una vez en Italia.
◆ **Once upon a time...** Érase una vez...
◆ **once in a while** de vez en cuando
◆ **once and for all** de una vez por todas
◆ **at once** enseguida

one [wʌn] NUMERAL, PRONOUN
uno MASC
una FEM

*Use **un** before a masculine noun.*

◇ *I've got one brother and one sister.* Tengo un hermano y una hermana. ◇ *I need a smaller one.* Necesito uno más pequeño.
◆ **one by one** uno a uno
◆ **One never knows.** Nunca se sabe.
◆ **one another** unos a otros ◇ *They all looked at one another.* Se miraron todos unos a otros.

oneself [wʌn'sɛlf] PRONOUN
1 (*reflexive*)
se ◇ *to hurt oneself* hacerse* daño ◇ *to wash oneself* lavarse
2 (*after preposition, for emphasis*)
uno mismo MASC
una misma FEM
◇ *It's quicker to do it oneself.* Es más rápido si lo hace uno mismo.

one-way ['wʌnweɪ] ADJECTIVE
◆ **a one-way street** una calle de sentido único
◆ **a one-way ticket** un billete de ida

onion ['ʌnjən] NOUN
la cebolla

online ['ɒnlaɪn] ADJECTIVE
en línea

only ['əunlɪ] ADVERB
see also **only** ADJECTIVE, CONJUNCTION
sólo ◇ *How much was it? – Only £10.* ¿Cuánto valía? – Sólo 10 libras. ◇ *We only want to stay for one night.* Sólo queremos quedarnos una noche. ◇ *It's only a game!* ¡Es sólo un juego!

only ['əunlɪ] ADJECTIVE
see also **only** ADVERB, CONJUNCTION
único ◇ *She's an only child.* Es hija única. ◇ *Monday is the only day I'm free.* El lunes es el único día que tengo libre.

only ['əunlɪ] CONJUNCTION
see also **only** ADJECTIVE, ADVERB
pero
◆ **I'd like the same sweater, only in black.** Quería el mismo jersey, pero en negro.

onwards ['ɔnwədz] ADVERB
en adelante ◇ *from July onwards* de julio en adelante

open ['əupn] ADJECTIVE
see also **open** VERB
abierto ◇ *The shop's open on Sunday mornings.* La tienda está abierta los domingos por la mañana.
◆ **Are you open tomorrow?** ¿Abre mañana?
◆ **in the open air** al aire libre

to **open** ['əupn] VERB
see also **open** ADJECTIVE
1 abrir* ◇ *What time do the shops open?* ¿A qué hora abren las tiendas? ◇ *Can I open the window?* ¿Puedo abrir la ventana?
2 abrirse* ◇ *The door opens automatically.* La puerta se abre automáticamente.

opening hours ['əupnɪŋauəz] PL NOUN
el horario de apertura

opera ['ɔpərə] NOUN
la ópera

to **operate** ['ɔpəreɪt] VERB

☞

operar (*machine*)
◆ **to operate on someone** operar a alguien

operation [ɔpə'reɪʃən] NOUN
la operación (PL las operaciones)
◆ **I've never had an operation.** Nunca me han operado.

operator ['ɔpəreɪtəʳ] NOUN
el operador
la operadora

opinion [ə'pɪnjən] NOUN
la opinión (PL las opiniones) ◊ *in my opinion* en mi opinión
◆ **What's your opinion?** ¿Tú qué opinas?

opinion poll [ə'pɪnjənpəul] NOUN
el sondeo de opinión

opponent [ə'pəunənt] NOUN
el adversario
la adversaria

opportunity [ɔpə'tju:nɪtɪ] NOUN (PL **opportunities**)
la oportunidad ◊ *I've never had the opportunity to go to Spain.* No he tenido nunca la oportunidad de ir* a España.

opposed [ə'pəuzd] ADJECTIVE
◆ **to be opposed to something** oponerse a algo ◊ *I've always been opposed to violence.* Siempre me he opuesto a la violencia.

opposing [ə'pəuzɪŋ] ADJECTIVE
contrario ◊ *the opposing team* el equipo contrario

opposite ['ɔpəzɪt] ADJECTIVE, ADVERB, PREPOSITION
1 contrario ◊ *It's in the opposite direction.* Está en dirección contraria.
2 opuesto ◊ *the opposite sex* el sexo opuesto
3 enfrente ◊ *They live opposite.* Viven enfrente.
4 frente a ◊ *the girl sitting opposite me* la chica sentada frente a mí

opposition [ɔpə'zɪʃən] NOUN
la oposición ◊ *There is a lot of opposition to the new law.* Hay una fuerte oposición a la nueva ley.

optician [ɔp'tɪʃən] NOUN
el óptico
la óptica
◆ **He's gone to the optician's.** Ha ido a la óptica.

optimist ['ɔptɪmɪst] NOUN
el/la optimista

optimistic [ɔptɪ'mɪstɪk] ADJECTIVE
optimista

option ['ɔpʃən] NOUN
1 la opción (PL las opciones) ◊ *I've got no option.* No tengo otra opción.
2 (*at school*)
la asignatura optativa ◊ *I'm doing geology as my option.* Tengo geología como asignatura optativa.

optional ['ɔpʃənl] ADJECTIVE
1 optativo (*subject*) ◊ *Biology was optional at my school.* La biología era optativa en mi colegio.
2 opcional (*feature*) ◊ *Fog lights are available as optional extras.* Los faros antiniebla son opcionales.

or [ɔ:ʳ] CONJUNCTION
1 o ◊ *Would you like tea or coffee?* ¿Quieres té o café?
*Use **u** before words beginning with "o" or "ho".*
◊ *six or eight* seis u ocho ◊ *men or women* mujeres u hombres
◆ **Hurry up or you'll miss the bus.** Date prisa, que vas a perder* el autobús.
2 ni ◊ *I don't eat meat or fish.* No como carne ni pescado. ◊ *She can't dance or sing.* No sabe bailar ni cantar.

oral ['ɔ:rəl] ADJECTIVE
see also **oral** NOUN
oral ◊ *an oral exam* un examen oral

oral ['ɔ:rəl] NOUN
see also **oral** ADJECTIVE
el examen oral (PL los exámenes orales) ◊ *I've got my Spanish oral soon.* Tengo el examen oral de español pronto.

orange ['ɔrɪndʒ] NOUN
see also **orange** ADJECTIVE
la naranja
◆ **orange juice** el zumo de naranja (el jugo de naranja *LatAm*)

orange ['ɔrɪndʒ] ADJECTIVE
see also **orange** NOUN
naranja MASC, FEM, PL

orchard ['ɔ:tʃəd] NOUN
el huerto

orchestra ['ɔ:kɪstrə] NOUN
la orquesta

order ['ɔ:dəʳ] NOUN
see also **order** VERB
1 (*arrangement*)
el orden ◊ *in alphabetical order* por orden alfabético
2 (*command*)
la orden (PL las órdenes) ◊ *to obey an order* obedecer* una orden
◆ **The waiter took our order.** El camarero tomó nota de lo que íbamos a comer.
◆ **in order to** para ◊ *He does it in order to earn money.* Lo hace para ganar dinero.
◆ **"out of order"** "averiado"

to **order** ['ɔ:dəʳ] VERB
see also **order** NOUN
pedir* ◊ *We ordered steak and chips.* Pedimos un filete con patatas fritas. ◊ *Are you ready to order?* ¿Han decidido qué van a pedir?

to **order about** [ɔ:dəʳə'baut] VERB

* Verbs marked with this symbol are irregular. See pages 380-382 for further details

dar* órdenes a ◊ *She was fed up with being ordered about.* Estaba harta de que le dieran órdenes.

ordinary ['ɔːdnrɪ] ADJECTIVE
normal y corriente ◊ *He's an ordinary man.* Es un hombre normal y corriente. ◊ *an ordinary day* un día normal y corriente

organ ['ɔːgən] NOUN
el órgano (*instrument*)

organic [ɔː'gænɪk] ADJECTIVE
biológico (*fruit, vegetables*)

organization [ɔːgənaɪ'zeɪʃən] NOUN
la organización (PL las organizaciones)

to **organize** ['ɔːgənaɪz] VERB
organizar*

origin ['ɔrɪdʒɪn] NOUN
el origen (PL los orígenes)

original [ə'rɪdʒɪnl] ADJECTIVE
original

originally [ə'rɪdʒɪnəlɪ] ADVERB
al principio

Orkneys ['ɔːknɪz] PL NOUN
♦ **the Orkneys** las Islas Órcadas

ornament ['ɔːnəmənt] NOUN
el adorno

orphan ['ɔːfn] NOUN
el huérfano
la huérfana

ostrich ['ɔstrɪtʃ] NOUN (PL **ostriches**)
el avestruz (PL los avestruces)

other ['ʌðə^r] ADJECTIVE, PRONOUN
otro MASC
otra FEM
◊ *Have you got these jeans in other colours?* ¿Tienen estos vaqueros en otros colores? ◊ *on the other side of the street* al otro lado de la calle
♦ **the other one** el otro (FEM la otra) ◊ *This one? – No, the other one.* ¿Éste? – No, el otro.
♦ **the others** los demás (FEM las demás) ◊ *The others are going but I'm not.* Los demás van, pero yo no.

otherwise ['ʌðəwaɪz] ADVERB, CONJUNCTION
1 si no (*if not*) ◊ *Note down the number, otherwise you'll forget it.* Apúntate el número, si no se te olvidará.
2 por lo demás (*in other ways*) ◊ *I'm tired, but otherwise I'm fine.* Estoy cansado, pero por lo demás estoy bien.

ought [ɔːt] VERB

*To translate **ought to** use the conditional tense of **deber**.*

◊ *I ought to phone my parents.* Debería llamar a mis padres. ◊ *You ought not to do that.* No deberías hacer* eso. ◊ *He ought to win.* Debería ganar.

*For **ought to have** use the conditional tense of **deber** plus **haber** or the imperfect of **deber**.*

◊ *You ought to have warned me.* Me deberías haber avisado. ◊ *He ought to have known.* Debía saberlo.

ounce [auns] NOUN
la onza

> *In Spain measurements are in grams and kilograms. One ounce is about 28 grams.*

our ['auə^r] ADJECTIVE
nuestro ◊ *our house* nuestra casa ◊ *Our neighbours are very nice.* Nuestros vecinos son muy simpáticos.

***Our** is usually translated by the definite article **el/los** or **la/las** when it's clear from the sentence who the possessor is or when referring to clothing or parts of the body.*

◊ *We took off our coats.* Nos quitamos los abrigos. ◊ *They stole our car.* Nos robaron el coche.

ours [auəz] PRONOUN
1 el nuestro MASC (PL los nuestros) ◊ *Your car is much bigger than ours.* Vuestro coche es mucho más grande que el nuestro. ◊ *Our teachers are strict. – Ours are too.* Nuestros profesores son estrictos. – Los nuestros también.
2 la nuestra FEM (PL las nuestras) ◊ *Your house is very different from ours.* Vuestra casa es muy distinta a la nuestra.
3 nuestro MASC (PL nuestros) ◊ *Is this ours?* ¿Esto es nuestro? ◊ *a friend of ours* un amigo nuestro
4 nuestra FEM (PL nuestras) ◊ *Sorry, that table is ours.* Disculpen, esa mesa es nuestra. ◊ *Isabel is a close friend of ours.* Isabel es muy amiga nuestra.

ourselves [auə'sɛlvz] PRONOUN
1 (*reflexive*)
nos ◊ *We really enjoyed ourselves.* Nos divertimos mucho.
2 (*after preposition, for emphasis*)
nosotros mismos MASC
nosotras mismas FEM
◊ *Let's not talk about ourselves any more.* No hablemos más de nosotros mismos. ◊ *We built our garage ourselves.* Nos construimos el garaje nosotros mismos.
♦ **by ourselves** solos (FEM solas) ◊ *We prefer to be by ourselves.* Preferimos estar* solos.

out [aut] PREPOSITION, ADVERB
see also **out** ADJECTIVE

*There are several ways of translating **out**. Scan the examples to find one that is similar to what you want to say. For other expressions with **out**, see the verbs **go, put, turn** etc.*

☞

O

fuera ◊ *It's cold out.* Fuera hace frío. ◊ *It's dark out there.* Está oscuro ahí fuera.
♦ **She's out.** Ha salido.
♦ **She's out for the afternoon.** No estará en toda la tarde.
♦ **to go out** salir* ◊ *I'm going out tonight.* Voy a salir esta noche.
♦ **to go out with somebody** salir* con alguien ◊ *I've been going out with him for two months.* Llevo dos meses saliendo con él.
♦ **a night out with my friends** una noche por ahí con mis amigos
♦ **"way out"** "salida"
♦ **out of town** fuera de la ciudad ◊ *He lives out of town.* Vive fuera de la ciudad.
♦ **three kilometres out of town** a tres kilómetros de la ciudad
♦ **to take something out of your pocket** sacar* algo del bolsillo
♦ **out of curiosity** por curiosidad
♦ **We're out of milk.** Se nos ha acabado la leche.
♦ **in nine cases out of ten** en nueve de cada diez casos

out [aut] ADJECTIVE
see also **out** PREPOSITION, ADVERB
1 apagado (*lights, fire*) ◊ *All the lights are out.* Todas las luces están apagadas.
2 eliminado (*eliminated*)
♦ **That's it, Liverpool are out.** Ya está, Liverpool queda eliminado.
♦ **The film is now out on video.** La película ya ha salido en vídeo.

outbreak ['autbreɪk] NOUN
1 la epidemia ◊ *a salmonella outbreak* una epidemia de salmonelosis
2 el comienzo ◊ *the outbreak of war* el comienzo de la guerra

outcome ['autkʌm] NOUN
el resultado

outdoor [aut'dɔːʳ] ADJECTIVE
al aire libre ◊ *an outdoor swimming pool* una piscina al aire libre

outdoors [aut'dɔːz] ADVERB
al aire libre

outfit ['autfɪt] NOUN
el traje ◊ *a cowboy outfit* un traje de vaquero

outgoing ['autgəuɪŋ] ADJECTIVE
extrovertido

outing ['autɪŋ] NOUN
la excursión (PL las excursiones) ◊ *to go on an outing* ir* de excursión

outline ['autlaɪn] NOUN
1 el esquema (*summary*)
Although **esquema** *ends in* **-a**, *it is actually a masculine noun.*
◊ *This is an outline of the plan.* Aquí tienen un esquema del plan.
2 el contorno (*shape*) ◊ *We could see the outline of the mountain.* Veíamos el contorno de la montaña.

outlook ['autluk] NOUN
1 la actitud (*attitude*)
2 las perspectivas (*prospects*)

outrageous [aut'reɪdʒəs] ADJECTIVE
1 escandaloso (*behaviour*)
2 exorbitante (*price*)
3 extravagante (*clothes*)

outset ['autsɛt] NOUN
♦ **at the outset** al principio

outside [aut'saɪd] NOUN, ADJECTIVE
see also **outside** PREPOSITION, ADVERB
1 el exterior ◊ *the outside of the house* el exterior de la casa
2 exterior ◊ *the outside walls* las paredes exteriores

outside [aut'saɪd] PREPOSITION, ADVERB
see also **outside** NOUN, ADJECTIVE
1 fuera ◊ *It's very cold outside.* Hace mucho frío fuera.
2 fuera de ◊ *outside the school* fuera del colegio ◊ *outside school hours* fuera del horario escolar

outsize ['autsaɪz] ADJECTIVE
♦ **outsize clothes** ropa de tallas muy grandes

outskirts ['autskəːts] PL NOUN
las afueras ◊ *on the outskirts of town* en las afueras de la ciudad

outstanding [aut'stændɪŋ] ADJECTIVE
excepcional

oval ['əuvl] ADJECTIVE
ovalado

oven ['ʌvn] NOUN
el horno

over ['əuvəʳ] ADJECTIVE, ADVERB, PREPOSITION
When something is located over something, use **encima de**. *When there is movement over something, use* **por encima de**.
1 encima de ◊ *There's a mirror over the washbasin.* Encima del lavabo hay un espejo.
2 por encima de ◊ *The ball went over the wall.* La pelota pasó por encima de la pared.
♦ **a bridge over the Thames** un puente sobre el Támesis
3 más de ◊ *It's over 20 kilos.* Pesa más de 20 kilos.
♦ **The temperature was over 30 degrees.** La temperatura superaba los 30 grados.
4 durante ◊ *over the holidays* durante las vacaciones ◊ *over Christmas* durante las Navidades
5 terminado
♦ **I'll be happy when the exams are over.** Estaré feliz cuando se hayan terminado los exámenes.

* Verbs marked with this symbol are irregular. See pages 380-382 for further details

♦ **over here** aquí
♦ **It's over there.** Está por allí.
♦ **all over Scotland** en toda Escocia
♦ **The shop is over the road.** La tienda está al otro lado de la calle.
♦ **I spilled coffee over my shirt.** Me manché la camisa de café.

overall [əuvər'ɔːl] ADJECTIVE
see also **overall** ADVERB
general ◊ *What was your overall impression?* ¿Cuál fue tu impresión general?

overall [əuvər'ɔːl] ADVERB
see also **overall** ADJECTIVE
en general ◊ *Overall, we played very well.* En general jugamos muy bien.

overalls ['əuvərɔːlz] PL NOUN
el mono (el overol *LatAm*) (*for work*)

overcast ['əuvəkɑːst] ADJECTIVE
cubierto ◊ *The sky was overcast.* El cielo estaba cubierto.

to **overcharge** [əuvə'tʃɑːdʒ] VERB
cobrar de más ◊ *They overcharged us for the meal.* Nos cobraron de más por la comida.

overcoat ['əuvəkəut] NOUN
el abrigo

overdone [əuvə'dʌn] ADJECTIVE
1 recocido (*vegetables*)
2 demasiado hecho (*steak*)

overdose ['əuvədəus] NOUN
la sobredosis (PL las sobredosis)

overdraft ['əuvədrɑːft] NOUN
el descubierto

to **overestimate** [əuvər'ɛstɪmeɪt] VERB
sobreestimar ◊ *We overestimated how long it would take.* Sobreestimamos el tiempo que se tardaría.

overhead projector [əuvəhɛdprə'dʒɛktər] NOUN
el retroproyector

to **overlook** [əuvə'luk] VERB
1 tener* vistas a ◊ *The hotel overlooked the beach.* El hotel tenía vistas a la playa.
2 pasar por alto ◊ *He had overlooked one important problem.* Había pasado por alto un problema importante.

overseas [əuvə'siːz] ADVERB
en el extranjero (*live, work*) ◊ *I'd like to work overseas.* Me gustaría trabajar en el extranjero.

oversight ['əuvəsaɪt] NOUN
el descuido

to **oversleep** [əuvə'sliːp] VERB (**overslept, overslept**)
quedarse dormido ◊ *I overslept this morning.* Me quedé dormido esta mañana.

to **overtake** [əuvə'teɪk] VERB (**overtook, overtaken**)
adelantar (rebasar *LatAm*)

overtime ['əuvətaɪm] NOUN
las horas extras
♦ **to work overtime** trabajar* horas extras

overweight [əuvə'weɪt] ADJECTIVE
♦ **to be overweight** tener* exceso de peso

to **owe** [əu] VERB
deber ◊ *How much do I owe you?* ¿Cuánto te debo?

owing to ['əuɪŋtə] PREPOSITION
debido a ◊ *owing to bad weather* debido al mal tiempo

owl [aul] NOUN
el búho

own [əun] ADJECTIVE, PRONOUN
see also **own** VERB
propio ◊ *This is my own recipe.* Ésta es mi propia receta. ◊ *I wish I had a room of my own.* Me gustaría tener mi propia habitación.
♦ **on his own** él solo ◊ *on her own* ella sola ◊ *on our own* nosotros solos

to **own** [əun] VERB
see also **own** ADJECTIVE
tener*

to **own up** [əun'ʌp] VERB
confesarse* culpable
♦ **to own up to something** confesar* algo

owner ['əunər] NOUN
el propietario
la propietaria

oxygen ['ɔksɪdʒən] NOUN
el oxígeno

oyster ['ɔɪstər] NOUN
la ostra

ozone layer ['əuzəunleɪər] NOUN
la capa de ozono

O

P

PA [piːˈeɪ] NOUN (= *personal assistant*)
el secretario de dirección
la secretaria de dirección
◊ *She's a PA.* Es secretaria de dirección.
♦ **the PA system** (*public address*) la megafonía

pace [peɪs] NOUN
el ritmo ◊ *the frantic pace of life in London* el frenético ritmo de vida de Londres

Pacific [pəˈsɪfɪk] NOUN
♦ **the Pacific** el Pacífico

pacifier [ˈpæsɪfaɪəʳ] NOUN US
el chupete

to **pack** [pæk] VERB
see also **pack** NOUN
hacer* las maletas (empacar *LatAm*)
◊ *I'll help you pack.* Te ayudaré a hacer las maletas.
♦ **I've already packed my case.** Ya he hecho mi maleta.
♦ **Pack it in!** ¡Vale ya!

pack [pæk] NOUN
see also **pack** VERB
el paquete ◊ *a pack of cigarettes* un paquete de tabaco
♦ **a pack of cards** una baraja

package [ˈpækɪdʒ] NOUN
el paquete
♦ **a package holiday** unas vacaciones organizadas

packed [pækt] ADJECTIVE
abarrotado ◊ *The cinema was packed.* El cine estaba abarrotado.

packed lunch [pæktˈlʌntʃ] NOUN (PL **packed lunches**)
♦ **I take a packed lunch to school.** Me llevo la comida al colegio.

packet [ˈpækɪt] NOUN
el paquete ◊ *a packet of cigarettes* un paquete de tabaco
♦ **a packet of crisps** una bolsa de patatas fritas

pad [pæd] NOUN
el bloc

to **paddle** [ˈpædl] VERB
see also **paddle** NOUN
1 chapotear (*swim*)
2 remar ◊ *to paddle a canoe* remar en canoa

paddle [ˈpædl] NOUN
see also **paddle** VERB
la pala
♦ **to go for a paddle** mojase los pies

padlock [ˈpædlɔk] NOUN
el candado

page [peɪdʒ] NOUN
see also **page** VERB
la página ◊ *on page 13* en la página 13

to **page** [peɪdʒ] VERB
see also **page** NOUN
♦ **to page somebody** llamar a alguien al busca

pager [ˈpeɪdʒəʳ] NOUN
el busca
*Although **busca** ends in **-a**, it is actually a masculine noun.*

paid [peɪd] VERB *see* **pay**

paid [peɪd] ADJECTIVE
1 remunerado ◊ *to do paid work* realizar* trabajo remunerado
2 pagado ◊ *three weeks' paid holiday* tres semanas de vacaciones pagadas

pail [peɪl] NOUN
el cubo

pain [peɪn] NOUN
el dolor ◊ *a terrible pain* un dolor tremendo
♦ **I've got a pain in my stomach.** Me duele el estómago.
♦ **She's in a lot of pain.** Tiene muchos dolores.
♦ **He's a real pain.** Es un auténtico pelmazo. (*informal*)

painful [ˈpeɪnful] ADJECTIVE
***doloroso** is used when talking about what causes pain, and **dolorido** for the person or thing that feels pain.*
1 doloroso ◊ *a painful injury* una herida dolorosa
2 dolorido ◊ *Her feet were swollen and painful.* Tenía los pies hinchados y doloridos.
♦ **Is it painful?** ¿Te duele?

painkiller [ˈpeɪnkɪləʳ] NOUN
el analgésico

paint [peɪnt] NOUN
see also **paint** VERB
la pintura

to **paint** [peɪnt] VERB
see also **paint** NOUN
pintar ◊ *to paint something green* pintar algo de verde

paintbrush [ˈpeɪntbrʌʃ] NOUN (PL **paintbrushes**)
1 el pincel (*for an artist*)
2 la brocha (*for decorating*)

painter [ˈpeɪntəʳ] NOUN
el pintor
la pintora

* Verbs marked with this symbol are irregular. See pages 380-382 for further details

◊ *The painters made a real mess of the windows.* Los pintores dejaron las ventanas hechas un desastre.

painting ['peɪntɪŋ] NOUN
1 el cuadro ◊ *a painting by Picasso* un cuadro de Picasso
2 la pintura ◊ *My hobby is painting.* Mi hobby es la pintura.

pair [pɛəʳ] NOUN
el par ◊ *a pair of shoes* un par de zapatos
◆ **a pair of scissors** unas tijeras
◆ **a pair of trousers** unos pantalones
◆ **in pairs** por parejas

pajamas [pə'dʒɑːməz] PL NOUN US
el pijama (el piyama *LatAm*) ◊ *my pajamas* mi pijama
◆ **a pair of pajamas** un pijama

Although ***pijama*** *ends in* ***-a****, it is actually a masculine noun.*

Pakistan [pɑːkɪ'stɑːn] NOUN
Paquistán MASC

Pakistani [pɑːkɪ'stɑːnɪ] ADJECTIVE
see also **Pakistani** NOUN
paquistaní (PL paquistaníes)

Pakistani [pɑːkɪ'stɑːnɪ] NOUN
see also **Pakistani** ADJECTIVE
el/la paquistaní (PL los paquistaníes)

pal [pæl] NOUN
el amiguete
la amigueta

palace ['pæləs] NOUN
el palacio

pale [peɪl] ADJECTIVE
1 pálido ◊ *She still looks very pale.* Está todavía muy pálida.
◆ **to turn pale** ponerse* pálido
2 claro ◊ *pale green* verde claro
◆ **pale pink** rosa pálido
◆ **pale blue** azul celeste

Palestine ['pælɪstaɪn] NOUN
Palestina FEM

Palestinian [pælɪs'tɪnɪən] ADJECTIVE
see also **Palestinian** NOUN
palestino

Palestinian [pælɪs'tɪnɪən] NOUN
see also **Palestinian** ADJECTIVE
el palestino
la palestina

palm [pɑːm] NOUN
la palma ◊ *the palm of your hand* la palma de la mano
◆ **a palm tree** una palmera

pamphlet ['pæmflət] NOUN
el folleto

pan [pæn] NOUN
1 (*saucepan*)
la cacerola
2 (*frying pan*)
la sartén (PL las sartenes)

pancake ['pænkeɪk] NOUN
la crepe (el panqueque *LatAm*)

panic ['pænɪk] NOUN
see also **panic** VERB
el pánico ◊ *The shouting caused quite a panic.* El griterío provocó el pánico.

to **panic** ['pænɪk] VERB
see also **panic** NOUN
◆ **He panicked as soon as he saw the blood.** Le entró pánico en cuanto vio la sangre.
◆ **Don't panic!** ¡Tranquilo!

panther ['pænθəʳ] NOUN
la pantera

panties ['pæntɪz] PL NOUN
las bragas

pantomime ['pæntəmaɪm] NOUN

> ℹ ***Pantomime*** *es una obra de teatro musical para niños representada por Navidad, que suele narrar un cuento tradicional en clave de humor, con mucha participación del público.*

pants [pænts] PL NOUN
1 las bragas (*for women*)
2 los calzoncillos (*for men*)
3 los pantalones US

pantyhose ['pæntɪhəuz] PL NOUN US
las medias

paper ['peɪpəʳ] NOUN
1 el papel ◊ *a paper bag* una bolsa de papel
◆ **a piece of paper** un papel (una hoja *LatAm*)
◆ **an exam paper** un examen
2 el periódico ◊ *I saw an advert in the paper.* Vi un anuncio en el periódico.

paperback ['peɪpəbæk] NOUN
el libro de bolsillo

paper boy ['peɪpəbɔɪ] NOUN
el repartidor de periódicos

> ℹ *En Gran Bretaña los periódicos se reparten a domicilio a petición. Generalmente, los repartidores son niños y niñas de hasta unos quince años.*

paper clip ['peɪpəklɪp] NOUN
el clip (PL los clips)

paper girl ['peɪpəgəːl] NOUN
la repartidora de periódicos

> ℹ *En Gran Bretaña los periódicos se reparten a domicilio a petición. Generalmente, los repartidores son niños y niñas de hasta unos quince años.*

paper round ['peɪpəraund] NOUN
◆ **to do a paper round** repartir los periódicos a domicilio

paperweight ['peɪpəweɪt] NOUN
el pisapapeles (PL los pisapapeles)

P

paperwork ['peɪpəwəːk] NOUN
el papeleo ◊ *I've got a lot of paperwork to do.* Tengo un montón de papeleo que hacer.

parachute ['pærəʃuːt] NOUN
el paracaídas (PL los paracaídas)

parade [pə'reɪd] NOUN
el desfile

paradise ['pærədaɪs] NOUN
el paraíso

paraffin ['pærəfɪn] NOUN
el queroseno
◆ **a paraffin lamp** una lámpara de petróleo

paragraph ['pærəgrɑːf] NOUN
el párrafo

parallel ['pærəlɛl] ADJECTIVE
paralelo

paralysed ['pærəlaɪzd] ADJECTIVE
paralizado

paramedic [pærə'mɛdɪk] NOUN
el auxiliar sanitario
la auxiliar sanitaria

parcel ['pɑːsl] NOUN
el paquete

pardon ['pɑːdn] NOUN
◆ **Pardon?** ¿Cómo?

parents ['pɛərənts] PL NOUN
los padres (los papás *LatAm*)

*Be careful not to translate **parents** by **parientes**.*

Paris ['pærɪs] NOUN
París MASC

park [pɑːk] NOUN
see also **park** VERB
el parque
◆ **a national park** un parque nacional
◆ **a theme park** un parque temático
◆ **a car park** un aparcamiento (un estacionamiento *LatAm*)

to **park** [pɑːk] VERB
see also **park** NOUN
aparcar* ◊ *Where can I park my car?* ¿Dónde puedo aparcar el coche?
◆ **"no parking"** "prohibido aparcar"

parking lot ['pɑːkɪŋlɔt] NOUN US
el aparcamiento

parking meter ['pɑːkɪŋmiːtəʳ] NOUN
el parquímetro

parking ticket ['pɑːkɪŋtɪkɪt] NOUN
la multa de aparcamiento

parliament ['pɑːləmənt] NOUN
el parlamento
◆ **the Spanish Parliament** las Cortes

parole [pə'rəul] NOUN
◆ **on parole** en libertad condicional

parrot ['pærət] NOUN
el loro

parsley ['pɑːslɪ] NOUN
el perejil

part [pɑːt] NOUN
see also **part** VERB
1 la parte ◊ *The first part of the play was boring.* La primera parte de la obra fue aburrida.
2 el papel ◊ *She had a small part in the film.* Tenía un pequeño papel en la película.
3 la pieza ◊ *spare parts* piezas de repuesto
◆ **to take part in something** participar en algo ◊ *Thousands of people took part in the demonstration.* Miles de personas participaron en la manifestación.

to **part** [pɑːt] VERB
see also **part** NOUN
◆ **to part with something** desprenderse de algo ◊ *I hate to part with this lamp.* Me fastidia tener que desprenderme de esta lámpara.

particular [pə'tɪkjuləʳ] ADJECTIVE
1 concreto (*definite*) ◊ *I can't remember that particular film.* No recuerdo esa película concreta.
2 especial (*special*) ◊ *He showed a particular interest in the subject.* Mostró un interés especial en el tema.
◆ **in particular** en concreto ◊ *Are you looking for anything in particular?* ¿Busca algo en concreto? ◊ *nothing in particular* nada en concreto

particularly [pə'tɪkjuləlɪ] ADVERB
especialmente ◊ *a particularly boring lecture* una clase especialmente aburrida

parting ['pɑːtɪŋ] NOUN
la raya

partly ['pɑːtlɪ] ADVERB
en parte ◊ *It was partly my own fault.* En parte fue culpa mía.

partner ['pɑːtnəʳ] NOUN
1 el socio
la socia
◊ *He's a partner in a law firm.* Es socio de un bufete de abogados.
2 la pareja ◊ *That doesn't mean you don't love your partner.* Eso no significa que no quieras a tu pareja. ◊ *my dancing partner* mi pareja de baile

part-time ['pɑːt'taɪm] ADJECTIVE, ADVERB
a tiempo parcial ◊ *a part-time job* un trabajo a tiempo parcial ◊ *She works part-time.* Trabaja a tiempo parcial.

party ['pɑːtɪ] NOUN (PL **parties**)
1 la fiesta ◊ *a birthday party* una fiesta de cumpleaños
2 el partido ◊ *the Conservative Party* el partido conservador
3 el grupo ◊ *a party of tourists* un grupo de turistas

pass [pɑːs] NOUN (PL **passes**)
see also **pass** VERB

1 el pase (*in football*) ◊ *a short pass* un pase en corto
2 el puerto ◊ *The pass was blocked with snow.* El puerto estaba bloqueado por la nieve.
3 el aprobado ◊ *She got a pass in her piano exam.* Sacó un aprobado en el examen de piano.
♦ **a bus pass** un abono para el autobús

to **pass** [pɑːs] VERB
see also **pass** NOUN
1 pasar ◊ *Could you pass me the salt, please?* ¿Me pasas la sal, por favor? ◊ *The time has passed quickly.* El tiempo ha pasado rápido.
2 adelantar ◊ *We were passed by a huge lorry.* Nos adelantó un camión enorme.
3 pasar por delante de ◊ *I pass his house on my way to school.* Paso por delante de su casa de camino al colegio.
4 aprobar* ◊ *Did you pass?* ¿Has aprobado? ◊ *to pass an exam* aprobar un examen

to **pass out** [pɑːs'aut] VERB
desmayarse

passage ['pæsɪdʒ] NOUN
1 el pasaje ◊ *Read the passage carefully.* Lea el pasaje con atención.
2 el pasillo ◊ *a narrow passage* un estrecho pasillo

passenger ['pæsɪndʒəʳ] NOUN
el pasajero
la pasajera

passion ['pæʃən] NOUN
la pasión (PL las pasiones) ◊ *Football is a passion of his.* El fútbol es una de sus pasiones.

passive ['pæsɪv] ADJECTIVE
pasivo
♦ **a passive smoker** un fumador pasivo

Passover ['pɑːsəuvəʳ] NOUN
la Pascua judía

passport ['pɑːspɔːt] NOUN
el pasaporte ◊ *passport control* el control de pasaportes

password ['pɑːswəːd] NOUN
la contraseña

past [pɑːst] ADJECTIVE, ADVERB, PREPOSITION
see also **past** NOUN
pasado ◊ *This past year has been very difficult.* Este año pasado ha sido muy difícil.
♦ **The school is 100 metres past the traffic lights.** El colegio está a unos 100 metros pasado el semáforo.
♦ **to go past** pasar ◊ *The bus went past without stopping.* El autobús pasó sin parar.
♦ **It's half past ten.** Son las diez y media.
♦ **It's a quarter past nine.** Son las nueve y cuarto.
♦ **It's ten past eight.** Son las ocho y diez.
♦ **It's past midnight.** Es pasada la medianoche.

past [pɑːst] NOUN
see also **past** ADJECTIVE, ADVERB, PREPOSITION
el pasado ◊ *I try not to think of the past.* Intento no pensar en el pasado.
♦ **This was common in the past.** Antiguamente esto era normal.

pasta ['pæstə] NOUN
la pasta

paste [peɪst] NOUN
el engrudo (*glue*)

pasteurized ['pæstʃəraɪzd] ADJECTIVE
pasteurizado

pastime ['pɑːstaɪm] NOUN
el pasatiempo

pastry ['peɪstrɪ] NOUN
1 la masa (*dough*)
2 el pastel (*cake*)

to **pat** [pæt] VERB
acariciar (*dog, cat*)

patch [pætʃ] NOUN (PL **patches**)
el parche ◊ *a patch of material* un parche de tela
♦ **He's got a bald patch.** Tiene una calva incipiente.
♦ **They're going through a bad patch.** Están pasando una mala racha.

patched [pætʃt] ADJECTIVE
♦ **a pair of patched jeans** unos vaqueros con remiendos

pâté ['pæteɪ] NOUN
el paté

path [pɑːθ] NOUN
el sendero

pathetic [pə'θɛtɪk] ADJECTIVE
penoso ◊ *That was a pathetic excuse.* Fue una excusa penosa.

patience ['peɪʃns] NOUN
1 la paciencia ◊ *He hasn't got much patience.* No tiene mucha paciencia.
2 el solitario (*game*) ◊ *She was playing patience.* Estaba haciendo un solitario.

patient ['peɪʃnt] NOUN
see also **patient** ADJECTIVE
el paciente
la paciente

patient ['peɪʃnt] ADJECTIVE
see also **patient** NOUN
paciente

patio ['pætɪəu] NOUN (PL **patios**)
el patio

patriotic [pætrɪ'ɔtɪk] ADJECTIVE
patriótico

patrol [pə'trəul] NOUN
la patrulla
♦ **to be on patrol** estar* de patrulla

patrol car [pə'trəulkɑːʳ] NOUN
el coche patrulla (PL los coches patrulla)

pattern ['pætən] NOUN
1 el motivo (*design*) ◊ *a geometric pattern* un motivo geométrico

P

☞

2 el patrón (*for sewing*)

pause [pɔːz] NOUN
la pausa

pavement ['peɪvmənt] NOUN
la acera

paw [pɔː] NOUN
la pata

pay [peɪ] NOUN
see also **pay** VERB
el sueldo ◊ *a pay rise* un aumento de sueldo

to **pay** [peɪ] VERB (**paid, paid**)
see also **pay** NOUN
pagar* ◊ *They pay me more on Sundays.* Me pagan más los domingos. ◊ *Can I pay by cheque?* ¿Puedo pagar con cheque?
♦ **to pay money into an account** ingresar dinero en una cuenta
♦ **I'll pay you back tomorrow.** Mañana te devuelvo el dinero.
♦ **to pay for something** pagar* algo ◊ *I paid for my ticket.* Pagué el billete.
♦ **I paid £50 for it.** Me costó 50 libras.
♦ **Does your current account pay interest?** ¿Le rinde intereses su cuenta corriente?
♦ **to pay somebody a visit** ir* a ver a alguien ◊ *Paul paid us a visit last night.* Paul vino a vernos anoche.

payable ['peɪəbl] ADJECTIVE
♦ **Who's the cheque payable to?** ¿A nombre de quién extiendo el cheque?

payment ['peɪmənt] NOUN
el pago ◊ *mortgage payments* los pagos de la hipoteca

payphone ['peɪfəun] NOUN
el teléfono público

PC [piː'siː] NOUN (= *personal computer*)
el PC

PE [piː'iː] NOUN (= *physical education*)
la educación física ◊ *We do PE twice a week.* Tenemos educación física dos veces a la semana.

pea [piː] NOUN
el guisante

peace [piːs] NOUN
la paz
♦ **peace talks** conversaciones de paz
♦ **a peace treaty** un tratado de paz

peaceful ['piːsful] ADJECTIVE
1 pacífico (*non-violent*) ◊ *a peaceful protest* una manifestación pacífica
2 apacible (*restful*) ◊ *a peaceful afternoon* una tarde apacible

peach [piːtʃ] NOUN (PL **peaches**)
el melocotón (PL los melocotones)

peacock ['piːkɔk] NOUN
el pavo real

peak [piːk] NOUN
1 la cumbre ◊ *the snow-covered peaks* las cumbres nevadas
2 el apogeo ◊ *She's at the peak of her career.* Está en el apogeo de su carrera profesional.
♦ **in peak season** en temporada alta

peak rate [piːk'reɪt] NOUN
la tarifa máxima ◊ *You pay peak rate for calls before one.* Si llamas antes de la una pagas la tarifa máxima.

peanut ['piːnʌt] NOUN
el cacahuete (el maní (PL los maníes) *LatAm*)

peanut butter ['piːnʌtbʌtəʳ] NOUN
la crema de cacahuete

pear [pɛəʳ] NOUN
la pera

pearl [pəːl] NOUN
la perla

pebble ['pɛbl] NOUN
el guijarro

peckish ['pɛkɪʃ] ADJECTIVE
♦ **to feel a bit peckish** tener* un poquito de hambre

peculiar [pɪ'kjuːlɪəʳ] ADJECTIVE
raro ◊ *He's a peculiar person.* Es una persona rara. ◊ *It tastes peculiar.* Sabe raro.

pedal ['pɛdl] NOUN
el pedal

pedestrian [pɪ'dɛstrɪən] NOUN
el peatón (PL los peatones)

pedestrian crossing [pɪ'dɛstrɪən'krɔsɪŋ] NOUN
el paso de peatones

pedestrianized [pɪ'dɛstrɪənaɪzd] ADJECTIVE
♦ **a pedestrianized street** una calle peatonal

pedigree ['pɛdɪgriː] ADJECTIVE
de raza ◊ *a pedigree dog* un perro de raza ◊ *a pedigree labrador* un labrador de pura raza

pee [piː] NOUN
♦ **to have a pee** hacer* pis

peek [piːk] NOUN
♦ **to have a peek at something** echar una ojeada a algo ◊ *I had a peek at your dress and it's lovely.* Le eché una ojeada a tu vestido y es muy mono.

peel [piːl] NOUN
see also **peel** VERB
la piel

to **peel** [piːl] VERB
see also **peel** NOUN
pelar ◊ *Shall I peel the potatoes?* ¿Pelo las patatas?
♦ **My nose is peeling.** Se me está pelando la nariz.

peg [pɛg] NOUN
1 el gancho (*for coats*)

* Verbs marked with this symbol are irregular. See pages 380-382 for further details

[2] la pinza (*clothes peg*)
[3] la estaca (*tent peg*)

Pekinese [piːkɪ'niːz] NOUN
el pequinés (PL los pequineses)

pellet ['pɛlɪt] NOUN
(*for gun*)
el perdigón (PL los perdigones)

pelvis ['pɛlvɪs] NOUN (PL **pelvises**)
la pelvis (PL las pelvis)

pen [pɛn] NOUN
[1] el bolígrafo (*ballpoint pen*)
[2] la pluma (*fountain pen*)
[3] el rotulador (*felt-tip pen*)

penalty ['pɛnltɪ] NOUN (PL **penalties**)
[1] la pena ◊ *The penalty for this offence is life imprisonment.* La pena por este delito es cadena perpetua.
◆**the death penalty** la pena de muerte
[2] (*in football*)
el penalty (PL los penaltys)
[3] (*in rugby*)
el golpe de castigo
◆**a penalty shoot-out** una tanda de penaltys

pence [pɛns] PL NOUN
◆**24 pence** 24 peniques

pencil ['pɛnsl] NOUN
el lápiz (PL los lápices)
(el lapicero *LatAm*)
◆**to write in pencil** escribir* a lápiz

pencil case ['pɛnslkeɪs] NOUN
el estuche

pencil sharpener ['pɛnslʃɑːpnəʳ] NOUN
el sacapuntas (PL los sacapuntas)

penfriend ['pɛnfrɛnd] NOUN
el amigo por correspondencia
la amiga por correspondencia

penguin ['pɛŋgwɪn] NOUN
el pingüino

penicillin [pɛnɪ'sɪlɪn] NOUN
la penicilina

penis ['piːnɪs] NOUN (PL **penises**)
el pene

penitentiary [pɛnɪ'tɛnʃərɪ] NOUN (PL **penitentiaries**) US
la cárcel

penknife ['pɛnnaɪf] NOUN (PL **penknives**)
la navaja

penny ['pɛnɪ] NOUN (PL **pence**)
el penique

pension ['pɛnʃən] NOUN
la pensión (PL las pensiones)

pensioner ['pɛnʃənəʳ] NOUN
el/la pensionista

pentathlon [pɛn'tæθlən] NOUN
el pentatlón

people ['piːpl] PL NOUN
[1] la gente ◊ *The people were nice.* La gente era simpática. ◊ *a lot of people* mucha gente
[2] las personas ◊ *six people* seis personas ◊ *several people* varias personas
◆**People say that...** Dicen que...
◆**How many people are there in your family?** ¿Cuántos sois en tu familia?
◆**Spanish people** los españoles

pepper ['pɛpəʳ] NOUN
[1] la pimienta ◊ *Pass the pepper, please.* ¿Me pasas la pimienta?
[2] el pimiento (el chile *LatAm*) ◊ *a green pepper* un pimiento verde

peppermill ['pɛpəmɪl] NOUN
el molinillo de pimienta

peppermint ['pɛpəmɪnt] NOUN
el caramelo de menta
◆**peppermint chewing gum** el chicle de menta

per [pəːʳ] PREPOSITION
por ◊ *per person* por persona ◊ *30 miles per hour* 30 millas por hora
◆**per day** al día
◆**per week** a la semana

per cent [pəː'sɛnt] ADVERB
por ciento ◊ *50 per cent* 50 por ciento

percentage [pə'sɛntɪdʒ] NOUN
el porcentaje

percolator ['pəːkəleɪtəʳ] NOUN
la cafetera de filtro

percussion [pə'kʌʃən] NOUN
la percusión ◊ *I play percussion.* Toco la percusión.

perfect ['pəːfɪkt] ADJECTIVE
perfecto ◊ *Dave speaks perfect Spanish.* Dave habla un español perfecto.

perfectly ['pəːfɪktlɪ] ADVERB
◆**You know perfectly well what happened.** Sabes perfectamente lo que ocurrió.
◆**a perfectly normal child** un niño completamente normal

to **perform** [pə'fɔːm] VERB
representar (*a play*) ◊ *to perform "Hamlet"* representar "Hamlet"
◆**The team performed brilliantly.** El equipo tuvo una brillante actuación.

performance [pə'fɔːməns] NOUN
[1] el espectáculo ◊ *The performance lasts two hours.* El espectáculo dura dos horas.
[2] la interpretación (PL las interpretaciones) ◊ *his performance as "Hamlet"* su interpretación de "Hamlet"

perfume ['pəːfjuːm] NOUN
el perfume

perhaps [pə'hæps] ADVERB
quizás ◊ *Perhaps they were tired.* Quizás estaban cansados.

*Use the present subjunctive after **quizás** to refer to the future.*

◊ *Perhaps he'll come tomorrow.* Quizás venga mañana.

P

☞

◆ **perhaps not** quizás no

period ['pɪərɪəd] NOUN
1 el periodo ◊ *for a limited period* por un periodo limitado
2 la clase ◊ *Each period lasts forty minutes.* Cada clase dura cuarenta minutos.
3 la época ◊ *the Victorian period* la época victoriana
4 la regla ◊ *I'm having my period.* Estoy con la regla.

perm [pəːm] NOUN
la permanente ◊ *She's got a perm.* Lleva permanente.

permanent ['pəːmənənt] ADJECTIVE
1 permanente ◊ *a permanent state of tension* un estado permanente de tensión
2 fijo ◊ *a permanent job* un trabajo fijo

permission [pə'mɪʃən] NOUN
el permiso ◊ *Could I have permission to leave early?* ¿Tengo permiso para salir antes?

permit ['pəːmɪt] NOUN
el permiso ◊ *a work permit* un permiso de trabajo

Persian ['pəːʃən] ADJECTIVE
◆ **a Persian cat** un gato persa

persistent [pə'sɪstənt] ADJECTIVE
persistente

person ['pəːsn] NOUN
la persona ◊ *She's a very nice person.* Es muy buena persona.
◆ **in person** en persona

personal ['pəːsnl] ADJECTIVE
personal ◊ *Those letters are personal.* Son cartas personales. ◊ *he's a personal friend of mine* es amigo íntimo mío

personal column ['pəːsnlkɔləm] NOUN
la sección de anuncios personales

personality [pəːsə'nælɪtɪ] NOUN (PL **personalities**)
la personalidad

personally ['pəːsnəlɪ] ADVERB
personalmente ◊ *Personally I don't agree.* Yo personalmente no estoy de acuerdo.
◆ **I don't know him personally.** No lo conozco en persona.
◆ **Don't take it personally.** No te lo tomes como algo personal.

personal stereo [pəːsnl'stɛrɪəu] NOUN
el walkman ®

personnel [pəːsə'nɛl] NOUN
el personal

perspiration [pəːspɪ'reɪʃən] NOUN
la transpiración

to **persuade** [pə'sweɪd] VERB
convencer*

*Use the subjunctive after **convencer de que** when translating "to persuade somebody to do something".*

◊ *to persuade somebody to do something* convencer a alguien de que haga algo ◊ *She persuaded me to go with her.* Me convenció de que fuera con ella.

Peru [pə'ruː] NOUN
Perú MASC

Peruvian [pə'ruːvjən] ADJECTIVE
see also **Peruvian** NOUN
peruano

Peruvian [pə'ruːvjən] NOUN
see also **Peruvian** ADJECTIVE
el peruano
la peruana

pessimist ['pɛsɪmɪst] NOUN
el/la pesimista

pessimistic [pɛsɪ'mɪstɪk] ADJECTIVE
pesimista ◊ *Don't be so pessimistic!* ¡No seas tan pesimista!

pest [pɛst] NOUN
el pesado
la pesada
◊ *He's a real pest!* ¡Es un pesado!

to **pester** ['pɛstər] VERB
dar* la lata a ◊ *He's always pestering me.* Siempre me está dando la lata.

pesticide ['pɛstɪsaɪd] NOUN
el pesticida

pet [pɛt] NOUN
el animal doméstico
◆ **Have you got a pet?** ¿Tenéis algún animal en casa?
◆ **She's the teacher's pet.** Es la enchufada del profesor.

petition [pə'tɪʃən] NOUN
la petición (PL las peticiones)

petrified ['pɛtrɪfaɪd] ADJECTIVE
◆ **She's petrified of spiders.** Las arañas le dan terror.

petrol ['pɛtrəl] NOUN
la gasolina
◆ **unleaded petrol** gasolina sin plomo

petrol station ['pɛtrəlsteɪʃən] NOUN
la gasolinera

petrol tank ['pɛtrəltæŋk] NOUN
el depósito de gasolina

phantom ['fæntəm] NOUN
el fantasma

*Although **fantasma** ends in **-a**, it is actually a masculine noun.*

pharmacy ['fɑːməsɪ] NOUN (PL **pharmacies**)
la farmacia

> ℹ *Pharmacies in Spain are identified by a special green cross outside the shop.*

* Verbs marked with this symbol are irregular. See pages 380-382 for further details

pheasant ['fɛznt] NOUN
el faisán (PL los faisanes)

philosophy [fɪ'lɔsəfɪ] NOUN
la filosofía

phobia ['fəubjə] NOUN
la fobia

phone [fəun] NOUN
see also **phone** VERB
el teléfono
◆ **by phone** por teléfono
◆ **to be on the phone (1)** (*talking*) estar* al teléfono ◊ *She's on the phone at the moment.* Ahora mismo está al teléfono.
◆ **to be on the phone (2)** (*to have a phone*) tener* teléfono ◊ *We're not on the phone.* No tenemos teléfono.
◆ **Can I use the phone, please?** ¿Puedo hacer una llamada?

to **phone** [fəun] VERB
see also **phone** NOUN
llamar ◊ *I'll phone you tomorrow.* Mañana te llamo. ◊ *Could you phone me a taxi, please?* ¿Me puedes llamar a un taxi, por favor?

phone bill ['fəunbɪl] NOUN
la factura del teléfono

phone book ['fəunbuk] NOUN
la guía telefónica

phone box ['fəunbɔks] NOUN (PL **phone boxes**)
la cabina telefónica

phone call ['fəunkɔ:l] NOUN
la llamada de teléfono
◆ **There's a phone call for you.** Tienes una llamada.
◆ **to make a phone call** hacer* una llamada

phonecard ['fəunkɑ:d] NOUN
la tarjeta telefónica

phone number ['fəunnʌmbə^r] NOUN
el número de teléfono

photo ['fəutəu] NOUN (PL **photos**)
la foto
*Although **foto** ends in **-o**, it is actually a feminine noun.*
◆ **to take a photo** hacer* una foto ◊ *I took a photo of the bride and groom.* Les hice una foto a los novios.

photocopier ['fəutəukɔpɪə^r] NOUN
la fotocopiadora

photocopy ['fəutəukɔpɪ] NOUN (PL **photocopies**)
see also **photocopy** VERB
la fotocopia

to **photocopy** ['fəutəukɔpɪ] VERB (**photocopied, photocopied**)
see also **photocopy** NOUN
fotocopiar

photograph ['fəutəgræf] NOUN
see also **photograph** VERB
la fotografía
◆ **to take a photograph** hacer* una fotografía ◊ *I took a photograph of the bride and groom.* Les hice una fotografía a los novios.

to **photograph** ['fəutəgræf] VERB
see also **photograph** NOUN
fotografiar*

photographer [fə'tɔgrəfə^r] NOUN
el fotógrafo
la fotógrafa
◊ *She's a photographer.* Es fotógrafa.

photography [fə'tɔgrəfɪ] NOUN
la fotografía ◊ *My hobby is photography.* Mi hobby es la fotografía.

phrase [freɪz] NOUN
la frase

phrase book ['freɪzbuk] NOUN
el manual de conversación

physical ['fɪzɪkl] ADJECTIVE
see also **physical** NOUN
físico

physical ['fɪzɪkl] NOUN US
see also **physical** ADJECTIVE
el reconocimiento médico

physicist ['fɪzɪsɪst] NOUN
el físico
la física
◊ *a nuclear physicist* un físico nuclear

physics ['fɪzɪks] NOUN
la física ◊ *She teaches physics.* Enseña física.

physiotherapist [fɪzɪəu'θɛrəpɪst] NOUN
el/la fisioterapeuta

physiotherapy [fɪzɪəu'θɛrəpɪ] NOUN
la fisioterapia

pianist ['pi:ənɪst] NOUN
el/la pianista

piano [pɪ'ænəu] NOUN (PL **pianos**)
el piano ◊ *I play the piano.* Toco el piano.

pick [pɪk] NOUN
see also **pick** VERB
◆ **Take your pick!** ¡Elige el que quieras!
*Replace **el que** with **la que, los que** or **las que** as appropriate to agree with the thing or things you can take your pick of.*

to **pick** [pɪk] VERB
see also **pick** NOUN
1 elegir* (*choose*) ◊ *I picked the biggest piece.* Elegí el trozo más grande.
2 seleccionar (*for team*) ◊ *I've been picked for the team.* Me han seleccionado para el equipo.
3 recoger* (*fruit, flowers*)
◆ **to pick on somebody** meterse con alguien ◊ *She's always picking on me.* Siempre se está metiendo conmigo.

to **pick out** [pɪk'aut] VERB
escoger* ◊ *I like them all – it's difficult to pick one out.* Todos me gustan, es difícil escoger uno.

to **pick up** [pɪk'ʌp] VERB

P

☞

1 recoger* ◊ *We'll come to the airport to pick you up.* Iremos a recogerte al aeropuerto. ◊ *Could you help me pick up the toys?* ¿Me ayudas a recoger los juguetes?
2 aprender ◊ *I picked up some Spanish during my holiday.* Aprendí un poco de español en las vacaciones.

pickpocket [ˈpɪkpɔkɪt] NOUN
el/la carterista

picnic [ˈpɪknɪk] NOUN
el picnic (PL los picnics)
♦ **to have a picnic** irse* de picnic

picture [ˈpɪktʃəʳ] NOUN
1 la ilustración (PL las ilustraciones) ◊ *Children's books have lots of pictures.* Los libros para niños tienen muchas ilustraciones.
2 la foto
*Although **foto** ends in **-o**, it is actually a feminine noun.*
◊ *My picture was in the paper.* Mi foto salió en el periódico.
3 (*painting*)
el cuadro ◊ *a picture by Picasso* un cuadro de Picasso
♦ **a picture of his wife** un retrato de su mujer
4 (*drawing*)
el dibujo
♦ **to draw a picture of something** dibujar algo
♦ **to paint a picture of something** pintar algo
♦ **the pictures** el cine ◊ *Shall we go to the pictures?* ¿Vamos al cine?

picturesque [pɪktʃəˈrɛsk] ADJECTIVE
pintoresco

pie [paɪ] NOUN
1 la tarta (*sweet*) ◊ *an apple pie* una tarta de manzana
2 el pastel (*of meat*) ◊ *a meat pie* un pastel de carne

piece [piːs] NOUN
1 el trozo ◊ *a piece of cake* un trozo de tarta
♦ **A small piece, please.** Un trocito, por favor.
2 pieza (*individual*) ◊ *a 500-piece jigsaw* un puzzle de 500 piezas
3 pedazo (*of something larger*) ◊ *A piece of plaster fell from the roof.* Un pedazo de yeso se cayó del tejado.
♦ **a piece of furniture** un mueble
♦ **a piece of advice** un consejo
♦ **a 10p piece** una moneda de 10 peniques

pier [pɪəʳ] NOUN
el muelle

pierced [pɪəst] ADJECTIVE
♦ **I've got pierced ears.** Tengo los agujeros hechos en las orejas.

pig [pɪg] NOUN
el cerdo

pigeon [ˈpɪdʒən] NOUN
la paloma

piggyback [ˈpɪgɪbæk] NOUN
♦ **to give somebody a piggyback** llevar a alguien a cuestas

piggy bank [ˈpɪgɪbæŋk] NOUN
la hucha

pigtail [ˈpɪgteɪl] NOUN
la trenza

pile [paɪl] NOUN
1 (*untidy heap*)
el montón (PL los montones) ◊ *a pile of dirty laundry* un montón de ropa sucia
2 (*tidy stack*)
la pila
♦ **Put your books in a pile on my desk.** Apilad vuestros cuadernos en mi mesa.

piles [paɪlz] PL NOUN
las almorranas

pile-up [ˈpaɪlʌp] NOUN
el accidente en cadena

pill [pɪl] NOUN
la píldora
♦ **to be on the pill** tomar la píldora

pillar [ˈpɪləʳ] NOUN
el pilar

pillar box [ˈpɪləbɔks] NOUN
el buzón (PL los buzones)

pillow [ˈpɪləu] NOUN
la almohada

pilot [ˈpaɪlət] NOUN
el/la piloto ◊ *He's a pilot.* Es piloto.

pimple [ˈpɪmpl] NOUN
el grano

pin [pɪn] NOUN
el alfiler
♦ **pins and needles** el hormigueo ◊ *I've got pins and needles.* Tengo hormigueo.

PIN [pɪn] NOUN (= *personal identification number*)
el número secreto

pinafore [ˈpɪnəfɔːʳ] NOUN
el pichi

pinball [ˈpɪnbɔːl] NOUN
la máquina de bolas
♦ **They're playing pinball.** Juegan a la máquina.

to **pinch** [pɪntʃ] VERB
1 pellizcar* ◊ *He pinched me!* ¡Me ha pellizcado!
2 birlar* (*informal*) ◊ *Who's pinched my pen?* ¿Quién me ha birlado el bolígrafo?

pine [paɪn] NOUN
el pino ◊ *a pine table* una mesa de pino

pineapple [ˈpaɪnæpl] NOUN
la piña

pink [pɪŋk] ADJECTIVE
rosa MASC, FEM, PL

pint [paɪnt] NOUN
la pinta

In Spain measurements are in litres and centilitres. A pint is about 0.6 litres.

◆ **to have a pint** tomarse una cerveza ◊ *He's gone out for a pint.* Ha salido a tomarse una cerveza.

pipe [paɪp] NOUN
1 la tubería ◊ *The pipes froze.* Se helaron las tuberías.
2 la pipa ◊ *He smokes a pipe.* Fuma en pipa.
◆ **the pipes** la gaita ◊ *He plays the pipes.* Toca la gaita.

pirate ['paɪərət] NOUN
el/la pirata

pirated ['paɪərətɪd] ADJECTIVE
pirata MASC, FEM, PL
◊ *a pirated video* un vídeo pirata

Pisces ['paɪsiːz] NOUN
el Piscis (*sign*) ◊ *I'm Pisces.* Soy Piscis.
◆ **a Pisces** un/una Piscis

pissed [pɪst] ADJECTIVE
mamado (*rude*)

pistol ['pɪstl] NOUN
la pistola

pitch [pɪtʃ] NOUN (PL **pitches**)
see also **pitch** VERB
el campo (la cancha LatAm) ◊ *a football pitch* un campo de fútbol

to **pitch** [pɪtʃ] VERB
see also **pitch** NOUN
montar ◊ *We pitched our tent near the beach.* Montamos la tienda cerca de la playa.

pity ['pɪtɪ] NOUN
see also **pity** VERB
la compasión ◊ *They showed no pity.* No demostraron ninguna compasión.
◆ **What a pity!** ¡Qué pena!

to **pity** ['pɪtɪ] VERB (**pitied**)
see also **pity** NOUN
compadecer ◊ *I don't hate him, I pity him.* No lo odio, lo compadezco.

pizza ['piːtsə] NOUN
la pizza

place [pleɪs] NOUN
see also **place** VERB
1 el lugar ◊ *It's a quiet place.* Es un lugar tranquilo.
2 la plaza ◊ *Book your place for the trip now.* Reserve ya su plaza para el viaje. ◊ *a university place* una plaza en la universidad
3 el puesto (*in sports*) ◊ *Britain won third place in the games.* Gran Bretaña consiguió el tercer puesto en los juegos.
◆ **a parking place** un sitio para aparcar
◆ **to change places** cambiarse de sitio
◆ **to take place** tener* lugar ◊ *Elections will take place on November 25th.* Las elecciones tendrán lugar el 25 de noviembre.
◆ **at your place** en tu casa ◊ *Shall we meet at your place?* ¿Nos vemos en tu casa?
◆ **Do you want to come round to my place?** ¿Quieres venir a mi casa?

to **place** [pleɪs] VERB
see also **place** NOUN
colocar* ◊ *He placed his hand on hers.* Colocó su mano sobre la de ella.

plain [pleɪn] ADJECTIVE, ADVERB
see also **plain** NOUN
1 liso (*not patterned*) ◊ *a plain tie* una corbata lisa
2 sencillo (*not fancy*) ◊ *a plain white blouse* una blusa blanca sencilla
◆ **It was plain to see.** Era obvio.

plain [pleɪn] NOUN
see also **plain** ADJECTIVE, ADVERB
la llanura

plain chocolate [pleɪn'tʃɔklɪt] NOUN
el chocolate amargo

plait [plæt] NOUN
la trenza ◊ *She wears her hair in plaits.* Lleva trenzas.

plan [plæn] NOUN
see also **plan** VERB
1 el plan ◊ *What are your plans for the holidays?* ¿Qué planes tienes para las vacaciones?
◆ **to make plans** hacer* planes
◆ **Everything went according to plan.** Todo fue según lo previsto.
2 el plano ◊ *a plan of the campsite* un plano del camping
◆ **my essay plan** el esquema de mi trabajo

to **plan** [plæn] VERB
see also **plan** NOUN
1 planear (*make plans for*) ◊ *We're planning a trip to France.* Estamos planeando hacer un viaje a Francia.
2 planificar* (*schedule*) ◊ *Plan your revision carefully.* Tienes que planificar bien el repaso.
◆ **to plan to do something** tener* la intención de hacer algo ◊ *I'm planning to get a job in the holidays.* Tengo la intención de encontrar un trabajo para las vacaciones.

plane [pleɪn] NOUN
el avión (PL los aviones) ◊ *by plane* en avión

planet ['plænɪt] NOUN
el planeta

Although ***planeta*** *ends in* ***-a****, it is actually a masculine noun.*

planning ['plænɪŋ] NOUN
◆ **The trip needs careful planning.** Hay que planear bien el viaje.
◆ **family planning** la planificación familiar

P

plant [plɑːnt] NOUN
see also **plant** VERB
la planta ◊ *I water my plants every week.* Riego las plantas todas las semanas.
◆ **a chemical plant** una planta química

to **plant** [plɑːnt] VERB
see also **plant** NOUN
plantar ◊ *We planted fruit trees and vegetables.* Plantamos árboles frutales y hortalizas.

plant pot ['plɑːntpɔt] NOUN
la maceta

plaque [plæk] NOUN
1 la placa conmemorativa (*to famous person, event*)
2 el sarro (*on teeth*)

plaster ['plɑːstəʳ] NOUN
1 la tirita ◊ *Have you got a plaster, by any chance?* ¿No tendrás una tirita, por casualidad?
2 la escayola
◆ **Her leg's in plaster.** Lleva la pierna escayolada.

plastic ['plæstɪk] NOUN
see also **plastic** ADJECTIVE
el plástico ◊ *It's made of plastic.* Es de plástico.

plastic ['plæstɪk] ADJECTIVE
see also **plastic** NOUN
de plástico ◊ *a plastic bag* una bolsa de plástico

plate [pleɪt] NOUN
el plato

platform ['plætfɔːm] NOUN
1 el andén (PL los andenes)
2 (*for speaker, performer*)
el estrado

play [pleɪ] NOUN
see also **play** VERB
la obra de teatro
◆ **a play by Shakespeare** una obra de Shakespeare
◆ **to put on a play** montar una obra

to **play** [pleɪ] VERB
see also **play** NOUN
1 jugar* ◊ *He's playing with his friends.* Está jugando con sus amigos.
2 jugar contra ◊ *Spain will play Scotland next month.* España juega contra Escocia el mes que viene.
3 jugar a ◊ *Can you play pool?* ¿Sabes jugar al billar americano?
4 tocar* ◊ *I play the guitar.* Toco la guitarra. ◊ *What sort of music do they play?* ¿Qué clase de música tocan?
5 poner* ◊ *She's always playing that record.* Siempre está poniendo ese disco.
6 hacer* de ◊ *I would love to play Cleopatra.* Me encantaría hacer de Cleopatra.

to **play down** [pleɪ'daun] VERB
quitar importancia a ◊ *He tried to play down his illness.* Trató de quitarle importancia a su enfermedad.

to **play up** [pleɪ'ʌp] VERB
◆ **The engine's playing up again.** El motor está haciendo de las suyas otra vez.

player ['pleɪəʳ] NOUN
1 el jugador
la jugadora
◊ *a game for four players* un juego para cuatro jugadores
◆ **a football player** un futbolista
2 (*musician*)
el músico
la música
◆ **a piano player** un pianista
◆ **a saxophone player** un saxofonista

playful ['pleɪful] ADJECTIVE
juguetón MASC
juguetona FEM

playground ['pleɪgraund] NOUN
1 el patio de recreo (*at school*)
2 los columpios (*in park*)

playgroup ['pleɪgruːp] NOUN
la guardería

playing card ['pleɪɪŋkɑːd] NOUN
el naipe

playing field ['pleɪɪŋfiːld] NOUN
el campo de deportes (la cancha de deportes *LatAm*)

playtime ['pleɪtaɪm] NOUN
el recreo

playwright ['pleɪraɪt] NOUN
el dramaturgo
la dramaturga

pleasant ['plɛznt] ADJECTIVE
agradable ◊ *We had a very pleasant evening.* Pasamos una tarde muy agradable.

please [pliːz] EXCLAMATION
por favor ◊ *Two coffees, please.* Dos cafés, por favor.

> ***por favor** is not as common as **please** and can be omitted in many cases. Spanish speakers may show their politeness by their intonation, or by using **usted**.*

◆ **Can we have the bill please?** ¿Nos puede traer la cuenta?
◆ **Please come in.** Pase.
◆ **Would you please be quiet?** ¿Quieres hacer el favor de callarte?

pleased [pliːzd] ADJECTIVE
◆ **My mother's not going to be very pleased.** A mi madre no le va a hacer mucha gracia.
◆ **It's beautiful: she'll be very pleased with it.** Es precioso: le va a gustar mucho.
◆ **Pleased to meet you!** ¡Encantado!

pleasure ['plɛʒəʳ] NOUN

el placer ◊ *I read for pleasure.* Leo por placer.

plenty ['plɛntɪ] PRONOUN
♦**Fifteen minutes is plenty.** Quince minutos es más que suficiente.
♦**I've got plenty.** Tengo de sobra.
♦**That's plenty, thanks.** Así está bien, gracias.
♦**I've got plenty to do.** Tengo un montón de cosas que hacer.
♦**plenty of (1)** (*lots of*) mucho ◊ *He's got plenty of energy.* Tiene mucha energía.
♦**plenty of (2)** (*more than enough*) de sobra ◊ *We've got plenty of time.* Tenemos tiempo de sobra.

pliers ['plaɪəz] NOUN
los alicates

plot [plɔt] NOUN
see also **plot** VERB
1 (*of story, play*)
el argumento
2 (*conspiracy*)
el complot (PL los complots) ◊ *a plot against the president* un complot contra el presidente
3 (*for vegetables*)
el huerto

to **plot** [plɔt] VERB
see also **plot** NOUN
conspirar

plough [plau] NOUN
see also **plough** VERB
el arado

to **plough** [plau] VERB
see also **plough** NOUN
arar

plug [plʌg] NOUN
1 (*electrical*)
el enchufe
2 (*for sink*)
el tapón (PL los tapones)

to **plug in** [plʌg'ɪn] VERB
enchufar ◊ *Is the iron plugged in?* ¿Está enchufada la plancha?

plum [plʌm] NOUN
la ciruela

plumber ['plʌməʳ] NOUN
el fontanero
la fontanera
◊ *He's a plumber.* Es fontanero.

plump [plʌmp] ADJECTIVE
rechoncho

to **plunge** [plʌndʒ] VERB
zambullirse* ◊ *He plunged into the water.* Se zambulló en el agua.

plural ['pluərl] NOUN
el plural

plus [plʌs] PREPOSITION, ADJECTIVE
más ◊ *4 plus 3 equals 7.* 4 más 3 son 7.
♦**three children plus a dog** tres niños y un perro
♦**I got a B plus.** Saqué un notable alto.

p.m. [piː'ɛm] ABBREVIATION
♦**at 2 p.m.** a las dos de la tarde
♦**at 9 p.m.** a las nueve de la noche

Use ***de la tarde*** *if it's light and* ***de la noche*** *if it's dark.*

pneumonia [njuː'məunɪə] NOUN
la pulmonía

to **poach** [pəutʃ] VERB
♦**a poached egg** un huevo escalfado

pocket ['pɔkɪt] NOUN
el bolsillo ◊ *He had his hands in his pockets.* Tenía las manos en los bolsillos.

pocket calculator [pɔkɪt'kælkjuleɪtəʳ] NOUN
la calculadora de bolsillo

pocket money ['pɔkɪtmʌnɪ] NOUN
la paga ◊ *How much pocket money do you get?* ¿Cuánto te dan de paga?

poem ['pəuɪm] NOUN
el poema

Although ***poema*** *ends in* ***-a,*** *it is actually a masculine noun.*

poet ['pəuɪt] NOUN
el poeta
la poetisa

poetry ['pəuɪtrɪ] NOUN
la poesía

point [pɔɪnt] NOUN
see also **point** VERB
1 el punto ◊ *a point on the horizon* un punto en el horizonte ◊ *They scored five points.* Sacaron cinco puntos.
2 el momento ◊ *At that point, we decided to leave.* En aquel momento decidimos marcharnos.
3 la punta ◊ *a pencil with a sharp point* un lápiz con la punta afilada
4 el comentario ◊ *He made some interesting points.* Hizo algunos comentarios de interés.
♦**They were on the point of finding it.** Estaban a punto de encontrarlo.
♦**Sorry, I don't get the point.** Perdona, pero no lo entiendo.
♦**a point of view** un punto de vista
♦**That's a good point!** ¡Tiene razón!
♦**That's not the point.** Eso no tiene nada que ver.
♦**There's no point.** No tiene sentido. ◊ *There's no point in waiting.* No tiene sentido esperar.
♦**What's the point?** ¿Para qué? ◊ *What's the point of leaving so early?* ¿Para qué salir tan pronto?
♦**Punctuality isn't my strong point.** La puntualidad no es mi fuerte.
♦**two point five (2.5)** dos coma cinco (2,5)

to **point** [pɔɪnt] VERB
see also **point** NOUN
señalar con el dedo ◊ *Don't point!* ¡No señales con el dedo!
♦**to point at somebody** señalar a alguien con el dedo ◊ *She pointed at Anne.* Señaló a Anne con el dedo.

☞

◆ **to point a gun at somebody** apuntar a alguien con una pistola

to **point out** [pɔɪnt'aut] VERB

1 señalar ◊ *The guide pointed out the Alhambra to us.* El guía nos señaló la Alhambra.

2 indicar* ◊ *I should point out that...* Me gustaría indicar que...

pointless ['pɔɪntlɪs] ADJECTIVE

inútil ◊ *It's pointless arguing.* Es inútil discutir.

poison ['pɔɪzn] NOUN

see also **poison** VERB

el veneno

to **poison** ['pɔɪzn] VERB

see also **poison** NOUN

envenenar

poisonous ['pɔɪznəs] ADJECTIVE

1 venenoso (*animal, plant*)

2 tóxico (*chemical*) ◊ *poisonous gases* gases tóxicos

to **poke** [pəuk] VERB

◆ **He poked me in the eye.** Me metió un dedo en el ojo.

poker ['pəukə^r] NOUN

el póker ◊ *I play poker.* Juego al póker.

Poland ['pəulənd] NOUN

Polonia FEM

polar bear [pəulə'bɛə^r] NOUN

el oso polar

Pole [pəul] NOUN

(*person*)

el polaco

la polaca

pole [pəul] NOUN

el poste ◊ *a telegraph pole* un poste de telégrafos

◆ **a tent pole** un mástil de tienda

◆ **a ski pole** un bastón de esquí

◆ **the North Pole** el Polo Norte

◆ **the South Pole** el Polo Sur

pole vault ['pəulvɔ:lt] NOUN

◆ **the pole vault** el salto con pértiga

police [pə'li:s] PL NOUN

la policía ◊ *We called the police.* Llamamos a la policía.

police car [pə'li:ska:^r] NOUN

el coche de policía

policeman [pə'li:smən] NOUN (PL **policemen**)

el policía (el agente *LatAm*)

police station [pə'li:ssteɪʃən] NOUN

la comisaría

policewoman [pə'li:swumən] NOUN (PL **policewomen**)

la policía (la agente *LatAm*)

polio ['pəulɪəu] NOUN

la polio

Although ***polio*** *ends in* ***-o****, it is actually a feminine noun.*

Polish ['pəulɪʃ] ADJECTIVE

see also **Polish** NOUN

polaco

Polish ['pəulɪʃ] NOUN

see also **Polish** ADJECTIVE

el polaco (*language*)

polish ['pɔlɪʃ] NOUN (PL **polishes**)

see also **polish** VERB

1 el betún (*for shoes*)

2 la cera (*for furniture*)

to **polish** ['pɔlɪʃ] VERB

see also **polish** NOUN

limpiar (*shoes, glass*)

◆ **to polish the furniture** sacar* brillo a los muebles

polite [pə'laɪt] ADJECTIVE

educado ◊ *a polite child* un niño educado

◆ **It's not polite to point.** Es de mala educación señalar con el dedo.

politeness [pə'laɪtnɪs] NOUN

la cortesía

political [pə'lɪtɪkl] ADJECTIVE

político

politician [pɔlɪ'tɪʃən] NOUN

el político

la política

politics ['pɔlɪtɪks] NOUN

la política ◊ *I'm not interested in politics.* No me interesa la política.

poll [pəul] NOUN

el sondeo de opinión

pollen ['pɔlən] NOUN

el polen

to **pollute** [pə'lu:t] VERB

contaminar

pollution [pə'lu:ʃən] NOUN

la contaminación

polo-necked sweater ['pəuləunɛkt'swɛtə^r] NOUN

el suéter de cuello alto

polo shirt ['pəuləuʃə:t] NOUN

el polo

polythene bag [pɔlɪθi:n'bæg] NOUN

la bolsa de plástico

pond [pɔnd] NOUN

1 la charca (*natural*)

2 el estanque (*artificial*)

pony ['pəunɪ] NOUN (PL **ponies**)

el poney

ponytail ['pəunɪteɪl] NOUN

la coleta ◊ *He's got a ponytail.* Lleva coleta.

pony trekking ['pəunɪtrɛkɪ[mg]] NOUN

◆ **to go pony trekking** ir* de excursión en poney

poodle ['pu:dl] NOUN

el caniche

pool [pu:l] NOUN

1 el estanque (*pond*)

2 la piscina (*swimming pool*)

3 el billar americano (*game*)
♦ **a pool table** una mesa de billar
♦ **the pools** las quinielas ◊ *I do the pools every week.* Juego a las quinielas todas las semanas.

poor [puəʳ] ADJECTIVE
1 pobre
pobre goes after the noun when it means that someone has not got very much money. It goes before the noun when you want to show that you feel sorry for someone.
◊ *a poor family* una familia pobre ◊ *Poor David, he's very unlucky!* ¡Pobre David, tiene muy mala suerte!
♦ **the poor** los pobres
2 malo
Use mal before a masculine singular noun.
◊ *He's a poor actor.* Es un mal actor. ◊ *a poor mark* una mala nota

poorly ['puəlɪ] ADJECTIVE
◊ *She's feeling a bit poorly.* No se siente muy bien.

pop [pɔp] ADJECTIVE
pop MASC, FEM, PL
◊ *pop music* la música pop ◊ *a pop star* una estrella pop
♦ **a pop group** un grupo de música pop

to **pop in** [pɔp'ɪn] VERB
entrar un momento

to **pop out** [pɔp'aut] VERB
salir* un momento

to **pop round** [pɔp'raund] VERB
♦ **I'm just popping round to John's.** Voy a pasarme por casa de John.

popcorn ['pɔpkɔ:n] NOUN
las palomitas de maíz

Pope [pəup] NOUN
♦ **the Pope** el Papa
Although Papa ends in -a, it is actually a masculine noun.

poppy ['pɔpɪ] NOUN (PL **poppies**)
la amapola

Popsicle® ['pɔpsɪkl] NOUN US
el polo

popular ['pɔpjuləʳ] ADJECTIVE
popular ◊ *Football is the most popular game in this country.* El fútbol es el deporte más popular de este país.
♦ **She's a very popular girl.** Es una chica que cae bien a todo el mundo.
♦ **This is a very popular style.** Este estilo está muy de moda.

population [pɔpju'leɪʃən] NOUN
la población (PL las poblaciones)

porch [pɔ:tʃ] NOUN (PL **porches**)
el porche de entrada

pork [pɔ:k] NOUN
la carne de cerdo (la carne de puerco *LatAm*)
♦ **a pork chop** una chuleta de cerdo

porn [pɔ:n] NOUN
see also **porn** ADJECTIVE
el porno

porn [pɔ:n] ADJECTIVE
see also **porn** NOUN
porno MASC, FEM, PL
◊ *a porn film* una película porno

pornographic [pɔ:nə'græfɪk] ADJECTIVE
pornográfico ◊ *a pornographic magazine* una revista pornográfica

pornography [pɔ:'nɔgrəfɪ] NOUN
la pornografía

porridge ['pɔrɪdʒ] NOUN
las gachas de avena

port [pɔ:t] NOUN
el puerto ◊ *a fishing port* un puerto pesquero

portable ['pɔ:təbl] NOUN
portátil ◊ *a portable TV* un televisor portátil

porter ['pɔ:təʳ] NOUN
1 (*in hotel*)
el portero
la portera
2 (*at station*)
el mozo de equipajes
la moza de equipajes

portion ['pɔ:ʃən] NOUN
1 (*of food*)
la ración (PL las raciones) ◊ *a large portion of chips* una ración grande de patatas fritas
2 (*part*)
la porción (PL las porciones) ◊ *a small portion of your salary* una pequeña porción de tu salario

portrait ['pɔ:treɪt] NOUN
el retrato

Portugal ['pɔ:tjugl] NOUN
Portugal MASC

Portuguese [pɔ:tju'gi:z] ADJECTIVE
see also **Portuguese** NOUN
portugués MASC (PL portugueses)
portuguesa FEM

Portuguese [pɔ:tju'gi:z] NOUN
see also **Portuguese** ADJECTIVE
el portugués (*language*)
♦ **the Portuguese** los portugueses

posh [pɔʃ] ADJECTIVE
de lujo ◊ *a posh car* un coche de lujo

position [pə'zɪʃən] NOUN
la posición (PL las posiciones) ◊ *an uncomfortable position* una posición incómoda

positive ['pɔzɪtɪv] ADJECTIVE
1 positivo ◊ *a positive attitude* una actitud positiva
2 seguro (*sure*) ◊ *I'm positive.* Estoy completamente seguro.

to **possess** [pə'zɛs] VERB
poseer* ◊ *She lost everything she possessed.* Perdió todo lo que poseía.

P

possession [pəˈzɛʃən] NOUN
♦ **Have you got all your possessions?** ¿Tienes todas tus pertenencias?

possibility [pɔsɪˈbɪlɪtɪ] NOUN (PL **possibilities**)
la posibilidad ◊ *There were several possibilities.* Había varias posibilidades.

possible [ˈpɔsɪbl] ADJECTIVE
posible
♦ **as soon as possible** lo antes posible

es posible que has to be followed by a verb in the subjunctive.

♦ **It's possible that he's gone away.** Es posible que se haya ido.

possibly [ˈpɔsɪblɪ] ADVERB
tal vez ◊ *Are you coming to the party? – Possibly.* ¿Vas a venir a la fiesta? – Tal vez.
♦ **... if you possibly can.** ... si es que puedes.
♦ **I can't possibly go.** Me es del todo imposible ir.

post [pəust] NOUN
see also **post** VERB
1 el correo ◊ *Has the post arrived yet?* ¿Ha llegado ya el correo?
♦ **by post** por correo
♦ **Is there any post for me?** ¿Tengo alguna carta?
2 el poste ◊ *The ball hit the post.* El balón dio en el poste.

to **post** [pəust] VERB
see also **post** NOUN
mandar por correo ◊ *You could post it.* Puedes mandarlo por correo.
♦ **I've got some cards to post.** Tengo que mandar algunas postales.
♦ **Would you post this letter for me?** ¿Me echas esta carta al correo?

postage [ˈpəustɪdʒ] NOUN
el franqueo

postbox [ˈpəustbɔks] NOUN (PL **postboxes**)
el buzón (PL los buzones)

postcard [ˈpəustkɑːd] NOUN
la postal

postcode [ˈpəustkəud] NOUN
el código postal

poster [ˈpəustəʳ] NOUN
1 (*public*)
el cartel ◊ *There are posters all over town.* Hay carteles por toda la ciudad.
2 (*personal*)
el póster (PL los pósters) ◊ *I've got posters on my bedrooms walls.* Tengo pósters en las paredes de mi cuarto.

postman [ˈpəustmən] NOUN (PL **postmen**)
el cartero ◊ *He's a postman.* Es cartero.

postmark [ˈpəustmɑːk] NOUN
el matasellos (PL los matasellos)

post office [ˈpəustɔfɪs] NOUN
la oficina de correos ◊ *Where's the post office, please?* ¿Sabe dónde está la oficina de correos?
♦ **She works for the post office.** Trabaja en correos.

to **postpone** [pəusˈpəun] VERB
aplazar* ◊ *The match has been postponed.* El partido ha sido aplazado.

postwoman [ˈpəustwumən] NOUN (PL **postwomen**)
la cartera ◊ *She's a postwoman.* Es cartera.

pot [pɔt] NOUN
1 el tarro (el pote *LatAm*) ◊ *a pot of jam* un tarro de mermelada
♦ **a pot of paint** un bote de pintura
2 la tetera (*teapot*)
♦ **a coffee pot** una cafetera
3 la maría (*informal*) ◊ *to smoke pot* fumar maría
♦ **the pots and pans** las cacerolas

potato [pəˈteɪtəu] NOUN (PL **potatoes**)
la patata (la papa *LatAm*)
♦ **mashed potatoes** el puré de patatas
♦ **a baked potato** una patata asada

potential [pəˈtɛnʃl] NOUN
see also **potential** ADJECTIVE
♦ **He has great potential.** Promete mucho.

potential [pəˈtɛnʃl] ADJECTIVE
see also **potential** NOUN
posible ◊ *a potential problem* un posible problema

pothole [ˈpɔthəul] NOUN
el bache

pot plant [ˈpɔtplɑːnt] NOUN
la planta de interior

pottery [ˈpɔtərɪ] NOUN
la cerámica

pound [paund] NOUN
see also **pound** VERB
1 la libra

In Spain measurements are in grams and kilograms. One pound is about 450 grams.

◊ *a pound of carrots* una libra de zanahorias
2 la libra esterlina
♦ **20 pounds** 20 libras
♦ **a pound coin** una moneda de una libra

to **pound** [paund] VERB
see also **pound** NOUN
latir con fuerza ◊ *My heart was pounding.* El corazón me latía con fuerza.

to **pour** [pɔːʳ] VERB
1 echar ◊ *She poured some water into the pan.* Echó un poco de agua en la olla.
2 llover* a cántaros ◊ *It's pouring.* Está lloviendo a cántaros.

♦ **in the pouring rain** bajo una lluvia torrencial

poverty ['pɒvətɪ] NOUN
la pobreza

powder ['paudəʳ] NOUN
el polvo
♦ **a fine white powder** un polvillo blanco

power ['pauəʳ] NOUN
1 la corriente (*electrical*) ◊ *The power's off.* Se ha ido la corriente.
2 la energía ◊ *nuclear power* la energía nuclear ◊ *solar power* la energía solar
3 el poder ◊ *They were in power for 18 years.* Estuvieron 18 años en el poder.
♦ **a power point** un enchufe

power cut ['pauəkʌt] NOUN
el apagón (PL los apagones)

powerful ['pauəful] ADJECTIVE
1 poderoso (*person, organization*) ◊ *the most powerful country in the world* el país más poderoso del mundo
2 potente (*machine, substance*) ◊ *a powerful computer system* un potente sistema informático

power station ['pauəsteɪʃən] NOUN
la central eléctrica

practical ['præktɪkl] ADJECTIVE
práctico ◊ *a practical suggestion* un consejo práctico ◊ *She's very practical.* Es muy práctica.

practically ['præktɪklɪ] ADVERB
prácticamente ◊ *It's practically impossible.* Es prácticamente imposible.

practice ['præktɪs] NOUN
1 la práctica ◊ *You'll get better with practice.* Mejorarás con la práctica.
♦ **in practice** en la práctica
♦ **It's normal practice in our school.** Es lo normal en nuestro colegio.
2 el entrenamiento ◊ *football practice* entrenamiento de fútbol
♦ **I'm out of practice.** Estoy desentrenado.
♦ **I've got to do my piano practice.** Tengo que hacer los ejercicios de piano.
♦ **a medical practice** una consulta médica

to **practise** ['præktɪs] VERB (US **practice**)
1 practicar* ◊ *I ought to practise more.* Debería practicar más. ◊ *I practise the flute every evening.* Practico flauta todas las tardes. ◊ *I practised my Spanish when we were on holiday.* Practiqué el español cuando estuvimos de vacaciones.
2 entrenarse (*train*) ◊ *The team practises on Thursdays.* El equipo se entrena los jueves.

practising ['præktɪsɪŋ] ADJECTIVE
practicante ◊ *She's a practising Catholic.* Es católica practicante.

to **praise** [preɪz] VERB
elogiar ◊ *Everyone praises her cooking.* Todo el mundo elogia cómo cocina.

pram [præm] NOUN
el cochecito de niño

prawn [prɔːn] NOUN
la gamba

prawn cocktail [prɔːn'kɔkteɪl] NOUN
el cóctel de gambas (el cóctel de camarón *LatAm*)

to **pray** [preɪ] VERB
rezar* ◊ *to pray for something* rezar por algo

prayer [prɛəʳ] NOUN
la oración (PL las oraciones)

precaution [prɪ'kɔːʃən] NOUN
la precaución (PL las precauciones)
♦ **to take precautions** tomar precauciones

preceding [prɪ'siːdɪŋ] ADJECTIVE
anterior

precinct ['priːsɪŋkt] NOUN
♦ **a shopping precinct** un centro comercial
♦ **a pedestrian precinct** una zona peatonal

precious ['prɛʃəs] ADJECTIVE
precioso ◊ *a precious stone* una piedra preciosa

precise [prɪ'saɪs] ADJECTIVE
preciso ◊ *at that precise moment* en aquel preciso instante
♦ **to be precise** para ser exacto

precisely [prɪ'saɪslɪ] ADVERB
precisamente ◊ *That is precisely what it's meant for.* Para eso precisamente está hecho.
♦ **Precisely!** ¡Exactamente!
♦ **at 10 a.m. precisely** a las diez en punto de la mañana

to **predict** [prɪ'dɪkt] VERB
predecir*

predictable [prɪ'dɪktəbl] ADJECTIVE
previsible

prefect ['priːfɛkt] NOUN

> *Alumno que está en el último curso de la escuela y tiene a su cargo mantener la disciplina entre los pequeños.*

to **prefer** [prɪ'fəːʳ] VERB
preferir* ◊ *Which would you prefer?* ¿Tú cuál prefieres? ◊ *I prefer chemistry to maths.* Prefiero la química a las matemáticas.

preference ['prɛfrəns] NOUN
la preferencia

pregnant ['prɛgnənt] ADJECTIVE
embarazada ◊ *She's six months pregnant.* Está embarazada de seis meses.

prehistoric ['priːhɪs'tɔrɪk] ADJECTIVE
prehistórico

prejudice ['prɛdʒudɪs] NOUN
el prejuicio ◊ *That's just a prejudice.* Eso no es más que un prejuicio.
♦ **There's a lot of racial prejudice.** Hay muchos prejuicios raciales.

P

prejudiced ['prɛdʒudɪst] ADJECTIVE
♦ **to be prejudiced against somebody** tener* prejuicios contra alguien

premature ['prɛmətʃuəʳ] ADJECTIVE
prematuro ◊ *a premature baby* un bebé prematuro

Premier League [prɛmɪə'li:g] NOUN
la primera división

premises ['prɛmɪsɪz] PL NOUN
el local ◊ *They're moving to new premises.* Se cambian de local.

premonition [prɛmə'nɪʃən] NOUN
el presentimiento

preoccupied [pri:'ɔkjupaɪd] ADJECTIVE
preocupado

prep [prɛp] NOUN
los deberes ◊ *history prep* los deberes de historia

preparations [prɛpə'reɪʃənz] PL NOUN
los preparativos ◊ *Preparations are being made for the visit of the Queen.* Se están realizando los preparativos para la visita de la reina.

to **prepare** [prɪ'pɛəʳ] VERB
preparar ◊ *He was preparing dinner.* Estaba preparando la cena.
♦ **to prepare for something** hacer* los preparativos para algo ◊ *We're preparing for our holiday.* Estamos haciendo los preparativos para las vacaciones.

prepared [prɪ'pɛəd] ADJECTIVE
♦ **to be prepared to do something** estar* dispuesto a hacer algo ◊ *I'm prepared to help you.* Estoy dispuesto a ayudarte.

prep school ['prɛpsku:l] NOUN
el colegio privado (*de enseñanza primaria*)

Presbyterian [prɛzbɪ'tɪərɪən] ADJECTIVE
see also **Presbyterian** NOUN
presbiteriano

Presbyterian [prɛzbɪ'tɪərɪən] NOUN
see also **Presbyterian** ADJECTIVE
el presbiteriano
la presbiteriana

to **prescribe** [prɪ'skraɪb] VERB
recetar ◊ *The doctor prescribed a course of antibiotics for me.* El doctor me recetó antibióticos.

prescription [prɪ'skrɪpʃən] NOUN
la receta ◊ *a prescription for penicillin* una receta de penicilina
♦ **on prescription** con receta médica

presence ['prɛzns] NOUN
la presencia
♦ **presence of mind** presencia de ánimo

present ['prɛznt] ADJECTIVE
see also **present** NOUN, VERB
1 presente ◊ *He wasn't present at the meeting.* No estuvo presente en la reunión.
2 actual ◊ *the present situation* la situación actual
♦ **the present tense** el presente

present [prɪ'zɛnt] NOUN
see also **present** ADJECTIVE, VERB
1 el regalo
♦ **to give somebody a present** hacer* un regalo a alguien ◊ *He gave me a lovely present.* Me hizo un precioso regalo.
2 el presente ◊ *to live in the present* vivir el presente
♦ **at present** actualmente
♦ **for the present** por el momento
♦ **up to the present** hasta el momento presente

to **present** [prɪ'zɛnt] VERB
see also **present** ADJECTIVE, NOUN
♦ **to present somebody with something** entregar* algo a alguien ◊ *The Mayor presented the winner with a medal.* El alcalde le entregó una medalla al vencedor.
♦ **He agreed to present the show.** Aceptó presentar el espectáculo.

presenter [prɪ'zɛntəʳ] NOUN
el presentador
la presentadora

presently ['prɛzntlɪ] ADVERB
1 enseguida ◊ *You'll feel better presently.* Enseguida te sentirás mejor.
2 actualmente ◊ *They're presently on tour.* Actualmente están de gira.

president ['prɛzɪdənt] NOUN
el presidente
la presidenta

press [prɛs] NOUN
see also **press** VERB
la prensa ◊ *The story appeared in the press last week.* La historia salió en la prensa la semana pasada.

to **press** [prɛs] VERB
see also **press** NOUN
apretar* ◊ *Don't press too hard!* ¡No aprietes muy fuerte!
♦ **He pressed the accelerator.** Pisó el acelerador.

press conference ['prɛskɔnfərəns] NOUN
la rueda de prensa

pressed [prɛst] ADJECTIVE
♦ **We are pressed for time.** Andamos mal de tiempo.

press-up ['prɛsʌp] NOUN
♦ **to do press-ups** hacer* flexiones

pressure ['prɛʃəʳ] NOUN
la presión (PL las presiones)
♦ **a pressure group** un grupo de presión
♦ **to be under pressure** estar* presionado ◊ *She was under pressure from the management.* Estaba presionada por la dirección.

◆**He's been under a lot of pressure recently.** Últimamente ha estado muy agobiado.

to **pressurize** [ˈprɛʃəraɪz] VERB
◆**to pressurize somebody to do something** presionar a alguien para que haga algo ◊ *My parents are pressurizing me to stay on at school.* Mis padres me están presionando para que siga estudiando.

prestige [prɛsˈtiːʒ] NOUN
el prestigio

prestigious [prɛsˈtɪdʒəs] ADJECTIVE
prestigioso

presumably [prɪˈzjuːməblɪ] ADVERB
◆**Presumably she already knows what's happened.** Supongo que ya sabe lo que ha pasado.

to **presume** [prɪˈzjuːm] VERB
suponer* ◊ *I presume so.* Supongo que sí. ◊ *I presume he'll come.* Supongo que vendrá.

to **pretend** [prɪˈtɛnd] VERB
◆**to pretend to do something** fingir* hacer algo
◆**to pretend to be asleep** hacerse* el dormido

*Be careful not to translate **to pretend** by **pretender**.*

pretty [ˈprɪtɪ] ADJECTIVE, ADVERB
1 bonito ◊ *She wore a pretty dress.* Llevaba un vestido bonito.
2 guapo ◊ *She's very pretty.* Es muy guapa.
3 bastante ◊ *That film was pretty bad.* La película era bastante mala.
◆**The weather was pretty awful.** Hacía un tiempo horroroso.
◆**It's pretty much the same.** Es más o menos lo mismo.

to **prevent** [prɪˈvɛnt] VERB
evitar ◊ *Every effort had been made to prevent the accident.* Se había hecho todo lo posible para evitar el accidente.

***evitar que** has to be followed by a verb in the subjunctive.*

◊ *to prevent something happening* evitar que pase algo ◊ *I want to prevent this happening again.* Quiero evitar que esto se repita.

***impedir a alguien que** has to be followed by a verb in the subjunctive.*

◊ *to prevent somebody from doing something* impedir* a alguien que haga algo ◊ *My only idea was to prevent him from speaking.* Mi única idea era impedirle que hablara.

previous [ˈpriːvɪəs] ADJECTIVE
anterior ◊ *the previous night* la noche anterior
◆**He has no previous experience.** No tiene experiencia previa.

previously [ˈpriːvɪəslɪ] ADVERB
antes

prey [preɪ] NOUN
la presa
◆**a bird of prey** un ave rapaz

price [praɪs] NOUN
el precio ◊ *What price is this painting?* ¿Qué precio tiene este cuadro?
◆**to go up in price** subir de precio
◆**to come down in price** bajar de precio

price list [ˈpraɪslɪst] NOUN
la lista de precios

to **prick** [prɪk] VERB
pinchar ◊ *I've pricked my finger.* Me he pinchado un dedo.

pride [praɪd] NOUN
el orgullo

priest [priːst] NOUN
el sacerdote

primary school [ˈpraɪmərɪskuːl] NOUN
la escuela primaria

prime minister [praɪmˈmɪnɪstəʳ] NOUN
el primer ministro
la primera ministra

primitive [ˈprɪmɪtɪv] ADJECTIVE
primitivo

prince [prɪns] NOUN
el príncipe ◊ *the Prince of Wales* el príncipe de Gales

princess [prɪnˈsɛs] NOUN (PL **princesses**)
la princesa ◊ *Princess Victoria* La princesa Victoria

principal [ˈprɪnsɪpl] ADJECTIVE
see also **principal** NOUN
principal

principal [ˈprɪnsɪpl] NOUN
see also **principal** ADJECTIVE
el director
la directora

principle [ˈprɪnsɪpl] NOUN
el principio ◊ *the basic principles of physics* los principios básicos de física
◆**in principle** en principio
◆**on principle** por principio

print [prɪnt] NOUN
1 la foto

*Although **foto** ends in **-o**, it is actually a feminine noun.*

◊ *colour prints* fotos a color
2 la letra ◊ *in small print* en letra pequeña
3 la huella ◊ *The policeman took his prints.* El policía le tomó las huellas.
4 el grabado ◊ *a framed print* un grabado enmarcado

printer [ˈprɪntəʳ] NOUN
la impresora

printout [ˈprɪntaut] NOUN
la copia impresa

priority [praɪˈɔrɪtɪ] NOUN (PL **priorities**)
la prioridad ◊ *My family takes priority over my work.* Mi familia tiene prioridad sobre mi trabajo.

prison ['prɪzn] NOUN
la cárcel ◊ *to send somebody to prison for 5 years* condenar a alguien a 5 años de cárcel
◆ **in prison** en la cárcel

prisoner ['prɪznəʳ] NOUN
1 (*in prison*)
el preso
la presa
2 (*captive*)
el prisionero
la prisionera
◆ **to take somebody prisoner** hacer* prisionero a alguien

prison officer ['prɪznɔfɪsəʳ] NOUN
el funcionario de prisiones
la funcionaria de prisiones

privacy ['prɪvəsɪ] NOUN
la intimidad ◊ *in privacy* en la intimidad

private ['praɪvɪt] ADJECTIVE
1 privado ◊ *a private school* un colegio privado
◆ **private life** la vida privada
◆ **private property** la propiedad privada
2 particular (*for one person only*)
◊ *private lessons* clases particulares
◊ *She has a private secretary.* Tiene secretaria particular.
◆ **a private bathroom** un baño individual
◆ **"private"** "confidencial" (*on envelope*)
◆ **in private** en privado

to **privatize** ['praɪvɪtaɪz] VERB
privatizar*

privilege ['prɪvɪlɪdʒ] NOUN
el privilegio

prize [praɪz] NOUN
el premio ◊ *to win a prize* ganar un premio

prize-giving ['praɪzgɪvɪŋ] NOUN
la entrega de premios

prizewinner ['praɪzwɪnəʳ] NOUN
el premiado
la premiada

pro [prəu] NOUN (PL **pros**)
◆ **the pros and cons** los pros y los contras

probable ['prɔbəbl] ADJECTIVE
probable

probably ['prɔbəblɪ] ADVERB
probablemente ◊ *He'll probably come tomorrow.* Probablemente vendrá mañana.

problem ['prɔbləm] NOUN
el problema

Although ***problema*** *ends in* ***-a****, it is actually a masculine noun.*

◊ *the drug problem* el problema de la droga
◆ **No problem! (1)** ¡Por supuesto! ◊ *Can you repair it? – No problem!* ¿Lo puedes arreglar? – ¡Por supuesto!
◆ **No problem! (2)** ¡No importa! ◊ *I'm sorry about that – No problem!* Lo siento – ¡No importa!
◆ **What's the problem?** ¿Qué pasa?

proceeds ['prəusi:dz] PL NOUN
la recaudación ◊ *All proceeds will go to charity.* Toda la recaudación se destinará a obras benéficas.

process ['prəuses] NOUN (PL **processes**)
el proceso ◊ *the peace process* el proceso de paz
◆ **We're in the process of painting the kitchen.** Ahora mismo estamos pintando la cocina.

procession [prə'sɛʃən] NOUN
la procesión (PL las procesiones)

to **produce** [prə'dju:s] VERB
1 producir* (*manufacture, create*)
2 montar (*on stage*)

producer [prə'dju:səʳ] NOUN
1 (*of film, record, TV programme*)
el productor
la productora
2 (*of play, show*)
el director
la directora

product ['prɔdʌkt] NOUN
el producto

production [prə'dʌkʃən] NOUN
1 la producción (PL las producciones)
◊ *They're increasing production of luxury models.* Están aumentando la producción de modelos de lujo.
2 el montaje ◊ *a production of "Hamlet"* un montaje de "Hamlet"

profession [prə'fɛʃən] NOUN
la profesión (PL las profesiones)

professional [prə'fɛʃənl] NOUN
see also **professional** ADJECTIVE
el/la profesional

professional [prə'fɛʃənl] ADJECTIVE
see also **professional** NOUN
profesional ◊ *a professional musician* un músico profesional ◊ *a very professional piece of work* un trabajo muy profesional

professionally [prə'fɛʃnəlɪ] ADVERB
◆ **She sings professionally.** Es cantante profesional.

professor [prə'fɛsəʳ] NOUN
el catedrático
la catedrática

Be careful not to translate ***professor*** *by the Spanish word* ***profesor****.*

profit ['prɔfɪt] NOUN
los beneficios ◊ *to make a profit* sacar* beneficios ◊ *a profit of £10,000* unos beneficios de 10.000 libras

profitable ['prɔfɪtəbl] ADJECTIVE
rentable

program ['prəugræm] NOUN

see also **program** VERB
el programa
*Although **programa** ends in **-a**, it is actually a masculine noun.*
◊ *a computer program* un programa informático
♦ **a TV program** US un programa de televisión

to **program** ['prəugræm] VERB
see also **program** NOUN
programar

programme ['prəugræm] NOUN
el programa
*Although **programa** ends in **-a**, it is actually a masculine noun.*
◊ *a TV programme* un programa de televisión

programmer ['prəugræməʳ] NOUN
el programador
la programadora
◊ *She's a programmer.* Es programadora.

programming ['prəugræmɪŋ] NOUN
la programación

progress ['prəugrɛs] NOUN
el progreso ◊ *You're making progress!* ¡Estás haciendo progresos!

to **prohibit** [prə'hɪbɪt] VERB
prohibir* ◊ *Smoking is prohibited.* Está prohibido fumar.

project ['prɔdʒɛkt] NOUN
1 el proyecto ◊ *an international project* un proyecto internacional
2 el trabajo (*research*) ◊ *I'm doing a project on the greenhouse effect.* Estoy haciendo un trabajo sobre el efecto invernadero.

projector [prə'dʒɛktəʳ] NOUN
el proyector

promenade [prɔmə'nɑːd] NOUN
el paseo marítimo

promise ['prɔmɪs] NOUN
see also **promise** VERB
la promesa ◊ *He made me a promise.* Me hizo una promesa.
♦ **That's a promise!** ¡Lo prometo!

to **promise** ['prɔmɪs] VERB
see also **promise** NOUN
prometer ◊ *He didn't do what he promised.* No hizo lo que prometió.
♦ **She promised to write.** Prometió que escribiría.
♦ **I'll write, I promise!** ¡Escribiré, lo prometo!

promising ['prɔmɪsɪŋ] ADJECTIVE
prometedor MASC
prometedora FEM
◊ *a promising tennis player* un tenista prometedor

to **promote** [prə'məut] VERB
ascender* (*employee, team*) ◊ *She was promoted six months later.* La ascendieron seis meses después.

promotion [prə'məuʃən] NOUN
el ascenso

prompt [prɔmpt] ADJECTIVE, ADVERB
1 rápido ◊ *a prompt reply* una rápida respuesta
2 puntual ◊ *He's always very prompt.* Siempre es muy puntual.
♦ **at eight o'clock prompt** a las ocho en punto

promptly ['prɔmptlɪ] ADVERB
1 puntualmente (*on time*) ◊ *We left promptly at seven.* Nos marchamos puntualmente a las siete.
2 enseguida (*immediately*) ◊ *He sat down and promptly fell asleep.* Se sentó y se quedó dormido enseguida.

pronoun ['prəunaun] NOUN
el pronombre

to **pronounce** [prə'nauns] VERB
pronunciar ◊ *How do you pronounce that word?* ¿Cómo se pronuncia esa palabra?

pronunciation [prənʌnsɪ'eɪʃən] NOUN
la pronunciación (PL las pronunciaciones)

proof [pruːf] NOUN
la prueba
♦ **I've got proof that he did it.** Tengo pruebas de que lo hizo.

proper ['prɔpəʳ] ADJECTIVE
1 de verdad (*genuine*) ◊ *It's difficult to get a proper job.* Es difícil conseguir un trabajo de verdad.
2 adecuado (*suitable*) ◊ *You have to have the proper equipment.* Tienes que tener el equipo adecuado.
♦ **If you had come at the proper time...** Si hubieras llegado a tu hora...

properly ['prɔpəlɪ] ADVERB
correctamente ◊ *You're not doing it properly.* No lo estás haciendo correctamente. ◊ *Dress properly for your interview.* Vaya correctamente vestido a la entrevista.

property ['prɔpətɪ] NOUN
la propiedad
♦ **"private property"** "propiedad privada"
♦ **stolen property** objetos robados

proportional [prə'pɔːʃənl] ADJECTIVE
proporcional ◊ *proportional representation* la representación proporcional

proposal [prə'pəuzl] NOUN
la propuesta

to **propose** [prə'pəuz] VERB
proponer* ◊ *I propose a new plan.* Propongo un cambio de planes. ◊ *What do you propose to do?* ¿Qué te propones hacer?
***proponer que** has to be followed by a verb in the subjunctive.*
◊ *He proposed that we stay at home.* Propuso que nos quedáramos en casa.

P

☞

♦ **to propose to somebody** (*for marriage*) declararse a alguien

to **prosecute** ['prɔsɪkju:t] VERB
♦ **They were prosecuted for murder.** Les procesaron por asesinato.

prospect ['prɔspɛkt] NOUN
la perspectiva ◊ *His future prospects are good.* Tiene buenas perspectivas de futuro.

prospectus [prə'spɛktəs] NOUN (PL **prospectuses**)
el prospecto

prostitute ['prɔstɪtju:t] NOUN
la prostituta
♦ **a male prostitute** un prostituto

to **protect** [prə'tɛkt] VERB
proteger*

protection [prə'tɛkʃən] NOUN
la protección

protein ['prəuti:n] NOUN
la proteína

protest ['prəutɛst] NOUN
see also **protest** VERB
la protesta ◊ *He ignored their protests.* Ignoró sus protestas.
♦ **a protest march** una manifestación

to **protest** [prə'tɛst] VERB
see also **protest** NOUN
protestar

Protestant ['prɔtɪstənt] NOUN
see also **Protestant** ADJECTIVE
el/la protestante ◊ *I'm a Protestant.* Soy protestante.

Protestant ['prɔtɪstənt] ADJECTIVE
see also **Protestant** NOUN
protestante

protester [prə'tɛstə^r] NOUN
el/la manifestante

proud [praud] ADJECTIVE
orgulloso ◊ *Her parents are proud of her.* Sus padres están orgullosos de ella.

to **prove** [pru:v] VERB
probar* ◊ *The police couldn't prove it.* La policía no pudo probarlo.

proverb ['prɔvə:b] NOUN
el proverbio ◊ *a Chinese proverb* un proverbio chino
♦ **a Spanish proverb** un refrán español

to **provide** [prə'vaɪd] VERB
proporcionar
♦ **to provide somebody with something** proporcionar algo a alguien ◊ *They provided us with maps.* Nos proporcionaron mapas.

to **provide for** [prə'vaɪdfɔ:r] VERB
mantener* ◊ *He can't provide for his family any more.* Ya no puede mantener a su familia.

provided [prə'vaɪdɪd] CONJUNCTION
siempre que

***siempre que** has to be followed by a verb in the subjunctive.*

◊ *He'll play in the next match provided he's fit.* Jugará el próximo partido siempre que esté en condiciones.

prowler ['praulə^r] NOUN
el merodeador
la merodeadora

prune [pru:n] NOUN
la ciruela pasa

to **pry** [praɪ] VERB
inmiscuirse* ◊ *He's always prying into other people's affairs.* Siempre está inmiscuyéndose en asuntos ajenos.

pseudonym ['sju:dənɪm] NOUN
el seudónimo

psychiatrist [saɪ'kaɪətrɪst] NOUN
el/la psiquiatra

psychoanalyst [saɪkəu'ænəlɪst] NOUN
el/la psicoanalista

psychological [saɪkə'lɔdʒɪkl] ADJECTIVE
psicológico

psychologist [saɪ'kɔlədʒɪst] NOUN
el psicólogo
la psicóloga

psychology [saɪ'kɔlədʒɪ] NOUN
la psicología

PTO [pi:ti:'əu] ABBREVIATION (= *please turn over*)
sigue

pub [pʌb] NOUN
el bar

public ['pʌblɪk] NOUN
see also **public** ADJECTIVE
♦ **the public** el público ◊ *open to the public* abierto al público
♦ **in public** en público

public ['pʌblɪk] ADJECTIVE
see also **public** NOUN
público
♦ **a public holiday** un día festivo (un día feriado *LatAm*)
♦ **public opinion** la opinión pública
♦ **to be in the public eye** ser* un personaje público

publican ['pʌblɪkən] NOUN
♦ **He's a publican.** Es dueño de un pub.

publicity [pʌb'lɪsɪtɪ] NOUN
la publicidad

public school [pʌblɪk'sku:l] NOUN
el colegio privado

public transport [pʌblɪk'trænspɔ:t] NOUN
el transporte público

to **publish** ['pʌblɪʃ] VERB
publicar*

publisher ['pʌblɪʃə^r] NOUN
1 (*person*)
el editor
la editora
2 (*company*)

* Verbs marked with this symbol are irregular. See pages 380-382 for further details

la editorial

pudding ['pudɪŋ] NOUN
el postre ◊ *What's for pudding?* ¿Qué hay de postre?
◆ **rice pudding** el arroz con leche
◆ **black pudding** la morcilla

puddle ['pʌdl] NOUN
el charco

puff pastry [pʌf'peɪstrɪ] NOUN
el hojaldre

to **pull** [pul] VERB
1 tirar (*to make something move*) ◊ *Pull as hard as you can.* Tira con todas tus fuerzas.
2 tirar de (jalar LatAm) (*to tug at something*) ◊ *She pulled my hair.* Me tiró del pelo.
◆ **He pulled the trigger.** Apretó el gatillo.
◆ **I pulled a muscle when I was training.** Me dio un tirón mientras entrenaba.
◆ **You're pulling my leg!** ¡Me estás tomando el pelo!
◆ **Pull yourself together!** ¡Tranquilízate!

to **pull down** [pul'daun] VERB
echar abajo ◊ *The old school was pulled down last year.* El año pasado echaron abajo la vieja escuela.

to **pull out** [pul'aut] VERB
1 sacar* (*remove*) ◊ *to pull a tooth out* sacar una muela
2 echarse a un lado (*car*) ◊ *The car pulled out to overtake.* El coche se echó a un lado para adelantar.
3 retirarse (*from competition*) ◊ *She pulled out of the tournament.* Se retiró del torneo.

to **pull through** [pul'θruː] VERB
recuperarse ◊ *They think he'll pull through.* Creen que se recuperará.

to **pull up** [pul'ʌp] VERB
parar (*car*) ◊ *A black car pulled up beside me.* Un coche negro paró a mi lado.

pullover ['puləuvəʳ] NOUN
el jersey (PL los jerseys)

pulse [pʌls] NOUN
el pulso ◊ *The nurse took his pulse.* La enfermera le tomó el pulso.

pulses ['pʌlsəz] PL NOUN
las legumbres

pump [pʌmp] NOUN
see also **pump** VERB
1 la bomba ◊ *a bicycle pump* una bomba de bicicleta
◆ **a petrol pump** un surtidor de gasolina
2 la zapatilla (*de deporte*) ◊ *She was wearing a black leotard and black pumps.* Llevaba malla y zapatillas negras.

to **pump** [pʌmp] VERB
see also **pump** NOUN
bombear
◆ **to pump up a tyre** inflar una rueda

pumpkin ['pʌmpkɪn] NOUN
la calabaza

punch [pʌntʃ] NOUN (PL **punches**)
see also **punch** VERB
1 el puñetazo (*blow*)
2 el ponche (*drink*)

to **punch** [pʌntʃ] VERB
see also **punch** NOUN
dar* un puñetazo a ◊ *He punched me!* ¡Me ha dado un puñetazo!

punch-up ['pʌntʃʌp] NOUN
la pelea

punctual ['pʌŋktjuəl] ADJECTIVE
puntual

punctuation [pʌŋktju'eɪʃən] NOUN
la puntuación

puncture ['pʌŋktʃəʳ] NOUN
el pinchazo ◊ *I had a puncture on the motorway.* Tuve un pinchazo en la autopista.

to **punish** ['pʌnɪʃ] VERB
castigar* ◊ *They were severely punished for their disobedience.* Les castigaron severamente por su desobediencia.
◆ **to punish somebody for doing something** castigar a alguien por haber hecho algo

punishment ['pʌnɪʃmənt] NOUN
el castigo

punk [pʌŋk] NOUN
el/la punki
◆ **a punk rock band** un grupo punk

pupil ['pjuːpl] NOUN
el alumno
la alumna

puppet ['pʌpɪt] NOUN
el títere

puppy ['pʌpɪ] NOUN (PL **puppies**)
el cachorro

to **purchase** ['pəːtʃɪs] VERB
adquirir*

pure [pjuəʳ] ADJECTIVE
puro ◊ *He's doing pure maths.* Estudia matemáticas puras.

purple ['pəːpl] ADJECTIVE
morado

purpose ['pəːpəs] NOUN
el objetivo ◊ *What is the purpose of these changes?* ¿Cuál es el objetivo de estos cambios?
◆ **his purpose in life** su meta en la vida
◆ **It's being used for military purposes.** Se está usando con fines militares.
◆ **on purpose** a propósito ◊ *He did it on purpose.* Lo hizo a propósito.

to **purr** [pəːʳ] VERB
ronronear

purse [pəːs] NOUN
1 el monedero (*for money*)
2 el bolso (*handbag*) US

pursuit [pə'sjuːt] NOUN
la actividad ◊ *outdoor pursuits* actividades al aire libre

P

push [puʃ] NOUN (PL **pushes**)
see also **push** VERB
el empujón (PL los empujones)
◆ **to give somebody a push** dar* un empujón a alguien

to **push** [puʃ] VERB
see also **push** NOUN
empujar ◊ *Don't push!* ¡No empujes!
◆ **to push a button** pulsar un botón
◆ **to push drugs** pasar droga
◆ **I'm pushed for time today.** Hoy ando fatal de tiempo.
◆ **Push off!** ¡Lárgate!
◆ **Don't push your luck!** ¡No tientes a la suerte!

to **push around** [puʃə'raund] VERB
dar* órdenes a ◊ *He likes pushing people around.* Le gusta dar órdenes a la gente.

to **push on** [puʃ'ɔn] VERB
seguir* ◊ *There's a lot to do, so I must push on now.* Hay mucho que hacer, así que ahora tengo que seguir.

to **push through** [puʃ'θruː] VERB
◆ **I pushed my way through.** Me abrí camino a empujones.

pushchair ['puʃtʃɛəʳ] NOUN
la silla de paseo

pusher ['puʃəʳ] NOUN
el camello (*of drugs*)

to **put** [put] VERB (**put, put**)
poner* ◊ *Where shall I put my things?* ¿Dónde pongo mis cosas? ◊ *Don't forget to put your name on the paper.* No te olvides de poner tu nombre en la hoja.
◆ **She's putting the baby to bed.** Está acostando al niño.

to **put across** [putə'krɔs] VERB
comunicar* ◊ *He finds it hard to put his ideas across.* Le cuesta comunicar sus ideas.

to **put aside** [putə'saɪd] VERB
apartar ◊ *Can you put this aside for me till tomorrow?* ¿Me lo puede apartar hasta mañana?

to **put away** [putə'weɪ] VERB
1 guardar ◊ *Can you put the dishes away, please?* ¿Guardas los platos?
2 encerrar* (*in prison*) ◊ *I hope they put him away for a long time.* Espero que lo encierren por muchos años.

to **put back** [put'bæk] VERB
1 poner* en su sitio (*in place*) ◊ *Put it back when you've finished with it.* Ponlo en su sitio cuando hayas terminado.
2 aplazar* (*postpone*) ◊ *The meeting has been put back till 2 o'clock.* La reunión ha sido aplazada hasta las 2.

to **put down** [put'daun] VERB
1 soltar* ◊ *I'll put these bags down for a minute.* Voy a soltar estas bolsas un momento.
2 apuntar (*note*) ◊ *I've put down a few ideas.* He apuntado algunas ideas.
◆ **to have an animal put down** sacrificar* a un animal ◊ *We had to have our dog put down.* Tuvimos que sacrificar a nuestro perro.
◆ **to put the phone down** colgar*

to **put forward** [put'fɔːwəd] VERB
adelantar (*clock*)

to **put in** [put'ɪn] VERB
poner* (*install*) ◊ *We're going to get central heating put in.* Vamos a poner calefacción central.
◆ **He has put in a lot of work on this project.** Ha dedicado mucho trabajo a este proyecto.
◆ **I've put in for a new job.** He solicitado otro empleo.

to **put off** [put'ɔf] VERB
1 apagar* (*light, TV*) ◊ *Shall I put the light off?* ¿Apago la luz?
2 aplazar* (*delay*) ◊ *I keep putting it off.* No hago más que aplazarlo.
3 distraer* (*distract*) ◊ *Stop putting me off!* ¡Deja ya de distraerme!
4 desanimar (*discourage*) ◊ *He's not easily put off.* No es de los que se desaniman fácilmente.

to **put on** [put'ɔn] VERB
1 ponerse* (*clothes, lipstick*) ◊ *I put my coat on.* Me puse el abrigo.
2 poner* (*tape, record*) ◊ *Put on some music.* Pon algo de música.
3 encender* (*light, TV*) ◊ *Shall I put the heater on?* ¿Enciendo el radiador?
4 representar (*play, show*) ◊ *We're putting on "Bugsy Malone".* Estamos representando "Bugsy Malone".
◆ **I'll put the potatoes on.** Voy a poner a hacer las patatas.
◆ **to put on weight** engordar ◊ *He has put on a lot of weight.* Ha engordado mucho.
◆ **She's not ill: she's just putting it on.** No está enferma: es puro teatro.

to **put out** [put'aut] VERB
apagar* ◊ *It took them five hours to put out the fire.* Tardaron cinco horas en apagar el incendio.
◆ **He's a bit put out that nobody came.** Le sentó mal que no viniera nadie.

to **put through** [put'θruː] VERB
poner* (comunicar* *LatAm*) ◊ *Can you put me through to the manager?* ¿Me pone con el director? ◊ *I'm putting you through.* Le pongo.

to **put up** [put'ʌp] VERB

1 colgar* (*on wall*) ◊ *The poster's great. I'll put it up on my wall.* El póster es genial. Lo colgaré en la pared.
2 montar ◊ *We put up our tent in a field.* Montamos la tienda en un prado.
3 subir ◊ *They've put up the price.* Han subido el precio.

♦ **My friend will put me up for the night.** Me quedaré a dormir en casa de mi amigo.

♦ **to put one's hand up** levantar la mano ◊ *If you have any questions, put your hand up.* Quien tenga alguna pregunta que levante la mano.

♦ **to put up with something** aguantar algo ◊ *I'm not going to put up with it any longer.* No pienso aguantarlo más.

♦ **to put something up for sale** poner* algo en venta ◊ *They're going to put their house up for sale.* Van a poner la casa en venta.

puzzle ['pʌzl] NOUN
el rompecabezas (PL los rompecabezas)

puzzled ['pʌzld] ADJECTIVE
perplejo ◊ *You look puzzled!* ¡Te has quedado perplejo!

puzzling ['pʌzlɪŋ] ADJECTIVE
desconcertante

pyjamas [pə'dʒɑːməz] PL NOUN
el pijama (el piyama *LatAm*) ◊ *my pyjamas* mi pijama

♦ **a pair of pyjamas** un pijama

*Although **pijama** ends in **-a**, it is actually a masculine noun.*

pyramid ['pɪrəmɪd] NOUN
la pirámide

Pyrenees [pɪrə'niːz] PL NOUN

♦ **the Pyrenees** los Pirineos

P

Q

quaint [kweɪnt] ADJECTIVE
pintoresco (*house, village*)

qualification [kwɔlɪfɪ'keɪʃən] NOUN
el título ◇ *He left school without any qualifications.* Dejó la escuela sin sacarse ningún título. ◇ *vocational qualifications* los títulos de formación profesional ◇ *a teaching qualification* un título de profesor

qualified ['kwɔlɪfaɪd] ADJECTIVE
1 cualificado ◇ *a qualified driving instructor* un profesor de autoescuela cualificado
2 titulado ◇ *a qualified teacher* un profesor titulado
♦ **She was well qualified for the position.** Estaba suficientemente capacitada para el puesto.

to **qualify** ['kwɔlɪfaɪ] VERB (**qualified, qualified**)
1 sacarse* el título (recibirse *LatAm*) ◇ *She qualified as a teacher last year.* Se sacó el título de profesora el año pasado.
2 clasificarse* ◇ *Our team didn't qualify for the finals.* Nuestro equipo no se clasificó para la final.

quality ['kwɔlɪtɪ] NOUN (PL **qualities**)
1 la calidad ◇ *a good quality of life* una buena calidad de vida ◇ *good-quality paper* el papel de calidad
2 la cualidad ◇ *She's got lots of good qualities.* Tiene un montón de buenas cualidades.

quantity ['kwɔntɪtɪ] NOUN (PL **quantities**)
la cantidad

quarantine ['kwɔrntiːn] NOUN
la cuarentena ◇ *in quarantine* en cuarentena

quarrel ['kwɔrl] NOUN
see also **quarrel** VERB
la pelea (*discusión*) ◇ *We had a quarrel.* Nos peleamos.

to **quarrel** ['kwɔrl] VERB
see also **quarrel** NOUN
pelearse (*discutir*)

quarry ['kwɔrɪ] NOUN (PL **quarries**)
la cantera (*for stone*)

quarter ['kwɔːtəʳ] NOUN
el cuarto
♦ **three quarters** tres cuartos
♦ **a quarter of an hour** un cuarto de hora
♦ **a quarter past ten** las diez y cuarto
♦ **a quarter to eleven** las once menos cuarto

quarter-finals [kwɔːtə'faɪnəlz] PL NOUN
los cuartos de final

quartet [kwɔː'tɛt] NOUN
el cuarteto ◇ *a string quartet* un cuarteto de cuerda

quay [kiː] NOUN
el muelle (*embarcadero*)

queasy ['kwiːzɪ] ADJECTIVE
♦ **I feel queasy.** Tengo náuseas.

queen [kwiːn] NOUN
1 la reina ◇ *Queen Elizabeth* la reina Isabel
2 la dama ◇ *the queen of hearts* la dama de corazones
♦ **the Queen Mother** la reina madre

query ['kwɪərɪ] NOUN (PL **queries**)
see also **query** VERB
la pregunta

to **query** ['kwɪərɪ] VERB
see also **query** NOUN
poner* en duda ◇ *No one queried my decision.* Nadie puso en duda mi decisión.
♦ **They queried the bill.** Pidieron explicaciones sobre la factura.

question ['kwɛstʃən] NOUN
see also **question** VERB
1 la pregunta ◇ *Can I ask a question?* ¿Puedo hacer* una pregunta?
2 la cuestión (PL las cuestiones) ◇ *That's a difficult question.* Ésa es una cuestión complicada. ◇ *It's just a question of...* Tan sólo es cuestión de...
♦ **It's out of the question.** Es imposible.

to **question** ['kwɛstʃən] VERB
see also **question** NOUN
interrogar* ◇ *He was questioned by the police.* Lo interrogó la policía.

question mark ['kwɛstʃənmɑːk] NOUN
el signo de interrogación

questionnaire [kwɛstʃə'nɛəʳ] NOUN
el cuestionario

queue [kjuː] NOUN
see also **queue** VERB
la cola ◇ *People were standing in a queue outside the cinema.* La gente hacía cola a las puertas del cine.

to **queue** [kjuː] VERB
see also **queue** NOUN
hacer* cola ◇ *We had to queue for tickets.* Tuvimos que hacer cola para comprar los billetes.

quick [kwɪk] ADJECTIVE, ADVERB
rápido ◇ *a quick lunch* un almuerzo rápido ◇ *It's quicker by train.* Se va más rápido en tren.
♦ **She's a quick learner.** Aprende rápido.

◆**Quick, phone the police!** ¡Rápido, llama a la policía!

◆**Be quick!** ¡Date prisa!

quickly ['kwɪklɪ] ADVERB
rápidamente ◊ *It was all over very quickly.* Se acabó todo muy rápidamente.

quiet ['kwaɪət] ADJECTIVE
1 callado ◊ *You're very quiet today.* Estás muy callado hoy. ◊ *She's a very quiet girl.* Es una chica muy callada.
2 silencioso ◊ *The engine's very quiet.* El motor es muy silencioso.
3 tranquilo ◊ *a quiet little town* un pueblecito tranquilo ◊ *a quiet weekend* un fin de semana tranquilo

◆**Be quiet!** ¡Cállate!

◆**Quiet!** ¡Silencio!

quietly ['kwaɪətlɪ] ADVERB
1 en voz baja ◊ *"She's dead" he said quietly.* "Está muerta" dijo en voz baja.
2 sin hacer ruido ◊ *He quietly opened the door.* Abrió la puerta sin hacer ruido.

quilt [kwɪlt] NOUN
el edredón (PL los edredones)

to **quit** [kwɪt] VERB
1 dejar ◊ *I quit my job last week.* Dejé mi trabajo la semana pasada.
2 marcharse ◊ *I've been given notice to quit.* Me han dado el aviso para que me marche.

quite [kwaɪt] ADVERB
1 bastante ◊ *It's quite warm today.* Hoy hace bastante calor. ◊ *It's quite a long way.* Está bastante lejos. ◊ *I quite liked the film, but it was too long.* La película me gustó bastante, pero fue demasiado larga.

◆**How was the film? – Quite good.** ¿Qué tal la película? – No está mal.
2 totalmente ◊ *It's quite different.* Es totalmente distinto. ◊ *I quite agree with you.* Estoy totalmente de acuerdo contigo.

◆**It's quite clear that this plan won't work.** Está clarísimo que este plan no va a funcionar.

◆**not quite...** no del todo... ◊ *I'm not quite sure.* No estoy del todo seguro.

◆**It's not quite the same.** No es exactamente lo mismo.

◆**quite a...** todo un ◊ *It was quite a shock.* Fue todo un susto. ◊ *That's quite an experience.* Eso es toda una experiencia.

◆**quite a lot** bastante ◊ *I've been there quite a lot.* He estado allí bastante. ◊ *quite a lot of money* bastante dinero ◊ *It costs quite a lot to go abroad.* Es bastante caro ir* al extranjero.

◆**There were quite a few people there.** Había bastante gente allí.

quiz [kwɪz] NOUN (PL **quizzes**)
el concurso (*de preguntas*) ◊ *a quiz show* un programa concurso

quota ['kwəutə] NOUN
el cupo

quotation [kwəu'teɪʃən] NOUN
la cita ◊ *a quotation from Shakespeare* una cita de Shakespeare

quotation marks [kwəu'teɪʃənmɑːks] PL NOUN
las comillas

quote [kwəut] NOUN
see also **quote** VERB
1 la cita ◊ *a Shakespeare quote* una cita de Shakespeare
2 el presupuesto ◊ *Can you give me a quote for the work?* ¿Puede darme un presupuesto por el trabajo?

◆**quotes** las comillas ◊ *in quotes* entre comillas

to **quote** [kwəut] VERB
see also **quote** NOUN
citar

Q

R

rabbi ['ræbaɪ] NOUN
el rabino
la rabina
rabbit ['ræbɪt] NOUN
el conejo
♦ **rabbit hutch** la conejera
rabies ['reɪbi:z] NOUN
la rabia ◇ *a dog with rabies* un perro rabioso
race [reɪs] NOUN
see also **race** VERB
1 la carrera
♦ **a cycle race** una carrera ciclista
2 la raza
♦ **race relations** las relaciones interraciales
♦ **the human race** el género humano
to **race** [reɪs] VERB
see also **race** NOUN
1 correr ◇ *We raced to get there on time.* Corrimos para llegar allí a tiempo.
2 echarle una carrera a
♦ **I'll race you!** ¡Te echo una carrera!
racecourse ['reɪskɔ:s] NOUN
el hipódromo
racehorse ['reɪshɔ:s] NOUN
el caballo de carreras
racer ['reɪsəʳ] NOUN
la bicicleta de carreras
racetrack ['reɪstræk] NOUN
1 el circuito (*for cars*)
2 el velódromo (*for cycles*)
racial ['reɪʃl] ADJECTIVE
racial ◇ *racial discrimination* la discriminación racial
racing car ['reɪsɪŋkɑ:ʳ] NOUN
el coche de carreras
racing driver ['reɪsɪŋdraɪvəʳ] NOUN
el/la piloto de carreras
racism ['reɪsɪzəm] NOUN
el racismo
racist ['reɪsɪst] ADJECTIVE
see also **racist** NOUN
racista
racist ['reɪsɪst] NOUN
see also **racist** ADJECTIVE
el/la racista ◇ *He's a racist.* Es racista.
rack [ræk] NOUN
(*for luggage*)
el portaequipajes (PL los portaequipajes)
racket ['rækɪt] NOUN
1 la raqueta (*for sport*) ◇ *my tennis racket* mi raqueta de tenis
2 el jaleo (*informal: noise*) ◇ *They're making a terrible racket.* Están armando muchísimo jaleo.
racquet ['rækɪt] NOUN
la raqueta
radar ['reɪdɑ:ʳ] NOUN
el radar
radiation [reɪdɪ'eɪʃən] NOUN
la radiación
radiator ['reɪdɪeɪtəʳ] NOUN
el radiador
radio ['reɪdɪəu] NOUN (PL **radios**)
la radio

*Although **radio** ends in **-o**, it is actually a feminine noun.*

♦ **on the radio** por la radio
♦ **a radio station** una emisora de radio
radioactive ['reɪdɪəu'æktɪv] ADJECTIVE
radiactivo
radio cassette ['reɪdɪəukæ'sɛt] NOUN
el radiocasete
radio-controlled ['reɪdɪəukən'trəuld] ADJECTIVE
teledirigido
radish ['rædɪʃ] NOUN (PL **radishes**)
el rábano
RAF [ɑ:reɪ'ɛf] ABBREVIATION (= *Royal Air Force*)
las fuerzas aéreas británicas
raffle ['ræfl] NOUN
la rifa ◇ *a raffle ticket* una papeleta de rifa
raft [rɑ:ft] NOUN
la balsa
rag [ræg] NOUN
el trapo ◇ *a piece of rag* un trapo
♦ **dressed in rags** cubierto de harapos
rage [reɪdʒ] NOUN
rabia ◇ *mad with rage* loco de rabia
♦ **to be in a rage** estar* furioso
♦ **It's all the rage.** Es el último grito.
raid [reɪd] NOUN
see also **raid** VERB
1 el asalto ◇ *a bank raid* un asalto de banco
2 la redada ◇ *a police raid* una redada policial
to **raid** [reɪd] VERB
see also **raid** NOUN
1 asaltar (*bank*)
2 hacer* una redada en ◇ *The police raided a club in Soho.* La policía hizo una redada en un club del Soho.
rail [reɪl] NOUN
1 la barandilla (*on stairs, bridge, balcony*)
2 el riel (*for curtains*)
♦ **by rail** por ferrocarril
♦ **railcard** la tarjeta de descuento para viajes en tren
railroad ['reɪlrəud] NOUN US

el ferrocarril
♦ **railroad line** la línea ferroviaria
♦ **railroad station** la estación de ferrocarril

railway ['reɪlweɪ] NOUN
el ferrocarril
♦ **railway line** la línea ferroviaria
♦ **railway station** la estación de ferrocarril

rain [reɪn] NOUN
see also **rain** VERB
la lluvia ◊ *in the rain* bajo la lluvia ◊ *It looks like rain.* Parece que va a llover.

to **rain** [reɪn] VERB
see also **rain** NOUN
llover* ◊ *It rains a lot here.* Aquí llueve mucho.
♦ **It's raining.** Está lloviendo.

rainbow ['reɪnbəu] NOUN
el arco iris (PL los arco iris)

raincoat ['reɪnkəut] NOUN
el impermeable

rainfall ['reɪnfɔːl] NOUN
las precipitaciones

rainforest ['reɪnfɔrɪst] NOUN
la selva tropical

rainy ['reɪnɪ] ADJECTIVE
lluvioso

to **raise** [reɪz] VERB
1 levantar ◊ *He raised his hand.* Levantó la mano.
2 mejorar ◊ *They want to raise standards in schools.* Quieren mejorar el nivel escolar.
3 aumentar ◊ *to raise interest rates* aumentar los tipos de interés
♦ **to raise money** recaudar fondos ◊ *The school is raising money for a new gym.* El colegio está recaudando fondos para un gimnasio nuevo.

raisin ['reɪzn] NOUN
la pasa

rake [reɪk] NOUN
el rastrillo

rally ['rælɪ] NOUN (PL **rallies**)
1 (*of people*)
la concentración (PL las concentraciones) ◊ *There was a rally in Trafalgar Square.* Hubo una concentración en Trafalgar Square.
2 (*sport*)
el rally (PL los rallys) ◊ *a rally driver* un piloto de rally
3 (*in tennis*)
el peloteo

to **ram** [ræm] VERB
embestir* contra ◊ *The thieves rammed a police car.* Los ladrones embistieron contra un coche de la policía.

ramble ['ræmbl] NOUN
♦ **to go for a ramble** ir* de excursión (*de marcha*)

rambler ['ræmblər] NOUN
el/la excursionista

ramp [ræmp] NOUN
la rampa

ran [ræn] VERB *see* **run**

ranch [rɑːntʃ] NOUN (PL **ranches**)
el rancho

random ['rændəm] ADJECTIVE
♦ **a random selection** una selección hecha al azar
♦ **at random** al azar ◊ *We picked the number at random.* Elegimos el número al azar.

rang [ræŋ] VERB *see* **ring**

range [reɪndʒ] NOUN
see also **range** VERB
la variedad ◊ *There's a wide range of colours.* Hay una gran variedad de colores.
♦ **It's out of my price range.** Está fuera de mis posibilidades.
♦ **a range of mountains** una cadena montañosa

to **range** [reɪndʒ] VERB
see also **range** NOUN
♦ **to range from...to...** oscilar entre...y... ◊ *Temperatures in summer range from 20 to 35 degrees.* En verano las temperaturas oscilan entre los 20 y los 35 grados.
♦ **Tickets range from £2 to £20.** El precio de las entradas va de 2 a 20 libras esterlinas.

rank [ræŋk] NOUN
see also **rank** VERB
♦ **a taxi rank** una parada de taxis

to **rank** [ræŋk] VERB
see also **rank** NOUN
♦ **He's ranked third in the United States.** Está clasificado tercero en los Estados Unidos.

ransom ['rænsəm] NOUN
el rescate

rap [ræp] NOUN
el rap

rape [reɪp] NOUN
see also **rape** VERB
la violación (PL las violaciones)

to **rape** [reɪp] VERB
see also **rape** NOUN
violar

rapist ['reɪpɪst] NOUN
el violador

rare [rɛər] ADJECTIVE
1 raro (*unusual*)
2 poco hecho (*steak*)

rash [ræʃ] NOUN (PL **rashes**)
see also **rash** ADJECTIVE
el sarpullido ◊ *I've got a rash on my chest.* Tengo un sarpullido en el pecho.

rash [ræʃ] ADJECTIVE
see also **rash** NOUN
precipitado

rasher ['ræʃər] NOUN

R

◆**a rasher of bacon** una loncha de bacon

raspberry ['rɑːzbərɪ] NOUN (PL **raspberries**)
la frambuesa

rat [ræt] NOUN
la rata

rate [reɪt] NOUN
see also **rate** VERB
1 la tarifa ◊ *There are reduced rates for students.* Hay tarifas reducidas para estudiantes.
2 el tipo ◊ *a high rate of interest* un tipo de interés elevado ◊ *the divorce rate* el porcentaje de divorcios ◊ *the birth rate* la tasa de natalidad

to **rate** [reɪt] VERB
see also **rate** NOUN
considerar ◊ *He was rated the best.* Era considerado el mejor.

rather ['rɑːðər] ADVERB
bastante ◊ *I was rather disappointed.* Quedé bastante decepcionado. ◊ *£20! That's rather a lot!* ¡20 libras esterlinas! ¡Es bastante caro!
◆**rather a lot of** mucho ◊ *I've got rather a lot of homework to do.* Tengo muchos deberes que hacer*.
◆**I'd rather...** Preferiría... ◊ *Would you like a sweet? – I'd rather have an apple.* ¿Quieres un caramelo? – Preferiría una manzana. ◊ *I'd rather stay in tonight.* Preferiría no salir esta noche.
***preferiría que** has to be followed by a verb in the subjunctive.*
◊ *I'd rather he didn't come to the party.* Preferiría que no viniera a la fiesta.
◆**rather than...** en lugar de... ◊ *We decided to camp, rather than stay at a hotel.* Decidimos acampar, en lugar de quedarnos en un hotel.

rattle ['rætl] NOUN
el sonajero

to **rave** [reɪv] VERB
poner* por las nubes
◆**They raved about the film.** Pusieron la película por las nubes.

raven ['reɪvən] NOUN
el cuervo

raving ['reɪvɪŋ] ADJECTIVE
◆**to be raving mad** estar* loco como una cabra

raw [rɔː] ADJECTIVE
crudo (*food*)
◆**raw material** la materia prima

razor ['reɪzər] NOUN
la maquinilla de afeitar
◆**razor blade** la hoja de afeitar

RE [ɑːr'iː] ABBREVIATION (= *Religious Education*)
la religión

reach [riːtʃ] NOUN
see also **reach** VERB
◆**out of reach** fuera del alcance ◊ *Keep medicine out of reach of children.* Guárdense los medicamentos fuera del alcance de los niños.
◆**within easy reach of** a poca distancia de ◊ *The hotel is within easy reach of the town centre.* El hotel está a poca distancia del centro de la ciudad.

to **reach** [riːtʃ] VERB
see also **reach** NOUN
1 llegar* a ◊ *We reached the hotel at seven o'clock.* Llegamos al hotel a las siete. ◊ *We hope to reach the final.* Esperamos llegar a la final. ◊ *Eventually they reached a decision.* Finalmente llegaron a una decisión.
2 ponerse* en contacto con (*get in touch*) ◊ *How can I reach you?* ¿Cómo puedo ponerme en contacto contigo?

to **react** [riː'ækt] VERB
reaccionar

reaction [riː'ækʃən] NOUN
la reacción (PL las reacciones)

reactor [riː'æktər] NOUN
el reactor
◆**a nuclear reactor** un reactor nuclear

to **read** [riːd] VERB (**read, read**)
leer* ◊ *I don't read much.* No leo mucho. ◊ *Read the text out loud.* Lee el texto en voz alta.

to **read out** [riːd'aut] VERB
leer* (*en voz alta*) ◊ *I was reading it out to the children.* Se lo estaba leyendo a los niños.

reader ['riːdər] NOUN
(*person*)
el lector
la lectora

reading ['riːdɪŋ] NOUN
la lectura ◊ *I'll see you in the reading room.* Te veo en la sala de lectura.
◆**I like reading.** Me gusta leer.

ready ['rɛdɪ] ADJECTIVE
preparado ◊ *The meal is ready.* La comida está preparada.
◆**She's nearly ready.** Está casi lista.
◆**He's always ready to help.** Siempre está dispuesto a ayudar.
◆**to get ready** prepararse
◆**to get something ready** preparar algo ◊ *He's getting the dinner ready.* Está preparando la cena.

real [rɪəl] ADJECTIVE
1 verdadero ◊ *the real reason* el verdadero motivo ◊ *It was a real nightmare.* Fue una verdadera pesadilla.
◆**In real life these things don't happen.** Estas cosas no pasan en la vida real.
2 auténtico ◊ *It's real leather.* Es piel auténtica.

realistic [rɪə'lɪstɪk] ADJECTIVE
realista

reality [riː'ælɪtɪ] NOUN
la realidad

to **realize** ['rɪəlaɪz] VERB
♦ **to realize that...** darse* cuenta de que... ◊ *We realized that something was wrong.* Nos dimos cuenta de que algo iba mal.

really ['rɪəlɪ] ADVERB
de verdad ◊ *I'm learning German. – Really?* Estoy aprendiendo alemán. – ¿De verdad?
♦ **Do you really think so?** ¿Tú crees?
♦ **She's really nice.** Es muy simpática.
♦ **Do you want to go? – Not really.** ¿Quieres ir*? – La verdad es que no.

realtor ['rɪəltɔːʳ] NOUN US
el agente inmobiliario
la agente inmobiliaria

rear [rɪəʳ] ADJECTIVE
see also **rear** NOUN
trasero ◊ *the rear wheel* la rueda trasera

rear [rɪəʳ] NOUN
see also **rear** ADJECTIVE
la parte trasera ◊ *at the rear of the train* en la parte trasera del tren

reason ['riːzn] NOUN
la razón (PL las razones) ◊ *There's no reason to think that he's dangerous.* No hay razón para pensar que es peligroso.
♦ **for security reasons** por motivos de seguridad
♦ **That was the main reason I went.** Fui mayormente por eso.

reasonable ['riːznəbl] ADJECTIVE
1 razonable ◊ *Be reasonable!* ¡Sé razonable!
2 bastante aceptable ◊ *He wrote a reasonable essay.* Escribió una redacción bastante aceptable.

reasonably ['riːznəblɪ] ADVERB
bastante ◊ *The team played reasonably well.* El equipo jugó bastante bien.
♦ **reasonably priced accommodation** alojamiento a precios razonables

to **reassure** [riːə'ʃuəʳ] VERB
tranquilizar*

reassuring [riːə'ʃuərɪŋ] ADJECTIVE
tranquilizador

rebel ['rɛbl] NOUN
el/la rebelde

rebellious [rɪ'bɛljəs] ADJECTIVE
rebelde

receipt [rɪ'siːt] NOUN
1 el ticket (*for goods bought*)
2 el recibo (*for work done*)

*Be careful not to translate **receipt** by **receta**.*

to **receive** [rɪ'siːv] VERB
recibir

receiver [rɪ'siːvəʳ] NOUN
el auricular
♦ **to pick up the receiver** descolgar*

recent ['riːsnt] ADJECTIVE
reciente ◊ *recent scientific discoveries* los recientes descubrimientos científicos
♦ **in recent weeks** en las últimas semanas

recently ['riːsntlɪ] ADVERB
últimamente ◊ *I haven't seen him recently.* No lo he visto últimamente. ◊ *I've been doing a lot of training recently.* Últimamente he estado entrenando mucho.
♦ **until recently** hasta hace poco

reception [rɪ'sɛpʃən] NOUN
la recepción (PL las recepciones) ◊ *Please leave your key at reception.* Por favor dejen la llave en recepción. ◊ *The reception will be at a big hotel.* La recepción tendrá lugar en un gran hotel.

receptionist [rɪ'sɛpʃənɪst] NOUN
el/la recepcionista ◊ *She's a receptionist in a hotel.* Es recepcionista en un hotel.

recession [rɪ'sɛʃən] NOUN
la recesión (PL las recesiones)

recipe ['rɛsɪpɪ] NOUN
la receta

to **reckon** ['rɛkən] VERB
creer* ◊ *What do you reckon?* ¿Tú qué crees?

reclining [rɪ'klaɪnɪŋ] ADJECTIVE
♦ **a reclining seat** un asiento reclinable

recognizable ['rɛkəgnaɪzəbl] ADJECTIVE
reconocible

to **recognize** ['rɛkəgnaɪz] VERB
reconocer*

to **recommend** [rɛkə'mɛnd] VERB
recomendar* ◊ *What do you recommend?* ¿Qué me recomienda?

to **reconsider** [riːkən'sɪdəʳ] VERB
reconsiderar

record ['rɛkɔːd] NOUN
see also **record** VERB
1 el disco
2 el récord (PL los récords) ◊ *the world record* el récord mundial
♦ **in record time** en un tiempo récord
♦ **criminal record** los antecedentes penales ◊ *He's got a criminal record.* Tiene antecedentes penales.
♦ **There is no record of your booking.** No tenemos constancia de su reserva.
♦ **records** los archivos ◊ *I'll check in the records.* Miraré en los archivos.

to **record** [rɪ'kɔːd] VERB
see also **record** NOUN
grabar ◊ *They've just recorded their new album.* Acaban de grabar su nuevo álbum.

*Be careful not to translate **to record** by **recordar**.*

R

recorded delivery [rɪkɔːdɪddɪˈlɪvərɪ] NOUN
♦ **to send something recorded delivery** enviar* algo por correo certificado

recorder [rɪˈkɔːdəʳ] NOUN
la flauta dulce (*musical instrument*)
♦ **cassette recorder** el cassette
♦ **video recorder** el vídeo

recording [rɪˈkɔːdɪŋ] NOUN
la grabación (PL las grabaciones)

record player [ˈrɛkɔːdpleɪəʳ] NOUN
el tocadiscos (PL los tocadiscos)

to **recover** [rɪˈkʌvəʳ] VERB
recuperarse
♦ **He's recovering from a knee injury.** Se está recuperando de una lesión de rodilla.

recovery [rɪˈkʌvərɪ] NOUN
la mejora
♦ **Best wishes for a speedy recovery!** ¡Que te mejores pronto!

rectangle [ˈrɛktæŋgl] NOUN
el rectángulo

rectangular [rɛkˈtæŋgjuləʳ] ADJECTIVE
rectangular

to **recycle** [riːˈsaɪkl] VERB
reciclar

recycling [riːˈsaɪklɪŋ] NOUN
el reciclaje

red [rɛd] ADJECTIVE
rojo ◊ *a red rose* una rosa roja ◊ *red meat* la carne roja
♦ **Gavin's got red hair.** Gavin es pelirrojo.
♦ **to go through a red light** saltarse un semáforo en rojo
♦ **red wine** vino tinto

Red Cross [rɛdˈkrɔs] NOUN
la Cruz Roja

redcurrant [ˈrɛdkʌrənt] NOUN
la grosella

to **redecorate** [riːˈdɛkəreɪt] VERB
1 volver* a pintar (*with paint*)
2 volver* a empapelar (*with wallpaper*)

red-haired [rɛdˈhɛəd] ADJECTIVE
pelirrojo

red-handed [rɛdˈhændɪd] ADJECTIVE
♦ **to catch somebody red-handed** coger* a alguien con las manos en la masa (agarrar a alguien con las manos en la masa *LatAm*)

*Be very careful with the verb **coger**: in most of Latin America this is an extremely rude word that should be avoided. However, in Spain this verb is common and not rude at all.*

redhead [ˈrɛdhɛd] NOUN
el pelirrojo
la pelirroja

to **redo** [riːˈduː] VERB (**redid, redone**)
rehacer*

to **reduce** [rɪˈdjuːs] VERB
reducir* ◊ *at a reduced price* a precio reducido
♦ **"reduce speed now"** "disminuya la velocidad"

reduction [rɪˈdʌkʃən] NOUN
la reducción (PL las reducciones)
♦ **a five per cent reduction** un descuento del cinco por ciento
♦ **"huge reductions!"** "¡grandes rebajas!"

redundancy [rɪˈdʌndənsɪ] NOUN (PL **redundancies**)
el despido ◊ *a redundancy payment* una indemnización por despido

redundant [rɪˈdʌndnt] ADJECTIVE
♦ **to be made redundant** ser* despedido

reed [riːd] NOUN
el junco

reel [riːl] NOUN
el carrete (*of thread*)

to **refer** [rɪˈfəːʳ] VERB
♦ **to refer to** referirse* a ◊ *What are you referring to?* ¿A qué te refieres?

referee [rɛfəˈriː] NOUN
el árbitro
la árbitra

reference [ˈrɛfrəns] NOUN
1 la referencia ◊ *He made no reference to the murder.* No hizo referencia al homicidio.
2 las referencias ◊ *Would you please give me a reference?* ¿Me podría facilitar referencias?
♦ **a reference book** un libro de consulta

to **refill** [riːˈfɪl] VERB
volver* a llenar ◊ *He refilled my glass.* Volvió a llenarme el vaso.

refinery [rɪˈfaɪnərɪ] NOUN (PL **refineries**)
la refinería

to **reflect** [rɪˈflɛkt] VERB
1 reflejar (*image*)
2 reflexionar (*think*)

reflection [rɪˈflɛkʃən] NOUN
el reflejo (*image*)

reflex [ˈriːflɛks] NOUN (PL **reflexes**)
el reflejo

reflexive [rɪˈflɛksɪv] ADJECTIVE
reflexivo ◊ *a reflexive verb* un verbo reflexivo

refresher course [rɪˈfrɛʃəkɔːs] NOUN
el curso de reciclaje

refreshing [rɪˈfrɛʃɪŋ] ADJECTIVE
1 refrescante ◊ *a refreshing drink* una bebida refrescante
2 estimulante ◊ *It was a refreshing change.* Fue un cambio estimulante.

refreshments [rɪˈfrɛʃmənts] PL NOUN
el refrigerio

refrigerator [rɪˈfrɪdʒəreɪtəʳ] NOUN
el frigorífico

to **refuel** [riːˈfjuəl] VERB

repostar ◇ *The plane stops in Boston to refuel.* El avión hace escala en Boston para repostar.

refuge ['rɛfju:dʒ] NOUN
el refugio

refugee [rɛfju'dʒi:] NOUN
el refugiado
la refugiada

refund ['ri:fʌnd] NOUN
see also **refund** VERB
el reembolso

to **refund** [rɪ'fʌnd] VERB
see also **refund** NOUN
reembolsar

refusal [rɪ'fju:zəl] NOUN
la negativa ◇ *her refusal to accept money* su negativa a aceptar dinero

to **refuse** [rɪ'fju:z] VERB
see also **refuse** NOUN
negarse*
♦ **He refused to comment.** Se negó a hacer comentarios.

refuse ['rɛfju:s] NOUN
see also **refuse** VERB
la basura
♦ **refuse collection** la recogida de basuras

to **regain** [rɪ'geɪn] VERB
♦ **to regain consciousness** recobrar el conocimiento

regard [rɪ'gɑ:d] NOUN
see also **regard** VERB
♦ **with regard to** con respecto a
♦ **Give my regards to Alice.** Dale recuerdos a Alice.
♦ **"with kind regards"** "un cordial saludo"

to **regard** [rɪ'gɑ:d] VERB
see also **regard** NOUN
♦ **They regarded it as unfair.** Lo consideraron injusto.
♦ **as regards...** en lo que se refiere a...

regarding [rɪ'gɑ:dɪŋ] PREPOSITION
referente a ◇ *the laws regarding the export of animals* las leyes referentes a la exportación de animales
♦ **Regarding John,...** En cuanto a John,...

regardless [rɪ'gɑ:dlɪs] ADVERB
♦ **to carry on regardless** continuar* como si nada

regiment ['rɛdʒɪmənt] NOUN
el regimiento

region ['ri:dʒən] NOUN
la región (PL las regiones)

regional ['ri:dʒənl] ADJECTIVE
regional

register ['rɛdʒɪstəʳ] NOUN
see also **register** VERB
el registro (*in hotel*)
♦ **to call the register** pasar lista

to **register** ['rɛdʒɪstəʳ] VERB
see also **register** NOUN
inscribirse* (*to enrol*)
♦ **The car was registered in his wife's name.** El coche estaba matriculado a nombre de su esposa.

registered ['rɛdʒɪstəd] ADJECTIVE
♦ **a registered letter** una carta certificada

registration [rɛdʒɪs'treɪʃən] NOUN
el número de matrícula
♦ **Registration starts at 8.30.** La inscripción empieza a las ocho y media.

regret [rɪ'grɛt] NOUN
see also **regret** VERB
♦ **I've got no regrets.** No me arrepiento.

to **regret** [rɪ'grɛt] VERB
see also **regret** NOUN
arrepentirse* ◇ *Try it, you won't regret it!* ¡Pruébalo! ¡No te arrepentirás!
♦ **to regret doing something** arrepentirse de haber hecho algo ◇ *I regret saying that.* Me arrepiento de haber dicho eso.

regular ['rɛgjuləʳ] ADJECTIVE
1 regular ◇ *at regular intervals* a intervalos regulares
♦ **to take regular exercise** hacer* ejercicio con regularidad
2 normal ◇ *a regular portion of fries* una porción normal de patatas fritas

regularly ['rɛgjuləlɪ] ADVERB
con regularidad

regulations [rɛgju'leɪʃənz] PL NOUN
el reglamento ◇ *It's against the regulations.* Va en contra del reglamento.
♦ **safety regulations** las normas de seguridad

rehearsal [rɪ'hə:səl] NOUN
el ensayo
♦ **dress rehearsal** el ensayo general

to **rehearse** [rɪ'hə:s] VERB
ensayar

reindeer ['reɪndɪəʳ] NOUN
el reno

reins [reɪnz] PL NOUN
las riendas

to **reject** [rɪ'dʒɛkt] VERB
1 rechazar* (*proposal, invitation*)
2 desechar (*idea, advice*)
♦ **I applied but they rejected me.** Presenté una solicitud, pero no me aceptaron.

relapse [rɪ'læps] NOUN
la recaída
♦ **to have a relapse** tener* una recaída

related [rɪ'leɪtɪd] ADJECTIVE
♦ **We're related.** Somos parientes.
♦ **Are you related to her?** ¿Eres pariente suyo?
♦ **The two events are not related.** Los dos sucesos no están relacionados.

relation [rɪ'leɪʃən] NOUN
1 el/la pariente ◇ *He's a distant relation.* Es un pariente lejano mío.
2 la relación (PL las relaciones) ◇ *It has no relation to reality.* No guarda ninguna relación con la realidad.

R

☞

♦ **in relation to** con relación a

relationship [rɪ'leɪʃənʃɪp] NOUN
la relación (PL las relaciones) ◊ *Their relationship is over.* Su relación ha acabado.
♦ **We have a good relationship.** Tenemos una buena relación.
♦ **I'm not in a relationship at the moment.** No tengo relaciones sentimentales con nadie en este momento.

relative ['rɛlətɪv] NOUN
el/la pariente

relatively ['rɛlətɪvlɪ] ADVERB
relativamente

to **relax** [rɪ'læks] VERB
relajarse ◊ *I relax listening to music.* Me relajo escuchando música.
♦ **Relax! Everything's fine.** ¡Tranquilo! No pasa nada.

relaxation [ri:læk'seɪʃən] NOUN
el esparcimiento
♦ **I don't have much time for relaxation.** No tengo muchos momentos de esparcimiento.

relaxed [rɪ'lækst] ADJECTIVE
relajado

relaxing [rɪ'læksɪŋ] ADJECTIVE
relajante ◊ *Having a bath is very relaxing.* Darse* un baño es muy relajante.
♦ **I find cooking relaxing.** Cocinar me relaja.

relay ['ri:leɪ] NOUN
♦ **a relay race** una carrera de relevos

to **release** [rɪ'li:s] VERB
see also **release** NOUN
1 poner* en libertad (*prisoner*)
2 hacer* público (*report, news*)
3 sacar* a la venta (*record, video*)

release [rɪ'li:s] NOUN
see also **release** VERB
la puesta en libertad ◊ *the release of Nelson Mandela* la puesta en libertad de Nelson Mandela
♦ **the band's latest release** el último trabajo del grupo

relegated ['rɛləgeɪtɪd] ADJECTIVE
♦ **to be relegated** bajar de división (*sport*)

relevant ['rɛləvənt] ADJECTIVE
pertinente (*documents*)
♦ **That's not relevant.** Eso no viene al caso.
♦ **to be relevant to something** guardar relación con algo ◊ *Education should be relevant to real life.* La educación debería guardar relación con la vida real.

reliable [rɪ'laɪəbl] ADJECTIVE
fiable ◊ *a reliable car* un coche fiable ◊ *He's not very reliable.* No es una persona muy fiable.

relief [rɪ'li:f] NOUN
el alivio ◊ *That's a relief!* ¡Es un alivio! ◊ *Much to my relief she made no objection.* Para mi gran alivio, no hizo objeción alguna.

to **relieve** [rɪ'li:v] VERB
aliviar ◊ *This injection will relieve the pain.* Esta inyección le aliviará el dolor.

relieved [rɪ'li:vd] ADJECTIVE
♦ **to be relieved** sentir* un gran alivio ◊ *I was relieved to hear he was better.* Sentí un gran alivio al saber que estaba mejor.

religion [rɪ'lɪdʒən] NOUN
la religión (PL las religiones) ◊ *What religion are you?* ¿De qué religión eres?

religious [rɪ'lɪdʒəs] ADJECTIVE
religioso ◊ *I'm not religious.* No soy religioso.

reluctant [rɪ'lʌktənt] ADJECTIVE
reacio
♦ **to be reluctant to do something** ser* reacio a hacer algo ◊ *They were reluctant to help us.* Eran reacios a ayudarnos.

reluctantly [rɪ'lʌktəntlɪ] ADVERB
de mala gana ◊ *She reluctantly accepted.* Aceptó de mala gana.

to **rely on** [rɪ'laɪɔn] VERB
confiar* en ◊ *I'm relying on you.* Confío en ti.

to **remain** [rɪ'meɪn] VERB
permanecer* ◊ *to remain silent* permanecer callado

remaining [rɪ'meɪnɪŋ] ADJECTIVE
restante ◊ *the remaining ingredients* los ingredientes restantes

remains [rɪ'meɪnz] PL NOUN
los restos ◊ *the remains of the picnic* los restos de la merienda ◊ *human remains* restos humanos
♦ **Roman remains** los restos romanos

remake ['ri:meɪk] NOUN
la nueva versión

remark [rɪ'mɑ:k] NOUN
el comentario

remarkable [rɪ'mɑ:kəbl] ADJECTIVE
extraordinario

remarkably [rɪ'mɑ:kəblɪ] ADVERB
extraordinariamente

to **remarry** [ri:'mærɪ] VERB (**remarried, remarried**)
volver* a casarse ◊ *She remarried three years ago.* Se volvió a casar hace tres años.

remedy ['rɛmədɪ] NOUN (PL **remedies**)
el remedio ◊ *a good remedy for a sore throat* un buen remedio para el dolor de garganta

to **remember** [rɪ'mɛmbə^r] VERB
1 acordarse* ◊ *I don't remember.* No me acuerdo.

2 acordarse* de ◊ *I can't remember his name.* No me acuerdo de su nombre. ◊ *I don't remember saying that.* No me acuerdo de haber dicho eso.

*In Spanish you often say **no te olvides** - **don't forget** - instead of **remember**.*

◊ *Remember your passport!* ¡No te olvides del pasaporte! ◊ *Remember to write your name on the form.* No te olvides de escribir tu nombre en el impreso.

Remembrance Day [rɪ'mɛmbrənsdeɪ] NOUN

En Gran Bretaña, domingo de Noviembre en que se conmemora la firma del armisticio de 1918, y se recuerda a todos aquellos que murieron en las dos guerras mundiales.

to **remind** [rɪ'maɪnd] VERB
recordar* ◊ *The scenery here reminds me of Scotland.* Este paisaje me recuerda a Escocia.

*When talking about reminding someone to do something, **recordar a alguien que** has to be followed by a verb in the subjunctive.*

◊ *Remind me to speak to Daniel.* Recuérdame que hable con Daniel.

remorse [rɪ'mɔːs] NOUN
el remordimiento ◊ *He showed no remorse.* No tenía ningún remordimiento.

remote [rɪ'məut] ADJECTIVE
remoto ◊ *a remote village* un pueblo remoto

remote control [rɪməutkən'trəul] NOUN
el mando a distancia

removable [rɪ'muːvəbl] ADJECTIVE
separable

removal [rɪ'muːvəl] NOUN
la mudanza
♦ **a removal van** un camión de mudanzas

to **remove** [rɪ'muːv] VERB
quitar ◊ *Please remove your bag from my seat.* Por favor, quite su bolsa de mi asiento. ◊ *Did you remove the stain?* ¿Quitaste la mancha?

rendezvous ['rɔndɪvuː] NOUN
la cita

to **renew** [rɪ'njuː] VERB
renovar* (*passport, licence*)

renewable [rɪ'njuːəbl] ADJECTIVE
renovable

to **renovate** ['rɛnəveɪt] VERB
renovar* ◊ *The building's been renovated.* Han renovado el edificio.

renowned [rɪ'naund] ADJECTIVE
renombrdo

rent [rɛnt] NOUN
see also **rent** VERB
el alquiler

to **rent** [rɛnt] VERB
see also **rent** NOUN
alquilar ◊ *We rented a car.* Alquilamos un coche.

rental ['rɛntl] NOUN
el alquiler ◊ *Car rental is included in the price.* El alquiler del coche está incluido en el precio.

rental car ['rentlkɑːʳ] NOUN
el coche de alquiler

to **reorganize** [riː'ɔːgənaɪz] VERB
reorganizar*

rep [rɛp] NOUN (= *representative*)
el/la representante

repaid [riː'peɪd] VERB *see* **repay**

to **repair** [rɪ'pɛəʳ] VERB
see also **repair** NOUN
reparar ◊ *Can you repair this for me?* ¿Me puede reparar esto? ◊ *I got the washing machine repaired.* Me repararon la lavadora.

repair [rɪ'pɛəʳ] NOUN
see also **repair** VERB
la reparación (PL las reparaciones)

to **repay** [riː'peɪ] VERB (**repaid, repaid**)
devolver* (*money*)
♦ **I don't know how I can ever repay you.** No sé cómo podré devolverle el favor.

repayment [riː'peɪmənt] NOUN
el pago ◊ *mortgage repayments* los pagos de la hipoteca

to **repeat** [rɪ'piːt] VERB
see also **repeat** NOUN
repetir*

repeat [rɪ'piːt] NOUN
see also **repeat** VERB
la reposición (PL las reposiciones) ◊ *There are too many repeats on television.* Hay demasiadas reposiciones en la tele.

repeatedly [rɪ'piːtɪdlɪ] ADVERB
repetidamente

repellent [rɪ'pɛlənt] NOUN
♦ **insect repellent** la loción anti-insectos

repetitive [rɪ'pɛtɪtɪv] ADJECTIVE
repetitivo

to **replace** [rɪ'pleɪs] VERB
1 sustituir* ◊ *Computers have replaced typewriters.* Los ordenadores han sustituído a las máquinas de escribir.
2 cambiar (*batteries*)

replay ['riːpleɪ] NOUN
see also **replay** VERB
♦ **There will be a replay on Friday.** El partido se volverá a jugar el viernes.

to **replay** [riː'pleɪ] VERB
see also **replay** NOUN
1 volver* a jugar (*match*)
2 volver* a poner (*tape*)

replica ['rɛplɪkə] NOUN

la réplica

reply [rɪ'plaɪ] NOUN (PL **replies**)
see also **reply** VERB
la respuesta

to **reply** [rɪ'plaɪ] VERB (**replied, replied**)
see also **reply** NOUN
responder

report [rɪ'pɔ:t] NOUN
see also **report** VERB
1 el informe (*of event*)
2 el reportaje (*news report*) ◊ *a report in the paper* un reportaje en el periódico
3 las notas (*at school*) ◊ *I got a good report this term.* He sacado buenas notas este trimestre.

to **report** [rɪ'pɔ:t] VERB
see also **report** NOUN
1 dar* parte de ◊ *I reported the theft to the police.* Di parte del robo a la policía.
2 presentarse ◊ *Report to reception when you arrive.* Preséntese en recepción cuando llegue.
♦ **I'll report back as soon as I hear anything.** En cuanto tenga noticias, te lo haré saber*.

reporter [rɪ'pɔ:tə^r] NOUN
el/la periodista

to **represent** [rɛprɪ'zɛnt] VERB
1 representar a (*client, country*)
2 representar (*change, achievement*)

representative [rɛprɪ'zɛntətɪv] ADJECTIVE
representativo

reproduction [ri:prə'dʌkʃən] NOUN
la reproducción (PL las reproducciones)

reptile ['rɛptaɪl] NOUN
el reptil

republic [rɪ'pʌblɪk] NOUN
la república

repulsive [rɪ'pʌlsɪv] ADJECTIVE
repugnante

reputable ['rɛpjutəbl] ADJECTIVE
acreditado

reputation [rɛpju'teɪʃən] NOUN
la reputación (PL las reputaciones)

request [rɪ'kwɛst] NOUN
see also **request** VERB
la petición (PL las peticiones)

to **request** [rɪ'kwɛst] VERB
see also **request** NOUN
solicitar

to **require** [rɪ'kwaɪə^r] VERB
requerir* ◊ *Her job requires a lot of patience.* Su trabajo requiere mucha paciencia.

requirement [rɪ'kwaɪəmənt] NOUN
el requisito ◊ *What are the requirements for the job?* ¿Cuáles son los requisitos para el puesto?
♦ **entry requirements** (*for university*) los requisitos para el acceso

to **rescue** ['rɛskju:] VERB
see also **rescue** NOUN
rescatar

rescue ['rɛskju:] NOUN
see also **rescue** VERB
el rescate ◊ *a rescue operation* una operación de rescate ◊ *a mountain rescue team* un equipo de rescate de montaña
♦ **to come to somebody's rescue** ir* en auxilio de alguien

research [rɪ'sə:tʃ] NOUN
la investigación (PL las investigaciones) ◊ *He's doing research.* Realiza trabajos de investigación.
♦ **She's doing some research in the library.** Está investigando en la biblioteca.

resemblance [rɪ'zɛmbləns] NOUN
el parecido

to **resent** [rɪ'zɛnt] VERB
♦ **I resent being dependent on her.** Me molesta tener que depender de ella.

reservation [rɛzə'veɪʃən] NOUN
la reserva ◊ *I've got a reservation for two nights.* Tengo una reserva para dos noches. ◊ *I'd like to make a reservation for this evening.* Quisiera hacer* una reserva para esta tarde.
♦ **I've got reservations about the idea.** Tengo mis reservas al respecto.

reserve [rɪ'zə:v] NOUN
see also **reserve** VERB
1 la reserva (*place*) ◊ *a nature reserve* una reserva natural
2 el/la suplente (*person*) ◊ *I was reserve in the game last Saturday.* Yo era suplente en el partido del sábado.

to **reserve** [rɪ'zə:v] VERB
see also **reserve** NOUN
reservar ◊ *I'd like to reserve a table for tomorrow evening.* Quisiera reservar una mesa para mañana por la noche.

reserved [rɪ'zə:vd] ADJECTIVE
reservado ◊ *a reserved seat* un asiento reservado ◊ *He's quite reserved.* Es bastante reservado.

reservoir ['rɛzəvwɑ:^r] NOUN
el embalse

resident ['rɛzɪdənt] NOUN
el vecino
la vecina
◊ *local residents* los vecinos del lugar

residential [rɛzɪ'dɛnʃəl] ADJECTIVE
residencial ◊ *a residential area* una zona residencial

to **resign** [rɪ'zaɪn] VERB
dimitir

resistance [rɪ'zɪstəns] NOUN
la resistencia

to **resit** [ri:'sɪt] VERB (**resat, resat**)

volver* a presentarse a ◊ *I'm resitting the exam in December.* Me vuelvo a presentar al examen en diciembre.

resolution [rɛzəˈluːʃən] NOUN
el propósito ◊ *Have you made any New Year's resolutions?* ¿Has hecho algún buen propósito para el Año Nuevo?

resort [rɪˈzɔːt] NOUN
el centro turístico ◊ *a resort on the Costa del Sol* un centro turístico en la Costa del Sol
◆ **a ski resort** una estación de esquí
◆ **as a last resort** como último recurso

resource [rɪˈzɔːs] NOUN
el recurso

respect [rɪsˈpɛkt] NOUN
see also **respect** VERB
el respeto
◆ **in some respects** en algunos aspectos

to **respect** [rɪsˈpɛkt] VERB
see also **respect** NOUN
respetar

respectable [rɪsˈpɛktəbl] ADJECTIVE
1 respetable ◊ *a respectable family* una familia respetable
2 decente ◊ *My marks were quite respectable.* Mis notas eran bastante decentes.

respectively [rɪsˈpɛktɪvlɪ] ADVERB
respectivamente ◊ *Spain and France came third and fourth respectively.* España y Francia llegaron en tercero y cuarto lugar respectivamente.

responsibility [rɪspɔnsɪˈbɪlɪtɪ] NOUN (PL **responsibilities**)
la responsabilidad

responsible [rɪsˈpɔnsɪbl] ADJECTIVE
responsable ◊ *You should be more responsible!* ¡Deberías ser más responsable!
◆ **to be responsible for something** ser* responsable de algo ◊ *He's responsible for booking the tickets.* Es responsable de reservar las entradas.
◆ **It's a responsible job.** Es un puesto de responsabilidad.

rest [rɛst] NOUN
see also **rest** VERB
1 el descanso ◊ *five minutes' rest* cinco minutos de descanso
◆ **to have a rest** descansar ◊ *We stopped to have a rest.* Nos paramos a descansar.
2 el resto ◊ *I'll do the rest.* Yo haré el resto. ◊ *the rest of the money* el resto del dinero
◆ **the rest of them** los demás ◊ *The rest of them went swimming.* Los demás fueron a nadar.

to **rest** [rɛst] VERB
see also **rest** NOUN
1 descansar ◊ *She's resting in her room.* Está descansando en su habitación.
◆ **He has to rest his knee.** Tiene que descansar la rodilla.
2 apoyar ◊ *I rested my bike against the window.* Apoyé la bicicleta en la ventana.

restaurant [ˈrɛstərɔŋ] NOUN
el restaurante ◊ *We don't often go to restaurants.* No solemos ir a restaurantes.
◆ **restaurant car** el vagón restaurante

restful [ˈrɛstful] ADJECTIVE
plácido

restless [ˈrɛstlɪs] ADJECTIVE
inquieto

restoration [rɛstəˈreɪʃən] NOUN
la restauración

to **restore** [rɪˈstɔːʳ] VERB
restaurar (*building, painting*)

to **restrict** [rɪsˈtrɪkt] VERB
limitar

rest room [ˈrɛstruːm] NOUN US
los servicios

result [rɪˈzʌlt] NOUN
el resultado ◊ *my exam results* los resultados de mis exámenes ◊ *The result was one-nil.* El resultado fue uno a cero.

résumé [ˈreɪzjuːmeɪ] NOUN US
el currículum vitae

to **retire** [rɪˈtaɪəʳ] VERB
jubilarse

retired [rɪˈtaɪəd] ADJECTIVE
jubilado ◊ *She's retired.* Está jubilada. ◊ *a retired teacher* un maestro jubilado

retirement [rɪˈtaɪəmənt] NOUN
◆ **since his retirement** desde que se jubiló

to **retrace** [riːˈtreɪs] VERB
◆ **I retraced my steps.** Volví sobre mis pasos.

return [rɪˈtəːn] NOUN
see also **return** VERB
1 el regreso ◊ *his sudden return home* su repentino regreso a casa
◆ **the return journey** el viaje de vuelta
◆ **a return match** un partido de vuelta
2 el billete de ida y vuelta ◊ *A return to Bilbao, please.* Un billete de ida y vuelta a Bilbao, por favor.
◆ **in return** a cambio ◊ *She helps me and I help her in return.* Me ayuda y yo la ayudo a cambio.
◆ **in return for** a cambio de
◆ **Many happy returns!** ¡Que cumplas muchos más!

to **return** [rɪˈtəːn] VERB
see also **return** NOUN
1 volver* ◊ *I've just returned from holiday.* Acabo de volver de vacaciones. ◊ *He returned to Spain the following year.* Volvió a España al año siguiente.
2 devolver* ◊ *She borrows my things and doesn't return them.* Toma prestadas mis cosas y no las devuelve.

reunion [riːˈjuːnɪən] NOUN

R

la reunión (PL las reuniones) ◇ *We had a big family reunion at Christmas.* Tuvimos una gran reunión familiar en Navidad.

to **reuse** [riː'juːz] VERB
reutilizar*

to **reveal** [rɪ'viːl] VERB
revelar

revenge [rɪ'vɛndʒ] NOUN
la venganza ◇ *in revenge* como venganza
◆ **to take revenge** vengarse* ◇ *They planned to take revenge on him.* Planearon vengarse de él.

to **reverse** [rɪ'vəːs] VERB
see also **reverse** ADJECTIVE
dar* marcha atrás (*car*) ◇ *He reversed without looking.* Dio marcha atrás sin mirar.
◆ **to reverse the charges** llamar a cobro revertido

reverse [rɪ'vəːs] ADJECTIVE
see also **reverse** VERB
inverso ◇ *in reverse order* en orden inverso
◆ **in reverse gear** en marcha atrás
◆ **reverse charge call** llamada a cobro revertido

review [rɪ'vjuː] NOUN
1 (*of policy, salary*)
la revisión (PL las revisiones)
2 (*of subject*)
el repaso

to **revise** [rɪ'vaɪz] VERB
estudiar para un examen ◇ *I haven't started revising yet.* Todavía no he empezado a estudiar para el examen.
◆ **I've revised my opinion.** He cambiado de opinión.

revision [rɪ'vɪʒən] NOUN
◆ **Have you done a lot of revision?** ¿Has estudiado mucho para el examen?

to **revive** [rɪ'vaɪv] VERB
resucitar ◇ *The nurses tried to revive him.* Las enfermeras intentaron resucitarlo.

revolting [rɪ'vəultɪŋ] ADJECTIVE
repugnante

revolution [rɛvə'luːʃən] NOUN
la revolución (PL las revoluciones)

revolutionary [rɛvə'luːʃənrɪ] ADJECTIVE
revolucionario

revolver [rɪ'vɔlvə^r] NOUN
el revólver

reward [rɪ'wɔːd] NOUN
la recompensa

rewarding [rɪ'wɔːdɪŋ] ADJECTIVE
gratificante ◇ *a rewarding job* un trabajo gratificante

to **rewind** [riː'waɪnd] VERB (**rewound, rewound**)
rebobinar ◇ *to rewind a cassette* rebobinar una cinta

rheumatism ['ruːmətɪzəm] NOUN
el reumatismo ◇ *I've got rheumatism.* Tengo reumatismo.

rhinoceros [raɪ'nɔsərəs] NOUN
el rinoceronte

rhubarb ['ruːbɑːb] NOUN
el ruibarbo

rhythm ['rɪðm] NOUN
el ritmo

rib [rɪb] NOUN
la costilla

ribbon ['rɪbən] NOUN
la cinta

rice [raɪs] NOUN
el arroz
◆ **rice pudding** el arroz con leche

rich [rɪtʃ] ADJECTIVE
rico
◆ **the rich** los ricos

to **rid** [rɪd] VERB
◆ **to get rid of** deshacerse* de ◇ *I want to get rid of some old clothes.* Quiero deshacerme de algunas ropas viejas.

ridden ['rɪdn] VERB *see* **ride**

ride [raɪd] NOUN
see also **ride** VERB
◆ **to go for a ride (1)** (*on horse*) montar a caballo
◆ **to go for a ride (2)** (*on bike*) dar* un paseo en bicicleta ◇ *We went for a bike ride.* Fuimos a dar un paseo en bicicleta.
◆ **It's a short bus ride to the town centre.** El centro de la ciudad queda cerca en autobús.

to **ride** [raɪd] VERB (**rode, ridden**)
see also **ride** NOUN
montar a caballo ◇ *I'm learning to ride.* Estoy aprendiendo a montar a caballo.
◆ **to ride a bike** ir* en bicicleta ◇ *Can you ride a bike?* ¿Sabes ir en bicicleta?

rider ['raɪdə^r] NOUN
1 el jinete ◇ *She's a good rider.* Ella monta muy bien a caballo.
2 el/la ciclista (*cyclist*)

ridiculous [rɪ'dɪkjuləs] ADJECTIVE
ridículo

riding ['raɪdɪŋ] NOUN
la equitación (*as sport*) ◇ *a riding school* una escuela de equitación
◆ **to go riding** montar a caballo

rifle ['raɪfl] NOUN
el rifle

rig [rɪg] NOUN
◆ **oil rig** la plataforma petrolífera

right [raɪt] ADJECTIVE, ADVERB
see also **right** NOUN

*There are several ways of translating **right**. Scan the examples to find one that is similar to what you want to say.*

1 correcto ◊ *the right answer* la respuesta correcta
2 adecuado (*place, time*) ◊ *We're on the right train.* Estamos en el tren adecuado. ◊ *It isn't the right size.* Ésta no es la talla adecuada.
♦ **Is this the right road for Ávila?** ¿Vamos bien por aquí para Ávila?
♦ **to be right (1)** (*person*) tener* razón ◊ *You were right!* ¡Tenías razón!
♦ **to be right (2)** (*statement, opinion*) ser* verdad ◊ *That's right!* ¡Es verdad!
♦ **Do you have the right time?** ¿Tienes hora?
3 bien ◊ *It's not right to behave like that.* No está bien comportarse así. ◊ *Am I pronouncing it right?* ¿Lo pronuncio bien?
♦ **I think you did the right thing.** Creo que hiciste bien.
4 derecho (*not left*) ◊ *my right hand* mi mano derecha
5 a la derecha (*turn, look*) ◊ *Turn right at the traffic lights.* Cuando llegues al semáforo dobla a la derecha.
♦ **Right! Let's get started!** ¡Bueno! ¡Empecemos!
♦ **right away** enseguida ◊ *I'll do it right away.* Lo haré enseguida.

right [raɪt] NOUN
see also **right** ADJECTIVE
1 el derecho ◊ *You've got no right to do that.* No tienes derecho de hacer* eso.
2 la derecha
♦ **on the right** a la derecha ◊ *on the right of Mr. Yates* a la derecha del Sr. Yates
♦ **right of way** la prioridad ◊ *We had right of way.* Teníamos prioridad.

right-hand ['raɪthænd] ADJECTIVE
♦ **the right-hand side** la derecha
♦ **It's on the right-hand side.** Está a la derecha.

right-handed [raɪt'hændɪd] ADJECTIVE
diestro

rim [rɪm] NOUN
la montura ◊ *glasses with metal rims* las gafas con montura metálica

ring [rɪŋ] NOUN
see also **ring** VERB
1 el anillo ◊ *a gold ring* un anillo de oro
♦ **a wedding ring** una alianza
2 el círculo ◊ *to stand in a ring* formar un círculo
3 el timbrazo (*at door*)
♦ **After three or four rings the door was opened.** Después de tres o cuatro timbrazos la puerta se abrió.
♦ **There was a ring at the door.** Se oyó el timbre de la puerta.
♦ **to give somebody a ring** llamar a alguien por teléfono
♦ **ring binder** la carpeta de anillas
♦ **ring road** la carretera de circunvalación

to **ring** [rɪŋ] VERB (**rang, rung**)
see also **ring** NOUN
1 llamar ◊ *Your mother rang this morning.* Tu madre llamó esta mañana.
♦ **to ring somebody** llamar a alguien
2 sonar* ◊ *The phone's ringing.* El teléfono está sonando.
♦ **to ring the bell** tocar* el timbre
♦ **to ring back** volver* a llamar ◊ *I'll ring back later.* Volveré a llamar más tarde.
♦ **to ring up** llamar por teléfono

ring binder ['rɪŋbaɪndər] NOUN
la carpeta de anillas (la carpeta de anillos *LatAm*)

ring road ['rɪŋrəud] NOUN
la carretera de circunvalación

rink [rɪŋk] NOUN
1 la pista de hielo (*for ice-skating*)
2 la pista de patinaje (*for roller-skating*)

to **rinse** [rɪns] VERB
enjuagar*

riot ['raɪət] NOUN
see also **riot** VERB
el disturbio

to **riot** ['raɪət] VERB
see also **riot** NOUN
causar disturbios

to **rip** [rɪp] VERB
rasgar* ◊ *I've ripped my jeans.* Me he rasgado los vaqueros. ◊ *My shirt's ripped.* Mi camisa está rasgada.

to **rip off** [rɪp'ɔf] VERB
timar (*informal*) ◊ *The hotel ripped us off.* En el hotel nos timaron.

to **rip up** [rɪp'ʌp] VERB
hacer* pedazos ◊ *He read the note and then ripped it up.* Leyó la nota y la hizo pedazos.

ripe [raɪp] ADJECTIVE
maduro

rip-off ['rɪpɔf] NOUN
♦ **It's a rip-off!** ¡Es un timo! (*informal*)

rise [raɪz] NOUN
see also **rise** VERB
1 la subida (*in prices, temperature*) ◊ *a sudden rise in temperature* una repentina subida de las temperaturas
2 el aumento (*pay rise*)

to **rise** [raɪz] VERB (**rose, risen**)
see also **rise** NOUN
1 subir (*increase*) ◊ *Prices are rising.* Los precios están subiendo.
2 salir* ◊ *The sun rises early in June.* En junio el sol sale temprano.

riser ['raɪzər] NOUN
♦ **to be an early riser** ser* madrugador

risk [rɪsk] NOUN

R

☞

see also **risk** VERB

el riesgo

♦ **to take risks** correr riesgos

♦ **It's at your own risk.** Es a tu propia cuenta y riesgo.

to **risk** [rɪsk] VERB

see also **risk** NOUN

arriesgarse* ◊ *You risk getting a fine.* Te arriesgas a que te multen. ◊ *I wouldn't risk it if I were you.* Yo en tu lugar no me arriesgaría.

risky ['rɪskɪ] ADJECTIVE

arriesgado

rival ['raɪvl] NOUN

see also **rival** ADJECTIVE

el/la rival

rival ['raɪvl] ADJECTIVE

see also **rival** NOUN

1 rival ◊ *a rival gang* una banda rival

2 competidor MASC competidora FEM ◊ *a rival company* una empresa competidora

rivalry ['raɪvlrɪ] NOUN

la rivalidad

river ['rɪvəʳ] NOUN

el río

♦ **the river Tagus** el río Tajo

Riviera [rɪvɪ'ɛərə] NOUN

♦ **the French Riviera** la Costa Azul

♦ **the Italian Riviera** la Riviera

road [rəud] NOUN

1 la carretera ◊ *There's a lot of traffic on the roads.* Hay mucho tráfico en las carreteras. ◊ *a road accident* un accidente de carretera

2 la calle ◊ *They live across the road.* Viven al otro lado de la calle.

road map ['rəudmæp] NOUN

el mapa de carreteras

Although ***mapa*** *ends in* ***-a****, it is actually a masculine noun.*

road rage ['rəudreɪdʒ] NOUN

la conducta agresiva al volante

road sign ['rəudsaɪn] NOUN

la señal de tráfico

roadworks ['rəudwəːks] PL NOUN

las obras ◊ *There are roadworks on the motorway.* Hay obras en la autopista.

roast [rəust] ADJECTIVE

asado ◊ *roast chicken* pollo asado

♦ **roast pork** el asado de cerdo

♦ **roast beef** el rosbif

to **rob** [rɔb] VERB

♦ **to rob somebody** robar a alguien ◊ *I've been robbed.* Me han robado.

♦ **to rob somebody of something** robar algo a alguien ◊ *He was robbed of his wallet.* Le robaron la cartera.

♦ **to rob a bank** asaltar un banco

robber ['rɔbəʳ] NOUN

el ladrón

la ladrona

♦ **a bank-robber** un asaltante de bancos (FEM una asaltante de bancos)

robbery ['rɔbərɪ] NOUN (PL **robberies**)

el robo

♦ **a bank robbery** un asalto a un banco

♦ **an armed robbery** un asalto a mano armada

robin ['rɔbɪn] NOUN

el petirrojo

robot ['rəubɔt] NOUN

el robot (PL los robots)

rock [rɔk] NOUN

see also **rock** VERB

1 la roca ◊ *They tunnelled through the rock.* Abrieron un túnel a través de la roca. ◊ *I sat on a rock.* Me senté encima de una roca.

2 la piedra ◊ *The crowd started to throw rocks.* La multitud empezó a lanzar piedras.

3 el rock ◊ *a rock concert* un concierto de rock

♦ **rock and roll** el rock and roll

♦ **a stick of rock** una barra de caramelo

to **rock** [rɔk] VERB

see also **rock** NOUN

1 mecer ◊ *to rock a baby* (*in one's arms*) acunar a un bebé

2 sacudir ◊ *The explosion rocked the building.* La explosión sacudió el edificio.

rocket ['rɔkɪt] NOUN

el cohete (*spacecraft, firework*)

rocking chair ['rɔkɪŋtʃɛəʳ] NOUN

la mecedora

rocking horse ['rɔkɪŋhɔːs] NOUN

el caballo de balancín

rod [rɔd] NOUN

la caña de pescar (*for fishing*)

rode [rəud] VERB *see* **ride**

role [rəul] NOUN

el papel ◊ *to play a role* hacer* un papel

role play ['rəulpleɪ] NOUN

el juego de roles ◊ *to do a role play* hacer* un juego de roles

roll [rəul] NOUN

see also **roll** VERB

1 el rollo ◊ *a toilet roll* un rollo de papel higiénico

♦ **a roll of film** un carrete de fotos

2 el panecillo ◊ *a cheese roll* un panecillo de queso

♦ **Roll call is at 8.30.** Pasan lista a las ocho y media.

to **roll** [rəul] VERB

see also **roll** NOUN

rodar* (*ball, bottle*)

to **roll out** [rəul'aut] VERB

extender* (*pastry*)

roller ['rəulər] NOUN
el rulo (*for hair*)

Rollerblade ® ['rəuləbleɪd] NOUN
el patín en línea

rollercoaster ['rəuləkəustər] NOUN
la montaña rusa

roller skates ['rəuləskeɪts] PL NOUN
los patines de ruedas

roller-skating ['rəuləskeɪtɪŋ] NOUN
el patinaje sobre ruedas

♦ **to go roller-skating** ir* a patinar (*sobre ruedas*)

rolling pin ['rəulɪŋpɪn] NOUN
el rodillo

Roman ['rəumən] ADJECTIVE, NOUN
romano ◊ *the Roman empire* el imperio romano

♦ **the Romans** los romanos

Roman Catholic [rəumən'kæθəlɪk] NOUN
el católico
la católica
◊ *He's a Roman Catholic.* Es católico.

romance [rə'mæns] NOUN
1 las novelas románticas (*novels*) ◊ *I read a lot of romance.* Leo muchas novelas románticas.
2 el romanticismo ◊ *the romance of Paris* el romanticismo de París

♦ **a holiday romance** un romance de verano

Romania [rəu'meɪnɪə] NOUN
Rumania FEM

Romanian [rəu'meɪnɪən] ADJECTIVE
rumano

romantic [rə'mæntɪk] ADJECTIVE
romántico

roof [ru:f] NOUN
el techo

roof rack ['ru:fræk] NOUN
la baca

room [ru:m] NOUN
1 la habitación (PL las habitaciones) ◊ *She's in her room.* Está en su habitación.

♦ **a single room** una habitación individual

♦ **a double room** una habitación doble
2 (*in school*)
sala ◊ *the music room* la sala de música
3 el espacio ◊ *There's no room for that box.* No hay espacio para esa caja.

roommate ['ru:mmeɪt] NOUN
el compañero de cuarto
la compañera de cuarto

root [ru:t] NOUN
la raíz (PL las raíces)

rope [rəup] NOUN
la cuerda

rose [rəuz] VERB *see* **rise**

rose [rəuz] NOUN
la rosa (*flower*)

to **rot** [rɔt] VERB
pudrirse* ◊ *As far as I'm concerned he can rot in jail.* Por mí, que se pudra en la cárcel.

♦ **The wood had rotted.** La madera se había podrido.

♦ **Sugar rots your teeth.** El azúcar pica los dientes.

rotten ['rɔtn] ADJECTIVE
podrido ◊ *a rotten apple* una manzana podrida

♦ **rotten weather** un tiempo asqueroso

♦ **That's a rotten thing to do!** ¡Eso está fatal!

♦ **to feel rotten** sentirse* fatal

rough [rʌf] ADJECTIVE, ADVERB
1 áspero ◊ *My hands are rough.* Tengo las manos ásperas.
2 violento ◊ *Rugby's a rough sport.* El rugby es un deporte violento.
3 peligroso ◊ *It's a rough area.* Es una zona peligrosa.
4 agitado ◊ *The sea was rough.* El mar estaba agitado.
5 aproximado ◊ *I've got a rough idea.* Tengo una idea aproximada.

♦ **to feel rough** sentirse* mal

♦ **to sleep rough** dormir* en la calle ◊ *A lot of people sleep rough in London.* Mucha gente duerme en la calle en Londres.

roughly ['rʌflɪ] ADVERB
aproximadamente ◊ *It weighs roughly 20 kilos.* Pesa aproximadamente 20 kilos.

round [raund] ADJECTIVE, ADVERB, PREPOSITION
see also **round** NOUN
1 redondo ◊ *a round table* una mesa redonda
2 alrededor de ◊ *We were sitting round the table.* Estábamos sentados alrededor de la mesa. ◊ *She wore a scarf round her neck.* Llevaba una bufanda alrededor del cuello.

♦ **It's just round the corner.** Está a la vuelta de la esquina.

♦ **to go round to somebody's house** ir* a casa de alguien

♦ **to have a look round** echar un vistazo ◊ *We had a look round the record section.* Echamos un vistazo a la sección de discos.

♦ **to go round a museum** visitar un museo

♦ **round here** por aquí cerca ◊ *He lives round here.* Vive aquí cerca. ◊ *Is there a chemist's round here?* ¿Hay alguna farmacia por aquí cerca?

♦ **all round** por todos lados ◊ *There were vineyards all round.* Había viñedos por todos lados.

♦ **all year round** todo el año

♦ **round about** alrededor de ◊ *It costs round about £100.* Cuesta alrededor de 100 libras esterlinas.

♦ **round about eight o'clock** hacia las ocho

round [raund] NOUN
see also **round** ADJECTIVE, ADVERB, PREPOSITION
1 (*of tournament*)
la vuelta
2 (*of boxing match*)
el round (PL los rounds)
♦ **a round of golf** una vuelta de golf
♦ **a round of drinks** una ronda de bebidas ◊ *He bought them a round of drinks.* Les invitó a una ronda de bebidas.
♦ **I think it's my round.** Creo que me toca pagar.

roundabout ['raundəbaut] NOUN
1 la rotonda (*at junction*)
2 el tiovivo (*at funfair*)

rounders ['raundəz] SING NOUN

ℹ *El* ***rounders*** *es un juego similar al béisbol.*

round trip [raund'trɪp] NOUN US
el viaje de ida y vuelta
♦ **a round-trip ticket** un billete de ida y vuelta

route [ruːt] NOUN
el itinerario ◊ *We are planning our route.* Estamos planeando el itinerario.
♦ **bus route** el recorrido del autobús

routine [ruː'tiːn] NOUN
la rutina ◊ *my daily routine* mi rutina diaria

row (1) [rau] NOUN
1 el jaleo ◊ *What's that terrible row?* ¿Qué es ese jaleo tan tremendo?
2 la pelea
♦ **to have a row** pelearse ◊ *They've had a row.* Se han peleado.

row (2) [rəu] NOUN
see also **row** VERB
1 la hilera ◊ *a row of houses* una hilera de casas
2 la fila (*of people, seats*) ◊ *in the front row* en primera fila
♦ **five times in a row** cinco veces seguidas

to **row** [rəu] VERB
see also **row (2)** NOUN
remar

rowboat ['rəubəut] NOUN US
la barca de remos

rowing ['rəuɪŋ] NOUN
el remo ◊ *My hobby is rowing.* My hobby es el remo.
♦ **rowing boat** la barca de remos

royal ['rɔɪəl] ADJECTIVE
real ◊ *the royal family* la familia real

to **rub** [rʌb] VERB
1 frotar (*stain*)
2 restregarse* (*part of body*) ◊ *Don't rub your eyes.* No te restriegues los ojos.

to **rub out** [rʌb'aut] VERB
borrar

rubber ['rʌbəʳ] NOUN
1 la goma ◊ *rubber soles* suelas de goma
2 la goma de borrar (*eraser*) ◊ *Can I borrow your rubber?* ¿Me prestas la goma?
♦ **a rubber band** una goma elástica

rubbish ['rʌbɪʃ] NOUN
see also **rubbish** ADJECTIVE
1 la basura ◊ *When do they collect the rubbish?* ¿Cuándo recogen la basura? ◊ *They sell a lot of rubbish at the market.* Venden mucha basura en el mercado.
♦ **That magazine is rubbish!** ¡Esa revista es una porquería! (*informal*)
2 las estupideces ◊ *Don't talk rubbish!* ¡No digas estupideces!
♦ **That's a load of rubbish!** ¡Son puras tonterías!
♦ **rubbish bin** el cubo de la basura
♦ **rubbish dump** el vertedero

rubbish ['rʌbɪʃ] ADJECTIVE
see also **rubbish** NOUN
♦ **They're a rubbish team!** ¡Es un equipo que no vale nada!

rucksack ['rʌksæk] NOUN
la mochila

rude [ruːd] ADJECTIVE
grosero ◊ *He was very rude to me.* Fue muy grosero conmigo.
♦ **It's rude to interrupt.** Es de mala educación interrumpir.
♦ **a rude joke** un chiste verde
♦ **a rude word** una palabrota

rug [rʌg] NOUN
1 la alfombra (*carpet*)
2 la manta de viaje (*travelling rug*)

rugby ['rʌgbɪ] NOUN
el rugby ◊ *He enjoys playing rugby.* Le gusta jugar* al rugby.

ruin ['ruːɪn] NOUN
see also **ruin** VERB
la ruina ◊ *the ruins of the castle* las ruinas del castillo
♦ **in ruins** en ruinas

to **ruin** ['ruːɪn] VERB
see also **ruin** NOUN
1 estropear ◊ *You'll ruin your shoes.* Te vas a estropear los zapatos. ◊ *It ruined our holiday.* Nos estropeó las vacaciones.
2 arruinar (*financially*)

rule [ruːl] NOUN
see also **rule** VERB
1 la regla ◊ *the rules of grammar* las reglas de la gramática
♦ **as a rule** por regla general
2 la norma ◊ *It's against the rules.* Va en contra de las normas.

to **rule** [ruːl] VERB
see also **rule** NOUN

* Verbs marked with this symbol are irregular. See pages 380-382 for further details

gobernar*

to **rule out** [ruːl'aut] VERB
descartar (*possibility*)

ruler ['ruːləʳ] NOUN
la regla

rum [rʌm] NOUN
el ron

rumour ['ruːməʳ] NOUN (US **rumor**)
el rumor ◊ *It's just a rumour.* Es sólo un rumor.

run [rʌn] NOUN
see also **run** VERB
♦**to go for a run** salir* a correr ◊ *I go for a run every morning.* Salgo a correr todas las mañanas.
♦**I did a 10-kilometre run.** Corrí 10 kilómetros.
♦**The criminals are still on the run.** Los delincuentes están todavía en fuga.
♦**in the long run** a la larga

to **run** [rʌn] VERB **(ran, run)**
see also **run** NOUN
1 correr ◊ *I ran five kilometres.* Corrí cinco kilómetros. ◊ *to run a marathon* correr un maratón
2 dirigir* ◊ *He runs a large company.* Dirige una gran empresa.
3 organizar* ◊ *They run music courses in the holidays.* Organizan cursos de música en las vacaciones.
4 llevar (*by car*) ◊ *I can run you to the station.* Te puedo llevar a la estación.
♦**Don't leave the tap running.** No dejen el grifo abierto. (No dejen la llave abierta. LatAm)
♦**to run a bath** llenar la bañera
♦**The buses stop running at midnight.** Los autobuses dejan de funcionar a medianoche.

to **run away** [rʌnə'weɪ] VERB
huir* ◊ *They ran away before the police came.* Huyeron antes de que llegara la policía.

to **run out** [rʌn'aut] VERB
♦**to run out of something** quedarse sin algo
♦**Time is running out.** Queda poco tiempo.
♦**We ran out of money.** Nos quedamos sin dinero.

to **run over** [rʌn'əuvəʳ] VERB
atropellar
♦**to get run over** ser* atropellado

rung [rʌŋ] VERB *see* **ring**

runner ['rʌnəʳ] NOUN
el corredor
la corredora

runner beans ['rʌnəbiːnz] PL NOUN
las judías verdes (las habichuelas verdes LatAm)

runner-up [rʌnər'ʌp] NOUN (PL **runners-up**)
el subcampeón (PL los subcampeones)
la subcampeona

running ['rʌnɪŋ] NOUN
el footing ◊ *Running is my favourite sport.* El footing es mi deporte favorito. ◊ *to go running* hacer* footing

runway ['rʌnweɪ] NOUN
la pista de aterrizaje

rural ['ruərl] ADJECTIVE
rural

rush [rʌʃ] NOUN
see also **rush** VERB
la prisa ◊ *I'm in a rush.* Tengo prisa. ◊ *There's no rush.* No corre prisa.
♦**to do something in a rush** hacer* algo deprisa

to **rush** [rʌʃ] VERB
see also **rush** NOUN
1 correr ◊ *Everyone rushed outside.* Todos corrieron hacia fuera.
2 precipitarse ◊ *There's no need to rush.* No hay por qué precipitarse.

rush hour ['rʌʃauəʳ] NOUN
la hora punta (la hora pico LatAm)

rusk [rʌsk] NOUN
la galleta para bebés

Russia ['rʌʃə] NOUN
la Rusia

Russian ['rʌʃən] ADJECTIVE
see also **Russian** NOUN
ruso

Russian ['rʌʃən] NOUN
see also **Russian** ADJECTIVE
1 (*person*)
el ruso
la rusa
◊ *the Russians* los rusos
2 (*language*)
el ruso

rust [rʌst] NOUN
el óxido

rusty ['rʌstɪ] ADJECTIVE
oxidado

ruthless ['ruːθlɪs] ADJECTIVE
despiadado

rye [raɪ] NOUN
el centeno
♦**rye bread** el pan de centeno

S

sack [sæk] NOUN
see also **sack** VERB
el saco ◊ *a sack of potatoes* un saco de patatas
♦ **to give somebody the sack** despedir* a alguien
♦ **He got the sack.** Lo despidieron.

to **sack** [sæk] VERB
see also **sack** NOUN
♦ **to sack somebody** despedir* a alguien ◊ *He was sacked.* Lo despidieron.

sacred ['seɪkrɪd] ADJECTIVE
sagrado ◊ *sacred places* lugares sagrados
♦ **sacred music** música sacra

sacrifice ['sækrɪfaɪs] NOUN
el sacrificio

sad [sæd] ADJECTIVE
triste

saddle ['sædl] NOUN
1 la silla de montar (*for horse*)
2 el sillín (*on bike*)

saddlebag ['sædlbæg] NOUN
1 la cartera (*on bike*)
2 la alforja (*for horse*)

sadly ['sædlɪ] ADVERB
1 con tristeza ◊ *"She's gone", he said sadly.* "Se ha ido" dijo con tristeza.
2 desgraciadamente ◊ *Sadly, it was too late.* Desgraciadamente, era ya demasiado tarde.

safe [seɪf] NOUN
see also **safe** ADJECTIVE
la caja fuerte (PL las cajas fuertes)

safe [seɪf] ADJECTIVE
see also **safe** NOUN
1 seguro ◊ *This car isn't safe.* Este coche no es seguro.
2 a salvo ◊ *You're safe now.* Ya estás a salvo.
♦ **to feel safe** sentirse* protegido
♦ **Is the water safe to drink?** ¿Es agua potable?
♦ **Don't worry, it's perfectly safe.** No te preocupes, no tiene el menor peligro.
♦ **safe sex** el sexo sin riesgo

safety ['seɪftɪ] NOUN
la seguridad
♦ **safety belt** el cinturón de seguridad
♦ **safety pin** el imperdible (el seguro *LatAm*)

Sagittarius [sædʒɪ'teərɪəs] NOUN
el Sagitario (*sign*) ◊ *I'm Sagittarius.* Soy Sagitario.
♦ **a Sagittarius** un/una Sagitario

Sahara [sə'hɑːrə] NOUN
♦ **the Sahara Desert** el Sáhara

said [sɛd] VERB *see* **say**

sail [seɪl] NOUN
see also **sail** VERB
la vela
♦ **to set sail** zarpar

to **sail** [seɪl] VERB
see also **sail** NOUN
1 navegar* ◊ *to sail around the world* dar* la vuelta al mundo navegando
2 zarpar ◊ *The boat sails at eight o'clock.* El barco zarpa a las ocho.

sailing ['seɪlɪŋ] NOUN
la vela (*sport*)
♦ **to go sailing** hacer* vela
♦ **sailing boat** el barco de vela
♦ **sailing ship** el velero

sailor ['seɪlə^r] NOUN
el marinero ◊ *He's a sailor.* Es marinero.

saint [seɪnt] NOUN
el santo
la santa

*When used before a man's name, the word **Santo** is shortened to **San**, the exceptions being **Santo Tomás** and **Santo Domingo**.*

◊ *Saint John* San Juan

sake [seɪk] NOUN
♦ **for the sake of argument** pongamos por caso
♦ **for the sake of the children** por el bien de los niños
♦ **For goodness sake!** ¡Por el amor de Dios!

salad ['sæləd] NOUN
la ensalada
♦ **salad cream** la mayonesa
♦ **salad dressing** el aliño para la ensalada

salami [sə'lɑːmɪ] NOUN
el salami

salary ['sælərɪ] NOUN (PL **salaries**)
el sueldo

sale [seɪl] NOUN
1 las rebajas ◊ *There's a sale on at Harrods.* En Harrods están de rebajas. ◊ *the January sales* las rebajas de enero
2 la venta ◊ *Newspaper sales have fallen.* Ha descendido la venta de periódicos.
♦ **on sale** a la venta
♦ **The house is for sale.** La casa está en venta.
♦ **"for sale"** "se vende"

sales assistant ['seɪlzəsɪstənt] NOUN
el dependiente
la dependienta

salesman ['seɪlzmən] NOUN (PL **salesmen**)
1 el representante (*commercial*) ◊ *an insurance salesman* un representante de seguros
2 el dependiente (*sales assistant*)
♦ **a car salesman** un vendedor de coches

sales rep ['seɪlzrɛp] NOUN
el/la representante

saleswoman ['seɪlzwumən] NOUN (PL **saleswomen**)
1 la representante (*commercial*) ◊ *an insurance saleswoman* una representante de seguros
2 la dependienta (*sales assistant*)

salmon ['sæmən] NOUN
el salmón (PL los salmones)

salon ['sælɔn] NOUN
el salón (PL los salones) ◊ *hair salon* salón de peluquería ◊ *beauty salon* salón de belleza

saloon car [sə'lu:nkɑ:ʳ] NOUN
el turismo

salt [sɔ:lt] NOUN
la sal

salty ['sɔ:ltɪ] ADJECTIVE
salado

to **salute** [sə'lu:t] VERB
saludar

Salvation Army [sælveɪʃən'ɑ:mɪ] NOUN
el Ejército de Salvación

same [seɪm] ADJECTIVE
mismo ◊ *the same model* el mismo modelo
♦ **It's not the same.** No es lo mismo.
♦ **They're exactly the same.** Son exactamente iguales.
♦ **The house is still the same.** La casa sigue igual.

sample ['sɑ:mpl] NOUN
la muestra ◊ *a free sample of perfume* una muestra gratuita de perfume

sand [sænd] NOUN
la arena

sandal ['sændl] NOUN
la sandalia ◊ *a pair of sandals* unas sandalias

sand castle ['sændkɑ:sl] NOUN
el castillo de arena

sandwich ['sændwɪtʃ] NOUN (PL **sandwiches**)
1 (*with sliced bread*)
el sandwich (PL los sandwiches)
2 (*with French bread*)
el bocadillo

sandwich course ['sændwɪtʃkɔ:s] NOUN

> *Curso que alterna periodos de estudio teórico con periodos de formación práctica en empresas o fábricas.*

sane [seɪn] ADJECTIVE
cuerdo ◊ *She was as sane as you or me.* Está tan cuerda como tú o como yo.

> *Be careful not to translate **sane** by **sano**.*

sang [sæŋ] VERB *see* **sing**

sanitary napkin [sænɪtərɪ'næpkɪn] NOUN
US
la compresa

sanitary towel ['sænɪtərɪtauəl] NOUN
la compresa

sank [sæŋk] VERB *see* **sink**

Santa Claus [sæntə'klɔ:z] NOUN
Papá Noel MASC

sarcastic [sɑ:'kæstɪk] ADJECTIVE
sarcástico

sardine [sɑ:'di:n] NOUN
la sardina

sat [sæt] VERB *see* **sit**

satchel ['sætʃl] NOUN
la cartera

satellite ['sætəlaɪt] NOUN
el satélite ◊ *by satellite* vía satélite
♦ **a satellite dish** una antena parabólica
♦ **satellite television** la televisión vía satélite

satisfactory [sætɪs'fæktərɪ] ADJECTIVE
satisfactorio

satisfied ['sætɪsfaɪd] ADJECTIVE
satisfecho

Saturday ['sætədɪ] NOUN
el sábado (PL los sábados) ◊ *I saw her on Saturday.* La vi el sábado. ◊ *every Saturday* todos los sábados ◊ *last Saturday* el sábado pasado ◊ *next Saturday* el sábado que viene ◊ *on Saturdays* los sábados
♦ **I've got a Saturday job.** Tengo un trabajo los sábados.

sauce [sɔ:s] NOUN
1 la salsa ◊ *tomato sauce* salsa de tomate
2 la crema ◊ *chocolate sauce* crema de chocolate

saucepan ['sɔ:spən] NOUN
el cazo

saucer ['sɔ:səʳ] NOUN
el platillo

Saudi Arabia [saudɪə'reɪbɪə] NOUN
Arabia Saudí FEM

sauna ['sɔ:nə] NOUN
la sauna

sausage ['sɔsɪdʒ] NOUN
la salchicha
♦ **a sausage roll** un pastelito de salchicha

to **save** [seɪv] VERB
1 ahorrar ◊ *I saved money by staying in youth hostels.* Ahorré dinero yendo a albergues juveniles. ◊ *I've saved £50 already.* Ya llevo ahorradas 50 libras. ◊ *It saved us time.* Nos ahorró tiempo.
♦ **We went in a taxi to save time.** Para ganar tiempo fuimos en taxi.

☞

[2] salvar ◊ *Doctors saved her from cancer.* Los médicos la salvaron del cáncer.
♦ **Luckily, all the passengers were saved.** Afortunadamente, todos los pasajeros se salvaron.
[3] guardar ◊ *I saved the file onto a diskette.* Guardé el archivo en un disquete.

to **save up** [seɪv'ʌp] VERB
ahorrar ◊ *I'm saving up for a new bike.* Estoy ahorrando para una bici nueva.

savings ['seɪvɪŋz] PL NOUN
los ahorros ◊ *She spent all her savings on a computer.* Se gastó todos sus ahorros en un ordenador.

savoury ['seɪvərɪ] ADJECTIVE
salado ◊ *Is it sweet or savoury?* ¿Es dulce o salado?

saw [sɔː] VERB *see* **see**

saw [sɔː] NOUN
la sierra

sax [sæks] NOUN (PL **saxes**)
el saxo

saxophone ['sæksəfəun] NOUN
el saxofón (PL los saxofones)

to **say** [seɪ] VERB **(said, said)**
decir* ◊ *to say yes* decir que sí ◊ *What did he say?* ¿Qué dijo él?
♦ **Could you say that again?** ¿Podrías repetir eso?
♦ **The clock said four minutes past eleven.** El reloj marcaba las once y cuatro minutos.
♦ **It goes without saying that...** Ni que decir tiene que...

saying ['seɪɪŋ] NOUN
el dicho

scale [skeɪl] NOUN
la escala ◊ *a large-scale map* un mapa a gran escala
♦ **He underestimated the scale of the problem.** Ha subestimado la envergadura del problema.

scales [skeɪlz] PL NOUN
[1] el peso (*in kitchen*)
[2] la báscula (*in shop*)
♦ **bathroom scales** la báscula de baño

scampi ['skæmpɪ] PL NOUN
las gambas rebozadas

scandal ['skændl] NOUN
[1] el escándalo (*outrage*) ◊ *It caused a scandal.* Causó escándalo.
[2] las habladurías (*gossip*) ◊ *It's just scandal.* No son más que habladurías.

scar [skɑː] NOUN
la cicatriz (PL las cicatrices)

scarce [skɛəs] ADJECTIVE
escaso ◊ *scarce resources* recursos escasos
♦ **Jobs are scarce.** Escasean los trabajos.

scarcely ['skɛəslɪ] ADVERB
apenas ◊ *I scarcely knew him.* Apenas lo conocía.

scare [skɛə[r]] NOUN
see also **scare** VERB
el susto ◊ *We got a bit of a scare.* Nos pegamos un susto.
♦ **a bomb scare** una amenaza de bomba

to **scare** [skɛə[r]] VERB
see also **scare** NOUN
asustar ◊ *You scared me!* ¡Me has asustado!

scarecrow ['skɛəkrəu] NOUN
el espantapájaros (PL los espantapájaros)

scared ['skɛəd] ADJECTIVE
♦ **to be scared** tener* miedo ◊ *Are you scared of him?* ¿Le tienes miedo?
♦ **I was scared stiff.** Estaba muerto de miedo.

scarf [skɑːf] NOUN (PL **scarfs** *or* **scarves**)
[1] la bufanda (*woollen*)
[2] el pañuelo (*light*)

scary ['skɛərɪ] ADJECTIVE
♦ **It was really scary.** Daba verdadero miedo.
♦ **a scary film** una película de miedo

scene [siːn] NOUN
[1] la escena ◊ *love scenes* las escenas de amor ◊ *It was an amazing scene.* Era una escena asombrosa.
[2] el lugar ◊ *at the scene of the crime* en el lugar del crimen ◊ *The police were soon on the scene.* La policía no tardó en acudir al lugar de los hechos.
♦ **to make a scene** montar el número

scenery ['siːnərɪ] NOUN
el paisaje

scent [sɛnt] NOUN
el perfume

schedule ['ʃɛdjuːl] NOUN
el programa

*Although **programa** ends in **-a**, it is actually a masculine noun.*

◊ *a production schedule* un programa de producción
♦ **There's a tight schedule for this project.** Este proyecto tiene un calendario muy justo.
♦ **a busy schedule** una agenda muy apretada
♦ **on schedule** sin retraso
♦ **to be behind schedule** ir* con retraso

scheduled flight ['ʃɛdjuːld'flaɪt] NOUN
el vuelo regular

scheme [skiːm] NOUN
el plan ◊ *a road-widening scheme* un plan de ensanchamiento de calzadas ◊ *a crazy scheme he dreamed up* un plan descabellado que se le ocurrió

* Verbs marked with this symbol are irregular. See pages 380-382 for further details

scholarship ['skɔləʃɪp] NOUN
la beca
school [sku:l] NOUN
1 el colegio (*for children*) ◊ *at school* en el colegio ◊ *to go to school* ir* al colegio
♦ **after school** después de clase
2 la facultad (*at university*) ◊ *art school* la facultad de bellas artes
schoolbook ['sku:lbuk] NOUN
el libro de texto
schoolboy ['sku:lbɔɪ] NOUN
el colegial
schoolchildren ['sku:ltʃɪldrən] PL NOUN
los colegiales
schoolgirl ['sku:lgə:l] NOUN
la colegiala
science ['saɪəns] NOUN
la ciencia
science fiction ['saɪəns'fɪkʃən] NOUN
la ciencia ficción
scientific [saɪən'tɪfɪk] ADJECTIVE
científico
scientist ['saɪəntɪst] NOUN
el científico
la científica
scissors ['sɪzəz] PL NOUN
las tijeras ◊ *a pair of scissors* unas tijeras
to **scoff** [skɔf] VERB
1 mofarse ◊ *My friends scoffed at the idea.* Mis amigos se mofaron de la idea.
2 zamparse (*informal*) ◊ *My brother scoffed all the sandwiches.* Mi hermano se zampó todos los sandwiches.
scone [sɪɔn] NOUN

> *Un **scone** es un bollo de masa dura que suele tomarse con mantequilla o nata y mermelada.*

scooter ['sku:tə^r] NOUN
1 la Vespa ® (*motorcycle*)
2 el patinete (*child's toy*)
score [skɔ:^r] NOUN
see also **score** VERB
1 la puntuación (PL las puntuaciones) ◊ *the highest score by an English batsman* la puntuación más alta de un bateador inglés
2 el resultado ◊ *The score was three nil.* El resultado fue de tres a cero.
♦ **What's the score?** ¿Cómo van?
to **score** [skɔ:^r] VERB
see also **score** NOUN
1 marcar* ◊ *to score a goal* marcar un gol
♦ **to score a point** anotar un punto
♦ **to score six out of ten** sacar* una puntuación de seis sobre diez
2 llevar el tanteo ◊ *Who's going to score?* ¿Quién va a llevar el tanteo?

Scorpio ['skɔ:pɪəu] NOUN
el Escorpión (*sign*) ◊ *I'm Scorpio.* Soy Escorpión.
♦ **a Scorpio** un/una Escorpión
Scot [skɔt] NOUN
(*person*)
el escocés
la escocesa
Scotch tape ® [skɔtʃ'teɪp] NOUN US
el celo
Scotland ['skɔtlənd] NOUN
Escocia FEM
Scots [skɔts] ADJECTIVE
escocés MASC
escocesa FEM
◊ *a Scots accent* un acento escocés
Scotsman ['skɔtsmən] NOUN (PL **Scotsmen**)
el escocés (PL los escoceses)
Scotswoman ['skɔtswumən] NOUN (PL **Scotswomen**)
la escocesa
Scottish ['skɔtɪʃ] ADJECTIVE
escocés MASC (PL escoceses)
escocesa FEM
◊ *a Scottish accent* un acento escocés
scout [skaut] NOUN
el boy scout
la girl scout
scrambled eggs [skræmbld'ɛgz] PL NOUN
los huevos revueltos
scrap [skræp] NOUN
see also **scrap** VERB
1 el trocito ◊ *a scrap of paper* un trocito de papel
2 la pelea ◊ *There was a scrap outside the pub.* Hubo una pelea a la salida del pub.
♦ **scrap iron** la chatarra
to **scrap** [skræp] VERB
see also **scrap** NOUN
desechar ◊ *In the end the plan was scrapped.* Al final se desechó el plan.
scrapbook ['skræpbuk] NOUN
el álbum de recortes (PL los álbumes de recortes)
to **scratch** [skrætʃ] VERB
see also **scratch** NOUN
1 rascarse* (*when itchy*) ◊ *Stop scratching!* ¡Deja de rascarte!
2 arañar (*cut*) ◊ *He scratched his arm on the bushes.* Se arañó el brazo con las zarzas.
3 rayar (*scrape*) ◊ *You'll scratch the worktop with that knife.* Vas a rayar la encimera con ese cuchillo.
scratch [skrætʃ] NOUN (PL **scratches**)
see also **scratch** VERB
el arañazo (*on skin, floor*)
♦ **to start from scratch** partir de cero
♦ **a scratch card** una tarjeta de "rasque y gane"
scream [skri:m] NOUN

S

see also **scream** VERB
el grito
to **scream** [skri:m] VERB
see also **scream** NOUN
gritar
screen [skri:n] NOUN
la pantalla (*television, cinema, computer*)
screensaver ['skri:nseɪvəʳ] NOUN
el salvapantallas
screw [skru:] NOUN
el tornillo
screwdriver ['skru:draɪvəʳ] NOUN
el destornillador
to **scribble** ['skrɪbl] VERB
garabatear
to **scrub** [skrʌb] VERB
fregar*
sculpture ['skʌlptʃəʳ] NOUN
la escultura
sea [si:] NOUN
el mar

*The word **mar** is masculine in most cases, but in some set expressions it is feminine.*

◊ *by sea* por mar ◊ *a house by the sea* una casa junto al mar
♦ **The fishermen put to sea.** Los pescadores se hicieron a la mar.
seafood ['si:fu:d] NOUN
el marisco ◊ *I don't like seafood.* No me gusta el marisco.
♦ **a seafood restaurant** una marisquería
seagull ['si:gʌl] NOUN
la gaviota
seal [si:l] NOUN
see also **seal** VERB
1 la foca (*animal*)
2 el sello (*on letter*)
to **seal** [si:l] VERB
see also **seal** NOUN
sellar
seaman ['si:mən] NOUN (PL **seamen**)
el marinero
to **search** [sə:tʃ] VERB
see also **search** NOUN
1 buscar* ◊ *They're searching for the missing climbers.* Están buscando a los alpinistas desaparecidos.
2 registrar ◊ *The police searched him for drugs.* La policía lo registró en busca de drogas.
♦ **They searched the woods for the little girl.** Rastrearon el bosque en busca de la niña.
search [sə:tʃ] NOUN (PL **searches**)
see also **search** VERB
1 la búsqueda ◊ *The search was abandoned.* Se abandonó la búsqueda.
♦ **to go in search of** ir* en busca de
2 el registro ◊ *a search of the building* un registro del edificio
search engine ['sə:tʃɛndʒɪn] NOUN
el buscador
search party ['sə:tʃpɑ:tɪ] NOUN (PL **search parties**)
el equipo de búsqueda
seashore ['si:ʃɔ:ʳ] NOUN
la orilla del mar ◊ *on the seashore* a la orilla del mar
seasick ['si:sɪk] ADJECTIVE
♦ **to be seasick** marearse en barco
seaside ['si:saɪd] NOUN
la playa
♦ **a seaside resort** un lugar de veraneo en la playa
season ['si:zn] NOUN
la estación (PL las estaciones) ◊ *What's your favourite season?* ¿Cuál es tu estación preferida?
♦ **out of season** fuera de temporada
♦ **during the holiday season** en la temporada de vacaciones
♦ **a season ticket** un abono
seat [si:t] NOUN
1 el asiento ◊ *I was sitting in the back seat.* Yo iba sentada en el asiento trasero.
♦ **Are there any seats left?** ¿Quedan localidades?
2 el escaño ◊ *to win a seat at the election* conseguir* un escaño en las elecciones
seat belt ['si:tbɛlt] NOUN
el cinturón de seguridad (PL los cinturones de seguridad)
seaweed ['si:wi:d] NOUN
el alga marina FEM

*Although it's a feminine noun, remember that you use **el** and **un** with **alga**.*

second ['sɛkənd] ADJECTIVE, ADVERB
see also **second** NOUN
segundo ◊ *the second time* la segunda vez
♦ **to come second** llegar* en segundo lugar
♦ **to travel second class** viajar en segunda
♦ **the second of March** el dos de marzo
second ['sɛkənd] NOUN
see also **second** ADJECTIVE, ADVERB
el segundo ◊ *It'll only take a second.* Es un segundo nada más.
secondary school ['sɛkəndərɪsku:l] NOUN
1 el instituto (*state*)
2 el colegio (*private*)
second-class ['sɛkənd'klɑ:s] ADJECTIVE, ADVERB
de segunda clase (*ticket, compartment*)
♦ **to travel second-class** viajar en segunda

♦ **second-class postage** un sello para correo normal

> ℹ *En Gran Bretaña se pueden usar sellos de primera y segunda clase para el correo, dependiendo de la urgencia con la que se desee enviar la carta.*

secondhand ['sɛkənd'hænd] ADJECTIVE
de segunda mano

secondly ['sɛkəndlɪ] ADVERB
en segundo lugar

secret ['si:krɪt] ADJECTIVE
see also NOUN
secreto ◇ *a secret mission* una misión secreta

secret ['si:krɪt] NOUN
see also ADJECTIVE
el secreto ◇ *Can you keep a secret?* ¿Me guardas un secreto?
♦ **in secret** en secreto

secretary ['sɛkrətərɪ] NOUN (PL **secretaries**)
el secretario
la secretaria

secretly ['si:krɪtlɪ] ADVERB
en secreto

section ['sɛkʃən] NOUN
la sección (PL las secciones)

security [sɪ'kjuərɪtɪ] NOUN
la seguridad ◇ *They are trying to improve airport security.* Intentan mejorar las medidas de seguridad en el aeropuerto. ◇ *They have no job security.* No tienen seguridad en el empleo.
♦ **security guard** el/la guarda jurado

sedan [sə'dæn] NOUN US
el turismo

to **see** [si:] VERB (**saw, seen**)
ver* ◇ *I can't see.* No veo nada. ◇ *I saw him yesterday.* Lo vi ayer.
♦ **You need to see a doctor.** Tienes que ir a ver a un médico.
♦ **See you!** ¡Hasta luego!
♦ **See you soon!** ¡Hasta pronto!

to **see to** ['si:tu:] VERB
encargarse* de ◇ *The shower isn't working. Can you see to it please?* La ducha se ha estropeado. ¿Podrías encargarte de eso?

seed [si:d] NOUN
la semilla ◇ *poppy seeds* semillas de amapola
♦ **sunflower seeds** pipas de girasol

to **seem** [si:m] VERB
parecer* ◇ *She seems tired.* Parece cansada. ◇ *That seems like a good idea.* Me parece una buena idea.
♦ **The shop seemed to be closed.** Parecía que la tienda estaba cerrada.
♦ **It seems that...** Parece que... ◇ *It seems you have no alternative.* Parece que no tienes otra opción.
♦ **It seems she's getting married.** Por lo visto se casa.
♦ **There seems to be a problem.** Parece que hay un problema.

seen [si:n] VERB *see* **see**

seesaw ['si:sɔ:] NOUN
el balancín (PL los balancines)

see-through ['si:θru:] ADJECTIVE
transparente

seldom ['sɛldəm] ADVERB
rara vez

to **select** [sɪ'lɛkt] VERB
seleccionar

selection [sɪ'lɛkʃən] NOUN
1 la selección (PL las selecciones) ◇ *a selection test* una prueba de selección
2 el surtido ◇ *the widest selection on the market* el más amplio surtido del mercado

self-assured [sɛlfə'ʃuəd] ADJECTIVE
seguro de sí mismo MASC
segura de sí misma FEM

self-catering [sɛlf'keɪtərɪŋ] ADJECTIVE
♦ **self-catering apartment** el apartamento

self-centred [sɛlf'sɛntəd] ADJECTIVE (US **self-centered**)
egocéntrico

self-confidence [sɛlf'kɔnfɪdns] NOUN
la confianza en uno mismo ◇ *I lost all my self-confidence.* Perdí toda la confianza en mí mismo.

self-conscious [sɛlf'kɔnʃəs] ADJECTIVE
1 cohibido ◇ *She was really self-conscious at first.* Al principio estaba muy cohibida.
2 acomplejado ◇ *She was self-conscious about her height.* Estaba acomplejada por su estatura.

self-contained [sɛlfkən'teɪnd] ADJECTIVE
independiente

self-control [sɛlfkən'trəul] NOUN
el autocontrol

self-defence [sɛlfdɪ'fɛns] NOUN (US **self-defense**)
la defensa personal ◇ *self-defence classes* clases de defensa personal
♦ **She killed him in self-defence.** Lo mató en defensa propia.

self-discipline [sɛlf'dɪsɪplɪn] NOUN
la autodisciplina

self-employed [sɛlfɪm'plɔɪd] ADJECTIVE
autónomo
♦ **to be self-employed** ser* autónomo
♦ **the self-employed** los trabajadores autónomos

selfish ['sɛlfɪʃ] ADJECTIVE
egoísta

self-respect [sɛlfrɪs'pɛkt] NOUN
el amor propio

self-service [sɛlf'sə:vɪs] ADJECTIVE
de autoservicio

to **sell** [sɛl] VERB **(sold, sold)**
vender ◊ *He sold it to me.* Me lo vendió.

to **sell off** [sɛl'ɔf] VERB
liquidar

to **sell out** [sɛl'aut] VERB
♦ **The tickets sold out in three hours.** Las entradas se agotaron en tres horas.

sell-by date ['sɛlbaɪdeɪt] NOUN
la fecha de caducidad

selling price ['sɛlɪŋpraɪs] NOUN
el precio de venta

Sellotape ® ['sɛləuteɪp] NOUN
el celo

semi ['sɛmɪ] NOUN
la casa adosada

semicircle ['sɛmɪsəːkl] NOUN
el semicírculo

semicolon [sɛmɪ'kəulən] NOUN
el punto y coma (PL los punto y coma)

semi-detached house [sɛmɪdɪtætʃt'haus] NOUN
la casa adosada ◊ *We live in a semi-detached house.* Vivimos en una casa adosada.
♦ **a street of semi-detached houses** una calle de casas pareadas

semi-final [sɛmɪ'faɪnl] NOUN
la semifinal

semi-skimmed milk [sɛmɪskɪmd'mɪlk] NOUN
la leche semidesnatada

to **send** [sɛnd] VERB **(sent, sent)**
mandar ◊ *She sent me a birthday card.* Me mandó una tarjeta de cumpleaños. ◊ *He was sent to London.* Lo mandaron a Londres.

to **send back** [sɛnd'bæk] VERB
devolver*

to **send off** [sɛnd'ɔf] VERB
1 enviar* por correo ◊ *We sent off your order yesterday.* Le enviamos el pedido por correo ayer.
2 expulsar ◊ *He was sent off.* Lo expulsaron.

to **send off for** [sɛnd'ɔffɔːʳ] VERB
1 escribir* pidiendo (*free*) ◊ *I've sent off for a brochure.* He escrito pidiendo un folleto.
2 pedir* por correo (*paid for*) ◊ *She sent off for the book.* Pidió el libro por correo.

to **send out** [sɛnd'aut] VERB
enviar*

to **send out for** [sɛnd'autfɔːʳ] VERB
pedir* por teléfono ◊ *Let's send out for a pizza.* Vamos a pedir una pizza por teléfono.

sender ['sɛndəʳ] NOUN
el/la remitente

senior ['siːnɪəʳ] ADJECTIVE, NOUN
alto ◊ *senior officials in the British government* altos cargos del gobierno británico ◊ *senior management* los altos directivos
♦ **She's five years my senior.** Es cinco años mayor que yo.
♦ **senior school** el instituto de enseñanza secundaria
♦ **senior pupils** los alumnos más mayores

senior citizen [siːnɪəʳ'sɪtɪzn] NOUN
la persona de la tercera edad

sensational [sɛn'seɪʃənl] ADJECTIVE
sensacional

sense [sɛns] NOUN
el sentido ◊ *the five senses* los cinco sentidos ◊ *Use your common sense!* ¡Usa el sentido común!
♦ **It makes sense.** Tiene sentido.
♦ **It doesn't make sense.** No tiene sentido.
♦ **a keen sense of smell** un olfato finísimo
♦ **sense of humour** sentido del humor

senseless ['sɛnslɪs] ADJECTIVE
1 sin sentido ◊ *senseless violence* violencia sin sentido ◊ *It is senseless to protest.* No tiene sentido protestar.
2 inconsciente ◊ *He was lying senseless on the floor.* Yacía inconsciente en el suelo.

sensible ['sɛnsɪbl] ADJECTIVE
sensato ◊ *Be sensible!* ¡Sé sensato! ◊ *It would be sensible to check first.* Lo más sensato sería comprobarlo antes.

*Be careful not to translate **sensible** by the Spanish word **sensible**.*

sensitive ['sɛnsɪtɪv] ADJECTIVE
sensible

sensuous ['sɛnsjuəs] ADJECTIVE
sensual

sent [sɛnt] VERB *see* **send**

sentence ['sɛntns] NOUN
see also **sentence** VERB
1 la oración (PL las oraciones) ◊ *What does this sentence mean?* ¿Qué significa esta oración?
2 la sentencia ◊ *to pass sentence* dictar sentencia
3 la condena ◊ *a sentence of 10 years* una condena de 10 años
♦ **the death sentence** la pena de muerte
♦ **He got a life sentence.** Fue condenado a cadena perpetua.

to **sentence** ['sɛntns] VERB
see also **sentence** NOUN
♦ **to sentence somebody to life imprisonment** condenar a alguien a cadena perpetua
♦ **to sentence somebody to death** condenar a muerte a alguien

sentimental [sɛntɪ'mɛntl] ADJECTIVE
sentimental

separate ['sɛprɪt] ADJECTIVE

* Verbs marked with this symbol are irregular. See pages 380-382 for further details

see also **separate** VERB
distinto ◊ *Men and women have separate exercise rooms.* Los hombres y las mujeres tienen salas de ejercicios distintas.
♦ **The children have separate rooms.** Los niños tienen cada uno su habitación.
♦ **I wrote it on a separate sheet.** Lo escribí en una hoja aparte.
♦ **on separate occasions** en diversas ocasiones

to **separate** ['sɛpəreɪt] VERB
see also **separate** ADJECTIVE
1 separar ◊ *Police moved in to separate the two groups.* La policía intervino para separar a los dos grupos.
2 separarse ◊ *Her parents separated last year.* Sus padres se separaron el año pasado.

separately ['sɛprɪtlɪ] ADVERB
por separado

separation [sɛpə'reɪʃən] NOUN
la separación (PL las separaciones)

September [sɛp'tɛmbəʳ] NOUN
septiembre MASC ◊ *in September* en septiembre ◊ *on 23 September* el 23 de septiembre

sequel ['si:kwl] NOUN
la continuación (PL las continuaciones)

sequence ['si:kwəns] NOUN
1 la serie ◊ *a sequence of events* una serie de acontecimientos
2 el orden (PL los órdenes) ◊ *in sequence* en orden
3 la secuencia ◊ *the best sequence in the film* la mejor secuencia de la película

sergeant ['sɑ:dʒənt] NOUN
1 el/la sargento (*army*)
2 el/la oficial de policía (*police*)

serial ['sɪərɪəl] NOUN
1 el serial (*on TV, radio*)
2 la novela por entregas (*in magazine*)

series ['sɪərɪz] NOUN
la serie

serious ['sɪərɪəs] ADJECTIVE
1 serio ◊ *You're looking very serious.* Estás muy serio.
♦ **Are you serious?** ¿Lo dices en serio?
2 grave ◊ *a serious illness* una grave enfermedad

seriously ['sɪərɪəslɪ] ADVERB
en serio ◊ *No, but seriously...* No, pero ya en serio... ◊ *to take somebody seriously* tomar en serio a alguien
♦ **seriously injured** gravemente herido
♦ **Seriously?** ¿De verdad?

sermon ['sə:mən] NOUN
el sermón (PL los sermones)

servant ['sə:vənt] NOUN
el criado
la criada

to **serve** [sə:v] VERB
see also **serve** NOUN
1 servir* ◊ *Dinner is served.* La cena está servida.
♦ **It's Agassi's turn to serve.** Al servicio Agassi.
♦ **Are you being served?** ¿Le atienden ya?
2 cumplir ◊ *to serve a life sentence* cumplir cadena perpetua
♦ **to serve time** cumplir condena
♦ **It serves you right.** Te está bien empleado.

serve [sə:v] NOUN
see also **serve** VERB
el servicio

server ['sɜ:vəʳ] NOUN
el servidor

to **service** ['sə:vɪs] VERB
see also **service** NOUN
revisar (*car, washing machine*)

service ['sə:vɪs] NOUN
see also **service** VERB
1 el servicio ◊ *Service is included.* El servicio está incluido. ◊ *the postal service* el servicio de correos
♦ **a bus service** una línea de autobús
2 la revisión (PL las revisiones) ◊ *The car needs a service.* Al coche le hace falta una revisión.
3 el oficio religioso ◊ *a memorial service* un oficio religioso conmemorativo
♦ **the armed services** las fuerzas armadas

service area ['sə:vɪsɛərɪə] NOUN
el área de servicios FEM

*Although it's a feminine noun, remember that you use **el** and **un** with **área**.*

service charge ['sə:vɪstʃɑ:dʒ] NOUN
el servicio ◊ *There's no service charge.* El servicio va incluido.

serviceman ['sə:vɪsmən] NOUN (PL **servicemen**)
el militar

service station ['sə:vɪssteɪʃən] NOUN
la estación de servicio (PL las estaciones de servicio)

serviette [sə:vɪ'ɛt] NOUN
la servilleta

session ['sɛʃən] NOUN
la sesión (PL las sesiones)

set [sɛt] NOUN
see also **set** VERB
1 (*of objects, tools*)
el juego ◊ *a set of keys* un juego de llaves
♦ **The sofa and chairs are only sold as a set.** El sofá y los sillones no se venden por separado.
♦ **a chess set** un ajedrez
♦ **a train set** un tren eléctrico
2 (*of ideas, actions*)
el conjunto ◊ *a set of calculations* un conjunto de cálculos
3 (*in tennis*)

S

el set (PL los sets)
◊ *She was leading 5-1 in the first set.* Iba ganando 5 a 1 en el primer set.

to **set** [sɛt] VERB (**set, set**)
see also **set** NOUN
1 poner* ◊ *I set the alarm for seven o'clock.* Puse el despertador a las siete.
2 establecer* ◊ *The world record was set last year.* El récord mundial se estableció el año pasado.
3 ponerse* ◊ *The sun was setting.* Se estaba poniendo el sol.
◆**The film is set in Morocco.** La película se desarrolla en Marruecos.
◆**to set something on fire** prender fuego a algo
◆**to set sail** zarpar
◆**to set the table** poner* la mesa

to **set off** [sɛt'ɔf] VERB
salir* ◊ *We set off for London at nine o'clock.* Salimos para Londres a las nueve.

to **set out** [sɛt'aut] VERB
salir* ◊ *We set out for London at nine o'clock.* Salimos para Londres a las nueve.

settee [sɛ'tiː] NOUN
el sofá (PL los sofás)

to **settle** ['sɛtl] VERB
1 zanjar ◊ *That should settle the problem.* Esto debería zanjar el problema.
2 pagar* ◊ *I'll settle the bill tomorrow.* Mañana pagaré la cuenta.

to **settle down** [sɛtl'daun] VERB
calmarse

to **settle in** [sɛtl'ɪn] VERB
adaptarse

to **settle on** ['sɛtlɔn] VERB
decidirse por

seven ['sɛvn] NUMERAL
siete ◊ *She's seven.* Tiene siete años.

seventeen [sɛvn'tiːn] NUMERAL
diecisiete ◊ *He's seventeen.* Tiene diecisiete años.

seventeenth [sɛvn'tiːnθ] ADJECTIVE
decimoséptimo
◆**the seventeenth floor** la planta diecisiete
◆**the seventeenth of April** el diecisiete de abril

seventh ['sɛvnθ] ADJECTIVE
séptimo ◊ *the seventh floor* el séptimo piso
◆**the seventh of August** el siete de agosto

seventy ['sɛvntɪ] NUMERAL
setenta ◊ *She's seventy.* Tiene setenta años.

several ['sɛvərl] ADJECTIVE, PRONOUN
varios ◊ *several schools* varios colegios ◊ *several times* varias veces

to **sew** [səu] VERB (**sewed, sewn**)
coser

to **sew up** [səu'ʌp] VERB
coser

sewing ['səuɪŋ] NOUN
la costura ◊ *I like sewing.* Me gusta la costura.
◆**sewing machine** la máquina de coser

sewn [səun] VERB *see* **sew**

sex [sɛks] NOUN
el sexo ◊ *the opposite sex* el sexo opuesto
◆**to have sex with somebody** tener* relaciones sexuales con alguien
◆**sex education** la educación sexual

sexism ['sɛksɪzəm] NOUN
el sexismo

sexist ['sɛksɪst] ADJECTIVE
sexista

sexual ['sɛksjuəl] ADJECTIVE
sexual ◊ *sexual discrimination* la discriminación sexual ◊ *sexual harassment* el acoso sexual

sexuality [sɛksju'ælɪtɪ] NOUN
la sexualidad

sexy ['sɛksɪ] ADJECTIVE
sexy (PL sexy)

shabby ['ʃæbɪ] ADJECTIVE
andrajoso (*person, clothes*)

shade [ʃeɪd] NOUN
1 la sombra ◊ *It was 35 degrees in the shade.* Hacía 35 grados a la sombra.
2 el tono ◊ *a beautiful shade of blue* un tono de azul muy bonito

shadow ['ʃædəu] NOUN
la sombra

to **shake** [ʃeɪk] VERB (**shook, shaken**)
1 sacudir ◊ *She shook the rug.* Sacudió la alfombra.
◆**"Shake well before use"** "Agítese bien antes de usarse"
2 temblar* ◊ *He was shaking with cold.* Temblaba de frío.
◆**Donald shook his head.** Donald negó con la cabeza.
◆**to shake hands with somebody** dar* la mano a alguien ◊ *They shook hands.* Se dieron la mano.

shaken ['ʃeɪkn] ADJECTIVE
afectado ◊ *I was feeling a bit shaken.* Estaba un poco afectado.

shaky ['ʃeɪkɪ] ADJECTIVE
tembloroso (*hand, voice*)
◆**I was feeling a bit shaky.** Estaba un poco débil.

shall [ʃæl] VERB
◆**Shall I shut the window?** ¿Cierro la ventana?

♦**Shall we ask him to come with us?** ¿Le pedimos que venga con nosotros?
***pedir que** has to be followed by a verb in the subjunctive.*

shallow ['ʃæləu] ADJECTIVE
poco profundo

shambles ['ʃæmblz] NOUN
el desastre ◊ *It's a complete shambles.* Es un desastre total.

shame [ʃeɪm] NOUN
la vergüenza ◊ *I'd die of shame!* ¡Me moriría de vergüenza!
♦**What a shame!** ¡Qué pena!
♦**It's a shame that...** Es una pena que...
***es una pena que** has to be followed by a verb in the subjunctive.*
◊ *It's a shame he isn't here.* Es una pena que no esté aquí.

shampoo [ʃæm'pu:] NOUN
el champú (PL los champús) ◊ *a bottle of shampoo* un bote de champú

shandy ['ʃændɪ] NOUN (PL **shandies**)
la clara (*de cerveza con gaseosa*)

shan't [ʃɑ:nt] = **shall not**

shape [ʃeɪp] NOUN
la forma ◊ *in the shape of a star* en forma de estrella
♦**to be in good shape** estar* en buena forma

share [ʃɛəʳ] NOUN
see also **share** VERB
1 la acción (PL las acciones) ◊ *They've got shares in many companies.* Tienen acciones en muchas empresas.
2 la parte ◊ *He refused to pay his share of the bill.* Se negó a pagar su parte de la factura.

to **share** [ʃɛəʳ] VERB
see also **share** NOUN
compartir ◊ *to share a room with somebody* compartir habitación con alguien

to **share out** [ʃɛəʳ'aut] VERB
repartir ◊ *They shared the sweets out among the children.* Repartieron los caramelos entre los niños.

shark [ʃɑ:k] NOUN
el tiburón (PL los tiburones)

sharp [ʃɑ:p] ADJECTIVE, ADVERB
1 afilado ◊ *Be careful, that knife's sharp!* ¡Cuidado con ese cuchillo que está afilado!
2 puntiagudo (*point, spike*)
3 listo (*intelligent*) ◊ *She's very sharp.* Es muy lista.
♦**at two o'clock sharp** a las dos en punto

to **shave** [ʃeɪv] VERB
afeitarse ◊ *He took a bath and shaved.* Se dio un baño y se afeitó.
♦**to shave one's legs** depilarse las piernas

shaver ['ʃeɪvəʳ] NOUN
♦**electric shaver** la maquinilla de afeitar eléctrica

shaving cream ['ʃeɪvɪŋkri:m] NOUN
la crema de afeitar

shaving foam ['ʃeɪvɪŋfəum] NOUN
la espuma de afeitar

she [ʃi:] PRONOUN
ella
***she** generally isn't translated unless it's emphatic.*
◊ *She's very nice.* Es muy maja.
*Use **ella** for emphasis.*
◊ *She did it but he didn't.* Ella lo hizo, pero él no.

shed [ʃɛd] NOUN
el cobertizo

she'd [ʃi:d] = **she had**, = **she would**

sheep [ʃi:p] NOUN (PL **sheep**)
la oveja

sheepdog ['ʃi:pdɔg] NOUN
el perro pastor (PL los perros pastores)

sheer [ʃɪəʳ] ADJECTIVE
puro ◊ *It's sheer greed.* Es pura codicia.

sheet [ʃi:t] NOUN
la sábana ◊ *to change the sheets* cambiar las sábanas
♦**a sheet of paper** una hoja de papel

shelf [ʃɛlf] NOUN (PL **shelves**)
1 el estante (*on wall, in shop*)
2 la parrilla (*in oven*)

shell [ʃɛl] NOUN
1 (*on beach, of tortoise, snail*)
la concha (el caracol *LatAm*)
2 (*of egg, nut*)
la cáscara
3 (*explosive*)
el obús (PL los obuses)

she'll [ʃi:l] = **she will**

shellfish ['ʃɛlfɪʃ] NOUN
el marisco

shell suit ['ʃɛlsu:t] NOUN
el chándal de nylon (PL los chándals de nylon)

shelter ['ʃɛltəʳ] NOUN
el refugio ◊ *a bomb shelter* un refugio antiaéreo
♦**to take shelter** refugiarse
♦**bus shelter** la marquesina de autobús

shelves [ʃɛlvz] PL NOUN *see* **shelf**

shepherd ['ʃɛpəd] NOUN
el pastor

sheriff ['ʃɛrɪf] NOUN
el sheriff

sherry ['ʃɛrɪ] NOUN
el jerez

she's [ʃi:z] = **she is**, = **she has**

shield [ʃi:ld] NOUN
el escudo

shift [ʃɪft] NOUN
see also **shift** VERB

S

el turno ◊ *the night shift* el turno de noche ◊ *His shift starts at eight o'clock.* Su turno empieza a las ocho.
♦ **to do shift work** trabajar por turnos

to **shift** [ʃɪft] VERB
see also **shift** NOUN
trasladar ◊ *I couldn't shift the wardrobe on my own.* No podía trasladar el armario yo solo.
♦ **Shift yourself!** ¡Quita de ahí! (*informal*)

shifty ['ʃɪftɪ] ADJECTIVE
sospechoso ◊ *He looked shifty.* Tenía una pinta sospechosa.
♦ **He has shifty eyes.** Tiene una mirada furtiva.

shin [ʃɪn] NOUN
la espinilla

to **shine** [ʃaɪn] VERB (**shone, shone**)
brillar ◊ *The sun was shining.* Brillaba el sol.

shiny ['ʃaɪnɪ] ADJECTIVE
brillante

ship [ʃɪp] NOUN
el barco ◊ *by ship* en barco
♦ **a merchant ship** un buque mercante

shipbuilding ['ʃɪpbɪldɪŋ] NOUN
la construcción naval

shipwreck ['ʃɪprɛk] NOUN
el naufragio

shipwrecked ['ʃɪprɛkt] ADJECTIVE
♦ **to be shipwrecked** naufragar*

shipyard ['ʃɪpjɑːd] NOUN
el astillero

shirt [ʃəːt] NOUN
la camisa

shit [ʃɪt] EXCLAMATION
¡Mierda! (*rude*)

to **shiver** ['ʃɪvəʳ] VERB
tiritar ◊ *to shiver with cold* tiritar de frío

shock [ʃɔk] NOUN
see also **shock** VERB
1 la conmoción (PL las conmociones) ◊ *The news came as a shock.* La noticia causó conmoción.
2 el calambre ◊ *I got a shock when I touched the switch.* Me dio calambre al tocar el interruptor.
♦ **an electric shock** una descarga eléctrica

to **shock** [ʃɔk] VERB
see also **shock** NOUN
1 horrorizar* (*upset*) ◊ *They were shocked by the tragedy.* Quedaron horrorizados por la tragedia.
2 escandalizar* (*scandalize*) ◊ *Nothing shocks me any more.* Ya nada me escandaliza.

shocking ['ʃɔkɪŋ] ADJECTIVE
escandaloso ◊ *It's shocking!* ¡Es escandaloso!

shoe [ʃuː] NOUN
el zapato ◊ *a pair of shoes* un par de zapatos

shoelace ['ʃuːleɪs] NOUN
el cordón (PL los cordones)

shoe polish ['ʃuːpɔlɪʃ] NOUN
el betún

shoe shop ['ʃuːʃɔp] NOUN
la zapatería

shone [ʃɔn] VERB *see* **shine**

shook [ʃuk] VERB *see* **shake**

to **shoot** [ʃuːt] VERB (**shot, shot**)
1 disparar (*fire a shot*) ◊ *Don't shoot!* ¡No disparen!
♦ **to shoot at somebody** disparar contra alguien
♦ **He shot himself with a revolver.** Se pegó un tiro con un revólver.
♦ **He was shot dead by the police.** Murió de un disparo de la policía.
2 fusilar (*execute*) ◊ *He was shot at dawn.* Lo fusilaron al amanecer.
3 rodar* ◊ *The film was shot in Prague.* La película se rodó en Praga.
4 chutar (*in football*)

shooting ['ʃuːtɪŋ] NOUN
1 los disparos ◊ *They heard shooting.* Oyeron disparos.
♦ **a shooting** un tiroteo
2 la caza ◊ *to go shooting* ir* de caza

shop [ʃɔp] NOUN
la tienda ◊ *a sports shop* una tienda de deportes

shop assistant ['ʃɔpəsɪstənt] NOUN
el dependiente
la dependienta

shopkeeper ['ʃɔpkiːpəʳ] NOUN
el/la comerciante (*tendero*)

shoplifting ['ʃɔplɪftɪŋ] NOUN
el hurto en las tiendas

shopping ['ʃɔpɪŋ] NOUN
la compra ◊ *Can you get the shopping from the car?* ¿Puedes sacar la compra del coche?
♦ **to go shopping (1)** (*for food*) ir* a hacer la compra
♦ **to go shopping (2)** (*for pleasure*) ir* de compras
♦ **I love shopping.** Me encanta ir de compras.
♦ **shopping bag** la bolsa de la compra
♦ **shopping centre** el centro comercial

shop window [ʃɔp'wɪndəu] NOUN
el escaparate

shore [ʃɔːʳ] NOUN
la orilla ◊ *on the shores of the lake* a orillas del lago
♦ **on shore** en tierra

short [ʃɔːt] ADJECTIVE
1 corto ◊ *a short skirt* una falda corta ◊ *short hair* pelo corto ◊ *a short walk* un paseo corto ◊ *It was a great holiday, but too short.* Fueron unas vacaciones estupendas, pero demasiado cortas.
◆ **a short break** un pequeño descanso
◆ **a short time ago** hace poco
2 bajo ◊ *She's quite short.* Es bastante baja.
◆ **to be short of something** andar* escaso de algo
◆ **at short notice** con poco tiempo de antelación
◆ **In short, the answer is no.** En una palabra, la respuesta es no.

shortage ['ʃɔːtɪdʒ] NOUN
la escasez ◊ *a water shortage* escasez de agua

short cut ['ʃɔːtkʌt] NOUN
el atajo

shorthand ['ʃɔːthænd] NOUN
la taquigrafía

shortly ['ʃɔːtlɪ] ADVERB
dentro de poco ◊ *I'll be there shortly.* Estaré allí dentro de poco.
◆ **She arrived shortly after midnight.** Llegó poco después de la medianoche.

shorts [ʃɔːts] PL NOUN
los pantalones cortos ◊ *a pair of shorts* unos pantalones cortos

short-sighted [ʃɔːt'saɪtɪd] ADJECTIVE
miope

short story [ʃɔːt'stɔːrɪ] NOUN
el cuento

shot [ʃɔt] VERB *see* **shoot**

shot [ʃɔt] NOUN
1 el tiro ◊ *to fire a shot* disparar un tiro ◊ *a shot at goal* un tiro a puerta
2 la foto

Although ***foto*** *ends in* ***-a****, it is actually feminine noun.*

◊ *a shot of Edinburgh castle* una foto del castillo de Edimburgo
3 (*vaccination*)
la inyección (PL las inyecciones)

shotgun ['ʃɔtgʌn] NOUN
la escopeta

should [ʃud] VERB

When ***should*** *means "ought to", use the conditional tense of* ***deber****.*

deber ◊ *You should take more exercise.* Deberías hacer más ejercicio. ◊ *He should be there by now.* Ya debería estar allí. ◊ *That shouldn't be too hard.* Eso no debería ser muy difícil.

tener que* *is also a very common way to translate* ***should****.*

◊ *I should have told you before.* Tendría que habértelo dicho antes.

When ***should*** *means "would", use the conditional tense.*

◆ **I should go if I were you.** Yo que tú, iría.
◆ **I should be so lucky!** ¡Ojalá!

shoulder ['ʃəuldəʳ] NOUN
el hombro ◊ *I looked over my shoulder.* Miré por encima del hombro.
◆ **shoulder bag** el bolso de bandolera

shouldn't ['ʃudnt] = **should not**

to **shout** [ʃaut] VERB
see also **shout** NOUN
gritar ◊ *Don't shout!* ¡No grites!

shout [ʃaut] NOUN
see also **shout** VERB
el grito

shovel ['ʃʌvl] NOUN
la pala

show [ʃəu] NOUN
see also **show** VERB
1 el espectáculo ◊ *to stage a show* montar un espectáculo
2 el programa

Although ***programa*** *ends in* ***-a****, it is actually a masculine noun.*

◊ *a radio show* un programa de radio
◆ **fashion show** el pase de modelos
◆ **motor show** el salón del automóvil

to **show** [ʃəu] VERB (**showed, shown**)
see also **show** NOUN
1 enseñar
◆ **to show somebody something** enseñar algo a alguien ◊ *Have I shown you my hat?* ¿Te he enseñado ya mi sombrero?
2 demostrar* ◊ *She showed great courage.* Demostró gran valentía.
◆ **It shows.** Se nota. ◊ *I've never been riding before. – It shows.* Nunca había montado a caballo antes. – Se nota.

to **show off** [ʃəu'ɔf] VERB
presumir

to **show up** [ʃəu'ʌp] VERB
presentarse ◊ *He showed up late as usual.* Se presentó tarde, como de costumbre.

shower ['ʃauəʳ] NOUN
1 la ducha
◆ **to have a shower** ducharse
2 el chubasco ◊ *scattered showers* chubascos dispersos

showerproof ['ʃauəpruːf] ADJECTIVE
impermeable

showing ['ʃəuɪŋ] NOUN
el pase (*of a film*) ◊ *a private showing* un pase privado

shown [ʃəun] VERB *see* **show**

show-off ['ʃəuɔf] NOUN
el fantasmón (PL los fantasmones)
la fantasmona

shrank [ʃræŋk] VERB *see* **shrink**

to **shriek** [ʃriːk] VERB
chillar

shrimps [ʃrɪmps] PL NOUN
los camarones

to **shrink** [ʃrɪŋk] VERB (**shrank, shrunk**)

☞

encogerse* (*clothes, fabric*)

Shrove Tuesday [ʃrəuv'tju:zdɪ] NOUN
el martes de carnaval

> *En este día es tradición preparar crepes - **pancakes**.*

to **shrug** [ʃrʌg] VERB
◆ **to shrug one's shoulders** encogerse* de hombros

shrunk [ʃrʌŋk] VERB *see* **shrink**

to **shudder** ['ʃʌdəʳ] VERB
estremecerse*

to **shuffle** ['ʃʌfl] VERB
◆ **to shuffle the cards** barajar las cartas

to **shut** [ʃʌt] VERB (**shut, shut**)
cerrar* ◊ *What time do you shut?* ¿A qué hora cierran? ◊ *What time do the shops shut?* ¿A qué hora cierran las tiendas?

to **shut down** [ʃʌt'daun] VERB
cerrar* ◊ *The cinema shut down last year.* El cine cerró el año pasado.

to **shut up** [ʃʌt'ʌp] VERB
callarse ◊ *Shut up!* ¡Cállate!

shutters ['ʃʌtəz] PL NOUN
las contraventanas

shuttle ['ʃʌtl] NOUN
◆ **space shuttle** el transbordador espacial
◆ **I'll get the shuttle.** Tomaré el puente aéreo.

shuttlecock ['ʃʌtlkɔk] NOUN
el volante (*de bádminton*)

shy [ʃaɪ] ADJECTIVE
tímido

Sicily ['sɪsɪlɪ] NOUN
Sicilia FEM

sick [sɪk] ADJECTIVE
1 enfermo ◊ *She looks after her sick mother.* Cuida de su madre enferma.
2 de mal gusto ◊ *That's really sick!* ¡Eso es de muy mal gusto!
◆ **to be sick** devolver* (arrojar *LatAm*) ◊ *I was sick twice last night.* Anoche devolví dos veces.
◆ **I feel sick.** Tengo ganas de devolver.
◆ **to be sick of something** estar* harto de algo ◊ *I'm sick of your jokes.* Estoy harto de tus bromas.

sickening ['sɪknɪŋ] ADJECTIVE
repugnante

sick leave ['sɪkli:v] NOUN
la baja por enfermedad

sickness ['sɪknɪs] NOUN
la enfermedad

sick note ['sɪknəut] NOUN
1 el justificante de ausencia (*from parents*)
2 la baja médica (*from doctor*)

sick pay ['sɪkpeɪ] NOUN
la prestación por enfermedad MASC (PL las prestaciones por enfermedad)

side [saɪd] NOUN
1 el lado (*of object, building, car*) ◊ *He was driving on the wrong side of the road.* Iba por el lado contrario de la carretera.
◆ **a house on the side of a mountain** una casa en la ladera de una montaña
◆ **We sat side by side.** Nos sentamos uno al lado del otro.
2 el borde (*of pool, bed, road*) ◊ *The car was abandoned at the side of the road.* El coche estaba abandonado al borde de la carretera.
◆ **by the side of the lake** a la orilla del lago
3 la cara (*of paper, record, tape*) ◊ *Play side A.* Pon la cara A.
4 el equipo (*team*) ◊ *He's on my side.* Está en mi equipo.
◆ **I'm on your side.** Yo estoy de tu parte.
◆ **to take somebody's side** ponerse* de parte de alguien
◆ **to take sides** tomar partido
◆ **the side entrance** la entrada lateral

sideboard ['saɪdbɔ:d] NOUN
el aparador

side-effect ['saɪdɪfɛkt] NOUN
el efecto secundario

side street ['saɪdstri:t] NOUN
la calle lateral

sidewalk ['saɪdwɔ:k] NOUN US
la acera

sideways ['saɪdweɪz] ADVERB
◆ **to look sideways** mirar de reojo
◆ **to move sideways** moverse* de lado
◆ **sideways on** de perfil

sieve [sɪv] NOUN
1 el colador (*for liquids*)
2 la criba (*for solids*)

sigh [saɪ] NOUN
see also **sigh** VERB
el suspiro

to **sigh** [saɪ] VERB
see also **sigh** NOUN
suspirar

sight [saɪt] NOUN
1 la vista ◊ *I'm losing my sight.* Estoy perdiendo la vista.
◆ **at first sight** a primera vista
◆ **to know somebody by sight** conocer* a alguien de vista
◆ **in sight** a la vista
2 el espectáculo ◊ *It was an amazing sight.* Era un espectáculo asombroso.
◆ **Keep out of sight!** ¡Que no te vean!
◆ **the sights** las atracciones turísticas
◆ **to see the sights of London** hacer* turismo por Londres

sightseeing ['saɪtsi:ɪŋ] NOUN
◆ **to go sightseeing** hacer* turismo

sign [saɪn] NOUN
see also **sign** VERB
1 el letrero ◊ *There was a big sign saying "private".* Había un gran letrero que ponía "privado".
2 la señal ◊ *She made a sign to the waiter.* Le hizo una señal al camarero. ◊ *There's no sign of improvement.* No hay señales de mejoría.
◆**road sign** la señal de tráfico
◆**What sign are you?** ¿De qué signo eres?

to **sign** [saɪn] VERB
see also **sign** NOUN
firmar

to **sign on** [saɪn'ɔn] VERB
apuntarse al paro

to **sign on for** [saɪn'ɔnfɔːʳ] VERB
matricularse en ◊ *I've signed on for a driving course.* Me he matriculado en la autoescuela.

signal ['sɪgnl] NOUN
see also **signal** VERB
la señal

to **signal** ['sɪgnl] VERB
see also **signal** NOUN
◆**to signal to somebody** hacer* señas a alguien

signalman ['sɪgnlmən] NOUN
el guardavía
*Although **guardavía** ends in **-a**, it is actually a masculine noun.*

signature ['sɪgnətʃəʳ] NOUN
la firma

significance [sɪg'nɪfɪkəns] NOUN
la importancia

significant [sɪg'nɪfɪkənt] ADJECTIVE
significativo

sign language ['saɪnlæŋgwɪdʒ] NOUN
el lenguaje por señas

signpost ['saɪnpəust] NOUN
la señal

silence ['saɪləns] NOUN
el silencio

silencer ['saɪlənsəʳ] NOUN
el silenciador

silent ['saɪlənt] ADJECTIVE
1 silencioso (*place*) ◊ *a silent room* una habitación silenciosa
2 callado (*person*)
◆**to be silent (1)** estar* callado ◊ *He was silent during the visit.* Estuvo callado durante la visita.
◆**to be silent (2)** ser* callado ◊ *He was a serious, silent man.* Era un hombre serio y callado.

silicon chip [sɪlɪkən'tʃɪp] NOUN
el chip de silicio (PL los chips de silicio)

silk [sɪlk] NOUN
la seda ◊ *a silk scarf* un pañuelo de seda

silky ['sɪlkɪ] ADJECTIVE
sedoso

silly ['sɪlɪ] ADJECTIVE
tonto

silver ['sɪlvəʳ] NOUN
la plata ◊ *a silver medal* una medalla de plata

similar ['sɪmɪləʳ] ADJECTIVE
parecido
◆**similar to** parecido a

simple ['sɪmpl] ADJECTIVE
1 sencillo ◊ *It's very simple.* Es muy sencillo.
2 simple ◊ *He's a bit simple.* Es un poco simple.

simply ['sɪmplɪ] ADVERB
sencillamente

simultaneous [sɪməl'teɪnɪəs] ADJECTIVE
simultáneo

sin [sɪn] NOUN
see also **sin** VERB
el pecado

to **sin** [sɪn] VERB
see also **sin** NOUN
pecar*

since [sɪns] PREPOSITION, ADVERB, CONJUNCTION
1 desde ◊ *since Christmas* desde Navidad ◊ *since then* desde entonces
◆**I haven't seen him since.** Desde entonces no lo he vuelto a ver.
2 desde que ◊ *I haven't seen her since she left.* No la he visto desde que se fue.
◆**It's a few years since I've seen them.** Hace varios años que no los veo.
3 como ◊ *Since you're tired, let's stay at home.* Como estás cansado podemos quedarnos en casa.

sincere [sɪn'sɪəʳ] ADJECTIVE
sincero

sincerely [sɪn'sɪəlɪ] ADVERB
◆**Yours sincerely...** Atentamente...

to **sing** [sɪŋ] VERB (**sang, sung**)
cantar

singer ['sɪŋəʳ] NOUN
el/la cantante

singing ['sɪŋɪŋ] NOUN
el canto ◊ *singing lessons* clases de canto
◆**flamenco singing** el cante flamenco

single ['sɪŋgl] ADJECTIVE
see also **single** NOUN
1 individual ◊ *a single room* una habitación individual ◊ *a single bed* una cama individual
2 soltero ◊ *a single mother* una madre soltera
3 solo ◊ *She hadn't said a single word.* No había dicho una sola palabra.
◆**not a single thing** nada de nada

single ['sɪŋgl] NOUN
see also **single** ADJECTIVE
1 el billete de ida
2 el single ◊ *a CD single* un single en CD

single parent [sɪŋgl'pɛərənt] NOUN
♦ **She's a single parent.** Es madre soltera.
♦ **a single parent family** una familia monoparental

singles ['sɪŋglz] PL NOUN
los individuales (*in tennis*) ◇ *the women's singles* los individuales femeninos

singular ['sɪŋgjulər] NOUN
singular ◇ *in the singular* en singular

sinister ['sɪnɪstər] ADJECTIVE
siniestro

sink [sɪŋk] NOUN
see also **sink** VERB
1 el fregadero (*in the kitchen*)
2 el lavabo (*in the bathroom*)

to **sink** [sɪŋk] VERB (**sank, sunk**)
see also **sink** NOUN
1 hundir ◇ *We sank the enemy's ship.* Hundimos el buque enemigo.
2 hundirse ◇ *The boat was sinking fast.* El barco se hundía rápidamente.

sir [sər] NOUN
el señor ◇ *Yes sir.* Sí, señor.

siren ['saɪərn] NOUN
la sirena

sister ['sɪstər] NOUN
1 la hermana ◇ *my little sister* mi hermana pequeña
2 la enfermera jefe (*nurse*)

sister-in-law ['sɪstərɪnlɔː] NOUN (PL **sisters-in-law**)
la cuñada

to **sit** [sɪt] VERB (**sat, sat**)
sentarse* ◇ *He sat in front of the TV.* Se sentó frente a la tele.
♦ **to be sitting** estar* sentado ◇ *He was sitting in front of the TV.* Estaba sentado frente a la tele.
♦ **to sit an exam** presentarse a un examen

to **sit down** [sɪt'daun] VERB
sentarse* ◇ *He sat down at his desk.* Se sentó en su escritorio.

sitcom ['sɪtkɔm] NOUN
la telecomedia

site [saɪt] NOUN
1 el lugar ◇ *the site of the accident* el lugar del accidente
2 (*campsite*)
el camping (PL los campings)
♦ **building site** la obra

sitting room ['sɪtɪŋrum] NOUN
la sala de estar (PL las salas de estar)

situated ['sɪtjueɪtɪd] ADJECTIVE
♦ **to be situated...** estar* situado... (estar* ubicado... *LatAm*)

situation [sɪtju'eɪʃən] NOUN
la situación (PL las situaciones)

six [sɪks] NUMERAL
seis ◇ *He's six.* Tiene seis años.

sixteen [sɪks'tiːn] NUMERAL
dieciséis ◇ *He's sixteen.* Tiene dieciséis años.

sixteenth [sɪks'tiːnθ] ADJECTIVE
decimosexto
♦ **the sixteenth floor** la planta dieciséis
♦ **the sixteenth of August** el dieciséis de agosto

sixth [sɪksθ] ADJECTIVE
sexto ◇ *the sixth floor* el sexto piso
♦ **the sixth of August** el seis de agosto

sixty ['sɪkstɪ] NUMERAL
sesenta ◇ *She's sixty.* Tiene sesenta años.

size [saɪz] NOUN
1 el tamaño (*of object, place*) ◇ *plates of various sizes* platos de varios tamaños

> ℹ *Spain uses the European system for clothing and shoe sizes.*

2 la talla (*of clothing*) ◇ *What size do you take?* ¿Qué talla usas?
3 el número (*of shoes*)
♦ **I take size five.** Calzo un treinta y ocho.

to **skate** [skeɪt] VERB
patinar

skateboard ['skeɪtbɔːd] NOUN
el monopatín (PL los monopatines)

skateboarding ['skeɪtbɔːdɪŋ] NOUN
♦ **to go skateboarding** montar en monopatín

skates [skeɪts] PL NOUN
los patines

skating ['skeɪtɪŋ] NOUN
el patinaje ◇ *to go skating* ir* a patinar
♦ **skating rink** la pista de patinaje

skeleton ['skɛlɪtn] NOUN
el esqueleto

sketch [skɛtʃ] NOUN (PL **sketches**)
see also **sketch** VERB
el boceto

to **sketch** [skɛtʃ] VERB
see also **sketch** NOUN
esbozar*

to **ski** [skiː] VERB
see also **ski** NOUN
esquiar*

ski [skiː] NOUN
see also **ski** VERB
el esquí ◇ *a pair of skis* unos esquís
♦ **ski boots** las botas de esquí
♦ **ski lift** el telesilla

> *Although **telesilla** ends in **-a**, it is actually a masculine noun.*

♦ **ski pants** los pantalones de esquí
♦ **ski pole** el bastón de esquí (PL los bastones de esquí)
♦ **ski slope** la pista de esquí

◆**ski suit** el traje de esquí
to **skid** [skɪd] VERB
patinar
skier ['skiːəʳ] NOUN
el esquiador
la esquiadora
skiing ['skiːɪŋ] NOUN
el esquí ◊ *I love skiing.* Me encanta el esquí.
◆**to go skiing** ir* a esquiar
◆**to go on a skiing holiday** irse* de vacaciones a esquiar
skilful ['skɪlful] ADJECTIVE
hábil
skill [skɪl] NOUN
la habilidad ◊ *It requires a lot of skill.* Requiere mucha habilidad.
skilled [skɪld] ADJECTIVE
◆**a skilled worker** un trabajador cualificado
skimmed milk [skɪmd'mɪlk] NOUN
la leche desnatada
skimpy ['skɪmpɪ] ADJECTIVE
1 mínimo (*clothes*)
2 escaso (*meal*)
skin [skɪn] NOUN
la piel
◆**skin cancer** el cáncer de piel
skinhead ['skɪnhɛd] NOUN
el/la cabeza rapada (PL los/las cabezas rapadas)
skinny ['skɪnɪ] ADJECTIVE
flaco
skin-tight ['skɪntaɪt] ADJECTIVE
muy ajustado
skip [skɪp] NOUN
see also **skip** VERB
el contenedor de basuras
to **skip** [skɪp] VERB
see also **skip** NOUN
saltarse ◊ *You should never skip breakfast.* No debes saltarte nunca el desayuno.
◆**to skip school** hacer* novillos
skirt [skəːt] NOUN
la falda
skittles ['skɪtlz] PL NOUN
los bolos
to **skive** [skaɪv] VERB
escaquearse (*informal*)
◆**to skive off school** hacer* novillos
skull [skʌl] NOUN
1 la calavera (*of corpse*)
2 el cráneo (*in anatomy*)
sky [skaɪ] NOUN (PL **skies**)
el cielo
skyscraper ['skaɪskreɪpəʳ] NOUN
el rascacielos (PL los rascacielos)
slack [slæk] ADJECTIVE
1 flojo (*rope*)
2 descuidado (*person*)
to **slag off** [slæg'ɔf] VERB
poner* verde a (*informal*)
to **slam** [slæm] VERB
cerrar* de un portazo ◊ *She slammed the door.* Cerró la puerta de un portazo.
◆**The door slammed.** La puerta se cerró de un portazo.
slang [slæŋ] NOUN
el argot
slap [slæp] NOUN
see also **slap** VERB
la bofetada
to **slap** [slæp] VERB
see also **slap** NOUN
dar* una bofetada a
slate [sleɪt] NOUN
la teja de pizarra
sledge [slɛdʒ] NOUN
el trineo
sledging ['slɛdʒɪŋ] NOUN
◆**to go sledging** ir* en trineo
sleep [sliːp] NOUN
see also **sleep** VERB
el sueño ◊ *lack of sleep* falta de sueño
◆**I need some sleep.** Necesito dormir.
◆**to go to sleep** dormirse*
to **sleep** [sliːp] VERB (**slept, slept**)
see also **sleep** NOUN
dormir* ◊ *I couldn't sleep last night.* Anoche no podía dormir.
to **sleep around** [sliːpə'raund] VERB
irse* a la cama con cualquiera
to **sleep in** [sliːp'ɪn] VERB
dormir* hasta tarde
to **sleep together** ['sliːptəgɛðəʳ] VERB
acostarse* juntos
to **sleep with** ['sliːpwɪð] VERB
acostarse* con
sleeping bag ['sliːpɪŋbæg] NOUN
el saco de dormir
sleeping car ['sliːpɪŋkɑːʳ] NOUN
el coche cama (PL los coches cama)
sleeping pill ['sliːpɪŋpɪl] NOUN
el somnífero
sleepy ['sliːpɪ] ADJECTIVE
◆**to feel sleepy** tener* sueño
◆**a sleepy little village** un pueblecito tranquilo
sleet [sliːt] NOUN
see also **sleet** VERB
el aguanieve FEM

Although it's a feminine noun, remember that you use **el** *with* **aguanieve**.

to **sleet** [sliːt] VERB
see also **sleet** NOUN
◆**It's sleeting.** Está cayendo aguanieve.
sleeve [sliːv] NOUN
la manga (*of shirt, coat*)
sleigh [sleɪ] NOUN
el trineo
slept [slɛpt] VERB *see* **sleep**

S

slice [slaɪs] NOUN
see also **slice** VERB
1 la rebanada (*of bread*)
2 el trozo (*of cake*)
3 la rodaja (*of lemon, pineapple*)
4 la loncha (*of ham, cheese*)

to **slice** [slaɪs] VERB
see also **slice** NOUN
cortar

slick [slɪk] NOUN
see also **slick** ADJECTIVE
♦**oil slick** la marea negra

slick [slɪk] ADJECTIVE
see also **slick** NOUN
impecable ◊ *a slick performance* una actuación impecable

slide [slaɪd] NOUN
see also **slide** VERB
1 (*in playground*)
el tobogán (PL los toboganes)
2 (*photo*)
la diapositiva
3 (*hair slide*)
el pasador

to **slide** [slaɪd] VERB **(slid, slid)**
see also **slide** NOUN
deslizarse* ◊ *Tears were sliding down his cheeks.* Las lágrimas se deslizaban por sus mejillas.
♦**She slid the door open.** Corrió la puerta.

slight [slaɪt] ADJECTIVE
ligero ◊ *a slight improvement* una ligera mejoría
♦**a slight problem** un pequeño problema

slightly ['slaɪtlɪ] ADVERB
ligeramente ◊ *They are slightly more expensive.* Son ligeramente más caros.

slim [slɪm] ADJECTIVE
see also **slim** VERB
delgado

to **slim** [slɪm] VERB
see also **slim** ADJECTIVE
adelgazar* ◊ *I'm trying to slim.* Estoy intentando adelgazar.
♦**I'm slimming.** Estoy a régimen.

sling [slɪŋ] NOUN
el cabestrillo ◊ *She had her arm in a sling.* Llevaba el brazo en cabestrillo.

slip [slɪp] NOUN
see also **slip** VERB
1 (*mistake*)
el desliz (PL los deslices)
2 (*underskirt*)
la combinación (PL las combinaciones)
♦**a slip of paper** un papelito
♦**a slip of the tongue** un lapsus

to **slip** [slɪp] VERB
see also **slip** NOUN
resbalar ◊ *He slipped on the ice.* Resbaló en el hielo.

to **slip up** [slɪp'ʌp] VERB
equivocarse*

slipper ['slɪpəʳ] NOUN
la zapatilla

slippery ['slɪpərɪ] ADJECTIVE
resbaladizo

slip-up ['slɪpʌp] NOUN
el desliz (PL los deslices)

slope [sləup] NOUN
1 la cuesta (*surface*) ◊ *The street was on a slope.* La calle era en cuesta.
2 la pendiente (*angle*) ◊ *a slope of 10 degrees* una pendiente del 10 por ciento

sloppy ['slɔpɪ] ADJECTIVE
descuidado

slot [slɔt] NOUN
la ranura

slot machine ['slɔtmə'ʃiːn] NOUN
1 (*for gambling*)
la máquina tragaperras (PL las máquinas tragaperras)
2 (*vending machine*)
la máquina expendedora

slow [sləu] ADJECTIVE, ADVERB
lento ◊ *He's a bit slow.* Es un poco lento. ◊ *to go slow* ir* lento
♦**Drive slower!** ¡Conduce más despacio!
♦**My watch is slow.** Mi reloj se atrasa.

to **slow down** [sləu'daun] VERB
reducir* la velocidad ◊ *The car slowed down.* El coche redujo la velocidad.

slowly ['sləulɪ] ADVERB
lentamente

slug [slʌg] NOUN
la babosa

slum [slʌm] NOUN
el barrio bajo

slush [slʌʃ] NOUN
la nieve medio derretida

sly [slaɪ] ADJECTIVE
astuto ◊ *She's very sly.* Es muy astuta.
♦**a sly smile** una sonrisa maliciosa

smack [smæk] NOUN
see also **smack** VERB
el cachete

to **smack** [smæk] VERB
see also **smack** NOUN
dar* un cachete a

small [smɔːl] ADJECTIVE
pequeño (chico *LatAm*) ◊ *two small children* dos niños pequeños
♦**small change** el dinero suelto

smart [smɑːt] ADJECTIVE
1 elegante ◊ *a smart navy blue suit* un elegante traje azul marino
2 listo ◊ *He thinks he's smarter than Sarah.* Se cree más listo que Sarah.

smash [smæʃ] NOUN (PL **smashes**)
see also **smash** VERB
el accidente de coche

* Verbs marked with this symbol are irregular. See pages 380-382 for further details

to **smash** [smæʃ] VERB
see also **smash** NOUN
1 romper* ◊ *They smashed windows.* Rompieron ventanas.
2 romperse* ◊ *The glass smashed into tiny pieces.* El vaso se rompió en pedazos.

smashing ['smæʃɪŋ] ADJECTIVE
estupendo ◊ *That's a smashing idea.* Me parece una idea estupenda.

smell [smɛl] NOUN
see also **smell** VERB
el olor ◊ *a smell of lemon* un olor a limón
◆ **the sense of smell** el olfato

to **smell** [smɛl] VERB (**smelled** *o* **smelt, smelled** *o* **smelt**)
see also **smell** NOUN
oler* ◊ *That dog smells!* ¡Cómo huele ese perro! ◊ *I can't smell anything.* No huelo nada.
◆ **I can smell gas.** Me huele a gas.
◆ **to smell of something** oler a algo ◊ *It smells of petrol.* Huele a gasolina.

smelly ['smɛlɪ] ADJECTIVE
maloliente ◊ *The pub was dirty and smelly.* El pub era sucio y maloliente.
◆ **He's got smelly feet.** Le huelen los pies.

smile [smaɪl] NOUN
see also **smile** VERB
la sonrisa

to **smile** [smaɪl] VERB
see also **smile** NOUN
sonreír*

smoke [sməuk] NOUN
see also **smoke** VERB
el humo

to **smoke** [sməuk] VERB
see also **smoke** NOUN
fumar ◊ *I don't smoke.* No fumo.

smoker ['sməukəʳ] NOUN
el fumador
la fumadora

smoking ['sməukɪŋ] NOUN
◆ **to stop smoking** dejar de fumar
◆ **Smoking is bad for you.** Fumar es malo para la salud.
◆ **"no smoking"** "prohibido fumar"

smooth [smu:ð] ADJECTIVE
liso ◊ *a smooth surface* una superficie lisa

smudge [smʌdʒ] NOUN
el borrón (PL los borrones)

smug [smʌg] ADJECTIVE
engreído

to **smuggle** ['smʌgl] VERB
◆ **to smuggle in** meter de contrabando
◆ **to smuggle out** sacar* de contrabando

smuggler ['smʌgləʳ] NOUN
el/la contrabandista

smuggling ['smʌglɪŋ] NOUN
el contrabando

smutty ['smʌtɪ] ADJECTIVE
◆ **smutty jokes** chistes verdes

snack [snæk] NOUN
◆ **to have a snack** picar* algo

snack bar ['snækbɑ:ʳ] NOUN
la cafetería

snail [sneɪl] NOUN
el caracol

snake [sneɪk] NOUN
la serpiente

to **snap** [snæp] VERB
partirse ◊ *The branch snapped.* La rama se partió.
◆ **to snap one's fingers** chasquear los dedos

snapshot ['snæpʃɔt] NOUN
la foto FEM
*Although **foto** ends in **-o**, it is actually a feminine noun.*

to **snarl** [snɑ:l] VERB
gruñir*

to **snatch** [snætʃ] VERB
arrebatar
◆ **to snatch something from somebody** arrebatar algo a alguien ◊ *He snatched the keys from my hand.* Me arrebató las llaves de la mano.
◆ **My bag was snatched.** Me robaron el bolso.

to **sneak** [sni:k] VERB
◆ **to sneak in** entrar a hurtadillas
◆ **to sneak out** salir* a hurtadillas
◆ **to sneak up on somebody** acercarse* sigilosamente a alguien

to **sneeze** [sni:z] VERB
estornudar

to **sniff** [snɪf] VERB
1 sorberse la nariz ◊ *Stop sniffing!* ¡Deja de sorberte la nariz!
2 olfatear ◊ *The dog sniffed my hand.* El perro me olfateó la mano.
◆ **to sniff glue** esnifar pegamento

snob [snɔb] NOUN
el/la esnob (PL los/las esnobs)

snooker ['snu:kəʳ] NOUN
el billar

snooze [snu:z] NOUN
la cabezadita (*informal*) ◊ *to have a snooze* echar una cabezadita

to **snore** [snɔ:ʳ] VERB
roncar*

snow [snəu] NOUN
see also **snow** VERB
la nieve

to **snow** [snəu] VERB
see also **snow** NOUN
nevar* ◊ *It's snowing.* Está nevando.

snowball ['snəubɔ:l] NOUN
la bola de nieve

snowflake ['snəufleɪk] NOUN
el copo de nieve

snowman ['snəumæn] NOUN (PL **snowmen**)

el muñeco de nieve ◊ *to build a snowman* hacer* un muñeco de nieve

so [səu] CONJUNCTION, ADVERB

1 así que (*therefore*) ◊ *The shop was closed, so I went home.* La tienda estaba cerrada, así que me fui a casa. ◊ *So, have you always lived in London?* Así que, ¿siempre has vivido en Londres?

♦ **So what?** ¿Y qué?

2 para que (*so that*)

***para que** has to be followed by a verb in the subjunctive.*

◊ *He took her upstairs so they wouldn't be overheard.* La subió al piso de arriba para que nadie los oyera.

3 tan (*very, as*) ◊ *He was talking so fast I couldn't understand.* Hablaba tan rápido que no lo entendía. ◊ *He's like his sister but not so clever.* Es como su hermana pero no tan listo.

♦ **It was so heavy!** ¡Pesaba tanto!

♦ **How's your father? – Not so good.** ¿Cómo está tu padre? – No muy bien.

♦ **so much** tanto ◊ *I love you so much.* Te quiero tanto. ◊ *She's got so much energy.* Tiene tanta energía.

♦ **so many** tantos ◊ *I've got so many things to do today.* Tengo tantas cosas que hacer hoy.

♦ **That's not so.** No es así.

4 también (*also*)

♦ **so do I** y yo también ◊ *I work a lot. – So do I.* Trabajo mucho. – Y yo también.

♦ **I love horses. – So do I.** Me encantan los caballos. – A mí también.

♦ **so have we** y nosotros también ◊ *I've been waiting for ages! – So have we.* ¡Llevo esperando un siglo! – Y nosotros también.

♦ **I think so.** Creo que sí.

♦ **... or so** ... o así ◊ *at five o'clock or so* a las cinco o así ◊ *ten or so people* diez personas o así

to **soak** [səuk] VERB

1 poner* en remojo ◊ *Soak the beans for two hours.* Ponga las judías en remojo dos horas.

2 empapar ◊ *Water had soaked his jacket.* El agua le había empapado la chaqueta.

soaked [səukt] ADJECTIVE

♦ **to get soaked** empaparse

soaking ['səukɪŋ] ADJECTIVE

empapado ◊ *By the time we got back we were soaking.* Cuando regresamos estábamos empapados.

♦ **Your shoes are soaking wet.** Tienes los zapatos calados.

soap [səup] NOUN

el jabón

soap opera ['səupɔpərə] NOUN

la telenovela

soap powder ['səuppaudəʳ] NOUN

el detergente en polvo

to **sob** [sɔb] VERB

sollozar*

sober ['səubəʳ] ADJECTIVE

sobrio

to **sober up** [səubər'ʌp] VERB

♦ **He sobered up.** Se le pasó la borrachera.

soccer ['sɔkəʳ] NOUN

el fútbol ◊ *to play soccer* jugar* al fútbol

♦ **soccer player** el/la futbolista

social ['səuʃl] ADJECTIVE

social ◊ *social problems* problemas sociales

♦ **I have a good social life.** Tengo mucha vida social.

socialism ['səuʃəlɪzəm] NOUN

el socialismo

socialist ['səuʃəlɪst] ADJECTIVE, NOUN

socialista

social security [səuʃlsɪ'kjuərɪtɪ] NOUN

la seguridad social

♦ **to be on social security** cobrar de la seguridad social

social worker ['səuʃlwəːkəʳ] NOUN

el asistente social

la asistenta social

society [sə'saɪətɪ] NOUN (PL **societies**)

1 la sociedad ◊ *a multi-cultural society* una sociedad pluricultural

2 la asociación (PL las asociaciones) ◊ *a drama society* una asociación de amigos del teatro

sociology [səusɪ'ɔlədʒɪ] NOUN

la sociología

sock [sɔk] NOUN

el calcetín (PL los calcetines)

(la media *LatAm*)

socket ['sɔkɪt] NOUN

el enchufe

soda ['səudə] NOUN

la soda

soda pop ['səudəpɔp] NOUN US

el refresco

sofa ['səufə] NOUN

el sofá (PL los sofás)

soft [sɔft] ADJECTIVE

1 suave ◊ *a soft towel* una toalla suave

2 blando ◊ *The mattress is too soft.* El colchón es demasiado blando.

♦ **to be soft on somebody** ser* blando con alguien

♦ **soft cheeses** los quesos tiernos

♦ **a soft drink** un refresco

♦ **soft drugs** las drogas blandas

♦ **soft option** la alternativa fácil

software ['sɔftwɛəʳ] NOUN

el software

soggy ['sɔgɪ] ADJECTIVE

1 revenido (*bread, biscuits*)
2 pasado (*salad*)

soil [sɔɪl] NOUN
la tierra

solar power [səuləˈpauəʳ] NOUN
la energía solar

sold [səuld] VERB *see* **sell**

sold out [səuldˈaut] ADJECTIVE
agotado ◊ *The tickets are all sold out.* Están agotadas todas las entradas.

soldier [ˈsəuldʒəʳ] NOUN
el soldado

solicitor [səˈlɪsɪtəʳ] NOUN
1 (*for lawsuits*)
el abogado
la abogada
2 (*for wills, property*)
el notario
la notaria

solid [ˈsɔlɪd] ADJECTIVE
sólido ◊ *a solid wall* un muro sólido
♦**solid gold** oro macizo
♦**for three solid hours** durante tres horas seguidas

solo [ˈsəuləu] NOUN
el solo ◊ *a guitar solo* un solo de guitarra

solution [səˈluːʃən] NOUN
la solución (PL las soluciones)

to **solve** [sɔlv] VERB
resolver*

some [sʌm] ADJECTIVE, PRONOUN
When ***some*** *refers to something you can't count, it usually isn't translated.*
◊ *Would you like some bread?* ¿Quieres pan? ◊ *Have you got some mineral water?* ¿Tiene agua mineral? ◊ *Would you like some coffee? – No thanks, I've got some.* ¿Quiere café? – No gracias, ya tengo.
♦**I only want some of it.** Sólo quiero un poco.
When ***some*** *refers to something you can count, use* ***alguno****, which is shortened to* ***algún*** *before a masculine singular noun.*
◊ *some day* algún día ◊ *some books* algunos libros ◊ *You have to be careful with mushrooms: some are poisonous.* Cuidado con las setas: algunas son venenosas.
♦**I'm going to buy some stamps. Do you want some too?** Voy a por sellos. ¿Quieres que te traiga?
♦**some day next week** un día de la semana que viene
♦**Some people say that...** Hay gente que dice que...
♦**some of them** algunos ◊ *I only sold some of them.* Sólo vendí algunos.

somebody [ˈsʌmbədɪ] PRONOUN
alguien ◊ *I need somebody to help me.* Necesito que me ayude alguien.

somehow [ˈsʌmhau] ADVERB
de alguna manera
♦**I'll do it somehow.** De alguna manera lo haré.
♦**Somehow I don't think he believed me.** Por alguna razón me parece que no me creyó.

someone [ˈsʌmwʌn] PRONOUN
alguien ◊ *I need someone to help me.* Necesito que me ayude alguien.

something [ˈsʌmθɪŋ] PRONOUN
algo ◊ *something special* algo especial ◊ *Wear something warm.* Ponte algo que abrigue.
♦**It cost £100, or something like that.** Costó 100 libras, o algo así.
♦**His name is Peter or something.** Se llama Peter o algo por el estilo.

sometime [ˈsʌmtaɪm] ADVERB
algún día ◊ *You must come and see us sometime.* Tienes que venir* a vernos algún día.
♦**sometime last month** el mes pasado

sometimes [ˈsʌmtaɪmz] ADVERB
a veces ◊ *Sometimes I drink beer.* A veces bebo cerveza.

somewhere [ˈsʌmwɛəʳ] ADVERB
en algún sitio ◊ *I left my keys somewhere.* Me he dejado las llaves en algún sitio.
♦**I'd like to go on holiday, somewhere exotic.** Me gustaría irme de vacaciones, a algún sitio exótico.

son [sʌn] NOUN
el hijo

song [sɔŋ] NOUN
la canción (PL las canciones)

son-in-law [ˈsʌnɪnlɔː] NOUN (PL **sons-in-law**)
el yerno

soon [suːn] ADVERB
pronto ◊ *very soon* muy pronto
♦**soon afterwards** poco después
♦**as soon as possible** cuanto antes

sooner [ˈsuːnəʳ] ADVERB
antes ◊ *Can't you come a bit sooner?* ¿No puedes venir* un poco antes?
♦**sooner or later** tarde o temprano
♦**the sooner the better** cuanto antes mejor

soot [sut] NOUN
el hollín

soppy [ˈsɔpɪ] ADJECTIVE
sentimentaloide

soprano [səˈprɑːnəu] NOUN
la soprano
Although ***soprano*** *ends in* ***-o****, it is actually a feminine noun.*

sore [sɔːʳ] ADJECTIVE
see also **sore** NOUN
♦**It's sore.** Me duele.
♦**I have a sore throat.** Me duele la garganta.
♦**That's a sore point.** Ése es un tema delicado.

sore [sɔːʳ] NOUN

see also **sore** ADJECTIVE
la llaga

sorry ['sɔrɪ] ADJECTIVE
◆ **I'm sorry.** Lo siento. ◇ *I'm very sorry.* Lo siento mucho. ◇ *I'm sorry, I haven't got any change.* Lo siento, no tengo cambio.
◆ **I'm sorry I'm late.** Siento llegar tarde.
◆ **Sorry!** ¡Perdón!
◆ **Sorry?** ¿Cómo?
◆ **I'm sorry about the noise.** Perdón por el ruido.
◆ **You'll be sorry!** ¡Te arrepentirás!
◆ **to feel sorry for somebody** sentir* pena por alguien

sort [sɔːt] NOUN
el tipo ◇ *What sort of bike have you got?* ¿Qué tipo de bicicleta tienes?
◆ **all sorts of...** todo tipo de...

to **sort out** [sɔːt'aut] VERB
1 ordenar ◇ *Sort out all your books.* Ordena todos tus libros.
2 arreglar ◇ *They have sorted out their problems.* Han arreglado sus problemas.

so-so ['səusəu] ADVERB
así así ◇ *How are you feeling? – So-so.* ¿Cómo te encuentras? – Así así.

soul [səul] NOUN
1 el alma FEM

*Although it's a feminine noun, remember that you use **el** and **un** with **alma**.*

2 el soul ◇ *a soul singer* una cantante de soul

sound [saund] NOUN
see also **sound** VERB, ADJECTIVE
1 el ruido ◇ *Don't make a sound!* ¡No hagas ruido! ◇ *the sound of footsteps* el ruido de pasos
2 el sonido ◇ *at the speed of sound* a la velocidad del sonido
◆ **Can I turn the sound down?** ¿Puedo bajar el volumen?

to **sound** [saund] VERB
see also **sound** NOUN, ADJECTIVE
sonar* ◇ *That sounds interesting.* Eso suena interesante.
◆ **It sounds as if she's doing well at school.** Parece que le va bien en el colegio.
◆ **That sounds like a good idea.** Eso me parece buena idea.

sound [saund] ADJECTIVE, ADVERB
see also **sound** NOUN, VERB
válido ◇ *His reasoning is perfectly sound.* Su argumentación es perfectamente válida.
◆ **Julian gave me some sound advice.** Julian me dio un buen consejo.
◆ **sound asleep** profundamente dormido

soundtrack ['saundtræk] NOUN
la banda sonora

soup [suːp] NOUN
la sopa

sour ['sauəʳ] ADJECTIVE
agrio

south [sauθ] ADJECTIVE, ADVERB
see also **south** NOUN
1 del sur ◇ *a south wind* un viento del sur
◆ **the south coast** la costa meridional
2 hacia el sur ◇ *We were travelling south.* Viajábamos hacia el sur.
◆ **south of** al sur de ◇ *It's south of London.* Está al sur de Londres.

south [sauθ] NOUN
see also **south** ADJECTIVE
el sur ◇ *the South of France* el sur de Francia

South Africa [sauθ'æfrɪkə] NOUN
Sudáfrica FEM

South America [sauθə'mɛrɪkə] NOUN
Sudamérica FEM

South American [sauθə'mɛrɪkən] ADJECTIVE
see also **South American** NOUN
sudamericano

South American [sauθə'mɛrɪkən] NOUN
see also **South American** ADJECTIVE
el sudamericano
la sudamericana
◇ *South Americans* los sudamericanos

southbound ['sauθbaund] ADJECTIVE
◆ **Southbound traffic is moving very slowly.** El tráfico que se dirige hacia el sur avanza muy despacio.

southeast [sauθ'iːst] NOUN
el sudeste
◆ **southeast England** el sudeste de Inglaterra

southern ['sʌðən] ADJECTIVE
◆ **the southern hemisphere** el hemisferio sur
◆ **Southern England** el sur de Inglaterra
◆ **southern cuisine** la cocina sureña

South Pole [sauθ'pəul] NOUN
el Polo Sur

South Wales [sauθ'weɪlz] NOUN
Gales del Sur MASC

southwest [sauθ'wɛst] NOUN
el sudoeste

souvenir [suːvə'nɪəʳ] NOUN
el recuerdo ◇ *souvenir shop* la tienda de recuerdos

soya ['sɔɪə] NOUN
la soja

soy sauce [sɔɪ'sɔːs] NOUN
la salsa de soja

space [speɪs] NOUN
el espacio ◇ *There isn't enough space.* No hay espacio suficiente. ◇ *in space* en el espacio
◆ **a parking space** un sitio para aparcar

spacecraft ['speɪskrɑːft] NOUN

la nave espacial

spade [speɪd] NOUN
la pala
♦ **spades** (*at cards*) las picas ◊ *the ace of spades* el as de picas
*Be careful not to translate **spade** by **espada**.*

Spain [speɪn] NOUN
España FEM

Spaniard ['spænjəd] NOUN
(*person*)
el español
la española

spaniel ['spænjəl] NOUN
el perro de aguas

Spanish ['spænɪʃ] ADJECTIVE
see also **Spanish** NOUN
español

Spanish ['spænɪʃ] NOUN
see also **Spanish** ADJECTIVE
el español

*The official name for the Spanish language in Spain and Latin America is **el castellano** and is also the term many Spanish speakers prefer to use. Despite controversies, both **español** and **castellano** are perfectly acceptable.*

◊ *Spanish lessons* las clases de español
♦ **the Spanish** los españoles

to **spank** [spæŋk] VERB
zurrar

spanner ['spænəʳ] NOUN
la llave inglesa

spare [speəʳ] ADJECTIVE
see also **spare** VERB, NOUN
1 de repuesto ◊ *Take a few spare batteries.* Llévate unas pilas de repuesto. ◊ *spare wheel* la rueda de repuesto
2 de sobra ◊ *Have you got a spare pencil?* ¿Tienes un lápiz de sobra?
♦ **spare part** el repuesto
♦ **spare room** el cuarto de los huéspedes
♦ **spare time** el tiempo libre

to **spare** [speəʳ] VERB
see also **spare** ADJECTIVE, NOUN
♦ **Can you spare a moment?** ¿Tienes un momento?
♦ **I can't spare the time.** No tengo tiempo.
♦ **They've got no money to spare.** No les sobra el dinero.
♦ **We arrived with time to spare.** Llegamos con tiempo de sobra.

spare [speəʳ] NOUN
see also **spare** ADJECTIVE, VERB
♦ **I've lost my key. – Have you got a spare?** He perdido la llave. – ¿Tienes una de sobra?

sparkling ['spɑːklɪŋ] ADJECTIVE
con gas ◊ *a sparkling drink* una bebida con gas ◊ *sparkling water* agua con gas
♦ **sparkling wine** vino espumoso

sparrow ['spærəu] NOUN
el gorrión (PL los gorriones)

spat [spæt] VERB *see* **spit**

to **speak** [spiːk] VERB (**spoke, spoken**)
hablar
♦ **Do you speak English?** ¿Hablas inglés? ◊ *Have you spoken to him?* ¿Has hablado con él? ◊ *She spoke to him about it.* Habló de ello con él.
♦ **Could I speak to Alison? – Speaking!** ¿Podría hablar con Alison? – ¡Soy yo!

to **speak up** [spiːk'ʌp] VERB
hablar más alto ◊ *You'll need to speak up – we can't hear you.* Habla más alto que no te oímos.

speaker ['spiːkəʳ] NOUN
1 (*loudspeaker*)
el altavoz (PL los altavoces)
2 (*at conference*)
el orador
la oradora
♦ **French speakers** los hablantes de francés

special ['speʃl] ADJECTIVE
especial

specialist ['speʃəlɪst] NOUN
el/la especialista

speciality [speʃɪ'ælɪtɪ] NOUN (PL **specialities**)
la especialidad

to **specialize** ['speʃəlaɪz] VERB
especializarse* ◊ *She specialized in Russian.* Se especializó en ruso.
♦ **We specialize in skiing equipment.** Estamos especializados en material de esquí.

specially ['speʃlɪ] ADVERB
especialmente ◊ *It can be very cold here, specially in winter.* Llega a hacer mucho frío aquí, especialmente en invierno. ◊ *It's specially designed for teenagers.* Está especialmente pensado para adolescentes. ◊ *Do you like opera? – Not specially.* ¿Te gusta la ópera? – No especialmente.

species ['spiːʃiːz] NOUN
la especie

specific [spə'sɪfɪk] ADJECTIVE
1 específico ◊ *certain specific issues* ciertos temas específicos
2 concreto ◊ *Could you be more specific?* ¿Podrías ser más concreto?

specifically [spə'sɪfɪklɪ] ADVERB
1 específicamente ◊ *It's specifically designed for teenagers.* Está específicamente pensado para adolescentes.
2 concretamente ◊ *in Britain, or more specifically in England* en Gran Bretaña, o más concretamente en Inglaterra
♦ **I specifically said that...** Especifiqué claramente que...

specs, spectacles [speks, 'spektəklz] PL NOUN

S

☞

las gafas (los anteojos *LatAm*)
spectacular [spɛk'tækjulər] ADJECTIVE
espectacular
spectator [spɛk'teɪtər] NOUN
el espectador
la espectadora
speech [spiːtʃ] NOUN (PL **speeches**)
el discurso ◊ *to make a speech* dar* un discurso
speechless ['spiːtʃlɪs] ADJECTIVE
♦ **I was speechless.** Me quedé sin habla.
speed [spiːd] NOUN
la velocidad ◊ *at top speed* a toda velocidad
♦ **a three-speed bike** una bicicleta de tres marchas
to **speed up** [spiːd'ʌp] VERB
acelerar
speedboat ['spiːdbəut] NOUN
la lancha motora
speeding ['spiːdɪŋ] NOUN
el exceso de velocidad ◊ *He was fined for speeding.* Lo multaron por exceso de velocidad.
speed limit ['spiːdlɪmɪt] NOUN
el límite de velocidad
♦ **to break the speed limit** saltarse el límite de velocidad
speedometer [spɪ'dɔmɪtər] NOUN
el velocímetro
to **spell** [spɛl] VERB (**spelled** *or* **spelt, spelled** *or* **spelt**)
see also **spell** NOUN
deletrear ◊ *Can you spell that please?* ¿Me lo deletrea, por favor?
♦ **How do you spell "library"?** ¿Cómo se escribe "library"?
♦ **I can't spell.** Cometo faltas de ortografía.
spell [spɛl] NOUN
see also **spell** VERB
el hechizo ◊ *to be under somebody's spell* estar* bajo el hechizo de alguien
♦ **to cast a spell on somebody** hechizar* a alguien
spelling ['spɛlɪŋ] NOUN
la ortografía ◊ *My spelling is terrible.* Cometo muchas faltas de ortografía.
♦ **a spelling mistake** una falta de ortografía
to **spend** [spɛnd] VERB (**spent, spent**)
1 gastar ◊ *They spend enormous amounts of money on advertising.* Gastan cantidades enormes de dinero en publicidad.
2 dedicar* ◊ *He spends a lot of time and money on his hobbies.* Dedica mucho tiempo y dinero a sus aficiones.
3 pasar ◊ *He spent a month in France.* Pasó un mes en Francia.
spice [spaɪs] NOUN
la especia
spicy ['spaɪsɪ] ADJECTIVE
picante
spider ['spaɪdər] NOUN
la araña
to **spill** [spɪl] VERB (**spilled** *or* **spilt, spilled** *or* **spilt**)
♦ **You've spilled coffee on your shirt.** Se te ha caído café en la camisa.
spinach ['spɪnɪtʃ] NOUN
las espinacas
spin drier ['spɪndraɪər] NOUN
la centrifugadora
spine [spaɪn] NOUN
la columna vertebral
spinster ['spɪnstər] NOUN
la solterona
spire ['spaɪər] NOUN
la aguja
spirit ['spɪrɪt] NOUN
1 el espíritu ◊ *a youthful spirit* un espíritu joven
2 el valor ◊ *Everyone admired her spirit.* Todos admiraban su valor.
3 el brío ◊ *They played with great spirit.* Jugaron con mucho brío.
spirits ['spɪrɪts] PL NOUN
los licores ◊ *I don't drink spirits.* No bebo licores.
♦ **to be in good spirits** estar* de buen ánimo
spiritual ['spɪrɪtjuəl] ADJECTIVE
espiritual
spit [spɪt] NOUN
see also **spit** VERB
la saliva
to **spit** [spɪt] VERB (**spat, spat**)
see also **spit** NOUN
escupir
to **spit out** [spɪt'aut] VERB
escupir ◊ *I spat it out.* Lo escupí.
spite [spaɪt] NOUN
see also **spite** VERB
♦ **in spite of** a pesar de
♦ **out of spite** por despecho
to **spite** [spaɪt] VERB
see also **spite** NOUN
fastidiar ◊ *He just did it to spite me.* Lo hizo sólo para fastidiarme.
spiteful ['spaɪtful] ADJECTIVE
1 rencoroso (*person*)
2 malintencionado (*action*)
to **splash** [splæʃ] VERB
see also **splash** NOUN
salpicar* ◊ *Don't splash me!* ¡No me salpiques!
♦ **He splashed water on his face.** Se echó agua en la cara.
splash [splæʃ] NOUN (PL **splashes**)

see also **splash** VERB
el chapoteo ◊ *I heard a splash.* Oí un chapoteo.
♦**a splash of colour** una mancha de color
splendid ['splɛndɪd] ADJECTIVE
espléndido
splint [splɪnt] NOUN
la tablilla
splinter ['splɪntəʳ] NOUN
la astilla
to **split** [splɪt] VERB (**split, split**)
1 partir ◊ *He split the wood with an axe.* Partió la madera con un hacha.
2 partirse ◊ *The ship hit a rock and split in two.* El barco chocó con una roca y se partió en dos.
3 dividir ◊ *a decision that will split the party* una decisión que dividirá al partido
♦**They decided to split the profits.** Decidieron repartir los beneficios.
to **split up** [splɪt'ʌp] VERB
separarse
to **spoil** [spɔɪl] VERB (**spoiled** *or* **spoilt, spoiled** *or* **spoilt**)
1 estropear ◊ *It spoiled our holiday.* Nos estropeó las vacaciones.
2 mimar ◊ *Grandparents like to spoil their grandchildren.* A los abuelos les encanta mimar a los nietos.
spoiled [spɔɪld] ADJECTIVE
mimado ◊ *a spoiled child* un niño mimado
spoilsport ['spɔɪlspɔːt] NOUN
el/la aguafiestas (PL los/las aguafiestas)
spoke [spəuk] VERB *see* **speak**
spoke [spəuk] NOUN
el radio
spoken ['spəukn] VERB *see* **speak**
spokesman ['spəuksmən] NOUN (PL **spokesmen**)
el portavoz (PL los portavoces)
(el vocero *LatAm*)
spokeswoman ['spəukswumən] NOUN (PL **spokeswomen**)
la portavoz (PL las portavoces)
(la vocera *LatAm*)
sponge [spʌndʒ] NOUN
la esponja
♦**sponge bag** la bolsa de aseo
♦**sponge cake** el bizcocho
sponsor ['spɔnsəʳ] NOUN
see also **sponsor** VERB
el patrocinador
la patrocinadora
to **sponsor** ['spɔnsəʳ] VERB
see also **sponsor** NOUN
patrocinar ◊ *The tournament was sponsored by local firms.* El torneo fue patrocinado por empresas locales.
spontaneous [spɔn'teɪnɪəs] ADJECTIVE
espontáneo
spooky ['spuːkɪ] ADJECTIVE
♦**The house is really spooky at night.** La casa te pone los pelos de punta de noche.
spoon [spuːn] NOUN
la cuchara
spoonful ['spuːnful] NOUN
♦**a spoonful** una cucharada
sport [spɔːt] NOUN
el deporte
♦**sports bag** la bolsa de deporte
♦**sports car** el coche deportivo
♦**sports jacket** la chaqueta de sport
sportsman ['spɔːtsmən] NOUN (PL **sportsmen**)
el deportista
sportswear ['spɔːtswɛəʳ] NOUN
la ropa de deporte
sportswoman ['spɔːtswumən] NOUN (PL **sportswomen**)
la deportista
sporty ['spɔːtɪ] ADJECTIVE
deportista ◊ *I'm not very sporty.* No soy muy deportista.
spot [spɔt] NOUN
see also **spot** VERB
1 la mancha ◊ *There's a spot on your shirt.* Tienes una mancha en la camisa.
2 el lunar ◊ *a red dress with white spots* un vestido rojo con lunares blancos
3 el grano ◊ *He's covered in spots.* Está lleno de granos.
4 el sitio ◊ *It's a lovely spot for a picnic.* Es un sitio precioso para un picnic.
♦**on the spot (1)** en el acto ◊ *They gave her the job on the spot.* Le dieron el trabajo en el acto.
♦**on the spot (2)** en el mismo sitio ◊ *Luckily they were able to mend the car on the spot.* Afortunadamente consiguieron arreglar el coche en el mismo sitio.
to **spot** [spɔt] VERB
see also **spot** NOUN
notar ◊ *I spotted a mistake.* Noté un error.
spotless ['spɔtlɪs] ADJECTIVE
inmaculado
spotlight ['spɔtlaɪt] NOUN
el foco
spotty ['spɔtɪ] ADJECTIVE
con granos
spouse [spaus] NOUN
el/la cónyuge
to **sprain** [spreɪn] VERB
see also **sprain** NOUN
torcerse* ◊ *She's sprained her ankle.* Se ha torcido el tobillo.
sprain [spreɪn] NOUN
see also **sprain** VERB
la torcedura
spray [spreɪ] NOUN

S

see also **spray** VERB
(*spray can*)
el spray (PL los sprays)
to **spray** [spreɪ] VERB
see also **spray** NOUN
1 rociar* ◊ *She sprayed perfume on my hand.* Me roció perfume en la mano.
2 fumigar* ◊ *to spray against insects* fumigar contra los insectos
♦ **There was graffiti sprayed on the wall.** Había pintadas de spray en la pared.
spread [sprɛd] NOUN
see also **spread** VERB
♦ **cheese spread** el queso para untar
♦ **chocolate spread** la crema de chocolate
to **spread** [sprɛd] VERB (**spread, spread**)
see also **spread** NOUN
1 extender* ◊ *She spread a towel on the sand.* Extendió una toalla sobre la arena.
2 untar ◊ *Spread the top of the cake with whipped cream.* Unte la parte superior de la tarta con nata montada.
3 propagarse* ◊ *The news spread rapidly.* La noticia se propagó rápidamente.
to **spread out** [sprɛd'aut] VERB
1 dispersarse ◊ *The soldiers spread out across the field.* Los soldados se dispersaron por el campo.
2 desplegar* ◊ *He spread the map out on the table.* Desplegó el mapa sobre la mesa.
spreadsheet ['sprɛdʃiːt] NOUN
la hoja de cálculo
spring [sprɪŋ] NOUN
1 la primavera ◊ *in spring* en primavera
2 el muelle (*metal*)
3 el manantial (*of water*)
♦ **spring onion** la cebolleta
spring-cleaning [sprɪŋ'kliːnɪŋ] NOUN
la limpieza general
springtime ['sprɪŋtaɪm] NOUN
la primavera
sprinkler ['sprɪŋklə^r] NOUN
el aspersor
sprint [sprɪnt] NOUN
see also **sprint** VERB
la carrera de velocidad
♦ **the women's 100 metres sprint** los cien metros lisos femeninos
to **sprint** [sprɪnt] VERB
see also **sprint** NOUN
correr a toda velocidad ◊ *She sprinted for the bus.* Corrió a toda velocidad para coger el autobús.

*Be very careful with the verb **coger**: in most of Latin America this is an extremely rude word that should be avoided. However, in Spain this verb is common and not rude at all.*

sprinter ['sprɪntə^r] NOUN
el/la velocista
sprouts [sprauts] PL NOUN
♦ **Brussels sprouts** las coles de Bruselas
spy [spaɪ] NOUN (PL **spies**)
el/la espía
spying ['spaɪɪŋ] NOUN
el espionaje
to **spy on** ['spaɪɔn] VERB
espiar*
to **squabble** ['skwɔbl] VERB
reñir* ◊ *Stop squabbling!* ¡Vale ya de reñir!
square [skwɛə^r] NOUN
see also **square** ADJECTIVE
1 el cuadrado ◊ *a square and a triangle* un cuadrado y un triángulo
2 la plaza ◊ *the town square* la plaza mayor
square [skwɛə^r] ADJECTIVE
see also **square** NOUN
cuadrado ◊ *two square metres* dos metros cuadrados
♦ **It's two metres square.** Mide dos por dos.
squash [skwɔʃ] NOUN
see also **squash** VERB
el squash (*sport*)
♦ **squash court** la cancha de squash
♦ **squash racket** la raqueta de squash
♦ **orange squash** la naranjada
♦ **lemon squash** la limonada
to **squash** [skwɔʃ] VERB
see also **squash** NOUN
aplastar ◊ *You're squashing me.* Me estás aplastando.
to **squeak** [skwiːk] VERB
1 chillar (*mouse, child*)
2 chirriar* (*door, wheel*)
3 crujir (*shoes*)
to **squeeze** [skwiːz] VERB
1 exprimir ◊ *Squeeze two large lemons.* Exprima dos limones grandes.
2 apretar* ◊ *She squeezed my hand.* Me apretó la mano.
♦ **The thieves squeezed through a tiny window.** Los ladrones se colaron por una pequeña ventana.
to **squeeze in** [skwiːz'ɪn] VERB
hacer* un hueco a ◊ *I can squeeze you in at two o'clock.* Te puedo hacer un hueco a las dos.
squint [skwɪnt] NOUN
el estrabismo
♦ **He has a squint.** Es estrábico.
squirrel ['skwɪrəl] NOUN
la ardilla
to **stab** [stæb] VERB

apuñalar

stable ['steɪbl] NOUN
see also **stable** ADJECTIVE
la cuadra

stable ['steɪbl] ADJECTIVE
see also **stable** NOUN
estable ◊ *a stable relationship* una relación estable

stack [stæk] NOUN
la pila ◊ *There were stacks of books on the table.* Había pilas de libros sobre la mesa.
♦ **They've got stacks of money.** Tienen cantidad de dinero.

stadium ['steɪdɪəm] NOUN
el estadio

staff [stɑːf] NOUN
1 el personal (*in company*)
2 el profesorado (*in school*)

stage [steɪdʒ] NOUN
1 la etapa ◊ *in stages* por etapas
♦ **at this stage in the negotiations** a estas alturas de las negociaciones
2 el escenario ◊ *The band came on stage late.* El grupo salió tarde al escenario.
♦ **I always wanted to go on the stage.** Siempre quise dedicarme al teatro.

to **stagger** ['stægəʳ] VERB
tambalearse

stain [steɪn] NOUN
see also **stain** VERB
la mancha

to **stain** [steɪn] VERB
see also **stain** NOUN
manchar

stainless steel [steɪnlɪs'stiːl] NOUN
el acero inoxidable

stain remover ['steɪnrɪmuːvəʳ] NOUN
el quitamanchas (PL los quitamanchas)

stair [steəʳ] NOUN
el escalón (PL los escalones)

staircase ['steəkeɪs] NOUN
la escalera

stairs [steəz] PL NOUN
las escaleras

stale [steɪl] ADJECTIVE
♦ **stale bread** el pan duro

stalemate ['steɪlmeɪt] NOUN
el punto muerto ◊ *to reach a stalemate* llegar* a un punto muerto
♦ **The game ended in stalemate.** (*in chess*) La partida terminó en tablas.

stall [stɔːl] NOUN
el puesto ◊ *He's got a market stall.* Tiene un puesto en el mercado.
♦ **the stalls** la platea (*in theatre*)

stamina ['stæmɪnə] NOUN
la resistencia física

stammer ['stæməʳ] NOUN
el tartamudeo
♦ **He's got a stammer.** Es tartamudo.

stamp [stæmp] NOUN
see also **stamp** VERB
el sello (la estampilla *LatAm*) ◊ *My hobby is stamp collecting.* Mi afición es coleccionar sellos.
♦ **stamp album** el álbum de sellos (PL los álbumes de sellos)

to **stamp** [stæmp] VERB
see also **stamp** NOUN
sellar ◊ *The file was stamped "confidential".* El archivo iba sellado como "confidencial".
♦ **The audience stamped their feet.** El público pateaba.

stamped addressed envelope [stæmptədrest'envələup] NOUN
♦ **please enclose a stamped addressed envelope** adjunte un sobre franqueado con su nombre y dirección

to **stand** [stænd] VERB (**stood, stood**)
1 estar* de pie ◊ *He was standing by the door.* Estaba de pie junto a la puerta.
♦ **What are you standing there for?** ¿Qué haces ahí de pie?
♦ **They all stood when I came in.** Se pusieron de pie cuando entré.
2 soportar ◊ *I can't stand all this noise.* No soporto todo este ruido.

to **stand for** ['stændfɔːʳ] VERB
1 significar* ◊ *"EU" stands for "European Union".* "EU" significa "European Union".
2 consentir* ◊ *I won't stand for it any more!* ¡No pienso consentirlo más!

to **stand in for** [stænd'ɪnfɔːʳ] VERB
sustituir*

to **stand out** [stænd'aut] VERB
destacar*

to **stand up** [stænd'ʌp] VERB
1 ponerse* de pie ◊ *I stood up and walked out.* Me puse de pie y me fui.
2 estar* de pie ◊ *She has to stand up all day.* Tiene que estar todo el día de pie.

to **stand up for** [stænd'ʌpfɔːʳ] VERB
defender* ◊ *Stand up for your rights!* ¡Defiende tus derechos!

standard ['stændəd] ADJECTIVE
see also **standard** NOUN
normal ◊ *the standard procedure* el procedimiento normal
♦ **standard equipment** el equipamiento de serie

standard ['stændəd] NOUN
see also **standard** ADJECTIVE
el nivel ◊ *The standard is very high.* El nivel es muy alto.
♦ **She's got high standards.** Es muy exigente.
♦ **standard of living** el nivel de vida

stand-by ticket ['stændbaɪ'tɪkɪt] NOUN
el billete en lista de espera

standpoint ['stændpɔɪnt] NOUN
el punto de vista

stands [stændz] PL NOUN
la tribuna SING

stank [stæŋk] VERB *see* **stink**

staple ['steɪpl] NOUN
see also **staple** ADJECTIVE
la grapa

staple ['steɪpl] ADJECTIVE
see also **staple** NOUN
básico ◇ *their staple food* su alimento básico

stapler ['steɪpləʳ] NOUN
la grapadora

star [stɑːʳ] NOUN
see also **star** VERB
la estrella ◇ *a TV star* una estrella de televisión
♦ **the stars** el horóscopo

to **star** [stɑːʳ] VERB
see also **star** NOUN
♦ **to star in a film** protagonizar* una película
♦ **The film stars Sharon Stone.** La protagonista de la película es Sharon Stone.
♦ **...starring Johnny Depp** ...con Johnny Depp

to **stare** [stɛəʳ] VERB
mirar fijamente ◇ *Andy stared at him.* Andy lo miraba fijamente.

stark [stɑːk] ADVERB
♦ **stark naked** en cueros

start [stɑːt] NOUN
see also **start** VERB
1 el principio ◇ *at the start of the film* al principio de la película ◇ *from the start* desde el principio
♦ **for a start** para empezar
♦ **Shall we make a start on the washing-up?** ¿Nos ponemos a fregar los platos?
2 la salida (*of race*)

to **start** [stɑːt] VERB
see also **start** NOUN
1 empezar* ◇ *What time does it start?* ¿A qué hora empieza?
♦ **to start doing something** empezar a hacer algo ◇ *I started learning Spanish two years ago.* Empecé a aprender español hace dos años.
2 montar (*business, organization, campaign*) ◇ *He wants to start his own business.* Quiere montar su propio negocio.
3 arrancar* ◇ *He couldn't start the car.* No conseguía arrancar el coche. ◇ *The car wouldn't start.* El coche no arrancaba.

to **start off** [stɑːt'ɔf] VERB
ponerse* en camino ◇ *We started off first thing in the morning.* Nos pusimos en camino pronto por la mañana.

starter ['stɑːtəʳ] NOUN
el primer plato (*first course*)

to **starve** [stɑːv] VERB
morirse* de hambre ◇ *People are starving.* La gente se muere de hambre.
♦ **I'm starving!** ¡Me muero de hambre!

state [steɪt] NOUN
see also **state** VERB
el estado ◇ *It's an independent state.* Es un estado independiente. ◇ *She was in a state of depression.* Se encontraba en un estado de depresión.
♦ **He wasn't in a fit state to drive.** No estaba en condiciones de conducir.
♦ **Tim was in a real state.** Tim estaba de los nervios.
♦ **the States** Estados Unidos MASC

to **state** [steɪt] VERB
see also **state** NOUN
declarar ◇ *He stated his intention to resign.* Declaró que tenía intención de dimitir.
♦ **Please state your name and address.** Por favor indique su nombre y dirección.

stately home [steɪtlɪ'həum] NOUN
la casa señorial

statement ['steɪtmənt] NOUN
1 la declaración (PL las declaraciones) ◇ *statements by witnesses* las declaraciones de testigos
2 la afirmación (PL las afirmaciones) ◇ *Andrew now disowns the statement he made.* Ahora Andrew desmiente la afirmación que hizo.
♦ **a bank statement** un extracto de cuenta

station ['steɪʃən] NOUN
la estación (PL las estaciones)
♦ **bus station** la estación de autobuses
♦ **police station** la comisaría
♦ **radio station** la emisora de radio

stationer's ['steɪʃənəz] NOUN
la papelería

station wagon ['steɪʃənwægən] NOUN US
la ranchera

statue ['stætjuː] NOUN
la estatua

stay [steɪ] NOUN
see also **stay** VERB
la estancia ◇ *my stay in Spain* mi estancia en España

to **stay** [steɪ] VERB
see also **stay** NOUN
quedarse ◇ *Stay here!* ¡Quédate aquí! ◇ *I'm going to be staying with friends.* Me voy a quedar en casa de unos amigos.
♦ **Where are you staying? In a hotel?** ¿Dónde estás? ¿En un hotel?

* Verbs marked with this symbol are irregular. See pages 380-382 for further details

◆**to stay the night** pasar la noche
◆**We stayed in Belgium for a few days.** Pasamos unos días en Bélgica.

to **stay in** [steɪ'ɪn] VERB
quedarse en casa

to **stay up** [steɪ'ʌp] VERB
quedarse levantado ◊ *We stayed up till midnight.* Nos quedamos levantados hasta las doce.

steady ['stɛdɪ] ADJECTIVE
1 fijo ◊ *a steady job* un trabajo fijo
◆**a steady boyfriend** un novio formal
2 firme ◊ *a steady hand* un pulso firme
3 constante ◊ *a steady pace* un ritmo constante
◆**Steady on!** ¡Calma!

steak [steɪk] NOUN
el filete

to **steal** [sti:l] VERB **(stole, stolen)**
robar

steam [sti:m] NOUN
el vapor ◊ *a steam engine* una máquina de vapor

steel [sti:l] NOUN
el acero

steep [sti:p] ADJECTIVE
empinado

steeple ['sti:pl] NOUN
la aguja

steering wheel ['stɪərɪŋwi:l] NOUN
el volante

step [stɛp] NOUN
see also **step** VERB
1 el paso ◊ *He took a step forward.* Dio un paso adelante.
2 el peldaño ◊ *She tripped over the step.* Tropezó con el peldaño.

to **step** [stɛp] VERB
see also **step** NOUN
dar* un paso ◊ *I tried to step forward.* Traté de dar un paso adelante.
◆**Step this way, please.** Pase por aquí, por favor.

to **step aside** [stɛpə'saɪd] VERB
hacerse* a un lado

to **step back** [stɛp'bæk] VERB
retroceder

stepbrother ['stɛpbrʌðəʳ] NOUN
el hermanastro

stepdaughter ['stɛpdɔ:təʳ] NOUN
la hermanastra

stepfather ['stɛpfɑ:ðəʳ] NOUN
el padrastro

stepladder ['stɛplædəʳ] NOUN
la escalera de tijera

stepmother ['stɛpmʌðəʳ] NOUN
la madrastra

stepsister ['stɛpsɪstəʳ] NOUN
la hijastra

stepson ['stɛpsʌn] NOUN
el hijastro

stereo ['stɛrɪəu] NOUN (PL **stereos**)
el equipo de música

sterling ['stə:lɪŋ] ADJECTIVE
◆**pound sterling** la libra esterlina
◆**one hundred pounds sterling** cien libras esterlinas

stew [stju:] NOUN
el estofado (el guisado *LatAm*)

steward ['stju:əd] NOUN
1 el auxiliar de vuelo (*on plane*)
2 el camarero (*on ship*)

stewardess ['stjuədɛs] NOUN (PL **stewardesses**)
1 la auxiliar de vuelo (*on plane*)
2 la camarera (*on ship*)

stick [stɪk] NOUN
see also **stick** VERB
el palo
◆**a walking stick** un bastón (PL unos bastones)

to **stick** [stɪk] VERB **(stuck, stuck)**
see also **stick** NOUN
1 pegar* ◊ *Stick the stamps on the envelope.* Pegue los sellos en el sobre.
2 pegarse* ◊ *The rice stuck to the pan.* El arroz se pegó a la olla.
3 meter ◊ *He picked up the papers and stuck them in his briefcase.* Recogió los papeles y los metió en el maletín.
◆**I can't stick it any longer.** Ya no lo aguanto más.

to **stick out** [stɪk'aut] VERB
sacar* ◊ *The little girl stuck out her tongue.* La niña sacó la lengua.

sticker ['stɪkəʳ] NOUN
la pegatina

sticky ['stɪkɪ] ADJECTIVE
1 pegajoso ◊ *to have sticky hands* tener* las manos pegajosas
2 adhesivo ◊ *a sticky label* una etiqueta adhesiva

stiff [stɪf] ADJECTIVE, ADVERB
rígido
◆**to have a stiff neck** tener* tortícolis
◆**to feel stiff** estar* agarrotado
◆**to be bored stiff** estar* aburrido como una ostra
◆**to be frozen stiff** estar* tieso de frío
◆**to be scared stiff** estar* muerto de miedo

still [stɪl] ADVERB
see also **still** ADJECTIVE
1 todavía ◊ *I still haven't finished.* No he terminado todavía. ◊ *Are you still in bed?* ¿Todavía estás en la cama?
◆**Do you still live in Glasgow?** ¿Sigues viviendo en Glasgow?
◆**better still** mejor aún
2 aun así (*even so*) ◊ *She knows I don't like it, but she still does it.* Sabe que no me gusta, pero aun así lo hace.
3 en fin (*after all*) ◊ *Still, it's the thought that counts.* En fin, la intención es lo que cuenta.

still [stɪl] ADJECTIVE
see also **still** ADVERB
quieto ◊ *He stood still.* Se quedó quieto.
◆ **Keep still!** ¡No te muevas!
sting [stɪŋ] NOUN
see also **sting** VERB
la picadura ◊ *a bee sting* una picadura de abeja
to **sting** [stɪŋ] VERB **(stung, stung)**
see also **sting** NOUN
picar*
stingy ['stɪndʒɪ] ADJECTIVE
tacaño
to **stink** [stɪŋk] VERB **(stank, stunk)**
see also **stink** NOUN
apestar ◊ *You stink of garlic!* ¡Apestas al ajo!
stink [stɪŋk] NOUN
see also **stink** VERB
el tufo ◊ *the stink of beer* el tufo a cerveza
to **stir** [stəːʳ] VERB
agitar
to **stitch** [stɪtʃ] VERB
see also **stitch** NOUN
coser
stitch [stɪtʃ] NOUN (PL **stitches**)
see also **stitch** VERB
1 la puntada (*in sewing*)
2 el punto (*in knitting, in wound*) ◊ *I had five stitches.* Me pusieron cinco puntos.
stock [stɔk] NOUN
see also **stock** VERB
1 la reserva ◊ *stocks of ammunition* reservas de munición
2 las existencias ◊ *the shop's stock* las existencias de la tienda
◆ **Yes, we've got your size in stock.** Sí, nos quedan existencias de su número.
◆ **out of stock** agotado ◊ *I'm sorry, they're both out of stock.* Lo siento, están los dos agotados.
3 el caldo ◊ *chicken stock* caldo de pollo
to **stock** [stɔk] VERB
see also **stock** NOUN
vender ◊ *Do you stock camping stoves?* ¿Venden infiernillos?
to **stock up** [stɔk'ʌp] VERB
abastecerse* ◊ *to stock up with something* abastecerse de algo
stock cube ['stɔkkjuːb] NOUN
la pastilla de caldo
stocking ['stɔkɪŋ] NOUN
la media
stole [stəul] VERB *see* **steal**
stolen ['stəuln] VERB *see* **steal**
stomach ['stʌmək] NOUN
el estómago
stomach ache ['stʌməkeɪk] NOUN
el dolor de estómago
◆ **I have a stomach ache.** Me duele el estómago.
stone [stəun] NOUN
1 la piedra ◊ *a stone wall* un muro de piedra
2 el hueso ◊ *an apricot stone* un hueso de albaricoque

> *In Spain measurements are in grams and kilograms. One stone is about 6.3 kg.*

◆ **I weigh eight stone.** Peso unos cincuenta kilos.
stood [stud] VERB *see* **stand**
stool [stuːl] NOUN
el taburete
to **stop** [stɔp] VERB
see also **stop** NOUN
1 parar ◊ *The bus doesn't stop there.* El autobús no para allí.
2 pararse ◊ *The music stopped.* Se paró la música.
◆ **This has got to stop!** ¡Esto se tiene que acabar!
◆ **I think the rain's going to stop.** Creo que va a dejar de llover.
◆ **to stop doing something** dejar de hacer algo ◊ *to stop smoking* dejar de fumar
3 acabar con ◊ *a campaign to stop whaling* una campaña para acabar con la caza de ballenas
◆ **to stop somebody doing something** impedir* que alguien haga algo
***impedir que** has to be followed by a verb in the subjunctive.*
◊ *She would have liked to stop us seeing each other.* Le hubiera gustado impedir que nos siguiéramos viendo.
◆ **Stop!** ¡Alto!
stop [stɔp] NOUN
see also **stop** VERB
la parada ◊ *a bus stop* una parada de autobús
◆ **This is my stop.** Yo me bajo aquí.
stopwatch ['stɔpwɔtʃ] NOUN (PL **stopwatches**)
el cronómetro
store [stɔːʳ] NOUN
see also **store** VERB
1 la tienda ◊ *a furniture store* una tienda de muebles
2 el almacén (PL los almacenes) ◊ *a grain store* un almacén de grano
to **store** [stɔːʳ] VERB
see also **store** NOUN
1 guardar ◊ *They store potatoes in the cellar.* Guardan patatas en el sótano.
2 almacenar ◊ *to store information* almacenar información

storey ['stɔːrɪ] NOUN
la planta ◊ *a three-storey building* un edificio de tres plantas

storm [stɔːm] NOUN
la tormenta

stormy ['stɔːmɪ] ADJECTIVE
tormentoso

story ['stɔːrɪ] NOUN (PL **stories**)
1 el cuento (*tale*)
2 la historia (*account*)

stove [stəuv] NOUN
1 la cocina (*in kitchen*)
2 el infiernillo (*camping stove*)

straight [streɪt] ADJECTIVE, ADVERB
1 recto ◊ *a straight line* una línea recta
2 liso ◊ *straight hair* pelo liso
3 heterosexual (*not gay*)
♦ **He looked straight at me.** Me miró directamente a los ojos.
♦ **straight away** enseguida
♦ **I'll come straight back.** Vuelvo enseguida.
♦ **Keep straight on.** Siga todo recto.

straightforward [streɪt'fɔːwəd] ADJECTIVE
1 sencillo ◊ *It's very straightforward.* Es muy sencillo.
2 sincero ◊ *She's very straightforward.* Es muy sincera.

strain [streɪn] NOUN
see also **strain** VERB
la tensión (PL las tensiones)
♦ **It was a strain.** Fue muy estresante.

to **strain** [streɪn] VERB
see also **strain** NOUN
♦ **to strain one's eyes** forzar* la vista
♦ **I strained my back.** Me dio un tirón en la espalda.
♦ **to strain a muscle** sufrir un tirón muscular

strained [streɪnd] ADJECTIVE
♦ **a strained muscle** una distensión muscular

stranded ['strændɪd] ADJECTIVE
♦ **We were stranded on the motorway.** Nos quedamos tirados en la autopista.

strange [streɪndʒ] ADJECTIVE
raro ◊ *That's strange!* ¡Qué raro!
***es raro que** has to be followed by a verb in the subjunctive.*
◊ *It's strange that she doesn't talk to us anymore.* Es raro que ya no nos hable.

stranger ['streɪndʒəʳ] NOUN
el desconocido
la desconocida
*No confundir **stranger** con **extranjero**, que a su vez se traduce como **foreigner**.*
◊ *Don't talk to strangers.* No hables con desconocidos.
♦ **I'm a stranger here.** Yo no soy de aquí.

to **strangle** ['stræŋgl] VERB
estrangular

strap [stræp] NOUN
1 el tirante (*of bra, dress*)
2 la correa (*of watch, camera, suitcase*)
3 el asa FEM (*of bag*)
*Although it's a feminine noun, remember that you use **el** and **un** with **asa**.*

straw [strɔː] NOUN
1 la paja ◊ *a straw hat* un sombrero de paja
2 la pajita ◊ *He was drinking his lemonade through a straw.* Se bebía la gaseosa con pajita.
♦ **That's the last straw!** ¡Eso es la gota que colma el vaso!

strawberry ['strɔːbərɪ] NOUN (PL **strawberries**)
la fresa (la frutilla *LatAm*)

stray [streɪ] ADJECTIVE
extraviado ◊ *a stray cat* un gato extraviado

stream [striːm] NOUN
el riachuelo

street [striːt] NOUN
la calle

streetcar ['striːtkɑːʳ] NOUN US
el tranvía
*Although **tranvía** ends in **-a**, it is actually a masculine noun.*

streetlamp ['striːtlæmp] NOUN
la farola

street plan ['striːtplæn] NOUN
el plano de la ciudad

streetwise ['striːtwaɪz] ADJECTIVE
♦ **to be streetwise** sabérselas* todas
♦ **a streetwise kid** un pillo

strength [strɛŋθ] NOUN
la fuerza ◊ *with all his strength* con todas sus fuerzas

to **stress** [strɛs] VERB
see also **stress** NOUN
recalcar* ◊ *I would like to stress that...* Me gustaría recalcar que...

stress [strɛs] NOUN
see also **stress** VERB
el estrés ◊ *She's under a lot of stress.* Está pasando mucho estrés.

to **stretch** [strɛtʃ] VERB
1 estirarse ◊ *The dog woke up and stretched.* El perro se despertó y se estiró.
♦ **I went out to stretch my legs.** Salí a estirar las piernas.
♦ **My jumper stretched after I washed it.** Se me dio de sí el jersey al lavarlo.
2 tender* ◊ *They stretched a rope between two trees.* Tendieron una cuerda entre dos árboles.

to **stretch out** [strɛtʃ'aut] VERB
tumbarse ◊ *They stretched out on the beach.* Se tumbaron en la playa.
♦ **to stretch out one's arms** extender* los brazos

stretcher ['strɛtʃəʳ] NOUN
la camilla
stretchy ['strɛtʃɪ] ADJECTIVE
elástico
strict [strɪkt] ADJECTIVE
estricto
strike [straɪk] NOUN
see also **strike** VERB
la huelga
♦ **to be on strike** estar* en huelga
♦ **to go on strike** hacer* huelga
to **strike** [straɪk] VERB (**struck, struck**)
see also **strike** NOUN
golpear ◇ *She struck him across the mouth.* Le golpeó en la boca.
♦ **The clock struck three.** El reloj dio las tres.
♦ **to strike a match** encender* una cerilla
striker ['straɪkəʳ] NOUN
1 (*person on strike*)
el/la huelguista
2 (*footballer*)
el delantero
la delantera
striking ['straɪkɪŋ] ADJECTIVE
1 asombroso ◇ *a striking resemblance* un parecido asombroso
2 en huelga ◇ *striking miners* mineros en huelga
string [strɪŋ] NOUN
la cuerda
♦ **a piece of string** una cuerda
to **strip** [strɪp] VERB
see also **strip** NOUN
desnudarse
strip [strɪp] NOUN
see also **strip** VERB
la tira
♦ **strip cartoon** la tira cómica (la historieta *LatAm*)
stripe [straɪp] NOUN
la franja
striped [straɪpt] ADJECTIVE
a rayas
♦ **a striped skirt** una falda de rayas
stripper ['strɪpəʳ] NOUN
el/la artista de striptease
stripy ['straɪpɪ] ADJECTIVE
de rayas
to **stroke** [strəuk] VERB
see also **stroke** NOUN
acariciar
stroke [strəuk] NOUN
see also **stroke** VERB
el derrame cerebral ◇ *to have a stroke* sufrir un derrame cerebral
♦ **a stroke of luck** un golpe de suerte
stroll [strəul] NOUN
♦ **to go for a stroll** ir* a dar un paseo
stroller ['strəuləʳ] NOUN US
la silla de paseo
strong [strɔŋ] ADJECTIVE
fuerte
strongly ['strɔŋlɪ] ADVERB
♦ **We strongly advise you to...** Te aconsejamos encarecidamente que...
♦ **He smelt strongly of tobacco.** Olía mucho a tabaco.
♦ **strongly built** corpulento
♦ **I don't feel strongly about it.** Me da un poco igual.
struck [strʌk] VERB *see* **strike**
to **struggle** ['strʌgl] VERB
see also **struggle** NOUN
forcejear ◇ *He struggled, but he couldn't escape.* Forcejeó, pero no pudo escapar.
♦ **to struggle to do something (1)** (*fight*) luchar por hacer algo ◇ *He struggled to get custody of his daughter.* Luchó por conseguir la custodia de su hija.
♦ **to struggle to do something (2)** (*have difficulty*) pasar apuros para hacer algo ◇ *They struggle to pay their bills.* Pasan apuros para pagar las facturas.
struggle ['strʌgl] NOUN
see also **struggle** VERB
la lucha ◇ *a struggle for survival* una lucha por la supervivencia
♦ **It was a struggle.** Nos costó mucho.
stub [stʌb] NOUN
la colilla
stubborn ['stʌbən] ADJECTIVE
terco
to **stub out** [stʌb'aut] VERB
apagar*
stuck [stʌk] VERB *see* **stick**
stuck [stʌk] ADJECTIVE
atascado ◇ *This lid is stuck.* La tapadera está atascada.
♦ **to get stuck** quedarse atascado
♦ **We got stuck in a traffic jam.** Nos metimos en un atasco.
stuck-up [stʌk'ʌp] ADJECTIVE
creído (*informal*)
stud [stʌd] NOUN
1 el pendiente (*earring*)
2 el taco (*on football boots*)
student ['stju:dənt] NOUN
el/la estudiante
studio ['stju:dɪəu] NOUN
el estudio ◇ *a TV studio* un estudio de televisión
♦ **a studio flat** un estudio
to **study** ['stʌdɪ] VERB (**studied, studied**)
estudiar
stuff [stʌf] NOUN
las cosas ◇ *Have you got all your stuff?* ¿Tienes todas tus cosas? ◇ *There's some stuff on the table for you.* En la mesa hay unas cosas para ti.

◆ **I need some stuff for hay fever.** Me hace falta algo para la alergia al polen.

stuffy ['stʌfi] ADJECTIVE
◆ **a stuffy room** una habitación mal ventilada
◆ **It's stuffy in here.** Hay un ambiente muy cargado aquí.

to **stumble** ['stʌmbl] VERB
tropezar*

stung [stʌŋ] VERB *see* **sting**

stunk [stʌŋk] VERB *see* **stink**

stunned [stʌnd] ADJECTIVE
pasmado ◊ *I was stunned.* Me quedé pasmado.

stunning ['stʌnɪŋ] ADJECTIVE
pasmoso

stunt [stʌnt] NOUN
◆ **It's a publicity stunt.** Es un truco publicitario.

stuntman ['stʌntmæn] NOUN (PL **stuntmen**)
el especialista

stupid ['stju:pɪd] ADJECTIVE
estúpido

to **stutter** ['stʌtəʳ] VERB
see also **stutter** NOUN
tartamudear

stutter ['stʌtəʳ] NOUN
see also **stutter** VERB
el tartamudeo
◆ **He's got a stutter.** Es tartamudo.

style [staɪl] NOUN
el estilo ◊ *That's not his style.* No es su estilo.

subject ['sʌbdʒɪkt] NOUN
1 el tema

*Although **tema** ends in **-a**, it is actually a masculine noun.*

◊ *The subject of my project is the internet.* El tema de mi trabajo es Internet.
2 la asignatura ◊ *What's your favourite subject?* ¿Cuál es tu asignatura preferida?
3 el sujeto ◊ *"I" is the subject in "I love you".* "I" es el sujeto en "I love you".

submarine [sʌbmə'ri:n] NOUN
el submarino

subscription [səb'skrɪpʃən] NOUN
(*to paper, magazine*)
la suscripción (PL las suscripciones)
◆ **to take out a subscription to** suscribirse* a

subsequently ['sʌbsɪkwəntlɪ] ADVERB
posteriormente

to **subsidize** ['sʌbsɪdaɪz] VERB
subvencionar

subsidy ['sʌbsɪdɪ] NOUN (PL **subsidies**)
la subvención (PL las subvenciones)

substance ['sʌbstəns] NOUN
la sustancia

substitute ['sʌbstɪtju:t] NOUN
see also **substitute** VERB
1 (*replacement*)
el sustituto
la sustituta
2 (*in football, rugby*)
el/la suplente

to **substitute** ['sʌbstɪtju:t] VERB
see also **substitute** NOUN
sustituir* ◊ *to substitute A for B* sustituir a B por A

subtitled ['sʌbtaɪtld] ADJECTIVE
subtitulado

subtitles ['sʌbtaɪtlz] PL NOUN
los subtítulos ◊ *a Spanish film with English subtitles* una película española con subtítulos en inglés

subtle ['sʌtl] ADJECTIVE
sutil

to **subtract** [səb'trækt] VERB
restar ◊ *to subtract 3 from 5* restar 3 a 5

suburb ['sʌbə:b] NOUN
el barrio residencial ◊ *a London suburb* un barrio residencial de Londres
◆ **They live in the suburbs.** Viven en las afueras.

suburban [sə'bə:bən] ADJECTIVE
◆ **a suburban train** un tren de cercanías
◆ **a suburban shopping centre** un centro comercial de las afueras

subway ['sʌbweɪ] NOUN
1 el metro (*underground*)
2 el paso subterráneo (*underpass*)

to **succeed** [sək'si:d] VERB
1 tener* éxito ◊ *to succeed in business* tener éxito en los negocios
2 salir* bien ◊ *The plan did not succeed.* El plan no salió bien.
◆ **to succeed in doing something** lograr hacer algo

success [sək'ses] NOUN (PL **successes**)
el éxito

*Be careful not to translate **success** by **suceso**.*

successful [sək'sesful] ADJECTIVE
de éxito (exitoso LatAm) ◊ *a successful lawyer* un abogado de éxito
◆ **a successful attempt** un intento fructífero
◆ **to be successful** tener* éxito
◆ **to be successful in doing something** lograr hacer algo

successfully [sək'sesfəlɪ] ADVERB
con éxito

successive [sək'sesɪv] ADJECTIVE
consecutivo ◊ *He was the winner for a second successive year.* Fue el ganador por segundo año consecutivo.

such [sʌtʃ] ADJECTIVE, ADVERB
1 tan ◊ *such clever people* gente tan lista ◊ *such a long journey* un viaje tan largo
2 tal ◊ *I wouldn't dream of doing such a thing.* No se me ocurriría hacer tal cosa.

S

☞

◊ *The pain was such that...* El dolor era tal que...
◆**such a lot** tanto ◊ *such a lot of work* tanto trabajo ◊ *such a long time ago* hace tanto tiempo
◆**such as** como ◊ *a hot country, such as India...* un país caluroso, como la India...
◆**as such** propiamente dicho ◊ *She's not an expert as such, but...* No es una experta propiamente dicha, pero...
◆**There's no such thing.** Eso no existe. ◊ *There's no such thing as the yeti.* El yeti no existe.

such-and-such ['sʌtʃənsʌtʃ] ADJECTIVE
tal ◊ *such-and-such a place* tal lugar

to **suck** [sʌk] VERB
chupar
◆**to suck one's thumb** chuparse el pulgar

sudden ['sʌdn] ADJECTIVE
repentino ◊ *a sudden change* un cambio repentino
◆**all of a sudden** de repente

suddenly ['sʌdnlɪ] ADVERB
de repente

suede [sweɪd] NOUN
el ante (la gamuza *LatAm*) ◊ *a suede jacket* una chaqueta de ante

to **suffer** ['sʌfəʳ] VERB
sufrir ◊ *She was really suffering.* Sufría de verdad.
◆**to suffer from something** padecer* de algo ◊ *I suffer from hay fever.* Padezco de alergia al polen.

to **suffocate** ['sʌfəkeɪt] VERB
ahogarse*

sugar ['ʃʊgəʳ] NOUN
el azúcar

to **suggest** [sə'dʒest] VERB
1 sugerir*
*Use the subjunctive after **sugerir que**.*
◊ *She suggested going out for a pizza.* Sugirió que saliéramos a tomar una pizza.
2 aconsejar
*Use the subjunctive after **aconsejar que**.*
◊ *I suggested they set off early.* Yo les aconsejé que salieran pronto.
◆**What are you trying to suggest?** ¿Qué insinúas?

suggestion [sə'dʒestʃən] NOUN
la sugerencia ◊ *to make a suggestion* hacer* una sugerencia

suicide ['suɪsaɪd] NOUN
el suicidio
◆**to commit suicide** suicidarse

suit [su:t] NOUN
see also **suit** VERB
1 el traje (*man's*)
2 el traje de chaqueta (*woman's*)

to **suit** [su:t] VERB
see also **suit** NOUN
1 venir* bien a ◊ *What time would suit you?* ¿Qué hora te vendría bien?
◆**That suits me fine.** Eso me viene estupendamente.
2 sentar* bien a ◊ *That dress really suits you.* Ese vestido te sienta la mar de bien.
◆**Suit yourself!** ¡Haz lo que te parezca!

suitable ['su:təbl] ADJECTIVE
1 conveniente ◊ *a suitable time* una hora conveniente
2 apropiado ◊ *suitable clothing* ropa apropiada

suitcase ['su:tkeɪs] NOUN
la maleta (la valija *LatAm*)

suite [swi:t] NOUN
la suite ◊ *a suite at the Paris Hilton* una suite en el Hilton de París
◆**a bedroom suite** un dormitorio completo
◆**three-piece suite** un tresillo

to **sulk** [sʌlk] VERB
estar* de mal humor

sulky ['sʌlkɪ] ADJECTIVE
malhumorado

sultana [sʌl'tɑ:nə] NOUN
la pasa de Esmirna

sum [sʌm] NOUN
la suma ◊ *to do sums* hacer* sumas ◊ *a sum of money* una suma de dinero

to **summarize** ['sʌməraɪz] VERB
resumir

summary ['sʌmərɪ] NOUN (PL **summaries**)
el resumen (PL los resúmenes)

summer ['sʌməʳ] NOUN
el verano ◊ *summer clothes* ropa de verano ◊ *the summer holidays* las vacaciones de verano ◊ *a summer camp* un campamento de verano

summertime ['sʌmətaɪm] NOUN
el verano

summit ['sʌmɪt] NOUN
la cumbre ◊ *the NATO summit* la cumbre de la OTAN ◊ *the summit of Mount Everest* la cumbre del Everest

to **sum up** [sʌm'ʌp] VERB
resumir
◆**To sum up...** Resumiendo...

sun [sʌn] NOUN
el sol ◊ *in the sun* al sol

to **sunbathe** ['sʌnbeɪð] VERB
tomar el sol

sunblock ['sʌnblɔk] NOUN
la crema solar de protección total

sunburn ['sʌnbə:n] NOUN
la quemadura

sunburnt ['sʌnbə:nt] ADJECTIVE
quemado por el sol
◆**Mind you don't get sunburnt!** ¡Cuidado de quemarte con el sol!

Sunday ['sʌndɪ] NOUN

el domingo (PL los domingos) ◇ *I saw her on Sunday.* La vi el domingo. ◇ *every Sunday* todos los domingos ◇ *last Sunday* el domingo pasado ◇ *next Sunday* el domingo que viene ◇ *on Sundays* los domingos

Sunday school ['sʌndɪsku:l] NOUN
la catequesis

*The Spanish equivalent of **Sunday school** takes place during the week after school rather than on a Sunday.*

sunflower ['sʌnflauəʳ] NOUN
el girasol

sung [sʌŋ] VERB *see* **sing**

sunglasses ['sʌnglɑ:sɪz] PL NOUN
las gafas de sol

sunk [sʌŋk] VERB *see* **sink**

sunlight ['sʌnlaɪt] NOUN
la luz del sol

sunny ['sʌnɪ] ADJECTIVE
soleado ◇ *a sunny morning* una mañana soleada
♦ **It's sunny.** Hace sol.
♦ **a sunny day** un día de sol

sunrise ['sʌnraɪz] NOUN
la salida del sol

sunroof ['sʌnru:f] NOUN
el techo corredizo

sunscreen ['sʌnskri:n] NOUN
el protector solar

sunset ['sʌnset] NOUN
la puesta de sol

sunshine ['sʌnʃaɪn] NOUN
el sol ◇ *in the sunshine* al sol

sunstroke ['sʌnstrəuk] NOUN
la insolación (PL las insolaciones)

suntan ['sʌntæn] NOUN
el bronceado
♦ **to get a suntan** broncearse
♦ **suntan lotion** la crema bronceadora
♦ **suntan oil** el aceite bronceador

super ['su:pəʳ] ADJECTIVE
estupendo

superb [su:'pə:b] ADJECTIVE
magnífico

supermarket ['su:pəmɑ:kɪt] NOUN
el supermercado

supernatural [su:pə'nætʃərəl] ADJECTIVE
sobrenatural

superstitious [su:pə'stɪʃəs] ADJECTIVE
supersticioso

to **supervise** ['su:pəvaɪz] VERB
supervisar

supervisor ['su:pəvaɪzəʳ] NOUN
el supervisor
la supervisora

supper ['sʌpəʳ] NOUN
la cena

supplement ['sʌplɪmənt] NOUN
el suplemento

supplies [sə'plaɪz] PL NOUN
las provisiones
♦ **medical supplies** material médico

to **supply** [sə'plaɪ] VERB (**supplied, supplied**)
see also **supply** NOUN
suministrar
♦ **to supply somebody with something** suministrar algo a alguien ◇ *The centre supplied us with all the equipment.* El centro nos suministró todo el material.

supply [sə'plaɪ] NOUN (PL **supplies**)
see also **supply** VERB
el suministro ◇ *the water supply* el suministro de agua
♦ **a supply of paper** una remesa de papel

supply teacher [sə'plaɪti:tʃəʳ] NOUN
el profesor interino
la profesora interina

to **support** [sə'pɔ:t] VERB
see also **support** NOUN
1 apoyar ◇ *My mum has always supported me.* Mi madre siempre me ha apoyado.
2 mantener* ◇ *She had to support five children on her own.* Tenía que mantener a cinco niños ella sola.
♦ **What team do you support?** ¿De qué equipo eres?

*Be careful not to translate **to support** by **soportar**.*

support [sə'pɔ:t] NOUN
see also **support** VERB
el apoyo

supporter [sə'pɔ:təʳ] NOUN
1 el/la hincha ◇ *a Liverpool supporter* un hincha del Liverpool
2 el partidario
la partidaria
◇ *a supporter of the Labour Party* un partidario del partido laborista

to **suppose** [sə'pəuz] VERB
suponer* ◇ *I suppose he'll be late.* Supongo que llegará tarde. ◇ *Suppose you win the lottery...* Supón que te toca la lotería...
♦ **I suppose so.** Supongo que sí.
♦ **You're supposed to show your passport.** Tienes que enseñar el pasaporte.
♦ **You're not supposed to smoke in the toilet.** No está permitido fumar en el servicio.
♦ **It's supposed to be the best hotel in the city.** Dicen que es el mejor hotel de la ciudad.

supposing [sə'pəuzɪŋ] CONJUNCTION
♦ **Supposing you won the lottery...** Suponiendo que te tocara la lotería...

***suponiendo que** has to be followed by a verb in the subjunctive.*

surcharge ['sə:tʃɑ:dʒ] NOUN
el recargo

sure [ʃuəʳ] ADJECTIVE

seguro ◊ *Are you sure?* ¿Estás seguro?
♦**Sure!** ¡Claro!
♦**to make sure that...** asegurarse de que... ◊ *I'm going to make sure the door's locked.* Voy a asegurarme de que la puerta está cerrada con llave.

surely ['ʃuəlɪ] ADVERB
♦**Surely you don't believe that?** ¿No te creerás eso, no?

surf [sə:f] NOUN
see also **surf** VERB
la espuma de las olas

to **surf** [sə:f] VERB
see also **surf** NOUN
hacer* surf

surface ['sə:fɪs] NOUN
la superficie

surfboard ['sə:fbɔ:d] NOUN
la tabla de surf

surfing ['sə:fɪŋ] NOUN
el surf ◊ *to go surfing* hacer* surf

surgeon ['sə:dʒən] NOUN
el cirujano
la cirujana

surgery ['sə:dʒərɪ] NOUN (PL **surgeries**)
1 el consultorio médico (*room*)
2 la cirugía (*treatment*)
♦**surgery hours** las horas de consulta

surname ['sə:neɪm] NOUN
el apellido

surprise [sə'praɪz] NOUN
la sorpresa

surprised [sə'praɪzd] ADJECTIVE
♦**I was surprised to see him.** Me sorprendió verlo.
♦**I'm not surprised that** ... No me sorprende que...

surprising [sə'praɪzɪŋ] ADJECTIVE
sorprendente

to **surrender** [sə'rɛndəʳ] VERB
rendirse*

to **surround** [sə'raund] VERB
rodear ◊ *surrounded by trees* rodeado de árboles

surroundings [sə'raundɪŋz] PL NOUN
el entorno ◊ *a hotel in beautiful surroundings* un hotel en un hermoso entorno

survey ['sə:veɪ] NOUN
la encuesta ◊ *They did a survey of a thousand students.* Hicieron una encuesta a mil estudiantes.

surveyor [sə'veɪəʳ] NOUN
1 (*of buildings*)
el perito tasador
la perito tasadora
2 (*of land*)
el agrimensor
la agrimensora

to **survive** [sə'vaɪv] VERB
sobrevivir

survivor [sə'vaɪvəʳ] NOUN
el/la superviviente ◊ *There were no survivors.* No hubo supervivientes.

to **suspect** [səs'pɛkt] VERB
see also **suspect** NOUN
sospechar

suspect ['sʌspɛkt] NOUN
see also **suspect** VERB
el sospechoso
la sospechosa

to **suspend** [səs'pɛnd] VERB
1 expulsar temporalmente (*from school*)
2 excluir* (*from team*)
3 suspender (*from job*)

suspenders [səs'pɛndəz] PL NOUN US
(*braces*) los tirantes

suspense [səs'pɛns] NOUN
1 la incertidumbre ◊ *The suspense was terrible.* La incertidumbre era terrible.
2 el suspense ◊ *a film with lots of suspense* una película llena de suspense

suspension [səs'pɛnʃən] NOUN
1 la expulsión temporal (*from school*)
2 la exclusión (*from team*)
3 la suspensión (*from job*)

suspicious [səs'pɪʃəs] ADJECTIVE
1 receloso (*mistrustful*) ◊ *He was suspicious at first.* Al principio estaba receloso.
2 sospechoso (*suspicious looking*) ◊ *a suspicious person* un individuo sospechoso

to **swallow** ['swɔləu] VERB
tragar*

swam [swæm] VERB *see* **swim**

swan [swɔn] NOUN
el cisne

to **swap** [swɔp] VERB
cambiar ◊ *to swap A for B* cambiar A por B
♦**Do you want to swap?** ¿Quieres que cambiemos?

to **swat** [swɔt] VERB
aplastar

to **sway** [sweɪ] VERB
balancearse

to **swear** [swɛəʳ] VERB (**swore, sworn**)
1 jurar ◊ *to swear allegiance to* jurar fidelidad a
2 decir* palabrotas ◊ *It's wrong to swear.* No se deben decir palabrotas.

swearword ['swɛəwə:d] NOUN
la palabrota

sweat [swɛt] NOUN
see also **sweat** VERB
el sudor

to **sweat** [swɛt] VERB
see also **sweat** NOUN

sudar

sweater ['swɛtəʳ] NOUN
el jersey (PL los jerseys)
(el suéter *LatAm*)

sweaty ['swɛtɪ] ADJECTIVE
1 sudoroso (*hands, face*)
2 sudado (*clothes*)

Swede [swi:d] NOUN
(*person*)
el sueco
la sueca

swede [swi:d] NOUN
el nabo

Sweden ['swi:dn] NOUN
Suecia FEM

Swedish ['swi:dɪʃ] ADJECTIVE, NOUN
sueco

to **sweep** [swi:p] VERB (**swept, swept**)
barrer ◊ *to sweep the floor* barrer el suelo

sweet [swi:t] NOUN
see also **sweet** ADJECTIVE
1 el caramelo ◊ *a bag of sweets* una bolsa de caramelos
2 el postre ◊ *Are you going to have a sweet?* ¿Vas a tomar postre?

sweet [swi:t] ADJECTIVE
see also **sweet** NOUN
1 dulce ◊ *a sweet wine* un vino dulce
2 amable ◊ *That was really sweet of you.* Fue muy amable de tu parte.
♦ **sweet and sour pork** el cerdo agridulce

sweetcorn ['swi:tkɔ:n] NOUN
el maíz dulce

sweltering ['swɛltərɪŋ] ADJECTIVE
♦ **It was sweltering.** Hacía un calor asfixiante.

swept [swɛpt] VERB *see* **sweep**

to **swerve** [swə:v] VERB
girar bruscamente ◊ *I swerved to avoid the cyclist.* Giré bruscamente para esquivar al ciclista.

swim [swɪm] NOUN
see also **swim** VERB
♦ **to go for a swim** ir* a nadar

to **swim** [swɪm] VERB (**swam, swum**)
see also **swim** NOUN
nadar ◊ *Can you swim?* ¿Sabes nadar?
♦ **She swam across the river.** Cruzó el río a nado.

swimmer ['swɪməʳ] NOUN
el nadador
la nadadora

swimming ['swɪmɪŋ] NOUN
la natación ◊ *swimming lessons* clases de natación
♦ **Do you like swimming?** ¿Te gusta nadar?
♦ **to go swimming** ir* a nadar
♦ **swimming cap** el gorro de baño
♦ **swimming costume** el traje de baño
♦ **swimming pool** la piscina
♦ **swimming trunks** el bañador

swimsuit ['swɪmsu:t] NOUN
el traje de baño

to **swing** [swɪŋ] VERB (**swung, swung**)
see also **swing** NOUN
1 columpiarse (*on a swing*)
2 balancearse ◊ *Her bag swung as she walked.* El bolso se balanceaba según iba andando.
♦ **He was swinging on a rope.** Se balanceaba colgado de una cuerda.
3 colgar* ◊ *A large key swung from his belt.* Le colgaba una gran llave del cinturón.
4 balancear ◊ *He was swinging his bag back and forth.* Balanceaba la bolsa de un lado al otro.
♦ **Roy swung his legs off the couch.** Con un movimiento rápido, Roy quitó las piernas del sofá.
♦ **The canoe suddenly swung round.** De repente la canoa dio un viraje.

swing [swɪŋ] NOUN
see also **swing** VERB
el columpio

Swiss [swɪs] ADJECTIVE, NOUN
suizo
♦ **the Swiss** los suizos

switch [swɪtʃ] NOUN (PL **switches**)
see also **switch** VERB
el interruptor

to **switch** [swɪtʃ] VERB
see also **switch** NOUN
cambiar de ◊ *We switched partners.* Cambiamos de pareja.

to **switch off** [swɪtʃ'ɔf] VERB
apagar* (*TV, machine, engine*)

to **switch on** [swɪtʃ'ɔn] VERB
encender* (prender *LatAm*) (*TV, machine, engine*)

Switzerland ['swɪtsələnd] NOUN
Suiza FEM

swollen ['swəulən] ADJECTIVE
hinchado ◊ *My ankle is very swollen.* Tengo el tobillo muy hinchado.

to **swop** [swɔp] VERB
cambiar ◊ *to swop A for B* cambiar A por B
♦ **Do you want to swop?** ¿Quieres que cambiemos?

sword [sɔ:d] NOUN
la espada

swore [swɔ:ʳ] VERB *see* **swear**

sworn [swɔ:n] VERB *see* **swear**

swot [swɔt] NOUN
see also **swot** VERB
el empollón
la empollona

to **swot** [swɔt] VERB

S

☞

see also **swot** NOUN

empollar ◊ *I'll have to swot for the maths exam.* Para el examen de matemáticas me va a tocar empollar.

swum [swʌm] VERB *see* **swim**

swung [swʌŋ] VERB *see* **swing**

syllabus ['sɪləbəs] NOUN (PL **syllabuses**)
el programa de estudios

*Although **programa** ends in **-a**, it is actually a masculine noun.*

symbol ['sɪmbl] NOUN
el símbolo

sympathetic [sɪmpə'θetɪk] ADJECTIVE
comprensivo

*Be careful not to translate **sympathetic** by **simpático**.*

to **sympathize** ['sɪmpəθaɪz] VERB

◆ **to sympathize with somebody (1)** (*feel sorry for*) compadecerse* de alguien

◆ **to sympathize with somebody (2)** (*understand*) comprender a alguien

sympathy ['sɪmpəθɪ] NOUN
1 la compasión (*sorrow*)
2 la comprensión (*understanding*)

symptom ['sɪmptəm] NOUN
el síntoma

*Although **síntoma** ends in **-a**, it is actually a masculine noun.*

syringe [sɪ'rɪndʒ] NOUN
la jeringuilla

system ['sɪstəm] NOUN
el sistema

*Although **sistema** ends in **-a**, it is actually a masculine noun.*

T

table ['teɪbl] NOUN
la mesa
♦ **to lay the table** poner* la mesa
tablecloth ['teɪblklɔθ] NOUN
el mantel
tablespoon ['teɪblspuːn] NOUN
la cuchara de servir
tablespoonful ['teɪblspuːnful] NOUN
♦ **a tablespoonful of sugar** una cucharada grande de azúcar
tablet ['tæblɪt] NOUN
la pastilla
table tennis ['teɪbltɛnɪs] NOUN
el tenis de mesa ◊ *to play table tennis* jugar* al tenis de mesa
tabloid ['tæblɔɪd] NOUN
♦ **the tabloids** la prensa amarilla
tackle ['tækl] NOUN
see also **tackle** VERB
[1] la entrada (*in football*)
[2] el placaje (*in rugby*)
♦ **fishing tackle** el equipo de pesca
to **tackle** ['tækl] VERB
see also **tackle** NOUN
♦ **to tackle somebody (1)** entrar a alguien (*in football*)
♦ **to tackle somebody (2)** placar* a alguien (*in rugby*)
♦ **to tackle a problem** abordar un problema
tact [tækt] NOUN
el tacto
tactful ['tæktful] ADJECTIVE
diplomático
tactics ['tæktɪks] PL NOUN
la táctica SING
tactless ['tæktlɪs] ADJECTIVE
poco diplomático ◊ *He's so tactless!* ¡Es tan poco diplomático!
♦ **a tactless remark** un comentario con poco tacto
tadpole ['tædpəul] NOUN
el renacuajo
tag [tæg] NOUN
la etiqueta (*label*)
tail [teɪl] NOUN
[1] la cola (*of horse, bird, fish*)
[2] el rabo (*of dog, bull, ox*)
♦ **Heads or tails?** ¿Cara o cruz?
tailor ['teɪləʳ] NOUN
el sastre ◊ *He's a tailor.* Es sastre.
to **take** [teɪk] VERB (**took, taken**)
[1] tomar ◊ *Do you take sugar?* ¿Tomas azúcar?
♦ **He took a plate out of the cupboard.** Sacó un plato del armario.
[2] llevar ◊ *He goes to London every week, but he never takes me.* Va a Londres todas las semanas, pero nunca me lleva. ◊ *Don't forget to take your camera.* No te olvides de llevarte la cámara. ◊ *It takes about one hour.* Se tarda más o menos una hora. ◊ *It won't take long.* No tardará mucho tiempo.
♦ **That takes a lot of courage.** Hace falta mucho valor para eso.
♦ **It takes a lot of money to do that.** Hace falta mucho dinero para hacer eso.
[3] soportar ◊ *He can't take being criticized.* No soporta que le critiquen.
[4] hacer* ◊ *Have you taken your driving test yet?* ¿Ya has hecho el examen de conducir? ◊ *I decided to take French instead of German.* Decidí hacer francés en vez de alemán.
[5] aceptar ◊ *We take credit cards.* Aceptamos tarjetas de crédito.
to **take after** [teɪk'ɑːftəʳ] VERB
parecerse* a ◊ *She takes after her mother.* Se parece a su madre.
to **take apart** [teɪkə'pɑːt] VERB
♦ **to take something apart** desmontar algo
to **take away** [teɪkə'weɪ] VERB
[1] llevarse ◊ *They took away all his belongings.* Se llevaron todas sus pertenencias.
[2] quitar ◊ *She was afraid her children would be taken away from her.* Tenía miedo de que le quitaran a los niños.
♦ **hot meals to take away** platos calientes para llevar
to **take back** [teɪk'bæk] VERB
devolver* ◊ *I took it back to the shop.* Lo devolví a la tienda.
♦ **I take it all back!** ¡Retiro lo dicho!
to **take down** [teɪk'daun] VERB
quitar ◊ *She took down the painting.* Quitó el cuadro.
to **take in** [teɪk'ɪn] VERB
[1] comprender ◊ *I didn't really take it in.* La verdad es que no lo comprendí.
[2] engañar ◊ *They were taken in by his story.* Se dejaron engañar por la historia que les contó.
to **take off** [teɪk'ɔf] VERB
[1] despegar* ◊ *The plane took off 20 minutes late.* El avión despegó con 20 minutos de retraso.
[2] quitar ◊ *Take your coat off.* Quítate el abrigo.
to **take out** [teɪk'aut] VERB
sacar* ◊ *He opened his wallet and took out some money.* Abrió la cartera y sacó dinero.

◆**He took her out to the theatre.** La invitó al teatro.

to **take over** [teɪk'əuvəʳ] VERB
hacerse* cargo de ◊ *He took over the running of the company last year.* Se hizo cargo del control de la empresa el año pasado.
◆**to take over from somebody (1)** sustituir* a alguien (*replace*)
◆**to take over from somebody (2)** relevar a alguien (*in shift work*)

takeaway ['teɪkəweɪ] NOUN
la comida para llevar (*meal*)

> ℹ *A **takeaway** es también un establecimiento que vende comida para llevar.*

takeoff ['teɪkɔf] NOUN
el despegue (*of plane*)

talcum powder ['tælkəmpaudəʳ] NOUN
los polvos de talco

tale [teɪl] NOUN
el cuento

talent ['tælnt] NOUN
el talento ◊ *He's got a lot of talent.* Tiene mucho talento.
◆**to have a talent for something** tener* talento para algo
◆**He's got a real talent for languages.** Tiene verdadera facilidad para los idiomas.

talented ['tæləntɪd] ADJECTIVE
◆**She's a talented pianist.** Es una pianista de talento.

talk [tɔ:k] NOUN
see also **talk** VERB
1 la conversación (PL las conversaciones) ◊ *We had a long talk about her problems.* Tuvimos una larga conversación acerca de sus problemas.
◆**I had a talk with my Mum about it.** Hablé sobre eso con mi madre.
◆**to give a talk on something** dar* una charla sobre algo ◊ *She gave a talk on ancient Egypt.* Dio una charla sobre el antiguo Egipto.
2 (*gossip*)
las habladurías ◊ *It's just talk.* Son sólo habladurías.

to **talk** [tɔ:k] VERB
see also **talk** NOUN
hablar ◊ *What did you talk about?* ¿De qué hablasteis?
◆**to talk to somebody** hablar con alguien
◆**to talk to oneself** hablar consigo mismo
◆**to talk something over with somebody** discutir algo con alguien

talkative ['tɔ:kətɪv] ADJECTIVE
hablador MASC
habladora FEM

tall [tɔ:l] ADJECTIVE
alto
◆**to be two metres tall** medir* two metros

tame [teɪm] ADJECTIVE
domesticado (*animal*)

tampon ['tæmpɔn] NOUN
el tampón (PL los tampones)

tan [tæn] NOUN
el bronceado
◆**to get a tan** broncearse

tangerine [tændʒə'ri:n] NOUN
la mandarina

tank [tæŋk] NOUN
1 el depósito (*for water, petrol*)
2 la cisterna (*on truck*)
3 el tanque (*military*)
◆**a fish tank** un acuario

tanker ['tæŋkəʳ] NOUN
1 (*ship*)
el petrolero
2 (*truck*)
el camión cisterna (PL los camiones cisterna)
◆**an oil tanker** un petrolero
◆**a petrol tanker** un camión cisterna

tap [tæp] NOUN
1 el grifo (la llave *LatAm*) (*for water*) ◊ *the hot tap* el grifo de agua caliente
2 el golpecito (*gentle knock*) ◊ *I heard a tap on the window.* Oí un golpecito en la ventana.
◆**There was a tap on the door.** Llamaron a la puerta.

tap-dancing ['tæpdɑ:nsɪŋ] NOUN
el claqué ◊ *I do tap-dancing.* Bailo claqué.

to **tape** [teɪp] VERB
see also **tape** NOUN
grabar ◊ *Did you tape that film last night?* ¿Grabaste la película de anoche?

tape [teɪp] NOUN
see also **tape** VERB
1 la cinta ◊ *a tape of Sinead O'Connor* una cinta de Sinead O'Connor
2 la cinta adhesiva (*sticky tape*)

tape deck ['teɪpdɛk] NOUN
la pletina

tape measure ['teɪpmɛʒəʳ] NOUN
la cinta métrica

tape recorder ['teɪprɪkɔ:dəʳ] NOUN
1 el casete (*large*)
2 la grabadora (*hand-held*)

target ['tɑ:gɪt] NOUN
1 la diana (*board*)
2 el objetivo (*goal*)

Tarmac ® ['tɑ:mæk] NOUN
el asfalto (*on road*)

tart [tɑ:t] NOUN

la tarta ◊ *an apple tart* una tarta de manzana

tartan ['tɑːtn] ADJECTIVE
escocés MASC (PL escoceses)
escocesa FEM
◊ *a tartan scarf* una bufanda escocesa

task [tɑːsk] NOUN
la tarea

taste [teɪst] NOUN
see also **taste** VERB
1 el sabor ◊ *It's got a really strange taste.* Tiene un sabor muy extraño.
2 el gusto ◊ *His joke was in bad taste.* Su broma fue de mal gusto.
◆ **Would you like a taste?** ¿Quiere probarlo?

to **taste** [teɪst] VERB
see also **taste** NOUN
probar* ◊ *Would you like to taste it?* ¿Quiere probarlo?
◆ **to taste of something** saber* a algo ◊ *It tastes of fish.* Sabe a pescado.
◆ **You can taste the garlic in it.** Se le nota el sabor a ajo.

tasteful ['teɪstful] ADJECTIVE
de buen gusto MASC, FEM, PL

tasteless ['teɪstlɪs] ADJECTIVE
1 (*food*)
soso
2 (*in bad taste*)
de mal gusto MASC, FEM, PL
◊ *a tasteless remark* un comentario de mal gusto

tasty ['teɪstɪ] ADJECTIVE
sabroso

tattoo [tə'tuː] NOUN
el tatuaje

taught [tɔːt] VERB *see* **teach**

Taurus ['tɔːrəs] NOUN
el Tauro (*sign*) ◊ *I'm Taurus.* Soy Tauro.
◆ **a Taurus** un/una Tauro

tax [tæks] NOUN (PL **taxes**)
los impuestos ◊ *I pay a lot of tax.* Pago muchos impuestos.
◆ **income tax** el impuesto sobre la renta

taxi ['tæksɪ] NOUN
el taxi
◆ **a taxi driver** un/una taxista

taxi rank ['tæksɪræŋk] NOUN
la parada de taxis

TB [tiː'biː] ABBREVIATION (= *tuberculosis*)
la tuberculosis ◊ *He's got TB.* Tiene tuberculosis.

tea [tiː] NOUN
1 té ◊ *Would you like some tea?* ¿Te apetece un té?
◆ **a cup of tea** una taza de té
2 la merienda (*afternoon tea*)
◆ **to have tea** merendar* ◊ *We had tea at the Savoy.* Merendamos en el Savoy.
3 la cena (*evening meal*)
◆ **to have tea** cenar ◊ *We're having sausages and beans for tea.* Vamos a cenar salchichas con alubias.

tea bag ['tiːbæg] NOUN
la bolsita de té

to **teach** [tiːtʃ] VERB (**taught, taught**)
1 enseñar ◊ *My sister taught me to swim.* Mi hermana me enseñó a nadar.
2 dar* clases de (*subject*) ◊ *She teaches physics.* Da clases de física.
◆ **That'll teach you!** ¡Así aprenderás!

teacher ['tiːtʃəʳ] NOUN
1 (*in secondary school*)
el profesor
la profesora
◊ *a maths teacher* un profesor de matemáticas ◊ *She's a teacher.* Es profesora.
2 (*in primary school*)
el maestro
la maestra
◊ *He's a primary school teacher.* Es maestro.

team [tiːm] NOUN
el equipo ◊ *a football team* un equipo de fútbol

teapot ['tiːpɔt] NOUN
la tetera

tear [tɪəʳ] NOUN
see also **tear** VERB
la lágrima
◆ **She was in tears.** Estaba llorando.

to **tear** [tɛəʳ] VERB (**tore, torn**)
see also **tear** NOUN
1 romper* ◊ *Be careful or you'll tear the page.* Ten cuidado que vas a romper la página.
◆ **He tore his jacket.** Se rasgó la chaqueta.
◆ **Your shirt is torn.** Tu camisa está rota.
2 romperse* ◊ *It won't tear, it's very strong.* No se rompe, es muy resistente.

to **tear up** [tɛər'ʌp] VERB
hacer* pedazos ◊ *He tore up the letter.* Hizo pedazos la carta.

tear gas [tɪəgæs] NOUN
el gas lacrimógeno

to **tease** [tiːz] VERB
1 atormentar ◊ *Stop teasing that poor animal!* ¡Deja de atormentar al pobre animal!
2 tomar el pelo a ◊ *He's teasing you.* Te está tomando el pelo.
◆ **I was only teasing.** Lo decía en broma.

teaspoon ['tiːspuːn] NOUN
la cucharita

teaspoonful ['tiːspuːnful] NOUN
◆ **a teaspoonful of sugar** una cucharita de azúcar

teatime ['tiːtaɪm] NOUN
la hora de cenar (*in evening*) ◊ *It was nearly teatime.* Era casi la hora de cenar.

♦ **Teatime!** ¡A la mesa!

tea towel ['ti:tauəl] NOUN
el paño de cocina

technical ['tɛknɪkl] ADJECTIVE
[1] técnico
♦ **a technical college** el centro de formación profesional
[2] la escuela politécnica *LatAm*

technician [tɛk'nɪʃən] NOUN
el técnico
la técnica

technique [tɛk'ni:k] NOUN
la técnica

techno ['tɛknəu] NOUN
el tecno

technological [tɛknə'lɔdʒɪkl] ADJECTIVE
tecnológico

technology [tɛk'nɔlədʒɪ] NOUN (PL **technologies**)
la tecnología

teddy bear ['tɛdɪbɛəʳ] NOUN
el osito de peluche

teenage ['ti:neɪdʒ] ADJECTIVE
♦ **a teenage magazine** una revista para adolescentes
♦ **She has two teenage daughters.** Tiene dos hijas adolescentes.

teenager ['ti:neɪdʒəʳ] NOUN
el/la adolescente

teens [ti:nz] PL NOUN
♦ **She's in her teens.** Es adolescente.

tee-shirt ['ti:ʃə:t] NOUN
la camiseta

teeth [ti:θ] PL NOUN *see* **tooth**

to **teethe** [ti:ð] VERB
echar los dientes

teetotal ['ti:'təutl] ADJECTIVE
abstemio

telecommunications ['tɛlɪkəmju:nɪ'keɪʃənz] PL NOUN
las telecomunicaciones

telephone ['tɛlɪfəun] NOUN
el teléfono ◊ *on the telephone* al teléfono
♦ **a telephone box** una cabina telefónica
♦ **a telephone call** una llamada telefónica
♦ **a telephone directory** una guía telefónica
♦ **a telephone number** un número de teléfono

telesales ['tɛlɪseɪlz] NOUN
las televentas

telescope ['tɛlɪskəup] NOUN
el telescopio

television ['tɛlɪvɪʒən] NOUN
la televisión ◊ *The match is on television tonight.* Ponen el partido en televisión esta noche.
♦ **television licence**

> *En el Reino Unido, para tener derecho a recibir los canales de la BBC hay que pagar una licencia anual.*

to **tell** [tɛl] VERB (**told, told**)
decir*
♦ **to tell somebody something** decir* algo a alguien ◊ *Did you tell your mother?* ¿Se lo has dicho a tu madre? ◊ *I told him I was going on holiday.* Le dije que me iba de vacaciones.
♦ **to tell somebody to do something** decir* a alguien que haga algo
Use the subjunctive after ***decir a alguien que*** *when translating "to tell somebody to do something".*
◊ *He told me to wait a moment.* Me dijo que esperara un momento.
♦ **to tell lies** decir* mentiras
♦ **to tell a story** contar* un cuento
♦ **I can't tell the difference between them.** No puedo distinguirlos.
♦ **You can tell he's not serious.** Se nota que no se lo toma en serio.

to **tell off** [tɛl'ɔf] VERB
regañar

telly ['tɛlɪ] NOUN (PL **tellies**) (*informal*)
la tele ◊ *to watch telly* ver* la tele ◊ *on telly* en la tele

temper ['tɛmpəʳ] NOUN
el genio ◊ *He's got a terrible temper.* Tiene muy mal genio.
♦ **to be in a temper** estar* de mal humor
♦ **to lose one's temper** perder* los estribos

temperature ['tɛmprətʃəʳ] NOUN
la temperatura
♦ **to have a temperature** tener* fiebre

temple ['tɛmpl] NOUN
[1] el templo (*building*)
[2] la sien (*on head*)

temporary ['tɛmpərərɪ] ADJECTIVE
temporal

to **tempt** [tɛmpt] VERB
tentar* ◊ *I'm very tempted!* ¡Tienta mucho!
♦ **to tempt somebody to do something** tentar* a alguien a hacer algo

temptation [tɛmp'teɪʃən] NOUN
la tentación (PL las tentaciones)

tempting ['tɛmptɪŋ] ADJECTIVE
tentador MASC
tentadora FEM

ten [tɛn] NUMERAL
diez ◊ *She's ten.* Tiene diez años.

tenant ['tɛnənt] NOUN
el inquilino
la inquilina

to **tend** [tɛnd] VERB

♦**to tend to do something** tener* tendencia a hacer algo ◊ *He tends to arrive late.* Tiene tendencia a llegar tarde.

tender ['tɛndəʳ] ADJECTIVE
tierno

tennis ['tɛnɪs] NOUN
el tenis ◊ *to play tennis* jugar* al tenis
♦**a tennis ball** una pelota de tenis
♦**a tennis court** una pista de tenis
♦**a tennis racket** una raqueta de tenis

tennis player ['tɛnɪspleɪəʳ] NOUN
el/la tenista ◊ *He's a tennis player.* Es tenista.

tenor ['tɛnəʳ] NOUN
el tenor

tenpin bowling [tɛnpɪn'bəulɪŋ] NOUN
los bolos ◊ *to go tenpin bowling* jugar* a los bolos

tense [tɛns] ADJECTIVE
see also **tense** NOUN
tenso

tense [tɛns] NOUN
see also **tense** ADJECTIVE
el tiempo
♦**the present tense** el presente
♦**the future tense** el futuro

tension ['tɛnʃən] NOUN
la tensión (PL las tensiones)

tent [tɛnt] NOUN
la tienda de campaña
♦**a tent peg** una estaquilla
♦**a tent pole** un mástil de tienda

tenth [tɛnθ] ADJECTIVE
décimo ◊ *the tenth floor* el décimo piso
♦**the tenth of August** el diez de agosto

term [tə:m] NOUN
1 el trimestre (*at school*) ◊ *It's nearly the end of term.* Ya casi es final de trimestre.
2 el plazo ◊ *in the long term* a largo plazo
♦**to come to terms with something** aceptar algo ◊ *He hasn't yet come to terms with his disability.* Todavía no ha aceptado su invalidez.

terminal ['tə:mɪnl] ADJECTIVE
see also **terminal** NOUN
terminal (*illness, patient*)

terminal ['tə:mɪnl] NOUN
see also **terminal** ADJECTIVE
el terminal (*of computer*)
♦**airport terminal** la terminal del aeropuerto
♦**bus terminal** la terminal de autobuses
♦**oil terminal** la terminal petrolera

terminally ['tə:mɪnlɪ] ADVERB
♦**to be terminally ill** estar* en fase terminal

terrace ['tɛrəs] NOUN
1 la terraza (*patio*) ◊ *We were sitting on the terrace.* Estábamos sentados en la terraza.
2 la hilera de casas adosadas (*row of houses*)
♦**the terraces** (*in stadium*) las gradas

terraced ['tɛrəst] ADJECTIVE
♦**a terraced house** una casa adosada

terrible ['tɛrɪbl] ADJECTIVE
espantoso ◊ *This coffee is terrible.* Este café es espantoso.
♦**I feel terrible.** Me siento fatal.

terrier ['tɛrɪəʳ] NOUN
el/la terrier (PL los/las terriers)

terrific [tə'rɪfɪk] ADJECTIVE
estupendo (*wonderful*) ◊ *That's terrific!* ¡Estupendo!
♦**You look terrific!** ¡Estás guapísima!

terrified ['tɛrɪfaɪd] ADJECTIVE
aterrorizado ◊ *I was terrified!* ¡Estaba aterrorizado!

terrorism ['tɛrərɪzəm] NOUN
el terrorismo

terrorist ['tɛrərɪst] NOUN
el/la terrorista
♦**a terrorist attack** un atentado terrorista

test [tɛst] NOUN
see also **test** VERB
1 la prueba ◊ *a spelling test* una prueba de ortografía ◊ *nuclear tests* pruebas nucleares
2 (*on blood, urine*)
el análisis (PL los análisis)
◊ *a blood test* un análisis de sangre
♦**an eye test** un examen de la vista
3 (*driving test*)
el examen de conducir ◊ *He's just passed his test.* Acaba de aprobar el examen de conducir.

to **test** [tɛst] VERB
see also **test** NOUN
probar*
♦**to test something out** probar* algo
♦**He tested us on the new vocabulary.** Nos hizo una prueba del vocabulario nuevo.
♦**She was tested for drugs.** Le hicieron la prueba antidoping.

test match ['tɛstmætʃ] NOUN (PL **test matches**)
el partido internacional

test tube ['tɛsttju:b] NOUN
la probeta

tetanus ['tɛtənəs] NOUN
el tétano
♦**a tetanus injection** una inyección contra el tétano

textbook ['tɛkstbuk] NOUN
el libro de texto ◊ *a Spanish textbook* un libro de texto de español

textiles ['tɛkstaɪlz] NOUN
los tejidos

Thames [tɛmz] NOUN
el Támesis

than [ðæn, ðən] CONJUNCTION
1 que ◊ *She's taller than me.* Es más alta que yo. ◊ *I've got more CDs than tapes.* Tengo más CDs que cintas.

T

[2] de ◊ *more than once* en más de una ocasión ◊ *more than 10 years* más de 10 años

to **thank** [θæŋk] VERB

dar* las gracias a ◊ *Don't forget to write and thank them.* Acuérdate de escribirles y darles las gracias.

♦ **thank you** gracias

♦ **thank you very much** muchas gracias

thanks [θæŋks] EXCLAMATION

¡Gracias!

♦ **thanks to** gracias a ◊ *Thanks to him, everything went OK.* Gracias a él, todo salió bien.

that [ðæt, ðət] ADJECTIVE

see also **that** PRONOUN, CONJUNCTION, ADVERB

[1] ese MASC
esa FEM
◊ *that man* ese hombre ◊ *that road* esa carretera

To refer to something more distant, use ***aquel*** *and* ***aquella.***

[2] aquel MASC
aquella FEM
◊ *Look at that car over there!* ¡Mira aquel coche! ◊ *THAT road there* aquella carretera

♦ **that one** ése MASC
ésa FEM
◊ *This man? – No, that one.* ¿Este hombre? – No, ése. ◊ *Do you like this photo? – No, I prefer that one.* ¿Te gusta esta foto? – No, prefiero ésa.

To refer to something more distant, use ***aquél*** *and* ***aquélla.***

[3] aquél MASC
aquélla FEM
◊ *That one over there is cheaper.* Aquél es más barato. ◊ *Which woman? – That one over there.* ¿Qué mujer? – Aquélla.

that [ðæt, ðət] PRONOUN

see also **that** ADJECTIVE, CONJUNCTION, ADVERB

[1] ése MASC (FEM ésa, NEUTER eso)

♦ **Who's that?** (*who is that man*) ¿Quién es ése?

♦ **Who's that?** (*who is that woman*) ¿Quién es ésa?

♦ **Who's that?** (*on the telephone*) ¿Con quién hablo? ◊ *That's impossible.* Eso es imposible. ◊ *What's that?* ¿Qué es eso?

To refer to something more distant, use ***aquél, aquélla*** *and* ***aquello.***

[2] aquél MASC (FEM aquélla, NEUTER aquello) ◊ *That's my French teacher over there.* Aquél es mi profesor de francés. ◊ *That's my sister over by the window.* Aquélla de la ventana es mi hermana. ◊ *That was a silly thing to do.* Aquello fue una tontería.

♦ **Is that you?** ¿Eres tú?

[3] (*in relative clauses*)

que ◊ *the man that saw us* el hombre que nos vio ◊ *the dog that she bought* el perro que ella compró ◊ *the man that we saw* el hombre que vimos

After a preposition ***que*** *becomes* ***el que, la que, los que, las que*** *to agree with the noun.*

◊ *the man that we spoke to* el hombre con el que hablamos ◊ *the women that she was chatting to* las mujeres con las que estaba hablando

that [ðæt, ðət] CONJUNCTION

see also **that** ADJECTIVE, PRONOUN, ADVERB

que ◊ *He thought that Henry was ill.* Creía que Henry estaba enfermo. ◊ *I know that she likes chocolate.* Sé que le gusta el chocolate.

that [ðæt, ðət] ADVERB

see also **that** ADJECTIVE, PRONOUN, CONJUNCTION

♦ **It was that big.** Era así de grande.

♦ **It's about that high.** Es más o menos así de alto.

♦ **It's not that difficult.** No es tan difícil.

thatched [θætʃt] ADJECTIVE

♦ **a thatched cottage** una casita con tejado de paja

the [ðə, ðiː] DEFINITE ARTICLE

[1] el MASC (PL los) ◊ *the boy* el niño ◊ *the cars* los coches

a *+* ***el*** *changes to* ***al*** *and* ***de*** *+* ***el*** *changes to* ***del.***

◊ *They went to the theatre.* Fueron al teatro. ◊ *the soup of the day* la sopa del día

[2] la FEM (PL las) ◊ *the woman* la mujer ◊ *the chairs* las sillas

theatre ['θɪətəʳ] NOUN (US **theater**)

el teatro

theft [θɛft] NOUN

el robo

their [ðɛəʳ] ADJECTIVE

su (PL sus) ◊ *their father* su padre ◊ *their house* su casa ◊ *their parents* sus padres ◊ *their sisters* sus hermanas

Their *is usually translated by the definite article* ***el/los*** *or* ***la/las*** *when it's clear from the sentence who the possessor is, particularly when referring to clothing or parts of the body.*

◊ *They took off their coats.* Se quitaron los abrigos. ◊ *after washing their hands* después de lavarse las manos ◊ *Someone stole their car.* Alguien les robó el coche.

theirs [ðɛəz] PRONOUN

[1] el suyo MASC (PL los suyos) ◊ *Is this their car? – No, theirs is red.* ¿Es éste su coche? – No, el suyo es rojo. ◊ *my parents and theirs* mis padres y los suyos

* Verbs marked with this symbol are irregular. See pages 380-382 for further details

2 la suya FEM (PL las suyas) ◊ *Is this their house? – No, theirs is white.* ¿Es ésta su casa? – No, la suya es blanca. ◊ *my sisters and theirs* mis hermanas y las suyas

*Use **de ellos** (masculine) or **de ellas** (feminine) instead of **suyo** if you want to be specific about a masculine or feminine group.*

◊ *It's not our car, it's theirs.* No es nuestro coche, es suyo. ◊ *The suitcase is theirs.* La maleta es suya. ◊ *Whose is this? – It's theirs.* ¿De quién es esto? – Es de ellos.

♦ **Isobel is a friend of theirs.** Isobel es amiga suya.

them [ðɛm, ðəm] PRONOUN

1 los MASC
las FEM

*Use **los** or **las** when **them** is the direct object of the verb in the sentence.*

◊ *I didn't know them.* No los conocía. ◊ *Have you seen my slippers? I'd left them here.* ¿Has visto mis zapatillas? Las había dejado aquí. ◊ *Look at them!* ¡Míralos! ◊ *I had to give them to her.* Tuve que dárselos.

2 les

*Use **les** when **them** means **to them**.*

◊ *I gave them some brochures.* Les di unos folletos. ◊ *You have to tell them the truth.* Tienes que decirles la verdad.

3 se

*Use **se** not **les** when **them** is used in combination with a direct-object pronoun.*

◊ *Give it to them.* Dáselo.

4 ellos MASC
ellas FEM

*Use **ellos** or **ellas** after prepositions, in comparisons, and with the verb **to be**.*

◊ *It's for them.* Es para ellos. ◊ *My sisters didn't go. My mother stayed with them.* Mis hermanas no fueron. Mi madre se quedó con ellas. ◊ *We are older than them.* Somos mayores que ellos. ◊ *It must be them.* Deben de ser ellos.

♦ **They were carrying them on them.** Los llevaban consigo.

theme [θi:m] NOUN

el tema

*Although **tema** ends in **-a**, it is actually a masculine noun.*

theme park ['θi:mpɑ:k] NOUN

el parque temático

themselves [ðəm'sɛlvz] PRONOUN

1 (*reflexive*)
se ◊ *Did they hurt themselves?* ¿Se hicieron daño?

2 (*after preposition*)
sí mismos MASC
sí mismas FEM
◊ *They talked mainly about themselves.* Hablaron sobre todo de sí mismos.

3 (*for emphasis*)
ellos mismos MASC
ellas mismas FEM
◊ *They built it themselves.* Lo construyeron ellos mismos.

♦ **by themselves** por sí mismos MASC (FEM por sí mismas) ◊ *The girls did it all by themselves.* Las chicas lo hicieron todo por sí mismas.

then [ðɛn] ADVERB, CONJUNCTION

1 después (*next*) ◊ *I get dressed. Then I have breakfast.* Me visto. Después desayuno.

2 pues (*in that case*) ◊ *My pen's run out. – Use a pencil then!* Se me ha acabado el bolígrafo. – ¡Pues usa un lápiz!

3 en aquella época (*in those days*) ◊ *There was no electricity then.* En aquella época no había electricidad.

♦ **now and then** de vez en cuando ◊ *Do you play chess? – Now and then.* ¿Juegas al ajedrez? – De vez en cuando.

♦ **By then it was too late.** Para entonces ya era demasiado tarde.

therapy ['θɛrəpɪ] NOUN (PL **therapies**)

la terapia

there [ðɛəʳ] ADVERB

1 ahí (*near you*) ◊ *Put it there, on the table.* Ponlo ahí, en la mesa.

2 allí (*further away*) ◊ *I lived there in 1997.* Viví allí en 1997.

♦ **over there**

♦ **in there** ahí dentro

♦ **on there** ahí encima

♦ **down there** ahí abajo

♦ **There he is!** ¡Ahí está!

♦ **there is** hay ◊ *There's a factory near my house.* Hay una fábrica cerca de mi casa.

♦ **there are** hay ◊ *There are 20 children in my class.* Hay 20 niños en mi clase.

♦ **There has been an accident.** Ha habido un accidente.

therefore ['ðɛəfɔ:ʳ] ADVERB

por lo tanto

there's ['ðɛəz] = **there is**, = **there has**

thermometer [θə'mɔmɪtəʳ] NOUN

el termómetro

Thermos ® ['θə:məs] NOUN

el termo

these [ði:z] ADJECTIVE

see also **these** PRONOUN

estos MASC
estas FEM
◊ *these shoes* estos zapatos ◊ *THESE shoes* estos zapatos de aquí ◊ *these houses* estas casas

these [ði:z] PRONOUN

see also **these** ADJECTIVE

éstos MASC
éstas FEM

◊ *I want these!* ¡Quiero éstos! ◊ *I'm looking for some sandals. – Can I try these?* Quiero unas sandalias. – ¿Puedo probarme éstas?

they [ðeɪ] PRONOUN
ellos MASC
ellas FEM
***they** generally isn't translated unless it's emphatic.*
◊ *They're fine, thank you.* Están bien, gracias.
*Use **ellos** or **ellas** as appropriate for emphasis.*
◊ *We went to the cinema but they didn't.* Nosotros fuimos al cine pero ellos no. ◊ *I spoke to my sisters. THEY agree with me.* Hablé con mis hermanas. Ellas estaban de acuerdo conmigo.
♦ **They say that...** Dicen que... ◊ *They say that the house is haunted.* Dicen que la casa está embrujada.

they'd [ðeɪd] = **they had**, = **they would**

they'll [ðeɪl] = **they will**

they're [ðeəʳ] = **they are**

they've [ðeɪv] = **they have**

thick [θɪk] ADJECTIVE
1 grueso (*wall, slice*) ◊ *Give him a thick slice.* Dále una rebanada gruesa.
♦ **The walls are one metre thick.** Las paredes tienen un metro de grosor.
2 espeso (*soup*) ◊ *My soup turned out too thick.* La sopa me quedó demasiado espesa.
3 corto (*informal: stupid*)

thief [θiːf] NOUN (PL **thieves**)
el ladrón (PL los ladrones)
la ladrona

thigh [θaɪ] NOUN
el muslo

thin [θɪn] ADJECTIVE
1 fino ◊ *a thin slice* una rebanada fina
2 delgado ◊ *She's very thin.* Está muy delgada.

thing [θɪŋ] NOUN
la cosa ◊ *beautiful things* cosas bonitas ◊ *Where shall I put my things?* ¿Dónde pongo mis cosas?
♦ **How's things?** ¿Qué tal?
♦ **What's that thing called?** ¿Cómo se llama eso?
♦ **You poor thing!** ¡Pobrecito!
♦ **The best thing would be to leave it.** Lo mejor sería dejarlo.

to **think** [θɪŋk] VERB (**thought, thought**)
1 pensar* ◊ *What do you think about it?* ¿Qué piensas? ◊ *Think carefully before you reply.* Piénsalo bien antes de responder. ◊ *What are you thinking about?* ¿En qué estás pensando?
♦ **I'll think it over.** Lo pensaré.
2 creer* ◊ *I think you're wrong.* Creo que estás equivocado.
♦ **I think so.** Creo que sí.
♦ **I don't think so.** Creo que no.
3 imaginar ◊ *Think what life would be like without cars.* Imagínate cómo sería la vida sin coches.

third [θəːd] ADJECTIVE, ADVERB
see also **third** NOUN
tercero
*Use **tercer** before a masculine singular noun.*
◊ *the third prize* el tercer premio ◊ *the third time* la tercera vez ◊ *Rachel came third in the race.* Rachel quedó la tercera en la carrera.
♦ **the third of March** el tres de marzo

third [θəːd] NOUN
see also **third** ADJECTIVE, ADVERB
el tercio (*fraction*)
♦ **a third of the population** una tercera parte de la población

thirdly ['θəːdlɪ] ADVERB
en tercer lugar

Third World [θəːd'wəːld] NOUN
el Tercer Mundo

thirst [θəːst] NOUN
la sed

thirsty ['θəːstɪ] ADJECTIVE
♦ **to be thirsty** tener* sed

thirteen [θəː'tiːn] NUMERAL
trece ◊ *I'm thirteen.* Tengo trece años.

thirteenth [θəː'tiːnθ] ADJECTIVE
decimotercero
♦ **the thirteenth floor** la planta trece
♦ **the thirteenth of January** el trece de enero

thirty ['θəːtɪ] NUMERAL
treinta ◊ *He's thirty.* Tiene treinta años.

this [ðɪs] ADJECTIVE
see also **this** PRONOUN
este MASC
esta FEM
◊ *this boy* este niño ◊ *this road* esta carretera
♦ **this one** éste MASC (FEM ésta) ◊ *Pass me that pen. – This one?* Acércame ese bolígrafo. ¿Éste? ◊ *This is my room and this one's my sister's.* Ésta es mi habitación y ésta es la de mi hermana.

this [ðɪs] PRONOUN
see also **this** ADJECTIVE
éste MASC (FEM ésta, NEUTER esto) ◊ *This is my office and this is the meeting room.* Éste es mi despacho y ésta es la sala de reuniones. ◊ *What's this?* ¿Qué es esto?
♦ **This is my mother.** (*introduction*) Te presento a mi madre.
♦ **This is Gavin speaking.** (*on the phone*) Soy Gavin.

thistle ['θɪsl] NOUN
el cardo

thorough ['θʌrə] ADJECTIVE
minucioso ◊ *a thorough check* un control minucioso
♦**She's very thorough.** Es muy meticulosa.

thoroughly ['θʌrəlɪ] ADVERB
minuciosamente ◊ *I checked the car thoroughly.* Revisé el coche minuciosamente.
♦**Mix the ingredients thoroughly.** Mézclense bien los ingredientes.
♦**I thoroughly enjoyed myself.** Me divertí muchísimo.

those [ðəuz] ADJECTIVE
see also **those** PRONOUN
1 esos MASC
esas FEM
◊ *those shoes* esos zapatos ◊ *those girls* esas chicas
To refer to something more distant, use ***aquellos*** *and* ***aquellas.***
2 aquellos MASC
aquellas FEM
◊ *THOSE shoes* aquellos zapatos ◊ *those houses over there* aquellas casas

those [ðəuz] PRONOUN
see also **those** ADJECTIVE
1 ésos MASC
ésas FEM
◊ *I want those!* ¡Quiero ésos!
To refer to something more distant, use ***aquéllos.***
2 aquéllos MASC
aquéllas FEM
◊ *Ask those children. – Those over there?* Pregúntales a esos niños. – ¿A aquéllos?

though [ðəu] CONJUNCTION, ADVERB
aunque ◊ *Though she was tired she stayed up late.* Aunque estaba cansada, se quedó levantada hasta muy tarde.
♦**It's difficult, though, to put into practice.** Pero es difícil llevarlo a la práctica.

thought [θɔːt] VERB *see* **think**

thought [θɔːt] NOUN
la idea ◊ *I've just had a thought.* Se me ocurre una idea.
♦**He kept his thoughts to himself.** No le dijo a nadie lo que pensaba.
♦**It was a nice thought, thank you.** Fue muy amable de tu parte, gracias.

thoughtful ['θɔːtful] ADJECTIVE
1 pensativo (*deep in thought*) ◊ *You look thoughtful.* Pareces pensativo.
2 considerado (*considerate*) ◊ *She's very thoughtful.* Es muy considerada.

thoughtless ['θɔːtlɪs] ADJECTIVE
desconsiderado ◊ *She's very thoughtless.* Es muy desconsiderada.
♦**It was thoughtless of her to mention it.** Fue una falta de consideración por su parte mencionarlo.

thousand ['θauzənd] NUMERAL
♦**a thousand** mil ◊ *a thousand pesetas* mil pesetas
♦**two thousand pounds** dos mil libras
♦**thousands of people** miles de personas

thread [θrɛd] NOUN
el hilo

threat [θrɛt] NOUN
la amenaza

to **threaten** ['θrɛtn] VERB
amenazar* ◊ *He threatened me.* Me amenazó.
♦**to threaten to do something** amenazar con hacer algo (*person*)

three [θriː] NUMERAL
tres ◊ *She's three.* Tiene tres años.

three-dimensional [θriːdɪ'mɛnʃənl] ADJECTIVE
tridimensional

three-piece suite ['θriːpiːs'swiːt] NOUN
el tresillo

threw [θruː] VERB *see* **throw**

thrifty ['θrɪftɪ] ADJECTIVE
ahorrativo

thrill [θrɪl] NOUN
la emoción (PL las emociones)
◊ *I remember the thrill of Christmas as a child.* Recuerdo la emoción que sentía de niño en Navidades.
♦**It was a great thrill to see my team win.** Fue muy emocionante ver ganar a mi equipo.

thrilled [θrɪld] ADJECTIVE
♦**I was thrilled.** Estaba emocionada.

thriller ['θrɪlə^r] NOUN
1 la película de suspense (la película de misterio LatAm) (*film*)
2 la novela de suspense (la novela de misterio LatAm) (*novel*)

thrilling ['θrɪlɪŋ] ADJECTIVE
emocionante

throat [θrəut] NOUN
la garganta ◊ *I have a sore throat.* Me duele la garganta.

to **throb** [θrɔb] VERB
♦**My arm's throbbing.** Tengo un dolor punzante en el brazo.
♦**a throbbing pain** un dolor punzante

throne [θrəun] NOUN
el trono

through [θruː] ADJECTIVE, ADVERB, PREPOSITION
1 a través de ◊ *to look through a telescope* mirar a través de un telescopio ◊ *I know her through my sister.* La conozco a través de mi hermana.
♦**I saw him through the crowd.** Lo vi entre la multitud.
♦**The window was dirty and I couldn't see through.** La ventana estaba sucia y no podía ver nada.
2 por ◊ *The thief got in through the kitchen window.* El ladrón entró por la ventana de la cocina. ◊ *to go through*

☞

Birmingham pasar por Birmingham ◊ *to walk through the woods* pasear por el bosque
◆ **to go through a tunnel** atravesar* un túnel
◆ **He went straight through to the dining room.** Pasó directamente al comedor.
◆ **a through train** un tren directo
◆ **"no through road"** "calle sin salida"
◆ **all through the night** durante toda la noche
◆ **from May through to September** desde mayo hasta septiembre

throughout [θruː'aut] PREPOSITION
◆ **throughout Britain** en toda Gran Bretaña
◆ **throughout the year** durante todo el año

to **throw** [θrəu] VERB (**threw, threw**)
tirar ◊ *He threw the ball to me.* Me tiró la pelota.
◆ **to throw a party** dar* una fiesta
◆ **That really threw him.** Eso lo desconcertó por completo.

to **throw away** [θrəuə'weɪ] VERB
[1] tirar (*rubbish*)
[2] desperdiciar (*chance*)

to **throw out** [θrəu'aut] VERB
[1] tirar (*throw away*)
[2] echar (*person*) ◊ *I threw him out.* Lo eché.

to **throw up** [θrəu'ʌp] VERB
devolver*

thug [θʌg] NOUN
el matón (PL los matones)

thumb [θʌm] NOUN
el pulgar

thumb tack ['θʌmtæk] NOUN US
la chincheta

to **thump** [θʌmp] VERB
◆ **to thump somebody** pegar* un puñetazo a alguien

thunder ['θʌndəʳ] NOUN
los truenos

thunderstorm ['θʌndəstɔːm] NOUN
la tormenta

thundery ['θʌndərɪ] ADJECTIVE
tormentoso

Thursday ['θəːzdɪ] NOUN
el jueves (PL los jueves) ◊ *I saw her on Thursday.* La vi el jueves. ◊ *every Thursday* todos los jueves ◊ *last Thursday* el jueves pasado ◊ *next Thursday* el jueves que viene ◊ *on Thursdays* los jueves

thyme [taɪm] NOUN
el tomillo

tick [tɪk] NOUN
see also **tick** VERB
[1] la señal ◊ *Place a tick in the appropriate box.* Marque con una señal la casilla correspondiente.
[2] el tictac ◊ *The clock has a loud tick.* El reloj tiene un tictac muy fuerte.
◆ **in a tick** en un instante

to **tick** [tɪk] VERB
see also **tick** NOUN
[1] marcar* ◊ *Tick the appropriate box.* Marque la casilla correspondiente.
[2] hacer* tictac (*clock*)

to **tick off** [tɪk'ɔf] VERB
[1] marcar* (*on form, list*) ◊ *The teacher ticked the names off in the register.* El profesor marcó los nombres de la lista con una señal.
[2] regañar (*scold*) ◊ *He was ticked off for being late.* Le regañaron por llegar tarde.

ticket ['tɪkɪt] NOUN
[1] (*for bus, train, tube, plane*)
el billete (el boleto *LatAm*) (el pasaje *LatAm: for plane only*)
[2] (*for cinema, theatre, concert, museum*)
la entrada
[3] (*for baggage, coat, parking*)
el ticket (PL los tickets)
◆ **a parking ticket** (*fine*) una multa por estacionamiento indebido

ticket inspector ['tɪkɪtɪnspɛktəʳ] NOUN
el revisor MASC
la revisora FEM

ticket office ['tɪkɪtɔfɪs] NOUN
la taquilla

to **tickle** ['tɪkl] VERB
hacer* cosquillas a ◊ *She enjoyed tickling the baby.* Le gustaba hacer cosquillas al niño.

ticklish ['tɪklɪʃ] ADJECTIVE
◆ **to be ticklish** tener* cosquillas

tide [taɪd] NOUN
la marea
◆ **high tide** la marea alta
◆ **low tide** la marea baja

tidy ['taɪdɪ] ADJECTIVE
see also **tidy** VERB
ordenado ◊ *Your room is very tidy.* Tu habitación está muy ordenada. ◊ *She's very tidy.* Es muy ordenada.

to **tidy** ['taɪdɪ] VERB (**tidied, tidied**)
see also **tidy** ADJECTIVE
ordenar (*room*)

to **tidy up** [taɪdɪ'ʌp] VERB
recoger* (*toys*) ◊ *Don't forget to tidy up afterwards.* No os olvidéis de recoger las cosas después.

tie [taɪ] NOUN
see also **tie** VERB
[1] la corbata (*necktie*)
[2] el empate (*in sport*)

to **tie** [taɪ] VERB
see also **tie** NOUN
[1] atar (*shoelaces, parcel*)

♦**to tie a knot in something** hacer* un nudo en algo
[2] empatar ◊ *They tied three all.* Empataron a tres.

to **tie up** [taɪ'ʌp] VERB
[1] atar (*person, shoelaces, parcel*)
[2] atracar* (*boat*)

tiger ['taɪgəʳ] NOUN
el tigre

tight [taɪt] ADJECTIVE
[1] ceñido (*fitting*) ◊ *tight jeans* vaqueros ceñidos
[2] estrecho (*too small*) ◊ *This dress is a bit tight.* Este vestido es un poco estrecho.

to **tighten** ['taɪtn] VERB
[1] tensar (*rope*)
[2] apretar* (*screw*)

tightly ['taɪtlɪ] ADVERB
♦**tightly closed** fuertemente cerrado
♦**She held his hand tightly.** Le agarró la mano con fuerza.

tights [taɪts] PL NOUN
las medias ◊ *a pair of tights* unas medias

tile [taɪl] NOUN
[1] la teja (*on roof*)
[2] el azulejo (*for wall*)
[3] la baldosa (*for floor*)

tiled [taɪld] ADJECTIVE
[1] de tejas (*roof*)
[2] alicatado (*wall*)
[3] de baldosas (*floor*)

till [tɪl] NOUN
see also **till** PREPOSITION, CONJUNCTION
la caja

till [tɪl] PREPOSITION, CONJUNCTION
see also **till** NOUN
[1] hasta ◊ *I waited till 10 o'clock.* Esperé hasta las 10.
♦**till now** hasta ahora
♦**till then** hasta entonces
♦**It won't be ready till next week.** No estará listo hasta la semana que viene.
[2] hasta que ◊ *We stayed there till the doctor came.* Nos quedamos allí hasta que vino el médico.

__hasta que__ has to be followed by a verb in the subjunctive when referring to an event in the future.

◊ *Don't go till I arrive.* No te vayas hasta que llegue yo. ◊ *Wait till I come back.* Espera hasta que yo vuelva.

time [taɪm] NOUN
[1] la hora ◊ *What time is it?* ¿Qué hora es? ◊ *What time do you get up?* ¿A qué hora te levantas? ◊ *It was two o'clock, Spanish time.* Eran las dos, hora española.
♦**on time** a la hora ◊ *He never arrives on time.* Nunca llega a la hora.
[2] el tiempo ◊ *I'm sorry, I haven't got time.* Lo siento, no tengo tiempo. ◊ *We waited a long time.* Esperamos mucho tiempo. ◊ *Have you lived here for a long time?* ¿Hace mucho tiempo que vives aquí?
♦**from time to time** de vez en cuando
♦**in time** a tiempo ◊ *We arrived in time for lunch.* Llegamos a tiempo para el almuerzo.
♦**just in time** justo a tiempo
[3] el momento ◊ *This isn't a good time to ask him.* Éste no es buen momento para preguntarle.
♦**for the time being** por el momento
♦**in no time** en un momento ◊ *It was ready in no time.* Estuvo listo en un momento.
[4] la vez (PL las veces) ◊ *this time* esta vez ◊ *How many times?* ¿Cuántas veces?
♦**at times** a veces
♦**two at a time** de dos en dos
♦**in a week's time** dentro de una semana
♦**Come and see us any time.** Ven a vernos cuando quieras.
♦**to have a good time** pasarlo bien ◊ *Did you have a good time?* ¿Lo pasaste bien?
♦**two times two is four** dos por dos son cuatro

time bomb ['taɪmbɔm] NOUN
la bomba de relojería

time off [taɪm'ɔf] NOUN
el tiempo libre

timer ['taɪməʳ] NOUN
el reloj automático (*of video, oven*)
♦**an egg timer** reloj de arena

time-share ['taɪmʃɛəʳ] NOUN
♦**a time-share apartment** un apartamento en multipropiedad

timetable ['taɪmteɪbl] NOUN
[1] el horario (*for train, bus, school*)
[2] el programa (*schedule of events*)

Although __programa__ ends in __-a__, it is actually a masculine noun.

time zone ['taɪmzəun] NOUN
el huso horario

tin [tɪn] NOUN
[1] la lata ◊ *a tin of beans* una lata de alubias ◊ *a biscuit tin* una lata de galletas
[2] el estaño (*metal*)

tinned [tɪnd] ADJECTIVE
enlatado (*food*) ◊ *tinned products* productos enlatados
♦**tinned peaches** melocotones en lata

tin opener ['tɪnəupnəʳ] NOUN
el abrelatas (PL los abrelatas)

tinsel ['tɪnsl] NOUN
el espumillón

tinted ['tɪntɪd] ADJECTIVE
ahumado (*glasses, window*)

tiny ['taɪnɪ] ADJECTIVE
minúsculo

tip [tɪp] NOUN
see also **tip** VERB
1 la propina (*money*) ◊ *to leave a tip* dejar propina
2 el consejo (*advice*) ◊ *a useful tip* un consejo práctico
3 la punta (*end*) ◊ *It's on the tip of my tongue.* Lo tengo en la punta de la lengua.
◆ **a rubbish tip** un vertedero de basuras
◆ **This place is a complete tip!** ¡Esto es una pocilga!

to **tip** [tɪp] VERB
see also **tip** NOUN
dar* una propina a ◊ *Don't forget to tip the waiter.* No te olvides de darle una propina al camarero.

tiptoe ['tɪptəu] NOUN
◆ **on tiptoe** de puntillas

tired ['taɪəd] ADJECTIVE
cansado ◊ *I'm tired.* Estoy cansado.
◆ **to be tired of something** estar* harto de algo

tiring ['taɪərɪŋ] ADJECTIVE
cansado

tissue ['tɪʃu:] NOUN
el Kleenex ® (PL los Kleenex)

title ['taɪtl] NOUN
el título (*of novel, film*)

title role ['taɪtlrəul] NOUN
el papel principal

to [tu:, tə] PREPOSITION
1 a
***a* + *el* changes to *al*.**
◊ *to go to school* ir* al colegio ◊ *to go to the doctor's* ir* al médico ◊ *Let's go to Anne's house.* Vamos a casa de Anne. ◊ *to go to Portugal* ir* a Portugal ◊ *I sold it to a friend.* Se lo vendí a un amigo. ◊ *the answer to the question* la respuesta a la pregunta ◊ *the train to London* el tren a Londres
◆ **from...to...** de...a... ◊ *from nine o'clock to half past three* de las nueve a las tres y media
2 de ◊ *It's easy to do.* Es fácil de hacer*. ◊ *something to drink* algo de beber ◊ *the key to the front door* la llave de la puerta principal
◆ **It's difficult to say.** Es difícil saberlo.
◆ **It's easy to criticize.** Criticar* es muy fácil.
◆ **I've never been to Valencia.** Nunca he estado en Valencia.
◆ **ten to nine** las nueve menos diez
3 hasta ◊ *to count to ten* contar* hasta diez
4 para (*in order to*) ◊ *I did it to help you.* Lo hice para ayudarte. ◊ *She's too young to go to school.* Es muy pequeña para ir al colegio. ◊ *ready to go* listo para irse ◊ *ready to eat* listo para comer
5 con ◊ *to be kind to somebody* ser* amable con alguien ◊ *They were very kind to me.* Fueron muy amables conmigo.
◆ **Give it to her!** ¡Dáselo!
◆ **That's what he said to me.** Eso fue lo que me dijo.
◆ **I've got things to do.** Tengo cosas que hacer.

toad [təud] NOUN
el sapo

toadstool ['təudstu:l] NOUN
la seta venenosa

toast [təust] NOUN
1 (*bread*)
el pan tostado
◆ **a piece of toast** una tostada
2 (*speech*)
el brindis (PL los brindis)
◆ **to drink a toast to somebody** brindar por alguien

toaster ['təustə^r] NOUN
la tostadora

tobacco [tə'bækəu] NOUN
el tabaco

tobacconist's [tə'bækənɪsts] NOUN
el estanco (la tabaquería *LatAm*)

toboggan [tə'bɔgən] NOUN
el trineo

tobogganing [tə'bɔgənɪŋ] NOUN
◆ **to go tobogganing** deslizarse* en trineo

today [tə'deɪ] ADVERB
hoy

toddler ['tɔdlə^r] NOUN
el niño pequeño
la niña pequeña (*que empieza a caminar*)

toe [təu] NOUN
el dedo del pie (PL los dedos de los pies) ◊ *The dog bit my big toe.* El perro me mordió el dedo gordo del pie.

toffee ['tɔfɪ] NOUN
el caramelo

together [tə'geðə^r] ADVERB
1 juntos ◊ *Are they still together?* ¿Todavía están juntos?
2 a la vez (*at the same time*) ◊ *Don't all speak together!* ¡No habléis todos a la vez!
◆ **together with** junto con

toilet ['tɔɪlət] NOUN
1 los servicios (*in public place*)
2 el wáter (*in house*)

toilet paper ['tɔɪlətpeɪpə^r] NOUN
el papel higiénico

toiletries ['tɔɪlətrɪz] PL NOUN
los artículos de perfumería

toilet roll ['tɔɪlətrəul] NOUN
el rollo de papel higiénico

token ['təukən] NOUN
♦**a gift token** un cheque-regalo (PL los cheques-regalo)
told [təuld] VERB *see* **tell**
tolerant ['tɔlərnt] ADJECTIVE
tolerante
toll [təul] NOUN
el peaje (*on bridge, motorway*)
tomato [tə'mɑːtəu] NOUN (PL **tomatoes**)
el tomate ◊ *tomato soup* sopa de tomate
tomboy ['tɔmbɔɪ] NOUN
el marimacho
tomorrow [tə'mɔrəu] ADVERB
mañana ◊ *tomorrow morning* mañana por la mañana ◊ *tomorrow night* mañana por la noche
♦**the day after tomorrow** pasado mañana
ton [tʌn] NOUN
la tonelada ◊ *a ton of coal* una tonelada de carbón
♦**That old bike weighs a ton.** Esa bici vieja pesa una tonelada.
tongue [tʌŋ] NOUN
la lengua
♦**to say something tongue in cheek** decir* algo en plan de broma
tonic ['tɔnɪk] NOUN
la tónica
♦**a gin and tonic** un gin-tonic
tonight [tə'naɪt] ADVERB
esta noche ◊ *Are you going out tonight?* ¿Vas a salir* esta noche? ◊ *I'll sleep well tonight.* Esta noche dormiré bien.
tonsillitis [tɔnsɪ'laɪtɪs] NOUN
la amigdalitis ◊ *She's got tonsillitis.* Tiene amigdalitis.
tonsils ['tɔnslz] PL NOUN
las amígdalas
too [tuː] ADVERB
1 (*as well*)
también ◊ *My sister came too.* Mi hermana también vino.
2 (*excessively*)
demasiado ◊ *The water's too hot.* El agua está demasiado caliente. ◊ *We arrived too late.* Llegamos demasiado tarde.
♦**too much** demasiado ◊ *too much noise* demasiado ruido ◊ *too much butter* demasiada mantequilla ◊ *At Christmas we always eat too much.* En Navidades siempre comemos demasiado. ◊ *£50? – That's too much.* ¿50 libras? – Eso es demasiado.
♦**too many** demasiados MASC (FEM demasiadas) ◊ *too many problems* demasiados problemas ◊ *too many chairs* demasiadas sillas
♦**Too bad!** ¡Qué pena! (*what a pity*)
took [tuk] VERB *see* **take**
tool [tuːl] NOUN
la herramienta
♦**a tool box** una caja de herramientas
tooth [tuːθ] NOUN (PL **teeth**)
el diente
toothache ['tuːθeɪk] NOUN
el dolor de muelas ◊ *These pills are good for toothache.* Estas pastillas son buenas para el dolor de muelas.
♦**I've got toothache.** Me duele una muela.
toothbrush ['tuːθbrʌʃ] NOUN (PL **toothbrushes**)
el cepillo de dientes
toothpaste ['tuːθpeɪst] NOUN
el dentífrico
top [tɔp] NOUN
see also **top** ADJECTIVE
1 la parte de arriba ◊ *at the top of the page* en la parte de arriba de la página
2 (*of mountain*)
la cima
3 (*of box, jar*)
la tapa
4 (*of bottle*)
el tapón (PL los tapones)
♦**a bikini top** la parte de arriba del bikini
♦**the top of the table** el tablero de la mesa
♦**on top of the cupboard** encima del armario
♦**There's a surcharge on top of that.** Hay un recargo, además.
♦**from top to bottom** de arriba abajo ◊ *I searched the house from top to bottom.* Busqué en la casa de arriba abajo.
top [tɔp] ADJECTIVE
see also **top** NOUN
1 de arriba (*shelf*) ◊ *it's on the top shelf* está en la estantería de arriba
♦**the top layer of skin** la capa superior de la piel
♦**the top floor** el último piso
2 eminente ◊ *a top surgeon* un eminente cirujano
♦**a top model** una top model
♦**a top hotel** un hotel de primera
♦**He always gets top marks in French.** Siempre saca excelentes notas en francés.
♦**at top speed** a máxima velocidad
topic ['tɔpɪk] NOUN
el tema
*Although **tema** ends in **-a**, it is actually a masculine noun.*
◊ *The essay can be on any topic.* La redacción puede ser sobre cualquier tema.
topical ['tɔpɪkl] ADJECTIVE
de actualidad MASC, FEM, PL
◊ *a topical issue* un tema de actualidad
topless ['tɔplɪs] ADJECTIVE
topless MASC, FEM, PL
♦**to go topless** ir* en topless
top-secret ['tɔp'siːkrɪt] ADJECTIVE
de alto secreto MASC, FEM, PL

☞

◊ *top-secret documents* documentos de alto secreto

torch [tɔːtʃ] NOUN (PL **torches**)
la linterna (*electric*)

tore, torn [tɔːʳ, tɔːn] VERB *see* **tear**

tortoise ['tɔːtəs] NOUN
la tortuga

torture ['tɔːtʃəʳ] NOUN
see also **torture** VERB
la tortura ◊ *It was pure torture.* Fué una tortura.

to **torture** ['tɔːtʃəʳ] VERB
see also **torture** NOUN
torturar ◊ *Stop torturing that poor animal!* ¡Deja de torturar al pobre animal!

Tory ['tɔːrɪ] ADJECTIVE (PL **Tories**)
see also **Tory** NOUN
conservador MASC
conservadora FEM
◊ *the Tory government* el gobierno conservador

Tory ['tɔːrɪ] NOUN (PL **Tories**)
see also **Tory** ADJECTIVE
el conservador
la conservadora
◊ *the Tories* los conservadores

to **toss** [tɔs] VERB
◆ **to toss pancakes** dar* la vuelta a las crepes en el aire
◆ **Shall we toss for it?** ¿Nos lo jugamos a cara o cruz?

total ['təutl] ADJECTIVE
see also **total** NOUN
total ◊ *The total cost was very high.* El coste total fue muy alto.
◆ **the total amount** el total

total ['təutl] NOUN
see also **total** ADJECTIVE
el total
◆ **the grand total** la suma total

totally ['təutəlɪ] ADVERB
totalmente

touch [tʌtʃ] NOUN
see also **touch** VERB
◆ **to get in touch with somebody** ponerse* en contacto con alguien
◆ **to keep in touch with somebody** mantenerse* en contacto con alguien
◆ **Keep in touch! (1)** ¡Escribe de vez en cuando! (*write*)
◆ **Keep in touch! (2)** ¡Llama de vez en cuando! (*phone*)
◆ **to lose touch** perder* el contacto
◆ **to lose touch with somebody** perder* el contacto con alguien

to **touch** [tʌtʃ] VERB
see also **touch** NOUN
tocar* ◊ *Don't touch that!* ¡No toques eso!

touchdown ['tʌtʃdaun] NOUN
el aterrizaje (*of plane*)

touched [tʌtʃt] ADJECTIVE
emocionado ◊ *I was really touched.* Estaba muy emocionada.

touching ['tʌtʃɪŋ] ADJECTIVE
conmovedor MASC
conmovedora FEM

touchline ['tʌtʃlaɪn] NOUN
la línea de banda

touchy ['tʌtʃɪ] ADJECTIVE
susceptible ◊ *She's a bit touchy today.* Hoy está un poco susceptible.

tough [tʌf] ADJECTIVE
1 difícil ◊ *It was tough, but I managed okay.* Fue difícil, pero me las arreglé.
◆ **It's a tough job.** Es un trabajo duro.
2 duro ◊ *The meat is tough.* La carne está dura.
3 resistente ◊ *tough leather gloves* guantes de cuero resistentes
◆ **He thinks he's a tough guy.** Le gusta hacerse el duro.
◆ **Tough luck!** ¡Mala suerte!

tour ['tuəʳ] NOUN
see also **tour** VERB
1 el recorrido turístico ◊ *We went on a tour of the city.* Hicimos un recorrido turístico por la ciudad.
◆ **a package tour** un viaje organizado
◆ **a bus tour** un viaje en autobús
2 la visita (*of building, exhibition*)
3 la gira
◆ **to go on tour** ir* de gira

to **tour** ['tuəʳ] VERB
see also **tour** NOUN
◆ **Paul Weller is touring Europe.** Paul Weller está haciendo una gira por Europa.

tour guide ['tuəʳgaɪd] NOUN
el guía turístico
la guía turística

tourism ['tuərɪzm] NOUN
el turismo

tourist ['tuərɪst] NOUN
el/la turista
◆ **tourist information office** la oficina de información y turismo

tournament ['tuənəmənt] NOUN
el torneo

tour operator ['tuərɔpəreɪtəʳ] NOUN
el operador turístico (PL los operadores turísticos)

towards [tə'wɔːdz] PREPOSITION
hacia ◊ *He came towards me.* Vino hacia mí. ◊ *my feelings towards him* mis sentimientos hacia él

towel ['tauəl] NOUN
la toalla

tower ['tauəʳ] NOUN

la torre
tower block ['tauəblɔk] NOUN
[1] el bloque de pisos (*of flats*)
[2] el bloque de oficinas (*of offices*)
town [taun] NOUN
la ciudad ◊ *a town plan* un plano de la ciudad ◊ *the town centre* el centro de la ciudad
town hall ['taunhɔ:l] NOUN
el ayuntamiento
tow truck ['təutrʌk] NOUN US
la grúa
toy [tɔɪ] NOUN
el juguete
♦ **a toy shop** una juguetería
♦ **a toy car** un coche de juguete
trace [treɪs] NOUN
see also **trace** VERB
el rastro ◊ *There was no trace of the robbers.* No había rastro de los ladrones.
to **trace** [treɪs] VERB
see also **trace** NOUN
[1] trazar* (*draw*)
[2] encontrar* (*locate*)
tracing paper ['treɪsɪŋpeɪpəʳ] NOUN
el papel de calco
track [træk] NOUN
[1] (*dirt road*)
el camino ◊ *a mountain track* un camino de montaña
[2] (*railway line*)
la vía ◊ *A woman fell onto the tracks.* Una mujer se cayó a la vía.
[3] (*in sport*)
la pista ◊ *two laps of the track* dos vueltas a la pista
[4] (*song*)
la canción (PL las canciones)
◊ *This is my favourite track.* Ésta es mi canción preferida.
[5] (*trail*)
la huella ◊ *They followed the tracks for miles.* Siguieron las huellas durante millas.
to **track down** [træk'daun] VERB
encontrar* ◊ *The police never tracked down the killer.* La policía nunca encontró al asesino.
tracksuit ['træksu:t] NOUN
el chándal (PL los chándals)
tractor ['træktəʳ] NOUN
el tractor
trade [treɪd] NOUN
el oficio ◊ *to learn a trade* aprender un oficio
trade union [treɪd'ju:njən] NOUN
el sindicato
trade unionist [treɪd'ju:njənɪst] NOUN
el/la sindicalista
tradition [trə'dɪʃən] NOUN
la tradición (PL las tradiciones)
traditional [trə'dɪʃənl] ADJECTIVE
tradicional
traffic ['træfɪk] NOUN
el tráfico ◊ *There was a lot of traffic.* Había mucho tráfico.
traffic circle ['træfɪksə:kl] NOUN US
la rotonda
traffic jam ['træfɪkdʒæm] NOUN
el atasco
traffic lights ['træfɪklaɪts] PL NOUN
el semáforo
traffic warden ['træfɪkwɔ:dn] NOUN
el/la guardia de tráfico ◊ *I'm a traffic warden.* Soy guardia de tráfico.
tragedy ['trædʒədɪ] NOUN (PL **tragedies**)
la tragedia
tragic ['trædʒɪk] ADJECTIVE
trágico
trailer ['treɪləʳ] NOUN
[1] (*for luggage, boat*)
el remolque
[2] (*of film*)
el tráiler (PL los tráilers)
train [treɪn] NOUN
see also **train** VERB
el tren
to **train** [treɪn] VERB
see also **train** NOUN
entrenar ◊ *to train for a race* entrenar para una carrera
♦ **to train as a teacher** estudiar magisterio
♦ **to train an animal to do something** enseñar a un animal a hacer* algo
trained [treɪnd] ADJECTIVE
cualificado (calificado *LatAm*) ◊ *highly trained workers* los trabajadores altamente cualificados
♦ **She's a trained nurse.** Es enfermera diplomada.
trainee [treɪ'ni:] NOUN
(*apprentice*)
el aprendiz (PL los aprendices)
la aprendiza
◊ *He's a trainee plumber.* Es aprendiz de fontanero.
♦ **She's a trainee teacher.** Es profesora de prácticas.
trainer ['treɪnəʳ] NOUN
[1] (*sports*)
el entrenador
la entrenadora
[2] (*of animals*)
el amaestrador
la amaestradora
trainers ['treɪnəz] PL NOUN
las zapatillas de deporte
training ['treɪnɪŋ] NOUN
[1] la formación ◊ *a training course* un curso de formación
[2] el entrenamiento (*in sport*)
♦ **He strained a muscle in training.** Se hizo un esguince entrenando.
tram [træm] NOUN

☞

el tranvía

*Although **tranvía** ends in **-a**, it is actually a masculine noun.*

tramp [træmp] NOUN
el vagabundo
la vagabunda

trampoline ['træmpəliːn] NOUN
la cama elástica

tranquillizer ['træŋkwılaızəʳ] NOUN
el sedante ◊ *She's on tranquillizers.* Está tomando sedantes.

transfer ['trænsfəʳ] NOUN
1 la transferencia ◊ *a bank transfer* una transferencia bancaria
2 la calcomanía (*sticker*)

transfusion [træns'fjuːʒən] NOUN
la transfusión (PL las transfusiones)

transistor [træn'zıstəʳ] NOUN
el transistor

to **translate** [trænz'leıt] VERB
traducir* ◊ *to translate something into English* traducir* algo al inglés

translation [trænz'leıʃən] NOUN
la traducción (PL las traducciones)

translator [trænz'leıtəʳ] NOUN
el traductor
la traductora
◊ *Anita's a translator.* Anita es traductora.

transparent [træns'pærnt] ADJECTIVE
transparente

transplant ['trænsplɑːnt] NOUN
el trasplante ◊ *a heart transplant* un trasplante de corazón

transport ['trænspɔːt] NOUN
see also **transport** VERB
el transporte ◊ *public transport* el transporte público

to **transport** [træns'pɔːt] VERB
see also **transport** NOUN
transportar

trap [træp] NOUN
la trampa

trash [træʃ] NOUN US
la basura
◆ **the trash can** el cubo de la basura

trashy ['træʃı] ADJECTIVE
malísimo ◊ *a trashy film* una película malísima

traumatic [trɔː'mætık] ADJECTIVE
traumático ◊ *It was a traumatic experience.* Fue una experiencia traumática.

travel ['trævl] NOUN
see also **travel** VERB
◆ **Air travel is relatively cheap.** Viajar en avión es relativamente barato.

to **travel** ['trævl] VERB
see also **travel** NOUN
viajar ◊ *I prefer to travel by train.* Prefiero viajar en tren.
◆ **I'd like to travel round the world.** Me gustaría dar la vuelta al mundo.
◆ **We travelled over 800 kilometres.** Hicimos más de 800 kilómetros.
◆ **News travels fast!** ¡Las noticias vuelan!

travel agency ['trævleıdʒənsı] NOUN (PL **travel agencies**)
la agencia de viajes

travel agent ['trævleıdʒənt] NOUN
◆ **She's a travel agent.** Es empleada de una agencia de viajes.

traveller ['trævləʳ] NOUN (US **traveler**)
el viajero
la viajera

traveller's cheque [trævləz'tʃɛk] NOUN (US **traveler's check**)
el cheque de viaje (PL los cheques de viaje)

travelling ['trævlıŋ] NOUN (US **traveling**)
◆ **I love travelling.** Me encanta viajar.

travel sickness ['trævlsıknıs] NOUN
el mareo

tray [treı] NOUN
la bandeja

to **tread** [trɛd] VERB (**trod, trodden**)
pisar
◆ **to tread on something** pisar algo ◊ *He trod on her foot.* Le pisó el pie.

treasure ['trɛʒəʳ] NOUN
el tesoro

treat [triːt] NOUN
see also **treat** VERB
◆ **As a birthday treat, I'll take you out to dinner.** Como es tu cumpleaños, te invito a cenar.
◆ **She bought a special treat for the children.** Les compró algo especial a los niños.
◆ **I'm going to give myself a treat.** Me voy a dar un gusto.

to **treat** [triːt] VERB
see also **treat** NOUN
tratar ◊ *The hostages were well treated.* Los rehenes fueron tratados bien.
◆ **She was treated for a minor head wound.** La atendieron de una leve herida en la cabeza.
◆ **to treat somebody to something** invitar a alguien a algo ◊ *I'll treat you!* ¡Te invito yo!

treatment ['triːtmənt] NOUN
1 el tratamiento (*medical*) ◊ *an effective treatment for eczema* un tratamiento efectivo contra el eccema
2 el trato (*of person*) ◊ *We don't want any special treatment.* No queremos ningún trato especial.

to **treble** ['trɛbl] VERB

triplicarse* ◊ *The cost of living has trebled.* El coste de la vida se ha triplicado.

tree [triː] NOUN
el árbol

to **tremble** ['trɛmbl] VERB
temblar*

trend [trɛnd] NOUN
1 la tendencia ◊ *There's a trend towards part-time employment.* Existe una tendencia hacia el empleo a tiempo parcial.
2 la moda (*fashion*) ◊ *the latest trend* la última moda

trendy ['trɛndɪ] ADJECTIVE
moderno

trial ['traɪəl] NOUN
el juicio (*in law*)

triangle ['traɪæŋgl] NOUN
el triángulo

tribe [traɪb] NOUN
la tribu

trick [trɪk] NOUN
see also **trick** VERB
1 la broma ◊ *to play a trick on somebody* gastar una broma a alguien
2 el truco ◊ *It's not easy: there's a trick to it.* No es fácil: tiene un truco.

to **trick** [trɪk] VERB
see also **trick** NOUN
♦ **to trick somebody** engañar a alguien

tricky ['trɪkɪ] ADJECTIVE
peliagudo (*problem*)

tricycle ['traɪsɪkl] NOUN
el triciclo

trifle ['traɪfl] NOUN
el bizcocho borracho

to **trim** [trɪm] VERB
see also **trim** NOUN
recortar

trim [trɪm] NOUN
see also **trim** VERB
♦ **to have a trim** cortarse las puntas

trip [trɪp] NOUN
see also **trip** VERB
el viaje ◊ *to go on a trip* ir* de viaje
◊ *Have a good trip!* ¡Buen viaje!
♦ **a day trip** una excursión de un día

to **trip** [trɪp] VERB
see also **trip** NOUN
tropezarse* (*stumble*) ◊ *He tripped on the stairs.* Se tropezó en las escaleras.
♦ **to trip up** tropezarse*
♦ **to trip somebody up** poner* la zancadilla a alguien

triple ['trɪpl] ADJECTIVE
triple

triplets ['trɪplɪts] PL NOUN
los trillizos MASC
las trillizas FEM

trivial ['trɪvɪəl] ADJECTIVE
insignificante

trod, trodden [trɔd, trɔdn] VERB *see* **tread**

trolley ['trɔlɪ] NOUN
el carrito

trombone [trɔm'bəun] NOUN
el trombón (PL los trombones)

troops [truːps] PL NOUN
las tropas

trophy ['trəufɪ] NOUN (PL **trophies**)
el trofeo

tropical ['trɔpɪkl] ADJECTIVE
tropical

to **trot** [trɔt] VERB
trotar

trouble ['trʌbl] NOUN
el problema
*Although **problema** ends in **-a**, it is actually a masculine noun.*
◊ *The trouble is, it's too expensive.* El problema es que es demasiado caro.
♦ **What's the trouble?** ¿Qué pasa?
♦ **to be in trouble** tener* problemas
♦ **stomach trouble** problemas de estómago
♦ **to take a lot of trouble over something** poner* mucho cuidado en algo
♦ **Don't worry, it's no trouble.** No te preocupes, no importa.

troublemaker ['trʌblmeɪkəʳ] NOUN
el alborotador
la alborotadora

trousers ['trauzəz] PL NOUN
los pantalones ◊ *a pair of trousers* unos pantalones

trout [traut] NOUN (PL **trout**)
la trucha

truant ['truənt] NOUN
♦ **to play truant** hacer* novillos

truck [trʌk] NOUN
el camión (PL los camiones)

truck driver ['trʌkdraɪvəʳ] NOUN
el camionero
la camionera
◊ *He's a truck driver.* Es camionero.

trucker ['trʌkəʳ] NOUN
el camionero
la camionera

true [truː] ADJECTIVE
verdadero (*love, courage*)
♦ **It's true.** Es verdad.
♦ **to come true** hacerse* realidad ◊ *I hope my dream will come true.* Espero que mi sueño se haga realidad.

trumpet ['trʌmpɪt] NOUN
la trompeta

trunk [trʌŋk] NOUN
1 el tronco (*of tree*)
2 la trompa (*of elephant*)
3 el baúl (*luggage*)
4 el maletero (*of car*) US

trunks [trʌŋks] PL NOUN
♦ **swimming trunks** el traje de baño

trust [trʌst] NOUN

☞

see also **trust** VERB
la confianza ◊ *to have trust in somebody* tener* confianza en alguien

to **trust** [trʌst] VERB
see also **trust** NOUN
◆ **Don't you trust me?** ¿No tienes confianza en mí?
◆ **Trust me!** ¡Confía en mí!
◆ **I don't trust him.** No me fío de él.

trusting ['trʌstɪŋ] ADJECTIVE
confiado

truth [tru:θ] NOUN
la verdad

truthful ['tru:θful] ADJECTIVE
1 sincero (*person*) ◊ *She's a very truthful person.* Es una persona muy sincera.
2 verídico (*account*)

try [traɪ] NOUN (PL **tries**)
see also **try** VERB
el intento ◊ *his third try* su tercer intento
◆ **to give something a try** intentar algo
◆ **It's worth a try.** Vale la pena intentarlo.
◆ **Have a try!** ¡Inténtalo!

to **try** [traɪ] VERB (**tried, tried**)
see also **try** NOUN
1 intentar ◊ *to try to do something* intentar hacer algo
◆ **to try again** volver* a intentar
2 probar* ◊ *Would you like to try some?* ¿Quieres probar un poco?

to **try on** [traɪ'ɔn] VERB
probarse* (*clothes*)

to **try out** [traɪ'aut] VERB
probar* (*product, machine*)

T-shirt ['ti:ʃə:t] NOUN
la camiseta

tube [tju:b] NOUN
el tubo
◆ **the Tube** el Metro (*underground*)

tuberculosis [tjubə:kju'ləusɪs] NOUN
la tuberculosis ◊ *He's got tuberculosis.* Tiene tuberculosis.

Tuesday ['tju:zdɪ] NOUN
el martes (PL los martes) ◊ *I saw her on Tuesday.* La vi el martes. ◊ *every Tuesday* todos los martes ◊ *last Tuesday* el martes pasado ◊ *next Tuesday* el martes que viene ◊ *on Tuesdays* los martes

tug-of-war [tʌgəv'wɔ:ʳ] NOUN
el juego de la cuerda

tuition [tju:'ɪʃən] NOUN
las clases ◊ *private tuition* clases particulares

tulip ['tju:lɪp] NOUN
el tulipán (PL los tulipanes)

tumble dryer [tʌmbl'draɪəʳ] NOUN
la secadora

tummy ['tʌmɪ] NOUN (PL **tummies**)
la tripa (*informal*)
◆ **he has a tummy ache** le duele la tripa

tuna ['tju:nə] NOUN (PL **tuna** *or* **tunas**)
el atún (PL los atunes)

tune [tju:n] NOUN
la melodía (*melody*)
◆ **to play in tune** tocar* bien
◆ **to sing out of tune** desafinar

Tunisia [tju:'nɪzɪə] NOUN
Túnez MASC

tunnel ['tʌnl] NOUN
el túnel

Turk [tə:k] NOUN
el turco
la turca
◊ *the Turks* los turcos

turkey ['tə:kɪ] NOUN
el pavo

Turkey ['tə:kɪ] NOUN
Turquía FEM

Turkish ['tə:kɪʃ] ADJECTIVE
see also **Turkish** NOUN
turco

Turkish ['tə:kɪʃ] NOUN
see also **Turkish** ADJECTIVE
el turco (*language*)

turn [tə:n] NOUN
see also **turn** VERB
la curva (*bend in road*)
◆ **"no left turn"** "prohibido girar a la izquierda"
◆ **to take turns** turnarse
◆ **It's my turn!** ¡Me toca a mí!

to **turn** [tə:n] VERB
see also **turn** NOUN
1 girar ◊ *Turn right at the lights.* Gira a la derecha al llegar al semáforo.
2 ponerse* (*become*) ◊ *When he's drunk he turns nasty.* Cuando se emborracha se pone desagradable.
◆ **The weather turned cold.** Empezó a hacer frío.
◆ **to turn into something** convertirse* en algo ◊ *The holiday turned into a nightmare.* Las vacaciones se convirtieron en una pesadilla.

to **turn back** [tə:n'bæk] VERB
volver* hacia atrás ◊ *We turned back.* Volvimos hacia atrás.

to **turn down** [tə:n'daun] VERB
1 rechazar* ◊ *He turned down the offer.* Rechazó la oferta.
2 bajar ◊ *Shall I turn the heating down?* ¿Bajo la calefacción?

to **turn off** [tə:n'ɔf] VERB
1 apagar* (*light, radio*)
2 cerrar* (*tap*)
3 parar (*engine*)

to **turn on** [tə:n'ɔn] VERB
1 encender* (*light, radio*)

2 abrir* (*tap*)
3 poner* en marcha (*engine*)

to **turn out** [tə:n'aut] VERB
resultar ◊ *It turned out to be a mistake.* Resultó ser un error. ◊ *It turned out that she was right.* Resultó que ella tenía razón.

to **turn round** [tə:n'raund] VERB
1 dar* la vuelta (*car*)
2 darse* la vuelta (*person*)

to **turn up** [tə:n'ʌp] VERB
1 aparecer* ◊ *She never turned up.* No apareció. ◊ *The lost dog turned up in the next village.* El perro extraviado apareció en el pueblo vecino.
2 subir ◊ *Could you turn up the radio?* ¿Puedes subir la radio?

turning ['tə:nɪŋ] NOUN
♦ **We took the wrong turning. (1)** (*in the country*) Nos equivocamos de carretera.
♦ **We took the wrong turning. (2)** (*in the city*) Nos equivocamos de bocacalle.

turnip ['tə:nɪp] NOUN
el nabo

turquoise ['tə:kwɔɪz] ADJECTIVE
turquesa MASC, FEM, PL

turtle ['tə:tl] NOUN
la tortuga de mar

tutor ['tju:təʳ] NOUN
(*private teacher*)
el profesor particular
la profesora particular

tuxedo [tʌk'si:dəu] NOUN (PL **tuxedos**)
US
el esmoquin (PL los esmóquines)

TV [ti:'vi:] NOUN
la tele

tweezers ['twi:zəz] PL NOUN
las pinzas ◊ *a pair of tweezers* unas pinzas

twelfth [twɛlfθ] ADJECTIVE
duodécimo ◊ *the twelfth floor* el duodécimo piso
♦ **the twelfth of August** el doce de agosto

twelve [twɛlv] NUMERAL
doce ◊ *She's twelve.* Tiene doce años.
♦ **twelve o'clock** las doce

twentieth ['twɛntɪɪθ] ADJECTIVE
vigésimo
♦ **the twentieth floor** la planta veinte
♦ **the twentieth of May** el veinte de mayo

twenty ['twɛntɪ] NUMERAL
veinte ◊ *He's twenty.* Tiene veinte años.

twice [twaɪs] ADVERB
dos veces ◊ *He had to repeat it twice.* Tuvo que repetirlo dos veces.
♦ **twice as much** el doble ◊ *He gets twice as much pocket money as me.* Le dan el doble de paga que a mí.

twin [twɪn] NOUN
el mellizo
la melliza
◊ *my twin brother* mi hermano mellizo
◊ *her twin sister* su hermana melliza
♦ **identical twins** gemelos
♦ **a twin room** una habitación con dos camas

twinned [twɪnd] ADJECTIVE
hermanado ◊ *Nottingham is twinned with Minsk.* Nottingham está hermanada con Minsk.

to **twist** [twɪst] VERB
1 torcer*
♦ **He's twisted his ankle.** Se ha torcido el tobillo.
2 tergiversar* ◊ *You're twisting my words.* Estás tergiversando lo que he dicho.

twit [twɪt] NOUN
el/la imbécil (*informal*)

two [tu:] NUMERAL
dos ◊ *She's two.* Tiene dos años.
♦ **The two of them can sing.** Los dos saben cantar.

type [taɪp] NOUN
see also **type** VERB
el tipo ◊ *What type of camera have you got?* ¿Qué tipo de cámara tienes?

to **type** [taɪp] VERB
see also **type** NOUN
escribir* a máquina ◊ *Can you type?* ¿Sabes escribir a máquina? ◊ *to type a letter* escribir* una carta a máquina

typewriter ['taɪpraɪtəʳ] NOUN
la máquina de escribir

typical ['tɪpɪkl] ADJECTIVE
típico ◊ *That's just typical!* ¡Típico!

tyre ['taɪəʳ] NOUN
el neumático
♦ **tyre pressure** la presión de los neumáticos

U

UFO ['juːɛfəu] ABBREVIATION (PL **UFOs**) (= *Unidentified Flying Object*)
el OVNI (= el Objeto Volador No Identificado)

ugh [əːh] EXCLAMATION
¡puf!

ugly ['ʌglɪ] ADJECTIVE
feo

UK [juː'keɪ] ABBREVIATION (= *United Kingdom*)
el RU (= el Reino Unido)

ulcer ['ʌlsəʳ] NOUN
la úlcera
◆**a mouth ulcer** una llaga en la boca

Ulster ['ʌlstəʳ] NOUN
el Ulster

ultimate ['ʌltɪmət] ADJECTIVE
máximo ◇ *the ultimate challenge* el máximo desafío
◆**the ultimate in luxury** el no va más del lujo

ultimately ['ʌltɪmətlɪ] ADVERB
a fin de cuentas ◇ *Ultimately, it's your decision.* A fin de cuentas, es tu decisión.

umbrella [ʌm'brɛlə] NOUN
el paraguas (PL los paraguas)

umpire ['ʌmpaɪəʳ] NOUN
el árbitro
la árbitra

UN [juː'ɛn] ABBREVIATION (= *United Nations*)
la ONU (= la Organización de las Naciones Unidas)

unable [ʌn'eɪbl] ADJECTIVE
◆**to be unable to do something** no poder* hacer algo ◇ *Unfortunately, he was unable to come.* Desafortunadamente, no ha podido venir.

unacceptable [ʌnək'sɛptəbl] ADJECTIVE
inaceptable

unanimous [juː'nænɪməs] ADJECTIVE
unánime

unattended [ʌnə'tɛndɪd] ADJECTIVE
◆**Please do not leave your luggage unattended.** Por favor, no abandonen su equipaje.

unavoidable [ʌnə'vɔɪdəbl] ADJECTIVE
inevitable

unaware [ʌnə'wɛəʳ] ADJECTIVE
◆**I was unaware of the regulations.** Ignoraba el reglamento.
◆**She was unaware that she was being filmed.** No se había dado cuenta de que la estaban filmando.

unbearable [ʌn'bɛərəbl] ADJECTIVE
insoportable

unbeatable [ʌn'biːtəbl] ADJECTIVE
inmejorable (*quality, price*)

unbelievable [ʌnbɪ'liːvəbl] ADJECTIVE
increíble

unborn [ʌn'bɔːn] ADJECTIVE
◆**the unborn child** el feto

unbreakable [ʌn'breɪkəbl] ADJECTIVE
irrompible

uncanny [ʌn'kænɪ] ADJECTIVE
extraño ◇ *That's uncanny!* ¡Es extraño!
◆**an uncanny resemblance** un asombroso parecido

uncertain [ʌn'səːtn] ADJECTIVE
incierto ◇ *The future is uncertain.* El futuro es incierto.
◆**to be uncertain about something** no estar* seguro de algo
◆**She was uncertain how to begin.** No sabía muy bien cómo empezar.

uncivilized [ʌn'sɪvɪlaɪzd] ADJECTIVE
poco civilizado (*behaviour*)

uncle ['ʌŋkl] NOUN
el tío
◆**my uncle and aunt** mis tíos

uncomfortable [ʌn'kʌmfətəbl] ADJECTIVE
incómodo

unconscious [ʌn'kɔnʃəs] ADJECTIVE
inconsciente

unconventional [ʌnkən'vɛnʃənl] ADJECTIVE
poco convencional

under ['ʌndəʳ] PREPOSITION

> *When something is located under something, use* **debajo de.** *When there is movement involved, use* **por debajo de.**

1 debajo de ◇ *The cat's under the table.* El gato está debajo de la mesa. ◇ *The tunnel goes under the Channel.* El túnel pasa por debajo del Canal.
◆**under there** ahí debajo ◇ *What's under there?* ¿Qué hay ahí debajo?
2 menos de ◇ *under 20 people* menos de 20 personas
◆**children under 10** niños menores de 10 años

underage [ʌndər'eɪdʒ] ADJECTIVE
◆**He's underage.** Es menor de edad.

undercover [ʌndə'kʌvəʳ] ADJECTIVE, ADVERB
secreto ◇ *an undercover agent* un agente secreto ◇ *She was working undercover for the FBI.* Trabajaba como agente secreto para el FBI.

to **underestimate** ['ʌndər'ɛstɪmeɪt] VERB
subestimar ◇ *You shouldn't underestimate her.* No la subestimes.

to **undergo** [ʌndə'gəu] VERB (**underwent, undergone**)
someterse a (*operation*)

underground ['ʌndəgraund] ADJECTIVE

* Verbs marked with this symbol are irregular. See pages 380-382 for further details

see also **underground** ADVERB, NOUN
subterráneo ◊ *an underground car park* un parking subterráneo

underground ['ʌndəgraund] ADVERB
see also **underground** ADJECTIVE, NOUN
bajo tierra ◊ *Moles live underground.* Los topos viven bajo tierra.

underground ['ʌndəgraund] NOUN
see also **underground** ADJECTIVE, ADVERB
el metro ◊ *Is there an underground in Barcelona?* ¿Hay metro en Barcelona?

to **underline** [ʌndə'laɪn] VERB
subrayar

underneath [ʌndə'ni:θ] PREPOSITION, ADVERB
When something is located underneath something, use ***debajo de****. When there is movement involved, use* ***por debajo de****.*
1 debajo de ◊ *underneath the carpet* debajo de la moqueta ◊ *I got out of the car and looked underneath.* Bajé del coche y miré debajo.
2 por debajo de ◊ *I walked underneath a ladder.* Pasé por debajo de una escalera.

underpaid [ʌndə'peɪd] ADJECTIVE
mal pagado ◊ *Teachers are underpaid.* Los profesores están mal pagados.

underpants ['ʌndəpænts] PL NOUN
los calzoncillos ◊ *a pair of underpants* unos calzoncillos

underpass ['ʌndəpɑ:s] NOUN (PL **underpasses**)
el paso subterráneo

undershirt ['ʌndəʃə:t] NOUN US
la camiseta

underskirt ['ʌndəskə:t] NOUN
las enaguas

to **understand** [ʌndə'stænd] VERB (**understood, understood**)
entender* ◊ *Do you understand?* ¿Entiendes? ◊ *I don't understand the question.* No entiendo la pregunta.
♦ **Is that understood?** ¿Está claro?

understanding [ʌndə'stændɪŋ] ADJECTIVE
comprensivo ◊ *She's very understanding.* Es muy comprensiva.

understood [ʌndə'stud] VERB *see* **understand**

undertaker ['ʌndəteɪkə^r] NOUN
el empleado de una funeraria
la empleada de una funeraria
♦ **the undertaker's** la funeraria

underwater ['ʌndə'wɔ:tə^r] ADJECTIVE, ADVERB
1 subacuático ◊ *underwater photography* fotografía subacuática
2 bajo el agua ◊ *This sequence was filmed underwater.* Esta secuencia se filmó bajo el agua.

underwear ['ʌndəwɛə^r] NOUN
la ropa interior

underwent [ʌndə'wɛnt] VERB *see* **undergo**

to **undo** [ʌn'du:] VERB (**undid, undone**)
1 desabrochar (*button, blouse*)
2 desatar (*knot, parcel, shoe laces*)
3 abrir* (*zipper*)

to **undress** [ʌn'drɛs] VERB
desnudarse (*get undressed*) ◊ *The doctor told me to undress.* El médico me dijo que me desnudase.

uneconomic ['ʌni:kə'nɔmɪk] ADJECTIVE
♦ **an uneconomic factory** una fábrica poco rentable
♦ **It's uneconomic to put on courses for so few students.** No es rentable organizar cursos para tan pocos alumnos.

unemployed [ʌnɪm'plɔɪd] ADJECTIVE
parado (desempleado *LatAm*)
♦ **He's been unemployed for a year.** Lleva parado un año.
♦ **the unemployed** los parados (los desempleados *LatAm*)

unemployment [ʌnɪm'plɔɪmənt] NOUN
el desempleo

unexpected [ʌnɪks'pɛktɪd] ADJECTIVE
inesperado ◊ *an unexpected visitor* una visita inesperada

unexpectedly [ʌnɪks'pɛktɪdlɪ] ADVERB
de improviso

unfair [ʌn'fɛə^r] ADJECTIVE
injusto ◊ *This law is unfair to women.* Esta ley es injusta para las mujeres.

unfamiliar [ʌnfə'mɪlɪə^r] ADJECTIVE
desconocido ◊ *I heard an unfamiliar voice.* Oí una voz desconocida.

unfashionable [ʌn'fæʃnəbl] ADJECTIVE
pasado de moda

unfit [ʌn'fɪt] ADJECTIVE
♦ **I'm unfit at the moment.** En este momento no estoy en forma.

to **unfold** [ʌn'fəuld] VERB
desplegar* ◊ *She unfolded the map.* Desplegó el mapa.

unforgettable [ʌnfə'gɛtəbl] ADJECTIVE
inolvidable

unfortunately [ʌn'fɔ:tʃənətlɪ] ADVERB
desafortunadamente

unfriendly [ʌn'frɛndlɪ] ADJECTIVE
antipático ◊ *The waiters are a bit unfriendly.* Los camareros son un poco antipáticos.

ungrateful [ʌn'greɪtful] ADJECTIVE
desagradecido

unhappy [ʌn'hæpɪ] ADJECTIVE
infeliz (PL infelices) ◊ *He was very unhappy as a child.* De niño fue muy infeliz.
♦ **to look unhappy** parecer* triste

unhealthy [ʌn'hɛlθɪ] ADJECTIVE
1 malo para la salud (*food*)
2 con mala salud (*ill*)
3 malsano (*atmosphere*)

uniform ['ju:nɪfɔ:m] NOUN
el uniforme

☞

◆**school uniform** el uniforme de colegio

uninhabited [ʌnɪn'hæbɪtɪd] ADJECTIVE
1 deshabitado (*house*)
2 despoblado (*island*)

union ['ju:njən] NOUN
el sindicato (*trade union*)

Union Jack [ju:njən'jæk] NOUN
la bandera del Reino Unido

unique [ju:'ni:k] ADJECTIVE
único

unit ['ju:nɪt] NOUN
la unidad ◇ *a unit of measurement* una unidad de medida

◆**a kitchen unit** un módulo de cocina

United Kingdom [ju:naɪtɪd'kɪŋdəm] NOUN
el Reino Unido

United Nations [ju:naɪtɪd'neɪʃənz] NOUN
las Naciones Unidas

United States [ju:naɪtɪd'steɪts] NOUN
los Estados Unidos

universe ['ju:nɪvə:s] NOUN
el universo

university [ju:nɪ'və:sɪtɪ] NOUN (PL **universities**)
la universidad ◇ *She's at university.* Está en la universidad. ◇ *Do you want to go to university?* ¿Quieres ir a la universidad? ◇ *Lancaster University* la Universidad de Lancaster

unleaded petrol ['ʌnlɛdɪd'pɛtrəl] NOUN
la gasolina sin plomo

unless [ʌn'lɛs] CONJUNCTION
a no ser que

> ***a no ser que*** *has to be followed by a verb in the subjunctive.*

◇ *I won't come unless you phone me.* No vendré a no ser que me llames.

◆**Unless I am mistaken, we're lost.** Si no me equivoco, estamos perdidos.

unlike [ʌn'laɪk] PREPOSITION
a diferencia de ◇ *Unlike him, I really enjoy flying.* A diferencia de él, a mí me encanta viajar en avión.

unlikely [ʌn'laɪklɪ] ADJECTIVE
poco probable ◇ *That's possible, but unlikely.* Es posible pero poco probable. ◇ *He's unlikely to come.* Es poco probable que venga.

> ***es poco probable que*** *has to be followed by a verb in the subjunctive.*

unlisted ['ʌn'lɪstɪd] ADJECTIVE US

◆**an unlisted number** un número que no figura en la guía telefónica

to **unload** [ʌn'ləud] VERB
descargar* ◇ *We unloaded the furniture.* Descargamos los muebles.

to **unlock** [ʌn'lɔk] VERB
abrir* ◇ *He unlocked the door of the car.* Abrió la puerta del coche.

unlucky [ʌn'lʌkɪ] ADJECTIVE

◆**to be unlucky (1)** (*be unfortunate*) tener* mala suerte ◇ *Did you win? – No, I was unlucky.* ¿Ganaste? – No, tuve mala suerte.

◆**to be unlucky (2)** (*bring bad luck*) traer* mala suerte ◇ *They say thirteen is an unlucky number.* Dicen que el número trece trae mala suerte.

unmarried [ʌn'mærɪd] ADJECTIVE
soltero ◇ *an unmarried mother* una madre soltera

◆**an unmarried couple** una pareja no casada

unnatural [ʌn'nætʃrəl] ADJECTIVE
poco natural

unnecessary [ʌn'nɛsəsərɪ] ADJECTIVE
innecesario

unofficial [ʌnə'fɪʃl] ADJECTIVE
no oficial

to **unpack** [ʌn'pæk] VERB
deshacer* ◇ *I unpacked my suitcase.* Deshice la maleta. ◇ *I went to my room to unpack. (1)* (*one suitcase*) Fui a mi habitación a deshacer la maleta. ◇ *I went to my room to unpack. (2)* (*more than one suitcase*) Fui a mi habitación a deshacer las maletas.

◆**I haven't unpacked my clothes yet.** Todavía no he sacado la ropa de la maleta.

unpleasant [ʌn'plɛznt] ADJECTIVE
desagradable

to **unplug** [ʌn'plʌg] VERB
desenchufar

unpopular [ʌn'pɔpjulə^r] ADJECTIVE
impopular ◇ *It was an unpopular decision.* Fue una decisión impopular.

◆**She's an unpopular child.** Tiene muy pocos amigos.

unpredictable [ʌnprɪ'dɪktəbl] ADJECTIVE
imprevisible

unreal [ʌn'rɪəl] ADJECTIVE
increíble ◇ *It was unreal!* ¡Fue increíble!

unrealistic ['ʌnrɪə'lɪstɪk] ADJECTIVE
poco realista

unreasonable [ʌn'ri:znəbl] ADJECTIVE
poco razonable ◇ *I think her attitude is unreasonable.* Creo que su actitud es poco razonable.

unreliable [ʌnrɪ'laɪəbl] ADJECTIVE
poco fiable ◇ *The car was slow and unreliable.* El coche era lento y poco fiable.

◆**He's completely unreliable.** Es muy informal.

to **unroll** [ʌn'rəul] VERB
desenrollar

unsatisfactory ['ʌnsætɪs'fæktərɪ] ADJECTIVE
insatisfactorio

to **unscrew** [ʌn'skru:] VERB

1 desestornillar (*screw*)
2 desenroscar* (*lid*)

unshaven [ʌn'ʃeɪvn] ADJECTIVE
sin afeitar

unskilled [ʌn'skɪld] ADJECTIVE
♦ **an unskilled worker** un trabajador no cualificado MASC (FEM una trabajadora no cualificada) (un trabajador no calificado *LatAm*)

unstable [ʌn'steɪbl] ADJECTIVE
inestable

unsteady [ʌn'stɛdɪ] ADJECTIVE
1 inestable (*chair*)
2 vacilante (*walk, voice*)
♦ **He was unsteady on his feet.** Caminaba con paso vacilante.

unsuccessful [ʌnsək'sɛsful] ADJECTIVE
fallido (*attempt*)
♦ **to be unsuccessful in doing something** no conseguir* hacer algo
♦ **an unsuccessful artist** un artista sin éxito

unsuitable [ʌn'su:təbl] ADJECTIVE
inapropiado (*clothes, equipment*)

untidy [ʌn'taɪdɪ] ADJECTIVE
1 desordenado (*disorganized*) ◊ *Your bedroom is really untidy.* Tu cuarto está muy desordenado.
2 descuidado (*writing*)
♦ **She always looks so untidy.** Siempre va tan desaliñada.

to **untie** [ʌn'taɪ] VERB
1 deshacer* (*knot, parcel*)
2 desatar (*shoelace, animal*)

until [ən'tɪl] PREPOSITION, CONJUNCTION
1 hasta ◊ *I waited until 10 o'clock.* Esperé hasta las 10. ◊ *It won't be ready until next week.* No estará listo hasta la semana que viene.
♦ **until now** hasta ahora ◊ *It's never been a problem until now.* Hasta ahora nunca ha sido un problema.
♦ **until then** hasta entonces ◊ *Until then I'd never been to Italy.* Hasta entonces no había estado nunca en Italia.
2 hasta que ◊ *We stayed there until the doctor came.* Nos quedamos allí hasta que vino el médico.

***hasta que** has to be followed by a verb in the subjunctive when referring to a future event.*

◊ *Don't go until I arrive.* No te vayas hasta que llegue yo. ◊ *Wait until I come back.* Espera hasta que yo vuelva.

unusual [ʌn'ju:ʒuəl] ADJECTIVE
1 poco común ◊ *an unusual shape* una forma poco común
2 raro

***es raro que** has to be followed by a verb in the subjunctive.*

◊ *It's unusual to get snow at this time of year.* Es raro que nieve en esta época del año.

unwilling [ʌn'wɪlɪŋ] ADJECTIVE
♦ **He was unwilling to help me.** No estaba dispuesto a ayudarme.

to **unwind** [ʌn'waɪnd] VERB (**unwound, unwound**)
relajarse (*relax*)

unwise [ʌn'waɪz] ADJECTIVE
imprudente ◊ *That was unwise of you.* Lo que hiciste fue imprudente.

unwound [ʌn'waund] VERB *see* **unwind**

to **unwrap** [ʌn'ræp] VERB
abrir* ◊ *After the meal we unwrapped the presents.* Después de comer abrimos los regalos.

up [ʌp] PREPOSITION, ADVERB

*For other expressions with **up**, see the verbs **come, put, turn** etc.*

arriba ◊ *up on the hill* arriba de la colina ◊ *up here* aquí arriba ◊ *up there* allí arriba
♦ **up north** en el norte
♦ **They live up the road.** Viven en esta calle, un poco más allá.
♦ **to be up** estar* levantado ◊ *We were up at six.* A las seis estábamos levantados. ◊ *He's not up yet.* Todavía no se ha levantado.
♦ **What's up?** ¿Qué hay?
♦ **What's up with her?** ¿Qué le pasa?
♦ **to go up** subir ◊ *The bus went up the hill.* El autobús subió la colina.
♦ **to go up to somebody** acercarse* a alguien ◊ *She came up to me.* Se me acercó.
♦ **up to** hasta ◊ *to count up to 50* contar* hasta 50 ◊ *up to three hours* hasta tres horas ◊ *up to now* hasta ahora
♦ **It's up to you.** Depende de ti.

upbringing ['ʌpbrɪŋɪŋ] NOUN
la educación

uphill ['ʌp'hɪl] ADJECTIVE
♦ **It was an uphill struggle.** Fue una tarea muy difícil.

upper ['ʌpəʳ] ADJECTIVE
superior

upright ['ʌpraɪt] ADJECTIVE
♦ **to stand upright** tenerse* derecho

upset ['ʌpsɛt] NOUN
see also **upset** ADJECTIVE, VERB
♦ **I had a stomach upset.** Tenía mal el estómago.

upset [ʌp'sɛt] ADJECTIVE
see also **upset** NOUN, VERB
disgustado ◊ *She's still a bit upset.* Todavía está un poco disgustada.
♦ **Don't get upset.** No te enfades.
♦ **I had an upset stomach.** Tenía mal el estómago.

to **upset** [ʌp'sɛt] VERB (**upset, upset**)
see also **upset** NOUN, ADJECTIVE
♦ **to upset somebody** disgustar a alguien

☞

◆**Don't upset yourself.** No te enfades.

upside down [ʌpsaɪd'daun] ADVERB
al revés ◇ *The painting was hung upside down.* El cuadro estaba colgado al revés.

upstairs [ʌp'stɛəz] ADVERB
arriba ◇ *Where's your coat? – It's upstairs.* ¿Dónde está tu abrigo? – Está arriba.
◆**the people upstairs** los de arriba
◆**He went upstairs to bed.** Subió para irse a la cama.

uptight [ʌp'taɪt] ADJECTIVE
tenso ◇ *She's very uptight today.* Está muy tensa hoy.

up-to-date ['ʌptə'deɪt] ADJECTIVE
1 moderno (*car, stereo*)
2 actualizado ◇ *an up-to-date timetable* un horario actualizado
◆**to bring somebody up-to-date on something** poner* a alguien al corriente de algo
◆**to bring something up-to-date** actualizar algo

upwards ['ʌpwədz] ADVERB
hacia arriba ◇ *to look upwards* mirar hacia arriba

urgent ['ə:dʒənt] ADJECTIVE
urgente

urine ['juərɪn] NOUN
la orina

US [ju:'ɛs] ABBREVIATION (= *United States*)
los EEUU (= los Estados Unidos)

us [ʌs] PRONOUN
1 nos
*Use **nos** to translate **us** when it is the direct object of the verb in the sentence, or when it means **to us**.*
◇ *They helped us.* Nos ayudaron. ◇ *Look at us!* ¡Míranos! ◇ *They gave us some brochures.* Nos dieron unos folletos.
2 nosotros MASC
nosotras FEM
*Use **nosotros** or **nosotras** after prepositions, in comparisons, and with the verb **to be**.*
◇ *Why don't you come with us?* ¿Por qué no vienes con nosotras? ◇ *They are older than us.* Son mayores que nosotros. ◇ *It's us.* Somos nosotros.

USA [ju:ɛs'eɪ] ABBREVIATION (= *United States of America*)
los EEUU (= los Estados Unidos)

use [ju:s] NOUN
see also **use** VERB
el uso ◇ *"directions for use"* "modo de empleo"
◆**It's no use shouting, she's deaf.** Es inútil gritar, es sorda.
◆**It's no use, I can't do it.** No hay manera, no puedo hacerlo.
◆**to make use of something** usar algo

to **use** [ju:z] VERB
see also **use** NOUN
usar ◇ *Can I use your phone?* ¿Puedo usar tu teléfono?
◆**I used to go camping as a child.** De pequeño solía ir de acampada.
◆**I didn't use to like maths, but now I love it.** Antes no me gustaban las matemáticas, pero ahora me encantan.
◆**to be used to something** estar* acostumbrado a algo ◇ *He wasn't used to driving on the right.* No estaba acostumbrado a conducir por la derecha. ◇ *Don't worry, I'm used to it.* No te preocupes, estoy acostumbrado.
◆**a used car** un coche de segunda mano

to **use up** [ju:z'ʌp] VERB
◆**We've used up all the paint.** Hemos acabado toda la pintura.

useful ['ju:sful] ADJECTIVE
útil

useless ['ju:slɪs] ADJECTIVE
inútil ◇ *a piece of useless information* una información inútil
◆**You're useless!** ¡Eres un inútil!
◆**This computer is useless.** Este ordenador no sirve para nada.
◆**It's useless asking her.** No sirve de nada preguntarle.

user ['ju:zə^r] NOUN
el usuario
la usuaria

user-friendly ['ju:zə'frɛndlɪ] ADJECTIVE
fácil de usar

usual ['ju:ʒuəl] ADJECTIVE
habitual
◆**as usual** como de costumbre

usually ['ju:ʒuəlɪ] ADVERB
normalmente ◇ *I usually get to school at about half past eight.* Normalmente llego al colegio sobre las ocho y media.

U-turn ['ju:'tə:n] NOUN
el cambio de sentido
◆**to do a U-turn** cambiar de sentido
◆**"No U-turns"** "Prohibido cambiar de sentido"

V

vacancy ['veɪkənsɪ] NOUN (PL **vacancies**)
1 la vacante (*job*)
2 la habitación libre (*in hotel*)
♦ **"no vacancies"** "completo"
vacant ['veɪkənt] ADJECTIVE
libre ◊ *a vacant seat* un asiento libre
vacation [və'keɪʃən] NOUN US
las vacaciones ◊ *to be on vacation* estar* de vacaciones ◊ *to take a vacation* tomarse unas vacaciones
to **vaccinate** ['væksɪneɪt] VERB
vacunar
to **vacuum** ['vækjum] VERB
pasar la aspiradora ◊ *to vacuum the hall* pasar la aspiradora por el vestíbulo
vacuum cleaner ['vækjumkli:nər] NOUN
la aspiradora
vagina [və'dʒaɪnə] NOUN
la vagina
vague [veɪg] ADJECTIVE
1 vago ◊ *I've only got a vague idea what he means.* Tengo sólo una vaga idea de lo que quiere decir.
2 distraído ◊ *He's getting a bit vague in his old age.* Se está poniendo un poco distraído en su vejez.
vain [veɪn] ADJECTIVE
vanidoso ◊ *He's so vain!* ¡Es más vanidoso!
♦ **in vain** en vano
Valentine card ['væləntaɪnkɑ:d] NOUN
la tarjeta del día de los enamorados
Valentine's Day ['væləntaɪnzdeɪ] NOUN
el día de los enamorados (*el 14 de febrero, día de San Valentín*)
valid ['vælɪd] ADJECTIVE
válido ◊ *a valid passport* un pasaporte válido
♦ **This ticket is valid for three months.** Este billete tiene una validez de tres meses.
valley ['vælɪ] NOUN
el valle
valuable ['væljuəbl] ADJECTIVE
1 de valor MASC, FEM, PL
◊ *a valuable painting* un cuadro de valor
2 valioso ◊ *valuable help* una valiosa ayuda
valuables ['væljuəblz] PL NOUN
los objetos de valor
value ['vælju:] NOUN
el valor
van [væn] NOUN
la furgoneta
vandal ['vændl] NOUN
el vándalo
vandalism ['vændəlɪzəm] NOUN
el vandalismo
to **vandalize** ['vændəlaɪz] VERB
destrozar*
vanilla [və'nɪlə] NOUN
la vainilla ◊ *a vanilla ice cream* un helado de vainilla
to **vanish** ['vænɪʃ] VERB
desaparecer*
♦ **to vanish into thin air** esfumarse
variable ['vɛərɪəbl] ADJECTIVE
variable
varied ['vɛərɪd] ADJECTIVE
variado
variety [və'raɪətɪ] NOUN (PL **varieties**)
la variedad
various ['vɛərɪəs] ADJECTIVE
varios ◊ *We visited various villages in the area.* Visitamos varias aldeas de la zona.
to **vary** ['vɛərɪ] VERB (**varied, varied**)
variar*
vase [vɑ:z] NOUN
el jarrón (PL los jarrones)
VAT [væt] NOUN
el IVA
*Although **IVA** ends in **-A**, it is actually a masculine noun.*
VCR [vi:si:'ɑ:r] NOUN (= *video cassette recorder*)
el vídeo (*aparato*)
VDU [vi:di:'ju:] NOUN (= *visual display unit*)
el monitor
veal [vi:l] NOUN
la carne de ternera
vegan ['vi:gən] NOUN
el vegetariano estricto
la vegetariana estricta
vegetable ['vɛdʒtəbl] NOUN
1 la verdura (*to be cooked*) ◊ *vegetable soup* sopa de verduras
2 la hortaliza (*for salads*) ◊ *peppers, tomatoes and other vegetables* pimientos, tomates y otras hortalizas
vegetarian [vɛdʒɪ'tɛərɪən] ADJECTIVE
see also **vegetarian** NOUN
el vegetariano
la vegetariana
◊ *I'm a vegetarian.* Soy vegetariano.
vegetarian [vɛdʒɪ'tɛərɪən] NOUN
see also **vegetarian** ADJECTIVE
◊ *vegetarian lasagne* lasaña vegetariana
vehicle ['vi:ɪkl] NOUN
vehículo
vein [veɪn] NOUN
la vena
velvet ['vɛlvɪt] NOUN
el terciopelo
vending machine ['vɛndɪŋməʃi:n] NOUN
la máquina expendedora

Venetian blind [vɪniːʃən'blaɪnd] NOUN
la persiana
verb [vəːb] NOUN
el verbo
verdict ['vəːdɪkt] NOUN
el veredicto
vertical ['vəːtɪkl] ADJECTIVE
vertical
vertigo ['vəːtɪgəu] NOUN
el vértigo ◊ *I get vertigo.* Tengo vértigo.
very ['vɛrɪ] ADVERB
see also **very** ADJECTIVE
muy ◊ *very tall* muy alto
◆ **It's very cold.** Hace mucho frío.
◆ **not very interesting** no demasiado interesante
◆ **very much** muchísimo
◆ **We were thinking the very same thing.** Estábamos pensando exactamente lo mismo.
very ['vɛrɪ] ADJECTIVE
see also **very** ADVERBIO
mismo ◊ *in this very house* en esta misma casa ◊ *That's the very book I was talking about.* Ese es justamente el libro del que hablaba.
◆ **The very idea!** ¡Cómo se te ocurre!
vest [vɛst] NOUN
1 la camiseta (*underclothing*)
2 el chaleco (*waistcoat*) US
vet [vɛt] NOUN
el veterinario
la veterinaria
◊ *She's a vet.* Es veterinaria.
via ['vaɪə] PREPOSITION
1 por ◊ *We drove to Lisbon via Salamanca.* Fuimos a Lisboa por Salamanca.
2 vía ◊ *a flight via Brussels* un vuelo vía Bruselas
vicar ['vɪkə^r] NOUN
el párroco
vice [vaɪs] NOUN
el tornillo de banco (*tool*)
vice versa ['vaɪsɪ'vəːsə] ADVERB
viceversa
vicious ['vɪʃəs] ADJECTIVE
1 brutal ◊ *a vicious attack* una brutal agresión
2 feroz ◊ *a vicious dog* un perro feroz
◆ **He was a vicious man.** Era un hombre despiadado.
◆ **a vicious circle** un círculo vicioso
victim ['vɪktɪm] NOUN
la víctima ◊ *He was the victim of a mugging.* Fue víctima de un atraco.
victory ['vɪktərɪ] NOUN (PL **victories**)
la victoria
to **video** ['vɪdɪəu] VERB
see also **video** NOUN
grabar en vídeo (grabar en video LatAm) ◊ *They videoed the whole wedding.* Grabaron en vídeo toda la boda.
video ['vɪdɪəu] NOUN (PL **videos**)
see also **video** VERB
el vídeo (el video LatAm) ◊ *to watch a video* ver* un vídeo ◊ *It's out on video.* Ha salido en vídeo.
◆ **a video camera** una videocámara
◆ **a video cassette** una cinta de vídeo
◆ **a video game** un videojuego
◆ **a video recorder** un vídeo
◆ **a video shop** un videoclub
view [vjuː] NOUN
1 la vista ◊ *There's an amazing view.* La vista es magnífica.
2 la opinión (PL las opiniones) ◊ *in my view* en mi opinión
viewer ['vjuːə^r] NOUN
el telespectador
la telespectadora
viewpoint ['vjuːpɔɪnt] NOUN
el punto de vista
vile [vaɪl] ADJECTIVE
repugnante
villa ['vɪlə] NOUN
el chalet
village ['vɪlɪdʒ] NOUN
1 el pueblo (*large*)
2 la aldea (*small*)
villain ['vɪlən] NOUN
1 (*criminal*)
el/la maleante
2 (*in film*)
el malo
la mala
vine [vaɪn] NOUN
1 la vid (*trailing*)
2 la parra (*climbing*)
vinegar ['vɪnɪgə^r] NOUN
el vinagre
vineyard ['vɪnjɑːd] NOUN
el viñedo
viola [vɪ'əulə] NOUN
la viola
violence ['vaɪələns] NOUN
la violencia
violent ['vaɪələnt] ADJECTIVE
violento
violin [vaɪə'lɪn] NOUN
el violín (PL los violines)
violinist [vaɪə'lɪnɪst] NOUN
el/la violinista
virgin ['vəːdʒɪn] NOUN
la virgen (PL las vírgenes) ◊ *to be a virgin* ser* virgen
Virgo ['vəːgəu] NOUN
el Virgo (*sign*) ◊ *I'm Virgo.* Soy Virgo.
◆ **a Virgo** un/una Virgo

* Verbs marked with this symbol are irregular. See pages 380-382 for further details

virtual reality ['vəːtjuəlriː'ælɪtɪ] NOUN
la realidad virtual
virus ['vaɪərəs] NOUN (PL **viruses**)
(*also computing*)
el virus (PL los virus)
visa ['viːzə] NOUN
el visado (la visa *LatAm*)
visible ['vɪzəbl] ADJECTIVE
visible
visit ['vɪzɪt] NOUN
see also **visit** VERB
la visita ◊ *my last visit to my grandmother* la última visita que le hice a mi abuela
◆**I saw him on my latest visit to Spain.** Lo vi la última vez que estuve en España.
to **visit** ['vɪzɪt] VERB
see also **visit** NOUN
visitar
visitor ['vɪzɪtə^r] NOUN
1 el/la visitante (*tourist*)
2 la visita (*guest*) ◊ *to have a visitor* tener* visita
visual ['vɪzjuəl] ADJECTIVE
visual
to **visualize** ['vɪzjuəlaɪz] VERB
imaginar
vital ['vaɪtl] ADJECTIVE
vital
vitamin ['vɪtəmɪn] NOUN
la vitamina
vivid ['vɪvɪd] ADJECTIVE
vivo ◊ *vivid colours* colores vivos
◆**to have a vivid imagination** tener* una imaginación desbordante
vocabulary [vəu'kæbjulərɪ] NOUN (PL **vocabularies**)
el vocabulario
vocational [vəu'keɪʃənl] ADJECTIVE
◆**a vocational course** un curso de formación profesional
vodka ['vɔdkə] NOUN
el vodka
Although ***vodka*** *ends in* ***-a****, it is actually a masculine noun.*
voice [vɔɪs] NOUN
la voz (PL las voces)
voice mail ['vɔɪsmeɪl] NOUN
el buzón de voz
volcano [vɔl'keɪnəu] NOUN (PL **volcanoes**)
el volcán (PL los volcanes)
volleyball ['vɔlɪbɔːl] NOUN
el voleibol
volt [vəult] NOUN
el voltio
voltage ['vəultɪdʒ] NOUN
el voltaje
voluntary ['vɔləntərɪ] ADJECTIVE
voluntario
◆**to do voluntary work** hacer* voluntariado
volunteer [vɔlən'tɪə^r] NOUN
see also **volunteer** VERB
el voluntario
la voluntaria
to **volunteer** [vɔlən'tɪə^r] VERB
see also **volunteer** NOUN
◆**to volunteer to do something** ofrecerse* a hacer algo
to **vomit** ['vɔmɪt] VERB
vomitar
to **vote** [vəut] VERB
see also **vote** NOUN
votar ◊ *Who did you vote for?* ¿A quién votaste?
vote [vəut] NOUN
see also **vote** VERBO
el voto
voucher ['vautʃə^r] NOUN
el vale ◊ *a gift voucher* un vale de regalo
vowel ['vauəl] NOUN
la vocal
vulgar ['vʌlgə^r] ADJECTIVE
vulgar

W

wafer ['weɪfəʳ] NOUN
el barquillo
wage [weɪdʒ] NOUN
la paga ◇ *He collected his wages.* Recogió la paga.
waist [weɪst] NOUN
la cintura
waistcoat ['weɪskəut] NOUN
el chaleco
to **wait** [weɪt] VERB
esperar ◇ *I'll wait for you.* Te esperaré. ◇ *Wait a minute!* ¡Espera un momento!
◆**to keep somebody waiting** hacer* esperar a alguien ◇ *They kept us waiting for hours.* Nos hicieron esperar durante horas.
◆**I can't wait for the holidays.** Estoy deseando que lleguen las vacaciones.
◆**I can't wait to see him again.** Me muero de ganas de verlo otra vez.
to **wait up** [weɪt'ʌp] VERB
esperar levantado ◇ *My mum always waits up till I get in.* Mi madre siempre espera levantada hasta que llego.
waiter ['weɪtəʳ] NOUN
el camarero
waiting list ['weɪtɪŋlɪst] NOUN
la lista de espera
waiting room ['weɪtɪŋrum] NOUN
la sala de espera
waitress ['weɪtrɪs] NOUN (PL **waitresses**)
la camarera
to **wake up** [weɪk'ʌp] VERB (**woke up, woken up**)
despertarse* ◇ *I woke up at six o'clock.* Me desperté a las seis.
◆**to wake somebody up** despertar* a alguien ◇ *Please would you wake me up at seven o'clock?* ¿Podría despertarme a las siete, por favor?
Wales [weɪlz] NOUN
Gales MASC
◆**the Prince of Wales** el Príncipe de Gales
◆**I'm from Wales.** Soy de Gales.
to **walk** [wɔːk] VERB
see also **walk** NOUN
[1] andar* ◇ *Don't walk so fast!* ¡No andes tan deprisa! ◇ *We walked 10 kilometres.* Anduvimos 10 kilómetros.
[2] ir* a pie (*go on foot*) ◇ *Are you walking or going by bus?* ¿Vas a ir a pie o en autobús?
[3] pasear (*for fun*) ◇ *I like walking through the park.* Me gusta pasear por el parque.
◆**to walk the dog** pasear al perro

walk [wɔːk] NOUN
see also **walk** VERB
el paseo
◆**to go for a walk** ir* a pasear
◆**It's 10 minutes' walk from here.** Está a 10 minutos de aquí a pie.
walkie-talkie ['wɔːkɪ'tɔːkɪ] NOUN
el walkie-talkie
walking ['wɔːkɪŋ] NOUN
el senderismo ◇ *I did some walking in the Alps last summer.* El verano pasado hice senderismo por los Alpes. ◇ *Walking is good for your health.* Andar es bueno para la salud.
walking stick ['wɔːkɪŋstɪk] NOUN
el bastón (PL los bastones)
Walkman ® ['wɔːkmən] NOUN (PL **Walkmans**)
el walkman ®
wall [wɔːl] NOUN
[1] la pared (*of room, building*)
[2] el muro (*freestanding*)
[3] la muralla (*of castle, city*)
wallet ['wɔlɪt] NOUN
la cartera
wallpaper ['wɔːlpeɪpəʳ] NOUN
el papel pintado
walnut ['wɔːlnʌt] NOUN
la nuez (PL las nueces)
to **wander around** [wɔndərə'raund] VERB
pasear ◇ *I just wandered around for a while.* Estuve paseando un poco.
to **want** [wɔnt] VERB
querer* ◇ *Do you want some cake?* ¿Quieres un poco de pastel?
◆**to want to do something** querer hacer algo ◇ *What do you want to do tomorrow?* ¿Qué quieres hacer mañana?
◆**to want somebody to do something** querer que alguien haga algo ◇ *They want us to wait here.* Quieren que esperemos aquí.

***querer que** has to be followed by a verb in the subjunctive.*

war [wɔːʳ] NOUN
la guerra
◆**to be at war** estar* en guerra
ward [wɔːd] NOUN
la sala (*de un hospital*)
warden ['wɔːdn] NOUN
(*of youth hostel*)
el encargado
la encargada
wardrobe ['wɔːdrəub] NOUN
el armario
warehouse ['wɛəhaus] NOUN

el almacén (PL los almacenes)

warm [wɔ:m] ADJECTIVE

[1] caliente ◊ *warm water* agua caliente

[2] caluroso ◊ *a warm day* un día caluroso ◊ *a warm welcome* una calurosa bienvenida

♦ **warm clothing** ropa de abrigo

♦ **This jumper is very warm.** Este jersey es muy calentito.

♦ **He's a very warm person.** Es una persona muy afectuosa.

♦ **It's warm in here.** Aquí dentro hace calor.

♦ **I'm too warm.** Tengo demasiado calor.

to **warm up** [wɔ:m'ʌp] VERB

[1] hacer* ejercicios de calentamiento (*for sport*)

[2] calentar* (*food*)

to **warn** [wɔ:n] VERB

advertir* ◊ *Well, I warned you!* ¡Ya te lo había advertido!

♦ **to warn somebody to do something** aconsejar a alguien que haga algo

Use the subjunctive after ***aconsejar a alguien que.***

warning ['wɔ:nɪŋ] NOUN

la advertencia

Warsaw ['wɔ:sɔ:] NOUN

Varsovia FEM

wart [wɔ:t] NOUN

la verruga

was [wɔz] VERB *see* **be**

wash [wɔʃ] NOUN

see also **wash** VERB

♦ **to have a wash** lavarse

♦ **to give something a wash** lavar algo

♦ **The car needs a wash.** Al coche le hace falta un lavado.

to **wash** [wɔʃ] VERB

see also **wash** NOUN

[1] lavar ◊ *to wash the car* lavar el coche

[2] lavarse (*have a wash*) ◊ *Every morning I get up, wash and get dressed.* Todas las mañanas me levanto, me lavo y me visto.

♦ **to wash one's hands** lavarse las manos

♦ **to wash up** lavar los platos

washbasin ['wɔʃbeɪsn] NOUN

el lavabo

washcloth ['wɔʃklɔθ] NOUN US

la toallita para lavarse

washing ['wɔʃɪŋ] NOUN

la ropa lavada (*clean laundry*)

♦ **to do the washing** lavar la ropa

♦ **dirty washing** la ropa para lavar

♦ **Have you got any washing?** ¿Tienes ropa para lavar?

washing machine ['wɔʃɪŋməʃi:n] NOUN

la lavadora

washing powder ['wɔʃɪŋpaudəʳ] NOUN

el detergente

washing-up [wɔʃɪŋ'ʌp] NOUN

♦ **to do the washing-up** lavar los platos

washing-up liquid [wɔʃɪŋ'ʌplɪkwɪd] NOUN

el lavavajillas (PL los lavavajillas)

wasn't ['wɔznt] = **was not**

wasp [wɔsp] NOUN

la avispa

waste [weɪst] NOUN

see also **waste** VERB

[1] el desperdicio ◊ *It's such a waste!* ¡Qué desperdicio!

♦ **It's a waste of time.** Es una pérdida de tiempo.

[2] los residuos PL ◊ *nuclear waste* residuos radioactivos

to **waste** [weɪst] VERB

see also **waste** NOUN

desperdiciar (*food, space, opportunity*)

♦ **to waste time** perder* el tiempo ◊ *There's no time to waste.* No hay tiempo que perder.

♦ **I don't like wasting money.** No me gusta malgastar el dinero.

wastepaper basket ['weɪstpeɪpə'bɑ:skɪt] NOUN

la papelera

watch [wɔtʃ] NOUN (PL **watches**)

see also **watch** VERB

el reloj

to **watch** [wɔtʃ] VERB

see also **watch** NOUN

[1] mirar

♦ **Watch me!** ¡Mírame!

[2] ver* ◊ *to watch TV* ver la tele

[3] vigilar ◊ *The police were watching the house.* La policía vigilaba la casa.

to **watch out** [wɔtʃ'aut] VERB

tener* cuidado

♦ **Watch out!** ¡Cuidado!

water ['wɔ:təʳ] NOUN

see also **water** VERB

el agua FEM

Although it's a feminine noun, remember that you use ***el*** *with* ***agua.***

to **water** ['wɔ:təʳ] VERB

see also **water** NOUN

regar* ◊ *He was watering his tulips.* Estaba regando los tulipanes.

waterfall ['wɔ:təfɔ:l] NOUN

la cascada

watering can ['wɔ:tərɪŋkæn] NOUN

la regadera

watermelon ['wɔ:təmɛlən] NOUN

la sandía

waterproof ['wɔ:təpru:f] ADJECTIVE

impermeable

♦ **a waterproof watch** un reloj sumergible

water-skiing ['wɔ:təski:ɪŋ] NOUN

el esquí acuático ◊ *to go water-skiing* hacer* esquí acuático

wave [weɪv] NOUN

see also **wave** VERB

la ola

to **wave** [weɪv] VERB

W

see also **wave** NOUN

◆**to wave to somebody (1)** (*say hello*) saludar a alguien con la mano

◆**to wave to somebody (2)** (*say goodbye*) hacer* adiós con la mano

wavy ['weɪvɪ] ADJECTIVE
ondulado ◇ *He's got wavy hair.* Tiene el pelo ondulado.

wax [wæks] NOUN
la cera

way [weɪ] NOUN
1 la manera ◇ *She looked at me in a strange way.* Me miró de manera extraña.

◆**This book tells you the right way to do it.** Este libro explica cómo hay que hacerlo.

◆**You're doing it the wrong way.** Lo estás haciendo mal.

◆**in a way...** en cierto sentido...

◆**a way of life** un estilo de vida

2 el camino (*route*) ◇ *I don't know the way.* No sé el camino. ◇ *We stopped for lunch on the way.* Paramos a comer en el camino.

◆**Which way is it?** ¿Por dónde es?

◆**The supermarket is this way.** El supermercado es por aquí.

◆**Do you know the way to the hotel?** ¿Sabes cómo llegar al hotel?

◆**He's on his way.** Está de camino.

◆**It's a long way.** Está lejos. ◇ *It's a long way from the hotel.* Está lejos del hotel.

◆**"way in"** "entrada"

◆**"way out"** "salida"

◆**by the way...** a propósito...

we [wiː] PRONOUN
nosotros MASC
nosotras FEM

we generally isn't translated unless it is emphatic.

◇ *We were in a hurry.* Teníamos prisa.

*Use **nosotros** or **nosotras** as appropriate for emphasis.*

◇ *They went but we didn't.* Ellos fueron pero nosotros no.

weak [wiːk] ADJECTIVE
1 débil
2 poco cargado (*tea, coffee*)

wealthy ['wɛlθɪ] ADJECTIVE
rico

weapon ['wɛpən] NOUN
el arma FEM

*Although it's a feminine noun, remember that you use **el** and **un** with **arma**.*

to **wear** [wɛəʳ] VERB (**wore, worn**)
llevar ◇ *She was wearing a hat.* Llevaba un sombrero.

◆**She was wearing black.** Iba vestida de negro.

weather ['wɛðəʳ] NOUN
el tiempo ◇ *What's the weather like?* ¿Qué tiempo hace?

weather forecast ['wɛðəfɔːkɑːst] NOUN
el pronóstico del tiempo

Web [web] NOUN

◆**the Web** la Web

web browser ['wɛbbraʊzəʳ] NOUN
el navegador de Internet

webmaster ['wɛbmɑːstəʳ] NOUN
el administrador de Web
la administradora de Web

web page ['wɛbpeɪdʒ] NOUN
la página web

website [wɛbsaɪt] NOUN
el sitio web

webzine ['wɛbziːn] NOUN
la revista electrónica

we'd [wiːd] = **we had**, = **we would**

wedding [wɛdɪŋ] NOUN
la boda

◆**wedding anniversary** el aniversario de boda

◆**wedding dress** el vestido de novia

Wednesday ['wɛdnzdɪ] NOUN
el miércoles (PL los miércoles)
◇ *I saw her on Wednesday.* La vi el miércoles. ◇ *every Wednesday* todos los miércoles ◇ *last Wednesday* el miércoles pasado ◇ *next Wednesday* el miércoles que viene ◇ *on Wednesdays* los miércoles

weed [wiːd] NOUN
el hierbajo ◇ *The garden's full of weeds.* El jardín está lleno de hierbajos.

week [wiːk] NOUN
la semana ◇ *in a week's time* dentro de una semana

◆**a week on Friday** el viernes de la semana que viene

◆**during the week** durante la semana

weekday ['wiːkdeɪ] NOUN
el día entre semana

*Although **día** ends in **-a**, it is actually a masculine noun.*

◆**on weekdays** los días entre semana

weekend [wiːk'ɛnd] NOUN
el fin de semana

◆**next weekend** el próximo fin de semana

to **weep** [wiːp] VERB (**wept, wept**)
llorar

to **weigh** [weɪ] VERB
pesar ◇ *How much do you weigh?* ¿Cuánto pesas?

◆**to weigh oneself** pesarse

weight [weɪt] NOUN
el peso

* Verbs marked with this symbol are irregular. See pages 380-382 for further details

◆ **to lose weight** adelgazar*
◆ **to put on weight** engordar
weightlifter ['weɪtlɪftəʳ] NOUN
el levantador de pesas
la levantadora de pesas
weightlifting ['weɪtlɪftɪŋ] NOUN
el levantamiento de pesas
weird [wɪəd] ADJECTIVE
raro
welcome ['wɛlkəm] NOUN
see also **welcome** VERB
la bienvenida ◊ *They gave her a warm welcome.* Le dieron una calurosa bienvenida.
◆ **Welcome!** ¡Bienvenido!
If you're addressing a woman remember to use the feminine form: ***¡Bienvenida!*** *If you're addressing more than one person use the plural form* ***¡Bienvenidos!*** *or* ***¡Bienvenidas!.***
to **welcome** ['wɛlkəm] VERB
see also **welcome** NOUN
◆ **to welcome somebody** dar* la bienvenida a alguien
◆ **Thank you! – You're welcome!** ¡Gracias! – ¡De nada!
well [wɛl] ADJECTIVE, ADVERB
see also **well** NOUN
1 bien ◊ *You did that really well.* Lo hiciste realmente bien.
◆ **She's doing really well at school.** Le va muy bien en el colegio.
◆ **to be well** estar* bien ◊ *I'm not very well at the moment.* No estoy muy bien en este momento.
◆ **Get well soon!** ¡Que te mejores!
◆ **Well done!** ¡Muy bien!
2 bueno ◊ *It's enormous! Well, quite big anyway.* ¡Es enorme! Bueno, digamos que bastante grande.
◆ **as well** también ◊ *We worked hard, but we had some fun as well.* Trabajamos mucho, pero también nos divertimos.
◆ **as well as** además de ◊ *We went to Gerona as well as Sitges.* Fuimos a Gerona, además de Sitges.
well [wɛl] NOUN
see also **well** ADJECTIVE, ADVERB
el pozo
we'll [wiːl] = **we will**
well-behaved ['wɛlbɪ'heɪvd] ADJECTIVE
◆ **to be well-behaved** portarse bien
well-dressed ['wɛl'drɛst] ADJECTIVE
bien vestido
wellingtons ['wɛlɪŋtənz] PL NOUN
las botas de agua
well-known ['wɛl'nəun] ADJECTIVE
conocido ◊ *a well-known film star* un conocido actor de cine
well-off ['wɛl'ɔf] ADJECTIVE
adinerado
Welsh [wɛlʃ] ADJECTIVE
see also **Welsh** NOUN
galés MASC
galesa FEM
Welsh [wɛlʃ] NOUN
see also **Welsh** ADJECTIVE
el galés (*language*)
◆ **the Welsh** los galeses
Welshman ['wɛlʃmən] NOUN (PL **Welshmen**)
el galés (PL los galeses)
Welshwoman ['wɛlʃwumən] NOUN (PL **Welshwomen**)
la galesa
went [wɛnt] VERB *see* **go**
were [wəːʳ] VERB *see* **be**
we're [wɪəʳ] = **we are**
weren't [wəːnt] = **were not**
west [wɛst] NOUN
see also **west** ADJECTIVE, ADVERB
el oeste
west [wɛst] ADJECTIVE, ADVERB
see also **west** NOUN
1 occidental ◊ *the west coast* la costa occidental
◆ **west of** al oeste de ◊ *Stroud is west of Oxford.* Stroud está al oeste de Oxford.
2 hacia el oeste ◊ *We were travelling west.* Viajábamos hacia el oeste.
◆ **the West Country** el sudoeste de Inglaterra
western ['wɛstən] NOUN
see also **western** ADJECTIVE
el western
western ['wɛstən] ADJECTIVE
see also **western** NOUN
occidental ◊ *the western part of the island* la parte occidental de la isla
◆ **Western Europe** Europa Occidental
West Indian [wɛst'ɪndɪən] ADJECTIVE
see also **West Indian** NOUN
antillano
◆ **She's West Indian.** Es antillana.
West Indian [wɛst'ɪndɪən] NOUN
see also **West Indian** ADJECTIVE
el antillano
la antillana
West Indies [wɛst'ɪndɪz] PL NOUN
◆ **the West Indies** las Antillas
wet [wɛt] ADJECTIVE
mojado ◊ *wet clothes* ropa mojada
◆ **to get wet** mojarse
◆ **dripping wet** chorreando
◆ **wet weather** el tiempo lluvioso
◆ **It was wet all week.** Llovió toda la semana.
wetsuit ['wɛtsuːt] NOUN
el traje de buzo
we've [wiːv] = **we have**
whale [weɪl] NOUN
la ballena
what [wɔt] ADJECTIVE, PRONOUN
1 qué

*Use **qué** (with an accent) in direct and indirect questions and exclamations.*

◊ *What subjects are you studying?* ¿Qué asignaturas estudias? ◊ *What colour is it?* ¿De qué color es? ◊ *What's the matter?* ¿Qué te pasa? ◊ *What's it for?* ¿Para qué es? ◊ *I don't know what to do.* No sé qué hacer. ◊ *What a mess!* ¡Qué desorden!

*Only translate **what is** by **qué es** if asking for a definition or explanation.*

◊ *What is it?* ¿Qué es? ◊ *What's a tractor, Daddy?* ¿Qué es un tractor, papá? ◊ *I asked him what DNA was.* Le pregunté qué era el ADN.

[2] cuál MASC (FEM cuál, PL cuáles)

*Translate **what is** by **cuál es** when not asking for a definition or explanation.*

◊ *What's the capital of Finland?* ¿Cuál es la capital de Finlandia? ◊ *What's her telephone number?* ¿Cuál es su número de teléfono?

[3] lo que

*Use **lo que** (no accent) when **what** isn't a question word.*

◊ *I saw what happened.* Vi lo que pasó. ◊ *I heard what he said.* Oí lo que dijo.

♦ **What? (1)** ¿Cómo? (*what did you say?*)
♦ **What? (2)** ¿Qué? (*shocked*)
♦ **What's your name?** ¿Cómo te llamas?

wheat [wi:t] NOUN
el trigo

wheel [wi:l] NOUN
la rueda
♦ **steering wheel** el volante

wheelchair [ˈwi:ltʃɛəʳ] NOUN
la silla de ruedas

when [wɛn] ADVERB
see also **when** CONJUNCTION
cuándo

*Remember the accent on **cuándo** in direct and indirect questions.*

◊ *When did he go?* ¿Cuándo se fue? ◊ *I asked her when the next bus was.* Le pregunté cuándo salía el próximo autobús.

when [wɛn] CONJUNCTION
see also **when** ADVERB
cuando ◊ *She was reading when I came in.* Cuando entré ella estaba leyendo.

***cuando** has to be followed by a verb in the subjunctive when referring to an event in the future.*

◊ *Call me when you get there.* Llámame cuando llegues.

where [wɛəʳ] ADVERB
see also **where** CONJUNCTION
dónde

*Remember the accent on **dónde** in direct and indirect questions.*

◊ *Where do you live?* ¿Dónde vives? ◊ *Where are you from?* ¿De dónde eres? ◊ *She asked me where I had bought it.* Me preguntó dónde lo había comprado.
♦ **Where are you going?** ¿Adónde vas?

where [wɛəʳ] CONJUNCTION
see also **where** ADVERB
donde ◊ *a shop where you can buy coffee* una tienda donde se puede comprar café

whether [ˈwɛðəʳ] CONJUNCTION
si ◊ *I don't know whether to go or not.* No sé si ir o no.

which [wɪtʃ] ADJECTIVE, PRONOUN
[1] cuál MASC (FEM cuál, PL cuáles)

*Remember the accent on **cuál** and **cuáles** in direct and indirect questions.*

◊ *I know his sister. – Which one?* Conozco a su hermana. – ¿A cuál? ◊ *Which would you like?* ¿Cuál quieres? ◊ *Of the five pairs, which were sold?* De los cinco pares, ¿cuáles se vendieron?

[2] qué

*Use **qué** (with an accent) before nouns.*

◊ *Which flavour do you want?* ¿Qué sabor quieres?

[3] que ◊ *It's an illness which causes nerve damage.* Es una enfermedad que daña los nervios. ◊ *This is the skirt which Daphne gave me.* Ésta es la falda que me dio Daphne. ◊ *Our uniform, which is green, is quite nice.* Nuestro uniforme, que es verde, está bastante bien.

*After a preposition **que** becomes **el que, la que, los que, las que** to agree with the noun.*

◊ *That's the film which I was telling you about.* Ésa es la película de la que te hablaba.

[4] lo cual ◊ *The cooker isn't working, which is a nuisance.* La cocina no funciona, lo cual es un fastidio.

while [waɪl] CONJUNCTION
see also **while** NOUN
[1] mientras ◊ *You hold the torch while I look inside.* Aguanta la linterna mientras yo miro por dentro.
[2] mientras que ◊ *Isobel is very dynamic, while Kay is more laid-back.* Isabel es muy dinámica, mientras que Kay es más tranquila.

while [waɪl] NOUN
see also **while** CONJUNCTION
♦ **a while** un rato ◊ *after a while* después de un rato

◆ **a while ago** hace un momento ◇ *He was here a while ago.* Hace un momento estaba aquí.
◆ **for a while** durante un tiempo ◇ *I lived in London for a while.* Viví en Londres durante un tiempo.
◆ **quite a while** mucho tiempo ◇ *I haven't seen him for quite a while.* Hace mucho tiempo que no lo veo.

whip [wɪp] NOUN
see also **whip** VERB
la fusta (*for horse*)

to **whip** [wɪp] VERB
see also **whip** NOUN
1 fustigar* (*animal*)
2 azotar (*person*)
3 batir (*eggs, cream*)

whipped cream ['wɪptkriːm] NOUN
la nata montada

whisk [wɪsk] NOUN
el batidor

whiskers ['wɪskəz] PL NOUN
los bigotes (*of animal*)

whisky ['wɪskɪ] NOUN (PL **whiskies**)
el whisky (PL los whiskys)

to **whisper** ['wɪspəʳ] VERB
susurrar

whistle ['wɪsl] NOUN
see also **whistle** VERB
el silbato ◇ *The referee blew his whistle.* El árbitro tocó el silbato.

to **whistle** ['wɪsl] VERB
see also **whistle** NOUN
1 pitar (*with a whistle*)
2 silbar (*with mouth*)

white [waɪt] ADJECTIVE
blanco ◇ *He's got white hair.* Tiene el cabello blanco.
◆ **white wine** el vino blanco
◆ **white bread** el pan blanco
◆ **white coffee** el café con leche
◆ **a white man** un hombre blanco
◆ **white people** los blancos

Whitsun ['wɪtsn] NOUN
Pentecostés MASC

who [huː] PRONOUN
1 quién (PL quiénes)
*Remember the accent on **quién** and **quiénes** in direct and indirect questions.*
◇ *Who said that?* ¿Quién dijo eso? ◇ *Who is it?* ¿Quién es? ◇ *We don't know who broke the window.* No sabemos quién rompió la ventana.
2 que ◇ *the people who know us* las personas que nos conocen
*After a preposition **que** becomes **el que, la que, los que, las que** to agree with the noun.*
◇ *the women who she was chatting with* las mujeres con las que estaba hablando
*Note that **a** + **el que** becomes **al que**.*
◇ *the boy who I gave it to* el chico al que se lo di

whole [həul] ADJECTIVE
see also **whole** NOUN
entero ◇ *the whole class* la clase entera ◇ *two whole days* dos días enteros
◆ **the whole afternoon** toda la tarde
◆ **the whole world** todo el mundo

whole [həul] NOUN
see also **whole** ADJECTIVE
◆ **The whole of Wales was affected.** Todo Gales se vio afectado.
◆ **on the whole** en general

wholemeal ['həulmiːl] ADJECTIVE
integral ◇ *wholemeal bread* pan integral

wholewheat ['həulwiːt] ADJECTIVE US
integral

whom [huːm] PRONOUN
1 quién (PL quiénes)
*Remember the accent on **quién** and **quiénes** in direct and indirect questions.*
◇ *With whom did you go?* ¿Con quién fuiste? ◇ *Whom did you call?* ¿A quién llamaste?
2 quien ◇ *the man whom I saw* el hombre a quien vi ◇ *the woman to whom I spoke* la mujer con quien hablé

whose [huːz] ADJECTIVE
see also **whose** PRONOUN
1 (*in questions*)
de quién (PL de quiénes)
*Remember the accent on **quién** and **quiénes** in direct and indirect questions.*
◇ *Whose books are these?* ¿De quiénes son estos libros? ◇ *Do you know whose jacket this is?* ¿Sabes de quién es esta chaqueta?
2 (*relative*)
cuyo ◇ *the girl whose picture was in the paper* la muchacha cuya foto venía en el periódico ◇ *a neighbour whose sons go to that school* un vecino cuyos hijos van a ese colegio

whose [huːz] PRONOUN
see also **whose** ADJECTIVE
de quién (PL de quiénes)
*Remember the accent on **quién** and **quiénes** in direct and indirect questions.*
◇ *Whose is this?* ¿De quién es esto? ◇ *I know whose they are.* Yo sé de quiénes son.

why [waɪ] ADVERB
por qué
*Remember to write **por qué** as two words with an accent on **qué** when translating **why**.*
◇ *Why did you do that?* ¿Por qué hiciste eso?
◆ **Why not?** ¿Por qué no?
◆ **That's why he did it.** Por eso lo hizo.

wicked ['wɪkɪd] ADJECTIVE
1 malvado (*evil*)
2 sensacional (*really great*)

wicket ['wɪkɪt] NOUN
los palos (*stumps*)

wide [waɪd] ADJECTIVE, ADVERB
ancho ◊ *a wide road* una carretera ancha ◊ *How wide is the room? – It's five metres wide.* ¿Cómo es de ancha la habitación? – Tiene cinco metros de ancho.
♦ **wide open** abierto de par en par ◊ *The door was wide open.* La puerta estaba abierta de par en par.
♦ **wide awake** completamente despierto

widow ['wɪdəu] NOUN
la viuda ◊ *She's a widow.* Es viuda.

widower ['wɪdəuər] NOUN
el viudo ◊ *He's a widower.* Es viudo.

width [wɪdθ] NOUN
la anchura

wife [waɪf] NOUN (PL **wives**)
la esposa

wig [wɪg] NOUN
la peluca

wild [waɪld] ADJECTIVE
1 salvaje ◊ *a wild animal* un animal salvaje
2 silvestre ◊ *wild flowers* flores silvestres
3 loco ◊ *She's a bit wild.* Es un poco loca.

wildlife ['waɪldlaɪf] NOUN
la flora y fauna

will [wɪl] NOUN
see also **will** VERB
el testamento (*document*)

will [wɪl] VERB
see also **will** NOUN

***will** can often be translated by the present tense, as in the following examples.*

◊ *Come on, I'll help you.* Venga, te ayudo. ◊ *We'll talk about it later.* Hablamos luego. ◊ *Will you help me?* ¿Me ayudas?

*Use **voy a, va a**, etc + the infinitive to talk about plans and intentions.*

◊ *What will you do?* ¿Qué vas a hacer? ◊ *We'll be having lunch late.* Vamos a comer tarde.

Use the future tense when guessing what will happen or when making a supposition.

◊ *It won't take long.* No llevará mucho tiempo. ◊ *We'll probably go out later.* Seguramente saldremos luego. ◊ *I'll always love you.* Te querré siempre. ◊ *That will be the postman.* Será el cartero.

*Use **querer** for "to be willing" in emphatic requests, and invitations.*

◊ *Tom won't help me.* Tom no me quiere ayudar. ◊ *Will you be quiet!* ¿Te quieres callar? ◊ *Will you have some tea?* ¿Quieres tomar un té?

willing ['wɪlɪŋ] ADJECTIVE
♦ **to be willing to do something** estar* dispuesto a hacer algo

to **win** [wɪn] VERB (**won, won**)
see also **win** NOUN
ganar ◊ *Did you win?* ¿Ganaste? ◊ *to win a prize* ganar un premio

win [wɪn] NOUN
see also **win** VERB
la victoria

to **wind** [waɪnd] VERB (**wound, wound**)
see also **wind** NOUN
enrollar (*rope, wire*)

wind [wɪnd] NOUN
see also **wind** VERB
el viento
♦ **a wind instrument** un instrumento de viento
♦ **wind power** la energía eólica

windmill ['wɪndmɪl] NOUN
el molino de viento

window ['wɪndəu] NOUN
1 la ventana (*of building*)
2 la ventanilla (*in car, train*)
♦ **a shop window** un escaparate
3 el cristal (el vidrio *LatAm*) (*window pane*) ◊ *to break a window* romper* un cristal

windscreen ['wɪndskriːn] NOUN
el parabrisas (PL los parabrisas)

windscreen wiper ['wɪndskriːnwaɪpər] NOUN
el limpiaparabrisas (PL los limpiaparabrisas)

windshield ['wɪndʃiːld] NOUN US
el parabrisas (PL los parabrisas)

windshield wiper ['wɪndʃiːldwaɪpər] NOUN US
el limpiaparabrisas (PL los limpiaparabrisas)

windy ['wɪndɪ] ADJECTIVE
♦ **a windy day** un día de viento
♦ **Edinburgh's a very windy city.** En Edimburgo hace mucho viento.
♦ **It's windy.** Hace viento.

wine [waɪn] NOUN
el vino ◊ *white wine* el vino blanco ◊ *red wine* el vino tinto
♦ **a wine bar** un bar especializado en vinos
♦ **a wine glass** una copa de vino
♦ **the wine list** la carta de vinos

wing [wɪŋ] NOUN
el ala FEM

*Although it's a feminine noun, remember that you use **el** and **un** with **ala**.*

to **wink** [wɪŋk] VERB
♦ **to wink at somebody** guiñar el ojo a alguien

winner ['wɪnəʳ] NOUN
el ganador
la ganadora
winning ['wɪnɪŋ] ADJECTIVE
vencedor MASC
vencedora FEM
◊ *the winning team* el equipo vencedor
♦ **the winning goal** el gol de la victoria
winter ['wɪntəʳ] NOUN
el invierno
winter sports [wɪntə'spɔ:ts] PL NOUN
los deportes de invierno
to **wipe** [waɪp] VERB
limpiar
♦ **to wipe one's feet** limpiarse los zapatos (*en el felpudo*)
♦ **to wipe one's nose** limpiarse la nariz
♦ **Did you wipe up that water you spilled?** ¿Recogiste el agua que derramaste?
wire ['waɪəʳ] NOUN
el alambre
♦ **copper wire** el hilo de cobre
♦ **the telephone wire** el cable del teléfono
wisdom tooth ['wɪzdəmtu:θ] NOUN (PL **wisdom teeth**)
la muela del juicio
wise [waɪz] ADJECTIVE
sabio
to **wish** [wɪʃ] VERB
see also **wish** NOUN
♦ **to wish for something** desear algo ◊ *What more could you wish for?* ¿Qué más podrías desear?
♦ **to wish to do something** desear hacer algo ◊ *I wish to make a complaint.* Deseo hacer una reclamación.
♦ **I wish you were here!** ¡Ojalá estuvieras aquí!
♦ **I wish you'd told me!** ¡Me lo podrías haber dicho!
♦ **to wish somebody happy birthday** desear a alguien un feliz cumpleaños
wish [wɪʃ] NOUN (PL **wishes**)
see also **wish** VERB
el deseo ◊ *to make a wish* pedir* un deseo
♦ **"best wishes"** (*on birthday card*) "felicidades"
♦ **"with best wishes, Kathy"** "un abrazo, Kathy"
wit [wɪt] NOUN
el ingenio
with [wɪð, wɪθ] PREPOSITION
1 con ◊ *He walks with a stick.* Camina con un bastón. ◊ *Come with me.* Ven conmigo.
2 de ◊ *a woman with blue eyes* una mujer de ojos azules ◊ *green with envy* muerto de envidia ◊ *to shake with fear* temblar* de miedo ◊ *Fill the jug with water.* Llena la jarra de agua.
♦ **We stayed with friends.** Nos quedamos en casa de unos amigos.
within [wɪð'ɪn] PREPOSITION
dentro de ◊ *I want it back within three days.* Quiero que me lo devuelvas dentro de tres días.
♦ **The police arrived within minutes.** La policía llegó a los pocos minutos.
♦ **The shops are within easy reach.** Las tiendas están cerca.
without [wɪð'aut] PREPOSITION
sin ◊ *without a coat* sin abrigo ◊ *without speaking* sin hablar
witness ['wɪtnɪs] NOUN (PL **witnesses**)
el/la testigo ◊ *There were no witnesses.* No había testigos.
witty ['wɪtɪ] ADJECTIVE
ingenioso
wives [waɪvz] PL NOUN *see* **wife**
woken up [wəukn'ʌp] VERB *see* **wake up**
woke up [wəuk'ʌp] VERB *see* **wake up**
wolf [wulf] NOUN (PL **wolves**)
el lobo
woman ['wumən] NOUN (PL **women**)
la mujer ◊ *a woman doctor* una doctora
won [wʌn] VERB *see* **win**
to **wonder** ['wʌndəʳ] VERB
preguntarse ◊ *I wonder why she said that.* Me pregunto por qué dijo eso.
♦ **I wonder where Caroline is.** ¿Dónde estará Caroline?
wonderful ['wʌndəful] ADJECTIVE
maravilloso
won't [wəunt] = **will not**
wood [wud] NOUN
1 la madera ◊ *It's made of wood.* Es de madera.
2 la leña (*for fire*)
3 el bosque ◊ *We went for a walk in the wood.* Fuimos a pasear por el bosque.
wooden ['wudn] ADJECTIVE
de madera ◊ *a wooden chair* una silla de madera
woodwork ['wudwə:k] NOUN
la carpintería
wool [wul] NOUN
la lana ◊ *It's made of wool.* Es de lana.
word [wə:d] NOUN
la palabra
♦ **What's the word for "shop" in Spanish?** ¿Cómo se dice "shop" en español?
♦ **in other words** en otras palabras
♦ **to have a word with somebody** hablar con alguien ◊ *Can I have a word with you?* ¿Puedo hablar contigo?
♦ **the words** la letra (*lyrics*)
word processing ['wə:dprəusɛsɪŋ] NOUN
el procesamiento de textos
word processor ['wə:dprəusɛsəʳ] NOUN
el procesador de textos
wore [wɔ:ʳ] VERB *see* **wear**
work [wə:k] NOUN
see also **work** VERB

☞

el trabajo ◊ *She's looking for work.* Está buscando trabajo.

◆**It's hard work.** Es duro.

◆**at work** en el trabajo ◊ *He's at work until five o'clock.* Está en el trabajo hasta las cinco.

◆**He's off work today.** Hoy tiene el día libre.

◆**to be out of work** estar* sin trabajo

to **work** [wə:k] VERB

see also **work** NOUN

1 trabajar ◊ *She works in a shop.* Trabaja en una tienda. ◊ *to work hard* trabajar mucho

2 funcionar ◊ *The heating isn't working.* La calefacción no funciona. ◊ *My plan worked perfectly.* Mi plan funcionó a la perfección.

to **work out** [wə:k'aut] VERB

1 hacer* ejercicio (*exercise*) ◊ *I work out twice a week.* Hago ejercicio dos veces a la semana.

2 salir* (*turn out*) ◊ *I hope it will work out well.* Espero que salga bien.

3 calcular (*calculate*) ◊ *I worked it out in my head.* Lo calculé en mi cabeza.

4 entender* (*understand*) ◊ *I just couldn't work it out.* No lograba entenderlo.

◆**It works out at £10 each.** Sale a 10 libras esterlinas por persona.

worker ['wə:kə^r] NOUN

el trabajador

la trabajadora

◊ *She's a good worker.* Trabaja bien.

work experience ['wə:kıkspıərıəns] NOUN

◆**I'm going to do my work experience in a factory.** Voy a hacer las prácticas en una fábrica.

working-class ['wə:kıŋ'klɑ:s] ADJECTIVE

de clase obrera ◊ *a working-class family* una familia de clase obrera

workman ['wə:kmən] NOUN (PL **workmen**)

el obrero

works [wə:ks] NOUN

la fábrica

worksheet ['wə:kʃi:t] NOUN

la hoja de ejercicios

workshop ['wə:kʃɔp] NOUN

el taller ◊ *a drama workshop* un taller de teatro

workstation ['wə:ksteıʃən] NOUN

la terminal de trabajo

world [wə:ld] NOUN

el mundo

◆**the world champion** el campeón mundial

◆**the World Cup** la Copa del Mundo

worm [wə:m] NOUN

el gusano

worn [wɔ:n] VERB see **wear**

worn [wɔ:n] ADJECTIVE

gastado ◊ *The carpet is a bit worn.* La moqueta está un poco gastada.

◆**worn out** agotado ◊ *We were worn out after the long walk.* Estábamos agotados después de andar tanto.

worried ['wʌrıd] ADJECTIVE

preocupado ◊ *to be worried about something* estar* preocupado por algo ◊ *to look worried* parecer* preocupado

to **worry** ['wʌrı] VERB (**worried, worried**)

preocuparse

◆**Don't worry!** ¡No te preocupes!

worse [wə:s] ADJECTIVE, ADVERB

peor ◊ *It was even worse than mine.* Era incluso peor que el mío. ◊ *I'm feeling worse.* Me encuentro peor.

to **worship** ['wə:ʃıp] VERB

adorar

worst [wə:st] ADJECTIVE

see also **worst** NOUN

peor ◊ *the worst student in the class* el peor alumno de la clase ◊ *my worst enemy* mi peor enemigo

◆**Maths is my worst subject.** Las matemáticas es la asignatura que peor se me da.

worst [wə:st] NOUN

see also **worst** ADJECTIVE

◆**The worst of it is that...** Lo peor es que...

◆**at worst** en el peor de los casos

◆**if the worst comes to the worst** en el peor de los casos

worth [wə:θ] ADJECTIVE

◆**to be worth** valer* ◊ *It's worth a lot of money.* Vale mucho dinero. ◊ *How much is it worth?* ¿Cuánto vale?

◆**It's worth it.** Vale la pena.

would [wud] VERB

*The conditional is often used to translate **would** + verb.*

◊ *I said I would do it.* Dije que lo haría. ◊ *If you asked him he'd do it.* Si se lo pidieras, lo haría. ◊ *If you had asked him he would have done it.* Si se lo hubieras pedido, lo habría hecho.

*When **would you** is used to make requests, translate using **poder** in the present.*

◊ *Would you close the door please?* ¿Puedes cerrar la puerta, por favor?

◆**I'd like ... (1)** Me gustaría ... ◊ *I'd like to go to China.* Me gustaría ir a China.

◆**I'd like ... (2)** Quería ... ◊ *I'd like three tickets please.* Quería tres entradas.

◆**Would you like a biscuit?** ¿Quieres una galleta? ◊ *Would you like me to iron your jeans for you?* ¿Quieres que te planche los pantalones?

*Use the subjunctive after **querer que**.*

◆**Would you like to go to the cinema?** ¿Quieres ir al cine?

wouldn't ['wudnt] = **would not**

wound [waund] VERB *see* **wind**

to **wound** [wu:nd] VERB
see also **wound** NOUN
herir* ◇ *He was wounded in the leg.* Fue herido en la pierna.

wound [wu:nd] NOUN
see also **wound** VERB
la herida

to **wrap** [ræp] VERB
envolver* ◇ *She's wrapping her Christmas presents.* Está envolviendo los regalos de Navidad. ◇ *Can you wrap it for me please?* ¿Me lo puede envolver en papel de regalo, por favor?

to **wrap up** [ræp'ʌp] VERB
1 envolver* (*parcel*)
2 abrigarse* (*put on warm clothes*)

wrapping paper ['ræpɪŋpeɪpəʳ] NOUN
el papel de regalo

wreck [rɛk] NOUN
see also **wreck** VERB
el cacharro ◇ *That car is a wreck!* ¡Ese coche es un cacharro!
◆**After the exams I was a complete wreck.** Después de los exámenes estaba hecho polvo.

to **wreck** [rɛk] VERB
see also **wreck** NOUN
1 destruir* ◇ *The explosion wrecked the whole house.* La explosión destruyó toda la casa.
2 destrozar* (*car*)
3 echar por tierra ◇ *The bad weather wrecked our plans.* El mal tiempo echó por tierra nuestros planes.

wreckage ['rɛkɪdʒ] NOUN
1 los restos (*of vehicle*)
2 las ruinas (*of buildings*)

wrestler ['rɛsləʳ] NOUN
el luchador
la luchadora

wrestling ['rɛslɪŋ] NOUN
la lucha libre

wrinkled ['rɪŋkld] ADJECTIVE
arrugado

wrist [rɪst] NOUN
la muñeca

to **write** [raɪt] VERB (**wrote, written**)
escribir* ◇ *to write a letter* escribir* una carta

to **write down** [raɪt'daun] VERB
anotar ◇ *I wrote down her address.* Anoté su dirección. ◇ *Can you write it down for me, please?* ¿Me lo puedes anotar, por favor?

writer ['raɪtəʳ] NOUN
el escritor
la escritora

writing ['raɪtɪŋ] NOUN
la letra ◇ *I can't read your writing.* No entiendo tu letra.
◆**in writing** por escrito

written ['rɪtn] VERB *see* **write**

wrong [rɔŋ] ADJECTIVE, ADVERB
1 incorrecto ◇ *The information they gave us was wrong.* La información que nos dieron era incorrecta. ◇ *the wrong answer* la respuesta incorrecta
◆**You've got the wrong number.** Se ha equivocado de número.
2 mal ◇ *I think hunting is wrong.* Opino que está mal cazar. ◇ *You've done it wrong.* Lo has hecho mal.
◆**to go wrong** (*plan*) ir* mal ◇ *The robbery went wrong and they got caught.* El atraco fue mal y los pillaron.
◆**to be wrong** estar* equivocado ◇ *You're wrong about that.* En eso estás equivocado.
◆**What's wrong?** ¿Qué pasa? ◇ *What's wrong with her?* ¿Qué le pasa?

wrote [rəut] VERB *see* **write**

Xmas ['ɛksməs] NOUN (= *Christmas*)
la Navidad

to **X-ray** ['ɛksreɪ] VERB
see also **X-ray** NOUN
hacer* una radiografía de ◊ *They X-rayed my arm.* Me hicieron una radiografía del brazo.

X-ray ['ɛksreɪ] NOUN
see also **X-ray** VERB
la radiografía ◊ *I had an X-ray taken.* Me hicieron una radiografía.

yacht [jɔt] NOUN
el yate

yard [jɑːd] NOUN
1 la yarda

> *In Spain measurements are in metres and centimetres rather than feet and inches. A yard is about 90 centimetres.*

2 el patio (*of school, house*)

to **yawn** [jɔːn] VERB
bostezar*

year [jɪəʳ] NOUN
el año ◊ *last year* el año pasado
◆ **to be 15 years old** tener* 15 años
◆ **an eight-year-old child** un niño de ocho años
◆ **She's in the fifth year.** Está en quinto.

to **yell** [jɛl] VERB
gritar

yellow ['jɛləu] ADJECTIVE
amarillo

yes [jɛs] ADVERB
sí ◊ *Do you like it? – Yes.* ¿Te gusta? – Sí

yesterday ['jɛstədɪ] ADVERB
ayer ◊ *yesterday morning* ayer por la mañana ◊ *all day yesterday* todo el día de ayer

yet [jɛt] ADVERB
todavía ◊ *Have you eaten? – Not yet.* ¿Ya has comido? – Todavía no. ◊ *It's not finished yet.* Todavía no está terminado. ◊ *There's no news as yet.* Todavía no se tienen noticias.
◆ **Have you finished yet?** ¿Has terminado ya?

to **yield** [jiːld] VERB US
ceder el paso

yob [jɔb] NOUN
el gamberro (el vándalo *LatAm*)

yoghurt ['jɔugət] NOUN
el yogur

yolk [jəuk] NOUN
la yema

you [juː] PRONOUN

> *There are formal and informal ways of saying **you** in Spanish. As you look down the entry, choose the informal options if talking to people your own age or that you know well. Otherwise use the formal options. Note that subject pronouns are used less in Spanish - for emphasis and in comparisons.*

1 (*informal: 1 person*)
tú ◊ *What do YOU think about it?* ¿Y tú qué piensas? ◊ *She's younger than you.* Es más joven que tú.
◆ **You don't understand me.** No me entiendes.

2 (*informal: 2 or more people*)
vosotros MASC PL
vosotras FEM PL ◊ *You've got kids but we haven't.* Vosotros tenéis hijos pero nosotros no. ◊ *They're younger than you.* Son más jóvenes que vosotros. ◊ *I'd like to speak to you.* (*ie all female*) Quiero hablar con vosotras.
◆ **How are you?** ¿Qué tal estáis?

3 (*formal: 1 person*)
usted ◊ *They're younger than you.* Son más jóvenes que usted. ◊ *This is for you.* Esto es para usted.
◆ **How are you?** ¿Cómo está?

4 (*formal: 2 or more people*)
ustedes

> ***ustedes** is always used in Latin America instead of **vosotros**.*

◊ *They're younger than you.* Son más jóvenes que ustedes. ◊ *This is for you.* Esto es para ustedes.
◆ **How are you?** ¿Cómo están?

> *When **you** means "one" or "people" in general, the impersonal **se** is often used.*

◊ *I doubt it, but you never know.* Lo dudo, pero nunca se sabe.

*When **you** is the object of the sentence, you have to use different forms from the ones above. See translations 5 to 10 below.*

5 (*informal: 1 person*)
te ◊ *I love you.* Te quiero. ◊ *Shall I give it to you?* ¿Te lo doy?
◆ **This is for you.** Esto es para ti.
◆ **Can I go with you?** ¿Puedo ir contigo?

6 (*informal: 2 or more people:*)
os ◊ *I saw you.* Os vi. ◊ *I gave you the keys.* Os di las llaves.
◆ **I gave them to you.** Os los di.

7 (*formal: 1 person - direct object*)
lo MASC SING
la FEM SING ◊ *May I help you?* ¿Puedo ayudarlo? ◊ *I saw you, Mrs Jones.* La vi, señora Jones.

8 (*formal: 1 person - indirect object*)
le
*Change **le** to **se** before another object pronoun.*
◊ *I gave you the keys.* Le di las llaves.
◆ **I gave them to you.** Se las di.

9 (*formal: 2 or more people - direct object*)
los MASC PL
las FEM PL ◊ *May I help you?* ¿Puedo ayudarlos?

10 (*formal: 2 or more people - indirect object*)
les PL
*Change **les** to **se** before another object pronoun.*
◊ *I gave you the keys.* Les di las llaves.
◆ **I gave them to you.** Se las di.

young [jʌŋ] ADJECTIVE
joven MASC
joven FEM
(PL jóvenes)
◆ **young people** los jóvenes
◆ **He's younger than me.** Es menor que yo.
◆ **my youngest brother** mi hermano pequeño

your [jɔːr] ADJECTIVE
*Use **tu** and **vuestro/vuestra** etc with people your own age or that you know well, and **su/sus** otherwise.*

1 (*informal: 1 person*)
tu (PL tus)
*Remember there's no accent on **tu** meaning "your".*
◊ *your house* tu casa ◊ *your books* tus libros ◊ *your sisters* tus hermanas

2 (*informal: 2 or more people*)
vuestro
*Remember to make **vuestro** agree with the person or thing it describes.*
◊ *your dog* vuestro perro ◊ *These are your keys.* Éstas son vuestras llaves.

3 (*formal*)
su (PL sus)
*Use **su** when talking to **one** person or to a **group** of people. **su** is used in Latin America instead of **vuestro**.*
◊ *Can I see your passport, sir?* ¿Me enseña su pasaporte, señor? ◊ *your wife* su mujer ◊ *your uncle and aunt* sus tíos
*Use **el, la, los, las** as appropriate with parts of the body and to translate **your** referring to people in general.*
◊ *Have you washed your hair?* ¿Te has lavado el pelo? ◊ *Would you like to wash your hands?* ¿Queréis lavaros las manos?
◆ **It's bad for your health.** Es malo para la salud.

yours [jɔːz] PRONOUN
*Use **tuyo/tuya** etc and **vuestro/vuestra** etc with people your own age or that you know well, and **su/sus** otherwise.*

1 tuyo (*informal: 1 person*)
*Remember to make **tuyo** agree with the person or thing it describes.*
◊ *That's yours.* Eso es tuyo. ◊ *Is that box yours?* ¿Ésa caja es tuya?
*Add the definite article when **yours** means "your one" or "your ones".*
◆ **I've lost my pen. Can I use yours?** He perdido el bolígrafo. ¿Puedo usar el tuyo?
◆ **These are my keys and those are yours.** Éstas son mis llaves y ésas son las tuyas.

2 vuestro (*informal: 2 or more people*)
*Remember to make **vuestro** agree with the person or thing it describes.*
◊ *That's yours.* Eso es vuestro.
*Add the definite article when **yours** means "your one" or "your ones".*
◆ **These are my keys and those are yours.** Éstas son mis llaves y ésas son las vuestras.

3 suyo (*formal*)
*Use **suyo** in more formal situations with **one** person or a **group** of people, and remember to make it agree with the person or thing it describes. **suyo** is always used instead of **vuestro** in Latin America.*
◊ *That's yours.* Eso es suyo.
*Add the definite article when **yours** means "your one" or "your ones".*
◆ **I've lost my pen. Can I use yours?** He perdido el bolígrafo. ¿Puedo usar el suyo?
◆ **These are my keys and those are yours.** Éstas son mis llaves y ésas son las suyas.
◆ **Yours sincerely...** Le saluda atentamente...

yourself [jɔːˈsɛlf] PRONOUN
*Use **te, tú mismo** and **ti mismo** when you are talking to someone of your own*

*age or that you know well and **se** and **usted mismo** otherwise.*

1 (*reflexive*)
te ◊ *Have you hurt yourself?* ¿Te has hecho daño?
2 (*for emphasis*)
tú mismo MASC
tú misma FEM
◊ *Do it yourself!* ¡Hazlo tú mismo!
3 (*after a preposition*)
ti mismo MASC
ti misma FEM
◊ *You did it for yourself.* Lo hiciste para ti mismo.
4 (*reflexive*)
se ◊ *Have you hurt yourself?* ¿Se ha hecho daño?
5 (*after a preposition, for emphasis*)
usted mismo MASC
usted misma FEM
◊ *You did it for yourself.* Lo hizo para usted mismo. ◊ *Do it yourself!* ¡Hágalo usted mismo!

yourselves [jɔːˈsɛlvz] PRONOUN
*In Spain use **os** and **vosotros mismos** when talking to people your own age or that you know well, and **se** or **ustedes mismos** otherwise. In Latin America **se** and **ustedes mismos** replace both **os** and **vosotros mismos**.*

1 (*reflexive*)
os ◊ *Did you enjoy yourselves?* ¿Os divertisteis?
2 (*after a preposition, for emphasis*)
vosotros mismos MASC
vosotras mismas FEM
◊ *Did you make it yourselves?* ¿Lo habéis hecho vosotros mismos?
3 (*reflexive*)
se ◊ *Did you enjoy yourselves?* ¿Se divirtieron?
4 (*after a preposition, for emphasis*)
ustedes mismos MASC
ustedes mismas FEM
◊ *Did you make it yourselves?* ¿Lo han hecho ustedes mismos?

youth club [ˈjuːθklʌb] NOUN
el club juvenil (PL los clubs juveniles)

youth hostel [ˈjuːθhɔstl] NOUN
el albergue juvenil

Yugoslavia [ˈjuːgəuˈslɑːvɪə] NOUN
Yugoslavia FEM ◊ *in the former Yugoslavia* en la antigua Yugoslavia

Z

zany [ˈzeɪnɪ] ADJECTIVE
estrafalario

zebra [ˈziːbrə] NOUN
la cebra

zebra crossing [ziːbrəˈkrɔsɪŋ] NOUN
el paso de cebra

zero [ˈzɪərəu] NOUN (PL **zeros** *or* **zeroes**)
el cero

Zimbabwe [zɪmˈbɑːbwɪ] NOUN
Zimbabue MASC

Zimmer frame ® [ˈzɪməfreɪm] NOUN
el andador ortopédico

zip [zɪp] NOUN
la cremallera

zip code [ˈzɪpkəud] NOUN US
el código postal

zipper [ˈzɪpəʳ] NOUN US
la cremallera

zit [zɪt] NOUN
el grano

zodiac [ˈzəudɪæk] NOUN
el zodíaco ◊ *the signs of the zodiac* los signos del zodíaco

zone [zəun] NOUN
la zona

zoo [zuː] NOUN
el zoo

zoom lens [ˈzuːmlɛnz] NOUN (PL **zoom lenses**)
el zoom

zucchini [zuːˈkiːnɪ] NOUN (PL **zucchini** *or* **zucchinis**)
US
el calabacín (PL los calabacines)